Teaching English Abroad

Your expert guide
to teaching English
around the world

Susan Griffith

VACATION WORK
THE GAP YEAR EXPERTS

While every effort has been made to ensure that the information contained in this book was accurate at the time of going to press, some details are bound to change within the lifetime of this edition, especially those pertaining to visa requirements for teachers, exchange rates and the conditions offered by the schools listed in the country directories. Readers are invited to write to Susan Griffith, c/o Crimson Publishing, Westminster House, Kew Road, Richmond, Surrey TW9 2ND, or email her at info@crimsonpublishing.co.uk with any comments or corrections. The best contributions will be rewarded with a free copy of the next edition or any other Crimson title.

DISCLAIMER

The text that appears in this style of box has been supplied by the company or organisation featured in the heading.

NOTE: Most wages and prices are given in local currencies. For conversion to pound sterling and US dollars, use www.oanda.com.

British Council offices abroad are frequently referred to in these chapters. The Council's up-to-date address book can be accessed on www.britishcouncil.org/about/contact.

Teaching English Abroad

This twelfth edition published in Great Britain 2012 by Crimson Publishing Ltd, Westminster House, Kew Road, Richmond, Surrey TW9 2ND

First edition published 1991; twelfth edition 2012

© Crimson Publishing Ltd, 2012

Author Susan Griffith

The right of Susan Griffith to be identified as the author of this work has been asserted by her in accordance with the Copyright, Designs and Patents Act, 1988.

British Library Cataloguing in Publication Data
A catalogue record for this book is available from the British Library.

ISBN 978 1 78059 118 6

Typeset by IDSUK (DataConnection Ltd)
Printed and bound in the UK by Ashford Colour Press, Gosport, Hants

CONTENTS

TEACHING ENGLISH ABROAD

CONTENTS

PREFACE

Those of us who speak English as a first language tend to take for granted how universally dominant it has become. As the global language of pop songs, air traffic control and the Olympic Games, English has gradually conquered the world. Aspirational families everywhere perceive English as a route to prosperity and are willing to invest in language study even when times are tough. And there is no doubting that times are tough. The youth unemployment statistics in the so-called PIGS countries (Portugal, Italy, Greece and Spain) are horrific; yet there is no direct correlation between these and the availability of vacancies for native English-speaking graduates. Many private institutes in Mediterranean countries have confirmed for this edition that they want to hire appropriately qualified native speakers.

It is outside Europe that the market is really booming. English will be the lingua franca of the Winter Olympics in Sochi, Russia in February 2014, at the World Cup in Brazil in 2014 and at the Rio Olympics in 2016; and it is no coincidence that these are thriving BRIC countries (Brazil, Russia, India and China). These governments have assigned massive sums of money to provide English language training, which will have a knock-on effect on the wider English language market.

World events inevitably have an impact on the demand for English. At the moment, the post-Arab Spring nations of Egypt, Libya and Tunisia are struggling towards political stability. Although the increase in demand for language teachers has been modest so far, these are countries to watch.

An ability to teach the English language is the most globally mobile skill there is. Countries that continue to have a high demand for English teachers include Korea, China, Vietnam, Taiwan, Indonesia, Turkey, Saudi Arabia, Chile and Argentina. Programmes are always opening in new corners of the world, from Burma (whose recent softening towards democracy bodes well for an opening up to English) to Azerbaijan which has its own section in this edition for the first time.

No average profile of the travelling teacher can be identified. For this twelfth edition, I have received enthusiastic feedback from many world-roaming teachers, including an international travel blogger who supported an extended stay in Thailand by teaching; a young graduate who used her newly obtained TEFL certificate to secure a job teaching children in Tanzania; an ELT professional who moved easily to a good job in Dubai from one in Costa Rica; a Peace Corps volunteer to Central Asia who decided to stay on and teach in Baku; a young woman whom I met in a hostel in Seoul participating in a large-scale government-run teacher placement programme; and a man who walked in off the street in a pleasant northern Bulgarian town to enquire about teaching hours and was offered them.

The TEFL industry has spawned hundreds of specialist websites that cover teacher training forums and publicise vacancies worldwide. Some might wonder what a book can add. I have tried to create a hand-held tool that makes it easy for the reader to compare, at a glance, destinations for teachers, institute requirements, visa regulations, possible problems and rewards. This book aims for clarity to make sense of the overwhelming clutter of unsifted information online.

Note that the hundreds of language schools and teaching organisations that submitted details of their vacancies have not paid to be included in this book. Shaded, boxed text headed by a company name has been supplied by the relevant company, whereas boxed first-hand accounts by named teachers have been freely shared with readers.

In addition to all the hard information and vacancy listings that it includes, this book tries to convey a flavour of life as a teacher abroad by including first-hand descriptions of everything from banquet-induced hangovers in China to tips for renting accommodation in Buenos Aires. My aim from the first edition in 1991 has been to make the information as concrete and up to date as possible, and to cut the waffle. This book can be the stepping stone to a brilliant year or two of adventure abroad.

Susan Griffith, Cambridge, October 2012

ACKNOWLEDGEMENTS

The new revised edition of *Teaching English Abroad* would not have been possible without the help of scores of English teachers and the people who employ them. They have generously shared their wealth of information, insights and anecdotes. As well as all the people who helped with the 11 previous editions, the following should be thanked for their contributions, some of them substantial, to the research for this updated edition:

Travis Boyle – Russia
Ruain Burrows – Peru
Dan Casaletto – China
Anthony Cook – Kazakhstan, Finland
Miranda Crowhurst – Tanzania
Hans Durrer – Brazil
Lindsay Fair – Costa Rica
Martin Filla – Czech Republic
John Gahan – Azerbaijan
Gisela Giunti – Argentina (www.giselagiunti.com – Spanish courses in Buenos Aires)
Luke Harris – Chile
Alexis Heintz – Brazil
Katherine Hyvärinen – Russia
Shane Johnson – China
Bill Lehane – China
Amanda Middlecote – Korea
Ben Naismith – Dubai
Lillian Nyamuda – Finland
Barry O'Leary – The World
Amalia Pesci – Vietnam
Mandy Powell – Chile
Darren Quinn – Bulgaria
Joanna Radwanska-Williams – Macao
Serika Ramlall – Chile
Allen Tracey – Costa Rica
Mark Wiens – Thailand

PART 1

INTRODUCTION

INTRODUCTION

The British Council estimates that the number of English language learners will peak in the next decade at a staggering two billion. The statistics illustrate the extent to which English dominates our globalised world: three-quarters of the world's mail is written in English, 80% of the world's electronically stored information is in English and well over a third of users of the internet communicate in the language you are reading at this moment. Furthermore there are six million teachers of English working worldwide. Mind-boggling statistics aside, the demand for instruction at all levels given by people who happen to speak English as their mother tongue is enormous and set to continue increasing for the foreseeable future.

Just as Latin was the lingua franca of Europe in the Middle Ages, now it is English that is the language used to communicate between persons not sharing a mother tongue. When the newly liberated nations of eastern Europe sloughed off Russian, they turned in very large measure to English rather than to the other main European languages. In fact, countries as far-flung as Cambodia, Namibia and Turkmenistan are busy making English one of the keystones of their educational systems. In German-speaking Switzerland, there are signs that English is replacing French as the preferred second language at school. English is the international language of science, of air traffic control, and to a very large extent of trade and export. This is bad news for all those Germans, Swedes and French Canadians who would like to market their language skills to fund a short or long stay abroad. But it is English speakers, mainly from Britain, Ireland, North America, Australia and New Zealand who accidentally find themselves in possession of such a sought-after commodity.

SOME DEFINITIONS

The commonly used acronyms ELT, TEFL, TESL and TESOL can be confusing, especially since they are often used interchangeably. ELT, which stands for English Language Teaching, has come to be the mainstream expression in the UK (preferred by such august bodies as the University of Cambridge and by the publishers of the main journal in the field). But most people still refer to TEFL (pronounced 'teffle'), Teaching English as a Foreign Language. TESL stands for Teaching English as a Second Language, and TESOL means Teaching English to Speakers of Other Languages. People learn English as a second language when they need to use it in their day-to-day lives, for example emigrants to the UK and the USA or inhabitants of ex-colonies where English retains official status and may well be the medium of instruction in schools. (English is the official or joint-official language in more than 75 countries.)

As this book is for people who want to travel abroad to teach, the term TEFL is mainly used here, as well as ELT. Teachers of English as a Second Language (ESL) are usually involved with multicultural education. In the USA, the vast majority of English language teaching is of ESL because of the huge demand for English among those people who have emigrated to the USA and whose first language is not English. Therefore the term ESL dominates in American contexts, even when (technically) EFL is meant.

The acronym TESOL covers both situations, yet it is not widely used apart from in institutions, which favour the Trinity College London qualifications known as the Certificate and Licentiate Diploma in TESOL (see Training section later) and also in the context of the American organisation TESOL Inc., which is the largest English teachers' organisation in the world, claiming more than 13,000 members.

There is no shortage of other acronyms and sub-categories in the world of TEFL. One of the main ones is ESP which means English for Specific Purposes. ESP aims to match language teaching with the needs of various professions such as business, banking, tourism, medicine, aviation, science, technology, secretaries, etc. Business English is probably the most important in this category (and 'English for Shopping' as sometimes offered in Japan is the least important). Because a great many learners are motivated by a desire to use English at work, they want their teachers to adopt a functional rather than a structural approach.

In other words they want to have lessons in which they can pretend to be telephoning a client, recommending, applying, advising, agreeing, complaining and so on. They are certainly not interested in the subjunctive.

EAP stands for English for Academic Purposes, i.e. English at an advanced level usually taught to students who are planning to study at foreign universities or English-medium institutions in their own country. EAP is largely in the hands of government-funded programmes, such as those run by the British Council.

Note that the acronym TOEFL can cause confusion. The Test of English as a Foreign Language is a US-based standardised test administered to language learners. Passing a TOEFL exam is widely held to be a reliable indicator of how well an individual can communicate in English. The focus of many language schools abroad is to prepare candidates for the exam, and so may advertise for teachers with 'TOEFL' experience. The UK counterpart, sponsored by the British Council and Cambridge ESOL is IELTS (International English Language Testing System).

SCOPE OF OPPORTUNITIES

The range of locations and situations in which English is in demand covers an enormous spectrum. If TEFL is booming in Kazakhstan and Laos and Guatemala, there can be few corners of the world to which English has not penetrated. English has been called a 'barometer of Western influence' and only a handful of countries in the world have rejected Western influence outright (such as Burma and North Korea) and which therefore have no call for EFL teachers. More important nations with their own native English speaking population (such as India) are also not promising destinations for the aspiring teacher.

Many years have passed since the arrival of the single European market, which precipitated the greatest expansion of the English language than ever before in Europe's history. There has been an enormous increase in demand, especially from companies and professionals eager to participate in an integrated Europe. At least one German-based multinational has gone so far as to decree that all operations will be conducted in English. The attraction of European Union countries for British and Irish teachers is enhanced by the fact that they have the legal right to work.

The kinds of people who want to learn English are as numerous as the places in which they live. The worldwide recession saw a certain amount of cutting back in spending from Moscow to Madrid, for example on corporate training budgets, but it is remarkable how resilient the market has remained. In an even more competitive employment market, a command of English is considered so essential that individuals are prepared to fund themselves and their children. The area of the industry which seems to be booming almost everywhere is the teaching of children, known as Young Learners or YL in the trade. Kids as young as three are being sent to private English classes to improve their career prospects.

People around the world can think of a dozen reasons why they need to sign up for private English lessons:

- A Taiwanese student dreams of studying at UCLA.
- A Polish bus driver, proud to be from a member state of the EU, wants to work in Denmark where he will be able to communicate in English.
- The wife of the Peruvian ambassador in Islamabad wants to be able to speak English at official functions.
- A Greek secondary school student has to pass her English exams in order to proceed to the next year and, like most of her classmates, attends a private tutorial college for English lessons.
- A Turkish youth wants to be able to flirt with tourists from northern Europe.
- A Mexican waiter wants to get a job in the Acapulco Hilton.
- A Saudi engineer has to be able to read reports and manuals in English for his job.

The list is open-ended, and prospects for hopeful teachers are therefore excellent. There are also hundreds of international schools throughout the world where English is the medium of instruction for all subjects and there may be specific EFL vacancies. These will be of most interest to certified teachers who wish to work abroad.

But the situation is not all rosy for the prospective teacher. As the profile of the English language has risen, so has the profile of the profession which teaches it, and the number of qualified and experienced English teachers has increased along with the rise in demand. The difficult employment situation for new graduates in the UK and elsewhere has prompted some to look abroad, and to equip themselves with a TEFL certificate in order to get some work experience on their CV. The explosion in the availability of training courses means that a much higher proportion of job-seekers have a TEFL certificate than was the case a decade ago, and (quite rightly) foreign language schools are becoming more selective when hiring staff.

People who cruise into a country expecting to be hired as an EFL teacher simply on the basis of being a native speaker are in most cases (though not quite all) in for a nasty shock. Employers at all levels will ask for evidence of the ability to teach their language or at least a university degree as proof of a sound educational background. Certainly without a degree, a TEFL qualification or any relevant experience, the scope of opportunities shrinks drastically.

WHO IS ELIGIBLE TO TEACH?

Anyone who can speak English fluently and has a lively positive personality has a fighting chance of finding an opening as a teacher somewhere. Geordies, Tasmanians and Alabamans have all been known to be hired as English teachers (not to mention Norwegians and North Africans), though most employers favour native speakers of English without a heavy regional accent. Depending on the economic and cultural orientation of a country, schools will prefer British English or North American English. For obvious geopolitical reasons Europe and Africa incline towards Britain while Latin America and the Far East incline towards the USA and Canada. Many other countries have no decided preference, for example Indonesia and Turkey. Clear diction is usually more important than accent. On the American English versus British English debate, **Sab Will**, Course Director of TEFL Paris training courses says:

I'm not convinced it's a major concern. There are certainly French who find one flavour (or should that be 'flavor'?) easier to understand than the other, and some people want to be taught mainly in one 'accent' based on their intended future use of English. But overall I think it all evens out. Most students are happy with a friendly, competent and enthusiastic teacher who is able to adapt to their needs and supply them with materials and learning situations relevant to their situation. In relation to that, the origin of the teacher pales in comparison. Of course the teacher should be able to 'neutralise' their accent if necessary, whatever their origins, so that the student has a model which will be understood throughout the English-speaking world.

English language teaching is an industry which is seldom regulated, giving rise to the host of cowboy schools which are mentioned (usually disparagingly) throughout this book. The other side of the coin is the proliferation of cowboy teachers, who have no feel for language, no interest in their pupils and no qualms about ripping them off. The issue of qualifications must be considered carefully. It is obviously unwise to assume that fluency in English is a sufficient qualification to turn someone into an EFL teacher. Many experienced teachers of English come to feel very strongly that untrained teachers do a disservice both to their pupils and to their language. Certainly anyone who is serious about going abroad to teach English should turn to the relevant chapter to consider the training options. As Groucho Marx said, who would want to belong to a club that would want him as a member if he has no formal qualifications or experience? Among the army of teachers-cum-travellers, there are undoubtedly some lazy, spiritless and ungrammatical native speakers of English who have bluffed their way into a teaching job. Most books and journals about language teaching are unanimous in their condemnation of such amateurs. Yet there are some excellent teachers who have learned how to teach by practising rather than by studying. For certain kinds of teaching jobs, a background in business and commerce might be far more useful than any paper qualifications in teaching. Therefore we have not excluded the unqualified teacher-traveller from our account. As long as they take their responsibilities seriously and bear in mind that their pupils have entrusted them with significant quantities of time and money to help them learn, they need not bring the EFL profession into disrepute. Some untrained teachers we talked to during the research for this book found the responsibility so unnerving that they promptly enrolled in a TEFL course before unleashing themselves on an unsuspecting language-learning public.

Non-native speakers should not assume that their services will not be in demand outside their home countries. **Richard Ridha Guellala** was born in Holland, raised in Tunisia and partly educated in England, and now has one of the most highly respected qualifications in TEFL, the Cambridge Diploma. While teaching in Thailand, he wrote:

> *Most non-native speakers think that a position as an EFL teacher is impossible for them. However I came to the conclusion that even unqualified non-native speakers are often hired by Asian schools, as long as they project a professional image during the interview, speak clearly, are well-groomed, know the basics of English grammar and are fluent in the language. Scandinavians and Dutch are sometimes even more successful in finding teaching jobs at top schools than native speakers. True, we non-native speakers possess a rather 'heavy' or 'funny' accent but, believe it or not, some Asian employers favour our accents to the native speaker's because we speak more slowly and use very simple basic vocabulary.*

At an extreme opposite from the casual teacher-traveller is the teacher who makes ELT a career. Only a minority of people teaching English abroad are professional teachers. Career prospects in ELT are in fact not very encouraging. After teachers have achieved a certain level of training and experience, they can aspire to work for International House and then for the British Council. From there, they might become a director of studies at a private language institute, although one is unlikely to become a director without a primary interest in business and administration.

THE OLDER TEACHER

An increasing number of early-retired and other mature people is becoming interested in teaching English abroad for a year or two. Although it may be true that in certain contexts, language institutes are more inclined to employ a bright young graduate, if only for reasons of image and marketing, there are plenty of others who will value maturity, especially the growing number of establishments specialising in teaching young children. **Peter Beech**, Director of Anglo-Hellenic in Corinth, Greece, which trains and places teachers in jobs, has noticed an increasing interest from people who have already had a career in the UK, in teaching or in any field, who want to move abroad.

Whereas few companies openly impose an upper age limit, some age discrimination does regrettably take place, more noticeable in some countries than in others. For older job-seekers it will be a matter of spreading their net as widely as possible by contacting as many relevant organisations, including voluntary ones, as possible. Older applicants may have to work harder to demonstrate enthusiasm, energy and adaptability to prospective employers; but this should be no bar to someone committed to creating adventures later in life.

Australian journalists **Alexandra Neuman** and **John Carey**, aged 49 and 50 respectively, decided that having worked for 30-odd years it was time to do something different. They didn't want to do the sensible thing and wait until retirement so started saving and planning, and after a couple of years had saved enough to fund a year in Italy. At first Alex didn't work but when they decided to extend their stay, she needed to find work. The only work available was teaching English, which is what she is doing right now in the lovely town of Bergamo:

> *It won't matter what you read, who you speak to or how much planning you do once you arrive, your experience will be completely different. I have yet to meet one person who had a similar experience to mine, so above all you must bring with you tolerance, flexibility and an upbeat attitude. The rewards are well worth it. I love*

living here and I have never met such kindness. I know bureaucracy is terrible and I get paid badly but as I sit looking out of my hilltop apartment to the snow-capped Alps and the grapes ripening on the vine just below my bedroom window I think life is pretty wonderful!

WHAT EMPLOYERS ARE LOOKING FOR

Between the dodgy operators and the British Council is a vast middle ground of respectable English teaching establishments. Many would prefer to hire only qualified staff, yet they are not always available. On the whole these schools are looking for teachers with a good educational background, clear correct speech, familiarity with the main issues and approaches to TEFL, and an outgoing personality.

A bachelor's degree and/or TEFL certificate is no guarantee of ability as **Marta Eleniak** observed in Spain, where she taught during her gap year (after doing a one-week introductory TEFL course):

I've seen graduate teachers make such a mockery of the enterprise that it's almost criminal. TEFL is creative teaching. Forget about your educational experiences. In TEFL you have got to be able to do an impression of a chicken, you've got to be a performer. And you have to be flexible. If the pupils are falling asleep, conduct a short aerobics class and change tack to something more interesting. A good teacher builds a rapport with the class, and is enthusiastic, patient, imaginative and genuinely interested in the welfare of the pupils.

A sophisticated knowledge of English grammar is not needed since, in most cases, native speakers are hired to encourage conversation and practise pronunciation, leaving the grammar lessons to local teachers. On the other hand, a basic grasp is necessary if only to keep up with your pupils.

JERRY MELINN

Jerry Melinn enjoyed teaching English at an institute in Athens through Anglo-Hellenic so much that he has signed on for another year.

I suppose you could say I don't fit the profile of a TEFL teacher. Usually they are unattached, young and out to see the world after finishing their university studies. I worked in the telecommunications industry in Ireland for almost 40 years and took advantage of an early retirement scheme when I was 56 years old. I didn't want to stop working and, as my four children were grown up, I decided with the agreement of my wife, to try my hand at teaching English in Greece. I was interested in Greece because we have friends here and had been coming to Greece on holidays for many years.

MOTIVES FOR TEACHING ENGLISH

There are perhaps five main types of individual to be found teaching English from Tarragona to Taipei:

- The serious career teacher.
- The student of the prevailing language and culture who teaches in order to fund a longer stay.
- The long-term traveller who wants to prolong and fund his or her travels.

- The philanthropic or religious person sponsored by an aid organisation, charity or mission society.
- The misfit or oddball, perhaps fleeing unhappiness at home.

Experienced English teacher **Deryn Collins** wrote from Spain, identifying just three types of folk who teach abroad:

> *There are people who want to learn about how others live and take part, those who want to put a year out on their CV and those who leave their homeland because they cannot live with their 'own'. Which means you will on occasion work with a weirdo or maybe you are that weirdo. But mostly the mix of personalities is a marvellous thing. You can find good friends in teachers' rooms – some might even find love!*

In many countries, English teaching is the most easily attainable employment, in fact the *only* available employment for foreigners. Anyone who wants to transcend the status of mere tourist in a country such as Thailand, Bolivia or Japan will probably be attracted to the idea of teaching English. The assumption behind some thinking at the snobbish end of the EFL spectrum is that people who do it for only a year or two as a means to an end (e.g. learning Chinese, studying Italian art, eating French food) are necessarily inadequate teachers.

There are small pockets of people (mainly in the Far East) whose sole ambition is to earn as much money as possible to pay off student debts or fund further world travels. These are seldom good teachers if only because they take on so many hours of teaching that they can't possibly prepare properly for their lessons. But for most teachers, making a lot of money is not a priority or, if it was at the outset, they are soon disillusioned.

Salaries in popular tourist destinations (such as Paris, Barcelona, Chiang Mai) may actually be lower than in less appealing neighbouring towns, even though the cost of living is higher. Pay scales are relatively meaningless out of context. For example, the high salaries paid in Japan are usually eaten up by high rents and other expenses, at least in the first year. When converted into sterling a salary in Romania might sound pitiful but will be perfectly adequate there. In some countries such as Bolivia and Kenya, a TEFL salary may not be enough to fund anything beyond a very spartan lifestyle, and savings from home are essential to fund any travelling. Yet the majority of people who spend time abroad teaching English are able to afford to live comfortably and have an enjoyable time without feeling pinched, although they end up saving little.

A summary of **Barry O'Leary's** round-the-world history as a TEFL teacher might be inspiring to others considering a new direction:

> *The last time I counted, which was early November 2011, I'd taught more than 2300 students in my eight years as a TEFL teacher. That's a lot of lost-looking faces, funny English accents, and spur of the moment questions that I've had to answer. I'm not saying I'm the most intelligent TEFL teacher – only last week I really grasped the difference between subject and object questions – but I can offer some advice to those willing to learn. After doing a TEFL course in London with St Giles College, I bought a one-way ticket to Australia with a stop off in South America. I left alone and without any job prospects but I was pumping with adrenaline; my new life living abroad was about to start.*
>
> *My first job was in Quito, Ecuador, where I got paid $2 an hour for teaching feisty Ecuadorian teenagers. I wasn't interested in the money, teaching was fun and I got a buzz from helping them. It was so much better than the pressurised sales jobs I'd escaped from. After three months teaching in Quito I was hooked. I travelled overland to Salvador (getting robbed in Rio on the way) and was lucky enough to get more work just before the Carnival. I stayed for four months and really fell in love with teaching, and Brazil. My time in Sydney wasn't such an adventure, but I learnt a lot teaching vigorous Chinese students. I saved up enough (the pay was pretty good) for an amazing three-week trip up the east coast, and shot off to Bangkok where I'd lined up a job.*
>
> *I was met by a strict Catholic nun, my new boss, who pummelled me into shape, or at least she tried, and that's where I first learnt how to teach younger learners. Despite being in Thailand for the Tsunami, which I*

almost ended up in, my seven months teaching was amazing. I loved teaching tiny, funny kids who were smiling all day. I saved up enough for a six-week overland trip through Laos, Cambodia, Vietnam, China, and then to Moscow on the Trans-Mongolian Railway. I returned to England a new man. I'd travelled the world and had become a teacher, but my thirst for adventure continued. After the summer teaching in London, I headed for Seville, Spain, where I've been ever since. This year I married my Spanish wife who, incidentally, used to be my student (she was 21 and I was 25 before you ask). In my six years here I've really learned how to teach, thanks to some excellent training and a stiff hand from my boss. I know how to teach now, I get excellent results and my students like my classes, well, the majority of them who can be bothered to learn.

Barry is a blogger and has self-published a book *Teaching English in a Foreign Land* (http://teachingenglishinaforeignland.blogspot.com.es).

UK-TEFL

Rosie Smith

UK-TEFL Graduate – London Regents College, February 2012

Rosie turned her back on a career in the music industry to pursue a lifelong dream of exploring the world, whilst funding her travels through teaching.

'After 15 years spent working in the music industry, I decided that it was time for a change. One of my friends mentioned TEFL courses to me, which got me thinking about fulfilling my ambitions of travelling the world. I did my research and chose to enrol with UK-TEFL as the company is popular, established, reputable and respected.

'As a complete beginner to teaching, I found my two-day course well organised, covering all the fundamental elements of teaching and giving me the opportunity to try out my new skills through teaching practices. The trainer was patient, supportive and approachable, and she was happy to tell us all about her own teaching experiences in Asia which everyone found really inspiring. The course was intensive and thoroughly enjoyable, and I was genuinely surprised at the amount of confidence and knowledge I had acquired in just one weekend. I opted to be formally assessed in order to achieve the NCFE issued QCF Level 2 qualification (I thought any way of enhancing my employability would be worthwhile!), which proved to be a good decision, as it seemed to impress my potential employers.

'After my course, I was very keen to get some experience, so I spoke to a helpful advisor at UK-TEFL who talked me through the various options of where I could go. As I wanted to ease myself into my new career gently, I thought a short role would be the ideal first step and, with some great recommendations from past students on the UK-TEFL website, I applied for the 6 day voluntary role in Spain. I was offered a place soon after, and I had a brilliant experience where I met some great characters, made friends for life and put my knowledge of grammar through its paces! The location was amazing, and it was the perfect way to launch my TEFL career. Since returning to the UK, I've been accepted to work in Romania and Poland which I am really looking forward to, but my long term goals are to venture to more faraway places such as South America and explore locations I've only dreamt of visiting.

'My motivation for choosing TEFL was to gain more career satisfaction because I was convinced there was more to life than London. UK-TEFL has ensured that I definitely haven't been disappointed, and I would recommend them to others without hesitation!'

RED TAPE

The European Union (EU) now consists of the UK, Ireland, the Netherlands, Belgium, Luxembourg, Denmark, Sweden, Finland, Austria, Estonia, Latvia, Lithuania, Poland, Czech Republic, Slovakia, Hungary, Slovenia, Malta, Bulgaria, Romania, the Greek populated area of Cyprus, France, Germany, Italy, Greece, Spain and Portugal, the latter six of which have enormous EFL markets. Within the EU, the red tape should be minimal for all nationals of member states who wish to work in any capacity. Outside the EU, legislation varies from country to country. In theory there is also 'free reciprocity of labour' within the European Economic Area. The EEA takes in those western European countries that have decided to stay outside the Union, viz. Iceland, Liechtenstein, Norway and Switzerland.

All of this means that British and Irish nationals have a significant advantage over Americans, Canadians, Australians, New Zealanders and South Africans when job-hunting in Europe. Although not impossible for other nationalities, it is very difficult for them to find an employer willing to undertake the task of proving to the authorities that no EU national is available or able to do the job. **Brian Komyathy** from Long Island, New York, was disappointed when he made enquiries about moving to an EU country:

> European walls of regulations do not exactly bespeak, 'Americans welcome aboard'. I'm technically eligible to acquire Irish and hence EU citizenship through my grandparents, so as soon as various documentary records are located and processed I'll not have the problems I do now. A slew of phone calls convinced me of the necessity of taking this course.

Other Americans find ingenious ways to stay just about legal. **Rachel Beebe** worked in Portugal using *recibos verdes* (green receipts), which are intended for use by freelance workers in the country. In some cases non-Europeans with a student visa are permitted to work up to a certain number of hours (see chapter on France, for example). International and student exchange organisations may be able to assist. Some US-based organisations co-operate with partner agencies in various countries to place native speaker teachers in schools or institutes, often as volunteers or as live-in tutors. For particulars, see the section on *Opportunities for North Americans* on p.93.

The immigration authorities of many countries accord degree-educated English teachers special status, recognising that their own nationals cannot compete as they can for other jobs. Other countries may lack the mechanism for granting work visas to English teachers and so will often turn a blind eye to those who teach on tourist visas, since everyone knows that locals are not being deprived of jobs, rather they're being given an advantage by having the chance to learn English.

Some organisations have developed a study-and-teach solution. While you are learning Russian in Moscow or Spanish in Caracas, you do some English tutoring on the side. Since your status is primarily as a student, it is unnecessary to obtain a full work authorisation. Teachers who find a job before leaving home can usually sort out their visas or at least set the wheels in motion before arrival, which greatly simplifies matters. You can only start the process after finding an employer willing to sponsor your application, preferably one who is familiar with the processes. There is no point applying to the embassy or consulate until you have found an employer. The majority of countries will process visas only when they are applied for from outside the country. So if you have to visit your chosen country on a tourist visa in order to find a job (which is the usual process), you will have to leave the country to apply for the work visa, though often this can be done from a neighbouring country rather than your country of residence. The restrictions and procedures for obtaining the appropriate documentation to teach legally are set out in Part 2 of this book, country by country.

STAYING ON THE RIGHT SIDE OF THE LAW
Prospective teachers should contact the relevant consulate for the official line. If you do get tangled up in red tape, always remain patient with consular officials. If things seem to be grinding to a halt, it may be helpful to pester them, provided this is done with unfailing politeness.

REWARDS AND RISKS

The rewards of teaching abroad are mostly self-evident: the chance to become integrated in a foreign culture, the pleasure of making communication possible for your students, the interesting characters and lifestyles you will encounter, a feeling of increased self-reliance, a better perspective on your own culture and your own habits, a base for foreign travel, a good suntan... and so on.

Yasmin Peiris, away from home for the first time and teaching in China, sums up the highs and lows:

> *Looking back on the last 12 months, some experiences stand out very clearly. Unfortunately, that includes times when you fall ill or feel homesick, or even feel lonely. Homesickness is natural and is a phase that passes very quickly. This is my first time away from home and I feel like the past year has been a massive achievement personally and professionally. It's been great having my own apartment, making friends from all over the world, learning Chinese, and more importantly, realising my own strengths, limits and skills through my time here. The work experience gained and the friendships made will be the most precious souvenir – that I know won't get lost or confiscated by customs. I already knew that I had to come into this experience with an open mind, and I'm glad I did because China surprised me at every turn, constantly giving me something weird or wonderful to write home about.*

Good teachers often find their classes positively fun and place a high value on the relationships they form with their students. Teaching is a lot of fun when it's done right. One-to-one teaching can also be enjoyable since you have a better chance to get to know your students or clients. (By the same token, it can be a miserable experience if you don't get on, since there is no escape from the intimacy of the arrangement.) Off-site teaching provides glimpses into a variety of workplaces and private homes, perhaps even resulting in hospitality and friendship with your students.

As competition for jobs has increased, working conditions have not improved. There is a growing tendency for EFL teachers to be offered non-contract freelance work, with no guarantee of hours, making it necessary for them to work for more than one employer in order to make a living. Job security is a scarce commodity. Part-time freelancers of course miss out on all the benefits of full-time work such as bonuses, holiday pay, help with accommodation in some cases, and so on.

Uninitiated teachers run the risk of finding themselves working for a shark or a cowboy who doesn't care a fig about the quality of teaching or the satisfaction of the teachers, as long as pupils keep signing up and paying their fees. 'Client satisfaction' is their only criterion of success; business takes complete precedence over education. Exploitation of teachers is not uncommon since the profession is hampered by a lack of both regulation and unionisation.

The job of teaching English is demanding; it demands energy, enthusiasm and imagination, which are not always easy to produce when confronted with a room full of stonily silent faces. Instead of the thrill of communication, the drudgery of language drills begins to dominate. Instead of the pleasure of exchanging views with people of a different culture, teachers become weighed down by sheaves of photocopies and visual aids. Like most jobs when done right, teaching English is no piece of cake and is at times discouraging, but invariably it has its golden moments. It offers opportunities for creativity, learning about other cultures and attitudes, making friends and of course travelling. Not a bad job in many ways.

Roberta Wedge writes amusingly on a possible spin-off from a teaching contract abroad:

> *TEFL is one of the most sex-balanced job fields I know (though the Director of Studies is usually a man) and, for those who are interested, the possibilities of finding your one true love appear to be high. 'Thrown together in an isolated Spanish village, eating tapas in the bar, hammering out lesson plans together – we found we have so much in common.' And a year later they were married. (A true story.)*

On a more serious note, teachers should inform themselves about the political situation before offering their EFL services and take stock of their particular sensitivities concerning issues such as political freedom, democracy, human rights, religion, and so on. To take a couple of examples, teachers in China have been shocked by the overt racism. For instance a Ghanaian teacher working in a small city not that far from Beijing had to get used to the local people coming up to him to rub his skin to see if the black would come off. In the Central Asian Republics, home to ethnically diverse populations, certain groups are treated shamefully. If you are concerned by these matters, check the US-biased Freedom House website at www.freedomhouse.org for updates. Additional insight can be gained from Reporters Sans Frontieres (Reporters without Borders) at www.rsf.org. With regard to 'press freedom' their Worldwide Press Freedom Index rates countries according to the liberality of their press.

LANGUAGE LINK

Language Link was established in 1975 and is now one of the most successful international language training organisations. Our London schools are accredited by the British Council and are members of English UK. Our teacher training school is recognised by Cambridge ESOL. Language Link also has excellent links with a number of major UK Universities.

Language Link has partner schools throughout the world in China, Russia, Vietnam and Uzbekistan.

Here are some testimonials from some of our Language Link teacher trainees:

'I enjoyed the course very much and what I liked most about it was the actual practice teaching. It would be very useful and worthwhile experience for an aspiring teacher.' (Nicola Humphries – England)

'I thoroughly enjoyed the CELTA course I did in Language Link. I couldn't have asked for more approachable and helpful tutors. The support and encouragement enabled me to develop my career. It was a great experience and I would definitely recommend it to others.' (Cynthia P.A. – Spain)

And our graduate teachers have discovered new experiences through Language Link:

'I did my Celta with Language Link in 2001. It was a very good and enjoyable course. The tutors were wonderfully supportive and positive, and the course gave me everything I needed to start a career as a teacher. Afterwards I got a job in one of the language schools in London, and seven years later I went on to gain the Delta qualification. At present I am the Director of Studies at Language Link London – the very same school that helped me to get into the EFL world over 10 years ago.' (Gabi Kotlubaj)

'The support we have received is second to none. We want for nothing. We have facilities available to us that aren't even available to local teachers. Fantastic banquets! Plenty of opportunity to pursue our own interests. Supportive, modern, professional work environment. Fantastic kids on the whole.' (Shona McCarthy – Ireland)

'Language Link ensures the needs of their teachers are met. They provide everything you need to come to Beijing, teach and have fun. I would recommend this company to anyone who wants to have a positive and fulfilling teaching and cultural experience in China.' (Melanie Morgan – Canada)

'The teaching is a rewarding challenge and living in Beijing is great as there's always plenty to see and do.' (Craig Lennox – Scotland)

'It's a great opportunity to develop as a teacher. The students are spread across all levels, which pushes teachers to hone their skills and expand their store of activities and techniques. It's a challenge but also pleasurable and fun.' (Jim Radebaugh – USA)

TRAINING

THE VALUE OF ELT QUALIFICATIONS

Training in teaching English as a foreign language is not absolutely essential for successful job-hunting; but it makes the task easier by an order of magnitude. Anyone with the Cambridge Certificate (CELTA) or the Trinity Certificate in TESOL (both discussed in detail below) is in a much stronger position to get a job in any country where English is widely taught. These certificate courses provide a rigorous introduction to teaching English in just one month full-time (admittedly at considerable expense) or part-time over a period of months, and so anyone interested in spending some time teaching abroad should seriously consider enrolling in a certificate course. There are numerous other kinds of qualifications available, some obtainable after a weekend course and others after years of university study; many are described briefly in the Directory of Training Courses below.

However, the Cambridge and Trinity certificates should not be thought of as a magical passport to work. Increasingly, even certificate-holders are having to struggle to find a decent job, mainly because so many more people now have the qualification than a decade ago. Many language schools, especially in France and Germany, will not want to hire a novice teacher and are unlikely to be tempted to take on anyone who does not present a dynamic and energetic image. Still, the certificate training continues to give applicants an important edge over the competition.

Increasing your marketability is not the only reason to get some training. The assumption that just because you can speak a language you can teach is simply false. There may be plenty of people who have a natural flair for teaching and who can do an excellent job without the benefit of a certificate or any other ELT qualification. (As mentioned earlier, the term ELT has come to be preferred to TEFL in many contexts.) There are, however, many other people who, when faced with a class full of eager adolescents, would not have a clue where to begin. Doing a TEFL course cannot fail to increase your confidence and provide you with a range of ideas on how to teach and (just as important) how not to teach. Even a short introductory course can usually illustrate methods of making lessons interesting and of introducing the range of teaching materials and approaches available to the novice teacher. What is needed more than theory or academic attainment, is an ability to entertain and to dramatise, but not without a framework into which your classroom efforts can be placed.

A perpetual problem which a TEFL course solves is the general level of ignorance of grammar among native speakers. Native-speaker teachers often find that their pupils, who are much better informed on English grammar than they are, can easily catch them out with questions about verb tenses and subjunctives, causing embarrassment all round. Some training courses can also introduce you to the cultural barriers you can expect to encounter and the specific language-learning difficulties experienced by various nationalities (many of which will be touched on in the country chapters).

Some go so far as to see training almost as a moral obligation. Completely untrained teachers may end up being responsible for teaching people who have paid a great deal of money for expert instruction. This is of special concern in countries which have been inundated with 'tourist-teachers', while the ministries of education may be struggling to create all-graduate teaching professions. If you happen not to be a natural in the classroom, you may well fail to teach anything much to your pupils, whether they be young children in Hong Kong or businessmen in Portugal.

Not satisfied that a one-week course was enough to qualify him as a teacher, **Ian Abbott** went on to do the Cambridge Certificate at International House in Rome and summarises his view of TEFL training:

I wouldn't recommend teaching English as a foreign language without investing in a course first. You've got to remember that the people coming along to your lessons are desperate to learn your language and it is costing them a small fortune. It is only fair that you know what you are doing and can in the end take that money without guilt, knowing you haven't ripped them off to increase your travel funds.

One of the practical advantages of joining a TEFL course is that many training centres have contacts with recruitment agencies or language schools abroad and can advise on, if not find, a job abroad for you at the end of the course. Training centres differ enormously on how much help they can offer. If the 'after-sales service' is important to you, shop around before choosing which training course to patronise.

STAR-TEFL

TEFL is fun, rewarding and lets you travel pretty much anywhere in the world. But it's also tricky to know how to get started. Why not better understand your options with our quick guide to TEFL courses.

At the top of the pile are CELTA and Trinity. They are the courses that all others are judged against. We don't offer this course with Star-Tefl, but there is no doubting they are the 'cream of the TEFL crop' and anyone who tells you otherwise is either lying or trying to sell you something. They are classroom-based courses that you can take anywhere in the world. The only downside for some is the cost. At around £1,000 plus living expenses, they are seen as a serious investment by many.

Next are online courses. They are a cheaper alternative to CELTA and Trinity. They basically cover the same material as a CELTA or Trinity, but deliver it virtually rather than from a classroom. They normally range from 100 to 150 hours of study which you can work through in your own time. The big difference between them and a CELTA, besides the prestige, is they don't have teaching practice. This is normally the main obstacle when looking for a teaching job with some schools. On the other side of the coin, they are a lot cheaper. The average price for an online course is £200–£300 and they still meet the visa requirements in over 90% of the countries in the world.

For those 'fly by the seat of your pants' TEFLers, you can complete a weekend course. There are many people who happily take this route as a way of supporting their backpacking. You have to have a certain personality to go into the classroom with little training. Ok, so you're at the bottom of the food chain when it comes to finding work, but there are two billion people learning English and around 150,000 teachers so finding a job won't be a problem, especially in Asia.

At Star-Tefl we offer all these options, but for the first time you are now able to consider a fourth option. You can now take an online course with an added teaching practice component that gives you 10 hours teaching practice. This doesn't quite make it a CELTA or Trinity, but it makes the difference a lot smaller and it's only 60% of the price.

Basically, you have four options: CELTA or Trinity; Online + Teaching Practice; Online; and Weekend TEFL courses. All you need to do is decide which course suits your budget and needs.

Even in countries where it may be commonplace to work without a formal TEFL qualification (for example Thailand and Japan), teachers who lack a specific grounding in TEFL will often be at a disadvantage. In some cases, the jobs available to the unqualified tend to be at the cowboy end of the market and may therefore offer exploitative conditions. In some countries (such as Turkey) a TEFL certificate is a prerequisite for a work visa, which is yet another justification for doing some formal training before setting off.

RANGE OF COURSES

There is a bewildering array of courses available, at vastly different levels and costs, so it is wise to carry out some careful research before choosing. The British Council publishes introductory information on its website (see www.britishcouncil.org/teacherrecruitment-tefl-qualifications.htm). If you need help funding a training course, you may be eligible for a Professional and Career Development Loan, which is a bank loan where the government covers the interest for the duration of the course and for the first month after the course finishes. After that you have to pay it back in the normal way; further details can be found at www.direct.gov.uk/cdl or by phoning 0800 585505. Unfortunately, due to a change in UK government funding for adult courses in 2010, TEFL training courses are not currently eligible for funding.

When choosing a course, it is worth asking certain questions that will indicate how useful the qualification will be at the end of it, such as, is there any external validation of the course and how much opportunity is there for teaching practice. Also find out what size a class you will be in (10–12 is much better than 15–20) and what qualifications and experience the tutors have. Cactus TEFL (www.cactustefl.com) is a mine of information about all things TEFL-related. It offers a useful advice, orientation and admissions service for prospective TEFL teachers. The online and telephone support offers personal guidance on courses, and allows you to apply directly to a wide range of TEFL course providers worldwide. Cactus also has a jobs site at www.cactustefl.com/jobs/index.php. The Directory of Training Courses in this chapter organises the courses available under various headings: the 100+ hour certificate courses externally validated by the University of Cambridge and Trinity College London, 'Academic and Other Recognised Courses', which are primarily full academic courses offered at universities (this list is far from comprehensive), a few 'Distance Learning' courses, 'Short Introductory Courses in the UK' and, finally, a selection of courses offered worldwide: 'Training Courses in North America' and 'Training Courses Worldwide'.

CERTIFICATE COURSES

The most useful qualification for anyone intending to spend a year or more abroad as an English teacher is a Certificate in English language teaching validated by one of the two examination bodies active in the field of ELT: University of Cambridge ESOL Examinations and Trinity College London. The Certificate qualification is acquired after an intensive 120–130-hour course offered full-time over one month or part-time over several months. As of September 2011, Cambridge is now offering a CELTA course online which combines online study with live teaching practice (described below).

Most centres expect applicants to have the equivalent of university entrance qualifications, i.e. three GCSEs and two A levels and some require a degree. Admission to the course is at the discretion of the course organiser after a sometimes lengthy selection process. Places on courses at the well-established centres may be difficult to get because of high demand, especially in summer, so early application is advised.

Applicants must be able to demonstrate a suitable level of language awareness and convince the interviewer that they have potential to develop as a teacher. Some centres won't consider applicants under the age of 20. Past academic achievement is less important than aptitude; even a PhD does not guarantee acceptance. Most schools will send you a task sheet or grammar research activity as part of the application. Sample questions might be 'How would you convey the idea of regret to a language learner?' or 'Describe the difference in meaning between "I don't really like beetroot" and "I really don't like beetroot"'.

Courses are not cheap but should be viewed as an investment and a potential passport to a worthwhile profession in many different countries. In fact, prices have not risen much over the past few years, with many centres trying to survive amid keen competition. The range is about £950 to £1,300 for a full-time course. Most centres include the validation body's fee, variously called assessment, moderation or examination fee, which in 2011 was about £110 for both Trinity and Cambridge, though potentially more for courses abroad.

Many colleges of further education offer the Trinity or Cambridge certificate part-time and these are usually less expensive. Timetables for part-time courses vary, but the norm is to attend classes one or two evenings a week for one or two terms of the academic year plus occasional full days for teaching observation and practice. Once accepted onto a certificate course, you will usually be given a pre-course task to familiarise yourself with some key concepts and issues before the course begins. Full-time courses are very intensive and 100% attendance is expected, so you need to be in a position to dedicate yourself completely to the task in hand for four weeks. The standard of teaching is high, the course rigorous and demanding and the emphasis is on the practice of any theory taught. One of the requirements is that participants teach a minimum of six hours of observed lessons to authentic English language students.

Trinity's CertTESOL and the Cambridge CELTA are accredited by the UK Qualifications and Curriculum Authority, the national body for the regulation of vocational qualifications outside the higher education sector. On the National Qualifications Framework for England, both certificate courses have been accredited as a Level 5 qualification, which is considered equivalent in difficulty to the second year of an undergraduate degree course. CELTA and Trinity CertTESOL graduates may receive credits towards degree programmes at the discretion of the institution.

INTERNATIONAL HOUSE BARCELONA

'I had been working for several years as a massage therapist in London, and I really wanted to expand upon my teaching qualifications and experience in another field. Several of my friends were working as English Teachers in Spain at the time, and they suggested I look into getting a qualification in English Teaching.

'It was one of the best decisions I ever made in my life!

'I took my time researching various language academies and institutes, in a number of cities across Europe. International House (IH) in Barcelona ticked all the boxes – I love Spain, and had been to Barcelona several times on holiday (what an amazing city it is!).

'IH offers a superb training in English Teaching, and is authorised and accredited to run the Cambridge University teaching diplomas (CELTA and DELTA) - internationally recognised, and respected as one of the best qualifications around.

'The course provided everything I was hoping for, and more. At IH, they not only tutor you in becoming an English Teacher, but they also help to instil and nurture an invaluable set of skills around group facilitation and training delivery.

'From day one, I felt supported and encouraged to learn, grow and evolve as a teacher. The tutors were enthusiastic, knowledgeable, happy to help and advise, and provided informed and invaluable insights into our teaching practice sessions. Our fellow trainee teachers were also a great source of inspiration – we were encouraged to observe each other and offer both motivational and developmental feedback to one another. We also learned how to reflect objectively upon our own teaching practice sessions, and how to bring awareness and sensitivity to the preparation and planning of our lessons. Creativity, integrity and authenticity were encouraged at every moment, and I loved the fact that the course focused our awareness on the needs of the students, as well as the skills of the teacher – a lesson for life.

'Because of the high regard held world-wide for the CELTA, I had offers of work almost straight away, as did most of my fellow trainees. I now live in Spain, and am thoroughly enjoying teaching English in Barcelona.

'Thank you International House!'

Mark

CAMBRIDGE CELTA

Cambridge CELTA (Certificate in English Language Teaching to Adults) has established itself as a key passport to teaching opportunities overseas. It has a solid reputation in the international teaching community and high levels of recognition among employers around the world. CELTA is administered and regulated by University of Cambridge ESOL Examinations (Cambridge ESOL, 1 Hills Road, Cambridge CB1 2EU; +44 1223 553355; ESOLHelpdesk@CambridgeESOL.org; www.cambridgeESOL.org) and is sometimes referred to simply as the Cambridge Certificate. Many believe that CELTA is the most reliable route to jobs with better rates of pay and with employers who are willing to give more support to novice teachers.

You don't have to stay in the UK to take CELTA. Administered and regulated by University of Cambridge ESOL Examinations, CELTA courses are offered at more than 280 centres worldwide. For example, the British Council runs courses in Milan, Naples, Kuwait, Kiev, Dhaka, Mumbai, Casablanca and many others; CELTA courses are offered by 30 centres in Australia and New Zealand and in North America there are now 10 CELTA course providers in the USA and six in Canada. A full list is available at the Cambridge ESOL website – www.CambridgeESOL.org/teaching.

The newly launched CELTA Online course blends self-study with teaching practice. The course has been produced in partnership with International House, London and leads to the same internationally recognised certificate as the face-to-face CELTA course. It was piloted in 2011 in order to be launched properly in 2012. Cambridge ESOL is proceeding cautiously so as not to devalue its well regarded Certificate qualification. Candidates will still have to do at least six hours of observed teaching practice in person, and the course will be carried out over at least 10 weeks. Note that it is not going to be offered at a cheaper rate than the original; in fact there is likely to be an extra charge of about £80 for course materials. Of the 308 centres that offer the CELTA course worldwide, 62 offer the CELTA Online, including 21 in the UK, seven in Australia, five in Canada, four in Italy and others worldwide.

HAMBURG SCHOOL OF ENGLISH

The CELTA Teacher Training Centre in Hamburg has been offering high-quality, small-sized courses since 2003, training around 60 teachers each year. If you could ask them, what would they say about our course?

'I would recommend this class to anyone who is serious about advancing their career in EFL just because of the amount of practice and knowledge they would stand to gain by taking it.'

'Do it! It's very hard work but you get so much out of it.'

'I can't imagine how I taught without it – it really opened my eyes to the needs of students and the resources available and also what I am capable of!'

We consider it part of our job to provide you during your training with the best set of resources to help you develop yourself as a teacher, but we also never forget that the richest resource available is you, and the rich experience of teaching and learning that you already have within you.

After a CELTA course with us, teachers go on to posts internationally, from working one-to-one to teaching groups of 100-400 people, from preparing students for language exams to helping politicians hone their presentation skills.

The possible contexts for teaching English are unlimited and so we cannot afford to restrict your development by adhering to dogmatic beliefs of what 'best practice' may be; it is much more important to appreciatively explore and critically appraise actions taken in the classroom, so that, once you leave us, you are well-equipped to continue developing and adapting. Teaching is, after all, learning.

Securing a place on a CELTA course isn't automatic. Course providers are selective in order to ensure standards are kept high – and as a result, the pass rate is usually at least 90%. Grades available are Pass, Pass 'B' and Pass 'A', giving candidates the chance to distinguish themselves. CELTA provides a foundation of theory but focuses on effective teaching skills and practical tools for teaching English to adult learners. You'll gain hands-on teaching practice and the experience and support to build confidence in the classroom.

Many teachers believe that a CELTA plus some teaching experience is the perfect recipe for securing a good teaching job, as **Doug Burgess** wrote while teaching in Chile:

If you are interested in job security and acquiring a work visa, it is highly advisable that you complete the CELTA and try to get some experience as it will give you flexibility and options when you are here so that you can have the most comfortable and enjoyable time possible.

Some people have voiced surprise that a course which qualifies people to teach only adults is still so dominant, when much of the demand for English comes from young learners. Cambridge ESOL also offers an equivalent course for people who want to teach young learners – CELTYL (Certificate in English Language Teaching to Young Learners) at a selected number of centres in the UK and abroad.

TRINITY COLLEGE LONDON

The other principal initial Certificate in TESOL is awarded by Trinity College London (89 Albert Embankment, London SE1 7TP; +44 20 7820 6100; tesol@trinitycollege.co.uk; www.trinitycollege.co.uk). The Trinity Certificate (CertTESOL) has international recognition, is highly regarded by employers in the UK and around the world and is considered to have equal academic standing as CELTA. Currently there are 76 centres worldwide offering CertTESOL training full or part-time. Nearly a third are outside the UK, with three centres in Spain and New Zealand and centres in other countries such as Canada, Hong Kong, Czech Republic, Ireland, Italy, Japan, Argentina and Uruguay.

Trinity stipulates a minimum of 130 hours offered intensively over a minimum of four and often five weeks or part-time over a longer period. All intensive courses must have a pre-course learning component in addition to the minimum hours. The course content includes grammar and phonology, a range of teaching approaches and methodologies, classroom management and motivation, hands-on experience of teaching aids (from blackboards to computers), introduction to the learning of an unknown language (in which trainees receive four hours' instruction and lesson planning). In addition, they must complete a minimum of six hours of observed and assessed teaching practice and spend at least four further hours observing experienced teachers of English.

The CertTESOL is accepted by the British Council as an appropriate initial TESOL qualification in its accredited English language teaching organisations in the UK and its own teaching centres overseas. All courses meet the core Trinity requirements but there are variations in course delivery across the different providers to reflect the best of their in-house practice and philosophy. Trinity also works closely with QuiTE – Quality in TESOL Education (www.quality-tesol-ed.org.uk) to ensure that its qualifications are in line with those of other comparable awarding bodies – principally Cambridge ESOL. The Trinity CertTESOL can also be taken as an integral module within a bachelor's degree programme at some universities such as Central Lancashire (Preston) and the Open University.

A graduate of the Trinity Certificate course remembers her experience:

I got good grades for my five A-levels and wanted to take a year out abroad. I did some research on the net – found out a bit about teaching English ('TESOL') – but realised that a weekend course wouldn't be cheap, or actually give me the qualification for a decent job. I looked into online teacher training – but I really wanted the experience of meeting other would-be teachers and experienced trainers. I therefore chose a five-week intensive Trinity CertTESOL course – I could have done it part-time, but I was in a hurry! I was warned about how very intensive it would be – how I should tell my friends that I'd be really busy for five weeks… and sure enough when I was accepted for the course I had to start reading straightaway for some written tasks to complete beforehand.

The course itself was an extraordinary experience. I started (and finished!) by feeling very enthusiastic and energetic. There were written assignments ('journals') to prepare over the four weeks and I was corrected on my grammar, punctuation and spelling, which was a surprise at first. I had to plan my time carefully – what I would do in the evenings and at the weekend, how much I could read. The most demanding but exciting part was the teaching practice with real students from different nationalities. It had never occurred to me I would feel so nervous. The first time I stood up in front of them I realised they expected to learn something from me, and I kept forgetting that there was no point in explaining difficult words or ideas in English – I had to learn very specific techniques to teach my own language. Overall…my own communication skills improved enormously, my students were very kind and I learnt to respect their feelings, the other trainees were (all bar one) very supportive, I learnt to manage a heavy workload in and out of school, and finally I feel I developed as a teacher and as a person – all in five weeks!

CHOOSING A COURSE

It is up to prospective trainees to weigh up the pros and cons of the courses available to them and to establish how rigorously each course under consideration is monitored. One reservation that a few employers abroad have expressed is that the proliferation of providers of certificate courses, whether on behalf of Cambridge, Trinity or independents, has made it more difficult to maintain a uniform standard, especially since so much of the assessment of candidates is subjective. The general decline in standards of literacy in Britain and North America has also prompted some to complain of a decline in quality of TEFL training.

When it comes to workload, trainees in both CELTA and Trinity TESOL courses complain of a punishing schedule. But most come away claiming that the course elements are superb. At the time, participants sometimes feel as though they are drowning in information, but realise that the course has to pack a great deal of material into four brief weeks. When trying to identify differences between them, one view is that the CELTA concentrates more on the structure of language and classroom management, and Trinity on the use of authentic materials and practical teaching techniques. The majority who go on to teach abroad are very grateful for the training it gave them, as in the case of **Andrew Sykes**, teaching in Bordeaux:

> *As for the certificate course that I did at Leeds Metropolitan University, it was certainly one of the most stimulating, challenging and interesting things I have ever studied for. Initially I felt a bit out of place – I had a background of science A levels, a maths degree and two years as a (failed) accountant. The course was professionally run and there were good teacher-student relations. Most people had never taught anybody anything before in their life, but we were gradually eased into teaching by the supportive teaching staff who were refreshingly (and diplomatically) critical when required to be. A criticism which some students had was that there wasn't enough feedback about what was expected to gain a pass, let alone achieve an A or B. The best recommendation for the course is perhaps that I would never have felt comfortable teaching without it.*

So even if your social life disappears for a month and all you can talk about at weekends is phrasal verbs and English idioms, the consensus is that it is worthwhile.

Many certificate courses are offered by independent companies outside the Cambridge and Trinity folds and these are more difficult to assess. For many, one of the key factors will be cost. Generic certificate courses are available in dozens of countries and the cheapest ones are offered in the cheapest countries. **James Clarke** and his girlfriend **Sally** were looking for a course for under $1,000 inclusive in South America and ended up at one in Peru, which has since gone out of business, though that did not prevent them for thinking it gave them a good grounding:

> *We took (and both passed) a TEFL training course in Trujillo, Peru which cost $900 for four weeks including a homestay and all food – much cheaper than anywhere in Buenos Aires where we had been before. It was a very good experience, with only one other student on the course, unlike a rival course we observed in Cusco, Peru, where there were maybe 14 students. Every day of the first week we observed four hours of classes (with participation) as well as four hours of theory from 9am to 1pm. The second week, the observation turned into actual teaching of the classes with the same theory lessons. The third week was observation of a higher standard of classes and then the fourth week was teaching, but four hours per day instead of two hours in the second week. We taught grammar, conversation and pronunciation, all using games, activities, dynamics and motivational*

techniques using music. There was one drawback which we suspect was down to the price of the course – we did not receive any original textbooks, just photocopied pages from textbooks.

Possible advantages of doing a TEFL training course abroad are that you may already be teaching or living in that country and want to upgrade your qualifications locally; the course and cost of living may be cheaper than in your home country; and successful course participants will almost certainly be put in touch with local employers, making it much easier to land a job in that place.

Teaching practice is key. Busy colleges such as Ealing, Hammersmith and West London College offer an insight into the diversity of ELT work because they teach such a wide range of students, to whom their CELTA trainees are exposed during teaching practice sessions.

OTHER RECOGNISED QUALIFICATIONS

In 2005, Cambridge ESOL introduced the Teaching Knowledge Test (TKT), a new accessible test about teaching English to speakers of other languages, delivered to international standards. The test, which can be taken by both practising and aspiring teachers, involves three modules that cover the background to language learning and teaching, planning lessons/using resources and managing the teaching and learning process. TEFL training centres worldwide are offering short courses to candidates who want to prepare for TKT, which is more accessible than CELTA and does not include teaching practice as part of the assessment. A new module of interest to current teachers with no formal qualifications is called TKT Practical which requires no coursework but an assessment of practical teaching abilities. Further information is available at www.cambridgeesol.org/TKT.

Beyond CELTA is the Diploma. Whereas CELTA is considered an initial qualification, the Diploma (as distinct from any old diploma with a lower case) is an in-service course for experienced English language teachers. The Cambridge Diploma in English Language Teaching to Adults (DELTA) and the Trinity Diploma (Dip TESOL) are high-level qualifications usually open to graduates who have at least two years of recent ELT classroom experience. The Diploma course is available intensively over a minimum of eight weeks but more usually part-time over several months or a year. A Distance DELTA option supported by International House (IH) and the British Council is increasingly popular (www.thedistancedelta.com) because it can be combined with full-time teaching work. The fees of £2,200 are sometimes subsidised by employers. DTE(E) LLS focuses on teaching English as a second language and replaces the Cambridge ESOL Certificate in Further Education Teaching.

Universities (especially the former polytechnics) from Brighton to Belfast offer their own certificate or diploma in TEFL. Most are one- or two-year courses, full or part-time, and tend to be more theoretical than Cambridge and Trinity courses. It is important to do some research before committing yourself to a course so that you are sure that the qualification you obtain will be recognised by employers both in the UK and overseas. Once again find out if there is some form of external assessment and whether the course includes a reasonable amount of teaching practice.

Stephen Curry felt let down by the course he chose:

I called my local university to see what courses were available and was advised that they could provide a course consisting of two modules, one from the PGCE and one from the MEd programme which would be equivalent in status to a one-month certificate and would be 'recognised'. The course of study took from May to February to complete. It was a lot of hard work, research-based and absolutely no fun whatsoever. I did the course on the understanding that it would lead to a stand-alone TEFL certificate. I have since tried to get the university to confirm in writing that this module carries the recognition they claimed it would but they now say that they cannot do this. Unfortunately it was not until the latter stages of the course that I (and others) began to see that the eventual outcome would be a qualification that was unlikely to be recognised in the eyes of anyone outside the university, let alone as being equivalent to the Cambridge/Trinity certificate.

A number of undergraduate institutions offer TESL as part of an undergraduate course; the weighty *UCAS Handbook* lists all university courses in the UK and can be consulted online at www.ucas.com, or in any careers or general library. MA courses in ELT and Applied Linguistics are offered at dozens of universities and colleges. Some offer a master's by distance learning aimed at practising ELT teachers worldwide. Arguably, there is a world oversupply of MAs; however, an MA is a prerequisite for many posts in some countries, especially in the Middle East.

Anyone who wishes to specialise in the highly marketable field of Business English should enquire about specialist courses such as the Further Certificate for Teachers of Business English (FCTBE) validated by the London Chamber of Commerce & Industry (LCCI) and offered by several companies involved in this market, such as Inlingua Teacher Training in Cheltenham. An alternative is the Certificate in Teaching Business English from International House (IH-BET) which involves a 50-hour online course (£350 for non-IH participants).

TEFL ENGLAND

Fiona was a teacher in the UK who was really desperate for a change of scene. After a TEFL England course, she headed to South Korea for the sunshine and stress-free life she was craving.

'With six years of London supply teaching under my belt, I wanted to find a new way of teaching without all the stress! I eventually found a place called EPIK, which stands for English Programme in Korea. Within a couple of months I was hired to work at a school in Korea. It was not the easiest of processes, as I had to get forms notarised and apostilled and obtain first-hand letters from past employers. However, I had a feeling that this was what I needed.

'Pretty soon I was on a plane bound for Hong Kong! Next stop was Busan, Korea, where myself and 400 other EPIKers were given a 10-day orientation into the lifestyle, culture and norms of Korean society. We learnt to eat with chopsticks, work with money (called Won) which comes in 1000s of units and got used to eating rice with every meal – yes including breakfast!

'It is the teaching that brings in the Won – a good salary with free food (school lunches) and free accommodation. I had completed a TEFL course in London and the tips and things I learnt in that one weekend were absolutely sufficient for teaching over here. I do have a teaching degree as well, but the TEFL course added more fun and easy ways to get the subject matter across. The standard of English is surprisingly low here. I really spend most of my time just repeating key phrases or playing a game where they are 'forced' to use English in order to win.

'My weekends are so full now and everything is cheap, not only compared to the West but also compared to our wages. I have been paragliding, abseiling, river-rafting, mountain climbing – you name it, I am there. Also, with so many foreign teachers out here, there is a huge opportunity to make friends and explore places together.

'I did not know what I was letting myself in for. I did not know what to expect. All I know is, I came here with an open mind and have not regretted my decision to become an ESL teacher in the Far East.'

INTRODUCTORY COURSES

Although the Cambridge and Trinity certificates are referred to as 'introductory courses', there are many cheaper, shorter and less rigorous introductions. With the dramatic rise in the popularity of certificate courses, what might be considered as more amateurish courses has declined, though these do have a role to play, for example for school leavers who would not be accepted onto a Certificate course or for the curious who do not want to commit to a month-long course or pay over £1,000.

Because there are some commercial enterprises and 'cowboy' operators cashing in on the EFL boom, standards vary and course literature should be studied carefully before choosing. Most people who have done a TEFL training course claim that the most worthwhile part is the actual teaching practice, preferably to living breathing foreigners rather than 'peer-teaching' in mock lessons to fellow participants. The fact is most short introductory courses do not allow much chance to do teaching practice. On the other hand they can provide lots of original lesson ideas and some hand out useful manuals full of lesson plans. The more upmarket introductory courses often present themselves as an opportunity to sample the field to see whether you want to go on to do a certificate course at a later stage. Others make their course sound as if it alone will be sufficient to open doors worldwide. Some in the industry consider weekend courses to be money-spinning machines and their claims to dispense internationally recognised certificates to be highly contentious. It would be unreasonable to expect a weekend or five-day course to equip anyone to teach, but most participants do find them helpful. After seeing an advertisement in the New York subway advertising for English teachers, **Roger Blake** was prompted to seek out some training. Back in England, Roger, who admits to being a not particularly academic type, enjoyed the 'crash' weekend training he did with i-to-i so much that he enrolled in a home-study module of a further 20 hours. Later when he was asking about local teaching possibilities in Addis Ababa, he felt more confident being able to show two course certificates.

The majority of residential courses last a weekend or for four to five days and cost between £200 and £500, not counting accommodation. Almost all will issue some kind of certificate which can sometimes be used to impress prospective employers. Anyone who wants a job after doing a short course should aim to do it in the spring when the majority of jobs are advertised for the following academic year. Many people who complete an introductory or 'taster' course go on to do an intensive certificate, often at the same centre.

A number of private language centres offer their own short courses in TEFL, which may focus on their own method, developed specifically with the chain of schools in mind (for example Berlitz) or may offer a more general introduction. You may come across schools looking for teachers to teach the Callan Method. But many people in the industry are sceptical (to put it mildly) about its efficacy, including an American teacher who worked at a participating school in Poland, a country where the Callan Method is very popular:

> *The Callan Method is little more than a fraud. The material is so pedagogically and linguistically outdated that no well-informed student would ever use it. Further, the book is excessively morbid. I couldn't, in good faith, teach the Callan Method again.*

DISTANCE LEARNING

Some practising teachers of English who want to obtain a qualification are attracted to the idea of self-study by distance learning, partly because it will be cheaper than a conventional course and because it can be done in the candidate's own time and/or in any part of the world. Course providers are making increased use of electronic communications, doing away not only with the necessity of having physical access to a training course but of being dependent on the post, often unreliable in distant parts of the world. Some companies are delivering complete courses online.

THE ENGLISH TRAINING CENTRE

'I was very happy with my tutor. She provided clear, informative and valuable feedback on all my assignments. I'll never forget her tremendous support! A big THANK YOU to Dodie, Paul, Sarah and all others at ETC. Cheers!' *Aileen, UK*

'I found the course material clear and informative and found myself referring back to it often in the course of my teaching. I benefited enormously from the support of my tutor. His feedback was always positive, encouraging and motivating. I was very impressed by his thoroughness and found his helpful suggestions really useful in my on-going teaching practice. I'm very grateful for the solid grounding provided by both the TEFL and TBE courses!' *Janine, Germany*

'The quick responses of my tutor and her detailed, careful and informative comments were highly appreciated. I have already recommended the course to two friends and would be happy to continue to recommend ETC in the future. I have already been successful in securing my first English teaching post here in France, partly on the strength of the quality of the course I completed.' *Tracey, France*

'I was extremely surprised by how much information this course covered. Before starting I honestly thought that teaching my own language couldn't possibly be too difficult. I feel prepared and confident in my abilities now, thanks to this course. The best part about the whole experience was my tutor. He gave me great feedback and was always supremely pleasant. I think you're all doing a fantastic job. Thanks so very much!' *Erin, Italy*

'I wish to thank you for this fantastic course. The entire content has helped me in my teaching career. Because I was already teaching at the time of the course, I was able to directly apply everything I learnt. My tutor was excellent and his feedback was always constructive. Thank you again, and I look forward to the possibility of doing future courses, perhaps with a greater Business English orientation.' *Kay, Italy*

'I was delighted to find that the course was so practical. A friend of mine, who for many years was responsible for external study courses in Australia, rated it as probably the best external study course he has come across, in both content and tutor response. All I can say is that I found the material very clear and relevant and that I looked forward to your encouraging and helpful responses.' *Zsuzsanna, Australia*

Typically, distance courses at the professional end of the spectrum involve at least 150 hours of home study, as required for NQF5 of the National Qualification Framework. Some 'hybrid' courses like the brand new CELTA Online offer distance learning in combination with a residential element. A new entrant to the profession is faced with a bewildering array of distance courses to choose from but does not always possess the knowledge or experience to judge between them.

UNIVERSITY OF MANCHESTER

The School of Education at the University of Manchester in the UK was one of the first university departments in the world to offer a professional qualification in TESOL, which it began back in 1962. At that time it was a diploma, but a master's qualification soon followed. The courses have always been influential and innovative, and since the 1980s the degree has been offered both as on-site and as a distance learning version. The university prides itself on the reflective approach that is developed at Manchester and its courses are designed for people who want to progress in their profession – those who may have had a number of years of experience and are now seeking new ways of working, new ways of engaging in their practice. Graduates from these courses may continue as class teachers, but many go on to take other roles in the profession including design, book publishing, running their own schools, researching and other roles.

A further aspect of the courses at Manchester is their engagement with a wide variety of new technologies in education. These feature very strongly in the MA in Educational Technology and TESOL, but are also a required component on the MA TESOL in which all students take at least one baseline module in this area. Other features of the courses include modules in the field of intercultural language education, the psychology of language education and teacher education. Manchester also believes that its assessment processes reflect good practice in the field and, as well as writing essays about their own teaching, course participants are also asked to do presentations and engage in enquiry-based learning. Quite often coursework ends up being published in a variety of different places.

Whether you choose to study face to face at Manchester or in context via distance learning, the coverage of subjects and topic areas are the same and the university increasingly brings its on-site and distance students together using a range of educational technologies. The students consider the uses of technology in teaching very innovative. All of the members of the academic staff are active in the profession, attending conferences, being active in teacher organisations like IATEFL and TESOL as well as more specialist organisations such as EuroCALL. For more information on the range of activities and publications, visit the Manchester Uni blog: http://edtechand tesol.info.

A number of accrediting bodies and monitoring organisations exists, but competition between them does not make the task much easier. It is strongly recommended that you ensure that the certificate course for which you are applying is accredited by an independent body.

As a part of the general move within the profession to monitor standards and offer assurances of quality, the College of Teachers (www.collegeofteachers.ac.uk) is an important awarding body. It has a Royal Charter, is based within the Institute of Education in London and is a registered charity.

Among other accrediting bodies, which mostly operate as commercial enterprises, are the newly formed Accreditat (www.accreditat.com) which accredits TEFL/TESOL providers for both face-to-face and distance/online courses, and Ascentis (www.ascentis.co.uk) based in Lancaster, a new awarding body which has approved some short TESOL courses such as the one offered by Mente in Argentina, but whose remit is to assess courses only up to NQF level 3. The Open & Distance Learning Quality Council (www.odlqc.org.uk) visits and accredits providers offering a whole range of courses of which TEFL training is only one, so they lack specialist expertise in the field. The International Accreditation of TESOL Qualifying Organisations (IATQuO) is another monitoring organisation, which has been run by an individual in Bristol since 2005 and is gradually expanding its inspection role; details from IATQuO (Park View, Alveston Road, Bristol BS32 4PH; ADMoller@aol.com; www.iatquo.org).

ACTDEC, the Accreditation Council for TESOL Distance Education Courses, was established in 1993 to improve on standards of distance TESOL/TEFL programmes. A copy of the ACTDEC code of practice and other details, including a list of accredited members can be viewed online at www.ACTDEC.org.uk.

A NOTE ABOUT ACCREDITATION

Distance training varies enormously in quality. Some companies are successful primarily because of their advertising campaigns and skill with social media but offer very mediocre courses. Others offer good quality courses and receive excellent feedback on coursework. Careful research is needed before choosing where to spend your money on an online course.

People considering the distance learning route to TEFL training should be cautious. The most obvious disadvantage is the lack of face-to-face teaching practice, though some courses do provide opportunities for blocks of teaching practice and others provide plenty of tutor feedback. Be aware that some employers, including ones whose details are included later in this book, specify that they will not consider applications from people with on-line certificates. A new development for distance students of TESOL is that they may be able to get actual teaching practice online or via Skype. If you are not satisfied with the course but have paid your money (typically £400+ for a certificate course), you have little recourse, though some such as ETC (www.englishtc.co.uk) offer a 30-day full refund. One way of ascertaining the worth of a distance learning course you may be considering is to ask to be put in touch with past students. For example, Global English asks its trainees to complete appraisal forms, many of which are very positive, such as this one filled out by **Glyn Askey** from Yorkshire:

Having had an interest in TEFL for some time, I required a course which would give me an insight into TEFL at an affordable cost. I found that the Global English course made you think from the outset about your students, your lesson planning and the methods of teaching... A well put together course and positive friendly feedback.

Details of introductory, internet and distance training courses both in Britain and abroad are provided in the Directory of Training Courses which follows.

MANCHESTER
1824

The University of Manchester

MA TESOL and
MA Educational Technology & TESOL

for experienced professionals with high competence in English and serious professional commitment.

Our commitment is to your exploration of:
⇒ Pedagogy beyond methods
⇒ Technology as integral to your work
⇒ TESOL as an intercultural endeavour
⇒ Contextualised teacher-learning

Distance and onsite study options.

Progression to doctoral study is open for appropriately successful candidates.

Find us at:

http://edtechandtesol.info
http://www.education.manchester.ac.uk/

TRAINING IN THE USA

Most TESL training in the USA is integrated into university degree courses in Applied Linguistics at both the undergraduate and graduate levels. Until a decade or two ago, there were virtually no short intensive courses in TEFL available in North America. That has now changed. In addition to the 10 Cambridge CELTA providers in the USA, a number of independent TEFL training organisations offer four-week intensive courses (see Directory of Training Courses below). The major providers like Transworld are well connected with language schools abroad (particularly in Latin America and the Far East). Competition is keen among the schools, and prices remain fairly consistent at about $2,300–$2,800 for a four-week course, with the odd course available for less than $2,000.

The American Language Institute in San Diego has been praised by its graduates, like **Bryson Patterson** writing from Costa Rica:

The amTEFL course is a solid teacher training programme encompassing methodology, live classroom practice, grammar and job placement. A day at the amTEFL begins with four hours of methodology (the theory and practice of second language acquisition). Trainees are then instructed in the ins and outs of lesson planning, and annual planning. Mock classes are video taped, helping students to evaluate their own performance. Afternoons are spent working as assistants for mentor teachers in live EFL classrooms and rotating through all the levels of EFL classes at the ALI.

If one of your main criteria is the after-course job advice, make sure you investigate properly. **Melanie Twinning** felt let down by the choice she made:

Despite being at least $1,000 more expensive than the competition, the course I chose really didn't do everything they promised. They have really no job placement to speak of and the man in charge of job placement is actually rather mean. Luckily I had your book and a bit of confidence and was able to find positions on my own but if you're paying $3,000 for a TEFL course I think you should get what they promise. I have to say the course itself was incredibly well done and the director is phenomenal. They just won't help you at all unless you are going to Korea.

Increasingly, American universities and colleges are offering intensive TESL training including one-semester courses. It is easier to get practical experience of teaching English (without a qualification) by joining one of the many voluntary ESL programmes found in almost every American city, run by community colleges, civic organisations and literacy groups. For a first hand account see the chapter on North America at the end of this book. ProLiteracy Worldwide (www.proliteracy.org) operates in most states and offers volunteer tutors a 12-hour tutor training workshop and publishes specialist ESL materials.

DIRECTORY OF TRAINING COURSES

CAMBRIDGE CERTIFICATE (CELTA) COURSES IN THE UK

ACTION ENGLISH LANGUAGE TRAINING LLP: Leeds; ✆ +44 113 244 9403; www.aelt.co.uk; full-time; rough frequency 12 per year.

ACTION ENGLISH

'After finishing my Masters degree, I was left floundering as to what I should do next for the first time in my life. It then occurred to me that English language teaching would be the perfect opportunity to share my love for the language and my experiences as a former learner. After searching online for a suitable teaching course, I contacted Action English about CELTA and decided to enrol on their full-time course. The school attracted me because of its welcoming and friendly atmosphere and the organisation of their courses. Thus began my journey through phonemics, participles (past or otherwise) and teacher-student interaction.

'At first I couldn't believe I would be teaching on the second day of the course and I was frankly terrified of facing a real class with so little experience;

however, this course provides an excellent balance between theory and practice and I was soon used to brushing up on my grammar and learning about methodology in the mornings and teaching in the afternoons.

'There is, indeed, a lot of brushing up on grammar to be done throughout the course as you do need to know it inside out when teaching. Also, you should definitely do some revising before starting your teacher training just so you don't get impossibly tangled in the different uses of the present perfect. Another essential aspect of this course was the excellent support from the instructors, who were always understanding and able to provide some constructive criticism during feedback. This is a very intensive course and it is not unusual for students to feel pressured and stressed; it is at these times that a few kind words and vast supplies of tea make the difference. Classes were always challenging and engaging and I have left the course with a new-found love of teaching.

'Since finishing the course, I have been taken on by Action English and have been giving individual classes which have varied my experience: IELTS preparation, Business English and Academic Writing. Having a CELTA Certificate has made me much more confident and capable of teaching such a large range of subjects, something which I would have found incredibly daunting before. This was an immersive and really rewarding experience and I would recommend it to anyone who is considering teaching English as it will undoubtedly give you an excellent start to your new career.'

Action English, Leeds – Ana A, April 2012

ANGLIA RUSKIN UNIVERSITY: Cambridge; ✆ +44 1223 363271; www.anglia.ac.uk.

ANGLO-CONTINENTAL TEACHER TRAINING CENTRE: Bournemouth; ✆ +44 1202 557414; www.anglo-continental.com; full and part-time; rough frequency 5 per year.

BASIL PATERSON COLLEGE: Edinburgh; ✆ +44 131 225 3802; www.basilpaterson.co.uk; full-time; rough frequency 8 per year.

BELFAST METROPOLITAN COLLEGE: Belfast; ✆ +44 28 9026 5142; www.belfastmet.ac.uk; part-time; rough frequency 2 per year.

BELL LANGUAGE SCHOOL: Cambridge; ✆ +44 1223 278804; www.bell-centres.com/celta; 3 full-time, £1150; Part-time course offered at Bedgebury, Kent.

BLACKBURN COLLEGE: Blackburn; ✆ +44 1254 292903; www.blackburn.ac.uk; part-time.

BOLTON COLLEGE: Bolton; ✆ +44 1204 907333; www.boltoncollege.ac.uk; part-time.

BRASSHOUSE CENTRE: Birmingham; ✆ +44 121 3030114; www.birmingham.gov.uk/brasshouse; part and full-time; rough frequency 1 per year.

BRITISH STUDY CENTRES: Oxford; ✆ +44 1865 246620; full-time; rough frequency 12 per year.

BROMLEY COLLEGE OF FURTHER & HIGHER EDUCATION: Bromley (Kent); ✆ +44 20 8295 7000, ext 7127; www.Bromley.ac.uk; part-time.

BROOKLANDS COLLEGE: Weybridge (Surrey); ✆ +44 1932 797774; www.brooklands.ac.uk; full and part-time; rough frequency 1 per year.

CANTERBURY CHRIST CHURCH UNIVERSITY: Canterbury; ✆ +44 1227 767700, ext 2129; www.canterbury.ac.uk; full and part-time January to May; rough frequency 1 per year. £1,225 plus moderation fee.

CARDIFF COLLEGE INTERNATIONAL: Cardiff; ✆ +44 2920 908033; www.glan-hafren.ac.uk; 1 full-time, 2 part-time per year; £1,200.

CILC (Cheltenham International Language Centre): Cheltenham (Gloucestershire); ✆ +44 1242 714092; www.glos.ac.uk/cilc; full-time; rough frequency 3 per year.

CITY COLLEGE HANDSWORTH: Birmingham; ✆ +44 121 204 0000; www.citycol.ac.uk; part-time.

CITY OF BATH COLLEGE: Bath; ✆ +44 1225 312191; www.citybathcoll.ac.uk; Full-time in summer, and part-time, £1,155.

CITY OF BRISTOL COLLEGE: Bristol; ✆ +44 117 312 5886; www.cityofbristol.ac.uk; part-time.

CONCORDE INTERNATIONAL STUDY CENTRE: Canterbury; ✆ +44 1227 451035; www.concorde-international.com; full-time; 6 per year.

EALING, HAMMERSMITH & WEST LONDON COLLEGE: London; ✆ +44 800 980 2185/2175; www.wlc.ac.uk; Full-time; 7 times a year and part-time.

EMBASSY CES NEWNHAM: Cambridge; ✆ +44 1223 345650; www.embassyces.com; Full-time; roughly 4 per year.

ENGLISH LANGUAGE HOUSE: Milton Keynes; ✆ +44 1908 694357; www.englishlanguagehouse.co.uk; full and part-time; rough frequency 5 per year.

GLOUCESTER COLLEGE: Cheltenham; ✆ +44 1242 532144; www.gloscat.ac.uk; full and part-time; rough frequency 2 per year.

GREENWICH COMMUNITY COLLEGE: London; ✆ +44 20 8316 6610; www.gcc.ac.uk; full and part-time; rough frequency 6 per year.

ILS ENGLISH: Nottingham; ✆ +44 115 969 2424; www.ilsenglish.com; full-time, £1,100.

INTENSIVE SCHOOL OF ENGLISH & BUSINESS COMMUNICATION: Brighton and Hove; ✆ +44 1273 384800; www.ise.uk.com; full and part-time; rough frequency 5 per year.

INTERNATIONAL HOUSE BELFAST: ✆ +44 28 9033 0700; www.ihbelfast.com.

INTERNATIONAL HOUSE BELFAST

Paul McMullan, Director, International House Belfast

'I moved to A Coruña in Galicia in the North West of Spain in 1997. It was relatively easy back then to organise some work teaching English privately in people's homes, however, it was obvious to me almost immediately that I had no idea whatsoever in how to teach English as a foreign language. I did however want to continue to teach and to travel so I enrolled on a CELTA with International House Barcelona and took myself across Spain to do my course.

'I met some very cool people on the course, some of whom I am still in touch with. I taught for many years in Barcelona both in schools and as a freelance teacher before training as a business analyst and project manager. I moved back to Northern Ireland in 2006 and we opened International House Belfast in 2007. We now train around 100 new teachers a year and graduates from IH Belfast CELTA courses are teaching all over the world.

'From our most recent course, after only two weeks, trainees have found teaching posts in Italy, Spain, Hong Kong, South Korea and Chile. Other recent graduates are working all across Europe, South America, the Middle East and Asia.'

Ciaran, CELTA Trainee

'I have just completed the May–June 2012 CELTA at IH Belfast. It's been a great (and intense!) experience. The tutors on the course were extremely supportive throughout.

'Their tuition in the morning input sessions was outstanding, comprising excellent in-depth tutorials on a very wide range of teaching skills. We were guided from having basic or no knowledge of the subject to feeling confident starting a career in teaching.

'The teaching practice in the afternoons gave us the chance to put what we were learning in the mornings into practice. It was great to be able to practice teaching with real students from such a wide variety of nationalities, cultures and backgrounds. When I wasn't teaching myself, it was really interesting watching my classmates teach and gave me a more objective eye on the whole experience. The feedback meeting at the end of the day was useful – the constructive criticism we received from the tutors and from our peers opened my eyes to the value of getting constructive criticism.

'I'm exhausted but very happy to have done the course. I've learnt more on my four weeks on the CELTA than I did during my four years at university!'

INTERNATIONAL HOUSE LONDON: London; ✆ +44 20 7611 2400; www.ihlondon.com; infott@ihlondon.com; full-time, part-time and online; rough frequency 11 per year.

INTERNATIONAL HOUSE LONDON

A graduate from International House London reflects upon his experience studying for a CELTA qualification:

'Studying for a qualification to teach English as a foreign language was something I had always planned to do and when I was made redundant earlier in the year I decided it was now or never. It is a long time since I was in full time education, and methods and techniques have changed a lot, so it was with some trepidation that I signed up for my course.

'Everything I read and the people I spoke to all suggested that the CELTA course was very 'full on' and hard. Having worked in a variety of sales and marketing roles in IT and then in fundraising for an international charity, I wondered just how hard could it be?

'Well, it was like trying to drink from a fire hose – there was so much information to absorb and you didn't want to spill a drop. There is a large volume of work to do throughout the four weeks, with the assignments and lesson preparation, and it certainly required some organisational skills, that I didn't know I had.

'The combination of theory followed each day by teaching practice with real students allowed you to immediately try out what you were learning and get feedback. The feedback from the tutors was invaluable, allowing us to benefit from their vast experience, but the feedback from the students' faces was immediate and a good indicator of how the lesson was going. The opportunity to observe experienced teachers also gave a good insight as to how it should be done.

'There was a real mix of people on the course and you certainly get to know each other very well in a very short space of time! International House was a great place to do a CELTA course since they have great resources and support. It felt very slick, well organised and efficient.

'Getting a CELTA qualification feels a bit like passing your driving test, you think you know how to drive, but the real learning comes when you start driving. I am looking forward to teaching and building on this experience.'

INTERNATIONAL HOUSE NEWCASTLE UPON TYNE: Newcastle; ✆ +44 191 232 9551; www.ihnewcastle.com; full-time; rough frequency 6 per year.

INTERNATIONAL HOUSE NEWCASTLE

'I took the CELTA course in March 2010 at International House Newcastle. The course was an amazing opportunity to develop solid skills in teaching English to speakers of other languages. I found it incredibly intensive, but hugely rewarding. Teaching practice sessions began on the second day – and whilst this was at first a daunting prospect (!) – each lesson I taught provided a great learning experience – tutor and peer feedback was always very useful and it really felt like all students were making visible progress with each lesson they delivered.

'The input sessions were always engaging and informative and gave invaluable insights into diverse aspects of teaching, covering everything from lesson planning, to learning styles, the role of the teacher to specific learner needs, to phonetics and alternative teaching approaches. The course tutors were really supportive but also very inspiring throughout the course. For me, this was the best learning experience I'd had in years.

'Following the completion of the course I was offered a teaching position at International House, which I am really enjoying. I still often refer to my notes from the course throughout my teaching week – looking at everything from my own self-evaluation exercises, to individual input sessions on skills, grammar lessons, etc. The course tutors also made lots of recommendations for further reading – and I have found these books really useful now that I'm teaching full-time.

'I have recently been offered a position at a language school overseas, and therefore had to give my first interview for a teaching position. Whilst some of the interview questions were challenging, I felt confident in talking about TEFL practice as I could continually draw upon my experience of the CELTA at IH Newcastle.'

Hannah Barnes, Teacher

INTO TEFL at NILE (Norwich Institute for Language Education): Norwich; ✆ +44 1603 664473; www.nile-elt.com; full-time; rough frequency 10 per year.

INTO TEFL AT NILE

Thom talks about his career in ELT, which all started with a CELTA

'I was close to finishing a degree in Renaissance History, with little idea of where to go next when a friend of a friend mentioned TEFL courses and said that he had a friend who was "living in Portugal, playing football on the beach in the days and teaching English in the evenings". It sounded pretty good to me and I followed the CELTA course (which can be taken at INTO TEFL at NILE, Norwich Institute of Language Education), followed by two years' teaching in Lisbon.

'I still had the travel bug so I returned to Britain for a year, finding work in ESOL classes at higher education colleges, and saved money to travel to Australia. During a year there, I taught in Surfer's Paradise and Sydney, and started to understand how people were making an interesting and fulfilling career from TEFL, rather than doing it as a means to an end.

'I moved to Thailand from Australia, and after a year or so working at a university, I started at the British Council, where I was encouraged to think more long-term about teaching, and did the Delta by distance learning. This modular qualification is now also offered by INTO TEFL, and is done by distance learning with online and local supervision. I did really well with this qualification, and started to become involved in more and more interesting projects, and to develop an interest in teacher training.

'It was time to leave Thailand, however, and life next took me to Santiago de Chile where my work led me to take a Master's in Language Testing, and the opportunity to develop in the area of Educational Technology. I've been working in language testing, teacher training, technology in and out of the classroom, and language teaching and learning for the last six years and these days I also have the chance to work closely with the MA and professional development students at NILE.

'Somewhere along the way I stopped playing football on the beach, but I haven't missed it as much as I would once have thought!'

Thom is now an assistant academic director at NILE, where he can put his extensive experience to full use in the delivery of their renowned CELTA courses

ITTC: Bournemouth; ✆ +44 1202 397721; www.ittc.co.uk; full-time; rough frequency 12 per year; £1,187.

ITTC

'I originally come from Canada, but came to England in 2002 and got work in an office. The monotony got to me and I searched around for a CELTA course and decided on ITTC. I'm glad I chose ITTC as the course was so practical and the tutors on the course were really good role models who tried to get the best out of everyone.

'I was lucky to be offered work at BEET/ITTC straight after the course, and I worked the whole summer for them before I went to teach overseas. I've taught in private language schools, I've set up and organised English immersion camps for teenagers where I had to design the whole course as well as produce materials, I've worked in secondary schools overseas and also trained up to be an examiner for English language examinations. So far I've spent time in Switzerland, Italy and Colombia, and I come back to England regularly to work on summer programmes.

'Having the CELTA has given me an opportunity to use my brain more than I ever did working in an office. I love working with people from different cultures, and it has also allowed me to learn other languages more easily. I still don't like being asked to teach areas I haven't been trained for and I'm not much of a disciplinarian – but this hasn't really been a problem, as my students always seem so motivated.'

Lisa D – a not-so-average CELTA candidate wrote this while in Bournemouth, but who knows where she is now!

LANGUAGE LINK TRAINING: London; ✆ +44 20 3214 8250; www.languagelink.co.uk; 6 full and 1 part-time; £1,100.

LANGUAGE LINK

What is it really like to teach abroad? We decided to ask one of our Language Link teachers, Brad Kishel from America, about his experiences teaching in China.

'It's fairly accurate to say that many Americans don't really get the education about the outside world that those in Europe or other countries may get. Impressions of other cultures tend to come from movies and T.V. and stereotypes for us. However, as a kid, I knew I wanted to go out and explore and try to be another Indiana Jones.

'After graduating from university and teaching for two years in Japan, I still wasn't really sure about what I wanted to do with my life. However, I knew I still wanted to see more of the world. I had a sudden curiosity about Chinese culture and wanted to check it out. I took a chance, found a job, and just jumped right in. When I arrived in China, I knew nothing about it and couldn't speak a word of Chinese. I lived in the northeast of China and worked at a number of different public schools. Eventually, I grew to dislike the conditions in this part of China and moved to Beijing.

'Looking back at my experience, I've learned a lot about developing countries and plenty about myself and what I want to do with my life. I've even managed to become quite good at Chinese without ever having really studied it. Overall, life has been both challenging and incredibly fun.

'With the cost of living quite low, I've managed to have a decent salary, nice duplex apartment, and still have been able to travel and see places that I've never seen before. It is 100% true that an average teacher is able to save a fair amount of money and still have a fairly good lifestyle here. There are companies or schools that will even help pay for your housing or give you housing for free. I've been here for 8 years now, and while there may have been bumps in the road, I wouldn't take back my decision to come here for all the tea in China, and there's A LOT of tea.

'For anyone who is interested in checking out what is arguably the fastest developing country in the modern world or for anyone who wants to learn a new language or more about themselves, China is definitely a good choice. You may end up never wanting to leave. I'm here and I still can't pull myself away yet.'

LTC ENGLISH ACADEMY: Hove (East Sussex); ✆ +44 1273 735975; www.ltc-brighton.com; full-time; rough frequency 5 per year.

MANCHESTER ACADEMY TEACHER TRAINING (UK) LTD: Manchester; ✆ +44 161 2375619; www.manacad.co.uk; full and part-time; rough frequency 11 per year.

NEWCASTLE COLLEGE: Newcastle; ✆ +44 191 200 4467; www.ncl-coll.ac.uk; part-time.

NEW COLLEGE NOTTINGHAM: Nottingham; ✆ +44 115 910 4595; www.ncn.ac.uk; part-time. Also offers PTLLS (Preparing to Teach in the Lifelong Learning Sector).

NEW COLLEGE NOTTINGHAM

CELTA kick-starts Craig's career

A CELTA qualification can really improve your skills and increase your chances of employment, as **Craig** found out when he completed the intensive Cambridge CELTA/PTLLS course at New College Nottingham.

'I had taught conversational English classes in schools and businesses in Japan, but enrolled at New College Nottingham because I realised the need to gain a recognised qualification to build my TEFL career.

'It was the best move I have ever made. The course has brought so much to both my teaching and my career; I have learned how to plan and organise lessons, teaching techniques and methodologies, and have had the opportunity to observe experienced teachers in the classroom. I still use many of the techniques I learnt at college.

'Upon returning to Japan I felt energised and my teaching was much more effective. Teaching became enjoyable again.

'For anyone thinking about a career in TEFL/TESOL I cannot recommend the course at New College Nottingham more highly.'

For an information pack and application form call New College Nottingham on 0115 910 4595, email rose.underwood@ncn.ac.uk, or visit www.ncn.ac.uk.

OXFORD AND CHERWELL VALLEY COLLEGE: Oxford; ✆ +44 1865 551828; www.ocvc.ac.uk/about-teacher-training; part and full-time; rough frequency 4 per year.

OXFORD HOUSE COLLEGE: London; ✆ +44 20 7580 9785; www.oxfordhousecollege.co.uk; part and full-time; rough frequency 12 per year.

RANDOLPH SCHOOL OF ENGLISH: Edinburgh; ✆ +44 131 226 5004; www.randolph.org.uk; part and full-time; rough frequency 9 per year.

READING OPEN CENTRE: English Language & Teacher Training Centre, Reading (Berkshire); ✆ +44 118 9391833; www.efl-reading.co.uk; semi-intensive; rough frequency 3 per year.

ST GILES BRIGHTON: Brighton; ✆ +44 1273 682747; www.stgiles-international.com; full-time; rough frequency 10 per year.

ST GILES INTERNATIONAL LONDON HIGHGATE: London; ✆ +44 20 8340 0828; www.stgiles-international.com/teacher-training; full-time; rough frequency 10 per year.

SAXONCOURT TEACHER TRAINING: London; ✆ +44 20 7499 8533; www.saxoncourt.com; full and part-time; rough frequency 12 per year.

SKOLA TEACHER TRAINING: London; ✆ +44 20 7287 3126; www.skola.co.uk; part-time; 3 times a year, £999.

SOLIHULL COLLEGE: Solihull; ✆ +44 121 6787277; www.solihull.ac.uk; part-time.

SOUTH THAMES COLLEGE: London SW18; ✆ +44 20 8918 7366; www.south-thames.ac.uk; part-time.

STANTON TEACHER TRAINING: London; ✆ +44 20 7221 7259; www.stanton-school.co.uk; full-time; rough frequency 12 per year.

STEVENSON COLLEGE: Edinburgh; ✆ +44 131 535 4600; www.stevenson.ac.uk; part-time.

STOKE-ON-TRENT COLLEGE: Stoke-on-Trent; ✆ +44 1782 603637; www.stokecoll.ac.uk; full-time; rough frequency 1 per year.

STUDIO SCHOOL: Cambridge; ✆ +44 1223 369701; www.studiocambridge.co.uk; full-time; rough frequency 2 per year.

SUSSEX DOWNS COLLEGE: Eastbourne; ✆ +44 1323 637232/08452 601608; www.sussexdowns.ac.uk; intensive course offered over 22 days in the summer; also part-time, £947.

TORBAY LANGUAGE CENTRE: Devon; ✆ +44 1803 558555; www.lalschools.com/torbay; full-time; rough frequency 5 per year; £1,100.

UNIVERSITY OF GLASGOW, EFL Unit: Glasgow; ✆ +44 141 330 6521; www.gla.ac.uk/efl.

UNIVERSITY OF SHEFFIELD, ENGLISH LANGUAGE TEACHING CENTRE: Sheffield; ✆ +44 114 222 1799; www.sheffield.ac.uk/eltc.

WALTHAM FOREST COLLEGE: London; ✆ +44 20 8501 8091; www.waltham.ac.uk; part-time.

WESTMINSTER KINGSWAY COLLEGE: London SW1; ✆ +44 20 7802 8813; www.westking.ac.uk; full-time; rough frequency 1 per year.

CAMBRIDGE CERTIFICATE (CELTA) COURSES ABROAD

The following centres, listed alphabetically by country, offer the Cambridge Certificate in English Language Teaching to Adults.

AUSTRALIA

AUSTRALIAN TESOL TRAINING CENTRE (ATTC): Sydney; ✆ +61 2 8252 2821; www.attc.edu.au; full and part-time; rough frequency 12 per year; also offered at ATTC Brisbane.

CURTIN UNIVERSITY: Perth; ✆ +61 8 9266 4224; www.celta.curtin.edu.au; full-time; rough frequency 2 per year.

HOLMESGLEN LANGUAGE CENTRE: Chadstone (Victoria); ✆ +61 3 9564 1819; www.holmesglen.vic. edu.au; full and part-time; rough frequency 4 per year.

HOLMES INSTITUTE TEACHER TRAINING: Melbourne; ✆ +61 3 9662 2055; www.holmes.edu.au; full-time; rough frequency 6 per year.

INSEARCH UNIVERSITY OF TECHNOLOGY, SYDNEY (UTS): Sydney; ✆ +61 2 9218 8646; www. insearch.edu.au/courses/celta; full and part-time; rough frequency 4 per year.

INSTITUTE OF CONTINUING & TESOL EDUCATION (ICTE): Brisbane; ✆ +61 7 3346 6770; www.icte.uq. edu.au; full and part-time; rough frequency 4 per year.

INTERNATIONAL HOUSE SYDNEY: Sydney; ✆ +61 2 9279 0733; www.training.ihsydney.com; 4 full-time courses per year, 3 part-time; A$2,700 plus $250 Cambridge assessment fee.

KAPLAN INTERNATIONAL COLLEGE: Cairns; ✆ +61 7 4031 3466; www.kaplaninternational.com; full-time; 3 times per year; A$2,750.

LA TROBE UNIVERSITY LANGUAGE CENTRE: Melbourne; ✆ +61 3 9479 1722; www.latrobe.edu.au; full-time; rough frequency 6 per year.

MILNER INTERNATIONAL COLLEGE OF ENGLISH: Perth; ✆ +61 8 9325 5444; www.milner.wa.edu.au/CELTA; full and part-time; rough frequency 6 per year.

PHOENIX ENGLISH LANGUAGE ACADEMY: Perth; ✆ +61 8 9227 5538; www.phoenixela.com.au; 4 full-time; (130 hours), 3 part-time per year. A$2,900.

RMIT ENGLISH WORLDWIDE: Melbourne; ✆ +61 3 9657 5876; www.rmitenglishworldwide.com; full and part-time; rough frequency 3 per year.

SOUTH AUSTRALIAN COLLEGE OF ENGLISH (SACE Adelaide): Adelaide; ✆ +61 8 8410 5222; www.sacecoll.sa.edu.au; full-time; rough frequency 4 per year.

TASMANIAN COLLEGE OF ENGLISH (SACE Hobart and SACE Whitsunday): Tasmania; ✆ +61 3 6231 9911; www.tas.sace.com.au; full-time; rough frequency 4 per year.

UNIVERSITY OF TASMANIA ENGLISH LANGUAGE CENTRE: Hobart; ✆ +61 3 6226 2590; www.international.utas.edu.au; once a year full-time and part-time; A$2,500.

AUSTRIA

BFI VIENNA: Vienna; ✆ +43 1 811 78 10152; www.bfi.at/english/courses/celta; full-time 2 per year.

BANGLADESH

BRITISH COUNCIL BANGLADESH: Dhaka; ✆ +880 2 911 6171/6145; www.britishcouncil.org/bangladesh; full-time; rough frequency 1 per year.

BRAZIL

BRITANNIA INTERNATIONAL ENGLISH: Ipanema, Rio de Janeiro; ✆ +55 21 2511 0940; www.britannia.com.br; full-time and part-time; R$3,816 (£1,425).

S B C I RIO DE JANEIRO: Rio de Janeiro; ✆ +55 21 2528 1104; www.culturainglesa.net; full-time.

SEVEN ENGLISH: Sao Paulo; ✆ +55 2533 36111; www.sevenidiomas.com.br; full-time and part-time both twice a year; R$2,420 (US$1,320) plus US$160 Cambridge fee.

SOCIEDADE BRASILEIRA DE CULTURA INGLESA: Recife; ✆ +55 81 3228 6649; www.culturainglesa.com.br; full-time; rough frequency 1 per year; also offered in Rio, Tambauzinho and Mirrasol.

UP LANGUAGE CONSULTANTS: Terreo; ✆ +55 11 5105 0200; www.uplanguage.com.br; full-time.

BULGARIA

AVO-BELL SCHOOL OF ENGLISH: Sofia; ✆ +359 2 944 032; www.teflcertificates-avo.com; full-time; rough frequency 5 per year. £989 for course only, £1,239 including self-catering accommodation.

CANADA

GLOBAL VILLAGE: Calgary; ✆ +1 403 543 7300; www.celtacalgary.ca; full-time 3 times a year, part-time offered twice a year; C$2,500.

GLOBAL VILLAGE: Vancouver; ✆ +1 604 684 1010; www.gvenglish.com; part and full-time; rough frequency 6 per year.

INTERNATIONAL HOUSE SOL GROUP: Toronto; ✆ +1 416 322 3405; www.sol-group.net; 3 part-time courses offered per year, C$2,500.

INTERNATIONAL LANGUAGE INSTITUTE: Halifax; ✆ +1 902 429 3636; teach@ili.ca; www.celta.ca; full-time monthly; C$2,300.

INTERNATIONAL LANGUAGE SCHOOLS OF CANADA – MONTREAL: Montreal; ✆ +1 514 876 4572; www.celta.ilsc.ca; full-time; rough frequency 6 per year.

LANGUAGE STUDIES CANADA: Toronto; ✆ +1 416 488 2200; www.lsc-canada.com; full-time; rough frequency 9 per year.

CHINA

INTENSIVE SCHOOL OF ENGLISH: Wuhan; see entry for ISE in listings of CELTA courses in the UK.

LANGUAGE LINK CHINA TRADE CENTER: Beijing; ✆ +86 10 5169 5591/92/93; www.languagelink.com.cn; full-time; rough frequency 8 per year.

SYDNEY INSTITUTE OF LANGUAGE AND COMMERCE (SILC): Shanghai; ✆ +86 21 6998 0003; www.insearch.edu.au/international./silc; course is run once a year in August by Insearch in Sydney (entry above).

COLOMBIA

BRITISH COUNCIL BOGOTÁ: Bogotá; ✆ +57 1 325 9090; www.britishcouncil.org/colombia; full-time; rough frequency 5 per year.

INTERNATIONAL HOUSE BOGOTÁ: Bogotá; ✆ +57 1 336 4747; www.ihbogota.com; full-time twice a year; $1,500.

COSTA RICA

INSTITUTO BRITANICO: San José; ✆ +506 283 7059 ext 110; www.institutobritanico.co.cr; full-time; rough frequency 3 per year.

CZECH REPUBLIC

AKCENT INTERNATIONAL HOUSE: Prague; ✆ +420 261109; www.akcent.cz; full and part-time; rough frequency 10 per year; also offered in Bratislava from time to time.

MASARYK UNIVERSITY: Brno; ✆ +420 549 497785; part-time.

ECUADOR

SOUTHERN CROSS TEACHER TRAINING CENTREL: Guayaquil; ✆ +593 42 6844 04; www.celtaecuador.com; 7 times a year a beachside eco-resort; $2.250 all-inclusive.

EGYPT

BRITISH COUNCIL: Cairo; ✆ +20 2 300 1666; www.britishcouncil.org/egypt; full-time; frequency 4 per year; 10,000 Egyptian pounds ($1,750/£1,200).

FRANCE

ILC FRANCE (INTERNATIONAL LANGUAGE CENTRE): Paris; ✆ +33 1 44 41 80 20; www.ilcfrance.com; full-time; rough frequency 9 per year. Also offered part time. Distance DELTA studies can be supported.

POLE FORMATION CCI-CIEL DE STRASBOURG: Strasbourg; ✆ +33 6 37 43 33 35; www.esolstrasbourg.com; 4 times a year full-time; €1,450.

ILC FRANCE-IH PARIS

Lynsey Hodkinson from Perth (UK), Michael Gleeson from Christchurch (New Zealand) and Eleanor Hickey from Leeds (UK) did the CELTA course at ILC France-IH Paris, and now work at the school.

Why did you want to do the CELTA course?

Lynsey: The CELTA offered a well-rounded introduction to teaching English and the possibility to travel and work. The intensive element gave me confidence that can't be obtained through part-time or distance learning.

Michael: I had just left a career in the army in New Zealand and saw the CELTA as an opportunity for a new way of life in France.

Eleanor: I had some hands-on experience as an assistant teaching English to teenagers in France. I enjoyed it, but felt training was essential if I was to teach well.

Why did you choose to do the course at ILC France-IH Paris?

Lynsey: ILC France-IH Paris was my first choice; I wanted to teach abroad. Doing the course outside your own country shows prospective employers you can operate in a new environment.

Michael: I had heard of International House and felt confident that the course would be well run. The centre was situated in the heart of Paris too.

Eleanor: A friend had trained at ILC France-IH Paris and recommended it. I knew it would be challenging, but rewarding.

How did you benefit from the course?

Lynsey: I gained confidence, awareness and understanding of the English language and learnt different teaching methods.

Michael: The tutors had lots of experience to share and the course structure, with morning seminars and afternoon teaching practice, really helped learning.

Eleanor: I especially liked feedback immediately after teaching practice. It allowed all the trainees to develop their skills.

Who would you recommend to do the CELTA course?

Lynsey: I recommend the course to individuals who are thinking about travelling or relocating to another country, considering a career change or a new challenge.

Michael: I liked the fact that there were people from different backgrounds on the course, all really keen to learn and teach.

Eleanor: People who are genuinely interested in teaching and who recognise that it's a full-time job.

GERMANY

BERLIN SCHOOL OF ENGLISH: Berlin; ✆ +49 30 229 0456; www.berlin.school-of-english.de; 8 full-time per year and two part-time; €1,500.

HAMBURG SCHOOL OF ENGLISH: Hamburg; ✆ +49 40 480 21 19; www.hamburg.school-of-english.de; full and part-time 7 per year; €1,500.

MUNCHNER VOLKSHOCHSCHULE: Harthausen, Munich; ✆ +49 8106 300631; www.mvhs.de; full and part-time; rough frequency 2 per year; €1,550.

GREECE

CELT: Athens; ✆ +30 210 330 2406; www.celt.edu.gr; €1,450; also offers its own certificate course.

STUDY SPACE: Thessaloniki; ✆ +302310 269697; www.studyspace.gr.

HUNGARY

INTERNATIONAL HOUSE: Budapest; ✆ +36 1 345 7046; www.ih.hu; full and part-time; 8 full-time, 2 part-time per year; £749–£849.

INDIA

THE BRITISH COUNCIL ENGLISH LANGUAGE TEACHING CENTRE: New Delhi; ✆ +91 11 4219 9000; www.britishcouncil.org/india; full-time 6 times a year, including those offered in Mumbai and Chennai; Rs105,000 (£1,550).

INDONESIA

THE BRITISH INSTITUTE (TBI): Jakarta; ✆ +62 21 300 27988; www.tbi.co.id; full and part-time; rough frequency 2 per year.

IRELAND

INTERNATIONAL HOUSE: Dublin; ✆ +353 1 4759011/1 4759013; www.ihdublin.com; 9 full-time and 1 part-time course; €1,610 full-time, €1,695 part-time.

UNIVERSITY COLLEGE CORK, Language Centre: Cork; ✆ +353 21 490 2043/490 3883; www.ucc.ie/Esol; part-time and one intensive course in August; €1,680.

ITALY

BRITISH COUNCIL: Milan; ✆ +39 0 2 772 22242; www.britishcouncil.it.

BRITISH COUNCIL: Naples; ✆ +39 0 81 578 82 47; www.britishcouncil.it; full-time; rough frequency 1 per year.

THE CAMBRIDGE SCHOOL: Verona; ✆ +39 045 800 3154; www.cambridgeschool.it; full and part-time; rough frequency 2 per year.

INTERNATIONAL HOUSE: Milan; ✆ +39 02 527 9124; www.ihmilano.it; full and part-time; rough frequency 2 per year.

INTERNATIONAL HOUSE PALERMO: Palermo; ✆ +39 091 584954; www.ihpalermo.it; full and part-time; rough frequency 1 per year.

INTERNATIONAL HOUSE ROME/ACCADEMIA BRITANNICA: Rome; ✆ +39 06 704 76 894; www.ihromamz.it; full-time and semi-intensive 8 per year. Also run 1 intensive CELTYL course per year, 1 of each DELTA module, and BET, 1-2-1 and TKT courses.

TEACHERTRAINING: Milan; ✆ +39 328 887 3365; www.teachertraining.it; full and part-time; rough frequency 5 per year.

INTERNATIONAL HOUSE ROME

Some testimonials of graduates from the International House Rome:

'I am completely satisfied with the course and especially the course tutors. Their professionalism and expertise are admirable. The content of the seminars was incredibly educational and interesting. I have been given the tools for further self-improvement and I have been given the opportunity to improve my teaching skills. I have got what I hoped for! Thank you all for your effort!' **Rachel B.**

'These have been the most constructive and satisfying weeks of my professional life.' **Luke T.**

'It was challenging, fruitful and inspiring. I learned a completely new perspective on teaching and the structure of the course was absolutely perfect to make me achieve all that, especially the fact that we were immersed in teaching practice (mine or of my colleagues) every single day!' **Lisa E.**

'The course was far more difficult at the start than I'd expected, but it gradually became easier to follow. I thank my tutors Ian, Elizabeth and Deborah for having put all their effort to back me up through such a complex and energy consuming practice of teaching (learning how to teach), and I must say each did brilliantly, helping me to develop my teaching skills from quite different yet complementary points of view. Especial thanks to Deborah, who kept on encouraging us all, I must say, despite all our flaws and repeated difficulties, till the bitter end! It's been great to get to know lovely people throughout this singular experience.' **H. Shariat**

'I really enjoyed the course, although it was intense and sometimes stressful. I feel the support from the trainers was great, they were very encouraging and provided very constructive feedback. They also acted as good role models in terms of their attitudes and teaching styles. Thank you!' **Sarah F.**

'It was really what I was looking for. It was very concrete, and I learnt about many useful teaching methodologies I hadn't known before. The tutors were fantastic, especially responding to the students' needs. It will certainly be one of the best points in my curriculum.' **Matthew H.**

'The course was worth every penny, and I would recommend this specific language school to anyone else interested in taking a CELTA course. Thanks for the experience!' **Daniel B.**

JAPAN

LANGUAGE RESOURCES: Kobe; ✆ +81 78 382 0394; www.languageresources.org; part-time.

KOREA

THE BRITISH COUNCIL: Seoul; ✆ +82 2 3702 0646; www.britishcouncil.org/korea.htm; full-time; rough frequency 2 per year; 2,500,000 won (£1,375/$2,000).

LEBANON

ALLC INTERNATIONAL HOUSE BEIRUT: Beirut; ✆ +961 1 500 978; www.allcs.edu.lb; full-time; rough frequency 2 per year in the summer; $1,600.

MALAYSIA

THE BRITISH COUNCIL LANGUAGE CENTRE: Kuala Lumpur; ✆ +60 3 2723 7900; www.britishcouncil.org/malaysia; part-time over 20 weeks (every Sunday) or 10 weeks (Tuesdays and Thursdays); 8,000 ringgits (£1,660).

MALTA

NSTS ENGLISH LANGUAGE INSTITUTE: Valletta; ✆ +356 2558 8500; www.nsts.org; full-time; rough frequency 2 per year.

MOROCCO

BRITISH COUNCIL CASABLANCA: Casablanca; ✆ +212 22 520990; www.britishcouncil.org/morocco-english-teach-celta.htm; full-time; rough frequency 1 per year; 2,100 dirhams (£1,570).

THE NETHERLANDS

BRITISH LANGUAGE TRAINING CENTRE: Amsterdam; ✆ +31 20 622 3634; www.bltc.nl; full and part-time; rough frequency 1 per year.
BRITISH SCHOOL NETHERLANDS: Den Haag; ✆ +31 70 315 40 80; www.britishschool.nl.

NEW ZEALAND

ASPECT EDUCATION: Christchurch; ✆ +64 3 379 5452; www.kaplanaspect.com; full-time: rough frequency 2 per year.
AUCKLAND LANGUAGE CENTRE: Auckland; ✆ +64 9 303 1962; www.learnenglish.co.nz; full-time; rough frequency 4 per year.
CHRISTCHURCH COLLEGE OF ENGLISH: Christchurch; ✆ +64 3 343 3790; www.ccel.co.nz; full-time; rough frequency 5 per year.
CHRISTCHURCH POLYTECHNIC INSTITUTE OF TECHNOLOGY: Christchurch; ✆ +64 3 940 8296; www.cpit.ac.nz; part-time.
LANGUAGES INTERNATIONAL: Auckland; ✆ +64 9 309 0615; www.languages.ac.nz; full-time; rough frequency 6 per year.
ROTORUA ENGLISH LANGUAGE ACADEMY: Rotorua; ✆ +64 7 349 0473; www.rela.co.nz; full-time; rough frequency 2 per year.
UNIVERSITY OF WAIKATO LANGUAGE INSTITUTE: Hamilton; ✆ +64 7 858 5600; www.waikato.ac.nz; full-time; rough frequency 4 per year.

OMAN

BRITISH COUNCIL OMAN: Qaboos; ✆ +968 2468 1000; www.britishcouncil.org/me-oman.
CALEDONIAN COLLEGE OF ENGINEERING: Seeb; ✆ +968 2453 6165 ext 376; www.cce.edu.om; full-time; rough frequency 2 per year.

POLAND

BRITISH COUNCIL KRAKOW: Krakow; ✆ +48 12 428 5936; www.britishcouncil.org/poland-celta-krakow.htm.

ELS-BELL SCHOOL OF ENGLISH: Warsaw; ✆ +48 22 621 3836; www.bellschools.pl; 2 full-time in summer and 2 part-time; 4,900 zloty (£990).

INTERNATIONAL HOUSE INTEGRA: Katowice; ✆ +48 32 259 99 97; www.ih.com.pl.

INTERNATIONAL HOUSE WROCLAW: Wroclaw; ✆ +48 71 78 17 290; www.ttcentre.ih.com.pl; full-time; rough frequency 3 per year.

PORTUGAL

INTERNATIONAL HOUSE LISBON: Lisbon; ✆ +351 21 315 1493/4/6; www.ihlisbon.com; full and part-time; rough frequency 10 per year.

INTERNATIONAL HOUSE LISBON

'Taking the CELTA course at IH Lisbon has been a life-changing experience. It is, without a doubt, an incredibly intense course, but ultimately, very rewarding. No sooner have you observed a veteran teacher in the classroom, than you are teaching your first class. The tutors, however, provide you with all the advice, support and encouragement you need to get through those first few nerve-wracking lessons. Feedback is constant, fair and endlessly helpful. In addition, all the reference materials you could possibly need are either located in the school library, or accessible from the computer room. IH Lisbon provided me with the solid foundations on which to start my teaching career, and I would highly recommend the school to anyone wishing to undertake the CELTA certificate.'

Louise Marques

RUSSIA

BKC-INTERNATIONAL HOUSE MOSCOW: Moscow; www.bkcih-moscow.com; full-time; rough frequency 7 per year; £995.

SINGAPORE

THE BRITISH COUNCIL SINGAPORE: Napier Road; ✆ +65 64721010; www.britishcouncil.org/singapore; part-time.

SOUTH AFRICA

GOOD HOPE STUDIES: Cape Town; ✆ +27 21 683 1399; www.ghs.co.za; full-time; rough frequency 5 per year. 12,200 Rand.

INTERNATIONAL HOUSE JOHANNESBURG: Johannesburg; ✆ +27 11 339 1051; www.ihjohannesburg.co.za; full-time; rough frequency 6 per year.

CAMBRIDGE SCHOOL: Barcelona; ✆ +34 93 870 2001; www.cambridgeschool.com; full-time; rough frequency 6 per year.
CAMPBELL COLLEGE: Valencia; ✆ +34 96 362 8983; www.campbellcollege.com.

CAMPBELL COLLEGE VALENCIA

Before the course

'I thought the application procedure at Campbell College was very efficient. Some of the language tasks were challenging but it gave me a very clear idea of what to expect. It helped me focus on what I really needed to learn before starting the course. I was also provided with useful material to help me prepare for the course as well as a useful supplementary booklist. All in all, I think I was extremely well prepared for the course.' *David, UK*

On the course

'Teaching practice was the most interesting yet challenging area of the course. Here, I feel I was given excellent guidance and support from tutors throughout the course at both elementary and upper-intermediate levels. Once I had finished my teaching practice session, I particularly enjoyed reading tutor's appraisals of my lessons. Without doubt, I learnt a lot from these and they certainly helped me plan future lessons.

'My mid-course tutorial really helped me evaluate my progress on the course and put things into perspective; it focussed on key areas and ways to help me improve further.

By the end of the course at Campbell College my teaching was a lot more effective, my lessons were well-structured with a clear purpose and suitable learning objectives.' *Verónique, Belgium*

After the course

'The whole experience was really brilliant. I really loved the course and have learnt so much – I didn't think it was possible to take so much on board in just 4 weeks. Now I feel really confident that I can plan my lessons on my own and teach EFL anywhere in the world. I believe in fact that I can do quite a good job too! I was extremely impressed with both centre and the tutors. Moreover, I feel everything I have learnt at Campbell College in Valencia will be invaluable for my future teaching career.' *Abby, Canada*

CLIC INTERNATIONAL HOUSE SEVILLE

Emily Turner is a graduate of CLIC International House Seville

'When I arrived at CLIC International House Seville on the first day of the CELTA course, I was painfully aware of the weight of the decision that I had made; I had willingly given up a secure job in the middle of a recession to pursue a career in EFL teaching. My former colleagues thought that I was mad!

'Now my only regret is that I didn't take the leap earlier! I have a job that I love which is both challenging and rewarding and gives you the opportunity to travel all around the world... although why anyone would ever want to leave Seville is beyond me!

'I will always remember the first day of the CELTA course as the day that my new life began. All my nerves evaporated after the warm welcome that I received from the staff at CLIC International House Seville and I soon felt at home. The most memorable part of that day was watching our tutors teach a lesson, observing them filled me with the determination to study hard and to one day teach as inspirationally as them.

'And study hard I did! The CELTA course is demanding, after all you only have a few weeks to be moulded into the teachers of tomorrow. It is testament to the quality of the course that after a month I felt filled with the confidence to teach an engaging, informative lesson to students of any age and ability.

'This intensive nature of the CELTA means that it is a bond for life! My classmates and I became a family; we were all there to offer encouragement as each of us took our turn to stand in front of a class and teach for the first time. Although now we are scattered all over the world we all stay in touch and are planning a reunion.

'Equally, my tutors have remained important in my life and two months after the course has ended, they are regularly in contact, tracking my progress and continuing to offer support and advice.

'Now to my great delight, I work for CLIC IH and I couldn't be happier. CLIC International House Seville isn't just a language school it's a community of people that have made a commitment to learning and development. It is a lively place to study and work and is bursting with interesting people and ideas. Just ask anyone in Seville and they will tell you themselves.'

CLIC INTERNATIONAL HOUSE: Seville; ✆ +34 95 450 0316; www.tefl.es; full-time; rough frequency 12 per year; €1,490 plus €520 for 4 weeks' accommodation.

HYLAND LANGUAGE CENTRE: Madrid; ✆ +34 91 431 9757; www.hylandmadrid.com; 3 full-time (June, July and September) and part-time from January; €1,500.

INSTITUTO DE IDIOMAS: Santiago; ✆ +34 981 563 100; www.usc.es; full-time; rough frequency 2 per year.

INTERNATIONAL HOUSE BARCELONA: Barcelona; ✆ +34 93 268 3304; www.ihes.com/bcn; full and part-time; rough frequency 10 per year.

INTERNATIONAL HOUSE MADRID: Madrid; ✆ +34 91 319 7224 or 90 214 1517; www.ihmadridtraining.com/allaboutcelta; full and part-time; rough frequency 7 per year; €1,580.

INTERNATIONAL HOUSE MADRID

'Not being a native speaker of English, I had certain reservations and wondered how I would fit in with the others on the course. But my nerves disappeared after the first day's teaching practice when the tutor assured me that not only was my level of English good enough, I had a very important strength; my knowledge of Spanish students' problems in learning English – both the grammar and their difficulty with pronunciation.

'The training was pitched at just the right level and the support that both tutors gave me helped build my confidence to learn about teaching and enjoy it! The tutors never used the word 'weaknesses', they only spoke about more effective teaching. I thoroughly enjoyed the teaching practice and learned so much by watching others that I actually looked forward to feedback because I knew I would have something positive to say about my colleagues and whatever they had to say about my lessons it would only help me improve.

'IH Madrid's CELTA centre is right in the heart of the city and each classroom of the newly designed CELTA wing of this impressive three-storey building has video projector, WIFI and state-of-the-art equipment which allowed audio to be played straight from my mobile phone. Madrid can be hot in the summer so I was so glad they had air conditioning and a great library to do a bit of quiet studying in the evening before heading to a terraza for a cool drink.

'Everyone told me it was going to be intensive and it was. But I'm still amazed at how much I learnt in just four weeks. By the end of the course I really felt prepared to go into class, which was essential because I wanted to start work straight after the course.

'I suppose I could sum up my CELTA like this. I learnt that with the right support and training from people who know their business inside out, you can achieve anything. I arrived a trainee, made some great friends and left ready to start my own classes. No more feedback, no more support, just me – an English teacher!'

Violeta, Albacete.

INTERNATIONAL HOUSE PALMA: Palma; ✆ +34 971 726408; www.ihes.com/pal; full-time; rough frequency 7 per year.

LEWIS SCHOOL OF LANGUAGES: Barcelona; ✆ +34 93 411 1333; www.tesol-spain.com; full-time; rough frequency 8 per year.

UNIVERSITY OF SANTIAGO DE COMPOSTELO: La Coruna; ✆ +34 981 563100 ext. 16599; www.usc. es/ full-time July and September; €1,400.

SWITZERLAND

BELL SWITZERLAND: Geneva; ✆ +41 22 749 16 16; www.bell-school.ch; full and part-time; rough frequency 1 per year.

FLYING TEACHERS: Zurich; ✆ +41 44 1 350 3344; www.flyingteachers.biz; full-time; rough frequency 4 per year; SFr3,950 (£2,350).

TLC, THE LANGUAGE COMPANY: Baden; ✆ +41 56 205 51 78; www.tlcsprachschule.ch; 1 full-time over 5 weeks and 2 part-time courses over 12 weeks, starting January and September. Also offering CELTA Online; SFr4,200.

THAILAND

ECC (THAILAND): Bangkok; ✆ +66 2 655 1236; www.eccthai.com; full-time; rough frequency 8 per year; $1,600; also offered in Phuket and Chiang Mai.

INTERNATIONAL HOUSE BANGKOK: Bangkok; ✆ +66 2 632679; www.ihbangkok.com; also offered in Chiang Mai.

TURKEY

BILKENT UNIVERSITY: Ankara; ✆ +90 312 290 1912; www.bilkent.edu.tr/~busel; part-time.

BRITISH SIDE: Istanbul; ✆ +90 212 327 9403; www.britishside.com; 2 full-time in summer, 1 part-time in autumn; 2,300 Turkish lira (£1,000).

INTERNATIONAL TRAINING INSTITUTE: Levent, Istanbul; ✆ +90 212 283 6466 or 26; www.iti-istanbul.com; full and part-time; rough frequency 5 per year.

IZMIR UNIVERSITY OF ECONOMICS: Izmir; ✆ +90 232 279 2525; www.ieu.edu.tr; full-time; rough frequency 1 per year.

UKRAINE

BRITISH COUNCIL KIEV: Kiev; ✆ +380 44 490 5600/99 792 2832; www.britishcouncil.org/ukraine; full-time in July (plus August course in Odessa); 10,000 hryvnia (£850).

INTERNATIONAL HOUSE KYIV: Kiev; ✆ +380 44 238 9870; www.ih.kiev.ua; full-time; rough frequency 3 per year.

UNITED ARAB EMIRATES

THE BRITISH COUNCIL, ABU DHABI: Abu Dhabi; ✆ +971 2 691 0600; www.britishcouncil.org/me; full and part-time, 1 per year; also in Sharjah and Dubai.

HIGHER COLLEGES OF TECHNOLOGY: Many locations; ✆ +971 2 681 2070; www.hct.ac.ae.

INTERNATIONAL HOUSE DUBAI: Dubai; ✆ +971 4 321 3121; www.ihdubai.com.

UNIVERSITY OF WOLLONGONG: Dubai; ✆ +971 4 395 4422; www.uowdubai.ac.ae; full and part-time; rough frequency 1 per year.

USA

CY-FAIR COLLEGE: Cypress; ✆ +1 832 482 1024; www.lonestar.edu/celta; full and part-time; rough frequency 3 per year.

DENVER BRIDGE TEFL: Denver; ✆ +1 303 777 7783 ext 862; www.bridgetefl.com; full-time; rough frequency 6 per year.

INTERCULTURAL COMMUNICATIONS COLLEGE: Honolulu; ✆ +1 808 946 2445; www.icchawaii.edu; full-time; rough frequency 3 per year.

ST GILES INTERNATIONAL: San Francisco; ✆ +1 415 788 3552; www.stgiles-usa.com; full-time; rough frequency 8 per year.

TEACHING HOUSE BOSTON: Boston; ✆ +1 617 963 0215; www.teachinghouse.com; full and part-time; rough frequency: 8 full-time courses per year and 2 part-time courses per year.

TEACHING HOUSE MIAMI: Miami; ✆ +1 305 508 4904; www.teachinghouse.com; full-time; rough frequency 2 per year.

TEACHING HOUSE NEW YORK: New York; ✆ +1 212 732 0277; www.teachinghouse.com and www.thnewyork.com; full and part-time; rough frequency 28 per year.

TEACHING HOUSE

Opening doors to opportunities

Caolan, a Cambridge CELTA graduate from Teaching House, reflects on her experience teaching in Vietnam:

'Index finger outstretched, breath held, continents and bodies of water flashing before my eyes, fast at first then slower, as the outlines of countries became clearer, the oceans became visible. Slower still, as the spinning sphere began to reveal the names of places I'd learned long ago. Losing its momentum, the globe breathed one final breath, jerking to a stop, leaving the tip of my index finger trembling above the spot where I would spend the next year and a half of my life: Vietnam. I closed my eyes, submitted my resume, completed a phone interview, accepted their offer, bought a one-way ticket, packed up my life into two small suitcases, hugged my family goodbye, held back tears, and fell asleep on the 24-hour flight to the other side of the world. I opened my eyes to find myself struck by two very intense feelings: fear and heat. There I was, alone, scared, and sweating outside International Arrivals at Tan Son Nhat airport in Ho Chi Minh City. That was all it took to change my life: the blink of an eye ... and my CELTA.

'I was very grateful for everything that I learned during my CELTA course. The foundation it gave me allowed me not to feel like a total fraud as I stepped foot into my first real class. Whether I was teaching 3 year olds the ABC song, listening to the latest Taylor Swift single with my teenage students, or delving into the depths of American culture with adults, my CELTA course at Teaching House New York prepared me to be creative and retrospective. It helped me to develop into the teacher I am proud to have become.

'Like most people who uproot their lives to take on new and challenging adventures, I found myself in a state of constant self-discovery. I realised that I loved teaching English, and that I wisely (or unwisely) invested so much of myself into my classes that my students had the power to affect me long after I went home for the night. I realised that I had the ability to bridge cultural barriers; developing relationships with those I had very little in common with except the desire to grow. I realised that every choice I had made in my life had led me to that point, that time, that place, and I was happy.

'My departure came in late spring, just as the dark clouds of rainy season were descending upon Vung Tau. The heavy rains seemed to wipe my slate clean, leaving my future open to just about anything. I could once again take out my globe, give it a spin, and hold my breath as my future lies just under the tip of my index finger.'

TEACHING HOUSE SAN DIEGO: San Diego; ✆ +1 619 320 6192; www.teachinghouse.com; full-time; 4 courses per year.

VIETNAM

APOLLO EDUCATION: Hanoi and Ho Chi Minh City; ✆ +84 4 943 2053; www.apolloedutrain.com; $1,500.

INTERNATIONAL LANGUAGE ACADEMY (ILA): Ho Chi Minh City; ✆ +84 8 3838 6788, ext 1924; www.ilavietnam.com; full-time; rough frequency 9 per year.

LANGUAGE LINK VIETNAM: Hanoi; ✆ +84 4 3974 4999; www.llv.edu.vn; full-time; rough frequency 4 per year.

TRINITY COLLEGE LONDON CERTIFICATE (TESOL) COURSES IN THE UK

ABERYSTWYTH UNIVERSITY: Aberystwyth, Wales; ✆ +44 1970 622545; www.aber.ac.uk/tesol; full-time; rough frequency 2 per year; £1,300.

BASINGSTOKE COLLEGE OF TECHNOLOGY: Basingstoke, Hampshire; ✆ +44 1256 306350; www.bcot.ac.uk; full-time and part-time; rough frequency 1 per year.

BRACKNELL & WOKINGHAM COLLEGE: Bracknell, Berkshire; ✆ +44 1344 401638; www.bracknell.ac.uk; full-time and part-time; once each per year.

CITY COLLEGE PLYMOUTH: Plymouth; ✆ +44 1752 305859; www.cityplym.ac.uk; part-time; 1 per year.

COLCHESTER INSTITUTE: Colchester; ✆ +44 1206 712487; www.colchester.ac.uk; full-time, also part-time (twice of 8 weeks, once of 21 weeks); £1,155.

DARLINGTON COLLEGE OF TECHNOLOGY: Durham; ✆ +44 1325 503275; www.darlington.ac.uk; part-time.

EAST BERKSHIRE COLLEGE LANGLEY: Slough, Berkshire; ✆ +44 1753 793000; www.eastberks.ac.uk; part-time.

GATESHEAD COLLEGE: Gateshead, Tyne and Wear; ✆ +44 191 490 0300; www.gateshead.ac.uk; part-time over 33 weeks.

GOLDERS GREEN COLLEGE TEACHER TRAINING CENTRE: London; ✆ +44 208 731 0963; www.englishlanguagecollege.co.uk; full-time; 9 times per year; part-time twice.

INLINGUA: Cheltenham; ✆ +44 1242 250493; www.inlingua-cheltenham.co.uk; full-time; 8 times a year. £995 + £120 moderation fee.

INTERNATIONAL HOUSE BRISTOL: Bristol; ✆ +44 117 9090 911; www.ihbristol.com; full-time; rough frequency 6 per year.

INTERNATIONAL HOUSE BRISTOL

'It was in September 2009 that I found myself, all of a sudden, at Bergamo train station in Lombardy, North Italy, bound for Lecco, a small town on the foot of the trailing leg of Lake Como. And as I stood alone on that platform in the early evening sunshine, with barely a word of the mother-tongue and not entirely sure whether I definitely had somewhere to stay when I arrived there, I reflected on how I had got myself into this situation.

'It had all started on 2 November 2008 and I was sat with my fellow fresh Tefl-ites awaiting the beginning of our 5 week TESOL guidance into the heady world of international EFL teaching. To cut a long story short, the course was as challenging and fulfilling as anything I had ever done. Along the way, amongst other things, I taught students from no less than 20 different countries, learnt rudimentary Japanese, taught, reflected, analysed, learnt about different languages and cultures, taught again, made a Facebook-page-worth of new friends, played the most international games of football ever, taught again and had a marvellous time whilst doing it all.

'As chance would have it, I was soon offered a job at the very place where I had received my expert guidance: The Language Project, Bristol (now IH Bristol). What followed remains the happiest period of my tax-paying life I have ever had. TEFL teaching was, without a doubt, the shoe that fitted. So why, 8 blissful months down the line, did I find myself alone on a train platform in North Italy? I had caught the bug.

'Now at the end of my 8 month tenure here in Italy I have had a chance to reflect once again on how it has developed me as a teacher. Teaching abroad swept me, as it has swept countless before me, out of a comfort zone and into a situation which has unequivocally allowed a deeper connection with the plight of the language learner. I was the fish out of water this time. Professionally, it has stretched and challenged me, with my having to integrate and, perhaps more essentially, assimilate into a new professional set up and 'way of doing things'; less skills-based and more grammar-focused lessons, variable hours, different protocol and standards expected from a foreign employer etc. It has been tough at times indeed, and a zeal for the job at hand, i.e. teaching, is essential. But, in short, by making the idealistic and slightly naïve leap into the unknown of international EFL teaching, I have come out head and shoulders a more fulfilled and, dare I say, better teacher than when I stood, alone and discombobulated on the platform of Bergamo train station.

'So go home and spin that globe and decide where it is you'd like to go next.'

Dominic Harris

INTERNATIONAL TRAINING NETWORK: Christchurch, Dorset; ✆ +44 1202 475956; www.itnuk.com; full and part-time; rough frequency 3 per year; Christian organisation; £990 plus £110 Trinity moderation fee.

ISIS GREENWICH SCHOOL OF ENGLISH: London; ✆ +44 208 293 1444; www.isisgroup.co.uk; full-time; rough frequency 9 per year.

KENT SCHOOL OF ENGLISH: Broadstairs, Kent; ✆ +44 1843 874 870; www.kentschoolofenglish. com; full-time.

LANGSIDE COLLEGE GLASGOW: ✆ +44 141 272 3776; www.langside.ac.uk; full and part-time; rough frequency 3 per year.

THE LANGUAGE INSTITUTE/TLI ENGLISH LANGUAGE TRAINING: Edinburgh; ✆ +44 131 226 6975; www.tlieurope.com; full time; rough frequency 4 per year; £995.

LANGUAGES TRAINING & DEVELOPMENT: Witney, Oxfordshire; ✆ +44 1993 708637; www.ltdoxford. com; full-time; rough frequency 6–12 per year.

MANCHESTER COLLEGE OF ARTS & TECHNOLOGY: Manchester; ✆ +44 161 953 5995; www.themanchestercollege.ac.uk; 2 full-time and 1 part-time per year.

NORTHAMPTON COLLEGE: Northampton; ✆ +44 1604 736225; www.northamptoncollege.ac.uk; part-time 1 per year.

NORTHBROOK COLLEGE: Northbrook, Sussex; ✆ +44 845 155 60 60; www.northbrook.ac.uk; part-time twice a year (evenings for 13 weeks); £901 (ask about discounts if on benefit).

OXFORDTEFL LONDON: London WC1; www.oxfordtefl.com; tesol@oxfordtefl.com; full-time and part-time throughout the year; £905.

ST BRELADE'S COLLEGE: St. Aubin, Jersey; ✆ +44 1534 741305; www.st-brelades-college.co.uk; full-time; rough frequency 2 per year; £1,000 plus £150 for books and exam fee.

ST GEORGE INTERNATIONAL: London; ✆ +44 20 7299 1700; www.tesoltraining.co.uk; 11 full-time and 4 part-time per year.

ST GEORGE INTERNATIONAL

'I completed my TESOL certificate at St George International one cold snowy day in January 2009, after a challenging but very rewarding four week course with a great bunch of people. It was definitely the best January I have ever spent in my career since leaving university 25 years ago. I had previously worked in retail and construction management, but wanted to find a more fulfilling and enjoyable career – and I have!

'After qualifying, I found a job very quickly and have been teaching in a school in Central London since then. I was amazed how relevant all of the course was, and how easy it was to move on from the training classroom to the real McCoy. My next step is to start teaching business classes, where I will be using my industry experience to help students to learn Business English.

'SGI prepared me well before starting the course, so I knew exactly what to expect and there were no surprises during the well coordinated course. It did require a lot of time commitment, but the four weeks passed in a very enjoyable flash of learning, comprehension and presentation. I think the best part was probably teaching a group of genuine students on the first afternoon. This represented a microcosm of the course as a whole: learn something, put it into practice, and observe others doing the same.

'The whole course ran like a well-oiled machine, with mentors and coaches providing positive support and enthusiasm in copious doses. The other trainees were all really interesting and there was a great spirit of helping each other through the course. The best thing about the course is, without doubt, the professionalism of the SGI team.'

Telford Wallace

ST GILES EASTBOURNE: Eastbourne; ✆ +44 1323 729167; www.stgiles-international.com; full-time; rough frequency 3 per year.

ST GILES LONDON CENTRAL: London; ✆ +44 20 7837 0404; www.stgiles-international.com; full-time; rough frequency 9 per year.

SHEFFIELD HALLAM UNIVERSITY TESOL CENTRE: Sheffield; ✆ +44 114 225 5515; www.shu.ac.uk/tesol/teaching; 4 full-time and 3 part-time courses offered per year.

SIDMOUTH INTERNATIONAL SCHOOL: Sidmouth, Devon; ✆ +44 1395 516754; efl@sidmouth-int.co.uk; www.sidmouth-int.co.uk; full-time; 3 per year; £1,040 including moderation fee; accommodation arranged on request.

SOUTH ESSEX COLLEGE: Southend-on-Sea, Essex; ✆ +44 1702 220400; www.southessex.ac.uk; part-time twice a year.

SUSSEX LANGUAGE INSTITUTE: University of Sussex, Brighton; ✆ +44 1273 678006; www.sussex.ac.uk; full-time; rough frequency 3–4 per year.

SUTTON COLLEGE OF LEARNING FOR ADULTS: Sutton, Surrey; ✆ +44 20 8770 6901; www.scola.ac.uk; part-time 1 per year.

TEFL LAB LONDON: London WC1; ✆ +44 20 7637 3813; www.tefllab.co.uk; full time.

TEFL LONDON: Bloomsbury International, 6-7 Southampton Place, London WC1A 2DB; ✆ +44 20 7242 2234; www.tefllondon.com; full-time offered monthly; £835 plus £110 moderation fee.

THE INSTITUTE: London N2; ✆ +44 20 8829 4141; www.hgsi.ac.uk; 3–4 times a year; part-time; £950.

UNIVERSAL LANGUAGE TRAINING (ULT): Woking, Surrey; ✆ +44 1983 853808; www.universal-language.co.uk; full-time monthly and part-time 2 per year.

UNIVERSITY OF CENTRAL LANCASHIRE: School of Languages and International Studies, Preston, PR1 2HE; ✆ +44 1772 894241; worldwise@uclan.ac.uk; www.uclan.ac.uk/worldwisecourses; full-time in August, £1,295. Also offers university level courses in TESOL.

UNIVERSITY OF CHICHESTER: Bognor Regis Campus, West Sussex; ✆ +44 1243 812194; www.chiuni.ac.uk; part-time for 8 weeks; £1,110.

UNIVERSITY OF WOLVERHAMPTON: Wolverhampton; ✆ +44 1902 322484; www.wlv.ac.uk; part-time 1 per year.

ST GILES INTERNATIONAL

'I did my Trinity Cert. TESOL at St Giles London Central in September 2007. Afterwards I moved to Seville in Spain to teach English there. When I arrived, I realised that I was better equipped to teach than a number of my new colleagues who had trained elsewhere. My training at St Giles prepared me extremely well for teaching abroad, and I would recommend it to anyone considering a career in TEFL.'

Hugh Podmore, Trinity Cert. TESOL, London Central

'Three days after arriving in Mexico I landed a job with a language center. I cannot express to you how valuable the CELTA course has been in the classroom. Right from my very first class I have been confident and able to give effective language instruction.'

Steve Byrne, CELTA, San Francisco

'I trained to be a teacher at St Giles in Brighton. The course gave me a great insight into teaching and I left with a new found confidence in my ability to teach. On completion I was offered a job in Japan and I taught English there for three years. I then decided to teach in Bolivia for a year. On returning to England, I taught at St Giles in Eastbourne and I am now back teaching at St Giles Brighton!'

Vivienne Emery, CELTA, Brighton

'The CELTA course at St Giles was a major turning point in my life. It enabled me to teach English as a Foreign Language in Nagoya, Japan, Palma de Mallorca, Spain and in Bangalore, India.'

Nicole McFadden, CELTA, San Francisco

'I really enjoyed my TESOL course at St Giles. The four weeks were very intense, but the support and guidance from the Teacher Trainers was excellent throughout, and by the end of the course I really felt I'd learnt a lot. I'd never taught before so I was quite nervous at first, but the course gave me the knowledge and teaching techniques I needed to build my confidence. I was really happy to be offered a job at the end of my course, and I have been teaching at St Giles ever since.'

Talia Lash, Trinity Cert. TESOL, London Central

TRINITY COLLEGE LONDON CERTIFICATE (TESOL) COURSES ABROAD

ARGENTINA

CASA DE INGLÉS: Avenida Lavalle 188, Primer Piso, Oficina 7, 3500 Resistencia-Chaco; ✆+54 362 4572892; lauraalvarez@arnet.com.ar or casadeingles@ymail.com. Part-time course between April and October.

CANADA

COVENTRY HOUSE INTERNATIONAL: Ontario; ✆ +1 416 929 0227; www.study-at-coventry.com; full-time; rough frequency 2 per year; C$999 (with discount).

CZECH REPUBLIC

OXFORD TEFL: Prague; ✆ +420 226 211 900; www.teflprague.com; full-time; roughly 10 per year, €1,300.

HONG KONG

ENGLISH FOR ASIA: Sheung Wan, Hong Kong; ✆ +852 2366 3792; www.englishforasia.com; full and part-time; rough frequency 10–12 per year.

INDONESIA

IALF BALI (INDONESIA AUSTRALIA LANGUAGE FOUNDATION): Bali; ✆ +62 361 225243; www.tesolbali.com; full-time; rough frequency 4 per year; $1,800.

IRELAND

ATLANTIC SCHOOL OF ENGLISH AND ACTIVE LEISURE: Schull, County Cork; ✆ +353 28 28943; www.atlantic-english.com; full-time; rough frequency 3 per year. €1,450 plus accommodation can be arranged for €80–€150 per week.

ITALY

BYRON LANGUAGE DEVELOPMENT: Rome; ✆ +39 06 571 36632; trinity@byronschool.it; www.byronschool.it; 4 per year between April and October. €1,680.
VICTORIA INTERNATIONAL SCHOOL: Turin; ✆ +39 01119701242; v.i.s@fastwebnet.it.

JAPAN

SHANE ENGLISH SCHOOL: Tokyo; ✆ +81 3 5275 6756; sophia.mcmillan@shane.co.jp; www.tefljob-sinjapan.com.

NEW ZEALAND

ALPHA EDUCATIONAL INSTITUTE: Christchurch; ✆ +64 3 359 1525; www.alpha.school.nz; full-time; rough frequency 2 per year.
EDENZ COLLEGES: Auckland; ✆ +64 9 920 5920; www.teachertraining.co.nz; full and part-time; rough frequency 5 per year.
ENGLISH LANGUAGE ACADEMY: Auckland; ✆ +64 9 919 7695; www.ela.auckland.ac.nz; full and part-time 1 per year.
INTERNATIONAL PACIFIC COLLEGE: Queenstown; ✆ +64 6 354 0922; www.ipc.ac.nz/index.php; full-time 1 per year.

PARAGUAY

STAEL RUFFINELLI DE ORTIZ – ENGLISH: Asuncion; ✆ +595 21 226062/207017; www.stael.edu.py; part-time 1 per year.

SPAIN

CHESTER SCHOOL OF ENGLISH: Madrid; ✆ +34 91 401 97 29; www.chester.es; full-time; rough frequency 5 per year.

THE LANGUAGE INSTITUTE: Pontevedra; ✆ +34 986 104763/862461; www.tlieurope.com; full-time; rough frequency 4 per year.

OXFORDTEFL: Barcelona; ✆ +34 93 458 0111; www.oxfordtefl.com; full-time; rough frequency 12 per year.

UNIVERSAL LANGUAGE TRAINING (ULT): Woking; ✆ +44 1483 770911 or +44 1983 853808; www.universal-language.co.uk; TEFL training centre which offers summer school in Zamora.

URUGUAY

DICKENS INSTITUTE: Montevideo; ✆ +598 2 710 7555; www.dickens.edu.uy; part-time.

SHORT INTRODUCTORY COURSES

BERLITZ WORLDWIDE: http://careerservices.berlitz.com; all newly hired teachers (who must be university graduates) must join free 2-week training in-house in the Berlitz method.

EF ENGLISH FIRST TEACHER TRAINING: Cambridge/Brighton, UK; ✆ +44 207 341 8777; www.ef.com/master/tl/professional-development; approx £530 for 1 week, £1,010 for 2 weeks; cost varies depending on location.

INTENSIVE SCHOOL OF ENGLISH AND BUSINESS COMMUNICATIONS: Brighton, UK; ✆ +44 1273 384800; www.ise.uk.com; £250; frequency 1 per year; also offers CELTA in Wuhan China.

INTENSIVE TRAINING COURSES (ITC): Darlington, Co. Durham, UK; ✆ 0845 644 5464; www.tefl.co.uk; £210; various locations; frequency most weekends all year; optional part 2 is a distance component costing a further £135.

i-to-i: Leeds, UK; ✆ 0800 093 2552; 0800 352 1793; www.i-to-i.com or www.teflcourses.com; from £179; various locations; frequency most weekends all year.

ITTC: Bournemouth, UK; ✆ +44 1202 397721; www.ittc.co.uk; TEFL Taster day £55 including lunch; frequency 10 per year.

KRISTALL INTERNATIONAL, Camarthen, UK; ✆ +44 1944 231145; www.tefl-course.net; modularised 30-hour courses which combine on-site and home study. Weekend courses offered in various UK locations. Prices from £229 for Module 1.

SAXONCOURT TEACHER TRAINING: London; ✆ +44 20 7499 8533; www.saxoncourt.com; several 1-week courses throughout the year; £300.

SUSSEX DOWNS COLLEGE: Sussex, UK; ✆ +44 1323 637 111; www.sussexdowns.ac.uk; TEFL taster day 1 per year, £18.

SUSSEX LANGUAGE INSTITUTE: Sussex, UK; ✆ +44 1273 873234; www.sussex.ac.uk; £225; frequency 1 per year.

TEFL ENGLAND: info@teflengland.co.uk; www.teflengland.co.uk. Courses in England, details as for TEFL Scotland (next entry).

TEFL SCOTLAND: ✆ 0800 9 888 200; info@teflscotland.co.uk; www.teflscotland.co.uk. Classroom, online and combined TEFL courses in Scotland, from 20 to 130 hours.

TEFL WALES: info@teflwales.co.uk;www.teflwales.co.uk. Courses in Wales, details as for TEFL Scotland (previous entry).

TEFL TIME: Sussex, UK; ✆ +44 1903 708178; www.tefltime.com; £189 for weekend courses, often held at the Holiday Inn at King's Cross; frequency 9 per year.

TEFL WALES

23-year-old Michelle Size's TEFL certificate took her all the way to Japan.

'I took the TEFL 20-hour weekend course with TEFL Wales in April. I have been in Japan for a month now, based in a small town 30 minutes by bus from the northernmost city of Honshu. I had just finished university and wanted a way to see the world without it costing any money. I really wasn't interested in getting a graduate job and with the current economic climate I knew it would be really difficult anyway.

'I chose Japan as Asia was the continent I knew least about and I wanted to challenge myself and gain knowledge. The Japanese government luckily have the JET scheme which seemed ideal as I liked the idea of being employed by the government, as well as all the benefits that come with it – free flights, free travel to destination, free hotel accommodation in Tokyo for orientation and a welcome event at the British Embassy to name a few! It is a secure job with a contract for at least one year.

'I am teaching in 10 different schools, which is good as I have variety and work with children from ages 3–15 so it's a lot of fun. It's really good for cultural exchange as I get to tell them about the United Kingdom. They usually don't know much about it as in Japanese there is just one word for the UK, Britain and England!

'I have a rent-free house, which is great to have people over to and also saves me so much money that I can live comfortably and go travelling at the weekends and on holidays. The community I have been placed in is very friendly and welcomed me with a party where I got to meet the mayor of the town. They also took me to a Japanese tea ceremony and to visit temples and scenic mountains. I really like being the only westerner in my town. It's also great for immersion into the culture and language and also it makes me a sort of "celebrity" as everyone seems to know who I am.

'There are other English teachers in nearby towns and an English speaking community in Sendai, so I don't feel isolated. I guess another good point is that I get paid a decent wage so I am able to start paying off student debts as well as have a great time here.'

UK-TEFL: Lytham, Lancashire, UK; ✆ 0871 222 1231; www.uk-tefl.com. Intensive standard and advanced 2/3-day courses throughout the UK on weekends and weekdays, £200–£250.

UK-TEFL

UK-TEFL is the leading TEFL trainer in the UK, specialising in two and three-day classroom-based courses across England, Northern Ireland, Scotland and Wales. Since we began, we have transformed tens of thousands of people into successful EFL teachers and we remain determined to bring you the best TEFL courses on the market through our elite training team, skilled TEFL qualified advisors and ongoing support including unrivalled worldwide employment opportunities.

We are accredited by the national awarding organisation NCFE, and we are also an approved NCFE centre. UK-TEFL has been awarded the NCFE Investing in Quality (IIQ) Licence, which is based on six Quality Statements providing a quality assurance framework for the development, delivery and evaluation of our courses. Our NCFE accreditation provides you with peace of mind and a guarantee of the high standard of training you will receive through UK-TEFL. It is essential to ensure that your TEFL qualification is an accredited qualification, as employers are much more likely to employ you with this!

UK-TEFL are also one of the only TEFL providers in the UK to offer you the chance to upgrade your TEFL certificate into a Qualifications and Credit Framework (QCF) qualification, enhancing your employability to greater heights than ever before. By choosing this option, you will participate in a formal assessment during your UK-TEFL course, resulting in a QCF Level 2 (standard courses) or QCF Level 3 (advanced courses) qualification issued directly by the NCFE.

After your UK-TEFL course, we are here to help you find your dream career with an exclusive FREE trial membership to our unique VIP Jobs Club. We work with a carefully-selected range of recruiters who collectively hire over 5,000 teachers each year for various roles in businesses, schools, universities, charities and summer camps, so there is sure to be a perfect role for you! Our Jobs Club is a unique gateway to the world, offering an unrivalled range of paid and voluntary worldwide teaching opportunities, 1000+ up-to-date recruitment contacts, travel guides, and ongoing support from our expert jobs team to provide you with all the tools required to launch a successful TEFL career.

We are confident that once you have chosen UK-TEFL as your training provider, you won't look back. With so many opportunities to acquire new skills, explore new cultures and gain life changing experiences, in addition to the fantastic salaries, benefits and training and development on offer, who knows where your TEFL career could lead? There has never been a better time to become UK-TEFL qualified!

Start your TEFL career today by ordering a FREE brochure at www.uk-tefl.com/brochure.

For further information, call 0871 222 1231 to speak to an advisor, or visit us online at www.uk-tefl.com.

DISTANCE LEARNING ONLINE COURSES

AMERICAN TESOL INSTITUTE: Tampa, FL, USA; ℂ +1 813 975 7404; www.americantesol.com; from US$295.

EUROLINK COURSES: Sheffield, UK; ℂ +44 114 262 1522; www.eurolinkcourses.co.uk; £600 in instalments/£540 if paid in full; offers optional practical teaching placement; cost with practical teaching placement is £1,095 in instalments/£1,020 if paid in full.

AMERICAN TESOL INSTITUTE

American TESOL Institute (ATI) was incorporated in 2004 to meet the global demand for professionally trained English teachers, and provides TESOL certification courses. American TESOL Institute's mission is the standardising of an introductory English teacher training program for individuals wishing to teach English. American TESOL Institute also provides teacher placements in Asia, Africa, Latin America, the Middle East, Europe, or online after completing TESOL certification.

Teaching English abroad is a great way to experience the world while acclimatising yourself to the global economy. Connecting with and understanding cultures facilitates ATI member success while enabling individual progress through teaching and learning. Careers teaching abroad educate and challenge teachers through interaction and observation of foreign cultures.

TESOL is the acronym for teaching English to speakers of other languages. It is similar to teaching English as a foreign language, or TEFL certification. American TESOL certification programs provide a base knowledge in teaching English as a second language with focus on methods and approaches to TESOL. TESOL Certification Online allows you to create your own learning environment, complete studies at your own pace, and fit curriculum into a busy lifestyle.

With ATI, you can also consider a certification course specifically for teaching English to children. American TESOL for children online course focuses on teaching methods for age groups 2–17, and the different developmental stages of children. Instructors focus on a variety of TESOL methodologies, classroom disciplinary methods, and which combination of methods works best in TESOL classrooms.

After completing an American TESOL certification program, you can teach English as a second language all over the world. American TESOL graduates are provided with ESL job placement support teaching English abroad. American TESOL graduates support people who speak another language, such as Portuguese, Spanish, Japanese, Korean, or Mandarin, learn the basics of the English language in their home country. American TESOL teachers are trained to meet general, academic, and professional needs, giving many opportunities for our graduates to teach in all environments. ESL is offered in most public and private school systems throughout the world. It is always an honour for schools and universities to receive American TESOL teachers.

We look forward to supporting you in meeting your teaching goals.

Learn more by visiting ATI online at www.AmericanTESOL.com or give us a call at 1-877-748-7900.

GLOBAL ENGLISH: Exeter, Devon, UK; ✆ +44 1392 411999; www.global-english.com; from £195; offers specialist components in Young Learners and Business English; teaching practice can be arranged in Portugal, Thailand and Italy.

ICAL: London, UK; ✆ 0845 310 4104; www.teacher-training.net; £135; offers practical teaching placement; cost is £395.

i-to-i: Leeds, UK; ✆ 0800 093 3148 or +44 113 204 4610; www.i-to-i.com, www.onlinetefl.com; from £143.

INTESOL WORLDWIDE: 4 Higher Downs, Knutsford, Cheshire WA16 8AW, UK; ✆ 0800 567 7189/ +44 1565 621661; www.intesoltesoltraining.com; accredited by a national awarding body; online and offsite courses from £395 to £895; offers teaching practice in accredited schools; accredited for quality of service with a money back guarantee by ODLQC; branches worldwide.

LANGUAGES TRAINING & DEVELOPMENT: Witney, Oxfordshire, England; ✆ +44 1993 708637; www.ltdoxford.com; £350; does not offer practical teaching placement.

LINGUAEDGE: Beverly Hills, CA, USA; ✆ +1 888 944 3343; www.linguaedge.com; 50-, 100- or 150-hour online courses.

LONDON TEACHER TRAINING COLLEGE: London; ✆ +44 20 8133 2027; www.teachenglish.co.uk; £175; offers practical teaching placement; cost with practical teaching placement is £255.

MIDWEST EDUCATION GROUP: 4633 N. Western Ave., Suite 207, Chicago, IL 60625; ✆ +1 847 496 7919; contact@midwested.us; www.midwested.us. 120-hour online TESOL training programme certified by Illinois State Board of Education open to candidates with an associated degree. $300 or $450 with tutor support. Shorter options are 50 hours ($75) or 60 hours with tutor support ($150).

NORWOOD ENGLISH: Laois, Eire; ✆ +353 57 8756325; www.norwoodenglish.com; from €160 for 140-hour distance course; does not offer practical teaching placement. Other specialist courses on Grammar for EFL (€100), teaching Business English (€175), etc.

TEACHING ENGLISH IN ITALY: Florence, Italy; sheila@teachingenglishinitaly.com; www.teachingenglishinitaly.com. TEFL/TESOL grammar course (20 hours) with guided tutor support, US$101. Teaching Business English and Teaching English to Young Learners, both 30 hours, and both cost US$218.

TEFL CORP: www.teflcorp.com. Part of TEFL International (see below) which puts on its own certificate courses in more than 30 centres around the world. Online 60- and 120-hour TEFL certificate courses with tutor support (US$180 or $295). 50- and 100-hour courses without tutor support (US$150 or $190) assessed by final test. Longer diploma and specialised courses also available.

TEFL EXPRESS: ✆ 0800 0488861; www.teflexpress.co.uk. 120-hour online course (£369), 100-hour course (£299), and shorter courses. Affiliated to Language Link and course provides passport to jobs and internships in their network of 100+ schools in Britain, Central Europe, Russia, Uzbekistan, Kazakhstan, Vietnam and China. Also weekend courses from £99 in London, Cork and Dublin.

TEFLSTOP: www.teflstop.com; part of INTESOL WORLDWIDE (above); new accredited online course aimed at backpackers; £195; optional extra of doing teaching practice via Skype; assistance given on finding jobs at a large language chain in Turkey and to graduates in North America who are looking for online teaching jobs.

TEFL TRAINING: Devon, UK; ✆ +44 1271 371373; www.tefltraining.co.uk; 140 hours; £395 if paid in full/£420 in instalments.

TRAINING LINK ONLINE: Sheffield, UK; ✆ +44 114 235 2245; www.traininglinkonline.co.uk; £525 if paid in full/£585 in instalments; offers practical teaching placement.

UNIVERSITY OF BIRMINGHAM: Birmingham, UK; ✆ +44 121 414 5695/6; www.cels.bham.ac.uk; does not offer practical teaching placement.

WORDS LANGUAGE SERVICES: Dublin, Ireland; ✆ +353 1 6610240; www.wls.ie; £325; does not offer practical teaching placement.

ACADEMIC COURSES

This represents a small selection of university courses in TEFL/TESL in the UK. On the UCAS.com site, you can search by subject and find courses in TEFL/TESOL usually offered in combination with another subject such as a modern language or tourism.

ANGLIA RUSKIN UNIVERSITY: East Road, Cambridge CB1 1PT; ✆ +44 1245 493131; efl@anglia. ac.uk; www.anglia.ac.uk; offer BA in English Language teaching and an MA in Applied Linguistics and TESOL.

ASTON UNIVERSITY: Languages and Social Sciences Unit, Aston Triangle, Birmingham B4 7ET; ✆ +44 121 204 3762; lss_pgadmissions@aston.ac.uk; www.aston.ac.uk; MSc in Teaching English to Speakers of Other Languages (TESOL), MSc in Teaching English for Specific Purposes (TESP), MSc in Teaching English to Young Learners (TEYL), MSc in Educational Management in TESOL (EMT), part-time, 2–5 years, £6,950; MA in TESOL studies, MA in TESOL and Translation, MA in Applied Linguistics, all £3,630.

CANTERBURY CHRIST CHURCH UNIVERSITY COLLEGE: North Holmes Road, Canterbury CT1 1QU; ✆ +44 1227 767700 (Department of English and Language Studies); languagestudies@canterbury. ac.uk; www.canterbury.ac.uk; offers Diploma/MA in TESOL; full (12 months) or part-time; also offers the CELTA (see entry).

LONDON METROPOLITAN UNIVERSITY: 166–220 Holloway Road, London N7 8DB; ✆ +44 20 7133 4202; humanities@londonmet.ac.uk/admissions@londonmet.ac.uk; www.londonmet.ac.uk; MA International ELT & Applied Language Studies (for experienced teachers); MA TEFL (for newly qualified teachers). Full-time one-year course; fees £4,050 for EU students or £7,155 for non-EU students.

MIDDLESEX UNIVERSITY: The Burroughs, London NW4 4BT; ✆ +44 20 8411 5555; enquiries@mdx. ac.uk; www.mdx.ac.uk; BA (Hons) in Teaching English as a Foreign Language.

UNIVERSITY OF BEDFORDSHIRE: Park Square, Luton, Bedfordshire LU1 3JU; ✆ +44 1234 400400; www.beds.ac.uk; BA (Hons) in English Language Studies with TEFL, BA (Hons) in English Language for Business, BA (Hons)/Diploma in English for International Communication, MA in Applied Linguistics (TEFL), TEFL Certificate (summer school), TEFL Certificate (part-time evening).

UNIVERSITY OF BIRMINGHAM: Centre for English Language Studies, Westmere, Edgbaston Park Road, Edgbaston, Birmingham B15 2TT; ✆ +44 121 414 3239/5696; cels@bham.ac.uk; www.cels. bham.ac.uk; the Centre for English Language Studies specialises in language research, training and consultancy; CELS is part of the Department of English at the University of Birmingham; the department holds the highest possible ratings for both research and teaching, offers full-time or part-time courses on campus in TEFL/TESL, Applied Linguistics, English for Specific Purposes, Language and Lexicography, Special Applications of Linguistics, Translation Studies, Applied Corpus Linguistics, Critical Discourse, Culture and Communication; also offers distance learning courses in TEFL/TESL, Translation Studies and Applied Linguistics in addition to Postgraduate Research Degrees by distance learning; all campus-based courses last for one year and begin in October. Distance learning MA courses begin in April and October and typically take 30 months; possibility to study part-time, one term per year; accommodation available on campus; contact CELS administrator via www.cels.bham.ac.uk.

UNIVERSITY OF BRIGHTON: School of Languages, Falmer, Brighton, East Sussex BN1 9PH; ✆ +44 1273 643336; a.pickering@brighton.ac.uk; www.bton.ac.uk; offers Diploma and MA in TESOL; 1 year full-time or part-time; these are both post-graduate courses; applicants must have some English teaching experience for the MA and 2 years for the Diploma; also offers a MA in English Language Teaching, 1 year full-time or part-time, for teachers with a limited amount of experience.

UNIVERSITY OF CENTRAL LANCASHIRE: School of Languages and International Studies, Preston, PR1 2HE; ✆ +44 1772 893136; cenquiries@uclan.ac.uk; www.uclan.ac.uk; BA (Hons) in Teaching English to Speakers of Other Languages, BA (Hons) in TESOL and Modern Languages, MA in TESOL and Applied Linguistics.

UNIVERSITY OF EDINBURGH: Institute for Applied Language Studies (IALS), 21 Hill Place, Edinburgh EH8 9DP; ✆ +44 131 650 6200; ials.enquiries@ed.ac.uk; www.ials.ed.ac.uk; offers short intensive EFL teacher development courses of between 1 and 3 weeks' duration in July/August.

UNIVERSITY OF ESSEX: International Academy, Wivenhoe Park, Colchester, Essex CO4 3SQ; ✆ +44 1206 872217; dilly@essex.ac.uk; www.essex.ac.uk/internationalacademy. MA TESOL/Diploma TESOL/Certificate TESOL; the modular MA TESOL (180 credits) can be taken either within 1 year or over a period of 6 years with exit points at Diploma (120 credits) or Certificate (60 credits); also providing CELTA training in conjunction with Santiago de Compostela in Spain and specialist tailor made programmes.

UNIVERSITY OF EXETER: School of Education and Lifelong Learning, St Luke's Campus, Heavitree Road, Exeter EX1 2LU; ✆ +44 1392 264837; ed-student@exeter.ac.uk; EdD/PhD/MPhil/MEd/ PgDip/PgCertTESOL, full-time, part-time and intensive summer study.

UNIVERSITY OF MANCHESTER: Postgraduate Admissions Office, School of Education, Faculty of Humanities, Oxford Road, Manchester M13 9PL; ✆ +44 161 275 3463; education-enquiries@ manchester.ac.uk; www.manchester.ac.uk; offers MA TESOL or MA Educational Technology and TESOL in 3 modes of study: 1 year full-time (onsite), UK/EU £3,466 and Overseas £11,300; 27 months part-time (onsite), EU/UK £1,733; and 3 years distance, £2,100 a year; entry requirements include 3 years' teaching experience; the university also offers an introduction to TESOL as part of an undergraduate degree (one term).

UNIVERSITY OF READING: Department of Applied Linguistics, School of Languages and European Studies, Whiteknights, PO Box 218, Reading RG6 6AA; ✆ +44 118 378 8123; languages@reading.ac.uk; www.rdg.ac.uk/app_ling; MA ELT in both campus-based and distance-study modes, with an additional study track for novice teachers; also, MA in Applied Linguistics, BA in Applied English Language Studies.

UNIVERSITY OF STIRLING/CELT: Institute of Education (CELT), Stirling FK9 4LA; ✆ +44 1786 467934; celt@stir.ac.uk; www.celt.stir.ac.uk; MSc in TESOL (Teaching English to Speakers of Other Languages); MSc in TESOL and CALL (Computer Assisted Language Learning); and PhD and EdD in TESOL Education available; General English, IELTS Preparation, English for University Study, Short Courses for Teachers, and a Summer School in August are also offered.

UNIVERSITY OF SUSSEX: Admissions, Sussex House, Falmer, Brighton, East Sussex BN1 9RH; ✆ +44 1273678416; UG.Admissions@sussex.ac.uk (for bachelor's degree programme) or PG.Admissions@

sussex.ac.uk (for master's programmes); www.sussex.ac.uk; BA in English Language Teaching; 3- or 4-year joint major in ELT with English, English Language, Language(s) or Linguistics; includes opportunity to take Trinity TESOL Certificate as part of degree; MA in English Language Teaching; MA in International English Language Teaching and a Post-graduate Diploma in ELT (full-time 1 year, part-time 2 years).

UNIVERSITY OF WARWICK: Centre for Applied Linguistics, Coventry CV4 7AL; ✆ +44 24 7652 3200; appling@warwick.ac.uk; www2.warwick.ac.uk/fac/soc/al/; MA in ELT/ESP/English for Young Learners (all post-experience), English Language Teaching (Studies and Methods) (less than 2 years' experience), ELT (Multimedia) (either pre- or post-experience); one-term Post-graduate Certificate in any of the MA specialisms (January to March), 2 terms for a Post-graduate Diploma.

TRAINING COURSES IN NORTH AMERICA

USA

AMERICAN LANGUAGE INSTITUTE: San Diego State University, 5250 Campanile Drive, San Diego, CA 92182-1914; ✆ +1 619 594 5907; ali@mail.sdsu.edu or rhillier@mail.sdsu.edu; www.american language.com; well-known AMTEFL Certificate validated by SDSU Dept of Education (3 graduate credits); 4 weeks, 130 hours, offered 4 times a year (spring and summer); $2,650; dormitory/homestay/apartment accommodation can be arranged through the ALI housing office.

BOSTON ACADEMY OF ENGLISH: 59 Temple Place, 2nd Floor, Boston, MA 02111; ✆ +1 617 338 6243; info@bostonacademyofenglish.com; www.bostonacademyofenglish.com; 4 weeks intensive 120-hour CTEFL course, $2,450; part-time over 12 weeks, $2,300.

BOSTON LANGUAGE INSTITUTE: 648 Beacon St, Boston, MA 02215; ✆ +1 617 262 3500; info@ teflcertificate.com; www.teflcertificate.com; intensive 4-week TEFL Certificate course (120 hours) offered monthly; 12-week Saturday programmes also offered 3 times a year; special TEFL Certificate Programme for Non-Native Speakers of English also offered: course includes additional training on pronunciation, American culture and other relevant topics; tuition of $2,795 includes fees, all study materials and lifetime job assistance.

BOSTONTEFL.COM: admin@bostontefl.com; www.bostontefl.com; basic online training course ($295) can be supplemented by a 20-hour face-to-face weekend course (together $785) and a further opportunity to obtain 2 weeks teaching practice overseas ($1,745).

GLOBAL TEFL: ✆ +1 312 209 3660; mail@globaltefl.org; www.globaltefl.org; Full-time SIT TESOL Certificate courses offered by freelance certified trainers Ron and Ellen Bradley and other SIT certified trainers in Chicago, California, Grand Junction, Colorado, and Boston; Part-time courses offered at some locations; $2,295 inclusive; (for further details of course see website).

HAMLINE UNIVERSITY: TEFL Certificate Program, School of Education, 1536 Hewitt Avenue, St. Paul, MN 55104; ✆ +1 651 523 2429; education@hamline.edu; www.hamline.edu; intensive 1-month courses in July and January and part-time extensive courses autumn and spring; current tuition $3,230; focus is on developing communicative language teaching strategies; ongoing career counselling provided. Graduate credit granted; course can be used towards Hamline's MA in ESL; advanced TEFL option offered.

LCC (LANGUAGE, CULTURE COACHING): 3463 State Street, Suite 496, Santa Barbara, CA 93105; ✆ +1 800 868 1452; www.lccteach.com. 100-hour TESOL course over five weekends, held at North Seattle Community College in Seattle. $1,095 ($995 with early registration discount).

MIDWEST TEACHER TRAINING PROGRAM: 19 N. Pinckney Street, Madison, WI 53703 USA; ✆ +1 800 765 8577 or +1 608 257 8476; info@mttp.com; www.mttp.com; practical, hands-on 5-week TEFL Certificate Course (130 hours including 10 hours of teaching practice) in a progressive university city; 4 times a year; tuition and course materials $2,595; housing arranged if needed; integrated with an ESL school providing an international environment; job placement assistance including resource library, job search workshop and personal résumé editing; grads have found jobs in 40 countries.

OXFORD SEMINARS: Santa Monica and New York; ℂ +1 800 779 1779; www.oxfordseminars. com; TESOL/TESL courses held in cities around the USA, usually on university/college campuses; 60 hours over 3 consecutive weekends; US$1,095.

SCHOOL OF TEACHING ENGLISH AS A SECOND LANGUAGE: (affiliate programme with Seattle University College of Education), 9620 Stone Avenue. N., Suite 101, Seattle, WA 98103; ℂ +1 206 781 8607; STESLinfo@seattleu.edu; www.schooloftesl.com; 12-credit, 4-week intensive courses (offered monthly, US$2,900), non-intensive evening classes (quarterly), and online classes (quarterly); $290 per credit 2012 academic year; accommodation available on request; classes carry college credit and can be used as a portion of master's degrees at Seattle University (except online classes); counselling, monthly employment seminars, graduates' networking services and an onsite ESOL class.

TRANSWORLD SCHOOLS: TESOL Certificate (Teaching English to Speakers of Other Languages) training courses at Transworld Schools, 701 Sutter Street, 6th Floor, San Francisco, CA 94109; ℂ +1 800 357 9905/415 928 2835; transwd@aol.com; www.transworldschools.com; Comprehensive TESOL Certificate (4 weeks full-time, 14 weeks part-time, $2,000); TESOL Certificate (3 weeks full-time, 10 weeks part-time $1,800); Intensive TESOL Certificate (for experienced ESOL teachers – 2 weeks full-time; 7 weeks part-time, $1,600); Advanced TESOL Certificate (for experienced ESOL teachers – 1 week full-time; 4 weeks part-time, $900); Online TESOL Certificate with 1 week on-site residency $1,200; all courses internationally recognised; approved by State of California, BPPVE (Bureau for Private Postsecondary Education) and accredited by ACCET, Continuing Education Credits awarded; high quality training, low tuition, and lifetime job placement worldwide; accommodation ($165–$250 per week); courses include evaluated Teaching Practice, teaching children and adults, grammar, Business English, TOEFL and syllabus design. Facilities include multimedia lab, video and internet.

TRANSWORLD SCHOOLS

Why Transworld?

'Transworld was more than a piece of paper ... it gave me all of the preparation I needed to teach in the adult schools prior to my departure overseas, in an English language school in Chile, and in my current position teaching middle school Spanish in the San Francisco Bay Area. My students (and employers) have responded positively to the communicative approach trained at Transworld. Why? Because they learn while they're having fun.'
Jay Rhodes, Chile/USA

The Mission of Transworld's TESOL program is to produce well-trained, culturally aware teachers who are able to secure employment as teachers of English both in the USA and overseas, and who contribute to the ideals of the greater community.

'The instruction and follow-up support that I received at Transworld have been instrumental in finding, securing and performing great jobs in great locations around the world. Within one week of searching, I was offered two excellent job contracts, one in Chile and the other in the United Arab Emirates (my first choices) – I opted for the UAE first then Japan the following year.'
Joshua Kalish, UAE/Japan

What makes Transworld different?

- Comprehensive full-time and part-time TESOL Certificate courses offered on campus and online.
- Transworld is approved and accredited and all TESOL Courses earn State of California Continuing Education Credits.
- Evaluated Teaching Practice with international students.
- Courses in Grammar, Language Skills, Teaching Techniques and Lesson Planning, Curriculum Development, Business English, and Computer Assisted Learning.
- 90% of graduates are successfully placed in universities and schools worldwide and all receive lifetime job placement assistance.

'I chose the Transworld TESOL course because I had heard positive feedback about the program and the job placement assistance. I wasn't disappointed. I found the course to be challenging and I thoroughly enjoyed the teaching practice with international students. I am now teaching English in beautiful Barcelona.' Catherine Harper, Spain

'As the Director of Recruitment for EF, one of the largest international language school organizations in the world, I am constantly looking for well-qualified and professional teachers. Transworld Schools TESOL teachers consistently turn out to be the best trained and the most appropriate for our teaching positions.' Nicole Hayes, EF, Boston

WASHINGTON ACADEMY OF LANGUAGES: TESL Graduate Certificate/Endorsement Program, 2 Nickerson St., Suite 201, Seattle, WA 98109; ✆ +1 206 682 4463 or toll-free ✆ 888 682 4463; info@wal.org; www.wal.org; Graduate TEFL Certificate offered in conjunction with Seattle Pacific University; 8 courses for total of 24 quarter credits; offered intensively as 8-week summer course, online or in evening classes over academic year; tuition for each course is $510.

WESTERN WASHINGTON UNIVERSITY TESOL PROGRAM: Bellingham, WA 98225; ✆ +1 360 650 4949; Trish.Skillman@wwu.edu; ww.wce.wwu.edu/Resources/TESOL; Full-time and part-time university courses starting in September, with a summer intensive option; interdisciplinary coursework and practical experience lead to a certificate of achievement and a supporting endorsement in teaching ESL; distance education and overseas practicum experiences in Mexico available; fees $1,950–$2,200.

CANADA

Note that the website of TESL Canada (www.tesl.ca) has links to a large number of approved teacher training programmes across Canada.

ARCHER COLLEGE VANCOUVER: 525 Dunsmuir St, Unit 200, Vancouver, BC V6B 1Y4; ✆ +1 604 608 0538; VancouverESL@ArcherEducation.com; www.archereducation.com; TESL Canada recognised courses offered full-time for 1 month, or part-time over 14 weeks; all courses include practicum and are offered year-round.

GLOBAL TESOL: Suite 126, 10654-82 Avenue, Edmonton, Alberta T6E 2A7, Canada; ✆ +1 888 270 2941/780 438 5704; info@globaltesol.com; www.globaltesol.com; office/training centres across Canada, and in many countries worldwide; world's largest TESOL Certificate and Diploma granting programme as described in a free Travel-and-Teach information package; 40,000 graduates teaching English in 85 countries; range of Canada Government certified TESOL Certificate and Diploma courses held regularly in cities throughout Canada and other countries; 5-day intensive format, or online and correspondence study options available worldwide; overseas job guaranteed; prices range from C$695 to C$3,495; famous for its 16 specialisation course options; 120-hour to 600-hour programme available; other courses offered online or by correspondence include Teaching Business English, Teaching TOEFL Preparation, Teaching Grammar, Teaching Children, Teaching Adults, Tourism English, Teaching CALL Computer English and more; accommodation can be arranged; franchises available, email for details.

GLOBAL VILLAGE ENGLISH CENTRES: Calgary and Vancouver; info@gvenglish.com; www.gvenglish. com; TESOL Diploma course; 180 classes over 8 weeks, offered 5 times a year in Calgary; C$2,665; also offer the CELTA.

INTERNATIONAL HOUSE VANCOUVER: 200–215 West Broadway, Vancouver, BC V6H 1G7; ✆ +1 604 739 9836; http://tesl-vancouver.com; IH Career College offers IH Certificate (130 hours and online) starting monthly. C$1,400 (C$950 online).

INTERNATIONAL LANGUAGE ACADEMY OF CANADA (ILAC): Toronto (920 Yonge St, 4th floor, Toronto M4W 3C7; ✆ +1 416 961 5151) and Vancouver (688 West Hastings, 3rd floor, Vancouver, V6B 1P1; ✆ +1 604 484 6660; www.ilactesol.com); 4-week, 100-hour Certificate courses offered 6 times a year in both cities.

OXFORD SEMINARS: 131 Bloor St. West, Suite 200–390, Toronto, ON M5S 1R8 and 10405 Jasper Ave, Suite 16–21, Edmonton, AB T5J 3S2; ✆ +1 800 269 6719; info@oxfordseminars.com; www. oxfordseminars.com; 60-hour course held over 3 consecutive weekends; C$995 (plus GST) with various discounts available such as C$100 off for early booking.

PEAK TESOL: Rocky Mountain School District 6; ✆ +1 877 427 5114 or +1 250 427 5114; peak. tesol@gmail.com or gabbot@rmbc6.ca; www.sd6.bc.ca/peaktesol; 50 hours of in-class training with 50 hours of distance-learning; the course includes supervised practice teaching with real international students; C$1,250.

TRAINING COURSES WORLDWIDE

WORLDWIDE

BRIDGE: Head office: 915 South Colorado Blvd, Denver, Colorado 80246; ✆ +1 303 785 8864; toll free (USA and Canada): ✆ +1 888 827 4757/0808 120 7163 (UK); www.bridgetefl.com; intensive 140-hour TEFL courses offered in centres in Argentina, Brazil, Chile, Peru, Colombia, Costa Rica, Guatemala, Mexico, Czech Republic, UK (Northern Ireland and London), Greece, Italy, Spain, Hungary, Russia, Thailand, Turkey, Vietnam, Cambodia, UAE, South Africa and USA; on-site TEFL course tuition starts at US$1,695. Online and blended-learning courses also available worldwide starting at US$184.

GLOBAL TESOL COLLEGE: main website: www.globaltesol.com and headquarters in Canada: 7712, 104 St, Edmonton, Alberta T6E 4C5; in North America: ✆ +1 888 270 2941/+1 780 438 5704; tesol@globaltesol.com; US-East in North America: ✆ +1 866 837 6565; tesol@tesolworld.com; US-West in North America: ✆ +1 888 837 6587; info@globaltesol usa.com; Australia: ✆ +61 7 3221 5100; teachenglish@sarinarusso.com.au; China: ✆ +86 134 0508 0034; info@teflcour sechina.com; Greece: ✆ +30 274 302 9012; Georgia@globaltesol.gr; for accommodation: info@ linguisticlab.com; India: ✆ +91 172 2692682; info@tesolindia.com; Malaysia: ✆ +60 85 413778; joanne@globaltesol.com.my; Mexico: ✆ +52 818 368 2410; linda@engcanada.com; New Zealand: nz@globaltesol.co.nz; Philippines: ✆ +632 910 1438; global@edulynxcorp.com; Singapore: ✆ +65 6221 3957; info@globalelt.org; Taiwan: ✆ +886 2 2369 1181 (24 hrs); anne@globaltesol. com.

LANGUAGE CORPS: Stowe, Massachusetts; ✆ +1 978-562-2100; toll-free (North America): 1-877-216-3267; www.languagecorps.com. 4-week TESOL training course offered in many places worldwide, and then job placement in Southeast Asia, Latin America and Europe.

PARADISE TEFL: www.paradisetefl.com. Based in Cambodia with intensive courses offered in multiple locations in Cambodia, Vietnam, Laos, Malaysia, Thailand and Mexico. Frequent start dates.

SIT (SCHOOL FOR INTERNATIONAL TRAINING) GRADUATE INSTITUTE: Kipling Road, PO Box 676, Brattleboro, VT 05302; ✆ +1 800 257 7751; tesolcert@sit.edu; www.sit.edu/tesolcert; Full-time; 130-hour SIT TESOL Certificate course offered in various locations in the US and worldwide including Chicago, IL and Rohnert Park, CA (see Global TEFL above under USA), Quito (Ecuador), Oaxaca (Mexico), Bangkok and Chiang Mai (Thailand), Guatemala City and Quetzeltanango (Guatemala), Kharviv (Ukraine) and others; fees vary from $1,400 in Thailand to $2,295 in the US.

TEFL INTERNATIONAL: admin@teflinternational.org.uk; www.teflinternational.org.uk; USA Head office: 1200 Belle Passi Rd. Woodburn, OR 97071; TEFL International TESOL Certificate, 120-hour including observed Teaching Practice; available worldwide – full-time, part-time and Distance Learning; Special Projects with guaranteed work or internship (including volunteer projects); TEFL International World Wide Locations: Buenos Aires, Beijing, Hong Kong, Shanghai, Zhuhai, Manuel Antonio, Prague, Alexandria, Brittany, Corinth, Calcutta, Florence, Rome, Tokyo, Kathmandu, Cebu (Philippines), Lubin, Seoul, Barcelona, Seville, Ban Phe, Chiang Mai and Phuket, London, New York, Woodburn, Ho Chi Minh City; most centres offer the course every month; prices vary slightly from US$1,390 to US$1,790, but with regular specials and discount programmes.

VIA LINGUA: info@vialingua.org; www.vialingua.org. Proprietory 120-hour Certificate course (Via Lingua CTEFL) accredited by the College of Teachers and franchised to language institutes worldwide. Moderated by ELT Institute, Hunter College, City University of New York. Course available in Arequipa (Peru), Budapest, Buenos Aires, Guzmán (Mexico), Crete, Florence, Ho Chi Minh City, Istanbul, New York, Panama, Pattaya (Thailand), Phnom Penh (Cambodia), Porto (Portugal), Rio de Janeiro, Saint Petersburg, Santiago (Chile) and Sardinia. Prices vary according to location from €1,175 course fee in Florence to $2,100 in New York.

ARGENTINA

EBC SERVICIOS LINGÜÍSTICOS: Anchorena 1676, 1425 Capital Federal, Buenos Aires; ✆ +54 11 6379 9391; 0800 845 6719 (UK, free); ✆ +1 888 393 4015 (US free); info@ebc-tefl-course.com; www.ebc-tefl-course.com; US$2,300 including shared accommodation.

ÍBERO SPANISH SCHOOL: 150 Uruguay Street, Buenos Aires; ✆ +54 11 2057 1116; info@iberotefl. com; www.iberotefl.com; intensive 4-week TEFL certificate courses offered monthly; $1,100 plus course materials costing $45; can be combined with 3 weeks Spanish tuition for $1,475; followed by optional 4-day trip to Iguazu Falls. Claim that 99% of graduates find paid jobs after gaining certificate.

MENTE ARGENTINA: Av. Santa Fe 3192 piso 4'b', C1425, Buenos Aires; ✆ +54 11 3968 7861 (Argentina); +1 858 926 5510 (USA); +44 203 286 3438 (UK); info@menteargentina.com; www.menteargentina.com. 4-week TEFL certificate course offered monthly; 150 hours including 24 hours of teaching practice. All-in prices including accommodation from US$2,690 for student residence to $3,250 for private apartment, all in the best areas of Buenos Aires such as Palermo, Belgrano, Barrio Norte and Recoleta. Spanish course can also be arranged.

ROAD2ARGENTINA: Buenos Aires; ✆ +54 11 4826 0820; www.road2argentina.com/tefl-argentina. Partner of EBC above with follow-on volunteer teacher placement programme (for a fee).

TEFL INTERNATIONAL: Recoleta Institute, Ayacucho 1571, 1055 Buenos Aires; ✆ +54 11 6380 3134; admin@teflinternational.org.uk; www.teflinternational.org.uk; 120-hour TESOL; monthly start dates; course fee $1,790.

AUSTRALIA

AUSTRALIAN TESOL TRAINING CENTRE (ATTC): Sydney: Level 1, 31 Market Street, Sydney, NSW 2000; ✆ +61 2 9389 0249; Brisbane: Level 1, 295 Ann Street, Brisbane, QLD 4001; ✆ +61 7 3229 0350; train@attc.edu.au; www.attc.edu.au. CELTA centres that offer Foundation in TESOL course (4 weeks); full and part-time courses throughout the year; accommodation service available; internet enrolment $1,500.

ENGLISH LANGUAGE SERVICES: Adelaide Institute of Technical and Further Education (part of the Government Department of Education, Training and Employment), 5th Floor, Renaissance Centre, 127 Rundle Mall, Adelaide, South Australia 5000; ✆ +61 8 8207 8805; els.tesol@tafesa.edu. au; http://els.sa.edu.au; Certificate IV in TESOL; 315 curriculum hour course A$3,300; TESOL for overseas teachers and TESOL online.

GLOBAL TESOL AUSTRALIA: Sarina Russo Centre, 82 Ann Street, Brisbane, Queensland 4000; ✆ +61 7 3221 5100; teachenglish@sarinarusso.com.au; www.globaltesol.com; 120-hour to 600-hour programmes available; tuition fees A$995–A$2,300; all courses can be completed in-class, online or by correspondence; job overseas guaranteed.

LANGUAGE TRAINING INSTITUTE (LTi): PO Box 1061, Nambour, Queensland 4560 (+61 7 5442 3511; admin@LTi.edu.au; www.LTi.edu.au). Certificate IV in TESOL; 5 weeks full-time or up to 12 months part-time. Course can be completed on-site at several centres in Victoria, NSW and Queensland (and also Singapore and Tehran) or by distance education (either online or traditional using printed textbooks and workbooks). A$2,000–A$3,000.

TEACH INTERNATIONAL: Head Office, Level 2, 370 George Street, Brisbane, Queensland 4000; ✆ +61 7 3211 4633 ext 4; www.teachinternational.com; Foundation in TESOL, 100 hours, A$1,695; Certificate III in TESOL, 110 hours, A$2,295, and Certificate IV in TESOL, 220 hours, A$2,995, accredited by Australian government; offered throughout the year.

CAMBODIA

LANGUAGECORPS ASIA CO LTD: Phnom Penh, Cambodia; ✆ +855 23 211 087; +1 508 471 4852 (US); +44 203 287 4853 (UK); www.languagecorpsasia.com; also in Thailand and Vietnam; 4-week 140-hour TESOL courses available monthly in Cambodia, Thailand, Vietnam and special China/Taiwan programmes; $1,750 includes initial 2 weeks academic instruction at Panasastra University in Cambodia followed by final 2 weeks in country of choice with 20 hours of local language classes, 15 hours of teaching practice, and daily lesson planning and materials development workshops; also includes 3-day excursion to Angkor Wat; job placement assistance is provided in each country.

CHILE

THE TEFL ACADEMY: Av. Las Urbinas 68, Providencia, Santiago; ✆ +56 0245 36740; info@tefl-academy.com; www.tefl-academy.com; 120-hour certificate course; offered 7 times a year; US$1,699; life-long job assistance.

CHINA

BUSINESS ENGLISH SOLUTIONS INTERNATIONAL, LLC: Zhejiang China and 510 West Deming Place, Chicago IL 60614; ✆ +1 773 572 2473 (Chicago); ✆ +86 137 5725 2787 (China); Info@journeyeast.org; www.Journeyeast.org; TEFL Certification and iTEFL (Intensive TEFL China Certification); US$1,800–$2,800 including accommodation; ESL Job Placement Service.

TEFL INTERNATIONAL: At Gateway Language Village, Xiangzhou Culture Plaza, Ningxi Road, Zhuhai; ✆ +86 756 229 8967; admin@teflinternational.org.uk; www.teflinternational.org.uk; 120-hour accredited TESOL certificate course; good job and internship prospects all over China with the job placement assistance programme; course runs monthly and costs US$1,590 (including accommodation).

COLOMBIA

ISSO – INTERNATIONAL STUDENT SERVICES ORG: Calle 24N #5 BN-63, Cali; ✆ +57 2 680 2001; also in Bogotá: cra. 15 # 95–35; ✆ 2 218 1679; www.estudiosexterior.com; training centres in Bogotá, Cali, Medellin and Barranquilla. In the past ISSO offered TEFL, TEYL and TKT (preparation course) among others.

COSTA RICA

COSTA RICA TEFL: Heredia and Playa Samara; info@costaricatefl.com; www.costaricatefl.com; offers 10 TEFL Certification courses per year, 160 hours' contact time; costs $1,350, including job placement assistance, course materials, course portfolio and text and access to local cultural events as well as a 10% discount on Spanish classes at Intercultura; the core instructors all have Masters degrees and/or higher in Education and in teaching English as a second or foreign language with more than 22 years of professional teaching experience; Heredia courses affiliated to Intercultura Costa Rica; www.interculturacostarica.com; see entry in Central America chapter.

MÁXIMO NIVEL EXECUTIVE LANGUAGE CENTER: de la Farmacia la Bomba 75m sur, San Pedro, San Jose (HQ in Cusco, Peru); ✆ +1 800 866 6358; info@maximonivel.com; www.maximonivel.com. 150-hour TEFL/TESOL Certificate (over 4 weeks) for US$1,400–$1,700 offered monthly except December; 50-hour TEIB (Teaching English for International Business) Certificate and TIEEP (Teaching International English Exam Preparation) Certificate (over 3 days), US$400 each; rough frequency 4 times a year; housing arranged with families, in shared apartments, hostels, etc from US$225 for 4 weeks; lifetime job-finding assistance; an average of 5 graduates are employed by Máximo Nivel each month.

TEFL INTERNATIONAL: TEFL International, S.A. Apartado #161 Quepos, 6350 Costa Rica; admin@teflinternational.org.uk; www.teflinternational.org.uk; 120-hour TESOL; optional Spanish as a Second Language Course; monthly start dates; course fee $1,690.

TESOL TRAINING COSTA RICA: PO Box 33-4417, La Fortuna, Alajuela; ✆ +506 2468 0020 or in USA: ✆ +1 585 200 3091; tesoltrainingcostarica@hotmail.com; www.tesoltrainingcostarica.org; School for International Training's TESOL Certificate Course; 1-month intensive, 3-month extensive; US$1,950 tuition, US$600 room and board in local homes or rented houses plus materials; other teacher training courses designed and delivered based on demand. Contact Mary Scholl.

CYPRUS

INTESOL: Limassol; UK office: ✆ +44 1565 631 743; info@intesolinternational.com; www.intesol international.com; 4-week TESOL course with teaching practice; lifetime job guidance.

PAPANTONIOU INSTITUTE: 30a Ippocratous, Nicosia 2122; ✆ +357 2245 5724; papantoniouinstitute @yahoo.co.uk; www.papantoniou-institute.com; 4-week and 8-week TEFL training, mainly for Cypriot teachers. 2-week practical training course offered between September and May, for £650 or €985 including 14 nights of hotel accommodation. Certificates issued by LTTC (London Teacher Training College).

CZECH REPUBLIC

BOHEMIA TEFL: Ceská 20, 370 01 Ceské Budejovice; ✆ +420 387 426 753/✆ +420 734 481 587; info@tefl-course.eu; www.tefl-course.eu; 2 week courses (65 hours) with minimum 6 hours' observed teaching practice; free organised activities during the course from adventure sports to brewery tour; interview and job assistance on completion of the course. €750. Affiliated with Grant Language School (www.grant-langschool.com).

ITC INTERNATIONAL TEFL CERTIFICATE: Frantiska Křížka 1, Prague 7 170 00; ✆ +420 224 817 530; info@itc-training.com; www.itc-international.eu; ITC trains English speakers during a 4-week 135-hour intensive course offered monthly which includes Business English; tuition is €1300, which includes registration, lifetime TEFL career and job guidance, course manual, all materials, and housing and visa help.

ITTP TEFL PRAGUE: Narodni 21, Prague 110 00; ✆ +420 775 071 550; www.tefl-prague.com. Onsite & Online international TEFL/TESOL certification courses. Offered monthly. $1,299–$2,090 depending on season.

TEFL IN PRAGUE: Edua Languages U Pujcovny 2, 110 00 Prague 1; ✆ +420 739 54 0930; info@ teflinprague.com; www.teflinprague.com. 4-week TEFL courses with job guarantee and visa support in the Czech Republic. €1,550 including 39 days of accommodation. Under the umbrella of EDUA Group, the biggest private educational institution in the Czech Republic.

TEFL INTERNATIONAL: Prague; admin@teflinternational.org.uk; www.teflinternational.org.uk; 120-hour TESOL; optional Czech Language Course; monthly start dates; from €1,300 plus accommodation from €300.

TEFL WORLDWIDE PRAGUE: Freyova ul. 12/1, 190 00 Prague; ✆ +420 603 486 830; info@teflworld wideprague.com; www.teflworldwideprague.com; Teach & Travel Worldwide! 4-week accredited and internationally recognised TEFL course offered monthly. American-owned school. Lifetime job guidance provided during and after the course. TEFL Worldwide has over 1,500 graduates who have taught in 60+ countries. €1,300 plus accommodation.

THE LANGUAGE HOUSE: Education Center SPUSA, Na poříčí 1038/6, 110 00 Prague 1; ✆ +420 224 210 813; Info@thelanguagehouse.net; www.thelanguagehouse.net. 4-week course offered 10 times a year. €1300 or €1550 with housing included (€100 discount February–May and November).

TEFL WORLDWIDE

Ginny Thompson remembers her experiences from the October 2006 course with TEFL Worldwide.

'When I think back about my two years living abroad, it's amazing to realise how much my four-week experience with TEFL Worldwide Prague has impacted my life. With a bag packed for only those four weeks, I arrived in Prague with an open mind and a desire to experience a life and culture outside of the States. Little did I know, I would end up living in the Czech Republic for two years, working in Spain, South Korea and Peru, travelling the world, developing lifelong friendships and most importantly experiencing illuminating growth.

'Although I had travelled and studied abroad before, I still arrived in Prague full of anxiety, a pounding heart and thoughts like, 'How can I possibly teach English to someone who doesn't understand English?' These thoughts were quickly comforted by a lovely welcome to the city from TEFL Worldwide Prague from the moment I arrived at my accommodation. It was reassuring to arrive in a completely foreign place and feel so well cared for and encouraged by TEFL Worldwide to truly make the most of my certification experience.

'The instructors were patient, competent and extremely knowledgeable in the TEFL field. As I had never taught a class before in my life I was shocked at how by the end of the four weeks I felt confident to walk into any classroom anywhere in the world and teach an engaging, successful lesson.

'I will always treasure memories like cooking dinner with friends while laughing over creative lesson ideas, the smile on my Czech student's face when she finally understood a grammar point, and the clinking of champagne glasses at the end of an incredible experience. TEFL Worldwide provided a program that not only gave me an excellent skill-set but also the freedom to be creative in my teaching, the support to find a job and home, and the encouragement to go out and explore the world. I've always said the most difficult part of leaving your comfort zone and moving abroad is that initial decision to pack your bags and get on a plane. After that first step, the world you enter will be an exciting, adventure-filled place full of experiences you can't even imagine. From then on your world will expand horizons beyond horizons and you will be so thankful you took that initial risk. TEFL Worldwide Prague welcomed me into that world, taught me to embrace it and will forever hold a special place in my heart.'

www.teflworldwideprague.com

ECUADOR

CENTRO DE ESTUDIOS INTERAMERICANOS/CEDEI: Casilla 597, Cuenca; ✆ +593 7 283 9003; info@cedei.org; www.cedei.org; summer TEFL programme, $3,225 including accommodation.

EGYPT

AMERICAN UNIVERSITY IN CAIRO: PO Box 74, New Cairo 11835; ✆ +20 2 2797 4978; teflinfo@auc-egypt.edu; www.aucegypt.edu; US enquiries to 420 Fifth Avenue, 3rd Floor, New York, NY 10018 2729; ✆ +1 212 730 8800; offers MA in Teaching English as a Foreign Language (MA/TEFL); American-style education in an overseas setting.

TEFL INTERNATIONAL: 4, Shohdy Basha Street, Stanly, Alexandria; admin@teflinternational.org.uk; www.teflinternational.org.uk; 120-hour TESOL; monthly start dates; course fee $1,690; optional teaching Internship programme with Arabic language and cultural programme, 10 weeks US$1,990 (incl. accommodation); steady supply of jobs in Cairo.

FRANCE

THE LANGUAGE HOUSE: Montpellier, Espace Langues, 5 ter avenue Saint Lazare, 34000 Montpellier; ✆ +33 6 84 83 85 59; info@teflanguagehouse.com; www.teflanguagehouse.com. Affiliated schools in Nice (English American Center, 22 rue d'Alsace Lorraine, 06000 Nice), as well as in Marrakesh (Morocco) and Antalya (Turkey). 4-week TEFL Certificate Program and 1-week Teaching Business English Program (also offered online). French programmes validated by IATQuO. Offered monthly. Cert. course costs €1,290, and Business course €690 onsite, €390 online. Homestays, single studios and shared apartments can be arranged. Job assistance focuses on Mediterranean countries. Contact Gyl Golden.

TEFL INTERNATIONAL: Association Camina Kergall, 22570 Plélauff, Brittany; admin@teflinternational.org.uk; www.teflinternational.org.uk; 120-hour TESOL; monthly start dates; course fee €1,590.

TEFL PARIS: 8 rue des Carmes, 75005 Paris; ✆ +33 143 25 7966; www.teflparis.com; 4-week certificate course operating since 2004. 8 times a year. €1,200 plus accommodation €320–€400.

GERMANY

LANGUAGE SPECIALISTS INTERNATIONAL: Pfalzburger Strasse 83, 10719 Berlin; ✆ +49 30 3450 2180; info@lsi-berlin.de; www.tefl-germany.com; 4-week TESOL courses run every month; €1,375.

GREECE

ANGLO-HELLENIC TEACHER TRAINING: PO Box 263, Corinth 20100; ✆ +30 27410 53511; info@teflcorinth.com; www.teflcorinth.com. Delivers training course for TEFL International (see entry below).

ANGLO-HELLENIC

Established in 1997, over the past 15 years Anglo-Hellenic has become synonymous with English teaching in Greece. Anglo-Hellenic Director Peter Beech moved to Greece to take up his first teaching post as a young graduate in 1987, and 10 years later inaugurated Anglo-Hellenic to fill the need for a reliable service linking schools and teachers. It was the search for native-speaker teachers to staff his own school in Corinth that led to the realisation that there was no dependable agency to provide that service. Over the next few years, Anglo-Hellenic quickly expanded to the point where they were organising placements for around a hundred teachers each year, and to date have placed well over a thousand native-speaker teachers in jobs in Greece.

Having established a network of clients throughout the country, Anglo-Hellenic used their influence to spearhead improvements in conditions for teachers – one result of this is that it is now standard practice for schools to provide rent-free accommodation for their teachers. Anglo-Hellenic has also been at the forefront of the movement to protect the rights of English teachers in Greece, most recently in organising opposition to proposals that would require English teachers to be proficient in Greek language.

In addition to teacher recruitment, Anglo-Hellenic also offers a range of teacher training courses. The TEFL International certificate course, run every month in Corinth, is a four-week course designed primarily for native-speakers of English intending to work in Greece. Providing extensive observed teaching practice with Greek students, children and adults, this course is the most effective preparation for teaching in Greece. Anglo-Hellenic also organises seminars and training courses for schools throughout Greece, as well as participating actively in conferences both in Greece and internationally.

CELT: 77 Akademias St, 106 78 Athens; ✆ +30 210 330 2406; www.celt.edu.gr; €1,300; 100+ hour Certificate course offered intensively in the summer months and part-time starting October, January, March and April; also offer CELTA course, €1,450.

TEFL GREECE/VIA LINGUA CRETE Chrysanthou Episkopou 48, 73 132 Chania; ✆ +30 28210 574 38; maria@vialingua.org; www.tefl.greece.com or www.vialingua.org. Offered 9 times a year. €1625 including shared accommodation.

TEFL INTERNATIONAL: 20 Vasiliou Street, 20006 Vrahati, 20100 Peloponnese; admin@tefl international.org.uk or info@anglo-hellenic.com; www.teflinternational.org.uk; 120-hour TESOL course over 4 weeks; monthly start dates; course fee €1,295. 10 hours' teaching practice with Greek children and adults. Teacher placement service via Anglo-Hellenic Teacher Recruitment (www.anglo-hellenic.com). Same course to be offered in Athens and Santorini from April 2012.

GUATEMALA

MÁXIMO NIVEL EXECUTIVE LANGUAGE CENTER: 6a Avenida Norte #16 y 16A, La Antigua (HQ in Cusco, Peru); ✆ +1 800 866 6358; info@maximonivel.com; www.maximonivel.com. 150-hour TEFL/TESOL Certificate (over 4 weeks) for US$1,400–$1,700 offered monthly except December; 50-hour TEIB (Teaching English for International Business) Certificate and TIEEP (Teaching International English Exam Preparation) Certificate (over 3 days), US$400 each; rough frequency 4 times a year; housing arranged with families, in shared apartments, hostels, etc. from US$225 for 4 weeks; lifetime job-finding assistance; an average of 5 graduates are employed by Máximo Nivel each month.

HONG KONG

CHINESE UNIVERSITY OF HONG KONG: 23/F, Tower B, School of Continuing and Professional Studies, The Chinese University of Hong Kong, Mongkok Town Centre, 90 Shantung Street, Mongkok, Kowloon; ✆ +852 2209 0235; www.scs.cuhk.edu.hk/cuscs/landings/lang_progs_eng. php?lang=en; two courses on offer: Diploma Programme in Teaching English as a Second Language, 10 months, tuition fee HK$13,500 plus HK$100 enrolment fee; Master of Arts Programme in Teaching English to Speakers of Other Languages (jointly organised by School of Continuing and Professional Studies, The Chinese University of Hong Kong and Lancaster University), 2 years, tuition fee HK$ 89,800 plus HK$200 enrolment fee; contact Carol To, Programme Coordinator.

HUNGARY

VIA LINGUA BUDAPEST: Tavasz u. 3, 1033 Budapest; ✆ +36 1 368 11 56; Budapest@vialingua. org; www.via-lingua.hu; 4-week intensive Certificate in TEFL course offered 5 times a year. €1,300 plus €300 for accommodation. Course run by Tudomany Nyelviskola (see entry in Hungary directory).

INDIA

TEFL INTERNATIONAL: Golpark, Kolkata, Bengal; admin@teflinternational.org.uk; www.teflinternational.org.uk; 120-hour TESOL; monthly start dates; course fee $1,490; internship, volunteering and paid teaching work arranged.

IRELAND

ALPHA COLLEGE OF ENGLISH: 4, North Great George's Street, Dublin 1; ✆ +353 1 8747024; admin@alphacollege.com; www.alphacollege.com.

CENTRE OF ENGLISH STUDIES: 31, Dame Street, Dublin 2; ✆ +353 1 6714233; info@ces-schools. com; www.ces-schools.com.

CLARE LANGUAGE CENTRE: Erasmus Smith Building, College Road, Ennis, Co Clare; ✆ +353 65 6841681; clarelc@iol.ie; www.clarelc.ie.

CORK LANGUAGE CENTRE INTERNATIONAL: Wellington House, 16, St Patrick's Place, Wellington Road, Cork; ✆ +353 21 4551661; info@corklanguagecentre.ie; www.corklanguagecentre.ie.

DORSET COLLEGE: 66 Lower Dorset St, Dublin 1; ✆ +353 1 8309677; info@dorset-college.ie; www. dorset-college.ie.

DUBLIN SCHOOL OF ENGLISH: Dollard House, 2–5 Wellington Quay, Temple Bar, Dublin 2; ✆ +353 1 6773322; admin@dse.ie; www.dse.ie.

GALWAY LANGUAGE CENTRE: The Bridge Mills, Galway; ✆ +353 91 566468; info@galway language. com; www.galwaylanguage.com.

INTERNATIONAL HOUSE DUBLIN: 66, Lower Camden Street, Dublin 2; ✆ +353 1 4759011/3; info@ ihdublin.com; www.ihdublin.com.

MEI: 1 Lower Pembroke Street, Dublin 2; ✆ +353 1 618 0910/1 618 0909; info@mei.ie; www.mei. ie; is an association of recognised schools and a representative body (similar to English UK); many MEI-RELSA schools provide teacher training courses (TEFL) and ACELS-accredited courses.

NORTH MON LANGUAGE INSTITUTE: North Monastery Road, Cork; ✆ +353 21 4394458; info@nmli.ie; www.nmli.ie.

U-LEARN: 6 Gardiner Place, Dublin 1; ✆ +353 1 8787 339; info@u-learn.ie; www.u-learn.ie.

Other course providers in the Republic of Ireland include:

INTERNATIONAL TEFL COLLEGE OF IRELAND: 29 Northumberland Avenue, Dun Laoghaire, Co. Dublin; ✆ +353 1 280 7001; info@itci.ie; www.itci.ie; 100-hour TEFL training courses; several courses run throughout the academic year (September to May); €500; teaching practice with foreign students free of charge.

ISRAEL

TASP (TEACH AND STUDY PROGRAM): Kadima, Israel; ✆ +972 9 899 5644; www.tasp.org.il; MA in Teaching English as a Foreign Language combined with 15 hours a week of interning in schools and Hebrew language classes; US contact: Jewish Federation of Greater Los Angeles (Talia Scharlin, TScharlin@JewishLA.org); from US$11,000 per year.

ITALY

ACLE (ASSOCIAZIONE CULTURALE LINGUISTICA EDUCATIONAL): Via Roma, 54, 18038 Sanremo; ✆ +39 0184 506070; info@acle.org; www.acle.org; 5–6 day intensive TEFL-TP (Through Theatre and Play) introductory course with full board and lodging included; €150 course fee; successful students work as paid tutors, teaching English at camps throughout Italy (see Italy chapter); this project offers a combination of theory plus invaluable practical experience with emphasis on drama and child-centred learning activities; tutors receive an introductory TEFL Certificate at the end of the working period.

INTERLINGUE LANGUAGE SYSTEM: Via Ennio Quirino Visconti 20, 00193 Rome; ✆ +39 06 321 5740/321 0317; info@interlingue-it.com; www.interlingue-it.com; TEFL International PELT Certificate courses run monthly (tefl.rome@interlingue-it.com; www.teflinternationalrome.it). €1,300 without accommodation; accommodation from €400; jobs often available for the best students on the courses.

TEACHING ENGLISH IN ITALY: Florence; www.teachingenglishinitaly.com. 4-week intensive courses offered monthly in Florence, US$500 deposit plus €1,190. 3-day weekend course 6 times a year at Europass. Florence; €200. Online course also offered which can be supplemented with Teaching Practice Programme in Florence lasting 1 or 2 weeks.

THE LEARNING CENTER OF TUSCANY, LLC: Viale Corsica, 15c/17a, Florence 50134; ✆ +39 055 051 5035; Cell USA ✆ +1 831 917 4752; www.learningcentertuscany.com; CTEFL school affiliated with TEFL International, offering a 4-week course in the basic methods of English language teaching, mainly for native English speakers; offered monthly; deposit of €500 plus €960.

VIA LINGUA FLORENCE: Via Brunelleschi 1 50123 Florence; ✆ +39 055 283161; florence@vialingua. org; www.cteflflorence.com; 1-month intensive; approximately 10 a year; course fee €1,175 plus €400-€550 for accommodation.

JAPAN

TEFL INTERNATIONAL: Watanabe Students House, 18–15 Kamiyama-cho, Shibuya, Tokyo; admin@teflinternational.org.uk; www.teflinternational.org.uk; 120-hour TESOL; monthly start dates; course fee US$2,290; paid teaching work arranged.

MEXICO

DUNHAM INSTITUTE: Avenida Zaragoza 23, Chiapa de Corzo, Chiapas; ✆ +52 961 61 61498; academic-coordinator@dunhaminstitute.com; www.dunhaminstitute.com; 4-week TEFL course in conjunction with Spanish courses and language exchange and tutoring of local students; minimum commitment 8 weeks if tutoring local students or 5 months if teaching in schools; US$1,500 includes free homestay with local family.

INTERNATIONAL TEACHER TRAINING ORGANIZATION: Madero No. 469, Guadalajara, Jalisco 44100; ✆ +52 33 3658 3224/03614 3800; toll-free from UK: ✆ 0800 404 9800; toll-free from USA: ✆ +1 866 514 7479; info@www.teflcertificatecourses.com; www.teflcertificatecourses.com/guadalajara.html; offered monthly; US$1,400.

TEACHERS LATIN AMERICA: Avenida Cuauhtemoc 793, Colonia Narvarte, DF Del Miguel Hidalgo; ✆ +52 55 52564108; teachers@innovative-english.com; www.innovative-english.com; 80-hour plus TEFL Certificate Programme; 40 hours in-class study, 10–20 hours of instructor-assessed student teaching and at least 25 additional hours of self-study on grammar, lesson planning, etc. US$1,190 including accommodation; job assistance throughout Latin America; TEFL online certificate course US$350.

PERU

MÁXIMO NIVEL EXECUTIVE LANGUAGE CENTER: Avenida El Sol 612, Cusco; (see also Costa Rica and Guatemala); ✆ 800 866 6358 info@maximonivel.com; www.maximonivel.com; 150-hour

TEFL/TESOL Certificate (over 4 weeks) for US$1,400 offered monthly except December; 50-hour TEIB (Teaching English for International Business) Certificate and TIEEP (Teaching International English Exam Preparation) Certificate (over 3 days), US$400 each; rough frequency 4 times a year; housing arranged with families, in shared apartments, hostels, etc. from US$225 for 4 weeks; lifetime job-finding assistance; an average of 5 graduates are employed by Máximo Nivel each month.

SEPA DEL PERU: (Servicios Educativos Peruanos Americanos del Peru), Puente Bolognesi 114–116, Arequipa; ✆ +51 54 222390; educationalexcellence@gmail.com or sepa@perupass.com; www.perupass.com (click on the logo of SEPA del Peru); 13-week TEFL training and volunteer teaching programme ('World's Toughest TEFL/TESOL Program'); monthly start dates; US$2,955; possibility of extra Spanish classes (US$75 for 10 hours per week); homestay or alternative accommodation (US$40–$65 a week).

PORTUGAL

INTERNATIONAL HOUSE LISBON: Rua Marques Sá da Bandeira 16, 1050–148 Lisbon; ✆ +351 21 315 1493/4/6; ttraining@ihlisbon.com; 4 week (120 hours) CELTA courses (€1450); also part-time DELTA course (200 hours) and IH Younger Learners Certificate (€725).

SOUTH AFRICA

TEACHERS SA/ONE WORLD LANGUAGE SCHOOL: 5th Floor, 50 Long Street, Cape Town 8001; ✆ +27 21 422 4493; info@teacherssa.co.za; www.teachersSA.co.za; entry-level TEFL courses focusing on the fundamentals of communicative language teaching; run throughout the year; courses run in Cape Town and Pretoria.

SPAIN

ANGLO CENTRES: Calle Unió, 41, bajo, Tarragona 43007; ✆ +34 977 546 309; www.tefl.anglocentres.com. 4-week residential Certificate course, accredited by College of Teachers. Offered 6 times a year; €1,200. Also offer online and short courses. Contact Vince Ferrer.

CANTERBURY TEFL: Calle Covarrubias 22, 2° Derecha, 28010 Madrid; ✆ +34 91 125 01 09/610 266 427; www.canterburytefl.com; 40 hours of teaching theory supplemented by 40 hours of lesson planning, 20 hours class observation and 20 hours paid internship. Course fee €1,275 reduced by €280 for paid teaching. Contact James Clarke.

EBC SERVICIOS LINGÜÍSTICOS: Orense 16, 2E, 28020 Madrid; ✆ +34 91 555 3975; info@ebc-tefl-course.com; www.ebc-tefl-course.com; offered monthly; approx £915/€1,175.

EUROPE TEFL TEACHER TRAINING: Salvador Espriu 91, 08005 Barcelona; ✆ +34 932 215 515 info@europetefl.com; www.europetefl.com; 4-week intensive full-time; TEFL courses run throughout the year in Barcelona, Seville, and many other locations in Europe and Latin America; €1,300, including all course materials, expert job guidance, alumni network and more; accommodation in the city centre and close to the schools can be arranged, €400–500 a month; contact: Kevin Cline.

INTERNATIONAL HOUSE BARCELONA: Calle Trafalgar 14, 08010 Barcelona; ✆ +34 93 268 3304; training@bcn.ihes.com; www.ihes.com/bcn; Business English Teachers course, 36 hours over 2 weeks, July only, €450; also, Director of Studies Training Course and Trainer Training Course, both 1 week in July, €555; and the International Diploma in Language Teaching Management (IDLTM), 2-week on-site course in July followed by 8 months of on-line assignments, €3,150; help given with finding accommodation.

OXBRIDGE BARCELONA: Numancia 47 entl 2, 08029 Barcelona; ✆ +34 902 500 100; UK: +44 20 8133 0043; tefl@oxbridge.es; www.oxsite.com. Oxbridge International TEFL Certificate with employment opportunities. 120 hours including 20 hours of real teaching practice. Subsidised course price after a successful interview in Barcelona, with reduction of €400 from full price of €1,250.

OXBRIDGE MADRID: Corredera Baja de San Pablo 39, 28003 Madrid; ℭ +34 91 112 97. As above.

TEFL INTERNATIONAL: In Seville, Granada and Barcelona. admin@teflinternational.org.uk; www. teflinternational.org.uk; 120-hour TESOL; monthly start dates; course fee from €1,390.

TtMADRID: Calle General Yague 70, 1°, 28020 Madrid; ℭ +34 91 572 1999; info@ttmadrid.com; www.ttmadrid.com; 4-week intensive courses accredited by the College of Teachers; courses run monthly; course fee €1,375. Interviews with teaching agencies arranged on graduation; course emphasis on teaching Business English; real teaching experience with adults and elective inputs on how to teach children.

THAILAND

AYC INTERCULTURAL PROGRAMS: 9/197, 7th Floor, GOT Building Soi Ratchadaphisek 29, Ratchadaphisek Road, Chatuchak, Bangkok, 10900; ℭ +66 2556 1533 38; gettesol@ aycthailand.com; www.aycthailand.com; 120-hour TESOL certification validated by INTESOL; course runs every month and costs US$899; job guarantee for native English speakers under 52 years of age, holding a bachelor's degree.

CHICHESTER COLLEGE, THAILAND: 1st Fl., Muangthai Phatra Complex, 252/193 Rachadapisek Rd., Bangkok 10320; ℭ +66 2 693 2901; www.chichester.ac.th; TESOL certificate and diploma courses in cooperation with Chichester College UK; certificate runs 10 weeks part-time 5 times a year, or 4 weeks full-time (offered monthly); TESOL diploma course runs over 6 months beginning October and April; US$1,490 for full-time Certificate course, US$890 for part-time; US$1,800 for Diploma; accommodation offered at a private lodge near the Chichester Training Centre in Bangkok, and provided at a special subsidised rate of US$100 for the entire duration of the full-time course only; graduates are provided teaching placements in Thailand or Cambodia.

PARADISE TEFL THAILAND: ℭ +66 846 161609; info@teachinparadise.com; www.paradisetefl.com; 4-week courses in Chiang Mai in Northern Thailand; 4-week Certificate course (120 hours) plus 2-week and weekend intro course. 4-week course costs 40,000 Baht (£600) including guaranteed job placement.

SEE TEFL (Siam Educational Experience): Chiang Mai; ℭ +66 53 266295/6; info@seetefl.com; www.seetefl.com; 4 week training course. 10 times a year. US$1,495 (or $1,295 if booked early). Accommodation can be provided for extra $200-$300. Job guarantee.

THE TEFL INSTITUTE: United Educational Consultants Co. Ltd, 4th Floor, Silom Plaza, Silom Road corner Narathiwat Road, Bangkok 10500; ℭ +66 2 233 2388; info@teflthai.com; www.teflthai.com; 120 hours over 5 weeks with 10 start dates throughout the year; 44,500 Baht; course earns eligible graduates 9 US graduate credits in education, US Master's degree can be completed in 1 year while teaching in Thailand, also offers graduate diploma in teaching, 3.5 year part-time Bachelor degree in education, and weekend study for 1.5-year dual US and Thai accredited master's degree (www. uecthai.com), including required Thai teaching licence.

TEFL INTERNATIONAL: 38/53–55 Moo 1, Klaeng, Muang Rayong 21160; ℭ +66 38 652 280; admin@teflinternational.org.uk; www.teflinternational.org.uk; 120-hour TESOL certificate course at Ban Phe, Chiang Mai and Phuket; £8,980 excludes accommodation; job and volunteering prospects arranged throughout Thailand.

TESOL COURSE THAILAND: Bangkok and Phuket; www.tesolcoursethailand.com; 120 hours (3 weeks) in-class course followed by 4-5 months of teaching in Thailand with free accommodation. Course fee US$1,100. Affiliated to American TESOL Institute.

TEXT AND TALK ACADEMY: 1961 Phaholyothin Road (opposite Mayo Hospital), Lardyao, Chatuchak, Bangkok 10900; ℭ +66 2561 3443; info@TEFLTeachThai.com; www.teflteachthai.com; 6 week certificate courses (about US$1,495), upgrade and refresher course, 16 week diploma course, 8 week TEYL course, 8 week advanced skills course and home study course.

UNITEFL THAILAND: T. Suthep, A. Muang, Chiang Mai 50200; ✆ +66 88-402-8217; www.unitefl.com; 120-hour course offered monthly. 45,000 Baht (£900). Affiliated to TEFL International and TAFEs (vocational colleges) across Australia.

TURKEY

INTESOL TURKEY: Antalya and Istanbul; www.amerikankultur.org.tr/intesol; INTESOL Certificate in the Methodology and Practice of English Language Teaching. 4-week onsite face-to-face course, 9-week onsite face-to-face course (weekday evenings), 9-week onsite face-to-face course (weekends), or online TESOL Course. Assistance with accommodation available.

VIA LINGUA ISTANBUL: Kent English, Kirtasiyeci sok. no.1, Kadiköy, Istanbul; +90 216 3472791/2; istanbul@vialingua.org; www.tefl-turkey.com. 4-week CTEFL course offered 6 times a year. €1,300 plus €300 for accommodation.

VIETNAM

MIDWEST EDUCATION GROUP, 4633 N. Western Ave., Suite 207, Chicago, IL 60625 (✆ +1 847 496 7919; contact@midwested.us; www.midwested.us). 4-week classroom-based TESOL programme in Vietnam. MEG has satellite offices in the two major cities plus Can Tho south of Ho Chi Minh City; course cost is $1,100.

FINDING A JOB

You have only two choices: to search for a job from afar or go to the country of your choice and look around. Having a job arranged before departure obviously removes much of the uncertainty and anxiety of leaving home for an extended period. It also allows the possibility of preparing in appropriate ways: sorting out the right visa, researching the course books in use, etc. Others prefer to meet their employer and inspect the school before signing a contract. It is always an advantage to meet or make contact with other teachers to get the real lowdown on a particular employer and place, rather than accepting a job in complete ignorance of the prevailing conditions. But of course this is not always feasible.

Employers usually choose their staff several months before they are needed, so most schools advertise between April and July for jobs starting in September. If you want to look for a job in person, you will either have to go on a reconnaissance mission well in advance of your proposed starting date or take your chances of finding a last-minute vacancy.

FINDING A JOB IN ADVANCE
There are three ways of finding a teaching job in advance:

- *By answering an online advertisement*
- *Using a recruitment agency or the large international English teaching organisations such as International House*
- *Conducting a speculative job search, i.e. making contact by email or letter with all the schools whose addresses you can find in this book or on the internet.*

TEFL WEBSITES

For schools, a website advert offers an easy and instantaneous means of publicising a vacancy to an international audience. Teachers looking for employment can use search engines to look for all pages with references to EFL, English language schools and recruitment. CVs can be emailed quickly and cheaply to advertising schools, who can then use email themselves to chase up references. The internet has very quickly taken over as the primary means of recruitment.

Arguably it has become a little too easy to advertise and answer job adverts online. At the press of a button, your CV can be clogging up dozens, nay, hundreds of computers. It is interesting to remark that some of the schools that corresponded with this book said that they seemed to get a more reliable brand of teacher from readers of this book and that they are more impressed with a job-seeker who goes to the trouble of assimilating the information in a book than the ones who spend their days skating over the internet. But basically, recruitment via the internet is here to stay.

While opening up an enormous range of possibilities, the internet can be a bewildering place to job-hunt. A host of websites promises to provide free online recruitment services for English teachers. Because many sites are struggling on the margins, they often seem to offer more than they can deliver and you may find that the number and range of jobs posted are disappointing. You would hope that a site with a name like 'eflteachingjobs.com' would have more than unpromising links such as 'TV Cabinets for Teachers' and some general waffle. But everywhere you look on the internet, potentially useful links can be found. More than 100 websites are devoted to EFL/ESL jobs, many in Asia. For many years Dave Sperling's 'Dave's ESL Cafe' (www.eslcafe.com) dominated the field and it is still the first port of call for many to check job vacancies and investigate further. Often the job discussion forums are invaluable, for example if you are considering signing a contract with a training company in Kazakhstan; although some of these forums tend to be quite a few years old. In any case 'Dave' provides a mind-boggling amount of material and many links to specific institutes and chains in each country.

Another key international site is www.tefl.com, which has gained in authority and popularity over recent years. When subscribing (for free), you can specify whether you want to be notified of vacancies by email on a daily or weekly basis. The site claims to have more than 18,000 registered employers. At the time of writing the countries with the most vacancies listed were China (48) and Spain (43).

It is possible to register your details as a job-seeker. **Fergus Cooney** learned the hard way not to be too general:

> *I posted a message simply stating 'Qualified teacher seeking job'. Within two days I was inundated with many dozens of replies requesting my CV and, more surprisingly with job offers everywhere, although the majority were from Korea, Taiwan and China. 'Jackpot,' I thought (I have since realised that many schools/agents must have an automatic reply system which emails those who advertise in the way I did). I quickly began sifting through them, but not as quickly as they kept arriving in my inbox. Before a few more days had passed, I had become utterly confused and had forgotten which school was which, so I deleted them all, got a new email address and posted a second, more specific message on Dave's.*

These two giants of the TESL world (eslcafe.com and tefl.com) have pushed some other rivals out of business. Here is a brief survey of some of the key recruitment sites:

- http://tesljobs.com – current dated vacancies with archive of older postings, country by country, Afghanistan to Yemen.
- http://youcanteachenglish.com/jobs – clear list of worldwide vacancies. At the time of writing there were one or two vacancies listed for many countries and no less than 194 for China.
- www.ihworld.com – International House maintains a clear website with links to its 150 affiliated schools in 50 countries with email addresses of directors and directors of studies. The recruitment and training sections of the website are accessible to all.
- www.tefl.net/esl-jobs/index.htm – more limited choice than some, but carries some up-to-date vacancies.
- www.eslbase.com – reasonably reliable links to language schools, country by country. Also posts current vacancies on Facebook at www.facebook.com/eslbase.
- www.Totalesl.com – part of the Icon Group of Thailand (www.icongroupthailand.com), which also owns Tesall.com and ESL Job Feed. Strongest in vacancies in Asia.
- www.tefllogue.com – discursive site with links to blogs and other sites that might be useful (but no current vacancies).
- http://jobs.guardian.co.uk/jobs/education/tefl – job vacancy listings on the *Guardian* Unlimited website. In the olden days the Tuesday *Guardian* was a primary source of TEFL job ads but the online version is a shadow of its former self (only one advertiser outside the UK at the time of writing). www.guardian.co.uk/education/tefl has an archive of relevant articles and a directory provided by country-by-country experts.
- www.eslemployment.com – reasonably new site with a good selection of dated vacancies.
- www.eslteachersboard.com – free community for EL teachers with current job postings (dated and with email addresses revealed).
- www.eflweb.com – vacancies are undated.
- www.jobs.edufind.com – TEFL jobs board operating since 1995 with 35,000 registered teachers using the service. Shows a list of 'most applied for' positions.
- www.teflscotland.co.uk and www.teflengland.co.uk – some current vacancies; contact details available to trainees on their TEFL training course.
- www.footprintsrecruiting.com – Vancouver-based recruitment service showing the range of vacancies in Korea, Taiwan, China, Chile, etc. that they are trying to fill.
- www.onestopenglish.com – maintained by the educational publisher Macmillan.
- www.jobsabroadbulletin.co.uk – jobs board has a 'Teaching & TEFL' section, which remains archived.
- www.teflcourse.net/tefl-jobs is good – easy to navigate with historic dated vacancies (part of ITTT – International TEFL & TESOL Training).

TEFL SCOTLAND

Now teaching in Xinjiang, a former TEFL Scotland student shares her experience of living and working in China.

Why did you decide to take a TEFL course?

'I saw it as a great opportunity to work and travel. I really wanted to experience living in a different country, learn a new language and learn more about different cultures. Though I had a reasonably well paid job that I enjoyed, I wasn't tied down in any way and I needed a change from the daily grind. I felt that if I didn't do it now, it might never happen.'

Best experience in the classroom?

'I created a game using giant dice, where names are pulled from the hat and the student chosen must roll the dice. On the board I had numbers 2 to 12 written with a question or forfeit including "4 = sing an English song" and "12 = do a little dance". The class just loved it, all cheering each other on.'

Worst experience in the classroom?

'I arrived one morning, got everything set up for the movie I planned to show them then, as the class piled in, the school had a power cut! I had 50 students all looking at me expectantly and I didn't have a clue what to do. The lesson I learnt there was, always have a back-up option.'

What challenges have you faced so far?

'There was some civil unrest in this region last year which resulted in the internet and international calls being cut off for 10 months. This was a bit of a challenge for me as I was away from home, but it allowed me to really immerse myself in the culture here and form some close bonds with new friends.'

What do you do for fun?

'I go to yoga classes at the local gym or meet friends for dinner. I have a good mixture of friends, probably an equal mix of foreign, Chinese and Uighur. At weekends I'll often meet up with friends and go to the big bustling Uighur market, to the country for a picnic or into the mountains for a walk.'

How would you sum up your experience as a TEFL teacher?

'It has been inspirational. I have been working in a very supportive environment and watching the kids improve has been incredibly rewarding. I feel like teaching has come quite naturally to me, and it has helped me make some decisions about my long-term future.'

Do you have any useful pieces of advice?

'Just do it, don't hold back – you won't regret it! I'm yet to meet a single person who regrets moving abroad to teach. Make sure you research the job first; I suggest that you contact some current employees and ask for their opinion about the school and the area. The most important thing is to be positive.'

Other websites that are country-specific, e.g. www.ohayosensei.com (jobs in Japan) or www.ajarn.com (teaching in Thailand) are listed in the relevant country chapters.

RECRUITMENT FAIRS

In an ideal world, prospective teachers could meet a range of employers all at once. Certified classroom teachers looking for vacancies in international schools have access to this kind of event (see section on Certified Teachers below). But it is not very common in TEFL. The energetic **Aidan O'Toole**, long-time resident of Andalucia, describes the advantages of the annual job fair he has spearheaded in Cordoba, where Spanish language schools can meet job-seekers in May:

> Last year was the first Spain-wise recruitment fair which was a success with 226 teachers attending and 60 FECEI language schools. Each side invests a small amount of money into getting a job, which is far more efficient than teachers flying out from England for just one or two interviews. The chance to meet face to face is tremendously useful for both sides. Of course tefl.com (and similar) have transformed the recruitment process and the typed CV and letter box seem to belong to another era. But it is just too easy for newly qualified teachers to lean on the wrong button on their computer and send out hundreds of CVs, sometimes in answer to adverts they haven't even read.

Aidan thinks that meeting a range of job-seekers makes it much easier for language school owners to spot the best candidates than rifling through a pile of CVs from new CELTA graduates. Meeting face to face also allows candidates who do not fit the perfect profile a chance to shine.

The only other job fairs we have heard of specifically for TEFL teachers take place in China (see chapter).

RECRUITMENT ORGANISATIONS

Major providers of ELT and teacher placement organisations of various kinds may be able to assist prospective teachers in English-speaking countries to find teaching jobs. Some are international educational foundations; some are voluntary organisations such as the Peace Corps or charities; some are major chains of commercial language schools; and others are small agencies which serve as intermediaries between independent language schools abroad and prospective teachers. The companies and organisations listed in this chapter have been assigned to the following categories (though there is some blurring of distinctions):

- International ELT organisations (including the major language school chains).
- Commercial recruitment agencies.

- Voluntary, gap year and religious organisations.
- North American organisations, which cater primarily (though not exclusively) to citizens of the USA and Canada.
- Placement Services for British and American state-qualified teachers.

Note that agencies and organisations that operate only in one country or one region are described in the country chapters in the second part of this book.

It is hardly worthwhile for a family-run language school in northern Greece or southern Brazil to pay the high costs which most agencies charge schools just to obtain one or two native-speaker teachers. Vacancies that are filled with the help of agencies and recruitment consultants tend to be at the elite end of the ELT market. Jobs advertised by agencies are usually for specialised or high-level positions, for example in corporations with in-house EFL programmes or foreign governments.

HOW AGENCIES WORK

Agencies make their money by charging client employers; the service to teachers is usually free of charge. By law in the UK, no fee can be charged to job-seekers either before or after placement, except if a package of services is sold alongside (e.g. insurance, visas, travel, etc.) Note that different rules apply in other countries, so that placement fees are the norm in the USA. Some of the best recruitment organisations to deal with are ones that specialise in a single country and are located in situ, such as English Educational Services in Madrid or Anglo-Hellenic Recruitment in Corinth (see Spain and Greece chapters). They tend to have more first-hand knowledge of their client schools.

Bear in mind that the use of an intermediary by foreign language institutes is no guarantee of anything. Particularly in the American context, small independent recruiters are sometimes trying to fill vacancies that no-one in the country who is familiar with the employer would deign to fill. As the American **Rusty Holmes** said of his employer in Taiwan, 'The school was so bad it had to recruit from America.' If you are in any doubt about the reliability of an agency or the client he/she represents, it is a sensible precaution to search online and ask for the name of one or more current or recent teachers whom you can ask for a first-hand account. It is a bad sign if the agency is unable or reluctant to oblige.

The hiring of teachers for chain schools abroad is done either at a local level especially when they are franchises (so direct applications are always worthwhile) or centrally, if the school has trouble filling vacancies.

One way in which recruitment agencies work is to create a database of teachers' CVs and to try to match these with suitable vacancies as they occur. In order to be registered with such an agency it is almost always essential to have a relevant qualification, often at least the Cambridge or Trinity Certificate and very often much more since agencies tend to deal with high level, difficult-to-fill vacancies. Smaller agencies may have fewer vacancies on their books but they can often offer a more personal service. A good agency will provide a full briefing and information pack on the school in particular and the country in general, and will make sure that the contract offered is a reasonable one.

Volunteer English teachers are in demand by dozens of commercial sending agencies which routinely charge volunteers £800–£2,000+ for placement and related services. Before her final year at university, **Susannah Kerr** took up one of these placements in Thailand which she found to be less structured than the agency literature had promised. She felt that the school to which she was assigned did not really need English-speaking volunteers and she suspected that they invited foreigners merely as status symbols. With hindsight she felt that she had been naïve to assume that the school would be grateful for her efforts. She was allowed to teach whatever she liked, so naturally she concentrated on spoken English and taught no grammar and only occasional writing exercises. She was given no lesson plans and was not required to prepare the students for exams. When the teachers saw that the volunteers were coping, they took a holiday.

THE BRITISH COUNCIL

The British Council (www.britishcouncil.org) is the largest ELT (English Language Teaching) employer in the world. The Council represents the elite end of the English language teaching industry. At its own 130 or so teaching centres in 56 countries, it offers the highest quality language teaching available in those countries and employs the best qualified teachers, so it is important to understand that the British Council will not welcome applications from very inexperienced or unqualified teachers. The British Council is a very professional organisation and jobs with it tend to come with attractive terms and conditions.

The Council's offices abroad are usually well informed about opportunities for English language teaching locally. Most maintain a list of private language schools (while making it clear that inclusion does not confer recognition), which is often a useful starting point for a job search.

The Council publishes an Address Book of its offices worldwide which is updated quarterly, and an interactive map (www.britishcouncil.org/new/articles/maps), with links to its centres around the world. The charter of the British Council defines its aims as 'to promote Britain abroad, providing access to British ideas, talents and experience in education and training, books and periodicals, the English language, the arts, the sciences and technology'. It is non-profit-making and works non-politically (although that didn't stop President Putin pressuring it to suspend operations in Russia in December 2007). It employs just over 6,000 staff overseas, a good percentage of whom are involved with the teaching of the English language in some capacity. In some countries such as Hungary the British Council has closed its teaching centre and prefers to work with local organisations to promote the teaching of English. Partly because of government cutbacks, the British Council has closed more than 30 teaching centres in the past few years. Other work that the Council carries out includes the running of libraries, the organisation of cultural tours and exchanges, etc. But language teaching and teacher recruitment remain one of its central concerns.

A useful starting place for qualified EL teachers is to check the recruitment information at www.british council.org/teacherrecruitment.htm (10 Spring Gardens, London SW1A 2BN; +44 20 7389 4928; teacher. vacancies@britishcouncil.org). This links through to the list of current vacancies at www.britishcouncil.org/ learning-teachingjobs.htm. Further details can be obtained from the Resourcing Office (current contact is Jonathan Wix). British Council teaching centres recruit both through London and locally. They especially welcome applications from teachers with experience or an interest in specialist areas such as Young Learners, Business English, skills through English, IELTS exam preparation, etc.

Contracts are usually for two years and renewable. Although terms and conditions vary from centre to centre, the terms of employment with the British Council are generally favourable. Teachers recruited through the Teacher Recruitment Service have their airfares paid, an allowance for shipping their belongings and an attractive salary package. Many teachers value all the intangible benefits such as the security of working for an established institution, and encouragement of professional development with possible perks such as receiving a subsidy to study for a Diploma qualification or other training grants. Once you have secured one job with the Council, it is possible to move to other jobs in other places, since the Council regularly notifies its network of all vacancies.

A completely separate programme run by the British Council is the placement of language assistants in schools for an academic year. The Language Assistants Team administers exchange programmes with 18 countries worldwide. Applicants for assistant posts must be aged 20–30 and native speakers of English who have completed their secondary education and at least two years of degree-level study in the UK, usually but not necessarily in the language of the destination country. In some countries (especially China and countries in Latin America) posts are of particular interest to graduates interested in a career in TEFL. The website is open for applications from October and the deadline for submission is 1 December (for a job starting the following autumn), though the deadlines may be extended for posts in China. Contact the Assistants Team (10 Spring Gardens, London SW1A 2BN; +44 20 7389 4596; assistants@britishcouncil. org; www.britishcouncil.org/languageassistants). There are offices also in Scotland (British Council Scotland, The Tun, 4 Jackson's Entry, Holyrood Road, Edinburgh EH8 8PJ; +44 131 524 5735); and Northern Ireland (7 Fountain Street, Belfast BT1 5EG; +44 28 9024 8220).

In conjunction with the BBC, the British Council also maintain a website called Teaching English (www.teachingenglish.org.uk), which is a free resource for teachers and includes lesson plans, work sheets, teaching tips, etc.

The British Council is a large and complex institution with two headquarters: one at 10 Spring Gardens, London SW1A 2BN (+44 20 7930 8466) and the other at Bridgewater House, 58 Whitworth Street, Manchester M1 6BB (+44 161 957 7000). Telephone callers who do not know exactly which department they need should contact the Council's Information Centre in Manchester (+44 161 957 7755; general.enquiries@british council.org).

INTERNATIONAL ELT ORGANISATIONS

The Bell Educational Trust Worldwide Educational Services, Hillscross, Red Cross Lane, Cambridge CB2 0QU (+44 1223 275500; www.bell-worldwide.com/jobs). Bell recruits teachers for ELT posts in its associated schools in Thailand (deployment.thailand@bell-worldwide.com), and for many current overseas projects in the Middle East (Bahrain, Jordan, Qatar, Saudi Arabia and Libya), Asia (China and Vietnam) and Central Europe (Poland, Romania, Bulgaria, Ukraine and Azerbaijan). Candidates will be required to have a degree and a recognised TEFL qualification.

Bénédict Network International Sarl, www.benedict-international.com. Dozens of franchised business and language schools in Europe (mostly in Germany, Switzerland and Italy), plus several in Russia and Ecuador.

Berlitz, www.berlitz.com; links to vacancies worldwide (some of them past their sell-by date). Berlitz is one of the largest language training organisations in the world with about 550 franchised locations in at least 50 countries. It is also one of the oldest, founded in 1878. The company's core business is language and cultural training, and teacher vacancies occur most often in Germany, Turkey and Korea. All Berlitz teachers are native, fluent speakers and university graduates; all must undergo training in the 'Berlitz Method', a direct 'see-hear-speak' teaching approach that does not rely on translation. Berlitz is known for supervising their teachers' techniques very closely, and deviation from the method is not permitted. When Berlitz has urgent vacancies to fill, usually in southern Europe, it places an advertisement in British newspapers inviting any interested university graduates to attend interviews in London, Manchester, Edinburgh or Dublin. Usually, however, Berlitz schools abroad employ teachers directly, usually on a part-time basis initially, after they have completed a two-week Method course. Berlitz have been expanding their summer programmes for young learners in Germany, Spain, etc.

Cactus TEFL, (www.cactustefl.com) is a consultancy which advises on TEFL training courses but is of little help in job-finding.

CfBT Education Trust, 60 Queens Road, Reading RG1 4BS (+44 118 902 1000; www.cfbt.com). Has offices in Brunei, Malaysia and Oman which recruit for and manage EFL/EAP/ESP/Primary/Secondary teachers and instructors for various projects and contracts. The website contains contact details for each office and information on how to apply. CfBT's International Development Group (+44 118 902 1000; consultancydatabase@cfbt.com), at above address, with regional bases in Africa, South East Asia and the Gulf, recruits education consultants for donor-funded projects and programmes in developing countries.

EF English First Teacher Recruitment and Training, 666 Fuzhou Road, 1st Floor, Shanghai, China 200001 (+86 21 6133 6043; efrecruitment@ef.com; www.teachenglishfirst.com and for China only www.ef-teachers.com). Recruitment of teachers for 200 EF schools in China, Russia and Indonesia.

ICC – The European Language Network, Berner Heerweg 183, D-22159, Hamburg (+49 40 645 32963; info@icc-languages.eu; www.icc-languages.eu). Umbrella organisation for adult education associations (e.g. Volkshochschulen, folk high schools or Universities of Applied Sciences) in

17 European countries co-operating in the learning and teaching of foreign languages in Europe. Can provide enquirers with a list of member organisations and contact names. The ICC runs specialist training courses for foreign language teachers in adult, continuing and vocational education. A teacher certification scheme (EUROLTA: European Certificate in Language Teaching to Adults) is also in operation.

IH World Organisation, Unity Wharf, 13 Mill Street, London SE1 2BH (+44 20 7394 2147; worldrecruit@ihworld.co.uk; www.ihworld.com). International House (IH) is one of the largest and oldest groups of language schools, teaching English as a foreign language (and 25 modern languages) in 150 schools in 50 countries worldwide. IHWO Recruitment Services is based in London at the International House World Office, which is the co-ordinating body for all International House affiliated schools. It is responsible for managing the recruitment of teachers, trainers and senior staff for IH schools and annually expects to assist in the recruitment of between 350 and 400 teachers for International House schools worldwide. The minimum qualification requirement for teaching posts is the Cambridge CELTA, IH CYL or Trinity TESOL Certificate. All IH schools adhere to internal quality standards which provide strict guidelines on terms and conditions, working hours and working environment. For further information on teaching and senior posts abroad visit www.ihworld.com/recruitment. (Note: IH London, a language school and teacher training centre, is a separate company; see training directory.)

Inlingua (www.inlingua.com). International chain of 345 language centres that operate autonomously in 43 countries across Europe, Africa, Asia, North and South America. Link to jobs on website. At the time of writing there were vacancies in its schools in Italy, Germany, Ecuador and India.

Language Link, 21 Harrington Road, London SW7 3EU (+44 20 7225 1065; recruitment@language-link.co.uk; www.languagelink.co.uk). Training and recruitment agency which places about 200 qualified (including newly qualified) teachers in its network of affiliated schools in Russia, China, Vietnam and Uzbekistan. Usually minimum qualifications are TEFL Certificate or PGCE or experience but visit the website of the country you wish to work in as the agency may be running in-service training courses over the period of the contract. Employment contracts are from 36 weeks and some involve 24 contact hours per week. Local pay rates. Shared apartment accommodation is usually provided at no additional cost or deduction from the salary. Interested teachers should ring to arrange an interview (in the UK or in Russia, etc.), and then send CV and photo. (See Training chapter for details of Language Link's CELTA courses.)

Marcus Evans Linguarama, 7 Elm Court, 1 Arden Street, Stratford-upon-Avon CV37 6PA (+44 1789 203910; personnel@linguarama.com or dannycoughlan@linguarama.com; www.linguarama.com/employment). Linguarama specialises in providing language training for professionals. Applicants for jobs in Linguarama language schools abroad must have at least a degree and a Cambridge/Trinity Certificate (or equivalent). Linguarama finds placements for 50–100 teachers and has an office in London for teacher interviews as well as the above address, which deals with vacancies at 21 centres in six European countries including Germany, the Netherlands, Spain and Italy.

Richard Lewis Communications, Riversdown House, Warnford, Southampton, Hampshire SO32 3LH (+44 1962 771111; david.lewis@rlc.global.com; www.crossculture.com). RLC has a network of offices worldwide, especially in Finland, Sweden and Germany, specialising in cross-cultural training and language teaching.

Saxoncourt, 59 South Molton Street, London W1K 5SN (+44 20 7491 1911; recruit@saxoncourt.com; www.saxoncourt.com). One of the largest UK-based recruiters of EFL teachers, Saxoncourt places several hundred teachers per year in schools worldwide. Clients are based in Japan, Taiwan, China, Italy, Vietnam, Peru, Saudi Arabia and elsewhere. Applications are welcome, particularly from candidates with a Cambridge CELTA, Trinity TESOL or equivalent qualifications. Interviews are held in London, where possible. Interested candidates should register online at www.saxoncourt.com. The Saxoncourt website features a regularly updated current vacancies page, online registration and country-specific sections with downloadable information packs.

SAXONCOURT

Saxoncourt sends teachers to China most months of the year. From initial application to arrival the company does everything it can to make the process as simple and as smooth as possible. Here's an example of a teacher who chose to work at one of our schools.

Why China?

'Adventure! Where else can you go down to your local market to pick up fresh fruit and vegetables along with a bag full of live hedgehogs, toads and what I can only guess is some sort of grub. Or join in a mass public aerobics class held in the city's square every morning. Then have people literally gasp because you're the first westerner they've ever seen, followed quickly by a hundred shy "Hellos". I wanted to discover just how differently other people see the world, the way they live, their upbringing and ambitions. I've also found out how very similar everyone is when it comes to the simple mundane things in life. I can do all this here, without even mentioning how ripe this vast country is for exploring.'

How did your recruitment company help you?

'Saxoncourt made everything easy for me. No doubt there were lots of things going on behind the scenes to make it possible for me to come here. I had them to help me with each step of the process, from the interview and contracts, entry visa, booking flights and even after I touched down in Beijing. I think Saxoncourt were the first to ask if I'd arrived safely. Months after I often pop online for a catch up. As they have so much experience, it makes it easy to chat about how things are going, especially as they know or have experienced exactly what you're talking about.'

How is the teaching?

'I have a variety of classes and age groups which keeps things interesting for me and my brain constantly active. Chinese students are enthusiastic, curious – mostly about me – and motivated, which makes going to school enjoyable. It's refreshing when you've just finished a class and there's a line of students asking you for more or extra homework. I was weirded out the first time this happened, but you soon learn to get used to it.'

What are you doing now?

'Currently I'm working at a brand spanking new school in the Henan province. The team are great and the school is growing quickly. I'm the only foreign teacher here right now but we all muck in together and the other staff speak great English. I'm looking forward to welcoming some new teachers to the school very soon and can see myself being here for at least the next couple of years. Providing they'll have me, and don't replace me with a younger, updated model.'

Wall Street Institute (teach@wallstreetinstitute.com; www.wallstreetinstitute.com). With headquarters in Baltimore, WSI operates both company-owned and franchised centres, and employs more than 2,000 teachers in over 400 centres in 28 countries and territories in Asia (China, Indonesia, Hong Kong, South Korea, Taiwan, Thailand), Europe (France, Germany, Italy, Portugal, Spain, Switzerland, Russia, Turkey), Latin America (Argentina, Brazil, Chile, Colombia, Ecuador, Mexico, Nicaragua, Peru, Venezuela), the Middle East (Israel, Saudi Arabia) and Africa (Morocco). The countries with almost continuous vacancies are China, Russia, Ecuador and Indonesia. Applicants should have at least a bachelor's degree and the appropriate professional qualifications of a CELTA or equivalent TEFL certificate. One year's teaching experience is an advantage. Due to restrictions on visa legislation in many countries within the network, WSI prefers teachers from the UK, Ireland, USA, Canada, Australia, New Zealand and South Africa. The interview process is as follows: a first-round interview is a 'get to know you' interview that will probably last around 45 minutes. Some countries will consider doing this on the phone with offshore applicants. A second-round interview will involve discussing a lesson plan created by the applicant and giving a brief teaching presentation of approximately 15 minutes. This interview will also last approximately 45 minutes. Qualified applicants can apply online at www.wallstreetinstitute.com/jobSeekers/teachingStaff/teachingStaff.aspx.

COMMERCIAL AGENCIES

If you have a TEFL background, you can send a CV with covering letter via email or post to the relevant agencies. Agencies that specialise in a single country are not included in this chapter, but are mentioned in the country chapters.

Anglo-Pacific (Asia) Consultancy, Suite 32, Nevilles Court, Dollis Hill Lane, London NW2 6HG (+44 20 8452 7836/+44 20 8452 2826). Educational consultancy specialising in recruitment in Thailand, Taiwan, China, Japan and the rest of South East Asia. Also offers careers guidance to TEFL teachers returning from overseas. Welcomes approaches from graduates (or people with an HND/equivalent higher qualifications) who have a recognised TEFL certificate. Places teachers at all levels in the public and private sectors and provides teachers with background information about their destination country including teaching tips and cultural information.

ESLstarter, Scarborough (info@eslstarter.com; www.eslstarter.com). Official recruitment partner for international schemes such as EPIK in Korea and TLG in Georgia. Also offers jobs or volunteer placements in Thailand, China and India.

Evocation EFL, Bon Marché Centre, 241–251 Ferndale Road, Brixton, London SW9 8BJ (+44 20 7274 8441); efl@evocationefl.net; www.evocationefl.net). Annually recruit about 200 teachers from English-speaking countries, after a face-to-face interview in the UK. Candidates must have CELTA/Trinity TESOL, first degree and at least some relevant experience. Most clients are in the UK, though agency has recently sought teachers for Saudi Arabia and Russia.

Footprints Recruiting (www.footprintsrecruiting.com). A proactive and principled teacher recruitment agency based in Canada with vacancies mostly in Korea but also in Chile, Georgia and other countries.

Global Recruitment Solutions (+44 7790479238; grsteachers@gmail.com or alison.recruitment@ gmail.com; www.globalrecruitsolutions.co.uk). Sole proprietor, Alison Morgan, interviews and places 300+ teachers per year for the Middle East, Malaysia, Singapore, etc. University degree required plus a teaching qualification such as PGCE + QTS or CELTA/TEFL for ESL positions.

HuntESL (www.huntesl.com). Online recruiter operating out of Honduras, especially active in Korea. Sister site of www.intesolinternational.com, which promotes INTESOL's TEFL training courses.

Language Solutions International, 11 Coldbath Square, London EC1R5HL (+44 20 7689 1900/ +44 7725 497166; barry.shorten@langsols.com or info@langsols.com; www.langsols.com). Global network of privately owned schools that specialise in teaching working adults in the energy industry; welcomes applications from highly qualified and experienced EFL teachers: Milan, Madrid, Baku (Azerbaijan), Atyrau (Kazakhstan), Algeria, Qatar, Libya and Jubail Industrial City (Saudi Arabia). Minimum requirement is a CELTA certificate.

Oxford Vision Education Ltd, 2nd floor, 22 Bloomsbury St, London WC1B 3QJ (+44 20 7436 0278; info@oxfordvision.com; www.oxfordvision.com). London-based consultancy that recruits TEFL teachers for international network of 500 private schools and language centres, with partner offices in Turkey, Azerbaijan, Turkmenistan, Kazakhstan, Nigeria, Ghana, Germany and China.

Prime Education Consultancy, York Science Park, Heslington, York, YO10 5NP (+44 1904 567673; info@primeeducation.org.uk; www.primeeducation.org.uk). UK-based recruitment consultancy for the education sector with vacancies primarily in Turkey and the Middle East.

Reach to Teach, head office in Iowa, USA (+1 201 467 4612; UK +44 203 286 9794, Australia +61 2 8011 4516, New Zealand +64 9 889 0557; www.ReachToTeachRecruiting.com). Describes itself as one of the largest human resource companies for teachers in Asia, primarily Korea, China, Taiwan and Thailand. Reach to Teach also places teachers in Georgia, Eastern Europe and Chile. All services are free to teachers.

Teachaway, Toronto and Vancouver, New York and Queensland (www.teachaway.com). Recruits for employers in Korea, China, Taiwan, Saudi Arabia, Mexico and many others. Appointed recruiters for state-qualified teachers to work in the public school system of Abu Dhabi among others.

TEFL Express, London W6 (0800 048 8861; jobs@teflexpress.co.uk; www.teflexpress.co.uk). Assists in recruiting for short-notice vacancies with Language Link with which they are affiliated. Also year-round recruitment and internships in Russia, China, Thailand, Hong Kong, Czech Republic and Uzbekistan. Candidates must be TEFL/CELTA trained; for some positions in China 2 years of experience is required.

TEFLOne (www.teflone.com). Since 2006, TEFLOne has been recruiting TEFL-certified teachers for repu- table schools in Taiwan, Japan, throughout China (including Beijing and Shanghai) and Indonesia. Advice is also available for positions in Vietnam and Korea. Positions start every month in all coun- tries, and teachers can be placed many months in advance. All positions offer a competitive salary with full training, support and great opportunities for career progression. TEFLOne carries out the whole recruitment process from advertising to interviewing, reference checking, visa liaison and ar- ranging arrival time. Candidates are provided with as much information and support as possible. Due to the requirements of the schools, TEFLOne can proceed only with teachers who are native English speakers from the UK, USA, Canada, South Africa, Ireland, Australia or New Zealand and holders of a recognised degree and a TEFL qualification. Most successful candidates will have completed an intensive 120-hour classroom-based TEFL course that includes at least six hours observed teaching practice. Applicant details are also added to a newsletter distribution list, which is sent out every two months by email and contains information on positions in schools in Asia with articles written by teachers. Contact David Coles (david.coles@teflone.com or Skype teflonerecruitment2).

UIC Teachers, Language House, 76–78 Mortimer Street, London W1W 7SA (+44 20 7307 1983; www.uicteachers.com). Recruits qualified EFL teachers for well established employers abroad, e.g. Shane Schools in Japan.

VOLUNTARY, GAP YEAR AND RELIGIOUS ORGANISATIONS

Christians Abroad (0300 012 1201; recruit@cabroad.org.uk; www.cabroad.org.uk). Ecumenical charity providing information and advice to people of any faith or none who are thinking of working overseas, whatever their circumstances, whether short- or long-term, voluntary or paid. Occasional openings for TEFL teachers, e.g. in Tanzania.

VSO (Voluntary Service Overseas), 317 Putney Bridge Road, London SW15 2PN (+44 20 8780 7500; enquiry@vso.org.uk; www.vso.org.uk). VSO works in more than 34 countries in Africa, Asia and the Pacific, and receives requests, including some in EFL teaching and training, for example in Ethiopia, Rwanda and Vietnam. Volunteer requirements vary but the usual commitment is two years. Most placements are for skilled and qualified professionals aged 18–75 from a variety of backgrounds. VSO recognises the Trinity TESOL and Cambridge CELTA qualifications. The VSO package for its volunteers includes airfares, medical cover, National Insurance contributions, rent-free accommodation and a modest salary in line with local pay rates. VSO also provides full in-country support including pre-departure training and briefing, basic language and cultural orientation on arrival prior to starting placement.

A number of companies charge school-leavers and others to arrange volunteer placements abroad, many of which are in schools where volunteers teach English. Several of those listed here are founder members of the Year Out Group (www.yearoutgroup.org), formed to promote well-structured gap year programmes.

AIESEC (www.aiesec.co.uk). Acronym for the International Association for Students of Economics and Management, a student organisation with links to 90 countries. AIESEC can organise placements in any of its member countries for students and recent graduates in many fields including education.

Educators Abroad (www.educatorsabroad.org). Paying participants are sent to 25 countries on all continents for 4 or 10 weeks throughout the year to volunteer as a resource for a teacher of English in another country. US$500 placement fee plus US$2,300–$4,200 excluding travel. Host schools assist with accommodation.

Global Crossroad, Irving, Texas (+1 866 387 7816; www.globalcrossroad.com). Volunteer teaching and internships in 23 countries. Paid teaching in China (1–12 months). Placement fee of $799 for paid teaching in China; for volunteer programmes in many countries including Tibet, application fee of $350 plus weekly fee.

Global Nomadic, London (+44 20 7193 2652; www.globalnomadic.com). Tries to minimise costs in its placements worldwide, including paid teaching in Thailand and China, and volunteer teaching in many other countries.

Inspire Volunteering, Newbury (0800 323350; www.inspirevolunteer.co.uk). Volunteer teaching placements from two weeks to six months in India, Nepal, Cambodia, Romania, Ecuador, Chile, The Gambia and Tanzania. Prefer older candidates with teaching experience. Costs start from £800 for a 1-month placement. All accommodation and some meals are included.

IST Plus, Churcham House, 1 Bridgeman Road, Teddington TW11 9AJ (+44 20 7788 7877; www.istplus.com). Formerly CIEE UK, IST Plus administers the Teach in China and Teach in Thailand programmes (see respective chapters).

i-to-i TEFL, 261 Low Lane, Leeds, LS18 5NY (+44 113 205 4610; info@i-to-i.com; www.i-to-i.com or www.onlinetefl.com). i-to-i offers intensive TEFL/TESOL training weekends at venues in UK/Eire cities or online courses, with many teaching placements worldwide for paying volunteers.

Lattitude Global Volunteering, 42 Queen's Road, Reading, Berkshire RG1 4BB (+44 118 959 4914; volunteer@lattitude.org.uk; www.lattitude.org.uk). Overseas volunteering opportunities for 17–25 year olds, including teaching, in many countries. Posts are for between four and 12 months (six is average) and cost the volunteer between £1,750 and £2,300 depending on the programme, plus airfare, insurance and medical costs. Board, lodging and (sometimes) a living allowance are provided. A one-week teaching skills course is mandatory for those undertaking to teach English.

Projects Abroad, Aldsworth Parade, Goring, Sussex BN12 4TX (+44 1903 708300; info@projects-abroad.co.uk; www.projects-abroad.co.uk). Sends up to 5,000 people abroad annually on a variety of projects in developing countries, such as Bolivia, Cambodia, Mongolia and Senegal. Projects start from two weeks in length, with an average volunteer spending three months. Three-month placements cost between £1,395 and £2,595, depending on placement, excluding travel costs but including accommodation, food, insurance, placement and in-country support.

The Project Trust, Hebridean Centre, Ballyhough, Isle of Coll, Argyll PA78 6TE (+44 1879 230444; info@projecttrust.org.uk; www.projecttrust.org.uk). Sends school leavers (aged 17–19) to teach (often other subjects as well as English) in schools across Central and South America, Africa and Asia. Participants must fundraise to cover part of the cost of their 12-month placement, at present £5,100 (2012/3).

Travellers Worldwide, 2A Caravelle House, 17/19 Goring Road, Worthing, West Sussex, BN12 4AP (+44 1903 502595; info@travellersworldwide.com; www.travellersworldwide.com). Provides teaching as well as many other work experience and volunteer placements worldwide. Prices start from £695. Travellers also runs a weekend TEFL course in the UK as well as distance learning courses; for details, see www.tefltime.com.

Travel to Teach (T2T), Chiang Mai, Thailand (+66 84 365 4035; www.travel-to-teach.org). Thai-based organisation which provides volunteer teaching opportunities (among others) in Thailand, Cambodia, Laos, China, Bali, Nepal, Costa Rica, Ecuador, El Salvador and Mexico. Fees start at £490 for a month.

Travelworks, Münsterstr. 111, 48155 Münster, Germany; (+44 844 576 5411 (UK), +49 2506 830 3299 (from outside UK); www.travelworks.co.uk). Tour operator that offers gap year, volunteering projects and paid work programmes in over 30 countries around the world, including some English teaching.

USIT, 19/21 Aston Quay, Dublin 2, Ireland (+353 1 602 1742; volunteer@usit.ie; www.usit.ie). In addition to the paid teaching placements USIT has in Thailand and China, it also places paying volunteers who do not need to have qualifications to teach in developing countries: Nepal, Peru, India, Thailand, Indonesia, Mozambique, Ghana and South Africa. Prices are from €750 for a month.

Volunteering Solutions, (0800 014 8160; www.volunteeringsolutions.com/teaching-volunteer-projects). Teaching placements in many countries in Africa, Asia and South America, from teaching monks in Galle, Sri Lanka to aspiring tourism workers in Honduras. Agency is based in Delhi with an office in Singapore.

OPPORTUNITIES FOR NORTH AMERICANS

Although the companies, agencies and charities listed here are based in the USA and cater primarily to North Americans, some may be in a position to help overseas applicants. Recruitment agencies in the USA have stronger links with Latin America and the Far East than with Europe. As in Britain, some organisations are involved primarily with English-medium international schools following an American curriculum, and are looking to recruit state-certified teachers; these are listed separately at the end of this section.

AIDE (Association of International Development and Exchange) (+1 866 6-ABROAD; reinventyourself@aideabroad.org; www.aideabroad.org). Variety of overseas placements in volunteer, internship, work, and teach abroad programmes lasting two weeks to 12 months in Argentina, Chile, China, Costa Rica, Ecuador, Guatemala, India, Peru, Spain, etc. Participants pay a programme fee to cover placement, airport pick-up, accommodation, meals, local support, medical insurance and optional language courses.

Center for Intercultural Education and Development (CIED), Georgetown University, Washington, DC (http://elf.georgetown.edu). The English Language Fellow Program, administered by the CIED is a 10-month fellowship sponsored and funded by the US Department of State. Participants must be US citizens, have an MA in TESOL or a related field and at least two years' teaching experience. Participants receive a stipend, living allowance to cover food, housing, local transportation and utilities. Pre-departure briefings take place in August.

CIEE: (Council on International Educational Exchange), 300 Fore Street, Portland, ME 04101 (+1 800 40-STUDY; www.ciee.org/teach). Administers teaching in Chile, China, Spain, Dominican Republic, South Korea, Vietnam and Thailand. Participants are placed in local schools where they teach English and are compensated with a local salary and temporary or permanent housing.

Council for International Exchange of Scholars, 3007 Tilden St NW, Suite 5L, Washington, DC 20008 3009 (+1 202 686 4000; scholars@iie.org; www.cies.org). The Fulbright Scholar Program, administered by the US Department of State, provides grants for teaching English in over 30 countries. A doctorate is usually required, although a master's degree is sufficient in some countries. Applicants must be US citizens.

InterExchange, 161 Sixth Avenue, New York 10013 (+1 212 924 0446; info@interexchange.org; www.interexchange.org). Arrange homestays with 15 hours a week of English tutoring of the family in France, Spain, Italy, Austria and Germany ($695 for 1–3 months), plus paid EFL teaching posts in Chile and China and volunteer teaching in Ghana (for 1–8 months). Programme fees from $1,195 do not include airfare.

LanguageCorps, Stowe, Massachusetts; (+1 978-562-2100; toll-free (North America): +1-877-216-3267; www.languagecorps.com). Company offers 4-week TESOL training course offered in many places worldwide, and then job placement in Southeast Asia, Latin America, etc. TESOL Plus programme includes accommodation, insurance and travel and is available in Thailand, Cambodia, Vietnam, Ecuador and Mexico.

Office of English Language Programs (OELP), US Department of State, SA 44, Room 304, 301 4th Street, SW, Washington, DC 20547 (http://exchanges.state.gov/englishteaching). OELP creates and implements high-quality English language programmes in specific regions and countries around the world. OELP's programmes promote understanding of American language, society, culture, values and policies. Some Embassy Public Affairs Departments provide English language instruction as do binational centres, which work closely with American embassies. Most teachers for binational centres are hired directly by the centre in question; addresses are listed on the website given above. Teachers with an MA in TESL/TEFL may apply for the English Language Fellow Program, a 10-month fellowship programme that provides American professional expertise in teaching English as a foreign language. Qualified candidates who want to teach in US Department of State Cultural Centers should go to the website and follow the link to 'Employment Outside the United States'. The English Language Specialist programme recruits US academics in the fields of TEFL/TESL and Applied Linguistics for short-term (two to four weeks) assignments abroad.

Peace Corps, Washington, DC (+1 800 424 8580; www.peacecorps.gov). TEFL has historically been one of the major programme areas of the Peace Corps, which has programmes in more than 70 countries. One-third of the nearly 8,000 volunteers who serve work in the education sector, with the majority of them in ELT. Volunteers, who must be US citizens, over age 18 and in good health, are sent on 27-month assignments. All expenses, including airfare and health insurance, are covered. Peace Corps volunteers teach at both secondary and university level, and some become involved with teacher training and curriculum development. It can take up to a year between application and departure. Education volunteers must have a college degree (not necessarily in education) and a minimum of three months' experience of ESL tutoring one-to-one or classroom teaching.

TESOL (Teachers of English to Speakers of Other Languages), Alexandria, Virginia (+1 240 646 7048; info@tesol.org; www.tesol.org). A key organisation for professional ESL/EFL teachers worldwide, TESOL is a non-profit association offering various publications and services to 12,000 members in 120 countries. Full individual membership costs $95 ($33 for students) per year, there is also electronic membership. Members receive a listing of job vacancies worldwide, or can search jobs online. TESOL also organises the Job MarketPlace, an ESL/EFL job fair held during TESOL's annual convention.

WorldTeach, Cambridge, Massachusetts (+1 857 259 6646; www.worldteach.org). Non-profit organisation that provides college graduates with one-year contracts (EFL or ESL) to American Samoa, Bangladesh, Colombia, Costa Rica, Ecuador, Guyana, Namibia, the Marshall Islands, Panama, China, Chile, Pohnpei (Micronesia), Rwanda, Tanzania and Thailand. Eight-week summer programmes are available in China, Costa Rica, Ecuador, Poland, Namibia and South Africa. Participants pay a volunteer contribution ranging from zero to $5,990; several programmes are fully funded by the host country including Bangladesh and Micronesia.

CERTIFIED TEACHERS

Certified primary and secondary teachers who want to work in mainstream international schools abroad should be aware of the following agencies and organisations, which match qualified candidates with vacancies. Most of the hiring for primary and secondary schools abroad (often referred to in the American context as K-12 – kindergarten to grade 12) is done at recruitment fairs included on the list below. The files of job-seekers are added to a database that can be consulted by recruiters, who then choose whom they want to interview. Candidates who successfully land a job abroad with the help of a US agency may have to pay a placement fee of $300–$600, though in some cases the employer underwrites this expense.

Council of International Schools, 21a Lavant St, Petersfield, Hampshire GU32 3EL (+44 1730 263131; www.cois.org). Assists only teachers who have a BEd or PGCE with at least two years' teaching experience. The agency hosts two recruitment fairs in London every January and May, and in the USA and has a searchable database online of accredited international schools.

Gabbitas Educational Consultants, London (www.gabbitasrecruitment.com). Established for 137 years, Gabbitas maintains a register of qualified and experienced teachers available for teaching posts in South America, Europe, etc. Gabbitas generally recruits subject-specialist teachers for English-medium schools.

International Schools Services, Princeton, New Jersey, USA (www.iss.edu). Offers teaching opportunities for educators in private American and international schools around the world. ISS hosts three international recruitment centres (IRCs) annually, where interviews are conducted by international school administrators. Applicants must have a bachelor's degree and relevant K-12 experience. IRC registration materials are provided on approval of application.

Queen's University, Kingston, Ontario (ed.careers@queensu.ca; http://info.educ.queensu.ca/torf/index.php). Organises the Teachers' Overseas Recruiting Fair. Registration closes in January for fair held in February for international schools. Teacher certification required plus at least two years' K-12 teaching experience.

Search Associates, British branch: David Cope, Berry House, 41 High Street, Over, Cambridge CB24 5NB, UK (+44 1954 231130; dr.cope@virgin.net; www.search-associates.co.uk). Fully qualified primary and secondary teachers with some experience either in the UK or in a British-system international school overseas should use this contact. Teachers preferring to work in International Baccalaureate schools overseas should contact Harry Deelman, Search Associates, PO Box 168, Chiang Mai 50000, Thailand (+66 53 244322; deelman@loxinfo.co.th; www.search-associates.com). Search Associates is not usually appropriate for TEFL teachers who have no school experience but offers information and placement assistance for teachers with at least some mainstream school experience (with pupils aged 3–18). Long-term positions only (one- to three-year contracts, renewable). Recruitment fairs for candidates seeking jobs in international schools are held annually in London, Dubai, San Francisco, Sydney and others.

Teacher Recruitment International (Australia), Sydney, Australia (+61 2 9360 0458; www.triaust.com). Places teachers in primary and secondary school posts in international schools in Europe, Asia, the Middle East and, to a lesser extent, South America. Initial small registration fee but no placement fee.

University of Northern Iowa, Overseas Placement Service for Educators, Cedar Falls, Iowa (overseas.placement@uni.edu; www.uni.edu/placement/overseas). UNI is a non-profit organisation and it does not charge any placement fees to schools or teaching candidates. Educators must hold current certification in elementary or secondary education.

SPECULATIVE JOB HUNT

The vast majority of language schools do not publicise their vacancies internationally and instead depend on local adverts, word of mouth, personal contacts and direct approaches. Because there is quite a high turnover of staff in TEFL positions, a speculative job search has a better chance than in many other fields of employment. For a successful campaign, only two things are needed: a reasonable CV and a list of addresses of potential employers. But always bear in mind that the majority of language schools won't offer you work until they have interviewed you in person and in the opinion of some old hands, it's probably wise to avoid language schools that are prepared to offer work to candidates they haven't met.

APPLYING IN ADVANCE

Entire books and consultancy companies are devoted to showing people how to draw up an impressive curriculum vitae (CV, or résumé as it is called in the USA). But it is really just a matter of common sense. Obviously employers will be more inclined to take seriously a well-presented document than something scribbled on the back of a dog-eared envelope. Obviously any relevant training or experience should be highlighted rather than submerged in the trivia about your schooling and hobbies. If you lack any TEFL experience, try to bring out anything in your past which demonstrates your 'people skills', such as voluntary work, group counselling, one-to-one remedial tutoring, etc. and your interest in (and ability to adapt to) foreign countries. If you are targeting one country, it would be worth drawing up a CV in the local language; **Judith Twycross** was convinced that her CV in Spanish was a great asset when looking for teaching work in Colombia. If you get the job, however, be prepared for your new employer to expect you to be able to speak the vernacular.

School websites very often have a Recruitment or 'Work for Us' icon, and increasingly applications are invited online. The necessary steps and required documents should all be explained clearly. Customs differ. In France, for example, many companies ask for a 'motivation letter'.

Attitudes and personality are probably just as important as educational achievements in TEFL, so anything which proves an aptitude for teaching and an extrovert personality will be relevant. Because this is difficult to do on paper, some eager job-hunters have gone so far as to submit a little film of themselves, preferably a snippet of teaching. A simpler alternative might be to send a photo and a CD/audio file of your speaking voice, again assuming this will be a help rather than a hindrance.

The other essential ingredient is the names and contact details of language institutes. Each of the country chapters in this book provides such a list and recommends ways of obtaining other addresses, for example by contacting a federation of language schools (if there is one) or the British Council in your destination country. The most comprehensive source of addresses of language schools is usually the *Yellow Pages,* which in many cases can now be consulted online. Just type 'yellow pages' and your destination country into a search engine and then search for *Scuole di Lingue* in Italy, *Jazykova Skola* in the Czech Republic and so on. Some countries are much better than others, for example, the online Portuguese Yellow Pages are very helpful whereas the Turkish are not.

Of course it has to be stressed that it is difficult, and increasingly so, to set up a firm job offer simply by correspondence. A language school would have to be fairly desperate to hire a teacher they had never met for a vacancy that had never been advertised. It is a good idea to follow up any hint of interest with a phone call. The best time to phone language school directors is six or seven weeks before the beginning of term. Perhaps the school has a contact in your country who would be willing to conduct an informal interview on their behalf. Increasingly schools are using Skype to interview prospective staff, so that they can see you as you speak.

If your credentials are not the kind to wow school directors, it might still be worth sending off a batch of warm-up letters, stating your intention to present yourself in person a couple of weeks or months hence. Even if you don't receive a reply, such a strategy may stick in the mind of employers, as an illustration of how organised and determined you are.

INTERVIEWS

Whether you are interviewed at home or abroad, slightly different rules apply. For example, smart casual dress, neither flashy nor scruffy, is appropriate in Britain, while something more formal might be called for in certain cultures such as France or Japan. Even if all your friends laugh when you pack a suit before going abroad, you may find it a genuine asset when trying to outdo the competition. As **Steven Hendry**, who has taught English both in Japan and Thailand with none of the usual advantages apart from traveller's canniness, says:

> *You may not need a tailor-made suit but you definitely need to be able to present a conservative and respectable image.*

As with the CV, so at interview: highlight anything that is remotely connected with teaching even if it has nothing to do with the English language, and do it energetically and enthusiastically. Yet keenness will seldom be sufficient in itself. You don't have to be an intellectual to teach English; in fact the quiet bookish type is probably at a disadvantage. An amusing illustration of this is provided by **Robert Mizzi**'s description of his interview for the JET Programme in the Japan chapter.

DON'T HAVE A TEFL BACKGROUND?
Do a certain amount of research, e.g. acquaint yourself with some of the jargon such as 'notional', 'communicative-based', etc. It is not uncommon for an interviewer to ask a few basic grammar questions. To help you deal with this eventuality, see the list of recommended reading in the chapter on Preparation. Visit the ELT section of a bookshop to begin familiarising yourself with the range of materials on offer. Always have some questions ready to ask the interviewer, such as 'Do you favour the Oxford or Cambridge course books?', 'What audio materials do you have?', 'Do you encourage the use of songs?' or 'Do you teach formal grammar structures?' If you are looking for an opening in a business context, you might pick up a few tips from the section on Interviews in the chapter on Germany.

You will certainly be asked how long you intend to stay and (depending on the time of year) nothing less than nine months will be considered. They will also want to know whether you have had any experience. With luck you will be able to say truthfully that you have (at least) taught at a summer school in Britain (again, see chapter on Preparation). Some applicants who are convinced that they can do a good job make a similar claim, untruthfully, knowing that at the lower end of the TEFL spectrum this will never be checked. Similarly some candidates claim to have done a TEFL course and pretend to have left the certificate at home. A certain amount of bluffing is inevitable in most interviews, so you'll just have to decide how far you are prepared to go. Bear in mind that the true depths of your ignorance could easily be plumbed. Another skill you might be tempted to exaggerate is your knowledge of the local language. **Philip Dodd** was hired by a language teaching agency in Madrid on the understanding that he could speak fluent Spanish and on his first assignment was sent out to give English lessons to a young child living in a wealthy suburb. He was greeted at the door by the mother who wished to make sure of a few things before she entrusted her precious offspring to this stranger. Not able to follow her voluble stream, Philip nodded affably and said 'si' whenever he guessed it was appropriate. After one of his affable 'si's, the woman's face turned grey and she ordered him out of her house. He still doesn't know what he said that was so shocking. On the other hand, a certain inflation of your abilities may be expected, and will be met with distortions of the truth from the employer as you both decide whether you are going to hit it off.

Of course many applicants avoid potential embarrassment at interview by preparing themselves for a stint as a teacher. If you have done a TEFL course of any description, be sure to take along the certificate, however humble the qualification. Even schools in farflung places are becoming increasingly familiar with the distinctions between various qualifications and are unlikely to confuse a Cambridge certificate with an anonymous correspondence 'certificate'. In Asia especially, nothing short of the original will do, since there are so many counterfeit copies around.

If you have a university degree, be sure to take the certificate along. Even if the interviewer is prepared to take your word for it, the school administration may need the document at a later stage either to give you a salary increment or to obtain a work permit. **Adam Hartley**, who taught English in China, hadn't realised that his MA would have earned him a higher salary; although he arranged for two separate copies to be sent from Britain, neither arrived and he had to be content with the basic salary. Americans should take along their university transcripts; any school accustomed to hiring Americans will be familiar with these. Also take along any references; something written on headed paper will always impress, even if your previous jobs were not in teaching.

Once the interviewer indicates that you are a strong contender, it is your turn to ask questions. Ask about the details of pay, hours and conditions and take notes (see the section on Contracts below). Often there are disappointing discrepancies between what is promised in the early stages and what is delivered; at least if these things have been discussed at interview, you will be in a stronger bargaining position if the conditions are not met.

Unrealistic expectations are a genuine hazard when contemplating an exciting stint of working abroad. A recruitment consultant in the field offers the following sensible advice:

> *Teachers should be made aware that they are being employed to do a professional job and it is hard work and long hours. They should not underestimate the cultural differences even in countries they think they know. These often lead to misunderstandings and dissatisfied teachers. I am also constantly surprised by teachers who take jobs without knowing the first thing about the place, the job, the sort of classes they will have, etc. They should make a checklist of questions and if they are making applications on their own they should ask to speak to teachers who are there at the time or who have just left.*

Research is the key. You wouldn't apply for a job in the UK without knowing something about it so why do so when you're going to another country? If you are offered a job by an agent and are worried about what kind of employer the school will be, you could phone the local British Council office to find out whether the school enjoys a good local reputation. Occasionally an embassy or consulate will assist, as in the case of the US Embassy in Seoul, which keeps a file of language schools about which they have received persistent complaints. More commonly, someone will have set up a webpage where this kind of inside information can be obtained (again, common in Korea).

Professional English language teachers often try to attend a regional conference sponsored by TESOL Inc (www.tesol.org) or IATEFL (International Association of TEFL; www.iatefl.org). **Sandeha Lynch** describes the TESOL Arabia Conference he attended a couple of years ago in Al-Ain:

These are serious ELT conferences not only as marketing fairs for publishers, booksellers and software companies, but they are an open job shop for the local employers. Teachers from all over the Gulf try to get there to socialise, look for a new job or just absorb enough academic wisdom to last them another year. If teachers are looking for a job then most of the time they'll be making appointments, checking off their interview score cards and watching the clock. All of the local colleges and recruiting agencies have stands there, and they are busy from morning to night giving interviews to anyone who knows the local scene and has the right qualifications.

ON THE SPOT

It is almost impossible to fix up a job in advance in some countries, due to the way the TEFL business operates. For example, written applications to the majority of language schools in Ecuador or Peru (assuming you could compile a list of addresses) would be mostly a waste of time since the pool of expat teachers and travellers on the spot is usually sufficient. Even in countries such as Spain and Germany, for which adverts appear in the UK, the bulk of hiring is done on the spot.

When you arrive in a likely place, your initial steps might include some of the following:

- Checking craigslist, Gumtree, Kijiji or equivalent.
- Transcribing a list of schools from the *Yellow Pages*.
- Reading the classified column of the local newspapers, including local English language papers and magazines.
- Checking noticeboards in likely locations such as the British Council, US Embassy/Cultural Centres, universities, TEFL training centres, English language bookshops (where you should also check which EFL materials are stocked) or hostels which teacher-travellers frequent.

Once you have prepared a CV, email it to yourself as an attachment so it will always be accessible. That way you don't have to carry it around with you and you can easily modify it in any internet café. A reconnaissance trip is a good idea if possible, although **Andrew Whitmarsh** didn't even realise he was looking for a new job, when one found him in Indonesia:

As often happens, I didn't find my job, my job found me. I was standing on top of a volcano in Indonesia when a gentleman in my hiking group asked me what I did for a living. Upon my reply of 'English Teacher', he declared that this was wonderful news to hear and he had just the job for me. The gentleman just happened to be the President Director of Wall Street Institute – and he needed teachers.

With a little more purpose and a little less serendipity, **Fiona Paton** found a job teaching English in France. On her way back from a summer holiday in Spain, she broke her return journey in Vichy long enough to distribute her CV to several language schools, which resulted in a job for the academic year.

After obtaining a list of potential employers and before contacting them, get hold of a detailed map and guide to the public transport network so you can locate the schools. Phone the schools and try to arrange a meeting with the director or director of studies (DOS). Even if an initial chat does not result in a job offer, you may learn something about the local TEFL scene, which will benefit you at the next interview, especially if you ask lots of questions. You might also be able to strike up a conversation with one of the foreign teachers who could turn out to be a valuable source of information about that school in particular and the situation generally. It is very common to have to begin with just a few hours a week. Make it clear that you are prepared to stand in at short notice for an absent teacher. The longer you stay in one place, the more hours will come your way and the better your chances of securing a stable contract.

This gradual approach also gives you a chance to discover which are the cowboy schools, something which is difficult to do before you are on the scene. The British Council has called for an EU-wide recognition scheme for language schools, to force rogue schools out of business. But this is a long way off, and in the meantime disreputable schools flourish in Europe just as they do in other parts of the world. It is not always easy to distinguish them, though if a school sports a sign 'Purrfect Anglish' you are probably not going to need an MA in Applied Linguistics to get a job there. Working for a cowboy outfit may not be the end of the world, though it often spells trouble, as the chapter Problems will reveal. But without many qualifications you may not have much choice.

ADVERTISEMENTS

The monthly *EL Gazette* (www.elgazette.com) is a source of news and developments in the ELT industry for all interested individuals even though it is pitched at the professional end of the market and carries few job ads. An annual print subscription costs £33 in the UK, and £55 worldwide, though much of its content is available online. Job vacancies appear year round on the main TEFL websites, though schools that advertise in February or December are often advertising a very urgent vacancy, e.g. 'to start immediately, good salary, air fares, accommodation'; but these are exceptional.

Almost all adverts specify TEFL training/experience as a minimum requirement. But there is always a chance that this is merely rhetorical. Those who lack such a background should not feel defeated before they begin, since a TEFL background may turn out not to be essential. A carefully crafted CV and enthusiastic personality (not to mention a shortage of suitable applicants) could well persuade a school that they don't require a Cambridge or Trinity certificate with two years' experience after all.

Advertisements will sometimes include a contact name or company in the UK to which enquiries should be addressed for posts abroad. This may be a recruiting agency, TEFL training centre or a language school in the UK which is in contact with language schools abroad or it may just be an ex-employee who has agreed to do some recruitment for a commission fee. Note that none of these middle men is allowed to charge the job-seeker any fee. When discussing terms and conditions with an agent, bear in mind that the agent may be more interested in collecting a commission for finding someone to fill the vacancy than in conveying all the seamy facts.

Occasionally cases crop up of misleading or even fraudulent ads. A case a few years ago resulted in this headline in the *Times Educational Supplement*: 'Thousands conned by Botswana job hoax.' A conman placed adverts for teaching jobs in a fictitious school in Botswana, sent a letter of acceptance to all who applied and a request for $100 as a visa processing fee. Even if this sort of bare-faced fraud is rare, it is best to be sceptical when interpreting ads, including on the internet where promises of earning huge salaries, particularly in less than affluent countries, are usually pie-in-the-sky.

*Based on his experience of answering advertisements placed by Turkish language schools, cynical job-hunter **John Boylan** has drawn up a glossary of terms, helping new applicants to 'read between the lines':*

- *'Dollar-Linked Salary' – paid in the local currency and only linked to the dollar every three or six months.*
- *'Free Accommodation' – no way can you afford to rent a place of your own. You have no say in who your flatmates are.*
- *'Paid Flight' – this is usually for a one-way flight.*
- *'Leading School' – all the schools say this about themselves.*
- *'Provides In-Service Training' – could be weekly, monthly or annually.*
- *'Degree and Cert essential' – that's what the Ministry of Education wants. Will recruit anybody if desperate (good schools) or anybody at all (cowboys).*
- *'Central Location' – near all the good pubs.*
- *'Young and Dynamic Team' – be like a student again.*
- *'Teachers are encouraged to use their own materials and be creative' – there isn't much in the way of resources.*

ELT training centres often have numerous links with foreign schools and may have a noticeboard with posted vacancies. Unless you are a trainee at the relevant centre, it will probably be tricky consulting such a noticeboard, but a cooperative secretary might not mind a potential trainee consulting the board. University careers offices may also have contacts with schools abroad to which their graduates have gone in the past, so if you have a university connection, it is worth making enquiries.

FREELANCE TEACHING

Private English lessons are usually more lucrative than contract teaching simply because there is no middle-man. Learners may prefer them as well, not only because of the more personal attention they receive in a private lesson but because it costs them less. As a private tutor working from your own home or visiting pupils in theirs, you can undercut the big schools with their overheads. But at the same time you deprive yourself of the advantages of working for a decent school: access to resources and equipment, in-service training, social security schemes and holiday pay. The life of a freelance teacher can be quite a lonely one. Usually teachers working for a school take on a small amount of private teaching to supplement their income, provided this is allowed in their contract. Most employers do not mind unless your private teaching is inter-fering with your school schedule or (obviously) if you are pinching potential clients from your employer.

In order to round up private pupils, you will have to sell yourself as energetically as any salesperson. Turn to the section on 'Freelance teaching' in the Spain chapter for some ideas that have worked in Spain but could work anywhere. It might be possible to persuade companies to pay you to run English classes for employees during the lunch hour or siesta (if appropriate), though you would have to be a confident teacher and dynamic salesperson to succeed. You are far more likely to find one or two pupils by word of mouth and build from there.

> **SELF-PROMOTION IS ESSENTIAL**
> **Steven Hendry** *plastered neatly printed bilingual notices all over town in Chiang Mai in northern Thailand.*
> **Ian McArthur** *made a large number of posters (in Arabic and English) and painstakingly coloured in the Union Jack by hand in order to attract attention in Cairo. (Unfortunately these were such a novelty that many posters were pinched.)*

Putting a notice on appropriate noticeboards (in schools, universities, public libraries, popular supermarkets) and running an advertisement on gumtree/craigslist are good ideas; you will also need a reliable mobile phone and preferably frequent access to your email. These methods should put you in touch with a few hopeful language learners. Once you've made a good start, word will spread and more paying pupils will come your way, though it can be a slow process.

Counterbalancing the advantages of higher pay and a more flexible schedule are many disadvantages. Everyone, from lazy Taiwanese teenagers to busy Barcelona businessmen, cancels or postpones one-to-one lessons with irritating frequency. People who have taught in Latin countries complain that the problem is chronic. Cancellations among school and university students especially escalate at exam time. It is important to agree on a procedure for cancellations that won't leave you out of pocket. Although it is virtually impossible to arrange to be paid in advance, you can request 24 hours' notice of a cancellation and mention politely that if they fail to give due warning you will insist on being paid for the missed lesson. But you can't take too tough a line, since your clients are paying above the odds for your flexibility. Another consideration is the unpaid time spent travelling between clients' homes and workplaces.

Teaching by Skype or some other online system is now a common supplement or even full-time teaching possibility. There are even companies that recruit teachers anywhere in the world to teach remotely from their homes, for example see the US site www.gofluent.com/web/us/become-a-teacher-at-gofluent. With more and more people having fast internet connections and not enough time to attend in-person lessons, this is a growing market.

If you are more interested in integrating with a culture than in making money, exchanging conversation for board and lodging may be an appealing possibility. This can be set up by answering (or placing) small ads in appropriate places (the American Church in Paris noticeboard is famous for this). **Hannah Start**, a school-leaver from Merseyside, put up a notice at her local English language school indicating that she wanted to exchange English conversation for accommodation in Paris; a businesswoman on an intensive English course contacted her and invited her to stay with her.

PROJECTS ABROAD

Projects Abroad was established in 1992 to help those who wanted to learn conversational English in the lesser developed world. Language skills were still important but so was the Western approach to problem-solving and other aspects of work.

No TEFL, teaching qualifications or local languages are required, just good spoken English and enthusiasm. Placements are flexible, starting throughout the year and last from two weeks upwards.

Volunteers are needed in Argentina, Bolivia, Brazil, Burma, Cambodia, China, Costa Rica, Ecuador, Ethiopia, Fiji, Ghana, India, Jamaica, Kenya, Mexico, Moldova, Mongolia, Morocco, Nepal, Palestine and Jerusalem, Peru, Romania, Samoa, Senegal, South Africa, Sri Lanka, Tanzania, Thailand, Togo and Vietnam.

Teaching in Peru

'I spent four amazing months Teaching English to wonderful children in a school in Peru with Projects Abroad, which has been the most incredible experience of my life so far. The Projects Abroad staff were so helpful and caring that I never felt worried or alone. I was allowed two weeks holiday allowance which I used to travel to Buenos Aires through Bolivia and back into Peru. It was incredible to gain an invaluable Teaching experience, improve my Spanish and see more of South America as both Argentina and Bolivia were completely different to Peru, all of which I shall never forget.'
Katherine Wragg

Tel: +44(0)1903 708300; www.projects-abroad.co.uk; info@projects-abroad.co.uk

PREPARATION

The preceding chapters on ELT training and job-hunting set out ways in which you can make yourself more attractive to potential employers. One of the best ways in which to prepare for a stint of teaching abroad is to teach English locally. Relevant experience can usually be gained by volunteering to tutor language learners in your home town; this is particularly feasible in the USA, where literacy programmes take place on a massive scale. It might also be a good idea to contact the director of a local commercial language school and ask to sit in on some lessons and to talk to teachers. A polite note expressing your interest in TEFL would probably meet with a positive response. EFL teachers are like everyone else; they are experts at what they do and don't mind sharing that knowledge with interested outsiders.

More prolonged exposure to TEFL can best be gained by working at a language summer school. This not only provides a chance to find out whether you will enjoy English teaching for a longer period, but may put you in touch with people who are well informed on overseas possibilities.

UK SUMMER SCHOOLS

Language courses take place throughout the British Isles in the summer, especially in tourist areas. It is estimated that there are 600–800 English language schools in operation in Britain during July and August, mainly catering for foreign students, especially from France, Spain, Italy and other EU countries, and increasingly from further afield, such as Russia and Turkey. Many of these schools advertise heavily in the spring, e.g. 'Teach English on the English Riviera'. Quality varies of course. The British Council has an accreditation scheme and a searchable database at www.educationuk.org/english, which allows you to search by region and type e.g. junior vacation courses in southern England. A sister organisation English UK also has links to its 450 members at www.arels.org.uk. Schools are located throughout the UK including Wales and Scotland, but are concentrated in the South East, Oxford, Cambridge and coastal resorts such as Bournemouth and Hastings.

While waiting for VSO to find him a teaching placement in Mongolia, **Rabindra Roy** taught English for Pilgrims (listed below), which gave him further experience at the same time as earning him a tidy sum:

> *I worked two three-week courses back to back which left me very little time to myself but also no time to spend any money and of course food and accommodation were included in the deal. It was really intense and tiring but good experience with all the visits and sports and performances and producing videos and magazines and reports. Pilgrims provided a good stock of books and equipment to help teachers prepare their lessons. I'm still in touch with them and would like to work another summer when I'm back in Britain.*

At the other end of the spectrum are the entrepreneurs who rent space (possibly ill-suited to teaching) and will take on almost anyone to teach. You may find yourself thrown in at the deep end with little preparation and few materials. **Marta Eleniak** was not very happy with her employer:

> *I have got nothing good to say about my employer. We were expected to do nearly everything including perform miracles, with no support and pathetic facilities. I can only liken it to being asked to entertain 200 people for 4 hours with a plastic bowl. The pupils got a raw deal too because of false promises made to them.*

She does admit though, that it was on the basis of this three-week job that she got a job in a Madrid language school.

Recruitment of summer teachers gets underway in the new year and is usually well advanced by Easter. The short-term nature of the teacher requirements means that schools sometimes have difficulties finding enough qualified staff. Wages are higher than for most seasonal summer jobs. The average starting salary for teachers with a TEFL certificate is about £270-£300 per week in addition to board and lodging at residential schools, and some salaries top £400 a week. Time off is normally non-existent in these intensive summer schools, and you may be asked to sign a waiver form regarding the 48-hour maximum working week. Since most schools are located in popular tourist destinations, private accommodation can be prohibitively expensive and the residential option attractive. Without a TEFL certificate or any TEFL background it is easier to get taken on as a non-teaching sports and activities supervisor, which at least would introduce you to the world of TEFL. EFL teachers must expect a number of extracurricular activities such as chaperoning a group of over-excited adolescents to a West End theatre or on an art gallery visit. In most cases, you will be required to obtain an enhanced CRB disclosure.

Some of the major language course organisations that offer a large number of summer vacancies are listed below.

Anglo Continental Educational Group, 29–35 Wimborne Road, Bournemouth BH2 6NA (+44 1202 411813; jali@anglo-continental.com; www.anglo-continental.com).

Anglophile Academics, 140-144 Freston Road, London, W10 6TR (+44 20 7603 1466; www.anglophiles.com/uk). Teachers needed for summer camps and schools in Ireland, UK and possibly other countries.

Ardmore Language Schools, Hall Place, Berkshire College, Burchetts Green, Maidenhead, Berkshire SL6 6QR (+44 1628 826699; jobs@theardmoregroup.com; www.theardmoregroup.com or www.ardmore-language-schools.com/working_for_ardmore.aspx). Successful applicants will be CRB-checked.

Concorde International Summer Schools, Arnett House, Hawks Lane, Canterbury, Kent CT1 2NU (+44 1227 451035; recruitment@concorde-int.com; www.concorde-int.com/recruitment).

Discovery Summer, 33 Kensington High St, London W8 5EA (+44 20 7937 1199; www.discoverysummer.co.uk). EFL teachers for various locations in England such as Radley (Oxfordshire) and Shrewsbury (Shropshire).

EF Language Travel, 22 Chelsea Manor Street, London SW3 5RL (+44 20 7341 8500; Lt.recruitment@ef.com; www.ef.com/summerjobs); also in Oxford: Pullens Lane, Oxford OX3 0DT (+44 1865 759660; oxford.recruitment@ef.com).

EJO, Eagle House, Lynchborough Road, Passfield, Hampshire; GU30 7SB (+44 1428 751549; enquiries@ejo.co.uk; www.ejo.co.uk/workwithus.php).

Embassy CES (www.embassyces.com/about/summer_jobs.aspx). Teachers and other staff needed for up to 25 summer schools.

International Quest Centres, 7 Trinity, 161 Old Christchurch Road, Bournemouth BH1 1JU (+44 1202 296868; jobs@internationalquest.co.uk; www.internationalquest.co.uk).

ISIS Education & Travel, 259 Greenwich High Road, London SE10 8NB (+44 20 8293 1188; recruitment@isisgroup.co.uk www.isisgroup.co.uk).

Kent School of English, 10 &12 Granville Road, Broadstairs, Kent CT10 1QD (+44 1843 874870; enquiries@kentschool.co.uk; www.kentschoolofenglish.com).

LAL UK Summer Schools, Conway Road, Paignton, Devon TQ4 5LH (+44 1803 558555; mark.cook@lalgroup.com; www.lalschools.com/jobs). Summer schools held in Torbay, Tavistock, Winchester, Twickenham, etc. Maximum wage of £275 for a 48-hour week.

OISE Youth Language Schools, OISE House, Binsey Lane, Oxford OX2 0EY (+44 1865 258300; ylsrecruit@oise.com; www.oiserecruitment.com). 120 summer teaching jobs at 10 summer schools.

Pilgrims Young Learners, 38 Binsey Lane, Oxford, OX2 0EY (+44 1865 258332; recruitment@pilgrims.co.uk; www.pilgrimst.co.uk).

Plus International, 8 Celbridge Mews, London W2 6EU (+44 020 7229 4435; www.plus-ed.com). 120 summer positions in Ireland (Dublin, Maynooth and Galway) and UK.

Project International, 20 Fitzroy Square, London W1T 6EJ (+44 20 7916 2522; recruitment@ projectinternational.uk.com; www.projectinternational.uk.com).

Stafford House Study Holidays, 19 New Dover Road, Canterbury, Kent CT1 3AH (+44 1227 787730; recruitment@staffordhouse.com; www.staffordhouse.co.uk). Part of Cambridge Education Group.

SUL Language Schools, 31 Southpark Road, Tywardreath, Par, Cornwall PL24 2PU (+44 1726 814227; efl@sul-schools.com; www.sul-schools.com).

TASIS England American School, Coldharbour Lane, Thorpe, Surrey TW20 8TE (+44 1932 565252 ext 2313; jeffbarton@tasis.com (summer programmes); www.tasis.com). Of special interest to American EFL teachers.

Thames Valley Summer Schools, 13 Park Street, Windsor, Berkshire SL4 1LU (+44 1753 852001; recruit@thamesvalleysummer.co.uk; www.thamesvalleysummer.co.uk).

Roberta Wedge found that working for a large summer school organisation was not only good preparation for a teaching contract in Italy, but was fun for its own sake:

> *The big language mills in Britain are a good way to see the country. I signed up with OISE in Exeter because I wanted to tramp the moors. It's possible to spend the whole summer jumping around fortnightly from contract to contract, all arranged ahead of time through the same organisation.*

WHILE YOU'RE WAITING

After you have secured a job, there may be a considerable gap which will give you a chance to organise the practicalities of moving abroad and to prepare yourself in other ways. If you are going to a country that requires immigration procedures (the majority of cases unless you're an EU national planning to work in another member state) your employer can start the visa procedures. In addition to deciding what to take and how to get to your destination, you should think about your tax position and health insurance, plus find out as much as you can about the situation in which you will find yourself.

LINKING UP
The website www.eltlinkup.org serves as a base for anyone with an EFL/ESOL link – but mainly those with a more professional interest – with members from 92 countries, it can be useful for finding old contacts, jobs, EFL issues, conferences, etc. It's free to join.

ELT professionals should consider joining the International Association of Teachers of English as a Foreign Language (IATEFL, Darwin College, University of Kent, Canterbury, Kent CT2 7NY; +44 1227 824430; www.iatefl.org). Membership, which costs £46 to individuals or £145 to institutions, entitles teachers to various services including six newsletters annually and access to special interest groups, conferences, workshops and symposia.

The more information you can find out about your future employer the better. **Kathy Panton** thinks that she would have been a more effective teacher in her first year in the Czech Republic if she had asked more probing questions beforehand:

> *Now that I have a better idea of what to teach I think I could handle it, but a first year teacher should ask a lot of questions; such as, what books the students have used, teacher continuity, very detailed report of what the students can do (as opposed to what they have studied), and most of all what they will be expected to accomplish during the school year. If the report is vague, I don't think anyone should take the job unless they*

are really confident that they'll be able to develop the framework themselves. I would look for a school that said something like, 'You'll guide the students through Hotline 1 textbook, and also give them extra vocabulary and speaking exercises to supplement the text. You'll also work with a phonics text for a few weeks, because these students have poor pronunciation. You'll probably find it useful to bring some old magazines but the school has several ESL textbooks already.' This would show that the school takes both curriculum and organisation seriously.

An invaluable source of information is someone who has taught at the school before; ask your employer for a couple of email addresses or (better) phone numbers. Past teachers often pass on priceless minutiae, not only recommending pubs, bakeries, etc. but (if the accommodation is tied to the job) to arrive early and avoid the back bedroom because of the noisy plumbing or to take your wellies since winter rains turn the streets to rivers.

CONTRACTS

This is the point at which a formal contract or at least an informal agreement should be drawn up. Any employer who is reluctant to provide something in writing is definitely suspect. Horror stories abound of the young unsuspecting teacher who goes out to teach overseas and discovers no pay, no accommodation and maybe even no school. For this reason you should not only sign a contract but also have a good idea about what you are committing to.

WHAT A CONTRACT SHOULD COVER
The following items should be covered in a contract or at least given some consideration:

- *Name and address of employer.*
- *Details of the duties and hours of the job. (A standard load might be 24 contact teaching hours a week, plus three hours on standby to fill in for an absent teacher, fill all the board markers in the staff room, etc.)*
- *The amount and currency of your pay. Is it adequate to live on? How often are you paid? Is any money held back? Can it be easily transferred into sterling or dollars? What arrangements are there if the exchange rate drops suddenly or the local currency is devalued?*
- *The length of the contract and whether it is renewable.*
- *Help with finding and paying for accommodation. If accommodation is not provided free, is your salary adequate to cover this? If it is, are utilities included? Does the organisation pay for a stay in a hotel while you look for somewhere to live? How easy is it to find accommodation in the area? If it is unfurnished what help do you get in providing furniture? Can you get a salary advance to pay for this and for any rent deposits?*
- *Your tax liability.*
- *Provisions for healthcare and sick pay.*
- *Payment of pension or national insurance contributions.*
- *Bonuses, gratuities or perks.*
- *Days off, statutory holidays and vacation times.*
- *Paid flights home if the contract is outside Europe, and mid-term flights if you are teaching for two years.*
- *Luggage and surplus luggage allowance at the beginning and end of the contract.*
- *Any probationary period and the length of notice which you and the employer must give.*
- *Penalties for breaking the contract and circumstances under which the penalties would be waived (e.g. extreme family illness, etc.)*

Obviously any contract should be studied carefully before signing. It is a wise precaution to make a photocopy of it before returning to avoid what happened to **Belinda Michaels** whose employer in Greece refused to give her a copy when she started to dispute some points. In some cases the only contract offered will be in a foreign language (e.g. Arabic or Kazakh) and you will either have to trust your contact at the school for a translation or consider obtaining an independent English translation. **Amanda Moody** signed documents that were only in Japanese and later found out that she'd been diddled out of her end-of-year bonus.

HEALTH AND INSURANCE

Increasingly, the immigration authorities abroad will not grant a teacher a work permit until they have provided a medical certificate. Many countries such as Russia and Korea may insist on an HIV test and various other health checks, including for syphilis and tuberculosis. General practitioners (GPs) make a charge for carrying out these tests, whether you do it before you leave home or after arrival.

Reputable schools will make the necessary contributions into the national health insurance and social security scheme. Even if you are covered by a national scheme, however, you may find that there are exclusion clauses such as dental treatment, non-emergency treatment, prescription drugs, etc. or you may find that you are covered only while at work. Private travel insurance can be very expensive. Most insurance companies offer a standard rate that covers medical emergencies and a premium rate that covers personal baggage, cancellation, etc. On a 12-month travel policy, expect to pay roughly £20–£25 per month for barebones cover and £35–£40 for more extensive cover. Within Europe private insurance is not absolutely essential because European nationals are eligible for reciprocal emergency healthcare within the EEA. The European Health Insurance Card (EHIC) entitles EU nationals to emergency healthcare in any member state. Specialist expatriate policies might be worth investigating. Bespoke insurance policies can be drawn up by brokers such as Campbell Irvine (www.campbellirvine.com). Off-the-peg policies are of course cheaper – try Direct Travel Insurance (www.direct-travel.co.uk) or Ace Traveller Insurance (www.aceinsure.com), which covers work and study abroad, and includes a gap year policy for people up to age 44. Policies endorsed by American Citizens Abroad in Geneva are available from Abrams Insurance Agency in Virginia (www. aia-international-insurance.com).

The EHIC is valid throughout the EEA and Switzerland. You can apply online for it at www.ehic.org.uk. Even if your employer will be paying into a health scheme, cover may not take effect immediately and it is as well to have the ordinary tourist cover for the first three months.

No matter what country you are heading for, you should obtain the Department of Health leaflet T7.1 *Health Advice for Travellers*, which is available from post offices and doctors' surgeries. Alternatively you can request a free copy on the Health Literature Line 0300 123 1002 or read it online at www.dh.gov.uk, which also has country-by-country details. Increasingly, people are carrying out their own health research on the internet; check, for example, www.fitfortravel.scot.nhs.uk and www.travelhealth.co.uk. The website of the World Health Organization (www.who.int/ith) has some information, including a listing of the very few countries in which certain vaccinations are a requirement of entry. The BBC's Health Travel Site (www.bbc. co.uk/health/travel) is a solid source of information about travel health ranging from tummy trouble to water quality and snake bites.

A company that has become one of the most authoritative sources of travellers' health information in Britain is MASTA (www.masta-travel-health.com). It maintains a database of the latest information on the disease situation for all countries and the latest recommendations on the prevention of tropical and other diseases. This advice is provided via a personalised health brief based on your destinations and the nature of your trip, which is emailed to you from their website, for a charge of £3.99. MASTA's network of travel clinics administers inoculations and sells medical kits and other specialist equipment like water purifiers, mosquito nets and repellents. Note that arguably the advice errs on the side of caution (which means they also make more profit). A worldwide searchable listing of specialist travel clinics is maintained by the International Society of Travel Medicine (www.istm.org) although many countries are not included.

NATIONAL INSURANCE CONTRIBUTIONS, SOCIAL SECURITY AND PENSIONS

Nationals of the EEA countries working in another member state will be covered by European Social Security regulations. Information can be read online at http://dwp.gov.uk/international. Similarly, contributions made in any EEA country count towards benefit entitlement when you return home. The UK also has social security agreements with other countries including Croatia, Israel, Jamaica, Turkey and the USA. The international section of the Department for Work and Pensions at Newcastle (helpline 0845 915 4811; http://dwp.gov.uk/international) should be able to advise. The EUlisses website (pronounced Ulysses after the hero himself; http://ec.europa.eu/idabc/en/document/7158/5926.html) explains national social security arrangements throughout Europe.

If you don't make national insurance contributions while you are out of the UK in a country with no reciprocal agreement, you will forfeit entitlement to benefits on your return. You can decide to pay voluntary contributions at regular intervals or in a lump sum in order to retain your rights to certain benefits. Unfortunately this entitles you only to a retirement/widow's pension, and not to sickness benefit or unemployment benefit.

The question of pensions may seem irrelevant if you are just taking off for a year or two to teach English abroad. However, anyone who remains in the job for more than a couple of years should give some thought to starting or maintaining a pension. Because most English language teachers move between countries, it makes sense to pay into a personal pension scheme in your home country and also to maintain your right to a state pension by keeping up voluntary contributions. The question becomes vexed in those countries where state pension contributions are compulsory, as in Germany (see relevant chapter). Regulations of course vary from country to country so that, for instance, you are entitled to receive a pension after paying into the German scheme for five or more years but in Portugal you have to contribute for 17 years. If you pay into a scheme and leave before you are entitled to claim a pension, you will have to try to reclaim some of the money you paid in. In Germany you won't get back more than half. If you work in a number of countries you may find that you spend your retirement corresponding with national pension authorities. **John Sydes**, an expatriate teacher in Munich, has looked into the question of pensions and has been lobbying the European parliament to consider the predicament of peripatetic English teachers:

Social security regulations vary from country to country, so it is important to look into whether you will be entitled to a pension later if you intend spending any length of time in one place and have to pay pension contributions in a state scheme.

It's nice to hop around when you are young and full of energy and ideas. It's not so nice to find out that you have paid a lot of money into a scheme that won't pay you a pension later. English teachers are adventurers, but I'm afraid too many of us are forgetting a fundamental problem: how do we survive when we are old? We have managed to get the EU to realise that there is at least one group of professionals, i.e. TEFL teachers, who are living up to the European ideal of mobility of labour, but may well find they face a bureaucratic nightmare when they retire and apply for a state pension.

TAX

Calculating your liability to tax when working outside your home country is notoriously complicated so, if possible, check your position with an accountant. Everything depends on whether you fall into the category of 'resident', 'ordinarily resident' or 'domiciled'. Most EFL teachers count as domiciled in the UK since it is assumed that they will ultimately return. New legislation has removed the 'foreign earnings deduction' for UK nationals unless they are out of the country for a complete tax year. Since most teaching contracts operate from September, this means that the vast majority of EFL teachers, including teachers on high salaries in the Middle East or on the Japan Exchange and Teaching scheme which were formerly tax-free, will now be liable to UK tax. If you are out of the country for a tax year, you will be entitled to the exemption, provided no more than 62 days (i.e. one-sixth of the year) have been spent in the UK. Anyone who is present in the UK for more than 182 days during a particular tax year will be treated as resident with no exceptions. HM Revenue & Customs has set out the requirements in the document HMRC6 'Residence, Domicile and the Remittance Basis' (www.hmrc.gov.uk/cnr/hmrc6.pdf).

If the country in which you have been teaching has a double taxation agreement with Britain, you can offset tax paid abroad against your tax bill at home. But not all countries have such an agreement and it is not inconceivable that you will be taxed twice. Keep all receipts and financial documents in case you need to plead your case at a later date. For details of UK income tax while you are abroad contact HM Revenue & Customs (HMRC), Charity, Assets & Residency, St John's House, Merton Road, Bootle, Merseyside L69 9BB (0845 0700040 or from outside the UK +44 151 210 2222). HMRC has a good website if you have the patience to look for the information you need (www.hmrc.gov.uk/index.htm).

If US citizens can establish that they are resident abroad, full-time for 12 months less up to 35 days spent in the USA, the first $91,500 of overseas earnings is tax-exempt in the USA.

TRAVEL

London is the cheap airfare capital of the world and the number of online and office-based agencies offering discount flights to all corners of the world is seemingly endless. General websites such as www.cheapflights. co.uk, www.travelsupermarket.com, www.skyscanner.net, www.expedia.com and www.opodo.com are good starting points, though comparison shopping this way can be time-consuming and frustrating. Even after long hours of surfing, the lowest internet fares can often be undercut by a good agent, particularly if your proposed route is complicated, so don't hesitate to get on the phone. Alternatively, consult specialist travel magazines such as *TNT* (free in London) plus *Time Out* and the Saturday edition of *The Independent* or other national papers. The major student and youth travel agency STA Travel is usually a good starting place. For bookings and enquiries call STA Travel on 0871 230 0040 or log on at www.statravel.co.uk to find fares and check availability. You can request a quote by email or make an appointment at your nearest branch. Other reliable agencies specialising in long-haul travel include Trailfinders with 22 branches in UK cities plus Ireland and Australia (0845 054 6060 worldwide; 0845 050 5945 Europe; www.trailfinders.com.) and Travel Nation in Hove (+44 1273 320580; www.travel-nation.co.uk) which is staffed by real experts who specialise in finding the best deals on round-the-world flights, discounted long-haul flights and multi-stop tickets.

Within Europe, rail is often the preferred way of travelling, especially since the months of September and June when most teachers are travelling to and from their destinations are among the most enjoyable times to travel. Good discounts are available to travellers under 26. Websites to check include www.raileurope. co.uk, www.trainseurope.co.uk (0871 700 7722) or the marvellous site for train travellers everywhere – www.seat61.com.

Thousands of travel websites in the USA compete for custom. Discounted tickets are available, for example, from Air Treks in San Francisco (www.AirTreks.com). When **Cara McCain** was looking for a cheap flight from Texas to Korea to take up a teaching job, she booked one on www.vayama.com.

HOSPITALITY EXCHANGES

If you are planning to travel and conduct a speculative job hunt, you might want to take advantage of one of the hospitality exchanges that flourish over the internet, the best known of which is the Couchsurfing Project (www.couchsurfing.com). Like so many internet-based projects, the system depends on users' feedback, which means that you can check on a potential host's profile in advance and be fairly sure that dodgy hosts will be outed straightaway.

Roving English language teacher **Bradwell Jackson** had been mulling over the possibility of travelling the world for about a decade before he finally gave up his job as a drug abuse counsellor in Florida to take off. On his earlier travels he had discovered the benefits of joining Servas (www.usservas.org in the USA; www.servasbritain.u-net.com in the UK) and two other hospitality exchange programmes Global Freeloaders (www.globalfreeloaders.com) and the Hospitality Club (www.hospitalityclub.org). His first destination was Mexico, where to his amazement he found English teaching work at the first place he happened to enquire in Mexico City:

> *I really must say right away that Servas is not simply for freeloading in people's homes. However, once you take the plunge and commit to wandering the earth, things just start to fall into place. If you belong to clubs such as Global Freeloaders, Hospitality Club, or any of the other homestay organisations, don't be surprised if the family you stay with invites you for an extended stay. The first such family I stayed with in Mexico invited me to stay for six months. All they asked is that I help with the costs of the food they prepared for me and the hot water I used.*

Bradwell has continued his couchsurfing travels in some unlikely locations. His host in Bamako, Mali, let him stay for two months in exchange for two hours of English lessons a day. He was a wealthy man who gave Bradwell all his meals, internet access, laundry and so on. He commented that 'once one lands into a dream situation like this, you are apt to feel a bit guilty, and such hospitality takes time to get used to. Still, I am certainly not complaining'. More recently, en route to his teaching job in China, he stayed with a host in Hong Kong.

MAPS AND INFORMATION

Good maps and guides always enhance one's enjoyment of a trip. Most people you will meet on the road will probably be carrying a *Rough Guide* or a *Lonely Planet*. These are both excellent series, though try not to become enslaved by their advice and preferences. Rough Guides has a series of *First Time* titles which could be of interest to gap year students including *Around the World*, *Europe*, *Africa*, *Asia* and *Latin America*. Even though so much advance information is available over the internet, nothing can compete with a proper guidebook to pore over and take away with you. If you are going to be based in a major city, buy a map ahead of time. Visit the famous travel bookshop Edward Stanford, with branches in Bristol and Manchester as well as the mother-store in Covent Garden, London; its searchable catalogue is available online at www. stanfords.co.uk. The Map Shop in Worcestershire (0800 085 4080/+44 1684 593146; www.themapshop. co.uk) and Maps Worldwide in Wiltshire (+44 1225 707004; www.mapsworldwide.co.uk) both do an extensive mail order business in specialised maps and guidebooks.

The Foreign & Commonwealth Office regularly updates its travel advice for every country in the world and includes risk assessments of current trouble spots. You can contact the Travel Advice Unit by phone on 0845 850 2829 or check the website (www.fco.gov.uk/travel). If you are living in a country with poor security, you might like to register your details on the FCO's LOCATE service (www.fco.gov.uk/locate) in countries where embassy officials may need to track you down in the event of an emergency.

LEARNING THE LANGUAGE

GIVE AND TAKE
Even if you will not need any knowledge of the local language in the classroom, the ability to communicate will increase your enjoyment many times over. After a long hard week of trying to din some English into your pupils' heads, you probably won't relish the prospect of struggling to convey your requests to uncomprehending shopkeepers, neighbours, etc. A refusal to try to learn some of the local language reflects badly on the teacher and reinforces the suspicion that English teachers are afflicted with cultural arrogance.

If there is time before you leave home, you might consider learning the language of the place you are going to by enrolling in a part-time or short intensive course of conversation classes at a local college of further education or using a self-study programme with books and tapes or an online course. This will also have the salutary effect of reminding you how difficult it is to learn a language. Take a good dictionary and a language course at a suitable level, for example the *Take Off In...* series from Oxford University Press (www.askoxford. com/languages) for £25, including mp3 downloads, the BBC (bbc.co.uk/languages), Linguaphone (0800 136973; linguaphone.co.uk) and Audioforum (audioforum. com). Also, check out noticeboards in local cafés etc. or on Facebook for info about language exchanges. A great resource is www.gumtree.com, which has a skills/language swap section. If you're lucky, your conversation partner might also be able to help you with advice/contacts for your trip.

Of course it is much easier to learn the language once you are there. Some employers may even offer you the chance to join language classes free of charge or swap English lessons for those in the local language; if you are particularly interested in this perk, ask about it in advance. Some cities, such as Barcelona and Istanbul, have regular informal 'English café' evenings (*intercambio* in Spanish), although people you meet this way will be more interested in improving their English than your Spanish. Check out the site www. lingobongo.com, which focuses on language exchanges in Berlin, Madrid and Barcelona.

Minna Graber, who fell in love with the Romanian culture and language, has been trying to improve her Romanian while teaching English in Bucharest, but her colleagues and acquaintances are not making it easy for her:

> *My main problem was that the English teaching staff were completely unable to understand that my main reason for being there was to improve my Romanian. They, in the main, refused to converse with me in anything other than English and on frequent occasions made fun of my efforts. This is despite the fact that I am at around level C1 in this language. They seemed to believe that if you know English you don't have to learn other languages. The other assumption was that English speakers can't learn other languages. This attitude was often replicated elsewhere in the town and I had to fight quite hard to persuade my Romanian friends that I was not a walking English conversation lesson.*

Signing up for language classes on location is a good way of finding out about local teaching openings, as **Till Bruckner** found:

> *The first thing I do when I arrive somewhere new is to get myself language lessons. The teacher will have met many other foreigners, have local connections and speak some English. In other words he or she is the natural starting point in your job hunt. If you make clear that you can only continue paying for your lessons if you earn money too, you've found a highly motivated ally in your search for work.*

Surprisingly, it is not always an advantage to know the language as **Jamie Masters** discovered in Crete:

> *About speaking Greek. Well, no one told me. I assumed that they'd be quite pleased to have a Greek-speaking English teacher, best of both worlds. It's useful for discipline; the kids can't talk about you behind your back; you can tell when they're cheating on their vocab tests; and, I stupidly thought, you can explain things more clearly, really get them to understand... Well, I was wrong, and was laboriously reprimanded for it when they finally worked out what I was doing. But by that time it was too late: the kids knew I could understand Greek, and so they knew they didn't have to make the effort to speak to me in English. No amount of my playing dumb worked.*

WHAT TO TAKE

The research you do on your destination will no doubt include its climate, which will help you choose an appropriate range of clothing to take. But there is probably no need to equip yourself for every eventuality.

EFL teachers usually earn enough to afford to buy a warm coat or boots if required. Be sure to pack enough smart clothes to see you through the academic year; denim jeans are rarely acceptable in the classroom.

> **SAVE BEFOREHAND!**
> *Even though you are expecting to earn a decent salary, you should not arrive short of money. It is usual to be paid only at the end of the first month. Plus you may need sizeable sums for rent deposits and other setting-up expenses.*

A generous supply of passport photos and copies of your vital documents (birth certificate, education certificates, references) should be considered essential. Recreational reading in English may be limited, so you might consider acquiring a Kindle (or equivalent) since a supply of novels will weigh you down. It could take time to establish a busy social life, leaving more time for reading than usual. If you plan to take a laptop try to find out about the ease with which you can access the internet, which would allow you to access BBC news and sport, listen again to your favourite radio programmes and so on. The fantastic BBC iPlayer sadly isn't available when you're abroad at the moment, though that may change (and there are ways round it by using a secure proxy).

A WiFi-enabled smartphone will probably do everything that you need, i.e. send emails and browse the web, not to mention take photos, play music and of course telephone (though roaming charges will be astronomical). To avoid floating off into a news vacuum, some people subscribe to the BBC daily email service, which sends out a selection of news stories according to the interests you register (http://newsvote.bbc.co.uk/email). Others relish the prospect of no longer having a clue who is who in the Cabinet or what scandal has befallen footballers and their wives. A further advantage of having access to the BBC is that you can record programmes for use in the classroom.

Find out from returned travellers what items are in short supply or very expensive. Some items that recur on teachers' lists are their favourite cosmetics, vitamin tablets, a deck of cards, ear plugs and thermal underwear.

TEACHING MATERIALS

Try to find out which course your school follows and then become familiar with it. Depending on the circumstances, there may be a shortage of materials, so again enquire in advance about the facilities. (For example, English texts being used in a few places in Cambodia dated from 1938 and contained such useful sentences as, 'I got this suit in Savile Row'.) If you are going to have to be self-reliant, you may want to contact the major EFL publishers, primarily Oxford University Press, Cambridge University Press, Longman, Macmillan, Heinemann, Penguin and Phoenix to request details of their course books with a sample lesson if possible, and the address of their stockist in your destination country. For information, advice and free teaching resources, you can join the Oxford University Press Teachers Club at www.oup.com/elt.

Before leaving home, try to visit a specialist ELT bookshop or the EFL department of a bookshop and obtain a detailed catalogue of ELT materials. The online specialist KELTIC (www.keltic.co.uk) operates an international mail order service from Oxfordshire, offering an extensive range of materials. You can use its user-friendly website anywhere in the world to get information and advice or to order materials including the *Keltic Guide*. You can contact KELTIC by telephone (+44 1869 363589) or email (keltic@btol-uk.com).

Another major stockist is BEBC, the Bournemouth English Book Centre (Albion Close, Parkstone, Poole, Dorset BH12 3LL; +44 1202 712934; elt@bebc.co.uk; www.bebc.co.uk). The company supplies books, CDs and ELT software by mail order to teachers worldwide. For a list of recommended titles, see the following section.

In North America those looking for TEFL titles can resort to purchasing online from Barnes and Noble (www.barnesandnoble.com) or Amazon.com. Dave's ESL Café devotes a page to ESL publishers. The publisher Delta (www.deltapublishing.com) has a series of online catalogues that may be helpful.

Here is a list of items to consider packing which most often crop up in the recommendations of teachers of conversation classes in which the main target is to get the students talking. Teachers expecting to teach at an under-resourced school might think about taking some of the following:

- Good dual language dictionary, picture dictionary.
- Appropriate pop music downloaded on an iPod with speakers so that you can play songs with clear lyrics such as the Beatles or early Billy Bragg to your classes.
- Games and activities book.
- Illustrated magazines such as the *National Geographic* or unusual publications, for example old comic books, teen mags or the *Big Issue*.
- Maps (for example of London).
- Tourist guides to your home country, travel brochures, blank application forms.
- Flash cards (which are expensive if bought commercially; homemade ones work just as well).
- Grammar exercise book.
- Old Cambridge exam papers (if you are going to be teaching from their suite of exams).

Postcards, balloons, stick-on stars and photos of yourself as an infant have all been used to good effect. If you know that there will be a shortage of materials, it might even be worth taking general stationery such as notebooks, carbon paper, Blu-Tack, plastic files, large pieces of paper, coloured markers, etc. Most employers would be willing to pay the postage costs if you don't want to carry it all in your luggage. (If you are entering a country without a prearranged work visa, bear in mind that teaching aids in your luggage will alert immigration officers that you intend to work.)

Koober Grob spent an enjoyable time in Russia trying to hone the conversation skills of her highly motivated students. Her main regret was that she hadn't brought with her a 10-page list of possible discussion topics to help them practise their colloquial English, because she found that she was sometimes at a loss for topics (which may account for the conversation one day turning to chocolate-covered ants in Africa).

Richard McBrien, who taught English in China, recommends taking a collection of photos of anything in your home environment. A few rolls shot of local petrol stations, supermarkets, houses, parks, etc. can be of great interest to pupils in far-off lands. It may of course be difficult to anticipate what will excite your students' curiosity. The anthropologist Nigel Barley, who has written amusing books on his fieldwork, describes in his book *Not a Hazardous Sport* being enlisted to attend an impromptu English conversation club in a remote corner of Indonesia:

> *I answered questions about the royal family, traffic lights and the etiquette of eating asparagus, and gave a quick analysis of the shipbuilding industry. At the end of the evening, I fled back to the hotel.*

EFL teachers cannot escape so easily, so you should be prepared to be treated like a guru of contemporary British or American culture. If you know in advance that you will have to perform in this capacity, you might get hold of *Britain: For Learners of English* by James O'Driscoll (Oxford University Press, 2009; £26.50) which provides historical and cultural background of British society and institutions, as well as the private daily life of the British people.

ONLINE RESOURCES

Although TEFL and TESL teachers have been relatively slow to get net-savvy, these days more and more are getting online and making use of the vast number of resources available. Also more and more schools are installing electronic whiteboards in classrooms which can be a godsend for teachers. After getting used to using them at a well-equipped school in Kazakhstan, **Anthony Cook** concluded that 'they tend to inspire a lot of new ideas and approaches, especially in terms of incorporating video into lessons'. He says that it's like having a cinema screen in the classroom, which makes it so much nicer than getting 10 people to crowd around a laptop.

Teachers can access online a range of actual lesson plans and printable materials for immediate use with students as well as teacher forums and job sites. **Sab Will** is Course Director and main trainer on the TEFL Paris Certificate Course (www.teflparis.com). He has a special interest in English-learning websites and language blogs and has provided much of the information for this section. He started his first website for teachers in 1997 and currently runs www.hotchpotchenglish.com, which includes a teacher training forum, in-depth ELT book reviews and free interactive exercises for students.

One of the most useful types of website is that offering free teaching materials. Publisher Macmillan's *www.onestopenglish.com* is a good example, although practically all the major ELT publishers now offer something similar. Here you will find masses of materials, either linked in to existing coursebooks or stand-alone exercises, often with recordings, printable sheets, videos and teacher's notes. Along the same lines are websites which are not linked to publishers but which offer very much the same thing – masses of exercises of all types. Again, there is usually a surprisingly rich free section, and a more comprehensive paying option, often aimed at organisations. The British Council's *www.teachingenglish.org.uk* is a good place to start, while *www.eslprintables.com* and *www.enchantedlearning.com* offer wonderful printouts and worksheets. *www.esl.about.com* is also well worth a look. Then there are websites which are not specifically for English teachers or learners but which house much which teachers can make use of, such as the major newspaper and television sites. Some of these, such as the BBC, Voice of America and the *Guardian* even have special sections where they have created mini-websites full of exercises for English learners based on their own up-to-date content, which is great for keeping lessons fresh and stimulating. Check out www.bbc.co.uk/worldservice/learningenglish, www.voanews.com/learningenglish and www.guardian.co.uk/education/tefl.

Hot on the heels of the resources above comes a whole raft of websites which are not explicitly for English teaching, have no derived exercises for use in class, are not always appropriate, and yet they offer incredible potential for the innovative and adventurous English language teacher. These belong to the online world of YouTube (free videos), Flickr (free photos), Wikipedia (free knowledge), Deezer (free music), the BBC (free news) and Google Earth (free maps). Once you have learnt how to adapt real English to your classroom and to your students you will find these sites to be an absolute goldmine which will help you inject some marvellously unexpected and highly appreciated moments into your classes.

An abundance of free little programmes is available to make life easier, at least for tech-heads. With the legendary Hot Potatoes you can create your own interactive exercises such as gap-fills, crosswords and MCQs. Audacity allows you to record high-quality audio. Site Pal lets you send cute animated messages by email. And Snaggit lets you grab any image, or any part of your computer screen, or the contents of an entire window, or make a video of your screen actions, in a second. With Google's Blogger you and your students can create blogs and use them to extend their English learning to their outside class activities. The virtual world 'Second Life' is being used ever more creatively by teachers to hold 'in-world' English classes in a unique, fun environment. And sites such as Amazon and eBay can be used to assess buying opportunities, read product reviews, discover the auction process and why not spend a few pennies as a group to buy something for the class! The possibilities are endless.

Last, but not least, let's mention the many teacher forums and other sources of useful information for new and experienced teachers alike. These typically cover teaching techniques, difficult situations needing solutions, or simply mention useful new teaching resources which have come to light recently. An example of this is **Sab Will**'s friendly and lighthearted www.hotchpotchenglish.com, and many of the above websites also include sections on teacher training and development.

In reality, there is such an enormous amount of great stuff out there that the addresses given above are given purely as examples only. The best way to discover some of them for yourself is simply to type in 'TEFL courses Paris' or 'English teacher training forum' or 'English teaching jobs Taiwan' or 'free English teaching resources' or whatever it is you're interested in and start surfing away. Googling for something specific will also provide useful leads, anything from ideas for teaching young learners (http://esl4word.wordpress.com) to preparation for IELTS (www.ielts.org). A good source of links is provided by an experienced teacher in Spain at http://eflbytes.wordpress.com.

OXFORD UNIVERSITY PRESS

About to embark on her first week of lessons at a primary school in the Czech Republic, **Naomi Moir** wasn't entirely sure that the two-hour 'Teaching Young Learners' session in the penultimate week of her CELTA course had quite prepared her for the task that lay ahead.

Her class of seven-year-olds was indeed as unpredictable as she had assumed. Sometimes they came into the class full of energy and sometimes the opposite. Activities could be loved one lesson and then fall flat the next. But she quickly came to realise that what happened at the beginning of the lesson set up the way the rest of her lesson would progress. Creating an impact at the beginning, getting their attention, and getting them involved meant that the rest of the lesson often went much more smoothly. Likewise, after several weeks of lessons disintegrating as they neared the end (fading attention, chaotic departure) she came to realise that how she finished the lesson was also important – as simple as asking each child to tell her something they had learned during that lesson made them, even at such a young age, reflect and therefore learn more from the lesson.

Taking this experience, Naomi went on to author *Starting and Ending Lessons* in the *Oxford Basics for Children* series by Oxford University Press (2009). And this is really the root of the success of not only this series but of all the English Language teaching materials from Oxford University Press. The courses and resources have not only been researched and reviewed but lived and breathed. They have been written by teachers, based on their experiences in the classroom, and this is why they will work for you.

The *Oxford Basics* and the *Oxford Basics for Children* are a series of short and accessible books for teachers who are new to ELT or who are looking for creative ways of teaching with limited resources.

The *Oxford Basics* are also inexpensive, so if you take nothing else before embarking on your journey to teach English abroad, pack a couple of these (see the list that follows for more titles in the series). Oh, and teabags and Marmite of course.

There is such a plethora of books and materials that the choice can be daunting to the uninitiated. Every teacher should have a basic manual of grammar handy, such as:

Oxford English Grammar Course by Michael Swan and Catherine Walter (Oxford University Press, 2011; Basic: £20 ISBN 978 019 442077 8; Intermediate: £21 ISBN 978 019 442082 2; Advanced: £21 ISBN

978 019 431250 9). Short bite-sized grammar explanations with plenty of practice. 'Pronunciation for grammar' CD-ROM helps students with the rhythm, stress and intonation of grammar structures.

Practical English Usage by Michael Swan (3rd edition, Oxford University Press, 2005; £26.50; ISBN 978 019 442098 3). Intermediate to Advanced. The world's most trusted reference grammar. Indispensable guide to problem points in the English language as encountered by learners and their teachers with clear, practical information and examples.

Teaching Grammar by Jim Scrivener (Oxford University Press, 2003; £9.50; ISBN 978 019 442179 9). Part of *Oxford Basics* series.

Grammar for English Language Teachers by Martin Parrott (Cambridge University Press, 2010; £20.55).

Understanding and Using English Grammar by B Schrampfer Azar (Pearson Education, 2000; £14.60).

English Grammar in Use by Raymond Murphy (Cambridge University Press, 2004; Special price of £12 with answers available; plus supplementary exercises with answers: £9.45).

Advanced Grammar in Use by Martin Hewings (Cambridge University Press, 2005; £16.75 with answers).

English Grammar (Collins Gem, 2006; £4.99; Genuinely pocket-sized). Dubbed by at least one novice, 'the teacher's friend'.

Below is a selected list of recommended books and teaching aids which you could consider.

Oxford Advanced Learner's Dictionary (8th edition, Oxford University Press, 2010; £25; ISBN 978 019 4799003). The world's best selling advanced learner's dictionary. Helps develop all language skills with information on collocations, synonyms and writing. Available with new iWriter CD-ROM.

Collins Cobuild Advanced Learners English Dictionary (Collins, 2006; £19.50). Collins publishes a range of dictionaries for the language learner.

Cambridge Advanced Learners Dictionary (Cambridge University Press, 2008; £27). Also available as a CD-ROM (£18.45).

Freestanding by Maurice Jamall (Delta Systems; £13.95). Elementary to Upper Intermediate. Teachers' resource book suitable for children and young adults.

Grammar Practice Activities by Penny Ur (Cambridge University Press, 2009). Paperback with CD-ROM £22. Teaching classic for all levels and ages. Includes photocopiable worksheets and visuals.

More Grammar Games by M. Rinvolucri and P. Davis (Cambridge University Press, 1995; £20.85). Includes activities for all levels.

The Practice of English Language Teaching by Jeremy Harmer (4th edition, Longman, 2007). £29. A well-known core reference work for teachers from the author of *How to Teach English* (£27.70), a straightforward introduction to TEFL for new teachers.

Oxford Basics is a series of 11 short accessible books (see case study above) for teachers who are new to ELT or who are looking for new creative ways of teaching with limited resources. The series includes *Introduction to Teaching English* by Jill & Charles Hadfield (Oxford University Press, 2008; £15), a practical guide with lesson plans for new teachers of English; and *Simple Speaking Activities* by the same authors (Oxford University Press, 1999; £10).

The Standby Book by Seth Lindstromberg (Cambridge University Press, 1997; £19.40). Teacher's resource book of 110 language learning activities for all types of teaching situation.

Lessons from Nothing by Bruce Marsland (Cambridge University Press, 1998; £16.35). From the Cambridge Handbooks for Language Teachers series.

Children Learning English (Macmillan, 2005; £19.30). Introduces the theory behind good classroom practice with examples from around the world.

Learning Teaching (Scrivener, 2005; £21). Useful for teachers in training and as a quick resource of lively lesson ideas.

Resource Books for Teachers is a series of 30 titles giving practical advice and guidance, together with resource ideas and materials for use with secondary and adult learners, all £20.50. Titles include *Drama and Improvisation* by Ken Wilson (2009), *Teenagers* by Gordon Lewis (2007), *Games* *for Children* by Gordon Lewis with Günther Bedson (1999) and *Storytelling with Children* by Andrew Wright.

Oxford Basics for Children is a series of five titles for teachers of young learners which provides adaptable teaching ideas in an easy-to-follow format. Series includes *Starting and Ending Lessons* by Naomi Moir (Oxford University Press, 2009; £10), *Vocabulary Activities* by Mary Slattery (2008; £10); *English through Music* by Jane Willis and Anice Paterson (Oxford University Press, £11.50).

Ladybird Key Words Reading Scheme (Ladybird's Books for English Learning). Inexpensive series for teaching young children.

PROBLEMS

Potential problems fall into two broad categories: personal and professional. You may quickly feel settled and find your new setting fascinating but may discover that the job itself is beset with difficulties. On the other hand the teaching might suit but otherwise you feel alienated and lonely. Those who choose to uproot themselves suddenly should be fairly confident that they have enough resources to rely on themselves, and must expect some adjustment problems. Only you can assess your chances of enjoying the whole experience and of not feeling traumatised. Women may encounter special problems in countries where women have little status. An informative site is www.journeywoman.com among many others.

PROBLEMS AT WORK

Anyone who has done some language teaching will be familiar with at least some of the problems EFL teachers face. Problems encountered in a classroom of Turkish or Peruvian adolescents will be quite different from the ones experienced teaching French or Japanese business people. The country chapters attempt to identify some of the specific problems which groups of language learners present.

Although you are unlikely to be expected to entertain 200 people for four hours with a plastic bowl, there may be a fairly complete lack of facilities and resources. The teacher who has packed some of the teaching materials listed above will feel particularly grateful for his or her foresight in such circumstances. Some schools, especially at the cowboy end of the spectrum, go to the other extreme of providing very rigid lesson plans from which you are not allowed to deviate and which are likely to be uncongenial and uninspiring. Even when reasonable course texts are provided, supplementary materials for role play and games can considerably liven up classes (and teachers). You can obtain extra teaching aids after arrival from the nearest English language bookshop or make them yourself, for example record a dialogue between yourself and an English-speaking friend or cut up magazines or use postcards to make flashcards. If the missing facilities are more basic (e.g. tables, chairs, heating, paper, pens) you will have to improvise as best you can and (if appropriate) press the administration for some equipment.

PROBLEMS WITH PUPILS

A very common problem is to find yourself in front of a class of mixed ability with incompatible aims. How do you plan a lesson that will satisfy a sophisticated business executive whose English is fairly advanced, a delinquent teenager and a housewife crippled by lack of confidence? A good school of course will stream its clients and make life easier for its teachers. But this may be left to you, in which case a set of commercially produced tests to assess level of language acquisition could come in very handy. Alternatively you can devise a simple questionnaire for the students to describe their hobbies, studies, family or whatever. This will not only display their use of English but also give you some clues about their various backgrounds. One way of coping with gross discrepancies is to divide the class into compatible groups or pairs and give tasks which work at different levels. Subdividing a class is in fact generally a good idea especially in large classes.

In some places you may even have to contend with racial or cultural friction among pupils, as **Bryn Thomas** encountered in Egypt:

One of the problems I found in the class was the often quite shocking displays of racism by the Egyptians towards their dark-skinned neighbours from Somalia. Vast amounts of tact and diplomacy were required to ensure that enough attention was given to the Somalis (who tend to be shy, quiet and highly intelligent) without upsetting the sometimes rowdy and over-enthusiastic Egyptians.

Your expectations of what teaching is supposed to achieve may be quite different from the expectations of your students. Foreign educational systems are often far more formal than their British or American counterparts and students may seem distressingly content to memorise and regurgitate, often with the sole motivation of passing an exam. But this doesn't always operate. Many teachers have had to face a class that doesn't seem to care at all about learning any English and merely wants to be entertained.

In many countries free discussion is quite alien, whether because of repressive governments or cultural taboos. It is essential to be sensitive to these cultural differences and not to expect too much of your pupils straightaway. The only way of overcoming this reluctance to express an opinion or indeed express anything at all is to involve them patiently and tactfully, again by splitting them into smaller units and asking them to come up with a joint reply.

Discipline is seldom a serious problem outside Europe; in fact liberal teachers are often taken aback by what they perceive as an excess of docility, an over-willingness to believe that 'teacher is always right'. In some cases, classes of bored and rebellious European teenagers might cause problems (especially on Fridays), or children who are being sent to English lessons after school simply as an alternative to babysitting for working mothers. Unfortunately, a couple of troublemakers can poison a class. You may even have to contend with one or two downright uncontrollable students as **Jamie Masters** did in Crete:

At least two of my pupils were very malevolent. There was one, Makis, who used to bring a 'prop' to every lesson, some new way of disrupting the class – an air pistol, a piece of string with a banknote tied to it, a whistle, white paint. He used to slap my cheeks, hug me and lift me off the floor, was quite open about not wanting to work ... and then claimed I was picking on him when I retaliated. Well, call me a humourless unfeeling bastard, but ...

One teacher in Turkey found the majority of his students 'bouncy, bright, enthusiastic and sharp' but with one class he was always amazed that they walked upright when they got out of their chairs. It often turns out that each class develops a certain character.

Marta Eleniak, who taught in Spain, recommends taking a hard line:

Be a tyrant at the start. The kids can be very wicked and take advantage of any good nature shown. Squash anyone who is late, shouts, gossips, etc. the first time or it'll never stop. The good classes make you love teaching. The bad make you feel as if you want to go back to filing.

Each level and age group brings its own difficulties. Anyone who has no experience of dealing with young children may find it impossible to grab and hold their attention, let alone teach them any English. A lack of inhibition is very useful for teaching young children who will enjoy sing-songs, nursery rhymes, simple puzzles and games, etc. A firm hand may also be necessary if **Aine Fligg**'s experience in Hong Kong is anything to go by. She was bitten on the ankle by one of her less receptive students. When the headmaster came in and remonstrated (with Aine!), the child bit him on the nose. The brat was then incarcerated in a cupboard, and emerged somewhat subdued.

Blogger and world traveller **Travis Ball** from California gradually learned how to cope with young children at the rural language school at which he taught in Japan:

I was brand new to teaching, so it was really rough getting started. With very little training, I was thrown in and expected to swim. I had 27 classes a week, 18 of them on different lesson plans. My youngest student was five while my oldest was 61. The sheer diversity of age and language experience threw me for a loop. In the first two weeks, I made two separate children cry which I felt awful about. This was a cultural thing that I had to get used to. The first occasion involved my youngest student. We were doing a warm-up drawing activity and at the end I asked for the coloured pencils back so we could get onto the next game. The one word this child knew was 'no' which he kept repeating. I tried to take the pencil and move on with the class, which caused him to cry. I handed back the pencil and he basically coloured for the whole class.

The other instance involved this little boy's sister. I was attempting to teach the class the difference between the sound 'B' and 'V'. I started with one student and had her watch my lips as I said the word 'vanilla' and after a few attempts, succeeded in getting her to say the correct sound. Then I came to the next student and she tried twice and broke into tears on the third failed attempt. Not sure what to do, I kept going around the circle and the crying student calmed down after a few minutes, and was laughing with the next game minutes later. By the end of my nine months there, I was close to all my students, young and old. Leaving was especially rough with a few of the kids, and some of the adults as well.

Only 18 years old himself, **Sam James** had to teach a variety of age groups in Barcelona during his gap year and despite the problems, ended up enjoying it:

The children I taught were fairly unruly and noisy. The teenagers were, as ever, pretty uninterested in learning, though if one struck on something they enjoyed they would work much better. Activities based on the lyrics of songs seemed to be good. They had a tendency to select answers at random in multiple choice exercises. On the other hand they were only ever loud rather than very rude or disobedient. The young children (8–12) were harder work. They tended to understand selectively, acting confused if they didn't like an instruction. Part of the problem was that the class was far too long (three hours) for children of that age and their concentration and behaviour tended to tail off as the time passed.

Beginners of all ages progress much more rapidly than intermediate learners. Many teachers find adolescent intermediate learners the most difficult to teach. The original fun and novelty are past and they now face a long slog of consolidating vocabulary and structures. (The 'intermediate plateau' is a well-known phenomenon in language acquisition.) Adolescents may resent 'grammar games' (which are a standard part of EFL) thinking that games are suitable only for children.

The worst problem of all is to be confronted with a bored and unresponsive class. This may happen in a class of beginners who can't understand what is going on, especially a problem if you don't speak a word of their language. It can be extremely frustrating for all concerned when trying to teach some concept or new vocabulary without being able to provide the simple equivalent. If this is the case, you'll have to rely heavily on visual aids. Whole books have been written to show EFL teachers how to draw, for example *1,000+ Pictures for Teachers to Copy* by Andrew Wright (Pearson, £39.20). For a very low-level class, you may need to resort to your bilingual dictionary for lesson plans. But some enjoy the challenge: 18-year-old **Hannah Bullock** found teaching her class of Czech beginners good fun 'because each lesson was like an invigorating game of charades'. Many new teachers make the mistake of doing all the talking. During his year of teaching in Slovenia, **Adam Cook**, like many others before him, came to the conclusion that silence is one of the teacher's most effective tools.

TIPS FOR DEALING WITH A LETHARGIC CLASS
The best way to inject a little life is to get them moving around, for example get them to do a relaxation exercise or have them carry out a little survey of their neighbours and then report their findings back to the class. A reluctance to participate may be because the pupils do not see the point of it.

In many countries foreign teachers come to feel like a dancing bear or performing monkey, someone who is expected to be a cultural token and an entertainer. If the students are expecting someone to dance a jig or swing from the chandelier (so to speak) they will be understandably disappointed to be presented with someone asking them to form sentences using the present perfect. At the other extreme, it is similarly disconcerting to be treated just as a model of pronunciation, and you may begin to wonder whether your employer might be better off employing a tape recorder.

PROBLEMS WITH YOURSELF

Lessons can fizz or fizzle. The latter may be the fault of the students but more often it is down to the teacher. One of the most common traps into which inexperienced teachers fall is to dominate the class too much. Conversational English can only be acquired by endless practice and so you must allow your pupils to do most of the talking. Even if there are long pauses between your questions and their attempts to answer, the temptation to fill the silences should be avoided. Pauses have a positive role to play, allowing pupils a chance to dwell on and absorb the point you have just been illustrating. Avoid asking 'Do you understand?' since the answer is meaningless; it is much more useful to test their comprehension indirectly.

> *A native speaker's function is seldom to teach grammar, though he or she should feel comfortable naming grammatical constructions. You are not there to help the students to analyse the language but to use it and communicate with it. It has been said that grammar is the highway code, the catalogue of rules and traffic signs, quite useless in isolation from driving, which gets you where you want to go. Grammar is only the cookery book while talking is cooking for other people to understand/eat. Persuading some students whose language education has been founded on grammar rather than communication that this is the priority may be difficult, but try not to be drawn into detailed explanations of grammatical structures.*

Being utterly ignorant of grammar can result in embarrassing situations. You can only get away with bluffing for so long ('Stefan, I don't think it matters here whether or not it's a subjunctive') and irate pupils have been known to report to school directors that their teachers are grammar-illiterate. One useful trick suggested by **Roberta Wedge** is to reply, 'Very good question – we're going to deal with that in the next class.' Usually it will suffice to have studied a general grammar handbook such as *Practical English Grammar* or *Practical English Usage* (see the bibliography in the previous chapter). If you contradict yourself between one lesson and the next, and an eager student notices it, take **Richard Osborne**'s advice and say 'Ah yes, I'm sorry about that. You see, that's the way we do it at home. Bizness is often spelled with a z in Canada.'

The worst fate that can befall a teacher is to run dry, to run out of ideas and steam completely before the appointed hour has arrived. This usually happens when you fail to arrive with a structured lesson plan. It is usually a recipe for disaster to announce at the beginning of the lesson 'Tonight let's talk about our travels/hobbies/animals' or whatever. Any course book will help you to avoid grinding to a halt. Supplementary materials such as songs and games can be lifesavers in and out of a crisis. If you are absolutely stuck for what to talk about next, try writing the lyrics of a popular song on the board and asking the class to analyse it or even act it out (avoiding titles such as *I Want Your Body*). Apparently songs which have worked well for many teachers include George Michael's *Careless Whispers*, the Beatles' *Here Comes the Sun* and *When I'm 64* and *Perfect Day* by Lou Reed. The site http://lyricstraining.com/game2043.htm attempts to provide an easy method to learn and improve foreign languages skills through music and lyrics. Another way of stepping outside the predictability of a course book might be to teach a short poem that you like, or even a short story (e.g. by Saki) if the class is sufficiently advanced.

LESSON STRUCTURE
A very popular way to structure a lesson is in 'notions'; you take a general situation like 'praising' or 'complaining', teach some relevant vocabulary and structures and then have the class put them into practice in role-play situations. Unfortunately repetition is the key to language learning, though you have to avoid boring drills, which will kill any interest in the language.

When a lesson goes well, it can be deeply satisfying. **Philip Tomkins** did his TEFL training in Greece in 2010 and identified the high point of his teaching experiences, as sharing a joke in English with a class and all having a fit of the giggles. The low point was inadvertently using technical jargon in his first lesson which temporarily killed it dead, and being faced with blank looks.

Culture shock is experienced by most people who live in a foreign country in whatever circumstances (see below), but can be especially problematic for teachers. Unthinkingly you might choose a topic which seems neutral to you but is controversial to them. A little feature on the English pub, for example, would not be enjoyed in Saudi Arabia. A discussion about whaling might make a class of Norwegians uncomfortable. Asking questions about foreign travels would be tactless in many places where few will be able to afford international travel.

One of the more subtle problems is knowing how to approach teaching as **J W Arble** discovered:

> *I was caught up with trying to work out how to present myself to my students: whether to assume the role of friend, exotic or mentor: whether to be 'charismatic' or reserved, enthusiastic or dry, serious-minded or idiot savant. Given the limited time, I persuaded myself the aim was to make the subject interestingly different; with the hope a few might be triggered into curiosity. Less worthily, I just wanted to be liked.*

One of the hardest problems to contend with is teacher burn-out. If you invariably arrive just as the class is scheduled to begin, show no enthusiasm, and glance at the clock every 90 seconds, you will not be a popular teacher. Getting hold of some new authentic materials might shore up your flagging enthusiasm for the enterprise. If not, perhaps it is time to consider going home (bearing in mind your contractual commitments).

PROBLEMS WITH EMPLOYERS

All sorts of schools break their promises about pay, perks and availability of resources. The worst disappointment of all, however, is to turn up and find that you don't have a job at all. Because schools which hire their teachers sight unseen often find themselves let down at the last moment, they may over-hire, just in the way that airlines overbook their flights in the expectation of a certain level of cancellation. Even more probable is that the school has not been able to predict the number of pupils who will enrol and decides to hire enough teachers to cover the projected maximum. Whatever the reason, it can be devastating to have the job carpet whipped from under your feet. Having a signed contract helps. It may also be a good idea to maintain contact with the school between being hired and your first day of work. If the worst does happen, you could try losing your temper, threatening to tarnish their good name, and demand a month's pay and your return airfare. Or you could try playing on the guilt of the director and ask him or her to help you get a last-minute job in another school.

Just because a school does not belong to the EFL establishment does not mean that teachers will be treated badly (and vice versa). However, the back street fly-by-night school may well cause its foreign teachers anxiety. The most common complaints revolve around wages – not enough or not often enough or both. Either you will have signed a contract (possibly in ignorance of the prevailing conditions and pay levels) or you have nothing in writing and find that your pay packet does not correspond with what you were originally promised. It is probably not advisable to take up a confrontational stance straightaway since this may be the beginning of a year of hostility and misery. Polite but persistent negotiations might prove successful. Find out if there is a relevant teachers' union, join it and ask them for advice (though EFL is notorious for being non-unionised). As the year wears on, your bargaining clout increases, especially if you are a half-decent teacher, since you will be more difficult to replace mid-term.

One recourse is to bring your employer's shortcomings to the attention of the British Council or in extreme cases of exploitation, your embassy/consulate. If you are being genuinely maltreated and you are prepared to leave the job, delivering an ultimatum and threatening to leave might work. Remember that if there are cowboy schools, there are also cowboy teachers. Many honest and responsible employers have fallen victim to unreliable and undisciplined individuals who break their promises, show up late and abuse the accommodation they are given. Try not to let your employer down unless the provocation is serious.

Language schools must function as businesses as well as educational establishments and in some cases the profit motive overtakes everything else. In those cases, teachers soon realise that they matter less to the people in charge than the number and satisfaction of students. You may be asked to conduct a conversation class in a room not much smaller than the Albert Hall. Some employers leave you entirely to your own devices and even look to you for teaching ideas. Others interfere to an annoying degree; we've heard of one school director in Spain who bugged the classrooms to make sure the staff were following his idiosyncratic home-produced course outlines. **Jayne Nash** worked for a chain of schools in France that use their own method; clients learned basic phrases and words for everyday situations in parrot fashion:

The courses were aimed at local business people, therefore students learned mostly spoken English to intro-duce themselves, their company or product, language for meetings, telephone conversations, etc. The method seemed very effective, but can prove extremely tedious for the teacher. After you have repeated a word 10–20 times with 10 students, 4 times a day, 5 days a week...

One of the most commonly heard complaints from teachers concerns the schedule. Eager only to satisfy clients, employers tend to mess around with teachers' timetables, offering awkward combinations of hours or changing the schedule at the last moment, which is extremely stressful. A certain amount of evening work is almost inevitable in private language schools where pupils (whether of school or working age) must study English out of hours. Having to work early in the morning and then again through the evening can become exhausting after a while. It can also be annoying to have several long gruelling days a week and other days with scarcely any teaching at all (but still not days off).

HPW = HOURS PER WEEK
One trick to beware of is to find that the 24 hours a week you were told you would be working actually means 32x 45-minute lessons (which is much harder work than teaching 24 one-hour lessons). Even if the number of hours has not been exaggerated, you may have been deluded into thinking that a 24-hour week is quite cushy. But preparation time can easily add half as many hours again, plus if you are teaching in different locations, travel time (often unpaid) has to be taken into consideration.

In some situations teachers may be expected to participate in extra-curricular activities such as dreary drinks parties for pupils or asked to make a public speech. Make an effort to accept such invitations (especially near the beginning of your contract) or, if you must decline, do so as graciously as possible. There might also be extra duties, translating letters and documents, updating teaching materials, etc. for which you are unlikely to be paid extra.

PROBLEMS OUTSIDE WORK

Your main initial worry outside your place of employment will probably be accommodation. Once this is sorted out, either with the help of your school or on your own, and you have mastered the essentials of get-ting around and shopping for food, there is nothing to do but enjoy yourself, exploring your new surroundings and making friends.

CULTURE SHOCK

Enjoying yourself won't be at all easy if you are suffering from culture shock. Shock implies something which happens suddenly, but cultural disorientation more often creeps up on you. Adrenaline usually sees you through the first few weeks as you find the novelty exhilarating and challenging. You will be amazed and charmed by the odd gestures the people use or the antiquated way that things work. As time goes on, practical irritations intrude and the constant misunderstanding caused by those charming gestures – such as a nod in Greece meaning 'no' or in Japan meaning 'yes, I understand, but don't agree' – and the inconvenience of not being able to do simple tasks without the help of a local will begin to get on your nerves. Unless you can find someone to listen sympathetically to your complaints, you may begin to think you have made a mistake in coming in the first place.

Experts say that most people who have moved abroad hit the trough after three or four months, probably just before Christmas in the case of teachers who started work in September. A holiday over Christmas may serve to calm you down or, if you go home for Christmas, may make you feel terminally homesick and not want to go back. Teachers who survive this, often find that things improve in the second term as they cease to perceive many aspects of life as 'foreign'.

You're bound to suffer from low spirits occasionally, but remember not to broadcast your feelings randomly. Feeling contempt and hostility towards your host country is actually part of the process of adjusting to being abroad. If you feel you have to let off steam about the local bureaucracy or the dishonesty of taxi-drivers or the shockingly bad accent of the local English teachers, remember to do so in private, in emails or when there are no local people around. This is especially important if you have colleagues who are natives of the country. They may find some of the idiosyncrasies of their culture irritating too but, unlike you, they have to live with them forever.

The best way to avoid disappointment is to be well briefed beforehand, as emphasised in the chapter on Preparation. Gathering general information about the country and specific information about the school before arrival will obviate many of the negative feelings some EFL teachers feel. If you are the type to build up high hopes and expectations of new situations, it is wise to try to dismantle these before leaving home. English teaching is seldom glamorous.

TOP TIP

Don't go around saying 'In my country, we do this …'. You're not in your country now, so let go of the things that frustrate you, and just enjoy the journey.

Some native-speaker teachers have found an unpleasant rift between local and foreign staff, which in some cases can be accounted for by the simple fact that you are being paid a lot more than they are. Sometimes new foreign teachers find their local colleagues cliquey and uncommunicative. No doubt they have seen a lot of foreigners come, and make a lot of noise, and go, and there is no particular reason why they should find the consignment you're in wildly exciting and worth getting to know.

LONELINESS

Creating a social life from scratch is difficult enough at any time, but becomes even more difficult in an alien tongue and culture. You will probably find that many of your fellow teachers are lots of fun and able to offer practical help in your first few weeks (especially any who are bilingual). If you find yourself in a one-foreigner village, surely there's another lonely teacher across the mountaintop. You could meet for a drink at the weekend to commiserate and to draw up a charter and call yourselves 'The Wonga Plateau EFL Teachers' Association' (and remember to put yourself down as founder the next time you are revising your CV). You may even want to take some positive steps to meet people and participate in activities outside the world of English language instruction. This may require uncharacteristically extrovert behaviour, but overcoming initial inhibitions almost always pays worthwhile dividends.

If you are tired of conversations about students' dullness or your director of studies' evident lunacy, you could try to meet other expatriates who are not EFL teachers. The local English language bookshop might prove a useful source of information about forthcoming events for English speakers, as will be any newspapers or magazines published in English such as the *Bulletin* in Belgium or the *Athens News* in Greece. Seek out the overseas student club if there is a university nearby (though when they discover what line of work you are in they may well have designs on you). Even the least devout teachers have found English-speaking churches to be useful for arranging social functions and offering practical advice. If there is a bar in town which models itself on a British/Irish pub or American bar, you will no doubt find a few die-hards drinking Guinness or Budweiser, who might be more than willing to befriend you.

The most obvious way to meet other foreigners is to enrol in a language course or perhaps classes in art and civilisation. Even if you are not particularly serious about pursuing language studies, language classes are the ideal place to form vital social contacts. You can also join other clubs or classes aimed at residents abroad, for example some German cities have English amateur dramatics groups.

Making friends with locals may prove more difficult, though circumstances vary enormously according to whether you live in a small town or a big city, with some gregarious colleagues or by yourself, etc. The obvious source of social contact is your students and their friends and families (bearing in mind that in certain cultures, a teacher who goes out to a bar or disco with students risks losing their respect). As long as you don't spend all your free time moping at home, you are bound to strike up conversations with the locals, whether in cafés, on buses or in shops. Admittedly these seldom go past a superficial acquaintance, but they still serve the purpose of making you feel a little more integrated in the community. Local university students will probably be more socially flexible than others and it is worth investigating the bars and cafés frequented by students. If you have a particular hobby, sport or interest, find out if there is a local club where you will meet like-minded people; join local ramblers, jazz buffs, etc. – the more obscure the more welcome you are likely to be. You only have to become friendly with one other person to open up new social horizons if you are invited to meet their friends and family. Also make an effort to organise some breaks from work. Even a couple of days by the seaside or visiting a tourist attraction in the region can revitalise your interest in being abroad and provide a refreshing break from the tyranny of the teacher's routine.

COMING HOME

For some, teaching abroad can be addictive. The prospect of returning home to scour the local job adverts becomes distinctly unappealing as they drink Retsina, eat sushi or spend the weekend at a Brazilian beach. Once you have completed one teaching contract, it will be very much easier to land the next one, and it can be exhilarating to think that you can choose to work in almost any corner of the globe. By the same token, many people who go abroad to teach English get burned out after a year or two. The majority of English teachers do not think of TEFL as a long-term proposition. They talk about their colleagues who move on to other things as getting a 'proper job', i.e. one that does not require an early start followed by a long idle morning, where shabby treatment by bosses is not the norm and where you do not have to correct anyone's phrasal verbs.

Homesickness catches up with most EFL teachers and they begin to pine for a pub or bar where repartee is quick and natural and for all the other accoutrements of the culture of their birth. The bad news is that there are few jobs in EFL in Britain except at summer schools. Even professional English language teachers can find it difficult to land a reasonable job in the UK. American teachers will probably fare better due to the growth industry of ESL in the US, though the majority of openings are part-time with few fringe benefits and opportunities for career development. The good news is that a stint of teaching English abroad is an asset on anyone's CV/resumé. Employers of all kinds look favourably on people who have had the get-up-and-go to work at a respectable job in a foreign land. On returning home from teaching in Chile, **Heidi Resetarits** began looking for jobs and found that having international work experience on her resumé was invaluable. Potential employers were intrigued by the fact that she'd lived in Chile. Such experience can always be presented as valuable for increasing self-assurance, maturity, a knowledge of the world, communication skills and any other positive feature which comes to mind. Very few teachers have regretted their decision to travel the world, even if the specific job they did was not without its drawbacks and difficulties.

PART 2

COUNTRY BY COUNTRY GUIDE

WESTERN EUROPE
CENTRAL AND EASTERN EUROPE
THE REST OF EUROPE
MIDDLE EAST
AFRICA
ASIA
LATIN AMERICA
CENTRAL AMERICA AND THE CARIBBEAN
NORTH AMERICA
AUSTRALASIA

AUSTRIA

The attraction to English in Austria is proved by the number of English bookshops with names such as the British Bookshop and Shakespeare & Co. and the popularity of English language newspapers such as *Austria Today* (www.austriatoday.at) and *Austrian Times* (www.austriantimes.at). The market for ELT in Austria is largely dominated by English for the business community, so teachers with any kind of experience of the business world, even if just temping in an office, have a sharp advantage over those with experience only of teaching general English.

As in Germany and Switzerland, most private language institutes depend on freelance part-time teachers drawn from the sizeable resident international community. An estimated 90% of EFL teachers in Austria are freelancers, which means that they do not have a contract with just one school and must pay tax as self-employed workers.

FINDING A JOB

The British Council in Vienna has a list of 17 English language institutes in Vienna. This list is annotated so that the kind of English tuition in which the company specialises is given, e.g. executive training, conversation classes, etc. It can be consulted online (www.britishcouncil.org/austria-english-courses-in-austria.htm).

The online *Yellow Pages* for Austria are very straightforward to use (www.gelbeseiten.at). They are fully usable in English and links to potential employers can be found under the heading 'Language Schools and Language Instruction'.

Most *Volkshochschulen* offer English courses in their programmes of general adult education. The co-ordinating office for the provinces in Austria is situated in Vienna. Browse www.vhs.or.at/volkshochschulen for more information (there is an English summary). See the list of employers for details about salary/working conditions for Vienna's adult education centres.

More than 200 English language teaching assistants from the UK and USA are placed in Austrian secondary schools from 1 October to 31 May by the British Council and the Fulbright Commission. The British Council annually looks for about 120 assistants with a decent level of German to work 13 hours a week for €1,080 net per month (www.britishcouncil.org/languageassistants-austria.htm). The Fulbright Commission is responsible for recruiting American graduates with a working knowledge of German and interest in teaching for the same scheme. Detailed information and an application form (between mid-November and mid-January) can be downloaded from the Commission's website (www.fulbright.at).

New arrivals in Austria should visit a number of institutes and try to piece together a timetable. After working for three or four schools, it is better to cultivate just one or two since it is unrealistic to work for any more than this on a longer-term basis. A smart appearance and confident manner are always assets when looking for work teaching within the business community. Most Austrians will have an intermediate or higher level of English.

To give an idea of qualifications needed, MHC Business Language Training in Vienna asks for teachers who have some business background, ideally in a specialised area such as marketing, finance or law; they do not insist on a degree but welcome a teaching certificate such as the CELTA. By contrast English Connection in Salzburg requires a TEFL qualification plus at least three years' teaching experience, whereas experience and/or knowledge of business, law, medicine, tourism, etc. are seen as useful bonuses.

The rate at reputable institutes starts at €18–€20 per lesson (normally 45 minutes) and more for 60-minute lessons (€20–€30). This is none-too-generous when the high cost of living in Vienna is taken into account, although taking seminars can pay fairly well (between €300 and €400 per 7+ hour day). Life in the provinces is less expensive of course. At the interview stage, always find out whether quoted rates are gross or net, if travelling time is covered and when you will be paid. Some schools pay after the course has finished, which will leave you a pauper for an extended period.

TEACHING CHILDREN AND AT SUMMER CAMPS

The demand for teachers of children and young people is very strong in Austria as elsewhere in Europe. Summer camps provide scope for EFL teachers, as indicated in the entries for English for Children and English For Kids. Another major player is The Kids English Company (Kagraner Platz 8, 1220 Vienna; 1 263 8931; www.kidsco.at/working.htm) which mounts language courses for children aged 3–10. More than 30 native speaker teachers work at their language centre in Vienna plus teach lessons in kindergartens, private homes, etc. Recruitment takes place between May and September, and pay is generous, €28 per hour.

REGULATIONS

There is no problem for British and Irish teachers; however, applications for work permits for non-EU citizens (*Beschäftigungsbewilligung*) are almost never granted. All schools claim that they will not hire a non-EU national unless they already have a work permit. According to American **Tom Clark**, who has taught English all over the world:

> *Austria is a hard nut to crack with all its red tape and its xenophobic attitude. I have been trying to find a way for seven years to get a job, preferably in Feldkirch, where my daughter lives, but it is a nightmare.*

A language institute there told him he needed to be married to an Austrian before he could be eligible for a work permit.

One complication is the reciprocal social security arrangements within the EU. Contributions into a health and pension scheme are reciprocal with the UK. Because schools have to register their staff for a social security card and also pay part of the contributions on their behalf, they are generally not willing to hire someone who is ineligible. A hefty percentage of earnings (typically 17%) will be deducted at source (or should be) of any teacher who earns more than €366 per month. The only people entitled not to have these deductions made are licensed translators (certified in Austria), who are permitted to take care of their contributions independently.

Austria (again like Germany) has many bureaucratic layers. New arrivals need to register with the police, organise a bank account (into which their wages will be paid directly) and get a tax number from the local tax office. Everyone also needs a *Meldezettel* or registration of residence.

GEOFF NUNNEY

Geoff Nunney, knowing that his job at a language school in Slovakia would end with the academic year, was anxious to sort out a summer job and had positive responses to his enquiries to summer employers in Austria, Italy and Spain, mostly sourced through this book. He accepted an invitation to Vienna, which is as accessible from where he was located in Nitra, as London is from his native Birmingham.

I walked away with the job on the day, which is a good feeling, and you couldn't wipe the smile off my face. I have got 6 weeks work with English for Kids, two in Vienna, and four in Linz. The programme is a mixture of English teaching, sports coaching and lots of things. It was quite a detailed application process: 3 lesson plans, 2 references, and then the director invited me to interview in Vienna. So I have more work than I did last summer, more time between camps and will be working in a beautiful country. Also, they pay travel expenses to Austria, and there are four days of training, before you start. It's not even the end of April, but I have my summer sorted. I can highly recommend them. The employer also responded positively to an admission of a chronic health problem I have, asked a couple of questions, not unreasonable, and checked if I have private health insurance, which I do (with Ace Travel Insurance).

LIST OF EMPLOYERS

BERLITZ AUSTRIA GmbH
Troststrasse 50, 1100 Vienna
Other branches in Vienna: Graben 13, 1010 Vienna;
Mariahilferstrasse 27, 1060 Vienna; Schlosshoferstr.
13–15, 1210 Vienna
✆ +43 1 6043911
📧 birgit.seisenbacher@berlitz.at
🖥 www.berlitz.at

NUMBER OF TEACHERS: No fixed number, teachers work on a freelance basis.
PREFERENCE OF NATIONALITY: None but it is very hard for non-EU citizens to obtain work permits.
QUALIFICATIONS: Perfect command of English and a talent for teaching. Academic background preferred; paedagogical experience is helpful but not vital. Any other background (business, engineering, IT, etc.) is welcome.
CONDITIONS OF EMPLOYMENT: Freelance contract with no fixed hours. Schools are open Monday to Friday, 8am–8pm.
SALARY: Starting salary is €24 for a double unit (80 mins).

RECRUITMENT: Interviews are essential.
CONTACT: Mag. Birgit Seisenbacher, Centre Director.

COLE ENGLISH CENTRE FOR KIDS
Weingartnerstrasse 108, 6020 Innsbruck, Tirol
✆ +43 512 571040
📧 admin@cole.at
🖥 www.cole.at

NUMBER OF TEACHERS: 2 pre-school teachers or teaching assistants and 2 QTS primary school teachers.
PREFERENCE OF NATIONALITY: British.
QUALIFICATIONS: PGCE with English/German or BA in English Language/Education. Well spoken British English.
CONDITIONS OF EMPLOYMENT: 1 year contract with either 10 or 20 hours per week.
RECRUITMENT: Usually via adverts on teaching and TEFL websites. Interviews are essential and can be conducted by phone; 1 month probationary period.
CONTACT: Rosie Ladner-Cole, Proprietor.

131

DELPHIN SPRACHSERVICE
Getreidemarkt 17, 1060 Vienna
℃ +43 1 5855347
✆ ils@dolphin.at
🖥 www.dolphin.at

NUMBER OF TEACHERS: 17.
PREFERENCE OF NATIONALITY: British, Irish, American.
QUALIFICATIONS: Charisma and competence, experience and appearance, resourcefulness and reliability, diligence and dynamics.
CONDITIONS OF EMPLOYMENT: Stage 1: freelance contracts from 1 to 6 months, starting at 1 hour/week; Stage 2: fixed contract (including healthcare and pension), open ended, starting at 10 hours/week.
SALARY: Stage 1 €15–€35 per unit (55 mins); stage 2 €10–€25 per hour.
FACILITIES/SUPPORT: Centres provide preliminary accommodation for the first weeks and help teachers find a place on their own. Assistance with work permit only after a trial period.
RECRUITMENT: Interview essential. Face-to-face, over the phone, review of references.
CONTACT: Mr Adrian Krois, Recruitment Officer.

DIE WIENER VOLKSHOCHSCHULEN
Hollergasse 22, A – 1150 Vienna
✆ info@vhs.at
🖥 www.vhs.at

16 Vienna Adult Education Centres (VHS, life-long learning). English courses according to CEFR levels, 60 different languages offered, European language portfolio for adults, Cambridge Exams in collaboration with British Council Vienna, TELC Certificates.
NUMBER OF TEACHERS: Varies according to demand. All teachers are freelance.
PREFERENCE OF NATIONALITY: None but normally hire teachers living locally.
QUALIFICATIONS: EUROLTA (ICC, The European Language Network, Die Wiener Volkshochschulen), EUROLTA-EUROVOLT Diploma (ICC, The European Language Network, Die Wiener Volkshochschulen), CELTA, DELTA and/or university training, *or* varied extensive experience of language teaching in upper secondary/adult/university education (at least 2 years' work experience).
CONDITIONS OF EMPLOYMENT: Self-employed freelancers. Minimum commitment 15 weeks (one term). Teaching hours Monday–Saturday between 6am and 9pm.
SALARY: €18 per 50-minute lesson. Maximum: approx €540 per month.

FACILITIES/SUPPORT: Workshops and other in-service training courses available. Library and media facilities.
RECRUITMENT: Courses are planned 6 months in advance. European CV (google 'Europass' for information on the standard format), letter of intent and local interview essential.

ENGLISH CONNECTION
Am Rainberg 7, 5020 Salzburg
℃ +43 662 876210
✆ office@english-connection.at
🖥 www.english-connection.at

NUMBER OF TEACHERS: 4–6 teachers of Business English.
PREFERENCE OF NATIONALITY: British, preferably resident in Austria and plan to remain medium term.
QUALIFICATIONS: TEFL qualification plus 3+ years' teaching experience. Experience and/or knowledge of business, the law, medicine, tourism, etc. very useful. Technical, chemical or engineering experience also advantageous.
CONDITIONS OF EMPLOYMENT: Freelance contract. Variable hours: 20–30 per week. Longer term fixed contract possible.
RECRUITMENT: Face-to-face interview preferred; sometimes possible in UK.
CONTACT: Jim Thomson, Course and Company Director.

ENGLISH FOR CHILDREN (EFC)/ENGLISH LANGUAGE DAY CAMP (ELDC)
Weichselweg 4, 1220 Vienna
✆ scott.matthews@englishforchildren.com
🖥 www.englishforchildren.com

NUMBER OF TEACHERS: EFC – varies according to need. ELDC – about 25.
PREFERENCE OF NATIONALITY: None, but must be a native English speaker.
QUALIFICATIONS: Minimum age 20. Experience of teaching children is required.
CONDITIONS OF EMPLOYMENT: EFC – freelance 10-month contract (September to June). ELDC – the summer camp runs during July for 4 weeks.
FACILITIES/SUPPORT: For the EFC programme teachers need to be living in Austria. Full training given, free of charge, before and during contract. All course materials provided. Housing not provided. ELDC – 4-week summer camp programme, lunch provided during camp days, 5 days a week, housing not provided, however relevant contacts to student housing, hostels etc. available.

RECRUITMENT: Direct applications by email and telephone interviews.

CONTACT: Scott Matthews, Director.

ENGLISH FOR KIDS
Postgasse 11/19, 1010 Vienna
✆ +43 1 667 45 79
🖰 magik@e4kids.co.at
💻 www.e4kids.at.

NUMBER OF TEACHERS AND CAMP COUNSELLORS: 6–8 for residential summer camp in Lachstatt near Linz in Upper Austria; 8–12 for day camps in Vienna.

PREFERENCE OF NATIONALITY: EU or others with work permit for Austria.

QUALIFICATIONS: CELTA or Trinity Certificate (minimum grade B) and some formal teaching preferred/required. Camp counsellors require no formal training/experience but must be outgoing, enjoy working with children and should like outdoor activities and sports.

CONDITIONS OF EMPLOYMENT: Duration – mid-July to end August. 2 weeks in Vienna and 3 weeks in Upper Austria. Pupil groups aged from kindergarten to age 10, and 10–15. Full-immersion courses with in-house methods following carefully planned syllabus and teachers' manual, supplemented with CD-ROMs etc.

SALARY: Varies depending on qualifications. Up to €1,650 per month gross, plus travel costs within Austria, full board and accommodation.

FACILITIES/SUPPORT: Good standard of accommodation and full board provided for teachers. Computer room, internet and video room available.

RECRUITMENT: www.e4kids.at/txt/jobs/apply/job_opportunity.html.

CONTACT: Irena Köstenbauer, Principal.

ENGLISH IS FUN CAMP
Döblinger Hauptstr. 38/3, 1190 Vienna
✆ +43 1 369 68 33
🖰 claudia_millwisch@chello.at
💻 www.englishisfun.at

PREFERENCE OF NATIONALITY: English native speakers (also Spanish, Italian and French native speakers). Must have permission to work in Austria.

QUALIFICATIONS: Experience of working with children needed.

CONDITIONS OF EMPLOYMENT: Hours according to demand. Freelance basis.

RECRUITMENT: Personal interviews held.

CONTACT: Claudia Millwisch, Director.

MHC BUSINESS LANGUAGE TRAINING GmbH
Wiedner Hauptstrasse 54/13A, 1040 Vienna
✆ +43 1 60 30 563
🖰 office@mhc-training.com
💻 www.mhc-training.com

NUMBER OF TEACHERS: 50. Also operate business language training in Bratislava (see entry in Slovakia chapter).

PREFERENCE OF NATIONALITY: Any.

QUALIFICATIONS: MHC trainers have an understanding of business experience, often specialising in areas such as marketing, finance, pharmaceutical or law. A degree is not necessary, although a teaching certificate such as CELTA would be of value.

CONDITIONS OF EMPLOYMENT: Freelance, teaching 15–25 hours per week.

SALARY: €26–€32 per 60 minutes, depending on experience and development with MHC. Seminars pay between €300 and €400 per day (7–9 hours). Trainers are responsible for paying their own taxes (about 21%) and social security (variable).

FACILITIES/SUPPORT: Resource library, photocopying, trainer development, course books for courses supplied for trainers. Trainers from non-EU countries require working papers.

RECRUITMENT: Interviews are essential and usually take place at premises. Possibility of Skype interviews if the applicant is based abroad.

CONTACT: Mark Heather, Managing Director (mark.heather@mhc-training.com).

MIND & MORE, MANAGEMENT AND EDUCATION SERVICES GmbH
Goldschmiedgasse 10, 3rd floor, 1010 Vienna
✆ +43 1 535 9695
🖰 office@mindandmore.at
💻 www.mindandmore.at

Management and Education Services is also the Representative Office of the British Open University and OU Business School in Austria, south Germany, Slovenia and Hungary.

NUMBER OF TEACHERS: About 70 language trainers in Vienna and more in many locations around the country and across the borders, plus management skills faculty trainers.

PREFERENCE OF NATIONALITY: None.

QUALIFICATIONS: Minimum university degree plus CELTA or TESOL and teaching experience; preferably also business experience.

CONDITIONS OF EMPLOYMENT: Freelance contracts. Hours vary.

SALARY: Language training – minimum rate is €22 per unit for 45-minute units/€28 for 60-minute units; more for specialised language training and seminars; market rates for management skills training.

FACILITIES/SUPPORT: Support given.

RECRUITMENT: Via internet, personal recommendations, partner institutions including British Council, BFI and related institutions. Face-to-face interview essential.

CONTACT: Julie Warner, Director of Studies for ELT (j.warner@ mindandmore.at).

SPIDI SPRACHENINSTITUT

Franz-Josefs-Kai 27/10, 1010 Vienna

🖰 +43 1 236 17 17 0

🖎 office@spidi.at

🖥 www.spidi.at

NUMBER OF TEACHERS: About 50 English teachers.

PREFERENCE OF NATIONALITY: EU citizens.

QUALIFICATIONS: Minimum CELTA or equivalent. Business English and ESP teaching experience preferred.

CONDITIONS OF EMPLOYMENT: Freelance. Flexible hours.

SALARY: €26–€28 per hour, depending on qualifications and experience.

FACILITIES/SUPPORT: No assistance with accommodation. Library with PCs for trainers. Monthly teacher development sessions.

RECRUITMENT: Local interview essential.

BENELUX

Belgium

As one of the capitals of the EU, there is a huge demand for all the principal European languages in Brussels. Yet, despite the enormous amount of language teaching in Belgium, there are also a large number of well-qualified expatriate spouses who take up teaching. This may meet some demand, but not all. To find contact details for language schools in Belgium, the online *Yellow Pages* are a useful tool. A search for 'Language Schools' in the Brussels Region on www.goldenpages.be will turn up 85 institutes.

Newcomer is a bi-annual publication which remains in print, though its sister English language monthly magazine *The Bulletin* ceased publication in June 2012 in order to go entirely digital (www.TheBulletin.be). *Newcomer* contains information and contact addresses of interest to the newly arrived teacher including a listing of major language schools (look for it in newsagents). The casual teacher will encounter a lot of competition from highly qualified candidates in Brussels and other cities, and will probably steer clear of schools that teach senior EU bureaucrats. Telephone/Skype teaching is popular in Belgium, especially among French learners of English; for example see Phone Languages (www.phonelanguages.com).

Several language teaching organisations are represented in more than one Belgian city, especially Berlitz, which employs about 225 freelance teachers in 14 branches. Linguarama Belgium also recruits freelance native speaker teachers with a TEFL teaching qualification and at least two years' experience of teaching non-native adults. CVs and letters of application can be emailed to personnel@linguarama.com. CLL (Centre de Langues), based in Louvain-la-Neuve, employs about 100 teachers to work on a freelance basis.

As throughout continental Europe, children attend summer camps which focus on language learning. Companies such as Kiddy & Junior Classes (part of Language Studies International) and Ski Ten International organise holiday English courses. Pro Linguis is another company that arranges week-long residential language courses in Thiaumont, a remote southern corner of Belgium near Luxembourg (+32 63 22 04 62; www.prolinguis.be) and which employs some native English speaker teachers who must be willing to keep themselves amused. Courses are put on for all ages including children, so teachers may also be given pastoral duties patrolling dorms, etc.

Social security payments are very high in Belgium. A full-time teacher should expect to be charged about €800 every three months. The first €7000 can be earned free of tax, thereafter the rates are high.

FREELANCE TEACHING

It is quite feasible to put up notices in one of the large university towns (Brussels, Antwerp, Gent, Leuven, Liège, etc.) offering conversation practice. Almost all foreign teachers who begin to work for an institute do so on a freelance basis and will have to deal with their own tax and social security. Officially they should declare themselves *indépendants* (self-employed persons) and pay contributions that amount to up to one-third of their salary. In fact many English teachers take their gross salary without declaring it, and don't work long enough to risk being caught. Once a teacher has worked black (*en noir/in het zwart*), it is difficult to regularise his or her status, since they then have to declare all previous earnings. Therefore anyone who plans to spend more than a few months teaching in Belgium should consider this issue.

LIST OF EMPLOYERS

BERLITZ LANGUAGE CENTRES
Avenue Louise 306–310, 1050 Brussels
+32 2 626 95 93
www.berlitz.be

NUMBER OF TEACHERS: About 225 (for Brussels, Waterloo, Namur, Charleroi, Liège, Antwerp, Bruges, Mouscron-Tournai, Geel, Hasselt, Tienen, Mechelen and Hubs West Flanders and Wavre-Louvain-la-Neuve).
PREFERENCE OF NATIONALITY: British or Irish.
QUALIFICATIONS: University degree.
CONDITIONS OF EMPLOYMENT: Freelance – Flexible hours (mornings, evenings plus Saturday morning).
SALARY: €15 per 40-minute teaching unit.
FACILITIES/SUPPORT: No assistance with accommodation. In-house training lasts 8 days.
RECRUITMENT: Via adverts and direct applications.
CONTACT: Joke Van Daele, Country Manager of Instruction.

CALL INTERNATIONAL
Rue des Drapiers 25, 1050 Brussels
+32 2 644 95 95
brussels@callinter.com
www.callinter.com

Centre for Accelerated Language Learning in Belgium (Brussels, Waterloo, Tournai and Liège).

NUMBER OF TEACHERS: 150.
PREFERENCE OF NATIONALITY: None.
QUALIFICATIONS: Degree necessary. Experience an advantage. Good communication skills needed.
CONDITIONS OF EMPLOYMENT: Freelance with a car. Flexible hours.
FACILITIES/SUPPORT: No assistance with accommodation.
RECRUITMENT: All year through.
CONTACT: Sylvie Laurent.

CLL CENTRE DE LANGUES
Place de l'Université 25, 1348 Louvain-la-Neuve
+32 10/47 06 28; 10/47 06 29
jobs@cll.ucl.ac.be
www.cll.be

NUMBER OF TEACHERS: 100.
PREFERENCE OF NATIONALITY: From English-speaking countries.
QUALIFICATIONS: Experience in teaching English as a foreign language and, if possible, with a degree in languages.
CONDITIONS OF EMPLOYMENT: Freelance, variable hours (daytime, evenings, Saturdays, etc.)
SALARY: €22.10–€27.50 per hour according to experience.
FACILITIES/SUPPORT: None.
RECRUITMENT: Interviews in Belgium essential, followed by an integration session.
CONTACT: Sabine Thirion, Recruiting Officer.

NUMBER OF TEACHERS: 30–60.

PREFERENCE OF NATIONALITY: None.

QUALIFICATIONS: For the adult school: qualified university level teachers with TEFL experience. For the children's school: qualified teachers or would-be teachers with experience in children's entertainment.

CONDITIONS OF EMPLOYMENT: Freelance, although 1–2 month contracts during the summer. Adult school hours: 9am–8pm; children's school: 9am–5pm.

SALARY: Varies.

FACILITIES/SUPPORT: None, although for the 2-month summer contract assistance is given finding accommodation.

RECRUITMENT: Via internet, newspaper, universities, company brochure. Interviews essential unless excellent references received. Interviews are carried out in Brussels.

CONTACT: Sylvaine Drablier, Director.

NUMBER OF TEACHERS: 20 (for English).

PREFERENCE OF NATIONALITY: UK and USA.

QUALIFICATIONS: TEFL or TESL and experience.

CONDITIONS OF EMPLOYMENT: Freelance/flexible contracts and work hours.

SALARY: Flexible.

FACILITIES/SUPPORT: None.

RECRUITMENT: Direct application. Interview essential.

CONTACT: Annick Lombard, General Manager.

NUMBER OF TEACHERS: 14 (freelancers) to work near Arlon close to the Luxembourg border.

PREFERENCE OF NATIONALITY: British.

QUALIFICATIONS: Kindergarten teacher or summer camp counsellor, primary school teacher, EFL training, BA in English or any other language, in business, law or social studies.

CONDITIONS OF EMPLOYMENT: Minimum 1-year contract, or 2-month contract in summer; 7 hours per day, 4–5 days per week.

SALARY: €97–€115 per day plus free board and lodging on campus.

RECRUITMENT: Personal contacts. Phone interviews.

CONTACT: Christiane Maillart (secretariat@prolinguis.be).

NUMBER OF TEACHERS: 2 for English (plus 1 for tennis).

PREFERENCE OF NATIONALITY: None.

QUALIFICATIONS: Experience with children. Some knowledge of French useful.

CONDITIONS OF EMPLOYMENT: Student contract for July or August. 6 hours of work per day including teaching and 'animation', i.e. supervising camp activities.

SALARY: €1,200 per month.

FACILITIES/SUPPORT: Board and lodging provided at camp.

RECRUITMENT: University exchanges, word of mouth.

CONTACT: Martine Goffinet, Directrice or Stéphanie de Bellefroid, Manager.

Luxembourg

With only a handful of private language schools in the country, Luxembourg does not offer much scope for ELT teachers.

The national employment service (l'Administration de l'Emploi) at 10 rue Bender, L-1229 (+352 2 478 53 00; www.adem.public.lu) has a EURES adviser who may have information about language teaching openings.

Informal live-in tutoring jobs are possible. Luxembourg Accueil Information (10 Bisserwee, L-1238 Luxembourg-Grund; +352 241717; www.luxembourgaccueil.com) is a centre for new arrivals and temporary residents. It provides a range of services on its premises from October to May, including workshops and language courses, and might be able to advise on teaching and tutoring possibilities.

Inlingua has a centre in Luxembourg City (www.inlingua.lu), and the Prolingua Language Centre hires professionally turned out teachers with a driving licence to teach in businesses (www.prolingua.lu/en/prolingua/employment-at-prolingua). Prolingua also runs language summer schools for school children.

The Netherlands

Dutch people have a very high degree of competence in English after they finish their schooling. Educated Dutch people are so fluent in English that the Minister of Education once suggested that English might become the main language in Dutch universities, a suggestion which caused an understandable outcry. However, the schooling system has become increasingly international and university staff are being challenged to lecture and publish in English and to advance their English language skills.

Yvonne Dalhuijsen, project manager at UvA Talen (see list of employers), sees an increasing need for advanced levels of English within both companies and universities. She is always on the lookout for teachers who are native speakers of English. On the other hand, one longstanding employer of freelance corporate trainers, Suitcase Talen in Almere, has ceased its English teaching operations because there has been no demand since the Europe-wide economic downturn.

What private language schools there are tend to provide specific training in Business English and to be looking for language trainers with extensive commercial or government experience as well as a teaching qualification and – particularly outside the capital – some fluency in Dutch. Business English, Legal English and Academic English (writing papers, abstracts, etc) are subjects in high demand. So many native English speaking citizens have settled in the Netherlands, attracted by its liberal institutions, that most companies depend on long-term freelancers.

It might also be possible to fix up some freelance lessons with university students from non-Dutch backgrounds, including Spanish, whose level of English is less advanced than their local counterparts.

The *Yellow Pages* are easy to search online (www.detelefoongids.nl) or for the capital The Hague, you can look up *Taalonderwijs* (Language Training) in the online directory www.allebedrijvenindenhaag.nl. The site of VTN (Vereniging Taleninstituten Nederland) or the Dutch Association of Language Institutes links to a handful of English-teaching institutes. The British Language Training Centre in Amsterdam offers the CELTA course (see Training chapter) and may be able to give advice to qualified job-seekers and recommend other institutes to try for work. Linguarama Nederland has a sizeable operation in the business training field with centres in Amsterdam, The Hague and Soesterberg; enquiries may be sent to personnel@nl.linguarama.com. Only applicants with a full TEFL/TESOL or CELTA qualification will receive a response (www.linguarama.com/nl).

Outside the mainstream language institutes, it might be possible to arrange some telephone teaching. Try, for example, Dialogue Talen at Nieuwe Parklaan 44, 2597LD, The Hague (www.dialoguetalen.nl).

Another possibility for those not interested in a corporate atmosphere is the network of *Volksuniversiteit*, adult education centres. Branches that teach English can be found throughout the country, all listed at www.volksuniversiteit.nl.

LIST OF EMPLOYERS

BERLITZ LANGUAGE CENTRES The Netherlands
Amsterdam, Den Haag, Maastricht and Rotterdam
- info@berlitz.nl
- www.berlitz.nl

NUMBER OF TEACHERS: 39.
PREFERENCE OF NATIONALITY: None.
QUALIFICATIONS: Minimum Bachelor degree and if possible TEFL.
CONDITIONS OF EMPLOYMENT: 1 year contract. Working hours are between 7.30am and 9.45pm.
SALARY: From €1,000–€2,500 per month depending on qualifications and hours worked.
RECRUITMENT: Via the website or on the spot. Interviews essential.
CONTACT: Joke Van Daere, Country Manager of Instruction (joke. vandaere@berlitz.be).

BOGAERS TALENINSTITUUT B.V.
Ringbaan Zuid 42, 5022 PN, Tilburg
- +31 13 536 21 01
- info@bogaerstalen.nl
- www.bogaerstalen.nl

NUMBER OF TEACHERS: 5 foreign out of total of 50.
PREFERENCE OF NATIONALITY: British.
QUALIFICATIONS: Degree and TEFL certificate. Experience in teaching conversational and Business English preferred.
CONDITIONS OF EMPLOYMENT: From 1 week to 9 months.
SALARY: €22.50 per hour.
FACILITIES/SUPPORT: Will help with accommodation if needed.
RECRUITMENT: Speculative CVs and applications.
CONTACT: Marion Bernard, Training Coordinator.

LANGUAGE PARTNERS
Sarphati Plaza, Rhijnspoorplein 24, 1018 TX, Amsterdam
- +31 0900 1234565
- afke.derijk@languagepartners.nl
- www.languagepartners.nl

Offices also in The Hague, Rotterdam, Amersfoort, Zwolle, Breda and Nijmegen.
NUMBER OF TEACHERS: Approximately 200 (freelance and contract).

PREFERENCE OF NATIONALITY: None.
QUALIFICATIONS: Native speakers, CELTA or TEFL qualifications, and relevant experience in business-to-business training.
CONDITIONS OF EMPLOYMENT: 6-12 months. Variable hours.
FACILITIES/SUPPORT: No help with accommodation or visas.
RECRUITMENT: Online recruitment and word of mouth. Interviews are essential.
CONTACT: Afke de Rijk, HR Manager.

PCI – PIMENTEL COMMUNICATIONS INTERNATIONAL
Bachlaan 43, 1817 GH Alkmaar
- +31 72 512 11 90/515 65 18
- info@pcitalen.nl/info@pcilanguages.com
- www.pcitalen.nl or www.pcilanguages.com

NUMBER OF TEACHERS: 50+.
PREFERENCE OF NATIONALITY: Mostly British, Irish or North American. Australians, New Zealanders and South Africans also welcome.
QUALIFICATIONS: Experience in business and technical English. Cross-cultural communication skills and familiarity with modern teaching methods needed.
CONDITIONS OF EMPLOYMENT: Freelancers working mostly in-company nationwide.
SALARY: Starts at €27 per hour.
FACILITIES/SUPPORT: Most teachers are already living in the Netherlands.
RECRUITMENT: Advertisements, word of mouth and recommendations.
CONTACT: Ms Iona de Pimentel.

UvA Talen
Roetersstraat 25, NL-1018 WB Amsterdam
- +31 20 525 46 37
- trainers@uvatalen.nl
- www.uvatalen.nl

Independent language institute, affiliated to the Universiteit van Amsterdam, and consisting of a translation agency and a training centre.
NUMBER OF TEACHERS: Varies, only freelance.
PREFERENCE OF NATIONALITY: None, provided native English speaker (with widely understood dialect).

QUALIFICATIONS: Experience in teaching adults and registered at the Dutch Chamber of Commerce as a freelancer, with a VAR-WUO. Working knowledge of Dutch and/or the level system European Framework Reference (A-B-C) is required.

CONDITIONS OF EMPLOYMENT: Freelance assignments only.

SALARY: From €25 per hour, plus compensation for preparation work or corrections.

FACILITIES/SUPPORT: No assistance with accommodation or work permits. Project manager monitors contents of the courses and is happy to advise teachers on content and materials.

RECRUITMENT: Teachers submit CVs and cover letter; face-to-face interviews required on arrival.

CONTACT: Yvonne Dalhuijsen, Operational Manager (YDalhuijsen@uvatalen.nl).

FRANCE

The French used to rival the English for their reluctance to learn other languages. A Frenchman abroad spoke French as stubbornly as Britons spoke English. But things have changed, especially in the business and technical community. French telephone directories contain pages of English language training organisations and the law continues to put pressure on companies to provide ongoing training for staff. The *Droit Individuel à la Formation (DIF)*, meaning the individual's right to vocational training, stipulates that companies have to devote a minimum of 0.8% of their gross payroll to employee training. English and computing are the most popular objects of investment, and therefore many private language institutes cater purely to the business market. In fact a quick browse through the entries in the list of employers at the end of this chapter will lead you to the conclusion that the majority of adult language training in France is business-oriented, with most of it taking place on-site and the rest taking place in business and vocational schools. In this setting the term *formateurs* or 'trainers' is often used instead of English teachers. Private training companies involved with *formation* often produce very glossy brochures which look more like the annual report of a multinational corporation than an invitation to take an evening course. Most offer one-to-one tuition.

Many of the thousands of non-profit Chambres de Commerce et d'Industrie (CCI) around France have their own Centres d'Etude des Langues. Pariglotte is the Centre de Langues in Paris (6 Av de la Porte de Champerret, 75017 Paris; www.pariglotte.fr), but there are many centres all over France. In addition, a considerable number of town councils (*mairies*) offer simple English courses to locals for a reduced rate, or allow associations to offer courses using their premises, so you might be able to pick up a few hours of teaching this way.

Teaching young children is left mostly to French teachers of English, although foreign language assistants are typically placed in schools (see later). Teaching by Skype or some other online system is now a common supplement or even full-time teaching a possibility in this growing market.

Much of the information used in the revision of this chapter was provided by **Sab Will**, Director of TEFL Paris Ltd (www.teflparis.com) and resident of Paris for 16 years, for which the author is very grateful.

PROSPECTS FOR TEACHERS

Advanced ELT qualifications seem to be less in demand in France than solid teaching experience, particularly in a business context. Few schools accept candidates on the basis of being a native speaker and candidates may be asked to provide an *attestation de durée d'études* to show the educational level they have reached. However, anyone who has a university degree in any subject and who can look at home in a business situation (and possesses a suit/smart clothes) has a chance of finding teaching work, particularly if they have a working knowledge of French.

All respectable language schools in France now want to see solid evidence of experience and competence, or at least a strong drive to work in the teaching field. A good CV showing past experience and a TEFL certificate from a reputable training organisation are almost guaranteed tickets at least to the interview stage.

Ironically, more 'serious' qualifications such as a BEd, PGCE or even the DELTA are not always a help. The fact is that language schools fight for contracts on price, and ordinary clients tend not to differentiate and believe language lessons are the same from whichever school. Therefore a teacher's experience and qualifications have little to do with schools winning training contracts. How much language schools have to pay teachers is a major issue. In other words, an enthusiastic new teacher clutching a shiny new TEFL Certificate may actually be more attractive than someone with a weight of experience and qualifications who expects to be paid accordingly. Salary scales are relatively fixed in France, and experience and advanced qualifications don't really give you much bargaining power. The situation is made worse by the rapidity with which language teachers move on, and language schools know that there are plenty of other good candidates hungry for work and experience, and more or less ready to work for the basic rate.

In some circles it is fashionable to learn American English which means that, despite the visa difficulties for non-EU nationals, it is possible for Americans to find work as well. Many institutes claim to have no preference as to the country of origin of their native-speaker teachers though most expect to hire foreigners already resident in France with appropriate working papers. Most French students are happy with a friendly, competent and enthusiastic teacher, whatever their nationality, who is able to adapt to their needs and supply them with materials and learning situations relevant to their situation.

FINDING A JOB

IN ADVANCE

France is such a popular and obvious destination for British and Irish people and also for North Americans that a job hunt from abroad can be disappointing. Major language teaching organisations receive speculative CVs every day and can't promise anything until they meet the applicant.

A comprehensive list of English language institutes in France is hard to come by. One source of reputable language schools is the French Training Federation (*Fédération de la Formation Professionnelle* – FFP) (www. ffp.org). The *Pages Jaunes* (*Yellow Pages*; www.pagesjaunes.fr) are another possibility, if you search under the headings 'Ecoles de Langues'. One recent job-seeker suggests an alternative at least in Paris:

> *I got a list of schools from the British Council, as I found the Yellow Pages were basically useless. I marked on my map all the schools in each district (arrondissement) and each day visited as many schools as possible in the same district (this limits time spent on metros and also walking).*

The Centre Regional Information pour Jeunesse lists English language schools (www.crij.org), as does the Paris Anglophone website (www.paris-anglo.com), minus email addresses. The Parisian Expat website has a list of companies that most often advertise for English language trainers, with links to their recruitment information (www.theparisienexpat.com/2010/06/11/teaching-jobs-in-paris/).

The British Council in Paris (9 rue de Constantine, 75340 Paris; +33 1 49 55 73 00; www.britishcouncil.fr) teaches English to adults, and to children and teenagers during the school holidays and may have vacancies for well-qualified teachers. Sab Will worked at the British Council for several years and says to get in you will have to convince them you are good with relevant experience and qualifications. The Council has taken over English teaching to adults from the British Institute, with which it shares the same building, and so is a major language teaching centre in Paris. It also has a useful online teaching resource centre (www.britishcouncil.org/fr/france-english-teaching-english-teaching-resources.htm) which offers a weekly collection of links to free materials from British Council websites.

The Centre International d'Etudes Pédagogiques (CIEP) in France offers thousands of assistantships in France for students from many different countries (+33 1 45 07 60 00; www.ciep.fr). Undergraduates and graduates under the age of 30 (35 in the UK) can spend an academic year working as English language assistants in secondary and (increasingly) primary schools throughout France. In return for giving conversation classes 12 hours a week, providing classroom support and teaching pupils about their country, assistants receive a gross allowance of approximately €950 a month (€770 net) for seven months, beginning 1 October. Similar posts are also available in other francophone countries such as Belgium, Canada (Québec) and Switzerland.

Assistants must have a working knowledge of French so modern languages students are encouraged to apply. Applications are considered from students who have at least AS level, Higher Grade or equivalent in French. Some posts in primary schools require degree level French because any help offered by colleagues and all discussion of pupil progress, curriculum, lesson planning, etc. is likely to be in French. British applicants should contact the Language Assistants Team, British Council (10 Spring Gardens, London SW1A 2BN; +44 20 7389 4596; assistants@britishcouncil.org; www.britishcouncil.org/languageassistants). American students can participate in the scheme by applying through the Assistantship Program at the French Embassy in Washington; for further information contact assistant.washington-amba@diplomatie.gouv.fr or browse www.frenchculture.org/assistantshipprogram.

EMILY SLOANE

Emily Sloane from America was posted as an assistant to a small town in Lorraine (where the quiche comes from), unknown to any English language guidebook that she could find.

I taught English to about 170 students in three different primary schools, two 45-minute sessions per class per week, for a total of 12 hours of work each week. In general, the teaching and lesson planning were thoroughly enjoyable, although I wasn't given much guidance and received no feedback throughout the year, so I'm sure the fact that I was already comfortable and experienced with teaching and working with children made a big difference in my enjoyment. The kids, although adoring and very enthusiastic, were a lot rowdier than I had expected, and I was obliged to spend a lot more time on behavior management than I'd anticipated. The kids were never mean, just excitable and chatty, especially so because my class offered a break from their usual blackboard-and-worksheet style routine. The fact that I was the only assistant in my town meant that my French improved noticeably, especially my slang and listening comprehension, although it made for some lonely weekends, because I was forced to get by in French all the time.

In some cases the description language 'assistant' is a misnomer in schools where there isn't much support from the rest of the staff. Whereas some might relish the responsibility others might find this quite isolating. It can be instructive browsing the forum for language assistants at www.assistantsinfrance.com/forums.

The Alliance Française (AF) is a venerable organisation, analagous to the British Council, with a large teaching operation in London and centres worldwide. Sab Will has heard favourable reports of people getting useful information or contacts from them. Anyone who can converse in French might find it useful to make contact before leaving home. Most centres have a noticeboard where requests for tutors, au pairs, etc. are occasionally posted. In London, the Alliance Française of Grande Bretagne is located at 1 Dorset Square, London NW1 6PU (info@alliancefrancaise.org.uk); for the New York branch, see www.fiaf.org.

There is also demand for experienced English teachers from French universities, although you really need to be living in France to stand a chance of securing a job. The university has various systems of employment. For example Lyon 2 employs about 45 native English teachers by a system called '*vacataire*', which means you need to have a principal employer. There is also another system called '*travailleurs indépendants*' where the teachers can work at two/three/four universities, but are classed as self-employed and have to pay their own social security. The disadvantage of working at the university is that although they pay relatively well with good conditions of employment, they often pay late; you could be waiting for up to six months. Almost every day, the TESOL France jobs list sends out requests, some of them sounding desperate, for teachers. You can join for free at www.tesol-france.org/teachingjobs.php. Vacancies are notified in the university world and in the private sector, and keeping track of these is a good way to get a feel for what's available.

When applying to a training organisation, try to demonstrate your commercial flair with a polished presentation including a business-like CV (omitting your hobbies) preferably accompanied by a handwritten letter in impeccable French.

Although English teachers can still get away with more relaxed dress codes and a certain 'originality' is tolerated, you will still give yourself the best chance of employment if you follow typical French conventions: dress very smartly for interviews, be positive and enthusiastic, ask questions as well as answer them, and don't sell yourself too cheaply if you have a qualification or experience which is relevant to what they are looking for. Watch out for language schools trying to make you believe that working evenings or Saturdays is absolutely normal. You may not be able to get paid more for agreeing to do this, but you might be able to negotiate other concessions, such as more time off during the week.

The technique of making a personal approach to schools in the months preceding the one in which you would like to teach is often successful. On the strength of her Cambridge Certificate from International House, **Fiona Paton** had been hoping to find teaching work in the south of France in the summer but quickly discovered that there are very few opportunities outside the academic year. On her way back to England, she disembarked from the train in the picturesque town of Vichy in the Auvergne just long enough to distribute a few self-promotional leaflets to three language schools. She was very surprised to receive a favourable reply from one of them once she was home, and so returned a few weeks later for a happy year of teaching.

Make it really easy for language schools to contact you. For about €115 you can get a rechargeable mobile phone so that potential employers can contact you no matter where you are. Feature the number prominently on all your CVs and motivational letter (often requested by employers and recruiters). Teaching English in exchange for room and board is not uncommon though is normally combined with looking after the family's children or doing some domestic chores in order to pay for studies. The strings attached to a free room should be made very clear from the outset, or the candidate (quite often a young woman) might be in for unpleasant surprises once installed if the family starts heaping on some decidedly non-linguistic tasks (ironing, washing, taking the kids to school). The British Institute in Paris has a noticeboard advertising very occasional teaching vacancies as well as live-in tutoring and au pair jobs.

While looking for something to do in her gap year, **Hannah Start** was put in touch with a French bank executive who had done an English language course in Hannah's home town and who wanted to keep up

ANDREW SYKES

Andrew Sykes felt that he owed the success of his job-hunt to his misguided and unsuccessful accountancy training rather than to his TEFL certificate.

I wrote to move or less all the schools from your book in France and elsewhere that didn't stipulate 'experience required' and was fairly disheartened by the few, none-too-encouraging replies along the lines of 'if you're in town, give us a call.' Sitting in a very cheap hotel bedroom halfway down Italy in early November feeling sorry for myself and knowing that I was getting closer and closer to my overdraft limit and an office job back in the UK, I rang the schools that had replied and so picked up the phone and rang through to a company in Tours. 'Drop in,' the voice said, 'and we will give you an interview'. So I jumped on the next train, met the director on Monday and was offered a job on the Tuesday morning, initially on an hour-by-hour basis and then in December on a contract of 15 hours which was later increased to 20 hours a week.

OK, I was very lucky. I have since learned that the school receives several phone calls and letters per week; it's an employer's market. What got me the job was not my TEFL certificate nor my very good French. It was the fact that I was an ex-accountant. I had been one of the thousands enticed by the financial benefits of joining an accountancy firm after graduation. But I hated the job and failed my first professional exams. Ironically the experience gained during those two and a half years of hell was invaluable. Whereas in Italy they want teaching experience, in France they want business experience.

You will in the end be teaching people not objects, and any experience you can bring to the job (and especially the job interview) will help. However ashamed you may be of telling everyone in the pub back home that you were once a rat catcher, it may be invaluable if the school's main client is 'Rent-o-kil'.

her English at home in Paris by having someone to provide live-in conversation lessons. So, in exchange for three hours of speaking English in the evening (usually over an excellent dinner), Hannah was given free accommodation in the 17th arrondissement.

TEACHING CHILDREN

The state *Education Nationale* system is highly regimented and difficult to get into without passing a very challenging test called the *CAPES*, and later on the *Aggrégation*. Native teachers might be able to find an opening in a specialised school such as a Montessori school, often run by expats. The British Council has a large and successful English teaching operation in Paris. Individual tutoring is most likely to take place on Wednesdays (when state schools are closed) and Saturdays.

If you are hoping to work with kids, for example with the British Council, you must have relevant experience, aptitude and (ideally) qualifications, as the criteria are stricter than for teaching adults. They take most new teachers on just in advance of the school year so will probably be looking to replace people around June or July ready for *la rentrée* (start of the academic year) in September. Another possibility is holiday courses, of which there are many, and for which extra teachers are needed in summer, winter and at Easter.

French kids can be rowdy, though if you have a small class, 'crowd control' shouldn't be too much of an issue. If you are having trouble managing a private class, it is difficult to complain to parents because they won't be too impressed to hear that their little cherubs are messing around and wasting their money.

ON THE SPOT

Prospective teachers should not automatically head for Paris but bear in mind that provincial cities have many language schools too. Due to the many French companies that have decided it is far more cost effective to relocate in the provinces, many regional centres such as Orléans, Lyon, Marseilles, Toulouse, Lille and Rouen are crawling with medium and large international companies, all needing English-speaking staff. Not only is it hard to find work in Paris, but of course rents are very high in the capital.

If you do decide to give it a go in Paris, watch for adverts in the *metro* for English language courses, since these are usually the biggest schools and therefore have the greatest number of vacancies for teachers. Certain streets in the 8th arrondissement around the Gare St Lazare abound in language schools.

SARA BREESE

Sara Breese describes her job-hunt in Paris and the style of life teaching can pay for.

Finding work in France is a rather arduous process; however, with determination and zeal one can easily find work. I moved to Paris in September as a jeune fille au pair and doing side work teaching children English. The next year I decided to get my ESL teaching certificate at TEFL Paris which was one of the best decisions I ever made. Not only did I love the process of getting my certificate, but I also discovered a love for teaching. ESL is probably the number one industry for Anglophones and is your best investment in terms of success in the job search. In order to find a teaching job I looked in the FUSAC [mentioned below] and applied to every English teaching organisation in the magazine. After about two weeks, I received some calls asking for interviews. I interviewed with three different places, accepting a job where I still work. I am paid €20 per hour gross, 16 euros after taxes. I immediately signed a CDII which is the ideal type of contract for a Business English teacher in Paris. It translates to basically a long-term intermittent contract meaning that you will receive work when it is available but you will not stop being considered an employee.

I have not been able to save money because Paris is very expensive. I can make anywhere between €1,000 and €1,600 a month. Rent in Paris is very high and I have never heard of a teaching organisation providing housing for their teachers. When I first moved to Paris I lived in what they call a 'chambre de bonne' (maid's quarters). These are rented for about €450 per month, so as a teacher you can expect at least half your paycheque to go to rent.

With abundance also come cowboy outfits whose standards are not always what they should be. Again, schools which insist on a TEFL certificate and use a rigorous recruitment process are probably the safest bet. If you are desperate, you might want to go for less reputable or well-known schools but be ready to be disappointed.

FREELANCE TEACHING

Well-off parents of French school children often pay for private lessons for their kids. Business people with a pressing need for English, which they are reluctant to reveal to their employer, and worried exam students are other big markets for freelance English tutors. Private lessons are a very good supplement to an official contract and it is worth spending a bit of time putting notices up and spreading the word that you are available for this sort of work. Sab Will has charged €30 an hour for a minimum of two hours at a time and people seem to accept this if you can convince them you are well-qualified, experienced and pleasant to be with. In general €20 is considered a decent fee for an hour's private tuition, and should be the minimum charged in Paris by anyone with qualifications or experience. Many people advertise and then have to find a suitable public place to meet clients. Rather than choose a café where you might end up spending a couple of euros on a drink, the Luxembourg Gardens or other parks make a good meeting place in the summer.

A category of legal worker was introduced a couple of years ago, the 'Auto-entrepreneur', which is open to anyone officially based in France (i.e. with French bank account, working papers and French social security number). Individuals can set up as a one-man or one-woman company and sell their services. This is attractive to teachers because it can be accomplished quickly, including online, and also to employers because they do not have to pay social security contributions. The downside for teachers is that they become responsible for making contributions for their own pension, health insurance, taxes and so on, and of course no paid holidays or travel pass (information in English at www.anglais.urssaf.fr). But the independence is appealing and allows you to work for more than one employer much more easily.

Self-employed workers (*travailleurs indépendants*) are obliged to register at the social security office (www.urssaf.fr/general/les_urssaf/votre_urssaf/fiche.phtml). The hourly fees (*honoraires*) paid to freelance teachers should be significantly higher than to contract workers (*salariés*) since they are free of deductions. In addition to the British Institute noticeboard mentioned above, there are many other *panneaux* that might prove useful to someone looking for private tutoring. This is especially appealing to Americans who do this without worrying too much about visas.

As part of a well-organised teaching job hunt in Marseille, American **Bradwell Jackson** tried to arrange to teach some private lessons:

Besides searching for jobs in schools, I also tried my hand at the tutoring market. I put up petites annonces in the local boulangeries and bars, and I also put an ad in a free local paper called 13 (treize), also called Top Annonce (www.topannonces.fr). The cost of placing the ad was not free, but it wasn't expensive (maybe €10). This did turn out to be fruitful, as I did get responses. My big disadvantage was that I didn't have a cell phone, and I was told that the French are not inclined to respond to someone only by email. I decided to counteract this by putting in a very low asking price, only €10 per hour. With that price, I got several responses, even with only an email address advertised. The problem was that there was a time lag of two weeks between my placing the order and its appearance, by which time I had booked a plane ticket back to Mexico. I also advertised on a free website service called Kelprof (www.kelprof.com). It was indeed free, but to contact referrals you have to use a password and 08 numbers which, I learned the hard way, are very expensive.

There are expatriate grapevines all over Paris, very helpful for finding teaching work and accommodation. The noticeboard in the foyer of the Centre d'Information et de Documentation Jeunesse (CIDJ) at 101 Quai Branly; +33 1 44 49 12 00; www.cidj.com (métro Bir-Hakeim) is good for occasional student-type jobs, but sometimes there are adverts for a *soutien scolaire en Anglais* (English tutor). It is worth arriving early to check for new notices; the CIDJ opens at 10am except Thursdays at 1pm and Saturdays at 9.30am.

The other mecca for job- and flat-hunters is the American Church at 65 Quai d'Orsay (métro Invalides), which has very active noticeboards upstairs, downstairs and outside. There is a charge for posting a notice and they are kept up to date. In the basement, the free corkboard is much more chaotic; it can take about half an hour to rummage through all the notices.

The American Cathedral in Paris (23 Avenue George V; www.americancathedral.org) near the métro stations Alma Marceau and George V, also has a noticeboard featuring employment opportunities and housing listings. English language bookshops like the eccentric Shakespeare & Company at 37 rue de la Bâcherie opposite Notre-Dame, as well as cafés, restaurants, and bars popular with the English-speaking community all distribute the free bilingual newsletter *France-USA Contacts* or *FUSAC* (www.fusac.org), which comes out the first Tuesday of the month. It comprises mainly classified adverts which are best followed up on the day the paper appears. An advert under the heading 'Work Wanted in France' starts at €36. Sab Will recalls placing his own small ad in *FUSAC* when he first arrived in Paris and getting responses from prospective students. But it is more effective at providing ways to get into the English-speaking expat community.

It may be worth including a reminder here that anyone who advertises their services should exercise a degree of caution when arranging to meet prospective clients.

Outside the bigger cities, your chance of picking up freelance work is greatly improved. Working as a language assistant in a small town in Lorraine, **Emily Sloane** had no problem finding freelance work:

Through word of mouth and no active self-promotion, numerous townspeople contacted me about private English tutoring. By the middle of the school year I had 5 private students, whom I taught once a week each for €10, with sometimes a meal on top of that. It was nice to be able to work through more complicated material with older students and really nice to have an inside look into various French households. Plus, the tutoring sessions kept me busy. I also earned some extra cash by doing freelance writing work for the mother of one of my students, which helped to supplement my fairly meagre salary and allowed me to take long and stress-free vacations during the numerous school breaks.

REGULATIONS

EU NATIONALS

Since 2003, EU citizens have been free of the obligation to obtain residence permits to live and work in other EU countries so the *carte de séjour* is now obsolete for most. Long-stayers may choose to apply for one since it can be a useful piece of ID, but they will have to be prepared to provide a battery of translated documents.

Once you take up paid employment in France, your employer must complete all the necessary formalities for registering you with social security (*sécu*) and you will be issued with a registration card and then pay a percentage of your wages as contributions. French admin and red tape is a pain in the neck, but once you've got it over and done with you are into quite a nice system of benefits and help on anything from unemployment and housing aid to child benefit and income supplements if you don't earn much one year.

NON-EU NATIONALS

In France, it is much more difficult for Americans, Canadians, Australians and all other non-EU nationalities to get a work permit than it is for EU teachers. However, people with initiative are able to get at least some legal work, at least for a limited period. The easiest way (apart from marrying a French national) is to enrol in a French course of some sort and acquire a student visa which allows the holder to engage in up to 20 hours of paid work a week, which is a typical teaching contract anyway. Possibilities exist for Americans who want to act as counsellors and activity leaders at English immersion summer camps in France, for example with companies like NACEL International (www.americanvillage.fr/en/recruitment/recruitmentnews.php) and Telligo (www.telligo.fr).

The certificate course offered by TEFL Paris (see Training directory) attracts a considerable number of Americans, some of whom go on to find teaching work in France. One of them describes the outcome of a well-organised job-hunt:

I recently went to Paris on the big TEFL job hunt, and thought I might share my advice on how to get a job. They say it's 'almost impossible' for Americans to get a work visa or a good job in France, and I'd like to prove that theory wrong. Come prepared. Get a TEFL certificate. Bring your birth certificate and CV in both French and English, handwritten cover letters in both languages, passport photos and college transcripts. On the third day of my search, I got an interview. A few days later, I showed up and got the job. Overall I'd say it was not nearly as bad as I was warned it would be. Of course, I had to go back to the US for three months to get my work visa, but there's no other way to do it, besides working illegally (something I wasn't willing to do).

Another American aged 22 took the student route, but doesn't mention what fees were payable for enrolling in a university. This advice is of use mainly to Americans who genuinely want to study for an MA:

Initially I decided to pursue a Master's degree in a French university. Luckily, I had a professor who had studied at Paris III, so I emailed him and asked how I could apply, but if you contact the head of the department at any Parisian university and send a proposal (CV plus motivation letter), you can ask for an application. I started this process around March/April last year for the fall semester. Getting accepted into a French university should not be too hard if you have a bachelor's degree. It helps to speak French, but if you don't, there may be some universities with French classes or you can consider an Anglophone university such as the American University in Paris. If and when you are accepted, you will receive a letter of enrolment with which you can apply for a visa in the States. Since you can only get a student visa before going to France, this letter is very important. I received this in about June/July. A law requires you to go through CampusFrance (www.campusfrance.org) for which you will probably need a translation of your diploma, etc. Applying for a student visa requires a lot of patience and setting up an appointment at the consulate weeks in advance. The important thing is never to get discouraged, have a lot of patience and remember — when there's a will, there's a way.

More questions on long stay student visas will be answered on the French consulate website, for example at www.consulfrance-losangeles.org. One possibility open to some Americans with Irish or Greek ancestry is to obtain an EU passport. An easier route is to teach on a voluntary or occasional basis; or you can always work on the 'black market', which is not really easy or advisable, but is something that the French, as well as foreigners, continue to do all the same.

CONDITIONS OF WORK

Teaching 'beezneezmen' is not everyone's cup of tea, but it can be less strenuous than other kinds of teaching. Provided you do not feel intimidated by your pupils' polished manners and impeccable dress, and can keep them entertained, you will probably be a success. As mentioned above, one-to-one teaching is increasingly common — with some schools in Paris it constitutes 70% of their business — for which ELT training (including the CELTA or Trinity Certificate) does not prepare you. However, if you develop a rapport with your client, this kind of teaching can be most enjoyable as **Sara Breese** describes:

I have enjoyed teaching as most of my students are adults who have chosen to take English classes, either for pleasure or to advance their career. The majority of them are nice and very motivated, thus making my job a pleasure. The teaching is mostly one-on-one and you are allowed to teach in whichever style you please. I appreciate this freedom to be creative with my students. However, this freedom is becoming more and more rare as schools are imposing their personalised TEFL methods. I have friends who work for other companies and it makes them feel like robots repeating the same lesson over and over again. The only problems I have encountered in my time as a teacher have been in the planning. I am travelling constantly all over Paris which means your day is never dull, but also can make it rather stressful. As a mobile teacher I have to carry all of my teaching materials with me. I am often seen running through the metro with a backpack full of books, CDs and a stereo.

As mentioned earlier, language schools which offer this facility to clients, especially those in small towns rather than big cities, may well expect you to drive, perhaps even own, a car so that you can give lessons in offices and other workplaces. Most schools pay between €18 and €25 (gross) per lesson.

Salaried teachers should be covered by a nationally agreed and widely enforced Convention Collective which makes stable contracts, sick pay, holiday pay, etc. compulsory as well as guaranteeing a monthly salary. Until recently, there were two types of typical teaching contract with French language schools. The first was a CDD (*contrat à durée déterminée*), a fixed-length contract, and a CDI (*contrat à durée indéterminée*), a permanent contract. However, because employers were obliged to pay teachers for a minimum number of hours (typically 20), during the recent downturn clients were in short supply and many teachers were being paid for 20 hours although only working for five, which meant that some schools went bust. To tackle this problem a new kind of contract has emerged and is becoming the norm: a CDII (*contrat à durée indéterminée intermittent*). This guarantees a low minimum such as 10 hours and pays an hourly rate for hours worked above that. A good language school should be able to allocate 20–25 hours a week to those who want them, but they are protected against paying for hours not taught when times are tough.

Another legislated benefit when working for a French company is that 1%–1.5% of your salary is paid into a fund for your future training. You are entitled to use this after you have worked for the company for a year or two, as **Sab Will** did:

My TEFL Diploma was paid for this way. But once I got it my employer didn't give me an extra centime more for my efforts. The three of us who had done the diploma stayed the obligatory year after the qualification and then left. So the language school lost its three most qualified teachers. Language schools that pay significantly more for experience or advanced qualifications are rare beasts.

The annual holiday allowance for full-time teachers is five weeks plus an extra five days off.

Telephone and internet teaching are popular for their convenience and anonymity, and a growing number of companies such as Phonalangue and Telelangue specialise in this and employ native speaker trainers. For many people, making mistakes over the phone is less embarrassing than face to face, though the lack of personal contact is felt by some to be detrimental to the learning experience. Many have been surprised by the good results. It is not necessary to be able to speak French and possibly even an advantage to be monolingual, so you won't be tempted to break into French in frustration. The standard rate of pay for telephone teaching is about €10 for half an hour plus incidental expenses.

An unusual feature in France is that some schools calculate the salary according to a certain number of teaching hours per 9 or 12 months, and will pay overtime for hours worked in excess of this. Obviously the total can't be calculated until the end of the contract, which is a drawback for anyone considering leaving early.

Partly because of France's proximity to a seemingly inexhaustible supply of willing English teachers, working conditions in France are seldom brilliant. You can survive in France, and even Paris, on a typical 20-hour-a-week contract, but to live more than a basic existence you will need to supplement this with extra hours from somewhere else.

Although **Andrew Boyle** enjoyed his year teaching English in Lyon and the chance to become integrated into an otherwise impenetrable community, he concluded that even respectable schools treated teachers as their most expendable commodity. By contrast, **Fiona Paton** was well looked after and had no trouble finding a comfortable and affordable flat in Vichy (which is often easy in popular holiday resorts outside the summer season). Her impression was that flat-sharing is not as commonplace in France as in other countries.

EMILY SLOANE

Emily Sloane discovered that although the French do not often come across as the most approachable of people, having a slightly firmer sense of privacy than is common in some countries, they can be great company.

I joined the French Alpine Club, which had a thriving and spirited branch in my village. In addition to weekly indoor rock climbing sessions, I accompanied club members on various weekend hikes and climbing trips in the Jura and Vosges Mountains in France and Switzerland and even attended a 10-day climbing clinic in northern Provence. Learning French climbing vocabulary while suspended 100 feet above the ground, when misunderstandings could have pretty serious consequences, was an experience I won't soon forget. The club members were fantastic people who generously shared the tight space of their homemade 'camping cars' and handcrafted liqueurs. I even convinced them to dress as Americans and speak English one night at the climbing wall. In return for their effort, I provided American snacks and music and a cheat sheet of useful American slang and insults that they enthusiastically tried out on each other. Through the club I even found my very own French lover, which proved to be the most efficient way to improve my language skills.

LIST OF EMPLOYERS

ANGLESEY LANGUAGE SERVICES (ALS)

1 bis, 3 Avenue du Maréchal Foch, 78400 Chatou

📞 +33 1 34 80 65 15

✉ als@alschatou.com

💻 www.als-formationlangues.com

Company established 1978, located just outside Paris.

NUMBER OF TEACHERS: 50.

PREFERENCE OF NATIONALITY: Native speakers.

QUALIFICATIONS: CELTA or equivalent plus 2 years of experience preferred but possibilities for trainees. Intermediate level or above in French an advantage. Car owner/driver an advantage.

CONDITIONS OF EMPLOYMENT: 10-month renewable contract. 15–25 hours per week. Learners are adults and many are taught in their workplaces. Recent expansion, so group lessons at all levels offered in evenings and during the day. Some evening and Saturday work available.

SALARY: €18.50 per hour plus 12% on top for holiday pay. Travel expenses.

FACILITIES/SUPPORT: Some help with finding accommodation is available. No initial training but help with preparation provided plus ongoing professional development provided for teachers.

RECRUITMENT: Initial contact by email then one-to-one interviews held in school or in Anglesey Wales.

CONTACT: Mike Webster.

APPLILANGUE

16 E rue du Cap Vert, 21800 Quetigny

📞 +33 3 80 52 98 98

✉ contact@appli-langue.com

💻 www.appli-langue.com

NUMBER OF TEACHERS: 12+.

PREFERENCE OF NATIONALITY: None.

QUALIFICATIONS: TEFL diploma and/or business experience.

CONDITIONS OF EMPLOYMENT: Open-ended contracts. Hours of teaching between 8.30am and 7.30pm.

SALARY: €1,449 per month starting, less about 20% for contributions.

FACILITIES/SUPPORT: School has contact who rents rooms while teachers are looking for an apartment. Help given with work permit applications including recommending a registered translator.

RECRUITMENT: Spontaneous CVs, word of mouth from former teachers.

CONTACT: Karen Longley (Karen.Longley@appli-langue.com).

CITYLANGUES

Bât. C, Le Triangle de l'Arche, 11, cours du Triangle, Le Faubourg de l'Arche, Secteur Arche Nord, 92937 Paris La Défense Cedex; also 8 rue Louis Blériot, 92500 Rueil Malmaison

✆ +33 1 55 91 96 70 (La Défense) and +33 1 47 49 79 46 (Rueil Malmaison)

✎ sw@citylangues.com

💻 www.citylangues.com

NUMBER OF TEACHERS: 25.

PREFERENCE OF NATIONALITY: None, but employ only teachers resident in Paris with French working papers.

QUALIFICATIONS: Degree and TEFL certificate.

CONDITIONS OF EMPLOYMENT: Teaching represents 72% of total paid hours as per French law.

SALARY: According to profile, graded accorded to experience.

FACILITIES/SUPPORT: No assistance with accommodation. Training available in how the French system works, emphasis on team work in school.

RECRUITMENT: Local interviews essential.

CONTACT: Stefan Wheaton, president of the Language Commission of the French Training Federation.

ENGLISH POINT

Head Office: 14E rue Pierre de Coubertin, Parc de Mirande, Dijon, 21000

✆ +33 820 626064

✎ t.holland@englishpoint.fr

💻 www.englishpoint.fr

NUMBER OF TEACHERS: 14.

PREFERENCE OF NATIONALITY: British, New Zealander, American, Canadian, South African.

QUALIFICATIONS: Preferably a CELTA or equivalent and/or significant teaching experience plus business work experience. The majority of courses are business-based so knowledge of how a business works is essential. Also, being an objectives-based school you should be able to think from the client's perspective and adapt your teaching accordingly.

CONDITIONS OF EMPLOYMENT: Contracts are from 3 months – permanent. Teaching hours 8am–9pm, Monday–Friday (possible Saturday mornings).

SALARY: €20–24 per hour depending on age/experience/flexibility etc.

FACILITIES/SUPPORT: School can help find accommodation for teachers, from organising viewings to full accommodation management.

RECRUITMENT: Through websites, training schools, word of mouth, etc. Telephone interviews essential followed by face-to-face meeting.

CONTACT: Tony Holland, Director.

EXECUTIVE LANGUAGE SERVICES

50 rue Sainte Lazare, 75009 Paris

✆ +33 1 44 54 58 88

✎ info@els-paris.com

💻 www.els-paris.com

NUMBER OF TEACHERS: Trainers for one-to-one and group tuition.

PREFERENCE OF NATIONALITY: None, but must be a native English speaker.

QUALIFICATIONS: TEFL certificate and good teaching experience of adults and professionals. A background in law, finance or business would be a plus.

CONDITIONS OF EMPLOYMENT: 1 year minimum. Full-time and part-time positions available. Team teaching in school and on-site in company premises.

FACILITIES/SUPPORT: 2 fully equipped resource centres for staff. No help with accommodation.

RECRUITMENT: Interview after CV and letter of motivation (can be interviewed by telephone). Observation of a class and demo lesson for the same class the following day.

CONTACT: N Fairbrother (nfairbrother@els-paris.com).

FONTAINEBLEAU LANGUES & COMMUNICATION

47 Boulevard Marechal Foch, 77300 Fontainebleau

✆ +33 1 64 22 48 96

✎ recruitment@flc-int.com or dianne.riboh@flc-int.com

💻 www.flc-int.com

NUMBER OF TEACHERS: 12 English teachers, 35 in total.

PREFERENCE OF NATIONALITY: British/Irish. Australians, Canadians and Americans or other native English speakers with EU nationality or French working papers.

QUALIFICATIONS: TEFL training (e.g. CELTA). Must be dynamic, creative, versatile and able to work in a team. Previous business experience a plus.

CONDITIONS OF EMPLOYMENT: 1 year minimum. Majority of teaching takes place in company premises so owning a car is necessary (transport costs reimbursed at €0.45 approx. per km). Variety of teaching situations including groups, one-to-one lessons and Business English. Hours are grouped as much as possible between 9am and 7pm, Monday to Friday.

SALARY: Starting at €19 per hour which includes 12% holiday pay. Social security deductions are about 22%.

FACILITIES/SUPPORT: Training workshops held regularly. Large teachers' library.

RECRUITMENT: Interview essential – usually by phone.

CONTACT: Dianne Riboh, Director.

ICB EUROPE

45 rue d'Aboukir, 75002 Paris

+33 1 44 55 38 31

declankehoe@icbeurope.com

www.icbeurope.com

NUMBER OF TEACHERS: 50.

PREFERENCE OF NATIONALITY: None but native English speaker.

QUALIFICATIONS: Prefer candidates who are TEFL/TESOL/CELTA qualified with a couple of years of business experience, ideally within the financial/insurance sectors.

CONDITIONS OF EMPLOYMENT: Open-ended contracts. Trainers who can stay for at least 1 year are preferred. To teach during normal office hours Monday to Friday.

SALARY: Trainers who are available at all times can be guaranteed 800 teaching hours a year with an average remuneration of about €1,600 per month plus a monthly bonus programme based on student satisfaction and lesson observations. 21% deductions for tax and social security.

FACILITIES/SUPPORT: No assistance given with visas or accommodation.

RECRUITMENT: Group interview involves candidates introducing themselves, a grammar test and some group discussion about different teaching techniques. If successful at this stage the candidate then goes on to have a one-to-one interview with the owner of ICB Europe, Eric Wrobley.

CONTACT: Declan Kehoe, Recruitment Manager/Résponsable Pédagogique.

ILC FRANCE – IH PARIS (INTERNATIONAL LANGUAGE CENTRE)

13 Passage Dauphine, 75006 Paris

+33 1 44 41 80 20

info@ilcfrance.com

www.ilcfrance.com

NUMBER OF TEACHERS: 34.

QUALIFICATIONS: CELTA or approved equivalent. Experience of business world essential.

CONDITIONS OF EMPLOYMENT: Teaching hours between 8.30am and 7pm. Contracts according to French labour laws. 80% of teaching is in-company.

SALARY: Variable according to contract.

FACILITIES/SUPPORT: Assistance with finding accommodation, teacher development and training. ILC offers CELTA course full-time and part-time (see Training chapter). Candidates can also be supported while doing the distance DELTA programme.

RECRUITMENT: Spontaneous CVs and local adverts, although priority given to IH network. Interviews in Paris essential.

CONTACT: Marlene Regaya, Director (marlene.regaya@ilcfrance.com).

IMPAQT

Head Office: Téléport IV, Futuropolis IV, B.P. 10186, 86962 Futurscope Cedex

+33 5 49 49 63 80

siege@impaqt.net

www.impaQt.net

NUMBER OF TEACHERS: 30 for operations in Poitiers, Paris, Angouleme, Tours, Toulouse and Lyon.

PREFERENCE OF NATIONALITY: None.

QUALIFICATIONS: Degree, TEFL qualification and some additional experience other than in education. Minimum age 25–35, open-minded and curious with excellent communication skills and a working knowledge of French.

CONDITIONS OF EMPLOYMENT: Teaching hours are during normal office hours.

SALARY: €1,750 per month before tax.

RECRUITMENT: Usually through newspaper adverts.

CONTACT: Jane Le Goff, Director of Relations (jane@impaqt.net).

INLINGUA PARIS

109 rue de l'Université, 75007 Paris

+33 1 45 51 46 60

invalides@inlinguaparis.com

www.inlingua-paris.com/recrutements.php

NUMBER OF TEACHERS: Many teachers required for 7 branches in Paris area (others at Bastille, La Défense, Roissy, Etoilre, etc.) and Pau.

PREFERENCE OF NATIONALITY: None.

QUALIFICATIONS: TEFL plus minimum 2 years' experience preferably with professional adults. Preferred minimum age 25. Candidates must be creative, independent, flexible, of excellent appearance and with a good cultural background.

CONDITIONS OF EMPLOYMENT: Minimum 12 months; open-ended contracts. Flexible hours, with guaranteed minimum, mostly 20–30 hours per week.

FACILITIES/SUPPORT: Assistance with accommodation, work permits and training possible.

RECRUITMENT: Interviews essential in France.

CONTACT: Philippe Fouque.

LINGUARAMA
Tour Eve, 7è étage, 1 Place du Sud, La Défense 9, 92806 Puteaux Cedex
- +33 1 47 73 00 95
- paris@linguarama.com
- www.linguarama.com.

NUMBER OF TEACHERS: 30.

PREFERENCE OF NATIONALITY: Native speakers with working papers for the EU.

QUALIFICATIONS: Recognised TEFL qualification (CELTA or Trinity Cert) plus 1 year's teaching experience required. Driving licence useful.

CONDITIONS OF EMPLOYMENT: Full-time teachers work 25 hours per week, September to June. Part-time teachers work flexible hours. Teaching is Business English, taught in-company and at school.

SALARY: Approx. €1,725 per month.

FACILITIES/SUPPORT: Advice on finding accommodation. Regular training available.

RECRUITMENT: Via Linguarama in England and also locally.

CONTACT: Jo Dennison, Pedagogic Manager (JoDennison@linguarama.com).

SYNDICAT MIXTE MONTAIGU-ROCHESERVIERE
35 Avenue Villebois, Mareuil, 85607 Montaigu
- +33 2 51 46 45 45
- anglais@sm-montaigu.rocheserviere.fr
- www.gapyear-france.com

NUMBER OF TEACHERS: 5.

PREFERENCE OF NATIONALITY: British gap year students.

QUALIFICATIONS: Experience of and interest in teaching and a love of France.

CONDITIONS OF EMPLOYMENT: Standard contract length 9 months, to teach 20 hours per week.

SALARY: €207 per month.

FACILITIES/SUPPORT: Accommodation provided with local host families/resident project coordinator.

RECRUITMENT: Interview essential possibly in UK or in France (Vendée April–June).

CONTACT: Julie Legrée, Project Coordinator.

TELAB LANGUAGE COURSES BY TELEPHONE
Head Office, En Verdan, 71520 Saint Point
- +33 3 85 50 58 58
- s.evans@telab.com
- www.telab.com

NUMBER OF TEACHERS: 60.

PREFERENCE OF NATIONALITY: None but must be native English speaker, resident in France and with necessary working papers.

QUALIFICATIONS: Language teaching qualifications (TEFL or equivalent), at least 2 years' experience in teaching languages to company employees, work experience in or knowledge of a specific field (e.g. marketing, finance, medical, technical, etc.), excellent communication abilities, independent, organised and rigorous at work. Must have a computer and know how to use the internet.

CONDITIONS OF EMPLOYMENT: Teachers work from home, flexible hours between 7am and 9pm. There is a trend for more teachers to work full-time rather than part-time.

FACILITIES/SUPPORT: Assistance given with social security registration (about 20% of gross salary is taken at source as contributions). No help with work permits or accommodation.

RECRUITMENT: Referrals, internet, press.

CONTACT: Stephanie Evans, Manager.

TRANSFER
15 rue de Berri, 75008 Paris
- +33 1 56 69 22 30
- info@transfer.fr
- www.transfer.fr

ALSO: 20 rue Godot de Mauroy, 75009 Paris; 303 Square des Champs Elysees, Evry

NUMBER OF TEACHERS: 90.

PREFERENCE OF NATIONALITY: None.

QUALIFICATIONS: Either professional or technical experience (law, finance, etc.) or solid teaching experience, Cambridge CELTA or similar qualification and degree.

CONDITIONS OF EMPLOYMENT: Short-term, long-term or permanent. Teaching takes place generally from 9am to 6pm and some evenings.

SALARY: On application. About 20% deducted for tax and social security.

FACILITIES/SUPPORT: Americans must have their own work papers as no assistance is given with arranging these.

RECRUITMENT: Application and CV. Interview.

CONTACT: Marian Casey (mcasey@transfer.fr).

WALL STREET INSTITUTE

www.wallstreetinstitute.fr/recrutement/accueil-Recrutement

NUMBER OF TEACHERS: Varies; 68 franchised branches (email addresses linked from website above).

PREFERENCE OF NATIONALITY: None.

QUALIFICATIONS: CELTA or TESOL certificate.

CONDITIONS OF EMPLOYMENT: Permanent contracts offered. To work part-time hours or full-time if necessary up to 136 hours per month.

SALARY: €1470 per month plus bonuses.

RECRUITMENT: Via local advertising and the internet. Online application procedure via recruitment site www.keljob.com.

CONTACT: For Paris branch contact HR Manager, 2 Patio de la Pyramide, Puteaux 92800; +33 1 58 13 89 80; recrutement@wsiparis.com.

GERMANY

The excellent state education system in western Germany ensures that a majority of Germans have such a good grounding in English that very little teaching is done at the beginner level. However, the number of lower-level learners in the eastern part of Germany is higher. If German students want exposure to a native speaker they are far more likely to enrol in a language summer course in Britain (especially now with the pound so weak against the euro) than sign up for extra tuition at a local institute. Furthermore, many secondary schools in Germany (including the former East) employ native speakers of English to assist in classrooms (programme details below). English is also offered at *Volkshochschulen* or adult education centres where various subsidised courses are run.

Cities in the former East Germany such as Leipzig, Dresden and Erfurt are less popular destinations for job-seeking teachers than Munich, Berlin and Freiburg, and may therefore afford more opportunities, especially since provision of English in the schools lags behind that of western Germany.

The greatest demand for English in Germany continues to come from the business and professional community, and with the continuing strength of the German economy demand for English has held up well. That does not mean that it is easy to walk into a job. **John Sydes**, long-time resident of Munich who runs a small team of English teachers, wrote to say '*given the current economic situation here we should be able to cover all the courses we have with the EFL teachers who are already based in the Munich area*'. However, highly paid in-company positions for EFL and ESP teachers can still be found, and the agencies and consultancies which supply teachers to business clients have increased the number of native speaker freelance teachers they recruit. Demand is greatest outside cities such as Munich, where teachers complain about a lack of work.

PROSPECTS FOR TEACHERS

Many of the companies that market in-company English courses are desperate for good teachers and trainers, though there is no shortage of inexperienced teachers looking for teaching opportunities. Any graduate with a background in economics or business who can speak German has a good chance of finding work in a German city. A TEFL certificate and a university degree have less clout than relevant experience, as **Kevin Boyd** found when he arrived with his brand new Cambridge certificate at the beginning of the academic year:

I was persuaded by a teaching friend to go to Munich with him to try to get highly paid jobs together. As he spoke some German and had about a year's teaching experience, he got a job straightaway. Every school I went to in Munich just didn't want to know as I couldn't speak German and only had four weeks' teaching experience. After two days of this I decided to try my luck in Italy.

Experience in business is often a more desirable qualification than an ELT qualification. The question is not so much whether you know what a past participle is but whether you know what an 'irrevocable letter of credit' or a 'bank giro' is. Many schools offer *Oberstufe*, advanced or specialist courses in, for example, Banking English, Business English, or for bilingual secretaries, etc. Full-time, vocationally oriented courses in languages for business and commerce are called *Berufsfachschule* and this is by far the most buoyant part of the market. For none of these is a Cambridge or Trinity Certificate or even a Diploma the most appropriate training. However, the more serious schools and the regional English Language Teachers' Associations (ELTAs) have been moving to professionalise the industry and to offer and require more training in ELT skills. Qualifications such as a degree in physics may also impress and lead to scientific translation work, according to **Penny**, a teacher in Berlin.

Very few schools are willing to consider candidates who can't speak any German. Although the 'direct method' (i.e. total immersion in English) is in use everywhere, the pupils may expect you to be able to explain things in German. Penny was not put off so easily:

At the beginning they all expected me to talk to them in German. True to my CELTA training I insisted on English except in emergencies and they got used to it!

If the school prepares its students for the London Chamber of Commerce exams (LCCI), the teacher will be expected not only to understand the syllabus but to interpret and teach it with confidence. There is still a preference for British English, but the increasing number of course participants working for global or American companies prefer Canadian/American English.

Fees charged to companies by the most established and specialist teachers and trainers can be very high, which means few openings occur in this sought-after sector. These teachers also have high overheads and a staggeringly large percentage of their incomes will disappear in compulsory contributions (described below) and expenses. One further requirement of many employers is a driving licence, so that teachers can travel easily from one off-site assignment to another.

FINDING A JOB

Up to 400 posts as English language classroom assistants are available at secondary schools throughout Germany. Applications are encouraged from students who have at least AS level, Higher Grade or equivalent in German. UK applicants should contact the Language Assistants Team at the British Council (10 Spring Gardens, London SW1A 2BN; +44 20 7389 4596; assistants@britishcouncil.org, www.britishcouncil.org/languageassistants-ela.htm). The salary is €800 a month (net) for 12 hours of work a week. Language assistants such as **Sarah Davies** (who was sent to a small town in the east) advise against agreeing to teach in a small village where conditions may be basic and the sense of isolation strong.

Other nationalities can also participate through Pädagogischer Austauschdienst (PAD; www.kmk-pad.org). American students and graduates can apply for the English Teaching Assistantships programme through the Fulbright Program (administered by the Institute of International Education, 809 UN Plaza, New York, NY +1 10017-3580). Candidates planning to go on to become teachers of German are strongly preferred; contractual arrangements are as above plus help with travel and insurance. University students and graduates can often find out about possible employers from their university careers office or local English schools, as happened to **Catherine Rogers**. She wrote on spec to a number of local language schools to get some experience before working abroad and ended up being interviewed by two British contacts of a government scheme for teaching English to unemployed engineers and secretaries operating in the Dresden area.

Like so many embassies, the German Embassy in London is not noted for its helpful attitude to aspiring teachers or other job-seekers. Apart from directing students to enquire about the exchange programme run by the British Council and providing addresses of the state ministries of education, it recommends applying to the Zentrale Auslands und Fachvermittlung (International Placement Services), ZAV, part of the German Federal Employment Agency (Villemombler Strasse 76, 53123 Bonn; +49 228 713 1330; zav-bonn.ferien beschaeftigung@arbeitsagentur.de). All applications from abroad are handled by this office. Although people of any nationality can apply through the ZAV, only citizens of old EU countries (who have German language skills) are entitled to expect the same treatment as a German. As usual, it is much more difficult to arrange a job by sending written applications and CVs from the UK than by presenting yourself in person to language school directors and training companies, CV in hand. Determination, qualifications, experience and being on the spot are often deciding factors when an employer has to choose between large numbers of similarly qualified applicants.

The best source of language school addresses is once again the *Yellow Pages* (*Gelbe Seiten*) which can be consulted online (www.herold.at) or try www.goyellow.de and search for *Sprachschulen*. Another way of accessing potential employers is via the local English Language Teachers Association, a branch of which can be found in most major cities. The Munich association (MELTA) is especially vigorous and carries a few job vacancies and a page of employers (www.melta.de/jobs_employers.php). There is also a forum for English teachers in Germany, including advice for 'newbies', which can be found at http://elt.yuku.com. Look for English language magazines aimed at expats and you should come across some relevant adverts. For example, the English-language magazine *Munich Found* (www.munichfound.de) carries occasional TEFL vacancies.

All the major language school chains have a significant presence in Germany including Berlitz, Inlingua (with 70 training centres), Linguarama, specialising in language training for business in eight cities, and Wall Street Institute, which keeps expanding. Rates of pay vary, however, some employers pay inexperienced teachers in the range of €12–€16 for a 45-minute lesson, whereas more senior positions are paid €18–€30+ an hour.

Throughout Germany, more than 2,000 adult education centres or *Volkshochschulen* teach the English language (among many other courses) to adults. Native speakers with teaching experience might find a role within the Deutscher Volkshochschul-Verband e.V (www.vhs.de).

One of the easiest entrées to the TEFL world is as a tutor on a language summer camp. These have mushroomed in Germany, and take on lots of native speakers to help kids improve their English through interactive play, sports, music, etc. during the school holidays. Try for example:

Berlitz Kids – www.berlitz.de. See entry.

Camp Adventure – www.campadventure.de. English camps in various locations. Instructors must be over 19 and have training.

LEOLingo Sprachcamps – www.leo-lingo.de. Camps in north-eastern Germany 24 June–13 August (Hamburg, Baltic Sea, Mecklenburg-Vorpommern), and Bavaria 22 July–10 Sept. Eight-day compulsory training is unpaid. Staff are paid €200 a week plus room and board, either camping or with host families.

Oskar Lernt English – www.oskarlerntenglisch.de. Native speaker teachers and counsellors should have a working knowledge of German.

Penguin Camp – www.pinguincamp.de/jobs.

Sphairos – +49 89 18 70 31 56; www.sphairos.de.

Sunflower Sprachcamps – www.sunflower-sprachcamps.eu. Camps from mid-July to the beginning of September in the Düsseldorf area. Five-day training session.

INTERVIEWS

Most schools and institutes in Germany cannot, under normal operating circumstances, hire someone unseen merely on the basis of his/her CV and photo. Applicants should arrange for a face-to-face interview and should be prepared to make themselves available at a moment's notice. Professional presentation is even more important for securing work in the German business world than elsewhere. Vacancies occur throughout the year since businessmen and women are just as likely to start a course in April as in September. Germans tend to be formal, so dress appropriately and be aware of your manners at an interview. Also good references (*Zeugnisse*) are essential.

A good starting place is Frankfurt am Main, known to locals as 'Bankfurt' or 'Mainhattan'. Frankfurt has the highest concentration of major banks and financial institutions in the country and a correspondingly high number of private language schools. It is helpful, though not essential, to have some basic knowledge of German and business experience. In a job interview with a language school director, demonstrating a detailed knowledge of a handful of commonly used textbooks may be more important than business experience. A former teacher who spent two years teaching in dozens of banks and multinational companies recommends *Build Your Business Vocabulary* by J. Flower and *New International Business English* by L. Jones and R. Alexander.

You can also impress a potential employer by showing some familiarity with current major German business news (bank mergers, etc). This can easily be done by scanning the English language press or watching the BBC's *World Business Report*. Language schools are looking for teachers who can pose intelligent questions to business students about their jobs. There is a considerable demand from the business community for guidance on conducting 'small talk' in English, which is crucial in building rapport with clients and colleagues.

NINO HUNTER

Nino Hunter decided to go to Berlin, a city which is both exquisitely trendy and reassuringly relaxed, and one that appeals most to people in search of European culture at its finest. Despite his recent degree in modern languages from the University of Bath, he found it a struggle.

I did find it extremely difficult to find teaching posts in Berlin. I think the main reason would be the sheer number of English speakers in Berlin, many of whom wish to stay in this amazing city. Given the lack of industry, they have little alternative but to fall back on teaching English, with or without a CELTA/TEFL certificate. The English community is huge in Berlin (check the online Toytown Berlin at www.toytowngermany.com/berlin which has tons of new postings every day). There are of course a huge number of schools in Berlin but given the number of teachers and the decreasing demand over the last two years due to the global economic crisis many of them have become exceptionally picky about who they choose to take on, often asking for at least two years' experience, etc. There was a particular demand for English teachers able to teach advanced students (Cambridge levels 1 and 2) and a few schools simply wouldn't take people on who didn't have experience teaching higher level students.

All of which means that the market in Berlin is extremely saturated and sending a CV off to each and every school usually doesn't help. The best way of finding teaching positions in the city is putting on a suit and going to the schools with a CV, introducing yourself and trying your hardest not to get fobbed off by a secretary, but rather to get an actual interview where they offer you a course. This obviously requires a little courage and a fair amount of energy but is the only way of being sure your CV isn't deleted immediately and is in fact the only way I or any of my colleagues got jobs at private language schools.

The teachers at the Berlin School of English where I did my CELTA course assured me that no one would pay less than €15 for 45 minutes to a teacher with a CELTA. My first school paid me just €12 and it took me 10 weeks to get up to €14, which was not at all uncommon.

Two pieces of advice I could give would be firstly to try to get on the lists for the Volkshochschulen (I think there are about seven in Berlin), as these pay more (if you have a university degree even more) and the classes are large and quite fun. I would also recommend joining ELTABB (English Language Teacher's Association, www.eltabb.com/main/index.php) which costs €40 a year but is undoubtedly the best place to network and sometimes perfect positions come up. Basically one needs to be as proactive as possible and not be too fussy. If Wall Street or Berlitz offers you a course, take it.

FREELANCE TEACHING

The majority of native speakers teaching for commercial institutes are not on contracts, but are employed on a freelance contract basis (*Honorarvertrag*) to work for between 2 and 20 hours per week. Schools employing freelance teachers are not in a position to make deductions, because they cannot know a teacher's full expenses. Teachers may also work for several different schools. Freelance teachers are responsible for paying their own tax, pension insurance contributions and (crucially) health insurance.

Upon successful completion of a Trinity TESOL certificate course in England, **Ann Barkett** from Atlanta went to Munich to look for freelance work, but found it tough going:

> *During the period December to March, I was putting up flyers for private and group lessons but received no response. I finally answered an advert for a private student whom I taught for a few weeks, but there just wasn't enough work or money coming in and I was tired of trying at that point.*

Many freelance teachers find themselves for the first time required to design an ESP course (English for Specific Purposes), individually tailored to the needs of their business students. **Nathan Edwards** found that he got better at this:

> *Experience has shown me that such a syllabus must be flexible, open to change and short-term adjustment so as to accommodate the complex and evolving needs of students who are also full-time working professionals. Students and their employers must be given the assurance of a clearly structured course outline, but this must be partly generated by an ongoing negotiated process with all the participants. Finally don't forget that the students themselves can be a valuable source of ESP course material such as authentic English email messages, business letters and company brochures from their offices.*

REGULATIONS

EU nationals are free to travel to Germany to look for and take up work, but like all German citizens they must register their address with the relevant district authority (*Einwohnermeldeamt*) or local *Bürgeramt* within a week of finding permanent accommodation. For this they will need proof that they are living locally, e.g. a copy of a contract with a landlord, and possibly proof of employment or funding. This office will then liaise with the immigration authority which issues a certificate of free movement, *EU-Freizuegigkeitsbescheinigung*.

Useful guidance for the red tape affecting freelance teachers is available on the internet, for example on the relative forums of MELTA at http://elt.yuku.com. Also try www.expatica.com/de/main.html, which covers topics such as taxation, pensions and insurance.

NON-EU NATIONALS

Any non-EU national who wants to stay in Germany for more than 90 days must obtain a residence permit (*Aufenthaltsgenehmigung*). Citizens of the USA, Australia, Canada, Israel, Japan, New Zealand and Switzerland may apply for a residence permit within a week of arrival in Germany. Citizens of other countries are required to obtain a visa prior to entry at a German embassy or consulate in their country of residence. Residence permits are handled by the local immigration office *(Ausländerbehörde).*

The normal procedures would be to find a job and to obtain a work permit before applying for a residence permit.

To apply for a work permit you need a valid passport, a letter from your employer stating what the position you have been offered is, what your projected income will be and the completed application form for a work permit. Once you have the work permit you can then apply for a residence permit, for which you will need:

- The completed application form.
- Valid official ID or passport.
- An up-to-date passport photograph.
- Accommodation: proof of sufficient room for all members of the family and statement of rental costs (including heating, water and electricity) and mortgage (where applicable).
- Work permit.
- Employees: proof of employment (written statement by employer or a contract).
- Self-employed applicants: statement of registration of business.
- Proof of sufficient means to support yourself.
- Detailed statement and proof of regular income (wages for the past three months, wages of spouse and children, if they have an income).
- Proof of health insurance in Germany.
- Students: statement of matriculation and proof of sufficient means to support yourself (a written statement from your parents stating they will support you is sufficient).

According to a recent law (*Aufenthaltsgesetz* or *AufenthG*) that governs residence permits for non-EU citizens, applicants must prove that they have a secure and regular income which is next to impossible for freelance teachers. The only exceptions are if you can show that you can invest at least a million euros and/or create at least 10 new jobs and/or prove that the business will benefit the region economically.

German immigration laws require discretionary decisions from the individual authorities, so prospects for non-EU freelancers will differ from region to region. Only a work permit which has been issued by the district/city you live in is valid.

American and Canadian students or recent graduates who find an employer while still in North America might seek advice on documentation from Cultural Vistas (formerly CDS International in New York) (www.culturalvistas.org) which can facilitate the red tape for individuals to work in Germany for up to a year.

As soon as a teacher from outside the EU obtains a promise of salaried employment, he or she should take steps to get the necessary permits. The teacher must first register his or her name and address (as for EU nationals) and then report to the *Ausländersamt* (foreigners' office). There they must present a contract or letter from a school claiming that they are the best candidate for the job (difficult). Further requirements may include a certificate of good conduct (notarised by the US Embassy for a fee), proof of address and health insurance and also a health certificate from a German doctor. If approved, a one-year residence permit will be affixed to the passport, with a handwritten explanation that the bearer is allowed to work as an English teacher in private language schools only.

Unfortunately, Canadians, Australians, New Zealanders and other nationalities experience more difficulties since they require a residence visa which has been applied for in their country of origin. If within the three months of their tourist stay they manage to obtain a formal written offer of employment, they must return to their home country in order to apply for a working visa at the German Consulate. The application process takes up to one month and there is always a risk that the application will be refused. Successful applicants are issued with a one-year renewable work visa. Not all employers are willing to wait one month for a new teacher to begin working and may prefer to hire British or Irish teachers in the meantime.

BERLIN SCHOOL OF ENGLISH

We've been running CELTA courses since 2004 and train more than 100 teachers every year. Most of our graduates intend to work in Germany but others use the course as a stepping-stone to travelling elsewhere in the world. Recent graduates say the following about us.

'The balance struck between classroom input and hands-on teaching meant the course was never abstract, completely engaging, and skills and methods discussed were always relevant. The course was intensive, but never unmanageable, and the tutors were passionate and completely expert in their field.' (Kiruba)

'The constructive criticism and feedback (both peer to peer and tutor to trainee) was incredibly effective.' (Chloe)

What's it like working as an English teacher in Germany? Well, nearly all of the work is on a freelance basis (often via language schools) and you will need an entrepreneurial attitude. As for the work itself, you can find yourself teaching a wide range of students and courses.

'As a result (of the course), I have been teaching English for Specific Purposes for a year now – from the energy industry and the banking sector to real estate, journalism and tourism, at all levels.' (Kiruba)

'The fact that just six weeks after completing the CELTA course I was up and running in Berlin as a full time EFL teacher at companies, language schools and universities is testament to the Berlin School of English's impressive teacher-training standards.' (Chloe)

What will help you be successful teaching English in Germany? A recognised qualification will certainly give you an enormous advantage over unqualified 'native speakers', but it is also important to be flexible and open-minded, curious, and committed to the quality of your work.

TAX, HEALTH INSURANCE AND SOCIAL SECURITY CONTRIBUTIONS

About 95% of all the EFL teaching work in language schools and companies in Germany is offered on a freelance or self-employed basis. The hourly rates you are offered might sound good, but freelancers and self-employed teachers have to pay about 20% of their income after expenses and before tax into the German pension scheme. This is a compulsory contribution for all freelance teachers regardless of whether they already have a private pension scheme. Compulsory pension contributions and health insurance payments (also a must to obtain a work and residence permit) can easily make up 30%–35% of a freelance or self-employed teacher's 'expenses', and then there is still income tax to think about. **John Sydes** (mentioned above) says that these 'expenses' plus rent to be paid, mean that most hard-working teachers are left with very little disposable income. **Sylvia Weismiller**, Director of Euro-Lingua, based in Freiburg, writes:

> *Yes, it's very complicated, and lots of grey areas, unenforced requirements, etc. One of my American teachers is having problems getting his permits renewed. They said if he paid his pension contributions, they would renew it. What those two have to do with each other is a mystery! However, I don't know any foreigners who pay it, even though it is an official policy. At the moment (2012) the responsible government offices are swamped with applications from Eastern Europe so it's a huge plus if the applicant has an EU passport.*

Sylvia also mentions solidarity tax (about 1%) and church tax (about 1%), which you can avoid by registering as an atheist. However, medical insurance can be painful, particularly if you're a woman:

> *Official health insurance depends on age, sex, etc. Also complicated. Women pay about double. For instance as a woman in my 40s I was paying more than €400 per month. It doesn't depend on your income. If you are a registered student, however, you can get a much lower rate, I think €80 per month. As a student you can only work a limited number of hours, but as there aren't any tuition fees it's not a bad idea. There are also ex-pat programmes which charge, I believe, €90 per month. They are limited to 5 years. You have to have health insurance to get your residence permit extended.*

If you are a non-EU citizen you can ask the *Deutsche Rentenversicherung* (German pension authority) to repay the contributions you have made if you have paid into the state scheme for less than five years, i.e. have paid less than 60 pension contributions.

Foreigners working in Germany should obtain a *Lohnsteuerkarte* (tax card) if they are employees, or a *Steuernummer* (tax number) if they are self-employed or freelance from their local *Finanzamt* (tax office).

CONDITIONS OF WORK

You can almost guarantee that you will be teaching adults except at summer camps, since school children receive such a high standard of English tuition at school. Contracts for full-time work are usually at least a year long, often with a three-month probation period. But it is rare to be *Angestellt*, i.e. fully employed by a school with guaranteed minimum hours, sick pay, holiday pay, etc.

Hourly rates can be high: typically €17–€22 per lesson and double that and more for established teachers of Business English. Off-site teaching hours often incur a premium of €2–€5 to compensate for travel time, or sometimes employers pay 'three hours for two'. Freelancers who earn high incomes have normally been in Germany a long time, speak excellent German and have invested in acquiring relevant specialisations, resources, materials, etc. They have built up their clientele and reputation over years and defend their patch with understandable vigour. The majority of newcomers gain their initial experience at franchise language schools where the pay is much lower, sometimes on a par with cleaners, and where poor working conditions and no job security prevail. A 30-hour working week could consist of 40–45-minute lessons, which would be a very heavy workload.

However, after walking into a tiny English school on her street in Berlin and asking the owner if she needed any help, **Penny**, a British widow in her 50s, built up an enviable client base. She describes her experiences in Berlin:

> I do two classes a week, one in the morning and one in the evenings. The morning class is made up of retired ladies who come for fun and I have difficulty keeping them speaking English. I keep reminding them that I am being paid to teach them English and not to learn German from them. We have a good relationship and go out to the cinema occasionally. The members of the evening class are slightly more serious about learning English. Some of them sometimes join in the cinema outings.
>
> The classroom has a table with eight chairs, which limits the size of the class. There is a black board – I would dearly love a white board – and a CD/tape player. Most of my work, however, is one-to-one teaching, which I originally obtained through the school. I charge €14 and pupils come to me. Now, many pupils are recommended by a former or current pupil, so I have several German-Russians and several art historians together with some business ladies – there is a big demand for Business English.

Penny doesn't depend on her teaching, because otherwise her standard of living would be much lower than it is. If you are depending solely on one employer for your income try to find an institute which guarantees a monthly minimum number of hours. Monthly salaries for full-time *Angestellter* (employees) can be from €1,200 to €2,000 gross, with the possibility of paid overtime. Considering that a one-bedroom flat in one of the big cities can easily cost €450–€600 per month, excluding bills, salaries need to be high. Quite a few schools assist with accommodation. Teachers often turn to agencies though their fees can be very steep, as much as two or three months rent plus VAT. Try answering ads in the local paper, or look up *Wohnung* (apartments/flats) in the phone book or try the local *Mitwohnzentralen* which charges a more reasonable fee (usually one month's rent) for finding flats, though they may charge less if you end up renting a room or flat from owners who are temporarily absent. It is customary to pay your rent directly out of a bank account, so open a basic current account (*Girokonto*) as early as you can. By law, the deposit you pay (usually three months' rent) is put in a bank account, which should be a joint savings account in the tenant's and landlord's name, so that neither can withdraw money without the approval of the other.

LIST OF EMPLOYERS

ACADEMY OF BUSINESS COMMUNICATION (ABC)
ABC Franchise GmbH, Asperger Weg 14, 71732 Tamm
+49 7154 797 5044
info@abc-stuttgart.de
www.abc-stuttgart.de

PREFERENCE OF NATIONALITY: None.
QUALIFICATIONS: Teaching experience or business background plus university degree in any subject.
CONDITIONS OF EMPLOYMENT: Freelance only.
RECRUITMENT: Interviews preferred and are occasionally available in UK.

ACADEMY OF EUROPEAN LANGUAGES
Prinz-Albert-Str. 73, 53113 Bonn
+49 228 24 25 840
info@sprachakademie-bonn.de
www.sprachakademie-bonn.de.

NUMBER OF TEACHERS: 360.
PREFERENCE OF NATIONALITY: None.
QUALIFICATIONS: Advanced qualifications needed and much experience.
CONDITIONS OF EMPLOYMENT: Negotiable hours; open freelance contracts.
SALARY: €18 for a 45-minute lesson.

FACILITIES/SUPPORT: Help can be given with accommodation and work permits if necessary.

RECRUITMENT: Personal recommendations.

CONTACT: Tony Westwood, Director (t.westwood@sprachakademie-bonn.de).

BERLIN SCHOOL OF ENGLISH

Checkpoint Arkaden, Charlottenstrasse 81, 10969, Berlin

📞 +49 30 229 04 55

🖱 info@berlin.school-of-english.de

💻 www.berlin.school-of-english.de

NUMBER OF TEACHERS: 30–40.

PREFERENCE OF NATIONALITY: None, but must be a native English speaker.

QUALIFICATIONS: University degree plus TEFL/CELTA Certificate and minimum 1 year's experience.

CONDITIONS OF EMPLOYMENT: Minimum 1 year on freelance basis. Between 16 and 30 hours per week. Focus on Business English and ESP in a diverse range of professions and industries.

SALARY: Details given at interview stage.

FACILITIES/SUPPORT: In-house training provided: accredited Cambridge CELTA Centre, regular teaching workshops and seminars, internet access for teachers, school library.

CONTACT: John Wills, School Manager (john.wills@berlin.school-of-english.de).

BERLITZ DEUTSCHLAND GmbH

💻 www.berlitz.com/careers/33

Job vacancies and information about working conditions are posted on the Careers Services website. Hiring is done locally by one of the 67 schools in Germany. All contact information is provided on the above website or on www.berlitz.de. At the time of writing, more than 20 Berlitz schools had vacancies but most were open to people already residing in the vicinity or having the required documents to work in Germany (visa and work permit).

NUMBER OF TEACHERS: Varies depending on the size of the language centre. Over 1,000 instructors employed in Germany.

PREFERENCE OF NATIONALITY: Native English speakers preferred.

QUALIFICATIONS: Teaching abilities, a professional attitude, good communication skills, willing to work a flexible schedule, and preferably have a business background.

CONDITIONS OF EMPLOYMENT: Open-ended, freelance contracts. Flexible hours between 8am and 9.30pm.

FACILITIES/SUPPORT: Training in the Berlitz Method given

before start. Assistance with accommodation and work permits occasionally given.

RECRUITMENT: Adverts and personal referral.

CONTACT: Kristin Smith, Country Manager of Instruction.

BERLITZ KIDS & TEENS – BERLITZ DEUTSCHLAND GMBH

Konigin-Elisabeth Strasse 52, 14059 Berlin

📞 +49 30 3030 8479

🖱 laurie.castrocamargo@berlitz.de

💻 www.berlitz.de

NUMBER OF TEACHERS: 250.

PREFERENCE OF NATIONALITY: Native English speakers.

QUALIFICATIONS: Experience working with children aged 7–17 and also experience of teaching English preferred.

CONDITIONS OF EMPLOYMENT: Freelance work in English holiday camps during German school holidays (Easter 1–2 weeks, summer 4–8 weeks, autumn 2–4 weeks). Camp programmes run all day from 8am to 11pm.

SALARY: €450 per week. Freelancers have to deal with tax and health insurance independently.

FACILITIES/SUPPORT: No help with accommodation. If required an employer's letter of intent can be provided to non-EU nationals. Support will be given in dealing with the German authorities.

RECRUITMENT: Advertising in local magazines and word of mouth. Interviews are desirable and can be carried out over the telephone.

CONTACT: Laurie Camargo, Kids Director (Quality and Training).

CAMBRIDGE INSTITUT

Hildegardstr 8, 80539 München

📞 +49 89 22 11 15

🖱 info@cambridgeinstitut.de

💻 www.cambridgeinstitut.de

NUMBER OF TEACHERS: Approximately 30.

PREFERENCE OF NATIONALITY: British.

QUALIFICATIONS: PGCE essential (preferably in modern languages).

CONDITIONS OF EMPLOYMENT: 11-month contracts, renewable for a further 11 months. 26 hours per week. Lessons 9am–11.45am and 5.30pm–9.10pm.

SALARY: €2,600 per month less social security and income tax payments.

FACILITIES/SUPPORT: Assistance with accommodation. Induction course and ongoing workshops.

RECRUITMENT: Interview in UK or Munich essential.

CONTACT: Philip Moore, Principal.

CONTEXT SPRACHEN – UND MEDIENDIENSTE GmbH

Elisenstr 4–10, 50667 Cologne

☏ +49 221 925 456 0

✉ teaching@contextinc.com

🖥 www.contextinc.com.

NUMBER OF TEACHERS: 15–20.

PREFERENCE OF NATIONALITY: None.

QUALIFICATIONS: Must be native English speakers with academic education and experience.

CONDITIONS OF EMPLOYMENT: Freelance basis. Hours vary between 8am and 8pm, Monday to Friday.

SALARY: Varies according to qualifications/experience and degree of difficulty of class taught.

FACILITIES/SUPPORT: Accommodation and visas are responsibility of teachers. Some training given.

RECRUITMENT: Newspaper adverts, followed by local interviews.

CONTACT: Wendy Lautenschlaeger, School Director.

DAVID BERRY LANGUAGES

Weinbergsweg 3, 10119 Berlin

☏ +49 3044 99 025

✉ ped@dbl-berlin.de

🖥 www.dbl-berlin.de

NUMBER OF TEACHERS: 10–15.

PREFERENCE OF NATIONALITY: None.

QUALIFICATIONS: Minimum CELTA with preferably 2 years' experience.

CONDITIONS OF EMPLOYMENT: Freelance contract with flexible working hours.

SALARY: Negotiable depending on travel/course requirements.

FACILITIES/SUPPORT: Will refer teacher to the local ELTA for help with accommodation.

RECRUITMENT: Interviews are essential.

CONTACT: David Berry-Lichtenberg, Director of Studies.

DESK

Blumenstr. 1, 80331 München

☏ +49 89 26 33 34

✉ info@desk.sprachkurse.de

🖥 www.desk-sprachkurse.de

NUMBER OF TEACHERS: 30 native speakers (70 teachers in total).

PREFERENCE OF NATIONALITY: None.

QUALIFICATIONS: Degree with TEFL experience (adults).

CONDITIONS OF EMPLOYMENT: Duration of contract to suit. One of the few schools in Munich offering a full contract, rather than freelance conditions. Teaching hours mainly early mornings and evenings.

SALARY: €22 per 45-minute lesson.

FACILITIES/SUPPORT: No help with accommodation.

RECRUITMENT: CV and interview.

CONTACT: Erwin Schmidt-Achert, Owner.

DIE NEUE SCHULE

Gieselerstrasse 30a, D-10713 Berlin

☏ +49 30 873 03 73

✉ info@neueschule.de

🖥 www.neueschule.de

NUMBER OF TEACHERS: 80–110.

PREFERENCE OF NATIONALITY: British, American, Irish, Canadian.

QUALIFICATIONS: Cambridge or TEFL certificate and teaching experience needed. Mostly adults (ages 25–40) in small groups of no more than 8.

CONDITIONS OF EMPLOYMENT: Open-ended freelance contracts and some employed teachers. Variable hours in the daytime (9am–3pm) and evenings (6pm–9.15pm).

SALARY: Approx. €19 per hour.

FACILITIES/SUPPORT: Help with accommodation.

RECRUITMENT: Personal interview necessary, application link on website.

ENGLISH STUDIO

Hornschuchpromenade 7, D-90762 Fürth

☏ +49 911 950 990 00

✉ jobs@englishstudio.de

🖥 www.englishstudio.de

Also branches in Regensburg and Munich.

NUMBER OF TEACHERS: 15–20.

PREFERENCE OF NATIONALITY: Native English speakers. Work permit required.

QUALIFICATIONS: Minimum teaching/training qualification, e.g. PGCE, CELTA/Trinity, TEFL/TESOL certificate. Relevant business experience and commercial/industrial training experience also considered.

CONDITIONS OF EMPLOYMENT: Open-ended contract for freelancers; 24 contact hours per week; teaching hours between 7.30am and 8pm.

SALARY: Hourly rates to be negotiated.

FACILITIES/SUPPORT: May be able to advise on accommodation.

RECRUITMENT: Word of mouth. Interviews essential.

CONTACT: Thomas Hintze (thomas.hintze@english studio.de).

State-recognised vocational language college.

NUMBER OF TEACHERS: 25.

PREFERENCE OF NATIONALITY: British, American, Canadian.

QUALIFICATIONS: At least a bachelor's degree (main focus *must* be German). PGCE preferred. At least 3 years' experience.

CONDITIONS OF EMPLOYMENT: Permanent contracts. Part-time work possible. 30 hours per week.

SALARY: Based on German state salary scale.

FACILITIES/SUPPORT: Assistance given with accommodation and work permits.

RECRUITMENT: Interview in Ingolstadt necessary.

CONTACT: Stuart Wheeler.

Also has branch in Riehen near Basel, Switzerland.

NUMBER OF TEACHERS: 5.

PREFERENCE OF NATIONALITY: None, but native English speakers preferred.

QUALIFICATIONS: University degree, teaching experience, foreign language ability, preferably TOEFL or teacher training.

CONDITIONS OF EMPLOYMENT: Freelance.

SALARY: €15 per 45-minute lesson starting salary.

FACILITIES/SUPPORT: Advice given on local accommodation agencies. Non-EU teachers applying for a work permit outside Germany can be supplied with statement of projected income, etc. Support available as needed for lesson planning, books and other materials.

RECRUITMENT: Word of mouth, local ads, contact with schools abroad.

CONTACT: Sylvia Weismiller, Director.

NUMBER OF TEACHERS: 25.

PREFERENCE OF NATIONALITY: British, Canadian, American.

QUALIFICATIONS: University degree plus a teaching qualification, plus at least 2 years' relevant teaching experience. However, personality is more important than a stream of qualifications.

CONDITIONS OF EMPLOYMENT: Teachers work as freelancers. School is looking for teachers able to commit for at least 1 year. Most teachers have a weekly timetable of about 17 90-minute classes.

SALARY: Teachers invoice Finer English for hours worked. Typical monthly earnings are €2,200–€3,000. Freelancers are paid in full but must organise the payment of income tax and health insurance.

FACILITIES/SUPPORT: Full teacher support provided including finding accommodation and dealing with red tape. Teachers need to arrange a medical examination with a German doctor in order to obtain medical insurance which is a pre-condition of receiving a work permit.

RECRUITMENT: Via internet. Intensive telephone interviews conducted from Kassel, Germany.

CONTACT: Joe Finer, Director.

NUMBER OF TEACHERS: 20.

PREFERENCE OF NATIONALITY: American.

QUALIFICATIONS: College degree (minimum requirement BA or BSc). Applications from candidates holding a certificate in TESOL or TESL or TEFL are especially welcome.

CONDITIONS OF EMPLOYMENT: Freelance positions only. Average workload 3–9 hours per week, teaching adults and high school students.

SALARY: Hourly wage.

RECRUITMENT: Local interview required.

CONTACT: Judith von Falkenhausen, Language Program Co-ordinator (+49 7071 795 2614; judith.falkenhausen@dai-tuebingen.de).

NUMBER OF TEACHERS: 60–70.

PREFERENCE OF NATIONALITY: British, North American.

QUALIFICATIONS: University degree plus ELT certificate. Preferred minimum 1 year's experience.

CONDITIONS OF EMPLOYMENT: Minimum 1 year on freelance basis. Between 16 and 30 hours per week.

SALARY: Approx. €29–€45 for 90-minute teaching session.

FACILITIES/SUPPORT: Assistance given with finding accommodation and obtaining work permits. Cambridge ESOL CELTA course provider.

RECRUITMENT: Via local or telephone interviews.

CONTACT: Bill Cope, Director of Studies.

HARDIE INTERNATIONAL LANGUAGE TRAINING & COACHING

Feldbank 1-3, 44265 Dortmund

✆ +49 231 779300

✉ info@hardie-iltc.com

💻 www.hardie-iltc.com

Also has branch in Steinhude.

NUMBER OF TEACHERS: 15.

PREFERENCE OF NATIONALITY: None.

QUALIFICATIONS: Highest possible. Usually branch specialists are retrained as coaches, consultants or trainers.

CONDITIONS OF EMPLOYMENT: Open freelance contracts. Lessons take place 7 days a week between 7am and 10pm.

SALARY: Above average (depending on qualifications and experience).

FACILITIES/SUPPORT: Accommodation can be provided or at least advice given.

RECRUITMENT: Through partner organisations. Interviews compulsory and sometimes carried out in UK or by telephone.

CONTACT: James Hardie, Owner.

ICC SPRACHINSTITUT

Am Nordplatz 9, 04105 Leipzig

✆ +49 341 550 22 460

✉ info@icc-sprachinstitut.de

💻 www.icc-sprachinstitut.de

NUMBER OF TEACHERS: 50.

PREFERENCE OF NATIONALITY: None.

QUALIFICATIONS: University degree, CELTA and preferably TEFL experience.

CONDITIONS OF EMPLOYMENT: Fixed term or freelance. Teaching in-company business courses, intensive and evening courses.

SALARY: €15–€20 per 45-minute lesson.

FACILITIES/SUPPORT: Assistance with accommodation and work permits (if necessary). Induction and regular training included. Good career prospects throughout the ASSET group.

RECRUITMENT: Walk-ins mainly though email applications welcome. Local interview essential.

CONTACT: James Parsons, Director (james.parsons@icc-sprachinstitut.de) or Nicola Seaton-Clark, Director of Studies (nicola.seaton-clark@icc-sprachinstitut.de).

INLINGUA SPRACHSCHULE HANNOVER

Andreaestrasse 3, Ecke Schillerstrasse, D-30159 Hannover

✆ +49 511 324580

✉ info@inlingua-hannover.de

💻 www.inlingua-Hannover.de

NUMBER OF TEACHERS: 15.

PREFERENCE OF NATIONALITY: English, American, Canadian; other native English speakers.

QUALIFICATIONS: Minimum 1 year TEFL experience.

CONDITIONS OF EMPLOYMENT: Minimum 12 months. Average at least 25 school lessons (45 minutes each) per week.

SALARY: Approx. €15 per lesson.

FACILITIES/SUPPORT: Assistance finding accommodation.

RECRUITMENT: Newspaper adverts and internet.

INLINGUA SPRACHCENTER KIEL

Alter Markt 7, 24103 Kiel

✆ +49 431 981380

✉ catherine.beveridge@inlingua-kiel.de

💻 www.inlingua-kiel.de

NUMBER OF TEACHERS: Approximately 10.

PREFERENCE OF NATIONALITY: None.

QUALIFICATIONS: CELTA certificate and some teaching experience preferred.

CONDITIONS OF EMPLOYMENT: 6-month probationary period. Teaching hours Monday to Friday between 8am and 9pm and extra Saturday hours possible 8am–5pm. Full-time contract guarantees 100 teaching hours per month.

SALARY: €12 per teaching hour.

FACILITIES/SUPPORT: Information is provided about the best way to find accommodation in Kiel. Necessary paperwork is provided for non-EU employee to take to foreigners' office to obtain a work permit.

RECRUITMENT: Through online advertisements and by receiving spontaneous CVs.

CONTACT: Catherine Beveridge, Director of Studies.

NUMBER OF TEACHERS: 42.

PREFERENCE OF NATIONALITY: None.

QUALIFICATIONS: CELTA plus experience, business background.

CONDITIONS OF EMPLOYMENT: Various hours, Monday to Saturday, mornings and evenings.

SALARY: Approx. €18–23 per hour.

FACILITIES/SUPPORT: Assistance given with accommodation. Training. Access to internet/materials.

RECRUITMENT: Via adverts, agencies, internet and word of mouth.

CONTACT: Kerstin Hansen, Manager.

NUMBER OF TEACHERS: 50.

PREFERENCE OF NATIONALITY: None.

QUALIFICATIONS: University degree plus TEFL experience and/or certificate. Experience in ESP preferred.

CONDITIONS OF EMPLOYMENT: Freelance only. Can generally give good teachers as many lesson hours as they want.

FACILITIES/SUPPORT: No help with accommodation. Will write the necessary letter to the employment office to support work permit application. In-house training available.

RECRUITMENT: Local interviews.

CONTACT: Charles Arrigo, Director.

NUMBER OF TEACHERS: From 25 in the smaller Linguarama schools to 70 in the larger ones; Linguarama schools located in Berlin, Cologne, Düsseldorf, Frankfurt, Hamburg, Leipzig, Munich and Stuttgart. Vacancies at the time of writing in Hamburg and Bremen, and often vacancies in Munich at Sendlinger-Tor-Platz 7, 80336 Munich; 89 200 009 3 0; munich@linguarama.com.

PREFERENCE OF NATIONALITY: Native English speakers only who must have valid working papers for the EU.

QUALIFICATIONS: Minimum university degree or equivalent and a basic TEFL qualification (e.g. CELTA). Experience of teaching Business English is preferred with a keen interest in business at the minimum.

CONDITIONS OF EMPLOYMENT: Mixture of contract and freelance teachers. Freelance teachers work variable hours, usually early mornings and evenings. Contract teachers usually contracted for 1 year, extendable to 2 years, but occasionally shorter contracts available. 23 days' paid holiday per 12-month contract.

SALARY: Depends on experience.

FACILITIES/SUPPORT: Contract teachers are given an initial 2-week accommodation entitlement and assistance with finding permanent accommodation. Travel expenses to the city are paid from the UK if recruitment is through head office. Help is given with obtaining a residence permit, etc. All teachers are given an induction course and paid training is held monthly.

RECRUITMENT: Usually interviews locally for freelance teachers. Contract staff are sometimes recruited locally or via Linguarama Group Personnel Department, 1 Elm Court, Arden Street, Stratford-upon-Avon CV37 6PA (see introductory section, Finding a job).

CONTACT: Danny Coughlan, Personnel Manager, Linguarama.

NUMBER OF TEACHERS: 10 freelancers for branches throughout Germany.

PREFERENCE OF NATIONALITY: None.

QUALIFICATIONS: TEFL qualification and/or degree preferable, as are business experience and friendly, outgoing disposition.

CONDITIONS OF EMPLOYMENT: Travelling to companies to hold in-company courses on a freelance basis.

SALARY: Minimum €21 per teaching unit (45 minutes) plus travel.

FACILITIES/SUPPORT: No assistance with accommodation. Materials support given. Teachers' workshops held.

RECRUITMENT: Direct applications. Local interviews necessary.

CONTACT: Paul Bacon, Owner/Manager (paul.bacon@pet-sprachen.de).

SPRACHZENTRUM SUD

Bahnhofplatz 2, 83607 Holzkirchen

📞 +49 8024 1733

🖱 info@sprachzentrum-sued.de

💻 www.sprachzentrum-sued.de.

NUMBER OF TEACHERS: 15.

PREFERENCE OF NATIONALITY: British, Irish, American, Australian.

QUALIFICATIONS: Teaching certificate (e.g. CELTA, DELTA) or university degree. Teaching experience needed, especially in Business English.

CONDITIONS OF EMPLOYMENT: Freelance, employment possible after 1 year successful freelance.

SALARY: Between €15 and €25 per hour, depending on the qualification and contract.

RECRUITMENT: Telephone interviews possible. Candidates in Europe will be invited to interview and to teach practice lesson with volunteer students.

CONTACT: Dr. Karin Wiebalck-Zahn, Managing Director.

STEVENS ENGLISH TRAINING

Essen: Rüttenscheiderstr. 68, 45130 Essen

Cologne: Hohenstaufenring 29–37, 50674 Cologne

Dortmund: Westenhellweg 112, 44137 Dortmund

Dusseldorf: Am Wehrhahn 67, 40211 Dusseldorf

Münster: Olferstrasse 6, 48153 Münster

📞 +49 201 8770770

🖱 office@stevens-english.de

💻 www.stevens-english.de

NUMBER OF TEACHERS: Approx. 80 full and part-time.

PREFERENCE OF NATIONALITY: None but should be native English speakers.

QUALIFICATIONS: TEFL certificate or business experience.

CONDITIONS OF EMPLOYMENT: 2 year contracts. Hours between 7.30am and 8.45pm Monday to Friday. 80% of teaching is in-company with high element of ESP.

SALARY: Paid on points system per 45-minute session.

FACILITIES/SUPPORT: Furnished flats available at certain locations (e.g. Essen) for trainers recruited from the UK. Extensive workshop training programme for trainers. Opportunity to take the LCCI exam 'Further Certificate in Teaching Business English' (FTBE). Extensive library of teaching materials.

RECRUITMENT: Interviews essential and regularly held in Essen. Candidates receive €100 towards travel expenses and one night's accommodation provided.

CONTACTS: Sigrid and Michael Stevens, Managing Directors.

WALL STREET INSTITUTE / WSI EDUCATION GmbH

ZHd. Teacher Recruitment, Rosental 5, 80331 Munich or Postfach 330911, 80069 Munich

📞 +49 89 552 989 0

🖱 recruiting@wallstreetinstitute.de

💻 www.wallstreetinstitute.de

NUMBER OF TEACHERS: Approximately 150, at 27 locations.

PREFERENCE OF NATIONALITY: None, but it is easier to employ EU nationals or those who have citizenship due to visa restrictions.

QUALIFICATIONS: Teachers must be native English speakers with ESL/TEFL or equivalent qualification, experience in teaching English as a second language, ability to work within an existing, structured teaching method, excellent organisational and interpersonal skills, and be motivated, energetic and dedicated.

CONDITIONS OF EMPLOYMENT: Contracts of at least one year, usually unlimited (if residency permit has been obtained). No freelance contracts. Between 15 and 25 hours per week, plus paid overtime.

SALARY: Depends on the city. There is also the opportunity to earn bonuses and be paid commission.

FACILITIES/SUPPORT: Can help teachers find accommodation through informing them about various, reputable websites and organisations when they arrive in the city of employment. Also, if the applicant does not speak German, WSI may accompany them to the immigration office and help them register as a citizen and obtain their work permit. WSI gives a letter of intent to the employment authorities. Once the employment authorities have given their permission, the applicant receives a contract.

CONTACT: Human Resources.

GREECE

As has been well publicised, Greece has been engulfed by an economic crisis that threatens to undermine the country. Many in the EU have already dismissed Greece as a basket case, especially Germans who have contributed billions of euros to prop up the economy. Every business is suffering at the time of writing, especially private language schools because when money is tight, language learning is one of the first things to get the chop. Public sector workers are having to accept drastic pay cuts, job losses, and an end to favourable pension payouts. So travelling teachers should not pin too many hopes on easily stepping into paid employment in Greece at the moment. On the other hand, the statistics aren't all depressing. Ordinary Greeks have been upset by the way the media has presented their fiscal woes and resulting strikes and demonstrations, giving the false impression that Greece is on its knees. Schools continue to operate and the teacher recruitment agencies (see Directory) remain in business.

Despite the contraction of recent years, thousands of private language schools – the term *Kentra xenon glosson* has been replacing the term *frontisteria* – continue to supplement the language education of most children aged 6–16. A few years ago the state school system lowered the age when students began to learn English so parents want very young children to 'get ahead of the game' and have a good grounding in English before they start their state school lessons. Secondary school students are all in pursuit of higher scores in the Panhellenic exams that determine university entrance.

Greek language schools are often run by local entrepreneurs and because they are limited to three or four classrooms are often housed in buildings which were not purpose-built as schools. Secondary school pupils in Greece are obliged to study 15 subjects, all of which they must pass before being allowed to proceed to the next year. In most areas the teaching of English in state schools is considered inadequate so that the vast majority of pupils also attend *frontisteria*, and it is not uncommon for a 15-year-old to have two or three hours of lessons a day (in other subjects as well as English) in one or more private establishments to supplement the state schooling. Despite this gruelling timetable, the students are usually motivated and generally participate enthusiastically in their lessons, reaching a very high level of proficiency by age 16.

English language teaching in Greece has been described as an exam industry, and there is fierce competition among the international exam bodies. At one time Cambridge First Certificate and Cambridge Proficiency examinations ruled the roost only to be replaced a few years ago by University of Michigan exams. Recently, there has been intense competition between the London Tests of English and the English Speaking Board exams, eating into Michigan's share of the market. These are administered by two rival associations of language schools, PALSO and EUROPALSO. A newcomer has just arrived on the scene in Greece, the City & Guilds, which is aggressively marketing their exams. In fact, there are now 15 exams to choose from, all administered by different examining boards, and the terminology can be confusing. A certificate in one of these exams earns points to help the applicant get on the waiting list for a job in the civil service or in a state school. Some teachers and students still refer to the exams by exam board names such as First Certificate and Proficiency (Cambridge), Michigan and Michigan Proficiency, Edexcel, etc. A new structure for language learning and assessment has been laid down by the European Union (called the Common European Framework of Reference for Languages) which has been gradually gaining acceptance in Greece. B2 denotes someone who can function in English as an 'Independent User' and C2 denotes the highest level 'Mastery' of English.

PROSPECTS FOR TEACHERS

The employment situation for teachers is undeniably more difficult than it was in the boom years when schools were opening left, right and centre. Schools throughout Greece have been shutting down since 2009 and closures continue. **Jain Cook**, long-time Director of Studies at a successful language school in Patras paints a depressing picture (mid-2012):

> *After nearly 20 years at the Koutsantonis School, I'm not sure if I'm going back in September, because nobody knows how many students there will be. Things have changed a lot here, and it's much more difficult to find work. A lot of schools have shut down, so there are some very experienced teachers out there looking for work. The Koutsantonis school has been lucky because our student numbers haven't really dropped. The problem is parents not paying the fees, and this applies to all private schools. I finished at the school two weeks ago, and have already had 17 phone calls from ex-teachers or someone who is a friend of someone I know, asking me for work in September. I've had teachers asking for a job who are willing to work for two or three Euros an hour! People are desperate for work. This also applies to private lessons, which are practically non-existent now and if you do get a student, you cannot charge much more than €5 an hour – and that's if you are a native speaker.*
>
> *In some ways it's depressing here. Every time you go out another shop has shut down and people look miserable. It's really not the best place to come at the moment to work, especially when just under half of 18–25 year olds are unemployed and there is a lot of bad feeling towards foreigners, although more towards illegal immigrants.*

Yet prospects for EU nationals with a university degree and a TEFL qualification are not hopeless, particularly outside Athens. A fairly recent development is that ESP classes are becoming more popular in Greece and institutions organising company classes are sometimes on the lookout for professional, highly trained teachers.

A qualification is becoming essential, though not necessarily experience. The government stipulates that in order to obtain a teacher's licence, English teachers must have at least a BA in English Language and literature or education, so virtually all schools expect to see a degree certificate. Having a TEFL qualification, as always, will make the job hunt easier. Given the size of the ELT market in Greece, it is surprising that so few training centres offer the CELTA or the Trinity TESOL certificate in Greece. The main teacher training organisations in Greece tend to concentrate on training Greek speakers to become English teachers, though Anglo-Hellenic in Corinth and Via Lingua in Crete run courses mainly attended by native English speakers. The main ELT training organisations in Greece are listed below:

Anglo-Hellenic, PO Box 263, 201 00 Corinth (www.anglo-hellenic.com; www.tefl.gr). TEFL International Certificate course (www.teflcorinth.com) held monthly (see Directory of Training Courses). Fee is €1,295. Training centre is located in Vrahati on the seaside near Corinth.

CELT, 77 Akademias St, 10678 Athens (+30 210 330 2406/201 330 1455 info@celt.edu.gr; www.celt.edu.gr). Offers its own 4-week certificate course for €1,300, CELTA (€1,450) and range of other courses.

Study Space, D Gounari 21, 54622 Thessaloniki (+30 2310 269697; www.studyspace.gr). Cambridge-approved centre that specialises in CELTYL because the local market mainly comprises 7–16 year olds but also offers CELTA package which includes a promise to graduates of employment in their partner schools in Thessaloniki and throughout northern Greece.

Via Lingua Crete, Chrysanthou Episkopou 48, Chania, 73132 Crete (+30 28210 57438; www.teflgreece.com or www.vialingua.org).

Americans and other non-EU nationals will find it difficult to find a school willing to hire them, purely because of immigration difficulties. The government can impose stiff penalties on employers who break the rules, and few, at least in the major cities, will risk it, as **Tim Leffel** found out: '*We had planned on teaching in*

Greece, but as Americans, we were not exactly welcomed with open arms in Athens; they told us to try the countryside.' Tim moved on to Turkey instead.

A further complicating factor is the high number of Greek emigrés to North America and Australia who have returned (or whose children have returned) to Greece. In many cases, they are virtually native English speakers but are favoured because of their ancestry. Of course there will always be schools prepared to hire Americans and others if well qualified, such as the Hellenic American Union, which has one of the largest programmes in adult EFL in Athens.

One reason why EU nationals with basic qualifications can expect to land a job in Greece is that wages are not high enough to attract many highly qualified EFL teachers. Greece tends to be a country where people get their first English teaching job for the experience and then move to more lucrative countries. Also, few schools place any emphasis on staff development or provide in-house training, so serious teachers tend to move on quickly. The majority of advertised jobs are in towns and cities in mainland Greece. Athens has such a large expatriate community that most of the large central schools at the elite end of the market are able to hire well qualified staff locally. But the competition will not be so keen in Edessa, Larissa, Preveza or any of numerous towns of which the tourist to Greece is unlikely to have heard.

FINDING A JOB

IN ADVANCE

Unless you elect to register with one of the recruitment agencies (that deal primarily with Certificate-qualified teachers), it may not be worthwhile trying to find a job in advance, since so much in Greece is accomplished by word of mouth. Getting a list of language schools from outside Greece is not easy. A considerable proportion of *frontisteria* belong to the Pan-Hellenic Federation of Language School Owners (PALSO Headquarters, 2 Lykavitou St/Akademias St, 106 71 Kolonaki, Athens; +30 210 364 0792). There are local branches of PALSO all over Greece though they are unlikely to offer much help to job-seeking teachers until they are looking on the spot. Note that the Athens association of language school owners has split from PALSO and now calls itself EUROPALSO (Akademias 98–100, Athens 106 77; +30 210 3830 752; www.europalso. gr). EUROPALSO consists of more than 2,500 schools in the Athens area and it keeps a file of applications submitted by teachers (europalso@europalso.gr) or you can visit in person to see if any school owners have registered an interest in hiring teaching staff. PALSO-Chania has a separate web presence at www.palso-chania.gr (Partheniou Kelaidi 72, Chania 73136; +30 28210 92622) while the Heraklion branch is at www. palsoher.gr and only in Greek (+30 2810 322002).

An alternative association of language schools is QLS (Quality in Language Services), which aspires to be a Panhellenic Association of Accredited Language Schools. Overseeing its 20 member schools, the main office is in Volos (www.qls.gr) with secondary offices in Athens and Thessaloniki. It now operates an affiliated teacher recruitment service, QRS, mentioned below.

The internet is not as useful for the job-seeker in Greece unless you can read the Greek alphabet. Some of the main Greek internet service providers maintain lists of language schools; try http://dir.forthnet.gr and the Hellenic search engine www.robby.gr for language schools and foreign language education listings in English.

Most schools do their hiring for the following academic year between May and July. Obviously the major chains of schools offer the most opportunities, and it is worth sending your CV in the spring to organisations such as the Stratigakis Group, which has about a hundred schools in northern Greece (+30 2310 264263; www.stratigakis.gr). Another major group is The Scholars Group (www.the-scholars.gr).

Fortunately there are several active recruitment agencies that specialise in Greece with offices in Greece and/or Britain. These recruitment agencies are looking for people with at least a bachelor's degree and normally a TEFL qualification and/or experience (depending on the client school's requirements). All client employers provide accommodation. QRS (Quality Recruitment Services) is based at the English Language Centre Anafadis in Evia (Koukouli 6A, Halkida, Evia 34100; +30 22210 80130; www.qrservices.eu) and also has an office in Stockton-on-Tees in England. It places English teachers in private language schools around Greece. Long-established agencies Anglo-Hellenic Teacher Recruitment and Cambridge Teachers Recruitment both have entries in the Directory below. Hyphen, based in Thessaloniki (www.hyphen.gr), can occasionally help ELT professionals.

When discussing your future post with an agency, don't be lulled into a false sense of security. It is wise to check contractual details for yourself and verify verbal promises. Check to see whether you are entitled to any compensation if the employer breaks the contract and similarly whether you will have to compensate the school if you leave early. Find out if there will be any other native English speaking teachers in the area, and ask about the possibility of contacting your predecessor in the job.

After graduating from the TEFL Corinth certificate course, **Jerry Melinn** (aged 56) began working in Katsianos School of Foreign Languages in Athens:

> *Like all schools in Greece it's exam-oriented but I was aware of this before I started teaching so the system was no surprise to me. Everyone works very hard, including the students, and the school has a very high pass rate in all the exams, Cambridge and Michigan, Lower and Proficiency. The pay and conditions are the same as most schools beginning at €700 a month with accommodation provided and all bills paid as well as health insurance, which I thought was very good.*
>
> *I have read some horror stories on the internet about teaching in Greece but my experience has been great. The TEFL course in Corinth prepared me well for teaching. I have learned so much, made many new friends and grown very attached to the school and especially the students. I have nothing but admiration for them as they come to lessons twice a week after Greek school and the vast majority are well-behaved and good-humoured.*

Phil Tomkins graduated from the Corinth course last year and took up his first TEFL post on the small island of Kea in the Cyclades. His 'interview' with the Director of the Kea school simply involved catching a bus to Athens and meeting her for an informal chat over coffee at a street café.

IAN PARR

Ian Parr is yet another mature candidate who trained in Corinth and found work straight afterwards, in his case at a chain of three language schools in a suburb of Athens called Vyronas.

This has been my first job as an EFL teacher, having previously worked as a laboratory scientist in England for 10 years. I decided I wanted a new challenge and to travel so I completed the TEFL International course at Corinth. I first heard about this school in Athens through a contact I made on a Living in Greece website. I rang the school and spoke to the owner who asked me to come to Athens for an interview the same week. I met the school owner who was friendly and who checked my degree and teaching certificates, asked me a few questions about myself and told me that she expects her teachers to act professionally at all times whilst at the school. She then told me she would have work for me from January until the end of the school year in June, around 20 hours a week and that she would pay me €10 an hour. On returning to Greece after the Christmas holidays I soon found a small apartment to rent in the centre of Athens.

As is usual, the Greek teachers teach the younger children and also teach grammar to the older students. Native teachers teach everything except grammar. This is common in Greece apparently and is a little frustrating as teaching grammar was a challenge I was looking forward to. Altogether my hours only added up to 12 hours a week which was disappointing considering I'd been promised 20. Over the months I have worked extra hours covering classes, doing mock speaking tests and giving extra classes close to the exams. The biggest difficulty has been surviving financially in what is an expensive city. Eventually it has gotten easier as I now have a private lesson and do some editing work for a local English man who owns a publishing company. I have been offered a full-time contract to work at the same school for next year and will take it as I have enjoyed my time here and want to learn more of the culture and language here in Greece.

ON THE SPOT

So many *frontisteria* rely on agents to find teachers for them, that it can be difficult to walk into a job. After gaining a lot of on-the-ground experience of Greece, **Jane McNally** from County Derry in Ireland concluded that knocking on school doors can be discouraging.

The majority of schools have filled all their vacancies by July, so September is usually too late for prospective teachers to be looking for work. One of the best times to look is January. Greece is far less attractive in mid-winter than in summer, and many foreign teachers do not return to their posts after Christmas. Finding work in the summer is virtually impossible; most English language summer courses in resorts or on the islands are staffed by people who have taught for an academic year. **Will Brady** is one of the co-founders of Atlantis Books on the island of Santorini (www.atlantisbooks.org). He picked up a teaching job on the island:

> *It was just an opportunistic thing. I knew that I needed to earn some money so having recently got a TEFL qualification I thought I'd try my hand at a bit of TEFL teaching. I wandered around Fira and asked if there were any language schools, discovered that I was facing one, and walked in. I met a very strange man, who was the manager (the owner didn't speak English). This guy had studied psychology in England. I think he took a liking to me because I was English. I asked if I could do some work for them and he more or less told me straight away that I could, but kept things on very vague terms. Whilst I was back in England to arrange a few things, I negotiated with him over the phone. Then when I got back to the island I just went in and started. There was no interview whatsoever.*

Although Will had enquired about working legally, he concluded that advice from the Greek Embassy in London *'seemed to lead to no certain conclusions about what was the correct protocol'*. He ended up working under the table, an arrangement that suited both himself and the school owner, and was paid a wage equivalent to the British minimum. Work was part-time, teaching (or assisting in the classroom) about 2–3 hours a day, 3–4 times a week. The language school had never hired a native English speaker before and all the Greek teachers would defer to Will on grammatical points, something he found 'quite strange', because he was considerably younger.

Although **Jamie Masters** knew that October was not prime time for job-hunting, that is when he arrived in Heraklion to look for work, some years ago now:

> *I advertised (in Greek) in the Cretan newspapers, no joy. I lowered my sights and started knocking on doors of frontisteria. I was put onto some guy who ran an English-language bookshop and went to see him. Turned out he was a lynch-pin in the frontisterion business and in fact I got my first job through him. Simultaneously, I went to the PALSO office and was given a list of schools which were looking for people. The list, it turned out, was pretty much out of date. But I had insisted on leaving my name with them (they certainly didn't offer) and that's how I found my second job.*

The Lexis chain of bookshops throughout mainland Greece and some of the islands can be a useful place to enquire, since they are usually very well informed about who needs teaching staff or who wants a private teacher.

Once you arrange an interview, be sure to dress well and to amass as many educational diplomas as you can. This will create the right aura of respectability in which to impress the potential employer with your conscientiousness and amiability. Decisions are often taken more according to whether you hit it off with the interviewer than on your qualifications and experience. Jamie Masters found that no one cared a fig about his PhD in Latin.

Check the adverts in the English language weekly *Athens News* (www.athensnews.gr) where *frontisteria* very occasionally advertise but where you are more likely to see a listing for an informal arrangement: many Greek families are looking for live-in or part-time tutors for their children. You could also try placing your own advertisement in the situations wanted column. When you elicit interest from a language school owner or a family, take your time over agreeing terms. Greece is not a country in which it pays to rush, and negotiations can be carried out in a leisurely and civilised fashion. On the other hand, do not come to an agreement with an employer without clarifying wages and schedules precisely. Make sure you read your contract very carefully so that you are familiar with what you should be entitled to. Anglo-Hellenic provides a detailed four-page contract in Greek and English, a sample of which is available on its website (http://anglo-hellenic.com/teachers/contract.htm).

FREELANCE TEACHING

Private lessons are not as easy to find as they used to be. Established EFL teachers might now have three or four private pupils when before they had as many as 15. This is partly because of the falling birth rate in Greece and also because the middle classes have less disposable income and prefer to send their children to the local *kentro xenon glosson* or to someone they know locally who has passed the B2 level examination and who charges much less than a native English speaker, sometimes as little as €2–€3. This is a huge contrast with the going rate for qualified private tutors of €25 per hour for B2 tuition, and €30 per hour for C2, probably more in Athens.

Private tutoring jobs seem to materialise either from the language schools (whose directors seldom seem to mind their teachers earning on the side) or from conversations in a café-bar. It is a good idea to pin your card up at private schools, local shops and so on.

Trading English lessons for board and lodging is a common form of freelance teaching in Athens and elsewhere. Sometimes contracted teachers are offered free accommodation in exchange for tutoring their boss's children. In Athens, the rich suburbs of Kifissia and Kolonaki are full of families who can afford to provide private English lessons for their offspring. The suburbs of Pangrati and Filothei are also well-heeled. It is also possible to start up private classes for children, provided you have decent accommodation in a prosperous residential area, though this will usually be too expensive if your only source of income is private teaching. **Leah White** solved her accommodation problem in Athens by approaching managers of blocks of flats to see whether they could arrange for her to have a rent-free flat in exchange for teaching their children.

REGULATIONS

English teachers must first obtain a teacher's licence and then a residence permit (which is also a work permit) and the bureaucratic procedures involved can be stressful, even with a supportive employer. The two documents needed for a teacher's licence used to be a health certificate and a degree certificate. The Ministry of Education considers a BA or higher degree in English Literature or a degree in Education a sufficient qualification, though a TEFL certificate strengthens your application of course. You must have your degree certificate officially translated and notarised, either before you leave home (which is usually cheaper) or in Greece. The health certificate can be obtained only in Greece, and involves a chest X-ray and in some cases a blood or stool test.

Ongoing controversy rages over a blanket rule that proficiency in Greek is required by applicants for a teacher's licence. This seems to be in contravention to EU rules, since knowledge of Greek is not needed for the job of English teacher. In the face of opposition from the EU, this proposal has not been enforced (see http://anglo-hellenic.blogspot.com).

If teachers work illegally, they will not be paying insurance contributions so will not be eligible for unemployment benefits, bonuses, pension, etc. Teachers are advised to contact the Greek Ministry of National Education/Department of Private Education which issues the teaching licence: Andrea Papandreou 37, Marousi 15180 (http://archive.minedu.gov.gr/en_ec_page1537.htm).

English speakers of Greek ancestry find it much easier to obtain a teacher's licence and are generally more attractive prospects.

When the teacher's licence arrives from Athens, the teacher must take it along with his or her passport, photos and a lot of patience to the police station to apply for a residence permit, which should come through in about a month. The health certificate and residence permit must be renewed annually, though if you protest loudly enough you can usually get away with just having a chest X-ray. Keep photocopies of all forms.

Frontisteria usually tend to leave all the bureaucratic legwork to the teachers. Employers will take on the necessary transactions only if they are convinced that a candidate will be an asset to their school. Non-EU teachers often find that the Ministry of Education delays and then turns down their applications for a teacher's licence. Officially applicants must obtain a letter of hire from a language school which must be sent to an address outside Greece. The teacher takes the letter to the nearest Greek consulate and applies for a work permit; the procedures take at least two months.

It is mandatory for Greek employers to register full-time employees with the Greek national health insurance scheme, which has recently changed its name from IKA to EOPYY, which covers less than it used to. For example everyone has to pay more for medicines and contribute 15% to the cost of medical tests, treatments, etc. In the past, IKA dentists did most non-cosmetic dental work, but now will only do fillings and extractions. School owners have always been reluctant to pay IKA for their staff, especially when the rate of contribution rose to 30% of salary in the wake of Greece's financial catastrophe, while the employee's contribution of 16–20% should be deducted at source. Many Greeks no longer see the point of paying since it is much more expensive for them than it used to be and covers less. It is necessary to qualify for a pension but many are wondering if there will be any pensions in the future.

CONDITIONS OF WORK

Standards vary enormously among employers. Legislation that used to protect teachers is being watered down so that the government can cut its expenditure. Again **Jain Cook** provided a bleak account of recent changes and their impact on teachers:

> *There is no longer a legal minimum wage. Our teachers took a 15% pay cut in September 2011 and we've been told we will lose another 20–22% in September 2012. Married teachers used to get an extra 10% per hour, but*

this has been abolished. That means that the income of a married woman will have been reduced by 45% over two years. Things are not easy! As salaries have dropped, so have rents. Some rents in Patras have dropped from €350 per month to €150, and there are hundreds of empty flats. Everything else though, has gone up.

In general the large chains are better, probably for no other reason than that they have a longer history of employing native English speakers. You also have some back-up if you have been hired through a mediating agency. Some of the small one-man or one-woman schools are cowboy outfits run by barely qualified entrepreneurs who have had little contact with the English language; their teaching techniques involve shouting (usually in Greek) at their students and getting them to recite English irregular verbs parrot fashion. In fact this kind of school is on the decline, and standards have been rising.

The average number of hours assigned to teachers has been shrinking, to 18 per week or even as low as 12, which means reduced earnings and the possibility that the school will not be obliged to pay contributions. Teachers with superior training or experience may be able to ask for more hours and a higher rate. Schools that recruit from abroad tend to pay €600-€1000 a month in addition to free accommodation.

The custom in Greece has been to supplement low basic wages with a range of statutory benefits, e.g. holiday pay and bonuses. However, the recent austerity measures threaten the survival of many of these compensatory perks. So far the long-established compulsory bonuses paid at Christmas, Easter and at the end of a contract have not been abolished in the private sector, though they have been abolished in the public sector. There are also plans to abolish unemployment benefit for teachers who have worked for an eight-month academic year.

Teachers must find their rewards elsewhere, as 45-year-old recently qualified TEFL teacher **Phil Tomkins** did in 2011 while teaching on the small island of Kea:

> *Regarding finances, I long ago reconciled myself to the fact that I would never be a millionaire (certainly not from teaching!) and for some time have been re-adjusting what I want out of life. Peace and contentment, for me, far outweigh the benefits of the rat race and I am happy to live in comfortable 'poverty' on a sunny Greek island doing a job I enjoy, rather than working my fingers to the bone chasing the almighty dollar, and giving whoever is the current architect of our doom a big, fat slice of it. To measure one's successes solely in pounds, shillings and pence is a sure way to depression, disappointment and stress. Friends and family have all been very enthusiastic and supportive of me 'doing a Shirley Valentine' – and not a little jealous that even now, at the end of November, I'm still to be found at the beach most days. So far I have been thoroughly enjoying it, though I am missing my two main dietary requirements: curry and beer.*

A joke that might cheer up any Greek feeling discouraged at the state of their economy: 'The Greek Government has ordered a total suspension on the manufacture of hummus and taramasalata amidst fears of a double dip recession.'

The teaching year has been shrinking, so that an increasing number of schools now start their courses at the beginning of October and finish at the end of May. So some schools offer eight-month contracts rather than the nine months that used to be standard. Teachers should always check beforehand the date up to which they will be paid. Native English speakers are often employed to teach exam classes that finish before the end of May. Teachers should check that they will be paid until the end of the month if they are not going to continue at least a few hours a week doing oral work with their students. Schools have been known to break the contract by paying off teachers as soon as their classes have taken the exams.

> *All areas have a local workers' office, where you can go if you are in dispute with your employer or fear that you are being ripped off.*

Employers who have suffered from staff desertions in the past may hold back some of your monthly pay as a bond (*kratisi*) against an early departure. Teachers with insufficient hours are forced either to work at more than one school (which school owners are not keen on) or to take on private students. Split shifts are now very uncommon except in technical colleges or universities. Almost all teaching at *frontisteria* takes place between 5pm and 10pm.

It is not unusual to be expected to teach in two or more 'satellite' sites of the main school in villages up to 10 miles away. Local bus services are generally good and cheap but you could find yourself spending an inordinate amount of (unpaid) time in transit and standing around at bus stops.

PUPILS

Most native English speakers are employed to teach advanced classes, usually the two years leading to Cambridge exams. Because of the Greek style of education, pupils may not show much initiative and will expect to be tested frequently on what they have been taught. **Andrew Boyle** found the prevailing methodology of 'sit 'em down, shut 'em up and give 'em lots of homework' was moderately successful.

Another problem is that there is a great deal of pressure to assign pass marks just to retain the students' custom. Some school owners are so profit-motivated, they have euros for eyeballs. Students expect to be told the answers and bosses want their teachers to be lenient with the marking so that the students all pass and parents will re-enrol them.

Will Brady, teaching on the island of Santorini, found the pupils quite challenging, particularly the girls:

> *The job was littered with problems because the kids, for a start, were pretty uninterested. They were the offspring of hotel owners on the island, for the most part, whose only reason for having their kids learn English was so that they could be of use in the family business when the tourists came in summer. They had a level of MTV English but that was about it. They weren't motivated to learn and it was quite difficult to get them interested in the subject. I had a particular problem with a class of 15–16-year-old girls who were quite difficult to discipline. For some lessons I was alone and they took advantage of the fact that I didn't speak Greek. They were not even bothering to whisper, but talking openly to each other, and playing footsie with me under the table, and it was very difficult to know how to handle that. The manager took me aside and told me in no uncertain terms that I should not respond to any of the advances. Thankfully, I hadn't entertained the idea.*

ACCOMMODATION

Since most schools provide a flat or at least help in finding a flat, teachers are often not too concerned about their living arrangements. Placements arranged by the recruitment agencies offer free accommodation in addition to the full salary. It is definitely worth checking in advance about furnishings. Flats are sometimes quite spartan but some of the better ones are comfortably furnished and may have a washing machine and television in addition to the essentials. However, some flats, especially in Athens, are unfurnished which is a serious nuisance for someone on an eight-month contract.

Utility bills come every two months, and winters in Greece can be surprisingly cold. Even in a small flat, the electricity bill will run to hundreds of euros. Water bills are very cheap, however. Before taking over accommodation, try to find out if the bills have been paid. Changing the name is such a major hassle (involving tax returns, etc.) and unfortunately it is not uncommon for tenants to move on without paying their bills and the new tenant becomes liable. Non-payment of electricity and phone bills (but not water bills) will result in disconnection, and no final reminders are sent out.

LEISURE TIME

Teachers in Athens should have no trouble constructing a social life. The visitors' site www.breathtaking athens.com contains details of clubs and events of interest to expats. Outside Athens, the social order is still fairly conservative. A further problem is the enormous language barrier in a country where it will take some time to learn how to read the alphabet. Watching Greek television is a good way to learn the language plus Greek lessons are run free of charge in many locations. **Cassandra**, based in the north of Greece, found that '*teaching was a bit more difficult and isolating than I expected, but once I was used to the lifestyle I enjoyed it… with hindsight I would have enrolled in Greek lessons sooner and tried to get out and meet more people.*'

Most teachers find the vast majority of Greek people to be honest, friendly and helpful and are seldom disappointed with the hospitality they receive. As anyone who has visited Greece knows, the country has countless other attractions, not least the very convivial tavernas. Eating out is no longer the bargain it once was. With the increase in VAT, many goods and services have risen in price, and even wine which used to be exempt is now taxed. Travel, particularly ferry travel, is affordable and a pure delight out of season. Despite all the hassles, most people enjoy a year in Greece.

CELT ATHENS

Dina Dobrou reflects on her time with CELT Athens in 2011:

'Regardless of how experienced an EFL teacher you may be, attending a CELTA course will definitely turn your whole world upside down! You suddenly realise that there's a wealth of approaches to teaching you haven't even thought about and putting everything you learnt during the input sessions into practice can be quite a challenge; but attending this course at CELT was not as intimidating as it initially sounds.

'The tutors were supportive and inspiring throughout the whole course making the input sessions fly by and then, when time came for assisted lesson planning, they were always there to help bring the best out of you. The meticulous feedback and guidelines on do's and don'ts for your next Teaching Practice were among the most valuable things I got from the course. Their voices still echo in my head when I teach or prepare for my classes.

'What is more, the director, Marisa Constantinides, is committed to familiarising you with what the future of ELT is, and I'm referring to online teaching, PLNs (personal learning networks) and what you can do beyond that. The minute you enrol you are invited to the CELT wiki where you can get information about the course and download useful materials for study. It is only a matter of time before you start creating your own online learning platforms for your students.

'Even after you have completed the course you are still in touch through social networks and PLNs specially made for trainees, so the professional development does not stop when you get the certificate. At CELT, it is ongoing.

'My only regret? Not having done it earlier!'

LIST OF EMPLOYERS

ANGLO-HELLENIC TEACHER RECRUITMENT

PO Box 263, 201 00 Corinth

jobs@anglo-hellenic.com

www.anglo-hellenic.com or www.tefl.gr

NUMBER OF TEACHERS: About 80 vacancies every year in a wide choice of locations.

PREFERENCE OF NATIONALITY: British.

QUALIFICATIONS: University graduates with a TEFL certificate.

CONDITIONS OF EMPLOYMENT: Most vacancies are in September, several in January and a few throughout the year.

SALARY: 9-month contracts pay the going rate of about €900 per month plus bonuses and 4 weeks' paid holiday.

FACILITIES/SUPPORT: Accommodation in a furnished flat. A four-page contract will be provided by agency (specimen copy available beforehand). Anglo-Hellenic also take care of the bureaucratic essentials, and encourage meetings and exchange visits of their teachers and provide interactive web-based facilities for information, opinion and social chat. TEFL certificate courses (120 hours) are run every month, with shorter professional development courses also being offered throughout the year.

RECRUITMENT: Interviews are conducted in London, Athens or Corinth, throughout the summer.

CONTACT: Peter Beech.

BETSIS LANGUAGE SCHOOLS

Thivon 109, 18542 Piraeus

+30 210 4920871

Second site: Pyrgou 31, 18542 Piraeus

+30 210 4923475

abetsis@otenet.gr; abetsis@hol.gr; lmamas@yahoo.com

NUMBER OF TEACHERS: 15–20.

PREFERENCE OF NATIONALITY: British and Irish.

QUALIFICATIONS: Bachelor's degree and Cambridge exams.

CONDITIONS OF EMPLOYMENT: 8 month contracts. 18–24 hours per week. Also opportunities for teachers to work at the publishing company, Andrew Betsis ELT, specialising in ELT exam books. Positions are available in the editorial and marketing departments.

SALARY: €9,000–€10,000 per year.

FACILITIES/SUPPORT: School helps teachers find rental accommodation and with the bureaucracy involved in applying for a work permit.

CONTACT: Lawrence Mamas, Director of Studies.

CAMBRIDGE TEACHERS RECRUITMENT

17 Metron St, 143 42 Athens

+30 210 2585155 or (mob) +30 697 222 8893

UK contact address of main interviewer during August only, 53 Green Acres, Parkhill, Croydon CRO 5UX

+44 208 686 3733 (UK)

macleod_smith_andrew@hotmail.com

NUMBER OF TEACHERS: 25+ per year.

PREFERENCE OF NATIONALITY: British or EU.

QUALIFICATIONS: Degree and TEFL certificate, a friendly personality and conscientious attitude.

CONDITIONS OF EMPLOYMENT: Contracts usually between September and May, although some summer work. Usual hours are Monday to Friday between 4pm and 10pm (25 hours per week).

SALARY: Roughly €650–€800 net per month plus flat, bonuses, 4 weeks' holiday pay and pension contributions.

FACILITIES/SUPPORT: Accommodation is provided (not necessarily free) plus health insurance and pension. Holiday pay is given at Christmas and Easter. Applicants can expect to receive plenty of information about working in Greece.

RECRUITMENT: Comprehensive interviews are conducted between mid-June and the end of August. Interviews are held in hotels in central London.

CONTACT: Andrew Macleod-Smith.

KOUTSANTONIS SCHOOL OF LANGUAGES

35 Gounari Ave, 26221 Patras

+30 2610 273925

kapaflc@otenet.gr

NUMBER OF TEACHERS: Out of staff of 35 in 10 schools, only 1 is British.

PREFERENCE OF NATIONALITY: Native English speakers with Greek ancestry.

QUALIFICATIONS: University degree. Preferably a teaching qualification and some experience.

CONDITIONS OF EMPLOYMENT: 8 month contracts. 10–12 teaching hours per week, evenings only, Monday–Friday.

SALARY: The legal minimum of €9 gross has ben abolished so it is up to school owner and teacher to agree a rate.

FACILITIES/SUPPORT: School owner will help with search for an apartment and might be able to lend furniture.

RECRUITMENT: Generally teachers leave their CVs in person and are called back for interview when a vacancy occurs.

CONTACT: Cindy or Connie Koutsantoni (kapaflc@otenet.gr).

LAMBRAKI FOREIGN LANGUAGES CENTRES
El. Venizelou 194, Gazi, 71414 Heraklion, Crete
 +30 2810 822 292
 info@lambraki.gr
 www.lambraki.gr

NUMBER OF TEACHERS: 10.

PREFERENCE OF NATIONALITY: Britain.

QUALIFICATIONS: University degree and TEFL qualification.

CONDITIONS OF EMPLOYMENT: Most teachers stay 2–3 years. 18–25 hours per week.

SALARY: From €700 per month negotiable, less 16% deductions.

FACILITIES/SUPPORT: Assistance given in finding accommodation. School assists with residence permit after teacher provides a verified copy of his/her degree; official translation can be done in Heraklion.

RECRUITMENT: Via newspaper adverts, personal contact and PALSO Association. Telephone interviews.

CONTACT: Irene Lambraki, School Director.

THE LINGUISTIC LAB
PO Box 12, Xylokastro, 204 00 Corinthia
 +30 27430-22135/6945 580359
 filisbob@hotmail.com
 www.linguisticlab.com

NUMBER OF TEACHERS: 6.

PREFERENCE OF NATIONALITY: None, but EU passport preferred.

QUALIFICATIONS: Minimum BA plus TESOL certificate and experience. TESOL courses offered at Linguistic Lab.

CONDITIONS OF EMPLOYMENT: Standard contract period 2 years. To work 25 hours per week. Classes begin early September and finish in May/June. Summer classes may run in June and July.

SALARY: €700 a month; no deductions made.

FACILITIES/SUPPORT: Free accommodation is provided, furnished 2 bedroom apartments, to be shared between 2 teachers. Option to have a private apartment, with a lower salary.

RECRUITMENT: To apply send a CV, copies of diplomas and passport, reference letters and a recent photo to the above address.

CONTACT: Bob Filis, Owner.

LORD BYRON SCHOOL
104, Tsimiski St, Diagonbios, 54622 Thessaloniki
 +30 2310 278804
 school@lordbyron.gr or lordbyron@lordbyron.gr
 www.lordbyron.gr

NUMBER OF TEACHERS: 3–5 native English speakers for 4 schools in the greater Thessaloniki area.

PREFERENCE OF NATIONALITY: EU nationals.

QUALIFICATIONS: University degree, TEFL or CELTYL or CELTA and EFL teaching experience.

CONDITIONS OF EMPLOYMENT: Standard contract 8 months. 24–26 hours per week. 40% of clients are adults or university students.

SALARY: €800 to €1,000 according to qualifications. 17% deductions for tax and social security.

FACILITIES/SUPPORT: Assistance finding accommodation and obtaining a legal status/teaching permit.

RECRUITMENT: Via detailed CV, interview, model lesson (with lesson plan). Interviews are carried out in Thessaloniki every May and June.

CONTACT: Harry J. Nikolaides, School Director (harry@lordbyron.gr).

PAPAELIOU SCHOOLS OF FOREIGN LANGUAGES
111 Karaiskou Str, 18532 Piraeus-Athens
 +30 210 417 3892
 karaiskou@papaeliou.edu.gr
 www.papaeliou.edu.gr

Branches in Pireaus, Nikea and Glyfada.

NUMBER OF TEACHERS: 45.

PREFERENCE OF NATIONALITY: British. Majority are Greek-Americans or Greek. Must possess a valid visa.

QUALIFICATIONS: Minimum age 21. Bachelor's or master's degree and teacher training.

CONDITIONS OF EMPLOYMENT: 1–3 year contracts to teach at least 4 hours a day. Hours extend late into the evening.

SALARY: Approx. €850 net; €382 deductions.

FACILITIES/SUPPORT: No help with accommodation.

RECRUITMENT: Interviewees teach a demo lesson. Successful candidates must then complete the in-service training programme and sign a probationary 3-month contract.

CONTACT: Ino Panayotou, Director of Studies.

ITALY

The economic woes that have afflicted southern Europe have hit some sectors of the English language teaching market hard, especially among companies specialising in corporate training where budgets have been slashed. However, the younger end of the spectrum is holding up well, with many children and teenagers being entered for externally moderated exams like the Cambridge suite, for which they often turn to private tutoring companies. Few English language schools have actually closed, but they are not thriving as they were five or 10 years ago, so opportunities for qualified native English speaker teachers are not as abundant as they were. Chances are always better in towns and cities which cannot boast leaning towers, gondolas or coliseums. Small towns in Sicily and Sardinia, in the Dolomites and along the Adriatic have more than their fair share of private language schools and institutes, all catering to Italians who have failed to learn English in the state system. (English teaching in Italian schools is generally acknowledged to be inadequate.)

PROSPECTS FOR TEACHERS

A complete range of language schools can be found in Italy, as the *Yellow Pages* will confirm. At the elite end of the market, there are the 35 schools which belong to AISLi, the Associazione Italiana Scuole di Lingue (www.aisli.com). Prospective teachers can submit their CVs to AISLi who will circulate them round all member schools. Only ultra-respectable schools can become AISLi members so there are thousands of good schools outside the association. AISLi schools normally expect their teachers to have advanced qualifications and in return offer attractive remuneration packages and conditions of employment.

At the other end of the spectrum, there is a host of schools which some might describe as cowboy operations, though these are decreasing in number. The CELTA is widely recognised and respected in Italy (unlike in France, for instance) as are other certificates. The days of finding work without a qualification are all but over. US qualifications are less well known for the simple reason that work permits are very difficult for non-EU citizens to obtain. There are so many job-seekers with TEFL training that qualifications are necessary in order to compete with all those native English speakers so keen to live, work and teach in Italy. A healthy number of schools can be seen advertising on the main ELT websites and relevant journals.

To reiterate the decline in corporate language training, **Peter Anderson**, owner of Anderson House in Bergamo (see entry), reflected in July 2012 on changes in the market that he has noticed over the past two years:

> *Things have become tough here in Italy as in the world as a whole. The Quality First Group (QFG), a network of 40 schools that specialised in corporate language training (of which Anderson House was a founding member), has disappeared! However, we have increased Cambridge exams considerably and they account for over 50% of our turnover so far this year (last year they accounted for roughly 18%). The corporate market has plummeted, so thank god individuals and families are still investing in courses! We are also delivering management training courses which companies appreciate.*

Strict employment regulations and red tape in Italy make small companies reluctant to offer full-time contracts. Increasingly, schools are hiring teachers on a freelance basis only, whom they pay by the hour. For example Caledonian Communications in Milan told this book in July 2012: *'Unfortunately due to the economic situation in Europe we have had to change our staffing policy. We therefore no longer offer contracts, teachers are hired on a freelance basis.'* And this is proving a trend throughout the industry.

A few schools offer a British contract (i.e. one that is not subject to Italian legislation) in which the wages are lower than on an Italian contract but the benefits better and the red tape much less (see entries for *Alpha Beta*

Piccadilly and *Caledonian Communications* for example). Compulsory contributions for social security and expensive perks make hiring a permanent member of staff very costly so most of the jobs available are eight- or nine-month contracts, October to May. The majority of English teachers in Italy work on contract with no long-term job security, which is acceptable for those who want to spend only one or two years in the country. A lot of teaching work in Italy is paid under the table. Contracts shouldn't be expected at the start though they are more likely to be given by private language schools in smaller out of the way places. Many English teachers in the main cities work for more than one private language school and also do freelance teaching on the side.

EU-funded initiatives such as the Programma Operativo Nazionale (PON) have been implemented to bolster training, including language learning. These schemes are providing a lot of competition with private schools because courses are free to students, while wages to teachers are very generous, typically €50-€60 an hour. Some private schools are contracted to provide teaching staff to state schools, but are trying to get away with paying teachers the same low wage of €12. If you are offered off-site work in the state sector (normally available only if you know Italian) do plenty of research and try to negotiate an hourly wage of at least €25 and read any contract carefully before signing.

A useful starting place for information on training and teaching English in Italy is www.teachingenglish initaly.com, a site maintained by **Sheila Corwin**, an American resident in Florence who has been working and living as an English language teacher and teacher trainer in Italy (on and off) since 2002. Her website includes affordable online options in basic TEFL certification (from €200) and allows registration for on-site courses in TEFL/TESOL/CELTA and a Teaching Practice (TP) programme in Florence is also available (sheila@teachingenglishinitaly.com).

FINDING A JOB

IN ADVANCE

There is no single compendium of the hundreds of language school addresses in Italy. The relevant *Yellow Pages* (*Pagine Gialle*) are user friendly; go to www.paginegialle.it and choose the handy English version of the site. Typing in 'Language Schools' will produce more than 2,000 entries. The search engine allows you to search by city or more generally by region.

International language school groups such as Benedict Schools, Linguarama, Berlitz and Inlingua are major providers of English language teaching in Italy. International House has 13 affiliated schools throughout the country. Wall Street Institute now has more than 90 centres in Italy and actively recruits native English speakers. Occasional vacancies are posted at www.wallstreet.it/jobs; in most cases applications should be sent directly to the school, whereas other recruitment is done by head office in Milan (staff@wallstreet.it). Applications to Berlitz should be sent to the individual schools hiring, e.g. workinrome@berlitz.com and workinmilan@berlitz.com.

A considerable number of Italian schools advertise vacancies on www.tefl.com; for example there were 37 job postings at the time of writing (July 2011). Several Italian-based chains of language schools account for a large number of teaching jobs. Many operate as independent franchises. For example you can get contact details for all 200+ British Institutes on their website www.britishinstitutes.it (click on *Sedi*) or contact the personnel office at personale@britishinstitutes.it. A smaller chain to investigate is Millenium (sic) Language Schools (www.milleniumlanguage.it).

Other chains include the British Schools Group (www.britishschool.com) with more than 60 member schools, which carry out some of their recruitment through the London agency Saxoncourt (+44 20 7491 1911) and the Oxford Group (www.oxford.it) whose recruitment department is centralised (CVs with photos may be sent to igbolton@oxford it). Most language schools in Italy seem to incorporate the word British, English, Oxford or Cambridge randomly combined with Centre, School or Institute, which can result in confusion.

American citizens have a lot of problems finding work in Italy, largely because it is so difficult to obtain a work permit. However, a solution suggested by **Carla Valentine**, an English teacher in Venice, is to try working for one of the Department of Defense US army schools on the military bases in Italy. Under these circumstances, work permits are processed in the USA.

ON THE SPOT

The online *Yellow Pages* is probably still the best source of possible employers. Italians like face-to-face contact and, according to **Sheila Corwin**, director of www.teachingenglishinitaly.com, stopping by a school to meet the director often works better than blindly sending out resumés through snail or electronic mail. When **Bruce Nairne** and **Sue Ratcliffe** went job-hunting in Italy a few years ago, they relied on the *Yellow Pages* as a source of potential employers:

> *Rather unimaginatively we packed our bags and made for Italy in the middle of the summer holidays when there was no teaching work at all. Nevertheless we utilised the Yellow Pages while we were in Sicily and proceeded to make 30 speculative applications, specifying our status as graduates who had completed a short course in TEFL. By the end of September we had received four job offers without so much as an interview.*

Unfortunately, the jobs in Bari which they chose to accept never materialised and so they once again resorted to the *Yellow Pages*, this time in Milan railway station, where they managed to secure the interest of three or four establishments for part-time work.

ALEX NEUMAN

Alex Neuman, a globetrotting journalist, describes how she set about finding teaching work in the town of Bergamo where she and her partner had decided to spend a year or two.

The first step these days is to go online. I quickly found three or four English schools in Bergamo: Shenker, Wall Street, Inlingua and two small local firms run by individuals. I decided I should also look in Milan since it is only 45 minutes by train from Bergamo.

This is where you quickly realise this is not like job hunting in your own country and in your own language. Few Italians answer emails from strangers. You have to pick up the phone – a challenge when your language is rusty but as these were English schools most had an English speaking receptionist. Then I discovered the vagaries of the private teaching system which basically is out to make as much money as possible while paying as little as possible to teachers and expecting infinite flexibility on the teacher's part and no flexibility on the school's part!

You will need patience and a sense of humour at this stage. I quickly got an interview with Wall Street Institute and Shenker and was accepted at Shenker. Being accepted is not a problem it's actually getting onto the payroll and teaching that takes time. It was three months before I got on a two week training course where I was promised €150 a week. In fact I received this money in December – two months after I'd done the course and five months after the initial interview. So it is best to have plenty of spare cash to see you through the first six months of finding work.

Shenker was good for me because I had no formal teaching qualification and it is based around a system so all your lesson plans are provided, you simply turn up and teach the system. For this you will be paid about €13.50 an hour before tax. I get about 15 hours work a week, although they promised 20. But as I started working for them during the financial crisis their student numbers were considerably down.

They do offer 30 hour-a-week contracts but at a much reduced rate of pay. This will suit some people as it means you can stay in the country if you have a work contract. However, the pay is truly abysmal and you have to do the 30 hours a week, which can often involve split shifts including working till 8.30pm every evening and Saturday mornings. Plus these contracts only run from September to July so you don't get paid in August.

The upside to teaching is that the Italians working in the schools are great on the whole. Everyone knows that the system is bad and tries to help each other through it. The students are also great and if you have a class you get to know, teaching can be really fun. It's a good way to get to know people and the Italians are by and large extremely friendly and always willing to help you out if they can. It also gives you a sense of belonging and really getting involved.

Often a few hours teaching can gradually be built up into a full-time job by those willing to say 'Yes'. If you're there when they need you, you can usually get something. Most find that the longer they stay, the more hours they get, though there is still no job security working this way.

Melanie Drake has had much better luck in Bari:

> *Italy has been a very positive experience for the most part, though living in the south without knowing the language can be quite problematic! It is really pretty easy to get work in Italy once TEFL-qualified, as the English level here is low (in the south especially). Money isn't fantastic but it balances out as life is fairly cheap, particularly if like me, you can walk to work. Often accommodation is included with the contracts offered too. Ironically I am earning half of what I got in London, though here I can save fairly easily as my outgoings are halved. It works out pretty well.*

Scouring adverts in English language newspapers has worked for some. The fortnightly publication *Wanted in Rome* (www.wantedinrome.com) is very useful (particularly in the spring) as is www.kijiji.it and also the Italian-language classified ads paper *Porta Portese*. If you happen to see a request for 'mothers only', this means that they are looking for a teacher whose mother tongue is English *(Insegnanti madrelingua)*, not a female with small children. Other publications with useful classifieds include *The Florentine* and *Easy Milano*.

FREELANCE TEACHING

Another possibility is to set up as a freelance tutor, though a knowledge of Italian is even more of an asset here than it is for jobs in schools. A participant on a recent *Guardian* web forum on ELT careers wrote in an encouraging vein for older job-seekers:

I'm a career changer in my mid-50s and have had no problems here in Italy. I don't teach in language schools but contract direct with local state schools, libraries and private students, but that is based on having had means of support until I developed the requisite contacts.

Alex Neuman is another teacher in middle life who has found Italy and Bergamo in particular a welcoming place. She has been supplementing her hours at local academies with private students:

Italians are desperate to speak English so getting private students isn't that hard. The best students I have got are through word of mouth. A very friendly neighbour is always recommending me to friends and colleagues and I have managed to find myself three or four that keep me busy. I got my very first student by putting up a notice on the university noticeboard in Bergamo but have never had to do more than that. When writing an ad for private students you must always use the words 'mother-tongue speaker' – even though 'native English speaker' is more correct English! Rates for private students vary between €15 and €25 an hour.

You can post notices in supermarkets, tobacconists, primary and secondary schools, etc. In Rome, the noticeboard at International House's training centre (Accademia Britannica, Viale Manzoni 22, 00185 Rome) displays requests for teachers. Also in Rome, check out the noticeboards at English language bookshops such as the Lion Bookshop & Café in Via dei Greci, or frequent the right pubs such as Ned Kelly's near Palazzo Valdassini and Miscellanea near the Pantheon. The noticeboard at the English language Paperback Exchange in Florence can also be explored.

Most cities have an *Informagiovani* or Youth Information Centre, for example the one at Vicolo Santa Maria Maggiore 1 in Florence, which may be able to supply information about teaching work or where to search. Listings of private language schools are often kept and provided on request by local tourist offices in Italy. University students looking for private tuition might consult university noticeboards such as the one at the Citta Universitaria in Rome, main campus of the Sapienza University of Rome.

Porta Portese is also a good forum in which to advertise your availability to offer English lessons in Rome; adverts placed by women should not betray their gender and meetings with prospective clients should not take place in private homes. It cost **Dustie Hickey** about £15 to advertise in four editions of the free paper in Rimini. As long as you have access to some premises, you can try to arrange both individual and group lessons. Whatever way you decide to look for work, remember that life grinds to a halt in August, just as in France. Competition is keenest in Florence and Venice which are both saturated, so new arrivals should head elsewhere including Rome. **Peter Penn** recommends Trieste, where he was offered two jobs with no experience.

Freelance teaching can be very lucrative and you can expect to make around €20 an hour, which is still undercutting most of the language schools (which charge around €26 per hour and take over half themselves).

Universities throughout Italy employ foreigners as *lettori* (readers/lecturers), who teach English as well as other subjects such as business and science in English. For decades they have been locked in a dispute with Italian universities over pay and conditions, since they are assigned to a low employment grade and paid less than their Italian counterparts. There are probably around 1,000 *lettori* on yearly contracts (maximum three years) earning about the same as EFL teachers in private institutes.

SUMMER WORK

Paid work is available at a number of summer camps offering English instruction, a good opportunity for young people to spend a summer in Italy and learn more about teaching English to young learners. A number teach through the medium of theatre, so anyone interested in drama will be attracted by this idea. This opportunity is open to non-European nationalities, since the work period is so short. Some teacher training is often provided by the schools and companies that run these camp programmes. Some of these teaching programmes are listed on the website www.teachingenglishinitaly.com. Most of these companies pay about €200 a week (less for city day camps). Successful summer teachers are often offered contracts for the academic year.

See entries at the end of this chapter for ACLE, Lingue Senza Frontiere (also based in San Remo, but unrelated) and International House in Campobasso. Other summer employers include:

Berlitz Italy (louise.thorne@berlitz.it or summercamps@berlitz.it; www.berlitz.it). Candidates must be native English speakers and experienced with children to work at two camps in Tuscany. 2-week minimum stay in June/July.

Horizons Language Services, Largo Brindisi 18, int. 11; 00182 Rome (tel/fax +39 0677 201534; www.horizons.ie). Summer camp tutors needed mid-June and July. Ideally aged 20-35 with CELTA or CELTYL and experience with young children. Teachers already resident in Rome preferred.

Kids in the World, Via Provinciale Capena-Roma, 74, 00060 Capena (RM) (danila.monaco@ kidsintheworld.it; www.kidsintheworld.it). This company takes on motivated young actors, teachers, musicians and artists to join a team that operates English language weeks at summer centres in Capena, Rignano Flaminio and Riano. Programme operates in June, July and September. Staff must be native English speakers (or have passed a Cambridge Advanced or Proficiency exam) and have some experience teaching children. Training provided.

Kid's World (s.charlesworth@kidsworld.it; www.kidsworld.it). Runs residential summer camps from June to August, located 3 hours from Rome. Applicants should be dynamic, out-going and have experience working with children. Wages, board, lodging and training offered to successful applicants.

Scotia Personnel, 6045 Cherry St, Halifax, Nova Scotia B3H 2K4, Canada (+1 902 422 1455; info@ scotia-personnel-ltd.com; www.scotia-personnel-ltd.com). This North American agency runs an organised scheme whereby young North Americans are recruited to work on language and sports camps in Italy in exchange for pocket money.

Smile, Modena (www.smilemodena.com). Employs summer tutors to mount English language theatre productions with groups of children. Summer staff are chosen after auditioning, including in London in October.

REGULATIONS

The bureaucratic procedures for EU nationals are fairly straightforward and teachers don't need a work permit or a residence permit, although the latter can be helpful for long-stayers. To obtain one teachers must take their passport and other papers (including a declaration of residence/consular declaration from your country's consulate in Italy) to the local *Questura* (police department) to obtain a *permesso di soggiorno* (residence permit).

PHILIP LEE

Philip Lee from New Zealand wanted to spend his summers working in Europe. After a successful camp job in Switzerland, his attention turned to Italy. Although he didn't have direct experience of teaching English as a foreign language, he had worked with children and given tuition and revision classes. Here he describes the highs and lows of the job.

I searched online for work over the summer in Italy. There were a lot of random jobs that didn't really lead to anything and a lot of misleading job adverts. However I found some English teaching websites that were credible and I applied. After completing a written application on my background and experience in teaching, working with children and art/drama/games/sport and providing references, I was hired by Lingua Senza Frontieres. I taught English through various indoor and outdoor activities. About 90% of my time was spent playing a game/sport or completing an activity that was explained and conducted in English and there was very limited traditional 'classroom' teaching. The focus was to do as much as possible in English, including the instructions for each activity. Depending on the children's age and their familiarity with English, it was possible by using simpler words, shorter sentences and demonstrating my instructions at the same time. Teaching was very physical: I spent most of my day – about five hours of teaching and two of supervision - standing. Because a lot of the children were not very familiar/comfortable with English I had to be very energetic, positive and supportive throughout the day to keep them encouraged.

Lunch was up to two hours long and we were always treated to a good and big Italian lunch. Most schools were happy to cater to special diets as long as they were given prior notice. I stayed with the most hospitable and generous families, most of whom lived by the seaside. While living with the host families, who often had children in the camp as well, I was given my own room and sometimes my own bathroom. The families were very accommodating and understood that non-Italians did do some things differently, such as eating more than one biscuit for breakfast. They also understood that I wanted to experience as much of Italy as possible and took me out on numerous occasions. We went to vineyards, restaurants, farms, relatives' houses, shops, the beach, holiday homes, bars and clubs with the older host brothers and sisters, the pool, concerts and neighbouring towns and cities. They were also quite happy when I went out to socialise at night.

The wages are not high, however I considered the English camp as a working holiday and was not aiming to leave with many savings. The biggest problem was the language difficulties with the children and at the schools. This was because it was uncommon for any of the tutors to speak much Italian. Any tutor who spoke Italian was instructed not to make this known so that the children would not take advantage of it. The difficulty in communication made our job harder, but arguably it gave the children a better learning experience. The training sessions that the camp organisation provides are really vital and it would have been a great benefit if I had written down all the ideas for games and activities for future reference.

There were a few behavioural problems with some children but we were not expected to deal with these. Each camp had a local Italian teacher in charge of the camp and we would tell her of any problems. If she did not handle it, we could inform our employer who would communicate directly with the school.

Altogether it was a great opportunity to meet people from all over the world as well as Italians, to spend time in Italy not as a tourist, and incredible fun working with children, as all day is spent playing games or doing activities.

As mentioned above, non-EU citizens have very little chance of getting their papers in order unless they are dual nationals or receive a firm offer of a job while they are still in their home country. According to the Italian Embassy in Washington, language teachers from the USA need a visa for *lavoro subordinato*. To qualify they must first obtain from their employer in Italy an authorisation to work issued by the Ministry of Labour or a Provincial Office of Labour (*Servizio politiche del lavoro*) plus an authorisation from the local *Questura*. The originals of these plus a passport and one photo must be sent to the applicant's nearest embassy or consulate. These procedures can take up to a year to complete and as **Carla Valentine**, an English teacher in Venice points out, 'no school director in his right mind is going to bother going through that process when there are plenty of British teachers here who can work without visa red tape'. It is for this reason that so many Americans and other non-EU citizens work in Italy without work visas. However, there are two legal alternatives for US citizens. The first is to go to Italy as a student, which allows you to work for up to 20 hours a week (enough to live on). This is the route that Carla took:

Getting a student visa is very easy. I paid $500 to enrol for a year at Instituto Venezia to learn Italian. With a letter of enrolment from the school I was able to get a student visa from the Italian Consulate in Boston for one year (whether or not I attend class is irrelevant, although obviously I do).

The second option is to become an independent contractor. This involves getting a tax code number (*partita IVA*) from the local town government which you have to do once you are earning more than €5,000. To get this number, you need a *codice fiscale* (similar to a social security number), which is available from the local town hall upon presentation of a passport or may also be obtainable online from the Agenzia delle Entrate (Revenue Agency). With this number it is possible to obtain the *partita IVA* from the municipal authorities, though it will probably be necessary to use the services of an accountant. With these numbers you can find work and get paid, even though technically without a *permesso di soggiorno* you are still an illegal immigrant. Australians and New Zealanders can take advantage of working holiday schemes, which allow a 12-month stay, although holders are not meant to work for more than three months.

Tax is a further headache for long-stay teachers. As soon as you sort out the work documents, you should obtain a tax number (*codice fiscale*). The rate of income tax (*Ritenuta d'Acconto*) is usually about 23% in addition to social security deductions of 8–9%.

CONDITIONS OF WORK

A typical salary for a full-time timetable would be about €1,200 net per month (roughly £1,000) though novice teachers sometimes earn less than €1,000. Staff on a *contratto di collaborazione* are paid by the hour, normally ranging from €12 to €18 net. Always find out if pay scales are quoted net or gross, since the two figures are so different. Take-home pay is not as high as might have been expected because of the high cost of compulsory national insurance, social security and pension contributions. Salaries tend to be substantially higher in northern Italy than in the south to compensate for the much higher cost of living. Business English, as always, can be very lucrative. Intensive Business English, based in Milan (see list of employers) offers a gross salary of between €1,700 and €3,250. However, some teachers in Rome, Milan, Bologna, etc. have had to reconcile themselves to spending up to half their salaries on rent. Even for Italians, salaries are low when compared with the cost of living.

Only professional teachers will benefit from the industry-wide agreement or *Contratto Collettivo Nazionale del Lavoro* (CCNL), which sets a high salary for a regulation 100-hour working month. Because of the high costs of legal employment, there is a lot of dubious practice in Italy and prospective teachers should try to talk to an ex-teacher before committing themselves, especially if offered a job before arrival. **Rhys Sage** was disappointed at the discrepancy between what he had been promised by a language institute in Chivasso near Torino and what he found when he arrived:

They had given a glowing description of the locality and of the cost of living, of the flat they were offering and of the high wages. Upon arrival, it transpired that the wages were minimal, the prices quite high and the flat shoddy. The toilet didn't work and neither did the heating. The school also wanted a sizeable deposit in advance for the first month and would then deduct from my salary for the rent. When I discovered the extent to which I'd been told a tissue of lies, I regretted going to Chivasso and left. In the end my Italian trip turned into a holiday.

Few teachers complain about their students. Even when pupils attend English classes for social reasons (as many do in small towns with little nightlife) or are generally unmotivated, they are usually good-natured, hospitable and talkative in class. In contrast to Greece, many language school directors are British rather than local.

Compared to many languages, Italian is easy to learn, though courses are expensive. It may be possible to swap English lessons for Italian ones, which might lead to further freelance teaching.

LEISURE TIME

Italian culture and lifestyle do not need to have their praises sung here. A large number of teachers who have gone out on short-term contracts never come back – probably a higher proportion than in any other country. While rents are high, eating out is fairly cheap and public transport is quite affordable. Women teachers should be prepared to cope with some Mediterranean machismo, particularly in the south, and may have to contend with unwanted male attention.

LIST OF EMPLOYERS

A.C.L.E. – SUMMER & CITY CAMPS
Via Roma 54, San Remo 18038
+39 0184 506070
info@acle.org
www.acle.org

NUMBER OF TEACHERS: 600+ for both day camps and residential camps all over Italy from Sicily to the Dolomites.
PREFERENCE OF NATIONALITY: Native English speakers between 19 and 30 years of age.
QUALIFICATIONS: Minimum age 19. Must have experience working with children and the ability to teach English through the use of theatre and outdoor activities. A fun-loving personality and genuine interest in children, high moral standards and a flexible attitude to work required, preferably with some experience of living and travelling abroad.
CONDITIONS OF EMPLOYMENT: Camps start in June and run until September. Minimum of 3 weeks commitment required. The average tutor works for 4 weeks or more.

SALARY: €225 (city camp) and €275 (summer camp) per week, plus full board and accommodation. Transport between camps provided plus insurance.
FACILITIES/SUPPORT: Intensive 5/6-day introductory TEFL-TP (Teaching English to Foreign Learners through Theatre and Play) course is compulsory and provided for fee of €150 usually deducted from wages.
RECRUITMENT: Application online at www.acle.org. Recruitment season for following summer opens 1 October. Deadline for applications is the middle of March.

ALPHA BETA PICCADILLY
via Talvera/Talfergasse 1a 39100 Bolzano/Bozen
+39 0471 978600
marsh-hunn@alphabeta.it
www.alphabeta.it

NUMBER OF TEACHERS: 10–15.
PREFERENCE OF NATIONALITY: Must have EU passport.

QUALIFICATIONS: Minimum CELTA or equivalent. DELTA plus at least 2–3 years' TEFL experience preferred.

CONDITIONS OF EMPLOYMENT: 9-month contract with 18–22 contact hours per week.

SALARY: Around £1,530–£1,650 per month gross based on a British contract, depending on qualifications and experience. Standard UK income tax and social security deductions are made.

FACILITIES/SUPPORT: School has 2 flats available for teachers to share. Assistance given with work permits; however, these are relatively straightforward.

RECRUITMENT: Usually via www.tefl.com. Interviews are essential and are occasionally held in the UK.

CONTACT: Peter Marsh-Hunn, Director of Studies, English.

ANDERSON HOUSE

Via Bergamo 25, 24035 Curno (BERGAMO)

📞 +39 035 46 30 74

🖱 info@andersonhouse.it

🖥 www.andersonhouse.it

AH is a language school specialising in corporate language training and management training for companies (TIP, DPI, ICE and intercultural communication). It also offers courses to children and adults in preparation for Cambridge exams, and is a centre for language testing and certifications (CAMBRIDGE, BULATS, TOEIC and TOEFL). Anderson House is a founder member of SIETAR Italia (www.sietar-italia.org).

NUMBER OF TEACHERS: 4 full-time, 6 part-time for English. 10 part-time for other languages.

PREFERENCE OF NATIONALITY: British and Irish. European passport essential.

QUALIFICATIONS: Degree plus CELTA (minimum grade B), TESOL, DELTA or CertIBET (Trinity's Certificate in International Business Training) and minimum 3 years' experience.

CONDITIONS OF EMPLOYMENT: Couples with car a bonus. Contracts from October to June (8/9 months) or from January for 5 months. All contracts renewable. To work 25 hours per week, 8am–10pm (one period of the day free). Some Saturday morning work; some summer work (June, July, September).

SALARY: €1,300 net for qualified teachers with 3 years' experience. Salary negotiable for those with more experience.

FACILITIES/SUPPORT: Italian lessons at cost. 70% is company work (general and business) both on and offsite. School has 3 small company cars and helps teachers with accommodation. Excellent facilities, staff resource centre, free internet access.

RECRUITMENT: Via www.tefl.com and direct application.

CONTACT: Peter Anderson, Director and Owner. (p.anderson@andersonhouse.it).

ANGLO-AMERICAN CENTRE

Via Mameli 46, Cagliari 09124, Sardinia

📞 +39 070 654 955

🖱 angloamericancagliari@gmail.com

🖥 www.angloamericancentre.it

NUMBER OF TEACHERS: 20.

PREFERENCE OF NATIONALITY: Must be native speakers of English.

QUALIFICATIONS: 2 years post-CELTA, reasonable Italian language competence, experience with adults and younger learners, knowledge of Cambridge ESOL exams.

CONDITIONS OF EMPLOYMENT: 1st October to 30th June for new teachers. 25 hours contact time per week.

SALARY: €1,110–€1,300 per month (net of contributions).

FACILITIES/SUPPORT: School helps teachers to make contact with landlords and may accompany new arrivals to viewings. References can be provided to landlords and loans to cover initial deposit if necessary.

RECRUITMENT: Direct applications, via TEFL.com or the AISLi website. Interviews are held face to face in Cagliari or via Skype.

ASSOCIAZIONE ITALO BRITANNICA

Piazza della Vittoria 14/22, 16121 Genoa

📞 +39 010 591605

🖱 mzacco@italobritannica.it

🖥 www.italobritannica.it

NUMBER OF TEACHERS: Approximately 15.

PREFERENCE OF NATIONALITY: None.

QUALIFICATIONS: Degree and CELTA or equivalent.

CONDITIONS OF EMPLOYMENT: Teachers are freelancers with approximately 12–15 hours work per week.

SALARY: €14 per hour net, VAT is paid by the school.

FACILITIES/SUPPORT: Help may be given to find accommodation.

RECRUITMENT: Interviews may be held in London but preferably in Genoa.

CONTACT: Marina Zacco, Director.

BENEDICT SCHOOL

C. so Alberto Pio 68, 41012 Carpi (MO)

📞 +39 059 695921

🖥 www.serverbenedict.com

NUMBER OF TEACHERS: 10.

PREFERENCE OF NATIONALITY: British or American.

QUALIFICATIONS: Minimum TEFL (CELTA or equivalent certification).

CONDITIONS OF EMPLOYMENT: Mid-September until mid-July. Minimum 90 hours per month guaranteed (average 120 hours). 80% of work is with companies; 20% with private students.

SALARY: To be discussed at interview.

FACILITIES/SUPPORT: Accommodation provided by school. Assist non-EU and EU teachers with permits.

RECRUITMENT: Internet and recruitment agency.

CONTACT: Philippe Bernet, Owner.

BRITISH INSTITUTES – NEW SCHOOL
Via de Ambrosis 21, 15067 Novi Ligure (AL)
- +39 0143 2987
- noviligure@britishinstitutes.it
- www.newschool.it

NUMBER OF TEACHERS: 8.

PREFERENCE OF NATIONALITY: British, American.

QUALIFICATIONS: TEFL Diploma/degree plus 1 year's experience.

CONDITIONS OF EMPLOYMENT: 9 months, renewable. Average of 25 hours per week.

SALARY: €11 per hour net.

RECRUITMENT: Via www.tefl.com.

BRITISH LANGUAGE SERVICES/LINGUAVIVA
Via C. De Cristoforis 15, 20124 Milan
- +39 02 659 6401
- segreteria@linguaviva.net
- www.linguaviva.net

NUMBER OF TEACHERS: Approximately 20.

PREFERENCE OF NATIONALITY: British and Irish (EU only).

QUALIFICATIONS: Minimum CELTA or equivalent, degree plus some experience. Must be dynamic. Preference given to teachers with accommodation in the Milan area.

CONDITIONS OF EMPLOYMENT: October to June/July. 15–25 hours per week.

SALARY: Freelance rates.

RECRUITMENT: Adverts followed by personal interviews in Milan. Send full CV with photo and email addresses of 2 referees.

BRITISH s.r.l.
Via XX Settembre 12, 16121 Genoa
- +39 010 593591
- britishsrl@libero.it
- www.britishgenova.it

NUMBER OF TEACHERS: 12.

PREFERENCE OF NATIONALITY: EU, American, Australian and Canadian.

QUALIFICATIONS: Bachelor's degree plus CELTA and some experience.

CONDITIONS OF EMPLOYMENT: 25+ hours per week between mid-September and mid-June.

SALARY: Variable according to hours worked.

FACILITIES/SUPPORT: Assistance given with accommodation, teaching materials and course programming.

RECRUITMENT: Interviews essential, usually take place in Italy or by phone.

CALEDONIAN COMMUNICATIONS
Viale Vigliani 55, 20148 Milan
- +39 02 4802 0486/1086
- info@caledonian.it
- www.caledonian.it.

NUMBER OF TEACHERS: 15–20, depending on time of year.

PREFERENCE OF NATIONALITY: EU citizens or others with permits already. British nationals can be hired on UK contract and given help to find accommodation. First 2 weeks are provided free and in some cases up to 1 month.

QUALIFICATIONS: Degree (preferably in a business subject) followed by TEFL qualification.

CONDITIONS OF EMPLOYMENT: All teachers are freelancers, and paid on an hourly basis.

SALARY: Varies according to age and experience.

RECRUITMENT: Word of mouth, newspapers, magazines, internet and CVs sent on spec.

CONTACT: Maria McCarthy, Managing Director (maria@caledonian.it).

CLM-BELL
Via Pozzo 30, 38122 Trento
- +39 0461 981733
- clm-bell@clm-bell.it
- www.clm-bell.com

NUMBER OF TEACHERS: 25 approximately, also for Riva del Garda.

PREFERENCE OF NATIONALITY: Native English speakers.

QUALIFICATIONS: Minimum 2 years' experience with CELTA/DELTA qualification.

CONDITIONS OF EMPLOYMENT: 9-month contracts. To work 23 hours per week, can be extended. Positions also available at summer camp.

SALARY: From €1,350–€1,550 per month.

FACILITIES/SUPPORT: Single subsidised accommodation on a limited basis. Help provided with work permits. Workshops given by teacher trainers.

RECRUITMENT: Via TEFL.com or direct applications. Interview required.

CONTACT: Ivana Ferrari, Centre Manager; or Jane Nolan, Centre Manager for English.

DARBY SCHOOL OF LANGUAGES – ROME – MILAN
Via Mosca 51, Villino 14, 00142 Rome
Also: Via Concordia, 6 San Donato Milanese-Milano
Skype: 'darby school of languages rome'
☎ +39 06 51962205
🖱 darby@darbyschool.it
💻 www.darbyschool.it

NUMBER OF TEACHERS: 40–50.

PREFERENCE OF NATIONALITY: None, but must be native English speaker.

QUALIFICATIONS: TEFL certificate CELTA.

CONDITIONS OF EMPLOYMENT: Freelance. Teachers for both Rome and Milan can choose their hours which usually are an average of 20–25 hours per week. More hours available if wanted.

SALARY: The average salary of about €1,400 is sufficient and more to live on in Italy.

FACILITIES/SUPPORT: New teachers are helped to find accommodation.

RECRUITMENT: Relevant CVs and interviews.

CONTACT: Gilda Darby.

THE ENGLISH CAMP COMPANY LLC
Via Della Madonna Delle Grazie, Santa Maria Delgi Angeli, Assisi (PG) 06081
☎ +39 075 8041 402
🖱 info@theenglishcampcompany.com
💻 www.theenglishcampcompany.com

NUMBER OF TEACHERS: 8–15.

PREFERENCE OF NATIONALITY: None.

QUALIFICATIONS: Previous teaching experience or experience working at summer camps with children.

CONDITIONS OF EMPLOYMENT: 2-month contract. Working hours 9am–5pm. Compulsory 1-week orientation must be attended in early June.

SALARY: €175 per week.

FACILITIES/SUPPORT: All teachers are housed with host families.

RECRUITMENT: Closing date for applications end of March.

CONTACT: Ashleigh McLean and Nate Poerio, Founders and Directors.

THE ENGLISH CONVERSATION CLUB
Via XX Settembre 26/09, 16121 Genova
☎ +39 010540964
🖱 enquiry@thetrainingcompany.org or smurrell@thetrainingcompany.org
💻 www.thetrainingcompany.org

NUMBER OF TEACHERS: 12.

PREFERENCE OF NATIONALITY: None.

QUALIFICATIONS: CELTA/DELTA or equivalent. Online certificates are not acceptable.

CONDITIONS OF EMPLOYMENT: 10-month contract. 100 working hours per month.

SALARY: €1,100–€1,300 per month net.

FACILITIES/SUPPORT: Assistance given to find accommodation prior to arrival.

RECRUITMENT: Usually via the internet. Interviews are essential and can be carried out over the phone or occasionally in the UK.

CONTACT: Stephen Murrell, Director.

IIK ANCONA SCUOLA DI LINGUE
Scalo Vittorio Emanuele II, 1, 60121 Ancona
☎ +39 071 206610
🖱 info@iik.it
💻 www.iik.it

NUMBER OF TEACHERS: 5–6.

PREFERENCE OF NATIONALITY: British preferred; EU nationals.

QUALIFICATIONS: Minimum 3 years' teaching experience and TEFL/TESOL certificate. (Taster weekend courses and distance learning courses without observed and assessed teaching practice will not be considered.)

CONDITIONS OF EMPLOYMENT: Generally from September until end of June. Guaranteed minimum 25 hours per week. Teaching takes place between 8.45am and 9pm.

SALARY: €10 net per hour.

FACILITIES/SUPPORT: Assistance given with finding accommodation but teacher responsible for paying rent. School advises EU teachers on getting residence permit, fiscal code and enrolling in health services.

RECRUITMENT: Direct contact and www.tefl.com.

CONTACT: Maria Margherita Gargiulo, Director of Studies.

NUMBER OF TEACHERS: 40.

PREFERENCE OF NATIONALITY: British, Irish, Australian, New Zealander.

QUALIFICATIONS: Minimum 3 years' experience and relevant certificate/qualification.

CONDITIONS OF EMPLOYMENT: 12-month contract. Usual hours are 9am–7pm, Monday to Friday.

SALARY: Between €1,700 and €3,250 gross depending on type of contract and experience. 20–30% deductions for taxes.

FACILITIES/SUPPORT: Accommodation in flats owned by the school at very low rates.

RECRUITMENT: By the internet, advertising in local magazines and through the teacher network in Milan. Interviews essential.

NUMBER OF TEACHERS: 25.

PREFERENCE OF NATIONALITY: British, Irish, or any other native English speaker in possession of EU citizenship or Permesso di Soggiorno (work visa).

QUALIFICATIONS: For adult classes: CELTA/TESOL or any other TEFL qualification plus at least 1 year's experience with teaching groups at all levels. For children's classes: any qualification for teaching children (not necessarily as an EFL teacher) and experience with teaching children. Must have a driving licence. Other skills advantageous such as sports, music, arts or drama.

CONDITIONS OF EMPLOYMENT: Standard contract is 9 months or longer. Permanent teachers welcome. Sometimes teachers are employed shorter term and summer contracts from June to July are offered. Teachers work 25–35 hours per week.

SALARY: €12.50 net per hour.

FACILITIES/SUPPORT: Accommodation in flats owned by the school at very low rates.

RECRUITMENT: By direct contact or recruitment agencies. Interviews can be carried out on the phone or by internet. Occasionally interviews arranged in the UK or USA during the summer.

CONTACT: Mary Sposari, Director of Studies.

NUMBER OF TEACHERS: 20 for summer camp in Italy.

PREFERENCE OF NATIONALITY: British/American.

QUALIFICATIONS: CELTA qualification and experience teaching children and teenagers essential.

CONDITIONS OF EMPLOYMENT: Contract 2, 4 or 6 weeks from end of June to August. 6 hours teaching per day. Pupils aged 8–16.

SALARY: Approximately €650 per fortnight.

FACILITIES/SUPPORT: Accommodation and all meals provided.

RECRUITMENT: Direct application.

CONTACT: Mary Ricciardi, Director of Studies.

NUMBER OF TEACHERS: 9 plus 1 Director of Studies and 1 Children's Coordinator.

PREFERENCE OF NATIONALITY: British; others considered (only European passport).

QUALIFICATIONS: Degree, CELTA (minimum grade 'B'), DELTA. School interested in career teachers only.

CONDITIONS OF EMPLOYMENT: 8-month contracts. 25 hours per week, usually 1pm–9.30pm.

SALARY: From €1,200 plus increments.

FACILITIES/SUPPORT: Assistance with finding accommodation (rent €350–€400 per month). Weekly seminars and workshops. School will subsidise in-service diploma course by distance learning for suitable candidates. Italian survival lessons. CELTA courses offered in June every year.

RECRUITMENT: Via IH World Organisation or directly. Interviews essential.

An international group of schools that offers an English-medium education to children aged 3–18.

NUMBER OF TEACHERS: 200+.

PREFERENCE OF NATIONALITY: EU passport required.

QUALIFICATIONS: Degree + TEFL certificate (or equivalent, including a teaching certificate). Experience and/or willingness to teach the younger age ranges needed.

CONDITIONS OF EMPLOYMENT: Normal term is mid-September until the end of July. Working hours vary, but average at 25 contact hours per week.

SALARY: To be discussed.

FACILITIES/SUPPORT: Schools may help teachers find accommodation but teachers pay their own rent.

RECRUITMENT: Via recruitment agencies, websites and newspapers. Interviews can be arranged by video conferencing or occasionally in the UK.

CONTACT: Ian George Bolton, Head of Language Department (igbolton@oxford.it).

KEEP TALKING
Via Roma 60, 33100 Udine, Friuli-Venezia Giulia
+39 0432 501525
info@keeptalking.it
www.keeptalking.it

NUMBER OF TEACHERS: 10.

PREFERENCE OF NATIONALITY: None, but must be native speakers.

QUALIFICATIONS: University degree and CELTA or equivalent required plus minimum 1 year of experience. Driving licence essential to carry out work in local companies.

CONDITIONS OF EMPLOYMENT: 9-month contracts (*contratto di lavoro a progetto* which means an hourly-paid contract with a guaranteed minimum number of hours). Min. 750 contact hours over 9 months. 25 hours per week. Lessons mostly at lunchtimes and evenings till 9.30pm and Saturday mornings.

SALARY: Starting hourly wage of €14.50–€16.50 (net); monthly €1,200–€1,330 depending on qualifications and experience.

FACILITIES/SUPPORT: Training seminars once a month. Excellent facilities. Income tax, pension, medical/accident insurance paid by employer. Accommodation provided.

RECRUITMENT: Face-to-face interview normally essential in Udine or in London in late July. Candidates who are successful at interview will be told within about 2 weeks if they have been successful. Adverts via internet (www.tefl.com).

CONTACT: Kip Kelland, Director.

LANGUAGES INTERNATIONAL SRL
Via Macaggi 23/13, 16121 Genoa
+39 010 595 8889
robertson@languagesinternational.it
www.languagesinternational.it

NUMBER OF TEACHERS: 35–70 (depending on the time of year) in 3 schools around Italy.

PREFERENCE OF NATIONALITY: Native English speakers.

QUALIFICATIONS: Minimum 2 years' teaching experience, university degree and TEFL/TESOL certificate.

CONDITIONS OF EMPLOYMENT: Between 24 and 34 working hours per week, depending on which city the teacher is based in and their flexibility.

FACILITIES/SUPPORT: Assistance is given with accommodation, i.e. appointments to visit rooms are set up.

RECRUITMENT: Usually via the internet or word of mouth. Interviews are carried out over the phone if the candidate is not in Rome, Milan or Genoa.

CONTACT: Millica Robertson, Director of Studies.

LINGUE SENZA FRONTIERE
Corso Inglesi 172, 18038 – Sanremo (IM)
+39 0184 533661
info@linguesenzafrontiere.org
www.linguesenzafrontiere.org

NUMBER OF TEACHERS: Approximately 150 per summer for English immersion camps.

PREFERENCE OF NATIONALITY: Native English speaker.

QUALIFICATIONS: TEFL certificate or equivalent and/or relevant experience. Must have a genuine interest in working with children. Italian is not required but is useful.

CONDITIONS OF EMPLOYMENT: 2-week contract plus a free 4-day training course, which is compulsory. Working hours are 8.45am–4.15pm, Monday to Friday. Some English-speaking actors are employed for the academic year as well.

SALARY: €450 net per 2-week camp.

FACILITIES/SUPPORT: Accommodation is provided from beginning to end of contract. During the training period accommodation is in shared rooms, then with an Italian host family during the camp.

CONTACT: Emma Bosworth, Tutor Coordinator.

LIVING LANGUAGES SCHOOL
Via Magna Grecia 2, 89128 Reggio Calabria
Also: via Madonna, 21 Gallico, 89135 Reggio Calabria
info@livinglanguages.it
www.livinglanguages.it

NUMBER OF TEACHERS: 8.

PREFERENCE OF NATIONALITY: Native English speakers.

QUALIFICATIONS: TEFL, CELTA.

CONDITIONS OF EMPLOYMENT: 9-month renewable contracts. British contract. Teaching hours 3pm–9pm, Monday to Friday.

SALARY: Approx. €826 (net) per month for an inexperienced teacher.

FACILITIES/SUPPORT: Help given with accommodation.

RECRUITMENT: Via adverts. Interviews sometimes carried out in UK.

LONDON SCHOOL
Corso Rosmini, 66, 38068 Rovereto (TN)
 info@londonschoolrovereto.it
www.londonschoolrovereto.it

NUMBER OF TEACHERS: 4–5.

PREFERENCE OF NATIONALITY: British.

QUALIFICATIONS: Degree, and excellent command of English language. Pronunciation and grammar must be perfect. Teachers who also speak Italian are preferred. For summer work, training or experience in teaching young learners is preferred, e.g. online TESOL plus TEYL course (via www.teachingenglishinitaly.com).

CONDITIONS OF EMPLOYMENT: 1-year contract which may be renewed. 20–25 working hours per week. Summer vacancies are also available at children's courses held between mid-June and mid-August at the BluHotel in Folgaria in the mountains of northern Italy. Summer teachers work between 2 and 9 weeks.

SALARY: €12–€15 per hour. Summer teachers earn €300 (net) a week in addition to full board and hotel accommodation; wages are paid at the end of the contract.

FACILITIES/SUPPORT: Help is given to find accommodation. Work permits are taken care of by the school's accountant.

RECRUITMENT: References, detailed CV and interviews essential.

CONTACT: Gordana Marjanovic, Owner.

LORD BYRON COLLEGE
Via Sparano 102, 70121 Bari
+39 080 523 2686
johncredico@lordbyroncollege.com
www.lordbyroncollege.com

One of the largest independent language schools in Italy, with 40 years' experience and an annual attendance of nearly 2,000 students of all levels and ages. Authorised by the Italian Ministry of Education and member of EAQUALS (European Association for Quality Language Services).

NUMBER OF TEACHERS: 30 full-time, 30 part-time.

PREFERENCE OF NATIONALITY: UK nationals; Canadian, American and Australian applicants can be considered only if they have dual European citizenship.

QUALIFICATIONS: Degree, TEFL qualification, at least 1 year's teaching experience and knowledge of a foreign language.

CONDITIONS OF EMPLOYMENT: UK contracts for 8 months from October to June or 5 months from January, renewable. National insurance and pension coverage. 27.5 hours per week including paid training and development hours. Students of all ages and levels.

SALARY: Starting salary from €900 net per month. Paid orientation week. 5 weeks' paid holiday.

FACILITIES/SUPPORT: Free in-house DELTA course for teachers with minimum 1,200 hours' teaching experience. Teacher training and development programme for all teaching staff. Large self-access centre with video club, cinema, large TEFL resource centre and library and staff internet access. Participation in school's film dubbing and voiceover programme. Free Italian course. Assistance finding accommodation.

RECRUITMENT: Online application form in the Teaching Opportunities section of the website can be submitted by email or post with full CV, recent photograph, names and email addresses of two teaching-related references, copies of degree, TEFL qualification and EU passport. Interviews and hiring in June for October start and in December for January.

CONTACT: John Credico, Director of Studies (johncredico@lordbyroncollege.com).

MAC LANGUAGE SCHOOL
Formazione OK, Via Alessandro Cruto, 8 00146 Roma
+39 0683664460
info@maclanguage.it
www.formazioneok.com or www.maclanguage.it

NUMBER OF TEACHERS: 57.

PREFERENCE OF NATIONALITY: None if native English speaker.

QUALIFICATIONS: 3 years' experience or certified teachers.

CONDITIONS OF EMPLOYMENT: 4–8 hours per day.

FACILITIES/SUPPORT: None.

RECRUITMENT: Internet, newspapers, other. Interviews essential. Sometimes phone interviews can be arranged.

CONTACT: Carman Lora, Director of Studies.

MADRELINGUA SCHOOL OF ENGLISH
Via San Giorgio 6, 40121 Bologna
+39 051 267 822
info@madrelinguabologna.com
www.madrelinguabologna.com

NUMBER OF TEACHERS: Around 10.

PREFERENCE OF NATIONALITY: None, but must be eligible to work legally in Italy.

QUALIFICATIONS: Degree plus CELTA (or equivalent) essential, YL qualification and/or DELTA preferred. The school contributes to course fees for staff wishing to do the DELTA or CELTYL.

CONDITIONS OF EMPLOYMENT: Academic year is October to June. Teachers work evenings and Saturday mornings. Some permanent positions available.

SALARY: Depending on experience but above average for the local market. Minimum €20 an hour gross. Taxes are around 20%.

FACILITIES/SUPPORT: The school can arrange a 'homestay' on a temporary basis. English teachers may take subsidised Italian language courses.

RECRUITMENT: Speculative CVs.

CONTACT: Daniel Stephens, Director.

ONE TO THREE – INTERNATIONAL SCHOOL FOR TODDLERS
Viale Premuda 38/A, 20129 Milan
+39 02 7600 6795
info@onetothree.it
www.onetothree.it

NUMBER OF TEACHERS: 15–20.

PREFERENCE OF NATIONALITY: EU only.

QUALIFICATIONS: Degree in early children/early years education or psychology.

CONDITIONS OF EMPLOYMENT: 10 months. 36 hours per week.

SALARY: €1,000–€1,300 net per month.

FACILITIES/SUPPORT: No help with accommodation or visas.

RECRUITMENT: Interviews essential, can be by phone or Skype.

CONTACT: Antonella Manuli, Head of Recruitment.

OXFORD INSTITUTE
Via Adriatica 10/12, 73100 Lecce
+39 0832 390312
inglese@oxfordiamo.com
www.oxfordiamo.com

Part of the Oxford Group – see entry for International School of Europe.

OXFORD SCHOOL OF ENGLISH s.r.l.
Administrative Office, Via S. Pertini 14, 30035 Mirano, Venice
+39 041 570 23 55
oxford@oxfordschool.com
www.oxfordschool.com

NUMBER OF TEACHERS: 20–30 for 13 schools in northeast Italy; most are independent franchises (60–70 teachers employed altogether).

PREFERENCE OF NATIONALITY: British.

QUALIFICATIONS: Degree, TEFL and knowledge of Italian needed. Candidates must be holders of an EU passport.

CONDITIONS OF EMPLOYMENT: 9-month contracts or longer, 22 hours per week.

SALARY: Varies according to hours and length of contract. Tax deductions of about 23% give minimum health and welfare cover.

FACILITIES/SUPPORT: Accommodation at teacher's own expense, but school will help to find it.

RECRUITMENT: Interviews in London from mid-May or in Italy.

CONTACT: Philip Panter, Administrator.

QUAGI LANGUAGE CENTRE
Via Manzoni, 100/C, Erice C. Santa, 91100 Trapani, Sicily
quagi@quagi.com
www.quagi.org

NUMBER OF TEACHERS: 7.

PREFERENCE OF NATIONALITY: Native English speakers with an EU passport.

QUALIFICATIONS: Preferably 2 years' experience, a degree and CELTA or TESOL certificate are required.

CONDITIONS OF EMPLOYMENT: Usually 8 months, October to the end of May. 4-month contracts also offered (January to May).

SALARY: €1,200 guaranteed base salary per month.

FACILITIES/SUPPORT: Modern school offering training to become an official Cambridge ESOL oral examiner and/or invigilator. In-house training is provided before courses start. Perks include internet, a large range of resources and a return flight to the UK at the end of the contract term and holidays are fully paid. The school will also help teachers find fully furnished accommodation, arrange tax file numbers and medical visits.

RECRUITMENT: Direct. Telephone interviews possible.

CONTACT: Teresa Matteucci, quagi@quagi.com.

UNITED COLLEGE

Ronco a Via Von Platen 16/18, 96100 Siracusa, Sicily

info@unitedcollege.it or carolyn.davies@ unitedcollege.it

NUMBER OF TEACHERS: 10.

PREFERENCE OF NATIONALITY: British (work contracts for non-Europeans much more difficult to arrange).

QUALIFICATIONS: Degree plus Trinity or Cambridge certificate, plus 1 year's experience. Basic knowledge of Italian preferable.

CONDITIONS OF EMPLOYMENT: Mid-September to mid-June. Hours between 3pm and 9pm.

SALARY: Approximately £900 per month (depending on experience).

FACILITIES/SUPPORT: Accommodation arranged and paid for by school. Car available.

RECRUITMENT: Through www.tefl.com.

CONTACT: Carolyn Davies, Director of Studies.

WALL STREET INSTITUTE – LUCKY LION SCHOOL SRL

Via Libertà 191 c/d/e, Palermo, Sicily

+39 091 9865100

palermo@wallstreet.it

www.wallstreet.it/palermo/Lavora-con-noi

NUMBER OF TEACHERS: 4.

PREFERENCE OF NATIONALITY: None.

QUALIFICATIONS: Native English speakers with CELTA or equivalent.

CONDITIONS OF EMPLOYMENT: Contracts are generally less than 1 year but are renewable. Approximately 25 hours per week depending on the time of year.

FACILITIES/SUPPORT: Help provided to find private accommodation.

RECRUITMENT: Face-to-face interview and demonstration lesson essential.

CONTACT: Jacqueline Louise Scott, Service Manager (jlscott@ wallstreet.it).

WINDSOR SCHOOL OF ENGLISH

Via Molino delle Lime 4/F, 10064 Pinerolo (TO)

+39 0121 795555

windsor@vds.it or cv@windsorpinerolo.it

www.windsorpinerolo.it

NUMBER OF TEACHERS: 6–9.

PREFERENCE OF NATIONALITY: British or EU applicants only.

QUALIFICATIONS: Minimum Certificate in TEFL, experience of teaching Military English.

CONDITIONS OF EMPLOYMENT: 9–10 months (October to June).

SALARY: About €1,000 net per month.

CONTACT: Sandro Vazon Colla, Director.

PORTUGAL

As one of the weak Mediterranean economies in the Eurozone, Portugal has been struggling to stay afloat. Although its situation is not nearly as dire as that of Greece, unemployment is high: in 2011 it hit a record 11.1%, and even the northern region around Porto which has traditionally been the country's economic powerhouse has not been immune. This means that there is less disposable income around for English courses, though plenty of leisure time if one in four under-25s does not have a job.

Yet plenty of opportunities persist especially in the teaching of young learners. Relations between Portugal and Britain have always been warm and a preference for British teachers remains strong. Most schools cater for anyone over the age of seven, so you should be prepared to teach children. The Portuguese government has been pushing for English to be taught from first grade and as a result parents are eager to start their children very young in private English classes. The enrolment for children's courses continues strong and a number of language institutes serve a student body that is 90% under the age of 17. Schools often find it hard to recruit teachers who have experience of teaching children and a basic knowledge of Portuguese, which is useful when teaching young children. A new trend is for established institutes to offer intensive summer courses. Teaching on one of these is easier to secure and can provide a useful route into longer term teaching.

In fact, some schools organise courses in nursery/primary schools for children from the age of three, sometimes as part of the Ministry of Education's 'Teaching and Understanding of the first level of basic English' programme. For example the Windsor School in Ovar, south of Porto, offers courses to 'toddlers' (www.windsorschool.ws).

The vast majority of British tourists flock to the Algarve along the southern coast of Portugal, which means that many Portuguese in the south who aspire to work in the tourist industry want to learn English. Schools such as the Wall Street Institute in Faro and the Centro de Línguas in Lagos cater for just that market. But the demand for English teachers is greatest in the north and central Portugal. Jobs crop up in historic centres such as Coimbra, Braga and Viseu and in small seaside towns like Aveiro and Póvoa do Varzim. These can be a very welcome destination for teachers burned out from teaching in big cities, first-time teachers who want to avoid the rat race, or teachers who simply want to secure a steady wage and accommodation. The British Council (www.britishcouncil.org/portugal) has English language centres in Coimbra, Greater Lisbon and Porto, and recruits teachers, usually on a part-time basis initially. Candidates must have a degree, TEFL certificate and two years post-TEFL qualification EFL teaching experience; see www.britishcouncil.org/portugal-ensinar-informacao-professores.htm for information about teachers who are locally engaged rather than hired through the Council's Teacher Recruitment department in London.

FINDING A JOB

Most teachers in Portugal have either answered adverts or are working for one of the large chains. International House (www.international-house.com) has 11 affiliated schools in Portugal. Wall Street Institute (www.wsi.pt) is well represented with 33 centres, some of whom are always looking for dynamic teachers; CVs can be emailed to cv.com@wsi-portugal.com.

About three-quarters of all IH students in Portugal are children, so expertise with young learners is a definite asset and IH in Lisbon and Porto offer the specialist Cambridge training courses in teaching young learners. IH and the British Council, among others, also offer 'courses to help professionals', so expertise in law/finance and business should also prove helpful when trying to secure a job.

Outside the cities where there have traditionally been large expatriate communities, schools cannot depend on English speakers just showing up and so must recruit well in advance of the academic year (late

September to the end of June). The Bristol School Group (see entry) offers the only possibility of which we have heard for working in the Azores, so if you want to work in the most isolated islands in the Atlantic Ocean – more than 1,000km west of Portugal – this is your chance. Small groups of schools, say six schools in a single region, is the norm in Portugal. A number of the schools listed in the directory at the end of this chapter belong to such mini-chains. One of the most well-established is the Cambridge Schools group which every year imports up to 100 teachers.

A company that specialises in teaching children aged 3–13 is Fun Languages/Kids Club (www.fun languages.co.pt) with dozens of clubs throughout the country. It is possible to submit an online application form, which is circulated round all the clubs and any with vacancies will make contact.

Many schools are small family-run establishments with fewer than 10 teachers, so sending off a lot of speculative applications is unlikely to succeed. As is true anywhere, you might be lucky and find something on the spot. The Cambridge CELTA is widely requested by schools and can be obtained at IH in Lisbon.

REGULATIONS

The red tape for EU nationals working in Portugal is reasonably painless. All that is required (as throughout the EU) is to obtain a residence permit (*Autorizacao de Residencia*) after an initial 3-month stay by taking documents to show proof of accommodation, health insurance and means of support. If you are employed, you must show that you have been registered in the social security system and are not being paid less than the Portuguese minimum wage. These must be presented to the local authorities, i.e. any office of the Serviço de Estrangeiros e Fronteiras (SEF) or Aliens Office (regional addresses are given at www.sef.pt).

Non-EU residents will have a much more difficult time trying to work in Portugal, as **Rachel Beebe**, an American, discovered:

> I was not able to obtain a work visa of any kind: I found that this is very difficult for Americans living and work-ing in Portugal. I had to work on a freelance basis using recibos verdes ('green receipts'), which are intended for use by temporary workers in the country. This situation prevented me from securing a contract with my school; a contract would have allowed me a more permanent position as well as vacation time and other benefits. To get a work visa, you need a work contract in hand. While my school offered me a letter of their intent to employ me, you are required to have a legal contract when applying for the visa, which can then take upwards of a year (or more) to process. In the meantime, you are only allowed to stay in the country on a 'temporary stay visa,' which will allow you to stay up to nine months from the time of your arrival in Portugal. Needless to say, this period of time will expire before you are able to obtain a work visa. After the nine months, you would be expected to leave the Schengen area (which includes most Western European countries, with the notable excep-tion of the UK) for an equal period of time. Ostensibly, this would prevent most would-be American teachers from being able to teach long-term in Portugal. You could always try to secure a contract 12 months in advance of your planned arrival date, but I have never heard of a school hiring more than five or six months before the start date. In my case, I managed to get my hands on a book of green receipts and taught for a few months using those. However, many government offices will give you conflicting information, and I was only able to get the receipts with the help and direction of a friend who was able to tell me exactly where to go and what to say to whom.

The other alternative is to seek employment with schools that may prefer American speakers: any school with 'American' in the title is probably a good bet. Try the American School of Languages (Av. Duque de Loule, 22–1°, 1050 090, Lisbon; +351 21 314 6000; www.americanschooloflanguages.com) or CAA (Centro Anglo-Americano, in Chaves and Vila Real (www.caaenglish.com). The latter is a family-run school that prefers to hire EU citizens because they are cheaper, although they'd make an exception for qualified candidates (who rarely apply).

Since most teachers working for nine months are working on a freelance basis, they are responsible for paying their own taxes and contributions. There are seven income tax brackets ranging from 10.5% to 42% and an array of tax deductions, credits and special benefits. Tax laws and regulations are frequently subject to change, so it is best to check with the relevant authorities (Direcção-Geral dos Impostos, dsdsitarp@dgci. min-financas.pt).

CONDITIONS OF WORK

The consensus seems to be that wages are low, but the cost of living, at least outside the major cities, is reasonable. Imported consumer goods are taxed and expensive and the cost of domestic fuel and tolls on roads and bridges are high, but local produce such as olive oil, fruit, vegetables and wine are still relatively inexpensive. Public transport is quite cheap, as well as eating out. Working conditions are generally relaxed and students are generally helpful, as **Rachel Beebe** discovered:

> *Most students had a good attitude and tried very hard to speak the language. I spoke virtually no Portuguese in encounters or classes, and the students made every effort to use what they were learning to communicate with me.*

The normal salary range is €700–€1,000 net per month. Full-time contract workers are entitled to an extra month's pay after 12 months, which is partly why most teachers are employed on 9/10 month contracts. Some schools pay lower rates but subsidise or pay for flights and accommodation. Several provide free Portuguese lessons. Teachers being paid on an hourly basis should expect to earn €10–€17, but they will of course not be eligible for the 13th month bonus or paid holidays. Rates per hour can sink as low as €6.50, which isn't enough to live on unless you can also secure free accommodation. If you are living in an urban centre, then you'll also need to factor in any unpaid travel time to find out how much you are 'really' getting paid.

LIST OF EMPLOYERS

AMERICAN SCHOOL OF LANGUAGES
22 -1° Avenida Duque de Loulé, 1050-090 Lisbon
☏ +351 21 314 6000/96 790 7035
✉ admin.asl@mail.telepac.pt
🖥 www.americanschooloflanguages.com

NUMBER OF TEACHERS: 5–10.
PREFERENCE OF NATIONALITY: EU citizenship is a plus but not essential.
QUALIFICATIONS: University degree, TEFL training course (preferably CELTA), EFL experience with adults preferable but not essential.
CONDITIONS OF EMPLOYMENT: Contract runs from October to June with some summer work an option. Contract is renewable for the next academic year, 21–24 working hours per week.
SALARY: €1,200–€1,600 per month with adjustments for inflation and opportunities for advancement.

FACILITIES/SUPPORT: Some assistance given to find accommodation, i.e. help making phone calls to prospective landlords, etc.
RECRUITMENT: Interviews in Lisbon are essential.

BRISTOL SCHOOLS GROUP
Bristol School – Instituto de Línguas da Maia,
Trav. Dr. Carlos Pires Felgueiras, 12–3°, 4470 158 Maia
☏ +351 22 948 8803
✉ bsmaia@bristolschool.pt
🖥 www.bristolschool.pt

Comprises a group of 9 small schools: 4 in Oporto area, 2 in the Azores and 3 inland (Castelo Branco, Fundão and Colvilha). Addresses and email contacts all on website.
NUMBER OF TEACHERS: 25.

PREFERENCE OF NATIONALITY: British only (couples preferred).

QUALIFICATIONS: Bachelor's degree and TEFL qualification. 1 year's experience essential.

CONDITIONS OF EMPLOYMENT: Minimum period of work 15 September to 30 June, 25 hours per week. Pupils aged from 8 to Proficiency level.

SALARY: Basic salary plus Christmas bonus and end-of-contract bonuses plus tax rebate. Legal contract of work.

FACILITIES/SUPPORT: Assistance with accommodation given. No training.

RECRUITMENT: Direct application preferred.

CAMBRIDGE SCHOOL
Avenida da Liberdade 173, 1250 141 Lisbon
C +351 21 312 4600
info@cambridge.pt or av.liberdade@cambridge.pt
www.cambridge.pt

Portugal's largest private language school with 6 centres in Lisbon and one each in Porto, Coimbra and Funchal (Madeira).

NUMBER OF TEACHERS: 90–110.

PREFERENCE OF NATIONALITY: EU citizens or in possession of a Portuguese *Autorizacao de Residencia.*

QUALIFICATIONS: Bachelor's degree plus CELTA, Trinity CertTESOL or an equivalent EFL qualification. Online qualifications are not acceptable. EFL experience preferred; however, newly qualified applicants may be successful.

CONDITIONS OF EMPLOYMENT: All contracts are Permanent Employment Contracts for full-time work, with minimum commitment of 9 months from 1 October to 30 June.

COMPENSATION: In a typical month, most starting teachers (2012) will average between €1,200 and €1,300 after deductions and extras. All staff receive a monthly meal subsidy of €141 and are included in Portuguese National Health scheme. The school employs its own medical officers. Salaries are adjusted at the beginning of October.

FACILITIES/SUPPORT: All schools have 2–3 senior staff.

RECRUITMENT: Adverts on tefl.com. Applicants should send CV, recent photograph, contact telephone number and copies of degree and EFL certificate. Interviews are usually held in London in May and possibly mid-summer depending on require-ments. Visitors to Portugal can be interviewed in Lisbon by prior arrangement.

CONTACT: Jeffrey Kapke, Robert Hart, Tony Hilzbrich or Adrian Mather, Pedagogical Management.

CENTRO DE INGLES DE FAMALICAO
Edificio dos Correios, n° 116 – 4° Dto, Rua S. Joao de Deus, 4760–162 V.N. de Famalicao
C +351 252 374 233
centroinglesfam@gmail.com

NUMBER OF TEACHERS: 3.

PREFERENCE OF NATIONALITY: Native speakers from UK or Ireland.

QUALIFICATIONS: Degree and CELTA (or equivalent) essential; experience an advantage but not essential. Online qualifications are not accepted.

CONDITIONS OF EMPLOYMENT: 9-month renewable contracts from late September to end of June. 24 contact hours per week, Monday to Friday only.

SALARY: At least €948 per month (net). Paid holidays at Christmas, Easter and Carnival. Travel expenses of €150 paid at beginning and end of contract.

FACILITIES/SUPPORT: Fully furnished flat near school provided rent-free, sharing with other teacher(s). Help given with work permit procedures. Lessons are regularly observed and feedback given.

RECRUITMENT: Via adverts on the internet (www.tefl.com). Interviews essential, normally in London in July.

CONTACT: David Mills, Director of Studies.

CIAL – CENTRO DE LINGUAS
Avenida Republica 14–2, 1050 191 Lisbon
C +351 213 533 733; mob +351 918 500 300
linguas.estrangeiras@cial.pt
www.cial.pt

NUMBER OF TEACHERS: 15–17.

PREFERENCE OF NATIONALITY: EU nationals.

QUALIFICATIONS: University degree, CELTA, EFL teaching experience to adults (minimum 2 years); Business English teaching experience.

CONDITIONS OF EMPLOYMENT: Contracts October to June. Early morning, lunch-time and evening teaching hours.

SALARY: Depends on work agreement. Possibility of full-time, part-time or hourly basis. Monthly performance evaluation bonus paid as well as free Portuguese lessons and free health insurance as fringe benefits.

FACILITIES/SUPPORT: Family accommodation can be arranged for first 4 weeks if requested.

RECRUITMENT: Pre-selection through detailed CV; personal interviews compulsory.

CONTACT: Isabel Coimbra, Director (isabelcoimbra@cial.pt).

ENGLISH LANGUAGE CENTRE Cascais

Rua da Palmeira 5, 1A/B, Cascais

☎ +351 214830716/916060170

🖱 caroline.darling@elc-cascais.com

💻 www.elc-cascais.com

NUMBER OF TEACHERS: 9.

PREFERENCE OF NATIONALITY: Native speakers only, preferably from the UK.

QUALIFICATIONS: University degree and CELTA or equivalent.

CONDITIONS OF EMPLOYMENT: 10-month renewable contract from September 1st. 15–18 hours per week. Also part-time work teaching Young Learners from age 5.

SALARY: €850 per month (for teaching a basic 15 hours per week).

FACILITIES/SUPPORT: Recruitment locally; pedagogical support – regular training workshops.

RECRUITMENT: Through tefl.com/local adverts. Face-to-face interviews essential.

CONTACT: Caroline Darling, Director.

ESE – ENGLISH SCHOOL ÉVORA

Praça da Muralha, 12 – 1° esq. 7005 248 Évora

☎ +351 266743231/938512574

🖱 englishschoolevora@gmail.com

💻 www.englishschoolevora.com

NUMBER OF TEACHERS: 3.

PREFERENCE OF NATIONALITY: EU nationals, native English speakers.

QUALIFICATIONS: Degree, TEFL qualification, minimum 2 years' experience.

CONDITIONS OF EMPLOYMENT: 9-month renewable contract, 23 hours plus possible overtime.

FACILITIES/SUPPORT: Some assistance with finding accommodation.

RECRUITMENT: Through the internet. Interviews are often by Skype.

CONTACT: Michael W. Lewis, Director.

FUN LANGUAGES – KIDS CLUB VISEU

19 Rua Eng. Lino M. Rodrigues, Edificio Vasco da Gama, 3510-084 Viseu

☎ +351 232 426 978

🖱 sandy@funlanguagesviseu.net

💻 www.funlanguages.co.pt

One of 29 franchised branches throughout the country.

NUMBER OF TEACHERS: 9.

PREFERENCE OF NATIONALITY: Native speakers from Britain or North America.

QUALIFICATIONS: University education, teaching experience and teaching qualification preferred, although if a candidate shows potential, the employer is willing to train.

CONDITIONS OF EMPLOYMENT: Period of work September to July. 30 teaching hours per week.

SALARY: Variable, depending on rent, bills, qualifications and circumstances. Arrangement will be discussed during the interview process. Teachers work with green receipts which means deductions are not made at source.

FACILITIES/SUPPORT: Accommodation is always provided for teachers moving to Portugal. Rent and bills are included in salary. The school registers teachers and takes care of permits, bank accounts and other issues involved in relocation.

RECRUITMENT: Advertising and headhunting at EFL summer camps in Britain. Interviews are essential, and sometimes take place in the UK as well as Portugal.

CONTACT: Sandy Albuquerque, Director of Studies.

ILC CENTRO INTERACTIVO DE LINGUAS

Rua Mouzihno de Albuqerque 56 1° Esq., 2440 Leiria

☎ +351 244 765307

🖱 Sergio.g@il-c.com.pt

💻 www.il-c.com.pt

NUMBER OF TEACHERS: 12.

PREFERENCE OF NATIONALITY: None.

QUALIFICATIONS: Degree.

CONDITIONS OF EMPLOYMENT: Standard contract is 10 months with 25 working hours per week.

SALARY: €12 per hour.

RECRUITMENT: Interviews carried out in Portugal.

CONTACT: Sérgio Gomes, Director.

INSTITUTO DE LINGUAS DE S. JOAO DA MADEIRA

Rua Durbalino Laranjeira S/N, 3700 – 108 S. João da Madeira

☎ +351 256 833906

🖱 institutodelinguas@gmail.com or institutodelinguas@hotmail.com

NUMBER OF TEACHERS: 14 working in schools/companies outside the Institute; 5 working at the Institute.

PREFERENCE OF NATIONALITY: British.

QUALIFICATIONS: DELTA/COTE plus 2 years' experience.

CONDITIONS OF EMPLOYMENT: 9-month contracts from mid-September.

SALARY: Dependent on qualifications.

FACILITIES/SUPPORT: No help given with accommodation, work permits; training sessions, workshops, seminars at the British Council Oporto.
RECRUITMENT: Interview essential.
CONTACT: Dr. Helena Borges, Director.

INTERNATIONAL HOUSE LISBON
Rua Marquès Sá da Bandeira 16, 1050 148 Lisbon
+351 213 151 493/494/496
info@ihlisbon.com
www.ihlisbon.com

NUMBER OF TEACHERS: 18.
PREFERENCE OF NATIONALITY: Native English speakers.
QUALIFICATIONS: CELTA minimum.
CONDITIONS OF EMPLOYMENT: Standard length of stay 9 months. Flexible working hours to include evening and Saturday work. Pupils range in age from 8 to 80. Standard working week is 18 hours.
SALARY: €1,340 per month for first year teachers, based on 18 hours per week teaching.
FACILITIES/SUPPORT: Assistance with finding accommodation. CELTA and IHCYL courses offered regularly (see Training chapter).
RECRUITMENT: Local advertisements and by IH, London.
CONTACT: Colin McMillan, Director.

INTERNATIONAL HOUSE (PORTO)
Porto: Rua Marechal Saldanha 145–1°, 4150 655 Porto
+315 22 617 7641
info@ihporto.org or info@ihleca.com
www.ihporto.org or www.ihleca.com
Matosinhos: Leça da Palmeira, Rua Oliveira Lessa 350, 4450 Matosinhos
+351 22 995 9087
business@ihporto.org

NUMBER OF TEACHERS: 10.
PREFERENCE OF NATIONALITY: British, Canadian, Australian, New Zealander and American.
QUALIFICATIONS: CELTA/Trinity.
CONDITIONS OF EMPLOYMENT: 1-year contracts, 22 hours per week, pupils aged from 7.
SALARY: Depending on qualifications and experience.
FACILITIES/SUPPORT: Assistance with accommodation. Portuguese lessons available. Training provided.
RECRUITMENT: Direct application.
CONTACT: Shawn Severson, Business Services Manager.

INTERNATIONAL LANGUAGE SCHOOL
Av. Republica Guiné-Bissau, 26 A, 2900 588 Setubal
+351 26 522 7934
http://ils.pai.pt

NUMBER OF TEACHERS: 6.
PREFERENCE OF NATIONALITY: Native English speakers.
QUALIFICATIONS: CELTA or equivalent, 1 year's experience or more.
CONDITIONS OF EMPLOYMENT: October–July, 25 teaching hours per week.
SALARY: Approximately €1,300 per month (gross).
FACILITIES/SUPPORT: Accommodation provided.
RECRUITMENT: Via www.tefl.com. Interviews can be conducted by phone.

LANGUAGE PROJECT – INSTITUTO DE LINGUAS
Rua de Camões Lt 15, Quinta Nova de S Roque, 2670 Loures
+351 219 823084
www.language-project.com

NUMBER OF TEACHERS: 3.
PREFERENCE OF NATIONALITY: None.
QUALIFICATIONS: CELTA or equivalent, relevant degree and 2 years' experience including with young learners.
CONDITIONS OF EMPLOYMENT: Contract is 9 months (1 academic year) with 22–24 contact hours per week.
SALARY: €1,200 gross per month.
FACILITIES/SUPPORT: Assistance given with finding accommodation if necessary.
RECRUITMENT: Usually via adverts in schools, word of mouth or local websites. Interviews are essential either face-to-face or via Skype.

NOVO INSTITUTO DE LINGUAS
Avenida das Tulipas, N° 20B, 1495 159, Miraflores, Lisbon
+351 21 412 0929 or 21 943 5238
nilportugal@gmail.com or admin@nil.edu.pt
www.nil.edu.pt

NUMBER OF TEACHERS: 9 /10 English teachers for three schools in and around Lisbon; branches in Portela and Massima.
PREFERENCE OF NATIONALITY: British preferred.
QUALIFICATIONS: Experienced and inexperienced graduates who have successfully completed a recognised TEFL course.

CONDITIONS OF EMPLOYMENT: 9-month (1 October to 30 June) contract that is renewable, 24 contract hours per week (Monday–Friday).

SALARY: Depends on experience.

FACILITIES/SUPPORT: Secretarial and administrative help in finding and renting accommodation. The school can act as guarantor for rentals. Week-long orientation course end of September to aid teachers in the classroom.

RECRUITMENT: Website advertising (e.g. www.tefl.com) followed by possibility of UK interviews in June/July and September.

CONTACT: Nicholas Rudall, Director of Studies.

OXFORD SCHOOL

Lisbon: Rua D. Estefania, 165–1°, 1000 154 Lisbon

 +351 21 354 6586/796 6660

 info2@oxford-school.pt

Cacém: Av. Bons Amigos, 37–1° Dto, 2735 077 Cacém

 +351 21 914 6343

 www.oxford-school.pt

Member of AEPLE and ELITE (Excellent Language Institutions Teaching in Europe).

NUMBER OF TEACHERS: About 40 employed at two branches in Lisbon and one in Cacém; 6 new hires per year.

PREFERENCE OF NATIONALITY: British.

QUALIFICATIONS: Minimum TEFL course (e.g. CELTA), qualifications and some experience.

CONDITIONS OF EMPLOYMENT: October–June. Hours mainly 1pm–3pm and 5pm–9pm.

SALARY: Minimum €17 per 1 teaching hour or €1,400 per month for 20 teaching hours per week. Deductions for taxes and social security approx 15%.

FACILITIES/SUPPORT: Help given with finding a shared flat.

RECRUITMENT: Direct application. Interviews essential in Lisbon or London.

CONTACT: Zilda Amaro, Manager (zildamaro@oxford-school.pt).

ROYAL SCHOOL OF LANGUAGES – ESCOLAS DE LINGUAS, LDA

Rua José Rabumba 2, 3810 125 Aveiro

 +351 234 429 156 or 234 425 104

 rsl@royalschooloflanguages.pt

 www.royalschooloflanguages.pt

Schools also in Porto, Agueda, Guarda, Ovar, Viseu, Ilhavo and Viseu. Languages taught: English, French, German, Italian, Spanish and Portuguese.

NUMBER OF TEACHERS: 30–35 in the whole group.

PREFERENCE OF NATIONALITY: British, Australian, Canadian and American.

QUALIFICATIONS: University degree plus TEFL/TESOL certificate.

CONDITIONS OF EMPLOYMENT: 9-month contracts. 25–27 teaching hours per week.

FACILITIES/SUPPORT: Assistance with accommodation and working papers. 5-day training course with Global TESOL College.

RECRUITMENT: Via CVs or interviews, which sometimes take place in UK.

SELF ESCOLA DE LINGUAS

Bela de São Tiago n° 20, 9060–400 Funchal, Madeira

 +351 291 222 894 / +351 962192323

 info@e-self.net

 www.e-self.net

NUMBER OF TEACHERS: 2 full-time and 3 freelancers (working on green receipts).

PREFERENCE OF NATIONALITY: Native speakers of English with permission to work.

QUALIFICATIONS: Teachers with teaching or other degree, TEFL or formal teacher training or experience.

CONDITIONS OF EMPLOYMENT: Full-time teachers for 9-month contracts sometimes needed from beginning of academic year. Most vacancies are for part-time teachers to give short-term intensive courses.

SALARY: Variable.

FACILITIES/SUPPORT: School can assist teachers in finding accommodation and has been known to assist financially.

RECRUITMENT: CVs can be submitted by email in Microsoft Word or posted.

CONTACT: Rebecca Jardim, Director of Studies (rebecca.jardim@gmail.com).

SPEAKWELL ESCOLA DE LINGUAS

Head office: Praça Mário Azevedo Gomes, N 421, 2775 240 Parede

 +351 21 456 1771

 speakwell@speakwell.pt

 www.speakwell.pt

NUMBER OF TEACHERS: 12 full-time and 40 part-time.

PREFERENCE OF NATIONALITY: None, but must be native English speakers.

QUALIFICATIONS: TEFL certificate, preferably plus some business experience, or experience teaching children.

CONDITIONS OF EMPLOYMENT: Freelance, with the possibility of full-time hours. School opening times are weekdays and Saturdays. Business trainers and qualified school teachers also required.

SALARY: Above the average hourly rate for Portugal.

FACILITIES/SUPPORT: Good paedagogic and administrative support. Can help find accommodation through contacts, etc.

RECRUITMENT: Internet, local advertising, word-of-mouth.

CONTACT: Catherine Bright, Director (catherine.bright @speakwell.pt).

YORK SCHOOL, LISBOA
Travessa de Santa Quitéria 34B, 1250-212 Lisbon
℡ +351 213 869142
🖱 yorkschool@gmail.com
🖳 www.yorkschool-lisboa.com

NUMBER OF TEACHERS: 6.

PREFERENCE OF NATIONALITY: British.

QUALIFICATIONS: CELTA.

CONDITIONS OF EMPLOYMENT: Standard contract is 1 year with 6 working hours per day.

SALARY: Variable.

RECRUITMENT: Interviews are not essential.

SCANDINAVIA

Certain similarities exist in ELT throughout Scandinavia. The standard of English teaching in state schools is uniformly high, as anyone who has met a Dane or a Swede travelling abroad will know. Yet many ordinary Scandinavians aspire to fluency so keep up their English by attending evening classes, if only for social reasons. Sweden, Denmark and Norway have excellent facilities for such people, which are variations on the theme of 'folk university', a state-subsidised system of adult education. Classes at such institutions are the ideal setting for enthusiastic amateur teachers.

But as elsewhere in Europe the greatest demand for the English language comes from the business community, particularly in Finland. Enthusiastic amateurs tend to be less in demand in this setting than mature professionals. Yet Scandinavia is not a very popular destination for such teachers, despite its unspoilt countryside, efficient public transport and liberal society. So there is scope for most kinds of teacher to work in Scandinavia.

Since Finland and Sweden are EU members, red tape is straightforward for EU teachers. But even in Norway, whose people voted by a referendum not to join, the formalities are straightforward for EU nationals and language institutes employ foreign teachers.

Denmark

There is little recruitment of English teachers outside Denmark, apart from the Cambridge Institute Foundation, which is Denmark's largest EFL institution with a number of branches that specialise in Business English. The Danish government has tightened up the immigration laws making it virtually impossible for non-Europeans to get working permits. Many schools expect their teachers to speak Danish, and there seems to be almost enough fully bilingual candidates resident in Denmark to satisfy this requirement. It is worthwhile for any native English speaker with an appropriate background who is staying in Denmark to enquire about part-time openings.

Like Scandinavians generally, Danes are enthusiastic self-improvers which means that evening classes in English (and hundreds of other things) are very popular. These are purely recreational and are meant to be fun and informal (*hygge* in Danish). Folkehøjskoler (folk high schools) offer residential courses of varying lengths where working conditions are generally so favourable that there is very little turnover of teaching staff. The tradition of voluntary organisations including trade unions running courses is still strong in Denmark. It might be worth tracking down one of the voluntary organisations which run evening classes countrywide such as the Danish equivalent of Workers' Education, Arbejdernes Oplysnings Forbund or AOF (www.aof.dk). Addresses of the Danish Folkeuniversitet can be found on its website at www.folkeuniversitetet.dk.

Wages in Denmark are set by law and teaching English is no exception. The minimum is kr170, and that is what most new arrivals earn. However, once you're established you can expect to earn £25 an hour teaching in the state sector (which is much better funded and resourced than its UK counterpart). Denmark has among the highest taxes in the world, i.e. over 50% until you acquire a tax card (*frikort*) whereupon the rate drops and only earnings over a certain limit are taxed.

Finland

Although Finland's second language is Swedish, English runs a close second (or third). Finns are admirably energetic and industrious in learning foreign languages, possibly because their own language is so impenetrable (belonging to the Finno-Ugric group of languages along with Hungarian and Estonian). English is taught in every kind of educational institution from trade and technology colleges to universities, in commercial colleges (*Kauppaloulu*) and in Civic and Workers' Institutes. Private language schools flourish too and traditionally have not been too fussy about the paper qualifications of their native English speaker teachers. They seldom teach straight English courses but tailor-make courses for clients, e.g. 'English for presentation skills', so they are not looking for young first-timers to teach their wealthy corporate clients. Still, some private schools (such as Berlitz) may take on native English speakers without a teaching qualification.

Children start their primary education at age seven, and many children between the ages of three and seven are sent to private kindergartens, many of which are English (as well as German, American, etc.) These sometimes welcome a native English speaker with experience of teaching children. (The only skill which concerned one of these nurseries-cum-kindergartens looking to hire a young British graduate was singing.) Local teachers all have an MA degree since this is the minimum requirement. Provision of English is so good in state schools that there is little scope for picking up slack from disgruntled school leavers who feel they can't speak enough English. Neither is there a demand from an immigrant population since there are few foreigners or refugees in Finland compared with Denmark or Sweden.

FINDING A JOB

Finnbrit is the new name of the long established Federation of Finnish-British Societies, with an emphasis on language courses; its head office is at Fredrikinkatu 20 A 9, 00120 Helsinki (+358 9 687 70 230; www.finnbrit.fi). It takes on a few native English speakers, mostly experienced teachers, for their teaching operation.

Another big player in the provision of English language teaching is Richard Lewis Communications (RLC) with offices throughout Finland and Sweden as well as England (see entry). RLC draws most of its students from senior management in both the public and private sector, and also provides cross-cultural training. Of course not all the teaching takes place in the capital. There is a significant demand for freelance teachers for business in Turku, Oulu and other cities.

Teachers without European nationality will still encounter serious problems. American university students and recent graduates (within two years) over 21 can apply to the American-Scandinavian Foundation

(58 Park Avenue, New York, NY 10016; +1 212 779 3587; www.amscan.org/work.html) for work permits to cover a self-arranged internship. At one time there was a well-developed programme of teaching placements in Finland but that has all but disappeared. It might still be worth asking ASF about TEFOL positions in Finland for the academic year, from the end of August until the end of May.

The Nordic School based in St Petersburg (see entry) mounts an ambitious series of children's summer schools at 11 different colleges in Finland (several of them Christian establishments) plus one in Sweden, for Russian children aged 7–17 learning English (age range varies among camps). Up to 80 native English speakers are recruited to implement an intensive programme of conversation lessons, for 24 fortnight-long camps. Teachers are given free accommodation and meals plus a wage at the end of each camp, and also offered transport to another location for those working at consecutive camps. The programme has expanded into the other seasons as well as summer. **Anthony Cook** has now enjoyed three summers with Nordic School and hopes to do more in the future, which is a positive endorsement:

I heard about the job from a colleague in Moscow who had previously worked for Nordic School. Although I am an experienced EFL teacher, it took me a couple of attempts before a vacancy came up. Since then, however, the school has sent me a list of available camps every year. After applying, I was sent a list of available camps, and asked to choose my preferred dates and places. Some camps are more popular than others (because of desirable location or whatever), so there's a bit of negotiation about which camps are free versus your first preferences. Although I'm Australian and don't have an EU passport, there were no red tape problems; I suspect it's because staff are technically employed in Russia which nicely avoids the Eureaucracy.

There are opportunities to use different spaces – including the Finnish outdoors – as your classroom. You should keep things light and lively, but with older/higher level students, you can certainly throw in some grammar points, as long as the main focus is on communication. Topic-based vocabulary usually goes down quite well. The lack of a set syllabus makes it essential to bring your own 'bag of tricks'. After my first year I arrived with a large folder full of stuff that I thought might be useful for various ages and levels, which made the experience much easier and more enjoyable.

The biggest challenge is that you're dealing with four groups: the students of course, the Nordic School management (who are very approachable and helpful – though some of the managers on-site have limited English), the camp instructors, and the Finnish staff at the rural colleges where most camps take place. Some camps are very remote, and isolation can be an issue. Ruokolahti camp, for example, is situated far from any town, at the end of a long promontory miles from the mainland, surrounded by a lake. The location is gorgeous – you've never taught anywhere prettier than this – but the conveniences of city life are quite inaccessible.

I like the fact that Nordic School employs other professionals to look after the students outside of teaching hours. You'll never find yourself staying with a homesick child at night, dealing with minor injuries or removing a teenaged girl from a teenaged boy's sleeping quarters at 2am – that's someone else's job. If one of the camp instructors is a 'newbie', the school usually pairs them with a more experienced colleague, so there's generally someone there who knows how to deal with the tricky situations that can arise in camp.

As a place to spend part or all of your summer, Finland is hard to beat. I especially like Anjalankoski, because about five minutes from the camp there's a bicycle shop where you can rent a bike for €20–€25 a week, and spend your free time ambling through the idyllic countryside. Porvoo is also nice; you're walking distance from a stunning 14th century wooden town, and all the students are adults, so in the evenings you can go for a drink in the town and get to know them socially if you want to.

Another fan of Nordic School is **Lillian Nyamuda**. Because she is a student and English teacher in St Petersburg, it was easy for her to arrange to be interviewed by the St Petersburg-based company that runs language camps throughout Finland. The camps she applied for ran in two-week sessions during which she was expected to teach five academic hours a day, for eight days, with the other days free to explore or to join in the students' programme – mountain climbing, barbecuing, canoeing, swimming in the lake, etc.

She considered the wages to be more than satisfactory, given that they didn't have any outgoing expenses whatsoever. Everything she earned went into her pocket – and subsequently on a holiday to India at the end of her summer job. The kids and other staff were all friendly and easy going, so she felt as though she had gone on a very light working holiday. For her the kids were the highlight. Although some were spoilt because of their affluent backgrounds, the disciplinary back up at Nordic School was exemplary.

I taught a marvellous group who always did their work and were eager to learn. Yes, they had their times of being mischievous as all children do, but they were great. I soon realised they were all really afraid of their mothers, so if they misbehaved, I could simply threaten to call their mothers, and in no time at all, they would be upright, behaving well, and acting like angels. I made sure that I kept the classes exciting and engaging, and they left the camp having learnt some new stuff in English and had a great time doing it. I love kids, and spending time with them is something that I find very refreshing. I laughed so much on camp – kids really do say the darndest things! As someone whose future career is centred around Paediatrics and Child Health, this experience was valuable as well as enjoyable.

CONDITIONS OF WORK

Back in the corporate work of Finnish cities, freelance arrangements have largely replaced contracts. A teaching unit of 45 minutes is the norm, with less evening work than elsewhere. Wages are high, but so is the cost of living. Some schools compress the teaching into four days a week, leaving plenty of time for weekend exploration of the country.

Taxes are high and are usually the responsibility of the teacher, whereas contributions should be paid by the employer; social security and unemployment insurance deductions will amount to at least 6% of the salary. Note that there is virtually no possibility of accepting payment 'under the table'. The system is highly controlled and everybody pays his or her taxes.

The Finnish Embassy in London's website (www.finemb.org.uk) has limited information about living and working in Finland. Helsinki has about 35 museums and art galleries plus a high density of sports facilities, ice rinks, etc. The long dark winters are relieved by a wide choice of cheerful restaurants, cafés, bars and clubs in the cities, and saunas almost everywhere.

Norway

The trend in Norwegian EFL is similar to that in Denmark, and most schools rely on a pool of native English speakers already resident in Norway. The instructional supervisor for Berlitz Norway says that he finds it next to impossible to recruit teachers from abroad because '*they don't have a place to stay, a bank account, a work permit, can't attend interviews or training "next week". On top of this I have so many applicants who have all of these things in place and are in the Oslo area.*' Most jobs are for part-time work and of course do not offer accommodation. At least things are easier from an immigration point of view than they used to be. Although Norway is not a member of the EU, it does allow the free reciprocity of labour so that EU nationals are allowed to work in Norway without a work permit. Immigration restrictions on non-EU teachers remain stringent.

The *Yellow Pages* for Norway are available online at www.gulesider.no, though typing in *Sprakinstitut* produces only three results, of which one is Berlitz. As throughout Scandinavia, the Folkuniversity of Norway plays an important role in language tuition and hires native English speakers, mostly on an occasional basis for evening classes (www.folkeuniversitetet.no). There are branches in several hundred Norwegian municipalities with fairly major teaching operations in Stavanger, Skien, Kristiansand and Hamar. Berlitz (see entry) hires native English speakers with no TEFL background provided they are graduates and successfully complete the Berlitz Instructor Training.

The basic hourly wage is about kr160, though this can double for high-level business teaching. Expect to lose about a third in deductions.

Casual opportunities may crop up in unpredictable places. **David Moor** was simply intending to spend a month on holiday skiing in Norway, but then he saw an advert in a local supermarket for a native English teacher and jumped at the chance:

> *A teacher put me up and fed me. I'd intended to stay in the hostel or a cheap hotel, but was finding Norway expensive. I was just working for keep, teaching three days a week, so I had lots of spare time. I had a fantastic time, much better than a normal holiday.*

Sweden

For many years the EFL market has been in a slow but inexorable decline, as standards of English among school leavers have improved. The Folkuniversity of Sweden has a long-established scheme (since 1955) by which British and other native English speakers may be placed for nine months (one academic year) in a network of adult education centres throughout the country, but they no longer have a policy of actively recruiting applicants from abroad. They take on new staff who are already resident in Sweden and even then, the work is part-time, at least initially (www.folkuniversitetet.se).Originally the teaching at the Folkuniversity consisted of evening classes called a 'Study Circle', an informal conversation session. Circumstances have changed, however, and the range of pupils can be very varied from unemployed people to business executives, as well as people who want to prepare for Cambridge examinations or IELTS. People who need English at work are in the majority these days.

FINDING A JOB

Advertisements almost never appear in the educational press. Teachers with a solid ELT background might try the main state universities which put on English courses or the language schools listed in the *Yellow Pages* of Stockholm, Malmö, Gothenburg, Orebro and Uppsala. **Charlotte Rosen** decided to do a TEFL course in London before going to Sweden to be with her Swedish fiancé:

> *I had visited Sweden several times before going to Gothenburg to work. After I'd been in Sweden for about six weeks, I looked through the Yellow Pages for language schools and sent off my CV in English, which wasn't a problem because everyone speaks English really well. I was offered several interviews, including by the British Institute. Many of them said they were interested but the terms only start in September and January so you have to time your applications quite carefully.*

Another possibility is to try some of the private schools in Sweden (not fee paying, as in Britain), particularly if you are interested in staying in Sweden longer term. The Swedish school system has changed dramatically over recent years and private schools (*friskolor* – free schools) are now plentiful. There are a few English schools within the state system but most of them are independent. Internationella Engelska Skolan (www.engelska.se) is one of Sweden's leading independent English-medium schools, founded by an American, and branches have opened all over the country. The website has detailed information about teacher recruitment which applies primarily to certified subject teachers. The schools follow the Swedish curriculum, are authorised by Skolverket and are free for the students.

Cathryn Lock, who has a Swedish fiancé and a degree from an English university, started working at a secondary school a couple of years ago. She found the job through the national employment service Arbetsförmedlingen (www.ams.se), sent in a letter of application and was interviewed by the Headmaster. Cathryn has since gone on to pass a teacher exam in Sweden and she believes that it is quite possible to get a job if you come from the UK.

Although a business background will stand you in good stead, some of the private language schools accept certification, or even just a degree. The British Institute sometimes has vacancies for teachers with the CELTA. Making a breakthrough as a freelancer is difficult without a knowledge of the language, or the Swedish labour market and a functioning network of contacts.

CONDITIONS OF WORK

Teachers must pay tax in Sweden on a scale that varies according to the municipality. Swedish income tax is notoriously high, and the FU estimates that teachers lose about 30% in deductions. However, the upside of paying lots of tax is that Sweden is famous for the quality of its public services, its generous childcare and sick-day policies, and its efficient and moderately priced public transport system. Although Swedes groan about tax, they do not often express frustration that their money is 'wasted'. Constructing a lively social life can be a challenge. **Ann Hunter** points out that it can be difficult to make Swedish friends:

> *The only Swedes you meet regularly are your pupils and the professional relationship can make it awkward to socialise, though after your first term you can get to know ex-pupils quite well. Learning Swedish, if it is possible, is a good way to meet people, though your fellow students are foreigners of course.*

Andrew Boyle had mixed feeling about Sweden and Swedish people:

> *Sweden is a pleasant place to live, if a little dull at times. It is a generally liberal place, although the increasingly multicultural nature of society is causing Swedes to have to face up to their own prejudices. The students are generally of a high level and although initially quiet not unfriendly and even chatty after they know you a little better.*

Still, once you meet one outgoing Swede you'll find yourself quickly drawn into a group, which manages to avoid the horrific cost of dining out/drinks by sticking to meals and parties in people's homes, trips to free galleries and museums and various meetings of social clubs/interest groups. There are also of course cheaper places to eat out, which you'll discover once you're able to find your way around. Stockholm has a great vibe, although the stylishness of its inhabitants can sometimes be intimidating. Gothenburg has a younger feel, and is the city of choice for hip young Scandinavians (and other nationalities since the Swedish government is remarkably supportive of promising artists).

Outside the major cities, especially further north, you have to be independent and comfortable with your own company for long periods to enjoy Sweden. During the seven months of the winter the locals either hibernate or devote all their leisure to skiing. Anyone who enjoys outdoor activities will probably enjoy a stint in Sweden, especially ramblers and hill-walkers, who take advantage of the *Allemannsrätt*, the law which guarantees free access to the countryside for everyone. Island hopping around the (car free) Stockholm archipelago with a tent is an excellent and cheap way to enjoy nature, eat far too many cinnamon buns and lie around in the sun. Summers are usually very warm, certainly more so than in Britain, which is why so many Swedes have an enviable golden tan.

should find it fairly easy to land a job this way. With a knowledge of Spanish, you can also fill one of the many vacancies for teachers of children, or low-level adult classes, but speaking Spanish is not a must for most jobs. The usual process is to put together a timetable from various sources and be reconciled to the fact that some or all of your employers in your first year will exploit you to some degree. Those who stay on for a second or further years can become more choosy.

The situation for Americans has become almost impossible if they want to work legally (see section on Regulations below).

Companies such as ModLang in Zaragoza (www.modlang.es) cunningly interweave sport and language learning by running intensive English and sports summer courses for children aged 5–18. For these, native English speakers are recruited in large numbers before the end of March, to teach the language and coach sports and/or supervise swimming. Other companies to try include Red Leaf (www.redleaf.es), Eurobridge International (www.eurobridge.net), McGrogans Summer School (www.mcgroganschool.com) and TECS (see entry).

FINDING A JOB

Because schools run the whole gamut from prestigious to cowboy, every method of job-hunting works at some level. Many independent language schools are run by expatriate Britons and Irish people, and a few of these will offer guidance and support for newer teachers as well as opportunities for further professional development.

IN ADVANCE

Candidates who know that they want to teach in Spain should consider doing their TEFL training with an organisation with strong Spanish links such as OxfordTEFL in London with schools in Barcelona and Cadiz (see Training chapter: Trinity College TESOL courses). Better still, do your training in Spain, which will allow you to get to know the country, and the specific needs of the students, to take advantage of the job guidance of trainers that know the local job market well, as well as being on the spot for job vacancies. This option is often even cheaper than staying in the UK, given the lower cost of living and the fact that many centres offer a package that includes low-priced accommodation. International House has centres in Barcelona and Madrid offering the CELTA course, as does CLIC in Seville.

ANDY HEATH

Andy Heath describes how he made good use of the Spanish TEFL Jobs Fair.

Fresh out of my CELTA course and with very little idea of what to do next, I was lucky enough to hear about the Spainwise Recruitment Fair, a kind of one-stop shop for TEFL jobs across the country. The only problem was I had already booked a return ticket home. Attending the fair would involve travelling to and from Spain twice in a month, difficult on a teacher's salary, almost out of reach of an unemployed one. I was serious about teaching, though, and equally serious about finding a good place to *do it. I'd heard all the scare stories about exploitation, fly-by-night schools and shady operators. The chance to meet dozens of potential employers face to face and size them up while they did the same to me seemed too good to pass up.*

A month later, as I mulled over three job offers, each in a different province of Spain and each from someone I was sure I would enjoy working with, I knew I'd made the right decision. The school I chose, Academia Blue Door in Cordoba, eased me through all the red tape and helped me with accommodation, as all the schools involved in Spainwise had offered to do. The job itself involved longer hours than you would ever teach without a break in England, but I appreciated the way that teaching in the evenings left mornings and afternoons free to sleep or enjoy life in a new city. A 10 o'clock finish coincides with when most Spaniards finish their dinner and start thinking about which bar to visit afterwards, so you don't miss much nightlife.

For a listing of English language schools in Spain, the most complete source is the *Yellow Pages* which can be accessed on the internet (www.paginas-amarillas.es) – you simply type in 'Academias de Idiomas' and the city or town of interest. You can find a list of members of FECEI, the national federation of language schools (*Federación Española de Centros de Enseñanza de Idiomas*) on the Spainwise website (www.spainwise.net). Also on the Spainwise site you will find details of the annual Spanish TEFL Jobs Fair held in late May, which acts as a showcase for FECEI schools. For further details, contact Aidan O'Toole (info@spainwise.net).

FECEI is concerned with maintaining high standards, so its members are committed to providing a high quality of teaching and fair working conditions for teachers. FECEI schools represent the elite end of the market and are usually looking for well-qualified teachers. However, FECEI represents only a fraction of the thousands of language schools that exist, and there are many quality language institutions that are not members of FECEI.

British or Irish nationals with a TEFL qualification or PGCE might want to make use of a recruitment agency, whether a general one or one which specialises in Spain such as EES Madrid (see entry). The owner Richard Harrison has been interviewing, assessing and recommending teachers to client schools since 1986, charges no fee to teachers and can advise and help with all the red tape and in finding either short-term or long-term accommodation in Madrid. It is a big help for teachers with little or no Spanish to have the paperwork in place early which usually results in more doors opening for potential employment.

He suggests that candidates with just a degree and TEFL qualification should come to Spain in early September and contact his agency on arrival since he is at his busiest through September and well into October trying to satisfy requests for teachers from client schools all over Spain. However, schools continue to request teachers throughout the academic year and for summer intensive and residential courses and applications are welcome at any time. Richard Harrison also runs a small English-speaking theatre company based in Madrid called Moving Parts (richardinmadrid@gmail.com), which tours Spain throughout the academic year and offers paid work to young teachers with performance ability, especially those applying in pairs. Speculative applications are welcome at any time.

Successful candidates from TtMadrid (see entry in Directory of Training Courses Worldwide; www.ttmadrid.com) are directed to several Madrid agencies such as the English Teachers Collective (www.etcspain.com) and Pembroke Educational Consultants (www.peceducacion.com). Another teaching agency to try is Training Express (jobs@trainingexpress.es; www.trainingexpress.es), which also offers teaching by telephone and has its principal offices in Madrid, Bilbao and Barcelona.

ON THE SPOT

Most teaching jobs in Spain are found on the spot. Interlang Business Language Centre in Madrid (address below) is hardly unusual in stipulating that they meet all candidates in person before hiring so do all their interviewing in Madrid only. With increasing competition from candidates with solid TEFL qualifications it is more and more difficult for the under-qualified to succeed. The best time to look is between the end of the summer holidays and the start of term which falls in the first two weeks of October, although you can find jobs in late October too. Since a considerable number of teachers do not return to their jobs after the Christmas break and schools are often left in the lurch, early January may also be possible. Try outlying towns and suburbs if work is scarce in the city centres. In Madrid there are usually at least part-time jobs going most months of the academic year, though after Easter demand dies down. Many schools shut over the summer, but there is some work to be had in those that remain open, since most of their teachers disappear over the summer too, as well as teaching kids in a number of English summer camps dotted around the country.

Once in Spain, the local press is very useful, for example newspapers such as the twice-weekly *Cambalache* in Seville, the *Vanguardia* on Sunday and the daily *Segundamano*. In *El Pais* look in the classified section of the salmon-coloured supplement Negocios, under 'Idiomas', and in *Segundamano* under 'Ofertas de Empleo – Profesores'. The classified advert papers *Cambalache* and *Segundamano* are also good for flat hunting, as is the webpage www.loquo.com which also carries some teaching jobs in its employment listings (can be viewed in English).

In Madrid is a printed English language magazine that can be consulted online (www.in-madrid.com) including display adverts for teaching posts and free 'job wanted' adverts.

The website www.madridteacher.com is a comprehensive source of information about teaching opportunities in Madrid (specifically), and also in the rest of Spain. It is run by a group of freelance teachers who teach in small and mid-sized companies, academies, schools and with private students in Madrid. The Expatriate Café website (www.expatriatecafe.com/index.php?option=weblinks&Itemid=4&topid=7) contains an annotated list of potential employers, as well as useful information about TEFL training, certification and ESL.

Local magazines may advertise the possibility of *intercambio* which means an exchange of English for Spanish or Catalan conversation practice – a great way to meet locals. Some Irish pubs not only offer the opportunity to meet other expats but often organise weekly *intercambio* nights, which will be listed in the English-speaking press. English language bookshops sometimes have a noticeboard with relevant notices, as do the EOIs (*Escuelas Oficial de Idiomas*) in major cities (these are enormous state-sponsored official language schools with up to 10,000 students).

After finishing A levels, **Sam James** and **Sophie Ellison** decided to spend their gap year in Barcelona if possible. After acquiring their Trinity TESOL Certificates in their destination city, they did the rounds of the language schools:

> *Though tedious, this did work and we doubt we would have found work any other way. Job availability didn't seem that high in Barcelona when we were looking in October and we both accepted our only job offers. (Our age may have put off some employers.) Most schools seem to have recruited in September, so October was a bit of a lean month. I got my job by covering a class at two hours notice for a teacher who had called in sick. When this teacher decided to leave Barcelona, I was interviewed and offered her classes on a permanent basis. I got the job permanently about a fortnight after handing out CVs. Sophie was asked to her first interview after about three weeks of job-hunting. She was selected but then had to wait for several more weeks while her contract was finalised.*

Conventional wisdom says that the beginning of summer is the worst time to travel out to Spain to look for work since schools will be closed and their owners unobtainable. However, **Sam James** handed round his CV again in May (when his hours were cut) and was given some encouragement. He thinks that because so few teachers look for work just six weeks before the end of the academic year, employers are sometimes in need of replacements and this might well be a way for teachers to get ahead of the queue for September jobs. With so many no-frills cheap flights on the market, it might be worth a gamble.

When knocking on doors, bear in mind that most language academies will be closed between 2pm and 4pm when directors are invariably away from their desks. Leave a CV with your contact telephone number. It is a very good idea to buy a mobile or at least an inexpensive local SIM card with a local number for your own phone. A serious director will probe into claims of experience and will soon weed out any bogus stories. Other directors are just checking to see that you are a reasonable proposition or at least not a complete dud.

A more probable scenario for the untrained is that they will elicit some mild interest from one or two schools and will be told that they may be contacted right at the beginning of term and offered a few hours of teaching. The academies do not know how many classes they will offer and how many teachers they will need until students finish signing up in October. It can become a war of nerves; anyone who is willing and can afford to stay on has an increasingly good chance of becoming established.

The great cities of Madrid and Barcelona act as magnets to thousands of hopeful teachers. **Sam James** blamed his lack of job security and bitty hours on Barcelona's popularity, '*the result of the great supply of willing teachers here keeping working conditions down and making it hard to exert any leverage on an employer when one is so easily replaced*'. For this reason other towns may answer your requirements better. There are language academies all along the north coast and a door-to-door job hunt in September might pay off. This is the time when tourists are departing so accommodation may be available at a reasonable rent on a nine-month lease.

LIVE-IN POSITIONS

People from outside the EU who want to experience Spanish culture might like to consider a live-in position with a family who wants an English tutor for their children or a voluntary position as an English assistant on summer language/sports camps. Further details may be sought from Relaciones Culturales, the youth exchange organisation at Calle Ferraz 82, 28008 Madrid (+34 91 541 71 03; www.clubrci.es), which places native English speakers aged 18–40 with Spanish families who want to practise their English in exchange for providing room and board; the placement fee is €300.

FREELANCE TEACHING

As usual, private tutoring can pay better than contract teaching because there is no middle man. **Stuart Britton** easily found private pupils to supplement his school income in a small town in the untouristy north of Las Palmas de Gran Canaria. However when his employer found out, he was told to drop them or risk being sacked, even over the summer when the school was closed and Stuart had no other source of income. He resented this so much that he advises not bothering with small schools, and simply concentrating on obtaining private students.

MICHELLE MANION

Michelle Manion from Australia enjoyed taking part in an exchange programme. Several American organisations including InterExchange in New York (www.interexchange.org) and AIDE (www.aideabroad. org) arrange Teach in Spain programmes whereby fee-paying young Americans (mainly women) live with a family in exchange for speaking English and providing 15 hours of tutoring a week for 1–3 months; fees are from $700 to $1,000.

I would recommend live-in tutoring to anyone in my situation, i.e. anyone who wants to live in Spain but not as an au pair and is not entitled to a work permit. I was placed with a family with two boys aged 11 and 14. In the morning I went off for my Spanish lesson and then gave a lesson to the boys in turn. Spanish boys are notorious for being spoilt and impossible to control, but also for possessing wonderful personalities and great senses of humour. Carlos and César were typically Spanish and always managed to be both delightful and infuriating. Anyone interested in undertaking this venture should try to ascertain the children's level of English before arriving in Spain and to bring textbooks, magazines and children's books to work with, since English books are difficult to find in Spain. Also, when you arrive in Spain try to make as many friends and take up every opportunity you're given as this is the best way to learn Spanish.

As always, it is difficult to start up without contacts and a good knowledge of the language; and when you do get started it is difficult to earn a stable income due to the frequency with which pupils cancel. The problem is particularly acute in May when undergraduates and school pupils concentrate on preparing for exams and other activities fall by the wayside. Spaniards are fond of taking off the days between a mid-week fiesta and the weekend known as *puente*, meaning bridge.

Getting private lessons is a marketing exercise and you will have to explore all the avenues which seem appropriate to your circumstances. Obviously you can advertise on noticeboards at universities, EOIs, community centres (*centros cívicos*), public libraries, corner shops and wherever you think there is a market. Major stores are a good bet, for example Jumbo and Al Campo in Madrid. A neat notice in Spanish along the lines of '*Profesora Nativa da clases particulares a domicilio*' might elicit a favourable response. Introduce yourself at local state schools and ask them to pin up a notice broadcasting your willingness to ensure the children's linguistic future. Compile a list of addresses of professionals (e.g. lawyers, architects, etc.) as they may need English for their work and have the wherewithal to pay for it. Try export businesses, distribution companies, perhaps even travel agencies. Make the acquaintance of language teachers who will know of openings.

Because private classes can be so much better paid than institute teaching, they are much in demand, including by contract teachers, most of whom are engaged in some private tutoring. The ideal is to arrange a school contract with no more than 15 or 20 hours and supplement this with private classes, which are lucrative though unstable.

REGULATIONS

All EU citizens planning to live in Spain for more than three months are obliged to register in person at the Foreigners' Office (*Oficina de Extranjeros*) in the province of residence or at a designated police station. You will be issued with a Residence Certificate stating your name, address, nationality, identity number and date of registration. The number on your resident card is your NIE (*Número de Identidad de Extranjeros*), an identification number necessary for filing taxes, establishing a business, opening a bank account (not necessary for foreign accounts), and for almost any other form. Once you start work, your employer should apply for a social security (*Seguridad Social*) number on your behalf; if you are self-employed, this is your responsibility. All people with an address in Spain including foreigners are obliged to register at the *padrón* office in their local town hall which is free of charge.

Many long-stay foreigners engage a specialist lawyer called a *Gestoria Administrava* to assist in navigating the bureaucracy. The websites of the British Embassy in Spain (http://ukinspain.fco.gov.uk) and Spain Expat (www.spainexpat.com) have pages of useful information about living and working in Spain, while the online community www.eyeonspain.com has some busy forums. Alternatively teacher recruitment agencies like EES can advise.

The immigration situation for people from outside Europe is very difficult indeed. Most of the schools that once hired North Americans now refuse to tackle the lengthy procedures involved in obtaining work permits. Berlitz cautions, '*unfortunately, the European Union (EU), of which Spain is a part, seldom issues work permits to non-EU citizens unless they are married to an EU national.*' Americans with Irish or Italian ancestry often prefer to chase the papers that will get them an EU passport.

This pessimistic view of the chances for Americans and Canadians was voiced by so many schools that it seems almost superfluous to describe the procedures. Briefly, you need to submit a slightly dizzying array of documents to the *Subdelegación del Gobierno* in the city you are trying to move to and work in, including, but not restricted to, an official job offer form, original official company fiscal identity document, and official certification that the job on offer has already been advertised in the official Provincial Unemployment Office and that no suitable European candidate has applied. Then you need to make an appointment with the Spanish Consulate serving your official home address (in country of origin) in order to process all the documentation that they require for a work visa, including, among others, a formal job offer from an employer in Spain, a recent medical certificate, *antecedents penales* (police certificate of good character), notarised degree certificate and seven passport photographs. Once your home country's Spanish consulate has processed your work visa, you have to fetch it in person. It cannot be handed to anyone other than you. Then you can return to Spain and finalise applications for a work/residence permit. According to Institut Nord-America (www.ien.es) in Barcelona, which has a vested interest in employing people with a North American accent, visa processing takes 12–16 months. They go on to stipulate that they prefer '*applicants with Spanish/European work permit/citizenship*', for obvious reasons.

None of this means that there aren't any Americans or other nationalities teaching in Spain without permits. According to **Jon Loop**, many post-Hemingway Americans go to Spain for a year to learn Spanish and 'find themselves man' (or maybe even find themselves a man). The teacher-training schools in major cities are full of American as well as British trainees, and Americans, Australians and New Zealanders also find work, not just teaching private classes but through numerous intrepid academies who hire them off-contract and send them off to teach in companies rather than on school premises. Anyone who works on a Schengen tourist visa will have to leave after three months and is prohibited from returning for at least 90 days.

Social security (*seguridad social*) contributions are between 4% and 7% of earnings, typically 6.4%. Tax residents will need to pay income taxes in Spain and are generally defined as those who live in Spain for more than 183 days in each calendar year. However, www.spainexpat.com suggests that in many cases you only need to file a tax return in Spain when you make more than €22,000 per year, unlikely if you are a language teacher. Spain and Britain have a double taxation treaty: for more information follow the links from www.hmrc.gov.uk/cnr/form_spain.htm. Under EU legislation, language schools must give contracts and make contributions for all staff, whether full-time or part-time. In practice, this does not always happen. After a few months of teaching for one academy, Jon Loop asked for a contract and was given a special 11-hour contract (though at the time he was teaching 20 hours a week). Contracts for fewer than 12 hours a week do not require more than minimal social security contributions. **Joanna Mudie** from the Midlands describes the situation which results from this:

> There's a great deal of uncertainty and insecurity about all aspects of work: hours, days, rates of pay, insurance, etc. Contracts (if you're lucky enough to get one) are a load of rubbish because employers put down far fewer hours on paper to avoid paying so much insurance, and also to protect themselves if business dwindles. My advice is, forget your English sense of honesty and obeying the law. 'When in Rome…' Relax and simply don't worry about the legalities. It usually seems to work out okay, and if not, well, it's a nice life in the sun.

Schools that sidestep the regulations to maximise profits and who do not pay contributions to cover their employees' social security might well be the ones willing to employ non-Europeans and pay cash in hand.

CONDITIONS OF WORK

Salaries are not high in Spain and have not increased significantly over more than a decade. A further problem for teachers in Madrid and Barcelona is that there is not much difference between salaries in the big cities where the cost of living has escalated and salaries in the small towns. The minimum net salary is about €900 per month, though most schools offer €1,000–€1,150 after deductions for 25 hours of teaching a week. A standard hourly wage would start at €14, although some pay their starter teachers more. The very best paid hourly wages are paid to registered freelancers sent out to firms. Spanish TEFL is no different from TEFL in other countries in that there are lots of employers offering low pay, long hours and exploitative conditions. For example, teachers have discovered that pay has been deducted when they have been unavoidably absent or that their bonuses have been withheld with no explanation. **Sam James** was taken aback when his hours were drastically cut by his employer in Barcelona with no notice. The simple explanation was that Sam was working without a contract, which would have guaranteed a certain number of hours. He advises getting a contract if at all possible, even on a lower rate of pay, since contracts bring security, a reliable income and holiday pay (which he knows because his girlfriend Sophie had one).

As always, you can gain an idea of an employer's integrity by talking to other teachers as well as by using your intuition at the interview. Asking lots of questions is a good idea since then you can find out your pay and maximum hours so that you will be in a stronger position to argue should your employer try to mess you around. But realistically, most new arrivals feel exploited at least in some respects in their first year. **Laura Phibbs** was spared the possibility of being exploited, since her promised job evaporated overnight:

The Madrid school director rang me to inform me that I had got the job and I was to start nine days later. When, as instructed, I rang to confirm the arrival time of my plane, I was told that there was no job for me after all since the school had gone bankrupt. I think what really made me angry was that I had rung him rather than the other way round. He did not even say sorry or sound in the least remorseful.

It is possible that the bankruptcy was just an excuse in the face of insufficient pupils. Some schools tend to work their teachers hard, and a load of 25 contact hours plus is commonplace. Considering that preparation and travelling is extra, this can result in a gruelling schedule. The ideal full-time timetable is 24–26 teaching hours a week. **Dennis Bricault** refers to the notoriously uncongenial timetable of most EFL teachers (and not just in Spain) as a 'bookend schedule', whereby you might have to teach between 8am and 10am, then again through the evening. According to Spanish law, workers are not entitled to paid holiday until they have been working for 12 months, hence the near-universality of nine-month contracts. Most teachers find it impossible to save enough in nine months to fund themselves abroad for the rest of the year. Most pay agreements also already include the bonuses (*pagas extraordinarias*) which have already been pro-rated, of which there are two or three a year. Legal schools will pay *finiquito* (holiday pay) at the end of a contract which should be equivalent to the pay for two and a half days of every month worked, based on your base (not full) salary.

If the terms of a contract are being breached and the employer does not respond to the teacher's reminders, recourse can be taken by means of a *denuncia*, which involves informing the authorities (either in person or via a union, such as the *Commissiones Obreros*) that your school is not complying with, for example, tax and social security rules or fire regulations. The *denuncia* can effectively close a school if it is taken seriously and if the school does not have the proverbial friends in high places. In fact the procedure is complicated and time-consuming but the mere mention of it might improve your working conditions.

The experience of teaching at a summer camp can be entirely different. The pay is generally fair (say, €800 for a four-week stint plus free board and accommodation, rising to €1,200, including accommodation, if you're particularly fortunate) though some organisations offer little more than accommodation, meals and pocket money. **Glen Williams** describes his summer job at a summer language camp in Izarra in the Basque Country:

The children learned English for three hours in the morning with one half hour break (but not for the teacher on morning snack duty trying to fight off the hordes from ripping apart the bocadillos). Then we had another three or four hours of duties ranging from sports and/or arts to shop/bank duty. For many of us, inexperienced with dealing with groups of kids, there were a few problems of discipline. It was the kids' holiday and they quickly cottoned on that we English teachers in general were a bunch of hippie types.

BARRY O'LEARY

Barry O'Leary wrote from Seville in his third year of teaching there. In his first year he worked for a slightly disorganised and crafty academy where there was no mention of a contract, classes started at 8am and staggered throughout the day until 10pm and it was difficult to predict how much you would earn from month to month because of all the unpaid festivals in Spain. Luckily in his second year, after mingling with the other ex-pat teachers, he was able to land himself a job with a more professional establishment. He now works fixed hours from 4pm until 10pm, Monday to Thursday, leaving the mornings free, and there are excellent ongoing training sessions on Friday mornings. The language school is one of the most successful in Seville with 12 academies scattered throughout the city and it takes care of its teachers, offering fixed contracts for long-term prospects.

The students, who are often passionate and keen to learn English, range in age from six to 60 so there is never a dull moment. Classes have a maximum of 12, all material is provided and there is scope to move away from the syllabus now and then. A lot of extra work is necessary in February and June when the exams take place but it's worth the agony.

Life in Seville is fun and varied, with an abundance of festivals including the religious Semana Santa and the livelier Feria. The city is a great place to live and a base for exploring Andalucía. Evenings can be spent in the many bars enjoying tapas, watching flamenco or Sevillanas (a local dance) or just mingling with the locals. Seville is generally safe and with the year-round blue skies, it's a great place to brush up on your Spanish and experience a different way of life.

PUPILS

For reasons which remain obscure, Spaniards have the reputation for being somewhat challenged at learning languages. This is more tolerable in adults who are motivated, but often hard-going with children (unless you are especially fond of kids). This was one of **David Bourne**'s biggest problems and one which he thinks is underestimated, especially as a high proportion of English teaching in some academies is with children and teenagers:

> *I have found that a lot of the younger students only come here because their parents have sent them in order to improve their exam results. The children themselves would much rather be outside playing football. There are days when you spend most of the lesson trying (unsuccessfully in my case) to keep them quiet. This is especially true on Fridays. I have found it very hard work trying to inject life into a class of bored 10-year-olds, particularly when the course books provided are equally uninspiring.*

In such cases it might be a good idea to change your aim, from teaching them English to entertaining them (and paying your rent). If students don't want to learn, you will only break your heart trying to achieve the impossible.

Adults are usually an easier proposition, willing to listen and think and with a good sense of humour. In general the Spanish will welcome opportunities to speak animatedly in class and express their opinions. A good knowledge of Spanish is helpful if not essential when teaching junior classes as **Peter Saliba**, director of a language school in Malaga, explains:

> *We need teachers with a fluent command of Spanish, not the typical grasp of elementary phrases which may get them by in a social context. On a limited two or three hour per week teaching timetable, there simply is not time for cumbersome English explanations of English grammar and vocabulary. It is worse still with young learners and teens, who will 'run riot' or at the very least run circles round non-Castilian speaking teachers.*

Needless to say, Spaniards are a nation of talkers. If things seem to be going awry in your classes, for example students turning up late or being inattentive, don't hesitate to make your feelings known, just as Spaniards do.

ACCOMMODATION

Rents usually swallow up at least a quarter of a teacher's income, more in the big cities and much more if you don't share. In small towns, it is not uncommon for schools to arrange accommodation for their teachers at least for an initial period. Many Spanish students want to live with English students so check language school, EOI, and university noticeboards for flat shares, especially in the Facultad de Filologia, which includes the Department of English. Some teachers even arrange to share a flat rent-free in exchange for English lessons.

When renting a flat expect to pay a month's rent in advance, plus one or two months' rent as deposit. Since your first pay cheque may not arrive until November, you should arrive with £1,000+ to tide you over. Try to avoid using an *inmobiliaria* (property agency) which will charge a further month's rent (at least). Be aware of the agencies or associations with seedy premises that charge you a fee before showing you anything. You will quickly distinguish their ads from private ones in the classifieds. In Madrid and Barcelona many people use the free ads paper *Segundamano*; if you do decide to compete for a flat listed in this paper, get up early since most decent flats are gone by 8am. When **Barry O'Leary** was looking for a two-bedroomed apartment to rent in central Seville, he advertised in Spanish on the university noticeboard site http://sevilla.campusanuncios.com. It is easier flat hunting in July/August than in September/October or February.

LEISURE TIME

Once you acquire some Spanish, it is very easy to meet people, since Spaniards are so friendly, relaxed and willing to invite newcomers out with them. Of course there is also a strong fraternity of EFL teachers almost everywhere. With luck you will end up socialising with both groups in bars, at parties, *romerías* (pilgrimages), *fiestas*, etc.

If you're looking for traditional Spanish culture, don't go to Madrid, and certainly don't look for it in Barcelona which is not Spanish at all but Catalan. Seville, Granada and Valencia are lovely Spanish cities. While teaching in Andalucia, **Joanna Mudie** appreciated the chance to learn about the traditional but still very much alive dances of Spain, e.g. Sevillanas, Malagueras and Pasadoble.

Deryn Collins is clearly enjoying a good quality of life while teaching at the Academia Blue Door in Córdoba:

> *Living in Spain gives me freedom. I never have to get up with an alarm; I have my mornings free to enjoy my hobbies and attend classes myself, and go for lazy breakfasts with friends before work. Then I get another time for myself after my day's work is done. I can go to the cinema at midnight, meet friends for tapas and a beer, go to the pub quiz, dance my socks off or listen to some live blues in a dark and smoky dive. At weekends I get out into the country, or explore the rest of the province around Cordoba...*
>
> *Teaching in Spain has provided me with an easy and relaxed lifestyle with more job satisfaction than I've found in any other field. Remember never mind how brilliant or grotty the job is, nor how great or awful the pay, nor how marvellous the working conditions are or aren't, you will not be happy in Spain (or anywhere else) unless you come with the right attitude. Come with a desire to integrate into the culture, to learn the language and to develop both on a professional and personal level.*

Glen Williams describes his spare time activities in Madrid, a city with an enormous variety of nightlife where he was clearly enjoying himself to the full:

> *Madrid is a crazy place. We usually stay out all night at the weekend drinking and boogying. During the gaps in my timetable (10–2 and 4–7) I pretend to study Spanish (I'm no natural) and just wander the back streets. I suppose I should try to be more cultural and learn to play an instrument, write poetry or look at paintings, but I never get myself in gear. I think most people teach English in Spain as a means to live in Spain and learn the Spanish language and culture. But there is a real problem that you end up living in an English enclave, teaching English all day and socialising with English teachers. You have to make a big effort to get out of this rut. I am lucky to live with Spanish people (who do not want to practise their English!).*

A few schools offer free or subsidised Spanish lessons as a perk to teachers. Otherwise investigate the government-run *Escuela Oficial de Idiomas*.

If the idea of teaching in Spain appeals at all, it is almost always a rewarding and memorable way for people with limited work experience to finance themselves as they travel and live abroad for a spell.

CLIC INTERNATIONAL HOUSE SEVILLE

Damien Burton is a graduate of CLIC International House Seville

'In August 2006 I arrived in Seville, a city that had always appealed to me, beckoning to me across thousands of kilometres to come and sample its rich history, its dazzling architecture, its glorious cuisine and the heady atmosphere of its picturesque squares and narrow streets. A place to visit?

Sure. A place to stay a few weeks? Definitely. A place to build a life? I didn't plan it so, but Seville and the life here took my heart and nearly six years later it is within this city that it still beats.

'I had come to do my CELTA course at CLIC International House Sevilla. I would be lying if I said I hadn't been nervous that first morning. I had nearly got lost in the labyrinthine twists and turns of the city centre, but I managed to arrive on time. Just. My class mates were nervous too, but there was an energy there, a sense that we were all embarking on something significant together. And so it proved. The course was a whirlwind of new ideas, fresh focus, academic growth and the building of confidence. Friendships were forged that I still hold dear to this day. I came out of the four week intensive course ready to begin my work, a job that is primarily about people. You can learn many things from books, but it is the interaction with people that helps them to reach their full potential.

'Suddenly I had options, possibilities that I had never thought I would have. Should I go to Italy? Poland? China? South America? Teach back home in Britain? Go down under? The CELTA qualification I had just received had become so much more than a piece of paper; it had become a passport to a new life.

'In the end that was not to be my fate. Love and life intervened, but I am still living in the city that I had admired and experiencing a life that I could have only dreamt of back home in rainy Wales, staring at the water drops running sluggishly down the window pane. I guess it all comes down to decisions. I made the decision to change my life and through TEFL I have achieved that. Choosing to do the CELTA was like opening up a Pandora's box of possibilities.'

LIST OF EMPLOYERS

ACADEMIA BLUE DOOR
C/Alhaken II, 6, 14008 Cordoba
+34 957 491535
recruitment@bluedoorspain.com
or info@spainwise.net
www.bluedoorspain.com

NUMBER OF TEACHERS: 12.

QUALIFICATIONS: Native speakers of English with university degree and TEFL qualifications.

CONDITIONS OF EMPLOYMENT: Student groups no larger than 6. Contracts are from the end of September to the end of June.

SALARY: School offers a competitive package with salary above national pay agreements plus full national health and social security cover.

RECRUITMENT: Blue Door is a member of ACEIA and FECEI, and recruits at the Spainwise annual recruitment fair in May (www. spainwise.net).

CONTACT: Aidan O'Toole, Director (+34 692 613687).

ACADEMIA BRITANICA International House Cordoba
C/Rodriguez Sanchez, 15,14003 Cordoba
+34 957 470350
info-cordoba@acabri.com
www.acabri.com

NUMBER OF TEACHERS: 20, also for branch in Huelva.

PREFERENCE OF NATIONALITY: EU passport holders who can get residence permits easily.

QUALIFICATIONS: A or B in CELTA plus minimum 1 year's experience, especially in teaching younger learners.

CONDITIONS OF EMPLOYMENT: 9-month contracts, mid-September to mid-June, 22–25 hours per week.

SALARY: Monthly average around €1,600 gross. Average 12% tax; 6.5% social security deductions.

FACILITIES/SUPPORT: Help with finding accommodation. Residence permits are applied for by the school and the teacher is accompanied to the permits office soon after arrival.

RECRUITMENT: Through IH recruitment system, or locally. Interviews in the UK for teachers recruited through IH World.

CONTACT: Simon Armour, Director of Studies (simon@acabri.com).

ASTEX SERVICIOS LINGUISTICOS

C/Hermanos Bécquer 7–6°, 28006 Madrid

+34 91 590 3754

aslpedagogico@astex.es or jmcamacho@astex.es

www.astex.es

NUMBER OF TEACHERS: ASTEX employs around 350 ESL teachers at any one time, and usually hires 30 new teachers each September/October, with vacancies needing to be filled throughout the year. More than 50% of their classes are phone lessons which can be given from anywhere in the world.

PREFERENCE OF NATIONALITY: Native English speakers.

QUALIFICATIONS: Require CELTA or equivalent and minimum 2 years' EFL teaching experience. For telephone classes a specific training course (2 sessions of 3 hours) must be completed.

CONDITIONS OF EMPLOYMENT: 9-months contract/20–25 hours per week.

SALARY: Contracted teachers earn €17–€17.50 gross; freelancers earn €23–24 gross.

FACILITIES/SUPPORT: Teachers' room: library, computers (free internet) and printer. Free workshops for teachers.

RECRUITMENT: Interview required.

CONTACT: David Warner, Director Servicios Lingüísticos (dwarner@astex.es).

BERLITZ (ESCUELAS DE IDIOMAS BERLITZ DE ESPAÑA)

HQ, Enrique Granados 6, Complejo Empresarial IMCE, 28223 Pozuelo de Alarcón. Recruitment office: Calle Jose Ortega y Gasset 11, 1° Izq, Barrio de Salamanca, 28006 Madrid

+34 91 577 7259

teach@berlitz.es

www.berlitz.es

---

10 Centres in Spain: 5 in Madrid, 2 in Barcelona, 1 in Seville, 1 Palma de Majorca, and 1 in Valencia.

NUMBER OF TEACHERS: Berlitz Spain employs approx 100 native speakers.

PREFERENCE OF NATIONALITY: EU (for paperwork reasons).

QUALIFICATIONS: Degree level of education; no teaching qualification required as Berlitz provides training.

CONDITIONS OF EMPLOYMENT: 9-month contracts. Depending on contract type, hours range from an average of 9 (smallest part-time) to 28 hours (full-time) per week, but can vary. Schedules are also quite varied.

SALARY: Depends on which of six contract types. For first-year teachers, total deductions are around 8%.

FACILITIES/SUPPORT: No assistance with accommodation.

RECRUITMENT: Via adverts on various Spanish websites. Face-to-face interviews essential.

CONTACT: Simon Williamson, Country Manager of Instruction.

BRITISH SCHOOL

Plaza Ponent, 5–2nd floor, 43001 Tarragona

british@bstarragona.com

www.bstarragona.com

NUMBER OF TEACHERS: 5.

PREFERENCE OF NATIONALITY: Native English speakers with EU passport.

QUALIFICATIONS: University degree, CELTA or Trinity EFL teaching qualification and minimum 1 year's experience teaching English abroad.

CONDITIONS OF EMPLOYMENT: October to June, 21 class hours per week.

SALARY: Gross salary €1,158.34 per month for 21 class hours a week; new-year bonus €260 and end-of-contract holiday pay €662 and travel expenses €228.

FACILITIES/SUPPORT: First week's accommodation paid in hotel; school video and book libraries.

RECRUITMENT: Internet with telephone interview.

CONTACT: Bernard Tingle, Director.

BVRNS ACADEMY

Kalebarria 44–46 bajo, Durango, +34 48200 Vizcaya

+34 946 203 668

info@bvrnsacademy.com

www.bvrnsacademy.com

NUMBER OF TEACHERS: 5.

PREFERENCE OF NATIONALITY: British, native English speakers; also bilingual French-English.

QUALIFICATIONS: Degree, TEFL qualification and experience. Teachers should be cheerful, lively, genuinely interested in teaching and enjoy working with both children and adults. Some knowledge of Spanish preferable.

CONDITIONS OF EMPLOYMENT: Standard 9-month contract. Students vary from young children to mature adults. Courses are grouped according to their level and age and take place mainly in the afternoon and evening (some in the morning). Maximum 8 in a class. Number of teaching hours around 25.

SALARY: €1,400 per month for academic year. Bonus at Christmas of €200 and at the end of the course €400 on successful completion of contract.

FACILITIES/SUPPORT: Shared furnished room in a flat available for rent of about €270 monthly plus bills.

RECRUITMENT: Telephone interview required.

CONTACT: Ana Lopez, Director.

CAMBRIDGE ENGLISH STUDIES
Avenida de Arteijo 8–1°, 15004 A Coruña
+34 981 160 216
www.cambridgeenglishstudies.com

NUMBER OF TEACHERS: 12 teachers, 8 in Coruña and 4 in Ferrol.

QUALIFICATIONS: Teachers must be EU nationals and hold a recognised TESOL qualification (e.g. CELTA/Trinity College London/RELSA).

CONDITIONS OF EMPLOYMENT: Contracts run from mid-September to end June, teaching 25 hours per week.

SALARY: Basic net salary is €1,000 per month plus increments for experience and qualifications. Taxes and social security paid by the school.

RECRUITMENT: Interviews required, but telephone interview is acceptable.

CAMBRIDGE HOUSE
C/Lopez de Hoyos, 95 1°A, 28002 Madrid
+34 91 519 4603/81346677
teachers@cambridge-house.com
www.cambridge-house.com

NUMBER OF TEACHERS: 35.

PREFERENCE OF NATIONALITY: British or Irish teachers. In the case of non-EU teachers, they must already have their working papers.

QUALIFICATIONS: University degree, CELTA certificate and a minimum of 6 months teaching experience.

CONDITIONS OF EMPLOYMENT: The average length of contract is 9 months (October to June) but summer work is available to teachers who want to stay on. Contact hours are between 22 and 26 with 3 hours paid preparation.

FACILITIES/SUPPORT: Advice offered on accommodation and help in all matters of social security and residency application. Full social security payments and a work contract guaranteed. Workshops and staff meetings are held regularly to inform teachers of any extra courses available.

RECRUITMENT: Applications are received by email and acknowledged immediately. CVs are kept on file for future vacancies that crop up.

CONTACT: Penny Rollinson, Director of Studies.

CAMBRIDGE SCHOOL
Placa Manel Montanya 4, 08400 Granollers, Barcelona
+34 93 870 2001
admin@cambridgeschool.com
www.cambridgeschool.com

NUMBER OF TEACHERS: 65.

PREFERENCE OF NATIONALITY: Native English speakers who can legally work in Spain, i.e. EU members or non-EU members with a work permit.

QUALIFICATIONS: At least CELTA or equivalent.

CONDITIONS OF EMPLOYMENT: Contract length September to June or possibly July, 20 contact teaching hours per week.

SALARY: Average salary is €1,300 a month for 20 contact hours per week.

FACILITIES/SUPPORT: Assistance with accommodation, weekly seminars and workshops are part of the job, school library, teachers' room and extensive teachers' materials available.

RECRUITMENT: Teachers should send their CV to admin@cambridgeschool.com and will be interviewed either face to face or by phone.

CONTACT: Alistair Jones, Director. (alistair@cambridgeschool.com).

CANADIAN LANGUAGE INSTITUTE
C/ París No 25, Montequinto, 41089 Seville
+34 95 412 9016
vmantecon@formacionymedios.com
www.clisevilla.com; www.clisevilla.es

NUMBER OF TEACHERS: 10.

PREFERENCE OF NATIONALITY: Any English-speaking country. EU passport a must.

QUALIFICATIONS: BA in Linguistics or Education. Experience with TPRS (Teaching Proficiency through Reading and Storytelling) and CI-based approaches.

CONDITIONS OF EMPLOYMENT: 1 or more years. 20–25 hours a week.

SALARY: €1,300 per month.

FACILITIES/SUPPORT: Advice on accommodation given.

RECRUITMENT: Via posts on EFL boards. Local interview esssential.

CONTACT: Victoria Mantecon, Director of EFL Department.

CENTRO EDIMBURGO IDIOMAS
Edificio Edimburgo, Plaza Niña, 21003 Huelva
+34 959 263821/26382 or +34 959 250168
info@centroedimburgo.com
www.centroedimburgo.com

NUMBER OF TEACHERS: 20.

PREFERENCE OF NATIONALITY: Must be EU national or hold work permit for Spain.

QUALIFICATIONS: Degree, CELTA plus 1 year's experience. Must speak conversational Spanish.

FACILITIES/SUPPORT: School helps find flats.

RECRUITMENT: Recent photograph and 2 references must be sent with application. Interviews essential.

CIC
Via Augusta 205, 08021 Barcelona
+34 93 200 1133
idiomes@iccic.edu
www.iccic.edu

NUMBER OF TEACHERS: 80.

PREFERENCE OF NATIONALITY: Mix of native English speaking and teachers with 'native competence' from all around the world.

QUALIFICATIONS: Cambridge/Trinity certificate and 1 year's experience.

CONDITIONS OF EMPLOYMENT: Most new teachers are given a temporary 9-month contract running from October to June.

SALARY: Discussed during interview.

FACILITIES/SUPPORT: In-house training and professional development if funded by school.

RECRUITMENT: CVs via internet, all suitable candidates are interviewed.

EES MADRID (ENGLISH EDUCATIONAL SERVICES)
Calle Alcalá, 20–2°, 28014 Madrid
+34 91 531 4783 or +34 91 532 9734
richardinmadrid@gmail.com
www.eesmadrid.es.tl

NUMBER OF TEACHERS: 100–120 across Spain per year.

PREFERENCE OF NATIONALITY: EU passport holders.

QUALIFICATIONS: Degree level education and CELTA/TESOL certificate/PGCE, etc.

CONDITIONS OF EMPLOYMENT: 9-month contract from September to June. Alternatively, 1–2 month contracts available in summer (July and sometimes August). Working hours are between 4pm and 9.30pm.

FACILITIES/SUPPORT: Assistance given with finding accommodation. New arrivals are also given assistance in registering their address with local authorities, registering with the Seguridad Social and obtaining an NIE. State qualified teachers can be helped to validate their teaching/academic qualifications with the Ministry of Education.

RECRUITMENT: Interviews are essential and are usually held in Madrid but occasionally in the UK.

CONTACT: Richard Harrison, Director.

EIDE SCHOOL OF ENGLISH
Genaro Oraa 6, Santurce 48980
+34 94 493 7005
eide@eide.es
www.eide.es

NUMBER OF TEACHERS: 2.

QUALIFICATIONS: Bachelor's degree and some teaching experience.

CONDITIONS OF EMPLOYMENT: 9-month contract; 15 hours per week in the evenings.

SALARY: €12 per hour plus bonus for holidays at the end of contract; 8% tax and social security deduction.

FACILITIES/SUPPORT: Help finding accommodation.

RECRUITMENT: Interview essential.

CONTACT: Marisol Largo, Director.

EL CENTRO DE INGLES
C/Calderers 7, 23740 Andújar (Jaén)
dirección@elcentrodeingles.es
www.elcentrodeingles.es

NUMBER OF TEACHERS: 2–4 new teachers required every year for September start.

QUALIFICATIONS: CELTA/Trinity and 2 years' experience, especially valued if with children.

CONDITIONS OF EMPLOYMENT: 9.5-month contract. 21–24 contact hours per week (full-time 34 hour contract to cover class preparation, meetings, teacher training etc). Holiday bonus on completion of contract.

FACILITIES/SUPPORT: Help with accommodation, paperwork, settling in and induction. Full medical cover.

RECRUITMENT: Interviews in Spain or England (as notified on website). Also recruit via www.spainwise.net.

CONTACT: Julie Hetherington, Director.

ENGLISH 1
Marqués del Nervión 116, 41005 Seville
✆ +34 95 464 20 98
✉ info@english1sevilla.com
🖥 www.english1sevilla.com

NUMBER OF TEACHERS: 6.

QUALIFICATIONS: Degree and TEFL certificate (or diploma) and experience, especially with young learners preferred.

CONDITIONS OF EMPLOYMENT: 23 contact hours per week, Monday to Thursday only, teaching children, teenagers and adults. Nine-month contract from October to June.

SALARY: Starting salary € 1,100 gross plus extra payments for Cambridge exam preparation classes.

FACILITIES/SUPPORT: In-house training and great support in a very friendly and harmonious working atmosphere. Lots of assistance in finding accommodation.

CONTACT: Jennifer Fricker.

ENGLISH LANGUAGE TRAINING
Avd País Valencià, 129–131, 03820 Cocentaina (Alicante)
✆ +34 96 559 2204
✉ info@qeltcocentaina.com
🖥 www.qeltcocentaina.com

NUMBER OF TEACHERS: 3.

PREFERENCE OF NATIONALITY: British.

QUALIFICATIONS: CELTA or TESOL qualification (not short online introductory courses) and a minimum of 1 year teaching experience.

CONDITIONS OF EMPLOYMENT: 9 months October to June. 25 hours a week.

SALARY: €950–€980 (net) according to experience.

FACILITIES/SUPPORT: Assistance offered with finding accommodation. Assistance given with obtaining identification documents for Spain.

RECRUITMENT: Via online advertising. Interviews are usually carried out over the phone or on Skype, but if the candidate is in the area a face-to-face interview is preferable.

CONTACT: Michaela Aylott, Director.

ENGLISH TEACHERS COLLECTIVE (ETC)
C/ Joaquín Costa 15, Madrid 28002
✆ +34 91 5212592
✉ info@etcspain.com
🖥 www.etcspain.com

NUMBER OF TEACHERS: 35.

PREFERENCE OF NATIONALITY: None.

QUALIFICATIONS: TEFL qualification plus 1 year of experience.

CONDITIONS OF EMPLOYMENT: 9-month contracts. 18 hours per week.

SALARY: €1,000 per month, net.

FACILITIES/SUPPORT: No help with accommodation or work permits.

RECRUITMENT: Links with training schools in Madrid such as TtMadrid. Local interviews essential.

CONTACT: Paul Hevicon, Director General.

ESIC IDIOMAS
Sancho el Fuerte 38, Bajo, 31011 Pamplona
✆ +34 948 173011
✉ idiomas.pam@esic.es
🖥 www.esic.edu/idiomas

NUMBER OF TEACHERS: 28 (some part-time).

PREFERENCE OF NATIONALITY: Native English speakers.

QUALIFICATIONS: Recognised TEFL qualification and relevant experience.

CONDITIONS OF EMPLOYMENT: 9-month contract; 24 hours per week.

SALARY: €1,240–€1,320 depending on experience; €18 per hour self-employed.

FACILITIES/SUPPORT: Help is given to find accommodation and paperwork necessary to work in Pamplona. An initial induction course, with accompanying handouts, is given and various training and information sessions are given throughout the academic year.

RECRUITMENT: Sometimes interviewed by phone.

CONTACT: Fay Williams, Coordinator (fay.williams@esic.es).

EUROSCHOOLS

Plaza de la Independencia, Regueiro 2, 36211 Vigo

📞 +34 986 291748

📧 info@euroschools.eu

💻 www.euroschools.eu

NUMBER OF TEACHERS: 15.

PREFERENCE OF NATIONALITY: Must be EU.

QUALIFICATIONS: Good degree preferably in English, Spanish or modern languages, TEFL qualification, some experience preferred. Must have knowledge of Spanish and outgoing, friendly personality.

SALARY: Competitive plus allowances are paid for university degree and TEFL teaching qualifications in proportion to qualifications.

FACILITIES/SUPPORT: Assistance given with finding accommodation. Holiday entitlement is 2+ weeks at Christmas, 1 week at Easter, 2 days at *Carnaval*. Access to internet and school computer network available to teachers.

RECRUITMENT: Good references needed.

CONTACT: Mr. Moriarty, Managing Director.

IDIOMASTER LANGUAGE CENTRES

C/Juan Rico 8, Apartado de Correos 591, 14900 Lucena (Cordoba)

📞 +34 957 591678

📧 idiomaster@terra.es, recruitment@idiomaster.es

💻 www.idiomaster.es

NUMBER OF TEACHERS: 9.

QUALIFICATIONS: University degree, CELTA and at least 1 year's experience, preferably with children.

SALARY: Minimum monthly gross salary €1,250 plus end of contract bonus of 2.5 days salary per month worked. Full social security and national health insurance cover.

FACILITIES/SUPPORT: Ongoing internal teacher training and support plus external teaching conferences and courses. Digital classrooms with interactive whiteboards. Help with finding accommodation. Preparation centre for the Cambridge suite of exams. A registered Trinity College, London examination centre and member of ACEIA and FECEI.

INLINGUA SANTANDER

Avenida de Pontejos 5, 39005 Santander

📞 +34 942 278465

📧 inlingua.santander@inlingua.com

💻 www.inlinguasantander.com

NUMBER OF TEACHERS: 12.

PREFERENCE OF NATIONALITY: EU native English speakers or having a work permit for Spain.

QUALIFICATIONS: TEFL certificate and/or teaching experience, university degree.

CONDITIONS OF EMPLOYMENT: Contract for academic year or summer, full-time contract: up to 26 teaching hours a week.

SALARY: Minimum net €1,041.56.

FACILITIES/SUPPORT: Assistance with accommodation, inlingua Method course, workshops, school library.

RECRUITMENT: Via internet, interview by phone.

CONTACT: Ingrid Antons, Director.

INSTITUTE OF MODERN LANGUAGES

Puerta Real 1, 18009 Granada

📞 +34 958 225536

📧 director@imlgranada.com

💻 www.imlgranada.com

NUMBER OF TEACHERS: 20.

PREFERENCE OF NATIONALITY: British, other native English speakers.

QUALIFICATIONS: University degree, TEFL qualification and relevant experience.

CONDITIONS OF EMPLOYMENT: Contract for the academic year, contract for part-time work, national insurance, social security.

FACILITIES/SUPPORT: Good resources, Examination Centre for University of Cambridge ESOL Examinations in Granada, Almería and Málaga.

RECRUITMENT: EFL teachers are recruited from among the best qualified in Granada at the time. Initial short-list drawn up by director of studies from available CVs, then school owner carries out second interviews of short-listed candidates.

CONTACT: Jonathan Baum.

INTERLANG

C/Velázquez, 117, 1ª, Madrid

📞 +34 91 5158422

📧 empleo@interlang.es

💻 www.interlang.es

NUMBER OF TEACHERS: 90.

PREFERENCE OF NATIONALITY: None but must be native speaker and have EU working papers if non-EU citizen.

QUALIFICATIONS: CELTA plus 2 years' TEFL experience and sound knowledge of business English.

CONDITIONS OF EMPLOYMENT: Registered freelancers, or school offers standard 9-month contracts. Typical teaching hours 8.30am–10am/1pm–6pm.

SALARY: €18.50 per hour gross on contract, €24 per hour gross for registered freelancers. Tax deductions vary, but for freelancers there's a 7% deduction for the first two years and then 15%.

RECRUITMENT: Via the company website or via permanent advert at www.madridteacher.com. Candidates are asked to send recent CV and colour photo to empleo@interlang.es. A face-to-face interview in Madrid is essential before an offer of work can be made.

CONTACT: Sean O'Malley, Director of Studies.

THE LANGUAGE CLUB
C/Rosalia de Castro 63, 08025 Barcelona
gillian@thelanguageclub.org
www.thelanguageclub.org

Teachers hired for business and academic full-immersion courses for all ages, taught on school premises or in-company.

LINC, ENGLISH FOR LIVING
c/Polavieja 13, 41004 Seville (main school); Also: Calle Genaro Parladé, 4. Bajo B, 41013 Seville; Av. Ana de Viya, 5, 11009 Cadiz
+34 954 500 459
sevilla@linc.es
www.linc.es

NUMBER OF TEACHERS: 15–20.

PREFERENCE OF NATIONALITY: Must be an EU passport holder and native English speaker.

QUALIFICATIONS: Degree plus EFL qualification (CELTA or Trinity) and 1 year's teaching experience. Some knowledge of Spanish helpful.

CONDITIONS OF EMPLOYMENT: Standard contract is 9 months from October to June. Full and part-time contracts available. Full-time is 24 contact hours per week.

SALARY: €1,200 per month for full-time contracts.

FACILITIES/SUPPORT: Help is given with finding accommodation, particularly if the teacher can't speak Spanish. Regular in-service training programme. Free Spanish classes.

RECRUITMENT: Interviews held via Skype or phone.

CONTACT: Mick Lawson, Director of Studies (mick@linc.es).

MCGINTY SCHOOL OF ENGLISH
Avda, Cabo de Gata, 82, 04007 Almeria
dos@mcgintyschool.com
www.mcgintyschool.com

NUMBER OF TEACHERS: 10.

PREFERENCE OF NATIONALITY: None.

QUALIFICATIONS: Minimum CELTA or PGCE, preferably language graduate with 2 years' teaching experience.

CONDITIONS OF EMPLOYMENT: 1-year contract with the possibility to renew. Working hours between 4pm and 9.30pm, Monday–Friday.

SALARY: Starting full-time salary is €1,150 net per month but may increase depending on experience and qualifications.

FACILITIES/SUPPORT: Assistance provided with finding accommodation and applying for work permits.

RECRUITMENT: Usually via internet and newspaper advertising. Interviews are essential and can be conducted in Spain, the UK or over the phone.

MAUCAL SL
Pol. Argualas Nave 35, 50012 Zaragoza
+34 976 350 205
maucal@maucal.com
www.maucal.com

NUMBER OF TEACHERS: Approximately 4.

QUALIFICATIONS: EFL qualification and bachelor's degree (with honours) preferable.

CONDITIONS OF EMPLOYMENT: Contracts of 9–10 months; from 12 to 34 hours a week.

SALARY: Depends on hours a week.

RECRUITMENT: Application via www.tefl.com or CV. Interview essential.

MERIT SCHOOL
Campo Florido 54–56, 2a, 08027 Barcelona
+34 93 243 15 24
dos@meritschool.com
www.meritschool.com

NUMBER OF TEACHERS: 40–50.

PREFERENCE OF NATIONALITY: Native English speakers. Must have EU passport or current work permit for Spain.

QUALIFICATIONS: University degree, TEFL certificate, 1–2 years' experience. Classroom experience with young learners or teenagers an advantage.

CONDITIONS OF EMPLOYMENT: Most contracts run from October to June with the possibility of extension into July for summer courses. Number of teaching hours varies – part-time and full-time teachers are sought.

SALARY: €15–€18 per hour. Travelling fee for off-site classes.

FACILITIES/SUPPORT: Three centres plus in-company department: Campo Florido and Sant Cugat campuses (Young Learners, Teenagers, Adults), UPC campus (University students and staff) and in-company department (Business and General English for adults off-site in companies). Regular in-house workshops, financial assistance to attend external training events, good library of teaching resources, peer observation scheme, regular observations and feedback by senior staff. Spanish classes.

RECRUITMENT: Mostly local (internet sites like www.loquo.com) but sometimes on international sites like www.tefl.com. Applications from interested teachers are always welcome. Face-to-face interview required. Best time to apply is late May to July or in September.

CONTACT: Michael Terry, Director of Studies.

PREMIER SCHOOL OF ENGLISH
C/ Perafán de Rivera 1 – Local, 41710
Utrera (Sevilla)
📞 +34 955 861 951
📧 info@premierenglish.es
💻 www.premierenglish.es

NUMBER OF TEACHERS: 7.

PREFERENCE OF NATIONALITY: No real preference as long as they are native speakers and have EU residency permit.

QUALIFICATIONS: Must have a CELTA or Trinity TESOL + 1 year's experience.

CONDITIONS OF EMPLOYMENT: 9-month contracts. Hours of teaching mostly in the afternoons and evenings: 4pm–9.45pm Monday to Thursday, 4pm–6.15pm Friday.

SALARY: Starting salary €1,300 (gross) which could increase depending on experience and qualifications. Deductions total about €100 a month.

FACILITIES/SUPPORT: School actively helps teachers find flats and negotiate with landlords, etc. Help given with red tape (the procedures vary from year to year).

RECRUITMENT: Through recommendations, www.Spainwise.net and other internet sites. Interviews essential.

CONTACT: Francis Rodriguez, Director of Studies (premierenglish@hotmail.com).

PUEBLO INGLES
Madrid
📞 +34 91 391 3400
📧 anglos@puebloingles.com
💻 www.puebloingles.com or www.morethanenglish.
com/anglos/index.asp

Informal exchange of English conversation for 8 days in various holiday resorts in Spain, which are 'stocked' with native English speakers and Spanish clients who want to improve their English. Participants receive free room and board, and transport from Madrid.

SPEAK ENGLISH SCHOOL
Cimadevilla 17 Ent F, 33003 Oviedo, Asturias
📧 speakschool@hotmail.com
💻 www.speakoviedo.com

PREFERENCE OF NATIONALITY: British.

QUALIFICATIONS: TEFL certificate and a minimum of 2 years' experience.

CONDITIONS OF EMPLOYMENT: 9-month contracts, to work 25 hours per week.

SALARY: Net salary of €1,200 per month plus end of contract bonus.

FACILITIES/SUPPORT: The school can help with finding accommodation.

RECRUITMENT: Interviews essential, but can be carried out in the UK. Sometimes, telephone/Skype interviews can be arranged.

CONTACT: Mick Gordon, Director.

TECS (THE EDUCATIONAL CONSORTIUM OF SPAIN)
The English Centre, Apdo. Correos 85, 11500 El Puerto de Santa María, Cadiz
📞 +34 902 350 356
📧 tecscamp@tecs.es
💻 www.tecs.es (commercial) and http://recruit.tecs.es

NUMBER OF TEACHERS: 15–20 teachers required throughout the year. More than 130 staff employed in summer (40–50 teachers, 50–60 monitors and 20–30 management and support staff) at two residential camps in southern Spain, close to Cadiz in Andalucia.

QUALIFICATIONS: Employees must be team players who are young at heart and full of energy, with a mature and responsible personality.

CONDITIONS OF EMPLOYMENT: Minimum 1 month.

SALARY: Free board and lodging.

RECRUITMENT: Online.

CONTACT: Douglas Haines, Summer Camp Recruitment.

TENIDIOMAS

C/Caracuel 15, 11402 Jerez de la Frontera (Cadiz)

📞 +34 956 324 707

📧 info@tenidiomas.com

💻 www.tenidiomas.com

NUMBER OF TEACHERS: 6.

PREFERENCE OF NATIONALITY: British.

QUALIFICATIONS: TEFL certificate and university degree.

CONDITIONS OF EMPLOYMENT: 9-month contract, 22 teaching hours per week.

FACILITIES/SUPPORT: Monthly workshops run by DOS.

RECRUITMENT: Usually recruit new teachers via internet, telephone interview required.

CONTACT: Gerry Rylance, Director.

TRAINING EXPRESS S.L.

Plaza del Cordón N° 1, 28005 Madrid

📞 +34 91 521 1554

📧 marcy.murdoch@trainingexpress.es or jobs@ training-express.es

💻 www.training express.es (see Teaching in Spain page) or www.ispeakuspeak.com (Online virtual trainer)

Madrid-based language consultancy.

NUMBER OF TEACHERS: 200 in Spain, 150 virtual trainers worldwide.

PREFERENCE OF NATIONALITY: None.

QUALIFICATIONS: Minimum 2 years' experience plus TEFL.

CONDITIONS OF EMPLOYMENT: 9-month contracts in Spain, full-time and part-time. Virtual trainer contracts worldwide, full-time and part-time.

SALARY: €1,000–€1,200 per month gross. Standard deductions of about 6%.

FACILITIES/SUPPORT: Assistance given with accommodation through a relocation agency. Help given with obtaining the necessary permits, including liaising with local state ministry.

RECRUITMENT: Via international websites such as www.tefl.com and local sources. Interview required.

CONTACT: Marcy Murdoch, Recruitment Officer.

VAUGHAN SYSTEMS

Edificio Eurobuilding 2, Calle Orense 69–1° planta, 28020 Madrid

📞 +34 91 748 5950

📧 anglos@vaughantown.com

💻 www.vaughantown.com, www.vaughanenglishteachers.com

Intensive 6-day cultural exchange programme or 'talk-a-thon', from a Sunday to a Friday, held almost every week year round. 15 Spaniards and 17 English speakers are put together in a relaxed environment, accommodation in hotels all over Spain, to re-create an English-speaking village. The programme is based on both one-to-one sessions and group activities, as well as excursions, parties and walks in the countryside. They also hire English teachers and offer free training to people willing to spend a year being paid to teach in various parts of Spain. No previous teacheing experience required. 2-week training course in Madrid, Santander, Barcelona, Valencia vigo or Valladolid provided before job starts.

SALARY: None for one-week language exchange, but free food, accommodation, and transport from Madrid to hotel locations are provided.

CONTACT: Mayte Velasco Ziga, Coordinator, Vaughan Volunteers.

SWITZERLAND

The status of English is steadily rising in Switzerland. Partly in response to parental pressure, some cantons (including Zurich) decided in 2001 to teach English rather than French as the first-choice second language, to the consternation of many Swiss. According to the Superintendent of Education in Zurich, the decision was taken because children and young people are far more motivated to learn English than any other language and he believes that this should be the starting point for success in teaching. English became compulsory throughout the curriculum in all Swiss schools in 2010, which involved retraining of Swiss teachers on a massive scale and more demand for foreign teachers of English.

Yet prospects are gloomy for people who fancy the idea of teaching the gnomes of Zürich or their counterparts in other parts of Switzerland, unless they are ultra-qualified. Although immigration regulations are not as restrictive as they once were (see next section), Switzerland will not suddenly be welcoming an army of foreign language teachers. Teachers may also like to consider whether they wish to face the barrage of regulations that are part and parcel of living in Switzerland, from attempting to open a bank account without possessing a small fortune, to falling foul of strict rubbish disposal regulations.

The Swiss economy remains solid, but is not as invincible as it was once considered to be, as the director of a *Sprachschule* in Basel explained:

> As a small language school in a country and region which has been experiencing severe withdrawal symptoms (from full employment, job and financial security), it is unlikely that we will be recruiting staff from outside Switzerland, especially as there is a large reservoir of potential candidates here in the Basel region and work permits for staff from outside Switzerland are now a rarity.

This was corroborated more recently by **Estelle Bieri** of the chain of Migros Club Schools (www.ecole-club.ch):

> In order to teach English, we require teachers to be either native speakers or to have a C2 level of English, preferably with a good Cambridge Proficiency pass. Teachers must have a B residence permit. In addition, they require a qualification in teaching English as a foreign language to adults, for example a CELTA or equivalent, or higher. This is valid for any Swiss school which is Eduqua validated (Eduqua is an independent body for quality control). Many of our teachers have university qualifications. Teaching experience is welcome, particularly with regard to teaching certain levels and types of classes (ESP, etc.).

There are nine Wall Street Institutes and the same number of Bénédict Schools in Switzerland; a list of addresses is available at www.wallstreetinstitute.ch and www.benedict-international.com. One of the biggest Wall Street schools is the one in Lausanne at Rue du Simplon 34, 1006 Lausanne (+41 21 614 66 14; wsi.lausanne@wallst.ch). If you are hired by a Swiss language school, wages are high, ranging from SFr30 to SFr60 for a 50-minute lesson.

Private tutoring is a possibility for those who lack a permit as the American world traveller and free spirit **Danny Jacobson** discovered when he was living with his Swiss girlfriend in Bern:

> A Swiss friend advised me to apply at one of the English schools but I didn't think it would work without a permit. So I just made my own flyer and put it up around town and the next thing I knew I had a bunch of people calling me up to help with proofreading seminar papers/assignments and to give private lessons. I figured I'd go for quantity and low-ball the market, charging only CHF20 per hour. But I found a few adverts for people looking for teachers and with those, I went with their offered price, which was much more.

A qualified teacher can charge about SFr80 an hour in the cities, so even SFr40 might be considered a bargain.

The English Teachers' Association in Switzerland (www.e-tas.ch) operates a jobs board with a few vacancies, mainly for part-time trainers for business. Recently the company SL&C in Geneva (www.supercomm. ch) was advertising for language trainers to join their 200-strong team in Geneva, Nyon, Lausanne, Fribourg, Zurich and Bienne. The newsgroup http://groups.yahoo.com/group/swissenglish is aimed at EFL teachers already in Switzerland, not those enquiring about job opportunities.

REGULATIONS

No permit is needed for EU nationals who stay for less than three months. If they want to stay beyond that, e.g. to continue job-hunting or to do a seasonal job, they must apply for an L permit (short-term residence permit). The L-EC/EFTA permit (*Kurzaufenhalter/Autorisation de Courte Durée*) is issued for periods of work lasting less than 12 months and can be renewed once for a further year. EU nationals simply need to take their passport and contract of employment to the local cantonal office. L-permits are no longer tied to a particular job or canton.

If the contract of employment is going to extend beyond two years, it is possible to apply for a B-permit, valid for between one and five years. However, slowly, the Swiss are opening to the outside world. In a popular vote held in 2009, nearly 60% of the Swiss people voted in favour of the continuation of the agreement on the free movement of persons from the EEA. Detailed information about the regulations is published by the Federal Office of Migration (www.bfm.admin.ch). Detailed information in English is sometimes available from the cantonal authorities, for example downloadable brochures about living and working in Zurich are available at www.welcome.zh.ch. The canton of Zurich also allows foreigners to apply for a work permit online (in German language only), which shortens the application time. The searchable forum www.englishforum. ch can also be helpful on technical matters.

As a result of Switzerland moving towards integration with Europe, non-EU citizens are finding it harder to gain legal access to Switzerland's English-teaching market unless they apply in special categories like spouse or trainee. If a non-European does find an employer willing to sponsor their application, the applicant will have to collect the documents from the Swiss embassy in his or her home country.

VACATION WORK

More possibilities for teaching English exist at summer camps than in city language institutes, as can be seen from the programmes listed in the directory below. There are a number of international schools in Switzerland, some of which run English language and sports summer schools. The Swiss Federation of Private Schools produces a list of summer schools in Switzerland held at its member schools, indicating which ones teach English. This is available at www.swiss-schools.ch. Watch for occasional ads or, if you are in Switzerland, make local enquiries.

In addition to the organisations with entries below, the following organisations offer summer language courses between June and September and may need teachers or monitors (or some combination of the two):

Aiglon College Summer School, 1885 Chesières (+41 24 496 6128; www.aiglon.ch).
Collège Alpin Beau Soleil, Holiday Language Camp, Avenue Centrale, CH-1884 Villarssur-Ollon (www.beausoleil/ch).
ESL (Ecole Suisse de Langues), Grand-Rue 42, CP 1206, 1820 Montreux (jobs@esl.ch; www.esl-schools.org/en/language-courses/summer-camps/informations/jobs/index.htm). Holiday language courses in Leysin, Ascona and Zug, as well as France and Germany, for which they hire tutors and activity leaders for the summer season.
Institut Le Rosey, Camp d'Eté, CH-1180 Rolle (+41 21 822 5500; summercamp@rosey.ch; www. roseysummercamps.ch). Qualified or experienced EFL teachers over 20 for co-educational summer

camps with sports coaching on Lake Geneva. Teachers must be capable of carrying out boarding school duties.

Institut Monte Rosa, 57 Avenue de Chillon, CH-1820 Montreux-Territet (+41 21 965 4545; info@ monterosa.ch; www.monterosa.ch).

International Camp Suisse is a British-based language camp with an office in West Yorkshire and the camp held in Torgon (www.campsuisse.com). Activity leaders and language teachers are needed to fill many summer positions.

Les Elfes in Verbier (www.leselfes.com). Another camp operator looking for seasonal summer or winter staff, most of whom will be over 20, though younger candidates are eligible to do work experience.

Leysin American School in Switzerland, CH-1854 Leysin (+41 24 493 37 7; www.las.ch/summer/ staffhome.html). Contact the Director of Summer Programs.

St George's School in Switzerland, 1815 Clarens/Montreux (www.st-georges.ch).

Surval Mont-Fleuri, Route de Glion 56, CH-1820 Montreux 1 (www.surval.ch). For teenage girls.

TASIS (The American School in Switzerland), Summer Language Programs, Via Collina d'Oro, 6926 Montagnola-Lugano (+41 91 960 5151 http://switzerland.tasis.com). Hiring takes place between January and March. Net salaries are US$2,100 for counsellors and US$3,200 for teachers. American staff may be eligible for a SFr1,300 contribution to their transatlantic airfares and Europeans up to SFr500.

PHILIP LEE

Philip Lee from New Zealand spent his summers during university working at English language summer camps on the continent including one summer with Village Camps (see entry). The application for the position of counsellor involved a formal application and phone interview, plus he had to complete a basic first aid/CPR course at his own expense. This opportunity is open to non-European nationals as Philip reported in 2010.

There wasn't much of a visa problem as most tutors from outside the EU (US/Canada/Australia/NZ) had a three-month tourist visa I believe. I never encountered any problems in relation to my visa and working and even when I was working in Switzerland, where I expected more regulation and controls, there wasn't a problem at all. I worked in Switzerland for a two-week camp. But there were people who stayed there for up to 12 weeks working without problems.

I was paid cash in hand for the Swiss camps. I think payment was always a bit of concern for people working in this line of work for the first time, in the sense that there were no 'employment rights', but at the organisations I worked with, payment was always managed very professionally.

LIST OF EMPLOYERS

BERLITZ SCHOOL OF LANGUAGES AG
Gerbergasse 4, 4051 Basel
✆ +41 61 226 90 40
🖥 www.berlitz.ch

Centres in Basle, Bern, Biel, Geneva, Lausanne, Lucerne, Zug and Zurich.

NUMBER OF TEACHERS: 15.

PREFERENCE OF NATIONALITY: Must have work permit.

QUALIFICATIONS: Bachelor's degree or professional experience, e.g. business, banking. Berlitz is looking for motivated and enthusiastic employees who can openly engage with others, have a love of language and culture, and a positive disposition. Must have teaching skills and be a communicative person.

CONDITIONS OF EMPLOYMENT: No limit on contract length. Flexible hours of work. Pupils are adults whose average age is between 30 and 40.

SALARY: SFr22.50 per 40-minute lesson plus 10–20% supplements for some programmes.

FACILITIES/SUPPORT: No assistance with accommodation. Training provided.

RECRUITMENT: Through adverts. Local interviews essential.

THE CAMBRIDGE INSTITUTE
Seidengasse 6, 8001 Zurich
✆ +41 44 221 12 12
🖱 zuerich@cambridge.ch
🖥 www.cambridge.ch

PREFERENCE OF NATIONALITY: Native English speaker who is already resident in Zurich.

QUALIFICATIONS: English teaching certificate or diploma (e.g. CELTA or equivalent). The candidate must have already obtained the required permits to live and work in Switzerland.

CONTACT: Keith Daborn, Director of Studies.

HAUT-LAC INTERNATIONAL CENTRE
1669 Les Sciernes
✆ +41 26 928 42 00
🖱 info@haut-lac.com or jobs@haut-lac.com
🖥 www.myswisscamp.com

NUMBER OF TEACHERS: Teachers/monitors needed for summer, spring, autumn and winter language camps for adolescents.

PREFERENCE OF NATIONALITY: Native English speakers, preferably with EU passport.

QUALIFICATIONS: TEFL CELTA or equivalent plus it is useful to have experience in sports, drama, art or games organisation.

CONDITIONS OF EMPLOYMENT: Language and sports summer camp (mid-June to end of August); winter ski camp (end of December to early April); spring camp (early April to early May) and autumn camp (late September to mid-October).

FACILITIES/SUPPORT: Full board and lodging provided in single, twin or three-bedded rooms. Help given with travel expenses. Free laundry facilities and use of sports equipment.

RECRUITMENT: Send for an application form to jobs@haut-lac.com.

CONTACT: Steve McShane (stevie@haut-lac.ch or stephen.mcshane@haut-lac.com).

INLINGUA - BASEL
Dufourstrasse 50, 4052 Basel
✆ +41 61 278 99 33
🖱 sprachschule@inlingua-basel.ch; christian.ruetti@inlingua.com
🖥 www.inlingua.com

NUMBER OF TEACHERS: 20–25.

PREFERENCE OF NATIONALITY: Must be an EU citizen.

QUALIFICATIONS: University degree is essential. If the degree is not a teaching degree then CELTA or equivalent is also required (online courses are not accepted).

CONDITIONS OF EMPLOYMENT: Generally open-ended contracts but a two-year minimum commitment is expected. Lessons are held from 7am to 9pm and the teachers' work load depends on their availability.

SALARY: Starting full-time salary is approximately CHF 6,200.

FACILITIES/SUPPORT: All paperwork for work permits is handled by the school.

RECRUITMENT: Usually via ETAS (English Teachers' Association of Switzerland), advertising online or, most commonly, spontaneous applications. Interviews are essential. First round is conducted via telephone followed by two rounds of personal interviews at the school.

CONTACT: Christian Rütti, Personnel and Office Manager.

TLC – THE LANGUAGE COMPANY
Bahnhofstrasse 44, 5400 Baden
✆ +41 56 205 51 78
🖱 info@tlcsprachschule.ch
🖥 www.tlcsprachschule.ch

NUMBER OF TEACHERS: 25.

PREFERENCE OF NATIONALITY: Native English speakers.

QUALIFICATIONS: Minimum CELTA plus experience teaching English to adults. Some business experience is preferable.

CONDITIONS OF EMPLOYMENT: Open-ended contract. Classes start at 8am and finish at 9.30pm. If the teacher is flexible in terms of location and time they can work up to 26 hours per week.

SALARY: SFr60–SFr72 depending on qualifications, experience and range of teaching.

RECRUITMENT: Usually through ETAS (English Teachers' Association of Switzerland), adverts on websites such as www.jobs.ch or through word of mouth. Interviews are essential. Preliminary interview can be done by phone and successful candidate will need to take a trial lesson in Switzerland.

CONTACT: Andrea Merki, HR Manager (Andrea.Merki@tlcsprachschule.ch).

VILLAGE CAMPS

14 Rue de la Morâche, 1260 Nyon

 +41 24 493 3064

personnel@villagecamps.com

www.villagecamps.com/personnel

Language summer camp at Leysin near Lake Geneva in French-speaking Switzerland (also in York, England).

PREFERENCE OF NATIONALITY: European, North American, Australian, New Zealand passport holders may apply.

QUALIFICATIONS: Applicants must be at least 21 years of age, possess a recognised qualification in language teaching (minimum 4 weeks) and be a native English speaker of the language of instruction. A second language is desirable and experience in sports, creative and/or outdoor activities is essential. A valid first aid and cardiopulmonary resuscitation (CPR) certificate is required while at camp.

CONDITIONS OF EMPLOYMENT: Employment periods vary from 3 to 8 weeks between June and August.

SALARY: Room and board, accident and liability insurance and a weekly allowance provided.

RECRUITMENT: Starts in January. There is no deadline to submit applications, but positions are limited. Interviews are by telephone. For information on dates, locations, and positions available and to apply directly online, visit www.villagecamps.com.

CENTRAL AND EASTERN EUROPE

The transition to a market economy throughout the vast area of Eastern and Central Europe has resulted in a huge demand for professional assistance at all levels, especially when it comes to improving the skills of communication. The dramatic changes which have taken place in the former Communist Bloc since 1989 mean that in every hotel lobby, office boardroom and government ministry from Silesia to Siberia, deals are being struck, export partnerships forged and academic alliances developed between East and West. The eastern Europeans benefiting from this new commerce tend to be the ones who have acquired the English language.

While Russia and many of its former satellites have continued to wrestle with their political and economic demons, the more stable Central European states of Hungary, Poland, the Czech Republic, Slovakia, the Baltic States and most recently, Bulgaria and Romania, have been welcomed into the European fold by acceding to the EU.

In some quarters of Central Europe there has been a noticeable backlash against what has been seen as a selling out to the West, especially in the major capitals, which are now swarming with foreigners. School directors are now perfectly aware of the English-speaking foreigner who masquerades as a teacher but really intends to indulge in cheap beer and clubs. They are suspicious of anyone projecting this hidden agenda, disliking the fact that so many foreigners used the region as an extended playground early on.

Yet despite having moved past making 'Western' synonymous with 'desirable', the majority of Central European people are still remarkably welcoming to British and American ELT teachers. On most street corners, private language schools employ native English speaking teachers. Working in Central and Eastern Europe may not seem as attractive as it did just after the 'revolution', but thousands continue to fall under the spell of famous destinations such as Prague, Budapest, Kraków, as well as many other beautiful towns in Slovakia and Bulgaria. Even those who find themselves in the less prepossessing industrial cities usually come away beguiled by Central European charm.

Even if ordinary people no longer see English as an automatic passport to higher wages and a better life, they have not stopped wanting to learn it. The English language teaching industry in those countries has grown up, and is now much more likely to hire native speaker teachers with proven experience or an appropriate qualification. For qualified English teachers the market is now more stable, realistic and developed. Massive amounts of money have been invested in Poland, Hungary and the former Czechoslovakia in retraining local teachers for the teaching of English in state schools and these programmes have been largely successful. Thousands of young people from Central Europe move to English-speaking countries to earn some money and improve their English. Yet, demand continues for native English speakers in state schools, private language schools and universities, often for those with a sophisticated understanding of linguistic methodology.

Opportunities persist. While the wealthy elite can afford to pay for extra tuition in English (and other subjects), most citizens must endure fairly small education budgets in their local schools, particularly in countries such as the Slovak Republic where local teachers hardly earn enough to live on. It is worth bearing these issues in mind when considering where to head to teach EFL, as emphasised by **Steve Anderson** from Minneapolis who spent two years teaching in Hungary, the first in a well-resourced urban school, the second in an impoverished rural one but which he found much more fulfilling.

The explosion in the number of training centres for TEFL/TESL teachers in all English-speaking countries means that the pool of certified available teachers is fairly large. Teachers who can claim to specialise either in teaching Young Learners or in teaching Business English are especially attractive since both these areas of ELT are buoyant. Tourism training colleges in Hungary, the Czech & Slovak Republics and the Baltics are especially keen on encouraging conversational English, while some schools in Poland are offering practical conversation classes which teach pupils to fill in English forms and rent a flat. Failing that, the easiest way to become more employable is to acquire a TEFL qualification which could prove especially useful (and incidentally cheaper) if obtained in Eastern Europe. For example International House in Prague, Budapest, Bratislava, Katowice and Wroclaw all offer the CELTA course while ITC Prague offers a TESOL certificate (see the Directory of Training Courses) as do many others.

North Americans will find that the accession of some of the former Eastern bloc countries to the EU has resulted in immigration regulations favouring English teachers from Britain and Ireland. Language institutes understandably do not want to become involved with the delays and expense in supporting non-EU candidates to obtain a residence permit, though some are willing.

One of the first language teaching organisations to break into Eastern Europe has continued to be one of the most active and energetic in the region, International House. IH-affiliated schools are flourishing in Belarus, Lithuania, Latvia, Ukraine, Poland, Romania, Russia and Slovakia. The affiliation agreement with all IH schools states that the schools can employ only teachers who have passed the CELTA course. Similarly the British Council is often in need of suitable candidates to fill vacancies in its teaching centres in Bulgaria, Romania, Ukraine, etc.

Local salaries can seem absurdly low when translated into a hard currency. Some schools pay what is usually a generous salary by local standards but which can leave little after paying for food and accommodation. It is difficult to generalise but a typical package would include a monthly net salary of £500–£600 in addition to free accommodation and possibly some other perks such as a travel stipend. The best paid jobs are for firms which teach in-company courses, especially in Poland, though they are unlikely to offer accommodation.

A host of private language schools which are either independent or part of larger language teaching organisations are represented in Eastern and Central Europe. Most of the Central European schools listed in the directory are well established and offer above-average working conditions. Some mainstream schools in the stable democracies have delegated to specialist recruiters the task of finding teachers. But in the more volatile climate of Russia and former Soviet republics (which are several years behind the Central European nations), locally managed schools come and go, and tend to choose their teachers from the pool of native English speakers on the spot, who also come and go. Intrepid travellers visiting the Central Asian Republics with no intention to work are still often invited to stay a while and do some English teaching, as was happening in off-the-beaten-track towns in Poland and the former Czechoslovakia 15 years ago.

One interesting option for those who do not wish to commit themselves for a full academic year is to work at one of the many language summer camps which are offered to young people, usually in scenic locations from Lake Balaton in Hungary to Lake Baikal in Siberia to the Black Sea resorts of Bulgaria.

CONDITIONS OF WORK

The financial rewards of working in the old Russian Empire are usually so negligible that trained/experienced teachers cannot be enticed to teach there unless they have an independent interest in living in that part of the world or are supported by a voluntary organisation such as the Soros Foundation. Even the large language chains which offer reasonable working conditions (e.g. flat provided, plenty of support) do not pay high enough wages to allow ordinary EL teachers to save any money. Russia itself can offer reasonable wages, particularly now that the economy is performing better, but the cost of living can be very high in Moscow and St Petersburg and inflation continues to be a problem.

Volunteering programmes arrange for eager volunteers in search of a cultural experience to spend time in this part of the world, provided they don't mind being out-of-pocket at the end of a short stint of teaching. The role of native speaking volunteers is to conduct practical English classes (i.e. conversation classes) to supplement grammar taught by local school staff.

Most of the Central European cities and larger towns have sprouted Western-style supermarkets and other consumer outlets, often to the disgruntlement of the older generations who have a fondness for their local shops. Living in these cities begins to feel not so very different from living in France or Italy, particularly with the influx of international companies. Smaller towns and rural areas can still be a very different proposition (until you come across expats who have bought property on the cheap in Bulgaria, etc.).

FINDING A JOB

Fewer vacancies in Central and Eastern Europe are being advertised in the educational press and on the internet, even in Poland, but it is still worth checking the main EFL job sites such as www.tefl.com which at the time of writing carried job ads for about 35 different employers, with the majority of 15 being in the Russian Federation. The possibility of creating your own job in the more obscure corners of this region still exists. Much of what takes place happens by chance, and protocol is often given a back seat to friendly encounters. Obtaining work often comes down to the right (or wrong) hairstyle or whether you've got any Polish/Lithuanian/Slovak/Azerbaijani ancestry. Looking professional, being persistent and asking as many questions as you answer, rather than sitting back on your heels, usually pays off. EU teachers will have an advantage in securing 'on the spot' jobs in private language schools, although other nationalities do sometimes succeed in finding an employer willing to take on the expense and hassle of applying for the documentation.

Michael Todd from the USA describes a typical trajectory for the TEFL teacher taking his or her first tentative steps into Eastern Europe to becoming established. When he arrived, he had done one undergraduate course in teaching English and a tutoring seminar for volunteer teachers, both back in Michigan. Initially he spent nine months near Katowice in Poland teaching the Callan Method, then two years at the Technical University of Liberec in the Czech Republic, and after five years in Bratislava, he is now a Senior Teacher. Along the way he acquired a CELTA from International House Budapest (which he wishes he had done earlier), and a Business English Teaching Certificate (BET) from International House Bratislava:

> *I found my first job in Slovakia online. I don't remember which site. They turned out to be bloodsuckers, so after a year I moved to International House Bratislava. Another teacher and I walked into IH and asked for an interview. The DOS promptly interviewed us. Because I didn't have a CELTA, the DOS had me do a teaching demonstration a few days later. Having impressed her in the teaching demo, we discussed the contractual terms. I decided, stupidly, to return to my first employer, but IH was still willing to hire me for the following fall.*

As of 2011, he mainly teaches managers one-to-one at international businesses around Bratislava, which gives him lots of autonomy and variety. Some of his students just want to chat but most are looking for competently delivered lessons and they expect to be corrected often. Students over the age of 45 tend to be more difficult to teach, and they complain about how hard the language is. Michael lives in a flat provided by the school with rent deducted from wages. He thinks it would be easier to save a bit of money if it wasn't so tempting to visit nearby Vienna, Budapest, and Prague. Fortunately there is a healthy market for private lessons, so it is not difficult to supplement his income. If you want to arrange a position through a mediating organisation, here are the main ones in the UK which continue to recruit teachers for more than one country in the region. (Organisations that deal only with one country are included in the relevant chapter.) In addition to International House, the major chains have some franchise schools in the region, chief among them EF English First, which sends many teachers to Russia and elsewhere, and Language Link with affiliated schools in Russia and Central Asia (www.languagelink.co.uk). ITC International TEFL Certificate in Prague 1 (www.itc-training.com) offers TEFL training with job guidance (though they no longer claim to be able to guarantee immediate employment in Eastern Europe as they once did).

Sharing One Language (SOL), 2 Bridge Chambers, The Strand, Barnstaple, Devon EX31 1HB; (+44 1271 327319; info@sol.org.uk/sol@sol.org.uk; www.sol.org.uk). Non-profit-making organisation which annually recruits teachers with a degree (ideally in Education or Languages) plus at least an introductory TEFL/TESOL certificate to teach in schools in the state sector in some Eastern and Central European countries, especially Hungary, Slovakia and Romania. All posts include local salary and free independent housing thus giving enough to live reasonably. The teacher's only expense is the cost of getting there and back. The website provides contact details for country coordinators in Hungary, Poland, Slovakia, Bulgaria, Serbia, Croatia and Romania.

Projects Abroad, Aldsworth Parade, Goring, Sussex BN12 4TX (+44 1903 708300; info@projects-abroad.co.uk; www.projects-abroad.co.uk). Recruits volunteers to work as English language teaching assistants for the summer or during the academic year in Moldova and Romania among many other countries worldwide. No TEFL background required. Packages cost from £1,445 for one month and include placement, accommodation and three meals a days. Full medical and travel insurance and 24 hour staff support.

FOR NORTH AMERICANS

Fewer US organisations are actively involved in teacher recruitment for the region than was the case in the heady 1990s.

Central European Teaching Program (CETP) (www.cetp.info). Places approximately 75–80 native speakers of English in Hungary (see chapter) with a few positions in the Czech Republic.

Peace Corps, 1111 20th St NW, Washington DC 20526 (toll-free +1 800 424 8580; www.peacecorps. gov). Provides volunteer teachers on 27-month contracts to many countries in Eastern Europe, with the largest numbers in Ukraine, Bulgaria, Kyrgyz Republic and Romania. Must be US citizen, over 18 and in good health. All expenses, including airfare and health insurance, are covered. Recruits people to teach at both secondary and university level and to become involved with teacher training and curriculum development.

The rest of this chapter is organised by country. Bulgaria, Czech Republic, Slovak Republic, Hungary, Poland and Romania are followed by Russia and its former satellite states (the Baltic states, Ukraine and the Central Asian Republics). The former Yugoslav republics of Slovenia, Croatia, Macedonia, Serbia and Montenegro are included in the chapter 'The Rest of Europe' following this section, though some placement organisations mentioned here include them as part of Central and Eastern Europe.

BULGARIA

Since Bulgaria joined the EU in 2007 it has attracted more EU tourists as well as property speculators and foreign businesses. The demand for English teachers is substantial, although opportunities in the private sector are still very scarce. Almost all schools ask for at least a degree and teaching certificate.

FINDING A JOB

A Bulgarian agency of long standing appoints 60–80 native speakers to teach in specialist English language secondary schools for one academic year for which the deadline is the end of May. Details are available from Teachers for Central and Eastern Europe (21 V 5 Rakovski Boulevard, Dimitrovgrad 6400; +359 391 24787; tfcee@usa.net; www.tfcee.8m.com). Students, preferably with a TEFL background, are accepted from the USA, UK, Canada and Australia to spend an academic year teaching. The weekly teaching load is 19 40-minute classes per four-day week. The monthly salary in Bulgarian levs is equivalent to $100. Benefits include free furnished accommodation, 60 days of paid holiday, paid sick leave and work permit. A summer programme is also available at Black Sea resorts for which the application deadline is 20 June. TfCEE charges an application fee of $60. A number of other companies offer English language summer schools and camps at resorts near Varna. A recent advertisement for teachers was placed by the Orange House English Language Centre in Varna (www.orangehousevarna.com).

The British Council in Sofia has a thriving English centre, which offers courses for young learners, adults and businessmen and women; to enquire about any forthcoming teaching vacancies email learnenglish@britishcouncil.bg. Pharos is the biggest chain of foreign language schools in Bulgaria, and affiliated to the Strategakis Schools network of Northern Greece; however, this book has never heard of any native speakers being hired by a Pharos school (www.pharos.bg).

American teachers with at least a master's degree could try the AUBG, a private American-style liberal arts university located in Blagoevgrad (www.aubg.bg). All classes are in English and the university's English Language Institute prepares future AUBG applicants for the TOEFL and SAT exams, as well as teaching courses every semester to absolute beginners and intermediate students. Outside the official education system a reasonable number of language institutes and educational establishments are on the look out for well-presented, confident candidates.

One of the first private schools to be established after the revolution of 1990 was the AVO-3 School of English with two schools in Sofia (www.avo-bell.com) affiliated to Bell Worldwide. It runs CELTA courses (see entry in the Directory of Training Courses) and employs native English speaking staff who must have a degree, TEFL certificate and at least three months of teaching experience.

EFL vacancies hardly ever crop up on the internet, but this does not mean that they do not exist, as **Darren Quinn** reported at the end of the 2012 academic year:

> *Before I came to Bulgaria I had no idea what the job market was really like. All the information and advice I found online was negative. However, when I arrived here, even though I didn't speak the language very well, I walked into every school I could find and asked them for work. I landed the job I have at the moment just by walking in off the street and asking if they had any hours available. I had obtained my CELTA and had worked in South Korea for one year before I got the job here, though it would have been possible to work at some schools here without the CELTA. Within a few months I was working part-time at four different schools and had some private students. The application procedure in three out of the four schools among which I divide my time consisted of a short interview and one observed lesson. One of the schools (Real English School) employs only native teachers with qualifications, whereas the other three employ mostly Bulgarians. I found my work*

at these three schools quite trying at times. Bulgarian educators, for the most part, have not been exposed, or choose to ignore, many modern teaching practices. Many of them flatly deny that grammar can be taught by a native teacher, which can be very frustrating as someone whose job requires doing precisely that.

It is not easy to save money here. It is possible, but you have to work very hard. From October to April, it is not unusual for me to begin working at 8am and finish at 9pm, which is my choice. If you are not interested in saving, you can still lead a relatively comfortable life on a standard working week's wages. I would have to say that overall my experience has been a good one. The students are excellent and the Bulgarian people are very friendly and relaxed. Many people are put off coming to Bulgaria, I think because they think there are few job opportunities. From my own experience, I can say that this is not true: it's just that very few of the local schools advertise online. If you put in the legwork you can find work here and if you aren't worried about making a fortune, this is a very enjoyable place to teach English.

REGULATIONS

Bulgaria's accession into the EU has made it easier for teachers in terms of red tape. EU nationals only need a letter from their employer in order to get permission to stay for one year. It's a little time consuming, but basically unproblematic, and is done at the local police station. US citizens, on the other hand, need a visa obtained from the Bulgarian Embassy. For this reason the Real English School (see entry), among others, only employs EU citizens or non-EU citizens who have a right to stay for some other reason (e.g. marriage to a Bulgarian). The English Academy, however, will consider employing US citizens who are responsible for their own visas, although some assistance is given with paperwork.

LEISURE TIME

Vicky Williams, co-director of the Real English School based in Veliko Turnovo and Pleven, finds that living in Bulgaria is never dull:

As for living and working in BG, it is a country which is changing rapidly. There are still some vestiges of communism around in terms of architecture, cars, bureaucracy and lack of choice in shops, etc., but on the other hand there is a huge amount of building going on and many people now do have a lot of money. It's a fascinating place to live at the moment – it is a country of contrasts.

The current minimum wage in Bulgaria is 290 leva a month (about £115). Since a month's rent can cost about the same, the majority of Bulgarians live together in family units, often with several generations squashed together in one house. Most big cities are well equipped and Bulgaria is striving to meet the guidelines put in place since joining the European Union in 2007. In town, you'll find everything you would expect from a modern European city. In rural areas, on the other hand, wages are still much lower and living conditions can be more traditional, for example in the countryside you can still see peasants with donkeys and carts and stooped old ladies lugging branches of trees home to burn for firewood. In these areas indoor toilets may be something of a luxury. The Bulgarian countryside, especially mountain areas, is expansive and unspoilt, with plenty of affordable opportunities to hike or ski in the winter. The Black Sea coast is mostly built-up as holiday resorts and is a popular place for a cheap seaside break.

LIST OF EMPLOYERS

ENGLISH ACADEMY PLOVDIV
28 Gladston Street, Plovdiv 4000

© +359 32 623 457

plovdiv@englishacademybg.com

www.englishacademybg.com

NUMBER OF TEACHERS: 4.

PREFERENCE OF NATIONALITY: Only native English speakers.

QUALIFICATIONS: First degree and recognised teaching certificate such as the Cambridge CELTA.

CONDITIONS OF EMPLOYMENT: 3, 6 and 12-month contracts. Full-time: Tuesday to Friday, 5.40pm–9.40pm and Saturday 9am–1pm and 2pm–6pm. Part-time: less than 24 hours per week within the same time frame.

SALARY: 16 Bulgarian Leva per hour, 10% flat rate tax.

FACILITIES/SUPPORT: Arranges with local agents for accommodation viewings and assists with translation. Non-EU citizens are responsible for their own visas although assistance is given by the school.

RECRUITMENT: Telephone and/or in person interviews.

CONTACT: Mark A Faulkner, Director of Studies (markfaulkner@englishacademybg.com).

ENGLISH ACADEMY VARNA
48 Preslav Str, Nezavisimost Square, Varna 9000

© +359 52 622351

varna@englishacademybg.com

www.englishacademybg.com/jobs.php or www.varnaschool.com

NUMBER OF TEACHERS: 14.

PREFERENCE OF NATIONALITY: Only native English speakers.

QUALIFICATIONS: Degree in any subject and teaching certificate are essential, 3 years' experience preferred. Must be friendly and outgoing.

CONDITIONS OF EMPLOYMENT: 12-month contracts preferred starting in July (over 4 terms), 20-24 teaching hours a week, 5 days a week (Monday to Friday at summer school or Tuesday to Saturday during academic year, although a lot of teaching takes place at weekends). Part-time positions 12+ hours. July summer schools run in association with charitable foundation (www.arkutino-school.eu).

SALARY: 20 leva per hour (approximately €10), more for technical/non-standard teaching. 10% flat rate tax.

RECRUITMENT: Through the internet (mainly www.tefl.com). Interviews essential, either by telephone/skype or face-to-face. Non-EU citizens are responsible for their own visas, but assistance given with the relevant paperwork.

CONTACT: Mark Mctaggart, Director of Studies (mark@englishacademybg.com).

THE REAL ENGLISH SCHOOL
21 Hadji Dimitar Street, Veliko Turnovo 5000

© +359 62 605 749/886 171753

information@realenglishschool.eu

www.realenglishschool.eu

NUMBER OF TEACHERS: 6. Also 3 or 4 teachers for Pleven branch (Office no.1, Turgovski Complex Maxi, Ul. Tsar Boris III no. 12, 4th Floor, Pleven; tel +359 64 80 63 63).

PREFERENCE OF NATIONALITY: Must have EU passport, native English speakers only.

QUALIFICATIONS: CELTA or equivalent, prefer minimum 1 year's experience. Without CELTA, must have BA/MA in English or PGCE plus 2 years' TEFL experience. Experience teaching any exam courses (FCE, CAE, CPE, TOEFL, SAT, IELTS, ILEC) will be an advantage. The school teaches General and Business English (students are aged from 8 to adult).

CONDITIONS OF EMPLOYMENT: 1-year standard contract. 24 contact hours a week. Also summer vacancies on Black Sea coast between early July and late August.

SALARY: 1,000 Bulgarian Levs per month (net).

FACILITIES/SUPPORT: Free Bulgarian lessons. Assistance with locating accommodation and registering with the police, etc.

RECRUITMENT: Through tefl.com, eslbase.com, and local hire. Interviews are essential, and can be by phone. Very occasionally interviews are required.

CONTACT: Colin and Vicky Williams, Directors.

CZECH REPUBLIC

The proliferation of TEFL qualified teachers has allowed language schools to become far more discerning, especially in Prague. Language institutes generally do not accept online TEFL certificates, and adhere to the international standard of looking for teachers who have had at least 106 class hours in a four-week on-site programme, with at least six hours of observed teaching practice. Smaller Czech towns including some rather uninspiring places in the steel-producing heart of the country and the Moravian capital Brno offer interested teachers more scope for employment than the tourist-clogged capital. Be prepared for living and working conditions to change dramatically as soon as you leave the capital, especially for EFL teachers. Prague offers low pay, split shifts and intense competition between language schools that leads to job insecurity for teachers. Teaching private lessons is the most lucrative but the most difficult to fix up for new arrivals. Private lessons can be charged at 350+ crowns an hour, but most teachers working for a run-of-the-mill institute are paid 200-300 crowns. A good way to attract pupils initially is to charge at the lower end of the scale but to teach in groups of three or four.

FINDING A JOB

Most schools express no preference for nationality, and prefer a mixture of accents. Americans are still in the ascendancy (it has been estimated that there are between 20,000 and 30,000 in Prague alone), but Canadians, Britons, etc. are all welcome. Australians are generally well received partly because of the large number of Czechs (about 20,000) who emigrated to Australia, though they will encounter more visa difficulties than teachers from Britain, Ireland or the USA. The Czech Republic's entry into the EU also gives Britons a red-tape advantage. It is interesting to note that no schools in the list below stipulate that they hire only EU nationals.

STATE SCHOOLS

Qualified teachers are recruited to teach in Czech primary and secondary schools, usually on a one-year contract with low-cost or free accommodation and a salary of 15,000–25,000 Czech crowns net per month. The centralised contact is the Academic Information Agency (AIA) in Prague (see entry). AIA is part of the Ministry of Education, and distributes its literature through Czech Embassies abroad. Almost since the Velvet Revolution of 1991, the AIA has assisted native English speakers interested in teaching English at primary and secondary state schools. Far fewer schools turn to the AIA nowadays for help with filling posts. At the time of writing, only three secondary schools were publicising a vacancy for the 2011/2012 academic year. Any positions that are registered with the AIA are likely to be in smaller towns and very seldom in Prague. The school year runs for 10 months from 1 September to 30 June, though some vacancies occur in January between semesters. In some cases, TEFL qualifications are not required, though normally the minimum requirement is a BA/MA in English/Applied Linguistics, a teaching qualification and experience are expected. Applications should be submitted before the end of April. The AIA simply acts as a go-between, circulating CVs and applications to state schools that have requested a teacher. Schools then contact applicants directly to discuss contractual details. **Brian Farrelly** spent a very successful year teaching in state schools:

> *I taught in two state schools in the Czech Republic and had a really great time in both. I felt really privileged to teach the students there. In my first job in a 'gymnasium' secondary school in a small town called Sedlcany, south of Prague, the staff and students made me tremendously welcome. I also greatly enjoyed the freedom to*

teach as I saw fit, although I felt initially very daunted by the lack of guidance regarding what I should be doing with the students. My next job was found by the AIA in Prague. After visiting, I was offered a number of schools and I chose another gymnasium in another small town called Jevicko, north of Brno.

The growth of a free market economy means that the role of voluntary organisations has diminished, and in fact SOL (see introduction to Eastern Europe) is much less active in the Czech Republic than it once was. Although CETP is more active in Hungary (see chapter), it is hoping to expand into the Czech Republic to place volunteer EFL teachers in small Czech towns (not Prague).

PRIVATE INSTITUTES

A wide range of well-established schools offers high standards of instruction. The main international chains of language schools such as Berlitz have large established operations in the country. Most teachers are recruited locally, often through their TEFL training centre, such as ITTP TEFL Prague (www.tefl-prague.com) or via noticeboards, for example at the British Council and English language bookshops.

It is not difficult to find contact details for English language institutes in Prague and elsewhere. The most established schools which are externally vetted and their quality standards monitored belong to the Asociace Jazykovych Skol a Agentur CR (AJSCR) or Czech Association of Language Schools (www.ajsa.cz). Member schools could be worth approaching, though only a handful include teacher recruitment information in English on their websites:

Agentura Educo, s.r.o. – www.educo.cz
Albion jazyková a vzdělávací agentura, s.r.o. – www.jazykyalbion.cz
Centrum Cizích Jazyků a dalšího vzdělávání, s.r.o. – www.ccjskola.cz
Excellent Dokonalost v jazyce spol. s r.o. – www.excellentskola.cz
Gulliver Group s.r.o. – www.skolagulliver.cz
Hello Language School, s.r.o. – www.hello.cz
Hope - E.S., v.o.s. – www.jazykovyservis.cz
Irislingua, s.r.o. – www.irislingua.cz
James Cook Languages, s.r.o. – www.jamescooklanguages.cz (among the largest schools in the country, teaching in dozens of cities)
Lexis s.r.o. – www.lexis.cz
Lingua s.r.o. – www.eLingua.cz
Lingua Sandy s.r.o. – www.lingua-sandy.cz
Mezinárodní Jazykový Institut s.r.o. – www.mjimost.cz
Eva Camrdová Jazyková škola – www.jsk.camrdova.cz
Mk Jazykové Centrum – www.mkcentrum.cz
Oxford Jazyková škola – www.jazykove-sluzby.eu
Progress Language Institute s.r.o. – www.pli.cz
Sentia s.r.o. – www.sentia.cz
Skrivánek s.r.o. – http://skrivanek.jobs.cz
Slůně svět jazyků s.r.o. – www.slune.cz
Sophia jazykové služby s.r.o. – www.sophia-cb.cz/en/join-us/in-house
Soukromá Jazyková Škola Jana – www.janahk.cz
VAPC – Vzdělávací a překladatelské centrum – www.vapc.cz

Also the *Yellow Pages* (Zlaté Stránky) are an excellent source of addresses under the heading *Jazykove skoly* as is the Business Directory of the *Prague Post* (http://bol.praguepost.com/language-schools-and-agencies).

Of the institute websites that are available in English, a selection that provide teacher vacancy information and in some cases online application forms, include the Gulliver Group, James Cook, Lexis, Skřivánek, Sophia and Tutor (all listed above or in the directory) plus:

Cloverleaf Group, Ostrava – www.cloverleaf.cz/english
English Link s.r.o, Prague – www.englishlink.cz
Glossa Sskola jazyků – http://glossa.cz
International House, Brno – www.ilcbrno.cz
Tandem Jazykove, Prague – www.tandem.cz/work-for-tandem

Even though most schools in Prague claim to receive plenty of CVs on spec from which to fill any vacancies that arise, their willingness to describe their recruitment procedures online indicates that the demand for teachers is still very strong. Anyone who is well qualified or experienced should have few difficulties in finding a job on the spot, particularly if they are lucky with their timing. The market in Brno is booming too, with more than 80 language schools listed as operating in the country's second largest city (many will be one person outfits), catering to a population of just over 400,000. Most people wait until they arrive in Prague before trying to find teaching work, which is what **Linda Harrison** did:

> *The best time to apply is before June. I arrived in September which was too late, but if you persevere there are jobs around. A lot of teaching work here seems to be in companies. Schools employ you to go into offices, etc. to teach English (though not usually Business English). After a short job hunt, I was hired by a company called Languages at Work which paid well and provided food and travel vouchers as well as helping with accommodation.*

Languages at Work has since morphed several times and is now the Spevácek Education Centre (see entry). People end up teaching in Prague via the most circuitous routes as **Anne Morris** from the USA describes:

> *Although I'm near retirement age, I'm still a free spirit and am living in Prague now more or less by chance. I ran into an American couple at a jam-packed event in Old Town Square on a visit to Prague two years ago who said they were teaching English here. I've always loved this city so I asked how one would get a job like that and they scratched out a website on the back of an envelope (TEFL Worldwide). I lost them in the crowd but on return to the US came across the envelope in a coat pocket and decided to check it out – and now here I am teaching English. Just wish I'd made this discovery much earlier in my life!*

Outside of Prague, chances are reasonable of finding jobs in the private sector all year round, with the greatest selection available in late August through to November and in January/February. Those without qualifications or experience will find it very difficult. Unlike state schools, private schools in Prague do not offer accommodation, and will give preference when hiring to anyone who is already resident.

If you are stuck for a job during the summer months, then a good option is to work in a summer camp until the school year starts. There are a number of good summer camp options available, particularly teaching children, as well as intensive one-week courses for adults at holiday resorts. Children's camps do not generally pay very well, but food and accommodation are included, and many teachers use the camps as an opportunity to get to know a bit more of the country before going back to their city jobs in September. One to try is run by Grant Language School in Ceské Budejovice (www.grant-langschool.com).

There are a few advertisements for teaching jobs in the local English press, primarily the *Prague Post* (www.praguepost.com); the classifieds can be read online. At the time of writing there were more English teachers offering private lessons than jobs offered. It is very cheap to place your own lineage advert by contacting classifieds@praguepost.com. It may be worth advertising your speciality as an English tutor (e.g. marketing, law, etc.) ahead of time. **Kathy Panton** suggests enlisting the help of a Czech friend to translate 'Native speaker will tutor English to intermediate or advanced students', and send it to a newspaper like *MF Dnes* or *Annonce*.

REGULATIONS

Since accession, EU nationals no longer have to apply for a visa or work permit. As throughout the EU, those who intend to stay more than 90 days must obtain a residence certificate from the regional office of the Ministry of the Interior; see www.mvcr.cz for contact details or phone the information hotline ☎ +420 974 832 421.

Correspondingly it has become more problematic for non-EU nationals to obtain the necessary permission to live and work in the Czech Republic. The sought-after document is the blue card which entitles foreign nationals with good qualifications (minimum university degree) to both live and work in the country. This requires gathering a raft of documents including employment contract, proof of accommodation, health cover of at least €60,000, etc. and presenting it at the Czech embassy in your country or in some circumstances to the Ministry of the Interior. Foreigners do sometimes pick up work on their Schengen tourist visa but before it expires after 90 days, the holder must exit the country and is not allowed to return until a further 90 days has elapsed.

The Czech Republic has Working Holiday/Youth Mobility agreements with New Zealand and Canada which allow young people aged 18–35 who meet the acceptance criteria, to reside in the Czech Republic for up to 12 months (www.mzv.cz/ottawa and www.mzv.cz/sydney); the administration fee is currently 2,500 crowns.

EU nationals who want to set up as self-employed freelancers should obtain a Business Licence as **Martin Filla** did:

It took me about six months to get a business license. Before then some people took me on just as a temporary teacher and without a contract. After I got my business license, more schools were willing to give me work and also a (standard) contract with it. According to law, it took me about three years to get my permanent residence visa and this also shows schools I plan to live in the Czech Republic.

CONDITIONS OF WORK

People teaching at private institutes in Prague where there is a definite glut of foreign teachers, attracted by the cultural chic of the city, have been called the 'sweat shop labourers' of the TEFL world because of the low wages that employers can get away with paying. Salaries in the capital are sometimes lower than in smaller cities such as Brno, even though the cost of living is higher.

Working conditions in state schools are generally better than in private schools, though opportunities are far fewer than they used to be. The guaranteed salary at state schools, even if you're sick or there is a holiday, is a definite advantage. If you are lucky enough to be teaching mostly final year students, your working hours in the exam month of June will be minimal, even though the teaching day at a state school might start at 8am. This counts as a lie-in compared with teaching in private companies, which is often underway by 7am or 7.30am. And of course in state schools there is no evening or weekend work.

The monthly wage range in state schools of 20,000–35,000 crowns gross is catching up with wages in the private sector. Subsidised accommodation can make the package seem even more attractive. If you are on your own, for accommodation expect to spend between a fifth and a quarter of your earnings on simple accommodation. Hourly fees start at roughly 200 crowns net, though a more usual wage is 230–250 crowns. A full-time salary should be adequate to live on by local standards but will not allow you to save anything, unless you take on lots of private tutoring.

In Brno, wages nearly match those of Prague, but you should expect a few thousand less in smaller cities such as Olomouc, Xlin, Hradec Kralove, etc. However, outside the Czech Republic's major cities the cost of living drops dramatically and many teachers in smaller cities and towns find that they are able to save much more despite actually earning a lower monthly salary.

The majority of private language school clients are adults who are available for lessons after work, so most teaching takes place between 4pm and 8pm, Monday to Thursday. **Martin Filla** (originally from Australia but with an EU passport) encountered the problem familiar to all EFL teachers, trying to balance encouragement of students to speak with trying to get them to speak accurately, as he reported in June 2012 while working for David's Agency (see entry) in the Moravian spa town of Luhacovice:

> *Most of the teaching was conversation-based, to students who were intermediate or upper intermediate. One great challenge was to make it comfortable and interesting for everyone to speak, and help the students overcome their shyness. It was difficult to make every lesson interesting for everyone, and I was unsure about how much I should correct the students' bad grammar habits. Adult students especially have bad habits from earlier learning and these are very difficult to correct.*

Some schools specialise in teaching children, for which a basic knowledge of the Czech language, or a TEFL qualification which includes some training in teaching children is essential. One to try is a British company Wattsenglish with children's schools in Prague, Liberec, Usti nad Labem, Teplice, Karlovy Vary, Sokolov, Pardubice, Olomouc, Ostrava and Mlada Boleslav (www.wattsenglish.com/for-teachers/employment-opportunities).

Accommodation in Prague is more plentiful than it used to be. If you have a friend to translate for you, you can try the accommodation listings in *Annonce*, the Prague free ads paper, or craigslist in English (http://prague.craigslist.cz). Most employers are prepared to help newcomers to find accommodation, usually a room in a small shared flat or university hostel. In the rest of the country there is less competition for affordable accommodation. However, those moving to Brno or Zlin will find that the real-estate agents have taken over the market, so those without local support will find themselves having to pay one month's rent to the agent as a finder's fee. On the other hand, agents do offer the advantage of providing a wide selection of furnished flats covering a range of budgets and in a variety of neighbourhoods. Many people place an advert in the local *Inzert Expres* or other classifieds magazine, looking for accommodation. Many Czech students welcome the opportunity to share a flat with a native English speaker in order to practise their English for free.

Students are reported to be 'a delight to teach, alert, intelligent, fun-loving, keen and interested'. Many English teachers avail themselves of the excellent resource centres run by the British Council in Prague and Brno. The British Council's teaching centre in Prague has very occasional openings for teachers who are TEFL certified with two years' relevant experience. One of the strongest motivations among secondary school (*gymnasium*) students to learn English is the prospect of the 'Maturita' (school-leaver's) exam. At the beginning of the year they are given 25 topics (e.g. the British Royal Family, the influence of the media) and at the end of the year they must talk in English about one topic (chosen at random) for 15 minutes. This is a very good incentive for class participation.

LEISURE TIME

The cost of living in Prague continues to creep up, though most things are still affordable in other towns. For example a decent midday meal at a Brno restaurant (soup, main course and beer) will cost 80–90 crowns, whilst Brno rents are around 6,000 minimum a month. It is possible to survive on 500 crowns a day. Prague has a vibrant nightlife with clubs and cafés, cinema, opera, poetry and dance. There is so much expat culture, that a new arrival serious about getting into Czech culture will encounter difficulty. In Prague theft is a problem, though walking the streets is reasonably safe. In small towns, however, English teachers are still likely to be treated as honoured guests with many offers of hospitality and invitations, for example to join skiing trips (which are very cheap), as **Hannah Bullock** from Oxford discovered in her year out between school and university in the town of Strakonice:

> I've got some great Czech friends here. A colleague of mine has been very kind (as I've found most Czechs are) and has been like a mentor-cum-grandpa to me, taking me to visit castles, nearby towns, beautiful little villages and to walk in the mountains which border Germany. Most of this would have been very difficult without a car (the trains go very infrequently and at unsociable hours). I've spent many weekends in Prague since it's only one and a half hours by bus. I had to do double takes on hearing English spoken and seeing the Guardian being passed round the bars. Now instead of seeing Prague as the opening to Central Europe with its old-fashioned trams and cobbled streets as I did when I first arrived in September, I now think of it as the door back to Westernisation.

One final tip: if you play a musical instrument, take it with you since it's a great way to make local friends.

ANNE MORRIS

Anne Morris warns that it will take time to find your financial feet in the Czech Republic.

Do not plan on living on your income for several months at least. Schools usually only give you a few classes to start out. Also you are not paid when classes are cancelled for one reason or another or school is on vacation (I found this out the hard way in February when classes stopped during winter break) and there are a lot of initial expenses involved in housing, agency fees, health insurance, phone, internet, etc. so best to have a bit of a stash to fall back on.

One reward has been the opportunity to, if not totally assimilate, be a part of the native culture to some extent. An example was last night when I attended my high school's prom or 'ball' as they call it. Such fun to compare this universal ritual to a US prom! For starters, it was held in a palatial hall by any standards - not a crepe paper decorated basketball court as I remember high school dances and, heaven forbid, alcohol was served! A definite no-no in the US. And of course the kids outdid themselves with originality of style and sophistication. Really fun to be an onlooker.

LIST OF EMPLOYERS

A SCHOOL JAZYKOVÁ SKOLA
Obilní trh 2, Brno 602 00
+420 543 211 122
recepce@aschool.cz and info@aschool.cz
www.aschool.cz

NUMBER OF TEACHERS: 5.
PREFERENCE OF NATIONALITY: None.
QUALIFICATIONS: CELTA or TEFL.
CONDITIONS OF EMPLOYMENT: 1-year renewable contract. Working hours can be between 7am and 9pm, Monday to Friday.
FACILITIES/SUPPORT: Assistance provided with finding accommodation if necessary. Applications for work permits are coordinated on behalf of the teacher.
RECRUITMENT: Interviews and a demo lesson are essential. If necessary, the interview can be carried out via Skype.
CONTACT: Mgr. Michaela Sobotková, Director of Studies (misa.sobotkova@aschool.cz).

ACADEMIC INFORMATION AGENCY (AIA)
Centre for International Service, Ministry of Education Youth & Sports (Dum zahranicních sluzeb MSMT), Na Porící 1035/4, 110 00 Prague 1
+420 222 850 504
aia@dzs.cz
www.dzs.cz/scripts/detail.asp?id=599

NUMBER OF TEACHERS: Teachers needed for state primary and secondary schools throughout the Czech Republic though numbers have been decreasing over the years.
PREFERENCE OF NATIONALITY: Native English speakers from UK, Canada, USA, Australia.
QUALIFICATIONS: Professional teachers are preferred for teaching at primary and secondary schools. All candidates are required to have a college or university-level degree, preferably in English or in a related field. Additional qualification in teaching English as a foreign language (e.g. CELTA) is necessary for applicants who are graduates of courses in non-related subjects. Previous experience in teaching English in a classroom setting is greatly welcomed. High motivation is expected.
CONDITIONS OF EMPLOYMENT: 10-month contracts, 1 September to 30 June, 24 hours per week.
SALARY: 15,000–25,000 Czech crowns per month (before taxes and compulsory social insurance deductions).
FACILITIES/SUPPORT: Accommodation provided by schools (free or subsidised). Non-EU citizens – work and residence permits organised before arrival.

RECRUITMENT: Interested applicants register their availability with AIA, which circulates details to schools looking for a teacher. Actual vacancies with contact details are posted at www.dzs.cz/scripts/detail.asp?id=612.
CONTACT: Karla Benesová.

AKCENT INTERNATIONAL HOUSE PRAGUE
Bitovská 3, 140 00 Prague 4
+420 2 6126 16 38/6126 16 75
info@akcent.cz
www.akcent.cz

NUMBER OF TEACHERS: 100.
PREFERENCE OF NATIONALITY: None (need to comply with Czech immigration laws).
QUALIFICATIONS: Degree plus CELTA or equivalent (minimum).
CONDITIONS OF EMPLOYMENT: 10 or 12 months from September/October. Approximately 21 contact hours per week. Mostly teaching General English to adults, though some YL teaching. Teaching both on-site and in-company.
SALARY: 10,000–19,000 crowns (before tax) per month plus accommodation and other benefits.
FACILITIES/SUPPORT: Health insurance covered and 25 days' paid holidays per calendar year. Contribution made to cost of travelling to Prague. Offers CELTA/DELTA courses plus courses in teaching Young Learners and Business English.
RECRUITMENT: Helena Linková, Director of Studies (helena. linkova@akcent.cz).

THE BRITISH SCHOOL
Tisová 86, 25084 Kvetnice
+420 603 240 870
britishschool@britishschool.cz
www.britishschool.cz

NUMBER OF TEACHERS: 15–20.
PREFERENCE OF NATIONALITY: English-speaking country including Commonwealth countries.
QUALIFICATIONS: Certificate TEFLA (Trinity or Cambridge) and degree. Some experience teaching teenagers or adults.
CONDITIONS OF EMPLOYMENT: Teaching adults September/October to June. 21 hours per week, in Prague or Pilsen. Part-time work also available.
SALARY: Full-time: 21,000 crowns per month (fixed salary). Compulsory deductions about 4,000 crowns.
FACILITIES/SUPPORT: School will find furnished flat to be shared with another teacher. Health insurance provided. Computer access

and books. EU citizens can be employed immediately. For non-EU teachers, assistance with work permit application and visas provided; such teachers should bring their TEFL certificate, birth certificate, photos, passport and degree certificate.

RECRUITMENT: Send a CV with dates and a detailed covering letter to the above address – followed by interview in Prague.

CONTACT: David James Camidge, Principal.

BRNO ENGLISH CENTRE

Starobrnenska 16/18, 602 00 Brno

📞 +420 54121 2262

✉ hooper@brnoenglishcentre.cz

💻 www.brnoenglishcentre.cz

NUMBER OF TEACHERS: 16.

PREFERENCE OF NATIONALITY: Native English speakers.

QUALIFICATIONS: A university degree plus an internationally recognised TEFL/TESOL qualification (not online), together with a minimum of 1 year teaching with a similar institution.

CONDITIONS OF EMPLOYMENT: Standard contract is from September to May (9 months). Up to 24 lessons (45 minutes) per week, plus preparation, training and meetings. Contracts may be renewed.

SALARY: Around 24,600 crowns per month (gross) for average of 24 teaching hours a week. The average teacher would take home about 18,000–19,000 crowns.

FACILITIES/SUPPORT: Centre finds affordable accommodation (e.g. monthly rent of 7,000 crowns), pays the fees associated with this and advances the first month's rent. Work permits are generally not a major problem. It is more problematic gaining the residence permit needed for non-EU citizens, although the centre provides assistance.

RECRUITMENT: Normally by direct application. The centre does not go through agencies or intermediaries. Interviews are essential and can, in theory, be carried out in the UK or else by phone.

CONTACT: Simon Hooper, Director.

CALEDONIAN SCHOOL

Vltavská 24, 150 00 Prague

📞 +420 210 084 221

✉ jobs@caledonianschool.com

💻 www.caledonianschool.com

NUMBER OF TEACHERS: 100 in various locations in Prague and in schools around the Czech Republic (also in Slovakia).

PREFERENCE OF NATIONALITY: Teachers with EU nationality preferred due to visa requirements.

QUALIFICATIONS: Teachers must have TEFL/TESOL/CELTA qualification with or without teaching experience.

CONDITIONS OF EMPLOYMENT: 1-year contract, usually from September, with possibility of renewal. 22 to 26 45-minute lessons a week. School teaches adults and young adults, in-school and in-company.

SALARY: Approx 18,000–20,000 crowns per month (after 15% deduction for tax) for qualified teachers, depending on number of hours worked. Health insurance must be arranged independently.

FACILITIES/SUPPORT: Personal assistance in finding accommodation is not provided, however there are a few tips at www.caledonianschool.com/jobs-teaching-english-accomodation.html.

RECRUITMENT: Interviews carried out in person or via Skype. Applicants must complete a lesson plan task as part of the interview. School hires year round.

CONTACT: Tereza Pálková, HR Consultant.

CENTRAL EUROPEAN TEACHING PROGRAM

3800 NE, 72nd Avenue, Portland, Oregon 97213, USA

📞 +1 503 287 4977

✉ mary@cetp.info

💻 www.cetp.info

NUMBER OF TEACHERS: 3 for Czech Republic in 2012–13 though programme is well established in Hungary (see entry) and it is expected the Czech programme will expand.

PREFERENCE OF NATIONALITY: Native English speakers: USA, Canada, Australia, the UK and native English speaking Europeans.

QUALIFICATIONS: Minimum bachelor's degree plus 40-hour online TEFL certificate. Retired people welcome.

CONDITIONS OF EMPLOYMENT: Standard contract 1 school year, or sometimes winter semester only.

SALARY: $450–$750 per month after taxes, paid in local currency.

FACILITIES/SUPPORT: All teachers receive a furnished apartment with utilities paid. Apartments range from a small studio to a spacious 1 or 2 bedroom flat. All are equipped with TV and washing machine, among other amenities. CETP provides teachers with all necessary documents for residence visas. A week-long orientation is provided in Prague prior to the start of the school term. A Czech director oversees CETP teachers throughout the year.

RECRUITMENT: Via word of mouth, the internet and university placement offices. CETP programme fee is US$2,500.

CONTACT: Mary Rose, Director.

DAVID'S AGENCY

Dr. Veseleho 1042, 763 26 Luhacovice

📞 +420 603 346 618

✉ catto@davidsagency.cz

NUMBER OF TEACHERS: 2 in Zlin, 2 in Luhacovice spa town and 1 in Uherske Hradiste.

PREFERENCE OF NATIONALITY: British or other native English speakers.

QUALIFICATIONS: University degree and TEFL.

CONDITIONS OF EMPLOYMENT: 10-month contracts, 8am–noon and 1pm–4.30pm.

SALARY: 24,000 crowns (gross) less about 25% for tax, health insurance and social benefits.

FACILITIES/SUPPORT: Accommodation arranged for 5,000 crowns per month. Assistance with work visa process. Training given in Czech language and culture.

RECRUITMENT: Via email. Early application encouraged to allow visa processing time. Interviews are held in Britain in the summer.

CONTACT: David Catto, Director.

P.A.R.K. SCHOOL OF ENGLISH
8c Stankova, 60200 Brno
+420 5 41211900
infobrno@jspark.cz
www.jspark.cz

NUMBER OF TEACHERS: 15.

PREFERENCE OF NATIONALITY: None.

QUALIFICATIONS: Normally CELTA or Trinity CertTESOL plus a degree.

CONDITIONS OF EMPLOYMENT: 1-year contract. Teaching hours are between 7.30am and 8.30pm. School tries to avoid assigning split shifts.

SALARY: Varies according to experience. Deducted contributions usually amount to 10% of salary.

FACILITIES/SUPPORT: Office staff help teachers find the right flat or room. Assistance willingly given with obtaining visas, though it is a long process for non-EU teachers.

RECRUITMENT: Mostly local or direct approach from recently qualified TEFL teachers.

CONTACT: Ralph Davies, Director of Studies (ralph@jspark.cz).

THE PHILADELPHIA ACADEMY s.r.o.
T.G.M. 916/111, 293 01 Mladá Boleslav
+420 326 733 386
philadelphia@dragon.cz
www.philadel.com

Member of AJSA.

NUMBER OF TEACHERS: Approx. 40 in total (around 5 native teachers).

PREFERENCE OF NATIONALITY: None (though visas for Canadian and Australian citizens are problematic).

QUALIFICATIONS: BA/MA in English plus TEFL/TESOL/CELTA.

CONDITIONS OF EMPLOYMENT: 1 school year at least. About 25 hours per week (20 guaranteed – more is possible).

SALARY: 200 crowns per hour. Deductions depend on agreement.

FACILITIES/SUPPORT: Fully furnished flat with satellite dish, DVD player etc. located 15 minutes walking distance from the school building – paid for by school, except for utilities.

RECRUITMENT: Internet advertising. Interviews essential.

CONTACT: Dana Zbíralová, Owner.

POLYGLOT SPOL S.R.O.
Mecislavova 8, 140 00 Prague 4
+420 241 740 566
skola.praha@polyglot.cz
www.polyglot.cz

NUMBER OF TEACHERS: Approximately 50 for 7 branches throughout Prague.

PREFERENCE OF NATIONALITY: None.

QUALIFICATIONS: CELTA/TEFL or other certification of at least 120 hours of training plus experience.

CONDITIONS OF EMPLOYMENT: Between 7 and 20 hours teaching per week depending on whether the employee teaches in the morning or afternoon.

SALARY: 200–300 crowns per hour.

RECRUITMENT: Interviews are not always essential.

SPEVACEK EDUCATION CENTRE
Namesti Miru 15, 120 00 Prague 2
+420 222 517 869
centrum@spevacek.info
www.spevacek.info

Member of Czech Association of Language Schools (www.ajscr.cz). ISO 9001.

NUMBER OF TEACHERS: 150.

PREFERENCE OF NATIONALITY: Must be a native English or Czech/Slovak speaker. EU nationals only unless non-EU candidate already holds a valid visa.

QUALIFICATIONS: Minimum requirements are university degree and a recognised TEFL certificate. Online TEFL training is not acceptable unless combined with extensive experience. Formal EFL teaching experience is valued and rewarded. Professionalism, reliability, enthusiasm and smart appearance expected.

CONDITIONS OF EMPLOYMENT: 10-month renewable contracts. 80-90 teaching units per month (more if requested). Teaching adults only, mainly in-company General and Business English, small groups and individuals. Teaching kindergarten children, teenagers or (optional) public courses in a sister school. Hours normally 7.30am–10am and 3pm–7pm. Summer work also available.

SALARY: Approx. 23,000 crowns (gross) per month plus performance bonus and contract completion bonus.

FACILITIES/SUPPORT: Accommodation assistance, free internet access, well stocked library in the city centre. Full academic support with twice-monthly teacher development workshops. Travel pass allowance to facilitate travelling to clients' premises. Free Czech lessons.

RECRUITMENT: School recruits year-round but main recruiting time is July/August. Resumés/CVs and cover letter welcomed by email with 'Recruitment' in subject line. Interviews conducted in Prague or via Skype.

CONTACT: Ria Korcová, DOS (ria.korcova@spevacek.info).

STATE LANGUAGE SCHOOL BRNO
Jazyková skola s právem státní jazykové zkousky,
Kotlářská 9, 602 00 Brno
kucerova@sjs-brno.cz
www.sjs-brno.cz

NUMBER OF TEACHERS: 5.

PREFERENCE OF NATIONALITY: British.

QUALIFICATIONS: Must have TEFL qualification.

CONDITIONS OF EMPLOYMENT: 1 academic year (September to June). Approximately 20 hours per week.

SALARY: About 17,000 Czech crowns per month.

FACILITIES/SUPPORT: Assistance with finding accommodation, full help with work permits and training available at staff meetings.

RECRUITMENT: Liaise with other schools.

CONTACT: Iveta Kučerová, Deputy Head.

TUTOR SCHOOL
Vltavská 24, 150 00 Prague
+420 210 084 210
jobs@tutor.cz
www.tutor.cz

Part of EDUA Group (www.eduagroup.cz) and associated with Caledonian School (see above entry) though a separate legal entity.

NUMBER OF TEACHERS: Most vacancies in Prague and Brno.

PREFERENCE OF NATIONALITY: Teachers with EU nationality preferred due to visa requirements.

QUALIFICATIONS: Teachers must have TEFL/TESOL/CELTA qualification with or without teaching experience.

CONDITIONS OF EMPLOYMENT: One-year contract, usually from September, with possibility of renewal. 22 to 26 45-minute lessons a week. Most teaching takes place in-company.

SALARY: Approx 18,000–20,000 crowns per month (after 15% deduction for tax) for qualified teachers, depending on number of hours worked. Health insurance must be arranged independently.

FACILITIES/SUPPORT: Assistance in finding accommodation is not provided.

RECRUITMENT: Interviews carried out in person or via Skype. Applicants must complete a lesson plan task as part of the interview. School hires year round.

CONTACT: Tereza Pálková, HR Consultant.

VISTA WELCOME
Konevova 210, 130 00 Prague 3
+420 284 862 345
vista@iol.cz
www.vista-welcome.cz.

NUMBER OF TEACHERS: 6 native speakers. 32 Czech teachers.

PREFERENCE OF NATIONALITY: British, Canadian, American.

QUALIFICATIONS: TEFL certificate and/or proven ELS teaching experience. Mature teachers preferred, though enthusiasm important. School does not want to hire people who are just looking for a way to see the world. Experience in teaching business English a plus.

CONDITIONS OF EMPLOYMENT: 1-year contract minimum. Teaching hours vary. Full-time teachers guaranteed at least 20 lessons (45 minutes each) per week. Courses aimed at firms and organisations looking for in-house courses. Teachers often work for more than one school to get enough teaching hours.

SALARY: 230 crowns per hour plus medical and social insurance; or 320 crowns without insurance.

FACILITIES/SUPPORT: No accommodation provided though advice may be given to new arrivals.

RECRUITMENT: Adverts in the local English-language newspaper for expats (*Prague Post*), the internet and via other schools in Prague.

CONTACT: Ela Strůzková, Principal.

SLOVAK REPUBLIC

Slovakia has been somewhat neglected not only by tourists but by teachers as well. As one language school director put it a couple of years ago:

Many teachers head for Prague, which is why Slovakia stands aside of the main flow of the teachers. That's a pity as Prague is crowded with British and Americans while there's a lack of the teachers here in Slovakia.

Another wrote from a small Slovakian town, '*It would be wonderful if through your book more native speakers come to Slovakia*'. The density of private language schools in the capital Bratislava and in the other main cities such as Banska Bystrika makes an on-the-ground job-hunt promising.

IH Bratislava (entry below) is one of the largest private language schools in the Slovak Republic with over 40 teachers based in Bratislava and other towns around the country. They are looking for teachers with a TEFL certificate such as CELTA, Trinity CertTESOL, IHC, etc. Teaching experience and business work experience are an advantage, but not essential. In-company training is in high demand, as attested by the success of IH, which caters principally to the business market.

Once considered a backward part of Europe, huge resources have been poured into the country's development including into increasing access to English instruction. The European Social Fund has targeted groups who need English and provided subsidised or even free courses for people working in education or the civil service. As a result a substantial demand exists for native English teachers, although the wages are fairly low so many teachers tend to take on private students and/or economise. The salary range for teachers is €450–€500 net, €600–€800 gross. Many schools pay by the lesson which should be around €12, though the ones that provide free accommodation of course offer a lower wage, e.g. from €6. The flat rate of tax in Slovakia is 20%.

University students often leave Slovakia to work abroad during the summer (many in English-speaking countries). Although students can learn English by immersion, many will wish to be reasonably fluent so they can land a decent job in the first place.

It used to be a level playing field for English-speaking foreigners wanting to teach in Slovakia, but now EU citizens have a clear advantage, needing only to confirm residency for tax purposes. Registration can be done at the local police station. In order to obtain a trade licence, which may be necessary for self-employed freelancers, you will have to supply a sworn declaration that you have not been convicted of any crimes for the previous 10 years, something that can be done at the British Embassy in Bratislava for a fee of €66. Many teachers go freelance after one or two years working for a school which is advantageous for both schools and teachers. Freelancers may have less security but earn a lot more.

For candidates from outside the EU, the Slovak visa process is expensive and time-consuming. The main costs are getting a criminal record check from the teacher's home country (cost varies) and the visa fee. The applicant may need to submit a medical certificate, evidence of accommodation (i.e. a document from your landlord/lady) and so on. A blood test must be carried out within a couple of weeks of arriving as a prerequisite for a residence permit. All documents will have to be translated, notarised and/or apostilled. Most employers guide their teachers through the process but not many will cover the cost.

As well as the British Council at Panská 17 in Bratislava (info@britishcouncil.sk), there are five British Centres around the country with libraries and facilities of interest to English teachers. As always, much has moved online so that the Council in Slovakia offers lesson plans and materials to support English teachers and organises workshops and events. The only English language newspaper is the weekly *Slovak Spectator* published on Mondays, though it doesn't carry many adverts of interest to people looking for teaching work.

Although wages can be low, prices for food and meals out are not expensive, though they crept up when Slovakia joined the euro in 2009. Accommodation in Bratislava is about twice as expensive as in small towns in central Slovakia.

Budapest, Vienna and Prague are all within easy reach. Slovakia also offers good conditions for mountain walking along thousands of miles of hiking routes up to an altitude of 2,500m and for mountain cycling.

Michael Todd who is now a Senior Teacher at IH Bratislava has enjoyed living in Slovakia, but has a few reservations:

Typically, teachers stay one or two years and move on to another country. Bratislava is more a place to get experience. It's nice enough, well-located, but turnover is very high as Blava just doesn't have enough to hold teachers, unless of course, they start dating a local. I've met a lot of people from different countries, seen a lot of interesting places around Bratislava and have been introduced to literature I hadn't known about. It's rewarding that I'm helping people and can believe in my work rather than working for some company that sells some product. But the pay is low and the hours can be long. Accommodation is ok but it's kind of like being in university again as we share apartments with other teachers and tend to have hand-me-down furniture. Landlords/ladies are often controlling and seem to view your renting from them not as a business arrangement but as if they are doing you some personal favor. On a further note, I wouldn't have stayed in Slovakia as long as I have except that I've been dating an Austrian woman and, as an American, moving to Austria just wasn't an option. Bratislava is ok, it's not hard to live here but it's not in the league of Prague or Budapest. Usually when I visit some nearby city, I feel a little depressed coming back to Bratislava.

GEOFF NUNNEY

Geoff Nunney enjoyed a stint in Slovakia so much that he has stayed on until summer 2012. First he worked at Vages School (see entry), then at Lingua School (www.lingua-english.sk) in Nitra and the Rain School in nearby Šala (www.rainschool.sk), both east of the capital, and finally at a *gymnazium* or high school in Čadca, which had been arranged through the excellent UK-based organisation SOL (www.sol.org.uk).

It's thanks to your book that I found Slovakia. I teach at two local schools and two businesses here, including a brewery, in Nitra. The people here are great and were incredibly supportive when I lost both parents last year and also when I returned to England for treatment for a chronic health problem.

During the school's opening hours (7am-8pm) I teach kids, teenagers and adult conversation classes. The school provides good teaching resources, internet, copying and up-to-date text books. The recruitment processes were very thorough, consisting of a face-to-face interview with the headteacher, who was very informative, approachable and asked relevant questions.

The best thing you need in Slovakia is a sense of humour. I have been in school plays, and they are a very friendly nation of people. Their standard of English is very good, and they are great fun to teach. For example last Friday, a student stopped me and said, 'Geoff, the walls have ears' to demonstrate his mastery of an English idiom. Oh yes, I am even dating a Slovak teacher, who asked me out - very forward people the Slovaks - she stole my business card, rang my mobile, and we had a night out at the Irish Pub in Nitra. So things are definitely looking up.

Teaching wages in Slovakia allow you to cover the basic cost of living, but not much else. You can survive, pay the bills, but don't expect to save a lot. Although wages aren't great here, the locals and the scenery and the supportive staff make up for it. I speak a little Slovak, and if you immerse yourself, you will get the rewards. I love it out here, and it has stunning mountains and walking country. I would describe it all as a Slovak adventure!

LIST OF EMPLOYERS

ACADEMIA ISTROPOLITANA NOVA
Prostredna 47/A, 900 21 Svaty Jur
☎ +421 2 4497 0449
✉ ruth@ainova.sk
💻 www.ainova.sk

NUMBER OF TEACHERS: 6.

PREFERENCE OF NATIONALITY: UK citizens.

QUALIFICATIONS: University graduates preferably with pedagogical degree or holders of CELTA, TEFL or other internationally recognised certificate.

CONDITIONS OF EMPLOYMENT: 1-year contract, 80 teaching hours per month.

SALARY: By agreement.

FACILITIES/SUPPORT: Assistance giving in finding accommodation but teachers pay rent.

RECRUITMENT: Personal recommendation and ELT training centres. Phone interviews possible.

CONTACT: Ruth Zorvan, Head of Professional Communication and Language Programmes.

AKADEMIA VZDELAVANIA – ACADEMY OF EDUCATION
Gorkého 10, 81517 Bratislava
☎ +421 2 5441 0033
💻 www.aveducation.sk

Non-profit adult education association.

NUMBER OF TEACHERS: Approximately 20 full-time posts in 35 branches throughout Slovakia but mainly in Bratislava. Branches recruit individually.

PREFERENCE OF NATIONALITY: Native English speaker holding an EU passport.

QUALIFICATIONS: CELTA or TESOL qualification (or recognised equivalent) and degree. Energy, enthusiasm and an interest in people required. Must be willing to teach a range of classes, including teenagers or young learners.

CONDITIONS OF EMPLOYMENT: 1 academic year (mid-September to end of June). Teachers' contracts are for a maximum of 22.5 contact hours per week.

SALARY: Competitive salary plus accommodation allowance, local travel pass, health insurance, luncheon vouchers and contribution to airfares.

FACILITIES/SUPPORT: Work and residence permits arranged and paid for. Academic and pastoral support, regular seminars and workshops; orientation for new teachers.

CONTACT: Philip Brooks, Director of Studies.

CALEDONIAN SCHOOL
Vltavská 24, Prague 5
☎ +421 2 57 313 650
✉ jobs@caledonianschool.com
💻 www.caledonianschool.com

Teachers hired for schools in Slovakia as well as the Czech Republic – see entry in chapter on Czech Republic.

THE ENGLISH CLUB
Pri Suchom mlyne 36, 811 04 Bratislava
☎ +421 904 415 490
✉ oravecmartin@ba.telecom.sk
💻 www.theenglishclub.sk

NUMBER OF TEACHERS: 2–4.

PREFERENCE OF NATIONALITY: British.

QUALIFICATIONS: University degree plus TEFL/TESL/CELTA and 1 year's experience.

CONDITIONS OF EMPLOYMENT: 10-month contract from September to June. Working hours between 7am and 9.45pm, 30 hours per week.

SALARY: From €7 per 45 minutes.

FACILITIES/SUPPORT: Shared flat with wifi is available. All necessary paperwork for work permits is completed by the school.

RECRUITMENT: Usually via the internet. Interviews are essential.

CONTACT: Martin Oravec, Director.

EUROTREND 21
Namestie slobody 16, 81332 Bratislava
✉ info@eurotrend21.sk
💻 www.eurotrend21.sk

NUMBER OF TEACHERS: 4.

PREFERENCE OF NATIONALITY: None.

QUALIFICATIONS: Minimum university degree, TEFL certificate and experience.

CONDITIONS OF EMPLOYMENT: Minimum contract 6 months. Hours available mornings, afternoons and evenings.

SALARY: Dependent on experience. Starts at €12 per 45-minute lesson.

RECRUITMENT: Interviews are essential and are carried out on-site.

CONTACT: Lucia Zahubelová, Coordinator of Language Courses (lucia@eurotrend21.sk).

HARMONY SCHOOL
26 Kapitulska, 91701 Trnava
marketing@harmonyschool.sk
www.harmonyschool.sk

NUMBER OF TEACHERS: 2.
PREFERENCE OF NATIONALITY: EU citizens.
QUALIFICATIONS: CELTA/DELTA or equivalent.
CONDITIONS OF EMPLOYMENT: 1-year contract with 30 teaching hours and 10 admin hours per week.
SALARY: €1,000–1,500.
FACILITIES/SUPPORT: Assistance given with finding accommodation.
RECRUITMENT: Interviews are essential.
CONTACT: Jana Chynoradska, Managing Principal (jana@harmonyschool.sk).

INSTITÚT EURÓPSKYCH JAZYKOV
J. Borodaca 2, 071 01 Michalovce
+421 907 448 408
institut.ej@gmail.com
www.institut.sk

NUMBER OF TEACHERS: Rolling vacancies.
QUALIFICATIONS: Must be university graduate. School is looking for professionalism, strong educational background, experience, personality, and communication and people skills. Teachers should be patient, enthusiastic, good team players, with a sense of humour.
CONDITIONS OF EMPLOYMENT: Semesters start mid-September, early January and early April. 90-minute lessons. Many clients are graduates and civil servants, since the European Social Fund pays for free English courses for these categories.
FACILITIES/SUPPORT: Accommodation provided and help given with settling into local area.
CONTACT: Petra Gondkovicova, Owner/Manager.

INTERNATIONAL HOUSE BRATISLAVA
Namestie SNP 14, 811 06 Bratislava
+421 2 52 96 26 74
info@ihbratislava.sk
www.ihbratislava.sk

NUMBER OF TEACHERS: 20.
PREFERENCE OF NATIONALITY: EU.
QUALIFICATIONS: Minimum Cambridge CELTA/Trinity Cert.
CONDITIONS OF EMPLOYMENT: 10 months. Average 26.5 teaching hours per week.

SALARY: Depends on qualifications and experience. 20% deductions.
FACILITIES/SUPPORT: Full-time teachers are offered rent-free accommodation in shared flats. Assistance given with red tape.
RECRUITMENT: Via www.tefl.com. Interviews are essential and can be carried out by telephone/Skype.
CONTACT: Marja Juhola, Director of Studies.

JAZYKOVÁ SKOLA START
Kriva 23, 040 01 Kosice
+421 915 846 728
recruitment@jazykova.sk
www.jazykova.sk/jobs.php

NUMBER OF TEACHERS: 10.
PREFERENCE OF NATIONALITY: Native English speakers, mainly British, American, Australian.
QUALIFICATIONS: TEFL or previous experience is an advantage.
CONDITIONS OF EMPLOYMENT: 1 academic year, extendable to a permanent contract. Usual hours are 3pm–8pm with some morning lessons.
SALARY: By negotiation.
FACILITIES/SUPPORT: School finds accommodation for teachers. School assists logistically but not financially with visas (e.g. €170). EU nationals do not require visas.
RECRUITMENT: Via the internet. Also, a number of teachers come to Slovakia because they are in a relationship with a local and their partners make the initial contact in response to advertising. Interviews are carried out by phone or Skype. In the case of teachers already in Slovakia they are carried out in person.
CONTACT: Richard Swales, Director.

MHC BUSINESS LANGUAGE TRAINING s.r.o.
Zamocká 30, 81101 Bratislava
+43 43 1 60 30 563
office@mhc-training.com
www.mhc-training.com

Sister school of MHC in Austria.
NUMBER OF TEACHERS: 25.
PREFERENCE OF NATIONALITY: Any.
QUALIFICATIONS: MHC trainers have an understanding of business experience, often specialising in areas such as marketing, finance, pharmaceutical or law. A degree is not necessary, although a teaching certificate such as CELTA would be of value.
CONDITIONS OF EMPLOYMENT: Freelance, teaching 15–25 hours per week.
SALARY: €16–€20 per 60 minutes, depending on experience and development with MHC. Seminars pay between €200 and

€250 per day. Trainers are responsible for paying their own taxes (about 19%) and social security (variable).

FACILITIES/SUPPORT: Resource library in Vienna, photocopying at clients' premises, trainer development. Books required for courses. Trainers from non-EU countries require working papers.

RECRUITMENT: Interviews are essential and usually take place at premises. Possibility of Skype interview if the applicant is based abroad.

CONTACT: Mark Heather, Managing Director (mark.heather@ mhc-training.com).

S-CLUB
Vojenska 30, 934 01 Levice
+421 36 631 3224
info@sclub.sk
www.sclub.sk

NUMBER OF TEACHERS: 6.

PREFERENCE OF NATIONALITY: British, Irish.

QUALIFICATIONS: TEFL/TESOL and some experience.

CONDITIONS OF EMPLOYMENT: Academic year (September to the end of June), 25 teaching units of 45 minutes per week in the afternoons.

SALARY: €7.50 per lesson.

FACILITIES/SUPPORT: Support given with finding accommodation. No special permits needed for EU citizens.

RECRUITMENT: Via the internet. First contact by email. Telephone interviews.

CONTACT: Ing. Zuzana Sahligerová (sahligerova@sclub.sk).

VAGeS
Hodzova 25, 94901 Nitra
+421 37 652 4098
vages@vages.sk or vages@nextra.sk
www.vages.sk

NUMBER OF TEACHERS: 1.

PREFERENCE OF NATIONALITY: British, American.

QUALIFICATIONS: TEFL or university student preparing for a career in TEFL.

CONDITIONS OF EMPLOYMENT: 1 year (renewable), 20 lessons (45 minutes) per week.

SALARY: €8 per lesson, less 19% tax.

FACILITIES/SUPPORT: Room in the university students' hostel is paid for by the school.

RECRUITMENT: Through the local university, AIESEC programme, personal contacts and through sister city programme in the USA.

CONTACT: Elena Vargicova, Head Teacher/Owner.

HUNGARY

English is compulsory for all Hungarian students who wish to apply for college or university entrance, and university students in both the Arts and Sciences must take courses in English. The Hungarian education system has much to be proud of, not least the efficacy with which it retrained its Russian teachers as English teachers after the return to democracy in 1989. The network of bilingual secondary schools (*gimnazia*) has produced a large number of graduates with a sophisticated knowledge of English. In cities and even some small towns, bilingual schools now operate at the elementary level as well. From first grade onwards, students study basic subjects in English and Hungarian. The vast majority of private language schools are owned and run by Hungarians rather than expats. Even though the calibre of Hungarian teachers is very high, some schools still seem keen to employ native English teachers.

The invasion of foreigners in Budapest was never as overwhelming as it was (and is) in Prague, but still Budapest has a glut of teachers, among them some who have fled over-crowded Prague. The opportunities that do exist now are mostly in the provinces. Even in the more remote parts of the country, formal academic qualifications are important. It is a legal requirement that the bilingual schools employ a native English speaker as lector. Most *gimnazia* liaise with the Fulbright Commission or the Central European Teaching Program and take on Americans, though Britons are also eligible.

Teachers are poorly paid in Hungary, aside from in the top-notch private schools. Rents in Budapest are high and take a major proportion of a teacher's salary; some schools help by subsidising accommodation, or it may be possible to arrange accommodation in return for English lessons. Teachers through the Central European Teaching Program (see entry) have housing and utilities provided. Low as the salaries may seem, native English speakers can console themselves with the thought that they are usually better paid than Hungarian university lecturers.

FINDING A JOB

Very few jobs in Hungary are advertised in the UK and only one or two UK sending organisations (notably Sharing One Language; www.sol.org.uk) include Hungary in their list of destinations. A handful of teaching companies publish information for job-seekers on their sites, for example Cambridge Schools with two branches in the capital (www.cambridge.hu), M-Prospect (www.m-prospect.hu) and Berlitz (www.berlitz. hu). In the USA, recruitment of conversational English teachers and sometimes of other academic subjects as well takes place via the Central European Teaching Program (see entry). The programme offers 'cultural immersion through teaching' and is open to anyone with a university degree, preferably some experience of TEFL and overseas teaching/study experience and a willingness to pay the programme fee. CETP liaises with the relevant government department in Hungary to place teachers in state schools as well as in some parochial schools throughout the country. Hungary has a network of Dual Language Grammar Schools in which English is the medium of instruction for some subjects.

AFTER ARRIVAL

The British Council in Budapest (www.britishcouncil.org/hungary.htm) closed its teaching operations and library but continues to contribute to the professional development of teachers by organising courses and workshops with partner organisations across the country and by promoting online resources. Its partner libraries' GatewayUK information points house English language teaching and learning collections that members can borrow and host events for those interested in British culture and learning English. Partner libraries are located in Budapest, Békéscsaba, Debrecen, Eger, Gyor, Kecskemet, Szeged, Szekszard, Szolnok, Tatabanya and Veszprem. The British Council employs well-qualified native English speaking teachers to supervise exams.

A useful resource for native English speaking teachers is the 'Book of Lists' from the *Budapest Business Journal* which contains about 40 addresses of private language institutes. Try to find it in a library because it costs about €100 to buy.

Of interest to Americans is the Regional English Language Office located in the Public Diplomacy section of the US Embassy (Szabadság tér 7, 1054 Budapest; +36 1 475 4565; relomail@usembassy. hu). Like the British Council, the Regional office does not run its own English teaching programme but provides some assistance to Hungarian teacher training programmes by providing access to English language materials. A small lending/resource collection of professional ELT materials is available to professionals in the field in the Information Resource Center in the Embassy's Public Affairs section. Note that this office arranges the summer camp for young people on Lake Balaton, Teaching Tolerance Through English (see entry).

PRIVATE SCHOOLS

While it has become increasingly difficult for foreigners to find teaching jobs in Hungarian state schools, private institutes have mushroomed, primarily to meet the needs of the business community and also for children whose parents are keen for them to supplement the English teaching at state schools. It is estimated that there are over 100 private language schools in Budapest alone and 300 around the country, both very fluid numbers since schools open and close so quickly. Many private schools use native English speakers as live commercials for the schools, though nowadays they want to advertise the qualifications of their teachers too.

Anyone with a recognised TEFL Certificate and experience of the business world has a good chance of finding at least some hourly teaching after arrival in Budapest or elsewhere. British and American accents are both in demand. International House offers one-year contracts for qualified teachers of both adults and children and (according to a former teacher) has 'a wonderful social and professional atmosphere'.

To find the less-well-established schools on the spot, keep your eyes open for the flyers posted in the main shopping streets or check out the English language weeklies. To find out what new institutes have opened or expanded, look at Hungarian papers such as *Magyar Nemzet* or the free ads paper *Hirdetes* (www.hirdetes. ws) to see if any courses in *Angol* are being advertised at *Nyelviskola* (language schools).

Private tutoring provides one way of supplementing a meagre salary. Freelance teachers may find a developing market for their linguistic expertise in companies. Many executives need English for business as Hungary seeks to integrate with the economies of the West and attract foreign investors. The Department of Commerce, for example, employs teachers to train bankers, traders and top electrical engineers. Many professionals need English as part of their work and are both able and prepared to pay for it.

Another option is the Budapest-based agency SELTI founded in 2007, which provides English language training by native English speaking teachers to client companies and schools.

REGULATIONS

Since Hungary's accession to the EU in 2004, EU nationals no longer require a residence permit and immigration procedures have been much simplified. However, before the 93rd day of their stay, they should report their presence to their nearest regional Office of Immigration and Nationality. The office will issue a registration certificate, which permits indefinite stays. EU nationals working full-time in Hungary are subject to the same social security and pension obligations as Hungarians. Employees must make payments into the National Health Insurance Fund and into a pension fund.

Non-EU citizens must arrange work permits and residence permits before leaving their country of residence. A foreign employee cannot be legally paid until she or he has a work permit (which costs 5,000 forints). This fee has been waived for those applying to teach through the Central European Teaching Program. Those nationals who require a work permit must find a Hungarian employer who is entitled to apply for a work permit from the relevant Regional Employment Office. General information in English is available on the website of the Hungarian Ministry of Foreign Affairs (www.mfa.gov.hu).

CONDITIONS OF WORK

Salaries vary, but teachers at private institutes tend to earn about 2,000 forints (€7) an hour or 200,000 forints a month. It is essential to find out whether pay is net or gross since Hungarians lose more than a quarter of their already meagre wages on tax and contributions. It is also important to check whether your employer is taking out insurance on your behalf: an insurance mix-up turned **Ellen Parham**'s 'satisfactory' high-school salary into something worse than meagre.

American graduate and CETP participant **Genevieve Pierce**, found that teaching teenagers in a state school could be challenging:

> They are totally uninterested in learning, don't complete their homework, and lack any opinion or viewpoint. This is a result of the political situation in Hungary and the low salaries. I am sure my students overhear their parents complain about money and politics constantly which has to drain the students' hope for a future. I think they feel trapped in Hungary. One student even said, 'Why should I do my homework when I'm going to live in Hungary and be a shop clerk like my mother?'

On a more positive note, Genevieve found that going to class with a topic that everyone could talk about and allowing lessons to evolve was a more successful teaching strategy than following a strict lesson plan. In general students in the rural areas of eastern Hungary are better behaved than their counterparts in Budapest, though their level of English will be lower. This kind of problem won't arise if you are teaching in the business community. Freelance teachers can ask for 3,000 forints per lesson.

LEISURE TIME

The Opera House in Budapest is one of the most beautiful in the world, the Széchenyi thermal baths are the perfect place to unwind graciously and the coffee houses are ideal for watching the world go by. It is easy to make a strong argument for living in Budapest, but there are downsides, as long-stay American teacher **Ellen Parham** explains:

> Everything is convenient for me here in Budapest, but some of the others in the CETP programme who are teaching in smaller towns are treated like celebrities and everyone knows them. Living in a big city is hindering my ability to speak Hungarian, too. Everyone speaks English and I am never forced to speak Hungarian.

Being made to speak this notoriously difficult language, however, can be a mixed blessing, as **Genevieve Pierce** discovered while living in a quaint city on the Romanian border:

> Teaching in a place where you don't speak the language is difficult because you feel like a child. I seriously need a babysitter if I'm going to do anything of grave importance (i.e. visit the doctor, purchase a bicycle, arrange a postage delivery). Though, with all that said, teaching abroad has been the best experience of my life. I love to see students' faces when they finally realise what I'm talking about. I have enjoyed all the school functions such as dances, initiation ceremonies, and graduation. The best part has been learning about another culture, understanding their way of life. It's like nothing I could learn from a book.

LIST OF EMPLOYERS

AMEROPA LANGUAGE SCHOOL

Móricz Zs. Körtér 14, 1117 Budapest

📞 +36 1 209 5243

✉ nyelviskola@ameropa.hu

💻 www.ameropa.hu

NUMBER OF TEACHERS: 60.

PREFERENCE OF NATIONALITY: None.

QUALIFICATIONS: Minimum bachelor's degree and teacher training (TEFL, CELTA or equivalent).

CONDITIONS OF EMPLOYMENT: Ongoing contracts, usually between 6 and 24 months with 10–20 working hours per week.

SALARY: Competitive.

FACILITIES/SUPPORT: Assistance given with work permits.

RECRUITMENT: Interview and demonstration lesson are essential.

CONTACT: Andrea Rückne Koczka

CENTRAL EUROPEAN TEACHING PROGRAM

3800 NE, 72nd Avenue, Portland, Oregon 97213, USA

📞 +1 503 287 4977

✉ mary@cetp.info or hajni@cetp.info

💻 www.cetp.info

NUMBER OF TEACHERS: 75–80 (plus a small number in the Czech Republic, see entry).

PREFERENCE OF NATIONALITY: Native English speakers: USA, Canada, Australia, the UK, and native English-speaking Europeans.

QUALIFICATIONS: Minimum bachelor's degree plus 40 hour online TEFL certificate. Retired people welcome.

CONDITIONS OF EMPLOYMENT: Standard contract 1 school year, although teachers can sometimes be placed for winter semester only. To teach 22 hours per week.

SALARY: $450–$750 per month after taxes, paid in local currency.

FACILITIES/SUPPORT: All teachers receive a furnished apartment with utilities paid. Apartments range from a small studio to a spacious 1 or 2 bedroom flat. All are equipped with TV and washing machine, among other amenities. CETP provides teachers with all necessary documents for residence visas. A week-long orientation is provided in Budapest (and Prague) prior to the start of the school term. A Hungarian (or Czech) director oversees CETP teachers throughout the year.

RECRUITMENT: Via word of mouth, the internet and university placement offices. CETP programme fee is US$2,500.

CONTACT: Mary Rose, Director.

INTER-EX CENTRE

4/a Budaörsi Str. 1118 Budapest

📞 +36 1 361 0248

💻 www.interexcentrum.hu

NUMBER OF TEACHERS: 1–2.

PREFERENCE OF NATIONALITY: None.

QUALIFICATIONS: Any TEFL qualification and Cambridge CELS language exams.

CONDITIONS OF EMPLOYMENT: 20 hours per week, open-ended contract.

SALARY: 200,000–300,000 forints per month.

FACILITIES/SUPPORT: Possibility of some assistance with accommodation.

RECRUITMENT: Candidates must be interviewed in Hungary or occasionally UK.

CONTACT: George Gallo, Director.

INTERNATIONAL HOUSE BUDAPEST

Language School & Teacher Training Institute, Vermezo út 4, 1012 Budapest

📞 +36 1 212 4010

✉ dos@ih.hu

💻 www.ih.hu

NUMBER OF TEACHERS: 40.

QUALIFICATIONS: Minimum Cambridge CELTA.

CONDITIONS OF EMPLOYMENT: Contracts are for 25 contact hours per week including in-company teaching, teaching young learners, groups, one-to-one and special projects.

SALARY: 198,000 forints per month (net).

FACILITIES/SUPPORT: Assistance given with finding accommodation. In-service teacher development.

RECRUITMENT: Through direct application. Interviews essential, conducted if necessary by telephone or Skype.

CONTACT: Anna Csiky, Director of Studies.

KARINTHY FRIGYES GIMNAZIUM

Thököly ucta 7, Pestlorinc, 1183 Budapest

📞 +36 1 291 2072

✉ bognaraniko1@gmail.com

💻 www.karinthy.hu

NUMBER OF TEACHERS: About 70.

PREFERENCE OF NATIONALITY: Native English speakers.

QUALIFICATIONS: MA in English (preferred) or TEFL/TESL qualification.

CONDITIONS OF EMPLOYMENT: 1–2 year contracts, 22 lessons a week.

SALARY: National salary plus all costs of accommodation in a pleasant, fully furnished and equipped flat near the school. 10% taxes and social security deduction.

FACILITIES/SUPPORT: Assistance with work permits; authorised copies of degrees and/or certificates are needed by the end of June.

RECRUITMENT: Application directly through agencies and foundations. Interviews preferred and conducted via Skype, web cam or telephone.

CONTACT: Dr Anikó Bognár, Deputy Head.

KATEDRA LANGUAGE SCHOOL
Anker köz 1–3, 1061 Budapest
+36 1 700 0137
info@katedra.hu
www.katedra.hu

Has a presence in 37 towns.

NUMBER OF TEACHERS: 15.

PREFERENCE OF NATIONALITY: Native English speakers.

QUALIFICATIONS: CELTA, DELTA or equivalent.

CONDITIONS OF EMPLOYMENT: Standard contract is 6–12 months, 12–16 45-minute lessons per week.

SALARY: From 2,750 to 3,250 forints per lesson.

FACILITIES/SUPPORT: Assistance given with applying for work permits.

RECRUITMENT: Interview and mock lesson in Budapest is essential.

LIVING LANGUAGE SEMINAR
Eló Nyelvek Szemináriuma, Fejér György u. 8–10, 1053 Budapest
+36 1 317 9644
elonyelv@t-online.hu
www.elonyelvek.hu

NUMBER OF TEACHERS: 3–5 native English teachers.

PREFERENCE OF NATIONALITY: British, American, Canadian.

QUALIFICATIONS: A great deal of ESL teaching experience, registered City & Guilds, Local State Examinations centre. Preparation for City & Guilds, Cambridge and local ITK-Origó exams, TOEFL iBT, business English.

CONDITIONS OF EMPLOYMENT: Contracts from 3 months. Negotiable hours. Mainly teaching adults (aged 16–40).

SALARY: High by local standards.

FACILITIES/SUPPORT: No assistance with accommodation at present.

RECRUITMENT: Through adverts. Interviews required.

CONTACT: Paul Biró.

MANHATTAN LANGUAGE SCHOOL
Örs vezér tér 25/C, 1106 Budapest
+36 1 431 8630
info@manhattannyelvstudio.hu
www.manhattannyelvstudio.hu

NUMBER OF TEACHERS: 8–10 depending on the term.

PREFERENCE OF NATIONALITY: None.

QUALIFICATIONS: Teaching qualification (preferably CELTA or equivalent) and some teaching experience.

CONDITIONS OF EMPLOYMENT: Teachers work on freelance basis. Working hours depend on the type of course that is taught, e.g. company courses can start as early as 7am or in-house courses can finish after 8pm.

SALARY: €7–€11 per hour depending on the level taught and location of the course.

RECRUITMENT: Face-to-face interview although on rare occasions a phone interview may suffice. Candidates must also conduct a mock lesson.

CONTACT: Zsuza Orzoi (orzoi@manhattannyelvstudio.hu), Director of Studies.

SELTI INTERNATIONAL
Erzsébet Krt 20, III/4, Budapest 1073
+36 1 785 7743
vacancies@selti-international.com; info@selti-hungary.com
www.selti-international.com

Specialist provider to client schools and private companies of language teaching by native English teachers.

PREFERENCE OF NATIONALITY: Native English speakers including American, British, Canadian, Australian and New Zealander.

QUALIFICATIONS: Native English speakers with a post-secondary degree (or equivalent). A TEFL, TESOL or CELTA certificate is also needed.

CONDITIONS OF EMPLOYMENT: 8–12-month contracts. 20 contact hours per week plus preparation and travel time.

FACILITIES/SUPPORT: Company provides salary, monthly travel pass, access to office resources and gives assistance with immigration, accommodation and settling into Budapest.

RECRUITMENT: Main intakes are September and February, though they are continually looking for new teachers. Interviews are essential and can be conducted over Skype.

CONTACT: Ryan Peden, Managing Director (ryan.peden@selti-international.com) and Adelina Wong, Chief Operating Officer (adelina.wong@selti-international.com).

'TEACHING TOLERANCE THROUGH ENGLISH'
SUMMER CAMP

Camp Location: Kalória Kht. Gyermeküdülő, Úszó u. 5, 8638 Balatonlelle

(phone) +36 85 700 611

(email) relomail@usembassy.hu (Programme coordinator)

(web) http://teentolerance7.pbworks.com

NUMBER OF PARTICIPANTS: 8 regular camp counsellors and 1 junior counsellor.

PREFERENCE OF NATIONALITY: Native or near native English speakers.

QUALIFICATIONS: University graduate or undergraduate over the age of 21 with necessary camp skills.

CONDITIONS OF EMPLOYMENT: English summer camp held in first 2 weeks of August. Counsellors are responsible for organising sports, arts, leisure and intercultural activities.

SALARY: Modest stipend.

FACILITIES/SUPPORT: Full board accommodation is provided plus round trip travel from Budapest to the camp. Compulsory on-site training for camp counsellors takes place during the 2 days preceding the camp (e.g. July 26–27 in 2012).

RECRUITMENT: Main recruitment drive from April to May. Applicants should send in CV and letter of motivation.

CONTACT: Regional English Language Office for Central and Southeastern Europe, US Embassy, Budapest.

TUDOMANY NYELVISKOLA

Tavasz u.3, 1033 Budapest

(email) info@tudomanynyelviskola.hu

(web) www.tudomanynyelviskola.hu

Sister school is Európai Nyelvek Stúdiója at Tavasz ut 2 (www.europainyelvek.hu).

NUMBER OF TEACHERS: 10–15.

PREFERENCE OF NATIONALITY: British and American.

QUALIFICATIONS: TEFL/TESL preferred.

CONDITIONS OF EMPLOYMENT: 10-month contracts, hours vary.

FACILITIES/SUPPORT: Assistance with accommodation not usually given. Training sometimes available. Affiliated with ELT training centre Via Lingua Budapest (see Training listings).

RECRUITMENT: Local interviews essential.

CONTACT: Zsuzsanna Tölgyesi, Director of Studies (zsuzsa@tudomanynyelviskola.hu or dos@tudomanynyelviskola.hu).

VOCATIONAL ACADEMY

Puskas T u 8, 9027 Győr

(phone) +36 70 44 54 844

(email) nagyotto@vocational.hu

(web) ww.vocational.hu

NUMBER OF TEACHERS: 34.

PREFERENCE OF NATIONALITY: British, American, Canadian.

QUALIFICATIONS: TEFL and/or a master's degree. University degree needed, preferably in economics, travel and tourism, social study (nurses, etc.).

CONDITIONS OF EMPLOYMENT: Minimum 1 year. Hours of teaching 7.30am–4.30pm.

SALARY: €580 per month plus 4 weeks' paid holiday per year and extra benefits (e.g. flat, cheap meals, etc.). Deductions amount to about €65.

FACILITIES/SUPPORT: Student residence or block of flats owned by school, or employer helps teacher find other rental accommodation. School provides work and residence permit provided teacher passes medical test and has relevant documents and certificates to hand.

RECRUITMENT: Advertising. Face-to-face interview not essential.

CONTACT: Paul Rogerson, Principal (paul.rogerson@ihh.hu) or Tamás Vaniss, School Director (forlang@t-e-mail.hu).

INTERNATIONAL HOUSE BUDAPEST

'I chose to do my CELTA at IH Budapest because I had heard about its fantastic reputation as a teacher training centre, and it exceeded all my expectations. I had taught for a year before the CELTA and the course really helped me to develop as a teacher, both inside the classroom and out.'

Claire, now teaching in Malaysia

'Doing the course in Budapest in particular was enjoyable because the school has so much training experience and the city is so central for travelling to other cities in Central Europe.'

Sophie, now teaching in Budapest

'What made the course special for me was the great atmosphere created by the trainers and staff at the school. The trainers were always supportive and enthusiastic. The CELTA course was very hard work but immensely rewarding.'

Jill, now teaching in Morocco

'The staff and other teachers at IH Budapest were friendly and helpful, and the trainers were excellent. The school is a short tram ride from the city centre, so when you have a spare moment, you can get out there and explore one of the most exciting cities in the new Europe.'

Paul, now teaching in Australia

POLAND

Prospects for English teachers in Poland, western Poland in particular, remain reasonable, even if the seemingly insatiable demand for English teachers that has characterised the past 20 years is now a thing of the past. Poles are still keen to learn English, but with the explosion of cheap flights to and from Poland and the opening of borders, millions of Poles simply get on a plane and come to Britain or Ireland, mainly to work but sometimes to sign up for English language courses.

This is gradually having a knock-on effect on the quality of Polish English teachers working in their home country, although the reverence for 'native speakerhood' still runs very high. A famous Polish poet described (in perfect English) how his teenage daughter and her friends largely communicate in English, or at least a form of English picked up from TV shows and pop songs, and that some of the older generation are worried that Poland is becoming swamped by the English language and Western culture.

For now, certain types of English classes, largely taught by native English speakers are still popular; according to one director of studies: 'realistic' conversation classes teach Poles how to rent a flat or order a drink, while others teach students how to fill in forms (good luck to them).

Major cities such as Warsaw, Wroclaw, Krakow, Poznan and Gdańsk are possible destinations, especially for people with experience of preparing for Cambridge exams or those looking for in-company work. The smaller towns, for example in Silesia in southern Poland are more promising destinations, where the competition for jobs will be less intense and you may still receive preferential 'foreigner' treatment if you gain a dependable reputation as a teacher. Foreign teachers usually find their students friendly, open and keen to learn more about the world. Discussion classes are likely to be informed and lively, with students well up to date on developments and very well motivated to practise their English. In some companies, promotion depends on the level of English achieved, which spurs students from the business world to be especially committed. On the other hand, if the company is paying for an employee's lessons, there may be little incentive to attend regularly or with enthusiasm.

FINDING A JOB

Interested teachers should not expect to be snapped up unless they have at least a TEFL certificate and some sort of teaching experience. International House has a big presence in Poland with schools in Bielsko-Biala, Bydgoszcz, Katowice, Kielce, Koszalin, Opole, Torun and Wroclaw, some of which are listed in the directory. The Bell Educational Trust has an Associate Network of schools in Bydgoszcz, Gdańsk, Gdynia, Sopot, Szczecin, Warsaw, Poznan and Krakow. These high profile ELT organisations are founding members of PASE, the Polish Association for Standards in English which promotes ethical practices in the private sector. PASE has about 25 member schools which are linked from www.pase.pl. PASE members employ almost exclusively teachers with a recognised teaching qualification. Schools approved by the Polish Ministry of Education insist that their teachers have a university degree and a teaching qualification.

ON THE SPOT

Semesters begin on 1 October and 15 February, and the best time to arrive is a month beforehand. After arrival, try to establish some contacts, possibly by visiting the English department at the university. Although some school directors state a preference for British or American accents, many are neutral provided you are a native English speaker.

Private language schools can be found everywhere, catering for all kinds of English. The Warsaw *Yellow Pages* carries several pages under the heading *Jezykowe Kursy, Szkolenia*. Alternatively you can trawl databases such as www.ang.pl/szkoly_jezykowe.php. The very busy British Council in Warsaw (near Central station) and the smaller partner offices and libraries in other cities may be able to assist personal callers.

While some institutes have high standards in those they hire, others are looking more for personality, as a rather jaundiced poster on an online forum complained recently (www.polishforums.com/work-study-43/ ih-school-krakow-19621):

> *It's a sad fact that the English teaching market in Poland is driven by price not quality. School owners want bright and bouncy 21-year-olds straight off a degree, ideally with a CELTA, who are going to entertain the customers and not have an opinion on teaching. They'll complain that 'natives are unreliable' when these 21-year-olds stay in the pub till 2 in the morning on a weekday but it's a fair trade at the end of the day because they won't start demanding better standards like a more experienced teacher would (e.g. Being paid. On time. As agreed).*

If you base yourself in Warsaw and wish to advertise your availability for private English tuition, try placing a notice just to the right of the main gate of Warsaw University. A further idea is to visit Irlandzki Pub 3 at ul. Miodowa 3 near the castle which many English speakers use as their watering-hole.

Freelancing is very popular, and there has been a huge increase in demand for tailor-made one-to-one courses. When **Kathy Cooper** was based in the small town of Raciborz in Silesia she worked for three language schools over seven years and also freelanced on the side. She found that once her name was established around town, she had a waiting list of willing students. Banks are likely clients and often pay very well by Polish standards. Kathy also taught corporate clients (signed through the school) from many industries, including '*food/chocolate, cement, power plants, furniture, steel, industrial cleaning and sanitation, automotive, banking, industrial equipment, manufacturing, legal profession, doctors, and hotel industry. Yes, I am in Poland, land of opportunity for teachers*'.

Competent freelancers ask for at least 40 zloty an hour. As usual private students can be unreliable so try to get them to pay for, say, a month's lessons in advance. For this work, teachers should have enough ELT awareness to be able to devise their own syllabus. They will also have to put up with early or late hours (8am/9pm) and the inevitable cancelled lessons as business execs reschedule due to important meetings. Kathy Cooper got around this problem simply by calling another business client who wanted to make up lost hours.

ACADEMIC INSTITUTES

NKJOs are teacher training colleges specialising in training teachers of foreign languages. NKJOs are sometimes willing to hire qualified, experienced teachers. Virtually every institute of higher education (universities, medical academies, technical universities, economics academies, art schools, etc.) has a Studium Jazykow Obcych (Foreign Language Department) which is where the students who aren't language majors fulfil their foreign language requirements. The learners are less advanced and possibly less motivated in English than at the NKJOs, and they may be prepared to accept less well qualified native English speaker assistants while offering the attractions of an academic setting.

Jobs attached to universities usually offer stability and a light workload, say 12–15 classroom hours a week during the two 15-week semesters. The salary is paid over 12 months and includes full health insurance, housing perks and discounts on train travel. Bear in mind that if you are tutoring some of them privately, this income will vanish over the summer vacation.

HOLIDAY LANGUAGE CAMPS

Private language teaching organisations run short-term holiday courses in summer and sometimes winter, requiring English native speakers. ESCS (www.escs-katowice.pl) hires teachers for language schools in southern Poland and summer language camps at the Polish seaside. American **Alicia Wszelaki** was full of praise for ESCS after spending a year immersing herself in Polish culture in the southern town of Myslenice. Similarly **Will Gardner** greatly enjoyed his summer job with ESCS which he had fixed up from England in the spring:

> *I spent one month working for ESCS at their summer camp on Poland's Baltic Coast. The camps were well organised and great fun. As an experienced teacher who has worked in several different countries for a range of schools, I would just like to say what a pleasure it was to work with such a well organised group of people and for a school that completely lived up to its promises. The school supplied a wide range of resources to assist teachers, although a lot of emphasis was placed on originality. The focus was always on communication and fun. The camp facilities were perfect for the situation. Food and accommodation were supplied and the weather was beautiful. Although the students were attending lessons daily, a holiday atmosphere prevailed over all activities.*

To take one example, the Perfect English private language school (www.perfectenglish.pl) in the foothills of the Beskidy Mountains in Southern Poland was recently advertising vacancies for its summer courses as well as for the academic year. American young people might be interested in volunteering to work at one of the many English language immersion camps run by the Kosciuszko Foundation's Teaching English in Poland Program (www.thekf.org/kf/programs/summer/teaching_english_in_poland). The four-week programme takes place in July.

Short holidays in which paying language learners mingle and interact with native speakers being given free room and board are organised by AIP Angloville (see entry).

REGULATIONS

Poland's requirements for EU teachers are broadly in line with the rest of Europe. They no longer need to apply for a work permit, however teachers wishing to stay for more than three months must obtain a residence card from the regional governor of their chosen city/town. Applicants will need to justify their stay in Poland and confirm that they have sources of income (e.g. a statement from a bank account). Employers should assist with the documentation and the necessary translation of official documents into Polish.

Non-EU nationals who want to stay for more than 90 days and for less than a year will have to jump through the usual hoops prior to departure from their home country. The required documents must be presented in person to a Polish Consulate: a valid work permit certificate issued by the Office of Wojewoda in Poland or a promissory work permit from your Polish employer, your passport, two photos, a completed application form and the current fee for a work visa. In order for your employer to obtain permission to employ a foreign teacher, he or she will have to submit originals or notarised copies of your degree diploma and TEFL certificate (if applicable) with official translations. After arrival with the visa, you will need to obtain a work permit. Most schools will assist with the documentation but may not bear the financial cost (approximately 250 zloties including courier). When the initial visa expires (after three months), it is possible to apply for a residency card from inside Poland which will be valid for two years (fee 350 zl). Most employers who take on foreign teachers are well aware of the procedures which, according to one, could fill a book on their own. English language teachers planning to work in Poland at universities or colleges can submit a Certificate of Employment issued by the president of the hiring institution instead of a work permit certificate. The Polish Embassy in Washington can provide further details (www.polandembassy.org).

CONDITIONS OF WORK

Generally speaking, private language schools in Poland offer reasonable working conditions. Instead of hearing complaints from teachers of employers, it tends to be more often the other way round, as the Director of Studies of a private language school makes clear:

> My boss, who has been employing British native speakers for seven years and who has proved to be a very patient person, could provide you with some hair-raising stories of teachers signing their contracts and withdrawing at the very last minute (having probably found a more lucrative job in Japan), teachers returning a couple of days late after the Christmas break without presenting any adequate excuse (or not returning at all), not to mention the state of flats and equipment which, after being used for nine months, is often left in a wrecked condition.

Wages are higher than they used to be, but the cost of living has crept up too. The current average net salary in the private sector starts at about 2,100 zloties (£460) per month. Wages that look low on paper may come with free accommodation and in general the terms of service are seldom exploitative. It is not uncommon for overtime to be paid to teachers for hours worked in excess of the contracted number (typically 24) and for transport perks to be offered. Accommodation does not present as major a problem as it did in the early days because most employers either offer staff accommodation or will assist in a flat hunt. If you have to rent on the open market, expect to pay about 1,000 zloties a month, plus utilities will total about 150 zloties and internet access will add a further 80 zloties to your monthly outgoings.

Until recently, few foreigners in their first two years were asked to pay income tax, though a deduction was made for social security. However, now that Poland is in the EU, the Polish tax authorities are becoming increasingly tough on language schools, and so it is unwise to work 'black' and run the risk of being asked to pay unpaid tax even after you have returned to the UK.

Despite a considerable amount of disorganisation at many schools, no one complains of a lack of hospitality from the Poles. Poles even seem to have the ability to crack jokes in English when their English is very elementary, so lessons are not usually dull. On the whole they are also very well-motivated and hardworking, including adolescents.

HEIDI ROTHWELL-WALKER

Heidi Rothwell-Walker enjoyed company teaching, which was a contrast with the basic adult education she had been doing in Britain.

I was expected to work any time from 7am to 6pm. Sometimes the early hours (especially in the long winter) can get you down, but you will be rewarded financially for starting at 7am. There was a lot of travelling and waiting at bus stops, but working conditions in the companies were excellent. Not every company gave you access to a white board or overhead projector but they could be made available upon request.

LEISURE TIME

Poland offers no shortage of sights to see, pubs to visit, museums, theatres and parks to enjoy. Films are usually in English with Polish subtitles. Travelling is fairly cheap and easy. The transport system in Warsaw and some other cities looks complicated at first glance but is in fact straightforward. People in shops and so on can seem rude and abrupt, though this should not be taken personally.

Kathy Cooper has fallen for the food, '*Poland yields the most amazing hams, kielbasas and bacon that have ever melted in my mouth. Add the dense and daily purchased homemade breads that taste like my grandmother's, the variety of local and international cheeses, harvests of the freshest chemical-free fruits and vegetables that can be found, plus ice creams, baked goods, and phenomenal yogurts abound. Need I say more?*'... although she does go on to say that the Western plague of hypermarkets is starting to lead to the closure of traditional small shops.

Heidi Rothwell-Walker is convinced that she made the right decision when she chose to work for a school in Poland rather than at one of the other schools around the world that offered her a job:

> The language is difficult, comprising such wonderful names as, 'Sczcyrk,' a tiny ski village, but it can make for a good atmosphere in the classroom as you struggle with Polish pronunciation whilst your students try to get their tongues round English words.
>
> Poland can seem a bit of a backwater, but it's a tremendous experience. It'll change your thinking completely and you'll either love it (like 98% of people) or hate it, but you must try it. I have just renewed my contract for another year because I have been very impressed by them and am very happy here.

KATHY COOPER

Kathy Cooper is an American grandmother who suddenly decided to live in Europe. Immediately after obtaining a Trinity certificate in TESOL in the UK, she was offered a job in southern Poland and has fallen in love with her life there, the chemical-free foods, the teaching and the culture. She began her Polish teaching career in the town of Opole, where she was thrown in at the deep end. With time, she was able to refine her teaching schedule.

Teaching varies from school to school, and from classroom to classroom. Starting out, I was thrown immediately into a range of beginning children to executive business and British Council exam classes. It was either to be my death or destiny. I now specialise in only executive business and exam classes. Periodically I embark on a student who wants to attend either high school or university in America whence I teach TOEFL exams for both. SLEP (Secondary Level English Proficiency) testing is the new format for high school entrance in America, it is part of the TOEFL system. I can proudly relate that my last student attending a foremost university in the States has just been asked to return, and on scholarship, to obtain her MA in Graphic Design. She was their first Pole of several thousand foreign students. Teachers are a mix of English speaking nationalities; I have worked with all, including other Americans. It is most common you will tandem teach with Polish teachers. In my case, again, I have some executives and advanced students that require only native speakers because of their language level. Facilities vary; I've been lucky to have had beautifully renovated and comfortable buildings and classrooms. It's not always the norm. Depending on the age of the company, depends on your resource library. I am with a young school now, and we are stocking year by year.

LIST OF EMPLOYERS

AIP ANGLOVILLE
Al. Niepodleglosci 147/25, 02-555 Warsaw.
- +48 796 409 986
- info@angloville.com
- www.angloville.com

NUMBER OF TEACHERS: 20 a month.

PREFERENCE OF NATIONALITY: None.

QUALIFICATIONS: No experience/qualifications. Must be a native speaker of English and at least 18. Must be enthusiastic conversationalist willing to engage in English conversation for at least 12 hours a day.

CONDITIONS OF EMPLOYMENT: 1 week language exchange programme at a hotel in the Bug River National Park, with variable hours of English conversation time mainly with business executives.

SALARY: None, but free board and hotel accommodation are given. Hotel has swimming pools, spa, tennis courts and other facilities.

RECRUITMENT: Application process is online. Occasionally interviews take place by telephone.

CONTACT: Michal Zak, Programme Co-ordinator.

ANGLOSCHOOL
ul. Klaudyny 12, 01–684 Warsaw
- +48 22 833 21 00
- agnieszka@angloschool.com.pl
- www.angloschool.com.pl

NUMBER OF TEACHERS: 10–12 native English speakers in 6 centres in Warsaw.

QUALIFICATIONS: CELTA or equivalent and a university degree. Teaching experience preferred.

CONDITIONS OF EMPLOYMENT: 9-month contract from mid-September, up to 28 hours per week teaching 3pm–8.30pm Monday to Friday. Some morning classes 8.30am–10am.

SALARY: Competitive. School pays taxes and social security (45%).

FACILITIES/SUPPORT: Accommodation is provided by the school in the form of two or three roomed shared flats or single rooms in a house. Accommodation includes all necessary facilities, i.e. furniture, a phone, cable TV, a washing machine, kitchen with necessary equipment. Initial training course and ongoing workshops.

RECRUITMENT: Co-operates with schools running CELTA, TEFL courses, which provide a job placement service. Advertising in newspapers, internet (www.tefl.com) and recruitment agencies. Direct application with CV and photo welcomed.

CONTACT: Agnieszka Heintze, School Director.

BRITISH CENTRE S.C – ENGLISH LANGUAGE COURSES
Dabrowskiego 8/6, 42–200 Czestochowa
- +48 34 361 5914
- office@britishcentre.pl
- www.britishcentre.pl

NUMBER OF TEACHERS: 2.

PREFERENCE OF NATIONALITY: British.

QUALIFICATIONS: CELTA and experience with preparing students for Cambridge ESOL exams.

CONDITIONS OF EMPLOYMENT: 1-year contract with between 15 and 20 lessons per week.

SALARY: 35 Zloty per lesson (45 minutes). 26–25 Zloty after tax and social security deductions.

FACILITIES/SUPPORT: Room provided in English teacher's house.

CONTACT: Henryka Rabenda, Co-owner.

ELS-BELL EDUCATION
ul Budapesztańska 3/17, 80-244 Gdansk
- +48 58 341 34 87
- gdansk@bellschools.pl
- www.bellschools.pl

In association with Bell Educational Trust of Cambridge.

NUMBER OF TEACHERS: 90 for centres in Gdansk, Gdynia, Bydgoszcz, Szczecin and Warsaw. Other Bell affiliates are Program Bell in Poznan, and Gama Bell in Krakow.

PREFERENCE OF NATIONALITY: British and Irish. Non-EU considered with relevant experience.

QUALIFICATIONS: CELTA or Trinity TESOL plus university degree. Minimum 1 year experience.

CONDITIONS OF EMPLOYMENT: September to June, 20–26 hours a week. Annual workload is 680 hours. Part-time contracts also available. Also run summer camps for young learners (aged 9–17).

SALARY: 2,400–2,800 Zloty net, plus end-of-contract bonus of 1,000 Zloty. Warsaw wages are higher: 3,000–3,600 Zloty.

FACILITIES/SUPPORT: Accommodation assistance. Costs of obtaining work permits and visas are reimbursed by school. Health insurance taken out. In-house teacher development programme. Warsaw centre also runs CELTA and DELTA courses.

RECRUITMENT: Ads on internet. Interviews necessary, usually by phone.

CONTACT: Ludka Kotarska, Managing Director.

ENGLISH COLLEGE
ul. Zeromskiego 31, 26 600 Radom
- +48 385 80 33
- biuro@englishcollege.pl
- www.englishcollege.pl

Centres located in Radom and 4 nearby towns Kozienice, Ilza, Pionki and Zwoleń.

PREFERENCE OF NATIONALITY: Native speakers of English with clear standard British or North American accent.

QUALIFICATIONS: Degree (preferably in education or TESOL), TEFL/TESOL Certificate and experience. Should be enthusiastic, energetic, open-minded and enjoy contact with people and eager to learn new things.

CONDITIONS OF EMPLOYMENT: 9-month contracts (30 teaching weeks) from end of September. 22–24 hours per week, teaching all ages: children, teenagers and adults. Hours mainly 3pm–8.30pm.

SALARY: 20,000–22,000 zloty per contract depending on the hours. Monthly advance of 2,000 zloty plus contract completion bonus (up to 10% of salary).

FACILITIES/SUPPORT: Single furnished studio flat provided free, but not utilities. Cost of work permit covered by school (including courier delivery) but not visa if required. Transport paid for to off-site schools (30–40 minutes away from Radom) by bus or company car. Half of the cost of health insurance will be reimbursed.

RECRUITMENT: Application form, photo and copies of teaching certificates to be submitted and 2 references received directly before Skype interview is arranged.

CONTACT: Witold Machlarz, Director.

ENGLISH LANGUAGE CENTRE 'RIGHT NOW'
Pszczynska 17, 44–240 Zory, Silesia
- +48 32 434 2929
- info@rightnow.pl
- www.rightnow.pl/jobopp.php

NUMBER OF TEACHERS: 2–3.

PREFERENCE OF NATIONALITY: EU passport holder.

QUALIFICATIONS: TESOL certificate or equivalent, and at least 1 year's teaching experience to speakers of other languages.

CONDITIONS OF EMPLOYMENT: 9–10 months September to mid-June. 12 90-minute lessons per week.

SALARY: About 2,000 zloty per month after deductions and taxes.

FACILITIES/SUPPORT: Free accommodation in a two-person flat within walking distance of the school.

RECRUITMENT: Internet ads followed by interviews in person or by telephone.

CONTACT: Rafal Zurkowski, Owner/Manager.

ENGLISH UNLIMITED
ul. Podmlynska 10, 80–855 Gdansk
- work@eu.com.pl
- www.eu.com.pl

NUMBER OF TEACHERS: 4 for 4 centres around the Tri-City (Gdansk, Gdynia and Sopot). Also possibility of teaching at the Teacher Training College in Gdansk.

PREFERENCE OF NATIONALITY: None; must be native English speakers (EU citizens preferred).

QUALIFICATIONS: Bachelor's or master's degree and Cambridge certificate or diploma plus experience of overseas teaching.

CONDITIONS OF EMPLOYMENT: 9-month contracts from September. Varied hours of teaching. Courses offered in ESP (e.g. Business English).

SALARY: About £350 per month (net).

FACILITIES/SUPPORT: Help given with arranging accommodation. Training provided.

RECRUITMENT: Adverts on internet. Interviews essential.

GLOBAL VILLAGE
Al. Legionów 42, 25–035 Kielce
- office@gv.edu.pl
- www.gv.edu.pl

NUMBER OF TEACHERS: 7.

PREFERENCE OF NATIONALITY: EU nationals preferred.

QUALIFICATIONS: Bachelor's or master's plus a CELTA, DELTA or TEFL certificate.

CONDITIONS OF EMPLOYMENT: Standard contract length 1 academic year, to work 3pm–8pm, Monday to Friday.

SALARY: Competitive.

FACILITIES/SUPPORT: The school organises accommodation.

CONTACT: Urszula Szczepanczyk, Director.

GREENWICH SCHOOL OF ENGLISH
ul. Gimnastyczna 70, 02–632 Warsaw
- rekrutacja@greenwich.edu.pl, school@greenwich.edu.pl
- www.greenwich.edu.pl

NUMBER OF TEACHERS: 20 full-time, 10 part-time for 4 branches in Warsaw and 1 in Gdansk.

PREFERENCE OF NATIONALITY: British or any other native English speaker.

QUALIFICATIONS: Minimum bachelor's or master's degree and teaching certificate and experience preferred. Willing to consider enthusiastic people who like working with students, are creative, open-minded and good team players.

CONDITIONS OF EMPLOYMENT: One school year contract, e.g. 30 September to 30 June. Guaranteed minimum 80 hours per month plus up to 15 hours overtime. Full sick and holiday pay.

SALARY: Approx. £470–£600 basic per month (net guaranteed) depending on experience, qualifications and ability. Plus end of contract bonus.

FACILITIES/SUPPORT: Accommodation found by school, normally in shared flats. Rent is approximately £160 per calendar month. Fully-paid work visa. Regular programme of seminars.

RECRUITMENT: Interviews essential and held in various locations in the UK in July or by phone where necessary.

INTERNATIONAL HOUSE – WROCLAW
Ul. Leszczynskiego 3, 50–078 Wroclaw
biurowroc@ih.com.pl
www.ih.com.pl

NUMBER OF TEACHERS: 12.

PREFERENCE OF NATIONALITY: EU passport holders, but non-EU passport holders may also be considered.

QUALIFICATIONS: Minimum CELTA or Trinity certificate. One year's experience or CELTA Pass 'A' or 'B' preferred.

CONDITIONS OF EMPLOYMENT: 9-month standard contract, 21 contact hours per week.

SALARY: 2,600–3,400 zloties per month net (in first year) depending on qualifications and experience.

FACILITIES/SUPPORT: The school helps new teachers find suitable accommodation on arrival.

RECRUITMENT: Interviews are carried out by IH Human Resources in London or else directly in Wroclaw (wrocdos@ih.com.pl) in person or by phone.

CONTACT: John Fowler, Director of Studies.

LEKTOR SZKOLA JEZYKOW OBCYCH
ul. Olawska 25, 50–123 Wroclaw
biuro@lektor.com.pl
www.lektor.com.pl

NUMBER OF TEACHERS: 70.

PREFERENCE OF NATIONALITY: British, Irish, American, Canadian, Australian.

QUALIFICATIONS: Certificate in TEFL required (CELTA, DELTA or equivalent).

CONDITIONS OF EMPLOYMENT: Contracts for one or more years, 20–25 lessons per week. Students are young adults. Company organises intensive summer courses and language camps as well.

SALARY: From 55 zloties per hour.

FACILITIES/SUPPORT: Assistance with finding accommodation and obtaining work permit if necessary.

RECRUITMENT: Adverts on www.tefl.com. Personal interviews essential.

LINGUA NOVA
ul. Wspólna 41, p.II, 00519 Warsaw
+48 22 584 10 10/37; mob +48 668 041 650
Kursy@linguanova.com.pl
www.linguanova.com.pl

Branches in several other towns as well as Warsaw.

NUMBER OF TEACHERS: 16.

PREFERENCE OF NATIONALITY: British, American, New Zealander, Australian or Canadian.

QUALIFICATIONS: Bachelor's or master's degree, CELTA/DELTA or similar qualifications of teaching ESL.

CONDITIONS OF EMPLOYMENT: 1-year contract with working hours between 7am and 8pm.

SALARY: 45 Zloty per 45-minute lesson.

FACILITIES/SUPPORT: Assistance is given with finding accommodation and applying for work permits.

RECRUITMENT: Usually via online advertising. Interviews are essential and can be carried out by phone.

CONTACT: Marta Migala, Senior Teacher and Methodology Supervisor (m.migala@linguanova.com.pl).

MCGREGOR LANGUAGE SCHOOLS
Rynek 29/1, 32–400 Myślenice
+48 12 272 15 66
jobs@mcgregor.home.pl
www.mcgregor.home.pl

NUMBER OF TEACHERS: 8–10.

PREFERENCE OF NATIONALITY: None.

QUALIFICATIONS: A successful candidate must have completed an ESL/EFL course. Experience is not necessary but is an advantage.

CONDITIONS OF EMPLOYMENT: Length of stay October to June. 24 teaching hours per week between 3pm and 9pm.

SALARY: 2,800 zloties gross, less 19% for income tax and social security contributions.

FACILITIES/SUPPORT: Free fully furnished accommodation provided. The school takes care of all paperwork and covers the cost of the work permit, as well as providing full support to non-EU citizens to obtain a residence visa (though teachers cover the cost, currently 50 zloties).

RECRUITMENT: Skype or face-to-face interviews.

CONTACT: Maria Garczyńska Payne, Academic Manager.

MULTISCHOOL SZKOLA JEZYKOW OBCYCH
Ul. Olawska 5, 01–494 Warsaw
+48 22 638 23 39; mob +48 604 97 33 49
biuro@multischool.pl
www.multischool.pl

NUMBER OF TEACHERS: 70–80 in 7 branches in Warsaw.

QUALIFICATIONS: TEFL course, higher education; experience not necessary.

CONDITIONS OF EMPLOYMENT: 12 months. Teaching hours 8am–3pm and 3pm–8pm.

SALARY: $1,000 a month average, varies according to timetable. Less 10% for deductions.

FACILITIES/SUPPORT: Help given in finding a flat to rent and in obtaining a work permit.

RECRUITMENT: Prefer to interview candidates but can rely on CVs, letters of motivation and telephone conversations.

YORK SCHOOL OF ENGLISH
ul. Mackiewicza 12, 31–213 Krakow
+48 12 415 1818
info@york.edu.pl
www.york.edu.pl.

PASE (www.pase.pl) and Quality English (www.quality-english.com) recognised school, City & Guilds and LCCI approved examination centre. Has branches in Bochnia and Brzesko as well.

NUMBER OF TEACHERS: 30, including approximately 10 full-time native English speakers.

PREFERENCE OF NATIONALITY: British and Irish, also American, Canadian or Australian (EU visa holders).

QUALIFICATIONS: BA/MA (preferably in English or Linguistics). TEFL certificate (CELTA/Trinity or equivalents). ELT experience, references.

CONDITIONS OF EMPLOYMENT: Minimum 1-year contract (September to June). 28 hours per week. Excellent working conditions.

SALARY: Monthly average salary 3,000 zl gross depending on qualifications and experience.

FACILITIES/SUPPORT: Help given with accommodation. Bonuses. Professional development, regular workshops and conferences.

RECRUITMENT: Tefl.com.

CONTACT: Ewa Krupska, Director of Studies (e.krupska@york.edu.pl).

ROMANIA

English was barely taught before the downfall of Ceaucescu in 1989 and the collapse of communism, and there are few private language schools in Romania at present, though with Romania's admission to the EU in January 2007 and increased investment from Brussels, this is changing. Romania's economy has been slow to develop and since the recession, growth has been fragile, but is expected to improve in 2012.

The Ministry of Education in Bucharest does not recruit EFL teachers directly, though it co-operates with the British Council to improve standards of local teachers and place volunteers. The British Council (www.britishcouncil.org/romania) has been very active in promoting English in Romania at all levels and runs its own Teaching Centre in Bucharest at Calea Dorobantilor 14 (+40 21 307 9650; teachingcentre@british-council.ro). Further along the same street in the capital is the expanding Cambridge School at number 39 (www.cambridgeschool.ro), which advertises for experienced teachers when it has a vacancy. In the last few years the government has made a foreign language exam compulsory for graduating from school and university which has boosted demand for private tuition.

The vast majority of English teaching is carried out by Romanian teachers, who seem to do a splendid job judging from the extremely high pass rate their pupils achieve in the Cambridge exams. Teenagers are also motivated to learn English, at least according to one young person, because of the desire to live and work abroad.

QUEST Romania (www.quest.ro) is the Romanian Association for Quality Language Services, which operates as a quality control system on the basis of an inspection scheme. Its website seems to have stagnated and it is not known how reliable the members' contact details are. The Language Centre members of QUEST employ well-qualified teachers (most of them Romanian) and operate as private language schools registered as non-governmental organisations (NGOs) and recognised by the Ministry of Education. For example, the Access Language Centre in Cluj-Napoca (www.access.ro) is such an NGO supported by the British Council.

Some language schools are listed under the heading *Limbi Straine – Cursuri* in the *Golden Pages* (www.paginiaurii.ro) but these are unlikely to employ a native English speaker.

The arrival of Western investment and companies such as McDonald's and Hilton Hotels has created more demand for commercial English though not necessarily the prosperity to pay for it. Romanian language schools find it next-to-impossible to attract native English speaker teachers because they simply can't afford to pay them.

As the director of one QUEST member school wrote:

While we would welcome having native English teachers on our staff (we do occasionally receive enquiries from interested people), it is true that given how small our school is (approximately 400 students a year altogether) we cannot afford spending too much on employing them. For the moment, we only employ highly qualified local teachers on part-time contracts. I do not want to mislead people before we reach a more secure position and financial situation, in a very unstable country, economically speaking.

MINNA GRABER

Many years ago, Minna Graber arrived in Romania to celebrate the New Year and has been besotted with the country ever since.

We went straight into a Carpathian village at the top of a mountain complete with gypsy fiddlers and not an internal combustion engine for miles around. I fell for the place hook, line and sinker and haven't been able to kick the habit. I wanted to teach in the northeast of the country and so contacted the British Council in Iasi who in turn referred me to SOL [www.sol.org.uk] I met the director Grenville Yeo at a café and we talked for a long time about the challenges, rewards and requirements. In the end the job offer was with one of the best schools in Bucharest where the students all go on to university. (and a significant minority are these days applying for British university places) I work for 18 teaching periods a week. I am not supposed to teach grammar which at least in my school is seen as the Romanian English language teachers' prerogative partly, I fear, because they assume native speakers are not capable of this. This is despite the fact that I am fully trained to do so.

The wages sound terrible – 1,100 Lei a month after deductions for tax and National Insurance. The other teachers have to pay for accommodation out of this so in comparison I have a big advantage (the school's parents' association provides and pays for my very simple small studio flat and for the running costs). I am very good at living frugally but find that I still have to take on a couple of private students to make ends meet. The rest of the staff work long hours, giving these private lessons.

According to Minna, native speakers of English can command a high fee for giving private tuition. She charges around 60 Lei an hour ($20). If you work in a private kindergarten, as she did at one point, you can charge even more. Despite her modest earnings, she is far from discontent with her lifestyle.

I go to all the best concerts, have private lessons in Romanian, attend martial arts classes and choir every week and travel a lot. I am even able to put a little by at the end of the month. My students are all completely delightful. I love teaching them. They are respectful and talented. I do have to mother them a little over matters such as getting work in on time. Occasionally they, and occasionally their parents, try to exert pressure on me over marks. If a form tutor asks my help in rescuing a student who has problems or who might otherwise get expelled I always do so, otherwise I resist changing marks.

As for leisure time, many a Saturday has been spent haring up the mountains with Bucharest's enormous and enthusiastic mountain club. As a result of my wanderings over the mountains in the summer I made friends with some traditional shepherds and peasant farmers and am always welcome to visit. The times spent with these friends in the countryside are like a journey back into a far distant past. Of course, for all of this a command of the Romanian language is essential.

Nobody knows anything about Romania and the upside of this is that it is very tourist-free area and you enjoy status as a visitor from the outside world. People are interested and welcoming largely because there are so few visitors. Catch it whilst it still lasts.

A few British charities recruit volunteers for summer language camps, such as DAD International UK-Romania in Iasi (☎+40 788 473523; www.dad.ro) which sends volunteer teachers to five camps in mountain or seaside locations around Romania. British-Romanian Connections in Liverpool used to organise summer volunteer trips to Piatra Neamt, but its programme is on hold. Since the accession of Romania to the EU, red tape for Europeans has become simpler. Any teacher wishing to stay for longer than 120 days should apply for a temporary resident permit. Romania hopes to join the Schengen Area by 2012 which would mean that non-EU citizens would be allowed a maximum stay of 90 days within six months unless they obtained a work/resident's permit.

LIST OF EMPLOYERS

PROFESSIONAL LANGUAGE CENTRE

13 Campului St, Singeorgiu de Mures, 4/1 Semanatorilor St, Targu-Mures 4300

☎ +40 265 251180; +40 723 241042 (mob)

✉ acotoara@gmail.com

💻 www.professionalcentre.ro

Homes of QUEST, Romanian Association of Quality Language Schools.

NUMBER OF TEACHERS: 1.

QUALIFICATIONS: Bachelor's degree or equivalent.

CONDITIONS OF EMPLOYMENT: 1-year contract. To work 4pm–8pm, 5 days a week.

SALARY: $7 per hour. Taxes and social security paid by the school.

FACILITIES/SUPPORT: Assistance with finding accommodation and acquiring work permits.

RECRUITMENT: Interview required.

CONTACT: Angela Cotoara, Director.

RUSSIA

The Russian economy has bounced back after the global recession, and the demand for English, especially business English, is soaring to new heights. Many old and new language training businesses are eagerly recruiting teachers via advertisements abroad. In a tough job market, a knowledge of English is even more worth the time and money in acquiring.

Russians are still basically conservative and concerned by the need for good education, but there is a constant shortage of Russian English teachers in state schools so private language schools continue to be popular. The large chains such as Language Link, BKC-International House and EF English First are constantly recruiting teachers for their schools. Rather than employ an underqualified native English teacher, most language schools would rather turn to home-grown English teachers for whom teaching English is a profession and not simply a one to two year pastime. Russian English teachers are also far cheaper and do not require visa support and other costly add-on benefits such as accommodation, health care and travel allowances.

However, exceptions are made for qualified candidates, e.g. native English teachers with a CELTA or Trinity College TESOL certificate. Most schools will also accept applicants who hold TEFL certificates obtained on credible 100+ hour training courses with teaching practice. If you do not hold a certificate but have gained valuable experience teaching General English, Business English and/or international examination courses (IELTS, FCE, CAE and their like) and you have taught both adults and children, you should have little difficulty finding a job teaching English in Russia.

Robert Jensky, who kindly provided much of the information for this chapter, is convinced that high standards are essential:

> *I have personally seen many unqualified teachers fail because they did not fully realise the difference between speaking English and teaching English. Although Russians can vary in temperament and personality, they share a respect for education. Russians who under communism did not have to pay for education have come to accept the fact that it is now necessary to do so. There is little debate among Russians as to the significance of the English language both domestically and globally. Their only concern is that they get their full money's worth from each and every lesson. Russian students are demanding and place high expectations on their teachers, and so do the companies which employ them (including those that hire EFL teachers illegally). Given these circumstances, it is strongly recommended that any teacher coming to Russia has with him or her a good grammar book, a dictionary and a concise guide to TEFL methodology.*

Many young Russians are already fairly competent in the language and want to become more conversant with Western culture, not just for its own sake but to enhance their career prospects. Jobs in international firms are often advertised only in English. Russians young and not-so-young who want to work in advertising, banking, computing and so on need to speak English and therefore are drawn to the intensive English courses advertised all over the Moscow metro and on lamp-posts.

There are also plenty of jobs tutoring and looking after young children, as affluent parents hope to give their children a head start by showing off at the same time. This sector seems to be expanding, with several companies and individuals posting adverts in newspapers/websites such as www.expat.ru, for example one seen July 2012 for one-to-one tutoring jobs with the Native Speakers Club (hr@nativespeakers.ru). Kindergartens and specialist companies that offer tutors, nannies and governesses for children have also realised that native English speakers '*create a good image for your company*', according to **Sveta Kotwani**, Director of Little Angels Kindergarten in Moscow (see list of employers). Two other specialist agencies are Gouverneur International (www.guvernior.ru) and Bonne International with offices in London and Moscow (www.bonne-int.com). Both take on native English speakers for a number of vacancies, mainly in and around Moscow. ESL-qualified native candidates are needed to tutor children aged 4 to 10 years. MsPoppins (+7 495 744 0651; www.mspoppins.com) also advertises for native English tutors for children aged from 4 to 12.

FINDING A JOB

Finding a vacancy in Russia shouldn't be too difficult. Russia is, after all, the largest country on earth, spanning 11 time zones. You only need to decide where in Russia you'd like to settle down to teaching English. As a rule, salaries can drop the further you go from Moscow. A lower salary, however, is usually more than made up for by the lower costs of living found in many of the big away-from-Moscow cities of Russia; and a lower cost of living usually means a higher standard of living. Likewise, you're more likely to experience real Russia and real Russians.

Rob Jensky cautions against focusing your job hunt entirely around salary and perks:

> *For newly qualified teachers, academic support can mean the difference between success and failure as a teacher. And speaking of success as a teacher, having tons of personality is imperative. Students want to like their teachers and the way to gain their affection is by truly liking them back. Teachers who like their students will spend the time needed to prepare for their lessons adequately and this is where the value of proper academic support cannot be underestimated. The availability of a good Director of Studies and other experienced teaching staff who can help you with lesson preparation is a benefit that cannot be counted in terms of dollars and cents or pounds and pence.*

Teachers who are capable of performing in a variety of EFL classroom settings (Young Learners, adults, General, Business English, examination preparation) are in the greatest demand. Likewise, teachers who are prepared to be flexible with regard to teaching schedules will find a far greater number of employment opportunities. This is especially true in the great metropolitan areas where the number of both business and one-to-one clients is on the rise, many of whom want to be taught before or after the working day.

The two most popular websites used by Russian employers looking to hire English teachers are www.TEFL.com and www.ESLcafe.com. A typical advert might read: '*British owned and managed school based in the centre of Moscow is always looking to recruit teachers of English to work with large Russian and multinational companies from the oil and gas industry and other spheres such as finance, banking and investments, market research, IT and pharmaceuticals. We offer excellent rates of pay, ongoing academic support and a friendly, professional working environment. Contact administrator @bblc.ru.*'

When considering potential employers in Russia make sure that the company has the right to invite and employ teachers in Russia (see visa section for details), check whether the salary is net or gross and ask if accommodation is free/included. An estimated 900 tertiary institutes offer English courses, and many employ one or two highly educated native speakers to assist. Most universities and polytechnics offer free or subsidised accommodation and a civilised timetable but usually can't pay more than a couple of dollars an hour.

Some of the main language chains recruit abroad, including Language Link and EF English First, which recruits large numbers for 27 language schools in Russia on reasonable terms with return flight, medical insurance and visa costs included. Many foreign teachers prefer the security of working for a Western-owned company. Even if the wages are not brilliant, the support and fringe benefits usually make up for it. Language Link (see entry) offers an array of different employment opportunities designed to fit the needs of most EFL applicants from qualified to unqualified willing to be interns or volunteers. In addition to jobs for qualified EFL teachers, Language Link also recruits for its teacher internship, work-study and volunteer programmes.

Barry Robinson spent a number of years in Moscow working the EFL circuit and has provided a snapshot of the main employers. He admits that his opinions are totally subjective and are meant purely as a guide:

> *EFL in Moscow can often be more rewarding financially on a freelance basis, but for those who prefer to tie in with an all-inclusive contract, here is some info on what's on offer. BKC have an excellent reputation for teacher development and you get loads of professional support. They always pay on time and for work finished, and they are a decent company who will always look good on your CV. The same applies to Language Link who are friendly, fair, very supportive and will find you a flat. EF English First probably offer the best contract. They allow teachers to find their own flat (and pay for temporary accommodation during house-hunting) and their schools are always well-equipped. They insist that you stick to the EF book so there isn't much room for teacher development.*

A thriving English language press has established itself in Moscow and St Petersburg. Check adverts in the *Moscow Times* and the *St Petersburg Times* (www.sptimes.ru). Look out also for the free ads paper *Iz Ruk v Ruki* in about 15 towns in Russia and check the online messageboards community for English speakers living in Moscow on www.expat.ru, which at the time of writing carried lots of adverts for native English speaker teachers.

Since 1992 the Serendipity Russian-English Program has been sending Americans to work at the American Home in Vladimir, a city 200km east of Moscow. Not only do they teach English but also deliver lectures on American culture. Contracts last 8–9 months (renewable) starting in mid-August. The annual deadline for applications is 1st March. The project is located at the American Home (Ulitsa Letneperevozinskaya 3, 600000 Vladimir) though the programme is administered from the USA (www.serendipity-russia.com).

Jim Clost from Canada did not have a TEFL certificate when he went to Russia but he had studied the language at university and so joined a voluntary teaching scheme organised by a local travel agency:

> *I was required to work between four and six hours a day, only conversation and listening. Accommodation and meals were provided with a local family (normally one of the students) however no wages were paid as the position was voluntary. I met wonderful students, kids and adults and made friends that I go back to see regularly. The pupils were in general quite shy but some were ready to speak up and chat with me right away. Once we got to know one another conversation flowed more freely. Many of my students were quite eager to have me in their home for dinner. This is normal in Russian society where meeting with foreigners on a personal basis is a rarity. In my free time, I skated, swam, visited friends for tea and dinner, walked and talked.*

Students of Russian should investigate the programme run by the Pro-Ba Centre in St Petersburg where four or eight weeks of intensive study of Russian is followed by a period of work in schools, kindergartens or summer camps (www.studyrussian.spb.ru). Fees are from €2,750 for two months to €3,750 for four months. A Russian youth organisation called SFERA organises short voluntary teaching projects in the Russian Federation (http://dobrovolets.ru/eng.php).

The youth exchange company CCUSA (www.ccusa.co.uk or www.ccusa.com) runs a Summer Camp Russia Programme whereby teacher/counsellors from the UK and USA are placed on youth camps in Russia lasting four or eight weeks between mid-June and mid-August. Participants must be between the ages of 18 and 35, have experience of working with children and/or abroad, and have an interest in learning about the Russian language and culture. Camps are widely scattered from Lake Baikal in Siberia to the shores of the Black Sea. The programme fee of £999/$3,000 includes round-trip travel to Moscow, visa, insurance, orientation on arrival and room and board.

PAUL JONES

Australian Paul Jones spent the summer in Russia.

I worked as a counsellor in a summer camp near the city of Perm. When I first arrived, my heart sank because it looked like a gulag (for which the area around Perm is famous!). But you soon forget the physical conditions, mostly anyway. If I didn't like the food at the start, I definitely learnt to like it by the end and now reminisce about the worst of it! My job, as with American summer camps for kids, was to help lead a group of up to 30 children for their 3 weeks stay at the camp. Because I did not speak the language, I was placed with two other leaders so my services weren't really necessary. However, this region of Russia doesn't exactly get many international visitors so the role I played at camp sometimes felt more like being a rock star! The types of activities the kids did ranged from football, basketball and swimming (the colour of the pool was scary) to singing, dancing and crafts. But while I tried as best I could to lead my group of kids in their daily activities, every single kid in the camp wants a piece of you because you're the foreigner! So a lot of the job is to just be there and share a different culture with the kids (and their parents sometimes), other Russian counsellors and the Camp Director. I found that a few words in Russian go a long way to bridging the culture gap. And if possible take some souvenirs for the kids. Even a pack of cards with the British flag on them provides 52 little gifts.

CONDITIONS OF WORK

The unregulated housing market makes it difficult for foreign teachers to find independent accommodation. Furthermore rents in Moscow and St Petersburg are staggering relative to the quality on offer, though if you are willing to live a long way from the centre, prices quickly drop. Company-provided accommodation is easily a $600–$900 add-on benefit. Of course, as you leave the bright lights of Moscow and St Petersburg, rental costs come down. Employers normally arrange accommodation for their teachers in small shared flats. As single flats are much more expensive, your employer is unlikely to cover the extra cost of providing you with this luxury. Teachers might also lodge with landladies, of whom there is no shortage considering how many widows are trying to make ends meet on vanishingly small pensions.

Teachers need to be flexible in their approach to the working world in Russia and be prepared to compromise and adapt to an unfamiliar working environment. **Katherine Hyvärinen** found travelling around the vast city of Moscow to teach in different locations tiring but also exhilarating. She found the rhythm of life to be very fast but ended up enjoying her explorations of 'the mysterious, cultural and chaotic city of Moscow'.

A cultural difference which many newcomers find difficult to accept is the apparent unfriendliness of the Russian people. However, the cold face of Russian officialdom could not be in starker contrast to the warmth that will greet you when you get to know Russians better. **Elizabeth Bearman**, a teacher in Moscow, goes some way to unravelling the mystery of the cold Russian exterior:

The Russian man in the street does not smile unless he is happy, he does not engage complete strangers in meaningless conversation and he does not suffer fools gladly. There is a Russian proverb that perhaps sums it up: 'Only a fool smiles all the time'. However, while Russians can appear rude and unfriendly, when you get

*to know them they are considerate, helpful, generous and well ... friendly. The Russian concept of friendship is
much deeper and less superficial than elsewhere.*

The clichéd cold exterior of the Russian is nothing compared to the literal cold of the Russian winter as
described by **Travis Boyle** who works in Moscow (and is from Texas!):

*The hardest thing about my job is probably the weather. Because I work in-company, I have to trek to all of my
students' offices, and because this is Moscow, it means that nine months of the year are cold, snowy, and icy. But
the students almost always offer hot tea or coffee.*

Moscow winters last a good four or five months, when temperatures regularly fall below minus 15ºC.

Not surprisingly, the younger generation seems more willing to embrace new communicative teaching
methods than the older one, according to the director of the Sunny Plus English School in Moscow
(www.sunnyplus.ru) which has a constant need for native English speaker teachers:

*Adults cause headaches. They get upset with grammar. Many of them can't easily accept modern methods of
teaching. The progress is very slow. For many weeks they can't understand a teacher. They demand changing
him. Their pronunciation is terrible, but during classes they keep silent.*

By contrast, **Travis Boyle** was pleased with both the quality of his students and the working conditions at IPT
Moscow (see entry), as he reported in 2012:

*I wanted a part-time teaching contract, and that is what I got with IPT. I wanted time in the middle of the day
to study Russian, apply for graduate school, teach private students and so on, so this job has afforded me a
framework in which to pursue those tasks. All my students are educated, polite, middle- and upper-class busi-
nesspeople. I teach in-company, so their offices are, in some ways, my office. They are all well organised, clean,
well stocked, and quiet enough for lessons.*

One of his colleagues, **Katherine Hyvärinen**, was similarly delighted with her adult students in Moscow
whom she described as 'enthusiastic, motivated and with a positive and at time humorous attitude' towards
her lessons. Their boss **Tim Newton** MD at IPT, has no complaints about the intermediate and advanced
students he has taught in Moscow who are mostly sponsored by their companies and are committed, hard-
working and dedicated. He compares his school favourably with some of the alternatives:

*Don't be fooled into believing that just because you choose to work for a chain school, you are going to be work-
ing in either a large school or one staffed by native English speaking teachers. Many major chains operate small
teaching operations in far-flung locations. Proximity to good healthcare cannot be taken for granted, and could
be an issue for people with medical conditions. If proximity to cultural and recreational outlets such as theatres,
cinemas, museums, parks, circuses and other tourist attractions is important to you psychologically, then be
sure to investigate locations prior to accepting a job.*

REGULATIONS

Legalising your status as a teacher has always been fraught with difficulties, particularly for the companies
that employ foreigners who must keep abreast of constantly changing legislation.

Established employers registered with the Federal Migration Service as visa sponsors will know the procedures and make it as painless as possible for you, though you will have to collect your visa from the Russian

Embassy in your home country. Some teachers work on multiple entry business visas, though it is not legal to do so. Foreigners entering the country on one-year multiple entry business visas may remain on Russian soil for a maximum of three months before having to leave Russian territory for at least three months; in other words, they may remain in Russia for only three months during any six-month period.

Although some Russian sources state that an HIV test is not required for issuance of a visa, you will undoubtedly be required to submit proof of being HIV-negative. Specialist visa agencies may be able to advise such as Real Russia (www.realrussia.co.uk).

LIST OF EMPLOYERS

AAA SGI ENGLISH
Bldg 6/7, No 8 Staromonetniy Pereulok, Moscow 119180
- +7 495 951 7038
- enquiries@aaaenglish.ru
- www.aaaenglish.ru and www.stgeorges.co.uk/sgi-global-group

School is a joint venture between AAA English and St George International in London; both are British owned and managed.

NUMBER OF TEACHERS: Up to 15 for about 300 students (2012) at two locations in Moscow (second location at Building 2, No 16 Prospect Mira, Moscow 129090; +7 495 951 7038).

PREFERENCE OF NATIONALITY: British.

QUALIFICATIONS: 1 year minimum teaching experience, first degree, CELTA/TESOL/TEFL.

CONDITIONS OF EMPLOYMENT: 1 year. 40 academic hours per week. Also liase with Russian summer camp organisation to provide native speaker teachers for the vacation.

SALARY: 80,000 Roubles (€2,000) net per month for 160 academic hours (40 per week). However, salary does not depend on doing a minimum of 40 hours per week. The school policy is to find enough students to keep the teaching staff fully occupied. Hours taught above 40 are paid an overtime rate of 500 roubles.

FACILITIES/SUPPORT: Employer finds apartments for staff and pays the finder's fee and security deposit. First return flight from London to Moscow is also paid. Assistance with work permits given. AAA English are licensed by the Moscow City Government as an education establishment and authorised by the Russian Foreign Migration Service to invite and issue work permits and contracts direct to teachers. The cost of the issue of the work visa and permit is covered by the school.

RECRUITMENT: Via www.tefl.com. Interviews normally conducted by Webex video over the internet.

CONTACT: Michael Lang, General Director/Owner/Head Teacher.

BENEDICT SCHOOL
4 Admiraltejskaya Nabereznaya, St Petersburg 190000
- +7 812 325 7574
- benedict-adm@peterlink.ru
- www.eng.benedi.ct.ru

The biggest English Language school in St Petersburg and North-West Russia.

NUMBER OF TEACHERS: 18–20 for St Petersburg and the surrounding cities.

PREFERENCE OF NATIONALITY: British, American, Canadian, Australian.

QUALIFICATIONS: TEFL qualification preferred. Benedict school offers its own intensive 4-week training courses 4 times a year (in cooperation with Via Lingua).

CONDITIONS OF EMPLOYMENT: 3–12 months. 15–25 hours per week.

SALARY: $1,000–$1,500 per month.

FACILITIES/SUPPORT: Visa support and help with accommodation given. Library and resource centre.

CONTACT: Natalya Rostovtseva, Director.

BIG BEN LANGUAGE SCHOOL
Office 203, 2 Komsomolskaya Street, Ufa, 450003
- +7 347 293 2075
- bigbenschool@yandex.ru
- www.bigbenschool.ru

NUMBER OF TEACHERS: 2–3.

PREFERENCE OF NATIONALITY: British or Canadian.

QUALIFICATIONS: CELTA.

CONDITIONS OF EMPLOYMENT: 12-month contract with 30 academic hours per week.

SALARY: $1000–$1500 per month including travel and healthcare.

FACILITIES: Furnished flat is provided for each teacher and the school will assist with visas and work permits.

RECRUITMENT: Usually via internet advertisements. Interviews are essential and usually conducted via telephone but occasionally in the UK in the summer.

CONTACT: Martyn Judd, Academic Director.

BKC – INTERNATIONAL HOUSE Moscow
3–5 Gazetny Pereulok, Office No 8, 125009
Moscow
(phone) +7 495 737 5225
(email) recruit@bkc.ru
(web) www.bkcih-moscow.com

NUMBER OF TEACHERS: Approximately 200 contract and hourly paid teachers in Moscow, 50 teachers in the Moscow region.

PREFERENCE OF NATIONALITY: None.

QUALIFICATIONS: CELTA, Trinity TESOL, DELTA, BA/MA/PhD in TESOL/Applied Linguistics.

SALARY: $800–$1,450 net depending on qualifications and experience, plus end of contract bonus of up to $1,000.

FACILITIES/SUPPORT: The school provides visa support, shared accommodation (rent and all utilities except long-distance phone calls paid by BKC), airfare allowance, healthcare, paid holidays and up to 90% discount for Russian classes. Great opportunities for professional development – an active in-house training programme, consisting of regular monthly training seminars and different workshops. Currently also offers DELTA and IHCYL (International House Certificate in Teaching Young Learners) training.

CONDITIONS OF EMPLOYMENT: 3, 6 or 9-month contracts; 30 or 24 teaching periods (1 lesson = 45 min) per week. Typical timetable includes some teens' or children's classes as well as adult classes. Business English, conversational and exam classes also offered.

RECRUITMENT: All year round.

CONTACT: Julia Abyshkina or Anna Mitrofanova, Recruitment Managers.

EF ENGLISH FIRST
Citydel Business Center, Zemlyanoy Val 9, 3rd Floor 105064
Moscow
(phone) +7 495 937 3883
(email) efrecruitment@ef.com
(web) www.englishfirst.com/trt and
www.ef-russiateachers.com

NUMBER OF TEACHERS: About 40 for 35 schools in 20 cities (including 20 in Moscow and others in St Petersburg, 1 in Stavropol, Rostov, Tyumen, 2 Nizhny Novgorod, Novosibirsk etc.).

PREFERENCE OF NATIONALITY: British, North American, Australian, New Zealander.

QUALIFICATIONS: CELTA/TESOL/EF TEFL certificate plus a university degree, minimum 1 year ESL teaching experience.

CONDITIONS OF EMPLOYMENT: 9-months September–May or 12-month renewable contracts. Schools open 9am–9pm, Monday to Friday, and 9am–6pm, Saturday. 28 teaching hours per week within a 40-hour working week.

FACILITIES/SUPPORT: Modern classrooms all fitted with computers and LCD screens with online supplementary materials. Support with finding accommodation. Visas and work permits arranged. 21 days' paid holidays. Monthly flight allowance. Orientation upon arrival and ongoing training. Medical insurance provided.

RECRUITMENT: All online.

ENGLISH CENTRE ANGLETICA
Head office: 47 Ordzhonikidze Street, Krasnodar 350000
(phone) +7 952 832 54 80
(email) telc1@mail.ru
(web) www.angletica.ru

NUMBER OF TEACHERS: 3–9 per year, depending on contract duration.

PREFERENCE OF NATIONALITY: British.

QUALIFICATIONS: Candidates should be well-organised, enthusiastic, able to communicate with adults and children alike. Previous work experience is not necessary, as full training is provided on arrival.

CONDITIONS OF EMPLOYMENT: 3–9 months. Minimum 20 hours per week for the right candidates.

SALARY: From £5 per hour net.

FACILITIES/SUPPORT: Free accommodation provided. Candidate covers cost for Russian visa application process but visa support and letter of invitation are arranged. Cost of registration upon arrival is paid for by school.

RECRUITMENT: Via direct search, e.g. internet and newspaper adverts in the UK. Face-to-face interviews preferred but can be via Skype for global applicants.

CONTACT: Mr. Stanislav Sukhanov, General Manager.

GLOBUS INTERNATIONAL
Makarenko St, 5, building 1A, 3rd floor, Office 5, Moscow 105062
(phone) +7 495 645 2158
(email) info@globus-int.ru
(web) www.globus-int.ru/eng

NUMBER OF TEACHERS: 26 for branches in Moscow, St Petersburg, Pushkin, etc.

PREFERENCE OF NATIONALITY: British, Irish, Australian, New Zealander, Canadian, American.

QUALIFICATIONS: Minimum CELTA or equivalent, plus ideally 2 years' experience.

CONDITIONS OF EMPLOYMENT: 12-month standard contract, 26 academic hours per week.

FACILITIES/SUPPORT: A housing manager helps to accommodate all teachers based on what they would like. Centre organises a work visa invitation, then when the teacher is in Russia, organises all the necessary documents to make sure the teacher is fully registered and has all correct documentation.

RECRUITMENT: Through TEFL websites. Telephone interviews are essential. If possible the school tries to set up face-to-face interviews in London.

GLORY SCHOOL FOREIGN LANGUAGES
31/1, Ruzovskaya Street, St Petersburg 198013
☎ +7 812 316 55 43
✎ edu@gloryschool.ru
🖥 www.gloryschool.ru

NUMBER OF TEACHERS: 10.

PREFERENCE OF NATIONALITY: British, American or Canadian.

QUALIFICATIONS: Native speaker with higher education and some experience. Prefer candidates with 3 years or more EFL teaching experience or EFL certificate.

CONDITIONS OF EMPLOYMENT: 1-year contract. Part-time in-company classes available.

SALARY: $20 per hour.

FACILITIES/SUPPORT: Assistance is given with renting a flat and applying for work permits and visas. Russian language lessons can be exchanged for English conversation practice.

RECRUITMENT: Usually via the internet.

CONTACT: George Agababyan, Head of Education.

IPT RUSSIA
Office 207, Petrovka Ulitsa 15/13, 107031 Moscow
☎ +7 495 228 3513
✎ info@iptrussia.ru
🖥 www.iptrussia.ru

NUMBER OF TEACHERS: 30 native speakers out of total staff of 260 in Moscow and the regions.

PREFERENCE OF NATIONALITY: Native speaker (or Russian national).

QUALIFICATIONS: EFL Certification, plus minimum 2 years' EFL experience, ideally including Business English and/or Corporate Language Teaching. Previous experience in Russia or Eastern Europe preferred, but not essential. Experience of financial or legal presentations would be valuable.

CONDITIONS OF EMPLOYMENT: 12 months. Schedule of minimum 80 academic hours per month.

SALARY: Negotiable. All salaries are paid net of tax; employer pays all income taxes and social fees.

FACILITIES/SUPPORT: Free accommodation given on arrival, and assistance given in search for accommodation, with agents and transport provided. All teachers receive a 12-month, multiple-entry, fully legal teaching visa, which is registered through the company for the duration of the contract. IPT provides native teachers with free Russian lessons on teaching workshops on different themes.

RECRUITMENT: Telephone interviews (at least 3), references, qualifications check, receipt of sample lesson plans.

CONTACT: Tim Newton, Managing Director.

LANGUAGE LINK RUSSIA
Moscow
🖥 www.jobs.languagelink.ru

NUMBER OF TEACHERS: 200 for 50+ schools throughout Russia (Moscow, Moscow Region, St Petersburg, St Petersburg Region, Volgograd, Samara, Toliatti, Ufa, Rostov na Donu, Stavropol, etc.)

PREFERENCE OF NATIONALITY: British, American, Canadian, Australian, New Zealander and South African.

QUALIFICATIONS: CELTA or Trinity Certificate/Diploma (or equivalents) required unless teachers apply with relevant EFL/ESL experience. Candidates without a 100-hour TEFL qualification may enter Language Link's Teacher Internship Programme. Openings also available to those without experience or qualifications as volunteers or summer camp staff.

CONDITIONS OF EMPLOYMENT: 6, 9 or 12-month contracts, 25 teaching hours per week, usually 4 hours a day, 5 days a week. Adult classes, children's classes and in-company. Also runs a number of English language summer camps near major cities (camps@languagelink.ru) starting the beginning of June.

FACILITIES/SUPPORT: All teachers provided with free accommodation in 2-room flat (for 2 teachers). Paid time off, paid medical services, full work visa support and academic support.

RECRUITMENT: Application is online. Minimum 2 professional references. Telephone/Skype interviews are compulsory unless carried out by Language Link in London.

CONTACT: Robert Jensky, Director.

LITTLE ANGELS KINDERGARTEN

St Novocheremushkinskaya no 49, Office 12, Moscow

litang@mail.ru

www.littleangels.ru

NUMBER OF TEACHERS: 5.

PREFERENCE OF NATIONALITY: British, Canadian or Australian.

QUALIFICATIONS: A strong background in early childhood education and a TEFL qualification. Also he/she should have experience of teaching.

CONDITIONS OF EMPLOYMENT: Standard 1-year contract, usual hours are 9am–5pm.

SALARY: Depends on qualification and experience but at least $1,500. If the employee has a work permit from Little Angels, 13% of the tax is deducted from their salary.

FACILITIES/SUPPORT: No help with accommodation or work permit at the moment. Usually, teachers already have a work permit from a company or agency.

RECRUITMENT: By interview, filling in a questionnaire and taking a class. Interviews are essential.

CONTACT: Sveta Kotwani, Director.

PRAKTIKA

18/7 Bolshaya Posadaskay U1, St Petersburg 197046

+7 921 9376593

office@flpractice.com

www.flpractice.com

NUMBER OF TEACHERS: 20.

PREFERENCE OF NATIONALITY: British or American.

QUALIFICATIONS: DELTA, CELTA or equivalent.

CONDITIONS OF EMPLOYMENT: 6-month contract with average workload between 20 and 30 hours per week.

SALARY: $1,000 per month is the starting point for 20 hours per week contract.

RECRUITMENT: Usually via local advertising and word of mouth. Interviews are essential.

CONTACT: Gleb Evzikov, Director of Studies.

PREMIUM ENGLISH

Chistopolskaya 20A, Kazan, Republic of Tatarstan, Russian Federation

+7 843 518 60 60 / +7 843 518 65 65

info@premiumenglish.ru

www.premiumenglish.ru

NUMBER OF TEACHERS: 12–15.

PREFERENCE OF NATIONALITY: None.

QUALIFICATIONS: CELTA or equivalent plus one year's experience.

CONDITIONS OF EMPLOYMENT: September to July, or 12 months from September. 25 contact hours per week, 5 days a week (2 consecutive days off: Sat/Sun or Sun/Mon). To teach children and adults in the business and professional community both in-company and on school premises.

SALARY: Approx $1000 per month after tax.

FACILITIES/SUPPORT: Accommodation is provided by the school. Employer provides teachers with all the legal paperwork to work in Russia. Teachers need to provide apostilled copies of passport and qualification. An HIV test is required for the visa.

RECRUITMENT: Via www.tefl.com.

CONTACT: Steven Mott, Director of Education.

SUNHILL SCHOOL

Bankovskaya Street 6a, Solnechnogorsk, Moscow region 141506

+7 495 726 9617 (September to May); +7 962 973 7271 (summer)

sunhillschool@gmail.com

www.sunhillschool.ru

NUMBER OF TEACHERS: 4 for schools in Solnechnogorsk and Mendeleevo.

PREFERENCE OF NATIONALITY: British, Irish, American, Canadian, New Zealander.

QUALIFICATIONS: Degree holder plus TEFL Cert, preferably CELTA or Trinity. Previous teaching experience preferred, e.g. 1 year's EFL teaching abroad. Enthusiasm and desire to work essential.

CONDITIONS OF EMPLOYMENT: 9-month contracts from September. 24 teaching hours per week (lessons last 45 minutes) plus 2 hours on standby.

SALARY: From $1,200 or $1,300 a month, 23 days' paid holiday per year.

FACILITIES/SUPPORT: Free shared accommodation provided by school, close to work. Flight compensation and end-of-contract bonus from $40 per month. Visa fees at consulate plus HIV test paid at end of contract. Healthcare and insurance provided. Free internet.

RECRUITMENT: Telephone interview.

CONTACT: Mrs Natalia Kruglova, Director.

WINDSOR ENGLISH LANGUAGE SCHOOL

7 Komsomolsky Prospect, Moscow 119146

+7 495 221 0832

job@windsor.ru

www.windsor.ru/eng

NUMBER OF TEACHERS: Vacancies almost all year round, especially for people experienced with IELTS preparation.

PREFERENCE OF NATIONALITY: British, Canadian, Irish, American, Australian and New Zealander.

QUALIFICATIONS: Bachelor's degree or higher and a TEFL certificate (CELTA, Trinity College TESOL, etc.). 1–2 years' experience of teaching in Europe.

CONDITIONS OF EMPLOYMENT: Part-time teaching mainly but also contracts from September. Summer openings in Siberia (Abakan in the Republic of Khakasia).

SALARY: Hourly teaching pays 750 roubles for an academic hour (i.e. 45 minutes), so that an evening class earns 2,250 roubles. Starting salary for contract work 33,000 roubles per month (approx US$1,000), no deductions.

FACILITIES/SUPPORT: The school provides good quality shared accommodation and fully assists and pays for work visas. Employer pays for utilities, health insurance, monthly travel card and bonus. Full in-house academic support.

RECRUITMENT: Via adverts in www.expat.ru, etc. Interviews are absolutely essential, usually done by telephone or Skype.

CONTACT: Polina Romashkina, Recruitment Manager.

THE BALTICS

Arguably the most Westernised part of the old Russian Empire, the Baltic countries of Lithuania, Latvia and Estonia all became fully fledged members of the EU on 1 May, 2004. This has significantly eased the bureaucracy for EU passport holders, while other citizens will need to apply for a work permit which can take many months. For this reason and due to extra costs, most schools strongly prefer to employ EU citizens. A number of budget airlines as well as national carriers operate to the region (e.g. Ryanair to Kaunas and Riga) and ticket prices can be remarkably low. Despite new business and tourism links, the market for English language teachers has been shrinking and few vacancies are advertised abroad.

Latvia and Lithuania

Of the three Baltic states, Latvia has been slowest to embrace change, although its beautiful capital, Riga, has become a mecca for a certain type of British tourist (at the lager lout end of the spectrum). English is increasingly necessary for anyone working in the hospitality sector, although there are still relatively few commercial language schools and these vary widely in quality.

Qualified ELT teachers should make contact with the Latvian Association of Teachers of English (LATE) in Riga (www.late.lv) though it doesn't get involved with job assistance.

Even voluntary opportunities are few and far between, and one of the few volunteer and gap year agencies that dealt with Latvia, Changing Worlds, dropped Latvia from its list of destinations in 2011.

One Latvian language school that may be able to offer decent facilities is the Language Centre International House Riga-Satva (www.ihriga.lv), which can also help with visas, flat-finding and teaching support.

The market in Lithuania seems to have shrunk over the past few years with EF English First scaling back and the ILS franchise up for sale. The only vacancies being advertised at the time of writing were for English for Academic Purposes at a private Christian university in Klaidepa (www.lcc.lt) affiliated to the heavy-duty proselytising City Church.

Estonia

Estonia is arguably the most progressive of the three Baltic countries, and the British Council in Tallinn has a list headed 'Major Language Schools in Estonia' with a couple of dozen addresses of universities and private language schools. The demand for native English speaker teachers is not very high as illustrated by the language institute in Tallinn that communicated with this book to say that it already has plenty of native speaking English teachers in its database with few vacancies.

LIST OF EMPLOYERS

AMERICAN ENGLISH SCHOOL
Naugarduko 4, 01141 Vilnius, Lithuania
- +370 5 2 79 1011
- vilnius@ames.lt
- www.ames.lt

NUMBER OF TEACHERS: 40.

PREFERENCE OF NATIONALITY: None.

QUALIFICATIONS: TEFL certificate required.

CONDITIONS OF EMPLOYMENT: 5 days per week (mornings and afternoons). Other conditions negotiable. Students are teenagers, adults and corporate clients, private and public sector.

SALARY: $9–$12 per contact hour.

FACILITIES/SUPPORT: Initial in-house training provided; continuous in-house training and teacher support provided.

RECRUITMENT: Demo class to be taught after the interview.

CONTACT: Egle Kesyliene, Director.

INTERNATIONAL LANGUAGE SERVICES
Roosikrantsi 8B, 10119 Tallinn, Estonia
- +372 627 7170/1
- info@ilstallinn.com
- www.ilstallinn.com

NUMBER OF TEACHERS: 8–12.

PREFERENCE OF NATIONALITY: Native English speakers, non-EU teachers (native speakers) also welcome.

QUALIFICATIONS: Minimum CELTA or Trinity certificate; experience and some business knowledge preferred.

CONDITIONS OF EMPLOYMENT: 10-month or 22-month contracts, 96–120 45-minute lessons per month.

SALARY: About €775–€900 per month after deductions.

FACILITIES/SUPPORT: Travel allowance, all procedures for work permits handled by school. Regular seminars and teacher development programme leading to LCCI Further Certificate in Teaching Business English. Sponsorship for the Trinity DipTESOL by distance for teachers on longer contracts. No accommodation since plenty of rental accommodation is easily available (from €200 a month for a one-bedroom flat).

RECRUITMENT: Internet and TEFL/TESOL press. Phone interviews.

CONTACT: Phil Marsdale, Director (phil@ilstallinn.com).

UKRAINE

The vast republic of the Ukraine's EFL market is no longer in its infancy, as demand for English increases. The citizens are now coming to realise that they may be able to double their earning power by learning English and open up opportunities for their children by sending them to private tutors. This increase in demand has not been met by an influx of native English teachers, partly because its reputation persists for offering low wages and primitive conditions though much has improved in recent years.

Many native English speaking teachers in the Ukraine remark on the enthusiastic reception they receive from pupils. Many of the younger pupils express an adoration for the teachers, which can at first be quite overwhelming, and prospective teachers should be prepared for receiving occasional invitations to students' homes in order to meet their families. Although this can initially be a little unnerving, most teachers find that the generous hospitality is one of the things that makes teaching in the Ukraine such a worthwhile experience.

After more than a decade in Kiev, **John Hall** is full of the rewards of teaching in the Ukraine:

You may ask, why teach in this part of the world and not sunnier climes? Well, I did a degree in English Lit and Russian at the University of Westminster. For part of the course I enjoyed nine months in St Petersburg and got hooked on the Slavic mentality, people, culture, literature and general way of life. I guess that feeling has never left me. My situation in Ukraine is not typical, but not unusual either. I have worked for three private language schools since my arrival here, most recently the London School of English and now International House Kyiv where I have been promoted to Assistant Director of Studies. I have also been married to a lovely Ukrainian woman for the last eight years. The reason for my long stay and subsequent happiness in Kyiv is mainly down to the friendly atmosphere within the city and the pleasing and professional work conditions I have encountered here. The social life is quite lively, though to master the language is a life-long goal!

Please don't get me wrong. Ukraine is not the easiest place to live. There are many schools out there that are not as foreigner-friendly as my current school. Work permits and visas are a constant nightmare. But here at IH, everything is done legally, which is a major plus, which everyone admires and respects. The students are lovely, polite and hard working on the whole. There are some who fit the first two qualities, but not the latter, and that's to be expected everywhere in the world. They are generally inquisitive and have high expectations of their teachers, which comes out of the national character. They are paying – sometimes quite highly – for a service and expect the teachers to deliver top-notch lessons and answer all their questions confidently. This can be a bit daunting for some teachers, but a challenge and a happy one for most. Children aged 5–16 make up more than half of the overall student number and this has a huge bearing on planning, timetabling and recruitment as all teachers are expected to be capable of teaching all these groups.

For professional opportunities, well-qualified candidates can try the British Council in Kiev, which has a teaching centre and can also supply a list of nearly 50 English language institutes that provide exam preparation (www.britishcouncil.org/ukraine-exams-schools-list.pdf). In addition to the Kiev branch where John Hall works, International House has a strong presence in the country with vacancies from time to time at its schools in Dnipropetrovsk, Kharkiv, Odessa and Lviv (the latter has an entry below).

The British-owned Educational Solutions Group (www.educationalsolutions.com.ua) is Ukraine's largest privately owned chain of ELT schools with a centralised Human Resources Office; +380 5038 01390). The group comprises four London Schools of English and three Language Academies, in various cities. Teachers with a minimum of a degree, CELTA or equivalent and experience will not find it difficult to be hired on an 11-month contract. Like other employers, the group quotes salaries in dollars, in the range of US$800 to $1,200 depending on qualifications, plus return flights, a free flat and visa costs. US nationals must obtain the IM-1 visa, for which they will need a labour authorisation form (*dozvil na pratsevlashtuvannia*) from their employer.

As in Russia, the process for schools of getting permission to hire foreigners is both expensive and labyrinthine. Business visas for British teachers cost twice as much as for other nationalities. As a result many schools don't bother. They register the teachers (illegally) in someone's apartment and force them to enter as tourists. Every three months they must leave and re-enter the country which incurs a fine which the good companies underwrite, since it is far cheaper and simpler than making them legal. It's a crazy situation. Many teachers are uncomfortable with this state of affairs and stay for a short time, leaving with an unfairly negative impression of Ukraine.

As is noticeable throughout Europe and elsewhere where English is in high demand, English language summer camps have arrived on the scene. This huge country has many beautiful landscapes for hosting such camps, from the Carpathian Mountains to the Crimea. Two companies seen advertising for summer staff on www.tefl.com were Dec Camp Ltd (info@dec-camp.com) which runs an English-immersion camp in the Mezhgorskom region of mountainous Transcarpathia; and the Celyn-abc-camp in Novye Sanzhary, Poltava Province (www.celyn-abc-camp.com) which wanted native speaker teachers and counsellors to work for between two weeks and three months. The Dec Camp is run by the Dec Language Institute in Kyiv (www.dec-school.com/er) which hires teachers for the academic year.

Valuable information about teaching in the Ukraine may be found at www.tryukraine.com/work/english. shtml, a site maintained by an expat teacher who will post CVs on his site for a fee (e.g. $20 for one month).

LIST OF EMPLOYERS

INTERNATIONAL HOUSE – KYIV

7 Vandy Vasilevskoy Street, Kyiv 03055

☎ +380 44 238 98 70

✉ dos@ih.kiev.ua or info@ih.kiev.ua

🖥 www.ih.kiev.ua/en/vacancies

NUMBER OF TEACHERS: 27–30.

PREFERENCE OF NATIONALITY: Native English speakers.

QUALIFICATIONS: Minimum TEFL/CELTA certificate.

CONDITIONS OF EMPLOYMENT: 1-year contracts. Teach up to 25 hours per week.

SALARY: $1,000–$1,500 a month based on experience, paid in Ukrainian currency.

FACILITIES/SUPPORT: The school provides the teacher with a single room or shared apartment.

RECRUITMENT: Through IH London or locally.

CONTACT: Mark Alan Forehand, dos@ih.kiev.ua.

INTERNATIONAL HOUSE LVIV

3 Petrushevych Square, 79005 Lviv

☎ +380 32 22 55 190

✉ ihlviv@gmail.com

🖥 www.ihlviv.com

NUMBER OF TEACHERS: 15.

PREFERENCE OF NATIONALITY: None, but should be native English speakers.

QUALIFICATIONS: CELTA/TESOL/IHC/Trinity certificate.

CONDITIONS OF EMPLOYMENT: 10 months plus 3 weeks' paid holidays. 24 teaching hours per week plus one meeting/seminar.

SALARY: From 6,800 hryvnias ($800 approximately) per month depending on experience.

FACILITIES/SUPPORT: US$400 of return ticket covered by the school. Furnished accommodation is provided for up to $200. Half the cost of the D-type visa and apostille is covered. The cost of the work permit, translation and registration is fully covered by school.

RECRUITMENT: Locally, via the internet and through IHWO recruitment services.

CONTACT: Marianna Ilyina, Director (marianna.ilyina@gmail.com).

LARISA SCHOOL OF LANGUAGE

Sovietskaya and Shevchenko 63, Second Floor, Nikolaev

☎ +380 512 7171 96 +380 94 944 0196

✉ larisaschooloflanguages@gmail.com

🖥 www.larisaschooloflanguage.com or
www.larisaschooloflanguage.net

Main office and language school for the LSL Education Network.

NUMBER OF TEACHERS: 10.

PREFERENCE OF NATIONALITY: American, British or Canadian.

QUALIFICATIONS: TEFL/TESL/CELTA.

CONDITIONS OF EMPLOYMENT: Minimum 3-month contract depending on the time of year. Usual working hours are Monday to Saturday, late afternoons and evenings.

FACILITIES/SUPPORT: Assistance is given with finding accommodation and applying for work permits.

RECRUITMENT: Usually via the internet. Interviews are essential and can be carried out through Skype.

CONTACT: Larisa Nemchenko, Director.

CENTRAL ASIAN REPUBLICS

With ever increasing frequency, the former Soviet republics are taking on their own national and regional identities due to geographic, cultural and economic factors. The number of treaty organisations that have emerged since the 'civilised divorce' of the former Soviet Union took place in 1991 is mind boggling. Whereas the Baltic States (Estonia, Lithuania and Latvia) desire few if any ties with Russia, other former Soviet republics especially those in north Central Asia (Kazakhstan, Kyrgyzstan, Tajikistan, Turkmenistan, and Uzbekistan) have joined with Russia (and China) to form a number of economic and security-related treaty organisations. In between these two extremes are the eastern European states (Belarus, Moldova and the Ukraine) and Caucasian States (Armenia, Azerbaijan and Georgia) which drift from one side to the other depending upon the nature of the area of co-operation. Prospective EFL teachers seeking to find employment in any of these countries or areas would do well to investigate the prevailing influences affecting the particular country(ies) or area(s) in which they are interested at the time of their job search.

Though a decision concerning where to look for work will most likely depend upon a number of variables, prospective EFL teachers looking for teaching jobs in the former Soviet republics should give some thought as to whether they will be able to tolerate different attitudes to human rights, religious freedoms, etc. On the question of the religious flavour, not to say fervour, of the republic in question, as a general rule, the former western republics are mostly Eastern Orthodox Christian and the southern Central Asian Republics are Sunni Muslim, so there are noticeable differences between levels of tolerance in matters of sexual freedom, alcohol, dietary habits and even smoking.

Once an informed decision has been made to look for work in a former Soviet republic, the most obvious question is where to start. A search of the internet will yield a few results. Though most TEFL job sites include these countries in their indexes, teachers will be disappointed to find few entries for many of the countries designated as former Soviet republics. Many established schools operating in the various countries of the former Soviet republics either don't have websites or are simply not found by the search engines. That said, a number of universities will be listed, which do employ at various times native English speaking teachers. Given the university nature of these jobs, they will no doubt be in either high demand or have teacher requirements above those held by the usual TEFL teacher. Unfortunately as attested to by internet experience, English teaching is still delivered by the state, for example the list of English language institutions sent by the British Council in the Uzbek capital Tashkent comprises only state universities and pedagogical institutes (i.e. teacher training colleges). University faculties often have their own international relations office which may have two or three vacancies for highly educated language assistants; try, for example, Pavlodar State University in Kazakhstan.

Another source of TEFL employment can be the NGOs operating in a number of former Soviet republic countries. In response to the increase in demand for English, the Peace Corps sends a substantial number of volunteer English teachers to various nation states. Much of this demand has been spurred by the influx of businesses connected with the Caspian oil industry, which has particularly affected Kazakhstan, Uzbekistan, Turkmenistan and Azerbaijan. Opportunities with international companies exist for professional ELT teachers where the salaries are approaching those of the oil-rich states of the Middle East. A company called ETI (Language & Business Skills) operates in Georgia, Azerbaijan, Kazakhstan and Turkmenistan (www.eti.az) and may have jobs to teach oil company employees, NGO staff and others, especially in Baku, capital of Azerbaijan.

Chain schools such as Language Link, EF and International House can provide sources of TEFL employment. For example, Language Link operates a teaching centre in Atyrau, Kazakhstan and may in future open others as long as the petro dollars flow.

Both International House and the Soros Foundation have also been active in opening up the region to English language learners. IH's partner in Almaty, Kazakhstan is Interpress which does some of its own teacher hiring (see entry). Try also Study Innovations Language Schools (www.studyinn.kz) in Almaty,

Astana, Karaganda, Shymkent and others which were hiring in the summer of 2012. Belarus is another republic with various language teaching opportunities, for example at International House Minsk (www.ih.by) and SOL Minsk (www.sol.by). Two Soros institutes which might have openings for people with an MA in TESOL are the English Language School in Bishkek, Kyrgyz Republic and the International Language Training Center in Chisinau, Moldova. Another US-oriented school in Chisinau is the American Language Center (http://alc.md), though it tends to hire only local staff. Few foreigners would be able to survive on the low monthly stipend they offer.

A base in Central Asia allows you to explore this fascinating region, as **Anthony Cook** did when he was working in Almaty in Kazakhstan:

I tended to try and save up a bit, then splurge on one or two longer trips each year. Travelling around Central Asia is quite the adventure. To mention just two of the 'stans': Kazakhstan itself has a unique multicultural history and awe-inspiring, dramatic landscapes, with wide regional variation (though you have to make a real effort to get to the good bits, because they're separated by vast stretches of nothingness and the transport infrastructure is not the best!) Uzbekistan has some of the world's most impressive Islamic architecture, plus the desert of Karakalpakstan in the west, dotted with ancient, deserted fortresses. The Uzbek people are an added bonus; they're every bit as warm and eccentric as the Kazakhs, and a lot chattier and more inclined to strike up a conversation with strangers. So you meet a lot of 'characters' when you visit their country. If I were to go back to the region, I'd definitely want to continue exploring – the list of intriguing destinations is quite long.

In searching for a job, perhaps the best advice might be to limit your search to a couple of countries and thereafter do your research. A thorough understanding of the country, its culture and its regard for foreigners is absolutely essential. And be sure to check out the legality of any employment that you are thinking to engage in. As **William Kinsey** found out while working in Almaty, things are not always what they seem. '*Our school was raided by the police who demanded our visas and claimed incorrect registration. Our boss/owner was useless and two of my fellow teachers were brought to the police station and had their apartment raided. Further the boss asked us to lie on his behalf and say that we are not paid rather we are only English consultants not accepting salary. I can only speculate but I surmise it creates a tax escape for him.*' Given this, teachers are well advised to check with consulates rather than potential employers as to how legal working status is obtained. As laws change often, employers may not be lying to potential teachers, they may simply be out of date in their current thinking.

Georgia

In advance of the September start of the academic year, the Ministry of Education took the dramatic decision to fund a native English speaker teaching programme on a large scale. Funding has been approved to bring in up to 1,000 foreigners to teach in state schools throughout the country. Airfares, homestay accommodation, medical insurance and a round-trip ticket for one vacation are all covered by the programme. Although teachers are called volunteers, they are paid a stipend of 500 lari (about US$300) per month. Note the preposition in the name of the programme: Teach and Learn with Georgia, since this is intended to be a cultural exchange as well. Contact TLG at 52 Uznadze St, Tbilisi 0102, Georgia (+995 32 318959/77 782442; info@tlg.gov.ge; www.tlg.gov.ge). You can apply directly or via various recruitment companies around the world like Footprints in Canada (www.footprintsrecruiting.com), Norwood in Ireland (www.norwoodenglish.com) and Reach to Teach in the US (www.ReachToTeachRecruiting.com).

A TLG teacher provided some feedback on the Footprints Recruiting web forum, which gives a taste of how the programme operates:

I have been in Georgia for a month now and it has been an amazing experience. First of all, come with an open mind and remember that we are here to help this country and their children especially to learn to speak English.

Before I came, I thought that I would like to go to Tbilisi but I have been placed in a rural village very close to the Russian border. In fact, I have 30 border guards living in the houses next door so everyone tells me that I am very safe.

My host family are very poor but they are wonderful, friendly people and every night there are people from the village who come to meet me and to bring some delicacy like wine jelly, fresh pears, bilberries etc. When you are undergoing training at Kutaisi, the Georgian TLG team are closely observing you and they place people according to their willingness to learn and their behaviour. About 12 guys from our group who went partying every night ended up in very remote villages in Ajara because most Georgian families will not host people who want to be out partying all the time. Respect for their very religious nature is important. They will judge all Westerners by our behaviour.

Teachers are also employed in the private sector, e.g. by International House (www.ihtbilisi.ge) and the London School of English (www.londonschool.ge) both in Tbilisi; the latter hosts intensive English summer courses for young learners and professionals, for which it recruits native speaking teachers.

LIST OF EMPLOYERS

REACH TO TEACH

1606 80th Avenue, Algona, Iowa 50511, USA

☏ +1 201 467 4612 (USA)/ +44 203 286 9794 (UK & Ireland)/+61 2 8011 4516 (Australia)/+64 9 889 0557 (New Zealand)

✉ info@ReachToTeachRecruiting.com

🖥 www.ReachToTeachRecruiting.com/teach-english-in-georgia.htm

For contacts in other countries, see entries in Asia chapter.

NUMBER OF TEACHERS: 150 for Georgia and elsewhere in Eastern Europe.

PREFERENCE OF NATIONALITY: British, American, Canadian, Australian, New Zealander, Irish and South African are preferred, but Reach to Teach will consider teachers of any nationality who speak and write English fluently. In order to qualify for permission to work in Asia, you must be from one of the following countries: USA, Canada, UK, Ireland, South Africa, Australia or New Zealand.

QUALIFICATIONS: College or university degree needed. Teaching experience is not required. TEFL qualified teachers are preferred.

Through a partnership with a TEFL course provider, Reach To Teach can assist teachers in getting course discounts.

CONDITIONS OF EMPLOYMENT: All job placements are full-time positions. 4–15 month contracts available (and usually extendable). Teaching schedules vary but are generally through daytime hours Monday–Friday.

SALARY: US$300 monthly stipend, free return airfare paid upfront and free housing with a Georgian host family. Teachers who commit to a year-long contract receive an additional flight ticket equal in value to their tickets to and from Georgia.

FACILITIES/SUPPORT: Visa guidance, airport collection, teacher orientation, etc. are provided. Teachers have the option of continued support and contact with Reach to Teach throughout year-long placement.

RECRUITMENT: Applications submitted via Reach To Teach website. Interviews conducted over Skype, by phone or occasionally in person.

CONTACT: Stephanie Long, Director of Recruiting, Georgia (Stephanie@ReachToTeachRecruiting.com).

Azerbaijan

Tucked away between Georgia, Iran, and the Caspian Sea, the republic of Azerbaijan produces great oil wealth. Because of the capital Baku's key role in the production and distribution of oil and gas, language institutes have a lot of money to throw around, and have been offering more than comfortable salaries to teachers. Yet teacher retention is not very high, partly because of the hardships of living in Central Asia and because the employers have not provided enough pastoral support to new arrivals. Many teachers arrive in Baku with no idea how to do the job well or to adapt to the culture.

John Gahan had a head start since he had spent two years as a volunteer with the Peace Corps in Gumlag Village in the Oghuz Rayon of Azerbaijan before deciding to move to the big city:

While I was completing my last couple months in my village for Peace Corps, a friend of mine and I decided to seek employment in Baku because we heard the salaries were good, and we felt the adjustment wouldn't be terribly difficult. I found out about English First, arranged an interview, taught a trial lesson to a large group of children and was offered a job in 2011. EF had me working immediately, since my visa from Peace Corps hadn't expired and EF arranged my work visa for me within that time. Having completed Peace Corps, I was expecting to roll into Baku and live a comfortable, lucrative life with all the cultural bases already covered. It didn't exactly happen that way because, as many people can attest, there's a big difference between volunteer and 'real' work. I had to make that adjustment rather quickly.

Thus far, the working conditions have been pleasant (well-equipped classrooms with whiteboards and computers, and so on) and wages have been satisfactory for a single male on a modest budget. As long as my expenses haven't gotten out of hand, I've been able to save around a thousand dollars a month after student loan payments. I can count on one hand the number of times I've had to deal with behavioural problems, which were efficiently dealt with by the school. Nonetheless, the 'orientation period' at EF is essentially non-existent. Though I had two years of volunteer teaching in a village under my belt, I had no idea about the expectations in the classroom at EF, and I had not taught in a setting like this before. This made my first groups mediocre at best, and particularly scary towards the ends of the levels because I was in a panic that the paying students weren't prepared for their final tests. I was also unaware of what I needed to do to get tests effectively graded and student reports and certificates completed. At this point, however, those problems are water under the bridge, and I fully enjoy working here now. For my own work, help is always available if I ask for it.

When a group of students clicks, it's really wonderful, and the students are extremely grateful for what you do for them. The biggest issue with students here is getting them to think outside the box and discuss topics other than national meals and weddings. For most of them, they want English as a skill, so they can 'find a good job' or study abroad. Teaching here forces idealistic foreign teachers to face the reality of many places, namely that people wish to adopt a language ability from you, but that does not mean that they want to adopt ideas or culture from you. Any strong, independent-minded teacher who wants to save some money and be in a fascinating region can do well in Baku. It's not the liveliest city, but it is changing rapidly, with new buildings going up all the time.

Several British companies recruit qualified teachers for Azerbaijan, such as Language Solutions (barry. shorten@langsols.com; www.langsols.az) and Oxford Vision which is the official UK representative of a global schools network including in Azerbaijan (http://oxfordvision.com). A company in Baku seen advertising recently is Senator LLC (www.senator.az) with an October 2012 deadline for applications.

LIST OF EMPLOYERS

EF ENGLISH FIRST
Shafayat Mehdiyev 83/23, AZ 1141, Baku
☏ +994 12 430 33 96/97
✉ info.baku@ef.com or lala.talishli@ef.com
💻 www.englishfirst.com

NUMBER OF TEACHERS: 1.
PREFERENCE OF NATIONALITY: British, North American, Australian, New Zealander.
QUALIFICATIONS: EFL/ESL certificate.
CONDITIONS OF EMPLOYMENT: 9-month contract from October.

Schools open 9am–9pm, Monday to Saturday, 24 contact hours per week. Mainly adults students.
SALARY: $2,000 per month.
FACILITIES/SUPPORT: Modern facilities, teacher library, computer laboratory, guidance and support of academic coordinator, flights paid on completion of contract, paid holiday, orientation and ongoing seminars and development. Assistance given with finding flat (not shared). Medical insurance and visa provided.
RECRUITMENT: Applications through English First (EF) teacher recruitment in offices worldwide.
CONTACT: Lala Talishli (lala.talishli@ef.com).

Kazakhstan

Kazakhstan is another prospering Central Asian Republic where the demand for IELTS preparation continues to soar and the market among young learners is also expanding. Culturally, the country is changing away from the one that was spoofed in *Borat* (full title: *Borat: Cultural Learnings of America for Make Benefit Glorious Nation of Kazakhstan*). Yet Kazakhstan has not enjoyed a very positive reputation amongst the ELT community, something which **Anthony Cook** thinks is undeserved. Since obtaining his CELTA in 2005, Anthony (originally from Australia) has had three contracts with Interpress-IH which, on balance, he says is probably his favourite school, and Almaty is definitely one of his favourite places to live in.

ANTHONY COOK

I first went to KZ to work for Interpress IH the year after 'Borat' was released, with no specific expectations except that it probably wouldn't be quite what Sacha Baron-Cohen had depicted. I know the school often has trouble enticing teachers to Kazakhstan, so I'd like to say why I think they're worth considering as employers. There's no such thing as a perfect language school in this world, of course, but I really enjoyed working there and hope I might have the chance to go back one of these days.

When the school accommodates the timetable of its many individual students, especially those preparing for IELTS and TOEFL, this can do inconvenient things to teachers' schedules. Overall, though, the hours are pretty good, and it's a relief to discover that, unlike in some other countries, there are no Kazakh people mad enough to request lessons at 7.30 in the morning! It can be a bit scary for a teacher who has never taught exam prep before to be thrown in at the deep end, but the 'teachers' room culture' is generally very good, with people around who are willing to help you get your head around unfamiliar material.

In general the accommodation the school provides is decent and you can occasionally luck out and get something really great, with mountain views, etc. Wages are quite good. You won't 'live like a king', but you will be comfortable. Most teachers find they have enough extra cash to travel around Central Asia a bit during the year, and those from the UK and EU can usually afford to fly home for Christmas. The end-of-contract bonus also gives you a nice 'buffer' so that you can have some time off over summer. I've found the school is quite conscientious and concerned about improving from year to year. This takes a lot of different forms: for example, they moved over to the exclusive use of electronic whiteboards, which teachers then had to get their heads around. Then in 2011 they partly aligned their General English courses to Cambridge exams. Things like this mean that every so often there's a 'shake-up' for teachers, so things don't get boring.

Things tend to go quiet around New Year, as it is very cold and quite a few teachers (local and foreign) go home to see their families. People are often disinclined to go out, so the NY holiday can get boring and a bit lonely. I'd suggest you clear out of KZ for a week or two in January, especially in your first year when you haven't had time to establish a social circle. The school tends to suffer from a 'dip' in available native speakers around Feb-March each year. So at that time of year, teachers may find themselves shunted from class to class, as the school tries to 'spread the native speakers around.' The school usually has around 15-20 expats on its books, so there are always a few native speakers around to go for a drink with. At the same time, Almaty is not overrun with foreign teachers, so you don't have the sense of being trapped in a giant expat bubble.

The students in KZ are probably the best I've taught anywhere. They're lively and talkative, and noticeably more 'worldly' than students in other ex-Soviet republics I've worked in. That's probably because KZ was historically a dumping ground for the USSR's unwanted, from North Koreans to Azeris and everyone in between, so now it's a relatively multicultural place, and the people there like it that way. Kazakh students are also keen on the more technical sides of learning a language - they want to master the grammar of English, because they see a connection between speaking correctly and getting the respect of those they speak to. They're inclined to bond well with classmates and, if you've a capable teacher, they'll be grateful for your presence in the class-room and you'll feel their loyalty. Also, in contrast to some Asian countries, in KZ it's considered acceptable and even good to be outspoken, so you generally don't have to struggle to wring opinions out of your students (excluding the occasional surly teenager, of course!). They are also generally quite sociable, and the culture doesn't have the 'barriers' between teacher and student that limit out-of-classroom interaction elsewhere. So it's not difficult to hang out with Kazakhs and make some local friends *if you want to. In Almaty there are large numbers of both traditional and Western bars, restaurants and cafés. The capital Astana is also developing in that regard, though it's still pretty quiet by comparison.*

Around Almaty there are quite a few beauty spots, and I often found myself going on excursions, some school-organised, others not. Anyone who loves mountains will never be bored - the city is right next to a massive mountain range that fills the entire horizon, so there are lots of walking opportunities.

Visas and work permits need to be sorted out before arriving in Kazakhstan but the school should handle all or most of the paperwork. One thing that may present an obstacle is the relative scarcity of Kazakh embassies and consulates around the world, and their possible lack of co-operativeness. The one in London has a dreadful reputation: they randomly refused to renew one returning teacher's Kazakh visa, without offering any explanation, and the subsequent appeal process dragged on for weeks and weeks. Anthony Cook had better luck applying in Seoul and Bangkok.

LIST OF EMPLOYERS

INTERNATIONAL LEARNING INSTITUTE
Bukhar Jirau 46/24, City Karaganda County, 100008
Kazakhstan
📞 +7 721 290 9690
🖱 marcelo@ganuc.com

NUMBER OF TEACHERS: 2.
PREFERENCE OF NATIONALITY: British.
QUALIFICATIONS: CELTA/DELTA with at least one year experience.
CONDITIONS OF EMPLOYMENT: 1-year contract. Usual hours are 9am–12pm and 3pm–8pm.
SALARY: Equivalent of US$1,000 net.
FACILITIES/SUPPORT: Accommodation is provided. Full assistance given with obtaining permits. Teachers must send all documents including copy of passport, diplomas, certificates, medical report and letters of recommendation. The process takes about 6 weeks before the permit can be sent to the candidate who then takes it to the embassy and gets the visa.
RECRUITMENT: Interviews are essential and are sometimes carried out in the UK.
CONTACT: Marcelo Lopez Lara, Country Director.

INTERPRESS-INTERNATIONAL HOUSE – ALMATY
InterPress-International House, Keremet 7, Almaty
050013
📞 +7 727 315 2525
🖱 recruit@ihkazakhstan.com
🖥 www.ihkazakhstan.com

NUMBER OF TEACHERS: About 60 foreign and local teachers employed, 35–40 new ones taken on each year for 5 branches in Almaty, and 2 in Astana.
PREFERENCE OF NATIONALITY: Native English speakers from UK, the USA, Ireland, Canada, Australia.
QUALIFICATIONS: Cambridge CELTA, IHC, Trinity TESOL, MA in TESOL as a minimum and at least 1 year of post-qualification teaching experience preferred. Young learners qualification and experience in teaching for exam preparation (IELTS and TOEFL) is preferable.
CONDITIONS OF EMPLOYMENT: 9 or 12-month contracts from September/October. Teaching load 120 hours (or 100 teaching hours) monthly plus 8 hours per month set aside for teachers' meetings, workshops and standby hours.
SALARY: 180,000–210,000 tenge net ($1,200–$1,500) in

Almaty, and 210,000–240,000 tenge ($1,400–$1,600) in Astana, depending on qualifications and experience. Overtime hourly rates paid after 1,080 contracted hours. Bonus paid on completion of contract amounting to 150 tenge per hour taught (e.g. could be total of 216,000 tenge for 12-month contract). Paid holidays: 20 days in 12 months, 15 days in 9 months. Free survival Russian course.

FACILITIES/SUPPORT: Free shared accommodation, all bills paid by the school (excluding long distance telephone calls, cable TV and Internet) or accommodation reimbursement. Airfare allowance. The school assists and covers the costs of a multiple entry 1-year work visa. Limited healthcare and 24-hour hotline emergency assistance. Opportunities for promotion and transfer in one of the world's leading educational organisations.

RECRUITMENT: Direct applications to the school and through IHWO Recruitment Services (www.ihworld.com) and online advertising. Phone/Skype interviews essential.

CONTACT: Elmira Tursunkhanova, Central Office Manager & Recruitment Manager.

LANGUAGE LINK KAZAKHSTAN
1a Kulmanova St, 060002 Atyrau
© +7 7122 272907
jobs@languagelink.ru
www.jobs.languagelink.ru

CONDITIONS OF EMPLOYMENT: Similar to Language Link Russia mentioned above.

CONTACT: Svetlana Akhmetova, Administrator.

Kyrgyzstan

LIST OF EMPLOYERS

LONDON SCHOOL IN BISHKEK
Sovetskaya 39, 720005 Bishkek
© +996 312 54 44 74/54 21 92/54 54 30
bishkekschool@gmail.com
http://thelondonschool.org/en/tefl-jobs.php

NUMBER OF TEACHERS: 8.

PREFERENCE OF NATIONALITY: American, British or Canadian native English speakers.

QUALIFICATIONS: Degree, CELTA and at least 1 year's teaching experience. Teachers without experience also would be considered.

CONDITIONS OF EMPLOYMENT: Minimum 6 months starting all year round. 22 hours per week, 5 hours per day, 4 days a week plus 1-hour interview with new students four times a month.

SALARY: From $650 to $800 a month with free accommodation and monthly cultural excursions within the country all year round.

FACILITIES/SUPPORT: Free room provided plus all accommodation expenses. Help given with work permits for which teachers must have CELTA certificate and two references from previous teaching jobs.

RECRUITMENT: Online application at: www.tlsbi.com/Tefl.htm. Teachers hired on basis of CV and references.

CONTACT: David Maytum, HR or Kendje Aitikeeva, Director.

THE REST OF EUROPE

Outside the mainstream European nations, demand for native speakers of English obviously exists though immigration problems often occur. This chapter contains a miscellany of European opportunities in some quite obscure corners of the continent.

Albania

Information about teaching in this European country wedged between Greece, Macedonia, Serbia and Montenegro has not always been easy to find, but Albania is now fairly stable and offers some opportunities for teachers keen to escape the traditional EFL circuit. The number of paid teaching jobs is still limited by the country's poverty, but Albania is signatory to a Stabilisation and Association Agreement with the EU, so there is hope that demand will increase if the country's economy slowly continues to grow.

English is certainly the favoured foreign language and is compulsory from the fifth grade through to university. Language schools have begun to open and most at least aspire to employ a native English speaking teacher, although few can currently afford it. The Language Schools in Albania Foundation (LSIA) is the largest non-profit private language tuition provider in Albania, founded in April 1994 by a group of Albanian university teachers and students. It currently enrols around 3,500 students in 15 locations across Albania and Macedonia, with new branches in Gramsh and Koplik (www.lsiaal.com/employment/employment.htm).

Out of 120 English teachers a handful are native English speakers. These schools have very limited funding and have started trying to recruit volunteer teachers to come to Albania to expose children from deprived backgrounds to English spoken by a native. Volunteers are likely to be offered local accommodation and LSIA will also assist with the red tape. **Blerina Gjonaj**, Head of the Overseas Department at LSIA, suggests that volunteering might lead to a paid job:

> *The demand for native English speakers is increasing every day, and the same can be said for paid employment, although that is not yet at the level that everybody wants. It is still easier to find a teaching job if you are a volunteer (maybe at the beginning), and then you can get involved as a paid employee. Albanian people are very interested in learning English. Language schools in Albania enrol children, mature students, adults and even parents of the students.*

Albania is still considered to be close enough to a developing country to have a sizeable contingent of Peace Corps volunteers in place including a number who are teaching English at foreign language high schools and other institutes. **Margaret Sheridan** was a Peace Corps volunteer who says '*I had a terrific experience, teaching English in high school and to adults, then opening a TOEFL test site, the first in southern Albania, with a terrific Albanian colleague.*'

Other institutions that may be worth contacting are the Memorial International School of Tirana (Ish Shkolla Partise Rr. Dumes, Tirana; +355 4 223 7379; info@mistedu.net; www.mistedu.com) which currently employs one American, one Briton, and three Canadians. The school's minimum requirement is that teachers have some years of experience in their own fields, although the majority have completed university courses with components in education. A language school in Vlora was recently advertising an urgent vacancy (info@smartcenter-al.com) and offering a monthly salary of US$500 (compared to the €1,450 quoted by the Memorial School). The Abraham Lincoln Foundation offers English language courses for all levels and special English programmes for several professional institutions in Albania. It employs a few American teachers with English degrees at their three branches in Tirana.

Visa guidelines can be checked at the Embassy of the Republic of Albania in the UK or USA. If your stay is going to be less than 90 days, you do not need to apply for a visa in advance but you may be required to pay an entry tax of €10. You are not permitted to cross out of Albania and straight back in again to renew your tourist visa. If you intend to stay longer than 90 days, you must apply for a residency permit.

Living costs are very cheap by US and UK standards, though choice can be limited. One volunteer teacher complained that he had to travel five hours by bus to Tirana to buy ketchup. Albania has plenty of scenic attractions, including rugged mountains and a marvellous stretch of Adriatic coastline, blissfully free of package holiday tourists.

LIST OF EMPLOYERS

ABRAHAM LINCOLN PROFESSIONAL STUDIES CENTER
Rruga Qemal Stafa Nr. 184, Tirana; also at Rr
Ismail Qemali 31 and at Kompleksi Kika, Rr Komuna e
Parisit
☏ +355 42 230880
🖂 info@lincoln.org.al
💻 www.lincolnalbania.org

NUMBER OF TEACHERS: Few native English speakers for the three branches.
PREFERENCE OF NATIONALITY: American and others.
QUALIFICATIONS: Degree/TEFL Cert. MA preferred.
CONDITIONS OF EMPLOYMENT: Most teachers are part-time. Courses offered for all levels and special English programmes for several professional institutions in Albania.
RECRUITMENT: Mainly via www.anegino.gen.al.

LSIA - LANGUAGE SCHOOLS IN ALBANIA
P.O.Box 1400, RR. Bardhyl NR.76/1, Tirana
☏ +355 523 76740
🖂 info.lsia@yahoo.com
💻 www.lsiaal.com

New initiative to expose children in need to native English speakers, all over Albania.
NUMBER OF TEACHERS: 6.
PREFERENCE OF NATIONALITY: None, but have to be native English speakers.
QUALIFICATIONS: Master's degree in any specialisation, job experience.
SALARY: Mainly volunteer positions so no salary.
FACILITIES/SUPPORT: School provides accommodation and assists with work permit.
RECRUITMENT: Interviews are carried out depending on the occasion. If the teacher is in Albania, then a face-to-face interview will be possible.
CONTACT: Human Resources Division.

Andorra

Andorra lies in the heart of the Pyrenees between Spain and France, and can be seen as an extension of both countries, though it has its own elected government. It is too small to have many language schools, but the one listed here is a possibility (and you would be there over the skiing season).

LIST OF EMPLOYERS

CENTRE ANDORRA DE LLENGUES (CALL)
15 Carrer del Fener, Andorra-la-Vella
☏ +376 80 40 30
🖂 centrandorra.lang@andorra.ad
💻 www.call.ad

NUMBER OF TEACHERS: 2.
PREFERENCE OF NATIONALITY: British, Irish and North Americans.
QUALIFICATIONS: BA in English or a foreign language plus TEFL qualification and 2–3 years' experience abroad most welcome.

A good knowledge of Spanish and/or French can help. Non-smokers preferred.

CONDITIONS OF EMPLOYMENT: 9–10-month renewable contract which runs from October to June. 27 hours per week, 5 days a week. Teaching hours spread throughout the day. Teaching very young learners (6–7 years) and all other ages including professionals.

SALARY: €1,800 per month (plus overtime if any available).

FACILITIES/SUPPORT: Board and lodging available within walking distance costs from €550 per month. Work permit arranged and paid for by the school.

RECRUITMENT: Direct application with CV and photo by email.

CONTACT: Claude Benet.

Bosnia-Herzegovina

There are still few private language schools in Bosnia, and most operate on a small scale. As usual you could check the list provided at www.eslbase.com/schools/bosnia which includes one larger company, Seal, with schools in Dvorovi, Brcko, Zvornik and Novi Sad (www.seal-rs.com).

LIST OF EMPLOYERS

NEW ACADEMY
Muharem Suljanovic Street, 79101 Prijedor

© +387 65 586 469

📧 new_academy@yahoo.com

💻 www.new-academy.com

PREFERENCE OF NATIONALITY: None.

QUALIFICATIONS: 2 years' TEFL experience.

CONDITIONS OF EMPLOYMENT: 1-year contract with working hours between 4pm and 10pm. Also offer summer courses.

RECRUITMENT: Interviews are essential.

CONTACT: Zoran Beric, Principal.

Croatia

Building on its strong indigenous English teaching infrastructure, Croatia's private language schools flourish in Zagreb, Varazdin and Karlovac, as well as in other towns. For many schools, the idea of employing a native English speaker teacher is very attractive; particularly given Croatia's popularity as a British tourist destination, accessible by cheap flights. Teachers who go to work in Croatia are likely to find themselves being made welcome and treated well, certainly outside the usual tourist hot spots. Salaries are likely to be quoted in euros even though the national currency is still the kuna.

The market for private teaching is strong, however native English teachers need to be well qualified to secure a job. The Foreign Language School, Ziger, is fairly modest in size, with only one or two native teachers, but they still ask for a degree, at least one year's experience, and a CELTA or DELTA certificate.

Anyone wishing to work in Croatia must apply to the Embassy of the Republic of Croatia for a visa. An application form must be completed by your employer and returned together with a passport, two photographs and details of the job (e.g. a copy of your contract, length of employment, type of work, location and full address of employer).

The British Council in Zagreb can offer informal assistance to prospective teachers and should be able to put you in touch with the Association of Croatian Teachers of English (HUPE), which organises teacher development activities but can't help foreign teachers to find jobs. The voluntary placement organisation Sharing One Language (SOL) (see Central and Eastern Europe: Finding a job) sends a few teachers to Croatia but posts are dependent on an unpredictable Ministry.

With its beautiful coastline and accessibility, Croatia has developed summer camps, some of which teach English. The exchange company CCUSA sends volunteer teachers to Camp California in Savudrija, almost on the Slovenia border, though counsellor-teachers here pay a programme fee of £180 (www.ccusa.com) but get free room and board. **Geoff Nunney** wanted to find a summer job after the academic term finished at the language school in Slovakia where he had spent the year. He got a job at Euroclub on Öolta, an island off the coast near Split (www.euroclub.hr), the largest international youth camp on the Adriatic:

I have a return invitation for this year, to teach kids of all nationalities from 10 to 20. There's a big mixture of teachers – I was known as the 'Crazy Teacher'. Lots of sports, lessons and a holiday atmosphere. I did four weeks there, and the pay is enough to live on.

LIST OF EMPLOYERS

FOREIGN LANGUAGE SCHOOL – ZIGER
S. Vraza 37, 42000 Varazdin
✆ +385 42 330 385
✉ irena.ziger@vz.htnet.hr
🖥 www.skola-ziger.hr

NUMBER OF TEACHERS: 1–2.
PREFERENCE OF NATIONALITY: British, American, Canadian.
QUALIFICATIONS: At least 1 year's experience, CELTA/DELTA, university degree.
CONDITIONS OF EMPLOYMENT: Minimum 1-year contract, teaching hours are usually late afternoon and evenings.
FACILITIES/SUPPORT: Assistance with finding accommodation and work permit (school applies and translates necessary documents).
RECRUITMENT: Via email contact. Interviews by phone.
CONTACT: Irena Ziger, Principal (skype: irena.ziger).

MHC BUSINESS LANGUAGE TRAINING d.o.o.
Petra Hektorovića 2, 10 000 Zagreb, Croatia
✆ +385 99 793 63 63
✉ zagreb@mhc-training.com
🖥 www.mhc-training.com

NUMBER OF TEACHERS: 15.
PREFERENCE OF NATIONALITY: Any.
QUALIFICATIONS: MHC trainers have an understanding of business experience, often specialising in areas such as marketing, finance, pharmaceutical or law. A degree is not necessary, although a teaching certificate such as CELTA would be of value.
CONDITIONS OF EMPLOYMENT: Freelance, teaching 15–25 hours per week.
SALARY: €10–€15 per 60 minutes, depending on experience and development with MHC. Seminars between €100 and €150 per day. Trainers are responsible for paying their own taxes (12%–25%) and social security (variable).
FACILITIES/SUPPORT: Trainer preparation room, resource library, photocopying, trainer development, social networking events. Trainers require working papers.
RECRUITMENT: Interviews are essential and usually take place at premises. Possibility of Skype interviews if the applicant is based abroad.
CONTACT: Bashkim Fazliu, Regional Director South East Europe.

Cyprus

A visitor to the Republic of Cyprus will be struck by the similarities with Greece – cuisine, architecture, landscapes and culture – but then be surprised at the relative prominence of English. Signs are printed both in Greek and English, many (if not most) local people even outside the cities speak some English, and the British influence can be noticed everywhere. Because of the longstanding relationship between Cyprus and Britain, the English language is given much prominence in the state educational system. As a result the density of *frontisteria* is not as high as it is in Greece, though there are still a fair number of private institutes preparing children for external examinations.

Cyprus has a small population of less than a million and therefore opportunities are not extensive. Also a large number of Cypriot students leave the island each year to study in the UK and USA, although there are still a number of afternoon language schools in the cities and towns.

To find an ELT job in Cyprus before you arrive is extremely difficult because very few of the ELT schools actually advertise on the internet and there is a sizeable expat community, from which native English teachers can be drawn. Some expats will also informally help Cypriot friends with their English over a glass of beer.

Sending speculative CVs is unlikely to succeed. It is more fruitful to visit schools in person and hand it in. Furthermore, state school jobs are extremely hard to come by for foreigners as you need at least a three-year degree in the relevant subject (e.g. English literature for teaching English) as well as a good knowledge of Greek. Therefore, most foreign teachers aim to find a job in a language school in the private sector, which will probably mean working in the afternoons or evenings, although some schools also have morning classes. One freelance opportunity might be to approach businessmen and women in the property sector, who have (or would like to have) English and American clients. You'd need a solid business background to succeed, and would be required to provide specialist vocabulary ('grouting', anyone?).

Since Cyprus has joined the European Union, visas are no longer a major hurdle. Nationals of all the other 26 EU countries have the automatic right of residence in Cyprus. Those who intend to work and stay in the country are obliged to apply for a registration certificate within four months of arrival. In Nicosia this can be done at the Migration department; elsewhere applicants must visit the Immigration Police. The fee for registration is a modest €8.54; however, the fine for failing to register is in excess of €2,500. The country has also adopted the euro.

If you wish to advertise your services as a tutor in the English language press of Greek Cyprus, contact the *Cyprus Mail* (www.cyprus-mail.com) though its Classified Jobs section isn't up to much, or *Cyprus Weekly* published on Fridays by Cyweekly (PO Box 24977, 1306 Nicosia; +357 22–666047; www.cyprusweekly.com.cy). Major English institutes include the Papantoniou Institute founded in 1999, (www.papantoniou-institute.com) which offers English at all levels.

Most schools offer a contract of 20–25 working hours a week for the academic year September to May/June. The hourly pay is above average for southern Europe, starting at about €12–€13 per hour. As in Greece, there are usually two paid holidays during the academic year: two weeks over Christmas and two weeks for the Greek Orthodox Easter.

Most Cypriot schools have very good facilities, although they may be lagging behind somewhat in technology. Teacher support is readily available with regular free seminars organised by various publishers. In language classrooms, there is a wide range of levels for all ages. The majority of children enrol at language schools when they are about eight and finish around the age of 16, attending lessons twice a week. However, there is a growing demand for children as young as 4 to start learning English as a foreign language, so schools are introducing classes for younger children. A lesson can last from one to two hours for higher levels. Young students and adults are usually motivated and love interactive teaching. However, those teaching teenagers will need to be firm and to make lessons particularly interesting.

People move to Cyprus nowadays more for the lifestyle than for cheap living. The downside is that eating out etc. is not cheap; however, the improved infrastructure (like the very good motorways) makes life easier. Note there is no train service on the island. Government plans to take the country upmarket by building more marinas and golf courses have had to be set aside because of the recession. The global downturn has seen a sharp decline in the number of tourists arriving in Cyprus and many small businesses have been forced to close. If reunification with the Turkish north takes place on the island (a long way off but positive moves have been made) then the country could really flourish.

A decent studio apartment can be rented for about €350 per month. Eating out is not too ruinous at €17 per person. Public transport, on the other hand, is very sparse. By opening the English speaking newspapers, you will be able to find out what's on and where to meet new friends. If you want to find out more about life in Cyprus for ex-pats, visit the forums at www.cyprusliving.org and www.easterncyprus.com.

Turkish Cyprus

There are six private universities, four private schools and at least two language schools in the Turkish Republic of Northern Cyprus (TRNC). The main industry in Northern Cyprus is tourism, largely catering for an English-speaking clientele, so there is strong local demand to master the language for employment purposes. However, it should be pointed out that the expatriate community numbers more than 4,000 so there is already a substantial pool of native English speakers on hand to fill any teacher vacancies that occur.

Malta

Although somewhat off the beaten track and although English is the first language of the tiny island, EFL is booming in Malta. A number of private language schools cater to groups coming from other Mediterranean countries on short courses in the spring, summer and at other times. Even the National Tourist Office of Malta distributes a leaflet 'Learning English in the Sun' or check the list of language schools on www.visitmalta. com (which devotes a whole section to 'language learning'). The Ministry of Education also publishes a list of 36 language schools that it has licensed plus a few that operate only in the summer (see www.education. gov.mt/edu/schools/english_language.htm). The interests of the mainstream English language institutes are represented by FELTOM, the Federation of English Language Teaching Organisations Malta (+356 2131 0927; www.feltom.com); the site has good links to the 16 member schools and basic information about teaching on the island. One member school, EC English Language Centre in St Julians, offers summer jobs to unqualified teachers provided they are able to do an intensive induction course for the first half of June; for details see www.ecenglish.com/work-for-ec/vacancies/summer-english-teacher.

All EU nationals have the right to live and work in Malta, although it is necessary to obtain an EFL teaching permit from the EFL Monitoring Board of the Ministry of Education. In order to be eligible for the permit, a

JESSICA STONE

Jessica Stone decided to leave the States to embark on a Mediterranean adventure in 2011, even though she was older than most who entertain such dreams.

I feel extremely lucky. After carefully examining all the countries I was interested in visiting / teaching / travelling in, I selected Malta as my first choice. I sent out about 15 letters and resumés and received roughly six responses. Three of them asked me to touch base when I arrived saying they could probably give me part-time work in the summer. One made a definite appointment to meet and one asked if I could do a Skype interview. The latter ended up offering me an excellent position as the Executive Director of Academic Programme Development and Marketing, a far cry from the teaching job I'd originally applied for. Just happened to have the skill set they were looking for at the time. I should say that I am 58 years old and hold a Masters and PhD in Communications, and have taught Business and Business Communications at US universities for over 20 years. In preparation I did a 100-hour TESOL course with LCC in Seattle.

So now I'm living in Malta, have a great flat with a view of the Med and a super job. The school is going to get the work permit for me, which will result in a one year residency visa to follow on from the initial three months as a tourist. From my understanding, the issues with visas are the same everywhere – lots of paperwork and rubber stamps and moaning about not being able to get one but anyone who really wants one, gets one. And the schools hire people right and left even though you can't officially work without a work permit. The money you earn teaching English is not very good, especially for people my age. But the adventure and cultural experience are truly priceless.

307

candidate must have an Advanced Level Certificate in English from a recognised institution, and have completed a TEFL course such as a CELTA. A 60-hour TEFL Induction Course is offered by the majority of FELTOM schools and also satisfies the government requirement. All teachers also need a clean police conduct certificate. Note that self-employed freelancers do not need to obtain a work permit. Australians and New Zealanders under the ages of 25 and 30 respectively may apply for a working holiday visa to Malta valid for one year.

Wages are paid hourly and are in the €8–€12 bracket, with a steady average of €10. Many professional teachers join MATEFL, the Malta Association of TEFL (www.matefl.org). Membership costs a modest €12. The NSTS English Language Institute in Gzira (HQ, 220 St. Paul St, Valletta VLT07; 2558 8000 www.nstsenglishlanguagemalta.com) markets its English courses in conjunction with sports holidays for young tourists to Malta. NSTS run weekly vacation courses from June to August, and it might be worth approaching them for a job, particularly if you are a water sports enthusiast. NSTS was keen to hire **Robert Mizzi** from Canada once it learned that he was half-Maltese:

I was offered a job quite casually when NSTS found out I was volunteering conversational English in the main youth hostel in Valletta. Perhaps one reason they wanted to hire me was they knew the visa would not be a problem. However, I was surprised by how relaxed the offer was. It was just mentioned in passing rather than at an actual interview. I guess it is the Maltese way: once you are one of them, then everything is gravy.

LIST OF EMPLOYERS

AM LANGUAGE STUDIO
299 Manwel Dimech Street, Sliema SLM1054
+356 2132 42 42
info@amlanguage.com
www.amlanguage.com

NUMBER OF TEACHERS: 3.
PREFERENCE OF NATIONALITY: British.
QUALIFICATIONS: CELTA or CertTESOL.
CONDITIONS OF EMPLOYMENT: Teachers are employed on a freelance basis and are required to work from July to August with 22.5–30 hours per week.
SALARY: €11 per hour.
FACILITIES/SUPPORT: As teachers are freelance they just have to register as self-employed with the local authorities and do not need to apply for a work permit.
RECRUITMENT: CV and telephone interview.
CONTACT: Larissa Jonk, Director of Studies.

ELANGUEST ENGLISH LANGUAGE SCHOOL
Keating House, Ross Street, St Julian's STJ 3243
+356 21374 777
info@elanguest.com
www.elanguest.com

PREFERENCE OF NATIONALITY: British, Canadian and Australian.

QUALIFICATIONS: TEFL course plus A level in English. Applicants with CELTA or TESOL certificate are given preference.
CONDITIONS OF EMPLOYMENT: No contract, however applicants who can work all year round are given preference. Between 4.5 and 5.5 working hours per day.
FACILITIES/SUPPORT: Assistance given with work permits.
RECRUITMENT: CV and telephone interview.

GLOBAL VILLAGE ENGLISH CENTRE
St George's Street, St. Paul's Bay SPB 02
+356 21 573417
info@gvmalta.com
www.gvmalta.com

NUMBER OF TEACHERS: All staff are native speakers of English.
PREFERENCE OF NATIONALITY: None.
QUALIFICATIONS: Experience and TEFL qualification needed plus minimum 1 year's experience.
CONDITIONS OF EMPLOYMENT: Open-ended contracts. 15–20 hours per week in low season, 20+ hours per week in peak season.
SALARY: Varies according to experience and qualifications.
FACILITIES/SUPPORT: Advice given on rental accommodation in area.
RECRUITMENT: Mainly via teacher training courses run on-site. Interviews are essential and are usually carried out face-to-face with the Director of Studies and include analysis of lesson planning.
CONTACT: Mrs Gaby Huhn, Head of School.

NUMBER OF TEACHERS: 60.

PREFERENCE OF NATIONALITY: None.

QUALIFICATIONS: Minimum CELTA but no experience required.

CONDITIONS OF EMPLOYMENT: Open-ended contract with 15 or 22.5 working hours per week depending on preference and availability.

SALARY: €10.50 per hour.

FACILITIES/SUPPORT: Assistance given with work permits.

CONTACT: Angie Conti, Academic Manager.

NUMBER OF TEACHERS: 30 freelancers.

PREFERENCE OF NATIONALITY: EU citizenship preferred though willing to consider any CV as long as teachers are native English speakers.

QUALIFICATIONS: Minimum of a TEFL course and a high school level qualification in English Language (A level or equivalent). However, a CELTA/DELTA/TESOL certificate is preferable.

CONDITIONS OF EMPLOYMENT: Freelance basis only. Flexible timetable according to teacher's availability. Normally 15–30 class hours a week.

SALARY: €8–€12 per hour.

FACILITIES/SUPPORT: Non-local teachers are given assistance in finding housing as close to the school as possible and at the best rate possible.

RECRUITMENT: Face-to-face interview and on occasion class observation. Occasionally telephone interviews are conducted.

CONTACT: Pia Zammit, Director of Studies.

Serbia, Montenegro and Kosovo

With the short-lived union of Serbia and Montenegro breaking down in 2006, followed by Kosovo's declaration of independence from Serbia in 2008, the dissolution of the former Yugoslavia is complete, with much underlying tension remaining.

The nascent ELT industry looks set to develop if the region remains stable. Possible leads include the Bejza Education Centre (Ul. Vuka Karadzi'ca br.7 11000, Belgrade, Serbia; +381 11/328 14 49; www.bejza. edu.rs) and ELS Language School (www.els.rs).

In order to get a residence/work permit for Serbia, you must submit a contract of employment and a translated copy of your diploma. Further information on the regulations for entering and working in Serbia can be found at www.serbianembassy.org.uk.

The non-profit-making British organisation SOL (+44 1271 327319; www.sol.org.uk) has set up volunteer placements at private schools in Serbia. After an exploratory trip, SOL's director was struck by the need: '*I have just been in Serbia and we are looking to the future there as a new destination. To see the catastrophic effect of our sanctions on the people and industry there makes me quite ashamed – yet reading our media, I fully supported the sanctions at the time as it seemed simply a political decision.*'

LIST OF EMPLOYERS

NUMBER OF TEACHERS: 1–2.

PREFERENCE OF NATIONALITY: None.

QUALIFICATIONS: Bachelor's degree plus CELTA minimum. DELTA or MA in TESOL/Applied Linguistics and/or long standing experience preferred.

CONDITIONS OF EMPLOYMENT: Two 90-minute lessons per week in some cases.

FACILITIES/SUPPORT: Assistance may be available for accommodation, and work permits may be possible.

RECRUITMENT: Interviews arranged on basis of submitted CV.

CONTACT: Natasha Jovanovich.

MHC BUSINESS LANGUAGE TRAINING Sh.p.k.

Bregu i Diellit, Z Lindje 13, 10000 Prishtina, Kosovo

+386 492 49784

see@mhc-training.com

www.mhc-training.com

MHC has headquarters in Austria with teaching operations in Bratislava and Zagreb.

NUMBER OF TEACHERS: 5.

PREFERENCE OF NATIONALITY: Any.

QUALIFICATIONS: MHC trainers have an understanding of business experience, often specialising in areas such as marketing, finance, pharmaceutical, or law. A degree is not necessary, although a teaching certificate such as CELTA would be of value.

CONDITIONS OF EMPLOYMENT: Freelance, teaching 15–25 hours per week.

SALARY: €10–€12 per 60 minutes, depending on experience and development with MHC. Seminars between €100 and €150 per day. Trainers are responsible for paying their own taxes (0–10%) and social security (variable).

FACILITIES/SUPPORT: Trainer preparation room, resource library, photocopying, trainer development, social networking events. Trainers require working papers.

RECRUITMENT: Interviews are essential and usually take place at premises. Possibility of Skype interviews if the applicant is based abroad.

CONTACT: Bashkim Fazliu, Regional Director South East Europe; Dardan Velija (Local Director).

OXFORD CENTAR

64 Rimiski trg, 81000 Podgorica, Montenegro

+382 20 234 425

oxford@t-com.me

www.oxfordcentar.com

NUMBER OF TEACHERS: 6.

PREFERENCE OF NATIONALITY: British, American, Australian, New Zealander, Canadian.

QUALIFICATIONS: 3–5 years' practical experience.

CONDITIONS OF EMPLOYMENT: 4 or 9-month contract with 22 to 27 working hours per week.

SALARY: €750–850 per month plus flat allowance of €200 per month.

FACILITIES/SUPPORT: School pays for 2 nights in a hotel as teacher looks for accommodation. Assistance also given with applying for work permits.

RECRUITMENT: Usually via adverts on www.eslbase.com or www.tefl.com. Interviews are essential and can be via phone or Skype.

CONTACT: Dale Kiehl, Director of Studies.

Slovenia

As in Croatia, there are a good many private schools and many opportunities can be created by energetic native English speakers both as freelance teachers for institutes or as private tutors. Slovenia is a sophisticated little country with high standards of education and many well-qualified native teachers of English.

The English Studies Resource Centre at the British Council in Ljubljana has a list of private language schools throughout the country (see www.britishcouncil.org/slovenia-exams-list-of-language-schools.htm). The Council remains closely in touch with language schools and may be able to refer qualified candidates to possible employers, though the Ljubljana office is not open to the general public. The average hourly wage should start at €10.

As one of the countries that joined the EU in May 2004 and the Schengen Agreement in 2008, Slovenia now has fairly straightforward regulations for EU members. All EU nationals are able to work in Slovenia under the same conditions as Slovene citizens in their countries. However, teachers should obtain a temporary residence permit within three months of entering the country, and will need a valid passport whose expiry date exceeds by at least three months the intended period of stay, health insurance, sufficient means of subsistence and a legitimate purpose for their residence (like a job). The Embassy in London

(10 Little College Street, London SW1P 3SH; +44 20 7222 5700) handles external applications for both British and Irish nationals; the average processing time is one month. Your school should report that you are working for them to the Employment Service of Slovenia (Zavod za zaposlovanje) in Ljubljana within eight days of starting the job.

LIST OF EMPLOYERS

BERLITZ LANGUAGE CENTER
Gosposvetska 2, 1000 Ljubljana
- +386 1 433 13 25
- berlitz.ljubljana@berlitz.si or workinslovenia@berlitz.si
- www.berlitz.si

Also: Svetozarevska 6, 2000 Maribor; and centres in Kranj, Novo Mesto and Celje.

NUMBER OF TEACHERS: 60.

PREFERENCE OF NATIONALITY: EU or candidates already with permission to work in Slovenia.

QUALIFICATIONS: Tertiary educational background, good communication skills, professional attitude and appearance.

CONDITIONS OF EMPLOYMENT: Minimum 1 year. All work on freelance basis. Number of hours assigned on merit, no guaranteed minimum. Good teachers work 20–40 hours per week.

SALARY: From €10+ per unit (40 minutes).

FACILITIES/SUPPORT: No assistance with accommodation. Compulsory training in Berlitz method offered twice a year. Regular support through observations and workshops.

RECRUITMENT: Adverts and personal recommendation. Applications welcome at any time and are kept on file for 6 months. Face-to-face interviews are compulsory.

CONTACT: Luke Davis, Local Instructional Supervisor for Berlitz Slovenia.

EVROPA BLED d.o.o.
Finzgarjeva 15, 4260 Bled
- +386 4 57 41 563/64 49 88
- cilka@evropa-bled.com
- www.evropa-bled.com

NUMBER OF TEACHERS: 1–2.

PREFERENCE OF NATIONALITY: None.

QUALIFICATIONS: Experience essential. Teacher training course for TEFL required.

CONDITIONS OF EMPLOYMENT: School year from October to May. Minimum 30–40 lessons a month.

SALARY: Starting salary about €6.50 net per 45-minute lesson.

FACILITIES/SUPPORT: Help is given with finding accommodation but the rental charge is borne by the teacher.

RECRUITMENT: Contacts through the British Council.

CONTACT: Ms. Cilka Demsar, Director.

NISTA LANGUAGE CENTER
Smarska C.5D, 6000 Koper
- +386 5625 0400
- nista@siol.net; info@nista.si
- www.nista.si

Located on the Adriatic not far from Trieste, Italy.

NUMBER OF TEACHERS: 15.

PREFERENCE OF NATIONALITY: England, Scotland, New Zealand, Australia.

QUALIFICATIONS: Bachelor's degree (hons) and TEFL certificate plus a year's teaching experience. Business background useful.

CONDITIONS OF EMPLOYMENT: Minimum 10 months September to June (preferably longer). Usual 24–26 hours contact time per week.

SALARY: About €13 per lesson. No tax or social security deductions.

FACILITIES/SUPPORT: The school finds accommodation for teachers and provides necessary documents for them.

RECRUITMENT: Email, internet.

CONTACT: Alenka Rajčič.

PANTEON COLLEGE
Linhartova 11, 1000 Ljubljana
- +386 1 080 1042
- info@panteon.si
- www.panteon.si

NUMBER OF TEACHERS: 5.

PREFERENCE OF NATIONALITY: British.

QUALIFICATIONS: English teacher with a variety of TEFL experience (TEFL or CELTA certificate).

CONDITIONS OF EMPLOYMENT: Standard length of contract 1 year. 20–30 hours per week including morning, afternoon and evening lessons.

SALARY: €10 per hour (45 minutes of teaching).

FACILITIES/SUPPORT: Help is given with finding accommodation and acquiring the necessary permits.

RECRUITMENT: CV must be submitted. Successful applicants will be invited to attend an interview.

YURENA

Glavni Trg 11, 8000 Novo Mesto

+386 7 337 2100

yurena@siol.net

www.yurena.si

NUMBER OF TEACHERS: 2–3.

PREFERENCE OF NATIONALITY: English.

QUALIFICATIONS: TEFL qualification.

CONDITIONS OF EMPLOYMENT: 1-year contracts. 25–30 hours per week.

SALARY: Approximately €1,000 per month.

FACILITIES/SUPPORT: Accommodation and help with work permits provided.

RECRUITMENT: Interviews essential.

CONTACT: Kati Golobic, Director.

MIDDLE EAST

Oil wealth has meant that many of the countries of the Middle East have long been able to afford to at-tract the best teachers with superior qualifications and extensive experience. Most employers can afford to hire only professionals and there are few opportunities for newcomers to the profession. However, recent events in the wake of the Arab Spring have caused many teachers to look elsewhere. With a brutal civil war in Syria, and alarming reports of repression in Bahrain and Yemen rendering those countries virtually off-limits, this may not be the best time to be thinking of going to work in the Middle East. Ongoing tensions between Israelis and Palestinians and an escalation of anti-Western sentiment throughout the region have dampened enthusiasm for employment in the region. The Iraq and Afghanistan wars have undoubtedly destabilised the area and fanned the flames of Islamic distrust of the West. Many prospective teachers have been put off by fear for their personal security. The main exception is Turkey where thousands of na-tive English speaking teachers find work. Despite its adherence to Islam, Turkey does not fit comfortably into a chapter on the Middle East. But despite its aspirations to join the EU and its secular government, neither does it fit logically into a section on Europe. But whatever its geographical classification, Turkey is a very important country for EFL teachers, whatever their background, and is treated at length later in this chapter.

On the one hand, the wealthy countries of Saudi Arabia, Oman and the Gulf states generally employ teach-ers with top qualifications. On the other hand, countries such as Jordan may have more casual opportunities. Anyone interested in teaching English to the Palestinians scattered throughout the Arab World is likely to be working on a voluntary basis or for accommodation and a local stipend, rather than for expatriate salaries.

Teachers who sign contracts in a strict Islamic country should be aware of what they are letting them-selves in for. People usually spend a year or two teaching in Saudi Arabia to make some money, rather than because they enjoy the lifestyle (unless they are students of Arab culture). When the amount of money accumulating back home is the principal or only motivation, morale can degenerate. The situation can be especially discouraging for women. Yet not everyone is gasping to get home to freely available alcohol, etc. A high percentage of teachers are recruited locally from a stable expatriate community. Demand for native English teachers is increasing in Saudi Arabia, mainly due to the opening of new colleges and universities, both in the public and private sector, some of which employ scores of English language teachers and lectur-ers. Note that many of them accept only online applications, for example (to take just one) ALHOSN University in Abu Dhabi (www.alhosnu.ae/Site/JobOpenings.aspx). A useful list of institutes of higher education with, in some cases, links to current job vacancies can be found at www.university-directory.eu.

Middle Eastern language schools are also more likely to recruit non-native English speakers, specifically well-heeled teachers with pristine qualifications. **Ahad Shahbaz**, Director of Interlink Language Center in Riyadh, asks: '*If a non-native speaker is highly educated, has earned his credentials from the Harvards of ESL teacher training institutions, and has near-native and at times superior proficiency and eloquence in the language, should we not be hiring him or her?*'

FINDING A JOB

Unless you are more or less resident in the Middle East, it is essential in most cases to fix up a job in advance. Casual teaching is not a possibility in most countries for a number of reasons, including the difficulty of get-ting visas, the prohibitively high cost of staying without working and the whole tradition of hiring teachers. There are a few countries which can be entered on a tourist visa (i.e. Qatar, Yemen and the United Arab Emirates) if you want to inspect potential employers, but this would be an expensive exercise. Visa difficulties vary from country to country. In Jordan, for example, schools that would like to hire foreign teachers are

313

often put off by the cost of securing a work permit ($500 straight to the government and minimum $150 in lawyers' fees). The American ESL Center, based in Jordan, (see list of employers) employs foreigners as native English speaker teachers.

Single women, no matter how highly qualified, are at a serious disadvantage when pursuing high-paying jobs in Saudi Arabia and other strict Islamic countries. The majority of adverts specify 'single status male' or, at best, 'teaching couples'. Another requirement often mentioned in job details which excludes many candidates is experience of the Middle East, in acknowledgment of the culture shock that many foreigners encounter in adapting to life under Islam.

Job adverts regularly appear on websites such as www.tefl.com and in specialist journals. The largest display ads in the British educational press are quite often for Middle East vacancies, many placed by recruitment agencies on behalf of high-spending Saudi clients. It is always worth checking regional newspapers as well such as the *Khaleej Times* (www.khaleejtimes.com).

The British Council has teaching centres in Bahrain (Manama), Lebanon (Beirut), Oman (Muscat), Qatar (Doha), Saudi Arabia (Riyadh, Jeddah and Dammam), Kuwait and the United Arab Emirates (Abu Dhabi and Dubai). America-Mideast Educational & Training Services or Amideast is a private, nonprofit organisation with headquarters in Washington DC and provides English language and other professional training through its network of operations throughout the Middle East (and North Africa). Its website www.amideast.org carries lots of recruitment information.

The usual suspects are active in the region. International House has five schools in Saudi Arabia, one in Dubai, one in Iran, several in Lebanon and one in Oman. Berlitz has schools in Bahrain, Beirut, Oman, Qatar and UAE, among others.

RECRUITMENT AGENCIES

In theory, being hired by an established recruitment agency in your own country should offer some protection against problems. However, this is not always the case. A couple of years ago an educational consultancy with an office in Toronto recruited a large number of EFL teachers to work for the United Arab Emirates military. When a dispute arose between client and recruiter, the teachers were the ones to suffer since they weren't paid promised salaries and their contracts were not honoured.

A typical agency advert for corporate language instructors for the Middle East might read:

> *Client seeks applications from male instructors for its corporate training programmes in the petrochemicals, utilities and heavy industries sectors. We can consider UK, Canadian, American, Irish, New Zealand, South African, Egyptian, Jordanian and Filipino nationals. Applied language practice is more important than descriptive language or grammar-bound approaches to language teaching. Applications from enthusiastic candidates who are interested in multimedia are especially welcome. We have projects available in several cities.*

Reputable agencies to check out include Teachaway (www.teachaway.com), the UK-based M2r Global (see entry) and First Select International (www.fsi.jobs) with its head office in UAE and branches elsewhere.

LEISURE TIME

The majority of teachers live in foreigners' compounds provided by their employers. Most of these are well provided with sports facilities such as tennis courts and swimming pools. In some locations, such as Jubail in Saudi Arabia, water sports are a popular diversion. Some have described expat life in the Middle East as a false paradise.

The principal pastimes are barbecues, reading out-of-date copies of the *International Herald Tribune*, playing with computers (which are cheaply available) and complaining about the terrific heat and the lack of alcohol (Saudi Arabia and Kuwait are completely dry states.) Others of course try to learn some Arabic and make local friends, always taking care not to offend against local sensibilities. The constraints of living under Islam are well known. For example, in some countries anyone found drinking or smoking in a public place during the month of Ramadan could face a jail sentence, large fine and/or deportation.

LIST OF EMPLOYERS

BRITISH COUNCIL – MIDDLE EAST

Offices in Bahrain, Kuwait, Oman, Qatar, Saudi Arabia, Yemen, Iraq and United Arab Emirates

jobs@ae.britishcouncil.org

www.britishcouncil.org/me-contact-us-job-opportunities.htm

NUMBER OF TEACHERS: Fluctuating vacancies across the region, but mostly in Saudi Arabia (teach@sa.britishcouncil.org).

PREFERENCE OF NATIONALITY: British.

QUALIFICATIONS: Minimum CELTA or equivalent plus 2 years' full-time ELT experience for hourly teaching, DELTA may be needed for more senior posts.

CONDITIONS OF EMPLOYMENT: Range of opportunities, e.g. hourly teaching in Riyadh.

FACILITIES/SUPPORT: Accommodation arranged plus medical insurance.

RECRUITMENT: Via British Council Recruitment Unit in London.

ELS LANGUAGE CENTERS – MIDDLE EAST

PO Box 3079, Abu Dhabi, United Arab Emirates

+971 2 6426640 1516

info@elsmea.com

www.elsmea.com

NUMBER OF TEACHERS: 30 full-time plus many part-time in 12 centres throughout the Middle East including Hawally (Kuwait), Muscat, Salalah, Sur and Sohar (Oman), Jeddah, Riyadh and Dammam (Saudi Arabia), Dubai, Abu Dhabi, Al Ain and Fujairah (UAE) and Doha (Qatar).

PREFERENCE OF NATIONALITY: American, Canadian, British, New Zealander, Australian, though other nationalities are sometimes accepted.

QUALIFICATIONS: Preferred MA in TEFL/TESL and 2 years' experience with recognised TEFL certificate plus 3 years' experience. Minimum bachelor's degree plus TEFL plus experience.

CONDITIONS OF EMPLOYMENT: 1–2-year contracts; 30 contact hours plus 15 administrative hours per week for full-time teachers.

SALARY: Varies according to qualifications, experience and location. Some salaries are tax free and come with benefits such as housing, airfares and medical insurance.

FACILITIES/SUPPORT: Furnished accommodation provided, though teachers may choose to find their own within their housing allowance. Work and residence permits arranged in all countries, usually involving a medical examination and blood test and a notarised and attested copy of the teacher's degree and qualifications. Standard orientation for all new teachers and monthly workshops.

RECRUITMENT: Through TESOL USA and TESOL Arabia, and also via the internet. Telephone interviews sometimes sufficient. Face-to-face interviews arranged where possible.

m2r Ltd

Evans House, Monckton Rd, Wakefield, West Yorks. WF2 7AS

+44 1924 888185 or 0845 3884145

info@m2rglobal.com

www.m2rglobal.com

Global recruitment consultancy.

NUMBER OF TEACHERS: 50 per year, sent to various organisations and employers in the Gulf Cooperation Council (GCC) region, i.e. Bahrain, Kuwait, Oman, Qatar, Saudi and the UAE.

PREFERENCE OF NATIONALITY: Native speakers of English only.

QUALIFICATIONS: Minimum BA degree, ideally in English Language, recognised ESL qualification and 1 year experience. Overseas experience is preferred also.

CONDITIONS OF EMPLOYMENT: Minimum 1-year contract, renewable. 40 hours per week, though number of contact hours varies.

SALARY: Minimum US$30,000 plus benefits such as housing and flights.

RECRUITMENT: Video or telephone interview can be arranged if face-to-face interview in Yorkshire is not possible.

CONTACT: Mr Munir Mamujee, Managing Director (munir@m2rglobal.com).

THE AMERICAN ESL CENTER

PO Box 1240, Al Jubeiha, Amman, Jordan 11941

✆ +962 6 534 1421

✉ info@aeslc.com

🖳 www.aeslc.com

NUMBER OF TEACHERS: 10.

PREFERENCE OF NATIONALITY: Native English speakers.

QUALIFICATIONS: ESL qualification and teaching experience.

CONDITIONS OF EMPLOYMENT: Standard 1-year contract, mostly teaching afternoons and evenings (usually 12pm–8:30pm).

SALARY: $1,000–$1,500 per month (average salary in Jordan is $600–$700). No deductions.

FACILITIES/SUPPORT: Assistance in locating accommodation near the centre. The company lawyer has offered a very low fee to process work permits for foreign employees. Cost of work permit $500 (paid to government). Cost of lawyer's fees is $150.

RECRUITMENT: Through internet/newspaper. 1 minute recording of the applicant's voice to be sent by email to determine language ability and accent.

CONTACT: Kara Murphy, Academic Director.

AFGHANISTAN

This information may not be of interest to anyone of a nervous disposition. **Tom Clark** from the USA taught here a couple of years ago, and this information is largely based on his account (note that the situation may have changed since he was there). He concludes that Afghanistan is a great place '*for a journalist, spy or madman*'.

TOM CLARK

While teaching in Kuwait, Tom Clark saw an advert on Dave's ESL Cafe which he followed up much later. It turned out that the American University in Kabul (the only private university in the country) was desperate to get teachers in place for a summer project funded by USAID. Since the programme was controlled by the US government, his visa was sorted out quickly. According to Tom, you would hear a lot of rumours about the funding and where it was going and how it got disbursed... It wasn't so much red tape as corruption, but that is everywhere in Afghanistan. The job was teaching at the university prep programme plus he was doing extra work for the UN and a human rights organisation. Tom describes the job:

The contract with the university was the best I have had in the ESL world. It paid $5,000 a month with danger pay and other bonuses. It was better than Saudi. It offered holiday pay, housing, transportation, laptop, cellphone, we could fly on UN planes, etc. We stayed in a guesthouse with a beautiful garden, had security guards 24/7 and were fenced in, and we had electricity more than 4 hours a day. Our money went a long way, as the cost of living was so low there and the American dollar was welcome. Transferring money in and out was not easy, nor setting up bank accounts. Security was a problem, as we were not free to travel around or mix with the locals. If an aid worker was killed, we would be on lock down/house arrest for weeks at a time. Sometimes we wore bullet-proof vests, were always in the presence of security guards, had to be very careful associating with local people and would have to come up with colourful stories to get out and about into the 'field'.

The workplace was quite unorganised and a lot of people were disgruntled. We wanted to teach different subjects, but things were always censored there. My fellow teachers were of a higher calibre than I was used to. All had Masters in specialised areas and I had the feeling they all worked for organisations they did not mention on their CVs. They spoke multiple languages and seemed to have alternative agendas other than just teaching. Many of them had prior links to the State Department. It was an odd assortment at best.

The pupils were the cream of the crop. They were not from typical backgrounds, they were from high ranking military, intelligence and diplomatic families. Occupying our spare time was difficult since we always had to get permission to go anywhere, unless we hid under the radar. There were a handful of 'safe' establishments for foreigners, but after a while you got bored with those and had to find a way to entertain yourself. If it were not for the money, it would be quite hard to stay and live there, unless you really liked reading books all the time.

Employment information about the university can be found at www.auaf.edu.af. In such an unstable setting as Kabul, things change fast and anyone who stays teaching for more than a year is likely to move up quickly. The British Council has a teaching centre in Kabul. Needless to say Afghanistan has a rich and complex history and the people are friendly, warm and wonderfully hospitable once you have gained their trust.

ISRAEL

Because of the large number of English-speaking Jews who have settled in Israel from the USA, South Africa, etc. many native speakers of English are employed in the state education system and there is little active recruitment of foreign teachers. There are a number of private language schools, for example a number of Wall Street Institutes and Berlitz schools. The British Council maintains a presence in Israel and has teaching centres in Ramat-Gan (Tel Aviv), West Jerusalem and Nazareth, which recruit qualified EFL teachers mainly from the local English-speaking population.

TOM BALFOUR

Tom Balfour discovered there were openings in Israel, shortly after reacquainting himself with a girl he knew in Tel Aviv.

I sent emails with my CV to various English schools, mostly branches of the two big companies Berlitz and Wall Street Institute, explaining my situation - that I would be leaving Israel in a week to return to England for my summer job, but that I wanted to come back in September and teach English in Tel Aviv. Most of the schools simply sent me a reply saying 'get back to us when you return' but Wall Street Institute Tel Aviv invited me for an interview. In the interview I was asked various questions about teaching, and then the director pretended to be a low level student and asked me to explain various words to her. When she asked me what a model was, I said 'Naomi Campbell, Kate Moss' and then got up and did a pretend cat-walk round the room. Although I'm sure that my qualifications helped, I think that might be what got me the job: knowing how to keep explanations simple, and being prepared to look silly if it helped. She told me that if I came back I would be offered a contract.

I had heard (from this book in fact!) that with the high number of native English speaking immigrants in Israel there wasn't really a market for English teachers. I think, however, that my Trinity qualification and my planned work at the summer school made me stand out from the native candidates, some of whom were hoping for a job simply on the strength of being English speakers.

One difficulty that native English speakers may run into is getting a visa. You improve your chances by being in a relationship with an Israeli citizen, or Jewish foreigner.

Israel is an amazing country and Tel Aviv is a great, cosmopolitan city with a good beach and fantastic nightlife.

PALESTINIAN GOVERNED AREAS

Education is all but impossible for many Palestinians and the situation is very difficult for teachers. Although the demand is there, the circumstances do not allow the vast majority of Palestinians to achieve their ambition. Like most international organisations, the British Council has withdrawn from the Palestinian Territories and its educational activities in Nablus, Ramallah, Gaza and East Jerusalem have been halted.

The charity UNIPAL (Universities' Trust for Educational Exchange with Palestinians – see entry in Lebanon section) operates an educational and cultural exchange with Palestinian communities. The political situation has made it impossible for projects to continue in Gaza and even in the other Palestinian territories, so now its projects carry on only in Lebanon. Another charity which arranges for English tutors to spend the summer in Nablus or nearby refugee camps for Palestinians is Project Hope (see entry). Palestinian schools struggle on and anyone who supports their cause might be prepared to become a volunteer teacher. Senior people who can set up programmes would be especially welcome.

LIST OF EMPLOYERS

PROJECT HOPE (Humanitarian Opportunities for Peace and Education)
29 An-Najah, Al Qadin St, Nablus, Palestine
recruiter@projecthope.ps, noblus@projecthope.ps
www.projecthope.ps

Offices also in Nablus and Toronto. Non-profit volunteer organisation that supports children denied access to basic services in Nablus on the northern West Bank and the nearby refugee camps of Balata and Askar.

NUMBER OF VOLUNTEER TEACHERS: 15–30.

PREFERENCE OF NATIONALITY: None.

QUALIFICATIONS: Teachers must have a TEFL qualification or teaching experience along with experience of working with groups of children and young people. Minimum age 21.

CONDITIONS OF EMPLOYMENT: 5 weeks to 1 year, 20–25 hours of teaching a week, with 2 full days off. School uses Oxford Headway series.

SALARY: None. Volunteers must make financial contribution to cover accommodation and equipment (US$100).

FACILITIES/SUPPORT: Accommodation provided in a shared apartment for a contribution of US$150 per month.

RECRUITMENT: Teachers fill in an application form and are then interviewed over the telephone (the recruiter calls the teacher).

CONTACT: Jenny, International Volunteer Recruiter.

KUWAIT

Although teaching salaries are no longer in the stratosphere, as some were more than a decade ago, many organisations still seek to lure expat teachers with favourable terms. Educational standards are variable, as encountered by **B. P. Rawlins** in Kuwait:

> *There are simply too many schools in Kuwait acting like pigs at a trough, all of them out there for the money. They dare not criticise any anti-social behaviour by pupils, parents or adult students for fear of losing fees in a competitive market. Professionalism is viewed with hostile suspicion in some quarters.*

This negative view is not subscribed to by all who have spent time in the region. Many agree that English learners in Kuwait, as throughout the Arab world, can be a pleasure to teach because they are so eager to communicate, and so unhesitant to speak English in class.

As well as keeping an up-to-date list of the many international and English medium schools in Kuwait, the British Council (PO Box 345, Safat 13004; +965 2251 5512; info@kw.britishcouncil.org) employs teachers year round and for July/August summer courses.

LIST OF EMPLOYERS

AMIDEAST

Mail: PO Box 44818, Hawalli 32063, Kuwait.

Physical Address: Ahmed Al-Jabeer St, Opp. Al-Awadhi Mosque, Commercial Bank Building, 2nd Fl, Sharq

☏ +965 2247 0091

✎ kuwait@amideast.org, jobopportunities@amideast.org

🖥 www.amideast.org

NUMBER OF TEACHERS: All part-time.

PREFERENCE OF NATIONALITY: North American. AMIDEAST emphasises American style English.

QUALIFICATIONS: BA/BEd and MA in TESL is essential. 5 years of teaching experience is required.

CONDITIONS OF EMPLOYMENT: Hired as independent contractors. Contracts are usually 6 weeks long and renewable according to demand. Average 2 hours a day, 3 days a week; generally evenings.

SALARY: Depends on qualifications and experience.

RECRUITMENT: Newspaper ads and referrals.

CONTACT: Samar Khleif, Country Director.

LEBANON

Lebanon has traditionally been an important commercial hub for the Middle East, although the military campaign launched by Israel several years ago set back the progress of an otherwise forward-thinking, artistic and entrepreneurial country. There continues to be heavy UN presence in the south and many foreign embassies advise against non-essential travel to the area.

Most teaching jobs in Lebanon are found in Beirut. Locals are generally open-minded and many speak three languages: English, French and Arabic. Male and female teachers will find it relatively easy to adjust (compared to the major culture shock experienced in other Middle East destinations), although the pace of life is slower and more conservative outside Beirut.

Finding an English teaching job in Lebanon can be difficult as there is a local pool of qualified teachers. A few schools advertise abroad and recruit on teaching websites, but most do not. If you cannot find a posting, search online; find the contact information of any school and then start sending off your CV. Most full curriculum schools are English or French, with the other language plus Arabic taught as second languages, although English continues to gain ground over French, to the chagrin of the French. The popularity of English is increasing due to its status as the international language of business and also to a strong tradition of Lebanese emigration to the USA and Australia.

However, even schools that do not use English as the medium of instruction employ English teachers. The website www.schoolnet.edu.lb has links to some private schools around Lebanon; www.lebweb.com is an online directory for everything from banks to schools in Lebanon and the classified section of www.dailystar.com.lb carries occasional teaching vacancies (but check daily). For info about teaching English to adults try the American Lebanese Language Center (see entry) or the British Council (www.britishcouncil.org/lebanon). It's perhaps also worth trying the Lebanese American University (PO Box 13–5053, Chouran, Beirut 1102 2801; www.lau.edu.lb). While the demand for teachers exists, the wages can be low unless you are lucky enough to be hired by a large and foreign-operated school or university. The minimum wage is about $400 per month and local teachers earn about $700 per month as a starting salary. Foreign teachers can expect to earn about $900–$1500 a month, depending on credentials, experience and how the contract is negotiated. Contact hours are often high and teachers may be assigned additional tasks. Lebanon has 20 official holidays.

A few larger schools offer on-site housing and those that do not will help teachers find decent accommodation. Finding a flat from abroad is difficult, although some English websites and newspapers list private and shared accommodation.

RED TAPE

Schools will manage your work visa, but expect this to take time. Teachers generally arrive at the airport on a tourist visa. After arrival, the school begins processing work papers, which may take between two weeks and more than two months. Lebanon is a developing country, paperwork is not always straightforward and government offices are not easy to negotiate (if they ever are). Note that teachers from the UK and USA are sometimes preferred simply because their visas are half the price of Canadians and Australians. However, **Shelley Beyak-Tarabichi**, who works for International House in Beirut, provides words of reassurance: '*Canucks and Aussies still get hired!*' Shelley is originally from Canada and has provided much of the information for this chapter.

Increasingly it will be worthwhile investigating possibilities in this tiny but fascinating country. While accompanying her husband on a short-term contract in Lebanon, **Anne Cleaver** (an early-retired teacher) easily found work (albeit voluntary) at a new Special Needs Centre just outside Beirut:

Even during my short period there, I was tentatively offered a full-time post at a neighbouring school and even an opening in Abu Dhabi. There is a real eagerness to learn English in Lebanon. I found Lebanese educationalists, parents and children most welcoming and enthusiastic. Being a British teacher there made me feel more valued, I regret to say, than back in the UK.

Good education is extremely important and costly in Lebanon and families pay large sums to ensure their child attends a distinguished school and also invest in tutoring outside of school. Children are expected to study hard inside and outside of school, as government tests are difficult.

A very different experience would be to teach in the Palestinian refugee camps. As mentioned, the charity UNIPAL (Universities' Trust for Educational Exchange with Palestinians) operates a summer volunteer teaching programme for teenagers in Palestinian refugee camps located in Lebanon. Volunteers must be native English speakers, based in the UK and at least 20 years old. Previous work with children is essential, and previous teaching experience preferred. TEFL/TESL qualifications are an advantage, but not necessary. The approximate cost of the programme is £550 to cover airfare and insurance as well as food and accommodation for five weeks.

LEISURE

Shelley Beyak-Tarabichi has come to appreciate life in Lebanon:

Lebanese hospitality is renowned, the food is fantastic (healthy and vegetarian-friendly) and the weather is comfortable. You can swim at a beach resort in the summer, ski in the winter and hike all year round. There are gyms, malls, outdoor groups, concerts, art schools and mountain resorts along with traditional Arabic cafés, monasteries, mosques and historical sites dating back thousands, if not millions, of years. While the political situation in Lebanon is termed unstable, it is not evident on a day-to-day level as one would expect.

LIST OF EMPLOYERS

ALLC IH BEIRUT

American Lebanese Language Center – International House Beirut, PO Box 55463, Confidence Center, 7th Floor, Sin el Fil, Beirut
- +961 1 500978; 1 489166
- recruitment@allcs.edu.lb
- www.allcs.edu.lb.

CONTACT: Elaine Kniveton, Academic Director (elainek@allcs.edu.lb).

UNIPAL

BCM Unipal, London WC1N 3XX, UK
- info@unipal.org.uk
- www.unipal.org.uk

Branches also in Dbayeh, Jounieh, Byblos, Saida and Zahle.
NUMBER OF TEACHERS: Approx. 20.
PREFERENCE OF NATIONALITY: American, British.
QUALIFICATIONS: CELTA or approved equivalent, 2+ years' post-CELTA experience. Business English experience essential.
CONDITIONS OF EMPLOYMENT: 12-month standard contract. 26 contact hours per week, split shift between 9am and 9:30pm.
SALARY: $1,000–$1,500, depending on experience and qualifications. No deductions.
FACILITIES/SUPPORT: The Centre finds suitable accommodation but does not pay for it. The Centre deals with all paperwork relating to work and residency permits. Health insurance provided.
RECRUITMENT: Normally through IHWO recruitment page, unsolicited applications and emails. Interviews are essential, usually carried out via Skype.

NUMBER OF TEACHERS: 30.
PREFERENCE OF NATIONALITY: Native English speakers.
QUALIFICATIONS: Experience with children or teaching. TEFL a bonus. Volunteers should have sensitivity, tolerance and political awareness
CONDITIONS OF EMPLOYMENT: 5 weeks 12 June to 15 July (2012), 5 hours a day.
SALARY: None – volunteers pay £550 for flight, accommodation, food, insurance, etc.
FACILITIES/SUPPORT: Simple accommodation provided. Compulsory pre-departure training days held in UK.
RECRUITMENT: Application forms are downloadable from website and are due mid-February for interviews in March.
CONTACT: Brenda Hayward, Director.

OMAN

According to experienced American teacher **Tom Clark**, who has worked in Egypt, Syria, Turkey, Kuwait and Saudi, Oman is '*the best in the Middle East for being friendly and open and laid back*'. Tom thinks Oman is experiencing a boom now in tourism and employment and is growing and developing very fast. He feels that it is at its best now and, as more luxury hotels are built and local residents are moved from the beaches, it will become a different country, so urges people to go now. Technical colleges such as the Salalah College of Technology where Tom worked – alongside 59 other ESL teachers – have periods of hiring on a big scale.

Since the 1970s Oman has had to import the majority of its skilled labour including teachers. Teachers of English are employed from Sudan, Sri Lanka, India and North Africa which means that there is a much broader mix of accents than usual. Positions for native English speakers from the UK etc. become available each year with the British Council and Amideast in Muscat, and the major employers of Western teachers are the Ministry of Higher Education, Sultan Qaboos University and CfBT. CfBT Education Services LLC, Oman, supplies expertise in Education and Training for various public and private sector clients including the Ministry of Education, the Ministry of Higher Education and Petroleum Development Oman (PDO). With more than 26 years' experience in-country, CfBT LLC maintains a project office in Muscat and has expanded operations to the Gulf Region.

Despite an expanding EFL market, there's no room at all for visiting job-seekers, since a tight hold is kept on tourist visas. It will make it much easier to land a job if you have an MA in TESOL or Applied Linguistics (or at least be enrolled in a distance learning ELT Master's degree) with at least three years' experience, preferably at university level. IH Muscat (Polyglot Institute) in Oman asks for teachers with a BA (English major), CELTA or Trinity TESOL, plus three to five years' EFL experience post-CELTA. If the first degree is a BSc, the approving body require five years' experience post-CELTA. The main recruiting season begins in March just prior to the annual TESOL Arabia conference.

Exactly why an MA in TESOL should be necessary is not very clear, at least not to **Sandeha Lynch** who provided some of the information in this section. His wry description of students in higher education could apply equally to students throughout the Middle East:

> *Unfortunately there is a widespread idea that experts in linguistics and the like have what it takes to teach English. It can come as a bit of a shock, therefore, for teachers who have studied phonics, syllabus design, methodology and socio-linguistics to discover that they are teaching 'Headway Elementary' units 1 to 5 to groups of up to 40 students per class. Not exactly what the MA prepares you for. One could say that the school-leavers who come to the colleges and higher institutes are ill-prepared.*

On the other hand Tom Clark found his students to be polite and really engaged with their studies. This is not life in the fast lane of academic endeavour but something of an academic lay-by. If you choose to work in one of the colleges of higher education, you may find that the concept of rigorous academic standards is imperfectly understood, and therefore rarely applied.

Itinerant teacher **Bradwell Jackson** was kind enough to investigate possibilities at Polyglot and reported in 2011 that it is both the oldest and the largest school in Muscat. According to the school's marketing manager, Syed Kirmani, the market for English is ever-expanding, possibly as much as 13% year on year. The students prefer British English to American, partly for political reasons and also because they are more likely to go to Britain for further studies. Teachers are paid US$2,500 a month for working 4pm–9pm Saturday through Tuesday with no morning classes. Bradwell concludes: '*In the very short time I have been here, Oman strikes me as a very pleasant place to live. It seems a very well-kept secret. Everyone is talking about UAE, as Oman quietly and slowly gains more and more gravitas. The city is very clean and surprisingly modern. I would love to work here myself.*'

Tom Clark also described the favourable quality of life. Newly arrived teachers were presented with a choice of places to live, from villas in the mountains to plantations in the woods, luxury apartments in the suburbs to places on the beach. It is possible to acquire a drinking licence for the five bars in town. Other recreations include scuba diving, boating, desert camping Bedouin-style, picnicking in the mountain valleys, camel racing or just haring around in a 4WD. The countryside and coasts are stunning and if you can handle the heat and at times the humidity, mountain walking is popular. Just try not to get bored with these activities. There are no others, unless you happen to live near Muscat where you can indulge in wandering around glossy shopping malls, watching Hindi movies and eating sushi.

LIST OF EMPLOYERS

AMIDEAST OMAN

11 Fahoud Street, Al Qurum (Opposite Qurum Park),
PO Box 798, PC 116, Mina Al Fahal, Muscat

☏ +968 2456 1727

🖰 oman@amideast.org

💻 www.amideast.org

NUMBER OF TEACHERS: 5 full-time EFL instructors for on- and off-site assignments.

PREFERENCE OF NATIONALITY: Americans and other native English speakers.

QUALIFICATIONS: Bachelor's degree plus recognised international certificate in TEFL/TESL and a minimum of 2 years' successful experience teaching English to non-native speakers.

CONDITIONS OF EMPLOYMENT: General English classes for children, teenagers and adults held between 8am and 9pm. Business English and other ESP courses conducted for public and private sector organisations. 40-hour work week, including 24 contact hours.

SALARY: Commensurate with qualifications and experience.

FACILITIES/SUPPORT: AMIDEAST will offer assistance in locating affordable housing. All visa related fees and procurement will be managed by AMIDEAST upon arrival.

RECRUITMENT: Via www.amideast.org plus regional and international TEFL conferences.

CONTACT: Paul Steele, English Language Program Manager (psteele@amideast.org).

CfBT EDUCATION SERVICES

PO Box 2278, PC 112 Sultanate of Oman

☏ +968 24692004

🖰 gen@cfbtoman.com or cfbt@teachanywhere.com

💻 www.cfbt.com

NUMBER OF TEACHERS: About 12 in British Training Institute in Muscat; over 40 in projects with Ministries of Education and Higher Education.

PREFERENCE OF NATIONALITY: British, North American, Australian, New Zealander.

QUALIFICATIONS: Usually DELTA. Salary increments paid for MA and PhD.

CONDITIONS OF EMPLOYMENT: 1-year renewable, September 1 to August 31. Up to 25 teaching hours a week.

SALARY: Market-rate. Tax-free.

FACILITIES/SUPPORT: Free accommodation or accommodation allowance; work permit; annual return flight.

RECRUITMENT: Normally through advertisements on internet (www.tefl.com, www.jobs.edufind.com), agents abroad; CfBT database and www.cfbt.com.

CONTACT: Juliet Cowley (jcowley@cfbtoman.com).

SUR UNIVERSITY COLLEGE

PO Box 400, Postal Code 411, Sur, Oman

🖰 job@suc.edu.om

💻 www.suc.edu.om

PREFERENCE OF NATIONALITY: Native English speakers.

QUALIFICATIONS: Bachelor's or master's degree in English or related areas, TEFL or CELTA certificate plus minimum 2 years' experience of teaching adults.

CONDITIONS OF EMPLOYMENT: 1-year renewable. 21 hours per week. To teach on foundation course for Omani students who want to study business, IT or engineering at university.

SALARY: US $2,000–$2,500 per month basic salary, tax-free. 40 days' paid summer holiday.

FACILITIES/SUPPORT: Free furnished accommodation and assistance with work permit. Transport provided, medical insurance, utilities allowance and annual round trip air ticket.

CONTACT: Professor Ahmad Sharieh (ahmadsharieh@suc.edu.om).

QATAR

The tiny traditional emirate of Qatar is surrounded by Saudi Arabia, Bahrain, the United Arab Emirates and Iran, and has a stable ELT industry. Past reforms by the Emir of the state, Sheikh Hamad bin Khalifa Al-Thani, promoted English over Arabic as the medium of instruction in the state school curriculum, while trying to balance respect for the heritage and conservative nature of Qatar's people.

As a country high in natural gas and oil reserves, Qatar has a per capita income that exceeds some of the leading industrial countries of Western Europe, and as such offers some enticing expatriate packages to teachers. After completing a Master of Education in Canada, **Arshiya-Nageen Ahmed** went to Qatar to teach and to research education practice in the Middle East:

> *I was actively looking for careers related to my field while volunteering to gain additional experience. After receiving three job offers I had to decide my best option. The interview procedures were long, however, I got the job in Qatar and have been working ever since. Students are hesitant to speak English at times since they do not want to make mistakes. Thus the best way is to build good student-teacher rapport so that the students become comfortable in an English language environment. I was already aware that students would find some difficulty in adjusting to a foreign accent but from their feedback, they seem at ease in understanding a Canadian accent. Furthermore, it is important to encourage students to speak English with their peers so that they stay in practice.*

The main teaching opportunities are to be found in the state schools and post-secondary education institutes. There are also opportunities for in-company development of business English for those with the appropriate qualifications. The British Council has an office in Doha (93 Al Sadd Street, PO Box 2992, Doha; general.enquiries@qa.britishcouncil.org) offering English courses to adults and children and possible advice on finding teaching work.

There are also possibilities within private language institutes: Inlingua Qatar is partnered with Score Plus (careers@score-plus.com), which claims to be looking more for 'intra-preneurs' than teaching employees.

LIST OF EMPLOYERS

EDUCATE LEARNING CENTER
Aamal Tower, 1st Floor, West Bay, Doha (PO Box 24635, Doha)

✆ +974 4417 7103

✉ info@educate.com.qa

🖥 www.educate.com.qa

NUMBER OF TEACHERS: 8–10 as of July 2012 with intentions of expanding.

PREFERENCE OF NATIONALITY: Canada, US, UK, New Zealand, Australia.

QUALIFICATIONS: Must be a native English speaker with a diploma or degree for post-secondary education. Some knowledge of Arabic is preferred. Junior trainers with 6 months to 5 years' experience are generally preferred for their fresh approach. Employer is looking for candidates who are extroverts, highly organised, professional and with a positive attitude. They should have the ability to teach upper management in corporate settings.

CONDITIONS OF EMPLOYMENT: Minimum 1 year. 40 hours per week: 20–24 hours teaching time, the rest for lesson planning and preparation.

SALARY: 6,000–10,000 rials per month, depending on experience and qualifications. No deductions because Qatar is a tax-free country.

FACILITIES/SUPPORT: Accommodation is provided or an allowance in lieu if teachers choose to find their own accommodation. Employer covers costs and takes responsibility for the processes involved in obtaining a work permit after teachers provide the necessary documentation (i.e. proof of higher education, valid passport etc.) and pass the Qatar medical examination.

RECRUITMENT: Referrals, online advertising, via AIESEC International. Interviews are completed over Skype or by telephone.

CONTACT: Lauren Ruttle, Client Relations & Human Resources Manager.

QATAR AERONAUTICAL COLLEGE

PO Box 4050, Doha

☎ +974 4440 8813

✉ careers@qac.edu.qa or doha.hr@gmail.com

💻 www.qac.edu.qa

NUMBER OF TEACHERS: 35–40.

PREFERENCE OF NATIONALITY: Native English speakers.

QUALIFICATIONS: Bachelor's degree, CELTA, DELTA, TEFL certificate or master's plus minimum 3 years' experience.

CONDITIONS OF EMPLOYMENT: Length of contract 6–12 months. Working hours are 7am–2pm.

SALARY: US $3,600–US $4,000 per month.

FACILITIES/SUPPORT: Furnished accommodation, government health card and assistance with work permits provided.

RECRUITMENT: Interviews required, usually carried out in the UK.

CONTACT: Hester Drewry, Acting Head of Academic Bridge Programme (hdrewry@qac.edu.qa) or Human Resources.

SAUDI ARABIA

Recruitment of English teachers is booming and the recruitment websites are full of advertised vacancies. Whereas in the 1990s, employers had very high standards and expected their teachers to have many years of experience, now there are some teachers in the kingdom who don't even have a university degree. Part of the problem is that the country is so wealthy that many from the elite classes know that they will never have to work for a living and do not particularly value education. The teaching is not always very serious and there is an expectation that everyone will 'pass' no matter what. The days of fabulously high salaries are also over, and rising violence against foreigners has acted as a further disincentive. But expatriate packages are still very attractive, with substantial salaries, free airfares and accommodation plus generous holidays and other perks.

Teaching in a naval academy or petrochemical company while living in a teetotal expatriate ghetto is not many people's idea of fun, especially after a request for an exit visa has been denied. The rare woman who gets a job as a teacher (at a women's college) may live to regret it when she finds that Saudi women are prohibited by law from driving a car and must not appear in public without being covered from head to foot.

Bell Worldwide has occasional adverts for qualified staff for various Saudi clients (ksu.recruitment@bell-worldwide.com). The package offered is a salary of between 9,000 and 14,000 riyals per month, plus accommodation and transport allowance, private health insurance, 35 days' holiday entitlement plus national Saudi holidays, return airfare plus second flight allowance. Specialist ELT recruiters like Evocation EFL (www.evocationefl.net) based in London, Creative English in Cardiff (www.creativeenglish.net) and Education-Experts in Saudi Arabia (www.edu-experts.com) all advertise vacancies, sometimes urgently. Other recruiters active in Saudi include Footprints Recruiting in Canada (www.footprintsrecruiting.com/teaching-in-saudi-arabia) and Teachaway.com with jobs for certified teachers in a private school in Dammam. Experienced recruiters warn that mobilisation to Saudi Arabia takes three to four months from the interview.

TOM CLARK

Tom Clark has also taught in Saudi Arabia. He describes the interview process in the UK with a large group of recruiters who rush the applicants through like cattle and then make them wait around all day to hear the outcome as an 'awful experience'.

Saudi is by far the oddest place to get paperwork done. The embassy people are not friendly and really try your patience. Every day they told me to come back, which meant

I was paying for a hotel and paying for taxis and food, etc. waiting for nothing. Yet the company told me the visa was all ready and signed by the Ministry.

I have worked in Saudi on three separate occasions, with Aramco, M-Trading and most recently with the Bin Laden Group. The contract means nothing, as everything is done by favours and who you know. Accommodation is normally in a compound, some of which have pretty high security with maybe three different check points, jeeps with machine guns, barricades, etc. The job in Jeddah put us up in a hotel though where there was no security at all.

I hate to be negative about any place, but Saudi is not an easy place. Depending on where you are, you could be in a very conservative place where shops close for two hours every prayer time. You need to keep covered and to be careful about what you say about most topics, but especially religion, politics and even history. There is no drinking and forget talking to the opposite sex. It is a very regimented lifestyle and you need some pretty tough skin to stay there. The religious police are everywhere and as a foreigner in the kingdom you are always being watched by someone. I had an all-women's class which by law had to be in a separate building. The students could see me on a screen, but I couldn't see them. An official was present to censor my lesson and shut down the power if I got off topic, even talking about how some battles were fought and won.

Depending on where you are, it is pretty slim pickings to find things to do in your spare time. Even to go around the country is not easy without proof of being Muslim. To the best of my knowledge there is only one cinema in Riyadh for mothers and children only. Jeddah offers some variety with the beaches and old town and more liberal culture. If you are going to be anywhere try to be in Jeddah.

Professional teachers tempted by the money should bear in mind the drawbacks, as **Philip Dray** did:

I decided against Saudi Arabia. The money was most appealing, but I couldn't think myself into a situation where there was no nightlife and limited contact with women. A year may seem short when you say it fast, but you could get very depressed in a situation like that. Money is nearly everything but it can't buy you peace of mind. So I opted for a job at a school for boys in the UAE which, from the description, sounds sociable, inviting and accessible.

Morris Jensen working for Elite Training points to the good things about Saudi Arabia including the hospitality, ease of finding lucrative private work, excellent sports facilities, shopping and accessibility of places of interest in the Middle East. He also acknowledges the problems, such as the religious and cultural clashes which arise in the classroom and the frustrating bureaucracy.

Visas are not granted to people over the age of 55. Among the documents required for a work permit are a medical certificate notarised by the Foreign and Commonwealth Office in London, an authorisation from the Saudi Ministry of Foreign Affairs, copies of diplomas, a contract of employment and accompanying letter from the sponsoring company. The fee of 50 riyals payable before leaving your home country is only the beginning. Your passport is held by your sponsoring employer while you carry around an official copy as identification, at least until you are issued with an *iqama* (resident visa). Every time you want to leave the country you must request an exit and re-entry visa which is given at the discretion of your employer. Some foreign workers have reported having to pay a very substantial sum for an exit visa.

LIST OF EMPLOYERS

BERLITZ LANGUAGE CENTRES AL-AHSA
recruitment@berlitz-ksa.com
www.berlitz-ksa.com

NUMBER OF TEACHERS: Variable for 4 language centres (2 male, 2 female) in Al-Ahsa in the eastern province of the country.

PREFERENCE OF NATIONALITY: British preferred. Must be native speaker of English.

QUALIFICATIONS: Minimum PGCE/BEd/MA in Applied Linguistics (or similar) +1 year's teaching experience; or MA + CELTA/Cert TESOL + 2 years' experience; or BA + CELTA/CertTESOL + 3 years' experience. Experience of TOEFL preparation would be useful. Married couples preferred.

CONDITIONS OF EMPLOYMENT: Summer-only or 1-year renewable contracts. 8 hours per day, all but half an hour of timetabled teaching. At busy times, teachers may be required to work overtime (up to 11 hours per week) which will be paid at 1 and a half times normal salary.

SALARY: From 96,600 riyals to 123,000 riyals per year tax-free.

FACILITIES/SUPPORT: Furnished single person's or family accommodation provided rent-free. Travel allowance covers air travel to and from Saudi Arabia. Full training in Berlitz Method is given. Compulsory training workshops are held.

RECRUITMENT: Online application.

EUROPEAN CENTRE, AL RAJHI CO. FOR HRD
PO Box 60617, Riyadh 11555
+966 505363109
www.theeuropeancentre.com or www.al-rajhi4hrd.com

NUMBER OF TEACHERS: 20–40 in various cities across Saudi Arabia

PREFERENCE OF NATIONALITY: British, American, Irish, Canadian, New Zealander, South African.

QUALIFICATIONS: Bachelor's degree in a language related field as a minimum plus a teaching certificate with at least 1 year of previous experience.

CONDITIONS OF EMPLOYMENT: Standard 12-month contract, 7:45am–4:00pm, 5 days per week. Average load of 27 contact hours per week.

SALARY: As of February 2010 the range is from 8,400 SAR gross to 10,900 SAR gross with additional 3,600 SAR or 7,200 SAR per month overtime available in certain locations. Salary scales undergo periodic review.

FACILITIES/SUPPORT: Free, fully furnished accommodation and transport allowance provided. Company provides valid work visas and residence permits (*iqamas*) at company cost and medical cards (*Tawuniya*) for private medical cover with £80 approx of the annual fee paid by the employee. The company also refers candidates at point of hire to a visa broker who does all the necessary paperwork for visa processing. The company covers the broker and medical charges, as well as the cost of the actual visa. Prepaid flights are provided. British management. Centre uses labs, tactile learning and simulator facilities, plus Adobe format materials for projectors and smart boards. On-the-job training provided.

RECRUITMENT: In person or by telephone. CV with scanned copies of qualifications and a photo should be sent by email. A comprehensive pdf information pack is usually sent out to a candidate within 48 hours of receipt of a suitable application. Candidates may apply at any time of year.

INTERLINK LANGUAGE CENTER
Al Yamamah College, PO Box 45180, Riyadh 11512
www.interlink.edu

NUMBER OF TEACHERS: About 50, 80–85% of whom are native English speakers.

PREFERENCE OF NATIONALITY: The centre doesn't base its selection on whether teachers are native or non-native; rather on their philosophical orientation, linguistic and cross-cultural competence, past experience, and many other attributes determined through 'dialoguing', questionnaires, and final interviews.

QUALIFICATIONS: MA in TESL, at least 2 years of EFL/ESL teaching experience with adult learners, and good cross-cultural background, either working or living in another culture.

CONDITIONS OF EMPLOYMENT: Minimum 2-year contract, longer preferred. 20–25 hours per week plus participation in programme of activities.

SALARY: $38,000–$40,000, tax-free.

FACILITIES/SUPPORT: Free furnished housing, medical insurance and round-trip transport to Saudi Arabia.

RECRUITMENT: Resumés collected through multiple websites. Interviews are essential and can be organised by conference call.

CONTACT: Ahad Shahbaz, President; Dr Nebila Dhieb-Henia, General Director.

NUMBER OF TEACHERS: 25+.

PREFERENCE OF NATIONALITY: British, Irish, American, Canadian, South African, Australian, New Zealander.

QUALIFICATIONS: BA in English, Linguistics or TESOL; or bachelor's degree in any discipline from an internationally recognised Anglophone university plus a CELTA/Trinity TESOL certificate. All teachers must have at least 2 years of full-time ESL/EFL/EAP/ESP teaching experience at university/college level and be a native English speaker, or have near-native competency.

CONDITIONS OF EMPLOYMENT: Initially 2-year contracts, renewable annually thereafter. 40 hours per week (20 contact teaching hours, 10 prep hours, 10 office hours).

SALARY: Varies depending on qualifications and experience. Salary is tax-free.

FACILITIES/SUPPORT: Free furnished accommodation provided. Full details are supplied to teachers when salary offer accepted on how to get medical clearance and visa application.

RECRUITMENT: Web-based advertising. Interviews conducted by Skype or telephone.

CONTACT: Mike Creed, Academic Recruiting Officer.

NUMBER OF TEACHERS: 90 (further 24 teachers are employed in the University English Program).

PREFERENCE OF NATIONALITY: American, Australian, British, Canadian, Irish, New Zealander.

QUALIFICATIONS: Master's degree or full-time postgraduate diploma in TESOL/Applied Linguistics, or Cambridge DELTA, plus minimum 4 years' overseas experience. Cambridge CELTA or equivalent may be acceptable with particularly relevant experience.

CONDITIONS OF EMPLOYMENT: Male, native speakers of English. 2-year contracts starting September and February. 20 hour teaching week Sat–Wed. Pupils aged 18–20.

SALARY: 124,000–180,000 SAR ($30,000–$42,000).

FACILITIES/SUPPORT: On-campus furnished accommodation with all services available for married or single status. Annual airfares. Local education. Contract completion bonus.

RECRUITMENT: Send cover letter and CV by email to recruite@ kfupm.edu.sa. Video conference interviews are required.

CONTACT: Jeffrey Gibbons, Director of the Preparatory English Program.

NUMBER OF TEACHERS: 200+ for positions in Saudi Arabia.

PREFERENCE OF NATIONALITY: American, British, Canadian, South African and New Zealand.

QUALIFICATIONS: BA degree minimum. TEFL/TESL/CELTA qualification.

CONDITIONS OF EMPLOYMENT: 1-year contract, 20–25 contact teaching hours, total of 40 working hours per week.

SALARY: Tax-free salary of US$2,600–$3,500 per month.

FACILITIES/SUPPORT: Furnished shared accommodation provided or stipend for those who live independently. Recruiter manages the visa process and works with local visa agencies to get visas processed.

RECRUITMENT: Print media and internet. Interviews are essential and are conducted in the US.

CONTACT: Esllam Elghamry, International Recruitment Specialist.

UNITED ARAB EMIRATES

The oil-rich UAE consists of seven emirates or principalities, each governed by an hereditary emir (Muslim ruler). The most important are Abu Dhabi the capital, Dubai and Sharjah. The great draw for TEFL teachers is the money that can be made, as **Ben Naismith** admitted not long after moving to Dubai in 2012:

> *Having spent a number of years working in countries that English teachers typically flock to (Costa Rica, Thailand, etc.), my wife and I decided it was time to earn more than the usual ELT pittance. So after a brief look at the available options, we settled on the UAE and Dubai. As with many teaching professionals, this decision was made in the hopes of finding a balance between financial stability and quality of life. And, although we have been here only a relatively short time, our expectations have thus far been pleasantly exceeded.*
>
> *In terms of the schools, there are a number of the usual chains including Berlitz, the British Council, and International House (for whom I work). In addition, there are plenty of teachers working at high schools, colleges, and universities. Although I personally work full-time for one school, it seems that the majority of the teachers I have met freelance at a number of different places. Getting a work visa is a bit tricky though as you need to either be sponsored exclusively by one employer, or else be married to someone who is!*
>
> *Regarding the makeup of classes, Dubai truly is a modern cosmopolitan city, and the learners come from all over the world, with the majority either from around the Middle East, south Asia, or south east Asia. Due to the massive demand for English speakers, there are all types of classes ranging from young learners, to General English, to Business English, to ESP – truly something for everyone.*
>
> *One of our greatest fears moving here, a common one I'm sure, was how we would adapt to the local surroundings. Prepared for an extremely conservative society, we were amazed at how liberal it is here in terms of clothing, attitudes, etc. The people are also, by and large, extremely friendly, probably as they too are mostly immigrants in a foreign land! What did live up to the hype though was the heat, which is truly unlike anything I have experienced before, so be prepared.*

The huge diversity of nationalities that makes up the population of the Emirates means that English is the lingua franca, and almost everyone is eager to improve his or her knowledge of the language.

Most advertised jobs in the UAE, as throughout the Gulf, say that they require at least a master's degree, though five or more years of EFL teaching experience could be acceptable, especially if it covers exam preparation, Toefl-iBT, academic and Business English. When **Steph Fuccio** and her husband (met on the international EFL circuit) applied to universities and similar in Oman and the UAE, most places cited the lack of an MA as the reason their applications were not moved forward. In the end they were hired in any case by Abu Dhabi University:

> *This is the first place I've lived where the British Council does not pay the highest English teaching wage, although they have a nice location on the island and still offer their high standard of organisation and good professional development. The rule of thumb for getting on here, much like Italy and some other countries I've been in, is it depends on who you know, no matter w\hat your experience and education are. 'Wasta' is key here: it's who you know, your connections, that get things done, including internet service, speeding tickets and teaching jobs.*
>
> *The pace in the classroom, much like the pace of life here in general, is slower than most Western institutes. Adult students expect a lot of personal attention (not to be confused with correction) but usually this dedication is not expected of them in return, i.e. they rarely will do any work outside of class, and sometimes will come up*

with amazing reasons not to do work even in class. Overall, they are good humoured. Although their sense of humour is different from mine, there is always an intersection of silliness that is available. They will always be late for class and want many breaks. They will usually have their 3–4 cell phones on the seat next to them, ready to take a call at the first ring. Emiratis are very well taken care of by their government. Although 80% of the population of the UAE is comprised of foreign nationals, it is the Emiratis who get the best jobs with the highest salaries and best benefits.

I wish I could make it sound more glamorous and inviting. The weather is great for the region, the low humidity is a relief after living in South East Asia. The food is amazing. The money is spoiling and the lifestyle isn't as strict as in neighbouring Saudi and Bahrain. But this isn't for the faint at heart or first timer.

Once again, the financial rewards are the principal attraction and make the red tape hassles bearable. The lowest jobs pay about 10–11,000 Dirhams (nearly US$3,000) per month plus free housing. The cost of living is surprisingly inexpensive, so most people can save a lot of money. Abu Dhabi and Dubai look very Western and familiar, though these similarities are only skin deep. After **Philip Dray's** arrival at the Oasis Residence in Dubai, he was well pleased with his decision to move to the UAE, since living conditions in his luxury apartment complex, complete with pool, steam room, squash court and gym, were just as lavish as he would have been given in Saudi.

LIST OF EMPLOYERS

BERLITZ LANGUAGE CENTER
PO Box 41720, Abu Dhabi
+971 2 667 2287
berlitz@emirates.net.ae
www.berlitz.uae.com

Centres also in Dubai (PO Box 71453, Dubai; 4 344 0034; berlitz 2@eim.ae; and PO Box 71453, Sharjah; 6 572 1115; berlitz3@eim.ae).

NUMBER OF TEACHERS: 45.

PREFERENCE OF NATIONALITY: None.

QUALIFICATIONS: University graduates with teaching diplomas. CELTA/TEFL. For candidates with non-education or teaching university degrees, a CELTA or TEFL certificate is essential. All instructors need to undergo and successfully complete training in the Berlitz Method of instruction.

CONDITIONS OF EMPLOYMENT: Minimum contract is 2 years. Usual hours are Sunday to Thursday, between 7.30am and 9pm, Saturdays between 9am and 1:30pm. A weekly schedule is provided by the Centre Director specifying working days and hours.

FACILITIES/SUPPORT: Accommodation is provided in a shared teachers' apartment. A work visa and labour card are issued to new candidates on full-time contracts. Original degrees/diplomas and a reference describing the candidate's experience is necessary, with attestation from the UAE Embassy or Ministry of Foreign Affairs in country of origin, plus copy of passport and passport photos.

RECRUITMENT: Through email applications, referrals and adverts in newspapers or websites. Interviews are important; for international applicants phone interviews are carried out.

CONTACT: Manal Mahshi Azar, Director, Abu Dhabi (manal.mahshi@berlitz-uae.com); Reem Shehab, Director, Dubai; Sereen Masri, Director, Sharjah.

HIGHER COLLEGES OF TECHNOLOGY
recruit@hct.ac.ae
http://recruit.hct.ac.ae

NUMBER OF TEACHERS: Up to 450 English faculty teachers involved in teaching ESL in 16 colleges throughout the UAE.

PREFERENCE OF NATIONALITY: None.

QUALIFICATIONS: English Faculty minimum requirements are master's degree in TEFL (preferred) or bachelor's degree and TEFL diploma; 3 years' teaching experience (tertiary preferred); practical teaching qualification (CELTA, DELTA or PGCE); knowledge of contemporary teaching practices and computer-assisted learning.

CONDITIONS OF EMPLOYMENT: Teaching year is from September to June. To teach 20 classes a week (Sunday to Thursday).

SALARY: Tax-free income. Salary based on experience and education. Annual rises are given upon receiving positive performance evaluations.

FACILITIES/SUPPORT: Visa arranged by HCT. Singles and families welcome. Unfurnished accommodation and a furniture allowance, excellent benefit package offered – details provided upon request or to short-listed candidates.

RECRUITMENT: Online HCT application required. Interviews can be conducted via video teleconference.

YEMEN

While some people consider Yemen to be the most beautiful and interesting of all Middle Eastern states, others consider it to be the most unpredictable and dangerous. According to an article in the *Yemen Times*, more than a hundred ESL schools operate in the capital Sana'a. The US Embassy-backed YALI (Yemen-American Language Institute, www.yaliefl.org/employment.html) has the lion's share of the market; enquiries about vacancies should be sent to the administrator (suhayri.amri@yaliefl.org). Other professional schools include Amideast and the British Council which both recruit English teachers. MALI (see entry) is broadening its appeal by offering business, IT and tourism training alongside ESL courses. Teaching salaries at the respectable institutes allow a good lifestyle since the cost of living is so low. A few years ago, **Mary Hall** worked for an aid agency in Yemen and became familiar with the teaching scene:

> *There are more and more places teaching English here. The main ones recruit mostly qualified teachers from England or the US. Some others hire any old bod who turns up and don't pay very well. I had a lodger who was teaching at one place for a pittance as the boss took money out of her wages to pay for her lodgings, even after she moved in with me. I think she was getting a couple of dollars an hour. This is something you sort of get used to. It can be very cheap living here, with rent about $50 a month or less if you're not fussy.*

For a while Yemen was attracting a growing number of tourists, but unrest and violence has put paid to that, and at the time of writing the Foreign & Commonwealth Office advice was against all travel to Yemen, and British nationals already there were being strongly urged to leave. Al-Qaida is active and suicide bombings are not infrequent.

LIST OF EMPLOYERS

AMIDEAST YEMEN
Box 6009, 162 Miswat Street, Khormaksar, Aden, Yemen
Sana'a: Box 15508, Off Algiers St., Sana'a
- +967 1 400279/80/81
- sanaa@amideast.org
- www.yemenjobs.org

NUMBER OF TEACHERS: 4–8 for Sana'a and Aden with outreach operations in Mukalla/Sheher and Taiz.
PREFERENCE OF NATIONALITY: American mainly though other native English speaking nationalities accepted.
QUALIFICATIONS: Degree plus TESOL/CELTA certification and minimal teaching experience. Suitable for part-time and entry-level teachers.
CONDITIONS OF EMPLOYMENT: 1-year contracts. 7-week sessions with 1 week off between. 4–6 hours teaching per day, 5 days per week.
SALARY: $11–$14 per instructional hour.

FACILITIES/SUPPORT: Furnished housing or monthly housing allowance provided.
RECRUITMENT: Internet and word of mouth. Most recruitment now via dedicated website yemenjobs.org on which applicants can upload their documents. Interviews can be by phone/email.

MODERN AMERICAN LANGUAGE INSTITUTE (MALI)
44 Djibouti St, Hadda, PO Box 11727, Sana'a
- +967 1446103 ext 111
- mazen.luqman@mali-training.net
- www.mali-training.net

NUMBER OF TEACHERS: 60 for 3 branches in Sana'a, Aden and Taiz.
PREFERENCE OF NATIONALITY: British, Canadian, American, Australian, New Zealander, South African.

QUALIFICATIONS: University degree and CELTA or relevant ESL certification. Teaching experience is preferred and candidates should be enthusiastic, motivated and adaptable to a different culture.

CONDITIONS OF EMPLOYMENT: 1-year contracts. 26 hours per week teaching time.

SALARY: $1,500–$2,000 per term (5 weeks) depending on qualifications and experience.

FACILITIES/SUPPORT: Single room in an apartment (shared among three) provided free. Return airfare, subsidised Arabic classes and residency visa provided.

RECRUITMENT: Send CV and recent photo to Mazen Luqman (mazen.luqman@mali-training.net). Phone interview can be arranged with shortlisted candidates.

CONTACT: Mazen Luqman, Founder & Director.

TURKEY

Turkey is a wonderful country to travel in with a wealth of historic sites like Troy and Ephesus, and an economy in reasonable shape to such an extent that politicians are beginning to talk about *when* Turkey will join the European Union rather than *if*. Turkey's ELT industry still absorbs an enormous number of globe-trotting English teachers and the country is a good choice of destination for fledgling English teachers with a university degree. Over the years, pay and perks have been cut back to some extent. However, every teacher who has complained about employers breaking their promises, run-down accommodation, and so on, has concluded by saying that Turkish people are amazingly hospitable and the country fascinating. By describing below the problems which some teachers have encountered on short teaching contracts in Turkey, it is to be hoped that readers can guard against them.

PROSPECTS FOR TEACHERS

Turkey's prosperous classes are more eager than ever to learn English and furthermore seem to have the money to pay for it. The boom in English is not confined to private language schools (*dershane*) which have proliferated in the three main cities of Istanbul, Ankara and Izmir. In order to prepare students for an English language engineering, commerce, tourism or arts course, many secondary schools hire native speaker teachers. Hundreds of private secondary schools (*lises*) consider as one of their main priorities the teaching of the English language. Similarly at the tertiary level, some universities, both private and public, use English as the medium of instruction.

A number of schools still offer a package which includes free accommodation and free airfares (London-Istanbul) on completion of a contract. Virtually all of these employers want to see a university degree and a TEFL Certificate of some kind, preferably the Cambridge CELTA or equivalent. Both a degree and a special-ist qualification are required by the Turkish Ministry of Education before it will approve a work permit (see Regulations below).

The bias in favour of British English over American is not particularly strong. Many schools claim to have no preference and yet because they advertise on UK-based sites and are more familiar with British qualifica-tions, there is a preponderance of British teachers. Also, the requirement that work visas be applied for in the country of origin makes matters more difficult for teachers from the USA, Australia, etc.

FINDING A JOB

IN ADVANCE

The British Council offices in Istanbul and Ankara have lists of private language schools, primary schools and high schools and may even maintain a Job File where local institutions advertise for TEFL teachers. When they closed down their teaching operations in Turkey, some ex-Council teaching staff set up British Side (www.britishside.com) which enjoys a good reputation as an employer. International recruitment agencies sometimes seek entry-level and more experienced teachers for chains of private and public schools in Turkey, especially the capital Ankara. Try for example Oxford Vision (teachabroad@oxfordvision.com) with a partner office in Turkey and Prime Education Consultancy (www.primeeducation.org.uk) in York. English-medium universities employ considerable numbers of language instructors, such as Bilkent in Ankara (see entry) and Istanbul Sehir University (www.sehir.edu.tr). Occasional job alerts are emailed to people who subscribe to the ITI Job List (http://jobs.iti-istanbul.com) managed by the International Training Institute in Levent, Istanbul which offers the CELTA and other TEFL training courses. EFINST, Dilko English, English Time, British Side, the Turco-British Association and the City of London College (www.clc-turkiye.com) are all well established in Istanbul. Deulcom International (www.deulcom.com.tr) has 17 branches including in Ankara, Kayseri and Adana which hire native speaking teachers from the UK, while one of the largest companies is Amerikan Kultur Dernegi, which with 80 schools claims to have the biggest network in Turkey, with telephone teaching a large part of their business.

Quite a few ads for Turkish schools appear on the main TEFL job sites and the educational press in the spring and through the summer. Some ads specify that they are looking to hire teachers already in Turkey, though many offer travel expenses. If you are considering accepting a job with an advertiser, consider asking for the name and telephone number of a previous teacher for an informal reference before accepting. An even better indication is if they have been able to keep their teachers for two or more years. If the school is reluctant to provide this kind of information, be suspicious. It may also be worth phoning the British Council office in the relevant city, since they keep a file of complaints about language schools.

The Hocam Benim Educational Consultancy (www.hocambenim.com) matches experienced teachers with clients looking for individual or group tuition, from children to professionals. Demand outstrips supply so registered teachers in Istanbul have a good chance of being assigned courses (+90 534 849 20 11).

ON THE SPOT

Although not the capital, Istanbul is the commercial, financial and cultural centre of Turkey, so this is where most of the EFL teaching goes on. On the negative side, there may be more competition from other teachers here and also in Izmir than in Ankara or less obvious cities. **Daniel Eldridge** from Seattle spent four months teaching in Istanbul:

> *The English teaching scene in Istanbul is absolutely huge and insane. Without the necessary charisma and connections (and confidence, maybe) I stayed on the bottom rung. I also had no TEFL certification which seemed to be important to some and not to others.*

Given the huge demand for native speaker teachers, Turkey is one country where scouting out possibilities on the ground can pay off, rather than signing a contract at a school you have never seen. After **Bruce Lawson** had a terrible experience with a private language teaching organisation in Istanbul (*'their contract was a fiction that Tolstoy would have been proud of'*), he concluded that he could have earned half as much again if he had been hired by a school which hired its teachers in Turkey.

Tim Leffel and **Donna Marcus** from New Jersey were amazed by the contrast between job-hunting in Greece (where Americans encounter visa problems even when they have a Cambridge Certificate as Tim and Donna had) and Turkey:

> *There's a huge demand for teachers (any nationality really) in Istanbul. We lined up work on our second day of interviews. We interviewed at three schools and all of them offered us positions. We chose one in Bakirköy because there were two jobs available in the same place and we were allowed to wear anything within reason (no ties, no new clothes to buy). They were satisfied that we could only commit ourselves for four months. We did see a lot of applicants turned away, even when there was a need for new teachers, because they lacked TEFL credentials.*

Fewer and fewer schools are willing to employ people with no formal TEFL background.

FREELANCE TEACHING

The standard Ministry of Education contract prohibits private teaching outside the bounds of the signed contract. In fact, unless you are blatantly pinching students from the institution that employs you, most employers turn a blind eye. University English departments might be a place to look for private pupils. The top rate of pay goes up to £20 an hour, though a more usual hourly rate would be less than half that, i.e. 25 lira.

> *In Istanbul there is a flourishing English Spoken Café where Turkish language learners can meet up with native speakers informally (though with their dictionaries at the ready). Join the Facebook group to find out where and when events are being held.*

REGULATIONS

It is necessary to apply for a visa before arrival in Turkey as the Vice Consul at the Turkish Consulate General in London clearly explains:

> *Anyone who intends to work in Turkey has to obtain a work visa before departing for Turkey. Otherwise, he/she will not be permitted to take up employment in the country, unless he/she chooses to work illegally.*

The application by the candidate in his or her own country must happen simultaneously with the employer in Turkey submitting an application to the Department for Work Permits for Foreigners, part of the Ministry of Labour and Social Security. It is not unknown for a hopeful teacher to proceed with the visa application while the employer does not carry out his side of the bargain, in which case the effort and money will be wasted. The current work permit fee for Britons is £245. Employers may be willing to pay this expense but it is not usual.

Teachers are required to submit their degree and ELT certificate. These have to be translated into Turkish by an official Turkish translator and then notarised. The Turkish employer needs to send permission from the Ministry of Education that he or she is authorised to employ foreign teachers, among other documents. Once these have arrived, the teacher takes them with the original contract of employment and completed forms in person to the Consulate to apply for a work visa, preferably eight weeks before the proposed departure. Clarification may be requested from the Office of Labour and Social Security Attaché in London (+44 207 581 5988; www.turkishconsulate.org.uk/en/work_visa.asp).

The regulations allow you to leave and re-enter the country without having to pay again for a visa, as long as your work and residence permits are still valid. If you stay in Turkey longer term (i.e. longer than the tourist visa) you are meant to obtain a residence visa as well.

The complications involved in obtaining a work visa have created a rise in language teachers who are working on just a tourist visa. In fact the majority of transitory language teachers opt for this route and as a result are forced to make a trip to either the border or the immigration office every three months, in order to renew their tourist visa. On entry make sure you get a multiple entry visa which allows you to enter and exit the country more than once within a one-year period and you can stay in Turkey for a maximum of 90 days each time. The tourist visa fee payable at the border is £10 in sterling or $20 for US citizens. Normally people cross the border to Greece, though a trip to Northern Cyprus is more pleasant. If you do this too many times the border officials will become suspicious. If you have overstayed, you become liable for a hefty exit fine of about $250.

Before agreeing to work on a tourist visa, teachers should negotiate financial help or at least a subsidy for their border run. Schools are often willing to do this as it is still cheaper for them than arranging a work visa. All salaries in Turkey are quoted net of deductions which amount to about 25% for contributions and tax. If the school makes social security contributions on your behalf, you will have medical cover from your first day of work. The scheme pays all your doctor's bills and 80% of prescriptions. Once again it is prudent to confirm that your employer keeps any promises he or she makes. More than one teacher has realised at a critical moment that, despite assurances, insurance premiums have not been paid by the school.

A complication for people who intend to teach English in a *lise* or secondary school is that the Ministry of Education insists that teachers of English have a university degree in English, Linguistics or related degree and preferably a PGCE or a BEd with English as a main subject. **Barry Wade**'s degree in philosophy with a minor in English was deemed inadequate to teach English at an Istanbul secondary school, despite what he had been told by an agent in England, and he was fobbed off with having to work for less money at a private language school instead.

CONDITIONS OF WORK

The normal deal is a one-year contract with airfare out and back from London, free or subsidised shared accommodation and a starting monthly salary in Turkish lira equivalent to £800/US$1,300 in private language schools, more in primary and secondary schools. For example EFINST with three branches in Istanbul offers from 2,300 to 4,000 Turkish lira per month which is supplemented by a relocation allowance, free accommodation and insurance. Hourly employment used to be fairly unusual in Turkey, but increasingly employers are finding it more profitable to pay by the hour, especially during low seasons when the number of teaching hours decreases dramatically.

Over the years many employers have come in for criticism with words such as 'cowboy', 'unprofessional' and 'untrustworthy' being bandied about by disappointed teachers. Browsing the web will eventually bring you to sites which name and shame schools that sack their teachers to save money, slash wages, fail to honour contracts, withhold certificates to prevent staff from leaving prematurely and so on. It is not always easy to establish how current some of this information is. Conditions have not significantly improved, as **John Boylan** commented after seeing a recent ad on craigslist for an employer he once worked for in Istanbul:

More than 10 years ago, I was getting about £500 a month with free accommodation and bills paid. Now in 2011, the salary offered by the same employer works out at £620 and you have to pay for your accommodation and, obviously, bills. The hours have increased, the days off decreased, so I think I made a wise decision not to return. Beware if you are told you'll teach '24 hours a week', because this could be 32× 45-minute lessons. Two non-consecutive days off a week still seems to be the norm.

Although one individual's personal experience is not always a good basis for generalising, there has been a lot of duplication over the years in the litany of complaints made about language schools in Turkey which focus on contracts being ignored, late payment of wages, assigning inflated marks to students to keep or attract custom, and so on. It may be a mistake to expect Western attitudes towards employees to prevail. John Boylan recommends keeping informed about the good and bad employers by checking this link www.facebook.com/groups12411239094058. In Turkey the manager is the boss and in many cases does not feel it incumbent on him or her to work efficiently or to look out for the welfare of their staff. Nevertheless, some people in the ELT business believe that the situation is gradually improving, among them a director of studies at a major Istanbul school:

I have worked for approximately four years in Turkey, in Istanbul and in a small remote town in the south. Prospective teachers always hear many horror stories about working in Turkey and to an extent they are well founded. In the past, schools and employers openly abused teachers' rights. But this is definitely changing. There are many good, up-and-coming organisations which can be trusted. Teachers should ask around, be careful about contracts and conditions, and not agree to the first job they are offered without checking out the school, its size, reputation, etc.

Yet it seems that there are still many dodgy operators and swashbuckling and unscrupulous employers. So it is important to remember that some teachers have a marvellous time, as **Raza Griffiths** had at the first school he worked for, which was in the town of Ordu on the Black Sea coast:

It would be no exaggeration to say that as a native English person in a region of Turkey unused to foreigners, I enjoyed celebrity status, with lots of inquiring eyes and lots of invitations to dinner. Although the town did not exactly have a thriving cultural life as we would understand it, this was more than compensated for by the sociableness of the people and their deep desire for communication. Because it was a private school, money was not in short supply and the facilities were excellent with computers, etc. The free furnished flat I was given was large and very comfortable, and there was a free school minibus service that took teachers to the school. On either side of the school there were hazelnut gardens, behind there were mountains and in front the Black Sea, all quite idyllic, especially in summer. The other teachers (all Turkish) were very welcoming from day one, despite the fact that I was less experienced and was getting four times their salary. I could live very comfortably on my salary and still have a lot left over for spending on holidays and clothes.

Contracts are usually for 9, 10 or 11 months; some offer 3-month summer contracts. If you want to stay longer than a year you are normally paid over the summer holidays. Do not put too much faith in your contract. **Rabindra Roy** described his as a '*worthless and contradictory piece of paper*'. Private language schools will expect you to work the usual unsocial hours and may chop and change your timetable at short notice, while *lises* offer daytime working hours plus (sometimes onerous) extra-curricular duties such as marking tests, attending school ceremonies, etc.

The standard paid holiday allowance for teachers is 15 days. At inferior schools, national holidays must be taken out of this annual leave, including Muslim holidays such as Seker Bayrami, usually celebrated at the end of Ramadan and Kurban Bayrami. The former last three days, the latter four days, and it is customary to make the bridge to a full week. Christmas is not observed much and you may be offered very little time off, especially in smaller schools where the majority of the staff is Turkish. Big chains of schools, where native English speakers are in the majority in the staff-room, tend to close for a week or a bit more. Most things can usually be negotiated in Turkey, be it the price of a carpet, or the terms of a contract, so it is wise to shop around carefully before accepting a job.

THE PUPILS

The major schools are well equipped with computers, language labs and course materials. But better than the back-up facilities is the enthusiasm of the pupils who are usually motivated, conscientious and well-behaved, and enjoy group discussions. Teachers should not, however, expect too much interaction between teacher and pupil, as **Tara Dermot**, a teacher in Istanbul describes:

Walk into a classroom in Turkey and you are likely to find every kind of student that you would find all over the world: the eager, the shy, the lazy, the clever one... What sets Turkish students significantly apart in my experience is their passivity. Turks grow up in an incredibly teacher-centred learning environment so that is what they are expecting. Having them participate in a far more student-centred, communicative course can therefore be frustrating, but given time and perseverance they will soon see the benefits and the fun to be had.

'*Willing if unimaginative*' was one teacher's description of her students. One undesirable aspect of Turkish education is that many *lises* (high schools) are too strongly oriented to exam preparation and university entrance. On the whole, however, the friendly openness of young Turks may cause a foreign teacher to forget that Turkey is still an Islamic country where dress is conservative and where only a small percentage of women of university age actually attend (around 14%). Teachers are still regarded as important figures in society and as such are expected to dress fairly conservatively.

Student behaviour differs radically depending on what kind of institution you teach in. Private secondary schools tend to be populated with spoiled and immature kids who do not always respect their teachers. **Joan Smith** found this hard to stomach at the private school in Kayseri where she taught:

Turkish parents indulge their children something rotten. Rich spoilt students abound in my classroom and discipline goes out the window. Foreign teachers are regarded as inferior and are given even less respect than the Turkish teachers.

Joan did not think that she should have to tolerate some of the innuendos her male students were getting away with, but had little hope of justice if they and their friends denied her allegations.

DICK BIRD

Dick Bird's (and others') experiences have been very different. Dick, a veteran EFL teacher, taught in Turkey a long time ago but his description of his pupils is still apt.

I have found women students defer to a far higher level of male chauvinism than would be acceptable anywhere in the West. Turkish women also seem to have exceptionally quiet voices and I can't help feeling that this irritating characteristic is somehow related to their role in society - a case of being seen but not heard until you are very very close perhaps? Sometimes my students know too much grammar to be able to express themselves freely. As their own language is radically different to Indo-European languages they have a lot of difficulty adapting to the sentence structure of English: they regard relative clauses as a perversion and are baffled, if not mildly outraged, by the cavalier way English seems to use any tense it fancies to refer to future actions but is puritanically strict about how one may describe present and past events. Another difficulty Turks have is that we EFL teachers like to use a lot of words in our meta-language (i.e. language about language e.g. adjective, verb) which do not have cognates in Turkish as they do in other European languages, for example a teacher may inform their students that 'will' expresses probability, not intention; this will be readily understood by an elementary level Spaniard but is total gibberish to a Turk (as I suspect it is to a great many native speakers of English.)

Dick's analysis of Turkish EFL students ends with a light-hearted description of their irrepressible energy and enthusiasm:

Whenever the class is asked a question they would fain prostrate themselves at their teacher's feet were it not that years of instilled discipline keep them penned by invisible bonds within the confines of their desks until the ringing of the bell, whereat pandemonium breaks loose as a thousand berserk adolescents fling themselves across the (highly polished) corridor floors and down the (marble) steps headlong into the playground. (This phenomenon may help to explain why fire drills are not a regular feature of Turkish school life.)

Paul Gallantry, at one time Director of Studies at Dilko English in Bakirköy, agrees that Turkish students are fun to teach but identifies a few of the problems he has encountered:

They have several major problems with English, especially mastering the definite article, the third person singular and the present perfect, none of which exists in Turkish. On the whole, their pronunciation is good, but they do have difficulty with words that have three consonants back to back. (My own surname Gallantry inevitably gets pronounced 'Galilantiree'.) If I have to be critical of my students, it is that they neither listen to, nor read, instructions; five minutes into an exercise there is always someone asking 'What am I supposed to do?'. Also a recurring problem is that some students merely come to a language school in order to use it as a social club. They're more interested in meeting someone of the opposite sex than learning English, and this can have a demoralising effect in class.

ACCOMMODATION

If accommodation is provided as part of your contract, it may be located close to the school in a modern flat which you will have to share with another teacher or it may be some way away, possibly in an undesirable neighbourhood. Fortunately not many teachers are assigned accommodation as gruesome as **Philip Dray**'s in Izmir:

Cockroaches, centipedes, noisy neighbours, a filthy shower room and a fitted kitchen circa 1920 – I was slowly adjusting to it all. But one day, while I was having a shower, I saw a rat looking at me from the ventilation shaft and I knew that my patience had run out. I asked for a new flat but they said they couldn't get a new one before May. So, reluctantly (as there were some very nice people at the school) I had to leave.

If the school doesn't provide a flat they will certainly help you find one and act as go-between with the landlord. Most provide some kind of rent subsidy, since rents in Turkey are high relative to the cost of living. The situation in over-crowded Istanbul is especially tight. It is usual to bargain over the rent as if you were buying a second-hand car. Flats are advertised through *Hurriyet* newspaper, or there are estate agencies called *emlak* but these tend to charge a month's rent. Foreigners are usually considered an attractive proposition as they tend to be undemanding tenants.

In Istanbul, the nicest flats are along the Bosphorus where the air is clean, the views stunning and a lot of the buildings are older properties with a lot of character; this is why they have been snapped up by well-heeled diplomats and multinationals. The Asian side of the city might have less charm but it also has less pollution and many people prefer it.

Flats in Istanbul do not offer standards such as those in Europe or other Western countries, but things appear to have improved somewhat in recent years, and the horror stories of cockroaches, and freezing window-less rooms have been replaced with less drastic reports of leakages, small rooms, old facilities and untidy flatmates. **Ian McArthur**'s school was in a suburb on the Asian side, but he chose to stay in a cheap hotel in Sultanahmet, partly for the social life:

> *I had to commute (from Europe to Asia in fact) for an hour in the morning and evening, but the marvellous views of the sunrise over the domes and minarets from the Bosphorus ferry whilst sipping a much-needed glass of strong sweet tea, made the early rise worth it.*

LEISURE TIME

Even if you are earning a salary at the lower end of the scale, you should be able to afford quite a good life, especially if you eat a lot of bread, drink local wines and use public transport. Basic meals and food, transport, hotels and cinemas (most films are subtitled rather than dubbed) are still very reasonable, especially away from the seaside and Istanbul. With the benefit of hindsight, **John Boylan** decided the hassles weren't so bad after all:

> *Recognise why you are in Turkey – for the experience – and try to enjoy that. You have a chance to live in a fascinating city for a year on the basis of a one-month certificate. You may live near Taksim and let's be honest, could you afford to live a stone's throw from the equivalent in London or New York? Don't fall into the trap of mixing only with EFL teachers. Broaden your horizons and don't spend all your time in ex-pat bars with a clique of English teachers. Socialising all the time with the same teachers can lead to a climate of moaning. Constructive criticism/advice is fine but too many teachers become bitter and vengeful. Most Turks are OK. If you want to make Turkish friends, get involved in sport or something where you'll see the same people regularly.*

Dick Bird points out the advantages of living in Ankara:

> *It's safer than any European capital (except maybe Reykjavik) and although it may not hum at night, there are enough clubs etc. to keep you going for a year, plus very cheap classical concerts and cinemas. And the air pollution is not as bad as it was.*

Travel in Turkey is wonderfully affordable. The efficiency, comfort and low cost of Turkish bus travel put the coach services of most other countries to shame (though not their safety record). There is very little crime in Turkey. Women will have to learn to handle pestering, which is usually best ignored. **Paul Gallantry** tries to put the problem into perspective:

While Turkey is generally an exceptionally safe place, women teachers can expect a certain amount of harassment from a minority of Turkish men, who seem to believe that all foreign females are prostitutes. This attitude leaves a lot of teachers with a thoroughly negative attitude towards Turkey and Turkish people as a whole, which is unfair.

Turkey generally is a great place to live and work. It's a fascinating country, full of contradictions, as befits a land that is the bridge between East and West.

LIST OF EMPLOYERS

ABC DIL OKULLARI
Esra Sk. No: 11, 34337, Etiler, Istanbul

+90 212 287 43 51
yk@abc-languageschool.com
www.abc-okullari.com

NUMBER OF TEACHERS: 2–5.
PREFERENCE OF NATIONALITY: USA, UK.
QUALIFICATIONS: MA in TESOL, DELTA/CELTA and minimum
4 years of experience.
CONDITIONS OF EMPLOYMENT: 1 year contract. 20–25 hours
a week teaching General and Business English (all levels), TOEFL,
IELTS and organising an English Conversation club. Classes
conducted on and off-site.
SALARY: $1,000–$2,500 per month depending on qualifications
and experience. Deductions made for SKG (social security)
FACILITIES/SUPPORT: No assistance given with accommodation
or visas.
RECRUITMENT: Adverts in mass media and relevant internet
sites, e.g. www.iti-istanbul.com. Interviews and presentation
essential after submitting letters of reference.
CONTACT: Ms Yevgeniya Kim, Executive Director.

BEST ENGLISH
Bayindir (2) Sokak No. 53, 06650 Kizilay, Ankara

+90 312 417 1819/417 2536
management@bestenglish.com.tr
www.bestenglish.com.tr

NUMBER OF TEACHERS: 30 native English speakers.
PREFERENCE OF NATIONALITY: None.
QUALIFICATIONS: First degree plus CELTA or equivalent plus
minimum 2 years' experience.
CONDITIONS OF EMPLOYMENT: 1-year renewable contracts.
Teaching load is 25 hours per week. Variable hours between

9am and 9pm, 7 days a week, with 2 days off a week. Students
mostly young adults.
SALARY: Varies according to qualifications and experience.
FACILITIES/SUPPORT: Shared accommodation provided.
Health insurance. One way airfare paid on completion of
1 year, plus 3 weeks' paid leave; return airfare and
4 weeks' paid leave if teacher renews contract. In-house
training.
RECRUITMENT: Adverts and online application via website.
CONTACT: Mustafa Kutlay Yavuz, Director of Studies (mkyavuz@
bestenglish.com.tr).

BILKENT UNIVERSITY SCHOOL OF ENGLISH LANGUAGE
06800 Bilkent, Ankara

+90 312 290 5401
intrec@bilkent.edu.tr
www.bilkent.edu.tr/~busel

Privately funded not-for-profit English-medium university, part
of the national university system, within the Times Education
Worldwide Top 50 New Universities.
NUMBER OF TEACHERS: 280 EFL/ESP teachers in preparatory
and freshman programmes.
PREFERENCE OF NATIONALITY: Bilkent employs Turkish
nationals and native English speakers from Australia, Canada,
Britain, USA, South Africa and Ireland.
QUALIFICATIONS: Must be degree holder, preferably BEd or
language degree; previous teaching experience not essential but
a distinct advantage.
CONDITIONS OF EMPLOYMENT: Contracts from September to
August. 20 contact hours per week.
SALARY: Salary quoted net in US dollars and Turkish lira, starting
at approximately US$900 plus 1,450 Turkish lira per month.
FACILITIES/SUPPORT: Free accommodation on campus, private
health insurance, airfare and baggage allowance, residence

permit, work visa, etc. Good facilities and opportunities for career advancement, e.g. to study for an ICELT, DELTA and/or MA on full scholarship.

RECRUITMENT: Directly via www.bilkent.edu.tr/~busel/interrec/index.html. Recruitment process for EFL/EAP instructors begins in February each year.

CONTACT: Vanessa McDonagh, Head of Teacher Services.

DIALOGUE LANGUAGE SCHOOLS
Akdeniz Cad. no. 69, Fatih, Istanbul
✆ +90 212 621 70 62
Branch office: Istasyon Cad. Yakut Sk No. 8, Bakirkoy, Istanbul
✆ +90 212 570 30 60
Branch office: Halitaga Cad. Vahapbey Sk. No. 18, Kadikoy, Istanbul
✆ +90 216 550 13 17
✎ info@dialogue.com.tr
🖥 www.dialogue.com.tr

NUMBER OF TEACHERS: 30 in 3 branches in Istanbul, including Basaksehir and Mecidiyekoy.

PREFERENCE OF NATIONALITY: British, American, Canadian, Australian and New Zealander.

QUALIFICATIONS: Native English speaking teachers with a clear non-regional accent, who have completed university education, have communicative abilities and desire to teach, are available for at least a year and have a teaching certificate or experience.

CONDITIONS OF EMPLOYMENT: 12 months for full-time teachers; shorter periods for part-time teachers. Variable hours with classes 6 days a week in daytime and evenings.

FACILITIES/SUPPORT: Full-time teachers are given rent allowance to find their own accommodation. No help with work permits.

RECRUITMENT: Online application form. Interviews essential.

EARLY AMERICAN ENGLISH
Gaziosmanpasa Branch, Mevlana Mah. Sefa Cad. No: 37/B, Gaziosmanpasa, Istanbul
✆ +90 212 650 4 650
✎ gaziosmanpasa@erkeningilizce.com
🖥 www.erkeningilizce.com/gaziosmanpasa

NUMBER OF TEACHERS: Up to 3.

PREFERENCE OF NATIONALITY: Good clear accent for teaching young learners aged 7–14.

QUALIFICATIONS: Must be cheerful and communicative.

CONDITIONS OF EMPLOYMENT: 1-year contract. To work 6 days a week, 8.30am–4pm with some variation in weekday and weekend schedules.

SALARY: Depends on whether hired as a full or part-time teacher. School normally pays a retainer plus a fee per lesson taught.

FACILITIES/SUPPORT: No assistance with accommodation or visas.

CONTACT: Dincer Demir, Head Teacher of ELT Department.

EFINST– FLORYA BRANCH
Florya cad, Senlikkoy mah, No 46, Florya, Istanbul
✆ +90 212 571 6424/+90 212 554 857 4887
🖥 www.efinsthr.com

NUMBER OF TEACHERS: 10.

QUALIFICATIONS, CONDITIONS OF EMPLOYMENT, etc.: As for Levent branch below.

CONTACT: Tim Luckhurst, Director of Studies (tim@efdilokulu.com) or Mrs Zeynep Gunduzyeli (zgunduzyeli@efdilokulu.com).

EFINST– LEVENT BRANCH
Aydin Sok. F Blok No. 12/1, Levent, Istanbul
✆ +90 212 282 90 64/5
🖥 www.efinsthr.com

NUMBER OF TEACHERS: 30.

PREFERENCE OF NATIONALITY: Must be native speaker or Turk.

QUALIFICATIONS: Must be from a country where the primary official language is English. Minimum requirements: university degree and a CELTA/TESOL certificate. At least 1 year post-CELTA teaching experience desirable. Turkish teachers need degree as English teacher and pedagogy certification.

CONDITIONS OF EMPLOYMENT: 9, 10, or 12-month contracts based on a 5 day working week with 2 consecutive days off and 30 contact hours teaching per week. Half-time and three-quarter contracts are also available. Paid holiday, number of days depending on the length of the contract, plus state and religious holidays.

SALARY: 2,300–4,000 Turkish lira monthly, depending on experience and qualifications, including accommodation allowance of 500 Turkish lira. Relocation allowance of up to $750. Full private health and life insurance.

RECRUITMENT: Internet, direct application. Interviews essential but can be by telephone/Skype.

CONTACT: Dina Pazarbasi (Director of Studies), (dina@efdilokulu.com) or Mrs Zeynep Gunduzyeli (zgunduzyeli@efdilokulu.com).

NUMBER OF TEACHERS: 18.

QUALIFICATIONS, CONDITIONS OF EMPLOYMENT, etc: As above.

CONTACT: Deirdre Costello, Director of Studies (dos@efdilokulu. com) or Mrs Zeynep Gunduzyeli (zgunduzyeli@efdilokulu.com).

Group of schools in Izmir, Denizli, Kusadasi and Usak in western Turkey, affiliated to Deren & Koray International Tourism and Education Center.

NUMBER OF TEACHERS: 7.

PREFERENCE OF NATIONALITY: English, Scottish, American, Australian, Canadian and NZ.

QUALIFICATIONS: Schools licensed by the Ministry of Education require teachers to have at least a 2-year university/college degree, however, a 4-year bachelor's degree is preferred. Those with a 2-year degree or bachelor's degree in a non-relevant field require a TEFL/TESOL certificate. This can be obtained online (preferably TEFL/TESL certification module and a special grammar module). Outgoing personality needed, with the ability to work in a team. The Callan Method of teaching English requires a sense of urgency, the use of miming and gesticulation, and the presentation of a clear accent with excellent pronunciation skills.

CONDITIONS OF EMPLOYMENT: 1-year contract, renewable for a second year, 20–25 hours per week.

SALARY: Salary is calculated either on hourly or salary-package basis. This varies by school and location, and will be discussed with candidate. All teaching positions have a 6-month probationary period with an increase in pay provided after successfully competing the probationary period.

FACILITIES/SUPPORT: Free accommodation for at least a month. Once teacher finds own accommodation, accommodation allowance of 250 Turkish lira is paid. Help with work permits and expense met. Intensive 1-week teachers training programme via the Callan Method given at time of hire and before starting teaching.

RECRUITMENT: Via eslcafe.com and others.

CONTACT: Koray Altan M.Sc. (Manager) and Chuck Militello (Education Group Coordinator).

NUMBER OF TEACHERS: 6.

PREFERENCE OF NATIONALITY: English, Scottish, American, Canadian, New Zealand and Australian.

QUALIFICATIONS: Schools licensed by the Ministry of Education require teachers to have at least a 2-year university/college degree, however, a 4-year bachelor's degree is preferred. Those with a 2-year degree or bachelor's degree in a non-relevant field require a TEFL/TESOL certificate. This can be obtained online (preferably TEFL/TESL certification module and a special grammar module). Outgoing personality needed, with the ability to work in a team. The Callan Method of teaching English requires a sense of urgency, the use of miming and gesticulation, and the presentation of a clear accent with excellent pronunciation skills.

CONDITIONS OF EMPLOYMENT: 1-year contract, renewable for a second year, 20–25 hours per week.

SALARY: Salary is calculated either on hourly or salary-package basis. This varies by school and location, and will be discussed with candidate. All teaching positions have a 6-month probationary period with an increase in pay provided after successfully competing the probationary period.

FACILITIES/SUPPORT: Free accommodation for at least a month. Once teacher finds own accommodation, accommodation allowance of 250 Turkish lira is paid. Help with work permits and expense met. Intensive 1-week teachers training programme via the Callan Method given at time of hire and before starting teaching.

RECRUITMENT: Via eslcafe.com and others.

CONTACT: Koray Altan M.Sc. (Manager) and Chuck Militello (Education Group Coordinator).

NUMBER OF TEACHERS: 10.

PREFERENCE OF NATIONALITY: Native (or good) English speakers.

QUALIFICATIONS: Experience with children, workcamp or teaching experience is preferred.

CONDITIONS OF EMPLOYMENT: Volunteering for teaching English to children aged 12–17 at summer camps for 2 weeks, through outdoor activities, games and songs.

SALARY: Free board and lodging.

RECRUITMENT: Only through partner voluntary organisations abroad (e.g. IVS GB, Thorn House, 5 Rose Street, Edinburgh EH2 2PR; +44 131 243 2745; info@ivsgb.org; www.ivsgb.org).

CONTACT: Zafer Yilmaz (zafer.yilmaz@genctur.com).

ICEP (INTERNATIONAL CULTURAL EXCHANGE PROGRAMS)
81 Oxford Street, London W1D 2EU, UK
📞 +44 020 7580 3106
🖱 uk@icepworld.co.uk
💻 www.icep.org.tr/English/teach.asp

London office of Turkish exchange organisation with offices in Ankara (+90 312 418 44 60) and Istanbul.

NUMBER OF TEACHERS: Varying number for positions at language school, English-medium university, private company or with host family where you will teach English to the family members.

PREFERENCE OF NATIONALITY: British and others.

QUALIFICATIONS: TEFL qualification e.g. CELTA, Trinity CertTESOL or DELTA required. Experience in teaching university level preferred.

CONDITIONS OF EMPLOYMENT: 5-day work week, 27 teaching hours per week plus 3 curriculum hours.

SALARY: Typically $500 per month. Possibility of better paying positions.

FACILITIES/SUPPORT: Accommodation, medical insurance and meals are provided.

INKUR ENGLISH LANGUAGE INSTITUTE
Ankara Cad. No: 8 izmit, Kocaeli
📞 +90 262 321 53 25
🖱 inkur@inkur.com
💻 www.inkur.com

NUMBER OF TEACHERS: 3–8.

PREFERENCE OF NATIONALITY: EU and OECD countries are preferred (easier visa procedure).

QUALIFICATIONS: Minimum qualifications are a bachelor's degree and TEFL/TESOL certificate.

CONDITIONS OF EMPLOYMENT: 9-month contracts, 28 teaching hours per week.

SALARY: Between $500–$700 per month.

FACILITIES/SUPPORT: Free accommodation available. School applies for the work permit with teachers' academic document copies.

RECRUITMENT: Face-to-face and/or telephone interviews, sometimes carried out in the UK or USA.

CONTACT: Mrs N Gökçiçek Doğàn, Owner and Director.

ISTANBUL SEHIR UNIVERSITY SCHOOL OF LANGUAGES ENGLISH PREPARATORY PROGRAM
Istanbul Sehir University, Dogu Kampusu, Kusbakisi Cad. No:27, Altunizade, Uskudar, 34662 Istanbul
📞 +90 216 444 40 34
🖱 sepp@sehir.edu.tr
💻 www.sehir.edu.tr

NUMBER OF TEACHERS: 10–15 per year.

PREFERENCE OF NATIONALITY: None.

QUALIFICATIONS: BA + CELTA or TESOL certificate is minimum requirement. MA in ELT or Applied Linguistics is preferable.

CONDITIONS OF EMPLOYMENT: 1-year contracts. Hours of teaching 8.30am–5.30pm with an afternoon off in the week.

SALARY: 3,500–4,500 Turkish Lira (£1,230–£1,580) per month.

FACILITIES/SUPPORT: No assistance with accommodation. The Human Resources Department is in charge of work and residence permits.

RECRUITMENT: Via ads posted on International Training Institute (ITI) Istanbul Joblist (http://jobs.iti-istanbul.com) and British Council mailing lists. Face-to-face interviews are essential; Skype interviews are not possible.

CONTACT: Dr Ilke Buyukduman, Director (ilkebuyukduman@sehir.edu.tr).

KENT SCHOOL OF ENGLISH – ISTANBUL
Kirtasiyeci Sokak No.1, 34714 Kadiköy, Istanbul
📞 +90 216 347 2791 / +90 216 347 2792
🖱 info@kentenglish.com
For job applications:
🖱 dos@kentenglish.com
💻 www.kentenglish.com; www.tefl-turkey.com

NUMBER OF TEACHERS: 10+.

PREFERENCE OF NATIONALITY: Native speakers of English from the USA, UK, Canada and Australia.

QUALIFICATIONS: Bachelor's degree and TEFL certificate required. Priority given to candidates with teaching experience.

CONDITIONS OF EMPLOYMENT: 8, 10 or 12-month contracts. Weekend, weekday and evening classes in and away from school premises (in-company training programmes). Weekly teaching hours 25 +.

SALARY: Average $1,200 per month.

FACILITIES/SUPPORT: Work and residency permits arranged. Some training provided. Paid vacation. Health insurance. Intensive CTEFL course (Via Lingua) available for those without a teaching certificate.

RECRUITMENT: Local interviews, telephone, fax, mail.

OXFORD VISION EDUCATION & VISA CONSULTANCY

Inebolu Sokak Sozer Apt. No: 9/6 kat: 2, Kabatas-Istanbul

✆ +90 212 2938350

✉ ahmet.dastan@oxfordvision.com

💻 www.oxfordvision.com

NUMBER OF TEACHERS: 35.

PREFERENCE OF NATIONALITY: USA, UK, Canada, Australia, New Zealand.

QUALIFICATIONS: Minimum 3 years' experience in primary or secondary school with BA degree in any subject and TEFL, TESOL or CELTA certificate.

CONDITIONS OF EMPLOYMENT: 8–9 months. 25 hours a week.

SALARY: Approximately $1,600 per month net.

FACILITIES/SUPPORT: Assistance given in finding accommodation. Government requires employers to apply for work permits after submitting original degree and TEFL certificates.

RECRUITMENT: Via Skype or local interviews.

CONTACT: Ahmet Dastan, TEFL Recruitment Manager.

SDM LANGUAGE SCHOOL AND EDUCATION AGENCY

Halaskargazi Caddesi No: 336/1 Kat:3–4, Sisli, Istanbul

✆ +90 212 233 02 49; business mob
  +90 533 224 37 16

✉ akin@sdm.com.tr

💻 www.sdm.com.tr

PREFERENCE OF NATIONALITY: Native English speakers.

QUALIFICATIONS: University graduate and experience of teaching adults.

CONDITIONS OF EMPLOYMENT: 6-day working week (with Fridays off). Working hours between 10am and 10pm. To teach mainly professionals.

FACILITIES/SUPPORT: Assistance with work permit given.

CONTACT: Akin Isik, Owner.

TURCO-BRITISH ASSOCIATION

Bestekar Sokak No. 32, Kavaklidere, 06680 Ankara

✆ +90 312 419 18 44

✉ dos@tba.org.tr

💻 www.tba.org.tr

NUMBER OF TEACHERS: 20–30.

PREFERENCE OF NATIONALITY: British.

QUALIFICATIONS: Degree plus EFL qualification. Experience desirable.

CONDITIONS OF EMPLOYMENT: 2 years, 27 contact hours per week (45 minutes each lesson).

FACILITIES/SUPPORT: Shared, fully furnished accommodation, paid utilities, close proximity to school (about a 5-minute walk). Assistance with travel costs at the beginning and end of a 2-year contract. Residence and work permit procedures undertaken and costs met. 4 weeks' paid annual leave, Christmas holiday, national Turkish holidays. Settling-in bonus, national social security covered.

RECRUITMENT: Via the *Guardian*, internet and locally.

UKLA ACADEMY LANGUAGE SCHOOLS

Dikkaldirim MH. Zübeyde Hn Cd. 15/A Demir Apt 16090 Osmangazi – Bursa

✆ +90 224 232 1440

✉ english@ukla.com.tr

💻 www.ukla.com.tr

NUMBER OF TEACHERS: 15–20 per year.

PREFERENCE OF NATIONALITY: Must be native speakers as this is government policy for foreign English teacher employment.

QUALIFICATIONS: Bachelor's degree and CELTA or equivalent certification. Relevant experience is an advantage.

CONDITIONS OF EMPLOYMENT: One year contract with 20–30 teaching hours per week.

FACILITIES/SUPPORT: Fully furnished shared housing, work visa, residence permit, healthcare and professional development support given (seminars and workshops).

RECRUITMENT: Process involves an application essay, lesson plan and a final interview carried out over the phone/Skype.

CONTACT: Ms Canan Aktug, Director of Studies.

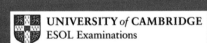

62-2012
ELEBRATING

50

EARS OF
EACHER
RAINING

ake the CELTA
et a job!

Cambridge **CELTA** is probably the most
rnationally recognised initial training
ification for teachers of English in the world.

offer CELTA in

vailable online

- Barcelona
- Beijing
- Belfast
- Bogotá

- Brussels
- Cape Town
- Palma de Mallorca
- Playa del Carmen

r Teacher Training courses in Barcelona: **DELTA,**
g Learners, CELTYL Extension. Also courses
oSs, Trainers, Managers and **Translators.**

Help and
advice finding
a job is part of
the package

International
House
IHLS Group

For more information:
www.ihls-group.com
training@bcn.ihes.com

UNIVERSITY *of* CAMBRIDGE
ESOL Examinations
Authorised Centre

HAMBURG SCHOOL OF ENGLISH

Teaching is learning

Keep learning

Be a teacher

- Learn to Teach English to Speakers of Other Languages

- Gain an internationally recognised qualification issued by Cambridge ESOL

- Experience Hamburg or Berlin - two of the most attractive cities in Europe

- Take your CELTA with us

HAMBURG SCHOOL OF ENGLISH
Teacher Training Centre

Isekai 19
20249 HAMBURG
GERMANY

Tel: +49 (0)40 4326 1686
Fax: +49 (0)40 4326 1687

Email: info@hamburg.school-of-english.de
Website: http://hamburg.school-of-english.de

BERLIN SCHOOL OF ENGLISH
Teacher Training Centre

Checkpoint Arkarden
Charlottenstr 81
10969 BERLIN
GERMANY

Tel: +49 (0)30 229 0455
Fax: +49 (0)30 229 0471

Email: info@berlin.school-of-english.de
Website: htto://berlin.school-of-enalish.de

BERLIN SCHOOL OF ENGLISH

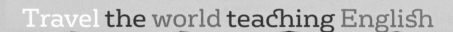

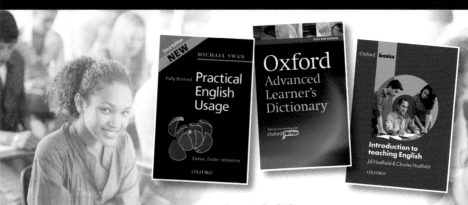

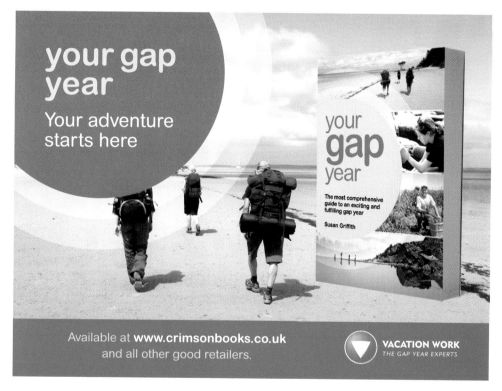

Work Your Way Around The World

Travel the world without getting into debt

15th edition

Work Your Way Around The World

"The globetrotter's bible"
The Independent

Susan Griffith

VOICE OF LANGUAGES

Ataşehir Bulvarl, 38 Ada Ata 3/3, Plaza Kat: 6, 57,
Ataşehir, Istanbul

© +90 216 455 08 16

🖳 www.volintr.com

NUMBER OF TEACHERS: 5.

PREFERENCE OF NATIONALITY: American, British, Australian, Canadian.

QUALIFICATIONS: University degree + CELTA /TEFL or equivalent certification + experience with adult learners.

CONDITIONS OF EMPLOYMENT: 12-month contracts. Mostly evening and Saturday classes, though there might be some morning classes if preferred.

SALARY: 25–50 Turkish lira (net), according to experience and level of preparation needed. Support given for obtaining work permits.

FACILITIES/SUPPORT: Help with accommodation may be negotiable.

RECRUITMENT: Networking, references, advertising. Face-to-face or Skype interviews.

 **AFRICA**

Contradictions abound in a continent as complex as Africa, and one of them pertains to the attitude to the English language. On the one hand the emergent nations of Africa want to distance themselves from their colonial past. On the other hand, they are eager to develop and participate in the world economy and so need to communicate in English. Yet, linguistic questions have been eclipsed at the time of writing by the humanitarian crisis looming in the Horn of Africa which may affect a staggering 10 million people. The ongoing conflict in the region is partly to blame, and is just one of many that beset the continent. Chaos in Congo and Somalia, the lunatic intransigence of Robert Mugabe in Zimbabwe, border tensions with the world's newest state South Sudan, fear of terrorism in the Maghreb, none of these add to Africa's allure. Scrolling through the Foreign & Commonwealth Office's travel warnings with repeated 'advice against all but essential travel' in many regions is enough to put off many. Of course there are some good news stories. The pro-democracy Arab Spring has given hope to many young Egyptians and Tunisians that their voices will be heard and their countries reformed. Social media played a key role in the success of the popular uprisings, and it is interesting to note that English is the language of choice in seven Arab countries, with French in five, and Arabic in three.

What makes much of Africa different from Latin America and Asia (vis-à-vis English teaching) is that English is the medium of instruction in state schools in many ex-colonies of Britain including Ghana, Nigeria, Kenya, Zambia, Zimbabwe and Malawi. As in the Indian subcontinent, the majority of English teachers in these countries are locals. But there is still some demand for native English speakers in the secondary schools of those countries. The only countries in which there is any significant scope for working in a private language school or institute are the Mediterranean countries of Morocco, Tunisia and Egypt.

The drive towards English extends to most parts of the continent. VSO supports ELT programmes in Rwanda and Ethiopia, among others. More than a decade ago, newly independent Namibia decided to make English its official language to replace the hated Afrikaans. A demand for hundreds of native English speakers, mainly at the advanced teacher-trainer level, was created overnight, which organisations such as the Department for International Development and VSO attempted to supply. Across southern Africa, the dominant language of business and commerce and the language of university textbooks is English, leaving Portuguese-speaking Mozambique out in the cold, which is why there are so many EFL teachers posted there by Skillshare Africa and VSO.

To balance the picture, it must be said that in some countries (such as Zambia, Nigeria, Sudan) the demand for English teachers has fallen off in favour of science, maths, technology and other languages. Even in ex-colonies of France (Morocco, Tunisia, Senegal, Mali, etc.) and of Portugal (Mozambique), English is a sought-after commodity. World traveller **Bradwell Jackson** discovered paid on-the-spot teaching opportunities in Mali, Mauritania and Senegal. The British Council has a few teaching centres in Africa, all apart from Egypt in francophone Africa, i.e. Cameroon, Morocco, Senegal and Tunisia.

PROSPECTS FOR TEACHERS

Few language schools exist in most African countries and even fewer can afford to employ expatriate teachers. The British Council maintains offices in most African countries and their assessment of the prospects for teachers tallies with that sent by the Information Manager of the British Council in Mbabane, Swaziland:

> *The English language is taught from a very early stage in Swaziland. As a result there are no institutes which specifically teach it. However, you may want to consider the university and colleges as institutions which teach English, even though it is at an advanced level.*

Because a high proportion of teaching opportunities in Africa is in secondary schools rather than private language institutes, a teaching certificate is often a prerequisite. Missionary societies have played a dominant role in Africa's modern history, so many teachers are recruited through religious organisations, asking for a Christian commitment even for secular jobs. Apart from work with aid or missionary agencies, there are quite a few opportunities for students and people in their gap year to teach in Africa. Students and other travellers have also stumbled upon chances to teach on an informal basis.

FINDING A JOB

Many organisations including a range of gap year agencies send people to Africa to teach English. These postings are normally regarded as 'voluntary' since if wages are paid at all they will be on a local scale though they often come with free housing. In some cases a substantial placement fee must be paid. See the chapter 'Finding a job' in Part I of this book for further details of the general agencies that send students such as **Sarah Johnson** from Cardiff to Zanzibar to teach English and geography at a rural secondary school. Once she started work Sarah discovered that:

> *The expectations which Zanzibari children have from school are worlds away from those of British school children. They expect to spend most of their lessons copying from the blackboard, so will at first be completely nonplussed if asked to think things through by themselves or to use their imagination. I found that the ongoing dilemma for me of teaching in Zanzibar was whether to teach at a low level which the majority of the class would be able to understand, or teach the syllabus to the top one or two students so that they would be able to attempt exam questions, but leaving the rest of the class behind. Teaching was a very interesting and eye-opening experience. I believe that both the Zanzibari teachers and I benefitted from a cultural exchange of ideas and ways of life.*

Networks like Couchsurfing (www.couchsurfing.com) have hosts registered all over Africa, who might be interested in exchanging hospitality for English lessons. **Bradwell Jackson** stayed with a couchsurfing host in Bamako, Mali, for two months:

> *He is a wealthy man who lives in a nice house, and I get all my meals, internet, my laundry, and a few other odds and ends done for free. I teach him two hours every day, which leaves me lots of time to explore Bamako and do whatever else I like.*

Just one word of caution about internet offers: if you see a job advertised that looks too good to be true, do not be tempted to investigate further. Although thankfully rare, scams aimed at 'greedy' foreigners can be sophisticated and seemingly plausible.

PLACEMENT ORGANISATIONS

Africa, Asia & Americas Venture, (www.aventure.co.uk). Offers students and recent graduates (aged 18–24) the chance to spend four–five months teaching a wide variety of subjects, especially English and sports in Africa (Uganda, Kenya, Tanzania, Malawi and South Africa). The 2011 participation fee is £3,505 for three–five months plus airfares.

Peace Corps, 1111 20th St NW, Washington DC 20526 (+1 800 424 8580 toll-free; www.peacecorps.gov). More than a third of Peace Corps volunteers are posted to Africa, many of whom teach on 27-month assignments in 27 African countries, ranging from Mali to Mozambique. Must be

US citizen, over 18 and in good health. All expenses, including airfare and health insurance, are covered.

Projects Abroad, (www.projects-abroad.co.uk.) Work placements in schools in Ethiopia, Ghana, Morocco, Senegal, South Africa and Tanzania.

Project Trust, (www.projecttrust.org.uk). Sends school leavers (aged 17–19) to teach (often other subjects as well as English) in schools across Africa including Namibia, Uganda, Botswana, Senegal and Swaziland. Participants must fund-raise to cover part of the cost of their 12-month placement, at present £5,100 (2012/3).

Skillshare International, (www.skillshare.org). Registered charity that recruits volunteer teachers to work for two years in southern Africa (Lesotho, Botswana, Mozambique, Swaziland, Namibia, Kenya, Tanzania, Uganda and South Africa). Pay approximately £500 per month plus flights, accommodation, insurance, etc. In 2011 Skillshare is looking to develop some shorter term opportunities lasting 3–12 months for suitable volunteers over 18.

Travellers (www.travellersworldwide.com). Teaching placements (English, Maths, Drama, etc.) and Sports Coaching placements in Ghana, Kenya, South Africa and Zambia.

VAE Teachers Kenya, (www.vaekenya.co.uk). three-month or preferably six-month gap year placements teaching in rural schools in the central highlands of Kenya. Inclusive fee of £2,235 or £3,155.

Village-to-Village, (http://v2vtanzania.wordpress.com/volunteers). Volunteers are sent to the Kilimanjaro region of Tanzania to assist on various projects including teaching English in primary schools and orphanages, teacher training as well as construction and sustainable agriculture projects. Typical 8-week placement requires a minimum donation of £1,800 (excluding international flights). The third and fourth months are charged at £300 each, and the following two months at £150 each. Accommodation is provided in volunteer centre or homestay.

Village Africa, (+44 239 2258 256; www.villageafrica.org.uk). Current initiatives are to provide volunteers to teach English for 3 or more months in Yamba village in the West Usambara Mountains of Tanzania, among other projects.

VSO, 317 Putney Bridge Road, London SW15 2PN (+44 20 8780 7500, www.vsointernational.org). Leading international development charity sends teachers to Ethiopia, Mozambique, Tanzania, Eritrea and Rwanda. Placements are usually for one or two years, and all costs and accommodation are covered.

WorldTeach, Cambridge, Massachusetts 02138, USA (+1 859 259 6646; www.worldteach.org). Nonprofit organisation that recruits volunteers to teach English in Namibia, Tanzania and South Africa, among other countries around the world.

ON THE SPOT

The best chances of picking up language teaching work on the spot are in North Africa, in Egypt, Morocco or Tunisia (treated separately below). Language schools are thriving in South Africa staffed in large measure by English-speaking South Africans but also by foreigners. Tourists can enter South Africa on a tourist visa for three months, renewable for a further three (for a fee) at an office of the Department of Home Affairs.

If teachers (British as well as American) are prepared to travel to an African capital for an interview with one of the US State Department-sponsored English teaching centres in Africa (often attached to American embassies), they may be given some freelance opportunities. Virtually all hiring of teachers in these government-run language programmes takes place locally, so speculative applications from overseas are seldom welcome. This is how one American got her foot in the door and went on to become the director:

Work in an American Cultural Center is a great way to start off. I myself did it five years ago and am now running a programme. It allows a person to work in Africa but also provides up-to-date material which teachers in the national programmes are often forced to go without. Classes are small and the hours are not too heavy but can usually be increased depending on the capabilities of the teacher. We also do outside programmes in specialised institutions and thus give teachers experience in ESP (hotels, oil companies, Ministries). People with degrees in EFL are very much in demand.

At the opposite end of the spectrum, grass roots voluntary organisations may have teaching positions. For example Ikando (www.ikando.org) is a volunteer and intern recruitment agency based in Accra which deals with education positions lasting up to eight weeks, as well as many others. Volunteers stay in the Ikando house in the centre of Accra and cover their living expenses (£92 per week after their initial fortnight at £531).

Till Bruckner is a veteran world traveller who has a decided preference for fixing up teaching and voluntary placements independently:

My advice to anyone who wants to volunteer in Africa (or anywhere else) is to go first and volunteer second. That way you can travel until you've found a place you genuinely like and where you think you might be able to make a difference. You can also check out the work and accommodation for yourself before you settle down. If you're willing to work for free, you don't need a nanny to tell you where to go. Just go.

Opportunities crop up in very obscure corners of the continent. For example EU nationals are entitled to work in Réunion, a département of France between Madagascar and Mauritius. Apparently there is a market for freelance teachers; consider advertising in the papers *Quotidien* and *SIR*.

PROBLEMS AND REWARDS

If teachers in Finland and Chile suffer from culture shock, teachers in rural Africa often find themselves struggling to cope at all. Whether it is the hassle experienced by women teachers in Muslim North Africa or the loneliness of life in a rural West African village, problems proliferate. Anyone who has fixed up a contract should try to gather as much up-to-date information as possible before departure, preferably by attending some kind of orientation programme or briefing. Otherwise local customs can come as a shock. On a more basic level, you will need advice on how to cope with climatic extremes. Even Cairo can be unbearably hot in the summer (and surprisingly rainy and chilly in January/February).

One unexpected problem is being accorded too much respect, as **Mary Hall** describes:

A white person is considered to be the be-all and end-all of everyone's problems for whatever reason. It's quite difficult to live with this image. Stare and stare again, never a moment to yourself. I'd like to say the novelty wore off but it never did. Obviously adaptability has to be one of the main qualities. We had no running water, intermittent electricity and a lack of such niceties as cheese and chocolate.

A certain amount of deprivation is almost inevitable; for example teachers, especially volunteers, can seldom afford to shop in the pricey expatriate stores and so will have to be content with the local diet, typically a staple cereal such as millet usually made into a kind of stodgy porridge, plus some cooked greens, tinned fish or meat and fruit. The cost of living in some African cities such as Libreville and Douala is in fact very high, and a teaching wage does not normally permit a luxurious lifestyle. **Peter Kent** taught in Tanzania and kept a journal throughout his stay:

Bit worried about the food situation, only seems to be tomatoes, onions and potatoes at the market so a pretty boring diet. Sijaona is, if I understand her right, going to show us where you can buy more exotic veg... Taught standard one (i.e. year 1) today for the first time since they started this term. There are 105 kids, 5 or 6 to a bench which fits 3 normally. Quite a sight really, 105 bright-eyed kids staring expectantly at you. Mrs Msigwa, their teacher, seems really nice, keen and capable. We may get somewhere between us. You get the impression that if you stuck with them for years to come they'd be speaking English.

But of course volunteer teachers can't stick around that long and after less than a year it was time for Peter Kent to bid farewell to his school amidst present-giving, choir singing and emotional speeches.

Health is obviously a major concern to anyone headed for Africa. The fear of HIV-contaminated blood or needles in much of central Africa prompts many teachers to outfit themselves with a complete expat medical kit before leaving home (see Introduction). Malaria is rife and there is an alarming amount of mosquito resistance to the most common prophylactics, so this too must be sorted out with a tropical diseases expert before departure.

The visa situation differs from country to country of course but is often a headache. Whereas in Cameroon it is not really necessary to obtain a work permit, in Ethiopia it is much more problematic.

If all that Africa could offer was a contest with malaria and a diet of porridge, no one would consider teaching there. But anyone who has seen movies such as *Out of Africa, Gorillas in the Mist* or *The English Patient* can imagine how the continent holds people in thrall. A chance to see the African bush, to climb the famous peaks of Kilimanjaro or Kenya, to frequent the colourful markets, these are the pleasures of Africa which so many people who have worked there find addictive.

TEFL training can lead to unexpected opportunities in Africa. After graduating from York University **Miranda Crowhurst** was pleased to be accepted for one of the 12 places on a CELTA course in her home town of Cambridge with the Bell School, and really enjoyed the course. While searching for jobs abroad she came across an intriguing opening in Tanzania, to teach the young children of two expat families, and secured the seven-month position. She set off from England in April 2012 and sent back descriptions of her life and adventures, divided between a prospering avocado farm and the nearby town of Mbeya, in a postcard perfect Africa:

> *The farm is just in front of Rungwe volcano and right up against the jungle – you would not believe how beautiful it is looking out over the mountains from my cottage. At dawn when we set off for town, the sun rises spectacularly, lighting up trucks piled with farm labourers, forested mountains silhouetted against the pink sky, and sweeps of mist lying lazily over the villages. I also love walking round town – lots of people say hello in Swahili, and hi, and good afternoon. I'm the only white person I ever see and it makes me feel a little bit like a lightbulb, but although people definitely notice me, no one hassles me, is pushy or unfriendly.*
>
> *Our first school outing with the five children is for an English assignment, and we walk up the hill with two false starts, one so Holly can run back to go to the toilet, and the other so Will can run back to tell Josie that Holly just broke the toilet. There's a beautiful old tree up towards the volcano, which the children draw and describe. The sun's out, and the scene makes me feel like a real English governess – except every so often, villagers with machetes stumble upon us looking a bit nervous of the dogs. On the way back the children play word games, and Hugh asks Will what a bachelor is. 'It's a spoon for cooking with' says Will.*

INTERNATIONAL HOUSE CAPE TOWN

Looking for a trusted institution to help you improve your English?

International House Cape Town (www.ihcapetown.com) is part of the renowned International House World Organisation (www.ihworld.com),a network of over 150 schools throughout the world committed to the highest quality of language learning and teacher training.

International House Cape Town offers a full range of English courses to suit your specific requirements, in addition to a variety of English Plus courses which include Study & Work, Study & Volunteer and university placement assistance to name a few. As a University of Cambridge ESOL authorised CELTA teacher training centre, one can expect highly qualified and experienced teachers using the latest technology to make your English lessons come alive.

Located in the heart of trendy Sea Point, IH Cape Town is ideally located being only five minutes from the city centre, V&A waterfront and the famous beaches of Clifton and Camps Bay. A wide range of accommodation options are available, all within walking distance to the school. These options include basic economy, superior self-catering apartments, host families, guesthouses and a range of hotels to suit your personal requirements.

An active social programme and a dedicated travel desk ensures that students are easily able to explore all of the amazing activities and tourist opportunities that Cape Town and the surrounding areas have to offer.

The IH Cape Town mission statement, summarized in the *IH Cape Town Way*, highlights the fact that all staff are personally involved in ensuring the well-being of students:

To have the spirit to succeed and the passion to work harder to be the best.

To be a respected company in terms of our professionalism, innovation, honesty, trust and integrity.

To take care in what we do and how we do it, always being fair and treating everybody with respect.

Our promise is that we will strive, through our personal involvement and commitment, to provide teachers and students an enjoyable, fulfilling learning experience that exceeds expectations.

For more information about International House Cape Town and the courses that we offer please visit www.ihcapetown.com or contact us on email: info@ihcapetown.com, tel: +27 21 4330546, fax +27 86 6286068.

EGYPT

The aftermath of the Arab Spring in 2011 has not yet brought about the radical improvements Egyptians were demonstrating to achieve, and a certain amount of cynicism and discontent have crept back in. Despite past attacks on tourists by Islamic fundamentalists, there is anything but hostility to the English language in Egypt. Of Egyptians who want to learn English, a large percentage is from the business community, though there is also a demand among university students and school children. Many young Egyptians who aspire to work in their country's computing or tourist industry want to learn English. Students at computer training schools or at tourism training centres like the one in Luxor might be looking for some private tuition from a native speaker.

Check the online *Yellow Pages* in English at www.egyptyellowpages.com.eg; a search for 'Language Schools & Instruction' reveals nearly 400. At one end of the spectrum there are the two British Council

Teaching Centres in Cairo (Agouza and Heliopolis) and the International Language Institute in Cairo affiliated to International House (www.arabicegypt.com). At the other there are plenty of dubious establishments. Whereas you will need a professional profile for the former, back street schools will be less fussy. The British Council in Cairo has a list of English medium schools in Cairo plus a short list of TEFL establishments, several of which are in the suburb of Dokki. The Council hires new teachers itself because of growth in the numbers signing up for General English and Corporate courses.

The British Council at 192 El Nil Street, Agouza, Cairo is probably the first place to check for work. The minimum requirements are native English speaker status, UK passport, CELTA or equivalent and two years' post-qualification teaching experience. You can pick up an application form from the British Council reception or by email at teacherapplications@britishcouncil.org.eg. You will be invited for an interview and demonstration lesson (having sat in on another class beforehand). If they think you are suitable they'll take you on, which is more likely during the summer when the regular teachers tend to go away to escape the heat. During exam time there is also a need for paid invigilators. The British Council (as always) has a great library and is a good place to teach. There is another British Council in Heliopolis which is quite a way from the centre of town and therefore has its own social world. The El-Alsson International School (PO Box 13, Embaba, 12411 Cairo; +20 202 3388 8510; info@alsson.com; www.alsson.com) out near the Pyramids employs a number of expat teachers.

Dan Boothby has spent time in Cairo and found it almost alarmingly easy to find work:

> *I taught one-to-one lessons to several people and got about 5 hours a week work and charged £10 an hour. Frankly this was much more than I was worth but if you charge less than the market rate then it is felt that you are an amateur. I taught an isolated and lonely five-year-old, son of the Georgian Consul, where I was more a babysitter than a tutor. I felt so guilty about the fee I was charging that I spent an hour trying to get him to learn something. I didn't feel so guilty charging to tutor the Georgian Ambassador since he probably passed the bill onto his government.*
>
> *I got a lot of students through friends that I made who were teaching at the international schools. The kids at these schools are often in need of extra tuition towards exam times when their parents realise that they've been mucking about all year and are close to failing. The problem is that the kids tend to be very uninterested and so it is difficult to make them concentrate. But I enjoyed one-to-ones. One could build up a large group of students and earn a decent wage but equally teach less hours and have more time – one of the reasons for getting out of England.*

Cairo seems to be a city where work seeks out the casual teacher rather than the other way round. Taxi drivers and hotel staff may ask you, unprompted, if you are available to teach. Most of these are genuine offers but it is best (especially for women) to be cautious. Most job-seekers find that potential bosses are not as interested in their educational background and experience as in how much confidence they can project. It is not unknown for an interview to take place over a game of chess and plenty of glasses of tea so that your general demeanour can be assessed. Jobs seem to be available year-round, so there is no right or wrong time to arrive.

Language schools are not all located in central Cairo but also in the leafy prosperous residential areas such as Heliopolis, Maadi or Zamalek. For example the Al Bashaer Language School is behind the bakery in District 9, New Maadi. Teachers must have A levels and three years' teaching experience and are paid a monthly base salary of 1,000 Egyptian pounds in addition to free accommodation and a food allowance. The school's mission is to 'apply western methods of teaching with Islamic ideas and etiquette'.

Residential areas are also the best areas to look for private clients as **Ian McArthur** found:

> *In Cairo I sought to work as a private English tutor. I made a small poster, written in English and Arabic, with the help of my hotel owner. I drew the framework of a Union Jack at the top, got 100 photocopies and then meticulously coloured in the flags. The investment cost me £3. I put the posters up around Cairo, concentrating on affluent residential and business districts. I ended up teaching several Egyptian businessmen, who were difficult to teach since they hated being told what to do.*

More recently an American traveller about to start law school posted the following on Lonely Planet's Thorn Tree forum:

Back in December I posted a message asking people if they thought it was possible to get short term jobs abroad or if it was a good idea to possibly make tutoring flyers to put up around town. Both were ideas to supplement the money I already had saved and to have some new adventures/meet locals while traveling. I got a ton of negative responses telling me those ideas wouldn't work, etc. etc. Just wanted to post back on here six months later that it IS possible and my friend and I just did it. We got teaching jobs in Egypt that paid fairly well, without having work permits, without having TEFL, and the classes were for business professionals and thus were short terms (five weeks). Also, we put up tutoring flyers all over Cairo and made a decent amount of money doing private tutoring.

The American University, centrally located at the eastern end of the now famous Tahrir Square, is a good place to find work contacts though teaching for the AUC itself is difficult; only five candidates a month are granted an interview so they can afford to be highly selective. Also try the noticeboards at the Community Services Association (CSA No. 4, Road 21, Maadi, Cairo; +20 358 5284) where a range of adult education courses for expats is offered. In fact beginners and conversational English are taught on the premises. If you do decide to advertise your services as a freelance tutor, it might be a good idea to rent a post office box from a business centre (e.g. the IBA Center in Garden City).

According to **Dan Boothby**, the best places to meet other expats and find out about work opportunities are Deals Bar, restaurants in Zamalek, café-bars near the American University and the BCA (British Community Association) in Mohandiseen where you can only go as the guest of a member.

STUDENTS

One former teacher describes his Egyptian pupils at a language institute in the northwest suburb of Sahafeyeen as 'rowdy and sometimes a little over-enthusiastic'. Having just obtained a Cambridge Certificate in London, he went to visit some friends in Cairo and was immediately offered a three-month summer contract where they were desperate for a teacher. He had to adapt his lessons to please both the ebullient Egyptian youths and a group of shy and industrious Somalis and describes his predicament with such a mixed class:

Different religions, different ways of thinking and (as I learnt in my first week at the school) different modes of dress must all be taken into consideration. One of the problems that English students in this area have difficulty with is hearing the difference between B and P. The exercise for this is to hold a piece of paper in front of the mouth and repeat the letters B and P. Since more air is exhaled during the sounding of the letter P than with B, the paper should fly up when P is said, and move only a little with B. The first time I made the students do this we went round the class, first Hamid the engineer from Alexandria, then Mona who was trying to get a job at the reception in the Hilton and then we came to Magda from Mogadishu (the capital of Somalia). All the Egyptians started to laugh – her whole face apart from her eyes was covered with a yashmak. I decided that this should not impede the exercise so if the yashmak moved it was a P, and not a B!

Living expenses are cheap in Egypt and taxes low (5%–7%). The CELTA course offered by the British Council in Cairo used to be one of the cheapest in the world; however, with the weak pound, the current fee of E£11,000 works out at an expensive £1,130.

Most teachers enter Egypt on a tourist visa and then ask their school to help them extend it. The tourist visa is valid for a maximum of three months. However, a business visa is issued for teachers to enter Egypt. This is valid for six months and schools will help to extend it. Work permits must be applied for from the Ministry of the Interior in Egypt, usually by your employer. UK citizens can find up-to-date visa information at www.egyptianconsulate.co.uk.

LIST OF EMPLOYERS

AMIDEAST EGYPT

Cairo Office: 23 Mossadak Street, Dokki-Giza, 12311 Cairo

☎ +20 2 19263; 2 333 20457

✆ egypt@amideast.org or akaram@amideast.org

💻 www.amideast.org

Alexandria Office: 3 El Pharana Street, Alexandria

✆ alexandria@amideast.org

💻 www.amideast.org

NUMBER OF TEACHERS: 15–22.

PREFERENCE OF NATIONALITY: North American, but all native English speakers are welcome to apply.

QUALIFICATIONS: Minimum CELTA or TESOL certification, and preferably 2 years of teaching adults.

CONDITIONS OF EMPLOYMENT: Local term-to-term hire agreements according to student numbers. 8–15 hours per week, 9 5-week sessions per year. Students are working adults and university students.

SALARY: US$5.50–$8 an hour (paid in local currency). Contracted teachers earn US$13, less 17.65% for tax and contributions.

FACILITIES/SUPPORT: Good teachers' resources, internet access, friendly working environment. Operates out of three historic mansions on the Mediterranean. No financial assistance with accommodation given, but temporary housing can be arranged at no cost. No assistance given with work permits.

RECRUITMENT: Pre-interview questions sent to applicants via email, and then a classroom demonstration.

CONTACT: Ahmed Karam, English Language Programmes Senior Coordinator.

SUDAN

According to the constitution of the Republic of Sudan drawn up in 2005, the two official languages are Arabic and English. After many years of diplomacy, South Sudan achieved national autonomy in July 2011 and its official language is only English, though most people speak Arabic or dialects of Arabic.

The long-established NGO, the Sudan Volunteer Programme, based in London and Khartoum (see entry), sends volunteers to help young Sudanese improve their English through contact with British volunteers. According to **Don Sloan**, writing in a recent *Newsletter*, English assignments include running discussion groups, providing support for teachers at universities, training for public servants, teacher-training course design, and developing course materials for English for legal purposes. Other volunteers have run General English courses and helped with English clubs, especially for pre-sessional and inter-sessional groups of university students. Some volunteers have recently produced and participated in radio programmes for learners of English and done editorial work for an English language newspaper, so there is plenty of scope for pursuing individual talents and interests.

This is all good news for a country in which the current government has shown little inclination to support the teaching of English as a second language and has instead promoted the Arabisation of the country's educational system. As a result, the general standard of English has sharply declined. Some are worried about their personal security based on media coverage and FCO travel warnings. The director of the Sudan Volunteer Programme describes what he sees as the FCO bias:

> We continue to be dogged by the negative and, I believe, misleadingly indiscriminate travel advice issued by the FCO which puts off potential volunteers, or more particularly their families. It stems it seems to me from the alarming experiences of embassy staff which induces them to put up ever higher fences to guard their premises and of course this siege mentality brings about an ever greater ignorance of the actual conditions. There was one threat to embassy security about 3 years ago and one murder of an American official in Khartoum in January 2008. There were otherwise no attacks in the recent years on foreigners in Khartoum or smaller northern towns. I do not belittle these outrages but they cannot be described as 'indiscriminate' as used in the FCO warning.

Travel to most parts of Sudan is straightforward, though it was not known what the land border formalities would be like with South Sudan. The development of the oil industry in South Sudan has been responsible for many changes such as new roads, more cars, more shops, and more building projects.

MARK TANNER

Mark Tanner, a New Zealand adventurer, found out about the Sudan Volunteer Programme by searching the web and was accepted onto the scheme.

While some volunteers were required to use the syllabus as a guide, I had a free rein over what I taught and how. This prompted me to ask the students to suggest topics that were of interest to them and allowed me freedom to encourage discussion about parts of the Sudanese culture I was interested in. The main objective was to provide the students with a native English speaker and get them used to conversation. We were encouraged to do less formal sessions called the English Club. For example we themed the cooking class as our university was all-female and cooking was something they considered important. Some classes stand out in my memory such as the one where we tried to teach the students to juggle. The classrooms could be quite hot and were equipped with blackboard and chalk, although we used teaching aids based on our own initiative.

The lodgings provided were basic, but by Sudanese standards good. The stipend was enough to subsist in Sudan, living like the Sudanese. As lovely as the Sudanese are, things are not as organised in the country as we would expect in the west. Yet it would be difficult to find more hospitable people than the Sudanese and there is never a shortage of offers for dinner or to visit a village, which provided a fantastic opportunity to experience the culture in a way many other NGO workers never saw.

There are many interesting things to see in Khartoum such as Nuba Wrestling, fish markets, Dervish dancing and museums. SVP has a deal with the Blue Nile Sailing Club which allows students to try their luck at sailing on the Nile. Many of the volunteers did other voluntary work for NGOs. I helped an NGO with marketing and to develop a website. My principal motivation for being in the Sudan was to paddle through Sudan on the Nile, and I spent a lot of my spare time trying to source permits for this.

One of the highlights for me was seeing the English of the students improve and the relationships develop from that. Teachers are greatly respected in the Sudan so volunteers are revered and treated with respect.

Not everyone is so positive about being placed by an agency, especially if their motives are strictly philanthropic. The placement that was fixed up for **Till Bruckner** in Sudan didn't live up to his expectations:

> They'd told me at my interview in London that I'd be teaching international politics but when I arrived the local branch didn't know what I'd come for and wanted me to teach conversational English at a university in Khartoum. I figured that if I was going to teach English to kids from well-off families while living in a city of outstanding natural ugliness, I might as well go elsewhere and get paid for it. There'd be no problem finding work as an English teacher in Sudan. There's great demand and little supply as nobody (including most Sudanese) wants to live there. In a country with poverty on that scale, there's more useful things you can do with £500 than pay for a scheme to tutor English. If you want fun, go elsewhere; if you want to help, put the £500 in an Oxfam charity box.

However, that is just one point of view and many people have felt that their contribution as a volunteerteacher has not been futile, either from the point of view of broadening their own horizons or helping others.

LIST OF EMPLOYERS

ALENEA RECRUITING

29–30 Windmill Street, London W1T 2JL, UK

📞 +44 020 7462 6481

📧 recruiting@alenea.com

💻 www.alenearecruiting.com.

Recruiting for a training institute in Khartoum.

QUALIFICATIONS: Must have CELTA/Trinity plus experience teaching young learners.

CONDITIONS OF EMPLOYMENT: 9 or 12-month contracts. Hours in primary schools are from 8am to 2pm and from 9am to 9pm in EFL institutes.

SALARY: $1,300 net per month.

FACILITIES/SUPPORT: Flights, accommodation, visas and in-country travel are all provided.

RECRUITMENT: Applications accepted all year round.

SUDAN VOLUNTEER PROGRAMME

34 Estelle Road, London NW3 2JY, UK

📞 +44 7910 940819

📧 david@svp-uk.com

💻 www.svp-uk.com

UK registered charity which promotes English teaching among university students and other adults.

NUMBER OF TEACHERS: 10–20 at any time in and around Khartoum including Omdurman.

PREFERENCE OF NATIONALITY: None but should be native speakers of English and if not, they should be qualified English language teachers.

QUALIFICATIONS: TEFL certificate, experience of travelling in developing countries and some knowledge of Arabic are helpful but not obligatory. Volunteers must be in good health and have some university education.

CONDITIONS OF EMPLOYMENT: Preferred minimum 8 months to tie in with university semesters: October–January or January–May.

SALARY: SVP pays subsistence, accommodation and insurance beyond the initial 3 months. Volunteers must raise the cost of the airfare to Sudan (currently £485) plus £65 (towards the cost of the first 3 months' insurance).

FACILITIES/SUPPORT: Accommodation with self-catering facilities is arranged, usually at the university where you are teaching.

RECRUITMENT: Applications accepted year round. Two referees are also required. Prior to departure, medical check-up required plus selection interviews, orientation and briefings take place. Volunteers are required to write a report of their experiences and to advise new volunteers.

CONTACT: David Wolton.

KENYA

Kenya is another country with a chronic shortage of school teachers. Since 2003 when the government kept its promise to abolish school fees for primary schools, there has been a surge in student numbers. The worst shortages are in Western Province. English is the language of instruction in many Kenyan primary schools, so foreign teachers not knowing Swahili need not be an insuperable barrier. The Kenyan Ministry of Education restricts jobs in the state sector to those who have a university degree, teaching certification and at least one year of professional teaching experience. The few private language institutes that there are in Nairobi are not subject to this restriction. The British Council in Nairobi at Upperhill Road (+254 20 283 6000; information@britishcouncil.or.ke) may be able to offer advice. One institute which carries information about year-round job openings on its website is The Language Center (PO Box 40661, Nairobi 00100; www.language-cntr.com); it hires native speakers with a degree and a recognised TEFL qualification.

According to the Kenyan High Commission in London (45 Portland Place, London W1B 1AS; +44 20 7636 2371), all non-Kenyan citizens who wish to work must be in possession of a work permit issued by the Principal Immigration Officer, Department of Immigration, PO Box 30191, Nairobi, before they can take up paid or unpaid work. The school should apply for work permits for the teachers even before they enter Kenya. Proof of professional qualifications is required. However, it is not certain that immigration regulations would be strictly enforced in the case of native English speakers looking for teaching work on the spot. Certainly in the past it was possible to fix up a teaching job by asking in the villages, preferably before terms begin in September, January and April. Be prepared to produce your CV and any diplomas and references on headed paper.

Also ascertain before accepting a post whether or not the school can afford to pay a salary, especially if it is a Harrambee school, i.e. non-government, self-help schools in rural areas. A cement or mud hut with a thatched or tin roof will usually be provided for the teacher's accommodation plus a local salary which would be just enough to live on provided you don't want to buy too much peanut butter or cornflakes in the city. Living conditions will be primitive, with no running water or electricity in the majority of cases. The Kenyan version of maize porridge is called *Ugali*. In Daisy Waugh's book *A Small Town in Africa* (no longer in print) she describes how when she arrived at the village of Isiolo (a few miles from Nairobi) where she had arranged to teach, she was told that they didn't need any teachers and there were no pupils. She patiently waited and five weeks into term, her class arrived.

People who choose to teach in Kenya do it for love not money. In the words of **Ermon O. Kamara**, PhD, former Director of the American Universities Preparation Institute in Nairobi:

> *Candidates must view being in Kenya as a holiday with pay. The cost of living and corresponding local salaries sound quite low to foreigners. Consequently they must think of the opportunities to enjoy Kenya's beaches, mountains and game parks as well as experiencing a new and interesting culture. During weekends and holidays, one can travel the breadth of Kenya. Also the proximity to other countries in East and Southern Africa permits a traveller to see a good deal of our continent.*

AVIF UK, administered from North Yorkshire (+44 777 171 2012; volunteer@avif.org.uk) sends volunteers to help at children's summer schools in Kenya, including with English lessons. Volunteers pay only the price of the airfare plus subsistence costs to spend the month of August in Kenya. At the end of each programme, AVIF can advise volunteers on how to join a safari from a base camp in Oropile, Maasai Mara or to climb Kilimanjaro with an experienced guide.

LIST OF EMPLOYERS

THE LANGUAGE CENTER LTD

P.O Box 40661, 00100 Nairobi

✆ +254 20 2641616/3870610/3870612/3869531

🖱 tlc@language-cntr.com

🖥 www.language-cntr.com

NUMBER OF TEACHERS: Approximately 6.

PREFERENCE OF NATIONALITY: British, American.

QUALIFICATIONS: Minimum first degree plus CELTA, TEFL or any other recognised teaching qualification.

CONDITIONS OF EMPLOYMENT: Standard length of contract is 2 years. Normal working hours 8.30am to 4pm.

SALARY: Around $8.50–$11 per hour for the first year plus medical insurance and gratuity. PAYE tax deductions of 20%–30% of salary.

FACILITIES/SUPPORT: Employer will handle the application process for work permits and pay half of the total expenses.

RECRUITMENT: Usually via internet or word of mouth. Interviews are essential and are conducted locally.

CONTACT: Mrs. Agnes W. Ngugi, Managing Director.

MOROCCO

Although Morocco is a Francophone country, English is a requirement for entrance to university or high-ranking jobs, and there is increasing demand from the business communities of the main cities. Like so many African countries, Morocco has sought to improve the standards of education for its nationals so that almost all teaching jobs in schools and universities are now filled by Moroccans. But outside the state system there is a continuing demand for native English speakers.

The Moroccan Ministry of Labour stipulates that the maximum number of foreign staff in any organisation cannot exceed 50%. It also insists that all foreign teachers have at least a university degree before they can be eligible for a work permit. Work permits are obtained after arrival by applying for authorisation from the Ministère de l'Emploi, Quartier des Ministères, Rabat. You will need copies of your diplomas, birth certificate and so on. Although a knowledge of French is not a formal requirement, it is a great asset for anyone planning to spend time in Morocco.

A number of commercial language schools employ native English speakers. The hourly rate of pay at most schools is less than £10 (equivalent in dirhams). The American Language Centers are located in the main cities of Morocco; see the website www.aca.org.ma for details. They are private institutes but are affiliated to and partially funded by the US State Department. Two are included in the list of employers. The Casablanca branch (http://casablanca.aca.org.ma/vacancies.asp) recruits native English speaker teachers from a number of courses including academic institutes in the USA such as the University of North Texas, which offers a graduate certificate in TESOL.

The workcamps movement is active in Morocco and some of these summer volunteer projects take place on English language camps for Moroccan adolescents, for example through Chantiers Sociaux Marocains (csm_incom@yahoo.fr).

LIST OF EMPLOYERS

AMERICAN LANGUAGE CENTER

1 Place de la Fraternité, Casablanca 20000
- +212 522 277765
- casa_dir@aca.org.ma
- www.aca.org.ma or http://casablanca.aca.org.ma

NUMBER OF TEACHERS: 12–15 full-time teachers (mostly native speakers) plus about 40 part-time Moroccan teachers.

PREFERENCE OF NATIONALITY: North American, but British teachers are also welcome to apply.

QUALIFICATIONS: Bachelor's degree, TEFL Certification (CELTA preferred) and a minimum of 1 year EFL overseas teaching experience.

CONDITIONS OF EMPLOYMENT: A standard contract is for 12 months from 1 October to 30 September. 18 contact hours a week are standard for the Adult Program. However, some teachers have additional classes including young learners.

SALARY: Based on qualifications and experience. For example a bachelor's degree, certification and 3 years of TEFL experience would expect the equivalent of $22 per hour. There is also a tax-free housing allowance of up to 3,000 Dhs per month plus a 10,000 Dhs settling in allowance (approx $850) which is also tax free. Taxes on a monthly salary of 12,120 Dhs are approximately 1,758 Dhs. Complete medical insurance (80% reimbursable) is provided for all full-time teachers. A ticket to the teacher's residence in the USA (for North Americans) or UK (for British teachers) is provided if a teacher successfully completes 1 year at the Center. There is also an end of contract bonus equal to one month's pay.

RECRUITMENT: Send CVs with photo, scanned copies of first page of passport and original diplomas and 2 letters of recommendation. All paperwork necessary for teachers to obtain work permits is done by administration staff. New teachers have to bring a copy of their birth certificate and their original University diplomas and certificates.

CONTACT: David Neuses (casa_dir@aca.org.ma).

AMERICAN LANGUAGE CENTER, RABAT

4 Zankat Tanja, Rabat 10000
- +212 37 767103
- dir@alcrabat.org

NUMBER OF TEACHERS: 20 full-time and 25 part-time teachers.

PREFERENCE OF NATIONALITY: Applicants should be from a country where English is the first language.

QUALIFICATIONS: BA in Education, TESOL, or related field; knowledge of French or Arabic highly desirable. TEFL certification required.

CONDITIONS OF EMPLOYMENT: 1-year renewable contracts. 20–25 hours per week full time. Hours of work generally between 2pm and 9pm weekdays (Tuesday to Friday) and 9am and 5pm on Saturdays. Pupils aged from 7, mostly aged 14–35.

SALARY: Approximately $1,500 per month (gross) for October to July school year. Possibility of paid overtime. Paid sick leave and medical insurance provided as well as vacation allowance and round-trip airfare upon completing 2 years.

FACILITIES/SUPPORT: Free housing/homestay provided for 2 weeks while permanent accommodation is sought. Pre- and in-service training fully supported. Free access to high-speed internet, free language classes (French and Arabic) and other benefits.

RECRUITMENT: Through TESOL convention and some local hiring. Video conference interviews are also used.

CONTACT: Michael McMillan, Director.

AMIDEAST

35 Rue Oukaimeden, Agdal, Rabat

C +212 37 67 50 75/81/82

Also: 3 Boulevard Al Massira Al Khadra, Maarif, Casablanca

C +212 5 22 25 93 93

knorris@amideast.org

www.amideast.org/morocco

NUMBER OF TEACHERS: Approximately 35.

PREFERENCE OF NATIONALITY: Must be native English speakers.

QUALIFICATIONS: TEFL qualification.

CONDITIONS OF EMPLOYMENT: 1-year contracts, preferably with a view to extending. To work around 70–100 hours per month.

FACILITIES/SUPPORT: Settling-in allowance. Assistance with apartment search and work visas, which must be acquired within 3 months of arrival.

RECRUITMENT: CV and cover letter to knorris@amideast.org. Telephone interview required.

CONTACT: Kenn Norris, Director of Studies for Morocco.

BUSINESS AND PROFESSIONAL ENGLISH CENTRE (BPEC)

74, Rue Jean Jaurès, Casablanca 20060

C +212 522 47 02 79 / 522 47 01 76

BPEC Academy, Rabat: Porte Verde, Imm N, 1 er etage, Mahaj Ryad, Hay Ryad, Rabat

C +212 537 57 07 57 / 537 57 07 77

info-rabat@bpec-english.com

www.bpec-english.com

NUMBER OF TEACHERS: 7 for both centres.

PREFERENCE OF NATIONALITY: British, American, Canadian.

QUALIFICATIONS: Bachelor's or master's degree plus CELTA and minimum of 3 years' experience in teaching adults and young learners.

CONDITIONS OF EMPLOYMENT: 9-month renewable contract, starting October. Limited openings in January. Split shifts spread over the day between 8am and 9pm (no more then 4.5 hours teaching per day). 22 contact hours in 5.5 days per week.

SALARY: 11,500 dirhams per month net.

FACILITIES/SUPPORT: Assistance given with finding housing and 2,500 dirham housing allowance. Return air fare and luggage allowance. Work permits are organised by the centre.

RECRUITMENT: Usually via www.tefl.com. Interviews are essential and can be carried out over the phone.

CONTACT: Mr Riyad Mugawer, Managing Director; Ms Kaoutar Lasmak (Centre Manager, BPEC Rabat) and Ms Leena Mugawer (Centre Manager, BPEC Casablanca).

TUNISIA

Like its neighbour in the Maghreb, Tunisia is turning away from the language of its former colonial master and embracing the dominant language of prosperous and democratic Europe. Although the young generation speaks fluent French because they have been taught it in school, many teenagers prefer English. Both Amideast (see entry) and the British Council Tunis Teaching Centre employ qualified native English speaker teachers. The latter runs a summer school in June and July with extra vacancies; teachers earn £1,800 for the whole period plus accommodation and flights.

The Bourguiba Institute in Tunis (47 Av. de la Liberté, 1002 Tunis; +216 71 832923; lblv@lblv.rnu.tn; www.iblv.rnu.tn) hires high-level teachers.

ROGER MUSKER

Roger Musker found that people would be interested in paying you for lessons, even though you plan to be in the country for a relatively short time. He was in Tunisia for one winter.

I decided to take a month off work as a kind of sabbatical and, if well planned, at no cost. I found all young people in Tunisia keen to practise and speak English whenever possible. I had one good contact in Sousse, who worked for the Tunisian Tourist Agency. I wrote to him from England and he replied that he could line up students on my arrival, which included himself and his 10-year-old daughter (who turned out to be my best student). At their house I was plied with extremely sweet tea and sticky cakes, which you are obliged to eat. Altogether I had eight keen fee-paying students including a blind telephone operator, a teacher of English on a revision course and students from the Bourguiba Institute at Tunis University. For the latter it was necessary to get permission from the Ministry of Education via the headmaster.

Every day I tutored 8–10am and 5–7pm. The hourly rate was about £8, allowing me to cover basic costs while having a working holiday. Even without the contact and knowing Arabic, work is there for the asking. It just takes initiative. Go to any official institute, the tourism or municipal offices, demonstrate your availability and enthusiasm, give them your contact number and await replies.

LIST OF EMPLOYERS

AMIDEAST TUNISIA
22 Rue Al Amine Al Abassi, B.P. 351, Cité Jardina 1002, Tunis

☎ +216 71 790 559/563, 841 488 or 842 523

✉ tunisia@amideast.org

🖥 www.amideast.org/tunisia

NUMBER OF TEACHERS: 25 full or part-time independent contract TEFL/TESL teachers. Also for Sousse.

PREFERENCE OF NATIONALITY: Native speakers of English.

QUALIFICATIONS: Ideally a degree and accredited 120-hour international certificate in TEFL/TESL. 1 year successful experience of teaching English to non-native speakers would be a plus. Should have knowledge of US standardised tests like TOEFL and GMAT.

CONDITIONS OF EMPLOYMENT: 1 year. Classes for children, teenagers and adults held between 8.30am and 9pm. Courses also run for public and private sector organisations.

SALARY: US$12–$13.50 per hour depending on qualifications and experience.

FACILITIES/SUPPORT: School will on request try to identify a Tunisian family willing to house the new teacher for an initial period until they find accommodation (with help of school). During the 4 months that American and Canadian citizens are allowed to stay as tourists, the school handles arrangements for getting a work permit and visa. A 500-dinar travel grant is paid at the end of the 1-year contract.

RECRUITMENT: Via www.amideast.org plus regional and international TEFL conferences.

CONTACT: Lorna Mgaieth,TEFL Program Manager (lmgaieth@amideast.org).

BRITISH COUNCIL TUNISIA
87 Avenue Mohamed V, BP 96 Le Belvédère 1002 Tunis

☎ +216 71 145 302

✉ Sarah.Rolph@tn.britishcouncil.org

🖥 www.britishcouncil.org/tunisia.htm

QUALIFICATIONS: Minimum certificate in EFL (CELTA or Trinity) plus two years' post-certificate teaching experience in EFL. Demonstrable ability to teach across the range of courses offered including adults and young learners. Experience of IELTS and Cambridge Exams desirable.

CONDITIONS OF EMPLOYMENT: 2-year full-time contracts. Also run summer school programme for which they need teachers for 8 weeks (June/July).

SALARY: Flights, baggage, medical insurance and pension contributions in addition to salary for full-time work. Salary for 2-month summer school is £2,000 plus flights, accommodation and medical insurance.

CONTACT: Sarah Rolph, Teaching Centre Manager.

ENGLISH CULTURAL CENTRE
Street of 7 November, immb El Itkan (Mez n°3) 3027 Sfax

☎ +216 74408949

✉ contact@englishculturalcenter.com

🖥 www.englishculturalcenter.com/www.english-tunisia.com

NUMBER OF TEACHERS: 4.

PREFERENCE OF NATIONALITY: British or American.

QUALIFICATIONS: 3 years' experience.

CONDITIONS OF EMPLOYMENT: 6 months or annual contract. Most classes are in the afternoon/evenings, 4pm–6pm and 6.30pm–8.30pm.

SALARY: 25 Tunisian dinars (£11) per 2 hour lesson.

FACILITIES/SUPPORT: Assistance given with applying for work permits.

RECRUITMENT: Interview is essential and can be conducted on the phone or Skype.

CONTACT: Mr Zayani, Administrative Officer.

LIBYA

On 23 October 2011, the National Transitional Council (NTC) proclaimed the liberation of Libya after more than 40 years under Colonel Gaddafi who had isolated himself and his country from the western world for so long. Already the English language has enjoyed increased favour, and a number of language schools, mostly on a small scale, have opened in Tripoli and other cities. Many are looking for staff among the many expat teachers who were evacuated from the country in February 2011, and among members of the huge diaspora of Libyans who have been living in exile since Gaddafi's coup in 1969. One of these returning expat teachers wrote on an expat blog in May 2012 that he had been offered three jobs within a couple of weeks of starting to search and that there are plenty of jobs coming up. Demand for native-speaking teachers is bound to increase over the coming years, both in the oil, gas and engineering sectors as well as the population at large.

There is now an English Teachers' Forum for Libya, with a page devoted to Teaching Jobs (which are sparse at the present time). Its member schools like IH-Elite (www.ihtripoli-elite.com) occasionally advertise vacancies. The American Libyan Education Training Center (www.aletc-libya.com/jobs.htm) is an expanding language centre looking for motivated teachers.

MAURITANIA

Mauritania is becoming a more popular overland route from Morocco to Senegal now that the tensions of the Western Sahara have cooled somewhat. The road from Nouadibou to Nouakchott is now paved, which makes travel considerably easier. When **Bradwell Jackson** visited he was surprised by how few Westerners he saw: '*It seems as though this country is up and coming as one of those unexplored gems that travellers haven't yet discovered.*'

Bradwell, who supplied all the information for this section, found a teaching job by a '*happy accident of fate*'. On striking up a conversation with a Westerner walking on the other side of the street, he asked her about English language schools, and was promptly taken to the front door of The English Language Centre:

> *I was lucky enough to speak with the owner right away. I was talking to her while she was busy doing some other things, so it was not a formal interview. I did not have to fill out an application, though she asked me to write a letter explaining why I wanted to work in Mauritania. She seemed very interested, and asked me to come back in a couple of days to do a mock class in front of her teachers. I was hired based on this.*

Bradwell's wages started at 50,000 ouguiyas ($180) a month and increased to 68,000 ($250) a month. He was told that a person hired from within the country is paid much less than a person hired from outside. Getting a work permit was refreshingly simple. The school simply took his passport to the employment office and paid for a one-year work permit.

Bradwell found the students to be a joy to work with, because they were 'serious' and hungry to learn. Native English teachers could try Nouakchott English Center (B.P. 4473 ILOT P-29; +222 529 25 42; sagna@univ-nkc.mr). The Coordinator of the Center (which is affiliated to the Université de Nouakchott) hires six to eight teachers, one or two of whom he would like to be native English speakers, although this would depend on the school's income. Teachers work four and half hours a week and are paid 1,500–2,500 ouguiyas per hour (about $5.50–$9/hour). British English is as popular as American English.

SENEGAL

The British Council has a flourishing teaching centre in Dakar (Rue AAB-68, Amitie Zone A et B, BP 6232; +221 869 2700; information@britishcouncil.sn) that hires well-qualified teachers. They will want to see your CV and certification, although Bradwell Jackson reports that they will consider hiring non-UK citizens and may leave you 'wriggle room' if you don't quite have the qualifications they officially require.

The British Senegalese Institute (Rue du 18 Juin BP: 35 Dakar; +221 822 28 70/40 23/77 8) is the oldest English teaching centre in the country. It does not require teachers to have a specific certificate or experience, although these are certainly desirable. The average hours per week are 15, and the pay is around 3,500 CFA per hour. Another possibility is the Centre Africain d'Etudes Superieres en Gestion (Boulevard du General De Gaulle, B.P. 3802, Dakar; +221 839 73 04 direct 839 74 39; moussa. dieng@cesag.sn). The school is located in a large, official complex and tends to cater for more affluent students. Bradwell Jackson spoke to Moussa Dieng, Chef du Departement Langues, who said that no specific certificate was required, just a good knowledge of the language. Moussa Dieng seemed to like the idea of hiring native English speakers.

The American Language Program in Senegal continues to recruit. Although Dakar is an interesting city of contrasts, Bradwell was not tempted to stay. He found the city sprawling and unwieldy, and a little too expensive.

LIST OF EMPLOYERS – OTHER AFRICAN COUNTRIES

GAMBIA

INSPIRE VOLUNTEERING
Town Hall, Market Place, Newbury RG14 5AA, UK
℘ 0800 032 3350
✉ info@inspirevolunteer.co.uk
💻 www.inspirevolunteer.co.uk

UK-based organisation sending volunteers to work on community-based teaching and other projects in Africa and worldwide.

NUMBER OF TEACHERS: Variable number of volunteers for teaching programmes in under-resourced primary and secondary schools in Gambia, and also in Tanzania.

PREFERENCE OF NATIONALITY: All native English speakers.

QUALIFICATIONS: Minimum qualification is A-level or equivalent in subjects to be taught. Must be able to cope with remote posting and to relate to people of other cultures.

CONDITIONS OF EMPLOYMENT: From 1 month.

SALARY: Unpaid. Volunteers pay a programme fee from £890 for 1 month which includes board and lodging in local family homes. Extra weeks cost £100.

GHANA

VOLUNTEER GHANA
Volunteer Programmes Department, BUNAC, 16 Bowling Green Lane, London EC1R 0QH, UK
℘ +44 20 7251 3472
✉ volunteer@bunac.org.uk
💻 www.bunac.org/voluteer/ghana

NUMBER OF TEACHERS: Varies each year.

PREFERENCE OF NATIONALITY: British or Irish.

QUALIFICATIONS: Applicants should be 18 or over. Previous classroom experience desirable.

CONDITIONS OF EMPLOYMENT: Placements available for 2–6 months, with monthly start dates.

SALARY: Placements are unpaid and applicants are expected to take sufficient spending money with them (approx. £175 per month). Programme costs from £880 for 2 months to £1,600 for 6 months, plus flights (£600–£800), comprehensive insurance, etc.

FACILITIES/SUPPORT: Most stay in homestay accommodation, which gives applicants a chance to become fully immersed in Ghanaian culture. Back up support and advice provided by BUNAC in the UK and the host organisation, Student & Youth Travel Organisation (SYTO) in Ghana. Applications are accepted year-round. Group flights depart every month.

RECRUITMENT: Send a completed application form (download-able from www.bunac.org), a deposit of £400 and other documentation as specified to BUNAC's Volunteering Department at least 10 weeks before departure date. All applicants are invited to attend an orientation interview as part of the application process.

MOZAMBIQUE

LYNDEN LANGUAGE SCHOOL
Av Zedequias Manganhela 267, JAT Building, 2nd Floor (PO Box 456), Maputo
 +258 21 360494
lynden@teledata.mz
www.lynden.co.mz

NUMBER OF TEACHERS: 5.
PREFERENCE OF NATIONALITY: British, Australian, South African, etc.
QUALIFICATIONS: CELTA or Trinity plus 2 years' experience.
CONDITIONS OF EMPLOYMENT: 1 year, 25 hours per week.
SALARY: US$1,000; half paid in the local currency (meticals).
FACILITIES/SUPPORT: School finds and pays for accommodation. School applies to Ministry of Labour for work permit once teachers gather necessary documents.
RECRUITMENT: *EL Gazette* or internet. References checked by phone.
CONTACT: Denise Lord or Lynne Longley, Co-Directors.

SOUTH AFRICA

INTERLINK SCHOOL OF LANGUAGES
Suite 501, The Equinox, 154 Main Road, Sea Point, Cape Town 8005
 +27 21 439 9834
 info@interlink.co.za
www.interlink.co.za

NUMBER OF TEACHERS: 10.
PREFERENCE OF NATIONALITY: South Africans preferred but will consider native English speakers with permission to work in South Africa.

QUALIFICATIONS: Recognised TEFL qualification CELTA preferred.
CONDITIONS OF EMPLOYMENT: Full-time contracts last for 1 year. Part-time contracts reviewed weekly according to demand.
SALARY: Varies according to experience and qualifications. Part-time salary R70 per hour.
RECRUITMENT: Interview required.
CONTACT: Luanne McCallum, Manager.

TANZANIA

SERIAN UK
PO Box 19, Monduli
 charley.nussey@gmail.com
www.serianuk.org.uk

Serian means 'Peace' in KiMaasai.
NUMBER OF TEACHERS: 15–20 teaching assistants and qualified teachers in ESL and other subjects placed at Serian UK Noonkodin Secondary School, in the rural Maasai village of Eluwai.
PREFERENCE OF NATIONALITY: All nationalities accepted. Non-native speakers of English should have IELTS 6.5 or above.
QUALIFICATIONS: Volunteers who want to be considered as independent class teachers of English should have the CELTA, TEFL or similar. Classroom assistants who work alongside a qualified Tanzanian teacher should ideally have completed a minimum of 1 year of undergraduate-level study in English, although school leavers with strong motivation and above-average qualifications will also be considered. Previous teaching experience in a school is strongly preferred, even if it is no more than a 2-week work experience placement. Maths and science teachers also needed.
CONDITIONS OF EMPLOYMENT: 2–3 months recommended for short-term volunteers though arrangements are flexible. Ideally 6–12 months from January or July for qualified teachers.
SALARY: Volunteers are asked to cover their living costs, $40–$50 per week, and are encouraged to carry out additional fundraising for the project.
FACILITIES/SUPPORT: Volunteers stay in a staff house. Volunteers can also take up (at reduced rates) a range of additional activities such as walking tours, homestays in traditional Maasai boma or Swahili tuition.
RECRUITMENT: Applications can be made online.
CONTACT: Ms. Charley Nussey, International Volunteer Coordinator (charley.nussey@gmail.com).

UGANDA

SOFT POWER EDUCATION (SPE)

UK: 55 Guildhall St, Bury St Edmunds, Suffolk IP33 1QF

Uganda: PO Box 1493, Jinja

📞 +256 774 162541

🖱 volunteering@softpowereducation.com or
info@softpowereducation.com

💻 www.softpowereducation.com

British registered non-religious charity improving quality of life through education. Among numerous other projects, SPE offers TEFL courses for men and women in the community.

NUMBER OF TEACHERS: 1 or 2 at a time based at the Amagezi Education Centre. Female teachers needed to work with women in Kyabirwa community near Bujagali Falls, Jinja.

QUALIFICATIONS: TEFL qualification and some experience preferable but not essential. Creativity and ability to work independently using one's own initiative essential.

CONDITIONS OF EMPLOYMENT: Minimum 3 months.

SALARY: None. Volunteers must cover their own living and travel expenses as well as a donation to the charity. Recommended amount is £75 a week.

FACILITIES/SUPPORT: Camping, dorms, private bandas or living within the local community. Guest houses in Jinja are also an option, but they are located some distance away from the Amagezi Education Centre so travel costs would be higher.

CONTACT: Sharon Webb, General Manager (sharon@softpowereducation.com).

ASIA

Although the English language is not a universal passport to employment, it can certainly be put to good use in many Asian countries where the demand for English teachers is substantial, even extraordinary, as is the case with China which was described as a 'black hole' for EFL teachers by a European director of studies.

Conditions and remuneration differ wildly between industrialised countries, such as Japan, Korea and Singapore with their Western-style economies, and developing countries, such as Nepal and Thailand, where both wages and the standard of living are lower. China combines rapidly industrialised cities with vast stretches of rural backwaters. A concerted job hunt in Asia will almost always turn up possibilities, and sometimes the difficulty comes in choosing among them. **Ross McKay** from Glasgow writes of his job hunt:

> *I was 50 and fed up for various reasons. So I wrote to about 500 institutions all over South East Asia. Whilst waiting for replies I did a distance TESOL course and College of Further Education teaching certificate. I got three offers, one in Hanoi, one in Bangkok and I chose Jakarta as I knew nothing about Indonesia. My colleagues come from all over the English-speaking world and often become great pals. But there are some head-cases. I guess one has to be a little crazy to live this life, and a few people crack up. The great thing about life in Indonesia is that every morning you wake up and have no idea what the heck is going to happen next.*

In contrast to Thailand and Indonesia with their strong demand for native English speaker teachers, other countries between Pakistan and the Philippines (with a few exceptions) are not easy places in which to find paid work as an English teacher. Poverty is the main reason why there is a very small market for expatriate teachers. Outside the relatively wealthy countries of Singapore, Malaysia and Brunei, there is no significant range of opportunities to earn money while teaching English. The largest growth area has been in Cambodia, Vietnam and Laos, where a number of joint ventures and locally owned language schools employ native English speaker teachers.

It may not be necessary to organise a mass mail-out in order to arrange a teaching stay in Asia. Recruitment organisations such as Saxoncourt (affiliated to Shane English Schools) and EF English First are very active in the region. Saxoncourt recruits for the group of Shane English Schools in Japan, China, Taiwan and Vietnam. The education broker Teach to Travel fills vacancies throughout the Far East, especially in South Korea, Thailand, Vietnam and China. Candidates with a university degree and TEFL qualification, but not necessarily experience, are invited to apply, as long as they have a British, Australian or New Zealand passport. TEFLOne is a free placement service for native English speaking EFL teachers with a degree and a 120-hour certificate qualification in TEFL for reputable schools throughout China, as well as Taiwan, Japan and Indonesia. Advice is available on positions in Vietnam and Korea. The package on offer normally consists of a monthly salary, end-of-contract bonus, paid return flight, free accommodation and welfare support (www.teflone.com).

In North America dozens of recruiters and agencies mediate between language schools in Asia and job-seekers, for example Footprints (www.footprintsrecruiting.com) and Reach to Teach (see entry below). Agencies can also be found in Australia and New Zealand, for example AA Circle (www.aacircle.com.au) which fills posts in China, Japan, Korea and Taiwan.

For American citizens and residents, both Princeton and Stanford universities have affiliated programmes which operate in various Asian countries and include TEFL teaching. VIA (Volunteers in Asia) has been providing international exchange opportunities since 1963. Each year VIA sends 30–40 volunteer English teachers to China, Vietnam, Indonesia, Thailand, Myanmar, Cambodia and Laos on short-term (summer) and longer term (1-year or 2-year) assignments. All programmes are open to college students or graduates over 18. Occasional exceptions can be made for people without a college degree. Applications are due in mid-February and the participation fee is between $1,500 and $3,000. Further information is available online at www.viaprograms.org (+1 415 904 8033; info@viaprograms.org).

For information about the Princeton-affiliated programme, contact Princeton-in-Asia, 194 Nassau Street, Suite 212, Princeton, NJ 08542 (+1 609 258 3657 pia@princeton.edu; http://piaweb.princeton.edu). They currently place about 150 full-year fellows in 17 Asian countries: Cambodia, China and Hong Kong, East Timor, India, Indonesia, Japan, Kazakhstan, Laos, Malaysia, Mongolia, Nepal, Philippines, Singapore, South Korea, Taiwan, Thailand and Vietnam. Applications, available on their website, are welcomed from college graduates from all universities. Suitable candidates will be invited to a compulsory interview in January or February and a weekend's orientation in late May, both on the Princeton campus. Teachers on the programme must also complete a TEFL training weekend in Princeton in April and/or at least 20 hours of TEFL/TESL preparation in the form of a course or experience before their fellowship begins.

Exposure to the radically differing cultures of Korea is fascinating. **Allison Williams** was writing from Korea about her exhilarating experiences and frustrations, but this could apply equally to much of Asia:

> *Among the highlights have been meeting and getting to know such awesome little people, by which I mean the kids! Some things here are so alien but then with other things you really do see that we are all pretty much the same. I've had quite a few of those wooah-man-I-live-in-Asia moments. For example you will have an old woman squatting on the road selling garlic right next to a couple that look like they just stepped out of Vogue magazine. I love eating all sorts of weird and wonderful things. Among the lowlights have been clothes that don't fit and being told you are a big size, lol. You get tired of not being able to do anything for yourself, liking banking or simple things like exchanging a product. Of course it gets better the longer you stay. Accepting the hierarchy and educational views has sometimes been tricky, and it has been frustrating not being allowed to do more teaching on my own. All in all I am really happy with the whole experience, but after two years I'll be ready to go home. I'm excited about clothes that fit, being able to understand everything and eating cheese!*

One issue that rears its ugly head from time to time is discrimination on the grounds of age and also race. For marketing reasons in Asia employers prefer their employees to look younger than 30 and many have complained that too much emphasis is placed on the photograph requested at the time of application. Racism is also a potential problem, as highlighted by a contributor to a *Guardian* TEFL forum in 2010:

> *Myself and my girlfriend, both in our mid-20s and university graduates with good work experience, have been looking into TEFL in Asia for over a year now. We've gotten so far as getting interviews, but on several occasions we've been denied a job as my girlfriend is mixed race (Chinese/British). This hasn't been the explicit reason for not getting a job, of course, but it's been heavily implied. For instance, my girlfriend was asked whether she could dye her hair blond in order to be considered for a job in a school in Hong Kong.*
>
> *I think that racism in Asia is hushed over by many, especially recruiting companies and advisors. It's a serious issue and one that affects many people applying for work in China, Hong Kong, Korea and Japan especially. If you don't 'look' Western, you'll struggle significantly compared to your Caucasian brethren.*

As one of the expert panellists sensibly replied, '*While some racism might be encountered, it doesn't mean the whole of Asia is inaccessible.*'

LIST OF EMPLOYERS

ASIAN CONSULTANTS INTERNATIONAL

182 N. Main Street, Concord, NH 03301, USA

✆ +1 978 228 5784

✉ hr@asianconsultants.com

💻 www.asianconsultants.com

NUMBER OF TEACHERS: 200–600 are interviewed each year.

PREFERENCE OF NATIONALITY: Native speakers only, mainly North Americans, but all are welcome.

QUALIFICATIONS: Bachelor's degree from a recognised university, passport from US, Canada, UK, Australia, New Zealand or South Africa, positive rapport with young people, professional attitude and an open mind. TESOL qualification preferred and teacher accreditation very desirable.

CONDITIONS OF EMPLOYMENT: 12-month contracts. Hours Monday–Friday 9am–6pm, 11am–8pm or 12pm–9pm. Some operations require half day on Saturdays, which means the working hours during the week will be shorter.

SALARY: Full-time monthly salary in Taiwan: NT$53,000–NT$80,000 and in China RMB6,500–RMB13,000. Some agency processing fees are applicable depending on position.

FACILITIES/SUPPORT: Local partner in Taiwan provides additional services such as relocation services (moving, apartment hunting, initial orientations, etc.), work permit application, etc.

RECRUITMENT: Online, referral, partnership. Online video Skype interviews are strongly preferred.

CONTACT: Candy, Consultant.

EXPERIENCE TEACHING ABROAD LTD

Helaman House, 49 Reed Way, St Georges, Weston-super-Mare, North Somerset, BS22 7RJ

✆ +44 208 1 333 885

✉ info@experienceteachingabroad.com

💻 www.experienceteachingabroad.com; www. teflheaven.com

TEFL Heaven is a division of Experience Teaching Abroad Ltd (ETA) a UK limited company which specialises in sending people to fill teaching positions abroad.

NUMBER OF TEACHERS: Around 250 English teachers to be placed in Thailand, South Korea, China, Vietnam and India.

PREFERENCE OF NATIONALITY: Teachers need to be of a native English speaking origin.

QUALIFICATIONS: Experience is not always necessary though an obvious advantage for some roles. For all paid teaching positions a Bachelor's degree is a requirement. Teaching-related qualifications and certificates are beneficial but not always required.

CONDITIONS OF EMPLOYMENT: 6–12 months is standard. 25–32 hours a week (with exceptions).

SALARY: Varies dramatically between countries and according to experience/qualifications.

FACILITIES/SUPPORT: If accommodation is not supplied as part of the package, assistance will be given in finding accommodation.

RECRUITMENT: Via direct marketing with universities, advertising online and word of mouth. Skype interviews mainly.

CONTACT: Ben Hesketh and the ETA Team.

REACH TO TEACH

1606 80th Avenue, Algona, Iowa 50511, USA. Also #319 Minsheng Road, Taipei, Taiwan

✆ +1 201 467 4612 (USA)/+44 203 286 9794 (UK & Ireland)/+61 2 8011 4516 (Australia)/+64 9 889 0557 (New Zealand)

✉ info@ReachToTeachRecruiting.com

💻 www.ReachToTeachRecruiting.com

Reach To Teach is one of the largest human resource companies for teachers in Asia and all services are free to teachers. See separate entries in chapters on China, Korea and Taiwan.

NUMBER OF TEACHERS: 500+ per year to work in Taiwan, Korea, China, Thailand and a few countries outside Asia.

PREFERENCE OF NATIONALITY: In order to qualify for permission to work in Asia, you must be from one of the following countries: USA, Canada, UK, Ireland, South Africa, Australia or New Zealand.

QUALIFICATIONS: A positive, enthusiastic, dedicated and flexible attitude is the most important qualification. Most positions in Asia require a 120-hour TEFL certification. Teaching experience is a plus.

CONDITIONS OF EMPLOYMENT: All job placements are full-time positions and for 1 full year. Teaching schedules vary but are generally either mornings and afternoons or afternoons and evenings.

SALARY: Competitive packages that reflect the local market rate. Ability to save depends on lifestyle. Some job placements (especially Korea and China) offer free flights, free accommodation and bonuses.

FACILITIES/SUPPORT: Recruiter offers personal attention to every job placement. Through a partnership with a TEFL course provider, Reach To Teach can assist teachers in getting course discounts. All placements come with guidance on visas, flights, accommodation, etc. and workplace teacher training. All teachers have the option of continued support throughout year-long placement.

RECRUITMENT: Applications submitted via Reach To Teach website. Interviews conducted over Skype, by phone or occasionally in person.

CONTACT: Carrie Kellenberger, Co-President (Carrie@ReachToTeachRecruiting.com).

CHINA

Recruitment of English teachers for the People's Republic of China is absolutely booming in the private sector. People inside and outside China keep wondering when this romance with the language will fade and when jobs won't be so easy to pluck from the vine, but so far the demand is only increasing. It seems that the number of applicants at both ends of the age spectrum is expanding, though schools prefer people between the extremes; the young tend to be unreliable and often don't show up after agreeing to be hired, while the old are looking for an adventure in their golden years and don't necessarily take the teaching very seriously.

In turn, native English speakers are heading to China in their thousands, barely bothering to look at teaching possibilities in Europe or even Japan. Cyberspace is a-buzz with new companies and organisations offering English language training from native English speakers. Western curiosity about this huge country, spurred on by a barrage of media stories, is rising exponentially. Thousands of native English speakers are teaching not only at schools and academic institutions around the country but in companies and (what would have been unthinkable not so long ago) private language institutes. Furthermore, the emerging middle class aspires to send its children for private tuition just as in the capitalist countries of Taiwan, Korea and Japan.

English is compulsory for school pupils from the age of nine. Although optional, English is now even taught from kindergarten. Many street and shop signs in the capital and other major cities are written in English as well as Chinese, though most Beijing citizens, especially the older generation, can say very little in English apart from 'McDonald's'. A great many students and teachers are very keen to improve their English to Cambridge Proficiency standard in the hope of being accepted to study overseas. Competition can be cut-throat although children from the wealthiest families may be less inspired, knowing that they'll be going abroad eventually, whether their English is fluent or not. But most are eager to learn, even if the style of learning to which they have become accustomed can be difficult for foreign teachers to adopt.

It is easy to forget, amid the well-reported stories of sprawling urban metropolises rising almost in the night, that about 80% of China's population still lives in the countryside. **Sam Meekings** was surprised to discover that although he headed off to Beijing every other weekend to stock up on Western foods and see the sights, most of his students had never left the small city of Hengshui; only 15 years previously it had all been farmland.

Bill Lehane was pleasantly surprised by his encounter with China:

I spent six months with my partner teaching teenagers at a school in Lishui City in Zhejiang province. As a journalist by trade with no prior interest in China or indeed teaching experience, I had perhaps an even steeper learning curve than most expat teachers in the Middle Kingdom. Undoubtedly switching the mild climes of Ireland for the hot and humid surrounds of provincial China is a big change, but I found the hours were good and the pay quite adequate as long as you stayed in-country. I would say the worst aspect for me was having to give a blood sample when I arrived, and the best was the ubiquitous, delicious street food. As a writer accustomed to hearing only bad things about communist China and its leaders in Beijing, I have to say I experienced a very different place on the ground. People are happy and friendly and have an interesting, varied and ancient culture.

PROSPECTS FOR TEACHERS

'With just a university degree and a little determination anyone can find an opportunity to challenge themselves somewhere in 21st century China,' writes **Sam Meekings**, who taught in a state-run normal college before accepting an editing job with Oxford University Press in Shanghai (and is now a published novelist). A degree is normally a minimum requirement these days and any teaching experience is useful, but not so much importance is attached to TEFL qualifications and quite often references are not taken up. However, the better schools have recently started to become more stringent in their recruiting methods and foreigners cannot simply walk into more lucrative jobs in the same way that they did in the early days. Nevertheless, there are still many schools so desperate that they will employ anyone simply to have a 'token foreigner' and hence enhance their status.

Theoretically the Chinese government classifies teachers either as foreign experts (FEs) or foreign teachers (FTs). FEs are expected to have a master's degree in a relevant area (English, Linguistics, TEFL/TESOL, etc.) and some teaching experience at the tertiary level. FTs are normally under 25 and have only a university degree. In practice, most teachers are classified as 'FEs', even if they only have a degree. Younger candidates including students on exchange schemes such as those run by gap year organisations, e.g. Lattitude and Project Trust, are usually placed in middle schools (public secondary schools, often boarding schools) or vocational schools. A large proportion of foreigners are employed in Beijing and (especially) Shanghai but there are many opportunities in the provinces as well, especially for FTs. The more remote the area or the more hostile the climate, the easier it will be to find a job. But there are also plenty of vacancies in comfortable cities such as Kunming and Dalian. Many vacancies for both FEs and FTs go unfilled. Specialist recruitment organisations are notified of more positions than they can find people to fill them.

Demand exists in the hundreds of universities, colleges, foreign language institutes, institutes of technology, teacher training colleges (called normal universities) and secondary schools, especially in the provinces. Normal universities often seem to be overlooked when FTs are assigned centrally, so they are a very promising bet for people applying directly or on the spot. China is the biggest market in the world right now for IELTS tests, so it is a good place to get trained and start testing. Once you are an official IELTS examiner, you can examine anywhere in the world, but have to keep your certification up to date by examining at least once every three months.

Applications can be made through various placement organisations, recruitment agencies (which don't charge teachers a fee) and voluntary bodies, or by applying directly to institutions advertised on the internet and elsewhere.

Even ordinary secondary schools employ native English speakers; applications can be made through provincial education bureaux. Writing direct to the Foreign Affairs Office (*waiban*) of institutes of higher learning may lead to a job offer. Chinese institutes seem to attach more weight to the letter of application than to the curriculum vitae, but the CV should still be sent and should emphasise any work or experience in education. Also enclose a photo, a photocopy of the first page of your passport, a copy of any education certificates and two references. **Jessie Levene** notes that schools seem to prefer female teachers, particularly for younger students, and as a result, she was given more and more classes, despite an already full timetable.

It is becoming increasingly common for schools to offer a job to an applicant but not guarantee employment until they arrive at the school. This is the result of foreigners having abused the system in the past, accepting numerous jobs in order to keep their options open. Many schools have also introduced a probationary period of between two and 10 weeks. Although this may sound a bit daunting if you have already paid for flight tickets, it can work in the applicant's favour, as it allows time to ensure that the school is suitable for you. It is always best, wherever possible, to visit a school before signing a contract and talk to other FTs, to make sure that the school is everything it says it is and to examine the accommodation.

Some schools and private language institutes which do offer contracts to unseen candidates rely on long-distance phone calls or Skype. Any university graduate travelling in China should be able to arrange a teaching contract just by asking around at the many colleges in the towns and cities on his or her itinerary.

Even when foreign travellers have not been looking for work, they have been approached and invited to teach English. The going rate in the big cities for private English tuition is £10–£15 an hour.

If you fix up a job at FT level on the spot, it may not be for an entire academic year and your pay may be calculated on an hourly basis.

FINDING A JOB

With the explosion in opportunities, the job hunt is far more straightforward than it was a few years ago when most teacher applications were for state institutes and had to go through the Chinese Education Association for International Exchange or one of its 37 provincial offices. Nowadays CEAIE leaves recruitment to online companies such as www.chinajob.com (see below) and other private recruiters, foundations or China-linked companies eager to sign up native English speakers (with or without relevant experience) for an academic year.

Some of the tried and tested old schemes are still in place and still work. The British Council's Language Assistants Programme, in co-operation with the Chinese Education authorities places graduates in schools across China. TEFL training is provided on a two-week course in Shanghai which is paid for by the British Council. Participants receive free accommodation, and utilities and a flight back to the UK. Teaching experience and/or qualifications are not necessary. Details of the application procedure can be obtained from the Language Assistants Team at the British Council (10 Spring Gardens, London SW1A 2BN; +44 20 7389 4596; assistants@britishcouncil.org) or at www.britishcouncil.org/languageassistants-china.htm. The British Council accepts applications up until the end of February (non-refundable placement fee £48). Applications are screened and then interviews conducted in April for positions starting in August. The minimum requirement is a university degree, though a TEFL certificate and/or teaching experience, preferably abroad, improve your chances of acceptance. Opportunities are available in a large variety of cities throughout mainland China, though initial training takes place for all participants in Shanghai in August. Wages are not brilliant on this programme, i.e. 3,000–4,000 Renminbi (net) per month, but all teachers are provided with free accommodation.

Any web search or a trawl of the major ELT job websites is bound to turn up plenty of contacts, such as www.jobchina.net and www.cathayteacher.com, which have long lists of jobs, all dated and described in detail. With an invitation letter or fax from an official Chinese employer, you will be able to obtain a Z visa to travel and work in China. Among the dozens of specialist online recruiters are Find Work Abroad (www.findworkabroad.com) based in Guangzhou in southern China, with a representative/interviewer in Poole (+44 1202 632756) which places many teachers in the cities of southern China such as Zhuhai, Foshan and Shenzhen as well as Guangzhou. Candidates who are not qualified are obliged to take a TEFL course (£210). Other places to look on the web include www.jimmychina.co.uk (a recruiter in Birmingham), www.networkesl.com, based in Wuhan City, and Gold Star TEFL Recruitment (www.GoldStarTeachers.com) which advertises salaries that are double the norm, i.e. 9,500 renminbi per month.

The www.chinajob.com job fairs have been running for more than a decade and offer a great (and free) opportunity for teachers to look for 'on the spot' opportunities in educational institutions, language training organisations, and private and national companies. Job fairs take place annually in April in Beijing, Shanghai and Guangzhou. For more information visit www.chinajob.com or the website of its partner, the State Administration of Foreign Experts Affairs (www.safea.gov.cn/english).

Some TEFL training courses offered in China also lead to jobs. Again chinajob.com is active and offers a seven-day training course to graduates which enables them to claim FE status. The course is offered frequently in Beijing and occasionally in Shenzhen and Zhuhai, and costs 3,000 RMB; further details at http://tefl.chinajob.com. Another company offering a training course combined with job placement is affiliated to the American exchange agency Journey East (www.journeyeast.org). A similar programme with guaranteed job placement is run by US-China Education and Culture Exchange Center (www.teachingin china.org).

Demand for qualified teachers is so high that any who advertise their services online may get an instantaneous response, as happened to a teacher writing from Shanghai last year:

I put my CV on TEFL.com and the DoS of EF Academic Partnerships contacted me by email enquiring about my current location and availability. I replied that I was at home and currently seeking employment and asked for some more information. He promptly replied and we arranged an interview for the following Saturday morning.

PRIVATE LANGUAGE TRAINING

Ever since the change in legislation allowing privatised companies to operate in the fields of media and education, a huge number of private language schools and training centres has opened. **Jane Pennington**, who taught for four years in China, carried out a little research and estimates that there are about 100 private language companies in Kunming, only about 15%–20% of which are officially licensed. These institutes are not allowed to invite FTs without a lot of red tape which is usually not worth their while. However, they are very eager to hire native English speakers on the spot, often people on a student visa at the university. Like private schools everywhere, a certain number of these are run by unscrupulous entrepreneurs interested only in profit. If considering working in the private sector, try to find out the degree of professionalism of the company that has expressed interest in hiring you, and talk to other foreigners working there, especially with regards to payment.

International ELT organisations such as EF English First or Wall Street Institute (see entries) are expanding quickly. **Yasmin Peiris** enjoyed working for the Wall Street Institute in Shenzhen, teaching different types of class 30 hours a week. Class sizes ranged from four to 15 people and the working environment was very good, '*with simple, modern classrooms and most teaching resources readily available*'.

The internet is a prolific source of possibilities and expanding all the time. According to a leading news agency, China has more people online than the USA. Any web search or a trawl of the major ELT job sites is bound to turn up plenty of contacts. Job China at www.jobchina.net, for example, publishes long lists of jobs, all dated and described. In the private sector, some large companies (e.g. hotel chains) have their own language training facilities for staff, especially if they are joint ventures with Western companies. Most recruitment of teachers by business and industry takes place locally, since they do not offer accommodation.

PLACEMENT AGENCIES AND ORGANISATIONS

Many organisations recruit teachers from abroad for China. Whereas many merely make the initial match, others have an ongoing relationship with their teachers. Australian **Shane Johnson** has been teaching all over China for the past seven years, and prefers to be hired through an agency, in his case Buckland International Education Group (see entry below), because they can sort out any problems that arise, as happened for the first time in 2011–12:

I have had a very smooth seven years and the only real problem was when I arrived at my current school to find that they wanted me to share an apartment and teach only Grades 1 and 2, even though they had assured me I would have my own apartment and my timetable would be Grades 3–6. It took only one phone call to my boss at Buckland before a second apartment was found and I had older classes added to my timetable. This is the reason I sign with a recruiter and not directly with a school. I have a contract with my boss/recruiter and they have a contract with each school.

A number of North American organisations involved in teacher placements in China have entries in the listings at the end of this chapter including the Colorado China Council, Appalachians Abroad and the US-China Educational Exchange. WorldTeach in Cambridge, Massachusetts (+1 857 259 6646; www.worldteach.org), is a non-profit organisation that sends volunteers to teach in secondary schools in Hunan province, for a full academic year (August to July) or for the summer. Volunteers pay $1,000 for the year and $4,490 for the summer; all of these include flights from the USA.

CONDITIONS OF WORK

With the rise of the free market the once rigid distinctions between FTs and FEs has become blurred since many reward packages are now open to negotiation. But there is still a strong tendency to heap more perks on anyone with a higher degree. They are more likely to have their airfares or shipping costs reimbursed and they usually earn more than FTs. The general monthly salary range for most ordinary native English speaker teachers should start from RMB4,500 ($700/£420) but can rise in the private sector (especially in sophisticated Shanghai and Beijing) to well over double that. Note that the renminbi is a non-convertible currency and foreigners have to negotiate a clause in their contract to be able to convert a certain percentage (up to a maximum 70%). When **Bradwell Jackson** arrived in Tangshan, he assumed that since so many foreigners are working in China as English teachers, it must surely be straightforward to deposit earnings in a bank at home (in the USA in his case). After some research he discovered that the Bank of China will make deposits into US bank accounts, albeit for a significant fee, especially if you don't have an account with them. An experienced teacher, **Megan Eaves**, wrote a book full of practical tips and insights, specifically aimed at teachers, *This Is China: A Guidebook for Teachers, Backpackers and other Lunatics* (2009, see www.meganeaveswriting.com). The experience of teachers in the big cities is very different for that of native speakers who go to more obscure locations. Be aware that what are called cities in China are more like counties or small states, so even when you think you are going to a big city, you could in fact end up in a small town with few recreational outlets as happened to **Dan Casaletto**:

> I was in a much smaller town than I had expected where there was no expat community. My fellow teachers were a bunch of Chinese men and women with whom I could not communicate. The few teachers who could speak English were friendly, but busy with their own lives. There was one other foreign teacher from the West and although we had little in common it was great to have a conversation in English and someone to commiserate with. The presence of a university nearby did give me a chance to make friends with English-speaking Chinese college students.
>
> I was living in a small town, where some of the more repugnant features of Chinese culture are brought to the fore (spitting including indoors, children defecating on the sidewalk, yelling in confined quarters and market sellers charging grossly inflated prices for inferior merchandise). The school curfew was terrible, school gates were locked from 11.30pm to 6am. If I could do it again I would have demanded to be placed in a larger city.

Although higher wages can be earned in the big cities of Beijing, Guangzhou, Shanghai, the megalopolis of Chongqing and in the Special Economic Zones such as Hainan, life in Chinese cities has many drawbacks in terms of crowds and pollution. **Kate Devlin** who taught at the China Agriculture University in Beijing, found the city 'polluted, very ugly and soulless'. For quality of life, south-western China is probably better than much of the east. Yunnan province has a particularly congenial climate. This area is also reputed to be less money-oriented than the east coast cities, which may have the drawback that it may be more difficult to find paying private students.

Shane Johnson is one teacher who has a decided preference for rural locations:

I'm now down south in Yangshuo in one of my favourite provinces Guangxi which is covered with huge lime-stone karst peaks, much like famous Halong Bay in Vietnam. But instead of a sea of water here there is a sea of rice fields. It has become touristy, but for good reason. I am so lucky as this is where my employer (Buckland) is based so I get free accommodation. My first year and a half here in China was in a very small rural farming town in western Guangxi Province. I taught primary school with up to one hundred students in some classes. Thankfully I had classroom assistants for each class in which I taught oral English by using games and songs along with the students' classroom books.

I usually stay in a school for a year and then I will change both schools and province as this enables me to really experience the true diversity of China, as each province has its own Minority Peoples who have their own culture, food, customs, etc. As I choose to teach only in small rural areas the money is much less than a more modern large city but it is still more than enough to both live and save to travel for up to four months each year. During the term when I'm not teaching I spend most of my time riding through bamboo-covered hills and lush green rice fields in search of small village temples to visit. Whilst on summer and winter break I usually travel through rural China visiting beautiful mountains, lakes, reserves, temples and friends.

Outside the major eastern cities you can live on RMB1,500 a month if your accommodation is provided, so it is important to be able to convert your saved yuan renminbi into a foreign currency. However, those living in the major eastern cities are more likely to spend RMB3,000–5,000 per month, depending on their lifestyle. One highly qualified teacher in Shanghai estimated the cost of living out of a salary of RMB10,500 per month: RMB2,000 for a flat (not shared), RMB500 to cover bills and RMB2,000–3,000 on food. Inflation is high in China so hanging out in expat bars and taking taxis is becoming more expensive. In Beijing, the automatic charge for a taxi is twice as much as it is in Tangshan (two hours east of the capital).

The three or four week holiday over Chinese New Year should be paid as should vacation periods in state schools if you are contracted to continue teaching after it. Companies in the private sector may not offer payment during enforced breaks from teaching. **Paul Carey** identified the sudden six-week break from working and earning with little notice given by the employer as one of the low points of his experience with EF English First in Shanghai which was otherwise '*a worthwhile experience both personally and professionally*'. Many employers offer free internet access and some offer free Chinese lessons. **Shane Johnson** appreciates the large number of holidays:

The Chinese are one of the most festive people I have ever known and they celebrate each festival with a lot of food, beer and a public holiday. In addition to all the school and statutory holidays, traditional festivals are celebrated such as Tomb Sweeping Festival and the Dragon Boat Festival. China is such a wonderful country to live in and life really is an amazing journey.

When you are first notified by your employer in China that you have a job, you should avoid the temptation to write back enthusiastically accepting it. Rather ask for more details such as your status, salary, timetable and other conditions. You could also ask for the names of any current foreign employees whom you can ask for inside information. What is agreed at this stage will set the terms of employment even though it is standard practice not to sign a contract until after two months' probation.

While teaching in a suburb of Shanghai, **Marybeth Hao** noticed many Chinese parents were more than willing to pay native English speaker tutors high fees to tutor their children outside school hours. For her, one of the main rewards of teaching in Shanghai was to experience a culture in the midst of such dramatic and hurried changes.

FTs can be expected to teach anything from 15 to 30+ hours a week. A load of 20 hours is typical though this sounds lighter than it actually is because there are bound to be extra duties. Often there is a heavy load of marking not to mention marketing. Teachers in the private sector are routinely asked to attend student recruitment events, for example to hand out flyers or to appear at drop-in evenings whose main purpose is to rope in new clients. Some teachers are expected to staff an 'English corner' or English club, or deliver a weekly lecture on Western culture. In out-of-the-way places, you might find yourself playing the part of 'token foreigner' at the many banquets you will be invited to when you first arrive. For **Dan Casaletto** one of the high points of his time in China was dancing at a night club on his birthday while a crowd chanted 'foreigner' and 'beautiful' in Chinese. He was enough of a rarity for one club to give him free drinks for four months on account of being a foreign. He was humbled and amazed at the generosity of many whom he encountered and befriended.

Sam Meekings describes how attendance at several Chinese banquets can lead to a succession of nasty hangovers:

> *Every foreigner in China quickly becomes familiar with baijiu, a sharp clear liquor with a cloying aftertaste, which is measured out into shot glasses in front of you at the start of a meal. Though beer is increasingly popular, no large event is complete without baijiu. At any large banquet, especially with officials or high-ranking teachers at the school or college, you will be encouraged to drink with them. Your glass will be topped up throughout the meal, and often many people will wish to toast you, meaning you must once again down your drink as a sign of mutual respect. This is why, by eight or nine in the evening, restaurants begin to clear out – many diners are too wasted to do anything but go home and sleep.*
>
> *It should be noted, however, that women are usually exempted from this custom, and though I would have liked to have been spared the attention (and the subsequent hangovers), my female colleagues were not impressed that they were simply expected to sit and slowly sip beer or Coca-Cola while all the men went through the intricate tradition of getting each other as drunk as possible.*
>
> *Similarly, while almost all the male teachers in the college were heavy smokers (one of the best gifts to present to someone is a box of cigarettes), women smoking was frowned upon. Though these attitudes cannot be found in big cosmopolitan cities, I am certain that they persist throughout the smaller towns that make up the bulk of this vast country.*

In cases where teachers are given a huge number of classes, the administration's main ambition is to maximise your exposure, which may have the effect of minimising your usefulness. On the whole **Michelle** enjoyed her time in China, but she thinks that FTs should be given more advice on what is required of them before they start teaching. It is not unusual for the school to leave it up to the FTs to find out if any national exams are looming for which you should be helping the students to prepare. Hours of teaching are unpredictable and the teaching days can be very long. Students get up at 6am and work at night in supervised sessions. Michelle was asked to take classes at weekends, which left little time for travel. If you want to keep your weekends free for travel and relaxation, firmly decline teaching hours on Saturday and Sunday, and be aware that it is all too easy to over-commit yourself in the first few weeks.

On the other hand, you may find your colleagues and bosses bend over backwards to help and support you, as **Bradwell Jackson** reported last year:

> *I was offered a job with Aston in China on the basis of a telephone interview and I am very happy with this. Aston is good to me, and my co-workers scramble to help me whenever I have even a mild matter that needs attention. For example, when I told them I was looking for a kung-fu school, they took this as a very important issue and had many long discussions-cum-negotiations with each other in order to come up with the best option for me. I think it might be hard to convince a Westerner to come and stay in an out-of-the-way city like Tangshan.*
>
> *Really, I'm living the life of Reilly here. I've got nothing to complain about. The school has given me a free apartment complete with cable TV, washing machine, toaster oven, microwave, and refrigerator. Whenever I'm hungry, I just mosey on down to the street vendors and get some proper Chinese food for a friendly budget price. Who can ask for more?*

THE PUPILS

'Big noses' (foreigners) are normally treated with respect, though idle Western ways are creeping in. In the early years of Western contact with China, English teachers outside the big cities found themselves lionised, unable to complete the simplest task in public without an enormous audience. There are not many corners of China these days into which foreigners, whether teachers or travellers, have not penetrated, although in Hengshui, three hours south of Beijing, **Sam Meekings** was amazed at the reaction he received from people in the town, who would stop and gape at him, as though they had seen 'dinosaurs or dragons'. **Yasmin Peiris**, based in Shenzhen, one of China's newest cities, agrees that the general attitude towards teachers is generally favourable, even though there is a language barrier. She chose to ask her students for advice on where to go at weekends and what to do (a foot massage, a little shopping and sampling tempting varieties of Chinese food were some of the suggestions). In Beijing, **Kate Devlin** reckoned that the students in her university classes came from very wealthy families and were spoiled rotten: '*Out of a class of 20–25 students, maybe five or six kids would listen to my lecture. Students would openly sleep, read, watch movies on their laptop or mostly talk. They were required to be in class so they were, but nothing more.*' As (censored) internet use continues to rise and more Chinese people come into contact with Westerners (in the ether or in person), it is unlikely that China's generally respectful attitude towards foreigners will continue unperturbed. **Bradwell Jackson** identified another interesting new trend in modern-day China from his experiences of teaching in a small city:

> There is another interesting phenomenon in China, which is the syndrome of the 'Little Emperor'. Chinese children are well behaved, but they were even better behaved 10 or 20 years ago. With the advent of the one-child policy, some interesting changes took place. It seems that with just one child in the house, and especially if it's a boy, the child is much more likely to be spoiled and accommodated. Any English teacher here will probably get his/her small share of little brats who just can't understand why they can't do what they want.
>
> I agree with the premise that a teacher has to be a bossy boots in order to establish the discipline straight off the bat. I certainly did this, maybe even a bit too much, so that now the (naughty) kids are just a tad bit resistant sometimes. The parents, on the other hand, are deliriously happy with me. They specifically love the fact that I'm strict with the kids.

Slowly, newer pedagogical methods are being accepted by students and administrators alike, although most teachers are warned not to stray into dangerous territory in their lessons, like politics and sex. **Bradwell Jackson** identified the three forbidden T topics: Tiananmen, Taiwan and Tibet. One recent teacher struggled with the contradictions: '*We're invited here to teach Western Culture, then instructed not to behave like Westerners*'. However it is impossible to generalise, because in one place, techniques that smack of innovation will be greeted with blank stares, while in another, there can be lively class discussions.

Bill Lehane from Ireland blogged while he was teaching in China (http://sillybilly.travellerspoint.com) and gave an amusing account of a less than triumphant lesson:

> The assignment, on the face of it, should have been simple. Choose your favourite foreign country, write seven sentences about it and then read your work out to the class the following week. The results were, well, pretty bad. Many of them obviously hadn't bothered to do the homework at all, and were just bluffing their way through about 2.5 sentences in the hope they would get away with it. And many couldn't even do that much – at least one stood up and said: 'USA. I like NBA. Thank you'. And promptly sat down. X is for fail, mister! The most popular country was Canada, but only because loads of students had found a stodgy piece about it in their English textbook. The result of this was that I must have heard the same spiel – 'My favourite country is Canada. It is north of the United States. It is the second largest country in the world. It has a population of only slightly over 30 million people' – about 40 or 50 times over the course of the week.
>
> Out of the 350-odd students, a few, to be fair, were quite good. One girl gave a presentation on Switzerland that could have doubled as a Wikipedia entry. One boy said his favourite country was South Africa because it

had lots of gold, and that when he found it he would be very rich. A few chose Ireland but seemed not to know what to say about it except to ply me with compliments. They all passed! Many more in the middle ground had perfectly acceptable mini-speeches. Even where they just regurgitated what I had said in my introduction, I felt that they had done their job for what was an Oral English assignment.

Culturally, the exercise was instructive despite the flawed results. Boys liking basketball and girls liking romance (or clothes!) seemed to be the benchmark of Chinese teenagerdom. In the end then, my first foray into assigning homework was a bit of a mixed bag. But lazy students aside, it's mostly a pleasant job being a foreign teacher in China I reckon. You draw up a simple lesson on PowerPoint and just run with it for a week, improvising and fine-tuning as you go along. And once you're plugged in to it, the work goes by really quickly, leaving plenty of time for fun.

Jessie Levene, reaching for some colourful similes, identifies the lowpoint of her first teaching job was feeling like a 'robot' and a 'teaching monkey'. It seems that you may have to work fairly hard to introduce modern teaching techniques into the classroom, as from a very early age Chinese children are taught in a very traditional style, as **Nina Capek** found while teaching in a primary school:

The teaching style does take a bit of getting used to. The children are used to learning by rote and the general ethos is: whatever the teacher says, we copy. Teaching 'my name is...' to 50 six-year-old children proved very entertaining as they all copied me and said 'My name is Nina'.

A teacher who started work at Shanghai Lixin University of Commerce last year was delighted with the standard of students:

Their attitude has been excellent on the whole. I have only a couple of disruptive students, but they all seem to be very motivated to learn English and realise how important it can be to their future careers. I know little of their real expectations other than most are concerned more with fluency than complexity or accuracy.

At university, students expect to pass, as it has been difficult for them to get in while some have paid to get in or used connections (*guanxi*), which means they expect to sail through. Don't be surprised if just before exam time your students ply you with gifts, expensive meals and even offer money. Teachers who accept these offers may find that their students expect high marks even if they do not turn up to the exam!

ACCOMMODATION

Every university has either a purpose-built hostel or similar. These differ enormously from place to place, though on the whole the standard is more acceptable to people with Western tastes than it was a few years ago. In some places (such as Chengdu University of Science & Technology) the accommodation can be airy and comfortable. In other places it is decidedly spartan and in some cases downright depressing, especially if electricity and heat/air-conditioning are rationed. Find out ahead of time whether you will have internet access.

SAM MEEKINGS

Sam Meekings, like some other teachers, found that there is a demand for any English, provided it is clearly enunciated. Imaginative interactive teaching methods can work, as Sam discovered when he had to teach a 60-strong class of university students, whose homework left something to be desired.

Each week I was supposed to go through the excerpts from Shakespeare or Dickens in the book, despite the fact that close to half of the class could barely communicate with me in English at all. Though the impulse was strong to follow the example of the Chinese teachers and teach only to the brighter students and hope the others kept quiet at the back, I soon found that it was much more enjoyable to try and work the material into games and activities that everyone could take part in. This took time, however, since some students were so used to either being ignored or simply learning by rote and repetition that they were too shy to speak up. This is a problem I have noticed even teaching in private school in bigger cities - students are often so heavily criticised for mistakes in their normal classes that they lack the confidence to risk answering a question or attempting to join a game or discussion in case they do something wrong.

It sometimes feels as if you are not only in a different country but also in a different century. None of the students I taught had any real concept of exploring or questioning an idea. When I set some homework essays for my literature class or set debate topics for my English speaking class to try to engage with, I was invariably met with 60 identical responses. Students are taught to pass exams in China, to memorise the single correct response and then repeat it when instructed - there is no concept of coming up with your own ideas. My students were all adamant that there was always one right answer and that everything else could therefore be discounted as wrong. This meant most essays and debates were very, very short. Coupled with the fact that we were not allowed to fail any students (even if they could not write more than their name on the biannual exam papers we had to set), it quickly became clear that we would have to set aside most of our preconceptions about education. Yet when students do finally open up or try something new, there is no better feeling.

REGULATIONS

Most institutes will issue teachers with an invitation or letter of appointment and other documents to be taken to the Chinese Consulate or Embassy to apply for a visa before leaving their country. You will need a medical report completed on official Chinese forms. In most cases with a 'Visa Notification Form' or letter of invitation you will obtain a Business (F) visa valid for 60 days. This is often referred to as a Visitor Visa, as distinct from a Tourist (L) Visa. After arrival in China this can be converted to a long-stay (Z) work visa. Processing should take four to eight weeks.

Many people enter China on a tourist (L) visa (one to three months), sign a contract with an employer, collect the documentation, then leave the country (to Hong Kong or Macao) to apply for the Z visa. Some employers will even cover the costs. Make sure this happens before your visitor visa expires, which is calculated according to the date of entry to China rather than the expiry date of the visa. Otherwise you will be liable to a fine. Since the Olympics the authorities have become more prickly about residence and related documentation.

As always happens in countries that initially welcome a huge influx of English teachers, the government regulations gradually tighten up, and this is what has been happening in China. It would be nice to provide a succinct summary of the visa rules, but that is not easy or even possible in a country as vast and diverse as China where rules are not enforced uniformly between regions or even municipalities. The toughest requirements for obtaining the Z visa are that candidates must have a degree plus TEFL plus two years' post-university teaching experience, as has been reported in Beijing and Shanghai. Elsewhere, the requirements seem not to be so tough, partly because schools that try to do things by the book are finding it difficult to recruit enough teachers. But the picture is not black and white and even within the most highly regulated regions, adverts can still be seen for teachers with minimal skills/qualifications. Any teacher considering answering an advert like this (e.g. for a no-degree-needed job) should find out in advance what visa the employer plans to get for them, Z or otherwise, and whether the school will provide them with basic employee benefits such as government health insurance.

The Z visa does not necessarily allow multiple entry so find out before you leave China. Everything has to be officially stamped. If you are found without the appropriate documents you will be harshly fined. For example, recently a teacher whose papers were mostly in order but hadn't got the resident's permit was fined RMB3,000 (more than half a month's wages). State institutes of education usually do everything by the book but you shouldn't expect the same of private language schools.

Last summer **John Ramage** answered an ad on Dave's ESL Café and describes the application process and red tape requirements in detail:

I sent the agent a statement of interest + the picture page of my passport + my CV + a reference letter + photos. The agent then set up an interview with the private university, Huanghe College of Science and Technology in Zhengzhou (Henan Province). They called me on my mobile during a lunch break in the office, in Scotland. This was amazingly quick and easy and I got the job fast. The agent then sent me a long contract in bits and pieces, which made it a bit awkward and finicky.

Before going to China, there were unexpected hiccups. Hiccup No. 1 was the medical. This is required for people teaching in China. A form is downloadable from the Chinese website which the doctor must complete. My GP flatly told me it was not NHS work. The MASTA Travel Clinic did help and promptly scheduled a comprehensive medical, exactly what the Chinese authorities were looking for, but it cost me £380.

The second hiccup was the elastic time taken over visa processes. The Chinese Consulate suggests one month, but it can take much longer. I gathered my documents and sent them to the Public Security Bureau in China for processing. The college sent me the invitation letter and work permit to take to the Consulate to apply for the visa. Getting the visa took one week after that. My documents spent far longer than expected in the PSB. The agent made it worse by promising it would be over in several weeks, so I left my UK job. As the weeks turned to months, I got really annoyed. The agency seemed to have a manana, manana attitude (although they were Australian). Surely he ought to have known! Fortunately I didn't book my flight until after I got my Z-Visa, otherwise I could have lost money.

Some schools (like English First) will reimburse the costs you incur in obtaining the visa. You will have to renew your residence permit every six months, which can be irksome.

LEISURE TIME

Foreigners who teach in Beijing can lead a standard expatriate life if they want to, socialising at expat bars and clubs. Life in the provinces will be very different. You may still be one of the very few foreigners that the local people have ever seen and are bound to be the object of curious stares (which will be even more persistent if you happen to be a non-white person).

The main way of socialising in China is going to restaurants, because a large banquet shared by many people is only marginally more expensive than cooking for yourself. However, as most people go out to eat around 6pm–7pm, restaurants do not usually stay open later than 10pm. Students in state institutions can be restricted by a strict curfew, but when everything closes at 10pm, native English teachers start to realise why the students are not so bothered.

In smaller settlements, there may be no restaurants even to rival the Chinese take-away in your home town; but the locals will be far more interested in you and perhaps even teach you to cook your own Chinese food. If there are several foreigners, communal dining facilities (often segregated) will usually be provided. Glutinous rice, soy beans and cabbage are staples and fresh produce may be in short supply in winter. In Tangshan, **Bradwell Jackson** reports that he can have a 'killer meal' of dumplings, quick and right off the street, for only 2 yuan (yuan is an alternative word for renminbi). Learning Chinese is the ambition of many teachers and is a great asset especially outside cosmopolitan areas. Take a good teach-yourself book and CD, since these are difficult to obtain outside Beijing and Shanghai. Mastering Chinese characters is a daunting business, though the grammar is straightforward. Others prefer to study Tai Chi, Wushu or other exotic martial arts.

Despite China's rapid 'Westernisation' in economic terms, its cultural differences remain a challenge. A teacher summed it up in 2010: '*I found it quite difficult to understand the Chinese mentality and even the simplest of tasks seemed to take a lot longer than they really should, due mostly to cross cultural misinterpretation I would say.*'

Be prepared for noise and air pollution even in small towns, though it is usually possible to escape into the countryside by bicycle or bus. Some universities with large contingents of FTs organise group excursions for them from time to time. School and college vacations take place over Spring Festival in or around February, when the trains are very crowded and the weather is cold. Often the holiday dates are not known until the very last minute which makes it difficult to plan vacation travels.

Some cities such as Kunming have a good expat community to which the Chinese cater with Western-style cafés and restaurants. There are plenty of films to watch (all pirated) and a couple of galleries to visit. Much of the time you will be responsible for your own amusement, so take plenty of reading matter, including *Wild Swans*, an astonishing account of life in the Cultural Revolution or perhaps *Under Fishbone Clouds* by Sam Meekings, quoted in this chapter, an interweaving of 20th-century Chinese history and folklore. **Jessie Levene** found lots to do in Chengdu: '*learn Chinese, take photos, enjoy the amazing Sichuan food, hang out with friends, go to bars…*'.

Bradwell Jackson would urge anybody to do TEFL in China:

> *My first impressions were that of a fascinating country with a splendid culture, and I wasn't even in a well-known city. The people are organised and respectful, and the food, of course, is a revelation. If you have just a little bit of travel experience to a non-Western country, you should be fine and have no worries at all. There is certainly no problem with safety. My school has been very good to me. You will find that most schools bend over backwards to get you here. All you need is a fair amount of teaching experience (and a college degree) and the whole new world of China awaits you.*

American **Ed Flok** is similarly enamoured of teaching in China and has just started his third year, this time at the North China University of Technology in Beijing:

Don't believe all the negative articles you read about China. Everywhere I taught (WECL-Qingdao and Yantai University) the people were awesome, and very polite, reaching out to make me their friend. I ate at personal dinner tables, swam in the Yellow Sea with students, ate at restaurants, went bike riding and socialised. The best of this experience was actually teaching the students English, and seeing how fast they learn. To this day I keep in contact with some of my first students. They really get attached to you as a role model, and want you as their friend.

LIST OF EMPLOYERS

AMITY FOUNDATION
71 Han Kou Road, Nanjing, Jiangsu 210008
+86 25 83260836
www.amityfoundation.org

NUMBER OF TEACHERS: 40–50 plus more for 1-month summer programme.
PREFERENCE OF NATIONALITY: None, but must be native English speaker or have a high level of proficiency in English and language teaching experience.
QUALIFICATIONS: Minimum bachelor's degree (though a handful accepted without a degree for summer programme). Teaching experience, a knowledge of Chinese or of living in Asia are useful but not essential. A Christian faith commitment is generally required, however, the 'mission' expected is to serve rather than to proselytise.
CONDITIONS OF EMPLOYMENT: Initial 2-year contract with possible year by year extensions to teach 12–16 in tertiary educational institutions in China, mostly small teacher training colleges in the western parts of China. Also SEP (Summer English Programme) for volunteers to provide oral English training to Chinese middle and primary school teachers of English in rural and minority areas, for 4 weeks from early July.
SALARY: Long-stay teachers receive $250 monthly plus RMB2,500. Expenses for travel, orientation, conferences and medical insurance are covered by the sponsoring agency. Summer volunteers pay fee of $1,200 to cover orientation, admin, etc.
FACILITIES/SUPPORT: Accommodation is usually provided in the form of an apartment on the school campus.
RECRUITMENT: Teachers are recruited primarily through church sending agencies, i.e. mission agencies of various denominations in a range of countries including the UK, Canada and the USA. See above website for contact details of these organisations. Interviews in person are expected and generally take place in the applicant's own country.
CONTACT: Ms. Ruhong Liu, Director, Education & International Exchange Division (liuruhong@amity.org.cn); SEP contact is Robert Ji, SEP Programme Coordinator (jixiaodong@amity.org.cn).

ANGLIA SCHOLARS EDUCATIONAL CONSULTANCY (ASEC)
24 Hampshire Terrace, Portsmouth, Hampshire PO1 2QF, UK
+44 02392 826636
liuweidan@hotmail.com; Info@angliascholars.co.uk
www.angliascholars.co.uk/www.teach-in-china.co.uk

NUMBER OF TEACHERS: 10–15.
PREFERENCE OF NATIONALITY: British, American, Canadian and Australian.
QUALIFICATIONS: Bachelor's or master's degree, TEFL.
CONDITIONS OF EMPLOYMENT: One academic year, 20 hours per week.
SALARY: RMB5,000–RMB6,000. The first RMB5,000 are tax-free.
FACILITIES/SUPPORT: Free accommodation provided.
RECRUITMENT: Newspaper adverts. Interviews held in the UK.
CONTACT: Ms. Weidan Liu, Secretary.

APPALACHIANS ABROAD TEACH IN CHINA PROGRAM
Center for International Programs, Marshall University, One John Marshall Drive, Huntington, West Virginia 25755, USA
+1 304 696 6265
gochina@marshall.edu
www.marshall.edu/gochina

NUMBER OF TEACHERS: 40–60 annually.
PREFERENCE OF NATIONALITY: American, Canadian and British.
QUALIFICATIONS: Bachelor's degree is essential; accepted ages range from new college graduates to early retirees.
CONDITIONS OF EMPLOYMENT: 10-month teaching contract from 1 September. Teaching 15–18 hours per week, at public and private primary and secondary schools and in institutes of higher education, mainly in Shanghai but other areas as well.
SALARY: RMB5,500–14,000 per month, up to 1 month paid winter school break and full international airfare paid on completion of teaching contract.

FACILITIES/SUPPORT: Accommodation provided free by hosting school. 4-day orientation in Shanghai in late August before arriving at Chinese host school.

RECRUITMENT: Internet adverts and phone or Skype-video interviews. Application deadline 31 March/16 April. Application fee is $100/£100; job placement and administrative fee is $1,250/£1,050 which includes 9 weeks of online China TEFL training and 4-day orientation in Shanghai and 1-year travel and medical insurance card.

CONTACT: QingQing Zhao, Director of China Projects.

ASIA INNOVATION INC

8F, 258, Sec.3, HePing East Road, Taipei, Taiwan

+886 2 2764 5784

twhr@asiainnogrp.com

www.asiainnogrp.com

NUMBER OF TEACHERS: 200 are interviewed per year, mainly for positions in China.

PREFERENCE OF NATIONALITY: Native speakers only from USA, Canada, UK, Ireland, Australia, NZ, and South Africa.

QUALIFICATIONS: Bachelor's degree with 2 years' working experience plus an acceptable passport as above.

CONDITIONS OF EMPLOYMENT: 12-month contracts. If working for kindergartens (3–6 years old) or academic institutions like public school system or universities: 9am–5pm Monday to Friday, with stable schedule of 16–22 hours per week. If working for language centres: schedule shifts vary greatly, but teachers mostly get 2 days off per week.

SALARY: RMB6,500–15,000 per month.

FACILITIES/SUPPORT: Agency communicates the needs of foreign teachers to employers however cannot fully assist with housing.

RECRUITMENT: Web, social media, referral, and partnership with other agencies or companies. Skype interviews are required. Sometimes a YouTube video is acceptable as well.

CONTACT: Ivan, Consultant.

ASTON ENGLISH SCHOOLS

Dalian Head Office, Room 2003, Yue Xiu Mansion, No. 82 Xin Kai Road, Xi Gang Dist. Dalian, Liaoning Province 116011

+86 411 8376 9995

www.astonrecruiting.com

NUMBER OF TEACHERS: 300+ annually for about 80 schools all over China (and Vietnam).

PREFERENCE OF NATIONALITY: American, Canadian, British, Irish, Australian, New Zealander and South African.

QUALIFICATIONS: University degree (any subject) and a TEFL certificate and/or TEFL experience. Candidates without a TEFL background can take a 1-week course in China which meets this requirement, at a cost of $315, which is part refunded on renewal of contract.

CONDITIONS OF EMPLOYMENT: Contract lengths of 6–7 weeks in summer or winter. Term-time contracts are for 6 or 12 months starting September and March; 7.5 or 13.5 months starting mid-January and mid-July. 19, 23 or 28 hours per week contracts.

SALARY: RMB7,000 for 28 hours, RMB6,000 for 23 hours and RMB4,800 for 19 hours per week. Varying flight allowances of up to RMB7,000 (approximately $1,100) based on hours and length of contract. Small deductions made for income tax.

FACILITIES/SUPPORT: Contracts provide teachers with private bedrooms in a 2- or 3-bedroom Chinese-style apartment. Teachers must pay for utilities. Proper documents provided for work visas before arrival and residence permit after. Chinese lessons provided.

RECRUITMENT: Via all methods such as internet, phone and drop-ins. Phone/Skype but not in-person interviews required.

CONTACT: Recruiter contact details in China and UK provided on website.

BELL PARTNER SCHOOLS

Hillscross, Red Cross Lane, Cambridge CB2 2QX, UK

+44 01223 275500

www.bell-worldwide.com

NUMBER OF TEACHERS: Varying for 4 language training centres in Shanghai, Beijing, Ningbo and Macao.

PREFERENCE OF NATIONALITY: None, but must have native-like fluency.

QUALIFICATIONS: Bachelor's degree and CELTA and 1 year's experience, preferably in China.

CONDITIONS OF EMPLOYMENT: 1-year renewable contracts. Normally 20 contact hours per week over 5 days.

SALARY: Varies but example of job teaching corporate clients in Beijing of RMB102,000–150,000 gross per year. Approximately 12% deductions.

FACILITIES/SUPPORT: Flights for teachers recruited outside China. Accommodation or accommodation allowance provided. Work permit and visas arranged. End of contract payment. 6 weeks' paid holiday per year plus public holidays. Local medical insurance cover provided. Commitment to in-service training and continued professional development.

RECRUITMENT: Internet, newspapers, personal interview, telephone interview through Bell Worldwide in the UK.

NUMBER OF TEACHERS: 100+.

PREFERENCE OF NATIONALITY: All major English-speaking
countries.

QUALIFICATIONS: Preferably those with TEFL/TESOL certificates
and college diploma and above.

CONDITIONS OF EMPLOYMENT: Usually a 6-month or 1-year
contract. The maximum weekly workload is about 20 hours.

SALARY: RMB6,400+ ($970) less RMB125 for tax.

FACILITIES/SUPPORT: Complimentary accommodation; usually
state-of-the-art fully-furnished apartment units equipped with
major domestic and electric appliances. Nationally accredited and
authorised to employ Western teachers and process work permits.

RECRUITMENT: By word of mouth and through partners throughout the world. Interviews are essential and are often carried out in
the UK and in North America.

CONTACT: Maria Wang, Recruiting Officer.

Cultural Exchange Teaching Programme.

NUMBER OF TEACHERS: 120+.

PREFERENCE OF NATIONALITY: Native English speakers –
British, American, Canadian, Australian, Irish or New Zealander.

QUALIFICATIONS: Bachelor's degree or TESOL certificate
preferable.

CONDITIONS OF EMPLOYMENT: 5 or 11-month renewable
contracts available. 15 teaching hours per week from Monday
to Friday.

SALARY: RMB4,000–5,500 after tax per month. Taxes paid by
the school. Bonus of RMB2,200 paid on completion of one year
contract.

FACILITIES/SUPPORT: Free housing provided: furnished, private
apartments with utilities (phone, TV, air-conditioning, Western
toilet, internet, etc.). Up to RMB200 per month utilities allowance.
Paid public holidays and up to 15 consecutive days of paid sick
leave. Free visa service: work visa invitation letters, work permit

and resident permit sponsorship and visa updates. Airfare reimbursement and assistance. Teacher training, cultural orientation
and post-training teacher assistance. Mandarin lessons provided.

RECRUITMENT: Usually via the internet. Interviews not essential.

CONTACT: Ping Wang (bucklandping@gmail.com) or Owen
Buckland (owenbuckland@gmail.com).

NUMBER OF PARTICIPANTS: 15–20 per year in the year-long
programme. Participants are placed at universities throughout
China.

PREFERENCE OF NATIONALITY: North American with no discern-
ible regional accent.

QUALIFICATIONS: Minimum bachelor's or higher degree (all
majors and professional backgrounds considered, though English,
TEFL, linguistics, business, accounting, economics and engineering especially welcome). Universities prefer that applicants have
some teaching/public speaking/tutoring/seminar presentation
background. People with a master's degree or PhD are strongly
encouraged to apply, as are couples. Must be 60 or under at time
of application and in excellent mental and physical health.

CONDITIONS OF EMPLOYMENT: Full academic year programme
runs from September to June/July. 16–20 hours per week;
2-week intensive TESL and Mandarin Training Institute in Sichuan
in August.

SALARY: Monthly stipend about RMB4,500–RMB11,000 per
month depending on university, and academic or professional
background. Free housing in FTs' complex, medical benefits, most
or all of round trip transportation costs reimbursed and 5–8 week
paid vacation over Chinese New Year.

FACILITIES/SUPPORT: CCC provides full support if any problems
or issues arise at any point. Most universities invite CCC's teachers to teach for a second year. Housing is adequate to excellent
depending on city and university. CCC is the oldest, non-religious,
China teaching, training and placement organisation in the USA
which accepts people from all over the country. CCC has just
published *Yin Yang: American Perspectives on Living in China*
(Rowman and Littlefield, 2012) which takes prospective applicants
through the entire process of teaching in China from attending
the Summer Institute, through the joys and frustrations of the
classroom, travel, making friends, and how families cope with this
challenging transition.

RECRUITMENT: Rolling admissions with fees rising every month after 1 January. For fees, application and detailed information, see www.asiacouncil.org.

CONTACT: Alice Renouf, Director.

CUBEL CULTURE & EDUCATION LIAISON UK LTD
8 Gwynant Crescent, Cardiff, CF23 6LT, UK
+44 29 2132 8693
j.song@cubel.co.uk or info@cubel.co.uk
www.cubel.co.uk

Recruiting partner of Suman Education International, 67 Ayres Road, Manchester, M16 9NH; (+44 161 209 8118; tong.fu@suman.uk.com; www.suman.uk.com), a joint venture since 2003 with Jiangsu Provincial Department of Education.

NUMBER OF TEACHERS: 4-year-long appointments and about 16 short summer placements.

PREFERENCE OF NATIONALITY: Native speakers of English to teach Suman's partners and clients in Jiangsu, Beijing and Jiangxi. Britons preferred for ease of interview and training.

QUALIFICATIONS: Anyone with a Bachelor's degree from a British or North American university can be considered. TEFL or teaching qualification preferred.

CONDITIONS OF EMPLOYMENT: Short contracts of 2–5 weeks at summer camps across China and longer contracts 6–12+ months available in Shanghai. Average 20 hours per week. Summer teachers get 1 day off per week.

SALARY: For summer positions, the cost of visa, plane tickets, accommodation and meals is provided by Suman Education International. Teachers are not paid for delivering lessons but will be given a £250 allowance for each week spent on the camp. For year-long jobs, 3,000–8,000 RMB (£300–£800 / US$470–$1,250) per month depending on the status of the schools/organisations. State schools or universities usually pay less than private language schools due to limited budget.

FACILITIES/SUPPORT: Accommodation provided in most cases.

RECRUITMENT: As soon as vacancies are notified by partners in China, they are advertised on website, TEFL forums, gumtree, etc. Interviews are essential; for summer positions these take place before 21 May. Skype interviews are possible.

CONTACT: Jane Song, TEFL Teacher Recruitment Consultant.

EF ENGLISH FIRST
Teacher Recruitment Office, 1F Jiu An Plaza, 258 Tongren Road, Shanghai 200040
+86 21 60395888
efrecruitment@ef.com
www.englishfirst.com/trt/

NUMBER OF TEACHERS: 1,000 a year for more than 100 EFL schools in China.

PREFERENCE OF NATIONALITY: Native English speakers.

QUALIFICATIONS: University degree, internationally recognised TEFL certification and teaching experience.

CONDITIONS OF EMPLOYMENT: 12-month contracts. Teaching 21 (real) hours between 9am and 9pm, 5 days a week.

SALARY: RMB12,350 (approx US$1,950) per month.

FACILITIES/SUPPORT: Shanghai, Beijing, Guangzhou and Shenzhen schools provide comprehensive benefits package including relocation assistance, flight allowance, health insurance, paid vacation, official working visa, Mandarin lessons, and ongoing training and professional development.

RECRUITMENT: Via EF's Online Recruitment Centre at www.englishfirst.com/trt or send resumé and qualification details to efrecruitment@ef.com.

GOLDEN APPLE CHILD EDUCATION (GROUP)
7 Xinguang Road, Gaoxin District, Chengdu, Sichuan 610041
+86 28 85133381/15 902804305
teachers@61bb.com
www.61bb.com/english

NUMBER OF TEACHERS: 20–25.

PREFERENCE OF NATIONALITY: American, British, Canadian, Australian, New Zealander, Irish and South African.

QUALIFICATIONS: Minimum bachelor's degree in any subject and 2 years' post-graduation work experience in any field.

CONDITIONS OF EMPLOYMENT: Standard 1-year contract. 15–25 hours per week.

SALARY: RMB4,000–RMB9,000 per month depending on hours and experience. (ESL Teachers) RMB6,000–RMB20,000 per month, qualified kindergarten, primary, IB teachers/coordinators. Taxes are deducted from salaries over RMB4,800 per month.

FACILITIES/SUPPORT: School provides accommodation or a stipend towards housing, and a FE's licence and working 'Z' visa. The procedure requires teachers to sign a contract with the school and the government, and get a medical in their own country on the official Chinese embassy paperwork. The school then applies for a government invitation letter using the paperwork, which takes about a month or so to receive. An invitation letter to the teacher is then posted and teachers apply for a Z visa from the Chinese embassy.

RECRUITMENT: Through internet adverts, word of mouth.

CONTACT: Nigel Jones, Director of English Education.

English-owned and managed, independent TEFL recruitment agent filling vacancies for a variety of English schools across China.

NUMBER OF TEACHERS: 25 a month.

PREFERENCE OF NATIONALITY: Native English speaker from UK, USA, Canada, Australia, New Zealand or South Africa.

QUALIFICATIONS: Bachelor's degree, TEFL certificate, plenty of passion and energy.

CONDITIONS OF EMPLOYMENT: 1 year. 20 hours per week (maximum 40).

SALARY: 6,500-16,000 RMB.

FACILITIES/SUPPORT: Schools provide accommodation, flight, insurance, etc.

CONTACT: Jim Althans, Recruitment Consultant.

NUMBER OF TEACHERS: 7 for three branches in Haikou.

PREFERENCE OF NATIONALITY: American, Canadian, British and Australian.

QUALIFICATIONS: Minimum – bachelor's degree, master's degree preferred. Considerable preference given to career educators with former relevant teaching experience in country of origin.

CONDITIONS OF EMPLOYMENT: 12-month renewable contract.

Starting SALARY: RMB5,500–8,000 per month net, contingent on education and experience with automatic annual increments, plus up to RMB15,000 per annum in bonuses paid semi-annually.

FACILITIES/SUPPORT: High standard single and married couple accommodation (close to the school) provided with furnishings and a Western, coiled-spring mattress. All teaching materials provided.

RECRUITMENT: Email correspondence and telephone interview.

NUMBER OF TEACHERS: 20.

PREFERENCE OF NATIONALITY: British, American, Canadian, Australian and New Zealander.

QUALIFICATIONS: Minimum bachelor's degree. ESL/EFL qualification and 2 years' teaching experience preferred.

CONDITIONS OF EMPLOYMENT: 1 year or longer. 18–26 hours per week.

SALARY: RMB5,600–RMB8,600 net, depending on qualifications and length of contract. International trip allowance, end-of-contract bonus, healthcare and travelling allowance all paid.

FACILITIES/SUPPORT: Accommodation offered free of charge. School applies for work permit from the provincial education administration on arrival. Free Mandarin lessons.

CONTACT: Maosi Yan, Programme Director; Manuel Gomez, Co-ordinator.

NUMBER OF TEACHERS: 10–15 each year.

PREFERENCE OF NATIONALITY: Native English speakers; non-native speakers must have near-native proficiency in English.

QUALIFICATIONS: University degree in any field essential. TEFL training or experience is not essential but preferred. Maximum age 65.

CONDITIONS OF EMPLOYMENT: 10-month renewable contracts starting in either August or February, teaching 16–18 classes a week, which works out at a working week of 30–35 hours.

SALARY: Minimum salary 3,500 yuan per month.

FACILITIES/SUPPORT: Free accommodation (usually on campus), all-inclusive 7-day orientation in Shanghai on arrival including basic TEFL training, accommodation, sightseeing and airport transfer. IST Plus arrange school/college placement, visa and work permit, insurance and 24-hour emergency hotline.

RECRUITMENT: Deadlines are mid-December for February departure and mid-June for August departure. Teach in China fees are

£1,095 for 10 months. All teachers who complete their contracts will receive a TEFL certificate.

CONTACT: Ralph Allemano, Director (rallemano@istplus.com).

LONGMAN SCHOOLS SHANGHAI
655 Fuzhou Road, 10th Floor, Huangpu District, Shanghai 200001
C +86 21 6351 5923
longmancareers.sh@pearson.com
www.longmancareers.com

Pearson bought the Wall Street English chain of language schools in China in 2009. An article in the *Guardian* in 2011 reported that Pearson intends to double its teaching capacity and has plans to open 50 new schools in cities such as Nanjing, Suzhou and Dongguan.

NUMBER OF TEACHERS: 50+.

PREFERENCE OF NATIONALITY: Native English speakers.

QUALIFICATIONS: Minimum bachelor's degree, TEFL and 2 years' teaching experience.

CONDITIONS OF EMPLOYMENT: One-year contract. Approximately 36 hours per week with a maximum of 20 teaching hours. Paid overtime available.

SALARY: RMB9,000–RMB13,000 base plus paid overtime and year end bonus.

FACILITIES/SUPPORT: Assistance provided with finding accommodation and applying for work permit.

RECRUITMENT: Usually via the internet and recruitment agencies. Candidates are asked to write a lesson plan prior to interview (carried out by phone if the candidate is not local).

REACH TO TEACH
1606 80th Avenue, Algona, Iowa 50511
C +1 201 467 4612
info@reachtoteachrecruiting.com
www.ReachToTeachRecruiting.com/teach-english-in-china.html

For contacts in other countries, see entry at beginning of Asia chapter.

NUMBER OF TEACHERS: 200+.

PREFERENCE OF NATIONALITY: British, American, Canadian, Australian and New Zealander, Irish, and South African.

QUALIFICATIONS: A full university degree (any discipline) is enough for most schools in the smaller cities or towns. Teachers in the bigger cities face much tougher requirements as the government will only issue work papers to those that have a TEFL qualification plus at least two years of work experience after

leaving university (with one of those years being in a teaching or training-related field). Through a partnership with a TEFL course provider, Reach To Teach can assist teachers in getting course discounts.

CONDITIONS OF EMPLOYMENT: All job placements are full-time positions and for 1 year (and usually extendable). Teaching schedules vary but are generally either daytime, or afternoons and evenings.

SALARY: Depends on school, but commonly: reimbursed flights to and from China, free furnished apartment, salaries between RMB7,000 and RMB16,000 per month depending on qualifications and location.

FACILITIES/SUPPORT: China visa guidance, airport collection, teacher orientation, etc. are provided. Teachers have the option of continued support and contact with Reach To Teach throughout their year-long placement.

RECRUITMENT: Applications submitted via website. Interviews conducted over Skype, by phone and occasionally in person.

CONTACT: Rick Goodman, Director of Recruiting – China (Rick@ReachToTeachRecruiting.com).

ROBERT'S EDUCATION CENTER (REC) BEIJING
8–2 Dong Dan San Tiao, #717, Beijing 100006
C +86 10 6526 1620
bobrec60@yahoo.com

NUMBER OF TEACHERS: 4–6.

PREFERENCE OF NATIONALITY: North American.

QUALIFICATIONS: College degree in English with a teaching credential.

CONDITIONS OF EMPLOYMENT: 1 year. Teaching hours 1pm–9pm.

SALARY: $1,000–$1,500 a month.

FACILITIES/SUPPORT: Fully furnished studio apartment for 1 is provided. Teachers can arrive on tourist visa and REC can organise visa upgrade after arrival.

RECRUITMENT: TESOL Conventions in North America. Otherwise via internet/email.

CONTACT: Robert H. Toomey, Director of Education.

TOSIC INTERNATIONAL EDUCATION GROUP
Suite 2A-2B, 525 Dundas St W, Toronto, Ontario, Canada M5T 1H4
C +1 416 356 8605
tosic@careerinchina.ca
www.careerinchina.ca

NUMBER OF TEACHERS: 500 recruited for various schools on TOSIC (Teach or Study in China) programme.

PREFERENCE OF NATIONALITY: Canadian, American, British and Australian.

QUALIFICATIONS: Minimum bachelor's degree.

CONDITIONS OF EMPLOYMENT: Standard length of contract is 1 year. 20 hours per week.

SALARY: RMB5,000+ net.

FACILITIES/SUPPORT: Free accommodation provided.

RECRUITMENT: Internet. Application can be made online.

CONTACT: Quartz Shi, Consultant.

US-CHINA EDUCATIONAL EXCHANGE

15 Locust St, Jersey City, New Jersey 07305, USA

+1 201 432 6861

edexchange@gmail.com

www.US-ChinaEdExchange.org

NUMBER OF TEACHERS: 200–300.

PREFERENCE OF NATIONALITY: Native English speakers: British, American, Canadian, Australian and New Zealander.

QUALIFICATIONS: Minimum bachelor's degree and commitment to teaching.

CONDITIONS OF EMPLOYMENT: 6 months or 1 year. 15 hours per week.

SALARY: Varies.

FACILITIES/SUPPORT: Schools provide free housing and send candidates visa approval documents.

RECRUITMENT: Internet and newspaper ads. Interviews always conducted by phone.

USIT IRELAND

19/21 Aston Quay, Dublin 2, Ireland

+353 1 602 1742

workandtravel@usit.ie

www.usit.ie/paid-teaching

PREFERENCE OF NATIONALITY: Native speakers of English from Ireland, UK, US, Canada, Australia, New Zealand or South Africa.

QUALIFICATIONS: Degree in any field preferred. Ages 22–45.

CONDITIONS OF EMPLOYMENT: Most placements are in Guilin. Minimum 6 months. Teaching minimum 20 hours per week.

FACILITIES/SUPPORT: Free 4-week TEFL certificate included in programme, during which meals and accommodation are provided free of charge. Otherwise, coordinator in China will assist with finding accommodation and obtaining work permits.

RECRUITMENT: Interviews essential and can be held using Skype. Cost of programme from €1,399.

WALL STEET ENGLISH

3f, Jin Mao Tower, 88 Century Avenue, Pudong, Shanghai 200121

+86 21 5047 0629

recruit_sh@wsi.com.cn

www.wsi.com.cn/career/en/index.aspx

NUMBER OF TEACHERS: Over 200.

PREFERENCE OF NATIONALITY: Must be native English speaker for visa requirements.

QUALIFICATIONS: Degree, CELTA or equivalent plus 2 years' post-graduation teaching experience.

CONDITIONS OF EMPLOYMENT: 1-year contract, with 2 options for working hours; 35 hours with 30 contact hours per week or 25 hours with 21 contact hours per week. All contracts include evening and weekend classes.

SALARY: Approximately $2,000 per month for 35 hour contract.

FACILITIES/SUPPORT: First week hotel accommodation is paid for. HR staff will help with accommodation thereafter as well as visa processing and general settling in. All visa costs are covered but teacher must pay rent and deposit for accommodation.

RECRUITMENT: Usually via online advertising and word of mouth. 2 rounds of interviews which can be conducted using Skype.

WECL ENGLISH COLLEGE QINGDAO

133 Fuzhou Road North, Building 4, Suite 322, Shibei District, Qingdao, 266034 Shandong Province

+86 532 85699787

nick@wallqd.com

www.weclqd.com

NUMBER OF TEACHERS: 10.

PREFERENCE OF NATIONALITY: American or Canadian.

QUALIFICATIONS: At least 1 year's teaching experience.

CONDITIONS OF EMPLOYMENT: 1-year contracts. 20/24 hours per week.

SALARY: RMB4,000–RMB6,000 per month.

FACILITIES/SUPPORT: Free apartment. School will apply for a FE certificate and residence permit for the teachers once they provide a resumé, passport copy, diploma and certificate, medical report, 2-inch photo, reference letter, etc.

RECRUITMENT: Via internet agencies. Interviews are required.

XI'AN JIAOTONG-LIVERPOOL UNIVERSITY ENGLISH LANGUAGE CENTRE

No.111 Ren'ai Road, Suzhou Dushu Lake Higher Education Town, Suzhou Industrial Park, Suzhou, Jiangsu 215123

✆ +86 512 88161300/1345

✉ elc.sec@xjtlu.edu.cn

💻 www.xjtlu.edu.cn/en/academic-departments/tc/english-language-centre

NUMBER OF TEACHERS: Approx 135.

PREFERENCE OF NATIONALITY: Local visa rules restrict employment to the following nationals only: UK, Ireland, Australia, New Zealand, Canada and the US.

QUALIFICATIONS: Tutors need an MA in TESOL/Applied Linguistics or equivalent, plus a teaching qualification (e.g. CELTA/DELTA or B.Ed) and at least two years of experience.

CONDITIONS OF EMPLOYMENT: Renewable contracts from 1–3 years. Office hours are between 9am and 5pm with 20 hours of teaching per week (Monday–Friday only). Currently around 47 days of paid holiday per year.

SALARY: RMB22,000 upwards per month for a qualified and experienced tutor. Some lower level tutor positions are available occasionally at tutor salaries ranging from RMB16,000.

FACILITIES/SUPPORT: Housing allowance of up to RMB3,000 per month and HR will assist with finding local accommodation and applying for work permits. Travel allowance of up to RMB15,000 per year. BUPA health insurance (basic) paid.

RECRUITMENT: Usually via adverts on www.jobs.ac.uk and other websites. Applications are welcome all year round but main recruitment drives are in March and May each year. Interviews and some pre-interview tasks are essential and can be carried out over the phone or internet.

CONTACT: Jack Parkinson, Deputy Director of the ELC.

XU BO ART AND CULTURE EXCHANGE

Room 2506, B Block, Lane 521, Wan Ping Road (South), Shanghai, 200032

✆ +86 21 54590999

✉ program.development@xubo.org

💻 www.xubo.org

NUMBER OF TEACHERS: 150 volunteers per year.

PREFERENCE OF NATIONALITY: None.

QUALIFICATIONS: None necessary.

CONDITIONS OF EMPLOYMENT: 1–3 months volunteer work. Between 10 and 15 lessons per week (40 minutes). Summer camp work available.

SALARY: None.

FACILITIES/SUPPORT: Accommodation is arranged. No working permits are needed.

RECRUITMENT: Via overseas volunteer organisations.

CONTACT: Jessie Duanmu.

Mongolia

LIST OF EMPLOYERS

NEW CHOICE MONGOLIAN VOLUNTEER ORGANIZATION

POB-159, Ulaanbaatar-210646 A

✉ info@volunteer.org.mn

💻 www.volunteer.org.mn

NUMBER OF TEACHERS: 5.

PREFERENCE OF NATIONALITY: None.

QUALIFICATIONS: Native speakers of English from UK, Ireland, USA or Australia with teaching skills.

CONDITIONS OF EMPLOYMENT: 4–12 weeks. 4–6 hours per day; 20–30 hours per week.

SALARY: Volunteers pay a fee of $945 for a month up to $2,045 for 3 months.. Some possibility of paid work.

FACILITIES/SUPPORT: Accommodation provided with host families or in apartment. New Choice will apply for teacher's work permission and long-term visa.

CONTACT: Bayarjargal Damdindagva, Programme Director.

HONG KONG

Since the former British colony became the Hong Kong Special Administrative Region (HKSAR) of the People's Republic of China on 23 June 1997, '*everything has changed and nothing has changed*', or so the saying goes. Only international schools and specialist 'ESF' (English Schools Foundation) primary schools offer a curriculum using English as the medium of instruction (EMI), although it's more common in secondary schools. There is ongoing pressure to review the EMI/CMI situation and the issue continues to be much in the news. The likelihood is that schools will be given more choice as to whether they switch to EMI, which may stem the decline of English as Putonghua (simplified Mandarin Chinese) has been pushed to the fore. Certainly, many parents are still willing to spend vast sums on English courses for their children and there is a high demand for native English speakers willing to teach children from as young as three years. Many of these companies have proprietary learning systems and systematic phonics programmes.

To meet the demand for English teaching, the Hong Kong government employs hundreds of English speakers to teach in the state education system and in non-government schools too as part of the NET scheme (native English teacher) described below.

It is illegal to enter Hong Kong as a tourist and take up work so that those graduates who arrive on holiday and want to change their status are out of luck. However, it is possible to visit the city, find a teaching job and then apply for a work permit from a neighbouring country; Macao is the most convenient. The authorities will expect to see a university degree, relevant work experience and a corporate sponsor. Teachers who satisfy these requirements should have no difficulty obtaining a work permit. Anyone who manages to find an employer before arrival can seek sponsorship to obtain a work permit. This is a major undertaking for any employer so teachers should try to honour their commitments instead of flitting off to a better-paying school after a month or two.

FINDING A JOB

NET SCHEME

The NET scheme is administered by the Hong Kong Education Bureau (EDB), formerly the Education and Manpower Bureau (NET Administration Team, Room 1321, 13th Floor Wu Chung House, 213 Queen's Road East, Wan Chai; netrecruit@edb.gov.hk; www.edb.gov.hk/index.aspx?nodeID=262&langno=1). The website carries full details of the scheme and an application form. Foreign Teachers known as 'NETs' can interview for any school with a vacancy and have some control over where they're placed. The NET community maintains an online 'blacklist' of schools to avoid. The reason the scheme is so popular is that salaries and benefits are generous.

The competition is becoming a lot keener for acceptance onto the scheme because there is no longer a shortage of applicants. Acceptance is easier if you have had teacher training, though the programme is open to university graduates of language-related subjects with a TEFL certificate. The salary range for primary NET is HK$19,835 (£1,500) to HK$40,290 (£3,130) per month and for secondary NET even higher, HK$22,985 (£1,800) to HK$48,400 (£3,800). Exact salaries are dependent on experience and qualifications. However, every NET whose home is outside Hong Kong gets a monthly cash housing allowance of HK$14,242 (£1,100) which really bumps up the salary. Also, there is a 15% gratuity on everything you earn, awarded at the end of the two-year contract, provided your conduct and performance have met with approval. Flights, medical allowance and baggage allowance are all additional perks.

Applications are usually accepted until mid-January and term begins around mid-August. After working in the private sector for the Chatteris Foundation (described below), **Tom Grundy** became a Netter and has posted useful information about living and working in Hong Kong on his website (www.globalcitizen.co.uk/wp/hong-kong-job-hunting-links) and has provided information for this chapter. In comparing the two, Tom concludes:

> *The government NET programme is more highbrow and demanding but offers a better package and wage. However, you don't get the 'instant social circle' you would with an employer like Chatteris. NET is ideal should you decide to remain in HK and great if you already have a TEFL or PGCE qualification.*

He recommends the 'NET Survival Guide' at http://en.wikibooks.org/wiki/NET_Teacher_Survival_Guide to answer any questions about the programme.

OTHER EMPLOYERS

Almost any English institute you locate on the internet will have a Recruitment or Careers page. The British Council has a teaching operation which has an ongoing need for certificate-qualified teachers with at least two years' experience; hiring takes place before mid-August via the Resourcing Office at the Council's HQ in London (www.britishcouncil.org/learning-teachingjobs.htm). One of the largest employers is the Chatteris Educational Foundation (see entry), which offers recent university graduates from English-speaking countries the opportunity to teach in Hong Kong. Like the government scheme, this scheme has become more difficult to enter, possibly because it is being scaled back or because the standard of applicant has risen. On the other hand, there were still some vacancies at the beginning of August 2011 for a 1 September deadline.

Tom Grundy completed the nine-month programme before he became a Netter:

> *The wages were just enough to live on and save some for travel. I saved hard and was able to travel for three months around South East Asia afterwards, and even afforded two laptops. Chatteris has its problems and its 'charitable' status is questionable, but they support and train you. You'll be placed with another British, Canadian or American in a primary or secondary school, there'll be several dozen others who you'll train with and so you'll immediately have a big social network. Chatteris has also started a somewhat experimental 'college programme', though the more traditional school placements are a better option. With Chatteris, your emphasis will be on oral English with a 'non-formal' approach, i.e. games, crafts and other 'fun' activities.*

The basic wage of HK$13,000 hasn't risen much in the past couple of years and by about Christmas many CNETs (Chatteris Native-speaking English Tutors) conclude that their wages are exploitative. A further problem is the interference from the scheme management requiring constant paperwork, workshops and meetings which can upset the balance of the relationship with the school.

Ready to Learn (www.readytolearn.com.hk) employs about 30–40 teachers for a number of centres, although it is not interested in '*travellers seeing the world with a TEFL qualification or similar*'. They are looking for teachers who will commit longer term and take an interest in the company and its methods.

Dramatic English (see list of organisations) employs drama graduates on 10- or 12-month contracts, who are able to use their arts degree and possible performance skills to help children learn English.

Demand is very strong for native English speakers to work in English-speaking kindergartens, for which a degree and a TEFL qualification are generally sufficient. English for Asia (www.englishforasia.com) in Kowloon is another major recruiter, though it can usually employ graduates of its own Trinity CertTESOL course (see Directory of Training Courses). Another reputable private language school which hires foreigners and also offers accredited TESOL certificates is Firstclass Intesol (http://intesol.firstclass.com.hk).

Both internet adverts and the more traditional print-based means of advertising jobs are still going strong. For example the bumper Saturday edition of the *South China Morning Post* might contain some useful leads;

its classified section often carries teaching posts and can be consulted online at www.classifiedpost.com. *HK Magazine* is a weekly listings paper aimed at the ex-pat community which is available every Thursday evening from branches of Pacific Coffee and other 'ex-pat friendly' outlets. *BC Magazine* is a similar monthly publication. The online community http://jobs.asiaxpat.com carries many ads for teachers and the main resource for jobs in HK is www.jobsdb.com. The *Yellow Pages* are an alternative source of institute addresses. Landline calls and faxes within the city limits are free, so by phoning around you can easily get an idea of the possibilities. Although hiring is continuous, the summer months bring even more openings, while the Chinese New Year in January/February is a bad time.

Some companies specialise in recruiting and outsourcing teachers, saving schools the administrative burden of employing a foreigner. Elton Educational Services (www.eltoneducation.com) provides English courses and English teachers to Hong Kong kindergartens and primary schools.

Freelance teaching can prove lucrative although it's always a risk for non-permanent residents, as work visas forbid foreigners to work for anyone other than their named sponsor. An attractive advertisement strategically placed in the letter boxes of the ritzy apartment estates in Mid Levels, Jardine's Lookout and Causeway Bay suburbs or in busy supermarkets might winkle out some private students. It is also possible to pick up tutoring work where you visit a family's home and help their child with homework/English games. The standard payment is £20–£30 an hour. Summer schools, English drama organisations and language schools are also options in Hong Kong, but all foreign workers doing paid or voluntary work require a work visa, so make arrangements with an employer beforehand.

Although Hong Kong is famous for its big city smog and vivacity, there are quieter places and it is worth researching the exact place where you will be living and working. **J.W. Arble** worked at a secondary school in the New Territories in a suburban town 30 miles to the north of Hong Kong Island. '*I lived alone in a 12 by 16ft flat, 17 floors above a colossal shopping centre of six hundred stores, 30 restaurants and a single bookshop that mainly stocked self-help guides and comics. Everything shut at 10pm.*'

REGULATIONS

British citizens may visit the HKSAR without a visa for up to 180 days provided they can satisfy the immigration officer on arrival that they are entering as bona fide visitors with enough funds to cover the duration of their stay without working and, unless in transit to the Mainland of China or the region of Macau, hold onward or return tickets. US citizens are given 90 days. The visa requirements are posted at www.immd.gov.hk/ehtml/hkvisas_4.htm. As already mentioned, visitors are not allowed to change their status after arrival.

Normally it will take about six weeks to process a visa application, assuming all accompanying documents are in order including the nomination of a local sponsor (usually the employer). Applicants should complete application form ID 990A and the employer should complete ID 990 B). The HKSAR Immigration Department is located on the 2nd Floor of Immigration Tower, 7 Gloucester Road, Wan Chai (+852 2824 6111; enquiry@immd.gov.hk).

CONDITIONS OF WORK

If you do not have an official contract and are picking up some teaching at a private institute, you are likely to be paid on an hourly basis and not very well. Erratic hours are also a problem, as **Leslie Platt** found out:

My institute was very vague as to what hours I would be working. I would arrive in the afternoon as instructed only to be informed that no students had turned up but that I had better hang around for a few hours just in case one did. If none did, it meant I didn't get paid.

PUPILS

Hong Kong children are usually well behaved, eager and well mannered, even though so many are under huge pressure from exams, extra tuition, band practice, kung fu, lion dancing and extra sports. It can be just as important for teachers to help their pupils enjoy English and gain confidence, as to instil the finer points of English grammar. Hong Kong's British past can also lead to some interesting situations as **J. W. Arble** discovered:

It is traditional for Hong Kong students to adopt an English name alongside their Chinese ones. These too have, in fact, become family names, passed down with little variation and as a result I found myself surrounded by ghosts from the Edwardian era, Sibyls and Mabels and Ethels and Normans and even an Algernon. Other students chose their own English names: King Kong was the moniker of one five-foot 14-year-old, School Bully was that of another, there was a Ferrari Vespa, an Ω – the student formerly known as Wong – and a Beckham, a 15-year-old covered in tattoos who literally slept through all my lessons undisturbed, who was rumoured to drive a minibus for the Triads. My favourite student name was Frozen Chicken Drumstick, belonging to a girl who had plucked it from a packet in the supermarket deep-freeze.

ACCOMMODATION

Hong Kong is Asia's most expensive city outside Japan and rents keep climbing. Serviced apartments, advertised in the *HK Magazine* and newspapers, are often a cheaper alternative. They are usually based in Jordan, Central, Wan Chai and Causeway Bay. The outlying islands such as Lamma and Lantau and the New Territories are still cheaper, often double the floor space for half the money. Even with HK's superb public transport system, the commute can be time-consuming, so living in Kowloon just north of Hong Kong island might be a happy medium. **Tom Grundy** suggests that the best deals are in old walk-up buildings without lifts where your money will buy comparatively more floor space. He goes on to recommend looking up flat shares on Asia Expat (the main expat community online – http://hongkong.asiaxpat.com), or Geo Expat (www.geoexpat.com) plus of course Facebook, Gumtree and similar.

Areas in Kowloon that are considered to be quite poor are becoming popular with foreigners, such as Sham Shui Po or Tai Kok Tsui, as they are cheaper and still on the MTR red line, which goes direct to Central on HK Island. A decent but standard shoebox-sized two-bedroom flat would set you back about HK$6,000 per month.

LEISURE TIME

Not surprisingly, culture shock is kept to a minimum in Hong Kong by the Western affluence and the lingering British bias. Hong Kong is famed as a shoppers' paradise in which the cheap food, clothing and travel help to alleviate the problem of expensive accommodation. **Tom Grundy** concludes that Hong Kong is an ideal place to live:

In Hong Kong, tax is low to non-existent, it's super clean, has a huge ex-pat community with lots of English clubs, activities, sports, events and the public transport is the world's best. It's very compact and all of Asia is on the doorstep (cheap flights and trains to China, Indonesia, Philippines, Thailand, Cambodia, Vietnam, Laos, etc). The territory has dozens of tropical beaches, temples, a mind-blowing metropolis at its heart, fantastic hiking and outdoor activities, 248 idyllic outlying islands, huge country parks (70% of HK's area is actually green) and everything's a good deal cheaper than home, what with China next door. It's an ideal balance of East and West, English is widely spoken and Western food and luxuries are available everywhere. Though Hong Kong is an aggressively consumerist, capitalist society, it is 'tempered' with Chinese tradition and Buddhist beliefs.

LIST OF EMPLOYERS

CHATTERIS EDUCATIONAL FOUNDATION

33 Sycamore Street, Tai Kok Tsui, Kowloon

📞 +852 2520 5736

✉ hr@chatteris.org.hk, info@chattteris.org.hk

🖥 www.chatteris.org.hk

NUMBER OF TEACHERS: 50–60 CNETs per year.

PREFERENCE OF NATIONALITY: British, American, Canadian, Australian and New Zealander. Composition of CNETS recently has been 36 Britons, 18 Americans and 2 Canadians.

QUALIFICATIONS: Bachelor's degree or higher qualification in any subject, no teaching experience necessary.

CONDITIONS OF EMPLOYMENT: 9-month contracts, 1 September–31 May (mandatory 2-week orientation begins mid-August). 8 hours per day with 1 hour lunch break, weekends free.

SALARY: HK$13,000.

FACILITIES/SUPPORT: Accommodation is provided free of charge by Chatteris during the first 2-week orientation period. During this time, flat-hunting workshops are provided to familiarise employees with the property system of Hong Kong. Chatteris office staff are also available for assistance with negotiation of rental agreements and any issues that may arise during this time. After acceptance into the programme comprehensive support is provided to applicants regarding the organisation and processing of work visa. Chatteris will request a number of documents such as original degree certificates, police clearance checks and references from accepted applicants in order for the visa to be processed.

RECRUITMENT: By word of mouth, seminars, online. Interviews are sometimes carried out in the UK/USA.

CONTACT: Grace Lee, Project Director.

DEBORAH INTERNATIONAL PRE-SCHOOL AND PLAY SCHOOL

G/F Shop 5–5B Site 9, Whampoa Garden, Kowloon

📞 +852 2994 8998

🖥 www.deborah-intl.edu.hk

NUMBER OF TEACHERS: More than 60 for all schools; 8 kindergartens in HK and 2 in Shenzen, China.

PREFERENCE OF NATIONALITY: Canadian, Australian, British or American. Must be native English speakers.

QUALIFICATIONS: Any university degree or an early childhood certificate plus minimum 6 months' teaching experience.

CONDITIONS OF EMPLOYMENT: 2-year contract. School hours from 8.30am to 5pm Monday to Friday plus occasional Saturdays

for special events. Must love children, since teaching children aged 2–6.

SALARY: HK$16,000 approx, depending on experience. Airfare, medical cover and 8–9 weeks approximately paid holiday provided.

FACILITIES/SUPPORT: Free shared accommodation per 2–3 teachers or HK$2,000 accommodation allowance.

RECRUITMENT: Via the internet, please send resumé/CV by email. Recruiting goes on year-round. Interviews not essential.

DRAMATIC ENGLISH

8/F, Breakthrough Centre, 191 Woosung Street, Jordan, Kowloon

📞 +852 2880 5080

✉ de@dramaticenglish.com

🖥 www.dramaticenglish.org

NUMBER OF TEACHERS: Around 40 full-time native-speaking teachers.

PREFERENCE OF NATIONALITY: None but must be native English speakers.

QUALIFICATIONS: Company largely deals with recent Drama and English graduates, as well as specialists in Early Childhood Development. Candidates should have a degree in theatre/drama, English or related field. ESL qualification/experience is preferred, but not essential.

CONDITIONS OF EMPLOYMENT: Contracts run for 10–12 months. Teachers may continue for another contract term. Working hours fall between 8.30am and 5pm with confirmed 22 contact teaching hours/week, depending on school programmes and timetabling.

SALARY: HK$16,000 per month starting salary plus airfare reimbursement and end-of-contract bonus. Employees are required to pay their own taxes at the end of each financial year. There are tax-free thresholds, and due to the timing of contracts, first year employees end up paying little, if any tax.

FACILITIES/SUPPORT: Temporary accommodation for new teachers can be organised. Local staff are happy to support teachers who experience communication problems with local real estate agents and/or property owners.

RECRUITMENT: Via direct contact with universities, referrals and some websites. Phone interviews are essential. The company very occasionally carries out interviews abroad.

CONTACT: Mr Leo Tai, Assistant Operations Manager (de.leotai@gmail.com).

British-owned and operated network of 9 schools around Hong Kong Island and Kowloon. The largest extra-curricular English school in Hong Kong.

QUALIFICATIONS: Degree and teaching certificate e.g. TEFL, CELTA. Applications from those without a teaching certificate will be considered if they have demonstrated experience of working with children in other capacities. Classes are limited to 4 students per class and are highly interactive, so potential teachers need to be energetic and friendly.

CONDITIONS OF EMPLOYMENT: To teach students aged 3–16. Minimum contract duration is 12–14 months. Generous completion gratuities reflect the importance of the contract. Saturday is a working day.

SALARY: Revealed to short-listed candidates.

FACILITIES/SUPPORT: Accommodation provided (about 90% accept this option). School applies for visas on behalf of the candidates before arrival in HK.

RECRUITMENT: Applications must include a cover letter and CV with photo. Recruitment is done via telephone interviews throughout the year.

NUMBER OF TEACHERS: 5.

PREFERENCE OF NATIONALITY: British or American.

QUALIFICATIONS: University degree, CELTA or equivalent ESL teaching certificate plus state teaching certifications e.g. PGCE.

CONDITIONS OF EMPLOYMENT: 1-year renewable contract with 20–25 contact teaching hours per week.

SALARY: HK$20,000 per month.

FACILITIES/SUPPORT: Accommodation provided for the first week then assistance is given to find suitable permanent accommodation. Sponsorship offered for work permits and all paperwork is taken care of.

RECRUITMENT: Usually via advertisements on corporate and professional websites. Interviews are essential.

NUMBER OF TEACHERS: 20.

PREFERENCE OF NATIONALITY: British, American, Australian and Canadian.

QUALIFICATIONS: 3 or 4-year full-time bachelor's degree plus TEFL/CELTA plus minimum 1 year teaching experience, preferably in Asia.

CONDITIONS OF EMPLOYMENT: 1-year contract. 110 contract hours per month.

SALARY: HK$20,000 per month (HK$240K per annum) subject to review after three-month assessment. A gratuity of HK$10,000 paid on satisfactory completion of 1-year contract.

FACILITIES/SUPPORT: Help finding an apartment provided, soft set up loan available to employees and also, visa sponsorship.

RECRUITMENT: Via internet with interviews in Hong Kong.

CONTACT: Ken Chu, Manager.

MACAO

The lesser known of China's two special administrative regions is Macao, a former Portuguese colony which lies west of Hong Kong across the delta of the Pearl River. The territory's economy is booming from its successful gambling and tourist industries. With a doctorate in Linguistics, **Joanna Radwanska-Williams** is an ELT professional at the Macao Polytechnic Institute and with MPI Bell (see entry) who makes Macao her home:

> *Macao is a very international city with a high standard of living. It's definitely a pleasant living environment, and the historic city centre is on the UNESCO World Heritage list. Macao feels like a 'happy place' and is welcoming to families and newcomers. Many people speak English as the international and regional lingua franca and there is a high demand for English. There is a lot of English-language local press. The health care is good. There are many churches, especially Catholic ones, and freedom of worship. It is basically a Western-type setting, though with lots of Chinese tourists from the mainland.*
>
> *The unusual factor – not necessarily a low – is the presence of the casino industry. This comes with incredibly luxurious shopping, good restaurants, etc. For the most part, we reap lots of benefits from this: good salaries, great public facilities funded by the government, such as parks, swimming pools, museums, cultural activities and tourist attractions. Macao has far surpassed Las Vegas in terms of revenue from the casino industry. To the extent that there is crime (much less so than in the US, I would think), it does not impact ordinary citizens. Macao is perfectly safe to walk in, day or night. The public transportation is great.*

LIST OF EMPLOYERS

ENGLISH FOR ASIA LTD (MACAO BRANCH)

10E, Edificio Comercial Rodrigues, No. 599 Av. Praia Grande, Macao, SAR PRC

📞 +853 2870 5784

✉ nathan@englishforasia.com

💻 www.englishforasia.com

NUMBER OF TEACHERS: 10–15 (at present).

PREFERENCE OF NATIONALITY: Native English speakers of any nationality.

QUALIFICATIONS: Minimum bachelor's degree and TESOL certificate (or other equivalent teaching certificate). Minimum of 2 years' experience preferred but not essential.

CONDITIONS OF EMPLOYMENT: 1-year rolling contracts (due to local labour laws). 27 teaching hours a week, plus an allocated 10 hours for preparation and admin work. Hours usually stretch over 6 days, with 1 full day off per week. Operational hours are 8am–9pm; teaching schedule can accommodate teacher's outside commitments.

SALARY: HK$18,000–$20,000 (depending on qualifications and experience). At current exchange rates, this is equivalent to £1,570–£1,750, about double the average wage in Macao. Deductions are made quarterly and are very low (approximately £45 per quarter).

FACILITIES/SUPPORT: Teacher trainer on hand to give on-the-job coaching and guidance. Reasonably priced temporary accommodation will be provided upon arrival until an employee finds a home in the territory. No housing allowance is given. Visa sponsorship is given; teachers provide a copy of their CV/resumé and original certificates for inspection. UK syllabus is followed. The process can take up to 3 months and teachers will be required to pay a fee of around £10 upon collection.

RECRUITMENT: Usually direct application for teachers already in the region. Interviews essential.

CONTACT: Nathan Fox, Centre Manager.

MPI-BELL CENTRE OF ENGLISH (BELL PARTNER SCHOOL)

Macao Polytechnic Institute, 3rd floor, Meng Tak Building, Rua de Luis Gonzaga Gomes, Macao

📞 +853 8599 3161

✉ mpibell@ipm.edu.mo

💻 www.ipm.edu.mo/bellcentre

NUMBER OF TEACHERS: 11 in Macao plus 3 in Xinjiang, China.

PREFERENCE OF NATIONALITY: None, but must be native-speaker of English.

QUALIFICATIONS: Minimum Bachelor's degree, CELTA and 5 years' experience, preferably in China.

CONDITIONS OF EMPLOYMENT: 2-year renewable contracts. Normally 20 contact hours per week over 5 days.

SALARY: Varies but approximately RMB400,000 gross per year. Approximately 8% deductions.

FACILITIES/SUPPORT: Accommodation or accommodation allowance provided. Work permit and visas arranged. End-of-contract payment. 22 days' paid holiday per year plus public holidays. Local medical insurance cover provided.

RECRUITMENT: Direct application to mpibell@ipm.edu.mo

CONTACT: David Quartermain, Deputy Director.

INDONESIA

Indonesia is the fourth most populous nation on earth. The country has been stable for the past few years, and it weathered the financial meltdown reasonably well with GDP on the increase. Schools are attracting professional ELT teachers from abroad with benefits packages and reasonable salaries of more than 11 million rupiah (£720). The best jobs continue to crop up in the oil company cities. Although oil production has been declining, the industry is still crucial to the country's economy. The so-called 'native English speaker schools' with multiple branches in Jakarta and the other cities continue to deliver English courses to the millions of Indonesians who still want to learn the language. These organisations can still afford to hire trained foreign teachers and pay them about 10 times the local wage. EF English First is the biggest and most well-known chain of the franchised language schools, with schools in Jakarta as well as on Sumatra, Java, Sulawesi and Bali. Wall Street Institute has four branches in Jakarta including a plush branch on Jalan Jend. Sudirman, the capital's most prestigious thoroughfare. WSI (jobs@wallstreet.ac.id) and Direct English, also on Jalan Sudirman, capture the market share by targeting office workers using a highly flexible schedule.

However, purely 'language' schools, as well as international schools, are feeling the heat from the burgeoning National Plus schools. According to the Sampoerna Foundation for improving education, there are now nearly 60 member schools of the Association of National Plus Schools. They tend to follow an international curriculum, often with some local content, and the medium of instruction is English, or a mix of Indonesian and English. They are favoured by middle-class Indonesians and expats who are not on oil company salaries and/or who don't get their children's education funded by their employer. Many schools tend to follow a religious path (usually Catholic), perhaps as a marketing tool that appeals to parents, and they tend to pay a little better than the language schools. They also tend to start lessons at 7am. Occasionally they advertise abroad, for example at the time of writing Prime One School (www.pos.sch.id) in Medan, North Sumatra, had posted an ad on www.tefl.com for two native English speaker teachers. Another source of work are the universities, although they don't always pay much more than small language schools.

FINDING A JOB

The CELTA is highly regarded in Indonesia and anyone who has acquired the certificate has a good chance of pre-arranging a job in Jakarta, Surabaya, Bandung or Yogyakarta (arguably the most interesting city in Indonesia). While some schools clearly favour either British or North American teachers, others express no preference, and there are also quite a few Australian and New Zealander EFL teachers in Indonesia. The government stipulates that teachers must be native English speakers from the UK, USA, Canada, Ireland, Australia or New Zealand in order to be awarded a work permit. Teachers are required to hold a bachelor's degree in a specified subject, i.e. Linguistics, English Language, English Literature or Education to satisfy government visa requirements, and this is now enforced, in spite of what other teaching or ELT qualifications the candidate might have. Among the main schools in Indonesia it is standard to reimburse airfares and visa costs at the end of a successful contract. A number offer medical insurance and others offer free housing.

ON THE SPOT

More and more teachers are being hired on the spot, which suits the major schools, who then don't have to pay for airfares. Local recruits can negotiate shorter contracts, for example six months, unlike teachers recruited abroad who usually have to commit for 12 months. Most teaching jobs start in July or September/October. With a Cambridge or Trinity Certificate and university degree your chances of being offered a job are high. Unqualified applicants would have to be extremely well presented (since dress is very important in Jakarta), able to sell themselves in terms of experience and qualifications and prepared to commit themselves for a longish spell or to start with some part-time work in the hope of building it up. Caution is advised at the interview stage, because promises are not always kept or the full extent of deductions mentioned.

Local schools staffed by Indonesians abound, many willing to hire a native English speaker at local wages. Some can even arrange a work permit. However, there is no 'easy answer' for how prospective teachers should try and sell themselves, as **Ross McKay**, a long-term teacher in Jakarta, is keen to point out:

> *Each school has it own ethos. One place likes lots of chat but others are sober-sides who keep students' noses to the grindstone. I went to one interview and kept the class happy for an hour, only to be told that 'we're educators, not entertainers'. But another school didn't call me for interview because I'd stated that I took the job seriously and didn't go easy on students who habitually arrived late. Jam Karet, rubber-time, is a bad habit here, and you either adjust to it or get driven nuts.*

Travellers have stumbled across friendly little schools up rickety staircases throughout the islands of Indonesia, as the German round-the-world traveller **Gerhard Flaig** describes:

> *In Yogyakarta you can find language schools listed in the telephone book or you just walk through streets to look for them. Most of them are interested in having new teachers. I got an offering to teach German and also English since my English was better than some of the language school managers. All of them didn't bother about work permits. The wages aren't very high but it is fairly easy to cover the costs of board and lodging since the cost of living is very low.*

The Indonesian *Yellow Pages* is online at www.yellowpages.co.id and searchable in English under the heading 'Language Schools'. Opportunities exist not only in the large cities but in small towns too. **Tim Leffel** from New Jersey, USA, noticed a large number of English schools in the Javanese city of Solo, and others have recommended Denpasar (Bali). At local schools unused to employing native English speaker teachers, teaching materials may be in short supply. One of the problems faced by those who undertake casual work of this kind is that there is usually little chance of obtaining a work permit (see below). It is also difficult for freelance teachers to become legal unless they have a contact who knows people in power. The problem of visas doesn't arise if you teach English on a completely informal basis as **Stuart Tappin** did:

> *In Asia I managed to spend a lot of time living with people in return for teaching English. The more remote the towns are from tourist routes the better, for example Bali is no good. I spent a week in Palembang, Sumatra, living with an English teacher and his family. You teach and they give their (very good) hospitality.*

If you get stuck job-hunting in Jakarta, go to Jalan Jaksa, a small but lively street where many teachers hang out.

REGULATIONS

The work permit regulations are rigidly adhered to in Indonesia and all of the established language schools will apply for a visa permit on your behalf. Some even employ a dedicated visa co-ordinator. The embassy's 'General Information for Foreigners Wishing to Work in Indonesia' starts with the warning, '*Please be informed that it is not easy for foreigners to work and stay in Indonesia since Indonesia has very strict and complicated immigration/visa requirements and regulations, and the process can be very long*' (www.indonesianembassy.org.uk). The Indonesian government limits work permits to teachers holding passports from the six main English-speaking countries and with degrees in an approved field as listed above, which one school director called 'nonsensical' but that is the situation.

If the job is arranged in plenty of time before you leave home, you may be sent a letter of sponsorship from your employer to take to the Indonesian Embassy in London and, subject to current visa requirements, they will issue you with an Employment Visa valid for a maximum of 60 days, £35 non-refundable. Alternatively, you may apply for a one-year Temporary Stay visa (VITAS), which costs £100.

It is possible to enter Indonesia on a tourist visa and after being hired, have the school arrange the work permit but for this you will have to leave the country after supplying your CV, TEFL course and university degree certificates, photocopies of your passport and application forms. Anyone without the necessary professional qualifications is unlikely to be granted the visa. The application is sent to the Indonesian Ministry of Education, the Cabinet Secretariat and the Immigration/Manpower Departments. If and when the application is approved, the work permit will be valid for one employer only and will be revoked and the offending teacher deported if work is undertaken outside the terms of the contract.

After your work permit and temporary stay permit have been granted (with a maximum validity of one year), the documentation will then be sent to the nearest Indonesian Embassy (normally Singapore) where the teacher can have it stamped in his or her passport. These visa runs only take a couple of days and should be paid for by your employer, although some, such as Berlitz, consequently withhold 10% of your salary for the first six months, then reimburse the 10% monthly, starting in the seventh month, to ensure that teachers fulfil the year's visa.

It is possible to renew your tourist status by leaving the country every two months (e.g. flying to Singapore, or by ferry to Penang in Malaysia) but the authorities might become suspicious if you did this repeatedly. Anyone found working on a tourist visa will be deported and blacklisted from entering Indonesia in the future. Also, the employer would be in serious trouble.

CONDITIONS OF WORK

Salaries paid by the 'native English speaker' schools can provide for a comfortable lifestyle including travel within Indonesia during the vacations. Most schools pay at least 9 million rupiah per month, after Indonesian tax of 10% (on earnings of up to Rp25 million) has been subtracted. Although salaries with Wall Street International are usually at the lower end, in Indonesia they offer Rp13,000-16,000 in addition to a travel subsidy. As mentioned, reimbursement for airfares is commonplace, as described by **Bruce Clarke**, who worked for EF English First:

In addition to a decent starting salary, my school also agreed to reimburse me at the end of my contract for both the price of my plane ticket and my work visa. Basic living is relatively cheap. I spend about half my salary on Western luxuries like beer, CDs, movies, etc. I bank the rest so at the end of my year I expect to head home with a few thousand dollars saved. Most of the teachers I meet are in their early 20s, and are generally still at the 'let's party every night' stage of their lives. They complain about constantly being broke because they tend to go clubbing two or three nights a week and waste a lot of money.

Many schools offer generous help with accommodation, ranging from an interest-free loan to cover initial rent payments or deposits, to free housing complete with free telephone, electricity and maid service. This perk may be at the expense of free choice though, and it is worth considering if you mind where you live/ who you live with. It is customary in the Jakarta housing market to be asked to pay the annual rent in a lump sum at the beginning of your tenancy, and so access to a loan from your employer is often essential. **Ross McKay** warns that housing contracts should not be undertaken lightly since one of his ex-colleagues who refused to pay a year's rent on a house he had occupied for two months ended up behind bars and subject to a huge payment of Rp20 million.

If you happen to work for a school which takes on outside contracts, you may have the occasional chance to work outside the school premises, possibly in a remote oil drilling location in Sumatra, for up to double pay. The majority of teachers, however, conduct lessons at their school through the usual peak hours of 3.30pm–8.30pm with some early morning starts as well. Many supplement their incomes with private pupils (provided their employer permits it). For example, Ross McKay was paid by a doctor to teach him while they drove into Jakarta in the morning, which boiled down to him being paid to be given a lift to work. Freelancers will have to get used to *jam karat* which means 'rubber time' or the Indonesian habit of appalling time-keeping.

THE PUPILS

Outside the big cities, the standard of English is normally quite low, with pupils having picked up a smattering from bad American television. Classes also tend to be large, with as many as 40 pupils, all expecting to learn grammar by the traditional rote methods. According to a VSO volunteer teaching in Western Java (as quoted in the *Times Educational Supplement*), '*If I want to do something interesting, the students complain that it isn't in the exam*'. As is the case elsewhere in the world, the average age of English learners is getting younger, so anyone with experience of teaching children or teenagers will be appreciated. **Andrew Whitmarsh**, a teacher for WSI in Jakarta, enjoyed being able to entice his students into university-style discussions:

> *As I look back over my experience, I would say that the best times have come during the classes when I almost forgot I was a teacher and they were my students, and instead felt like I was leading a discussion group back at university. At the other end of the scale there were certainly days that some classes felt repetitive, but I got through these by being sure to make creative and engaging social clubs to balance it all out.*

LEISURE TIME

Although Jakarta is a hot, dusty, overcrowded, polluted and poverty-stricken city, there is a great deal to see and do, and most teachers end up more than tolerating it. After quitting his job in information technology at age 37, **Bruce Clarke** obtained a TEFL certificate from Winfield College in Vancouver and immediately landed a one-year teaching contract with EF English First in Indonesia and concluded that Indonesia is 'okay', though not quite as glamorous as he had hoped. He liked his school and staff, but found Jakarta just another big, crowded city. On a happier note, a past Director of Studies at Executive English Programs (EEP) writes:

> *Jakarta has moved on in leaps and bounds in many ways since I first arrived. The traffic may be viler than ever, but while it still certainly isn't Hong Kong or Singapore food-wise, the variety of good quality, reasonably-priced restaurants is very impressive these days. Once you know your way around!*

Indonesia is a fascinating country and most visitors, whether short-term or long, agree that the Indonesian people are fantastic. Travel is cheap and unrestricted, and excursions are very rewarding in terms of scenery and culture. Travel by public transport can be time-consuming and limiting for weekend trips, so you might consider getting a motorcycle, although Jakarta's traffic problems make this too dangerous and unhealthy for many.

Internal flights are also within the range of most teachers. **Ross McKay** recommends using Bluebird or Express taxis in Jakarta as the most dependable and to use air-conditioned buses (but not after midnight). He also advises newcomers to arrive with crisp, new notes since banks are loath to handle creased or tatty foreign currency.

Predictably the community of expatriate teachers participates in lots of joint activities such as football and tennis matches, chess tournaments, beach excursions, diving trips and parties. Most teachers have DVDs but occasionally go out to see an undubbed American film. The pleasant city of Bandung might prove an attractive alternative to Jakarta and offers a good quality lifestyle to teachers, with a good mixture of rural and city life. Since the completion of the new toll road from Jakarta to Bandung a journey time of two hours is possible. It's choked at the weekends, but fine during the week.

Speaking of weekends, **Andrew Whitmarsh** has no problem finding something to do, often with the help of his students:

This is one of the wildest and most wonderful countries I've worked in, so a lot of my time is spent getting out and seeing the city or jumping a train to check out the surrounding countryside. The traffic in Jakarta is tough to deal with and the air quality isn't great, but the opportunity for adventure and excitement is always just around the corner. Many of my students-turned-friends are great guides to the sights and always know the best nightclubs to visit, when the concerts are and where the best food is.

Bahasa Indonesian, almost identical to Malay, was imposed on the people of Indonesia after independence in 1949 and is one of the simplest languages to learn both in structure and pronunciation.

LIST OF EMPLOYERS

AIM FOR ENGLISH
Jalan Padang 5C, Manggarai, Jakarta
+62 21 837 85 238
ian@aimjakarta.com/info@aimjakarta.com
www.aimjakarta.com

NUMBER OF TEACHERS: 11.

PREFERENCE OF NATIONALITY: British, American, Canadian, Australian, New Zealander and Indonesian.

QUALIFICATIONS: Must have a Bachelor's degree in English Language, English Literature, Linguistics or Education. At least CELTA, and at least 3 years' experience (teaching adults, test preparation, Business English and academic English).

CONDITIONS OF EMPLOYMENT: 12-month contracts. 24 hours contact. 7 hrs in the office 5 days a week. Some evening work. Teachers will also visit clients in their workplaces around Jakarta.

SALARY: 15 million Rupiah (after tax), equivalent to around US$1,600 per month.

FACILITIES/SUPPORT: Return tickets home, end-of-contract bonus, full health insurance. Ongoing career development. Visas and work permits taken care of: outsourced to a reliable agent.

RECRUITMENT: Through online advertising, word of mouth. Interviews essential, and can be via web-meeting (via Skype/Yahoo messenger with webcam). Face-to-face interviews preferred, as teaching a demonstration class is often necessary.

CONTACT: Ian Bishop, Managing Director.

BERLITZ LANGUAGE CENTRES
PT Berlitz, Hotel InterContinental MidPlaza Jakarta, Shopping Gallery R-26, Jl. Jendral Sudirman Kav. 10–11, Jakarta 10220
+62 21 251 4589
lincoln@berlitz.co.id, recruitment@berlitz.co.id
www.berlitz.co.id

NUMBER OF TEACHERS: 10.

PREFERENCE OF NATIONALITY: British, American, Canadian, Australian and New Zealander.

QUALIFICATIONS: Degree minimum. TEFL certificate (CELTA or equivalent) and/or experience preferred but not essential.

CONDITIONS OF EMPLOYMENT: 12-month contracts. School hours: 7.30am–9pm, Monday to Friday; 7.30am to 3pm Saturday. Lessons scheduled as available between these hours.

SALARY: Approximately $1,000–$1,200 (net) depending on qualifications and experience.

FACILITIES/SUPPORT: Housing allowance paid and first month's housing arranged. Berlitz Instructor Training free of charge. Visa agent assists with permits and school bears the cost.

RECRUITMENT: Word-of-mouth, newspapers and via internet. Interviews by phone or held at nearby language centre.

CONTACT: Lincoln Taylor (Manager of Instruction) and Cora Ramschie (Instructional Supervisor).

EF ENGLISH FIRST
Indonesian Head Office, Wisma Tamara Lt. 4, Suite 402,
Jl. Jend. Sudirman Kav. 24, Jakarta 12920
+62 21 520 6477
efrecruitment@ef.com
www.englishfirst.com/trt

NUMBER OF TEACHERS: More than 700 for 68 schools through-out Indonesia.

PREFERENCE OF NATIONALITY: British, Canadian, Australian, American or New Zealander only (due to work visa restrictions).

QUALIFICATIONS: TEFL/TESL certificate indicating 120 hours of class work, observations and evaluated practice teaching. Experience, bachelor's or master's degree and references may be submitted in lieu of the certificate.

CONDITIONS OF EMPLOYMENT: 12-month contracts. Usual hours are early afternoon until evening (1pm–9pm).

SALARY: Varies significantly between cities: 6–9 million Rupiah per month (no tax deduction).

FACILITIES/SUPPORT: Most schools provide shared housing free or a monthly housing allowance. Teachers preferring to live alone are given advice and help but bear the contractual responsibilities themselves. Schools provide and pay for necessary working papers. Orientation on arrival, ongoing training and development, medical insurance, paid holidays and completion bonus provided. All schools are well equipped with a variety of resources.

RECRUITMENT: Via EF's Online Recruitment Centre or approaching individual schools. Candidates are requested to register their details at www.teachenglishfirst.com.

CONTACT: Alan Davies (alan.davies@ef.com).

EXECUTIVE ENGLISH PROGRAMS (EEP)
Jalan Ir. H. Juanda 130B, Bandung
+62 22 250 3727
dos@eepbdg.com
www.eepbdg.com

PREFERENCE OF NATIONALITY: British, American, Canadian, Australian and New Zealander.

QUALIFICATIONS: CELTA/Trinity certificate plus university degree in English, English Literature or Linguistics (as laid out in the new Department of Education regulations) and at least a year's experience preferred.

CONDITIONS OF EMPLOYMENT: 1-year contracts to work a maximum of 28 hours per week.

SALARY: Minimum 10,000,000 Rupiah per month for in-centre training. Increments for higher duties, in-company work and specialised training projects. Contract renewal bonus operates. Salary includes 25 days' paid holiday per year and limited medical coverage.

FACILITIES/SUPPORT: Will provide documentation and assist in finding accommodation.

RECRUITMENT: Through local newspapers (*The Jakarta Post*). Candidates should send cover letter, CV and certification. Local interviews preferred, although online interviews are also acceptable.

KELT SURABAYA (formerly International Language Programs)
Jalan Jawa 34, Surabaya 63105, Jatim
+62 31 734 3535
simonb@k-elt.com or jawa@k-elt.com
www.k-elt.com

NUMBER OF TEACHERS: 25 in 3 schools.

PREFERENCE OF NATIONALITY: Must be classified native English speaker (to satisfy work permit requirements) i.e. British, American, Canadian, Australian and New Zealander.

QUALIFICATIONS: Recognised EFL qualification required, e.g. CELTA or Trinity; short intro courses and online courses not acceptable.

CONDITIONS OF EMPLOYMENT: 1-year contracts, e.g. from July. 20 hours per week, teaching 5 days a week, between 2.30pm/3.45pm/5pm and 7pm/9.15pm. Pupils from age 4. 8 weeks' holiday a year.

SALARY: Starting salary is 11,000,000 Rupiah (net) per month.

FACILITIES/SUPPORT: Accommodation provided including utilities and servants. Regular workshops held.

RECRUITMENT: Adverts on the internet (www.tefl.com). Recruitment 4 times a year.

CONTACT: Simon Bradshaw, Coordinator of Studies (simonb@k-elt.com).

LONDON CITY INSTITUTE
Jalan Danau Toba 104, Benhil, Jakata Pusat 1021
+62 21 870 1505
lci@londoncityinstitute.com
www.londoncityinstitute.com

NUMBER OF TEACHERS: 3.

PREFERENCE OF NATIONALITY: None.

QUALIFICATIONS: Accredited certificate such as TESOL or CELTA and experience teaching adults. Experience teaching in-company classes is preferred.

CONDITIONS OF EMPLOYMENT: Minimum 1-year contract with a maximum of 20 teaching hours per week.

SALARY: Starting salary is 10 million Rupiah per month plus bonus at the end of the contract. Taxes and social security are paid for.

FACILITIES/SUPPORT: Help given with finding accommodation and teachers are provided with all the necessary legal documents needed for a work visa.

RECRUITMENT: Usually via advertisements on websites such as www.eslbase.com and www.onestopenglish.com. Interviews are essential. If the candidate is outside the country telephone interviews can be arranged.

CONTACT: Richard Jackson, Academic Coordinator.

THE BRITISH INSTITUTE (TBI)
Menara Kuningan, Unit F1, Jl. HR. Rasuna Said Blok X7
Kav. 5, Jakarta 12940
📞 +62 21 300 27988/9
📧 recruit@tbi.co.id
💻 www.tbi.co.id

TBI has 16 schools across Indonesia (9 in Greater Jakarta, 3 in Bandung, one each in Medan, Surabaya, Semarang and Malang) and is the only CELTA centre in the country.

NUMBER OF TEACHERS: Approximately 150 expatriates and local teachers.

QUALIFICATIONS: CELTA or equivalent plus university degree minimum. TBI teachers must meet Indonesian education department criteria. Aspiring teachers with degrees in English disciplines approved by the Indonesian Department of Education may be considered for contracts that include CELTA sponsorship.

PREFERENCE OF NATIONALITY: British, American, Canadian, Australian and New Zealander only (for visa reasons).

SALARY: Base salaries vary and are based on relative cost of living and number of teaching hours per week (22–24). Monthly salary after tax ranges from 10,000,000 to 15,000,000 Rupiahs. End of contract bonuses and airfare contributions are also paid.

FACILITIES/SUPPORT: Free health insurance coverage, settling-in loan, work permits and documentation paid. Six weeks' paid leave per annum. Professional development programme of workshops and observed teaching with feedback. Good career development prospects, including supervisory positions.

RECRUITMENT: Local hire or distance. Local applicants must teach a demonstration lesson. Distance applicants must complete tasks and have a Skype/telephone interview.

CONTACT: Tuti Maryati, Human Resources Manager.

JAPAN

After stagnating for some years, the Japanese economy was dealt a grievous blow by the earthquake and tsunami of 2011. The marketplace in which English language academies are now competing is more desperate than it once was and it seems that the glory days for English teachers are over. Of the five largest chains of language schools, three have gone bankrupt or been sold off over the past few years. Yet groups of *eikaiwa* (conversation schools) remain in business, alongside thousands of independent English schools in Tokyo, Osaka and many other Japanese cities which hire *gaijins* (foreigners) to teach. Some are still willing to hire native speakers of English with no teaching qualification as long as they have a university degree and preferably some relevant experience.

The demand among Japanese people to learn English from native speakers will survive no matter what. One of the booming areas of the market is the teaching of English to pre-school and primary-aged children. English is about to become compulsory for fifth and sixth grade pupils throughout Japan, and many parents are sending their children to cram schools in order to prepare them for this change. Furthermore from 2013, some lessons in Japanese secondary schools are going to be taught using the medium of English. Japanese families devote a colossal percentage of their household income to promoting education, and English language schools are among the main beneficiaries.

The basic monthly salary of 250,000 yen for full-time EFL teachers may not have risen in well over a decade, but it is worth nearly £2,000/$3,100, considerably more than can be earned in most other countries. Wages are of course meaningless without balancing them against the local cost of living which is notoriously high. People used to say that you can't expect to break even and begin to save before you've been in Japan for about a year, but the cost of living has stabilised and many teachers who live frugally do manage to save. Developments such as the increase in the number of '100 yen shops' (the equivalent of 'pound shops') have made it far easier to outfit an apartment or buy teaching materials at reasonable prices.

A university degree is a prerequisite for getting a teaching job, simply because it is a requirement for a work visa. However, despite the increase in competition for teaching jobs, there is still surprisingly little emphasis on TEFL qualifications. Image is of paramount importance to the Japanese and many employers are more concerned to find people who are lively and a touch glamorous than they are to find people with a background in teaching.

As long as your expectations are realistic, Japan should turn out to be a rewarding choice of destination. Native English speakers are hired in a surprising range of contexts: in-house language programmes in steel or electronics companies, state secondary schools, hot-house crammers, 'conversation lounges' where young people get together for an hour's guided conversation, vocational schools where English is a compulsory subject, 'ladies' classes' (quaintly so-called) where courses called 'English for Shopping' are actually offered, and also classes of children from as young as two, since it has become a status symbol in Japan to send children of all ages to English classes. In fact, studying English for many Japanese is still more a social than an educational activity.

> *Culture shock grips most new arrivals to Japan. Incoming teachers are often so distracted by the mechanics of life in Japan and the cultural adjustments they have to make to survive that they devote too little energy to the business of teaching. On the other hand, anyone who has a genuine interest in Japan and who arrives reasonably well prepared may find that a year or two in Japan provides a wonderful experience.*

PROSPECTS FOR TEACHERS

Jobs teaching English in Japan can be looked for in a variety of establishments from kindergartens (increasingly popular) to universities (difficult to crack until you have been living in Japan for years). Most private language schools in Japan are looking for native English speakers with a bachelor's degree (any nationality) and possibly some TEFL experience. Although only a minority are looking for professional qualifications in their teachers, there has been a noticeable increase in the number of qualified EFL teachers (especially from Australia) looking for work, and naturally schools prefer to take them over complete novices. In fact if you can prove that you have three years of full-time experience teaching ESL, that will be accepted even if you don't have a degree.

Old Japan-hand **Joseph Tame** reported on his blog that he was interviewed by an agency recruiting teachers: '*CELTA was once again highlighted by the interviewers as one of the main reasons they'd contacted me in the first place – it's good to know that it has an impact in the real world recruitment.*' Many schools have no set intake dates and serious applications are welcome at any time of the year, though most contracts begin in April and finish the following March (i.e. one year) which corresponds to the academic year.

The demand for Business English and TOEIC (Test of English for International Communication) preparatory courses is also considerable. Japanese workers who have paid employment insurance for over three years are eligible to take courses with accredited learning institutions and claim a portion of the cost back from the government. The growth in the demand for Business English is also due to companies expecting new recruits to be able to communicate in English in an increasingly global marketplace.

The favoured accent is certainly American and to a lesser extent Canadian. In fact, not many Japanese can distinguish a Scot from a Queenslander, or an Eastender from an Eastsider. What can be detected and is highly prized is clear speech. Slow precise diction together with a smart appearance and professional bearing are necessary to impress some potential employers. One way round this is that telephone teaching has just penetrated the language teaching market, for example English Telephone Club (www.aoki.com/job/etc) hires telephone tutors part-time.

FINDING A JOB

With the decrease in vacancies at a sub-professional level, it is more difficult for university graduates to find a job before arrival, though this is preferable because it means the employer will sort out visas and help with initial orientation and housing. The disadvantage is that the salary and working conditions will probably compare unfavourably with those of teachers who have negotiated their job after arrival; but most new recruits (*nama gaijin* or raw foreigners) conclude that the trade-off is a fair one. Of course the pool of foreign job-seekers already in Japan is large enough that the jobs offering good conditions tend to be snapped up quickly. Some organisations do not welcome speculative applications from outside Japan, and quite a few advertisements specify that they will consider only candidates who already have the right visa.

One of the best ways of arranging a job in advance is to join the Japan Exchange and Teaching (JET) Programme, which is a prestigious government-sponsored programme that offers what many consider to be a 'dream job' for new graduates. Whereas at one time the majority of ALTs (Assistant Language Teachers) in the public school system entered Japan as JET participants, now many are hired by private language teaching companies known as 'dispatch companies' which do not always enjoy a favourable reputation. In fact **Del Ford**, with nine years' teaching experience in East Asian countries as of 2011, takes a decidedly dim view of this shift:

Now, many of the public school ALT jobs are filled by the poor saps who accept dispatch company contracts. These companies represent pure evil – low salaries, no benefits, no support system, no paid airfare, health insurance, etc. I really think a section in your next edition should include a blurb on the pitfalls of working for these gangsters. Some smaller eikaiwa *outfits have this type of nonsense for ads: '200,000 yen per month, prefer experience, basic Japanese language ability, TEFL Cert., International Driving Licence, etc'. Simply put, it's gotten grimmer over the last decade.*

Not everyone is so disillusioned with opportunities available through the mass-market schools like Interac, as **John Ramage** reported in 2011:

After several frustrating trips to London a few years ago, I did manage to get a job, which seemed like falling through an open door. Interac interviewed me in Edinburgh, rather close to home, and it was a positive experience. I arrived in Japan just in time for the cherry blossom, and I met many memorable people. I started learning to write Japanese. My experiences were so vivid that my life back home and in the West generally seemed less real.

THE JET PROGRAMME

JET is an official Japanese government scheme aimed at improving foreign language teaching in schools and fostering good relations between the people of Japan and the 44 participating countries. The programme has been in existence since 1987 and is now responsible for placing more than 2,000 native English speakers of English for a minimum contract of one year in state junior and senior high schools throughout Japan, with an increasing number in rural areas. Many consider the emphasis to be more on cultural exchange than on English teaching. The rumour is that the programme is in decline with the possibility that over the next decade or so it will be wound up entirely, though this has not been officially confirmed.

The majority of participants are from the USA (contact details below). Britain annually recruits graduates to the programme – this year's intake was 150 compared with 200 in previous years – making it among the largest employer of new graduates after the UK government. Acceptance has become much more competitive and the prospects for people who become assistant language teachers (ALTs) in English on the JET Programme are excellent. Any UK national who is under 40 with a bachelor's degree and an interest in Japan is eligible to apply.

In the UK the scheme is administered by the JET Desk at the Embassy of Japan, 101–104 Piccadilly, London, W1J 7JT (+44 20 7465 6668; info@jet-uk.org; www.jet-uk.org). Non-British applicants should contact the Japanese embassy in their country of origin for information and application forms. US applicants can obtain details from any of the 16 consulates in the USA or from the JET Office, Japanese Embassy, 2520 Massachusetts Avenue NW, Washington, DC 20008 (+1 202 238 6772/3; jet@embjapan.org; www.us.emb-japan.go.jp/JET).

The timetable for applicants from the UK is as follows: application forms are available online from late September; the deadline for applications is the last Friday in November; interviews are held in January and February; an intensive two-day orientation for successful candidates is held in London and Edinburgh at the start of July and departures for Japan take place in late July/August.

Robert Mizzi from Canada worked hard on his application, which paid off since he was called to an interview:

The interview was probably the most difficult interview I have ever had. It was only 20 minutes, but a painful 20 minutes. Besides the usual 'Why' and 'Tell us about yourself' questions, I was asked to teach a lesson on the spot using dramatic techniques I would use in class. Stunned, I managed to get out of my seat and draw some pictures of the stars and moon on the board, taught them the meaning of those words and then proceeded to ask the interview team to stand up and learn a little dance to the song **Twinkle twinkle little star.** *All I wanted to do was to create an impression and to stand out of the 300 people being interviewed. People remember you best when you are acting like a complete fool. When it is teaching English as a foreign language, the ability to act like a fool is one of the main requirements of the job. Getting Japanese men in suits up and dancing during a job interview with the prestigious JET programme was a half-crazed risk, but a successful one at that.*

Often government-run exchanges of this kind do not offer generous remuneration packages; however, pay and conditions on the JET scheme are excellent. In addition to a free return flight, JET participants receive 3,600,000 yen a year. This is the salary before income and inhabitant taxes have been paid (though some participants are exempt) and there are further social and medical insurance fees. The salary is standard for all JET participants. Contracts are with individual contracting organisations in Japan, so there can be discrepancies in working conditions. It is the luck of the draw that determines who goes where, although stated preferences will be taken into consideration. Pension regulations mean that JET teachers can reclaim money paid into the national insurance scheme as a lump sum equivalent to about one month's salary.

ALTs are theoretically expected to work a seven-hour day and quite often teachers are assigned an average of three classes a day; however, hours spent in the classroom will vary between placements. **Mark Elliot** feels that the JET programme is 'probably the best job in the world' and describes his situation:

> *I live on a wonderful island, three hours' ferry ride from Nagasaki, nearer Shanghai than Tokyo. There is lots more to the job than teaching. After all, the programme is just as much about meeting people and participating in cultural exchange as it is about teaching.*

All JET participants teach in partnership with a native Japanese teacher so those without significant teaching experience are not thrown in at the deep end. The degree of responsibility varies depending on the relationship built with the Japanese teacher with some ALTs effectively teaching the class in large part by themselves. Unfortunately this was not the case for **Charlotte Steggall** from Suffolk, who majored in Japanese and TESOL at university and is serious about pursuing TESOL at a master's level and as a career. She felt the ALT role to be of little actual value, but rather felt they were treated as '*singing, dancing white people to wheel out and show off in events in the town*'. This was not what she signed up for, yet she loved the students and so agreed to stay on for a second year:

> *What I do depends on which teacher I'm working with. Some ask me to do a 10-minute game in a lesson, some ask me to be a living tape recorder, some ask me to do full classes. Training Japanese teachers to work with ALTs is very hit and miss, and most have no idea what to do with us. What we do has little meaning to the kids, who see us and say 'Yey! She's here today so we get to play games!' They would never ask us to do a lesson to prepare for a test, or anything else with responsibility. I love teaching. But we are here mainly to allow country kids to interact with us and to overcome racism for when they are older. When I try to help or do something more because I have passion, I am batted down again.*
>
> *I have a lot of spare time at work. I study Japanese, read books, use the internet. After school, I earn more money and brush up my teaching skills by doing private lessons, which allows me to break free and try different teaching styles.*

Other teachers are delighted with the easy timetable. As **Rabindra Roy** wrote from Shizuoka prefecture, '*I can think of very few jobs where a freshly qualified graduate with an irrelevant degree and no experience can walk straight into such a big salary for this little work*'. He also describes the programme as '*desperately well organised*'. But partly because of the variety in locations and schools and partly because Japan is such a weird and wonderful place, it is impossible to predict what life will be like, no matter how many orientations you attend. About two-thirds of JET participants renew for a second year, which indicates its success. A third of the second years stay for a third year, with five years being the maximum a candidate can stay. The programme offers a tremendous amount of support and even those who are placed in remote or rural areas are usually within striking distance of other JET participants. In retrospect, **Susannah Kerr** was not too sorry to have been turned down by JET because their teachers have little control over where they are sent and end up in small towns (however, she wouldn't have minded a JET salary).

IN ADVANCE

There are many other ways to fix up a job in Japan ahead of time, though these will usually require more initiative than signing on with JET. Some Japanese language schools have formed links with university careers departments, particularly in the USA and Canada, so anyone with a university connection should exploit it. Another possibility for Americans is to explore the Japanese-American Sister City Program which assists some native English speakers to find teaching jobs in the city twinned with theirs.

One or two language training organisations operate on a huge scale, with many branches and large numbers of staff. For instance Aeon (see entry) has four offices outside Japan: New York, Los Angeles, Toronto and Sydney (down from six a few years ago) and Interac interviews in cities throughout English-speaking countries. They want to interview anyone with a university degree and a perfect command of English. Some chains have been described as factory English schools, where teachers are handed a course book and told not to deviate from the formula. They depend on a steady supply of fresh graduates who want the chance to spend a year or two in Japan. Often new recruits do not have much say in where they are sent and in their first year may be sent to the least desirable locations, as **John Ramage** discovered after a successful interview with Interac in the UK:

> *I was so keen to go to Japan that I accepted a job in a very rural location. I knew this could be problematic and I was right, it was. Coming with limited funds meant I could not afford to buy a laptop and have internet, which might have made things bearable. I tried to be frugal but found the isolation hard to take. Later I moved to Tokyo, with Shane English School and stayed for much longer. After suffocating small towns I found Tokyo positively exciting.*

Shane English Schools confines its recruitment to the UK through its partner Saxoncourt. An energetic agency operating mainly online is TEFLOne Recruitment (www.teflone.com), which recruits qualified teachers for posts in Japan as well as other countries in the Far East. A major employer is iTTTi Japan which trades as Peppy Kids Club. The head office is in Nagoya but it has recruiting representatives in the UK, USA, Canada and Australia (see www.ittti.com). The company hires 350 native English speakers to work all over Japan, with the exception of central Tokyo and the Islands of Okinawa. The giant Gaba Corporation (http://teaching-in-japan.gaba.co.jp) operates 36 Learning Studios around Tokyo, Osaka and in Nagoya where clients are taught individually, and have recently begun teaching corporate clients off-site. Gaba hosts recruitment fairs abroad, e.g. in London, Manchester and Glasgow in mid-June.

A steady trickle of adverts appear in newspapers, *EL Prospects, TESOL Placement e-Bulletin*, etc. placed by individual schools in Japan and agents. Quite often schools and groups of schools will appoint a foreign recruiter. Many schools have no need to advertise abroad since they receive so many speculative resumés (the American term for CV is used in Japan).

The internet is a valuable job search tool. Using any of the popular household search engines, type 'English Teaching in Japan' and dozens of job-related websites will appear. *O-Hayo-Sensei* (which means 'Good Morning Teacher') has pages of teaching positions across Japan at www.ohayosensei.com. Many ads specify that 'Candidates must currently reside in Japan'. *ELT News* (www.eltnews.com/jobs) lists ELT jobs around Japan and the online magazine carries news, classroom ideas, etc. for ELT teachers in Japan. It is a good idea to send your CV to the big employers before arrival, make some follow-up calls and hope to arrange some interviews in your first week. Professional teachers can make contact with JALT, the Japan Association for Language Teaching (www.jalt.org). JALT categorically cannot help with employment but it does run professional development activities through its local branches. Annual membership costs a hefty 40,000 yen.

Once you have some international experience of teaching, particularly of IELTS testing, you can aim to fix up short lucrative contracts as **Steph Fuccio** and her husband **Evan** did for the last three months of 2010:

> *Nagoya is a very livable city, a million times more so than Tokyo was. My love for bicycling was rekindled along with a craving for sushi. We worked for a company called Westgate Corporation both in Nagoya and Tokyo. It's*

a very reputable, trustworthy organisation. I would do this programme again in a heartbeat, it's that easy and lucrative.

The Westgate Corporation has been providing English language instruction programmes for corporations, residents, and public schools since 1983 and also operates an online application programme (www. westgate.co.jp).

ON THE SPOT

As has been mentioned, native English speakers with a bachelor's degree have a chance of landing a job as an English teacher on arrival in Japan. The crucial question is how long will it take. The murderous cost of living means that job-hunters spend hundreds of dollars or pounds very quickly while engaged in the time-consuming business of answering ads, sending round CVs, and going for interviews. If you're starting cold try to arrive on a weekend so you can buy the Monday edition of the English language *Japan Times*, which carries ads for English teachers. Note that ads often specify 'female' which usually indicates a job teaching young children. Male applicants for these posts may be expected to have prior experience of working with children.

Travis Ball from Los Angeles set off on what he intended to be five years of world travels and chose Japan as his first destination, because he had come to the conclusion that it would be one of the easier countries to find work teaching English without any experience or certificates:

I was basically sitting in my travellers' hotel room in Osaka sending out as many resumés as I could while attempting not to spend any money. I started by sending emails to every address listed in the chapter on Japan in your book and kept looking using the web and other resources. After filling out an online application and sending my resumé to a big chain, I was asked if I could attend an interview in Tokyo, which took place over two days and included a couple of tests and a mock 20-minute lesson we all had to prepare the evening before the second day. I was told that I had a job in a very small rural school (one other teacher who was Japanese and a manager). With hindsight I would probably have voiced my preference for a bigger city with more going on. That being said, I think it was my flexibility that helped me get the job in the first place.

Joseph Tame from Herefordshire arrived in Tokyo with two big advantages, a working holiday visa and a Japanese girlfriend with whom he could stay:

Having spent virtually all of my travel funds in my first 21 days in the city, I eventually decided to face the fact that I'd have to find a job, for a couple of months at least. What with all this talk of a global recession, I really didn't feel too positive. Furthermore I have virtually no experience teaching, have no teaching qualifications and indeed no university degree which all employers insist on. My first stop was the Japan Association for Working Holiday Makers. I was fortunate in that as I was being registered, a phone call came through from a private English school who were desperate for a teacher. Thirty minutes later I had a job paying £17 an hour. The catch was that it was only four hours per week, but that was my pocket money taken care of. I actually spent time surfing the web in an attempt to remember what pronouns and adjectives are; I only ever remember that a verb is a 'doing' word.

Later Joseph Tame made good use of GaijinPot.com which remains a superb resource for jobs, accommodation and news for foreign residents in Japan. GaijinPot is by far the largest job site for foreigners and has a near monopoly on the English teaching jobs in Japan, both in English conversation schools and among the dispatch companies (for teaching in the public schools). GaijinPot has over 150,000 resumés in the resumé bank with 130,000 allowing their information to be searched by employers. It is also a key portal site for foreigners in Japan with all the information needed for a foreigner to live, work and enjoy life. The forums are popular in offering a place where foreigners can share information, experiences, questions, etc.

Josph Tame also recommends www.findateacher.net for those wanting to teach English (or other languages); an alternative is www.findstudents.net. You simply enter the relevant information about what you teach, what area of Japan you teach in, how much you charge, etc. and the students will come to you. The free weekly English language magazine *Metropolis* (www.metropolis.co.jp) also has a good classifieds section which is worth checking for jobs, as is www.jobseekjapan.com. Another useful free publication is *Tokyo Notice Board* (www.tokyonoticeboard.co.jp). A typical advertisement randomly selected might read: *'We are seeking an energetic, gregarious and reliable job applicant who wishes to share their experience with Japanese Community. Part-time job (1,000–1,500 yen per hour free talk; 2,160 yen per hour for teaching a lesson; 3,000 yen for a dispatch lesson).'* A 'dispatch lesson' is a private lesson given at a company premises.

Few things could be more intimidating for the EFL teacher than to arrive at Narita International Airport with no job and limited resources. The longer the job-hunt takes, the faster the finances dwindle and the more nerve-racking and discouraging the situation becomes. One way to lessen the monumentality of the initial struggle would be to get out of Tokyo straightaway. Although there are more jobs in the capital, there is also more competition from other foreigners, to the point of saturation. Enterprising teachers who are willing to step off the conveyor belt which takes job-seekers from the airport to one of Tokyo's many '*gaijin* houses' (hostels for foreigners) may well encounter fewer setbacks. Osaka seems a good bet since it is within commuting distance of the whole Kansai area, including Kobe, which is 20 minutes away by train. In Osaka the cost of living is as much as a quarter less than it is in Tokyo. Another promising destination is Sapporo in the north, the fifth largest city in the country. **Ken Foye**, a reader of this book, chose to teach on Hokkaido, the northern island on which Sapporo is located:

> *I have been teaching here for a year and a half now and I would recommend Hokkaido to anyone, especially those who don't find living in a large urban metropolis very appealing. Here the people seem much friendlier than in Tokyo, the cost of living isn't as high, there's fresh air and the scenery is magnificent. And I probably would not have ended up here if not for your book.*

Susannah Kerr was made redundant by Nova when it collapsed and swiftly began 'on the spot' job-hunting courtesy of websites such as www.gaijinpot.com. She considered a large employer, Gaba (mentioned above), which specialises in one-to-one teaching and offers the advantage of being able to choose your hours. The disadvantage is that earnings are dependent on your popularity as a teacher since students vote with their feet. Susannah was interviewed by a company called Balloon Kids, which employs up to 20 teachers and pays 240,000–300,000 yen per month. Instead of working from its own institute, the company hires rooms in (for example) suburban shopping malls, where 12–15 kids show up. The teacher would be expected to go to an office to pick up teaching materials and a key, and then let him/herself into the room, so there would be no contact with other teachers. They also withhold 10,000 yen per month to be paid at the end of the contract.

The six-month contract that Susannah eventually accepted was with M.L.S (see entry), a school that uses a proprietary Drama Method to teach English. With 36 branches in Tokyo and Yokohama, it is a small company by Japanese standards. Susannah was impressed with the efficacy of the method, and because the teachers were '*interesting, creative, often musical types, the children were often engaged and excited, and their spoken English really did improve. The teachers were always trying to use attention-grabbing games like charades*'.

TOKYO

One of the most often recommended places to start a job hunt in Tokyo is the Kimi Information Center (Oscar Building, 8th Floor, 2 42 3 Ikebukuro, Toshima-ku, Tokyo 171 0014; +81 3 3986 1604; kimiinfo@kimiwillbe. com). Its website (www.kimiwillbe.com) carries teaching job adverts. Like so many postal addresses in Japan, it is difficult to find without a map (print one off from their website) or follow these detailed directions: from Ikebukuro station take the West Exit, walk straight past the McDonald's for one block and turn right when you see Marui Department Store. Go three blocks past Sumitomo Mitsui Bank. Kimi is on the right across from the post office.

The Kimi Center offers extensive services for foreigners such as internet café, photocopying, free guided tours with Japanese students as well as advising on cheap short and long-term accommodation, where tenants are not liable for key money. If you register with them online, you can receive information about new jobs daily. Their Teaching Job Search Register can be found at www.kimiwillbe.com/joboppo.htm. With this free service, Kimi can assist with searching for a suitable job and even setting up interviews.

Another useful source of guidance for new arrivals on a working holiday programme is the Japan Association for Working Holiday Makers (www.jawhm.or.jp/eng) whose services are available to those with the appropriate visa (see section on Regulations below). **Joseph Tame** was a satisfied customer when he was on the programme:

> *My first stop was the JAWHM, one of whose offices was 20 minutes by bicycle from where I was staying. They were very helpful. After registering I had access to their lists of jobs. Essentially it's a job centre for foreigners. They also have the latest copies of all the relevant magazines and newspapers with sits vacant columns. They will advise on housing, etc.*

Registration now costs 1,000 yen, which is a very worthwhile investment. When looking for accommodation, try to pick up a list of *gaijin* houses from an information or tourist office and look for ones which charge a monthly rather than a nightly rent since these are the ones which attract long-term residents. Apple House (www.applehouse.ne.jp) is recommended for being affordable, friendly and in a good location; it advertises that it is a good place to meet language exchange partners from all over the world. A good place to look is Fontana (+81 3 3382 0151; www.fontana-apt.co.jp) which provides an excellent service. Because it is so difficult to rent flats, some teachers continue living in *gaijin* houses after they find work. Many foreigners live and work in the Roppongi district of Tokyo which might therefore be a sensible place to base yourself.

A couple of years ago, **Susannah Kerr** rented a two-bedroom flat in a nice traditional Japanese neighbourhood of Kagurazaka for 160,000 yen a month, but when her flatmates moved on and she had to pay the rent by herself, she decided to move. Even when accompanied by a local, using a local rental agency proved impossible so she used an English-speaking rental agency to find a one-bedroom apartment for 80,000 yen in Okubo, a bustling 24-hour-a-day area known as Koreatown, with a mildly sleazy reputation but gradually improving. Foreign letting agencies offer the advantage of not insisting that you provide a local guarantor. The Sakura House agency, which caters for non-Japanese accommodation-seekers (www.sakura-house.com), has become a prominent feature of the accommodation landscape in Tokyo, but there are many others.

A free ads paper called *Tokyo Classifieds* is distributed in the Roppongi district on Fridays carrying job and accommodation ads. Even tourist offices such as the one at Hibuya station (exit A-3) have free noticeboards where private lessons may be sought or offered, as well as accommodation. **Amanda Searle** describes what she found in the newspapers when she was job-hunting:

> *Most companies give little idea in their adverts of the hours and salary, let alone the age and number of students or the textbooks used. They are not very willing to give that information over the phone, explaining that you will get the opportunity to ask questions if you are called for interview. I sent cover letters out with my resumé, explaining that I was looking only for full-time positions which offered visa sponsorship. I sent out about 20 applications and about 10 companies contacted me and I went to eight interviews. I ended up being offered two full-time positions and three part-time ones.*

The initial phone call is very important and should be considered as a preliminary interview. Since you may be competing with as many as 100 people answering the same ad, you have to try to stand out over the phone. Speak slowly, clearly, and be very *genki*, which means bubbly and fun. You may be asked to fax your CV to them; the cover letter should be short and intelligent, and the CV should be brief and interesting, emphasising any teaching experience. Always carry a supply of professional looking business cards (*meishi*).

Demonstration lessons form an integral part of most job interviews in Japan, regardless of one's qualifications. Try to prepare yourself as much as possible if only because travelling to an interview in Tokyo is a major undertaking which can take up to three hours and cost a lot of money; it would be a shame to blow your chances because of a simple oversight. Dress as impeccably and conservatively as possible, and carry a respectable briefcase, since books are often judged by their covers in Japan. Inside you should have any education certificates you have earned, preferably the originals since schools have long since realised that a lot of forgeries are in circulation. Your resumé should not err on the side of modesty.

REGULATIONS

Britons, Irish, Canadians, Australians and New Zealanders (among a few other non-English speaking countries) are eligible to apply for a working holiday visa for Japan; details can be found at www.uk.emb-japan. go.jp/en/visa/working-holiday.html. Applicants must be aged 18–30. Applicants must show that they have sufficient financial backing, i.e. savings of $2,500 or £1,500 and a return flight. Visa holders may accept paid work in Japan for up to 12 months, provided it is incidental to their travels. The quota of working holiday visas for Britons is 1,000. Note that applications are accepted from April and once the allocation has been filled, no more visas will be granted until April of the following year.

Some schools rely on a stream of Canadians, Australians and New Zealanders on working holiday visas which they must obtain in their home countries through the SWAP Japan Programme. SWAP allows students aged 18–30 to work for six months in the first instance but is extendable to 18 months. To qualify you must prove that you have $3,000 at your disposal.

For those ineligible for a working holiday visa, the key to obtaining a work visa for Japan is to have a Japanese sponsor. Documents which will help you to find a sponsoring employer are the original or notarised copy of your bachelor's or other degree and resumé. Most teachers are sponsored by their employers, although on rare occasions it is possible for the sponsor to be a private citizen. Not all schools by any means are willing to sponsor their teachers, unless they are persuaded that they are an ongoing proposition. If your visa is to be processed before arrival, you must have a definite job appointment in Japan. Your employer must apply to the Ministry of Justice in Tokyo for a Certificate of Eligibility which he or she then forwards to you. You must take this along with a photocopy of it, your passport, photograph and application form to any Consulate General of Japan. The regulations stipulate that anyone who works in Higher Education must have an MA in Education or TEFL. Sponsoring schools warn that the visa application process takes between three and five months.

The UK and US have a visa exemption arrangement with Japan (www.uk.emb-japan.go.jp/en/visa/general-info.html). British citizens can stay for up to six months without a visa, US citizens can stay for up to 90 days. It is possible to enter Japan, look for work and then apply for a work visa. Those found to be overstaying as tourists can be deported. Furthermore, employers who are caught employing illegal aliens as well as the foreign workers themselves are subject to huge fines, and both parties risk imprisonment.

Finding an employer to sponsor you for a work visa is very important. A number of schools advertising for teachers state in their ads that they are willing to consider only those who already have a work visa. Although immigration laws are being tightened, the government is making it easier for foreigners to get working visas. Whereas previously it was necessary for the teacher to leave the country, at great personal expense, to change their visa status (the Korean Visa Tour), these days the teacher need only take their Certificate of Eligibility into the local immigration office, where the visa will be processed. However, those on a student visa still need to leave the country to complete the visa process. According to **Alan Suter** the cheapest way is to take a ferry from Kobe to Busan, Korea. The work visa may be valid for six months, 12 months or three years. After you have worked for one year on a work visa, you can renew it for a further three years. When renewing, one of the most important requirements is a tax statement showing your previous year's earnings. It is difficult to obtain a new visa unless you can show that you have earned at least 250,000 yen per month. Cash-in-hand and part-time jobs may be lucrative but they do nothing to help your visa application. If you break your contract with your employer, you will have to find another sponsor willing to act as sponsor the following year.

You are permitted to work up to 20 hours a week on a cultural or student visa. Cultural visas are granted to foreigners interested in studying some aspect of traditional Japanese culture on a full-time basis. In this case you must find a teacher willing to sponsor you. Cultural visas are often granted for *shodo* (calligraphy), *taiko* (drumming), karate, aikido, *ikebana* (flower arranging) and *ochakai* (tea ceremony). At one time these study visas were liberally handed out but nowadays you must produce concrete evidence that you actually are studying.

Teachers usually have the basic rate of national income tax in Japan (6%–7%) withdrawn at source.

CONDITIONS OF WORK

Despite the high cost of living, most teachers seem to be able to save money without having to lead too frugal an existence. Some even save half their salary in their first year by avoiding eating out and going to the cinema. **Antoinette Sarpong** spent last year teaching in Osaka and preferred to enjoy herself to saving:

> *I enjoyed Osaka's nightlife thoroughly. I also opted to save for travel, so I only put a small dent in my student loans. Having said that, I lived very comfortably and had a lot of friends who did save quite a bit of money because they stuck to a budget. Japan is an expensive country but it is possible to save heaps of money if you stick to a budget. I would also suggest living rurally, if you can – less temptation than the big cities.*

The longer you work in Japan the higher the salary and better working conditions you can command. Rank beginners outside Tokyo and Osaka can earn as little as 200,000 yen a month, but the steady average of 250,000 yen persists almost everywhere. Perks such as increments for higher qualifications, end-of-contract bonuses, free Japanese lessons and travel tickets, etc. are in fairly wide evidence, although it is always worth making sure that your contract mentions these perks. Teaching schedules can be exhausting. Cost-cutting is a big part of the new Japanese economy, with some supermarkets charging customers for shopping bags, banks closing branches, companies hiring temps rather than full-time employees to save on benefits, and rural municipalities merging for greater efficiency. Language schools are not exempt from this movement and the majority are filling teachers' schedules with bigger classes in an effort to reduce teacher numbers. Teachers are also increasingly asked to work 'outside their job description', helping out with advertising, student retention and the sale of study materials.

Timetables may be announced at the last minute, though it is more difficult to opt out in Japan than in other countries because of the dedication Japanese workers show to their firms. (At best a Japanese worker gets 10 days' holiday a year and few take their full entitlement for fear of seeming lazy or disloyal to the company.) Some schools remain open all weekend and on public holidays too.

One of the advantages of working in state schools (as JET teachers do) is that they close for holidays, usually three weeks at Christmas and two weeks in August between semesters. Most schools offer one-week holidays (paid or unpaid or a combination of the two) at the beginning of May (the 'Golden Week') and in the middle of August ('O-bon vacation'). Holidays for those lucky enough to work in institutes of higher education are much more generous.

Private tutoring is still lucrative, paying between 3,000 and 6,000 yen an hour. **Susannah Kerr** managed to hold on to six hours of private teaching a week (teaching three children in one family) which netted her 18,000 yen, enough to eat. Occasionally you will meet someone who has been paid $100 just to have dinner with a language learner and converse in English, but these plums are few and far between.

THE PUPILS

The stereotype of the diligent Japanese pupil is becoming somewhat outmoded. The younger generation of Japanese is not always willing to play by the rules that their elders lay down, and there is increasing tension in schools which may manifest itself in (mildly) unruly behaviour. But mostly teachers find their students eager, attentive and willing to confer great respect on their teachers and in some out-of-the-way places even celebrity status. All teachers are expected to look the part and most schools will insist on proper dress (e.g. suits and dresses). But they do not want a formal approach to teaching.

Adults will have studied English at school for at least six years, and their knowledge of grammar is usually sound. They go to conversation schools in the expectation of meeting native English speaker teachers able to deliver creative and entertaining lessons. Yet some are crippled by diffidence or excessive anxiety about grammatical correctness. **Michael Frost** is one teacher who experienced a clash of cultures when trying to encourage discussion in his classroom:

> *It is very difficult for Japanese students to come out and express an individual opinion. The best tactic is to get them in pairs, so that together they can work something out. They are more productive and open in pairs, and it takes the pressure off them. Then get the pairs into fours, to express a mini-group opinion, then work for a total group agreement. The thing to avoid at all costs is to stroll into class, saying, 'OK, today we are going to discuss environmental issues. Tetsuya, you set the ball rolling: What do you think of pollution?' It will not work.*

It is a popular myth that Japanese students have good reading abilities in English and require only conversation practice. This was not the experience of **Nathan Edwards**, a diploma-qualified teacher from Canada:

> *I am currently teaching at the Tokyo YMCA College of English, a pioneer in English teaching in Japan, established in 1880. The fact is that both reading and speaking in English present major challenges even to students with years of English instruction in the Japanese school system. It is highly advisable for teachers to bring a good supply of realia with them (various English brochures, used tickets, maps, coins, etc.) and old lesson plans.*

Problems can arise in team teaching situations if your Japanese colleague has not attained a high enough level of English. While teaching in the JET programme, **Robert Mizzi** came to admire Japanese culture, but he did find some aspects of his job frustrating:

> *A lot of times I cannot introduce a game idea because, literally, it will take 20 minutes for the teacher to understand (never mind the students).*

Amanda Moody worked in a small school in Nagoya, where she taught preschool-aged children using a mixture of the 'Gentle Revolution' and Rosetta Stone software:

> *My pupils were very smart and the children of successful Japanese parents. Some were the products of brain surgeons or music producers. Others were businessmen's kids. But most of them were reading and writing around the age of three. Their parents expected the world of both us and their children.*

Amanda loved her students, but thought poorly of her employer, who fined teachers for 'infringements' such as 'smelled strange and suspicious acting: 500 yen fine'. Among the many strange aspects of Japanese culture is one which most foreigners find particularly disturbing. A native English speaker who happens to have non-Caucasian features will almost certainly be discriminated against.

ACCOMMODATION

It is not uncommon for teachers who are hired overseas to be given help with accommodation, which is a tremendously useful perk, even if the flat provided is small and over-priced, with poor insulation and a badly equipped kitchen. If you are on your own, you will be forced to use a foreigners' rental agency. Rental costs are likely to range from 40,000 yen to 70,000 yen per person per month (more in Tokyo, less in more distant prefectures). When you find a place through an agency, you will have to pay a commission of one month's rent.

A sizeable deposit called 'key money' is payable on signing a tenancy agreement, which can cause problems as it did to **John Ramage**:

> *A word of warning. I came to Japan with relatively little money. Interac will help you set up in a new place but they will offer you a loan because no one gets paid until they have been working for two months. It takes time for the loan to come through, and meanwhile there was a landlord on day one with his hand stretched out asking for £1,000 of key money. So, I used my credit card in an ATM. Bad move. My debt soared and this happened to other people too. Fortunately when I moved on to Tokyo, Interac returned part of the key money, and paid me the end of contract bonus which was a great help.*

According to John, housing is more likely to be subsidised in Korea, Taiwan and China.

A further problem is the near total absence of furnished apartments because Japanese people do not like to use belongings that have been used by other people, which means you may have to go shopping for curtains and cookers on top of all your other expenses. Again, schools which normally hire foreign teachers may keep a stock of basic furnishings which they can lend to teachers. If all this sounds too much hassle, perhaps staying in a *gaijin* house long term is not such a bad idea.

John Ramage paid an inflated rent for the convenience of staying in an apartment provided by Shane in Tokyo and suggests ways to keep the cost of living down:

> *In Tokyo internet cafés are expensive if you use them a lot, but an internet connection to your house is cheap. It took me a while to find the cheap shops. There are some, and people in Tokyo and its environs ought to try the 99 Shop, which has a green and orange logo. When I was there almost all the food cost around 100 yen, which was a blessing. The 100 yen shops sell cheap stuff for the house and the recycle shop is where you get second-hand electric goods which is helpful because Japanese flats tend to be unfurnished.*

Obviously it is to your advantage to live as close to your place of work as possible but, as noted above, many teachers are forced to spend a sizeable chunk of their earnings and a lot of time commuting. Ask your employer to pay for your travel, preferably in the form of a monthly travel pass which can be used for your leisure travel as well. If you're in Tokyo, bear in mind that city buses charge a flat fare of 200 yen.

LEISURE TIME

According to some veteran teachers, leisure time and how to spend it will be the least of your worries. Depending on your circumstances, you may be expected to participate in extra-curricular activities and social events which it would cause offence to decline and will eat up lots of your leisure time. Although **Bryn Thomas** enjoyed the sushi which his school provided for teachers still at work at 9pm, he was less keen on the '*office parties when teachers were required to dress up in silly costumes and be nice to the students*'. Most teachers are happy to accept occasional invitations to socialise with their Japanese colleagues or pupils, even if it does mean an evening of speaking very very slowly and drinking heavily. Many teachers find the socialising with students fun if expensive. Knowing a *gaijin* is a considerable status symbol for many Japanese, many of whom are willing to pay good money just for you to go to their houses once a week and eat their food.

But it is not like that everywhere. A glut of Westerners in Tokyo means that your welcome may be less than enthusiastic. In fact non-Japanese are refused entrance to some Tokyo bars and restaurants. Many people head straight out of Tokyo for the more appealing city of Osaka. **Julie Fast** describes the contrast:

I am still enamoured of Osaka; it is like a village after Tokyo. I am constantly amazed at the trees we see every-where. I never realised in Tokyo how much I hated being constantly surrounded by people. I never had personal space in Tokyo. No one does – which explains the distant, sour looks on most people's faces. What a difference in Osaka. Osaka people have the roughest reputation in all of Japan. From a Western point of view, they are the friendliest. I have been invited to houses for lunch, children say hello and people in shops actually talk to you. Which proves you can't judge a country by its largest city.

All cities are expensive. Any entertainment which smacks of the West such as going out to a fashionable coffee house or a night club will be absurdly expensive. However, if you are content with more modest indigenous food and pastimes, you will be able to save money. A filling bowl of noodles and broth costs £3, though you may never take to the standard breakfast of boiled rice and a raw egg. Staying home to listen to Japanese language CDs or to read a good book (e.g. *Pictures from the Water Trade*, a personal account of life in Japan) costs nothing. Obviously the more settled you become, the more familiar you will be with the bargains and affordable amusements. For example, while the Tokyo superclubs impose a cover charge of up to 4,000 yen (£30+), **Susannah Kerr** found much cheaper ones and in fact one where she got to know the DJs was free.

Learning to live cheaply is easier in small towns, but there will be fewer entertainments. **Travis Ball** had to depend on his own resources to fill his leisure time:

Unfortunately, due to the rural nature of where I was living, there wasn't really a whole lot to do with my spare time. In addition to a lack of activities, the weather was much colder than what I was used to at home in California and this limited my getting around via bike and on foot. I tried to use the time to work on personal projects such as teaching myself how to cook and working on my photography. I was occasionally able to organise day trips with my co-worker and some students, but found myself on my own more often than not, I took the time to develop a personal travel blog for flashpackers (www.flashpackerhq.com) that I'm still working on to this day.

Finding your way around is nothing if not a challenge in a country where almost all road and public trans-port signs are incomprehensible. What use is an A–Z if you can't read the alphabet? Many feel that it is worth making an effort to master at least something of the written language. There are three alphabets in Japanese: kanji (ancient pictograms), hiragana and katakana (the characters used to spell loan words from English). **Amanda Searle** is just one teacher who feels that kana can be learned through independent study so that at least you will be able to read station names and menus. Learning some of the script not only impresses students and shows that you are making an effort to absorb some of the culture, it also helps you to survive. **Joseph Tame** signed up for Japanese lessons so he could get beyond 'large beer please' and 'I don't understand' to a variety of expressions to exclaim 'HOW MUCH?' in disbelief.

Japanese addresses are mind-bogglingly complicated too: the numbers refer to land subdivisions: pre-fecture, district, ward, then building. When in doubt (inevitable) ask a friendly informant for a chizu (map). It is also a good idea to get a Japanese person to write your destination in both kanji and transliterated into roma-ji (our alphabet). Japanese people will sometimes go to embarrassing lengths to help foreigners. This desire to help wedded to a reluctance to lose face means that they may offer advice and instructions based on very little information, so keep checking. Young people in jeans are the best bets. Outside the big cities the people are even more cordial. Wherever you go, you don't have to worry about crime.

Travel is expensive. For example the bullet train from Tokyo to Sendai, a couple of hundred miles north, costs about £82 one way. Yet the pace of a teacher's life in Tokyo or another big city can become so stress-ful that it is essential to get on a local train and see some of the countryside. Tour operators do sometimes have special deals on train fares. For example, JR East (which operates in Kanto in northern Japan) has an unlimited one day Saturday/Sunday ticket for 2,300 yen and a five-day ticket for just over £150, which includes bullet trains (Shinkansen). Shopping around for package tours is another good way to get to see Japan at the lowest possible price. For example, a two to three day hotel/transportation package, could end up costing significantly less.

The alienness of Japanese culture is one of the main fascinations of the place. It is foolish to become bogged down worrying about transgressing against mysterious customs. The JET literature, for example, may be unnecessarily intimidating in its pointing up of possible cultural faux pas. But in fact Japanese people are more tolerant of foreigners than many give them credit for. For example **Claire Wilkinson** felt quite overwhelmed after reading the JET literature. One of the many prohibitions mentioned is 'never blow your nose in public', and so the heavy cold with which she arrived made her even more miserable than it would have otherwise. But she soon discovered that the Japanese allow foreigners a great deal of latitude and that she could relax and be herself without causing grave offence. **Antoinette Sarpong** got better at her encounters with the local people after she realised that Japanese people do not like to say 'No' or directly express disagreement so she gradually learned to read between the lines and to interpret their subtle communication style.

The expat scene is also not to everyone's taste, as **Antoinette Sarpong** from Canada described in 2010:

One aspect of being here in Japan that was a little difficult was dating and body image. A conversation with a female mate from England the other day reminded me that it can be difficult for women first arriving in Japan, which is so patriarchal, and experience the highs and lows of the dating scene. However, for foreign men, it is often thought of as being much easier to meet women for relationships.

Japan is a fascinating country, but don't expect to blend in or go incognito; it is very difficult to be 'accepted' by the Japanese.

LIST OF EMPLOYERS

ACC ENGLISH SCHOOL

252 Genjishinmei-Cho, Hekinan-Shi, Aichi-Ken 447 0872

C +81 566 422 332

info@acc-english.co.jp

www.acc-english.co.jp

PREFERENCE OF NATIONALITY: Native English speakers for chain of schools in Aichi Prefecture (Nagoya, Anjo, Kariya, Handa, Hekinan, Nishio, Toyota and Toyoake).

QUALIFICATIONS: University graduates. Teaching experience, basic Japanese language ability or TESOL training an advantage. Applicants must be prepared to teach all levels, from very young children to adults.

CONDITIONS OF EMPLOYMENT: 1 year full-time positions available to teach approximately 25 hours per week. Approximately 4 weeks of paid vacation. Part-time positions sometimes available.

FACILITIES/SUPPORT: One-week pre-service training provided. Subsidised furnished accommodation arranged (monthly rent is around 40,000 yen).

RECRUITMENT: Speculative applications should be emailed/posted to the above addresses with a photo of yourself in business attire.

AEON CORPORATION

222 Sepulveda Blvd., Suite # 2000, El Segundo, California 90245, USA

C +1 310 662 4706

aeonla@aeonet.com

Also: 230 Park Avenue, Suite 1000, NYC, NY 10169

C +1 212 808 3080

aeonnyc@aeonet.com

www.aeonet.com

One of the largest chains of English conversation schools in Japan with over 320 branches.

NUMBER OF TEACHERS: 800.

QUALIFICATIONS: Bachelor's degree in any subject and a perfect command of the English language.

CONDITIONS OF EMPLOYMENT: 1 year renewable contract. 5-days a week. 40 hours/week work schedule.

SALARY: 270,000 yen per month.

FACILITIES/SUPPORT: Single occupancy apartment furnished to Japanese standards. Subsidised monthly rent of 55,000 yen. Accident and sickness insurance provided under Japan's Socialised Health Insurance plan. 3 weeks of paid vacation and paid training.

RECRUITMENT: 2 full-time recruiting offices in the US as above. Group and personal interviews held on a regular basis in the USA, and 3 times a year in London, Toronto, Vancouver and Sydney. Positions start every month. Rolling deadlines. Initial applicants should send résumé and minimum 500-word essay entitled 'Why I want to live and work in Japan'. For up-to-date information regarding recruiting trips and application instructions see www.aeonet.com.

CONTACT: Lars Frank, Motoko Toki and Derek Johnson (Personnel Recruiters, New York office) and Andy Gadt, Yumiko Hamanaka and Tomoka Tsuchida (Personnel Recruiters, Los Angeles office).

ARK FOREIGN LANGUAGE ACADEMY

4519–4 Innoshima Takuma, Onomichi, Hiroshima
722–2324

📞 +81 845 22 8511
✉️ contact@arkgaigo.com
💻 www.arkgaigo.com/jobs

NUMBER OF TEACHERS: 3.
PREFERENCE OF NATIONALITY: None.
QUALIFICATIONS: Degree.
CONDITIONS OF EMPLOYMENT: 1-year contract with 6–8 working hours per day.
SALARY: 200,000 yen per month. US $20 per 40 minute lesson.
FACILITIES/SUPPORT: Accommodation provided and sponsorship given for work visas.
RECRUITMENT: Interviews are essential.
CONTACT: Matt Winfield, Owner-Manager (matt@arkgaigo.com).

BERNARD ENGLISH SCHOOL OF JAPAN

Shamotto Tsukuba 2F, 4–2-7 Matsushiro, Tsukuba City, Ibaraki-ken 305–0035

📞 +81 298 56 5093
✉️ recruitment@bernard.co.jp
💻 www.bernard.co.jp

NUMBER OF TEACHERS: 15+.
PREFERENCE OF NATIONALITY: American, Australian, British, Canadian.
QUALIFICATIONS: Must have a four-year university degree (any field), TESOL-type qualifications are a plus, must have a valid driver's licence (either a Japanese or an international licence).
CONDITIONS OF EMPLOYMENT: 1–2 year contracts, renewable on mutual agreement. Contracts are a salary/hourly hybrid. Full-time teachers average about 110 hours per month, spread over 44 weeks per year, with 8 weeks of school holidays spread throughout the year.

SALARY: First-year salaries for full-time work earn around 240,000 yen per month, depending on qualifications and experience. Monthly incentives are offered. Contract completion bonus of 60,000 yen.
FACILITIES/SUPPORT: Modern, fully equipped apartments are available through the company. Staff are free to choose other lodgings, if desired. Visa sponsorship can be provided. Company cars are available for lease. A vehicle is necessary for travel between schools. Weekly Japanese language classes available for all teachers free of charge.
RECRUITMENT: Usually takes about 2 months from initial contact. Telephone interviews will be conducted. References are also required.
CONTACT: Frank Pridgen, Foreign Staff Manager (cfpj@bernard.co.jp).

BERLITZ JAPAN

Shin Aoyama Bldg., East 16F, 1–1 Minami Aoyama 1-chome, Minato-ku, Tokyo 107–0062

💻 http://teach.berlitz.co.jp

NUMBER OF TEACHERS: Over 1,200 for 63 locations, about half of which are in Greater Tokyo.
PREFERENCE OF NATIONALITY: None, must be native English speaker. For many vacancies, only candidates already in Japan will be considered.
QUALIFICATIONS: Minimum university degree, business experience and/or teaching experience needed for some posts.
CONDITIONS OF EMPLOYMENT: Choice of 3 contracts: semi full-time is open to all applicants; part-time and hourly contracts available only to people already in Japan with current visa. Working hours vary.
SALARY: Starting salary of 250,000 yen, plus possibility of a contract completion bonus.
FACILITIES/SUPPORT: Visa assistance given in some cases but for part-time openings teacher must be already resident and in possession of a visa. All new hires must attend a 6-day Berlitz Instructor Qualification Programme (unpaid).
RECRUITMENT: Via the above website. Interviews are essential and are conducted in Japan or sometimes by telephone and Internet. Group interview sessions are organised at intervals.
CONTACT: Mark Richey, Manager.

THE BRITISH ENGLISH AND NEW DANCE ACADEMY

9–23 Hinodemachi, 3 chome, Sanyoonoda-shi, Yamaguchi-ken 756–0091

📞 +81 836 84 2390
✉️ englishbenda@yahoo.co.uk or ennutton@gmail.com
💻 http://bendaacademy.jimdo.com

NUMBER OF TEACHERS: 6.

PREFERENCE OF NATIONALITY: English Native speaking countries.

QUALIFICATIONS: At least a BA degree or 2-year college diploma. Experience is a plus.

CONDITIONS OF EMPLOYMENT: 12 months with option to renew. Teachers work a maximum of 24.5 teaching hours per week, with little or no office time.

SALARY: 235,000–255,000 yen per month. National tax is paid from the first year and city tax from the second year.

FACILITIES/SUPPORT: Academy covers key money expenses for teachers' apartments. Teachers pay for their own rent, usually 40,000–55,000 yen. Employer provides work visa sponsorship which is mainly carried out in Japan, but requires the teacher to complete the process in his/her home country.

RECRUITMENT: After receiving applicant's documents by email and airmail, school will arrange telephone interview.

CONTACT: Ted Nutton, Principal (ennutton@gmail.com).

CALIFORNIA LANGUAGE INSTITUTE
Yamaha Bldg 4F, Uomachi 1–1-1, Kokurakitaku, Kitakyushushi 802–0006
🖰 information@cli-kids.co.jp
🖵 www.cli-kids.co.jp

NUMBER OF TEACHERS: 40+ for branches in various cities such as Tokyo, Chiba, Fukuoka and Hiroshima.

PREFERENCE OF NATIONALITY: None.

QUALIFICATIONS: None, but must like children because most of the teaching is in kindergarten.

CONDITIONS OF EMPLOYMENT: 12-month contract from September; 32.5 hours per week per 5-day working week. Days off may not be consecutive.

SALARY: From 250,000 yen per month less income tax (7%) and rent.

FACILITIES/SUPPORT: Fully furnished single accommodation provided at rent of 67,500 yen. Work visa applications carried out through Japanese immigration. Airfare contribution paid at end of contract.

RECRUITMENT: Interviews essential, available in UK. Adverts appear in the *Guardian* and *TES* about 4 weeks before interviews held in London (e.g. mid-April for early May interviews). CV and photo must be submitted in advance.

ECC FOREIGN LANGUAGE INSTITUTE
General Headquarters: 3rd Floor, ECC Honsha Building, 1 10 20 Higashi-Temma, Kita-ku, Osaka 530–0044

🖵 http://recruiting.ecc.co.jp (for job applicants)
Kanto Management Centre Head Office:
9th Floor, Shinjuku Plaza Building, 1 3 14
Nishi-Shinjuku, Shinjuku-ku, Tokyo 160–0023
🖰 ganative@ecc.co.jp
Chubu Management Centre Head Office: 8th Floor
Kanayama Building, 1 16 16 Kanayama, Naka-ku,
Nagoya 460–0022
🖰 nhr@ecc.co.jp
Kinki Management Centre Head Office: 8th Floor,
ECC Honsha Building, 1 10 20 Higashi-temma, Kita-ku,
Osaka 530–0044
🖰 instruct@ecc.co.jp

NUMBER OF TEACHERS: 600+ at 165 schools throughout Japan.

PREFERENCE OF NATIONALITY: Applicants for whom English is their native language.

QUALIFICATIONS: Minimum bachelor's degree.

CONDITIONS OF EMPLOYMENT: 1-year contracts, ending yearly on 31 March; 29.5 total working hours per week, mostly evenings. To work 5 days a week with variable days off. 7 weeks' paid holiday per annum. Teachers work some Saturday or Sunday shifts. Opportunities for paid overtime are plentiful.

SALARY: From 252,000 yen per month.

FACILITIES/SUPPORT: Assistance with accommodation. Compulsory 50–70 hour pre-service training course over 2 weeks.

RECRUITMENT: Visit the website recruitment.ecc.co.jp for recruitment schedules. Main hiring period is September–November. *UK recruitment*: c/o ECC Recruitment (UK), PO Box 11985, Nayland, Colchester, CO6 4XB; ukhiring@ecc.co.jp. *Australia recruitment*: AMAC Recruitment, www.amacrecruitment.com.au (+61 8 8131 0027; ECC@amacrecruitment.com.au). *Canada and USA recruitment:* ECC Canada Office, Suite 1801, Toronto Star Building, 1 Yonge Street, Toronto, Ontario M5E 1W7, recruitment. ecc.co.jp (+1 416 703 3390; toronto@ecc.co.jp).

ENGLISH ACADEMY & HARVARD-KIDS ACADEMY
2–9-6 Ichibancho, Matsuyama 790–0001
📞 +81 89 931 8686
🖰 marinbu@post.harvard.edu or marinburch@
   hotmail.com
🖵 www.e8686.jp or www.eigo-academy.com

NUMBER OF TEACHERS: 7–9, including for new branch of Harvard-Kids Academy opening in Yokohama.

PREFERENCE OF NATIONALITY: None.

QUALIFICATIONS: Teachers with at least a 4-year degree. Some experience in teaching is also helpful although training is given.

Native English speakers preferred. Experience with young children is preferred for Harvard-Kids Academy which is an immersion kindergarten/pre-school.

CONDITIONS OF EMPLOYMENT: 18-month contracts. Hours 12pm–9pm, Tuesday to Friday, 10am–6pm on Saturday.

SALARY: Starting at 250,000 yen per month. Income tax is withheld and different arrangements are made for social security or health insurance depending on the circumstances of the teacher.

FACILITIES/SUPPORT: Help in finding accommodation and loan in making initial deposit. Academy has two apartments which require only minimal deposits. Help to apply for Certificate of Prior Permission for a work visa and in visa renewal when the time comes.

RECRUITMENT: Advertise in publications in Japan and sometimes at Ohayo-Sensei. Telephone and Skype interviews.

CONTACT: K Marin Burch Tanaka.

THE ENGLISH VILLAGE

4–2–1–113 Taihei, Sumida-ku, Tokyo 130 0013

+81 3 3624 3300

englishvillage@msg.biglobe.ne.jp

www.englishvillage.gr.jp

NUMBER OF TEACHERS: 7 for branches in Kinshicho (area of Tokyo) and Funabashi in Chiba.

PREFERENCE OF NATIONALITY: British.

QUALIFICATIONS: Degree (any discipline) and CELTA qualification or equivalent. Valid visa essential.

CONDITIONS OF EMPLOYMENT: One year renewable. 30–50-minute lessons per week and sessions supervising free conversation room. School specialises in teaching British English to adult learners.

SALARY: 250,000 yen per month plus 200,000 yen completion bonus.

FACILITIES/SUPPORT: Subsidised accommodation is arranged. New teachers are given a period of thorough training before they start teaching, followed by in-service training.

RECRUITMENT: British press adverts. Interviews in the UK.

CONTACT: Neil Pearson, Principal.

HEART ENGLISH SCHOOL

310-0805 Ibaraki-ken, Mito-shi, 2-6-10 Chuo

+81 29 226 8010

info@heart-school.jp

www.heart-school.jp

Places teachers in public schools to assist Japanese teachers of English.

NUMBER OF TEACHERS: 300 Assistant Language Teachers (ALTs) per year, but varies by season.

PREFERENCE OF NATIONALITY: Native or near-native English speakers. Visa sponsorship possible only for passport holders of the US, Canada, UK, Ireland, Australia and New Zealand.

QUALIFICATIONS: For visa sponsorship, a BA degree or equivalent is absolutely required. However applicants able to obtain a spouse or working holiday visa independently can also be considered. Key qualities are flexibility and a good personality with children. Experience is a plus but not essential if candidates have the right personality and are able to co-operate effectively with their Japanese co-teacher.

CONDITIONS OF EMPLOYMENT: Contracts are usually from the start date – normally April or September – through March, which is the end of Japan's public school year. If both parties agree, contract can be renewed in 1-year increments. Rarely, contract lengths are non-standard due to a specific school board request. Some positions offer only 180 or 210 days of work a year which is less than full-time (240 days). Typical hours are 8/8.45am to 3.30/5.30pm, though in most cases the number of contracted hours is just under 6 per day, with the rest of the time spent as break periods.

SALARY: Pay depends on the municipality, and on number of working hours and days. Range from 180,000 yen per month to 240,000 yen. After rent, taxes, utilities and other compulsory expenses, an ALT earns the equivalent of US$1,200–$2,400 in take home pay, with an average of about $1,850. No payment when school is closed (as in August). Some companies provide a 100,000 yen stipend in these fallow periods, which is enough to cover rent, taxes, utilities, and have enough left over for food, but not much else. Employees are expected to prepare for these lulls.

FACILITIES/SUPPORT: Housing can be arranged and subsidised in a private apartment, usually furnished. School co-operates with legalities, and does most of the leg-work in obtaining and renewing Instructor visa.

RECRUITMENT: Via Japan-specific recruitment websites or via university career fairs in North America, UK and Australia. Interviews are required in person or via phone or video connection online.

CONTACT: Kent Phillips, Recruiter.

INTERAC CO. LTD.

Fujimi West 3F, Fujimi 2–14–36, Chiyoda-ku, Tokyo 102 0071

+81 3 3234 7840

www.interacnetwork.com

Non-governmental provider of Assistant Language Teachers in Japan.

NUMBER OF TEACHERS: Over 2,000 full-time employees throughout Japan.

PREFERENCE OF NATIONALITY: None, though majority are Australian, New Zealander, Canadian, American, British, Irish and Jamaican.

QUALIFICATIONS: Minimum university degree, 12 years' education in the medium of English (all subjects taught in English at school for at least 12 years) plus a passion for teaching and a strong desire to live in Japan and work in Japanese public schools. Japanese language skills and teaching qualifications preferred but not a necessity. Drivers licence and willingness to drive are an advantage.

CONDITIONS OF EMPLOYMENT: 12-month contracts from early April to late March. Up to 29.5 teaching hours per week, Monday to Friday 8am–5pm; 7 months contract available from late August to following year late March.

SALARY: Average monthly minimum of 230,000 yen; 10% deducted in tax.

FACILITIES/SUPPORT: Comprehensive orientation programme on arrival with follow-up training sessions. Company acts as guarantor for apartment contracts and visa sponsor. Private health insurance cover available. Free Japanese lessons available in some locations.

RECRUITMENT: All recruitment is done through online system. Interviews may be conducted in Oxford, Toronto and elsewhere. Intakes in late August and late March.

INTERNATIONAL EDUCATION CONSULTANTS
Shin Yokohama, IK Bldg. 604, 2 12 12 Shin Yokohama, Kohoku ku, Yokohama shi, 222–0033
 +81 45 308 6280
 info@ieconsultants.co.jp
 www.ieconsultants.co.jp

NUMBER OF TEACHERS: 4.

PREFERENCE OF NATIONALITY: Native English speakers.

QUALIFICATIONS: University graduate. Must be in the country and have work visa already.

CONDITIONS OF EMPLOYMENT: Part-time only. Lessons take place between 6am and 9pm.

SALARY: Hourly rate. Local taxes deducted at source.

FACILITIES/SUPPORT: No assistance with accommodation or visas.

RECRUITMENT: Word of mouth. Face-to-face interview required.

CONTACT: Ulrich Kulz, CEO (ulikulz@ieconsultants.co.jp).

JAMES ENGLISH SCHOOLS
4–16–6 Teraoka Izumi, Sendai, Miyagi 981 3204
 +81 22 7720161
 jesliaison@james.co.jp
 www.JesJapan.com

NUMBER OF TEACHERS: 50–100 for 15 branches in the Tohoku region of northern Japan.

PREFERENCE OF NATIONALITY: None.

QUALIFICATIONS: Bachelor's degree and TESOL.

CONDITIONS OF EMPLOYMENT: 1-year contract. Expect teachers to stay at least 2 years. 30 teaching hours per week (average).

SALARY: 250,000–290,000 yen per month.

FACILITIES/SUPPORT: Loan provided for initial settling in costs. Visa sponsorship. Training and regular professional development offered.

RECRUITMENT: Adverts on GaijinPot.com, etc. Application process completed through website. Skype interviews.

CONTACT: Mr. Yoshi Kigawa, Owner and President..

JET PROGRAMME UK
JET Desk, Embassy of Japan, 101–104 Piccadilly, London W1J 7JT, UK
 +44 20 7465 6668
 info@jet-uk.org
 www.jet-uk.org

NUMBER OF TEACHERS: Approximately 150 each year from the UK going to educational institutions all over Japan.

PREFERENCE OF NATIONALITY: UK passport holders only.

QUALIFICATIONS: Must hold a bachelor's degree by the time of departure and be under 39 years of age. TEFL training or experience preferred but not essential.

CONDITIONS OF EMPLOYMENT: 12-month renewable contracts starting in August up to maximum of 5 years. Normal working hours are 35 hours per week, although teaching hours are between 15 and 20. Conditions of service vary according to the policies of different contracting organisations.

SALARY: Annual renumeration is about 3.6 million yen per year.

FACILITIES/SUPPORT: JET finds placement, organises visa and insurance, hosts 2-day pre-departure orientation day in London, beginners' TEFL training and basic Japanese language course, 2 day orientation in Tokyo, language books and return flights provided upon completion of contract.

RECRUITMENT: Deadline for application is the last week in November. Interviews in following January/February with decisions given in April. All application info is online or contact Jet Desk with any queries.

KENT SCHOOL OF ENGLISH

Shoppers' Plaza 706, 1–4-1 Irfune, Urayasu-shi, Chiba
Ken 279–0012

🖰 kentappli@aol.com

NUMBER OF TEACHERS: 8.

PREFERENCE OF NATIONALITY: None, but interviews held in London in July.

QUALIFICATIONS: Minimum university degree plus TEFL certificate or PGCE plus 2 years' TEFL experience. Must like children.

CONDITIONS OF EMPLOYMENT: 1-year contract. 23 contact hours per week. 5–6 weeks' paid holiday.

SALARY: From 260,000 yen per month (gross) plus outward flight provided. Tax and insurance deductions are less than 8%

FACILITIES/SUPPORT: Subsidised furnished flats available, some shared, some single. All deposits/key money/gratuities paid, so teachers pay only the rent and utilities charges.

RECRUITMENT: Adverts in the *Guardian* and via the internet (e.g. tefl.com). Interviews held in the UK in the summer. Once contract is signed, permits are arranged and issued in mid-September.

CONTACT: Liz Fuse, Director of Studies.

KEVIN'S ENGLISH SCHOOLS

Iizawa 242–23, Minamiashigara Shi, Kanagawa
Pref. 250-0122

📞 +81 465 74 4458
🖰 kevinsenglishschools@hotmail.com
💻 www.eikaiwa1.com

NUMBER OF TEACHERS: 3.

PREFERENCE OF NATIONALITY: None.

QUALIFICATIONS: College or university degree and some extra training in how to teach English. A TEFL certificate and experience are pluses.

CONDITIONS OF EMPLOYMENT: 1-year contract. Most teaching hours fall in the afternoon and evening up till 9pm.

SALARY: 250,000 yen per month.

FACILITIES/SUPPORT: Apartment is provided for a rent of about 60,000 yen per month. Assistance given with all official paperwork.

RECRUITMENT: Via www.how-to-teach-english-in-japan.com. Interviews by phone or in person are essential; many candidates are interviewed by phone.

CONTACT: Kevin R Burns, Owner.

MODEL LANGUAGE STUDIO (MLS)

2–31-8 Yoyogi, Shibuya-ku, Tokyo-to 151–0053

📞 +81 3 3320 1555
🖰 careers21@mls-etd.co.jp
💻 www.mls-etd.co.jp

NUMBER OF TEACHERS: 55 across 35 schools.

PREFERENCE OF NATIONALITY: All native speakers.

QUALIFICATIONS: Experience working with students aged 1–12. Valid Working Visa or minimum BA Certification in which case sponsorship is possible.

CONDITIONS OF EMPLOYMENT: 12-month contracts from April. Up to 30 hours per 5-day week (of which 25 are teaching hours).

SALARY: 255,000 yen (gross) per calendar month. Up to 80,000 yen end-of-contract bonus.

FACILITIES/SUPPORT: Company can temporarily house new arrivals. It has links to large number of apartments and can help staff source a suitable one (key money not required). Transport to and from work is paid. Various other monetary incentives. Long paid vacations and all national holidays paid. Company can help sponsor appropriate candidates for a visa before arrival in Japan.

RECRUITMENT: Via company website, gaijinpot and various Japanese recruitment agencies. Face-to-face interview essential. Non-Japan based applications must include an mpeg/DVD of the candidate in action.

CONTACT: David Flynn, Instructor Management.

RED ROOF ENGLISH SCHOOL

Okinawa Prefecture, Ginowan City, Samashita 175–1-102 (Kasa G2)

📞 +81 98 890 1228
🖰 job.info@redroof.jp
💻 www.redroof.jp

NUMBER OF TEACHERS: 3.

PREFERENCE OF NATIONALITY: None.

QUALIFICATIONS: University degree is essential for visa sponsorship. Experience working with children is preferred.

CONDITIONS OF EMPLOYMENT: 1-year contract. Usual teaching hours between 1pm and 9pm Monday to Friday or Tuesday to Saturday.

SALARY: Starting from 185,000 yen to 225,000 yen per month depending on expertise; 40,000 to 50,000 yen deducted per month for rent and utilities.

FACILITIES/SUPPORT: Apartment with modest furnishings is provided. Assistance is also given with setting up telephones and banking etc.

RECRUITMENT: Usually through the internet or word of mouth. Interviews are essential and can be held via web cam or occasionally in Canada.

CONTACT: Ken Nakamura-Huber, Director (ken@redroof.jp).

SHANE ENGLISH SCHOOL JAPAN (SESJ)

Kenkyusha Fujimi Building '4F, 2–11–3 Fujimi, Chiyoda-ku, Tokyo 102–0071

ⓒ +81 3 5275 6756

drp@shane.co.jp or teflrecruitment@shane.co.jp

www.tefljobsinjapan.com and www.saxoncourt.com/jobs-abroad/japan

Chain of language schools in the Greater Tokyo region which has been part of Japanese cram school company, Eikoh Inc, since November 2010.

NUMBER OF TEACHERS: 400+ in 180 schools.

PREFERENCE OF NATIONALITY: Native speakers of British English, i.e. from Commonwealth countries.

QUALIFICATIONS: University degree required plus CELTA or Trinity CertTESOL.

CONDITIONS OF EMPLOYMENT: 12-month renewable contracts. Maximum 29.5 contact hours per week. Students from age 2. 5–6 weeks' paid holiday.

SALARY: Starting salary 252,800 yen per month plus possible bonuses. Deductions for income tax work out at about 6.5% of gross income.

FACILITIES/SUPPORT: Accommodation, sub-lets provided for teachers who require it or information on guesthouses that accept long-stay foreigners. All documentation for work visas is provided.

RECRUITMENT: Via face-to-face interviews in Japan or via recruitment agencies in the UK, i.e. Saxoncourt International (www.saxoncourt.com), TEFLOne and UIC.

CONTACT: Director of Recruitment and Personnel (teflrecruitment@shane.co.jp).

VOLTA ASSOCIATES

Chiyoda Platform Square 1005, 3–21 Kanda Hishikicho, Chiyoda-ku, Tokyo 101–0054

info@volta-associates.com

www.volta-associates.com

NUMBER OF TEACHERS: 5.

PREFERENCE OF NATIONALITY: None.

QUALIFICATIONS: Bachelor degree with TESOL.

CONDITIONS OF EMPLOYMENT: 1-year contract. 4–6 lessons a day, 5 days a week.

SALARY: Approximately 230,00 yen.

FACILITIES/SUPPORT: Assistance given with finding accommodation (translating paperwork, finding estate agents etc). TESOL course is provided.

RECRUITMENT: Usually via the internet. Interviews are essential.

CONTACT: Benard Oppong-Kusi, President and CEO.

KOREA

Anyone who has witnessed the early morning scramble by students and businessmen to get to their English lessons before the working day begins in Seoul might be surprised to learn that the motto for South Korea is 'Land of the Morning Calm'. Because Korea's economy is so heavily dependent on export, English is a very useful accomplishment for people in business. The level of affluence in Seoul and the other major cities is striking, and many of these ambitious Koreans are not only keen but are able to afford English lessons. An English proficiency test must be passed by all aspiring university students which is why so many students of secondary school age study the language so feverishly. Both these groups have probably studied English for many years at school but need to practise conversation with native English speakers.

School and university vacations (July and January) often see a surge in student enrolment at private language institutes and at seasonal camps. The teaching of children is booming more than ever and there is a huge demand for English teachers to teach in schools where English is compulsory. This must be the only country in the world where it is possible to have your international airfare covered in return for teaching for a couple of weeks at a camp (see description below). Major language teaching organisations rely heavily on recruitment agencies abroad to fill their recurring vacancies for native English speaker staff. The market in Korea is ever changing. There are still lots of jobs around but it is becoming harder to find good positions. Partly because of the difficult employment situation in their home countries, many teachers are staying in their jobs in Korea longer or finding new ones there instead of returning home.

The bias is strongly in favour of North Americans, especially Canadians, and there are still relatively few British TEFLers in Korea, though this might be slowly changing with the activities of UK-based recruiters such as Flying Cows in Nottingham (see entry) which recruits for positions in both the private and public sectors. Note that in the case of Korea, 'schools' normally refer to the state sector whereas 'institutes' mean private language academies run as businesses. The number of small to medium sized *hagwons* (private language institutes) in all Korean cities interested in hiring a few native English speakers is massive. Identifying the good recruitment agencies interested in more than collecting their commission is tricky. The fact that recruiters come and go indicates that some are just out to make a fast buck. When dealing either with *hagwon* owners or recruiters, ask for the email address of a current English-speaking teacher and use it to ask about the school, students, the town/city and accommodation. If the school is reluctant to provide a contact, ask why.

Fortunately the language industry's bad reputation for shamelessly exploiting foreign teachers seems to be slowly improving. Of broader concern than the possible shark-like practices of some potential employers is the looming proximity of North Korea. Ongoing border incidents in 2012 have done nothing to calm nerves or keep the currency (the won) stable. **William Naquin**, a well-qualified American who taught in Kyunggi-Do, sums up the politics as he saw them when he was there:

> *Korea is a divided country. We were quite nervous that war might break out here between the two Koreas. The situation in the north is universally reported to be extremely bad, with summary executions and food riots. The North Koreans have nuclear missiles, nerve gas and chemical weapons, and are led by the most isolated, despotic lunatic and paranoid military strongmen in the world. Prospective teachers need to know that this is one of the most likely flashpoints for war on earth, and that coming here necessarily involves some degree of risk.*

For the curious, it is possible to visit the Demilitarised Zone (DMZ) between South and North Korea on a day trip (from about £27 in 2012). However, it is not possible to enter the reclusive Democratic Republic from the south.

PROSPECTS FOR TEACHERS

There are hundreds of *hagwons* in Seoul the capital, Busan (Korea's second city, less than four hours south of Seoul) and in smaller cities. The majority of these are run as businesses, where profit is the primary or even sole *raison d'être*. ELT training is superfluous in the majority of cases. Native-speaker status and a bachelor's degree are usually sufficient to persuade the owner of an institute to hire an English speaker. Education is greatly respected in Korea and degrees generally matter far more to potential employers than specialist qualifications. For now, a bachelor's is sufficient and a master's (no matter in what field) counts heavily in one's favour. Having a TEFL certificate and/or teaching experience usually attracts more job offers, although some schools are suspicious of candidates with experience because they view them as potentially picky, plus they don't want to pay more than a basic entry level salary.

If you wait until you get to Korea, it is easy to fix up a job, but the visa is more difficult to arrange (see section on regulations below). If you want to find a good job make sure you present yourself well. **Peter Burnside** offers three brief tips to people considering going to teach in Korea: '*follow your heart, trust your instincts and take insane risks*'.

FINDING A JOB

IN ADVANCE

The Korean government administers an official teacher placement programme in imitation of JET in Japan. EPIK (English Program in Korea) is run by the Ministry of Education and administered through Korean embassies and consulates in the USA, Canada, Australia and the UK, placing about 2,000 foreign graduates in state schools and education offices throughout the country. Private recruiters are also involved, such as www.tefljobplacement.com (part of Denver-based Bridge TEFL) and Toronto-based Teach Away (www.teachaway.com); using these mediating agencies will make things easier.

The author met a US teacher on the EPIK programme in Seoul in April 2012 who passed on a persistent rumour that the South Korean government is intending to reduce or even wind up EPIK over the next few years. They claim that Korean teachers of English are now ready to take over from native speakers, though many doubt this to be the case. **Amanda Middlecote**, director of the specialist recruitment company Flying Cows, corroborated this:

> *I know a lot of public school teachers have not had their contracts renewed and the school is not hiring any new 'foreigners'. This has led them to go directly to* hagwons *looking for work, which has had a knock-on effect on people outside Korea looking for work. We have had people accepted for positions then the job taken from them at the eleventh hour because someone already with a visa has walked in off the street ready to start work.*

For the time being the programme continues.

The annual salary offered on the EPIK programme is 1.8–2.7 million won per month (depending on qualifications) plus free furnished accommodation, visa sponsorship, flight costs (which are reimbursed on arrival in Korea), 50% contribution to medical insurance and an end-of-contract bonus. Applications for the autumn semester are accepted between 1 April and 1 June, but documents can be submitted all year round in case of openings.

Details of the programme are available from the EPIK website (www.epik.go.kr) or by contacting the local Korea government representative, e.g. in the UK the Education Director, Korean Embassy, 60 Buckingham Gate, London SW1E 6AJ (+44 20 7227 5547; edu@koreanembassy.org.uk). Americans should contact any of the 10 Korean consulates in the USA. Other nationalities can contact the EPIK office in Korea (EPIK Office, 81 Ihwajang-gil, Jongno-gu, Seoul 110–810; +82 2 3668 1400). Note that EPIK does not attract the same high praise that the JET Programme does, though it has been better organised in recent years.

EPIK/public school applicants need to have a TEFL qualification, unless they have a BA in Education, English or Linguistics or an MA or one or more years of full-time teaching experience. Applicants are no longer able to specify the location in which they would like to live/work and couples cannot apply together. You can select a preference of metropolitan, provincial or Seoul, but with no guarantee that your request will be honoured.

A subsidiary government programme is called TALK (talkkorea@gmail.com; www.talk.go.kr), which is open to people with at least two years of university education. The teaching here takes place in after-school clubs, the commitment is shorter (6 months instead of a year) and the pay is lower (1.5 million won a month). Otherwise the internet is awash with job vacancies. Try for example Seoul-based www.eslpro.com and www.teachkoreans.com. Check www.englishspectrum.com for current ads placed by recruiting companies such as Double S Edu (www.doublesedu.com), part-time work, etc.

Another option is to work for Gyeonngi English Villages (www.english-village.or.kr) where they try to simulate an English-speaking environment for learners without their having to travel abroad. You will see signs advertising this concept on the highway between Seoul and the DMZ, because the village is located in Paju City near the border between the Koreas.

RECRUITMENT AGENCIES

Most private recruiters offer one-year contracts to English speakers with a university or college diploma. Candidates with additional EFL/ESL qualifications and teaching experience should be able to negotiate higher monthly salaries than the standard 1.8–2.1 million won. Recruited teachers are asked to commit themselves to teach 120 hours a month which is a heavy load. Return airfares, free accommodation, paid holidays, contribution to medical insurance and completion bonus are all promised as a rule. Applicants who cannot be interviewed locally can do so by telephone or internet. Note that recruiters should not charge teachers any fee since they earn their commission from the schools and institutes. An agency in the UK called Flying Cows, formed in 2004, aims to be as honest as possible about the rewards and drawbacks of teaching in South Korea (see entry).

Here is a list of Korea-based recruiters active at the time of writing. The following list directs North American readers to recruiting contacts on their continent, all of whom are located in Canada.

Morgan Recruiting, Seoul (+82 2 2299 226; www.morganrecruiters.com).
Park English Recruitment Agency, Suite #402, 4th Floor Bomm Building, 124–7 Itaewon-dong Yong-san-gu, Seoul 140–858 (+82 2 749 1140; www.parkenglish.com).
People Recruit, Busan – www.peoplerecruit.com. Calls itself a 'Competent Persons Database.'
SeoulESL Recruiting, 1014, LGSeochoECLAT, 1599–2 Seocho-dong, Seocho-gu, Seoul 137–727 (+82 2 585 7871; esl@seoulesl.com; www.seoulesl.com).
Think Outside, Woongjin Thinkbig Overseas Education Department 535–1, Moonbai-Ri, Gyoha-Eup, Paju-Shi, Gyeonggi-Do (+82 31 9567326; www.thinkoutsiderecruiting.com).

The following Canadian agencies are willing to place more than just Canadians provide they meet the requirements:

Canadian Connection Consulting Agency (see entry).
English Beyond Borders, Toronto (www.englishbeyondborders.org). Linda Lee recruits for one-year jobs and also summer and winter camps run by Hankuk University, among other positions.
GMSC Recruiting (*Vancouver office:* toll-free +1 888 771 3350 or 778 786 2854; *Seattle office:* +1 425 949 7916; www.gmsc-recruiting.com).
Gone2Korea Employment Services, 25 Grenville Street, Toronto M4Y 2X5 (+1 416 928 0964; www. gone2korea.com). They fill positions in public schools for EPIK.
JC Canada Recruitment, Toronto (+1 416 226 9787; jccakr@yahoo.com; www.iloveesl.com). Korean ESL job placement agency. Offices in Toronto and Seoul. Opportunities to teach English at Korean schools available throughout the year.
Korea Connections, 211–3030 Lincoln Ave, Coquitlam, BC V3B 6B4 (admin@koreaconnections.net; www.koreaconnections.net). Recruit for EPIK among others.
Russell Recruiting, Vancouver (russell_recruiting@yahoo.ca; www.russellrecruiting.com). Caters to ESL teachers wishing to work in Korea. Agency made up of former and current teachers so all services provided are safe, secure and free for job applicants. Schools are inspected and recommended by the current teachers working in Asia.
Scotia Personnel, 6045 Cherry St, Halifax, NS B3H 2K4 (+1 902 422 1455; info@scotia-personnel-ltd. com; www.scotia-personnel-ltd.com). Refers Canadians with university degree to teaching English in schools in South Korea. Employer provides airfare, accommodation, competitive salary and more.

Cara McCain found a good way of dipping her toe in the water of teaching in Korea without committing herself for a whole year. Furthermore, the camp she worked for pays round-trip airfares from the US and provides accommodation, food and a wage of 800,000 won (£460), for a commitment of three to four weeks. In order to apply, you need to have a university degree, no criminal record and be willing to jump through all the bureaucratic hoops to prove it in order to qualify for a C4 (short-term work) visa:

I was looking for a way to finance my trip to Korea, and a winter camp seemed like a perfect opportunity. Don't bother to apply unless you already have the documents which include a notarised background check and an apostilled degree certificate. I contacted a couple of camps while I was waiting for my paperwork in the mail, but they turned me down flat because I didn't have the documents in hand. I was hired to teach a three-week intensive camp, seven hours a day with Sundays off. The camp that hired me was IHUFS through a recruiter in Australia who worked with me over Skype and email.

The next step was buying my plane ticket. It was the winter holiday season, so airfares came out at about US$1600. I told the recruiter that I didn't have the money to pay for my own ticket. He suggested that I just buy the ticket on a credit card, and the camp would transfer the money into my American bank account once I got to Korea. I took a leap of faith and it worked out fine. The camp went great. The staff was professional and took good care of all the teachers at the camp. We were picked up at the airport, and were given food and adequate accommodation. The students were great and enjoyed learning English. Couldn't ask for more. Overall the experience was a great way to jumpstart my ESL career. I gained relevant teaching experience, got to try the food, learned about the culture, and met people that I still keep in touch with to this day.

The internet is well equipped to keep track of the volatile English language market and many Korean employers rely exclusively on it. One that lists vacancies is www.findateacher.co.kr. More than one webpage lists good and bad employers along with a few horror stories.

Another possibility for anyone with an MA or advanced TEFL/TESL qualifications is to work for the language department of a Korean university (of which there are nearly 100). Universities probably offer the best paid and most stable employment. Serious teachers should enquire at their local Korean consulate for addresses.

JESSIE COX

After doing a two-week evening course on TESL teaching in her final term of university in Ontario, Jessie Cox, a Canadian, scoured the job forums at www.daveseslcafe.com to find some decent recruiters for Korea who would not renege on their agreements. Before long she was on her way to provincial Korea.

I taught at the only middle school in a small farming town, and the biggest problem I encountered was the extremely low English level of most of the students. Even simple directions were hard for me to give, so we had to spend some time learning simple instructions like 'open your book to page 22' or 'Repeat after me'. The language barrier also made discipline more of a challenge for me. If the Korean teacher wasn't in the room at the time, I was pretty much limited to 'Stop that' 'No!' and 'Be quiet please'. I was mostly responsible for leading pronunciation and speaking exercises, along with conducting memory tests in which the students had to recite a passage from the text book. The teaching was mostly textbook based. The best feature of working in a state school as the only non-Korean teacher was the chance to be completely immersed in Korean culture in a way that would never be possible as a tourist. The wages at public schools in Korea are quite good and the pay of 1.8 million won per month was more *than enough to cover expenses. Although I travelled quite a bit, including to Thailand and Mongolia, I still managed to save about C$10,000 over the year. The biggest reward of my experience in Korea was seeing the world from a different perspective. I was able to climb mountains, visit Buddhist temples, visit the border between North and South Korea, explore ancient palaces, and even eat a live octopus!*

ON THE SPOT

Under new visa regulations (15 December 2007) any person who arrives in Korea to teach English must get their final visa processing completed in their own home country. This means that entering on a tourist visa for job-hunting is simply not possible, at least this is the official line. There are all kinds of interesting conversations happening in Korea as to whether this regulation is really necessary.

REGULATIONS

For many years a number of Korean employers and agents asked English teachers to arrive on a tourist visa and do a Japan visa run. This is no longer allowed. Teachers must get their final visa processing completed in their home country if they are going to a *hagwon* job or even a short-term camp job, although some exemptions exist for visa processing in a third country if you are going to a public school job. Anyone working without a visa risks fines and possible deportation. Similarly, the schools which hire freelance foreigners without permits can be closed down by the government. So, if at all possible, obtain a work visa (E2), which is available only to people with a 3- or 4-year bachelor's degree. The alternative C4 visa valid for single entry and maximum 90 days is also available only to degree holders. All must be native speakers of English and nationals of the UK, Ireland, USA, Canada, Australia, New Zealand or South Africa. Unfortunately, some schools such as Berlitz want to hire only those with an F2 or F4 residency visa and will not accept E2 visas.

The procedures are ludicrously complicated, and seem to change every month. In the words of **Del Ford** who has taught throughout the Far East for nine years: *'The application and immigration documentation requirements, especially for jobs in public schools, have entered the realm of Kafkaesque absurdity.'* Recruiters and employers accustomed to the procedures will set them out as clearly as they can. For example Camp Korea has reams of information on its website (www.ck.co.kr/teacher). Here is a summary: You must gather together the contract of employment from your prospective employer, your passport, your original degree officially notarised, which must be from an approved institution in an English-speaking country, a notarised criminal record/CRB check, ID and forms. After mailing these and other documents to the employer in Korea, they are used to obtain a visa issuance number. With a visa issuance number, they can proceed to apply for the E-2 visa at the Korean consulate in their home country (the fee is £80 in the UK, usually US$30-50 in the US). The consulate officer may schedule a short interview which can be by phone and then stamp the passport with an E2 visa stamp.

You can then enter Korea and present your passport to an immigration officer: finally, your visa becomes valid and you may commence work immediately. A recent change means that in order to apply for an Aliens Registration Card after arrival, teachers must take medical tests at a designated hospital to check for HIV, TB and cannabis. So controversial is the compulsory HIV test that in 2011 the Secretary General of the United Nations, Ban Ki-moon, urged South Korea to drop the test for English teachers on the grounds that it is discriminatory and typecasts them as promiscuous drug-users.

Since September 2010, most Korean embassies and consulates are accepting only notarised degree certificates that have been affixed with the relevant 'apostille' (French for 'certification'). This can be done by specialist companies, for example in the UK see www.apostille.org.uk where the stamp will cost £90. Obtaining a criminal record check is another headache. US nationals must now have one issued by the FBI, so a state-level check is no longer sufficient, and these can take up to three months to process. Note that the authorities no longer return your submitted documents.

This palavar has discouraged many teachers from considering Korea as a destination. For example, blogger Johnny Ward gave up because of 'the stubbornness of the Korean Embassy in Australia' who told him that to get a visa he would have to fly back to his native Britain. When he questioned this, he was told to 'respect the Korean law', which he has done by going to Taiwan to teach instead.The E2 visa is valid only for employment with the sponsoring employer which means that if you change employers, you must have your E2 visa officially endorsed, which is much easier than applying from scratch. So if you have obtained an E2 and completed your contract, you can transfer the visa to a new employer with minimal fuss. Freelance teaching is not permitted under the terms of your work permit and can (and does) lead to fines and deportation. However, the extremely high rates of pay available for private lessons (40,000 won per hour is not uncommon) prove too much a temptation for the majority of teachers. Koreans who inform the authorities about illegal workers are rewarded, so working illegally is more risky than ever.

Teachers are liable to income tax from their first day of work. The rate of income tax for most teachers should be 3.3% so beware employers who try to hold back much more from earnings. Most teachers participate in the Korean National Medical Insurance Union; most employers pay half of the total leaving teachers to pay about 2% of earnings; total deductions will be less than 7%. The law permits foreigners to send up to two-thirds of their salary out of the country.

CONDITIONS OF WORK

Discontentment seems to be chronic among English teachers in Korea. So many American teachers have fallen foul of faulty contracts, that the US Embassy in Seoul issues a handbook offering guidance and tips for avoiding the pitfalls, which is currently being revised (check http://seoul.usembassy.gov/teach.html or visit the American Citizens Services Branch at 82 Sejongno Road, Jongno-gu, Seoul). Information about contracts in the Embassy's old edition is instructive:

> *Foreign instructors in Korea occasionally have contract disputes with their employers. Many have observed that in Korea, a contract appears simply to be a rough working agreement, subject to change depending on the circumstances. Many Koreans do not view deviations from a contract as a breach of contract, and few Koreans would consider taking an employer to court over a contract dispute. Instead, Koreans tend to view contracts as always being flexible and subject to further negotiation. Culturally, the written contract is not the real contract; the unwritten or oral agreement one has with one's employer is the real contract. However, many employers will view a contract violation by a foreign worker as serious, and will renege on verbal promises if they feel they can. Any contract should be signed with these factors in mind.*

Tim Leffel is one in a long line of American EFL teachers who came to the conclusion that '*nearly 100% of the* hagwon *owners are crooks or unbelievably inept – sometimes both and in Korea both oral and written contracts are a joke*'. He passes on the advice to record all interviews and meetings. By working for a big chain, he avoided most problems and was given a decent apartment, good wages and lots of support materials. He even got his post-contract bonus though he had to return to Korea six weeks after finishing work to insist on it. When there are conflicts over contracts, Tim advises teachers to choose their battles carefully and to remain civilised as long as possible.

The issue of severance pay is a sore point for many teachers. By law, anyone who completes a 52-week contract is entitled to one month's salary as severance pay. Employers have been known to make life quite unpleasant for their teachers near the end of their contracts, so that they're tempted to leave and forego the bonus.

Bear in mind the quality of *hagwons* varies enormously. Some are run by sharks who may make promises at interview which they can't fulfil, and overfill classes to maximise profits. Many schools do not use recognised course books but rely on home-made materials of dubious usefulness. On the other hand, standards are rising in some schools and the experience of teachers in the private sectors is not all bad.

The majority of Korean language learners are serious (some attend two-hour classes three or four times a week) and want to be taught systematically and energetically, though even those who have been studying for years often show precious little confidence in conversing. They also expect their teachers to direct the action and are not happy with a laid-back 'let's have a chit-chat' approach. Whereas **Judith Night** (a certified teacher) found her pupils in the public school system '*eager to learn and a joy to teach*', **Mark Vetare**, with no teaching background, found things very hard going, and concluded in the end that TEFL teaching was not for him:

> *The major drawback is teaching the sullen, bored, exhausted, precocious and* Mok Dong *spoiled children aged 14 to 16: torture. (*Mok Dong *means upper mid class, whatever that means.) They drain me of energy. What they want is a white monkey to entertain them and make them giggle. Trouble is they provide zero material to work from. No sports, no interests. Their stated hobbies are sleeping, TV and listening to music. Their parents want their kids to move up book by book as if that's a gauge of progress. 'Oh, you're in 10B, great.' Never mind that they still can't speak English.*

ACCOMMODATION

Most schools that recruit teachers from abroad will sort out accommodation for their teachers. If you are looking for accommodation independently, be prepared (as in Japan) to be required to pay a large deposit ('key money'). This should be returned to you at the end of your tenancy, though as in Japan, disagreements can arise. If you don't hear about available flats from your school or other foreigners, check the English language newspaper or find an English-speaking rental agent.

LEISURE TIME

Visitors are often surprised to discover the richness and complexity of Korean history and culture, partly because Japanese culture is far better known. Despite being a bustling metropolis of more than 10 million, Seoul has preserved some of its cultural treasures. Assuming your teaching schedule permits, you should be able to explore the country and, if interested, study some aspect of Korean culture such as the martial art Tae Kwon Do. The country's area is small, the public transport good, though traffic congestion at weekends is a problem.

Teachers often find that their students are friendly. Anyone homesick for the West will gravitate to the area of Seoul called Itaewon, where fast food restaurants and discos are concentrated, not to mention a jazz club, a decent bookstore and other expatriate forms of entertainment. Teachers in the provinces will have to become accustomed to a very quiet life.

A contributor to a recent *Guardian* web forum on TEFL reported the following:

> *Last year I worked in South Korea and it was the best year of my life. I have made friends all across the globe and loved every minute of my adventure in Busan, Korea's second largest city. It is a wonderful place and you can get to Seoul for a fun-filled weekend quite easily. The exchange rate is great and the free flights and accommodation allow for a high spending and saving lifestyle even though when the wage is measured against the pound it sounds fairly average. There are of course risks. But with Korea being a country unburdened by any large amount of crime and a love for Westerners, especially Brits, you are in good hands. Kids run around till midnight in the summer with no trouble. Old men drink* soju *all day and pass out on the benches at night;*

ajumas (old women) make you feel at home while joking about men and making harsh but delicious Korean treats. It's also wired up to the hilt with an extremely fast internet and a love for online gaming. Teaching can be challenging but it can also be a slacker's heaven, but I urge you to give it your all and you will feel better about yourself. Oh – and the beer is crap but you'll learn to love it.

ALLISON WILLIAMS

Allison Williams contacted a recruiter and was soon accepted onto the government's EPIK programme, which she thinks is vastly preferable to teaching for a commercial institute.

I applied through the agency Gone2Korea who accepted me on to the EPIK programme and gave me the opportunity to apply for whichever city or province I wanted. Getting all the paperwork was a bit of a slog but at the end of the day the whole process was fairly painless. We arrived on February 18 for a week-long orientation which covered tips on teaching and advice. I really found it very useful. I also was able to make contacts with other people teaching in Daegu. Since then I have taken an online 100hr TEFL course while in Korea, which has resulted in a $100 a month pay rise.

I co-teach, which in Korea can be one of three options: you do everything, you do nothing or you do about 50%. Many of the Korean teachers' English ability is very low so their own lack of confidence inhibits them from interacting or working with the native teachers. When co-teaching, the experience is very dependent on the teacher you work with. Last year I did the 50% option. I prepared worksheets and games for the lessons, I taught about half of the class, monitoring or assisting for the other half. Because this year our school has to improve on its national English test scores, I'm pretty much doing very little to nothing. I don't prepare games for lessons any more as they have cut down on the games in place of tests. This is not the norm but it can happen. It is a bit frustrating going from being so involved to doing so little, but I'm looking forward to being more involved next semester again. We follow the national curriculum and the teachers don't deviate from it, even if the grammar and/or phrases are incorrect or inappropriate, though they do add supplementary materials.

Working conditions are great! Since my accommodation is provided and paid for by the government, I have very few living costs and can save $1000–$1300 per month, without having to eat beans on toast or should I say instant noodles. The teachers and students are all fantastic, very welcoming and kind. From day one I felt like a celebrity and still do after 15 months at the same school. I have my own desk and computer and have been helped with everything from my personal bills to getting a cell phone. In terms of pay, hours, vacation and working conditions public schools are the way to go. If you are looking for autonomous teaching and complete control over what you teach then public schools are not always the best option. I think the biggest problem is that the government has come up with this idea to have native English speakers in every school, but at the level of the school they have little or no idea what to do with them.

LIST OF EMPLOYERS

BERLITZ KOREA

10F. KTUF Bldg, 35, Yeouido-Dong, Yeongdeungpo-gu, Seoul 150–980

☎ +82 6227 2777

✉ hiring@berlitz.co.kr

🖥 www.berlitz.co.kr

NUMBER OF TEACHERS: 60, for 3 Seoul branches: Samseong, City Hall and Yeouido.

PREFERENCE OF NATIONALITY: American, Canadian, British, Irish, Australian, New Zealand or South African. For most vacancies, only candidates already with a Korean work visa will be considered.

QUALIFICATIONS: Teachers mostly aged 22–60. Must have F2 or F4 visa (E2 visa is not acceptable).

CONDITIONS OF EMPLOYMENT: Mostly split shifts. Opening hours are 6.45am–9pm Monday–Friday, and 7.30am–6pm on Saturdays.

CONTACT: Alastair Middleton, Hiring Manager.

CANADIAN CONNECTION CONSULTING AGENCY

232 Merton Street, Suite 205, Toronto, Ontario M4S 1A1, Canada

☎ +1 416 203 2679

✉ esl@canconx.com

🖥 www.canconx.com

NUMBER OF TEACHERS: 300 per year.

PREFERENCE OF NATIONALITY: Canadian, American, British, Irish, Australian, New Zealander and South African.

QUALIFICATIONS: Bachelor's degree in an English-related field, EFL qualification and teaching experience minimum.

CONDITIONS OF EMPLOYMENT: 1-year contract. To teach 22–30 hours per week.

SALARY: 1.8–2.5 million Korean won per month.

FACILITIES/SUPPORT: Accommodation is supplied and paid for (teachers pay utilities). Agency handles all visa applications, teachers must supply documentation including notarised copy of their degree, criminal record check, 2 reference letters, passport photos, university transcripts, and valid passport.

RECRUITMENT: Interview required.

CONTACT: Shane Finnie, Director.

CHUNGDAHM LEARNING INC

Faculty Human Resources, 4F Kwangjung Bldg, 18–9 Hwayang-dong, Kwangjin-gu, Seoul 143–916

☎ +82 2 497 9470

✉ job@chungdahm.com or esljobs@aclipse.net

🖥 www.teachinkorea.com and www.aclipse.net

One of the largest private language institutes in South Korea, with 120+ campuses teaching English to children.

PREFERENCE OF NATIONALITY: Canadian, American, British, Australian, New Zealander, Irish and South African.

QUALIFICATIONS: College graduates, with clean criminal records, from English speaking countries. Candidates ideally have previous experience working with children, although previous teaching experience is not a requirement. Employer is looking for a professional, patient, flexible and outgoing demeanour. A strong desire to teach children overseas is required.

CONDITIONS OF EMPLOYMENT: 12 months. 4–5 days a week. Usual hours are 4–10pm for learners aged 10–16, or 1–7pm for younger learners aged 5–10. Hourly teachers work 120 hours per month, with a guarantee of 96 hours per month.

SALARY: Varies according to previous teaching experience, level of education and other factors, including performance on the Aclipse interview and evaluation. Standard salary for a teacher who performs well on the Aclipse evaluation and has a strong resumé is 27,000 won ($22.50) per hour. Hourly teachers earn 2.2 million won per month for 96–120 hours, with paid overtime at an hourly rate. Teachers on a monthly salary are taxed at a rate of 7–8% on their monthly income by the Korean government. Teachers on an hourly salary are taxed at rate of 3%.

FACILITIES/SUPPORT: With the monthly salary, housing is paid for by the school and set up for the teacher, typically before they arrive. On the hourly salary, ChungDahm Learning helps their teachers find housing either before they arrive or upon arrival, assists with the Key Money (security deposit), and the teachers then pay rent directly to their landlord each month. Aclipse in the US assists candidates with obtaining the E2 visa. Teachers are responsible for obtaining the necessary visa documents, such as a state-wide criminal background check and original diploma, which the Aclipse office in Boston checks and forwards to ChungDahm in Korea. The visa code is then emailed to candidate who takes it to their nearest Korean consulate and gets visa stamped in passport.

RECRUITMENT: Online advertisements, social media, career fairs, and campus events/information sessions. Interviews are essential: initial interviews are typically done over the phone, with recruiters from the Boston office or by US recruiter Aclipse (www.

aclipse.net) with offices in Boston (6 Beacon St, Boston, MA 02108; +1 617 960 8875; aclipseadmin@aclipse.net) and San Francisco as well as Seoul.

CONTACT: Rebecca McNeil, Marketing Manager at Aclipse (subsidiary of ChungDahm Learning/ChungDahm America).

FLYING COWS
26 Henry St, Beeston, Nottinghamshire NG9 2BE, UK
- +44 115 824 0824
- info@flying-cows.com
- www.flying-cows.com

Agency so-named because it aims to provide a service 'without the bull'.

NUMBER OF TEACHERS: Up to 30 teachers placed per month in schools throughout South Korea.

PREFERENCE OF NATIONALITY: Mostly British although can also be Canadian, American, Irish, Australian, New Zealander, and South African.

QUALIFICATIONS: Minimum degree in any discipline. Experience of teaching or working with kids is a bonus. TEFL not essential but can help attract job offers.

CONDITIONS OF EMPLOYMENT: 12-month contracts. 6 hours per day, with varying hours. Positions available in after-school academies and public schools.

SALARY: From 2.1 million won per month. Deductions made for health insurance and income tax.

FACILITIES/SUPPORT: School arranges and pays for the accommodation and flights. Assistance given for obtaining the relevant E2 visa. Support in all aspects of placement – contract negotiation, location advice, etc.

RECRUITMENT: Via ESL internet sites, university careers centres, media advertising and careers fairs. Applicants will be interviewed by an FC representative over the phone then by the school also by phone. FC staff have personal experience of teaching in Korea. They recruit for spring and autumn positions, with deadlines falling 5–6 months in advance of the start dates.

CONTACT: Amanda Middlecote, Director/Senior Consultant.

KOREACONNECTIONS EMPLOYMENT LTD
#71, 583–6 Tap-Rib-dong, Yoosung-gu Daejon, 305–510
- +82 2 2058 2888
- *North American office* : 211–3030 Lincoln Ave, Coquitlam, BC V3B 6B4, Canada
- +1 206 734 4863
- admin@koreaconnections.net/
  Jamie.koreaconnections@gmail.com
- www.koreaconnections.net

NUMBER OF TEACHERS: Approximately 150 annually.

PREFERENCE OF NATIONALITY: None; however, the Korean government only issues E2 visas to English teachers from UK, USA, Canada, Ireland, New Zealand, South Africa and Australia.

QUALIFICATIONS: Minimum bachelor's degree. BA in English, Education, Linguistics, TESOL or qualified teacher status is a plus though not mandatory. Clear spoken English and experience with working with young children.

CONDITIONS OF EMPLOYMENT: 1-year contract. Usual hours are 9am to 5pm Monday to Friday for public schools. Hours may be longer at private language institutes.

SALARY: Average basic salary is between 2 and 2.3 million won at franchised private schools and can be between 1.8 and 2.7 million won at public schools, depending on experience and qualifications.

FACILITIES/SUPPORT: Accommodation is provided by the schools. Usually the housing is single accommodation within walking distance of work. Sponsorship and assistance provided when applying for E2 visas and help is given with flight booking arrangements and airport pick up.

RECRUITMENT: Usually via word of mouth, university career centre and online advertising. Interviews are essential and can be held over the phone or Skype. Face-to-face interviews can be arranged internationally depending on where the consultants are located at that time. Interviews have also been arranged while visiting TESOL conventions and job fairs in USA, UK, Canada and Ireland.

CONTACT: Jamie Lee, HR Director.

PLANET ESL RECRUITING
#201 Bogwang-dong 3-154, Yongsan-gu, Seoul 140-822
- +82 10 9012 0579
- Jobs@PlanetESL.com
- www.PlanetESL.com

Recruiter for many schools in Korea.

PREFERENCE OF NATIONALITY: Teachers must be citizens of one of the seven designated English-speaking countries (Australia, Canada, Ireland, New Zealand, United Kingdom, United States and South Africa).

QUALIFICATIONS: Bachelor's degree from an accredited university in one of the seven designated English speaking countries.

CONDITIONS OF EMPLOYMENT: 1-year contracts are standard. Teaching hours range from 20 to 40 per week depending on whether it is a public or private institute. Private institutes normally operate an afternoon/evening schedule, while public schools have a 9.30-4.30pm schedule.

SALARY: Average salary range 2.0–2.3 million won depending on experience and qualifications.

FACILITIES/SUPPORT: Accommodation is provided.

RECRUITMENT: Via online job postings and through recommendations. Interviews can be carried out by skype or telephone.

CONTACT: Jiyeon Kim, CEO & President.

REACH TO TEACH (SOUTH KOREA)
1606 80th Avenue, Algona, Iowa 50511, USA
+1 201 467 4612
john@reachtoteachrecruiting.com
www.ReachToTeachRecruiting.com/Teach-English-in-Korea.html

Also has contacts in UK, Australia and New Zealand (see entry at beginning of Asia chapter).

NUMBER OF TEACHERS: 200+.

PREFERENCE OF NATIONALITY: Canadian, American, British, Australian, New Zealander, Irish and South African.

QUALIFICATIONS: Teaching experience is a plus, but not a requirement. A 120-hour TEFL certificate is a requirement for most positions, unless candidates have more than a year of teaching experience, an MA, or a BA in English or Education. The agency has a limited number of placements for non-TEFL qualified applicants.

CONDITIONS OF EMPLOYMENT: Public (EPIK, etc.) and private school positions. All job placements are full-time positions and for 1 year (and usually extendable). Schedules are generally either morning/afternoon (preschool or public elementary, middle or high school) or afternoon/evening (elementary school).

SALARY: 2–3 million won per month (from $1,720–$2,500) plus reimbursed flights to and from Korea.

FACILITIES/SUPPORT: Free housing always given in a furnished one-bedroom apartment or studio. Teachers pay a deposit which is reimbursed. Teachers are also helped with work permits from beginning to end. All teachers are welcome at various teacher social events and gatherings (often held in Seoul).

RECRUITMENT: Detailed Skype or telephone interviews are essential. The company also carries out in-person interviews periodically in the USA and UK. Public school positions start twice a year (March and September) and the application process ideally needs to start 6 months in advance. Private school positions can be applied for year round and the time between application and arriving in Korea is often much quicker.

CONTACT: John Kellenberger, Co-President (John@ReachToTeachRecruiting.com).

TEFA (THE ENGLISH FRIENDS ACADEMY)
733, Banghak-3 Dong. DoBong-gu, Seoul 132–855
+82 2 3493 6567
tefaenglish@yahoo.co.kr

NUMBER OF TEACHERS: Approximately 50 Western teachers in 16 franchises throughout Korea.

PREFERENCE OF NATIONALITY: None, but should be a native English speaker.

QUALIFICATIONS: Minimum 3 or 4-year bachelor's degree. Love of kids, mature interactive outlook.

CONDITIONS OF EMPLOYMENT: 12-month contract. Less than 30 hours' teaching. Return airfare, medical insurance, 10 days' vacation. End of contract bonus (1 month's salary).

SALARY: 2.2 million won per month.

FACILITIES/SUPPORT: Close to all amenities and the schools, free fully furnished, single or shared accommodation. Well-resourced schools, supportive work environment, job security.

RECRUITMENT: Via email and phone.

YBM EDUCATION ECC
YBM ECC Head Office, Jongro Place, 8th Floor, 28–2 Inui-dong, Jongno-gu, Seoul, 110–410
eccmain@ybmsisa.co.kr
www.ybmecc.co.kr

NUMBER OF TEACHERS: 200 at 31 company-owned ECC branches and about 450 at 74 franchise ECC schools that are not placed by YBM Head Office. YBM Language Institutes (see next entry) are for adults and offer slightly less advantageous terms of employment.

PREFERENCE OF NATIONALITY: Canadian, American, British, Australian, New Zealander, Irish and South African.

QUALIFICATIONS: Minimum bachelor's degree, criminal background check, academic transcripts. No teaching experience required but candidates must enjoy teaching young children using curriculum provided (training given).

CONDITIONS OF EMPLOYMENT: 12-month contracts. Schedule 1: 9:30am–6pm. Schedule 2: 1pm–8pm.

SALARY: 2 million to 2.4 million won per month.

FACILITIES/SUPPORT: YBM provides rent-free, furnished accommodation near the school plus prepaid airfare, medical, severance pay and pension compliance, guaranteed contracts backed by the YBM Head Office, and assistance with E2 visa.

RECRUITMENT: Job postings via internet, word of mouth referrals from previous teachers. Every applicant undergoes either a phone interview or a face-to-face interview if they are in Korea.

CONTACT: Danny J. Kim, HR Manager, YBM Education ECC Head Office.

YBM LANGUAGE INSTITUTES

YBM Building, 13th Floor, 820-8 Yeoksam-dong, Gangnam-gu, Seoul, 135-080

🖰 +82 2 3466 3519

🖱 gregstapleton@ybmsisa.com

💻 www.ybmhr.co.kr

NUMBER OF TEACHERS: Between 250 and 300.

PREFERENCE OF NATIONALITY: Canadian, American, British, Australian and New Zealand.

QUALIFICATIONS: Minimum bachelor's degree plus 1-year formal teaching experience with adult learners. Candidates with graduate degrees in applied linguistics or CELTA/TESOL certification are preferred.

CONDITIONS OF EMPLOYMENT: 1-year renewable contract, six 50-minute classes per day (30 hours per week).

SALARY: Depending upon academic qualifications and teaching experience, salaries range from 2.1 million won to 2.5 million won per month, plus 200,000 won housing allowance.

FACILITIES/SUPPORT: During the initial 5-day training period teachers are provided with accommodation in a motel near the training centre in Seoul. Upon completion of training instructors return to their school and are shown several apartments from which the teacher can choose. The school then provides up to 10 million won in key money (leasing) to secure the apartment plus a monthly housing stipend of 200,000 won. Instructor development and support is overseen by native-speaking English academic supervisors.

RECRUITMENT: Primarily through web-based job postings, followed by telephone/webcam interviews when candidates are outside South Korea. Candidates applying from within Korea must attend a face-to-face interview.

CONTACT: Greg Stapleton, National Acadmic Director.

INDIAN SUBCONTINENT

The fast growing economy of India has proved remarkably resilient to the global financial crisis. One of the most notable by-products of globalisation has been the outsourcing of services to countries with cheaper labour costs, which has been accelerated in India by the widespread knowledge of English, a legacy of the Raj in the educational system. After a long period in which nationalistic sentiment tended to view British colonial rule and therefore the English language as a tool of enslavement, there seems to be a softening of attitudes, partly in acknowledgment that India's technology boom owes a huge debt to the country's English medium education. The bias against English is weakening, and it is now taught in state schools from the age of six. Interestingly it is especially popular among the marginalised castes (once called 'untouchables' and now called Dalit) who see English as a job skill that will help them achieve social and financial emancipation.

This does not mean that there is a huge demand for native speaker teachers. Very few ordinary citizens in much of South Asia can dream of affording the luxury of English conversation classes. Few Westerners could manage on the wages earned by ordinary teachers in India, Nepal, Sri Lanka, Pakistan, etc. However, those foreigners prepared to finance themselves and volunteer their time can find eager students by asking around locally.

Mainstream voluntary organisations are active in the region, especially providing skilled volunteers to teachers' colleges and vocational colleges. Unskilled volunteers can be placed in the Indian subcontinent and beyond by the main commercial volunteer placement agencies like Travellers Worldwide and i-to-i. Grassroots organisations are also active, especially those concerned with improving literacy among women and children. Plenty of commercial language teaching also goes on, for example in business colleges, though usually with local teaching staff.

India

The emerging economy of India has some commentators predicting that together with China, its capacity and markets will before long overtake the West. High standards of education in the dominant class and an entrepreneurial spirit have helped India to flourish. English has been the medium of instruction in the elite schools and universities since India was a colony, and now is spreading to many ordinary middle class Indians who want to participate in the booming global economy. Much of the demand is met by English-speaking Indians rather than foreigners. For example, the British Council in Delhi that until recently looked to employ British English teachers now prefers Indian nationals.

Nevertheless, travelling English speakers have arranged to teach in the state sector, simply by entering a school and asking permission to sit in on an English class. Provided they do not expect a wage, some teaching role could probably be found for them. A volunteer from Derbyshire teaching in several village schools through VESL in Andhra Pradesh wrote that she and her teaching partner were in such demand that a busload of volunteers would find work. But it can be very challenging and discouraging. Facilities can be brutal with no teaching materials and no space. The majority of local English teachers, who have not really mastered the language, are very badly paid and can be transferred without appeal at any time; it is not too surprising to find that most are demoralised.

A number of organisations in the UK send volunteers to teach English in India, including the main gap year placement organisations. For example, Projects Abroad (+44 1903 708300; www.projects-abroad.co.uk) arranges placements around Madurai in South India; fees start at £900 for two weeks up to £1,700 for three months. Postings are mainly to English-medium primary schools. New academies such as Valuepoint (see directory) cater to the insatiable demand in many Indian businesses to compete on an equal footing with the West. Just before **Raymond George** (age 62) started his official retirement from his job as a university physics lecturer, he noticed an advertisement on a college noticeboard for volunteer teachers with Travellers Worldwide. They were offering teaching placements in southern India, a region he was keen to see, so he enrolled for a two-month placement teaching spoken English in a primary school. This proved to be hugely rewarding, giving him a wonderful opportunity to experience life in a family and local community with enough spare time to travel to see the amazing temples of South India. Cross-Cultural Solutions with offices in the USA and UK (www.crossculturalsolutions.org) organises volunteer vacations in India. Volunteers work alongside grassroots organisations doing a range of tasks including English teaching. The programme fees are expensive, e.g. US$4,768 for six weeks. **Jenna Bonistalli** from New York City found a much more inexpensive option. She decided to use a windfall to fund six months off work to volunteer in India as a teacher:

Colleagues, friends and family were surprised upon hearing my decision to take off for half a year, especially when they learned my destination. The first three months were spent in the Himalayan hill town of Kalimpong in West Bengal. My boyfriend and I volunteered through HELP, the Himalayan Education Lifeline Programme (www.help-education.org), an organisation that places teachers in primary schools throughout Indian and Nepali Himalayan regions. We chose to go through them for a number of reasons, mainly location (we were both interested in going to this region mainly due to religious and cultural interest) and cost (their fees and donation requirements were VERY reasonable compared to some other outrageously high prices). This was after months of searching online, in books, on www.idealist.org and through recommendations. We had some choice in where we wanted to be placed and were able to read descriptions and see photos of the school and family, so this was helpful. There were no real requirements for being accepted, aside from an application form and references. Both of us had experience as educators in different capacities, so this made us more confident. Our experience in the Himalayas was unsurpassed – the setting, our students, the people we met, everything (aside from a bout of dysentery) was utterly amazing.

The current combined admin fee and donation to HELP is £390, plus volunteers contribute £75 a month for host family or school hostel accommodation.

Jon Walker was surprised by how contented he felt living in rural India as a volunteer teacher, where the atmosphere struck him as entirely calm, peaceful and beautiful. He spent the month of January (2011) volunteering through Dakshinayan (www.dakshinayan.org), a grassroots development charity that works with tribal peoples in the hills of Rajmahal and nearby plains:

The children are of course what makes Dakshinayan so special. We were teaching Maths and English for 3 hours a day, and I really enjoyed the teaching. Although I had difficulties trying to translate to them what I wanted them to do, particularly to Class 2 whose English isn't so good, this was all part of the challenge. It was quite different from any teaching I had done before and meant that I really had to learn how to adapt lessons and make them the most beneficial. But we had some good fun along the way singing songs and playing games – educational of course! Their enthusiasm to learn is what motivates you every day and I miss their smiles and laughter that radiated around the school when they were there.

Life at Dakshinayan is very simple and a way of life that I adapted to very quickly. Waking up at 5.30am and being in bed by 9.30pm seemed very natural. Initially I was apprehensive that I would get bored when we weren't teaching. But after planning our lessons and helping with the chores around the school, it was very easy to fill our time and the days flew by. We also learnt some Hindi on the way and it was good fun having conversation exchanges with Bansi and Shanku.

LIST OF EMPLOYERS

BRITISH COUNCIL NEW DELHI
17 Kastuba Gandhi Marg, New Delhi
+91 11 2371 1401
careers.bcdelhi@in.britishcouncil.org
www.britishcouncil.org/india

NUMBER OF TEACHERS: 16 and increasing.
PREFERENCE OF NATIONALITY: Indian nationals preferred.
QUALIFICATIONS: Minimum CELTA qualification and 2 years' post-CELTA experience.

CONDITIONS OF EMPLOYMENT: Only hourly paid contracts are available at present.

SALARY: Starts at approximately Rs892 per hour for CELTA-qualified; Rs1,057 for DELTA qualified.

FACILITIES/SUPPORT: No help can be given with visas or accommodation.

RECRUITMENT: Interview required. May be conducted over the telephone.

CONTACT: June-Rose Davis, Head of Teaching Centres North India (+91 11 2371 1401 ext 225).

BRITISH LINGUA

1/48, Lalita Park, Laxmi Nagar, Vikas Marg, Delhi 110092

☎ +91 11 32585879/+91 11 43026787

✉ britishlingua@yahoo.com

💻 www.britishlingua.com

NUMBER OF TEACHERS: 2.

PREFERENCE OF NATIONALITY: None.

QUALIFICATIONS: University graduate.

CONDITIONS OF EMPLOYMENT: 1 year. 8 hours per day.

SALARY: Negotiable.

FACILITIES/SUPPORT: Assistance given with accommodation. No help with visas.

RECRUITMENT: Local interview necessary.

HELP (HIMALAYAN EDUCATION LIFELINE PROGRAMME)

30 Kingsdown Park, Whitstable, Kent CT5 2DF, UK

☎ +44 1227 263055

✉ jim.coleman@help-education.org

💻 www.help-education.org

HELP recruits volunteer teachers to work in poor communities in the Indian Himalayas (Sikkim, West Bengal, Ladakh and Uttarakhand) as well as Nepal. See entry in Nepal section.

LHA CHARITABLE TRUST

Temple Road, McLeod Ganj-176219, Dharamsala, Dist. Kangra, Himachal Pradesh

☎ +91 189 222 0992

✉ director@lhasocialwork.org; volunteercoordinator@lhasocialwork.org

💻 www.lhasocialwork.org

NUMBER OF VOLUNTEER TEACHERS: 5 at any one time.

PREFERENCE OF NATIONALITY: No preference, but fluency in English is required.

QUALIFICATIONS: Native speakers with prior teaching experience preferred, but non-native speakers with a high-level of English language skill and/or documented proof of completion of a TEFL course are accepted.

CONDITIONS OF EMPLOYMENT: Minimum 2 months, maximum 6 months. One or two hours of class time per day, Monday through Friday, plus any time needed for preparation and grading. Additional hours may be needed if teachers are also participating in Lha's one-on-one tutoring programme.

SALARY: None; these are voluntary positions.

FACILITIES/SUPPORT: Lha is unable to provide room and board for volunteer teachers, though advice and orientation are given.

RECRUITMENT: Volunteer applications through Lha website and via partner websites like Omprakash.org. In-person interviews are not essential. All communication prior to volunteers' arrival is carried out via email or telephone.

CONTACT: Ngawang Rabgyal, Director of Lha Charitable Trust.

MANJOORANS GROUP

Corporate Office: 3D, Metro Place, Opposite North Railway Station, Cochin, Kerala

☎ +91 4842396816; +91 9447080482

✉ info@manjoorans.com; ceo@manjoorans.com

💻 www.manjoorans.com

The group also has offices in Trivandrum, Kottayam, Thrissur and Kollam, and runs 10 schools with 15,000 students participating in an English language programme called 'Speak Perfect'.

NUMBER OF TEACHERS: 50+ in ELT centres throughout the state of Kerala.

PREFERENCE OF NATIONALITY: British, American, Canadian, Australian, etc.

QUALIFICATIONS: TEFL, TESOL, etc. with a passion for teaching. Anyone with a good command of spoken English is eligible even without professional qualifications.

CONDITIONS OF EMPLOYMENT: 6 month visas only are available. Hours of work are 9.30am–1pm and 2pm–4pm. To teach IELTS, TOEFL, conversational English.

SALARY: Rs10,000 plus accommodation.

FACILITIES/SUPPORT: Accommodation provided. Assistance given with sorting out visas.

RECRUITMENT: ESL websites. References needed. Interviews not essential.

CONTACT: Babu Manjooran, CEO.

ROSE PUBLIC SCHOOL (Rural Organization for Social Elevation)

Social Awareness Centre, Sunargon, PO Kanda, Bageshwar, Uttarakhand 263631

🖰 jlverma.rosekanda@gmail.com or jeevanverma@ rosekanda.org

🖳 www.rosekanda.org

PREFERENCE OF NATIONALITY: None.

QUALIFICATIONS: None required. Experience of teaching or living in a developing country useful. Flexibility, sense of humour and positive thinker.

CONDITIONS OF EMPLOYMENT: Grassroots development project which organises range of activities to help this rural community in the Himalayan foothills. Projects include teaching English in the school, office computer networking, and other social projects.

SALARY: None. Volunteers contribute to their living and food expenses as paying guests (about £9 or Rs700 per day). Also registration/admin fee Rs10,000.

FACILITIES/SUPPORT: Accommodation arranged in local homes as homestay. Hindi instruction. Cultural exchange available.

CONTACT: Jeevan Verma, Director.

VALUEPOINT ACADEMY

2nd floor, Shankar House, 1 RMV Extension Makhri Circle, Bangalore 560080

📞 +91 80 40793777

🖰 hr@valuepointacademy.com

🖳 www.valuepointacademy.com

PREFERENCE OF NATIONALITY: None.

QUALIFICATIONS: Degree, preferably MA or PhD, in English plus preferably 5 years of teaching experience. English language trainers must be passionate about the job.

CONDITIONS OF EMPLOYMENT: 1-year contract with maximum 8 working hours per day.

FACILITIES/SUPPORT: Assistance can be given with finding accommodation and applying for work permits.

RECRUITMENT: Interview and demonstration lesson.

CONTACT: Meenu Sood, Director.

Nepal

After a period when Maoist rebels made the country dangerous to visit, Nepal is once again a destination for casual English teachers and volunteers to consider. After a decade-long campaign against Nepal's constitutional monarchy, the Maoist party has formed the government. Nepal's political problems are not over, but foreigners need to no longer fear of being waylaid while trekking and forced to hand over money. Tourist visas (which can be purchased on arrival for $100 cash) are valid for 90 days (shorter stays for less money are also available) and can be extended for $2 a day thereafter, up to a maximum of five months normally. Note that a hefty fine or even prison sentence can be imposed on foreigners found overstaying their visas.

A range of organisations makes it possible for self-funding volunteers to teach. Of course living expenses are very low by Western standards, though the fees charged by mediating or gap year organisations such as i-to-i and Africa, Asia & Americas Venture as well as by Nepali agencies (some listed below) can increase the cost significantly. If you want to avoid an agency fee, you can make direct contact with schools on arrival.

Relevant organisations in addition to the ones in the directory are listed below:

Alliance Nepal (Krishnatimi@gmail.com; www.volunteerworkinnepal.org). Opportunities to teach English, help in an orphanage, etc. in the Pokhara Valley and Chitwan area for 2 weeks to 3 months. Prices from €200 for 2 weeks to €600 for 12 weeks.

Cultural Destination Nepal, Kathmandu (www.volunteernepal.org.np). Volunteer Nepal, a service work programme. Fee of €650 includes 2-week pre-service orientation and homestay throughout. Placements last 2–4 months starting February, April, June, August and October.

Experience Himalayan Nepal (www.experiencehimalayannepal.org/teaching.html). NGO based in Kathmandu offering low-cost volunteering including teaching and orphanage work. £560 for 8 weeks plus £80 admin fee.

KEEP (Kathmandu Environmental Education Project), Thamel, Kathmandu (www.keepnepal.org). KEEP is eager to recruit volunteers to help deliver English language training to Nepalis who work in the tourist and trekking industry, government schools, etc. Volunteers stay with a host family and must be self-funding.

RCDP Nepal Volunteer, GPO Box: 8957, Tasindole Marg 95/48, Kalaniki 14, Kathmandu, Nepal (www.rcdpnepal.org). Paying volunteers work on various programmes lasting 1–12 weeks, including teaching English. Volunteers stay with families in villages. Registration fee of $259 plus a weekly charge which goes down the longer you stay, up to US$780 for 12 weeks.

After **Melissa Evans**' placement in Kenya was cancelled at the last moment, her gap year agency, Adventure Alternative (www.adventurealternative.com), had to live up to their name and quickly find her an alternative adventure. They arranged for Melissa to fly a month later to Nepal where she taught in a school:

> *It was very, very rewarding, as the children really thrived off the teaching from a foreign teacher. I found the teaching a challenge as the children struggled with English, and also pronunciation. Sometimes, I found myself unable to understand the children and vice versa. However, familiarity over the three months allowed the language barrier to break down, and conversing with the children was easier by the end of my placement, as I had learned a little Nepali and they had grown used to my pronunciation. Before my gap year I had the ambition of being a teacher. However, after travelling for the first time my ambition changed, and now I aim to found an orphanage.*

Rachel Sedley spent six months between school and university as a volunteer teacher at the Siddartha School in Kathmandu, arranged through a UK gap organisation and conveys some of the flavour of the experience:

> *The sun is shining and the kids are running riot. New Baneshwar is a suburb of Kathmandu, very busy and polluted, but of course so friendly. I do get tired of being a novelty, especially when I'm swathed in my five metres of bright turquoise silk (we wear saris for teaching) but I'm really loving it here. Already after one month, the thought of leaving the kids and my simple lifestyle is terrible. I find it funny that as a Westerner I'm seen to represent infinite stores of knowledge and yet the servant girl is having to patiently teach me to wash my own clothes. And the general knowledge people have of the fundamentals of life makes me feel helpless and incapable. The children are so gorgeous (most of the time) and the Principal's family with whom I am living are lovely. It seems to me unnecessary to come to Nepal through an organisation. Everyone here is so keen to help.*

Rachel's main complaint about her situation was that she was teaching in a private school for privileged children when she had been led to believe that she would be contributing her time, labour and money to more needy children. While there, she met several people from various schools and orphanages who would love to have English volunteers.

LIST OF EMPLOYERS

HELP (HIMALAYAN EDUCATION LIFELINE PROGRAMME)
30 Kingsdown Park, Whitstable, Kent CT5 2DF, UK
(C) +44 1227 263055
jim.coleman@help-education.org
www.help-education.org

HELP enables young people from poor communities in the Indian Himalayas (Sikkim, West Bengal, Ladakh and Uttarakhand) and Nepal (Kathmandu Valley, Pokhara and Chitwan) to improve their employment opportunities through education by providing financial and volunteer resources to their schools.

NUMBER OF PLACEMENTS: HELP supports some 25 schools in Nepal and the Indian Himalayas. Also a women's weaving cooperative in Pokhara.

QUALIFICATIONS: Ages 19/20–60+. Appropriate teaching experience and/or a basic TEFL qualification is essential.

Volunteers should be mature and resourceful. Qualities needed include resilience and adaptability, an open mind and an interest in other cultures, good mental and physical health, plus tact and diplomacy. A love of and experience with children is vital.

CONDITIONS OF WORK: Minimum 1 month. Volunteers can stay for a maximum of 6 months (for visa reasons).

SALARY: None. Admin fee of £150, donation to project £250 plus contribution to board and accommodation of 11,000 Rupees per month. Accommodation is provided with host families or in school hostel.

FACILITIES/SUPPORT: Volunteers receive a briefing pack. Once in post, a local HELP representative is on hand to help with any problems.

RECRUITMENT: Applications accepted year round. Telephone interviews conducted after receipt of the online application form.

CONTACT: Jim Coleman, Executive Director.

HOPE AND HOME
Travel Program, PO Box 119, Kathmandu
+977 1 443 909
info@hopenhome.org; UK: aryal@hotmail.co.uk
www.hopenhome.org

Community-oriented volunteer opportunities for international volunteers with homestay and cultural exchange.

NUMBER OF PLACEMENTS PER YEAR: 55–60 in the Kathmandu Valley, Pokhara, Chitwan and Nawalparasi areas of Nepal.

QUALIFICATIONS: Ages 18–35. All that is needed is a desire to help people.

CONDITIONS OF WORK: Volunteer opportunities lasting 2 weeks to 3 months are in the fields of teaching English, as well as community, health and environmental programme.

SALARY: None. Volunteer fees entirely fund programme and include homestay accommodation and food. From $400 for 2 weeks to $1,000 for 12 weeks plus registration fee of $200.

FACILITIES/SUPPORT: Language class, cultural information and project information provided.

RECRUITMENT: Online applications accepted year round.

CONTACT: Rabyn Aryal, Director; Binay Aryal (Director Europe – aryal@hotmail.co.uk).

INSIGHT NEPAL
PO Box 489, Pokhara, Kaski
+977 61 530266
insightnepal@gmail.com
www.insightnepal.org.np

NUMBER OF TEACHERS: 60 volunteers accepted each year for development projects mainly in the Pokhara Valley.

PREFERENCE OF NATIONALITY: All.

QUALIFICATIONS: Minimum 'A' levels for UK volunteers, high school diploma for Americans. Age limits 18–65. Teaching or volunteering experience desirable but not necessary.

CONDITIONS OF EMPLOYMENT: Placements last 7 weeks or 3 months starting year round.

SALARY: None. Programme participation fee is $1,100 for 3 months, $840 for 7 weeks.

FACILITIES/SUPPORT: Accommodation and two meals a day provided, usually as homestay. Programmes include pre-orientation training, placement in a primary or secondary school in Nepal to teach mainly English or in community development projects, and a 1-week village or trekking excursion. The 3-month programme also includes 3 days jungle safari in Chitwan National Park.

RECRUITMENT: Application forms, 3 photos and introductory letter should be sent 3 months in advance of proposed starting date.

CONTACT: Naresh Shrestha, Programme Coordinator.

TREK TO TEACH
San Diego, CA, USA
+1 619 405 8818
Brad@trektoteach.org
www.trektoteach.org

Achieved NGO status March 2012.

NUMBER OF PLACEMENTS PER YEAR: 3–7 (because programme is new).

QUALIFICATIONS: Minimum age 22. Schools want teachers who can teach English, Math and Computers. The Nepali students want teachers who can teach them new hobbies and new ways of looking at the world. Candidates should be academically able with a degree or heading towards one and be passionate about life.

CONDITIONS OF WORK: Programme combines teaching in Himalayan Nepal with a family stay and trekking. Minimum 3 months, maximum 8.

SALARY: None because this is a volunteer programme. Programme costs: first 3 months US$3,100; fourth to eight months $500 each.

RECRUITMENT: No deadline. Applications must be in at least 1 month prior to expected teaching date. Nepali school year is March–December. Telephone interviews necessary.

CONTACT: Brad Hurvitz, Founder.

VOLNEPAL (Volunteer Nepal National Group)
Nayabazar, Kathmandu

℡ +977 984 1223127

✆ info@volnepal.org; UK: shekharbhattrai@volnepal.
org

🖳 www.volnepal.org/teaching_schools.php

Community-based non-profit organisation that coordinates teach-ing and care projects in Nepal.

NUMBER OF PLACEMENTS PER YEAR: 100 in Kathmandu Valley near the historic city of Bhaktapur.

QUALIFICATIONS: Minimum age 18.

CONDITIONS OF WORK: Placements for volunteers in schools, colleges and universities, lasting 2 weeks to 5 months, starting mid-February or August. Volunteers usually spend 2–3 hours a day teaching English to children aged 6–13, plus help with sports, music, extra-curricular activities and other administrative and social welfare work.

SALARY: None. Volnepal programme fees including pre-service training, language instruction, homestay and meals, trekking, rafting, jungle safari and volunteering, are from $400 for 2 weeks to $1,150 for 18 weeks.

RECRUITMENT: Application form, CV and references needed.

CONTACT: Anish Neupane, Director (anishn@volnepal.org).

Pakistan and Bangladesh

The need for English in Pakistan was replaced in 2010 by the desperate need for more basic aid, following the catastrophic floods, water contamination and resulting disaster. It will be years before the infrastructure can be repaired and schools rebuilt. When that happens, once again schools should be willing to take on native English speaker teachers, but the problems will still pertain: lack of remuneration and difficulty with visas. Most opportunities are available only to teachers willing to finance themselves and to work on a three-month tourist visa. Security clearance and visa processing can take months, and is very difficult unless you have someone to push for you.

The British Council employs qualified teachers at its own teaching centre in Dhaka, who are recruited in London. The centre also employs a number of hourly paid teachers who are recruited locally but the demand for courses fluctuates so much that steady employment cannot be guaranteed. People who are established in Dhaka (such as spouses of expat managers, etc.) manage to earn reasonable part-time wages teaching private classes.

Far fewer gap placement agencies and other educational charities send volunteers to Bangladesh than to Nepal. Few private language schools exist in Pakistan. The British Council organises exams, but does not run teaching courses. The US counterpart is the Pakistan American Cultural Center (PACC) with several branches throughout the country. Security concerns are largely confined to places like the Swat Valley rather than the big cities. Demand for English is strong among the young not least because (sad to say) working in a Western call centre probably pays better than an engineering job.

Opportunities for native English teachers are probably there for the taking, tutoring businessmen, university students and children, if teachers are respectful and resourceful. While loitering in a second-hand book-shop in Scotland, **Hannah Adcock** fell into conversation with a Pakistani university professor who promptly offered food and board in exchange for working at his wife's private school for children near Karachi. Having a native English speaker is apparently a real status symbol for a school (something you wouldn't guess from reading the British/American press).

LIST OF EMPLOYERS

BANGLADESH WORK CAMPS ASSOCIATION (BWCA)
289/2 Workcamp Road, North Shajahanpur, Dhaka 1217
✆ +880 2 935 8206/6814
✉ bwca@bangla.net
🖥 www.mybwca.org

BWCA organises workcamps and longer-term projects for volunteers in rural and urban areas of Bangladesh.

NUMBER OF TEACHERS: 5 per year (roughly equally divided male and female).

QUALIFICATIONS: Native English speakers aged 18–30.

CONDITIONS OF EMPLOYMENT: Volunteers work 30 hours per week on placements which last 2–6 months on the RTYP (Round the Year Programme). Work can include teaching and developing English speaking and writing to primary and secondary school teachers, as well as to students. For example, a recent project was in a Dhaka kindergarten.

SALARY: Voluntary work. Volunteers bear all expenses at a cost equivalent to $300 per month for the first 3 months and then $50 per month plus $2.50 a day for food. Homestay or other accommodation is provided.

CONTACT: Abdur Rahman, Director and Organisation Secretary.

Tibet

Tibet (known as Xizang province in Mandarin) in the far west of China, has fascinated people in the West for centuries and until 1986 was inaccessible to the outside world. On the highest plateau in the world and encompassing a large section of the Himalayan mountains, Tibet offers something quite different from the rest of China. While there is a certain appetite to communicate with the outside world and learn English, there is also anxiety about incursions into Tibetan culture. The recent opening of a rail link to Beijing has hastened and increased the influx of Han Chinese visitors and settlers, whereas the number of international tourists has been sadly decreased by the intermittent closure of Tibet's borders, most recently in June 2012. It is becoming increasingly difficult to get a visa just for a short visit in a group, and almost all NGOs who were active in the Tibetan (so-called) Autonomous Region have been expelled. The Chinese authorities have been made very nervous by the tragic spate of self-immolations by Tibetan monks as a final despairing act of protest against the occupation of their country and suppression of their culture. The security crackdown has been ferocious, particularly in Lhasa. So for the present time, there is very little chance of entering Tibet as a teacher.

Despite a decision taken some time ago to change the medium of instruction used in Tibetan schools in exile from English to Tibetan, there are plenty of volunteering opportunities in places such as Dharamsala in the Indian Himalayas. Try for example the Lha Charitable Trust (see entry above in India section).

LIZZI MIDDLETON

Lizzi Middleton's gap year was spent teaching English in a completely unexpected setting.

Not quite believing that I was embarking on what was to be the biggest adventure of my life so far, I arrived in Delhi and a few days later caught a 15-hour overnight bus to McLeodganj in north-west India, seat of the Tibetan government in exile and home of His Holiness the Dalai Lama. It was a further hour's hair raising bus journey down into the valley to my placement at the Jamyang Choeling Himalayan Institute for Buddhist women. The nunnery is in a very secluded area of the countryside, set in front of the stunning backdrop of the snow-capped foothills of the Himalayas. It was unbelievably picturesque and was a welcome relief after the madness of Delhi!

Finding out what we were meant to be doing, and where we were meant to be was our first major challenge. Tibetans are notoriously vague – we had been warned about this but it was vague on a level that I've never experienced vague before! This was one of the real cultural differences that I had to adapt to. Having just completed my A levels and the careful structuring of time that they had required, and coming from a family where we always let each other know where we are, life at Jamyang Choeling was quite a change. I had to learn to be very easy going, to not mind when a class just didn't turn up or when there was only half a class there.

My classes were loosely organised according to ability but to be honest that didn't mean much. Lessons were fun – I realised soon after I arrived that these women needed their hour with me to be educational but light-hearted. They get up at 5am every day and apart from an hour for lunch and an hour for dinner they don't stop until 10 or 11pm – they're studying Buddhism all day. My first few lessons were pretty diabolical as I tried to find my feet in a completely alien situation. I had no idea of how I was going to learn the names of 90 women, none of whom had any hair and who all wore exactly the same clothes!

So the teaching was the reason that I was there but there were lots of other things to be done at the nunnery too. Cooking for 90+ three times a day is no mean feat and so every day from 10am to noon I cut up vegetables with a small team of nuns. I found that it was a great time for the nuns to practise the English that they were sometimes too shy to use in front of each other in the classroom, and it was also an opportunity for me to learn some Tibetan and to listen to their stories – often of escape over the Himalayas from Tibet. I made some amazing friends. Together we had a huge amount of fun – riding on the roofs of local buses, swimming in the river, shopping for food for our leaving party, teaching each other national dances (I'm afraid we ended up opting to teach the Macarena), blowing up balloons, and a lot of the time just sitting and chatting about the similarities and most of all the differences between our lives, religions and cultures.

Of course, you can do some online research before arriving. The website www.volunteertibet.org carries teaching vacancies for which you must send an email to receive further information. All of the volunteer teaching positions are in Tibetan monasteries and nunneries in Himalayan India, mainly in and around Dharamsala.

Specialist tour operators may be able to advise. For example, Tibetan Wild Yak Adventures publishes a little information about volunteering on a page of its website (www.tibetanwildyakadventures.com/teach_english.htm) including in orphanages in Tibet, although it is likely the information pre-dates recent visa changes. The American-run Global Crossroads volunteer agency (www.globalcrossroad.com) used to offer volunteer teaching positions in Tibet but cannot at the moment.

Sri Lanka

In May 2009, the Sri Lankan government declared military victory over the Tamil Tigers, ending 26 years of civil war and there is free movement on the Jaffna peninsula. This opening up has fuelled a demand for English language education. English is sometimes seen as a neutral choice between rival Tamil and Sinhalese and, as in India, is used in some elite private schools.

The British Council at 49 Alfred House Gardens in Colombo (www.britishcouncil.org/srilanka) has offices with libraries and teaching centres in both Colombo and Kandy. The teaching centres offer classes to adults and young learners. Teachers need a minimum of two years' post-certificate experience to be considered. The Council runs part-time CELTA courses in Colombo April to June and October to December plus a full-time course in August, both costing £1,700.

Originally called Volunteers for English in Sri Lanka, VESL has branched out to Thailand and India, but continues to send teachers to Sri Lanka (see entry) Also the Senahasa Trust based in London (www.senahasa.org) has been working in rural state schools in southern Sri Lanka since 2005 and recruits a few volunteer English teachers for the four schools the charity rebuilt after the Tsunami.

LIST OF EMPLOYERS

SCHOOLHOUSE VOLUNTEERING

Schoolhouse, Anderson Road, Ballater, Aberdeenshire, Scotland AB35 5QW, UK

+44 1339 756333

info@school-house.org

www.school-house.org

Schoolhouse Volunteering offers well-researched and well-supported English teaching volunteering opportunities in a range of formal and informal situations in Sri Lanka and Tamil Nadu in India.

PREFERENCE OF NATIONALITY: Must be native or fluent English speaker. Ideally candidates can attend pre-placement training in Scotland.

QUALIFICATIONS: Teaching qualifications are not essential as there is a range of placements to match a range of skills and experience. However, newly qualified teachers seeking experience, those wishing to explore teaching with a view to training in the future, teachers seeking a refreshing sabbatical or holiday and retired teachers may be particularly interested. Volunteers must be good communicators, be enthusiastic and open to contributing to and learning from new and challenging experiences.

CONDITIONS OF EMPLOYMENT: Volunteer English teaching placements in government schools through the Ministry of Education in Colombo and other organisations in Sri Lanka and Tamil Nadu. Placements last 1 month to 1 year.

FACILITIES/SUPPORT: A free (optional) 2/3-day residential pre-departure training course is given at Schoolhouse premises in Scotland. The course aims to prepare volunteers and enable them to get the most out of their volunteer teaching experience, both in terms of contribution and self-development. Volunteers stay in campus accommodation, with selected host families or in a shared house or flat with other volunteers.

RECRUITMENT: Applications welcomed year round. After submitting the online application form (on the Schoolhouse site), Schoolhouse will develop a rapport with applicants to ensure an effective matching and good preparation.

COST: £650 for first month (covers placement admin, training, airport pick-up, accommodation, most meals and ongoing support during placement). Subsequent months go down to £550 and then £450.

CONTACTS: Alan and Cathy Low, Schoolhouse Volunteering.

VESL (VOLUNTEERS FOR EDUCATIONAL SUPPORT & LEARNING)

17 Silk Hill, Buxworth, High Peak, Derbyshire SK23 7TA, UK

0845 094 3727

info@vesl.org or enquiries@vesl.org

www.vesl.org.

VESL is a charity registered in the UK (no. 1117908) and as an NGO in Sri Lanka and Thailand and sends volunteers to work on projects in Asia.

NUMBER OF TEACHERS: Up to 60 (including placements in India and Thailand as well).

QUALIFICATIONS: Minimum age 18, though most volunteers are older. Volunteers should be enthusiastic, motivated and up for a challenge. TEFL experience and some experience overseas are helpful but not a requirement.

CONDITIONS OF EMPLOYMENT: 4–6 week summer programmes in July and August and 3–6 month projects throughout the year. Some volunteers are also required to help run teacher workshop programmes in August each year. Volunteers and qualified teachers are sent to run English language summer schools in remote communities.

RECRUITMENT: Applications accepted throughout the year. All candidates must be able to attend a selection day and training weekend (dates and places in the UK to be notified).

SALARY: Voluntary work. All applicants pay a programme fee ranging from £900 for summer placement to £1,350 for 3 months, which covers cost of setting up the projects, training, orientation, insurance, accommodation, food, in-country travel and comprehensive back up and support. VESL is run mainly by volunteers so costs are kept to a minimum.

CONTACT: Tom Harrison, Programme Director, and Lauren Pluss, Programme Manager.

Maldives

A country that is normally associated with celebrities' luxury holidays, the island nation of the Maldives in the Indian Ocean promotes the use of English and encourages native speakers to spend time working in schools. The Permanent Secretary of the Ministry of Education invites volunteers whose mother tongue is English, from all walks of life and different ages, to spend an academic year from January to November volunteering in the Maldives. People who are proficient in English and with some educational background are recruited by the High Commission in London. Participants are paid approximately US$500 a month to cover living expenses and are provided with accommodation with local families, but will have to cover their own airfares. Details of the government-sponsored International Volunteer Programme, whose principal aim is to improve exam results, can be found at www.maldiveshighcommission.org.

A privately run scheme affiliated to a travel agency is called Volunteer Maldives Pvt Ltd (Unimoo Building, Orchid Magu, Male; +960 3300609; www.volunteermaldives.com). The two company founders offer a structured volunteering programme in various locations in the Maldive Islands, mainly involved with teaching and sports programmes. Participants can stay for a month or a year, though the preferred minimum is two or three months. Possible extra activities include snorkelling trips, visits to uninhabited islands for swimming and sunbathing, and night fishing with the locals. Costs fall over time, so that the first month costs $950, and subsequent months $700 with substantial discounts for early booking and paying.

MALAYSIA

For the many Malaysian students who aspire to go to university in the UK, USA or Australia, intensive English language tuition is an essential part of their training. The government has increased the profile of English as a medium of instruction in the state education system so the demand is set to increase. CfBT (Centre for British Teaching) has been in Malaysia for about 30 years and is currently assisting the Malaysian Ministry of Education to improve the standard of English in rural schools. For details contact Chris Frankland, Senior Manager (Suite B-306, Block B, Phileo Damansara 1, No. 9 Jalan 16/11, Off Jalan Damansara, 46350 Petaling Jaya, Selangor; www.cfbt.com.my).

Positions include 32 District English Language Co-ordinators (DELCs) and 10 Project English Teachers (PETs). DELCs encourage and develop ELT in all aspects in target districts. DELCs work out of medium-sized provincial towns in Sabah, Sarawak and West Malaysia and liaise at district and schools levels, working closely with Heads, Heads of Departments and teachers. Applicants must have a degree, postgraduate qualification in ELT, a minimum of five years in ELT and a driving licence, since they will have the use of a project car. PETs teach in government residential schools for gifted students and provide native English speaker inputs for teachers and students, new ideas and approaches in the language classroom and encourage the use of English outside the language classroom. Applicants must have a degree, certificate in ELT and a minimum of two years' ELT experience. Benefits of a two-year package include a good local salary, return airfares, housing allowance, medical expenses and an end-of-contract bonus. The government issues work permits only to highly qualified applicants. People caught working on tourist visas can expect to be fined and deported.

Other education consultancies recruit teachers and senior trainers including the Kuala Lumpur-based Brighton Education Group (www.brightoneducation.org/recruitment.html). It has linked up with the UK company Nord Anglia Education to supply qualified teachers to participate in TELL (Teaching English Language and Literacy), a government initiative to be implemented in primary schools. The British Council has teaching centres in Kuala Lumpur and Penang (www.britishcouncil.org/malaysia) which recruit teachers (minimum age 27) on a rolling basis; the former offers the CELTA course part-time (price 8,500 ringgits). As an employer the British Council is highly regarded, as long-time TEFLer **Steph Fuccio** from the USA reported after a stint of teaching in Kuala Lumpur at a different institute:

My husband and I moved to Malaysia right after we got married and worked for different branches of the same language school. After a lot of pondering and trying to make it work, we left after six months. While we were there the government switched from using English as the primary language in the schools back to Bahasa Malay. This switch apparently happens often, and with an unfortunate effect on the kids in the school system. Thus, there weren't as many jobs open to us as initially thought.

The British Council was by far the best paying language school in town, pretty much doubling standard language school salaries, with more benefits to boot. We interviewed at many places and finally decided on another school because it offered set daytime hours, good pay (5,000 ringgits before tax), and they had locations near our apartment. Unfortunately, what we didn't bargain on was the materials that we were supposed to use, their own cut and paste versions of difficult grammar books, the method they wanted us to teach with (lecture, not communicative method) and just how penny pinching they were. My husband's school gave them a ream of paper each month for photocopies, my school had a copy tally. We were all 'talked to' monthly on lowering our copy numbers.

Work permits must be obtained and can take up to three months. You will need to produce your degree and TEFL qualification certificates, university transcripts, reference letter from previous employer, medical report and passport photos. Also enquire about a minimum age stipulation. While Steph and her husband Evan were teaching in Malaysia, the government was issuing work permits only to people over 30. As of 2011, foreign workers who have been granted the Visa Pass Temporary Employment (VPTE) must also obtain the Visa With Reference (VDR) from the Malaysian Embassy or the High Commission of Malaysia before entering the country. Without this, entry to Malaysia will be refused. Once you are earning, be sure to register at the tax office as soon as you start employment, and ensure your employer is taking taxes regularly from your pay. Otherwise you can be hit by a colossal bill when you leave, as happened to one of Steph's fellow teachers. Suddenly huge amounts were missing from his pay cheque with no itemisation, and they heard that this was not uncommon.

The Erican Language Centre (see entry) offers teachers willing to relocate to various parts of Malaysia to teach children or adults an attractive package.

New Zealanders are eligible for working holiday visas for Malaysia.

One aspect of life in Malaysia which can be difficult to accept is that racial Malays are accorded special privileges over other citizens of Chinese, Indian or tribal origins. For example, places at the universities are available exclusively to *bumiputeras* or 'bumis', which means literally 'sons of the soil', i.e. ethnic Malays. Otherwise Malaysia offers a pleasant multicultural environment and teachers usually experience less culture shock than they do in Thailand and Indonesia. Kuala Lumpur is a model of modernity and efficiency when compared with the neighbouring capitals of Jakarta and Bangkok.

LIST OF EMPLOYERS

ERICAN LANGUAGE CENTRE

C-19–4 Megan Avenue II, Jalan Yap Kwan Seng, 50450
Kuala Lumpur

 +60 3 2164 9999

career@erican.edu.my

www.erican.edu.my

Language education and training company with 20+ centres across the peninsula.

NUMBER OF TEACHERS: 5 full-time.

PREFERENCE OF NATIONALITY: British, American, Canadian, Australian or New Zealander.

QUALIFICATIONS: Minimum TEFL/TESOL or CELTA qualification and one year's teaching experience.

CONDITIONS OF EMPLOYMENT: 12–24-month contracts to teach children and adults. Usual working hours (25 per week) between 9am and 5pm Monday to Friday.

SALARY: Approximately $1,200 per month plus monthly performance incentive, less 10% deductions for tax and social security.

FACILITIES/SUPPORT: Free shared room in teachers' hostel is normally available or the teacher will be subsidised by the centre (typically 500 ringgits per month) for private accommodation. The centre applies for work permits and covers all required visa charges. The visa application process may take 2–3 months.

RECRUITMENT: Usually via online advertisements. Interviews are essential and are normally via online video conferencing.

CONTACT: Ki Chong, Human Resources Manager.

SINGAPORE

Malaysia's tiny neighbour clinging to the tip of the Malay peninsula is a wealthy and Westernised city-state in which there is a considerable demand for qualified English teachers on minimum one-year contracts. Once a teacher does get established in a school, freelance teaching is widely available paying from S$30 an hour (over US$25).

The Foreign Recruitment Unit of the Ministry of Education in Singapore (MOE_FRU@moe.gov.sg) recruits foreign teachers in English language/English literature, as well as Geography, History and Economics, on one to three-year contracts in secondary schools and junior colleges (Grades 7 to 12). The scheme is very competitive, so only suitably qualified applicants should consider this option. Candidates should possess a relevant and very good degree preferably with teaching/higher qualifications and experience. Details and application form can be found at www.moe.gov.sg/careers/teach. Salaries for degree-holders start at S$2,550 (gross) plus an end-of-year bonus and airfares into/out of Singapore.

The British Council at 30 Napier Road has a teaching operation that hires qualified teachers locally especially for teaching young learners (and can also provide a list of approved language schools). Many are located in the ubiquitous shopping centres, especially along Orchard Road, for example Berlitz (501), Geos (Thong Sia Building, just off Orchard Road), Linguarama (220), Ikomo (350) and Goro (60b). The majority of commercial language centres are Chinese-owned with a high proportion of teachers from Australia.

Not strictly an ESL programme, native English speakers are being recruited to teach literacy skills to children with a company called I Can Read. As with the government scheme, candidates must have either a university teaching qualification or a degree in a humanities subject such as English literature, linguistics or psychology, in order to qualify for the Employment Pass. Two-year contracts start in July/August (www.icanreadsystem.com).

Singapore is not a recommended destination for the so-called 'teacher-traveller' who, without qualifications but with a smart pair of trousers, hopes to be able to impress a language school owner. Even people who have qualifications cannot count on walking into a job. However, persistent enquiries have resulted in the offer of hourly work. If you would like to go to Singapore to look for work you can apply online (www.mom.gov.sg) for the Employment Pass Eligibility Certificate (EPEC), which allows foreigners who are holders of selected university qualifications (their list includes most respectable universities) to stay in Singapore for up to one year to facilitate their job search. Generally, if you have been granted an EPEC by the Ministry of Manpower (MOM), you are likely to qualify for an Employment Pass upon securing employment. If you are just a student or a trainee, you can investigate the Work Holiday Pass programme.

Once you have a sponsoring employer, the prospective employer must contact the Singapore Immigration and Checkpoints Authority (10 Kallang Road, ICA Building, Singapore 208718; www.ica.gov.sg) for an application form and approval letter, or simply apply online. The process usually takes between six and eight weeks, and it is necessary to wait for the approval letter before travelling as you will be required to present it at Immigration Control in Changi Airport.

Some teachers have reported that they have quickly tired of Singapore, coming to see it as one giant shopping mall. So if shopping malls and a repressive regime (for example there are signs threatening to fine you $150 if you jaywalk or fail to flush the loo) leave you cold, Singapore is perhaps best avoided.

LIST OF EMPLOYERS

INLINGUA SCHOOL OF LANGUAGES

1 Grange Road, Orchard Building #04–01, Singapore 239693

📞 +65 6737 6666

✉️ info@inlingua.edu.sg

💻 www.inlingua.edu.sg

NUMBER OF TEACHERS: 8 full-time English teachers (62 teachers in total in 13 language sections).

PREFERENCE OF NATIONALITY: Multinational team from the UK, USA, Canada and Australia. Teachers from the UK preferred.

QUALIFICATIONS: University degree and post-graduate teaching qualification required (CELTA, CELTYL, TESOL or TEFL). Experience is not necessary but candidates must be effective teachers who can work well in a team.

CONDITIONS OF EMPLOYMENT: Standard 18-month contract. 40 hours per week (8 hours per day maximum) on school premises. This includes up to 25 hours of teaching (30 lessons lasting 50 minutes each). Group lessons are usually Monday to Friday 9am–1pm but trainers may also have to teach until 9pm Monday to Friday and 8am–3pm on Saturdays.

SALARY: Starts at S$3,100 per month. After a 6-month probationary period and satisfactory performance, salary increases to S$3,300. 18-month contracts are taxed at around 3%. Teachers do not need to pay Central Provident Fund contributions.

FACILITIES/SUPPORT: Temporary homestay accommodation can be arranged for at least 1 month at a cost of S$900. Teachers are given help by school's admin when looking for more permanent accommodation.

RECRUITMENT: Please apply by email by sending detailed CV. Interview and demonstration lesson in Singapore preferred but not essential.

CONTACT: Graham Sage, School Director.

MORRIS ALLEN STUDY CENTRES

#B1–27, Park Mall, 9 Penang Road, Singapore 238459

📞 +65 6334 2623

✉️ principal@morris-allen.com.sg

💻 www.morris-allen.com.sg

NUMBER OF TEACHERS: 40+.

PREFERENCE OF NATIONALITY: British, Australian, New Zealand, Canadian, American and South African.

QUALIFICATIONS: Minimum 3 years' experience plus degree in education; or bachelor's degree plus teacher training specialising in English, primary or early childhood education. Most teachers have classroom experience with children whose mother tongue is English.

CONDITIONS OF EMPLOYMENT: 2 years (1 year is available, extensions welcome). 28 teaching hours per week out of total working week of 35 hours. To teach Singapore children aged 3 to 16 years, in an English-medium education system.

SALARY: S$3,500 per month, tax free plus bonus of S$3,000 at the end of 2-year contract.

FACILITIES/SUPPORT: S$700 per month per person provided for accommodation expenses in first year, S$900 second year, plus S$500 freight allowance. Medical insurance provided. Two weeks initial hotel accommodation and assistance given in finding an apartment. Employer will submit visa applications.

RECRUITMENT: Adverts in foreign teachers' journals. Face-to-face interview preferred; telephone interview possible.

CONTACT: Peter Scarrott, Principal.

NYU LANGUAGE CENTRE

The Adelphi 04–35, 1 Coleman St, Singapore 179803

📞 +65 338 3533

✉️ admin@nyu-online.com

💻 www.nyu-online.com

NUMBER OF TEACHERS: 5.

PREFERENCE OF NATIONALITY: American, British.

QUALIFICATIONS: Degree with teaching experience in English.

CONDITIONS OF EMPLOYMENT: 1-year contracts. Hours 9.30am–5.30pm, Monday to Friday.

SALARY: S$2,500–S$3,000.

FACILITIES/SUPPORT: Help given with work permits.

RECRUITMENT: Via advertisements or recommendation.

CONTACT: Nance Teo, Principal.

BRUNEI

Few people can locate Brunei Darussalam (Brunei, the Abode of Peace) on a map of the world, let alone anticipate that there is a steady demand for qualified English teachers there. This wealthy oil state on the north shore of Borneo can afford universal education for its population of less than 400,000. The Ministry of Education has been implementing a bilingual educational system which '*ensures the sovereignty of the Malay language while at the same time recognising the importance of the English language*'.

Brunei, mostly covered in luxuriant tropical rainforest, has a pollution free, healthy environment, few traffic jams and one of the lowest crime rates in the world. It provides a very pleasant place to live and work for those who like the outdoor lifestyle and don't crave a wide variety of nightlife. For watersports enthusiasts, the warm calm waters of the South China Sea provide an ideal environment for diving, sailing and power boating. Most expatriates join one of the many sports and social clubs which provide excellent facilities.

Brunei has a rich cultural heritage and still boasts the largest water village in the world in the capital, Bandar Seri Begawan. There are many opportunities to participate in colourful, cultural extravaganzas to mark national events such as the Sultan's birthday on 15 July and National Day on 23 February. In the rural areas there is an opportunity to see how the other indigenous groups celebrate their traditional harvest festivals. Although Brunei is a Malay Islamic monarchy, other religions are allowed to practise freely and Chinese New Year and Christmas Day are also national holidays, in addition to the numerous Islamic public holidays.

There are currently over 250 expatriate primary and secondary EFL teachers working in Brunei in state sector schools. CfBT Education Services (Locked Bag 50, MPC, Old Airport Road, Berakas BE3577, Brunei; hr@cfbt.org; www.cfbt.org) recruits suitably qualified and experienced individuals along guidelines set by the Brunei Ministry of Education. All teachers must have Qualified Teacher Status, e.g. PGCE or equivalent, plus a degree, a minimum three years' experience including EFL/ESL and be under 52 (primary) or 55 (secondary). The package currently includes tax-free salary, end-of-contract bonus, accommodation, flights, baggage allowance and other benefits. Contracts are usually for two years initially. A car driving licence is essential. CfBT also runs a range of courses for teachers and the public including Cambridge ICELT, General English and ESP, ICT and Malay. CfBT also administers IELTS. Borneo Outdoors is a division of CfBT in Brunei and runs Youth Enrichment and Environmental courses, GAP programmes and Professional Development programmes. They also cater to the corporate sector by providing Management Training/Team Building courses for clients in Brunei and Malaysia.

VIETNAM

The market in English language training has come off the boil to some extent, but is still very lively. With soaring inflation at the beginning of 2012, Vietnam is undergoing if not an economic crisis, at least a slow-down. As a result student numbers are down which makes it harder for the established language schools to ensure that teachers get a full-time timetable. Yet many people in the cities want to learn English with a view to joining a profession such as banking or tourism or to have a chance of acceptance at institutes of higher learning overseas. From Ho Chi Minh City (HCMC) in the south to Hanoi in the north, opportunities abound both for trained professionals and freshly certified CELTA/TESOL graduates.

Although Vietnam is still a one-party socialist republic (which has been accused of blocking Facebook), it bears all the trappings (complete with garish advertising hoardings and American pop music) of a capitalist society with an expanding young middle class, who invest in electronic goods, luxury items and English. The British Council offers many types of English course, from 'corporate training solutions' to 'English for study success'. Language Link Vietnam is holding steady and is looking to employ 100 native English speakers (see entry). Base pay for university degree and CELTA qualifications starts at $19 per teaching hour, and rises to about $24. This should allow a comfortable lifestyle since the cost of living remains low (for example, HCMC is much cheaper to live in than Bangkok), so Vietnam is a good country for those trying to save some money. Furthermore a law was recently passed that exempts ESL teachers from having to pay tax, so earnings should be net of deductions.

But times are not quite as good as they were when **Amalia Pesci** first went to Hanoi to teach for Language Link in 2008, and she was able to save a lot of her wages. Her teaching job gave her a lifestyle she could never have imagined in Europe, where she ate out most days, could afford anything she wanted and was able to travel around Southeast Asia during the holidays. In addition to perks such as health insurance, flight allowance, assistance with visa and accommodation, the students were great too. Amalia says that '*teachers are very highly respected in Vietnam, so we were treated extremely well. Students took any opportunity to bring us flowers, presents, or invite us out for dinner.*'

Accommodation in a shared house might be £125 a month out of total outgoings of £200, while teaching wages should net you at least £600. The cost of living is higher in Hanoi than Saigon – the old name for HCMC is still in wide use – with rents and wages following suit. There is a two-tier system for utilities and travel in Vietnam, which means foreigners pay substantially more than locals for almost everything.

Prospective teachers in Vietnam should be aware that the country is becoming increasingly savvy about qualifications. A degree is often no longer seen as sufficient and EFL teaching qualifications are very desirable. This attitude is reflected in the fact that there are now five CELTA course providers in Vietnam including Language Link, Apollo English and ILA Vietnam (see list of employers).

Steph Fuccio had no trouble getting work in Hanoi with Language Link after doing the CELTA course:

> *Language Link is a great place to do a CELTA and start working. They have all the usual trappings of an EFL job such as unpredictable schedules, weekend work and so on. BUT, they do have a huge amount of resources, keen students and there is real opportunity to build up your teaching skills quickly. In my second year I taught English for Academic Purposes and Toefl-iBT along with my regular Business and General English classes.*

Often the best way to find work is simply to arrive in Hanoi or HCMC and look around. Check out Craigslist for Vietnam or other community sites for expats such as http://tnhvietnam.xemzi.com which has info about jobs among accommodation and other listings. The demand for Young Learners' English is holding up well. On arrival at her job with Language Link Hanoi, **Amalia Pesci** was taken aback to be told that she would be mainly teaching young learners, because all of her extensive experience had been in teaching Adult English. She coped with teaching children for her first year but found the parental pressure hard to deal with: '*The parents wanted their children to learn English in about six months*'. A further problem she encountered was

the unsuitability of some of the teaching materials; she says: *'With coursebooks designed for European audiences, materials had to be adapted constantly, as the cultural references in the coursebook meant absolutely nothing to Asian learners.'*

The British Council has offices in both Hanoi and HCMC and the latter office should be able to provide a list of language schools in the city with prestigious centres such as ACET (which specialises in academic English), RMIT, ILA, Apollo (affiliated to International House), AUSP and the British Council schools. RMIT in HCMC (employment@rmit.edu.vn) often advertises for qualified and experienced English language tutors to fill positions in HCMC and Hanoi. Another frequent advertiser is VUS Language Schools with a number of centres run by the Vietnam-USA Society around HCMC (stevebaker@vus-etsc.edu.vn; www.vus-etsc.edu.vn). Newly certified ESL teachers are welcome to apply.

In her late 20s, **Dawn Wilkinson** decided to use some money she inherited to take a year off from her publishing job in the UK. After five months of travelling around Southeast Asia with friends, she felt she wasn't ready to go home, so decided to find out how far her BA and MA in English would get her in landing a teaching job. After meeting up with a uni friend in Saigon, and making friends with a few ex-pats and locals, she decided Saigon would be a good place to live. She proceeded to sort out her CV and started looking regularly online at the jobs on offer, specifically looking for any private tutoring jobs. After trawling through numerous ads placed by tutors looking for work, she finally stumbled across an ad placed by a wealthy French-Vietnamese woman looking for an English tutor for her seven-year-old daughter. Dawn began tutoring three afternoons a week for two hours at a time and then also supplemented these hours tutoring at the home of her employer's sister-in-law:

The family were lovely and, as the sessions were at their house, they always invited me to eat dinner with them afterwards. This family were what I would call middle class, so working for the two families gave me a great insight into Vietnamese life and I spent a lot of time chatting with the parents about their lives and to the girls about their hopes for the future (they were all keen to improve their English as a means to travel and work in Europe or America).

Initially, it was quite difficult to prepare for the lessons, but with a bit of advice from my teacher friends and a lot of borrowing of ideas and worksheets from the mountain of TEFL resources on the internet, I managed to devise lesson plans for each of my students and they really seemed to enjoy it. I always tried to make the lessons fun and, because we weren't in a formal school environment, I encouraged them to feel confident about suggesting topics or areas of English they wanted to learn or talk more about. In hindsight, I probably should have charged a higher hourly rate than the $12 we agreed on as, by the time I'd travelled the 30–60 minutes it took on my motorbike to get to their houses four times a week (which was often enough of a challenge in itself on Saigon's chaotic roads), I wasn't really making that much money.

After arranging for her mum to post out her original degree certificate, Dawn applied for a job at VUS, a large language school with a number of campuses across Saigon. As a new starter, she was landed with some of the worst shifts – Friday/Saturday nights and Saturday/Sunday mornings – but at $16 an hour the pay was good. She earned about $1,200 a month for 22 hours teaching a week. Topics for the lessons were already set, so it was just a case of using the textbooks and materials to plan how to deliver the lesson. She always tried to add in a few fun activities and games, which the kids enjoyed. As usual, the drawbacks of living in a large Asian city gradually began to intrude:

On the whole, I didn't find Saigon a particularly pleasant city to live in: it was either stiflingly hot or pouring down with rain, heavily crowded and polluted and had no green spaces at all. I tended to sleep through the day (directly in front of my fan!) or watch TV, then go out with friends late in the evenings after I'd finished working – Saigon does have a great, tight-knit ex-pat social scene. But after three months in Vietnam I felt I wasn't really enjoying it, so decided to move on to Thailand. Although I had signed a 12-month contract with VUS, they completely understood that circumstances change for people quite frequently out there. They said if I ever came back to Saigon they'd be able to find me another teaching position, which was nice to know.

SAMANTHA THORNLEY

Samantha Thornley shied away from joining the corporate world after graduation from college and was delighted to be accepted by Teachers for Vietnam in the USA (see entry), which has a well-run programme; unusually, funding is available for qualifying volunteers.

I have been living and teaching in Vietnam for almost five months now. I can honestly say that this has been the hardest, scariest, best and most rewarding months of my life. The people that I have met have been the nicest, friendliest people I have ever encountered, and I am continuously amazed at the generosity and hospitality of the Vietnamese people, especially my students.

On arrival I was continuously challenged by my surroundings. The first obvious problem I encountered was the language barrier. Simple things like ordering and paying for food, saying thank you or I'm sorry, it all got lost in translation. I took a crash course in learning Vietnamese - numbers, food, all the necessities for my daily needs. It turns out that I was capable of learning how to get by in a strange land. The more I explored Can Tho, the more I realised how fast English is becoming a second language for the locals.

My placement is as a volunteer English teacher at a university in Vietnam. I work about 20 hours a week in class, although with lesson preparation that's usually at least another 10 hours a week. I also teach at a private English school at nights, which was my choice (I'm not contracted) and just a way to meet more students and make some extra cash. In most places in Vietnam (especially Saigon and Hanoi) you can find private schools to work at and as long as you are certified or have experience you can teach there. Most of the smaller cities, such as mine (Can Tho) love to have a foreign teacher and are more than willing to find a way to accommodate you.

It is amazing to watch a country develop right in front of your eyes. The Vietnam I am experiencing is not the same as it was even two years ago, and I am convinced it will not be the same in two years from now. This is truly a once in a lifetime experience, to call this amazing, thriving country home for a few months.

The cities are wonderfully packed with cheap restaurants (Com Binh Dan) and fantastic street food. Soon you will be addicted to *bun cha* (pork patty), *pho* (noodle soup), banana flower salad and *bia hoi* (draught beer). International restaurants and cafés are more expensive but still affordable for the average teacher.

Exams are taking off in Vietnam and many students strive to obtain a good TOEFL score in the hope of going to America, while the Cambridge suite of exams and IELTS are popular with those wanting to take up scholarships to Australia and the UK.

Hanoi is smaller and more beautiful yet bustling and noisy whereas HCMC is a Bangkok in the making. This sophisticated, sprawling commercial centre boasts a skyline already dotted with fledgling skyscrapers. The main complaints thus are traffic, noise, pollution and street hassle. Vietnam is a developing country and although the wealth of the nouveau riche classes in the cities is very visible, the countryside is still desperately poor. Countryside and cities alike experience frequent power cuts and things in general don't always work as they are supposed to.

Travelling round the region is very affordable, and has become more so with the rise of low-cost airlines such as Jetstar based at HCMC airport and Malaysia's AirAsia which has a few flights now from Hanoi and Saigon so that Kuala Lumpur can be used as a cheap hub to the region. In 2010 AirAsia purchased a one-third stake in VietJet to create VietJet AirAsia based in Hanoi, with plans to fly to HCMC and Da Nang. The *Reunification Express* is a train that runs the full-length of the country (over 1,300km). The cheapest fare for the Hanoi–Saigon trip is about $30, though you will have to pay nearly three times that for an air-conditioned soft sleeper.

Bear in mind that what you see is not always what you get. Behind that charming Vietnamese smile is more often than not the intent to extract money. Of particular note are the numerous women in search of a foreign husband, a foreign passport and an airline ticket. Single men should beware. Internet access is widely available and improving although it is still unreliable, slow and censored. Government firewalls prohibit prying eyes from seeing anything they don't want you to see.

To simplify getting a work permit in Vietnam teachers need to bring with them from home the originals of their university degree, TEFL certification and police clearance or criminal history certificate. Everything else can be taken care of in Vietnam with the help of an employer, some of whom are willing to reimburse the fee of $300. The original or notarised documents are submitted to the immigration office with a medical report, and the work permit should be issued within about six weeks.

Dawn Wilkinson commented that the laws are not always strictly observed. Her employers assured her that it was fine to work on a tourist visa, as they were in the process of securing her a full work permit. In order to get this she would have to complete some kind of TEFL course, and was told that even a basic 60-hour, $200 online course would be enough to fulfil the criteria for a work permit. Although the Vietnamese authorities were supposedly cracking down on illegal work, a lot of other teachers in HCMC were working without a permit, sometimes on a long-term basis. It is so costly for schools to obtain full work permits for their teachers, that a lot of skullduggery takes place to avoid the hassle and expense, and rumours abound of schools paying off the authorities to turn a blind eye.

A degree certificate is obligatory for acquiring the permit, though the rules can be bent here too, as Dawn noticed:

Two friends in Saigon didn't have a degree but still managed to find long-term teaching positions. One of the guys had lied to a school that he had a degree and, I think, may have shown them a fake photocopy of a degree certificate (easily bought on Khao San Road in Bangkok) to get a job. He worked there for about 18 months with no problems and was considered a very good teacher. However, in 2010, the Vietnamese authorities became a lot stricter, so the school had to start applying for work permits, which meant teachers needed to submit their original documents. My friend had to admit to the school that he didn't actually have a degree. I don't think they were very pleased about it at first but, as he had always worked hard for them, the school somehow managed to secure him a work permit – although he had to pay for it himself (money does seem to buy you anything in Southeast Asian countries!).

LIST OF EMPLOYERS

APOLLO ENGLISH (INTERNATIONAL HOUSE)

3 branches in Hanoi, 2 in Ho Chi Minh City and one each in Danang and Haiphong.

- recruitment.vn@apollo.edu.vn
- www.teachatapollo.com or www.apollo.edu.vn

Established in 1994, Apollo is affiliated to International House and offers training in English, professional development and overseas study consultancy as well as teacher training (Cambridge CELTA). Apollo also has an increasing number of younger learner and corporate classes in addition to partnership contracts with local schools.

NUMBER OF TEACHERS: Approximately 100 nationwide, more in the summer months.

PREFERENCE OF NATIONALITY: None, but must be native English speaker.

QUALIFICATIONS: Teachers must have a CELTA or equivalent (i.e. 100 hours minimum with at least 6–8 hours of observed classroom teaching practice). Vietnamese work permit regulations (for contracts longer than 3 months) stipulate that teachers must also have a degree.

CONDITIONS OF EMPLOYMENT: 1-year contract (some 3-month short-term contracts are available, particularly for the summer programme). Teaching hours are between 7.30am and 9.45pm, Monday to Friday; 7.45am–8.15 pm, Saturday; 7.45am–6pm, Sunday.

SALARY: $1,360–$1,560 per month depending on qualifications and a competitive package including 20 days' holiday, 9 days' public holidays, contract completion bonus and re-signing bonus.

FACILITIES/SUPPORT: $550 contribution to medical insurance,

sponsorship plus visa and internal work permit costs. For short-term contracts, accommodation is provided. For 1-year contracts teachers are placed in Apollo-rented accommodation or given agents' names and/or a Vietnamese member of staff can visit accommodation with the teacher to assist with translation and negotiation.

RECRUITMENT: Through ihworld.com, local adverts and internationally using posters, websites etc. Interviews are essential, and are occasionally carried out in the UK/USA.

ASIAN INSTITUTE OF TECHNOLOGY IN VIETNAM

Education Management Section, Building B3, University of Transport and Communications, Hanoi

- +84 4 37669493 ext 120
- linh@aitcv.ac.vn
- www.aitcv.ac.vn

NUMBER OF TEACHERS: 2.

PREFERENCE OF NATIONALITY: None.

QUALIFICATIONS: At least 5 years' experience and preferably a master's degree.

CONDITIONS OF EMPLOYMENT: Hours vary according to course availability.

SALARY: US$20 per hour (Diploma in TEFL/TESOL or TESOL Certificate), US$25 per hour (Master's in TEFL or TESOL).

FACILITIES/SUPPORT: Some assistance with finding accommodation. No assistance with work permit.

RECRUITMENT: Word-of-mouth. Interviews.

CONTACT: Ms Pham Ngoc Linh, HR Administrator.

NUMBER OF TEACHERS: Many for schools in Vietnam but mainly in China (see entry in China chapter).

CONTACT: Recruiter contact details in China and UK provided on website.

NUMBER OF TEACHERS: 300+, with centres in Ho Chi Minh City, Danang, Vung Tau and Hanoi.

PREFERENCE OF NATIONALITY: None, but must be native English speakers.

QUALIFICATIONS: Minimum requirements are university degree (any discipline), plus a CELTA, Trinity or equivalent. Preference is given to applicants who have experience with young learners.

CONDITIONS OF EMPLOYMENT: Standard 12-month contract. Approximately 25 hours per week.

FACILITIES/SUPPORT: School provides an airport pickup and pays for initial accommodation at a guesthouse. Information and contact details for estate agents are provided. Other teachers are always on the lookout for flatmates and there is an accommodation board in each school. School provides a relocation bonus for overseas applicants as well as paying for and obtaining visas and work permits. Free health insurance and Vietnamese lessons plus quarterly social events are paid for by the school. Bonus paid on successful completion of contract.

RECRUITMENT: Via the internet (tefl.com; eslcafe.com) and recruiters. Telephone interviews for overseas hires; face-to-face interviews for applicants in Vietnam. Applicants must send CV with cover letter, supporting documents, passport details and realistic start date. Local applicants must also provide visa details.

CONTACT: Pierre Woussen, Teacher Recruitment Executives/ Expatriates Human Resources.

NUMBER OF TEACHERS: 100.

PREFERENCE OF NATIONALITY: Native English speakers.

QUALIFICATIONS: Bachelor's degree in any discipline plus 120-hour intensive teaching certificate with practicum (online certificates are not eligible).

CONDITIONS OF EMPLOYMENT: Minimum 1 year if hired from overseas, 6 months if already local. 70–100 contact hours per month.

SALARY: Hourly rate from $19 to $24; 70 hours minimum guaranteed after probationary period. Tax deductions 5%–30% on progressive scale.

FACILITIES/SUPPORT: Advice given on finding accommodation and assistance with obtaining work permit. CELTA course offered on premises.

RECRUITMENT: Internet advertising and local press. Local interviews necessary.

CONTACT: Justin Seton-Browne, Teacher Recruitment and Welfare Manager (justin.setonbrowne@languagelink.vn).

NUMBER OF TEACHERS: 15.

PREFERENCE OF NATIONALITY: UK, Canada.

QUALIFICATIONS: Professionally qualified teachers as they tend to be substantially better trained than ESL teachers.

CONDITIONS OF EMPLOYMENT: 9.5 month contracts. Minimum 18 hours a week.

SALARY: US$20–$25 an hour (net).

FACILITIES/SUPPORT: School advises on reliable landlords, helps negotiate issues and deals with local registration with the police. School covers two-thirds of the cost of obtaining the permits, but expects teachers to refund the difference if they leave after one year.

RECRUITMENT: Interviews essential.

CONTACT: Sean J McGough, BSc (H), PGCE, QTS, Director of Study (seanjoe1977@hotmail.co.uk).

TEACHERS FOR VIETNAM

PO Box 384, Piermont, New York 10968, USA

📞 +1 860 480 504 1

🖱 info@teachersforvietnam.org

💻 www.teachersforvietnam.org

NUMBER OF TEACHERS: About 5 teachers of ESL for university posts in Vietnam to further Vietnam's educational development by increasing fluency of spoken English and to build bridges between people in Vietnam and the West, particularly the USA.

QUALIFICATIONS: Must be university graduate so most volunteers are over 21. Some experience and/or training in TESL needed, plus eagerness to live and work in Vietnam.

CONDITIONS OF EMPLOYMENT: Academic year from late August to May.

SALARY: Programme application fee US$50. Programme pays for airfare, health insurance and travel during Tet holiday. Host universities pay a cost-of-living salary and in most cases provide free housing, usually a room or suite in a campus guesthouse.

FACILITIES/SUPPORT: In-country orientation session provided, which covers cultural issues as well as practical matters for foreigners newly arrived in Vietnam.

RECRUITMENT: Deadline for applications is 1 April. Face-to-face interviews preferred but can be done by phone.

CONTACT: John Dippel, Executive Director.

ILA VIETNAM

Emma Cragg, reflects on her experiences as an English teacher with ILA Vietnam:

'I decided to teach English as a foreign language when I was made redundant from my IT job in 2009. I had been travelling at the beginning of the year and had met several people who had taught in Asia. They all raved about the amazing lifestyle you could have, whilst saving money at the same time. It seemed too good to be true but on further investigation I realised that it was true!

'Originally, I was going to try my luck in South Korea, but I was unqualified at the time. Then, a friend suggested I use my redundancy money to do a CELTA course in Vietnam. I did some research on places to do the course and ILA came up. I already knew someone working for ILA in HCMC so I contacted her and asked a few questions about the company and the course. After receiving very positive feedback I completed the application form (which took me several days – they really want to be sure you've got what it takes) and was interviewed a few weeks later. Before I knew what was happening I'd been accepted on the course and was booking a one way ticket to Vietnam.

'Once I had completed the CELTA course, I was hired by ILA. They were very flexible and understanding of individual situations and offered me a part time contract to begin with so that I could visit family in Australia for Christmas. Then, when one became available, they offered me a full time teaching contract in March 2010. Since working for ILA I've progressed seamlessly from teaching children to adults to exam preparation classes. ILA's comprehensive academic support and continuous professional development has definitely helped. The wealth of experience I've gained in teaching a variety of ages and levels has set me in good stead for any future roles in the ELT business.

'I'm currently in the process of applying for next year's DELTA course which ILA runs every year. Gaining the DELTA certificate will open many doors through ILA's unique career pathway with ILA refunding the fee as I go. Perfect for my future career and prospects, as well as my bank account.'

CAMBODIA

Cambodia is a relatively stable country, having emerged from the shadow of its tragic past. The ELT market has been wide open to private enterprise in Cambodia ever since the UN ceased to be in charge. Foreign ministries and government offices are all keen to sign up for private lessons as are the diplomatic corps and their families as well as the military. The British Council does not maintain an office in Phnom Penh. On a visit to Phnom Penh a few years ago, **Mark Vetare** was impressed by the demand for English teachers:

Just rent yourself a moto for the day and have a spin around Phnom Penh. There's virtually a school on every corner. Not all schools employ native speakers since many poor Khmer can't afford them. Pay and hours are the main problems for teachers. Time was when you could get four hours a day. Now you've got to stick around for the better times and more hours. Things are becoming more stringent in the 'real' schools. That being said, it's backpacker heaven: young men with long hair, good (but not necessarily native) English and no high level education still get jobs.

Cambodia still operates on a dollar economy, so few wages are quoted in riels. Wages at the decent schools start at $15 an hour. Visa extensions are relatively easy to get and schools usually organise them for their teachers. Prospective teachers should arrive with extra passport photos and buy a Business B or Business E visa on arrival for $25.

One of the longest established schools is the Australian Centre for Education or ACE (see entry) which is flourishing. There are many other commercial institutes such as ELT (www.elt.edu.kh), New World Institute (www.nwi.edu.kh) and Home of English International (www.homeofenglish.edu.kh), all in Phnom Penh. When experienced teacher **Bradwell Jackson** from the US visited, he ascertained that the American Intercom Institute at 217 ABCD Mao Tse Tong Blvd (+855 23 223 295/ 2221 222 or +855 11 388 868; info@aii.edu.kh) is happy to hire foreign teachers who are in Phnom Penh.

Volunteers can offer to teach at Savong's School, near Siem Reap, which was set up by Svay Savong to give children who can't afford tuition fees the chance to learn a language and improve their job prospects. The school's website (www.savong.com) advises: '*There's an informal tradition of taking the school such things as soccer balls, volleyballs or Frisbees as well as stationery – just ask Savong to see what he needs from the book store in Siem Reap and, if you're up to it, try a spot of teaching*'. On her gap year **Pascale Hunter** from Cambridge noticed a flyer for Savong's School up in her hostel and spent a short time teaching teenagers and younger children there. Although she found the experience interesting, she felt it was '*fairly commercial, with the kids clamouring for Western souvenirs*'. However, plenty of other volunteers have enjoyed their visit and are impressed by the dedication of the students.

Another organisation to try is Volunteer in Cambodia (www.volunteerincambodia.org), which recruits volunteers to teach at Conversations With Foreigners (CWF), a local conversational English school in Phnom Penh (No 247C, Street 271, Toul Pumbung II). Money raised by the programme goes towards the Cambodian Rural Development Team, a local organisation working to improve livelihoods in rural communities. Volunteers stay three months (there are specific group starting dates) and pay for their accommodation and meals, which currently costs $850 for three months. Teaching qualifications/experience is an advantage, but not required.

LIST OF EMPLOYERS

AMERICAN EDUCATION CENTER

7E Mao Tse Tung Blvd, Sangkat Boeung Keng Kang I,
Khan Chamkarmorn, Phnom Penh

- +855 23 220 420
- contact@aec.edu.kh
- www.aec.edu.kh

NUMBER OF TEACHERS: 6.

PREFERENCE OF NATIONALITY: none.

QUALIFICATIONS: B.Ed, ESL experience.

CONDITIONS OF EMPLOYMENT: 1 year. 5 hours a day.

SALARY: Negotiable depending on experience.

FACILITIES/SUPPORT: No assistance with accommodation. AEC arranges for the processing of Business Visas.

RECRUITMENT: Via local advertisements in newspapers and on websites. Skype interviews are possible.

CONTACT: Janet English, Director.

AUSTRALIAN CENTRE FOR EDUCATION

46, Street 214, Sangkat Boeung Raing, Khan Daun Penh,
(PO Box 860), Phnom Penh, Cambodia

- +855 23 724204
- info.phnompenh@idp.com or info@acecambodia.org
- www.cambodia.idp.com/ace.aspx

NUMBER OF TEACHERS: 55 foreign teachers in Phnom Penh and Siem Reap.

PREFERENCE OF NATIONALITY: Any native English speaker is acceptable, though Australians preferred.

QUALIFICATIONS: Undergraduate degree plus CELTA or equivalent. 1 year teaching experience, with proven ability to work autonomously.

CONDITIONS OF EMPLOYMENT: 21–23 hours of classes a week, but teachers are expected to attend at the school 40 hours per week. Minimum commitment 6 months. Hours vary: the school is open 6am–8pm and on Saturday mornings. Teachers needed for general courses, English for Academic Purposes and ESP.

SALARY: $18–$25 per hour freelance, $1,700–$2,100 per month.

FACILITIES/SUPPORT: Advice given on affordable accommodation which is not hard to find in Phnom Penh (rents from $150 a month plus utilities). Assistance given before arrival on obtaining visas. The school is well equipped and resourced and a variety of professional development sessions are held at least once a month.

RECRUITMENT: Web advertisements, word of mouth. Interviews are required, but can be over the phone and are carried out in Australia from time to time. Professional references are checked.

CONTACT: Louise FitzGerald, Director (louise.fitzgerald@idp.com).

WESTERN INTERNATIONAL SCHOOL

Siem Reap Branch, #437 Lapaix Street, Svay Duangkum
Commune, Siem Reap

- +855 63 760 767
- jamesrath_siu@yahoo.com
- www.western.edu.kh/wis/index.php

NUMBER OF TEACHERS: 40.

PREFERENCE OF NATIONALITY: None.

QUALIFICATIONS: Degree holders are preferred, but positions for non-degree holders are also available. In-house training is offered, and professional development is encouraged under guidance of the team leaders.

CONDITIONS OF EMPLOYMENT: 12-month contract. Students study in 3 shifts: morning session 7.30–11.30am, afternoon session 1–5pm, and evening session 5.30–8pm. Teachers are offered a choice of classes within these time frames.

SALARY: US$7 per classroom hour. Teachers submit a 5% tax return.

FACILITIES/SUPPORT: School has a library, computer laboratory and large play area which teachers may use during class time. All classrooms are air-conditioned.

CONTACT: James Rath, School Director.

LAOS AND BURMA

Laos was the last country in the region to open its doors to foreigners. Over the past few years an amazing number of English schools have opened in the Laotian capital of Vientiane, ranging from well-established institutes to small, shop-front establishments, staffed with locals or expats passing through on tourist visas. When English institutes first started opening in Vientiane, most were fly-by-night operations. But there are now several international English-medium schools such as the Lao-American College and the Vientiane International School (www.vislao.com), and also better organised private language schools.

The visa procedures have settled down in Laos. If possible, a letter of invitation should be obtained from your employer before arrival which entitles the holder to enter Laos on a B2 visa (non-immigrant, business visa) instead of a tourist visa. The B2 visa costs around $300 for a year, although 6-month and 3-month visas are available at a reduced rate. To extend the B2 visa if you are working at the same school costs the same each time. Only the most elite schools will cover the cost of the visa, although most will assist you in obtaining it.

In order to obtain the invitation, your sponsor needs a copy of your passport and probably copies of any educational credentials. Otherwise it is possible to apply for a tourist visa outside of the country (Bangkok is the closest and easiest place) for around $30 and enter the country on a one-month tourist visa. After arrival, the employer will have to make the invitation for a B2 visa. Then the teacher will be required to leave the country (usually across the border to Thailand) and re-enter on the B2 visa for a further fee. In addition to visas, work permits can be arranged by reputable schools at a cost of $120 per year.

Salaries and conditions of work can vary as much as the schools themselves. Vientiane College (see entry below) provides the best working conditions, staff development programme and benefit package. The majority of language schools pay by the hour, from as little as $5 up to $15 at the higher end of the range.

Demand for native English speakers also occasionally comes from bilingual schools such as the Vientiane Pattana School, a small primary school in Laos that has advertised internationally in the past. Teaching opportunities also exist in the larger provincial centres such as Luang Prabang and Svannakhet and, in Vientiane, in larger companies and ministries as in-house teachers. Again, conditions vary greatly and there are often delays with payment in the local currency (kip). It is possible to advertise on noticeboards around the town, or in the English language newspaper, the *Vientiane Times* (www.vientianetimes.org.la), in order to pick up one or two private students.

Some volunteer opportunities exist in Laos, for example with the Thai organisation Openmind Projects (mentioned below in the chapter on Thailand) and with the Sunshine School (see entry).

Until very recently, there was almost no scope for teaching English in reclusive, repressive, Myanmar (Burma). However, with the recent election of Aung San Suu Kyi to the Burmese parliament, hopes are rising that military rule will slowly give way to a more open and pro-Western system that would support English language schools. At present, most of the English taught in Burma is via Buddhist monasteries. NGOs may be allowed to become more active in the country, for example Teach for Myanmar (www.teachmyanmar.org) has been recruiting graduates for the past few years to do a stint of volunteer teaching (and unlike many volunteer programmes, participants do not have to pay a fee). The British Council has a presence in Rangoon and Mandalay mainly to support local teaching efforts. A tiny handful of vacancies has been seen online in 2012, for example on the Thai teaching site www.ajarn.com, where the Horizon International School in Rangoon was trying to recruit teachers. Also the Kensington Academy of English in London was advertising for EFL teachers to work in its new school to open in Mandalay in the summer of 2012. They were offering free accommodation and meals and a return flight every six months in addition to a salary of £700 per month.

For information about teaching programmes for Burmese refugees in northern Thailand, see the chapter on Thailand.

LIST OF EMPLOYERS

21ST CENTURY SCHOOL OF ENGLISH

74/6 Sisangvone Rd. That Luang Tai, Vientiane Lao PDR,
PO Box 77

☎ +856 21 45 2500

✉ info@21centuryeducation.com

🖥 www.21centuryeducation.com

NUMBER OF TEACHERS: 13.

PREFERENCE OF NATIONALITY: American, British, Australian,
New Zealander.

QUALIFICATIONS: CELTA/TESOL/TEFL.

CONDITIONS OF EMPLOYMENT: 1-year or 6-month contracts
with 13.5+ teaching hours per week.

SALARY: $13–17 per hour.

FACILITIES/SUPPORT: School will arrange 6 or 12-month work
visas; payment terms vary.

RECRUITMENT: Usually via the internet or word of mouth.
Interviews are essential and can be carried out from the
UK or USA.

SUNSHINE SCHOOL

PO Box 7411, Vientiane

✉ sunshinelaos@gmail.com

🖥 http://sunshineschool.tumblr.com

NUMBER OF TEACHERS: Volunteers only.

PREFERENCE OF NATIONALITY: English-speaking countries.

QUALIFICATIONS: Creative approach to working with the kids is
important; experience in teaching or experience with young kids
are both good assets.

CONDITIONS OF EMPLOYMENT: 1–10 months (volunteers
needed September–July). School hours include 7 teaching periods
from 8am to 4pm on weekdays. Volunteers usually have 4–5
teaching periods a day (maybe less depending on the volunteer's

needs), in kindergarten, primary or junior secondary classes.
Volunteers may also be involved in creative activities with the
children or teachers' classes or teaching village children and
youth on the weekends.

SALARY: Voluntary basis only. Long-term volunteers staying 6–12
months may get a small living allowance (max $100 a month)
or help with housing, depending on the financial condition of the
school at the time.

FACILITIES/SUPPORT: Long-term volunteers will be supported
with working visas (which cost $250–$450). All volunteers get
a vegetarian lunch provided on school days. No accommodation
provided but local guest houses charge only $60–$90 per month.

RECRUITMENT: Direct application to school.

CONTACT: Cathy Lee, Director.

VIENTIANE COLLEGE

PO Box 4144 (Rue 23 Singha), Vientiane

☎ +856 21 414873/414052/412598

✉ info@vientianecollege.com

🖥 www.vientianecollege.com

NUMBER OF TEACHERS: 40.

PREFERENCE OF NATIONALITY: Native English speakers from
any region.

QUALIFICATIONS: Minimum bachelor's degree and CELTA. ESP/
EAP experience preferred.

CONDITIONS OF EMPLOYMENT: Sessional and contract.

SALARY: From $1,500–$2,800 per month less 10% income tax.

FACILITIES/SUPPORT: Assistance with finding accommodation.
School arranges and pays for work permit and residence visa.
In-house training programme.

RECRUITMENT: Personal interview necessary.

CONTACT: Denley Pike, Director.

TAIWAN

Taiwan remains a magnet for English teachers of all backgrounds and the ELT industry is booming. Part of the appeal of teaching in Taiwan is that the wages compare favourably with countries such as Japan, yet the cost of living is significantly lower. Equally important is that finding a job here is fairly easy. It used to be the case that schools were looking for only three things: a passport from an English-speaking country, a bachelor's degree and a pulse. These days, however, the better schools are becoming choosier, it is more difficult to get a working visa and many schools and local education departments are looking for an ELT qualification and prior experience. Nevertheless, the opportunities for teaching English in Taiwan are endless. For example, hundreds of private cramming institutes or *bushibans* continue to teach young children and high school students for university entrance examinations.

English language schools in Taiwan are becoming increasingly regulated. Only the reputable language schools, those who are fully licensed as foreign language schools, are permitted to employ English-speaking foreigners and sponsor them for visas, provided that they are willing to sign a one-year contract. Only native English speaker teachers with a university degree (in any subject) are eligible. Taiwanese consumers of English have a clear preference for the North American accent because of strong trading and cultural links between Taiwan and the USA. However, many schools will hire presentable native English speakers, whatever their accent. Few want their staff to be able to speak Chinese; in fact one teacher reported seeing a sign in a *bushiban* window boasting 'Teachers Not Speak Chinese'. Language teachers and tutors working in Taipei are predominantly American; native English speakers of other nationalities tend to gravitate to southern Taiwan. **Amanda Searle** from the UK felt only slightly discriminated against:

> *My employer claimed that they did not discriminate between people of different nationalities, but this is not what I have found. North Americans are the first choice when hours are allocated. I have had students complain that they wanted an American teacher because they wanted to learn 'real' English, though I have never had a student complain to me or the secretaries that my accent was difficult to understand.*

This has not been everybody's experience however, and some schools even boast 'English comes from England and so do our teachers'. Many non-Caucasians have experienced prejudice in Taiwan.

The market for teaching children from about age three seems boundless at the moment, so anyone who enjoys working with primary age children, i.e. likes to sing songs, play games and comfort little ones who miss their mums, may be able to find a job. However, recent government regulations require all kindergarten teachers to be fully qualified kindergarten specialists. While many CELTA trained teachers can no longer legally work in kindergartens, many still do so. English immersion kindergartens are all the rage and tend to pay their teachers very well. Women are often considered to have an advantage in this regard, and also tend to be preferred by the mothers of female pupils. Employers in this field generally provide detailed lesson plans which means that little time needs to be spent on lesson preparation.

FINDING A JOB

A few of the major organisations hire overseas either directly or via a North American agent. The Hess Educational Organization (see entry below), whose head office is in Taiwan, has a representative in North America who can send out information to enquirers (Christina Derwee at christina@hesseducation.ca). Interviews are conducted either in Taiwan or by telephone from Taiwan. The agency TEFLOne Recruitment (www.teflone.com) is one of many that recruits qualified teachers for posts in Taiwan as well as other countries in the Far East.

JAMES ROBINSON

James Robinson is one satisfied client of Teflone.com and he wrote last year from the small town of Taoyuan in Kaohsiung County in Taiwan's interior. After being made redundant as a welder/fabricator, he did a TESOL course which he describes as 'the best move I ever made'. Soon afterwards he met the chief recruiter for TEFLOne, David Coles, to hear about opportunities with the Shane School:

My interview was a very positive experience. I knew that Shane would offer peace of mind, a highly efficient service and above all a friendly interview. It is for these reasons that Shane stood out from amongst the rest. Many other interviewers from other organisations sounded a bit officious and none of them offered as realistic and honest information about life in Taiwan as Shane did. It also sorted out all the administrative requirements such as work permits and bank accounts and patiently answered questions they had probably been asked a hundred times before!

My hours are currently about 25 a week, a lot more if you include the preparation, but a million times more interesting than welding! Most of the children are so eager to learn and I was astonished how the really young children retained new information.

Entertainment is the key. Yes it was a learning curve and yes I made mistakes. But after a few weeks the preparation became far easier and it was a far more rewarding and positive experience. I think it's important to make things happen for yourself, e.g. to go climbing and cycling and participate in activities you like. This can be hugely rewarding for your inspiration as a teacher, to meet local people and get to know your new environment. As a result, my spare time is incredible. I still find it amazing that I can be out of the city and in the national park in 45 minutes, with its new aromas, wildlife and breathtaking scenery.

Another recruiter looking for candidates with a four-year degree is Asian Consultants International in Taipei (hr@asianconsultants.com; www.asianconsultants.com). Many websites contain a wealth of detail about Taiwan and what it's like to teach there. Jobs and lots of information about teaching in Taiwan can be found at www.tealit.com, www.taiwan-taipei.com and www.aacircle.com.au. Also have a look at www.englishintaiwan.com. The US-based recruiter for Asia Reach to Teach (www.reachtoteachrecruiting.com) is very active in Taiwan where its main centre is located. Another possibility is ESL Dewey (www.esldewey.com.tw) which posts some ads, as does the *Tainan Bulletin* (www.tainanbulletin.com).

If using a recruitment agency in Taiwan, it is best to proceed with caution. In years gone by there have been reports of teachers accepting jobs before arriving in Taiwan, only to find that they have been placed not in Taipei as they agreed, but in some three-goat mountain village. Discrepancies also sometimes occur between the contracts agents have given to teachers in English, and those given to employers in Chinese.

Many people arrive on spec to look for work. Finding a *bushiban* willing to hire you is not as difficult as finding a good one willing to hire you. If possible, try to sit in on one or two classes or talk to another teacher before signing a contract. (If a school is unwilling to permit this, it doesn't bode well.) Read the fine print of the contract to find out what the penalties are for breaking a contract.

On the strength of the TEFL course she had completed at the American Language Institute in San Diego and a year spent teaching in Poland, freelance photographer **Alicia Wszelaki** wanted a taste of teaching in the Far East. She joined a short summer teaching project in Taiwan for adolescent girls, run by the American Language Village (www.kidscamp.com.tw) that she had noticed on Dave's ESL Cafe. Teachers were housed in a hotel not far from the camp and she found working conditions to be very good although the hours were long over 10 straight days.

> *I realised a few days into the camp that this was indeed a summer camp and the kids were there not only to learn English but also to have fun. We played games, had lessons on pizza and hamburgers and other subjects that were more real world. The students really enjoyed these. There was lots of songs and dancing. If you choose to do a camp of this nature, bring lots of energy, smiles, optimism, an open mind, and water. It was a wonderful and rewarding experience. The students were great and the teachers were some of the most incredible people I have met – a truly great blend of personalities and experiences.*

The best time to arrive is at the beginning of summer (the end of the school year), when Chinese parents enrol their offspring in English language summer schools. Late August is another peak time for hiring, though there are openings year-round. Word-of-mouth is even more important in Taiwan than elsewhere because there is no association of recognised language schools.

As always travellers' hostels will be helpful as reported by **Bradwell Jackson** from his most recent trip to investigate the teaching scene in 2011:

> *I couldn't believe all the English schools in Taipei. I presumed that the market must be saturated by now and that it would be too difficult to find a job, but after talking to the people in the know at the Taipei Hostel (www. taipeihostel.com/teach.html), I found out that this was not the case. The hostel is English teaching central for foreigners and the common room is where all the newcomers meet to get the latest on the English teaching situation. Once you get the lowdown from the old hands there, just pick a direction and start walking. After passing about three corners, you'll definitely see an English school, probably two. Have your introduction ready, march on in there and sell yourself.*

Apparently some hostels feature blackboards on which job vacancies are chalked up as the hostel manager is notified.

A good noticeboard is located in the student lounge on the sixth floor of the Mandarin Training Center of National Taiwan Normal University at 129 Hoping East Road. You might also make useful expat contacts in Taipei at the Community Services Centre (www.community.com.tw).

Once you have decided to approach some schools for work, make contact by email or telephone in the first place. Next you must present yourself in person to the schools. Many schools in Taiwan are used to and expect cold-callers. In order to get around Taipei you should invest in the invaluable English language *Taipei Bus Guide* available from Caves Books (corner of Chung Shan Road and Minsheng E. Road) or Lucky Book Store in the university. Take along your university certificate and any other qualifications, and take the trouble to look presentable. **Peter McGuire** was told point blank that your appearance and how you conduct yourself at interview count for everything, and concluded that '*all your experience in life or teaching in other countries really doesn't mean a thing here*'. **David Hughes** specifically recommends paying attention to your feet:

> *Bring plenty of socks/tights. You have to leave your shoes at the door of Chinese homes, and it's difficult to appear serious and composed with a toe poking through.*

Anyone with a high level of education (i.e. a master's degree or PhD) might find work attached to one of the scores of universities and colleges, where working conditions are very good. Foreigners are also allowed to work in public high schools, though it is difficult to function without a knowledge of the language.

FREELANCE TEACHING

Work visas are valid only for employment with the sponsoring employer. However, many teachers teach private students, which pays handsomely from NT$700–$1,000 per hour. In a country where foreigners are sometimes approached in bars or on trains and asked to give English lessons, it is not hard to set up independently as an English tutor. **Peter McGuire** found the dream job of tutoring a travel agent three to six hours a day, seven days a week and then was invited to accompany his client on a trip to Hawaii:

> *Some of my lessons are given at private clubs, saunas, in taxicabs and fine restaurants. Actually, it's kind of unbelievable.*

Although it would be possible to make a good living by teaching privately, you will need to work for a school in order to obtain the visa. A helpful hint is to have business cards printed up, calling yourself 'English consultant'. It is even more lucrative if you can muster a small group of students and charge them, say, NT$300 per person. Women usually find this easier to set up than men. The main problem is finding appropriate premises.

Cancelled hours are a perennial problem. Freelancers will find it prudent to explain to students gently but forcefully that they will be liable to pay if they cancel without giving sufficient notice; most will not object. You can even request one month's fees in advance. Once you are established, other jobs in the English field may come your way such as correcting business faxes, transcribing lyrics from pop CDs or writing CVs and letters of application for Taiwanese students hoping to study overseas.

REGULATIONS

Tourists who arrive without any visa are allowed to stay in Taiwan no more than 14 days. People who intend to look for work can apply for the resident visa after arrival; however, they will need to enter the country on a visitor's visa valid for 60 days (an extension may be granted, but this isn't easy). To apply for this visa you need proof of a return air ticket and a document verifying the purpose of your visit, or a recent bank statement. During those 60 days, you must find a job and organise all the paperwork described in this section. If time runs out you will have to leave the country.

Information on visas should be requested from the Taiwan overseas office in your country of origin which is also where you apply for the visitor's visa. Do not reveal on any form that you are considering looking for work. You will have a choice of a single-entry visa (£32) and a multiple entry visa (£64), although to apply for the six-month multiple entry visa you need a letter of confirmation from your UK employer stating the purpose of your visit. The Taipei Representative Office in the UK is at 50 Grosvenor Gardens, London SW1W 0EB (+44 20 7881 2650; www.taiwanembassy.org/uk). Details may be obtained in the USA from TECRA (4201 Wisconsin Avenue NW, Washington, DC 20016–2137; +1 202 895 1800; www.roc-taiwan.org/us) and in Canada from the Taipei Economic & Cultural Offices in Vancouver and Toronto (www.taiwan-canada. org). To stay legally in the country, teachers need to obtain an Alien Resident Certificate (ARC) from one of the many national immigration offices. Once you arrive and find a school offering a one-year contract, your school applies to the local education authority for a working permit for which they will need a copy and translation of your degree diploma, contract, medical certificate (requiring various tests) and passport. Once that is processed you can apply for a resident visa at the Ministry of Foreign Affairs; the fee will be NT$1,000 (about £21). Up to two weeks later your resident visa will be stamped in your passport. You are then obliged to apply to the Foreign Affairs police within two weeks for an ARC and a multiple entry permit. Some schools may make a contribution towards permit costs when the contract is renewed for a further year. If your tourist visa is due to expire before you have arranged a resident visa, you will also have to leave Taiwan to renew your tourist visa, and have a plausible reason why you want to remain in the country. If you claim to need an extension because you are studying Chinese, you can expect a spot test in Mandarin. (It is not clear if the same applies if you're a student of Kung Fu.)

TAX

After the work visa has been issued, tax will be withheld from your pay. The tax rate for foreigners who stay in Taiwan for less than 183 days in one calendar year (category A) is 18%. After six months, the rate of tax drops to between 5% and 13% but only on income beyond the standard exemption of NT$76,000.

CONDITIONS OF WORK

Most jobs are paid by the hour, and for the past three or four years, the minimum hourly rate a teacher should expect is around NT$550 (approximately US$19). For a monthly salary you should expect to receive around NT$55,000 (approximately US$1,900) for 25 hours per week. Occasionally the rate for cushy morning classes drops below and unsociable hours are rewarded (if you're lucky) with a premium rate of NT$600–NT$700. Rates outside Taipei (where the cost of living is lower) tend to be slightly higher due to the relative scarcity of teachers.

As usual some schools are shambolic when it comes to timetabling their teachers' hours. In a profit-driven atmosphere, classes start and finish on demand and can be cancelled at short notice if the owner decides that there are too few pupils to make it economic. When you are starting a new job, ask your employer to be specific about the actual number of hours you will be given. It is not uncommon for teachers who have been promised a full timetable at the point of hiring to find themselves with fewer hours than promised and a considerably lower pay packet.

Although exploitation of teachers (and pupils) is not as rife as in Korea, you should be prepared for anything, as **Rusty Holmes** had to be:

> *The real reason there was such a high turnover rate of staff at one school was because of the supervisor's habit of barging into class at unpredictable moments and accusing the teacher (especially my Scottish colleague) of mispronouncing words, when she herself could barely speak English. The worst incidents occurred when she beat her own children in the face for getting poor grades, when she engaged a parent in a fistfight over a tuition dispute, and when she physically ran her husband out of the school, all right in front of our students.*

Having discovered the joys of world travel at age 30, **Steph Fuccio** from the USA took the plunge and fixed up a teaching job with an English school in Tainan via the internet. She found that good money could be earned and the cost of living was really low, which had the disadvantage that many of the foreigners there were focused on money to the exclusion of everything else. Her low overheads included US$200 a month for a small apartment all to herself and a used scooter bought (nowadays expect to pay between NT$15,000 and NT$20,000 for a second-hand scooter). Meanwhile she was earning US$17 an hour despite having no teaching certificate or experience. She stayed for most of an academic year but left a little early having tired of teaching only young children. She concludes that '*the whole country is simply gone mad with learning English*'.

The usual problems which bedevil TEFL teachers occur in Taiwan, such as split shifts, often ending at 10pm, and compulsory weekend work, especially if you are teaching children. Few schools provide much creative training or incentives to do a good job. Like the educational system of China and so many other countries, Taiwanese state schools rely heavily on rote learning, making it difficult to introduce a more communicative approach, especially at the beginner level. Whereas some schools offer no guidance what-soever, others leave almost nothing to the teacher. What is termed a 'training programme' often consists of a paint-by-number teaching manual. Here is an extract from the Teacher's Book of one major chain of schools:

> *How to teach ABCs (e.g. the letter K): Review A-J... Using the flash cards, say 'A – apple, B – boy, C – cat... J – jacket'. The whole class repeats after the teacher. Then say, 'A-B-C-D-E-F-G-H-I-J' and have the whole class repeat. Show the letter K flashcard. Say 'K' having the whole class repeat it each time you say it. Say 'K' 4 or 5 times.*

And so on. This certainly makes the inexperienced teacher's job easier but possibly also very boring. Not everyone will be comfortable with such a regimented curriculum.

LEISURE TIME

Flats are predictably expensive in central Taipei so many teachers choose to commute from the suburbs, where living conditions are more pleasant in any case. Rents tend to be in the region of NT$7,000–NT$12,000 per month. There are so many foreigners coming and going, and the locals are so friendly and helpful, that it is not too difficult to learn of flats becoming vacant. You will have to pay a month's rent in advance plus a further month's rent as a deposit; this bond or 'key money' usually amounts to £400+. Several schools will appoint a Chinese member of staff to chaperone new arrivals and translate on house-hunting trips.

Taipei has a rapid transit system which is far more enjoyable (and cheaper) than running a motorbike. Some teachers stay in hostels near the central station and commute to work in a satellite city where wages are higher than in Taipei (e.g. Tao Yuan and Chung Li). Without doubt, the biggest inconvenience and danger in Taiwan is on the roads. Taiwanese drivers often commit driving manoeuvres that would result in lynching in other countries. Red lights and traffic laws are more often than not ignored and foreigners compound the problem by riding too fast on scooters, with little experience, and often under the influence.

Not a single visitor to Taipei, which is one of the most densely populated cities in the world, fails to com-plain of the pollution, second only to that of Mexico City. Not only is the air choked with the fumes and noise of a million motorised vehicles, but there are occasional scares that chemicals have infiltrated the water table contaminating locally grown vegetables. One blogger maintains that you have to carry an umbrella to protect your skin and clothes from falling acid rain (www.roadjunky.com/article/654/teaching-english-in-taiwan). The weather is another serious drawback. The typhoon season lasts from July to October bringing stormy wet weather and mouldy clothes. The heat and humidity at this time also verge on the unbearable.

Taipei is not the only city to suffer from pollution; Taichung and Kaohsiung are also bad. Even Tainan with two-thirds of a million people has some pollution; 100 new cars are registered here every day adding to the problem. (This is a statistic which rather detracts from Tainan's appeal as the most historic city on the island with many old temples, etc.) Kaohsiung on the south-west coast is a large industrial city with a high crime rate but has the advantage of being near the popular resort of Kenting Beach and within reach of mountain campsites such as Maolin. The geographical advantage of Taichung further north is proximity to the mountains as well as a good climate and cultural activities. The east coast is more tranquil, though some find it dull.

Wherever you decide to teach, one of the highlights of living in Taiwan is the hospitality of the locals. In fact some people report being smothered by kindness, since the Taiwanese will not accept a refusal of any food or drink offered, and even paying for meals or drinks can be a struggle. In general, apart from some petty crime, corrupt politicians and fairly well hidden gang activity, Taiwan is virtually crime free, so you are free to pursue your leisure pursuits without worry. Taipei has a 24-hour social scene which can seriously cut into savings. Heavy drinking is commonplace. Films are usually shown in English with Chinese subtitles.

For the truly homesick there are some English-style pubs with pool tables and darts boards. For **Rusty Holmes**, the food was a highlight:

Eating out is just as much a pastime in Taiwan as it is in Hong Kong. There are countless little mom-and-pop restaurants which offer delicious and inexpensive food. My favourite is the US$4 black pepper steak. Considering the high price of food in supermarkets, it would be cheaper to eat out than to cook at home. Taiwan is also a fruit-lover's paradise, though most are expensive by American standards. My favourite is the outstanding sugarcane Taiwan produces.

LIST OF EMPLOYERS

GLORIA ENGLISH SCHOOL
262 Alley, 17–14, Lane 66, Huan-Nan Road, Ping-Jen City, Taoyuan
ⓒ +886 3 495 1751/2
✉ gloria@glo.com.tw
🖥 www.glo.com.tw

NUMBER OF TEACHERS: 100 for 18 branches in Taoyuan County (near Taipei).
PREFERENCE OF NATIONALITY: American or Canadian.
QUALIFICATIONS: Bachelor's degree, or 2-year college diploma and TESOL/TEFL certificate.
CONDITIONS OF EMPLOYMENT: 12-month contracts. Most classes are between 4pm and 9pm on weekdays and all day Saturday.
SALARY: NT$600 per hour for teachers without previous teaching experience (approximately US$18.50). Deductions vary from 0% to 10% depending on length of employment. End of contract bonus of NT$25,000 plus other bonuses given throughout the year.
FACILITIES/SUPPORT: Rent-free accommodation at one of the school's dormitories provided for 15 months. School will provide assistance with all related visa paperwork, but teachers are responsible for paying for their work permits. Training given.
RECRUITMENT: Online job postings, newspaper job postings, referrals by current or previous employees. Phone interviews are mandatory. If the applicant is already in Taiwan, in-person interviews are preferable.
CONTACT: Anita Yang, Hiring Manager.

HESS INTERNATIONAL EDUCATIONAL ORGANIZATION
No 107, Section 2, Minquan E Road, Zhongshan District, Taipei City 104
ⓒ +886 2 2592 6998
✉ hesswork@hess.com.tw
🖥 www.hess.com.tw/en

NUMBER OF TEACHERS: 600 native English speaking teachers in more than 150 branches throughout Taiwan. About 250 new teachers hired each year.
PREFERENCE OF NATIONALITY: American, Australian, British, Canadian, Irish, New Zealander and South African.
QUALIFICATIONS: Bachelor's degree (in any subject) plus desire to work with varied age groups and to experience Chinese culture. Those holding an Associate degree are welcome to apply provided they hold a TEFL/TESOL certificate as well.
CONDITIONS OF EMPLOYMENT: 1-year renewable contract. Three contract options are available to suit each teacher's preference. *20-hour Contract:* 20 hours a week guaranteed minimum. Teaching hours are generally between 1.30pm and 9pm, Monday to Friday and between 8.30am and 6.30pm on Saturdays. Students aged 5–16. Classes are 100 minutes. *20M Contract:* 20 hours a week guaranteed minimum. Teaching hours are generally between 8.30am and 9pm, Monday to Friday and between 8.30am and 6.30pm on Saturdays. Students are aged 2–16. *25-hour Contract:* Same as Contract *20M* except guaranteed minimum number of hours is 25 per week.
SALARY: NT$580 per hour (gross) starting salary. Tax rate is 18% for first six months then drops to 5%. A raise and bonus system is also part of the pay structure.
FACILITIES/SUPPORT: Airport pick-up and free hotel accommodation during initial 9-day training period. Full TEFL and curriculum training provided with four follow-up training sessions after 1, 3, 6 and 9 months. Assistance given to obtain work permits and accommodation. Application process should be started 3 months in advance to allow time to collect visa and work permit documents.
RECRUITMENT: Apply online through Hess website (www.hess.com.tw/en); 4 major new teacher intakes per year. Applications accepted all year round.
CONTACT: Amy Simpson, Applications and Interviews Consultant, English Human Resources Department (amy.simpson@hess.com.tw).

INTERNATIONAL AVENUE CONSULTING COMPANY

295 Wulhuan Rd, S, Taichung City 403

© +886 4 2285 5139

🖱 recruiting@iacc.com.tw

💻 www.iacc.com.tw

Recruitment agency with partner offices in Canada.

NUMBER OF TEACHERS: Dozens for elementary, high schools, private language schools and kindergartens in Tainan County, Taichung City, Chunghua County and Keelung City.

PREFERENCE OF NATIONALITY: Native English speakers: American, Canadian, British, Australian and New Zealander.

QUALIFICATIONS: Bachelor's degree. Government recognised provincial/state teaching certificate.

CONDITIONS OF EMPLOYMENT: 1-year contract, many starting July to September for the academic year. 25 teaching hours per week (approximately 40 working hours per week). IACC offers extra services for which a service charge is payable in instalments (which is refunded on successful completion of the contract).

SALARY: NT$60,000–NT$71,000 per month. Performance bonus.

FACILITIES/SUPPORT: Airport pick up and temporary accommodation for the first days. Assistance in finding an apartment and signing the contract with the landlord. Assistance in processing the work permit, ARC and NHI cards. Help in opening a bank account. Online teacher management system.

RECRUITMENT: All interviews carried out in Taiwan.

CONTACT: Apply online or email CV for the attention of Gina Wang.

JUMP START

6F, No. 3, Lane 334, JianGuo S Road, Sec 2, Taipei 106

© +886 2 2369 4128

🖱 eric@jumpstart.com.tw

💻 www.jumpstart.com.tw

English immersion schools for children aged 2–12.

QUALIFICATIONS: Native English speakers. Early childhood education/elementary teachers needed, e.g. with degree, preferably BEd (especially early childhood or elementary specialists). Must be enthusiastic and enjoy teaching children.

CONDITIONS OF EMPLOYMENT: To start mainly from 1 July or 1 September but other dates possible. Guaranteed hours with extra hours available. Planned curriculum with complete teaching materials. Teachers should arrive a week in advance in order to receive a 2–3 day induction.

SALARY: Depends on qualification and experience.

FACILITIES/SUPPORT: Work visa and health insurance. provided. Airport pick-up. Accommodation provided on arrival.

KANG NING ENGLISH SCHOOL

No. 39 Park Road, Jhudong310, Hsinchu County

© +886 3 594 3322

🖱 serenachutung@gmail.com

💻 www.kangning.com.tw

NUMBER OF TEACHERS: 13 native speaking teachers.

PREFERENCE OF NATIONALITY: British, American, Canadian, Australian, South African and New Zealander.

QUALIFICATIONS: Minimum bachelor's degree or two-year associate's degree (e.g. from US community colleges) and a TESOL certificate.

CONDITIONS OF EMPLOYMENT: 1-year contract. Working hours in the Language Department 1pm–9.30pm. Working hours in the Kindergarten Department 9am–6pm.

SALARY: NT$60,000–NT$68,000 per month depending on professional and academic qualifications, with end-of-contract bonus, perfect attendance bonus, performance bonus and additional overtime pay and bonus. Average tax rate 6%.

FACILITIES/SUPPORT: Free Chinese lessons, staff trips, free meals, health insurance, and paid national holidays/vacation. Fully formed curriculum cuts down on preparation time. Free accommodation for the first month during compulsory training and assistance to find suitable housing thereafter. KNES will also help teachers to obtain an Alien Residence Card (ARC) and open a bank account.

RECRUITMENT: Via website. Interview and reference check required. Occasional possibility of interviews in the US.

CONTACT: Serena Wen, Principal.

KNS LANGUAGE INSTITUTE

313 Wunxin Road, Gushan District, Kaohsiung

© +886 7550 5611

🖱 knsleon@yahoo.ca

💻 www.kns.com.tw

NUMBER OF TEACHERS: 45 teachers over 6 branches.

PREFERENCE OF NATIONALITY: North American, though all native English speakers accepted (American, Canadian, British, Irish, Australian, New Zealander and South African).

QUALIFICATIONS: At least a bachelor's degree. Teaching experience, TESOL certification or BEd preferred. Applicants must pass a medical examination.

CONDITIONS OF EMPLOYMENT: 1-year contracts. Full-time hours 2pm–9.10pm, Monday to Friday, in one location.

SALARY: NT$580 per hour plus end-of-contract bonus of NT$42,000.

FACILITIES/SUPPORT: Assistance with accommodation, no-interest loans, 2-week paid training, paid work permit fees, health insurance, 3-week summer vacation.

RECRUITMENT: Via internet, university placement offices, etc. Interviews in Taiwan or via Skype. Deadlines are 15 January for spring intake, 15 July for autumn start and 15 April for summer. Teachers must arrive at least 2 weeks early for training and set-up.

CONTACT: Leon Ranger, Recruitment Administrator.

KOJEN ELS

10F-2, No. 200, Roosevelt Road, Sec. 4, Taipei

📞 +886 2 8663 8287

✉ luisarecruit@hibox.hinet.net

💻 www.kojenenglish.com

NUMBER OF TEACHERS: Around 300 for 21 schools in Taipei plus 4 in Kaohsiung and 2 in Taichung.

PREFERENCE OF NATIONALITY: American, Canadian, British, Irish, Australian, New Zealander and South African.

QUALIFICATIONS: Minimum bachelor's degree. ESL experience and/or TESOL/TEFL certificate will increase chance of employment.

CONDITIONS OF EMPLOYMENT: 1-year contracts. Afternoon, evening and Saturday work. Pupils range in age from 4 to 13 in the children's department.

SALARY: Starting wage NT$580–NT$590 per hour. Bonuses paid at end of contract, calculated according to number of hours taught for hourly teachers.

FACILITIES/SUPPORT: 1 week free accommodation in shared apartments. Training provided. National health and labour insurance provided

RECRUITMENT: Direct application/walk-ins. Local interviews compulsory for some applicants. Applicants may be asked to teach a sample lesson. The original university degree certificate must be brought to Taiwan.

CONTACT: Luisa Sia, Recruiter/Consultant.

MICHAEL'S EFL SCHOOL

261 Tong-Nan Street, Hsin-Chu City

✉ michaelenglishschool@hotmail.com

💻 http://dl.dropbox.com/u/2560400/MES/Michaels_
English_School/Welcome.html

A small privately owned school managed by a Brit and his Taiwanese wife since 1985.

NUMBER OF TEACHERS: 3 Native English speakers.

QUALIFICATIONS: Native English speakers with recognised university degree. Teaching/coaching experience/EFL qualifications an advantage. References required. A genuine interest in teaching is essential. (Ideal for candidates considering teaching as a career.)

CONDITIONS OF EMPLOYMENT: Minimum 1-year contract. Afternoon and evening work only. Student-centred classes for 7–17 year olds with average class size 7–10 pupils. School aims to offer parents a family-focused approach to education in contrast to the franchise schools.

SALARY: NT$600 per teaching hour.

FACILITIES/SUPPORT: One month (paid) induction course. 10 days' paid holidays, 10 days unpaid. Gratuity fund. Free airport pick up. Assistance finding accommodation. Work visa, national healthcare, ARC, all available through school.

RECRUITMENT: Via UK education newspapers and the internet. In the first instance send dates of availability and photo plus CV. interview with Michael Weatherley (School Owner) by Skype or in person.

CONTACT: Michael Weatherley, Proprietor.

REACH TO TEACH

1606 80th Avenue, Algona, Iowa 50511, USA. Also #319 Minsheng Road, Taipei, Taiwan

📞 +1 201 467 4612

✉ info@reachtoteachrecruiting.com

💻 www.ReachToTeachRecruiting.com/teach-english-in-taiwan.htm

For contacts in other countries, see entry at beginning of Asia chapter.

NUMBER OF TEACHERS: 150+.

PREFERENCE OF NATIONALITY: American, Canadian, British, Irish, Australian, New Zealander and South African.

QUALIFICATIONS: Positive, enthusiastic, dedicated and flexible attitude are the most important qualifications. Teaching experience and/or a 120-hour in-class TEFL qualification will often lead to a higher salary or more job placement options. A TEFL certificate is often a requirement.

CONDITIONS OF EMPLOYMENT: 1 year full-time. Schedules are generally either morning/afternoon (preschool) or afternoon/evening (elementary school). Preschool positions start twice a year (February and August) and applications are needed 3 months in advance. Elementary school positions can be applied for year round.

SALARY: Salaries are competitive with most elementary and preschools in Taiwan. Salaries vary depending on teaching experience, qualification, location and benefits. Salaries usually range between NT$55,000 and NT$70,000 per month.

FACILITIES/SUPPORT: Taiwan visa guidance and airport collection are provided plus teacher orientation/training (when available). Teachers have the option of continued support and contact with

Reach To Teach throughout their year-long placement. Agency hosts teacher social events and gatherings (mostly in Taipei).

RECRUITMENT: Applications submitted via website. In-depth interviews conducted over Skype, by phone or occasionally in person.

CONTACT: Carrie Kellenberger, Co-President (Carrie@ ReachToTeachRecruiting.com).

SHANE ENGLISH SCHOOL

6F-1, 41 Roosevelt Road, Section 2, Taipei

(C) +886 2 2351 7755 ext 116

steve.lambert@shane.com.tw

www.shane.com.tw

NUMBER OF TEACHERS: 180 in 60 language schools and 3 English immersion kindergartens.

PREFERENCE OF NATIONALITY: Must be citizen of native English-speaking country.

QUALIFICATIONS: TEFL/CELTA/PGCE (dependent on position applied for).

CONDITIONS OF EMPLOYMENT: 1-year renewable contracts. Guaranteed salaries. 5 days per week schedule.

SALARY: NT$42,400–$65,000 per month depending on position, location and experience. Contract completion bonus also paid.

FACILITIES/SUPPORT: Up-to-date facilities and teaching resources. Work permits, assistance with accommodation, and comprehensive initial and ongoing training provided.

RECRUITMENT: Applicants can apply directly to arrange face-to-face or Skype interview. Saxoncourt in the UK (www.saxoncourt. net) also recruits for Shane Taiwan.

CONTACT: Steve Lambert, Academic Director.

THAILAND

Following a period of political and civil unrest in 2010, the situation in Thailand is once again generally calm and foreign teachers will be warmly welcomed. The same advice applies here as anywhere, that visitors should avoid demonstrations, specifically by anti-government ('Red Shirt') protestors which, even at the height of the crisis, was easy to do since they congregated in specific areas. Prospective teachers can keep abreast of the situation by checking the UK government's advice on http://ukinthailand.fco.gov.uk/en.

The English teaching scene is flourishing, especially in schools that teach English to children. For several years the government has been making efforts to extend the instruction of English in state schools, by introducing 'EP' (English Programme), a bilingual stream within Thai state schools which involves the teaching of English and other subjects, preferably by native speaker teachers willing to accept a modest wage.

A knowledge of English is eagerly sought by most urban young people and, in the context of Thailand, 'urban' is almost synonymous with 'Bangkok' which is more than 20 times larger than its nearest rival Nonthaburi. The *Bangkok Post* is a much less fruitful source of vacancies than Thai-specific websites such as www.teachingthailand.com and www.ajarn.com described below. The latter is a treasure trove of teaching information, contact details and job advertisements.

In its aim to improve the quality of English teaching in Thailand and to ensure that 'fake' teachers cannot be so easily accepted into the expat community, the government has tightened up the visa regulations and issuance of teachers' licences, which might provide an incentive for more people to consider joining one of the many volunteer teaching schemes that operate throughout the country.

PROSPECTS FOR TEACHERS

Only a small percentage of recruitment takes place outside Thailand. The major schools use foreign recruitment agencies and the internet to make contact with potential teachers, but most organisations depend on finding native-speaker teachers locally, including Thai universities and teachers' colleges, as well as private business colleges which all have EFL departments. Hundreds of foreigners graduate from one of the many

TEFL training courses offered in Thailand (see Directory of Training Courses) and many of them have links with local schools. One of the most active is See TEFL (Siam Educational Experience) (www.seetefl.com) which guarantees employment if job-seekers follow nine steps.

Thailand also appeals to English speakers who would like a career break and find that teaching is the best job going. **Ed Reinert** worked as a salesman for 25 years before becoming a teacher in Thailand; **Carlos Vega** was a computer technician who thinks that his teaching job is the best he can get in Thailand, '*there is nothing else you can do here but be a teacher, even if you are not a teacher*'. Whereas few language companies openly impose an upper age limit, some age discrimination does regrettably take place, especially with companies that specialise in the teenage market (a significant sector in summers).

Thais are exuberant and fun-loving people and their ideas about education reflect this. They seem to value fun and games (*sanuk*) above grammar, and an outgoing personality above a teaching certificate, although this attitude may be changing. Of course, there is already a nucleus of professional EFL teachers working at the most prestigious institutes in Bangkok. Many international and Thai bilingual schools look for individuals who can teach art, maths and science through the medium of English. Originally set up as teacher training colleges, there are about 40 Rajabhat Universities around Thailand which are autonomous and hire their own English teachers. Some schools and language institutes may be more keen to hire women on the assumption that they are less likely to become engrossed by the seamier side of Thailand's night life. However, all teachers now have to pay for a criminal background check, so this gender bias may be less relevant.

One thing to consider is that Thai salaries have not really increased in the last few years, even though the government wants to attract more professional teachers. This is something of a sticking point, and teachers who want to make a good living in Asia would be better off looking at Korea or Taiwan. However, living costs are still fairly low in Thailand (Bangkok and tourist resorts excepted) and many teachers have such an exciting time that they don't give a thought to savings, or indeed to coming home.

FINDING A JOB

IN ADVANCE

Among the many teacher placement agencies attempting to place suitably qualified candidates in schools throughout Thailand, try the following:

AYC Intercultural Programs Thailand, GOT Building, 9/197, 7th floor, Ratchadaphisek soi 29, 10900 Chatuchak, Bangkok (+66 2 556 1533; h_r@aycthailand.com; www.aycthailand.com). Native English speakers with a bachelor's degree are recruited for 80 schools in Thailand, and also for summer language camps.

BFITS (Bright Future International Training & Services), Suite 401–2, Chao Phraya Tower, 89 Soi Wat Suan Plu, New Road, Bangrak, Bangkok 10500 (+66 2 630 6622/3/4; hr@bfitsthailand.com; www.bfitsthailand.com). BFITS is an agency that runs educational programmes in both private and public schools, rather than a teacher recruiter.

JP Education (Thailand) (www.JPTEACHERS.com). JP Education's tagline is 'Your Gateway to Teaching in Thailand' and the company invites online applications. Sister company is TeachTeflThailand (www.teachteeflthailand.com).

Teach to Travel, Bangkok (+66 85 998 5900; teachtotravel@gmail.com; www.teach-to-travel.com). This Thai company recruits paid teachers, normally with a degree and a TEFL certificate, and volunteers. Placements to teach children are made in schools in central and northern Thailand and pay about 30,000 baht per month for 12 months. Guidance is given on obtaining a non-immigrant visa and most of the schools provide or assist with accommodation.

TLS Language School, 48/9 Ramkhamhaeng Road 60/3 Ramkhamhaeng Road, Bangkapi, Bangkok 10240 (+66 2 735 0956; tewiaeiou@hotmail.com; www.tlslanguageschool.com). Licensed teaching agency that either employs about 40 teachers directly or places them in educational establishments. Assistance is given with work permit applications. TLS has satellite offices in Nonthaburi and Pattaya. The company also offers cultural courses such as the 20-hour course that is a requirement for obtaining a teacher's licence, and also a 200-hour Thai language and culture course that facilitates another long-stay visa, the ED (Educational) Visa.

Training Consultant Center (TCC), Bangkok (+66 84 159 0088 or +66 83 704 3854; training_tcc@ yahoo.com). Part-time and full-time teachers recruited for 10-month contracts, for example in Phaya Thai area.

London-based exchange travel companies such as IST Plus (see entry) and Global Nomadic (www. globalnomadic.com) arrange paid teaching jobs in Thailand but charge an administrative fee for their services. Global Nomadic's programme involves a two-week TEFL training course in Singburi in northern Thailand and job placement package costing €750 plus a placement fee of £295.

The British Council (www.britishcouncil.org/en/thailand) stipulates that it will consider only candidates who have a degree and at least 200 hours post-CELTA experience teaching EFL to kids (7–11) and/or teens (12–16). The downside is that stricter regulations have been enforced with regard to the recruitment of foreign teachers. If you have a degree you should be able to find work, particularly as schools have had difficulty attracting foreign teachers because of the low wages and red tape issues. Certified teachers will fare even better.

The Anglo-Pacific (Asia) Consultancy (Suite 32, Nevilles Court, Dollis Hill Lane, London NW2 6HG; +44 20 8452 7836) is an educational consultancy which concentrates on recruiting teachers for schools, colleges and universities in Thailand as well as other Asian countries. Teachers are placed every month by APA, which welcomes graduates with a CELTA or Trinity certificate but also tries to place people with any TEFL background and/or appropriate personalities as long as they have a university degree. Their recruits are given briefing notes on their country of destination and a follow-up visit in their schools if possible. Recruits are guaranteed a salary, regardless of timetable fluctuations, something which can be incredibly valuable when schools and institutes promise to pay 35,000 baht for 28 teachings hours, which then fail to materialise.

One of the best all-round sources of information about teaching in Thailand with an emphasis on Bangkok and for inside information on the main hiring companies is the website www.ajarn.com – *Ajarn* is the Thai word for teachers – with stories and tips and current job vacancies posted on www.AjarnJobspace. com. The site is run and constantly updated by a teacher, Philip Williams, who has been in Thailand for many years. Various online recruitment sites such as www.totalesl.com carry current vacancies in Bangkok and beyond. It belongs to the Icon Group Thailand (IGT) of TEFL/TESOL websites providing educational resources and information to teachers, schools and students around the world with a special focus on Asia and the Middle East.

DAWN WILKINSON

In 2010, Dawn Wilkinson taught at St Joseph's Convent School in Silom, Bangkok, which she found through the BFITS agency advert on www. ajarn.com.

Although it wasn't my favourite part of Thailand, I had made a few friends in Bangkok, so thought this would be the best place to live and look for work. I was surprised to discover how low teaching wages were in comparison to Vietnam; Thailand is so much more developed as a country (and living costs are much higher), but teaching wages far from reflect this - something which is complained about regularly on internet forums. There seemed to be hundreds of teaching jobs available in Bangkok. I only really looked at www.ajarn.com and, although I didn't struggle to find a job, I knew I could have got a better and higher paid position if I had a TEFL qualification. After a successful Skype interview, I accepted a full-time position as a Prathom (Grade) 4 teacher in a prestigious Catholic girls' school in Silom. The agency arranged all my paperwork and visa, changing my tourist visa into a non-immigrant B visa which allows you to work while applying for your teaching licence (I wouldn't advise attempting to work in Thailand without the right visa - the authorities regularly catch and fine a lot of people).

Teaching in Thailand actually seemed much more formal and serious than Vietnam. The Convent School was particularly strict in their enforcement of the 'proper' conduct and dress code of the teachers (no trousers or skirts above the knee for women, no sleeveless tops, no tattoos on show, etc). I taught more than 250 eight- and nine-year-old girls, across eight classes, who were very sweet and affectionate, but who were also very hard to tell apart in their identical uniforms and French plaits (their self-styled nicknames, like Mint, Coffee and Bogey, gave the teachers a few giggles). I earned 35,000 baht (roughly £700) a month which, after 6,000 baht rent for a small studio apartment (I lived in a cheaper 'Thai' rather than an ex-pat area), plus bills (2,500 baht), as well as the cost of travelling to work on public transport and food, didn't leave as much as I had had in Saigon. However, on the plus side, during just five months at the school I had about seven weeks of paid holiday - which I thoroughly enjoyed on the Thai beaches and islands!

Melanie Drake is another young teacher who landed a job in Thailand with ease, this one with ECC (see entry), after gaining a TEFL qualification at TEFL International Corinth in Greece:

I was contacted by my soon-to-be boss after he had spotted my CV on tefl.com. After several emails and a simple visa application process I was in Thailand. Culture shock all round. My job required me to teach in businesses, poor government schools with cramped, sometimes a bit unsanitary conditions and also in a local private language school. My tiny, basic but clean apartment was free and came with the job. My wages were more than satisfactory to save some as life was incredibly cheap. I was pretty lonely before I got to meet the other members of staff. I was living alone quite far out from the school and was unable to communicate with anyone due to language difficulties. I was terrified of dogs and it turns out that my city, Ayutthaya, had some of the highest numbers of stray dogs in the country, and dealing with this was easily my biggest hurdle. Classes were also over-populated in the schools, sometimes 60 to a class - plus never air-conditioning. Students were for the most part quite lazy and more interested in the novelty of a foreigner than learning English. But, in hindsight, they showed more respect than the average British/American kid probably would.

VOLUNTEERING

For those who do not qualify for a salaried teaching position, the option of volunteering is attractive. Many worthy agencies operating internationally or at a grassroots level supply volunteer teachers to local schools who would otherwise not be exposed to native English speakers. To take one example, Gap Year Thailand (see entry) has a flourishing programme. The director, **David Lancaster**, explains: '*In our experience in Thailand, schools particularly want help from volunteers in spoken English. They usually have local teachers who are reasonably competent in grammar, vocabulary, spelling, teaching reading, etc, but value help from first-language speakers of English.*'

A charity founded by an American, Volunthai (www.volunthai.com) runs a teaching programme in rural north-eastern Thailand. Teachers' accommodation is provided as homestays, and the fee is a modest $325 for the first month and $150 thereafter. Small-scale charities such as this can respond flexibly to individual requirements. For example, not so long ago Volunthai was able to incorporate an American family with four children aged 3–13, all of whom participated in school activities. Looking back on their experiences of travelling around the world, the **Battye** family concluded that becoming part of a rural Thai village through Volunthai was the highlight of the year for them.

In rural parts of Thailand, schools cannot afford to pay salaries to foreign teachers, and local children have little or no exposure to fluent English. Yet the children who dream of going to university and into the professions need to achieve a certain standard of English. To meet this need various organisations such as Volunthai, Dragonfly and Thai-experience.org (see entries) enlist the help of volunteer teachers.

The Karen Hill Tribes Trust, York, UK (+44 1904 411891; www.karenhilltribes.org.uk) sends self-funding volunteers, including gap year students, to northwest Thailand to work in upland and hill communities of Karen tribespeople, sometimes as language teachers for two or five months (fees respectively £1,000 and £1,750).

Mundo Exchange Organization, 1435 NW 30th Ave, Portland, Oregon 97210, USA (+1 503 227 8442; www.mundoexchange.org). Volunteers teach English and computer skills to disadvantaged children and/or adults mainly in Isan province in north-eastern Thailand. Volunteers can be placed at short notice but 2–3 months' advance warning is preferred. The placement costs are €200 for 1 week, €750 for 12 weeks. Fees include orientation, pre-arranged accommodation, travel within the project and support before and during the stay.

Openmind Projects, 856/9 Moo. 15 Prajark Rd, Amphor Muang, 43000 Nong Khai (+66 42 413 678; www.openmindprojects.org). The fee range for this volunteer teacher programme is €380 for independent volunteers.

Starfish Ventures (0845 004 8010; www.starfishvolunteers.com). UK organisation that places volunteers of all nationalities in development projects in Surin, a town northeast of Bangkok and off the tourist trail. The current fee is from £400 for 2 weeks.

Travel to Teach, T2T, 47/1 Charunmuang Road, Soi 2, Muang Chiang Mai 50 000 (+66 84 365 4035; www.travel-to-teach.org). Thai-based organisation which provides volunteer teaching opportunities (among others) in various locations. Fees start at £490 for a month.

VESL (Volunteers For Educational Support & Learning), Derbyshire SK23 7TA, UK (0845 094 3727; www.vesl.org) is a charity with an expanding programme in Thailand. All applicants pay a programme fee ranging from £900 for summer placement to £1,350 for 3 months.

Volunteer Teacher Thailand, Khao Lak, Phang Nga 82190 (+66 845290616; www.volunteerteacherthailand.org). This charity continues the work of the now disbanded Tsunami Volunteer Centre. Registration fee of 3,000 baht and volunteers can join programme any Sunday.

Barbara Darragh also saw for herself how extremely popular English teachers are:

My first volunteer trip to Thailand was with an organisation set up after the tsunami. I then went to Chiang Mai for six months and after completing a month's TEFL course with SeeTEFL I offered my services to a local school. I loved working there and made many Thai friends who are always emailing me and asking me when I plan to return, which I hope to do again in September. It is very easy to find good cheap accommodation and the Thai people are so friendly. The children are a delight to teach and are so excited when you go into the school. The poorer schools where I volunteer would never normally be able to afford an 'English' English teacher. There is also plenty of paid work and I did have a private student and if I had wanted I could have had a lot more. As soon as people realise that you are an English teacher they want you to teach them or their family. I have never felt so rewarded in a job before and the fact that I want to go back every year and work for nothing must say something.

The Burma Education Partnership (www.burmaeducationpartnership.org) is a specialist British organisation involved with teacher training close to the Burmese border, in order to support education in refugee communities which have been affected by war, hardship and oppression. Volunteers can also work with displaced Burmese through the Burma Volunteer Programme (see entry below).

ON THE SPOT IN BANGKOK

Any new arrival in Bangkok would be well advised to spend a week getting his or her bearings and asking foreigners living in the city for inside information about possible employers. Many people say that the teaching scene has become somewhat exploitative and life in the city so unpleasant that it is better to leave Bangkok as quickly as you can.

For those who feel strong enough to survive in Bangkok, language schools are very easy to locate, to approach on spec. As a long-term traveller, **Mark Wiens** claims not to make lots of cash, but he has discovered ways to make enough money to live overseas, partly by blogging at http://migrationology.com, and one of the strings to his bow is English teaching. While he was in Bangkok he noticed a billboard for English courses at the Wall Street Institute and simply went into the school, and had a short friendly meeting with the human resources manager who just wanted to confirm that he would be someone that would respect and be patient with the students (though he did have a four-week TESOL certificate too).

My number one task was to elicit correct English from the students. The students studied the grammar using a computer programme and it was my job to confirm their comprehension of what they learned. I worked from 11am until 8pm, five days per week in a very nice air-conditioned facility located in a shopping centre. The other teachers were a cool group of recent university graduates who enjoyed other cultures and experiencing new things. The low point was having to teach the same material day after day. Like any job it became too much of a routine and I did get bored.

The best place to start is around Siam Square where numerous schools and the British Council are located. The Council has a list of private and public universities, institutes, teachers' colleges and international schools throughout the country which have English departments and therefore possible openings for a native English speaker, but most people rely on the *Yellow Pages*, which include dozens of language school addresses. Note that the Thai school year ends in mid-March and restarts the second week of May.

The English language daily newspaper, the *Bangkok Post*, is an excellent source of job vacancies, especially the site www.JobJob.co.th/en, which is supported by the *Bangkok Post* and *Post Today*. Craigslist (http://bangkok.craigslist.co.th/edu) serves Bangkok and publishes Situations Vacant.

DILYS EWART

Dilys Ewart discovered that the divide between voluntary and paid teaching is not absolute when she went as an unqualified volunteer to Thailand through Gap Year Thailand. Within two months Dilys had had three job offers for paid employment as a teacher.

During my introduction week in Thailand, we were shown many different aspects of the Thai culture. We were introduced to Thai food, Thai language, and Thai schools. On our fourth day in Thailand we went to a nursery school based in Bang Saen; there were eight classes in the school with 15-20 students in each class. When we arrived we were given ideas and examples to make a lesson plan for a class. I had only ever done one lesson plan before and it was for a different subject. After an hour of preparation time I was given a classroom of 16 students for 45 minutes. There were 3 assistant teachers there to help with the translation for the students. I got the students to play English games and write letters from the alphabet. At the end of the day I was invited into the Director's office and was offered a job as an English teacher, with a contract for 1 year; she told me how much she was willing to pay me and also discussed accommodation. As I was going to my placement as a volunteer teacher a few days later I declined her offer.

In my volunteer placement, during lunch breaks I helped a 6th year girl for an English speaking competition which she was entering. When competition day came I went along with her for support and last minute preparation. While she was being judged I was sitting outside on a bench when I was approached by a Thai teacher from another school. She asked what I was doing here in Thailand and where I was teaching. Then she asked me directly if I was interested in a job at her school as an English teacher. Once again she said how much they were willing to pay and said they would supply accommodation and some meals, with a six-month contract. I was very surprised, as she hadn't even seen me teach a class. As I was only a couple of weeks into my placement I declined the offer, but they insisted in giving me a number to call if I changed my mind.

I taught as a volunteer at Suan Pa Kao Cha Ang School for two months, through Gap Year Thailand. In my last week at the school I was offered a job with a year's contract with accommodation and reasonable pay, but again I declined the offer as I had plans for travelling. I feel if I need a job in Thailand I would be able to go out and use one of my job offers if I want. What can I conclude from this experience? Well, firstly, that there is massive enthusiasm in Thailand for learning English; secondly, that the schools are very keen to have first-language speakers of English as teachers; and thirdly that is it obviously possible to start as an unqualified volunteer teacher of English and easily get offers of employment. I had thought I would go to Thailand and get some teaching experience but I never thought I would come home with three job offers - and one of the best memories of my life.

If the Siam Square schools are not short of teachers, which may be the case in the slack season, you will have to try schools further afield. Travelling around this city of nearly 10 million is so time-consuming and unpleasant that it is important to plot your interview strategy on a city map before making appointments. Also be sure to pick up a map of the air-conditioned bus routes, particularly if you are contemplating a job which involves travelling to different premises.

It may not be necessary to do much research to discover the schools with vacancies. Many of the so-called back street language schools (more likely to be on a main street, above a shop or restaurant) look to the cheap hotels of Banglamphu, the favourite haunt of Western travellers in the northwest of Bangkok. There is such a high turnover of staff at many schools that there are bound to be vacancies somewhere for a new arrival who takes the trouble to present a professional image and can show a convincing CV supported with diplomas/certificates. As usual, it may be necessary to start with part-time and occasional work with several employers, aiming to build up 20–30 hours in the same area to minimise travelling in the appalling traffic.

The teaching of children is an expanding area; if you don't want to teach the alphabet, don't accept pupils under the age of 5. On the strength of her claim that she had experience of 'working with children', **Alison Eglinton** was soon earning a reasonable wage (and she suggests that anyone teaching young children should master at least one word of Thai: *hong nam*, which means toilet).

Ajarn (teachers) are respected in Thailand and are expected to look respectable. As well as dressing smartly for an interview, try to maintain a reserve in your manner while still projecting a relaxed and easy-going image. Too many gesticulations and guffawing are considered impolite and immature and will not earn you the respect of Thai people. When visiting a school, wear your posh clothes and carry CVs and passport photos to clip onto the application forms; otherwise you'll be asked to come back with the correct documents. Don't be surprised if the application form asks some weird questions, such as asking you to give the name, age and profession of every member of your family. You won't be hired on the spot but may well be contacted by phone within a day or two. Everyone who has ever had anything to do with teaching English in Thailand emphasises the need to dress smartly, as **Bruce Lawson** describes:

> The Thais like their pet farangs (i.e. foreign teachers) to look as much like currency dealers as possible. I bought a suit in Bangkok for £50 especially for the job hunt. Men should take out all earrings and wear a tie, thus risking asphyxiation in the heat and humidity of the hot season. Women should wear a decent skirt, not trousers.

Appropriate dress was also a problem for **Susannah Kerr** who had been told by her sending agency (i-to-i. com) that T-shirts and flip flops would be appropriate. But this was not the case at her school in Nakhon Nayok (pop. 25,000), and she was promptly taken on a compulsory shopping expedition and obliged to spend money on smarter clothes which she didn't care for.

> The busiest season for English schools is mid-March to mid-May during the school holidays, when many secondary school and university students take extra tuition in English. This coincides with the hot season. Vacancies continue to be advertised through June, July and August. The next best time to look for teaching work in private schools is October, while the quietest time is January/February.

ON THE SPOT IN CHIANG MAI

According to **Annette Kunigagon** who has made her home in Chiang Mai and is something of a resident expert in teaching in her adopted town, far more people have been coming to Chiang Mai to look for work than was the case a few years ago, since no one wants to live in Bangkok. She co-owns the Eagle Guesthouse at 16 Chang Moi Gao Road, Soi 3 (www.eaglehouse.com). She even organises unpaid teaching work as part of her Helping Hands Social Projects scheme (see her website).

Teaching opportunities crop up in branches of the big companies such as ECC and AUA and in academic institutes. There are lots of bilingual programmes at EP schools. Some of these schools are Anubaan Chiang Mai School, Wattano Payap School, Waree School and Fatih School. When approaching the bilingual schools, seek out the director for the 'bilingual' section of the schools. Teachers are recruited for all levels from nursery school to kindergarten, primary to secondary, though usually a master's degree in education or a teaching degree will be required. When applying for jobs, it is best to visit the schools directly as they don't have time or the aptitude to answer endless emails. Most schools do now have websites, though they are not always professional or helpful.

There are five international schools which employ English teachers, though most are recruited abroad e.g. at international teachers' fairs such as those sponsored by the thorough and professional Search Associates (www.search-associates.com) rather than locally. Other jobs are available in the school holidays at summer and weekend camps held at resort hotels or at Chiang Mai's international schools and attended by rich children from Bangkok and other parts of Thailand. Getting in to these and the summer camps run by the British Council and YMCA is by word of mouth, friends or advertisements. Annette's advice is to be brazen, knock on doors, try hotels, shops catering to tourists, companies which export or have to deal with foreigners, pubs, restaurants, computer shops, large shops in the Night Bazaar area, etc.

Many private language schools can be found in the vicinity of Chiang Mai University and also in the area near the prestigious Thai secondary schools such as Montfort, Paruethai, Regina, Dara and Prince Royal College. The expanding expat community in Chiang Mai comprises many nationalities, most of whom use English as their second language and want to improve their skills.

ON THE SPOT IN THE PROVINCES

The number of teaching opportunities outside Bangkok has escalated; however, not many foreigners show an interest since the pay is much less than in Bangkok. The estimated four-fifths of teachers who are single males enjoying the nightlife in Bangkok are unwilling to move to a less exciting country town.

Competition for work is almost non-existent in lesser known cities such as Nakhon Sawan, Khon Kaen, Udon Thani, Ubon Ratchathani and Pathumthani. For a job in a university you will probably have to show a higher degree or teaching certificate. The best places are Hat Yai and Songkhla. Hotels are always worth asking, since many hotel workers are very keen to improve their English. If you find a place which suits and you decide to stay for a while, ask the family who run your guesthouse about local teaching opportunities. Sometimes the happiest and most memorable experiences take place away from the cities and the tourist resorts. **Brian Savage** returned to England after a second long stint of teaching in Thailand and describes one of the highlights for him:

My most rewarding experience was my week teaching English conversation in a rural high school in Loei province in northeast Thailand. These children had rarely seen and had certainly never spoken to a farang (foreigner in Thai) before. My work during that week and a subsequent second visit was really appreciated by the pupils. The first visit came about after I was introduced to a teacher at the Chiang Mai school where I was teaching. If travellers get away from Bangkok and the resorts, they too can have experiences such as this, especially in the friendly towns of the north and northeast. A little voluntary teaching can really boost the confidence of students who are usually too poor to pay to study with native speakers.

REGULATIONS

The goal posts keep shifting on the question of visas, but enforcement is far stricter than it used to be. The preferred alternative for people who have already found a job is to apply for a non-immigrant B visa from any Thai Embassy. For this you will be asked to provide a copy of your degree certificate (now essential), various documents from your prospective employer in Thailand such as a contract of employment, and police clearance. With this visa, the applicant can stay in Thailand for no longer than 90 days unless his or her employer obtains a teacher's licence for which you will need a bona fide four-year university degree in education or any degree plus a TEFL certificate. A recent added requirement is that applicants must attend a 20-hour course with the unwieldy name 'Training Program for Foreign Teachers on Thai Culture and Teacher Professional Code of Ethics' which will cost between 4,000 and 8,000 baht. According to some, this is a means by which the government can add all teachers to a database in order to be able to check the legitimacy of work permit applications.

There may be exceptions to these strict requirements. For example **Nana Tosuwan**, Manager of the BR Language School (see entry), says that the small temple schools with which they work can submit requests to the education department for British, North American and Antipodean teachers to be granted a work permit just with a TEFL certificate. According to Nana (June 2012):

> *By law, teachers must have a degree to get a teacher license first and then the work permit. To apply for the teacher license, teachers must take the culture course from the University in Bangkok for a year and then pass the examination and apply for the visa which takes two to three months. Altogether it will take up to a year and a half before new teachers are able to teach in Thailand, which is not possible. As a language school, we have got an exemption from the Private Education department of Thailand for our teachers who have a degree to apply for the work permit without a teacher license.*
>
> *Many Europeans can travel to Thailand and get a visa at the airport because they have a visa exemption. So it is not always necessary to apply for a tourist visa or non-immigrant B before entry. After one month they can travel to a neighbouring country to get a two-month extension of the tourist visa. After they have got the approval from the education department and the labour department to apply for a work permit approved by the Mayor of the province, they can then apply for a Non-Immigrant B visa. It looks very complicated but it is possible to do it. The other option, if teachers do not mind, is that we can give our teachers the documents to apply for an education visa to learn Thai language and culture; with this visa our teachers can stay in Thailand for one year without a problem.*

To upgrade a tourist visa to a Non-Immigrant B you must have a guaranteed job, the correct paperwork, patience and 2,000 baht for the fee. It is usually easier to apply for the Non-Immigrant B at a Thai embassy in another country. In this case the applicant must stay overnight and pick up the visa the next day. Most people take the overnight bus from Bangkok and arrive at whichever border town they're going to early the next morning which makes the whole trip take at least three days. The visa forum of www.ajarn.com is a very good place to read about the evolving red tape situation and its practical (rather than theoretical) implications.

Once a work permit is granted, tax will be withdrawn at a very modest rate, sometimes as low as 2%. Thailand's national health scheme applies to visitors and so not all teachers worry about private insurance. Current Thai Labor Law demands that '*all people who work in The Kingdom of Thailand must be covered by The National Health Care Program, no exceptions, and regardless of nationality*'. Many employers may not even know this or keep it to themselves, in order not to have to pay any insurance fees. The monthly maximum an employer can charge you is 750 baht.

CONDITIONS OF WORK

In Thailand, the wages for *farang* teachers continue to be low. The basic hourly rate has risen only slightly over the past couple of years and is now in the 250–350 baht range (roughly £5–£7) while the monthly range is normally 30,000–35,000 baht in Bangkok, and on average 5,000 baht less in other cities.

Company work can pay more depending on location, but in-company contract work has greatly diminished. The norm is for schools to keep their staff on as part-time freelancers while giving them full-time hours; this is primarily to avoid taxes. Most language institutes pay weekly in cash, but beware of schools which turn pay day into a moveable feast.

The best remuneration is available from international schools such as the Bangkok Patana School (643 Soi Lasalle, Sukhumvit 105, Bangkok 10260; +66 2 398 0200; www.patana.ac.th). Note that the pay at international schools in Bangkok is as much as twice that paid by international schools elsewhere in the country. For a list of international schools in Thailand go to the website of the International Schools Association of Thailand (www.isat.or.th) which has an employment link.

Few employers help with accommodation which does not matter much since vacant apartments are not hard to locate and rental deposits not crippling as they are in Japan. Things are more relaxed in Chiang Mai where a group of people can rent a house or live Thai-style in a studio room with attached bathroom for very affordable rents.

Remember never to touch a student on the head, which is difficult if you are teaching children. In class a show of anger will soon lose the students' respect since the Thais value a 'cool heart' (*jai yen*) and go to great lengths to avoid displays of negative emotion. They are great adherents of a 'No worries' attitude, called '*mai pen lai*' in Thai. Calm, smiling and enthusiastic personalities make all the difference. **Carlos Vega** thinks that there are two types of pupils, '*Primary are nice and ready to learn every day. Secondary students mostly don't care and don't want to learn anything in a system that makes it impossible for any student to fail. No one really has to do any work in order to pass the grade, so why bother? Usually if the parents are involved with the school the student tends to do well.*'

LEISURE TIME

It has to be said that Bangkok may be an exciting and lively city but it is not beautiful. It has very few parks, bad traffic congestion and polluted air. There is also a great deal of what some might consider moral pollution, and there is a certain element of the teaching fraternity in Bangkok who are there primarily for the easy availability of sex in the notorious Patpong district (despite the AIDS crisis in Thailand). Thai Labor Law stipulates that '*any employees who comport themselves in a manner which would embarrass or cause serious damage to employers' reputation may be terminated immediately, by employer, with no legal recourse available to employee*'. This applies on AND off the clock. Many a *farang* man has been spotted in a 'night time establishment' and been fired the next day.

With the ratio of foreign men to women teachers at least six to one, many women (although in great demand as teachers) do not enjoy the atmosphere in the city and leave as quickly as they can. Fortunately for teachers earning a low wage, the more innocent pleasures of Thailand come cheap. **Felix Poon** wrote from Bangkok to say that the low cost of living makes even a low salary enough for a very comfortable lifestyle. You can eat a good street meal for about 45 baht and a beer is 35–65 baht in a supermarket (twice as much in bars). Even part-time teachers should be able to afford to travel round the country, visiting jungle attractions such as Kanchanaburi, where you can ride an elephant along the banks of the River Kwai, and islands such as Koh Samet, Koh Samui and Koh Phangan where life is slow and the beaches are wonderful. Try to learn a little Thai as **Bruce Lawson** did after getting fried battered banana when he thought he had ordered garlic chicken. He recommends organising word-swaps with students, which will also illustrate to them that they are not the only ones who have to struggle with alien sounds. Wherever you end up teaching you are sure to discover that Thailand is famously welcoming.

LIST OF EMPLOYERS

THE AMERICAN ENGLISH LANGUAGE SCHOOL

29/492 Moo 2, Ransit Klong 3, Klong Sahm, A.
Klongluang, Pathumthani 12120

℃ +66 89 922 4126

✎ americanenglishthailand@gmail.com

▣ www.americanenglishthailand.com

NUMBER OF TEACHERS: 30.

PREFERENCE OF NATIONALITY: American (but all nationalities welcome).

QUALIFICATIONS: At least a bachelor's degree from an internationally accredited academic institution. BEd (or higher) degree holders will receive preference.

CONDITIONS OF EMPLOYMENT: 1-year contract. To teach Monday to Friday, 8am–4pm.

SALARY: Starts at 35,000 baht per month with no real ceiling. The AELS sends teachers to many levels of schools where top earnings are 45,000 baht and up. Taxes are 1,000–2,000 baht per month and 750 baht per month for health care coverage and social security (compulsory under Thai law).

FACILITIES/SUPPORT: Company helps teachers find a place that has a good location, for a good rent, with good amenities, and takes them to all the necessary offices, every step of the way, to get the necessary papers. Teachers pay for Visa and Work Permit upfront, but will be reimbursed by AELS on completion of contract.

RECRUITMENT: By personal interviews and teaching demonstrations, followed by credential checks. Company rarely hires directly from overseas: three videoconferencing interviews have led to only one hire so far.

CONTACT: Jason Alavi, Owner.

AMERICAN UNIVERSITY ALUMNI LANGUAGE CENTER

Bangkok: 179 Rajdamri Road, Lumpini, Patumwan, Bangkok 10330

℃ +66 2 650 5040

✎ branches@auathailand.org

▣ www.auathailand.org

Chiang Mai branch: AUA, 73 Rajadamnern Road, Amphur Muang, Chiang Mai 50200

℃ +66 53 278407

✎ chiangmai@auathailand.org

17 branches throughout Thailand (5 in Bangkok, 12 provincial).

NUMBER OF TEACHERS: About 200 in total: 50–60 at main branch, up to 20 at other branches. Offers SIT TEFL certificate course in Bangkok and Chiang Mai.

PREFERENCE OF NATIONALITY: American, Canadian, British, Australian and New Zealander.

QUALIFICATIONS: Bachelor's degree and CELTA (or equivalent).

CONDITIONS OF EMPLOYMENT: 1-year commitment preferred. 4–6 hours teaching daily (considered to be full-time). Teaching year consists of 7 6-week terms separated by 1 free week (unpaid). Courses aimed at professionals aged 18–35.

SALARY: Starting rate is 330 baht+ per hour depending on experience/qualifications. Annual bonus paid after completion of Professional Development Program, free health insurance, work permit obtained but paid for by the teacher for first 2 years.

FACILITIES/SUPPORT: Participation in pre-service training session (32 hours) is preferred before teaching hours are assigned. Mentoring programme for new teachers, 15,000 titles in resource library.

RECRUITMENT: Adverts in the *Bangkok Post*, the internet and word of mouth. Apply online.

CONTACT: Stuart McMullan (Bangkok), Mike White (Provinces).

BELL EDUCATIONAL TRUST

UK: Hillscross, Red Cross Lane, Cambridge CB2 0QU

Thailand: 18th Floor, Wave Place, 55 Wireless Road, Lumpini, Pathumwan, Bangkok 10330

℃ +66 2 655 4901

✎ jobs.thailand@bell-worldwide.com

▣ www.bell-worldwide.com/locations/thailand

▣ www.bell-worldwide.com/jobs

NUMBER OF TEACHERS: 30+ for 3 independent language centres in Bangkok.

PREFERENCE OF NATIONALITY: None, but must be native English speaker.

QUALIFICATIONS: Bachelor's degree and CELTA (better still PGCE and/or DELTA). Experience of and/or interest in teaching English to young learners preferred. Candidates should be dependable and culturally sensitive team players.

CONDITIONS OF EMPLOYMENT: 1/2-year renewable contracts. Up to 21 contact hours per week (Monday to Friday or Tuesday to Saturday). Much of the work is with young learners.

SALARY: Gross salary 48,000 baht –58,000 baht per month (for degree and CELTA) or 54,000 baht –58,000 baht (PGCE).

FACILITIES/SUPPORT: Flight for teachers recruited outside Thailand. Hotel accommodation on arrival. Assistance in finding suitable accommodation. A loan for accommodation is made available, repayable over initial 3 months of employment. Work permit arranged. End of contract gratuity. 8 weeks' paid holiday per year plus public holidays. Health and medical insurance cover provided. Commitment to in-service training and professional development.

RECRUITMENT: Bell website (www.bell-worldwide.com/jobs), internet, newspapers, telephone and face-to-face interviews.

BRIGHT FUTURE INTERNATIONAL TRAINING & SERVICES (BFITS)

Units 401, 4th Floor, Chao Phraya Tower, 89 Soi Wat Suanplu, Bangrak, Bangkok 10500

✆ +66 2 630 6622 24
🖂 info@bfitsthailand.com/hr@bfitsthailand.com
🖥 www.bfitsthailand.com

NUMBER OF TEACHERS: 120+ for about a dozen full curriculum partner schools.

PREFERENCE OF NATIONALITY: American, Canadian, British, Australian and South African. Primarily looking for native English speakers; non-native English speakers must provide TOEFL/TOEIC score.

QUALIFICATIONS: Bachelor's and TEFL certification. TEFL certification is not required for licensed teachers, teachers with degrees in education or English, or for teachers teaching content subjects such as mathematics.

CONDITIONS OF EMPLOYMENT: 1 year. 20–25 teaching hours per week for English conversation.

SALARY: 33,000 baht –35,000 baht per month for English Conversation Teachers; 38,000 baht for English Programme (Content) Teachers. All positions come with yearly bonuses. Thai taxes are deducted at a rate of approximately 1,300 baht per month.

FACILITIES/SUPPORT: Assistance given in locating accommodation and translating/negotiating lease, if needed. Teachers are given necessary documents with instructions on how to obtain a non-immigrant B visa plus 2 paid working days to travel to obtain it. BFITS takes care of all costs and processing of the work permit.

RECRUITMENT: Via TotalESL.com, TESall.com, ESLjobfeed.com and TeachOverseas.ca, partner sites of BFITS. Applications with CV, photo, degrees/certificates and professional references can be emailed with contact information. Date of availability (or relocation date to Thailand) must be specified. Interviews by Skype or in person.

BR LANGUAGE SCHOOL

73–75 Old Petchakaseam Road, Klongkrachang, Muang, Petchaburi 76000

🖂 br.language@hotmail.com

NUMBER OF TEACHERS: 26 native English speakers.

PREFERENCE OF NATIONALITY: None.

QUALIFICATIONS: No preferences, though school recommends that candidates take at least an introductory TEFL course e.g. with UK-TEFL (www.uk-tefl.com). BR School hopes to offer its own TEFL training in future.

CONDITIONS OF EMPLOYMENT: 1-year contract. 18–25 teaching hours a week.

SALARY: 20,000 baht –35,000 baht a month for full-time teacher, less 3% for taxes.

FACILITIES/SUPPORT: Assistance given to teachers to find cheap accommodation (e.g. US $30–$120 per month) and to obtain work permit if eligible. Internet access provided at school. Some schools provide free accommodation and/or free lunches. Meals in temple schools cost less than $1. Free or cheap internet access provided.

RECRUITMENT: Interviews not always necessary or can be conducted by phone. Written applications sometimes acceptable.

CONTACT: Noavarat Tosuwan (Nana), Manager.

BRITISH-AMERICAN

1730–1732 Ladprao Road (Opposite Chokchai 4 Market), Wangtonlang, Bangkok 10310

✆ +66 2 933 5635/6/7/8 mob +66 89 482 3577
🖂 british_american2000@hotmail.com
🖥 www.british-american.ac.th

NUMBER OF TEACHERS: About 25.

PREFERENCE OF NATIONALITY: Native English speakers.

QUALIFICATIONS: Enthusiasm and positive attitude are essential.

CONDITIONS OF EMPLOYMENT: Usually part-time, 4–6 teaching hours per day.

SALARY: Earnings usually approximately 30,000+ baht per month. Local rent for an apartment is approximately 3,000 baht monthly.

FACILITIES/SUPPORT: Provide details of recommended apartments. All the visa paperwork is done by the school, but the teacher pays for visa and out-of-pocket expenses.

RECRUITMENT: Advertising in national newspapers.

CONTACT: Jack Downes.

BURMA VOLUNTEER PROGRAM (BVP)

PO Box 114, Mae Sot, Tak 63110

🖂 recruitment@burmavolunteers.org,
    bvp@burmavolunteers.org
🖥 www.burmavolunteers.org

NUMBER OF TEACHERS: Volunteers accepted year round.

PREFERENCE OF NATIONALITY: None.

QUALIFICATIONS: Teaching and/or international development experience preferred, independent and hardworking with a genuine interest in Burma issues. Minimum age 21 years.

CONDITIONS OF EMPLOYMENT: 3-month minimum commitment. Teaching approximately 3 hours per day, 5 days per week.

SALARY: Accommodation and food are generally provided.

RECRUITMENT: Application, reference and phone interview.

CONTACT: Vanessa Miller, Programme Manager.

DRAGONFLY
1719 Mookamontri Soi 13, A. Meuang Nakhon Ratchasima 30000
dan@thai-dragonfly.com
www.thai-dragonfly.com

NUMBER OF VOLUNTEER PLACEMENTS PER YEAR: 50.

QUALIFICATIONS: Good working knowledge of English (or Thai!), flexibility and an open mind.

CONDITIONS OF WORK: 2–4 months from May/June/July or November. On most projects, volunteers teach 15–20 hours a week but are expected to be in school 5 full days a week.

SALARY: None. Volunteers pay a fee of 3,000 baht to join 5-day training and Thai culture course in Korat.

FACILITIES/SUPPORT: Orientation in Thai language and culture given. Homestay accommodation provided.

RECRUITMENT: Preliminary contacts online; application forms processed by email.

CONTACT: Dan Lockwood.

ECC (THAILAND)
Teacher Service Centre (English & Computer College), ITEC House, Ist Floor, 9 Rajdamri Road, Lumpini, Patumwan, Bangkok 10330
+66 2 655 3333
jobs@ecc.ac.th
www.eccthai.com

50 schools in Bangkok and in most major centres outside Bangkok (including Chiang Mai and Phuket). Largest private language school in Thailand.

NUMBER OF TEACHERS: Around 500 native English speakers (usually recruit 10–15 new teachers each month).

PREFERENCE OF NATIONALITY: None.

QUALIFICATIONS: Bachelor's degree plus TEFL certificate (CELTA, Trinity or equivalent).

CONDITIONS OF EMPLOYMENT: 100–120 hours per month (average 25–30 hours per week), 6 day week, mostly in evenings and weekends. BUPA medical insurance, end of contract bonus, location allowance in Bangkok (4,000 baht –6,000 baht per month). 5 days' paid holiday plus 13 statutory holidays.

SALARY: Depending on qualifications and experience 32,000 baht–38,000 baht per month in Bangkok, 20,000 baht–30,000 baht in the provinces.

FACILITIES/SUPPORT: Work permit and 1-year visa applied for after arrival. Assistance (non-financial) given with finding accommodation. Professional development with regular workshops, including a number of short courses which are free to ECC teachers: Teaching English to Young Learners and Teaching Business English. ECC offer the Cambridge CELTA course and an Introduction to TESOL course.

RECRUITMENT: Adverts on the internet and qualified walk-ins.

CONTACT: Garth Marshal, Teacher Service Centre (jobs@ecc.ac.th).

GAP YEAR THAILAND
1 Vernon Avenue, Rugby CV22 5HL, UK
+44 1788 552617
david@gapyearthailand.org.uk
www.gapyearthailand.org.uk

Professional education organisation whose key team members have a background in teacher education in universities in UK or in the Rajabhat universities (teacher training universities) in Thailand. The programme is approved and endorsed by the South East Asian Ministers of Education.

NUMBER OF PLACEMENTS PER YEAR: 20+ volunteers to work as assistant teachers, teaching English (particularly conversational English) in schools or universities.

QUALIFICATIONS: Minimum age 18, average age 20s. Must speak English as a first language. Teaching qualification not needed.

CONDITIONS OF EMPLOYMENT: Minimum 2 months up to 6+ months.

SALARY: None. Programme cost: £980 including accommodation, which can be homestay with family or in a teacher's house.

RECRUITMENT: Applications accepted throughout the year. Telephone interviews. Pre-departure briefing weekend with some TEFL training, and further training in the orientation programme on arrival.

CONTACT: Dr. David Lancaster, Chief Executive.

PROGRAMME DESCRIPTION: Teaching English, computer skills or vocational skills to disadvantaged children and/or adults in north-eastern Thailand (Isan province). Maintaining computers.

NUMBER OF PLACEMENTS PER YEAR: 80.

QUALIFICATIONS: Minimum age 18. Good command of English language. Computer trainers need computer skills, open mind and patience to deal with the different environment. No TEFL certificate needed as volunteers do not replace teachers but assist them, encouraging students to use their English language skills to speak, practise and motivate them to learn more.

CONDITIONS OF PLACEMENT: 1 week to 1 year; typically 2–3 months.

RECRUITMENT: Application can be made online. Volunteers can be placed at short notice but 2–3 months' advance warning preferred.

COST: €350 for 1–2 weeks, €450 for 3 weeks, €500 for 1 month, $1,380 for 24 weeks. Fees include orientation, pre-arranged accommodation, travels within the project, cultural outings and support before and during the stay.

CONTACT: Sabine Lindemann, Project Manager.

NUMBER OF TEACHERS: 140 full-time, 100 part-time.

PREFERENCE OF NATIONALITY: Native English speakers: American, Canadian, British, Irish, Australian, New Zealander and South African.

QUALIFICATIONS: Candidates must have at least 2 of the following: bachelor's degree, TESOL/TEFL/CELTA, experience.

CONDITIONS OF EMPLOYMENT: 1 year. Children's classes are on Saturday/Sunday 9am–6pm. Teachers work a 6-day week or 5 for corporate work.

SALARY: Guaranteed minimum 35,000 baht for full-time contract teachers; possibly more, depending on workload.

FACILITIES/SUPPORT: Try to point staff in the direction of suitable accommodation. Full support given in work permit/visa applications. BUPA medical insurance.

RECRUITMENT: Internet adverts on www.ajarn.com. Applications welcomed on above email address. Mostly local hires.

CONTACT: Fraser Morrell, Director of Studies (fraserm@inlingua bangkok.com).

NUMBER OF TEACHERS: 20–30 each year for two programmes, one for paid teachers in state schools, supported by the Overseas Education Group (www.overseasedu.com), and the other voluntary.

PREFERENCE OF NATIONALITY: None, although non-native speakers of English must have near-native proficiency in English.

QUALIFICATIONS: University degree in any field essential. TEFL training or experience is not essential but preferred. Maximum age 65.

CONDITIONS OF EMPLOYMENT: 5- or 10-month renewable contracts starting in either May or October, teaching 22 classes a week, which works out at a working week of 35–40 hours.

SALARY: Minimum salary 14,000–18,000 baht per month.

FACILITIES/SUPPORT: Free accommodation (usually on-campus), all-inclusive 7-day orientation in Bangkok on arrival including basic EFL training, accommodation, sight-seeing and airport transfer. IST Plus arrange school placement, visa and work permit, insurance and 24-hour emergency hotline.

RECRUITMENT: Deadlines for application are mid-March for May departure and mid-July for October departure. Teach in Thailand Programme fees from £850 for 5 months, £900 for 10 months. Teachers who complete 10 month contracts starting in May will have their one-way flight home paid for by the host school. All teachers who complete their contracts will receive a TEFL certificate.

CONTACT: Ralph Allemano, Director (rallemano@istplus.com).

A group of 4 English language schools in Thailand.

NUMBER OF TEACHERS: 35–40.

PREFERENCE OF NATIONALITY: Native English speakers: British (majority), Canadian, American, Australian, New Zealander.

QUALIFICATIONS: University degree (any subject) plus CELTA or 120-hour equivalent. Preference given to applicants with qualifications or experience teaching young learners, and/or with experience at summer camps or primary schools. Support and extensive materials are supplied.

CONDITIONS OF EMPLOYMENT: 1-year contracts. Contractual arrangement is 112 contact hours per month; preparation time is extra. Saturday and Sunday are working days. 2 consecutive days off a week.

SALARY: Approximately 34,000 baht per month depending on qualifications and experience. Yearly increment, paid holidays (13 days plus 13 statutory public holidays). End-of-contract bonus of 25,000 baht.

FACILITIES/SUPPORT: Assistance with accommodation. Basic private health insurance provided by school. Free Thai language lessons plus Thai cookery and boxing programme.

RECRUITMENT: Local and web adverts and UK recruitment agency. UK applicants should send CV and photo in the first instance to John Hudson (john.hudson@firstwayforward.com). Interviews are usually by Skype and phone.

SIAM COMPUTER & LANGUAGE INSTITUTE
471/19 Ratchawithi Road, Bangkok 10400
C +66 2 247 2345 ext 200/204
✉ bhudeb@siamcom.co.th or recruitment@siamcom.co.th
💻 www.siamcom.co.th/english_teach.php

NUMBER OF TEACHERS: 37 at 35 school locations in the greater Bangkok area and 49 at 38 external locations in the greater Bangkok area.

PREFERENCE OF NATIONALITY: Native English speakers.

QUALIFICATIONS: College degree required; CELTA or equivalent and experience preferred.

CONDITIONS OF EMPLOYMENT: 1-year contracts. Full-time internal teachers 6 days per week in air-conditioned facilities; 15 or fewer students per class. All ages. Full-time external teachers 5 days per week in Thai classrooms. 50 students per class from kindergarten to high school level.

SALARY: 30,000+ baht per month based on experience. Bonus plans for external teachers. Hourly rates for part-time internal and external teachers.

FACILITIES/SUPPORT: Assistance with finding local accommodation. 15 paid Thai vacation days per year, assistance in obtaining a teacher's licence, work permit and 1-year visa. Complete teacher

orientation and teacher training before starting in the classroom, with bimonthly teachers' meetings.

RECRUITMENT: Adverts in the *Bangkok Post* and on the worldwide web, and contacts with schools in Australia and the USA. Interviews in Bangkok required.

CONTACT: Mr. Bhudeb.

SPENCER INTERNATIONAL
1st Fl., Muangthai Phatra Complex, 252/193
Rachadapisek Rd., Bangkok 10320
C +66 293 2901
✉ stephen.l@spencer.co.th
💻 www.spencer.co.th

NUMBER OF TEACHERS: 60.

PREFERENCE OF NATIONALITY: None.

QUALIFICATIONS: Degree holders are preferred, but positions for non-degree holders are also available. Inexperienced and unqualified teachers have opportunities to undergo formal or in-house training through a staff development programme.

CONDITIONS OF EMPLOYMENT: 10-month contract. Usual hours 7:30am–3:30pm Monday to Friday. Evening and weekend work are offered as overtime.

SALARY: Starting salary 32,000 baht with increments after 3 months, 6 months and 1 year. Tax is deducted at source.

FACILITIES/SUPPORT: Spencer International provides TEFL and TESOL courses in Bangkok, accredited through Chichester College, UK. Assistance given with finding accommodation in the school vicinity to suit teacher's lifestyle. School takes care of all work permit procedures for teachers holding the appropriate qualifications.

RECRUITMENT: Via TESOL training programmes or the internet. Spencer International provides TEFL and TESOL courses in Bangkok, accredited through Chichester College, UK. Interviews can be conducted by email, Skype or telephone.

CONTACT: Stephen Louw, Academic Coordinator.

SUPER ENGLISH
38/1–2 Bandon Rd., Talad, Muang, Surat Thani 84000
C +66 77 213395
✉ teach@superenglishsurat.com
💻 www.superenglishsurat.com

NUMBER OF TEACHERS: 14.

PREFERENCE OF NATIONALITY: American.

QUALIFICATIONS: University degree essential. Must have the right attitude: a willingness to learn, be flexible about living in an Eastern culture, able to think creatively and be patient. Must enjoy working with children and have a sincere desire to teach them English and to have an impact on their lives.

CONDITIONS OF EMPLOYMENT: Standard 1-year contract. Schedules vary greatly but usually less than 25 hours per week (and hours above 25 are paid overtime rate of 300 baht). Some teachers work in the morning and have their afternoons off; others prefer late mornings and continuing through the early evening. Classes finish at 6.30pm.

SALARY: 250–300 baht per hour. Current average salary is around 28,500 baht per month less tax deductions of about 200 baht per month.

FACILITIES/SUPPORT: Shared, furnished house in an ideal location of Surat Thani is provided for teachers, who all have a private bedroom. Paperwork provided pre-arrival for a 3-month non-immigrant B visa. School will process that visa into a 1-year non-immigrant visa and will obtain a 1-year labour permit and 3-year teacher's licence.

RECRUITMENT: Adverts on www.eslcafe.com and directly via website. Interviews via Skype.

CONTACT: Peter C. Meltzer, Owner and Founder.

USIT

19/21 Aston Quay, Dublin 2, Ireland

 +353 1 602 1742

workandtravel@usit.ie

www.usit.ie/paid-teaching

PREFERENCE OF NATIONALITY: Native speakers of English from Ireland, UK, US, Canada, Australia, New Zealand or South Africa.

QUALIFICATIONS: Degree in any field required. Ages 21–45.

CONDITIONS OF EMPLOYMENT: Minimum 5 months, starting April or October. Teaching 4–6 hours per day. Placements mainly in Hat Yai in the south and Chiang Mai in the north.

COST: From €999. Salary paid of 30,000 Baht (€750) per month.

FACILITIES/SUPPORT: Schools will organise accommodation for the teachers, free of charge. Otherwise coordinator in Thailand will assist with finding accommodation and obtaining work permits.

RECRUITMENT: Interviews essential and can be held using Skype.

LATIN AMERICA

Spanning 75 degrees of latitude, the mammoth continent of South America together with the Caribbean islands and the eight countries of Central America, offer an eclectic range of teaching opportunities. With the important exception of Brazil where Portuguese is spoken, South American countries have a majority of Spanish speakers and, as in Spain itself, there is a great demand for English teaching, from dusty Mexican towns near the American border to Punta Arenas at the southern extremity of the continent, south of the Falkland Islands.

The countries of most interest to the travelling teacher are Chile, Argentina, Colombia, Ecuador, Venezuela, Brazil and Mexico. Certain patterns emerged during the research for the various editions of this book, though sweeping generalisations are of limited value and will not apply to all countries and all situations. After problems with inflation, most countries (apart from Venezuela) have brought the problem under control, which means that salaries do not lose their value as quickly as they used to. Although pay scales are sometimes quoted in US dollars, wages are almost always paid in the local currency.

Urban life in the big cities of Brazil, Argentina and Chile is more like that of Europe than of developing countries. In such cities, the greatest demand for English comes from big business, and because of the strong commercial links between the two American continents, the demand tends to be for American English, though an increasing number of British and Australian teachers are finding work in these countries.

Among the most important providers of the English language are Bi-National Centers and Cultural Centers, the American counterpart of the British Council. There are scores of these centres in Latin America, including nearly 40 IBEUs (Instituto Brasil-Estados Unidos) in Brazil alone including the sub-network. Many of these centres are engaged in the teaching of English, some on quite a large scale employing upwards of 20 teachers. While some want a commitment from teachers to stay for two years, others are happy to take someone on for shorter periods or part-time. While the English Language Fellow Program administered from Washington requires teachers with an MA in TESL from a US university, there may be local opportunities for others. A good point of contact is the relevant Regional English Language Officer (http://exchanges.state.gov/englishteaching/reg-el-officers.html).

Britain also has cultural representatives in several Latin American countries; the longest established Culturas Inglesas are in Argentina (founded 1927) plus Brazil, Chile, Mexico, Paraguay, Peru and Uruguay. Among them, these *Culturas* teach English to a quarter of a million students. Usually they require their teachers to have specialised ELT training and experience. Only a few recruit abroad so it is worth making local enquiries on arrival.

Several South American nations have a number of British or American-style bilingual schools and *colegios*. Although this book is not centrally concerned with English-medium schools, which are usually looking for teachers with a PGCE or full teacher accreditation, international schools in South America are mainly for local nationals (rather than expatriates) who want a bilingual Spanish-English education and have a very strong emphasis on English language teaching. Despite the prestige of these schools, some are willing to consider EFL teachers who have not done teacher training. For example, many of them accept school leavers participating in gap year projects.

Finally, there are private and commercial language institutes from International House (Argentina, Chile, Colombia, Costa Rica, Mexico and Uruguay) through to Berlitz (which is strongly represented in Latin America) to the cowboy operations where standards and wages will be extremely low. **David Hewitt**, a computer programmer from Yorkshire with no TEFL training or experience, was surprised not only to walk into a teaching job in Brazil but also to find himself giving lessons to the director of the school. In whatever kind of school you teach, or if you just give occasional private lessons to contacts, you will probably find the local people extremely friendly and eager to help. The ethnic diversity and Latin warmth encountered by foreign teachers and travellers throughout the continent usually more than compensate for low wages and (in the big cities) a high crime rate.

PROSPECTS FOR TEACHERS

In a land where baseball is a passion and US television enormously popular, American (and also Canadian) job-seekers have an advantage. The whole continent is culturally and economically oriented towards the USA. There is a decided preference among language learners for the American accent and for American teaching materials and course books, which explains why so many language institutes are called Lincoln and Jefferson. Business English is gaining ground throughout the region, particularly in Argentina, Chile, Venezuela, Colombia, Brazil and Mexico, and anyone with a business background will have an edge over the competition.

The academic year begins in February or early March and lasts until November/December. In the southernmost nations of Chile and Argentina, January and February are very slack months for language schools; while further north in Bolivia, for example, the summer holiday consists of December/January. The best time to arrive to look for work is a few weeks before the end of the summer holidays. But many institutes run eight- to 12-week courses year round and will be eager for the services of a native English speaker whatever the time of year.

FINDING A JOB

Speculative enquiries from EFL teachers are much less likely to work if sent before arrival than after, although sending a 'warm-up' CV may help your job search. What the principal of a girls' school in Lima wrote is echoed by many other institutes. '*Anyone interested in a job is welcome to write to me at any time. If they happen to be in Lima they are equally welcome to come into school.*' Unless you are very well qualified or have met your prospective employer before, you are unlikely to be offered a contract while out of the country. This is unfortunate since work visas are best applied for in the country of origin of the teacher (see below).

IN ADVANCE

Not many Latin American language schools advertise internationally. Even the most prestigious schools complain of the difficulties they encounter recruiting teachers abroad, mainly due to the low salaries they can offer and the bureaucratic procedures for obtaining a work permit. Some British Council offices in South America keep lists of schools, as do some embassies and consulates in London and Washington. When 20-year-old **James Gratton** was making plans for his first trip to South America, he wrote to all the embassies in London and received quite a lot of literature, including a number of lists of language schools, for Paraguay, Uruguay, Peru, etc. He claims that the Argentinian embassy was particularly helpful and friendly at that time. Serious candidates might ask the cultural attaché for advice.

Language school chains and organisations which might be of assistance to qualified British TEFL teachers are International House, Berlitz, EF English First and Wall Street Institute. Saxoncourt Recruitment is occasionally active in Peru and one or two other countries of South America and sometimes recruits on behalf of Culturas Inglesas and international schools. For language school listings and teaching information check the splendid site http://thelajoblist.blogspot.com. TEFL training colleges in the USA often have close ties with Latin American language schools. The training centres in the USA such as Transworld Teachers send large numbers of their graduates to posts in South America.

The British Council arranges for language assistants to work in six Latin American countries for an academic year: Argentina, Chile, Colombia, Ecuador, Mexico and Paraguay; details at www.britishcouncil.org/languageassistants-latin-america.htm. Applicants must be undergraduates studying Spanish or graduates with a Spanish A level. The level of placements and the nature of the duties are more suited to graduates than undergraduates. Deadlines for application vary among the different countries.

The Association of American Schools in South America (AASSA, www.aassa.com) co-ordinates teacher recruitment for its 60+ full and invitational members, all American-international schools in 20 Latin

American countries. Candidates who attend a recruiting fair in December must have a degree and generally be state-certified teachers. There is a $110 registration fee and if you are hired your school pays a further placement fee to AASSA.

South American Explorers (formerly the South American Explorers Club) keeps lists of schools that employ English teachers. They have a volunteer database for members to access with information about volunteering opportunities throughout South America. Many of the organisations listed will take on English teachers without TEFL certification. Membership costs US$60 per year ($90 for a couple). Contact South American Explorers for further details (www.saexplorers.org).

Lots of commercial volunteer agencies have programmes in Latin America such as: i-to-i (www.i-to-i.com), which sends people to teach in Argentina, Brazil, Costa Rica, Ecuador and Peru; Travellers Worldwide (www.travellersworldwide.com) with a programme in Argentina, Brazil, Bolivia, Peru and Guatemala; and Africa, Asia & Americas Venture (www.aventure.co.uk) with a teaching scheme in Mexico. MondoChallenge (www.mondochallenge.co.uk) sends volunteer teachers to projects in the Elqui Valley of Chile, the Andes and on the coast of Ecuador as well as Quito. Knowledge of Spanish may be expected on some of these programmes and accommodation is usually with host families.

WorldTeach at Harvard (+1 857 259 6646; www.worldteach.org.) places paying volunteers as teachers of EFL or ESL in Costa Rica, Ecuador, Chile and (unusually) Guyana. AmeriSpan in Philadelphia (+1 215 751 1100; www.amerispan.com) is primarily a language training organisation but it arranges internships in education and other fields, lasting two weeks to six months, in many Spanish-speaking countries.

ON THE SPOT

The concept of 'job vacancy' is very fluid in many Latin American language institutes and, provided you are willing to work for local teaching wages, you should be able to create your own job almost anywhere. As throughout the world, local applicants often break into the world of language teaching gradually by teaching a few classes a week. Non-contractual work is almost always offered on an unofficial part-time basis. So if you are trying to earn a living you will have to patch together enough hours from various sources. Finding the work is simply a matter of asking around and knocking on enough doors. For those who speak no Spanish, the first hurdle is to communicate your request to the secretaries at language schools since they invariably speak no English. Try to memorise a polite request in Spanish to pass your CV (*hoja de vida*) and letter (in Spanish if possible) to the school director who will know at least some English. Check adverts in the English language press such as *The News* in Mexico City or the *Buenos Aires Herald*. English language bookshops are another possible source of teaching leads.

Ask in expatriate bars and restaurants, check out any building claiming to be an 'English School' however dubious-looking, and in larger cities try deciphering the telephone directory for schools or agencies which might be able to use your services. There is more competition as well as more opportunities in the major cities (for example, it is said that up to half a million Americans live in Mexico City), so if you are having difficulties rounding up work, you could try smaller towns and cities off the beaten track.

The crucial factor in becoming accepted as an English teacher at a locally run language school may not be your qualifications or your accent as much as your appearance. You must look as neat and well-dressed as teachers are expected to look, at least when you're job-hunting. Later your standards might slip a little; **Nick Wilson**, who taught for two years in Mexico, says that it is easy to spot the English teachers in banks and office buildings; they're the ones wearing jeans, T-shirts and carrying cassettes.

FREELANCE TEACHING

In most Latin American cities, there is a thriving market in private English lessons, which usually pay at least half as much again as working for an institute. It is not uncommon for teachers to consider the language school which hires them as a stepping stone to setting up as a private tutor. After they have familiarised themselves with some teaching materials and made enough contacts among local language learners, they strike out on their own, though this is far from easy unless you can get by in the local language and have access to suitable premises. Clients can be found by advertising in the quality press, by placing notices on strategic noticeboards or by handing out business cards. If the latter, use the local method of address and omit confusing initials such as BA after your name: teachers often call themselves '*Profesor*' or '*Profesora*'.

REGULATIONS

Of course requirements vary from country to country but the prospects are dismal for teachers who insist on doing everything by the book. It is standard for work visas to be available only to fully qualified and experienced teachers on long-term contracts. Often you will have to present an array of documents, from university certificates and transcripts to FBI police clearance, which have been authenticated by your consulate abroad or by the consulate of the host country. Although many schools will not offer a contract before interview and then will make it contingent on a work permit, the procedures should be started in the teacher's country of origin, which makes the whole business very difficult. All of this can take as long as six months and involve a great deal of hassle and expense, not least for the employer.

The upshot is that a high percentage of teachers works unofficially throughout Latin America. It is hardly an issue in some countries, for example virtually no one gets a work permit in Brazil, not even long-resident language school teachers and no one seems to worry about it. Teaching on a tourist visa or as a 'tourist' in countries where you don't need a visa, is a widespread practice in Mexico and Peru. There are ways round the regulations, for example to work on a student/trainee/cultural exchange visa (as in Ecuador or Venezuela).

CONDITIONS OF WORK

Very few schools offer perks such as an extra month's salary or return flights to teachers who stay for a two-year contract. Contracts are fairly hard to come by and always require a minimum commitment of a year. The advantages are that you are guaranteed a certain income and you have a chance of applying for a work permit. Teachers without the CELTA or Trinity certificate are not greatly disadvantaged, partly because this qualification is not as widely known in Latin America as it is in Europe, although you can take the Trinity TESOL course at the Casa de Ingles in Chaco (Argentina), the Dickens Institute in Montevideo (Uruguay), and Stael Ruffinelli de Ortiz English in Asuncion (Paraguay). Many institutes offer their own compulsory pre-job training (to be taken at the teacher's own expense), which provides a useful orientation for new arrivals.

One of the seldom-mentioned perks of teaching in Latin America is the liveliness and enthusiasm of the pupils. Brazilian students have been described as the 'world's most communicative students' and classrooms around the continent often take on the atmosphere of a party. You may also be dazzled by the level of knowledge of Western pop culture, and should be prepared to have your ignorance shown up. Also be prepared to lose their attention if a lesson coincides with a major sporting event.

LEISURE TIME

Whether you are a serious student of Spanish or a frivolous seeker after the excitement generated by Latin carnivals, South America is a wonderful place to live in and travel. Women teachers may find the machismo a little hard to take, but will soon learn how to put it in its place. If you want to travel around, the annually revised *South American Handbook* definitely justifies the initial outlay of £22.50.

ARGENTINA

The teaching market in Argentina is ticking over without being really buoyant. Hundreds of institutes operate at varying standards. The economy is recovering well, with government figures showing growth of nearly 5% (mid-2012). The exchange rate is quite convenient for both European and American citizens with more than 4 pesos to the US dollar and nearly 6 pesos to the euro. Language schools which specialise in the business market have fully recovered from the deep recession that engulfed Argentina more than 10 years ago, and there is plenty of cause for optimism. Teachers are far more likely to secure a job once they are in Argentina than by applying from their home country.

Cultural exchange programmes will appeal to those willing to teach as volunteers in rural areas, normally in state rather than private schools. For example, Connecting Schools to the World (see entry) invites university graduates to live for one or two semesters in a *pueblo* or city in the Argentinian province of Córdoba. The programme fee covers homestay accommodation with a local family and a modest monthly stipend. As with all these programmes, participants are encouraged to take up various extra-curricular activities such as tango lessons, cookery and photography.

Other possibilities include:

BAEnglish House (www.baenglishhouse.com.ar/eng/teach-english.html).Volunteer teachers assist permanent teachers by providing conversation practice. The language school is an institution where children from a variety of backgrounds attend English lessons.

BA Placements, Recoleta, Buenos Aires (www.baplacement.com/tefl.php). TEFL Certification Program provides training for aspiring English teachers, and helps with local job placement.

Connecting Worlds, Buenos Aires and Mar de Plata; (+54 11 5032 8136; www.connectingworlds.com.ar). ESL Argentina Program in Mar del Plata. Volunteers stay for 4–24 weeks. Registration fee of $75 plus varying costs for accommodation from $1,075 for 4 weeks.

EBC Servicios Lingüísticos, Buenos Aires (+54 11 6379 9391; toll-free numbers in English speaking countries listed on website www.teflgap.org or www.ebc-tefl-course.com). Offers a month-long TEFL training course for $1,599 followed by a job placement programme.

Expanish, Buenos Aires (+54 11 5252 3040 or 1 888 EXPANISH; www.expanish.com/volunteer). Spanish language school with Volunteer English teaching programme. Considered by some to be overly motivated by profit.

La Montana Spanish School, San Carlos de Bariloche, Patagonia (+54 2944 524212; volunteer-work@lamontana.com; www.lamontana.com/volunteer-work). Students who complete a Spanish course, usually lasting 4 weeks, can be placed in rural schools around Patagonia for at least a month but typically two. Modest placement fee is charged.

Pasantias Argentinas, Córdoba (+54 351 474 5947; www.pasantias-argentinas.com). Arranges professional internships in Córdoba including English teaching placements. Open to all native English speakers who have achieved a speaking knowledge of Spanish via a Pasantias language course; intensive course price from €120 per week. Donation to voluntary project €100.

Road2Argentina, Buenos Aires (+54 11 4826 0820; www.road2argentina.com). Places ESL interns for 2–16 weeks between March and November, as part of a cultural exchange and language immersion programme. International interns are accepted without relevant training or experience to help in private or public school classrooms. Programme fees start at $1,290 for one month and include accommodation in a student residence. (Road2Argentina also co-operate with EBC TEFL Course in Buenos Aires – see entry.)

Many companies are located in the outskirts of Buenos Aires, a city whose area is larger than London's. It can sometimes take more than an hour to reach some companies from downtown (where teachers might live) by bus, so make sure you negotiate a block of three hours minimum in one place, or it may not be worth your while. Language schools are linked from www.inglesnet.com, which also has a decent community section. Courses in Argentina tend to start in March and finish in December. The hourly wage for starting teachers is normally between 30 and 40 Argentine pesos, currently equivalent to $6.75–$9.

Job-seekers can try the *Buenos Aires Herald*, which accepts adverts for English teachers, or check community noticeboards such as Craigslist (http://buenosaires.en.craigslist.org). There is a useful notice-board in El Ateneo, the English language bookshop at 340 Calle Florida (the main shopping street). For information on other English language bookshops, often good places to meet native speakers and to discover informal opportunities, download *Buenos Aires' Brilliant Bookshops* (http://argentinastravel.com/downloads/bookstore-guide.pdf). Schools of Spanish abound and often prove good contact points for foreign residents who want to teach on the side.

Some of the 14 bi-national Centers or Instituto de Intercambio Cultural Argentino-Americano (listed at http://argentina.usembassy.gov/binational_centers.html) offer English courses, as do the three International House schools in the capital (located in Recoleta, Belgrano and San Isidro). To work at one of these, you usually have to have worked for IH before. A large number of full-curriculum private schools prepare students for Cambridge and other exams, such as the Belgrano Day School (Juramento 3035, (c1428doa) Ciudad de Buenos Aires; +54 11 4781 6011; www.bds.edu.ar), which has pupils from kindergarten to school leaving age.

If you want to cast your net wider you can move to smaller cities where there will be fewer vacancies but also fewer applicants competing for the jobs. For example, Bariloche in Patagonia in the deep south of Argentina has an unexpectedly large market for English teachers because of its role as an international ski resort.

It is commonplace for Americans and Britons to move from learning Spanish to teaching English as **Chris Moloney** from Queensland did (and along the way had a romance with a previous Miss Argentina) and also **Richard Ferguson**, a New Zealander who has travelled extensively in South America:

There are heaps of English schools in Buenos Aires and everyone wants to learn English. I made a few basic signs in Spanish advertising conversational classes, stuck them around Palermo (a wealthier suburb) and sometimes I'll stand on a busy corner and hand out leaflets. I'm charging about 30 pesos an hour and have a few students already so it's a good bet. I think any native speaker can teach here, better with experience and better still with qualifications. Either do as I did, approach some schools or look in the papers in the jobs section. I saw at least 15 in one edition of the **Buenos Aires Herald.**

Luke McElderry from Texas and his girlfriend **Jenny Jacobi** spent hours researching potential teaching employers in Buenos Aires on the internet. After completing a training course locally, he sent a mass email with CV attached to at least 40 addresses and waited for responses to trickle in, and ended up hearing from about a quarter. He describes his job-hunt:

The first interviews were varied, some in English, one in Spanish, but all fairly casual. Most take 30 minutes and they seem to care more about your availability than your experience. I was asked a couple of times if I had any visa/permit and said no, and the employers didn't seem to care at all. I have heard the biggest institutes are the ones who care, and ironically pay the least!

Before long, they were working for an institute, Speak Spanish, which, confusingly, also teaches English (www.speakspanish.com.ar). They were sent out to teach one-and-a-half-hour classes in businesses. Sometimes they were assigned to comfortable conference rooms with whiteboards, free photocopies, faxes and coffee. Luke and Jenny found that all went smoothly, apart from finding accommodation:

It is a real hassle finding an apartment as they want to charge you tourist rates and it is nearly impossible to get a lease as an ex-pat. Accommodation prices depend on your ability to find a rental agency that doesn't require a garantiá *from an Argentine property owner saying that you will pay the entire rental term in full; some places will let you pay everything up front, usually 6 months or more, but these places are very few and far between.*

Alicia Meta of ACM Business English, Buenos Aires, explains how the letting market works:

> *A one-bedroom apartment in a decent neighbourhood might now cost US$1,000 if it is furnished, if not, around US$600. If it is a short contract the agents will ask you to pay in full. For a short-term contract you also have to pay a commission to the real estate agency of about 8% of the total amount. For a one-year contract the commission is the equivalent of one and a half months of the rent to be paid. The deposit for a long-term contract (one year) is equal to two months rent. It is always returned once the deal is over.*
>
> *It is difficult for tourists to rent an apartment and unfortunately I believe that there is no other way out. My advice would be to get some feedback before coming to Argentina, go to a hostel and then calmly try to look for the best option. Usually, apartments in the outskirts of Buenos Aires can be cheaper but the payment method might not differ.*

RED TAPE

According to the Argentine embassies in London and Washington, UK and US nationals do not need a tourist visa to enter Argentina for up to 90 days, which can be extended for another 90 days at the *Dirección Nacional de Migraciones*. The tourist visa can also be renewed by crossing the border, most commonly by ferry to Uruguay for the weekend.

Working papers can be obtained from the National Direction of Migrations by employers, though a school will be willing only for long-term propositions. It will be necessary for the applicant to provide a contract of employment for a minimum of a year, and birth certificate (notarised by a notary public in Argentina), as well as passport. Non-British passport holders must also provide a certificate of good conduct from the police authorities in his or her country or countries of residence in the five years prior to applying.

Most teachers are paid hourly by the language institutes employing them. Self-employed people are obliged to register in the *monotributo* system with AFIP (tax office) and pay approximately 15% of their full-time earnings in tax.

LIST OF EMPLOYERS

ACM BUSINESS ENGLISH
Viamonte 2660, Buenos Aires
 +54 11 5025 4752
info@acmbusinessenglish.com.ar
www.acmbusinessenglish.com.ar

NUMBER OF TEACHERS: 3–4.

PREFERENCE OF NATIONALITY: American, British and Canadian. Note: A strong Australian accent is usually difficult for Latin Americans to understand.

QUALIFICATIONS: TEFL, ESL or equivalent. Experience teaching ESL to adults in companies needed. Candidates with a teaching degree are the most sought after. General knowledge and high intellectual level needed for training executives who will be dealing with native English speakers at headquarters.

CONDITIONS OF EMPLOYMENT: No contracts. Part-time work so people are self-employed. Most teachers intend to stay in the country for at least 1 year, starting in March. Courses in Argentina start in March and finish in December. Usually 2–3 hours twice a week teaching in different companies. Many companies are located on the outskirts of Buenos Aires, so it can take more than an hour to reach some companies from downtown (where most candidates live) by bus. In these cases, a block of 3 hours minimum in one place is offered.

SALARY: Around 70 pesos per hour, paid at the beginning of the following month.

FACILITIES/SUPPORT: No training given. No assistance with accommodation.

RECRUITMENT: Word of mouth/posting on international websites, and in *the Buenos Aires Herald* (local English newspaper). Interviews in Buenos Aires.

CONTACT: Alicia Meta, Director.

CIL – CENTRO INTEGRAL DE LENGUAS

Leon 1753, Maipu, Córdoba

☎ +54 351 458 1727

✉ info@cil-method.com.ar

💻 www.cil-method.com.ar

NUMBER OF TEACHERS: 3.

PREFERENCE OF NATIONALITY: None.

QUALIFICATIONS: Experience of teaching a second language or English.

CONDITIONS OF EMPLOYMENT: 9-month contracts. Teaching takes place in the afternoons.

SALARY: 45 pesos an hour. If the teacher can invoice school, social security contributions of about 200 pesos can be made.

FACILITIES/SUPPORT: No assistance with accommodation or visas.

RECRUITMENT: Via newspaper ads and local interviews.

CONTACT: Liliana Bellolio, Headmistress.

COLONIAS DE INMERSION AL IDIOMA (CII)

Av Forest 1213, Caba, 1427 Buenos Aires

☎ +54 11 4553 8445

✉ experienceargentina@ecolonias.com

💻 www.ecolonias.com

NUMBER OF TEACHERS: 25–35 TEFL interns per semester who spend 20 hours per week assisting with English in a local school, a few hours a week tutoring members of their host family and one weekend a month at a language camp for children and young people.

PREFERENCE OF NATIONALITY: Citizen of any English-speaking country.

QUALIFICATIONS: University students and graduates aged 20–26, no specific qualifications or experience required. Speaking knowledge of Spanish preferred and TEFL certificate.

CONDITIONS OF EMPLOYMENT: 3–12 months, preferably starting 10 March or 25 July. Most schools prefer applicants who can commit to at least a semester. Schedules vary from school to school. Total of 25 hours a week.

SALARY: Monthly stipend of 280–350 pesos plus 200 pesos for participating in weekend language camp. Early booking programme fees of $1,750 for up to 6 months, $2,000 for up to 12 includes homestay accommodation throughout with full board, Spanish coaching and opportunities to travel.

FACILITIES/SUPPORT: 60-hour Bridge TEFL online certificate course is compulsory for those who do not have a TEFL qualification (at a cost of $325).

RECRUITMENT: Through cooperating universities and the internet. Interviews sometimes carried out in the UK and Ireland.

CONTACT: Fernando Damian Carro, CII Director.

CONNECTING SCHOOLS TO THE WORLD

Luis Maria Campos 545 1 D; 1426 Buenos Aires

☎ +54 11 477 26724

✉ connectingschools@gmail.com

💻 www.connectingschools.com.ar

NUMBER OF TEACHERS: 20 teachers per year. All placed in different towns in the interior of Argentina for a period of one semester.

PREFERENCE OF NATIONALITY: People from any English speaking country.

QUALIFICATIONS: College graduates.

CONDITIONS OF EMPLOYMENT: Teaching periods of one or two semesters. Up to 25 hours of work per week. First semester mid-February to 9 July and second from 9 July to 15 December. Participants must wish to become part of the community and to make a contribution. They must also wish to learn the Spanish language.

SALARY: Homestay in Argentine family, private Spanish tutoring, round trip bus ticket from Buenos Aires to location, $100 monthly stipend after fortnight of training and 1 week placement. Programme fee is $1,300.

FACILITIES/SUPPORT: Two weeks of intensive ESL training on arrival in Buenos Aires while participants stay in a hostel (hostelpalermosuites.com). Supervision and help with lesson planning throughout the teaching period. 4 hours of private Spanish classes a week while teaching and homestay accommodation for 4 months arranged after initial 3 weeks. Volunteers teach on tourist visa (available at airport for $120 fee).

RECRUITMENT: Via internet. Resumé, list of references and a telephone interview with director required.

CONTACT: Cristina Rapela, Director.

GIC ARGENTINA

Av. de Mayo 1370, 3er piso of. 24, Buenos Aires C1085ABQ

☎ +54 11 5353–9497/USA: +1 202 552 1081/ UK: +44 20 7193 2270

✉ info@gicarg.org

💻 www.gicarg.org

GIC refers to Grupo de Intercambio Cultural Argentino.

NUMBER OF TEACHERS: 10.

PREFERENCE OF NATIONALITY: None.

QUALIFICATIONS: None. Participants normally have a working knowledge of Spanish.

CONDITIONS OF EMPLOYMENT: 3-month contracts offered. To work 20 hours per week.

SALARY: Unpaid (volunteers and interns).

FACILITIES/SUPPORT: Accommodation provided in a student dorm, with host families, shared apartments. 4-week Spanish language course is compulsory on the internship programme, starting at $1,200. TEFL/TESOL certification offered via TEFL International (teflinternational.org.uk/buenos_aires.htm).

RECRUITMENT: Interview required.

CONTACT: Graciela Cerquatti, Director.

HOME INTERCULTURAL LEARNING

Calle 37 nro 1091 PB La Plata, CP 1900, Buenos Aires

(C) +54 221 4833575

info@homeintercultural.com.ar

www.homeintercultural.com.ar

NUMBER OF TEACHERS: Variable.

PREFERENCE OF NATIONALITY: None.

QUALIFICATIONS: Teacher training (CELTA, TEFL) or university degree needed for regular courses, other university degrees for fluency and multi-discipline consultancy work.

CONDITIONS OF EMPLOYMENT: Flexible hours and length of stay, according to teacher's wishes. School uses dynamic teaching techniques that emphasise conversation and make use of acting, singing, playing games, reading comics, listening to podcasts, etc.

SALARY: About 60 pesos per teaching hour. Teachers need to be enrolled in *monotributo*.

FACILITIES/SUPPORT: Spanish classes (and other languages) are offered at partner schools for special rates. Home Intercultural Learning has agreements with local hostels, but teachers must arrange accommodation on their own. Teachers are responsible for arranging their own permits.

RECRUITMENT: Skype interviews can be arranged.

CONTACT: Andrea Assenti del Rio, Director of Studies.

INTERACTION LANGUAGE STUDIO

Av. L. N. Alem 428 6 I, Buenos Aires 1003

(C) +54 11 4311 7220

info@interactionls.com

www.interactionls.com

NUMBER OF TEACHERS: 5–8 foreign teachers and 40 local teachers.

PREFERENCE OF NATIONALITY: American and British.

QUALIFICATIONS: TEFL certificate and some teaching experience.

CONDITIONS OF EMPLOYMENT: Contracts from March to December. Usual hours from 3 to 20 a week.

SALARY: 31 pesos per hour (around $8).

RECRUITMENT: CV by mail, interview and mock lesson. Interviews essential.

CONTACT: Professor Virginia López Grisolia, Director of Studies and Owner.

NETWORK ENGLISH LANGUAGE TEACHING

Entre Ríos 265, Avellaneda (1870) Buenos Aires

(C) +54 11 4228 4900

info@networkinstitute.com.ar

www.networkinstitute.com.ar

NUMBER OF TEACHERS: 3–4 per year.

PREFERENCE OF NATIONALITY: none.

QUALIFICATIONS: TEFL.

CONDITIONS OF EMPLOYMENT: Minimum 9 months (March to November); renewable for the next school year. Hours of teaching 5.30pm–8.30pm for regular courses; mornings and lunchtimes for in-company courses.

SALARY: On application.

RECRUITMENT: Face-to-face interviews.

CONTACT: Cecilia Cicolini, Director.

PASANTIAS ARGENTINAS

Antonio del Viso 32, B° Alta Córdoba, CP 5001, Córdoba

(C) +54 351 474 5947

info@pasantias-argentinas.com

www.pasantias-argentinas.com

NUMBER OF VOLUNTEER TEACHERS: 1–2.

PREFERENCE OF NATIONALITY: none.

QUALIFICATIONS: Native English speaker.

CONDITIONS OF EMPLOYMENT: 2–6 months.

SALARY: none.

FACILITIES/SUPPORT: Accommodation provided in one of several volunteer houses, but must be paid for.

RECRUITMENT: Directly via website. Local interviews.

CONTACT: Mr. Kai Peter Weers, CEO/Owner.

SWITCH LANGUAGE SCHOOL
Avenida Presidente Roque Sáenz Pe–na 615, 7° Off. 716,
Buenos Aires
☏ +54 11 4393 4125
🖱 consultoraswitch@yahoo.com.ar or info@
switchschool.com.ar
💻 www.switchschool.com.ar/www.consultoraswitch.
com.ar

NUMBER OF TEACHERS: 25.
PREFERENCE OF NATIONALITY: None.
QUALIFICATIONS: Recognised TEFL Certificate.
CONDITIONS OF EMPLOYMENT: 9-month minimum contract.
SALARY: Around 40 pesos per hour.
FACILITIES/SUPPORT: No help given with work permits or finding accommodation.
RECRUITMENT: Interviews plus a mock class carried out at the school are essential.
CONTACT: Mara France Garcia, Headmistress.

WEBSTER SCHOOL OF ENGLISH
Libertad 1691, Florida (1602), Buenos Aires
☏ +54 11 4 797 9081
🖱 websterenglish@gmail.com

NUMBER OF TEACHERS: 3.
PREFERENCE OF NATIONALITY: British.
QUALIFICATIONS: Often recruit university students close to graduation for one semester. School is looking for a TESOL/TEFL Certificate and some teaching experience.
CONDITIONS OF EMPLOYMENT: 12–15 hours a week for one semester.
SALARY: $200–$400 a month, with no deductions.
FACILITIES/SUPPORT: Accommodation provided at school owner's house with spare bedrooms, garden and swimming pool. Work contract provided to assist with visas.
CONTACT: Nora Snitowski, Head of School.

BOLIVIA

Even the poorest of Latin American nations offers reasonable possibilities to EFL teachers, provided you are prepared to accept a low wage. In contrast to the standard hourly wage of $15–$20 per hour in Santiago or Brasilia, the wages paid by language schools in Bolivia are about 14 bolivianos ($2 at the time of writing). However, a lot of businesses choose to pay their employees in dollars. Many teachers touring South America prefer Bolivia to many other countries for cultural reasons. La Paz is a city with a low cost of living and a colourful social mix. The class structure is immediately apparent with the upper class consisting of people of Spanish descent, the middle class or *mestizos* of mixed Spanish/Bolivian ancestry and the underclass of Indians still wearing their traditional costume. Bolivia may have preserved its traditional culture more successfully than other Latin American countries, but the inequality of wealth distribution has led socialist president Evo Morales to implement stringent wealth distribution measures, including nationalising much of the energy industry. Four of the country's wealthiest regions, including Santa Cruz, have been threatening (or declaring) autonomy in protest.

Only a handful of language schools and a couple of *colegios* (private schools) are listed in the La Paz *Yellow Pages* (www.guia-amarilla.com) and they are unlikely to commit themselves to hiring a teacher without meeting them first. Terms normally last from early February to early September, resuming at the end of September to the beginning of December. The biggest language school in the country is the ultra respectable Centro Boliviano Americano or CBA (Parque Iturralde Zenón 121, La Paz; +591 2 243 0107; http://cba.edu.bo) with four other locations in La Paz, plus schools in other cities such as Sucre, Cochabamba (see entry below) and Santa Cruz (www.cba.com.bo). Despite its name it hires British and Irish native English speakers as well.

Colegios employ native English speakers for their English departments and tend to pay twice as much as the private language schools. Also, the hours of 8.30am–1.30pm are more convenient.

Mike Martin is one teacher who has fallen under the spell of Bolivia:

I love it here and get on very well with Bolivians. It's only fair to point out, though, that unrest is always here, and there are periodic protests and outbreaks of violence. I should also mention that I now teach free. I am in the fortunate position of being able to do this as I took early retirement and receive a pension, which goes a lot further here than at home. I reckon that you could live reasonably comfortably here for about $600 a month, allowing $150 for an apartment. But be prepared for lots of hassles with the immigration paperwork. When I was charging my students, I charged $3 an hour if they could afford it. A young woman joined and wanted 4 hours a week tuition. A few weeks later I asked her what she was earning and she was paying me about 70 percent of her salary as a part-time professional, so I halved her fees and later halved them again. It's because of stories like this that I eventually decided to teach free. I do think that if you advertised in the local press, you would have a plentiful supply of students as most want to learn English.

JONATHAN ALDERMAN

Jonathan Alderman was happy to put up with low pay in exchange for the excellent quality of life he found in Bolivia, which he says 'can feel like an idyllic paradise sometimes, because of the climate'. He did things that would be unimaginable at home such as swimming in a pool (in Oruro) whose waters were heated underground by a volcano, attending one of the many carnivals in February and throwing water balloons at the locals.

I first went to Cochabamba as a volunteer to give conversation classes in the city's public university, San Simon. This was through Projects Abroad (www.projects-abroad. co.uk). Everything was organised for me before I arrived, including accommodation and Spanish lessons. This was a great gentle introduction for someone new to the city and to teaching. In the university it is easy to settle in and make friends very quickly.

That only lasted for a few months, but I was sufficiently taken with Cochabamba to want to go back the following January. Before arriving, I had already fixed myself up with a job teaching at the Pan American English Center, which was a genuinely enjoyable place to work because of the relaxed atmosphere. But I became fed up with being paid late and left after only a couple of months to travel a bit. I wasn't breaking any contract, as there was none. I came back to Cochabamba after a little while exploring South America and took a job in another institute, El Britanico Boliviano de Cultura (BBC, Calle Espa~na 171, Cochabamba; 422 0936). This was much better paid, at $3.50 an hour. The lessons were mostly in the evening, but I was lucky to get some one-to-one classes through the school to teach during the day as well. This school was professionally run and the director paid me on the last day of the month without any hassle. In this school I also taught mostly adults rather than kids. One thing that makes this school stand out from the many others in Cochabamba is the strong emphasis on British rather than American English (as the name would suggest). This is the only institute in Cochabamba where students can take Cambridge exams. BBC often finds it quite hard recruiting teachers, simply because it is difficult to attract teachers to Bolivia due to the low salaries.

I would highly recommend staying and working in Bolivia – and if you are staying in Bolivia, it just has to be Cochabamba, because of the perfect spring-like climate. Teaching Bolivian students can be very fun, though the kids can be boisterous (I especially found teenage boys to be a pain in the arse). When teaching adults, it was nice to be able to establish friendships with the students. I obviously made a very positive impression with one class of students I taught for 4 months at the BBC, because when I left they presented me with a most ornate chess set (with many of the pieces in the shape of native Americans or llamas) – it was the best present I think I have ever received!

Later Jonathan went back to Cochabamba to concentrate on teaching private classes and doing some translation work, while still teaching an hour and a half a day in the Britanico. He concluded, 'if someone wants to earn a decent wage teaching English in Bolivia, one has to turn to private classes'. When he first arrived, he advertised in the local newspaper for private classes charging 30–35 Bolivianos an hour. He says you can expect to be approached in shops and restaurants as well as by your pupils and asked about private classes, but these will generally come from people who would find it a hardship to pay even $2 an hour. The best place to advertise private English lessons is the Sunday edition of the newspaper El Diario (www.eldiario.net).

Most teachers arrive on a tourist visa and should in theory apply for a work visa. As Jonathan admits, most simply continue to work on a tourist visa:

This is illegal, of course, but there doesn't tend to be a great problem with it, as you are allowed four 90-day stamps in a year. In fact, schools tend to encourage their teachers to work this way, from my experience. One simply has to leave the country and return to get another tourist stamp. If I were asked questions at immigration I would say that I was working on a voluntary project in Bolivia and they would accept it. Of the people I knew who did get a long-stay visa they did it off their own bat with no help from their school as far as I know.

The Bolivia Volunteers teaching project (www.boliviavolunteers.org) supports a number of schools in Cochabamba, La Paz or Santa Cruz that are often severely understaffed and rely on donations, small tuition payments from parents, and the assistance of volunteers who pay from US$750 for four weeks of volunteering.

Volunteering Solutions (www.volunteeringsolutions.com/bolivia/volunteer_teaching_english_bolivia.htm) is an agency based in India but with a global reach. It places volunteer teachers in kindergartens, primary and secondary schools all located in the city of Santa Cruz for up to six months. Inexperienced volunteers with little knowledge of Spanish work as classroom assistants alongside the regular teachers, but more adventurous people may be given a chance to teach a class independently. The application fee here is $200 plus approximately $200 a week to cover living and other expenses.

LIST OF EMPLOYERS

CAMBRIDGE COLLEGE

Residencias del Norte, Av. Beni entre 4to y 5to Anillos, Santa Cruz de la Sierra

℮ +591 3 3416541

✆ esolacademic@cotas.com.bo; direcciong@cotas. com.bo; cambridgecollege@cotas.com.bo

▭ www.cambridgebolivia.com.bo

NUMBER OF TEACHERS: 12.

PREFERENCE OF NATIONALITY: British.

QUALIFICATIONS: CELTA and 10 years' classroom experience.

CONDITIONS OF EMPLOYMENT: 2-year contract with working hours between 7am and 11am then 5pm and 9pm Monday to Friday.

FACILITIES/SUPPORT: Assistance given finding apartments near the school and the school organises all the relevant paperwork for work permits.

RECRUITMENT: Usually via adverts on TEFL websites. Candidates submit their CV and a model lesson plan and an interview is conducted through video conferencing.

CONTACT: Maria Renee Canedo Landivar, Headmistress.

CENTRO BOLIVIANO AMERICANO – COCHABAMBA

PO Box 1399, Cochabamba

℮ +591 4 425 6721/4 422 1288

✆ mblum@cbacoch.org

▭ www.cbacoch.org

NUMBER OF TEACHERS: 3.

PREFERENCE OF NATIONALITY: American and British.

QUALIFICATIONS: Proficiency in English. Work experience in schools/universities. International Examination Diplomas/TESOL/ TEFL certificates.

CONDITIONS OF EMPLOYMENT: 2-year renewable contract. 6 hours chosen from the following teaching hours: 7–8.30am, 8.30–11.45am, 1.45–5pm, 2.30–3.45pm, 3.45–5pm, 5–6.30pm, 6.45–8.15pm, 6.35–9.45pm.

SALARY: Average of $4 per hour. Varies depending on academic background and teaching experience. Income tax of 13% is not deducted when the teacher submits invoices for the same amount each month. Social security deductions 12.21%.

FACILITIES/SUPPORT: Help given on finding accommodation at orientation. Healthcare provided. Assistance given with work permits. Teachers should come with a *visa de objeto determinado* valid for 30 days to start the paperwork for a work visa. If the teacher comes with a tourist visa, he/she has to change it to a *visa de objeto determinado* at a Bolivian Consulate in a neighbouring country. After that he/she may start with the paperwork for a one- or two-year work visa. School also helps with additional procedure for a work permit which incurs an extra fee.

RECRUITMENT: Via adverts in newspapers. Local interview necessary.

CONTACT: Mery Blum de Schwarz, Academic Director.

SPEAKEASY INSTITUTE

Av. Arce 2047, La Paz

℮ +591 2 244 1779

✆ speakeasyinstitute@yahoo.com

▭ www.speakeasyinstitute.com

NUMBER OF TEACHERS: 8.

PREFERENCE OF NATIONALITY: None.

QUALIFICATIONS: Minimum CELTA qualification or equivalent plus 1 year's experience.

CONDITIONS OF EMPLOYMENT: 6-month to 1-year contracts available. Maximum 40 teaching hours per week. School open from 7.30am to 9pm Monday to Friday.

SALARY: Bs 3,200 (£225) per month.

FACILITIES/SUPPORT: Help provided with finding accommodation and getting visa.

RECRUITMENT: Via internet. No interview required.

CONTACT: Alix Shand, Coordinator.

BRAZIL

As tourism, business and a burgeoning middle class continue to expand throughout Brazil, so too has the demand for the English language. In the rush to prepare for the World Cup in 2014 and Olympics in 2016, the government has been offering subsidised language classes. The Ministry of Tourism introduced a programme called Olá Turista! which is bringing basic English (and Spanish) classes, free of charge to the 12 host states of the 2014 World Cup: Rio de Janeiro, Sao Paulo, Bahia, Amazonas, Ceara, Pernambuco, Mato Grosso, Parana, Minas Gerais, Rio Grande do Norte and Rio Grande do Sul, as well as the Federal District. This comes in the wake of a recent report published by the worldwide educational company English First (EF) that ranks Brazil among the countries with the worst English language competency in the world. So there is plenty of scope for native speaker English teachers to address the perceived problem. The phenomenal growth in Brazil's economy in recent years has encouraged the market for English teaching almost everywhere.

Dozens of Culturas Inglesas in the Associacao Brasileira de Culturas Inglesas (www.culturainglesa.com.br) and many IBEUs (Instituto Brasil-Estadios Unidos) scattered all over the fifth largest country in the world employ several hundred teachers to serve thousands of students. Qualified teachers can send their CVs to trabal.henoibeu@ibeu.org.br to find out about vacancies. Language teaching chains like Wizard, the largest in the country, are worth trying once you're in Brazil (www.wizard.com.br/en/Work-With-Us).

Schools in smaller places often notify co-operating institutes in the big cities of any job vacancies for native English speakers. But speculative visits to towns of any size are likely to succeed eventually. Any of the four British Council offices in Brazil (Brasilia, Recife, Rio and Sao Paulo) may be able to supply a list of Cultura Inglesas and other established schools to people who call on them. The distinguishing feature of Brazilian EFL is the high proportion of well-qualified Brazilian English teachers. Recruiting teachers from overseas is seen to be unjustifiably costly and also very difficult from the visa point of view. Only individuals with very specialised expertise are invited to work in very senior posts.

Visas are a major headache. You are permitted to stay no more than six months on a tourist visa after which you will have to leave the country (usually across the Paraguayan border) or get an extension from the Federal Police. Training visas are an option for some. The Administrative Director of one of Rio de Janeiro's upmarket schools describes the difficulties:

> *Unfortunately, teaching English is not an area the government considers a priority in issuing visas. There are only two situations in which foreigners can teach in Brazil. The first is to work illegally, since there are numerous small schools who can afford to run the risk of hiring illegal foreigners. As a result, pay is usually bad and employment unstable. The alternative is available only to specialists, and is extremely rare. Because we have a webpage, I get requests from foreigners all the time. I basically tell them that it is an adventure here, only for the strong of stomach, and you have to be willing to subject yourself to the unsavoury experiences that go along with working without proper papers. I have come across dozens of foreigners who have been promised work-related visas. In 27 years of living in Brazil, I have never, not once, seen this happen. The only cases I know of where a person has taught legally, it has been when they enter the country with visas issued at the Brazilian consulate in their country of residence.*

Occasionally language institutes in Brazil advertise on tefl.com and eslcafe.com. The latter is the site on which **Alexis Heintz** discovered that the Speaking School (see entry) had a vacancy which he filled in February 2012:

> *I contacted the school via email, then found them on Facebook and started chatting with the secretaries, teachers, and eventually the owner of the school, which included Q & A on both ends (from my side and theirs) about the job and my experience (I had volunteered as an English teacher a few months), and then I sent them my*

updated CV. The pupils all feel that English is very important for them to know and learn. However, since the majority are Engineering students at uni, they treat their uni studies as their number one priority and English falls into second place. The business professionals also have to put their career demands above their English studies, so I feel that most students do not spend much time studying outside of class. The low point for me is when you have a 7am class scheduled and your student does not show up and does not cancel in advance. You don't get paid for the 30 minutes which you have to spend waiting around for the student before you can confirm that the class is indeed cancelled.

If you wait until after arrival to look for work, use the *Yellow Pages*, expatriate networks or informative websites such as www.gringoes.com, run by expats based in Sao Paulo; the latter has a classified section in jobs for native speaker teachers. In Sao Paulo a good source of teaching jobs is the newspaper *Folha de São Paulo* on a Sunday. When job-hunting, expect to go through quite a rigorous interview procedure, as **Jon Cotterill** discovered:

When you drop your CV in, the school may ask you to take a written English test on the spot. This can consist of anything up to 100 questions plus a composition section. If you pass the test, you may get invited to a group interview, a 'dinamica de grupo'. This consists of a group of potential teachers (usually Brazilians) and you have to perform various tasks in small teams or pairs. If you are successful then you may be asked to do a two-week training course (usually unpaid). Only after all of this will you be offered work.

Richard Ferguson, a New Zealander who has learned Portuguese, spent time in Brazil but didn't pursue his idea of looking for teaching work since he decided to move on to Argentina. However, he did meet an American who gave private English lessons in São Paulo charging 50 reais an hour (more than $30 at that time). But he bemoaned the fact that the city was hard to get around (the Metro area has a population of about 20 million) and he insisted that you need to have the students pay in advance for a few lessons. This is because Brazilians are notorious for not showing up, being late or cancelling at the last minute (which they don't see as a problem) so you need to take some precautions so as not to waste your time.

Although he is Swiss by birth, and arrived in Brazil assuming the Swiss time was a universal standard, **Hans Durrer** slowly adjusted to a different rhythm. He became familiar with the Brazilian way of life, made Brazilian friends, learned Portuguese and felt generally enriched. He attributes this to his open, curious and eager-to-learn attitude, and also to the warm hospitality of the school owners. He describes how rewarding it can be to tutor students with whom you develop a rapport, even when their attendance is sporadic, as happened when he spent two long stints working with Schutz & Kanomata (see directory entry) in southern Brazil:

Two days ago, Reinaldo attended his last conversational English class in Santa Cruz do Sul. As usual, we talked about anything and everything, from corruption to the ways of perception, from travels to how best to live your life. He enjoyed my classes a lot and thought them interesting, stimulating and helpful, he said. He wasn't however too sure whether his English had improved, he laughed. Well, to be honest, it hasn't, I laughed back. Reinaldo is in his fifties and works in tourism. He's been around, from Bariloche to China, and often missed his private classes with me. But whenever he managed to attend, we had a ball. Among other things, I learned what a truly special place Easter Island is and that I really need to visit a certain fabulous hotel in the jungle near Manaus.

If you want to study Portuguese, you can apply for a student visa which would make it easier to stay on. For example, many foreigners register at the Pontificia Universidade Católica in Rio de Janeiro (Extension Department, Casa 15, Rua Marques São Vincente 225, Gávea, 22453–900 Rio; +55 21 529 9212). This is an excellent place to link up with students and advertise classes if you want to offer private lessons (which pay much better than working for an institute).

BARRY O'LEARY

Barry O'Leary, well-travelled TEFLer, arrived in Salvador (northern Brazil) just before Carnaval. (The best time to start work is following the Carnaval, which takes place during the week over Ash Wednesday every February.) He bought a map, borrowed a telephone directory from his hostel and walked round all the 25 language academies with his CV. His luck wasn't as quick as it had been in Ecuador (described later) because most academies couldn't tell how many students they would have until after Carnaval. But Barry managed to find an evening job at an academy outside Salvador and later found two other jobs.

I taught in three Institutes, PEC (www.pec.com.br), Okey Dokey and AEC Idiomas. The business academy sent me to various offices which were all fully equipped and well organised. Generally working conditions were excellent and so was the pay; I received about $8 an hour which was a good rate for Brazil. The pupils were a mixed bag, yet they all had a great sense of humour and participated in the lessons, though some students were there only because their boss wanted them to be and had little interest.

I worked at another academy one afternoon a week. The approach here was to teach English through music, followed by group conversation lessons. Each week the director would translate two or three songs for the students to sing along in English. The students enjoyed this immensely, and I thought it was a very original way to learn. Most students seemed to be more interested in asking me questions about England and my life rather than pay attention to the lessons, but it was a good way for them to improve their fluency. I found Brazilian students very happy-go-lucky people; they were always smiling and interested in learning English.

I was lucky enough to live in the old quarter of Salvador called Pelourinho, which was the hub of the nightlife, but also the hub of any trouble. I lived in a house with 15 people including Brazilians, Nigerians, French and Irish, for which I paid $20 a month and had a brilliant three months.

LIST OF EMPLOYERS

ENGLISH CAMP

Rua Barão de Capanema 220 - Cerqueira Cesar - 01411-010 São Paulo - SP

☎ +55 11 3062 6333

✉ englishcamp@englishcamp.com.br

🖥 www.englishcamp.com.br

NUMBER OF TEACHERS: 5 per vacation season.

PREFERENCE OF NATIONALITY: None provided they are fluent English speakers.

QUALIFICATIONS: Must have open mind, to teach international students.

CONDITIONS OF EMPLOYMENT: 2–4 weeks starting January and July. 6–8 hours a day.

SALARY: None, volunteer positions only for those travelling on tourist visas. Full room and board provided free.

FACILITIES/SUPPORT: Letter of invitation sent so that volunteer teachers can arrive with tourist visa.

RECRUITMENT: Word of mouth from other teachers. Interviews can be conducted by Skype. Applications should be made at least 2 months in advance of January and July start dates to give time for a visa to be issued.

CONTACT: Silvia Goulart, Interviewer.

ENGLISH ON DEMAND

Rua Pouso Alegre 2822, Santa Tereza, Belo Horizonte - MG 31010–330

☎ +55 31 3309 5590

✉ eod@mail.com

🖥 www.englishondemand.amawebs.br

NUMBER OF TEACHERS: 2.

PREFERENCE OF NATIONALITY: Native English speakers: American, British, Canadian and Australian.

QUALIFICATIONS: Minimum bachelor's degree. Must enjoy teaching even if lacking experience. Preference given to those with teaching experience.

CONDITIONS OF EMPLOYMENT: Minimum 12 months.

SALARY: Minimum $10 per hour. Extra payments depend on experience, attitude towards learning to teach and the commitment to the students.

FACILITIES/SUPPORT: One-bedroom house attached to the school can be made available to a qualified and approved teacher.

RECRUITMENT: Via internet. References will be taken up. Initial interview can be via Skype and also face-to-face interviews.

LINGUAE – PERSONAL LANGUAGE INSTITUTE

Rua Paraisopolis 52, Santa Tereza, Belo Horizonte – MG 31010–330 Rua Dom José de Barros, 152, 10th Floor, Centre, 01038-902 Sao Paulo-SP

☎ +55 11 3255 7975; +55 11 8784 4489 (Mob)

✉ plinio@linguae.com.br

🖥 www.linguae.com.br

PREFERENCE OF NATIONALITY: Native speakers.

CONDITIONS OF EMPLOYMENT: In-company, part-time work.

SALARY: Hourly rates from R$35 to R$45.

RECRUITMENT: Candidates should be living locally.

CONTACT: Plinio Gherardi Junior.

NEW START COMUNICACOES

Rua Uruguiana 10/1211, Centro, 20050–090 Rio de Janeiro

☎ +55 21 2508 6917

✉ newstart@newstart.com.br

🖥 ww.newstart.com.br

NUMBER OF TEACHERS: 15–20.

PREFERENCE OF NATIONALITY: Must be a native English speaker.

QUALIFICATIONS: Preferably CELTA or Trinity TESOL certificate and some classroom experience.

CONDITIONS OF EMPLOYMENT: Minimum 5 months' work.

SALARY: R$33 (£11.50) per hour.

FACILITIES/SUPPORT: Training in Business English.

RECRUITMENT: Direct application by CV via email and telephone.

CONTACT: Stephanie Crockett or Adam Reid.

SCHUTZ & KANOMATA ESL & PSL

Rua Galvao Costa 85, Santa Cruz do Sul 96810 012

☎ +55 51 3715 3366

✉ sk@sk.com.br

🖥 www.sk.com.br/guests/sk-lcb.html

NUMBER OF TEACHERS: 5 every semester on Brazilian Language and Culture Exchange Program.

PREFERENCE OF NATIONALITY: Canadian, American and British.

QUALIFICATIONS: Main qualification is personality; must be communicative, considerate and interested in making friends. ESL teaching experience desirable.

CONDITIONS OF EMPLOYMENT: 10–12-month contracts; semesters run March 1–July 20 or August 1–December 20. Occasionally one-semester positions are possible. 20 hours per week, mostly in the evenings.

SALARY: Average net income above the cost of living. Bonus of $400 paid per completed semester.

FACILITIES/SUPPORT: Programme provides accommodation, meals, Portuguese instruction and occasional weekend tours. Advice given on appropriate visas, e.g. visitor visa acceptable for 5-month programme and trainee visa for 10–12 month programme, for which course enrolment is a requirement.

RECRUITMENT: Strong internet exposure. Also former teacher in Canada acts as agent. Candidates are chosen 3–4 months before semester start date, plus short-notice vacancies sometimes available.

CONTACT: Ricardo Schütz, Principal.

SPEAKING - CENTRO DE CULTURA AMERICANA

R. Cel. Renno, 321 Centro, Itajuba, Minas Gerais 37500 050

📞 +55 35 3621 3354

📠 speakingidiomas@yahoo.com.br; administracao@speaking.com.br

💻 www.speaking.com.br

NUMBER OF ESL TEACHERS: 3–4 per year.

PREFERENCE OF NATIONALITY: American, Canadian and British.

QUALIFICATIONS: TESL or similar.

CONDITIONS OF EMPLOYMENT: Standard commitment February to December. 38 hours per week, Monday to Saturday.

SALARY: R$16 ($8) per hour net. Wage is enough for living in a small town in Brazil.

FACILITIES/SUPPORT: School provides a small furnished studio house; or help with living expenses.

RECRUITMENT: By email or via ESL websites such as www.jobstefl.com.

CONTACT: Dagmar Andrade, Director (dagmarandrade@yahoo.com.br).

THE GLOBAL ENGLISH

Avenida 23, # 1274, Ituiutaba, MG 38300-114

📞 +55 34 3261 2141

📠 iica@netsitecom.br

💻 www.iica.com.br

Number of teachers: 15.

Preference of nationality: USA, UK or Canada.

Qualifications: Should be aged 21–32 and either a student enrolled in last year of university or within 12 months of graduation at the time of application.

Conditions of employment: 12 months. 34 h.p.w. Monday–Saturday.

Salary: Allowance of R$1,050 reais ($300) per month plus free family homestay.

Facilities/Support: Programme eligible for special trainee visa status after participants sign a contract and provide documentation as required by Brazilian Immigration Service. The Global English will assist with visa process. Visa fees are US$420–$720 and cannot be refunded in the case of a visa being denied.

Recruitment: Screening based on candidate's CV.

Contact: Professor Jacy Pimenta, Coordinator.

CHILE

More than most other South American economies, Chile's is flourishing with a modest unemployment rate of 6.6% (2012) which is considerably lower than it was a year or two ago. In terms of market competitiveness, Chile ranks most highly among South American countries. As commercial, touristic and cultural contacts with the outside world have increased, so has the demand for the English language. The most booming market is for business English, though there is also demand for teachers of children, created largely by the Chilean government lowering the age at which English is taught in state schools from 7th grade to 5th grade.

The ongoing drive to raise the level of English language teaching throughout the country continues with the Chilean Ministry of Education's major initiative, the *Programa Inglés Abre Puertas* or English Opens Doors Program. This ambitious programme aims to improve English language education in state schools in cities and small towns throughout Chile, by enlisting the help of native and near-native English speakers. University graduates work alongside local teachers in classrooms to help improve listening and speaking skills among pupils. Participants must be university graduates (aged 21–35) and stay for one or two semesters, normally from March/April or end of July but dates vary. Volunteers receive a small monthly participation bonus of 60,000 pesos (US$120) in addition to free room and board with a Chilean host family and domestic travel. Health insurance is provided.

Prospective volunteers can apply directly via the Volunteer Centre in Santiago (+56 2 406 7191; Skype: EnglishOpensDoors; voluntarios@mineduc.cl or English.open.doors.applications@gmail.com; www.centrodevoluntarios.cl) or through partner organisations abroad which recruit for the programme such as Bridge Linguatec (www.bridgetefl.com), CIEE (www.ciee.org), BUNAC (www.bunac.org), the Experiment in International Living (www.experiment.cl), TeachAway Inc (www.teachaway.com), Reach to Teach (www.reachtoteachrecruiting.com) and TEFL Institute (www.teflinstitute.com). **Luke Harris** was so enthusiastic about the EODP that after finishing his stint of teaching he moved into the office to help recruit further volunteer teachers:

> *Before doing the programme I had only volunteered as a teaching assistant a few hours per week in an ESL classroom. The application process is fairly rigorous. In addition to the application form and writing two essays, you must submit various documents and photos which is followed with a Skype interview. Since you work in a public school, teachers and students are often not very motivated which can be frustrating. Living with a host family was awesome! It is a great way to get a feeling for the community and culture, not to mention it allows you to learn a ton of Spanish.*
>
> *My students were extremely enthusiastic to have a native speaker for a teacher. For that reason they always received me with a great deal of warmth and appreciation. This made for a very comfortable and positive environment. However, students have a very low level of English. Despite many years of English courses most are not at a conversational level. Also, discipline can be difficult if you are used to an orderly classroom. In Chile classes are large and students have more freedom. Chileans are generally much more open and gregarious than people in the US. I was lucky to make many Chilean friends and spent a lot of time making barbecues with them, playing football and travelling on the weekends. I had not expected to receive so much attention for being a foreigner. This was great at times and difficult at times. For me, this experience has been a life-changing and self-defining experience. If you are a professional teacher though and have your own ideas, styles and lesson plans this programme could be somewhat unsatisfying in the classroom. The cultural experience is unparalleled.*

Similarly **Serika Ramlall** from South Africa stayed on after her EOD volunteer period in Puerto Montt mid-2011:

> *I have always loved travelling in South America and I was keen to spend more time in a less well-known country, so I searched online for teaching opportunities. When I found out about the EOD programme in Chile, I was*

immediately interested. I applied through BridgeTefl (www.bridgetefl.com/english-opens-doors-chile) who accepted me as a volunteer within about a week of applying.

One of the advantages of the programme is that the Centro de Voluntarios explains the process for applying for the 'residencia temporaria' during orientation. It took about two months for my visa to be processed, but during that time, I was still able to teach. As a volunteer, you´re expected to teach 25 pedagogical hours (an hour is calculated as a 45-minute lesson in Chile) per week. In addition, you are required to spend 10 hours working on lesson planning with your head teacher as well as leading extracurricular activities. Sometimes it could be quite frustrating when students didn´t respond to lessons that I´d spent a lot of time working on and I had to modify my teaching methods and ideas quite a lot. Students loved games and more interactive lessons, so it was really rewarding when they learned vocabulary or grammar from these.

Apart from the EOD programme operating in state schools, most teaching opportunities in Chile are in the commercial sector and the majority of those are in the capital Santiago where there are scores of private language schools. Some relevant institutes can also be found in the Valparaiso-Viña del Mar area. There will be less competition for teaching vacancies and a lower cost of living in smaller places such as the aptly named La Serena in the dry north of the country, or other towns such as Arica, Iquique, Antofagasta, Talca, Concepción, Valdivia, Osorno and Punta Arenas, all of which have possibilities for teachers, albeit on a smaller scale. Some course providers in Santiago serve clients in Valparaiso and their teachers either commute to 'Valpo' twice a week or live there.

The Instituto Chileno-Británico de Cultura in Santiago (entry below) recruits only qualified teachers, and has a good library which incorporates the British Council's resource library for teachers; anyone prepared to pay the membership fee can borrow materials, though many schools in Santiago have good libraries themselves. Native English speaker teachers are also hired by the Institutos Chileno-Britanico de Cultura in Concepcion (www.ibritanico.com), Arica (www.britanicoarica.cl) and Viña del Mar (www.institutochilenobritanico.cl).

Mandy Powell from Cambridge noticed that there were relatively few teachers from Britain compared to North America and she speculated that this might have something to do with the high cost of the work visa for Britons. Perhaps because of their scarcity, the British accent is at a premium in Mandy's experience which makes work easier to find. She enjoyed the mixture of people, from students just out of university to people who had left work in search of a different pace of life.

South American language schools tend to prefer face-to-face meetings rather than emails and phone calls. **Heidi Resetarits** typed 'English schools in Santiago' into a search engine, came up with a huge list of language schools in areas she wanted to apply to and then dropped off resumés in person.

I actually got an interview on the spot at the second school I applied to... and I happened to just walk by it – it wasn't even on my list! Santiago is a very modern city and new schools are popping up all the time. It's worth it just to walk around town and see what's there. I know that South Americans appreciate face-to-face meetings rather than emails and phone calls, so I walked in and asked to meet with a director. I decided to stay and chat a bit with the receptionist, and he made me an appointment for the next day.

The interview was a face-to-face with the director of the school. After we talked about my resumé and a bit about my teaching experience, we set up a teaching practice (he chose a topic and a student) for the next day. I got the job within three days.

Doug Burgess went job hunting in Santiago, armed with a CELTA he had acquired at home in Cambridge and some experience. He had an interview with both Burford Corporate Training (www.burford.cl) and EF English First (see entry). Burford works exclusively from its own site, whereas about 60% of English First's classes are in offices. English First offered Doug a contract for 12 months with work visa and a rate of 5,500 pesos an hour, more if he had to travel more than two metro stations or worked at their other campus. Burford did not offer a contract: their rate of pay was 4,000 pesos an hour which would have gone up to 6,000 after a three-month probationary period. In the end, Doug accepted another offer from the prestigious Instituto Chileno-Británico de Cultura, paying 5,400 pesos an hour, more for high level classes, on Saturdays or in another branch of the British Institute. His contract was for 15 hours which was enough to secure a work visa, although he had the option of working up to 30 hours or more. Before Doug secured a full-time teaching job, he participated in an exchange programme run by the Woodward Institute in Providencia. For every Spanish lesson he received, he gave an English lesson, and went from being a complete beginner in the language to fairly competent.

A further possibility is to teach at English-medium *colegios*, where a longer commitment will be necessary and a reasonable salary paid. Although they employ mainly certified teachers, often hired at recruitment fairs and through international advertising, they do need some native English speakers for their English departments. For example, **Eleanor Padfield** from Cambridge was determined to work abroad after finishing her A levels but did not want to go through an agency where she would be with lots of other British students. After spending the first half of her year in Salamanca, Spain, she sent emails in Spanish all over the world to find something to do, preferably in Latin America. Of the many schools and language schools she contacted, one of the few to reply was the Redland School, an upmarket private school. Although they told her that they didn't usually accept gap year students (since so many previous gappers had left prematurely to travel), they made an exception for Eleanor when she promised to stick it out till the end of the term beginning in March and ending in August. When June rolled round, she was tempted to leave early but her conscience (or her mother's exhortations) persuaded her to keep her promise, trying to see as much of the country as she could in her days off.

Heidi Resetarits was an English teacher for both the Universidad de Las Americas and Comunicorp, Santiago simultaneously:

> *I had two sets of students. My students from the institute were mainly businessmen who needed to learn English for work. These men were preoccupied with work but used their lunch breaks to take classes. They do want to learn, but more often than not, work took priority. I had a few women who were very dedicated and learned rather quickly.*
>
> *I also taught 4th year college students how to write essays and give public speeches. They were at a different level than my business students (they were majoring in Teaching English) and they had a better grasp of the language. They were about 50–50 with effort and participation, but I could also have higher expectations for them. I really enjoyed working with these students.*

The commercial institutes in Santiago vary greatly in size, reliability in their treatment of employees and teaching methods. Newcomers to the city quickly learn which are the better schools and gradually acquire more hours with them. In-company teaching usually takes place early in the morning; middle-ranking staff tend to be taught before the official working day begins while directors and higher-ranking executives take their classes at a more civilised mid-morning hour. Most teachers enjoy the variety of off-site teaching rather than classroom teaching which tends to be more textbook-based.

After completing the TEFL certificate course at the American Language Institute in San Diego, **Brianna Antman** heard about vacancies teaching business people at Comunicorp in Santiago, Chile. She sent her CV to the director and after a phone interview was given a contract to work for the standard academic year:

> *Most of my classes were one-on-one with managers, CEOs and other employees of large companies held in their offices. We were given a course summary sheet for each level which described the grammar points and functions that we were supposed to cover. Since we worked in a business atmosphere we were required to dress formally and adapt to the professional/business world.*
>
> *I found accommodation in the local newspaper El Mercurio. However, most teachers found their accommodation through word of mouth and/or friends who were already here. Because the school is one of the higher paying institutes in Santiago, the wages of 6,000 pesos an hour were quite decent, enough to live off and travel. The school had a teacher's room filled with a plethora of resources, books, shared lessons on the computer, CDs, and incredibly experienced people in the field. All of the books were scanned onto the computer, thus making it quite easy to find/plan lessons.*

The academic year runs from March to December with a two-week winter holiday in July and one week recess in mid-September, so the best time to apply for a contract is the end of February. There are 19 British curriculum schools listed on the website of the Association of British Schools in Chile (www.absch.cl). The Santiago *Yellow Pages* are a useful source; look up Instituto de Idiomas or check online www.chilnet.cl/rc/port_select_companies.asp?acti_code=779.

Non-contractual work is usually paid by the hour, starting at 5,000 pesos and rising to 8,000 pesos. Established teachers working for universities such as UNIACC in Providencia can top 15,000 pesos but this is rare. The cost of living is higher than in many other places on the continent but teachers can still support themselves. **Heidi Resetarits** says that '*you won't be able to do much saving in South America in general*', and recommends that you don't move to Chile without savings if you want to have fun and money to travel. Normally 10% of earnings must be paid in tax, which in some cases can be reclaimed the following April/May. After taking the first job she was offered by Bridge Linguatec, **Mandy Powell** assumed that all jobs paid roughly the same. However, later when she was working for EES (see entry) she discovered that there is a huge variation and wishes that she had looked for a better paid teaching job sooner. It was especially tough trying to make ends meet in the quiet periods of January–February and July.

Usually the CELTA, Trinity or equivalent certificate is a minimum requirement for anyone considering working in the private sector. However, those looking to work within the state system of education will find that CELTA qualifications will not be accepted. In Chile a teaching degree takes five years, and school directors tend to look quite disparagingly upon one month/120 hour courses. A worthwhile volunteer teaching scheme is run by Voluntarios de Esperanza (VE; Carabineros de Chile 33, Santiago; +56 2 717 99 37; www.ve-global.org). VE works with partner institutions to place volunteers to work with at-risk children, including teaching English, for a minimum of four months beginning in September, January and May. The application process is competitive and no registration fee is charged.

RED TAPE

Most job-seekers arrive on a tourist visa valid for 90 days. Note that on entry by air some nationalities (not Britons) will have to pay a one-off 'reciprocity tax', e.g. $100 for Americans, $55 for Canadians. Once you find a job, the most common visa to apply for is the *Visa Sujeta a Contrato* (subject to contract visa) for which you will need to take a notarised copy of a contract from an employer that shows a minimum salary of 100,000 pesos a month to the *Departamento de Extrajería*. The cost varies among nationalities: in this case Americans get it for free whereas Britons have to pay $74. If you are able to commit yourself for a year, your employer may be willing to help you obtain the more flexible temporary resident visa. Some official sources say that this costs $350 for UK nationals, although **Mandy Powell**, writing in May 2012, said that the total expenses for her permits came to about £1,000 and took two months processing time. After you get your work visa, you then need to register your address with the immigration police and obtain your ID card or *cedula* which you require for joining the Chilean health care scheme, opening a bank account, etc.

Many teachers who enter the country on a tourist visa end up working for employers who will not assist, and these tend to be the less reputable schools. Before the 90-day validity of their tourist visa is up, they simply get a new tourist visa by crossing the border to Mendoza, Argentina. Good detailed visa information is available on the website of the TEFL training centre, the TEFL Academy, in Santiago (www.tefl-academy.com). If you are from New Zealand, Australia or Canada you can apply for a working holiday visa which allows you to work anywhere and to live and work without a contract for one year. Rarely, people are offered a job before arrival. If this is the case, there are two ways to obtain the appropriate visa permit. Either your employer submits the application at the Ministry of Foreign Affairs in Chile (Direccion de Asuntos Consulares y de Imigracion, Bandera 46, Santiago) or you apply at the Chilean Consulate in your country of origin. You will need a signed and notarised work contract and a full medical report. If granted, the visa will be valid for one year. After that you may be eligible for a *visacion de residencia* which allows an unlimited stay.

ADVERTISING FOR PRIVATE CLIENTS

The average rate for private lessons is about 10,000–12,000 pesos per hour. There are many ways to meet the expatriate community from playing cricket at the Prince of Wales Country Club to frequenting the English language bookshop Books and Bits on Av Apoquindo in Santiago (www.booksandbits.cl).

You can advertise for private clients in *El Mercurio*, the leading quality daily. Check ads on Craigslist (http://santiago.en.craigslist.org) or in the free ads paper *El Rastro*.

Advertising at your embassy has helped some teachers. A useful option is to find a supermarket which has a noticeboard for small advertisements in their entrance halls. For example the Lider and Jumbo chains of stores have such noticeboards. Lider is located on the corner of Avenida Pedro de Valdivia and Bilbao, while Jumbo is on the corner of Portugal and Diagonal Paraguay. If you can translate between English and Spanish, it will be worth advertising yourself as a translator as well. The best way to find private clients, however, is by word of mouth.

LEISURE TIME

Although Santiago is cosmopolitan and modern, there are pockets of poverty and the men can be aggressive, shouting across the street at women. However, Santiago is an interesting and safe city where young women can feel reasonably secure even if being out alone in the wee small hours. Pollution in the winter months can get a bit depressing. However, for the most part, the quality of life is enviable. **Mandy Powell** especially relished waking up after rain and seeing the fantastic mountains clearly against crystal blue skies. **Heidi Resetarits** managed to keep herself pleasantly busy in her spare time:

I planned trips all over Chile at least once a week. I wrote for a magazine. I joined a gym and a swim team. I bought a bike and rode around town. I also spent a lot of time drinking coffee, pisco sours and/or wine on patios, reading or just enjoying the day. Santiago is a great city to spend time in, and it is very easy to get around in and relatively safe. The people are friendly and want to know who you are and where you are from. My favourite days were spent walking to a random café, meeting a friend and letting that meeting go into a warm summer Santiago night.

LIST OF EMPLOYERS

ACADEMIA DE IDIOMAS DEL NORTE
Ramirez 1345, Iquique
℡ +56 57 411 827
✉ secretaria@languages.cl
🖳 www.languages.cl

Swiss owned.
NUMBER OF TEACHERS: 4.
PREFERENCE OF NATIONALITY: Native English speakers.

QUALIFICATIONS: Recognised TEFL certificate.
CONDITIONS OF EMPLOYMENT: 6–9-month contracts with 6 working hours per day.
FACILITIES/SUPPORT: Information on homestay families, flats, hotels, etc. is given. Shared apartments with other teachers sometimes available. Work contract provided in order to get work permits.
RECRUITMENT: Interviews are essential and usually held in Chile but can be conducted by telephone or Skype.

NUMBER OF TEACHERS: 15.

PREFERENCE OF NATIONALITY: None.

QUALIFICATIONS: TEFL-certified teachers with previous experience.

CONDITIONS OF EMPLOYMENT: Contract length is negotiable. Full-time is 25–30 hours per week with classes between 8am and 9pm, Monday to Friday. Some Saturday work available.

SALARY: Average 500,000 Chilean pesos per month.

FACILITIES/SUPPORT: Assistance given with work permits and guidance when filling in relevant paperwork.

RECRUITMENT: Interviews essential.

CONTACT: Craig Wilson, Director.

NUMBER OF TEACHERS: Approximately 30.

PREFERENCE OF NATIONALITY: None. Company prefers to have a wide variety of cultures and accents represented on the staff.

QUALIFICATIONS: At least one of the following: CELTA, TEFL certificate, MA in TESOL, MA in Education, MA in Communicative Disorders, and at least one year of classroom EFL experience, preferably with adult Business English students.

CONDITIONS OF EMPLOYMENT: New teachers are hired throughout the year, but most new positions begin in April, May, June, July and August. Hours are usually spread out during the day. Most business students prefer to have classes at the peak hours which are: 8:30–10am, 1–2:30pm, 6–7:30pm. Other students, who are more flexible, take classes during the off-peak hours from 10am to 11:30am and from 3pm to 4:30pm.

SALARY: Varies according to classroom experience, degree held, and time with the company. The lowest salary would be 500,000 Chilean pesos per month for 80 classroom hours. There are additional benefits such as a travel bonus at the end of the contract for those hired from abroad and a monthly transportation budget. Taxes are less than 5% and social security is not an issue if the teacher has a home pension plan.

FACILITIES/SUPPORT: Assistance with finding accommodation. School assists with processing the work visa. Spanish classes are available in exchange for English teaching hours.

RECRUITMENT: Internet and word of mouth.

CONTACT: Diane Greenstein, Academic & Human Resources Director.

NUMBER OF TEACHERS: 30–40.

PREFERENCE OF NATIONALITY: None.

QUALIFICATIONS: 4+ year degree, TESOL, CELTA or TEFL and 1+ year's experience preferred.

CONDITIONS OF EMPLOYMENT: Standard contracts are 6–12 months. The usual hours are mornings, lunch time and evenings, Monday to Friday.

SALARY: 7,000 to 8,000 Chilean pesos per hour, 25–30 hours per week. Deductions of 10% refundable with filing of tax return.

FACILITIES/SUPPORT: Company will provide proof of employment for lease and rental agreement. All foreign employees receive a Chilean work visa.

RECRUITMENT: In person interview.

CONTACT: Howard H. Spencer, Director of Studies.

Associate Member of International House.

NUMBER OF TEACHERS: Around 15.

PREFERENCE OF NATIONALITY: None.

QUALIFICATIONS: CELTA, Trinity TESOL or IH certificate are preferred and English for Life also offers its own teacher training programme. More experienced teachers have the possibility of moving into more senior roles or teacher training.

CONDITIONS OF EMPLOYMENT: Contract is initially for one academic year (9 months). The contract specifies an agreed number of contact (teaching) hours.

SALARY: Varies with number of contracted hours. Bonus may be paid depending on location of teaching in Santiago. Teachers are guaranteed a base salary, for example, for an 18-hour contract with extra hours and bonuses paid in addition. 7%

deduction for health insurance. Overtime paid on hours worked over 24 per week.

FACILITIES/SUPPORT: Accommodation and flights are not paid for by the school, although help and advice are given in finding suitable accommodation. Teachers enter on a tourist visa and then apply for a work permit/visa when they have signed the contract. Teachers are entitled to paid holiday and sick leave on a pro-rata basis. Full academic support is given, e.g. employer pays for teachers to attend meetings and teacher development sessions which are run once a week by in-house teacher trainer. The school is easily accessible by metro and bus. School has a garden available to staff for lesson preparation, barbecues, etc. Free wifi access and computers. DOS willing to supervise teachers who wish to do the online DELTA or other career development courses.

RECRUITMENT: Through IHWO (www.ihworld.com/recruitment), www.tefl.com or direct application throughout the year. CVs should be sent to the DOS (dos@englishforlife.cl) who will contact suitable candidates for interview.

CONTACT: Justine Robertson, School Manager.

FISCHER ENGLISH INSTITUTE
Calle Cirujano Guzmán 49 Providencia, Santiago de Chile
+56 2 235 6667/+56 2 235 9812
contacto@fischerinstitute.cl
www.fischerinstitute.cl

NUMBER OF TEACHERS: 30.
PREFERENCE OF NATIONALITY: USA.
QUALIFICATIONS: University degree and TEFL certificate or similar and 1 year's experience in teaching.
CONDITIONS OF EMPLOYMENT: Minimum 1-year contract, 20 hours a week.
FACILITIES/SUPPORT: None.
RECRUITMENT: References, preferably from school abroad. Interviews essential, carried out in Santiago.
CONTACT: Celsa Contreras, Academic Secretary.

INSTITUTO CHILENO-BRITANICO DE CULTURA
Huerfanos 554 (Santa Lucia), Santiago
+56 2 413 2350
edovas@britanico.cl
www.britanico.cl

Other branches in Las Condes, La Florida, Nuñoa, Maipu and Providencia.
NUMBER OF TEACHERS: 10.
PREFERENCE OF NATIONALITY: None, but should be native English speaker.

QUALIFICATIONS: A degree in English or Modern Languages, plus a TEFL qualification. However, experience is valued more than TEFL qualification.
CONDITIONS OF EMPLOYMENT: 1 year, March to February. 30 teaching hours per week mostly evenings.
SALARY: £700 per month.
FACILITIES/SUPPORT: Help with finding accommodation is provided. Teachers are provided with a settling-in grant towards their accommodation.
RECRUITMENT: Usually on the spot.

INSTITUTO CHILENO-NORTEAMERICANO DE CULTURA
Moneda No. 1467, Santiago
+56 2 696 3215 or +56 677 7070
englishteachers@norteamericano.cl
www.norteamericano.cl

NUMBER OF TEACHERS: 15–20.
PREFERENCE OF NATIONALITY: American and Canadian.
QUALIFICATIONS: BA in Education or TESL/TEFL and 6 months' teaching experience, or a bachelor's degree in related field with certificate in TESL/TEFL and 2 years' teaching experience.
CONDITIONS OF EMPLOYMENT: 1-year contracts starting in March. 30 hours per week. Peak hours of work early morning and early evening, and some Saturdays. Classes for adults, children, teens, business and academic English.
SALARY: Equivalent of US$1,100 per month in Chilean pesos.
FACILITIES/SUPPORT: Assistance given in obtaining visas. Training provided. Teacher's room with computers, email access and cafeteria privileges.
RECRUITMENT: Direct application by mail, email, phone or fax. Applicants should send cover letter, resumé, recent photo, copy of diplomas/certificates and letters of reference from recent employers.

REDLAND SCHOOL
Camino el Alba 11357, Las Condes, Santiago
+56 2 959 8500
secretaria_rector@redland.cl; jobs@redland.cl
www.redland.cl

NUMBER OF TEACHERS: 72 in total.
PREFERENCE OF NATIONALITY: British or other nationalities with English as a first language.
QUALIFICATIONS: University degree and teaching qualification. Pre- and post-university students also considered for gap year placements.

CONDITIONS OF EMPLOYMENT: 1–3-year contract, mostly starting late February for academic year March to December. Classes run from 8am to 3.30pm or 5pm. Pupils aged 4–18.

SALARY: On application. Increases are pegged to cost of living. 13th month salary given as a bonus.

FACILITIES/SUPPORT: Assistance finding accommodation can be offered. Professional development opportunities and free lunches provided.

RECRUITMENT: Via email in first instance. Recruitment starts in August for following academic year.

TEACHING CHILE

Av. Vitacura 3355, Dept 113, Santiago

+1 720 221 3831 (US phone number routes calls to Santiago office); +44 20 8150 6981 (UK phone number routes calls to Santiago office)

info@teachingchile.com

www.teachingchile.com

NUMBER OF TEACHERS: Approximately 90 native English-speaking teachers per year.

PREFERENCE OF NATIONALITY: None. To date, TeachingChile have placed teachers from Australia, Canada, England, Ireland, New Zealand, Scotland and the USA.

QUALIFICATIONS: Varies among schools. Overall, applicants should be a graduate of a university or in their final year of undergraduate studies, ESL/TEFL/TESOL certification and teaching experience are desired but not required. Spanish language skills are not required for classroom instruction but elementary conversational language skills are recommended for the teacher's cultural enjoyment.

CONDITIONS OF EMPLOYMENT: Minimum 6-month contract. The majority of teachers choose a 1-year contract. All contracts are renewable directly with the teaching institution assuming the school has positions available and the teacher has a good rapport with the employer and students.

SALARY: Minimum 400,000 Chilean pesos per month for a base of 15 hours of classroom time per week. For longer hours teachers can earn up to 450,000 pesos. Some schools deduct 13% for tax and an optional 7% for medical insurance, but salaries are adjusted accordingly and teachers make about the same net salary.

FACILITIES/SUPPORT: Guaranteed work contract, visa processing assistance, and accommodation arrangements are in place before the teacher leaves home. TeachingChile provides assistance with accommodation and a pre-paid transfer from Santiago airport to the first night's accommodation.

RECRUITMENT: Via the internet, universities and ESL/TEFL/TESOL job placement websites. Applicants submit an application package available from TeachingChile's website prior to arrival and will be interviewed by telephone. Placement fee for full service is US$1,295.

CONTACT: Bruce Thompson, Managing Director (bruce@teachingchile.com).

COLOMBIA

Since most people's only associations with Colombia are with crime and violence, it is not surprising to learn that teaching institutes in that country sometimes have trouble attracting qualified foreign teachers. Foreign teachers are extremely unlikely to become involved in any drug-inspired tensions but are guaranteed to be welcomed by the locals. Memories will be of a local carnival rather than of a neighbourhood shoot-out. **Dave Crowder** takes strong exception to knee-jerk negative reactions to his adopted country and to the warning contained in US and UK embassy literature:

> *I have found the people of Colombia to be universally friendly and helpful to strangers. Unlike the USA, the welcome here is genuine, open and amicable, and the people are genuinely interested in the novelty of a stranger among them. There is no more drug trafficking in Medellín where I live than in any other major city anywhere in the world (I used to live in Miami where there is much more drug gang activity). As a matter of fact, I will extend my comments about Medellín to every part of the nation that I have visited, which is everywhere but the few FARC/ELN-controlled areas in the boondocks.*

With the expansion of trade, interest in English has increased, as evidenced by the popularity of English language media like newspapers and radio stations. However, a local law prohibits more than a 30%+ participation of foreign nationals in a school, so jobs for native English speakers are fewer than demand would seem to suggest. First Class English (see list of organisations) employs about 24 teachers, but can only offer six jobs to native English speakers without dual citizenship.

Colombia is more strongly oriented towards the USA than elsewhere in South America, with an extensive network of Colombian-American Cultural Centers around the country. However, **Charles Seville** from Oxford, who spent a year as an English language assistant at the University de Los Llanos in Villavicencio, was struck by how keen Colombians were to learn British English. There is a British Council Teaching Centre in Bogotá, whose market is primarily university students and young learners (www.britishcouncil.org/colombia) but which also runs conversation clubs. From time to time it advertises teacher vacancies, offering a salary of between about 4,300,000 and 5,760,000 Colombian pesos per month.

It is possible to access the Colombian *Yellow Pages* on the internet (www.quehubo.com) which might provide a starting place for finding school addresses; search for *Instituto Idiomas*. The website www.poorbu thappy.com contains a list of language schools in Medellín, though the website is no longer maintained and is only useful as an archive. Some global EFL companies have a strong presence in Colombia. EF Education First in Bogotá is based at the Edificio EF (Carrera 9, No. 80-12, Oficina 702; +57 1 616 1130; www.ef.com.co) and Berlitz (www.berlitz.com.co) runs 13 centres, including five in Bogotá.

The main newspaper *El Tiempo* carries adverts for language schools in the capital. There are plenty of local language schools where untrained native English speakers can find work, but there are two main disadvantages. Wages and conditions can be very poor; many schools offer a few thousand pesos an hour (less than US$3), though the schools listed below offer more attractive salaries, with an upper limit of 18,500 Colombian pesos per hour (US$10). The second problem is the red tape. As usual, temporary working visas must be applied for in your country of residence. The Colombian Consulate in London has information about the requirements on their website (www.colombianconsulate.co.uk), which includes an undertaking by the employer to bear the cost of repatriation if the visa is cancelled and a letter from the Ministry of Work & Social Security testifying that the Colombian employer is not exceeding the legal limit on foreign employees. The visa fee is £130 and a personal interview is required. If a teacher intends to stay in Colombia longer than six months, he or she must register in person at DAS, the Colombian equivalent of the FBI, within 30 days of arrival. Approval will mean that you are entitled to acquire a *Cédula de Extranjería* (foreigners' ID).

LIST OF EMPLOYERS

FIRST CLASS ENGLISH

Carrera 12 # 93 - 78 Oficina 407, 407 Bogotá

+57 1 6232380

info@fcecolombia.com

www.fcecolombia.com

NUMBER OF TEACHERS: On average the school has space for at least 6 foreign national teachers.

PREFERENCE OF NATIONALITY: American and British.

QUALIFICATIONS: At least 1 year's teaching experience, preferably with executives/professionals. CELTA, ICELT certification is a plus. But the bottom line is that the candidate must have 3+ year college/university degree, hopefully in business or related areas.

CONDITIONS OF EMPLOYMENT: Minimum 1 year, if volunteering a minimum of 4 months. Up to 8 hours of teaching within the hours of 6am to 9pm.

SALARY: Contracted hourly pay from $15,000 to $18,500 Colombian pesos per hour, disbursed every 15 days. The *retencion* (tax) deduction, specific to this type of contract, is about 7% of income.

FACILITIES/SUPPORT: Can assist with accommodation if necessary on a case-by-case basis. School provides paperwork for working visa, however the teacher is required to activate the visa by travelling to a neighbouring country and going to the local consulate. This process can take up to 60 days in total from the moment the visa is requested.

RECRUITMENT: Email requests and walk-ins. An interview – possible by phone – is followed by 20-hour mandatory selection process. The process includes training, simulated class, teaching crash course and administrative instruction.

FUNDACION EDUCATIVA PERSONAL GROWTH

Transversal 25 No 53C-15 Bogotá

+57 1 5411503

info@pgrowth.com or admin@pgrowth.com

www.pgrowth.com

Private international organisation with headquarters in the Cayman Islands.

NUMBER OF TEACHERS: 45.

PREFERENCE OF NATIONALITY: UK, USA, Australia, Canada, South Africa.

QUALIFICATIONS: Native speakers with or without experience. Teachers can take on-site TEFL course if needed.

CONDITIONS OF EMPLOYMENT: 1 year. 30–48 hours per week to teach one-to-one and in small groups (adults, teenagers and children).

SALARY: 22,500 pesos ($12.50) per 90-minute class, before tax. Teachers are responsible for paying their own health insurance.

FACILITIES/SUPPORT: Accommodation arranged with choice of homestay for $250 per month to private furnished apartment for $700 (including furniture, bedding and internet connection). Help given to teachers who must submit documents to the Colombian consulate in their country.

RECRUITMENT: Usually via Craigslist. Local or skype interviews essential.

CONTACT: Sigfried Castell, International Academic Director.

INSTITUTO DE IDIOMAS (UNIVERSIDAD DEL NORTE)

Km 5 Via Pto Colombia, Barranquilla

+57 5 3509736/+57 5 3598852

idiomas@uninorte.edu.co

www.uninorte.edu.co/extensiones/idiomas

NUMBER OF TEACHERS: Around 5 a year.

PREFERENCE OF NATIONALITY: None.

QUALIFICATIONS: Master's degree in TESOL, Linguistics, Psychology, English, Elementary/Bilingual Education, or related areas. Must have certified experience teaching EFL, preferably outside the USA. Must be a native English speaker; be able to teach and evaluate students effectively; and have experience using language lab equipment.

CONDITIONS OF EMPLOYMENT: Minimum 1 year. 8 hours a day depending on classes assigned. Most likely 9am–5pm.

SALARY: Depends on qualifications. Other benefits include a living allowance of around $200 for rent, ticket and visa issuing costs. The university pays in Colombian pesos.

FACILITIES/SUPPORT: University recommends a rental agency and will serve as a guarantor. When teachers arrive, the university pays for a hotel for 1 week. The university also provides transport and documentation needed for the working visa.

RECRUITMENT: Via internet websites such as www.studyabroad.com. Interviews through Skype or videoconferencing are required. References are also checked.

CONTACT: Lourdes Rey, Academic Coordinator.

NATIVE TONGUE ENGLISH INSTITUTE

Cra. 4a Bis #35-05, Ibague, Tolima

+1 905 296 3562

smiranda@cogeco.ca

www.nativetongue.edu.co

Canadian-owned and operated company in its 10th year which operates schools in Ibague and Pereira, but is currently expanding throughout Colombia.

NUMBER OF TEACHERS: 10+.

PREFERENCE OF NATIONALITY: Canadian preferred, Americans accepted.

QUALIFICATIONS: Native speaker with at least one year overseas teaching experience. Spanish is an asset but not necessary.

CONDITIONS OF EMPLOYMENT: 11 months. Teaching hours 28 per week.

SALARY: Approx 1,500,000–2,000,000 pesos (from CAN$750) less deductions of about 40,000 pesos ($23) per month.

FACILITIES/SUPPORT: Assistance given with finding accommodation, guaranteeing contract and a stipend. Help given with obtaining work visa outside of Colombia.

RECRUITMENT: Via web postings. Phone interviews acceptable. Face-to-face interviews occasionally carried out in Canada.

CONTACT: Shawn Miranda, Canadian Operations.

TRAINING PEOPLE

Cra 15 No.98–42 Of 503, Bogotá

+571 6115009

sales@training-people.com

www.training-people.com

NUMBER OF TEACHERS: 5.

PREFERENCE OF NATIONALITY: British.

QUALIFICATIONS: TEFL certification (minimum 100 hours) such as CELTA, DELTA or even TESOL and TEFL (with approval of the Principal). Short courses such as TKT test are not acceptable. Candidates should be over 21. Degree plus TEFL preferred.

CONDITIONS OF EMPLOYMENT: 1 year. 40 hours a week, including business English to adults.

SALARY: Approx $1,000 per month.

FACILITIES/SUPPORT: Assistance given with obtaining a working visa, but teachers normally arrange their own accommodation.

RECRUITMENT: Via teflcourse.net and other advertisements.

CONTACT: Jorge Gil Gomez, Director (jgil@training-people.com or jorgilgo@hotmail.com).

ECUADOR

Ecuador's economy has benefitted since it was forced to adopt the US dollar as the national currency and it has been an oasis of political stability in the region for a long time. Teaching wages are still low, but obviously EFL teachers do not go to Ecuador to save money and it is still possible to live on the wages paid. For example, a night in a budget hotel costs from $9 and a tasty meal costs $5.

Demand for English continues to thrive, particularly for American English, in the capital Quito, the second city Guayaquil and in the picturesque city and cultural centre of Cuenca in the southern Sierra. The majority of teaching is of university students and the business community whose classes are usually scheduled early in the morning (starting at 7am) to avoid the equatorial heat of the day and again in the late afternoon and evening. Many schools are owned and run by expatriates since there are few legal restrictions on foreigners running businesses.

Wages are not as high as in Chile but higher than in Colombia, and usually allow teachers to enjoy a comfortable lifestyle since the cost of living is low. A qualified teacher can expect to earn about $700 a month. Accommodation is harder to find in Quito than in Cuenca. Qualified TEFLers should not accept less than US$6 an hour though the private institutes that accept unqualified teachers pay accordingly less. All teachers (both contract and freelance) have taxes withdrawn at source of between 5% and 12%. Quito is not as large and daunting a city as some other South American capitals and it should be easy to meet longer-term expats who may be able to give advice on teaching. The helpful British Council will give you a list of ELT schools throughout the country and will (unofficially) indicate which offer the best teacher support and modern teaching methods and resources. One possible source of information is the South American Explorers clubhouse (membership costs $60). In Quito the Club is at Jorge Washington 311 y Leonidas Plaza (Apartado 17 21 431). It includes language schools in Ecuador on its database and has a useful noticeboard.

As throughout the continent, charitable schools for children can always use voluntary help. The department of education in the country's poorest province runs a free volunteering scheme for native speakers with a basic knowledge of Spanish to teach in primary schools. If you want to spend at least four months between September and June in the Chimborazo region in the Andes, go to http://ecuador.teach-english-volunteer.com for details. You Volunteer (www.youvolunteer.org) is part of a small registered British charity that offers volunteers the opportunity to work and teach in schools in the Amazon jungle of central Ecuador as part of the Arajuno Road Project (see entry).

RED TAPE

Technically you shouldn't work on a tourist visa but there is little control. Britons and Americans can stay 90 days. If possible, teachers should get a 12-IX non-immigrant visa in their country of origin for stays of three to six months (fee $200), which can be extended by visiting a neighbouring country, usually Colombia. Most employers will help teachers who commit themselves for a reasonable stay to obtain a Cultural Exchange visa, (Category 12 VIII) valid for a year. The requirements are as follows: a notarised copy of a police report, doctor's certificate (including HIV test) and birth certificate, letter of invitation and various other documents from an Ecuadorian employer, letter of financial support from a backer/inviter and and so on. The visa fee for US citizens applying in the US is $50 plus a $30 application fee. The Centro de Educación Continua in Quito and CEDEI in Cuenca (see entries) both contract instructors as Cultural Exchange volunteers.

A new requirement for a proper teacher's work permit is a degree in English or Education plus a TEFL Certificate qualification.

BARRY O'LEARY

Barry O'Leary, on arriving in Quito, visited a tourist agency that had the addresses of all the possible academies and institutes. He started his first TEFL job-hunt armed only with a basic TEFL certificate and speaking very little Spanish. As luck would have it he found two jobs in 24 hours just by walking round the city with copies of his CV.

I can still remember the buzz I felt when José, my first employer, said 'yeah we're looking for someone to start next week.' I couldn't quite believe it. With this institute there wasn't really a formal interview or application process. With another school I had a basic interview to make sure I could speak and wasn't a monster, they didn't even ask for my TEFL certificate. In Ecuador everyone I knew was working without a work visa. I remember being worried about telling them I was only staying for three months but they were just happy to have a native speaker teaching their students.

The teaching varied. In one school I was responsible for conversation classes. I had no guidance with the type of lessons they wanted so had to use resources from my course, the internet and my imagination. In every lesson a local teacher was there to help with any language barriers. The working conditions were very relaxed, no lesson plans or meetings, I was just given a timetable and left to get on with it. As long as the students were smiling I was seen to be a good teacher.

I was lucky enough to find an apartment with an Ecuadorian family through an advertisement in an internet café. I made enough money to pay for my rent, food and some social activities and even managed to travel a bit with my last pay packet - and the dollars went much further in Peru. The students were all great, the teenagers tending to be cheeky, a few times they changed the theme of the lessons to 'make the teacher dance like a fool' before they did any work, but this was all part of the fun. It was a very relaxed atmosphere most of the time. I really enjoyed working with local teachers and they were all very open and friendly and interested in my life in England since many of them had never left Ecuador.

The highlight of Ecuador was helping my first students to prepare a presentation for the Directors on their chosen topics of hooliganism, pollution and anorexia. The looks on their faces when they received their certificates was definitely worth all the hours of hard work we put in. The low point of my experience was unfortunately when I was held at knife point outside my house. Luckily I was not hurt and they did not steal anything but it should be known that certain areas of Quito are dangerous.

SOUTHERN CROSS LANGUAGE CENTRE

Hannah McHugh on Southern Cross Teacher Training on the beach in Ecuador

'If there's one thing that got me through five weeks of one of the greatest educational challenges I've ever faced, it was the ability to take a moment and clear my head on the beautiful, endless beach on my doorstep. Starting each day with a run and a surf meant that it was possible at Kamala, like nowhere else, to stay healthy enough to deal with all the challenges the course presents. The food, as well as being delicious and nutritious, was a real bonus in terms of time. If I'd been working those hours and having to cook, I would have died of malnutrition halfway through the course.

'The course content was spot-on and delivered perfectly by two wonderful trainers. It was great to have two people with very different approaches on some things, but so united in others to get two different perspectives on teaching. I felt I came away with a good understanding of the basics, now just ready to buff them up and put them into practice.

'I do feel I got value for money from this course. I feel in a really confident position to start work in terms of my developing teaching abilities and the knowledge and tools I have to seek employment and be competitive in the workplace. I also felt that all the other aspects of the course; location, provisions etc. although basic, were sufficient for our needs. We all had private individual cabanas right on the beach with hot running water in an en suite bath, a big comfortable bed, a work desk; I was very happy with my accommodation.

'I would recommend the Southern Cross CELTA at Kamala without hesitation in terms of course content. For the location, I'd recommend it to the sort of person I think would deal well with that location and lifestyle, but I would acknowledge paradise for me is not paradise for everyone! I know you will have varying responses from my course mates, but I am really happy with everything I came away with.

'Thanks!'

LIST OF EMPLOYERS

ARAJUNO ROAD PROJECT

Casilla 16-01-710, Puyo-Pastaza, Ecuador

✆ +593 9 85 11 638

🖰 info@amazonvolunteerecuador.com

💻 www.amazonvolunteerecuador.com,
www.youvolunteer.org and www.facebook.com/
ArajunoRoadProject.

The Arajuno Road Project supports children and their families by providing quality English instruction, improving the infrastructure and environment of their schools, and working on community development and conservation programmes in the Ecuadorian Amazon.

NUMBER OF TEACHERS: 2 Teaching Coordinator positions, 6 Teaching Volunteer positions and interns are accepted on a case-by-case basis.

PREFERENCE OF NATIONALITY: All nationalities encouraged to apply, however all teachers must be proficient in English.

QUALIFICATIONS: Anyone over the age of 18 and in good physical/mental health is welcome to become a Teaching Volunteer. Teaching Coordinators must have a minimum of 1 year of work experience and must be bilingual in English and Spanish. It is highly preferred that applicants have previous experience working with children, working internationally, teaching and have a TESOL/TEFOL certificate. In addition, applicants should have excellent organisational skills, communication skills and people skills. Applicants should have the ability to adapt to diverse situations, and be tolerant, patient and understanding.

CONDITIONS OF EMPLOYMENT: Minimum stay 2 weeks for volunteers, 10 weeks for coordinators. The schools run from 7.30am to 12.30pm Monday–Friday, including approximately 4 hours of English instruction. In addition, teachers travel up to 45 minutes to reach the schools. Teachers are also welcome to participate in non-formal English instruction in the afternoons and run cultural exchange activities as time and interest permit.

SALARY: None. Teaching Volunteers pay an at-cost placement fee and weekly fee covering food, housing, materials and support.

FACILITIES/SUPPORT: All teachers stay at the Project's volunteer house, unless a host family is requested. No need for work permits; volunteers enter Ecuador with an automatic 90-day tourist visa, which can be renewed if needed.

RECRUITMENT: Via personal recommendations, social media/internet and partner volunteer organisations.

CONTACT: Laura Hepting, MSc, Director, Amazon Language & Conservation Exchange (laura.hepting@gmail.com).

CENTRO DE EDUCACIÓN CONTINUA DE LA ESCUELA POLITÉCNICA NACIONAL

Edificio Araucaria, Baquedano 222 y Reina Victoria, Quito

✆ +593 22 500068

🖰 henryguygooch@yahoo.com and linguist@cec-epn.edu.ec

💻 www.cec-epn.edu.ec

NUMBER OF TEACHERS: 160+.

PREFERENCE OF NATIONALITY: American, Canadian and British.

QUALIFICATIONS: BA in English, Applied Linguistics, TEFL, Drama, International Studies or a related field. TEFL certificate, one-year experience.

CONDITIONS OF EMPLOYMENT: Minimum 1 year (40 weeks of teaching). 6 hours per day.

SALARY: Volunteers are not paid a salary, but are provided with a monthly subsistence allowance of $665–$798 net as required by law and written agreement.

FACILITIES/SUPPORT: Teachers must find their own accommodation. Instructors are contracted as Cultural Exchange Volunteers under the agreement the university maintains with the Ecuadorian Ministerio de Relaciones Exteriores.

RECRUITMENT: Word of mouth. Telephone interviews are conducted.

CONTACT: Henry Guy Gooch, Director of Linguistics and Cultural Exchanges.

CENTRO DE ESTUDIOS INTERAMERICANOS/CEDEI

Casilla 597, Cuenca

✆ +593 7 2839003

🖰 English@cedei.org

💻 www.english.cedei.org

A non-profit institution dedicated to the study of American languages and cultures.

NUMBER OF TEACHERS: 50

PREFERENCE OF NATIONALITY: Native English speakers.

QUALIFICATIONS: Minimum university degree in related field and TEFL/CELTA/TESOL certificate or university degree in TESL/TEFL. Experience in teaching EFL/ESL.

CONDITIONS OF EMPLOYMENT: Minimum 9-month stay, preference given to year-long commitments. Courses run from January to mid-March, early April to early June, end of June to early September and mid-September to early December. Teachers teach on average 20 hours per week. Most classes meet Monday to Thursday and there are also Saturday Intensives. To teach both classroom courses and individuals. In addition to classroom classes, teachers may elect to give tutorials and conversation classes to supplement their income.

SALARY: Approximately $325 per teenage/adult course, $260 per children's course, and $300 per Saturday class. Courses are 40–50 hours long and teachers are given 3–4 courses per term (10 weeks). This is a high salary by Ecuadorian standards.

FACILITIES: Apartments are very reasonably priced. Cost of living is low. Average rent for a shared apartment/house is between $90 and $140 per month. Free Spanish classes, dance classes and internet access for teachers. Beautiful school building. Very charming city in an Andean setting. Extensive help given with visas.

RECRUITMENT: Via the website www.cedei.org.

CONTACT: Elisabeth Rodas, Academic Director of English Programs (erodas@cedei.org).

EF SCHOOL OF ENGLISH – QUITO

Catalina Aldaz No. N34–267 y Portugal, Quito

☎ +593 2 224 8651 ext 105

✉ steve.tomkins@ef.com

🖥 www.ef.com.ec/quito

NUMBER OF TEACHERS: 20.

PREFERENCE OF NATIONALITY: None; school aims to have a mixture of nationalities and accents.

QUALIFICATIONS: CELTA or equivalent teaching qualification.

CONDITIONS OF EMPLOYMENT: 6 months to 2 years. 35 hours per week.

SALARY: Average $700+ per month after deductions of 12% for tax.

FACILITIES/SUPPORT: Accommodation arranged in local hostel, EF residence or with host family. Pre-arrival pack contains detailed information about the options. Free transfers on arrival.

RECRUITMENT: Via internet or worldwide network of EF schools. Teachers also recruited locally. For senior positions and long-term posts applicants may be asked to present themselves at a local EF centre.

CONTACT: Steven Tomkins, English School Director.

INLINGUA

Sebastian Quintero N37–12 y Jose Correa (behind the Atahualpa Olympic Stadium), Quito

☎ +593 2 245 8763

✉ inlinguaquito@inlingua.com

🖥 www.inlinguaquito.com

NUMBER OF TEACHERS: 25–30.

PREFERENCE OF NATIONALITY: None, but native English speakers only.

QUALIFICATIONS: Recognised TEFL/CELTA and/or teaching experience (particularly Business English).

CONDITIONS OF EMPLOYMENT: Minimum 6-month part-time/full-time contracts. Hours vary. Full-time position totals 20/25 hours per week.

SALARY: $6.15–$7.35 per hour depending on experience and/or qualifications.

FACILITIES/SUPPORT: Full training on Inlingua's international programme and teaching resources provided. Spanish classes and health insurance offered at discounted rates for teachers.

RECRUITMENT: Applications by email, interview and induction in Quito upon arrival.

CONTACT: Danni Walters, Academic Coordinator (academic@inlingua.com)

NEXUS: LENGUAS Y CULTURAS

PO Box 01011013, Cuenca **(or Paseo 3de Noviembre entre Cedros y Jacaranda, Cuenca)**

☎ +593 7 409 0062

✉ mcarrasco@nexus.edu.ec or info@nexus.edu.ec

🖥 www.nexus.edu.ec

NUMBER OF TEACHERS: 3 or 4 teachers per term.

PREFERENCE OF NATIONALITY: None.

QUALIFICATIONS: Teaching certification (CELTA or similar at least). Teaching experience of at least 1 year.

CONDITIONS OF EMPLOYMENT: 6-month contracts. 3 regular terms per year plus a summer session. 18 hours per week.

SALARY: $288 per month.

FACILITIES/SUPPORT: Assistance given to teachers in getting cultural visas by sending them the necessary invitations and certificates. Spanish classes at special price.

RECRUITMENT: On-site interview or via email.

CONTACT: Marcela Carrasco, Director.

UNIDAD EDUCATIVA GÉNESIS

Genesis Net, Apartado Postal 13028, Bahía de Caráquez, Manabí,

☎ +593 5 269 1723 / +593 5 269 1823

✉ unidadeducativagenesis@hotmail.com; info@genesisecuador.org

🖥 www.uegenesis.blogspot.co.uk or www.gen-esisecuador.org

Non-profit organisation Fundacion Genesis del Ecuador.

NUMBER OF TEACHERS: 1–3.

PREFERENCE OF NATIONALITY: North American accent preferred but all accepted.

QUALIFICATIONS: Fluency in English, proficiency in Spanish, and a bachelor's degree, preferably related to linguistics, education, English or Spanish. TESOL/TEFL certificate needed if degree is in unrelated subject. Minimum one year of in-classroom teaching experience.

CONDITIONS OF EMPLOYMENT: 10–12 months with possible extension. School hours are 7am–3pm. Teachers generally spend 5–6 hours a day in the classroom with 2–3 hours prep time.

SALARY: US$400 per month.

FACILITIES/SUPPORT: One month transitional housing provided. Volunteer visa can be arranged in Ecuador. School provides all paperwork and transport to facilitate visa plus pays half the visa fee of $180.

RECRUITMENT: Word of mouth and ESL job postings. Interviews by phone or Skype.

CONTACT: Vladir Villagran, Director (vladir@childrenecuador.org).

MEXICO

The lure of the USA and its language is very strong in Mexico. The frenzy of American investment in Mexico after the North American Free Trade Agreement (NAFTA) saw a huge upswing in both the demand for English by businesses and the resources to pay for it. That boom is now over, but the market for English is still enormous in universities, in business, almost everywhere. Proximity to the USA and a tendency towards what Australians call the cultural cringe (in Mexico called Malinchism after the lover of Cortès who betrayed her people) means that there will always be an unquenchable thirst for English taught by native English speakers in Mexico. Foreign teachers are automatically respected and are often promoted almost immediately.

Companies of all descriptions provide language classes for their employees especially in the early mornings and evenings (but seldom on weekends or even Fridays). **Roberta Wedge** even managed to persuade a '*sleek head honcho in the state ferry service*' that he needed private tuition during the sacred siesta and that busy executives and other interested employees of a local company needed English lessons at the same time of day.

It is not surprising that enrolment in English courses is booming when some employees have been threatened with dismissal unless they master some English. A vet going to Dubai, a stockbroker doing deals with the New York Stock Exchange, housewives who have to go to parties with their executive husbands, teenagers with exam worries, all are keen to improve their English. After each six-year presidential term of office, the top layers of management in companies (especially oil and banking) are replaced by new staff who need new training, especially English. Elections always boost the demand for English not only in Mexico City and the border cities to which US industries looking for cheap labour have relocated, but throughout the country, including the Yucatan Peninsula and other unlikely places, at least one of which must remain nameless in order to preserve Roberta Wedge's dreams:

> After doing a 'taster' ESL course in Vancouver, I set out for Nicaragua with a bus ticket to San Diego and $500 – no guide book, no travelling companion, no Spanish. On the way I fell in love with a town in Mexico (not for worlds would I reveal its name – I want to keep it in a pristine timewarp so I can hope to return) and decided to stay. I found a job by looking up all the language schools in the phonebook and walking around the city to find them. The problem was that many small businesses were not on the phone. So I kept my eye out for English school signs. I had semi-memorised a little speech in Spanish, 'I am a Canadian teacher of English. I love your town very much and want to work here. This is my CV.' Within two days I had a job at a one-man school.

The British Council in Mexico City can provide the addresses of the 25 or so language centres attached to state universities. Also check the website of the Unión Nacional de Escuelas de Idiomas AC (www.unei.org. mx) which has links to all the major companies providing English tuition. The British Council runs English teaching centres in Mexico. For more information visit www.britishcouncil.org/mexico. Mexican-American bi-national centres employ scores of native English speakers, mostly on a local basis. The school year starts in early August and lasts for 11 months. The site of the Mexican Association of Teachers of English (www. mextesol.com.mx) carries very occasional job vacancies in universities and state schools.

With a TEFL qualification and a year's experience in Indonesia, Canadian **Bruce Clarke** was in a good position to make use of the Mexico forum on eslcafe.com, where he learned of the vacancy at a state university in Oaxaca which he went on to fill. He reports that his students were pleasant and fun-loving, though not particularly energetic or keen to complete homework. A further possibility is to work at English-medium schools modelled either on the American or British system. Many of these advertise internationally for certified teachers or recruit through recruiting fairs but, as in Chile, Peru and elsewhere, some are willing to interview native English speakers locally to work in the EFL department. Without a TEFL background or at least a solid university education you are unlikely to break into any of these more upmarket institutes.

THE PRIVATE SECTOR

A host of private institutes supplies language training to business either on their own premises or in-company. The norm is for teachers to freelance and work for a combination of companies. There are also full-time school-based jobs with teaching companies such as Harmon Hall and Interlingua which have a national network of branches; the latter's website has an online application procedure (www.interlingua. com.mx). Hours can be unpredictable and a lot of time is taken up travelling from office to office. Getting three hours of work a day (early morning and early evening) is easy. Anything above that is much trickier. Freelance teachers must be prepared for frequent holidays cutting into earnings. Normally institutes do not pay for public holidays, sickness or annual leave. For example, attendance goes into a sharp decline after Independence Day on 20 November in the month leading up to Christmas and there are no classes over Easter. Most courses run for three months and there may be a lapse of one or two weeks before another starts. Usually freelancers are paid cash in hand with no deductions for tax.

The spectrum of institutes varies enormously. At one extreme there is the employer who pays the equivalent of $5 an hour, never pays on time, and who employs only Mexicans with poor English or native English speakers who have just arrived with their backpacks and no interest in or knowledge of teaching. The top of the range pays $15–$18 an hour, offers free training and gives contracts that aren't cancelled. These institutes are of course a lot more choosy about their teachers. Whereas a few companies want to control their teachers completely and send inspectors into classes, most leave teachers alone as long as the clients are happy. The typical institute consists only of four people: the owner who gets the contracts, a teacher coordinator, a secretary and an office boy.

One company with an office in the USA offers prospective teachers a job in Hermosillo or Monterrey, a Mexican visa, room and board in secure area, paid travel and modest pay; try contacting teachers@ goenglish.com.mx. On arrival in Mexico City, a good place to meet foreigners is the famed Quaker-run peace and service centre in Mexico City, Casa de los Amigos, which has information on a variety of volunteering opportunities throughout Mexico City and Mexico. The Casa is at Ignacio Mariscal 132, 06030 Mexico, D.F., Mexico (+52 55 5705 0521; amigos@casadelosamigos.org) and provides simple accommodation starting from US$10 per night.

Obviously a TEFL qualification is an advantage though few employers are concerned about whether it is from a 130-hour or a 30-hour course. Business and financial experience is also beneficial, possibly more than a university degree. An ability to make a class interesting and patience are the two key qualities that many employers are looking for. As one of **Nick Wilson**'s bosses said, '*The most important thing is that the students enjoy* *their classes and think that they are learning English; don't just teach or we'll lose customers.'* Word-of-mouth recommendations are very important in Mexican culture, and jobs are seldom filled by postal applications.

Michael Tunison contacted half a dozen major teaching organisations from the *Yellow Pages* and was interviewed by Berlitz and Harmon Hall. Both offered tentative positions based more on his native English speaking than his American university degree and journalism background. The starting wage at both schools should be about 5000 pesos (US$400) per month which seems typical of the large chains. One problem here is that these organisations do not pay cash in hand and therefore they want to hire only teachers with working papers. Other international language companies represented in Mexico include International House with schools in eight cities and the Wall Street Institute (www.wallstreetinstitute.com.mx/empleo.html) with schools in Mexico City and Monterrey.

> *Guadalajara and resorts such as Puerto Vallarta, Cancun, Acapulco and Mazatlan are places where a great many locals need to master English before they can be employed in the booming tourist industry, though wages tend to be lower than in the capital and the cost of living higher. Several independent US training organisations have set up TEFL training courses in Mexico, for example Teachers Latin America (www.innovative-english.com) offers a job placement service to qualified candidates, especially graduates of its own 80-hour certificate course in Mexico City.*

American **Bradwell Jackson** is funding his round-the-world travels by teaching English:

> *After reading* **Work Your Way Around the World,** *I made the decision to quit my job, leave my home, give most of my belongings to charity and sell my car, so that I could wander the earth freely. I wondered if it was really possible to get a job teaching English so easily. Well I found out that it is. I was sitting at a metro stop in Mexico City, trying to figure out what school to go to for my first planned job enquiry. After I decided that the particular school I had in mind was too far away, I looked up and saw an English school right across the street. Providence, I thought. I was right. I sauntered on upstairs, cheerfully asked if they needed an English teacher, and about an hour and a half later, I was told when to start my training. It really was that easy.*
>
> *I teach a range of students including some teenage girls. For them I came up with the idea of asking them to talk about a popular television programme* **Rebelde.** *I also got them to pull out a teen magazine and tell me about the stars in it. I have also asked my students about popular Spanish songs and asked them to translate them into English for me.*
>
> *Mexico is the first country I have visited on my world wanderings and I can't believe how lucky I've been. The people are top-notch and I certainly must count my blessings.*

WORKING FOR YOURSELF

Private lessons are in great demand, and may be given informally in exchange for board and lodging. But it is also possible to teach on a more business-like footing. With so many clients seeking one-to-one tuition through institutes, it is worth considering setting up as an independent tutor and offering private lessons at a rate which undercuts the institutes. Teachers who are tempted to poach students from the organisation they work for should bear in mind that employers who find out have been known to set the immigration department on errant teachers. However, it is legitimate to advertise yourself in the press and distribute printed business cards. **Elizabeth Reid** based some of the material in her book *Native English Speaker: Teach English & See the World* (now out of print) on her experiences of teaching in a small Mexican city. She started by developing her own private classes in borrowed premises (a disused shop). She recommends approaching the local community centre (*casa de cultura*), chamber of commerce or public library and offering one free sample class before signing up paying students. To increase goodwill she offered 'scholarships' to a limited number of students who really couldn't afford to pay.

Teaching in companies sometimes produces lucrative spin-offs in the field of translation and editing documents in English. Clients may offer other kinds of work too; for example **Nick Wilson** was asked to set up a Mexican-British arts foundation through a bank trust by someone he tutored in English.

REGULATIONS

The red tape situation in Mexico is a difficult one. Visitors are not allowed to work or engage in any remunerative activity during a temporary visit, though plenty do work under the table. British citizens can stay in Mexico for 180 days without a visa as a tourist. The Free Trade Agreement makes it somewhat easier for Americans and Canadians but it's still not straightforward. Some employers may be willing to apply for an FM3 visa (a 'no immigrante') which will be valid for one-year and renewable thereafter. As has been mentioned, established schools are not usually willing to contract people without an employment visa, unlike private institutes. Among the required documents are a CV in Spanish, notarised TEFL and university certificates that have been certified by a Mexican consulate.

LIST OF EMPLOYERS

AHPLA INSTITUTE
Juan Escutia No. 97, Colonia Condesa, C.P. 06140 D.F.
+52 55 5286 9016
Kallen@ahpla.com
www.ahpla.com

QUALIFICATIONS: Educated, flexible, willing to work with a team and travel. People skills and personality are a must.
CONDITIONS OF EMPLOYMENT: Minimum period of work 6 months. To work 7am–9am and 5pm–7pm.
FACILITIES/SUPPORT: No help with accommodation or flights, but assistance given with working papers after teacher has shown commitment to the institute.
CONTACT: Karen Julie Allen, Operations Manager.

THE AMERICAN-IRISH SCHOOL OF ENGLISH
21 Poniente 111-6, Col. El Carmen 72530, Puebla, Pue.
+52 222 571 1459
info@AmericanIrishSchool.com
www.AmericanIrishSchool.com

New school opening late autumn 2012.
NUMBER OF TEACHERS: 10.
PREFERENCE OF NATIONALITY: Seeking a balance of teachers with British and American English backgrounds.
QUALIFICATIONS: CELTA or TEFL-certified teachers with a four-year college degree and at least one year of experience

teaching English abroad. Candidates should have strong personal character traits and a proven ability to work well in a team environment.
CONDITIONS OF EMPLOYMENT: 6–12 month contracts. One team teaches Monday to Friday morning to early afternoon. The other team works later afternoons to early evenings Tuesday to Friday plus Saturday mornings.
SALARY: Competitive.
FACILITIES/SUPPORT: Plenty of free time to allow foreign teachers to tour the local sites. School can advise teachers on where to find accommodation and can help them acclimatise to the Puebla community. Help given with obtaining necessary work permits.
RECRUITMENT: Via popular ESL websites and local marketing to attract Mexican English teachers. Skype interviews can be arranged.
CONTACT: Daniel Cotter, Director.

BERLITZ (CENTRO INTEGRAL DE IDIOMAS)
Av. Benito Juarez No. 2005, Local Sub Ancla M Plaza
Sendero, Colonia Estrella de Oriente, C.P. 78396
+52 444 166 35 70
elvia.rico@berlitzslp.com.mx
www.berlitzslp.com.mx

NUMBER OF TEACHERS: 20.
PREFERENCE OF NATIONALITY: None.
QUALIFICATIONS: TESOL, TEFL, CELTA certification or a university degree in education.

CONDITIONS OF EMPLOYMENT: Standard 1-year contract. Hours mainly 7am–9am and 6pm–9pm, Monday to Friday, 8am–2pm Saturday.

SALARY: 65–75 pesos per 45 minutes of class.

FACILITIES/SUPPORT: School makes sure that the applicant has a place to stay after arrival.

RECRUITMENT: By email and telephone interview.

CONTACT: Elvia Rico, Academic Supervisor.

CULTURLINGUA JALISCO

Reforma #31, Col. Centro, Tlaquepaque, Jalisco

☎ +52 33 33 44 91 39

✉ nfo@culturlinguagdl.com

🖥 www.culturlinguagdl.com/teaching

Franchise of the Culturlingua group of schools with branches throughout the states of Michoacán and Jalisco in the Highlands of Mexico.

NUMBER OF TEACHERS: 4.

PREFERENCE OF NATIONALITY: Native English speakers.

QUALIFICATIONS: TEFL/TESOL certificate is essential.

CONDITIONS OF EMPLOYMENT: Standard length of contract is 15 weeks with maximum 32 working hours per week.

SALARY: 4,500 pesos per month.

FACILITIES/SUPPORT: Fully furnished accommodation is provided for teachers and included in the salary.

RECRUITMENT: Via internet sites such as Dave's ESL Cafe. Candidates with successful CVs are asked to submit a sample lesson plan and then a telephone interview will be organised.

CONTACT: Greg Davies, Owner.

DUNHAM INSTITUTE

Avenida Coronel Urbina 30, Chiapa de Corzo, Chiapas 29160

☎ +52 961 61 61498

✉ academic-coordinator@dunhaminstitute.com

🖥 www.dunhaminstitute.com

NUMBER OF TEACHERS: 4.

PREFERENCE OF NATIONALITY: Native English speaker.

QUALIFICATIONS: ESL certified.

CONDITIONS OF EMPLOYMENT: Minimum 5 months. 3–4 hours in the afternoon and study Spanish in the mornings.

SALARY: None. Exchange of English teaching for free accommodation with a local family and 2 hours of Spanish tuition a day.

FACILITIES/SUPPORT: Work permits not required.

RECRUITMENT: Interviews are necessary.

CONTACT: Joanna Robinson.

EXPERIENCE MEXECO LTD

#59-2 Valentín Gómez Farías, San Patricio Melaque, Municipio de Cihuatlan, Jalisco CP 48980

☎ +52 1 315 355 7027

✉ info@experiencemexeco.com

🖥 www.experiencemexeco.com

Some volunteer opportunities on Pacific coast of Mexico.

QUALIFICATIONS: All nationalities and ages (average 19–26). All backgrounds welcomed as any necessary training is provided. Spanish is not a necessity as local staff speak English and Spanish.

CONDITIONS OF PARTICIPATION: 1–3 months.

SALARY: None. Programme fee £799–£899 for 1 month, £1,899–£1,999 for 3 months which covers accommodation (homestay or private) and food throughout placement plus insurance and 24-hour in-country support, but excludes flights.

CONTACT: Daniel Patman, Director.

FAST ENGLISH INSTITUTE

Tlalpan 1525, Col. Portales, Mexico City 03300

☎ Mobile +52 4455 4225 1840

✉ fastamericanenglish@yahoo.com.mx

NUMBER OF TEACHERS: 12.

PREFERENCE OF NATIONALITY: None.

QUALIFICATIONS: Ability to communicate effectively in English, spoken and written.

CONDITIONS OF EMPLOYMENT: Teachers may sign a contract after 3 months (no contract required at the beginning). Hours can fall any time between 7am and 10pm.

SALARY: From US$7 an hour. Maximum US$14 per hour.

FACILITIES/SUPPORT: Some teachers stay at school's residential facilities.

RECRUITMENT: Interview and written exam.

CONTACT: R. Alaiyo Moreno, Academic Director.

HELP! HESLINGTON LANGUAGE PROGRAMS

2 Norte 1210 Colonia Jacarandas Tehuacan, Puebla

☎ +52 238 384 6929

✉ instituto_heslington@hotmail.com

🖥 www.helpenglish.org

NUMBER OF TEACHERS: 20 per semester.

PREFERENCE OF NATIONALITY: None.

QUALIFICATIONS: TESOL/TEFL/CELTA Certification – no experience abroad required.

CONDITIONS OF EMPLOYMENT: 4 months. 25 hours per week.

SALARY: Monthly stipend of 4,000 pesos (US$300) plus free housing (rent and utilities paid by school).

FACILITIES/SUPPORT: Free housing or host family arrangement.

RECRUITMENT: Via internet adverts (e.g. eslteachersboard.com) and word of mouth. Interviews carried out by Skype.

CONTACT: Rachael Luna, Director of Education.

ROBINSON SCHOOL

Blvd. Everardo Marquez #200 Piso 2, Colonia Periodistas, Pachuca, Hidalgo 42060

USA mob +1208 241 6493 and 771 719 2247

luke@therobinsonschool.com

www.therobinsonschool.com

NUMBER OF TEACHERS: 3.

PREFERENCE OF NATIONALITY: None, must be native English speaker.

QUALIFICATIONS: ESL certificate preferred. Must be enthusiastic and politically and culturally open-minded.

CONDITIONS OF EMPLOYMENT: 10 weeks. Individual schedules vary. Classes begin at 7am and finish at 8:30pm.

SALARY: 2,000 Mexican pesos per week (net).

FACILITIES/SUPPORT: Housing and/or furnishings can be provided and monthly rent deducted from pay cheque. Teachers will be assisted in acquiring necessary documents.

RECRUITMENT: Internet, word-of-mouth, newspaper adverts. Interviews are sometimes carried out in person in the USA but mostly conducted by phone.

CONTACT: Luke Robinson, CEO & Head of Recruitment.

UNIVERSIDAD DEL MAR

Bahias de Huatulco, Oaxaca 70989

+52 958 587 2559

umarmxjob@yahoo.com

www.umar.mx

NUMBER OF TEACHERS: 16.

PREFERENCE OF NATIONALITY: None but must be native English speaker.

QUALIFICATIONS: Degree level education, TEFL teaching qualification (or an MA in TOEFL or related field) plus at least 1 year's experience working in a foreign country.

CONDITIONS OF EMPLOYMENT: 1 year commitment. Teaching hours are 8am–1pm and 4pm–7pm, Monday to Friday.

SALARY: 14,881 pesos gross (more for candidates with an MA in TEFL or Education plus 2 years' experience), plus free medical service, Christmas and vacation bonuses, savings scheme and monthly shopping vouchers. Monthly deduction of about 2,000 pesos for tax and social security.

FACILITIES/SUPPORT: Teachers must arrange their own accommodation. University files paperwork for work permit on arrival; processing can take up to 3 weeks and teachers cannot start work without work visa.

RECRUITMENT: Most via internet ads and emailed CVs. Telephone interviews essential; short-listed candidates are telephoned.

CONTACT: Caryl Coffey, Director of Languages (caryldelaney@ hotmail.com).

PERU

Lima has in the past been considered one of the most stressful and dangerous South American cities in which to live; however, threats from guerrilla groups are a thing of the past and Peru has returned to the mainstream of destinations for English language teachers. Modest wages and the difficulty of obtaining working papers mean that few professional teachers can be attracted to the private EFL sector. For those who are, it is worth sending a CV to the English Language Officer at the British Council, who may be able to provide a list of British schools and language teaching institutes to anyone sufficiently well qualified, or alternatively pass the CV to potentially interested institutions such as the 11 Lima branches of the British-Peruvian Cultural Association, known familiarly as Britanico (www.britanico.edu.pe).

Yet the range of opportunities in Lima is enormous and the stampede to learn English is unstoppable. Many company employees have been told by their bosses to learn English or risk demotion. Some employers organise a course at their place of work, but most expect their staff to fix up private lessons making the freelance market very promising at the moment. In-company training courses in all industries are often offered in English, so knowledge of the language is becoming essential for all ambitious Peruvians. The Peruvian economy is not in dire straits at present, as evidenced by the stability of its currency, the new sol.

A useful online resource is the LA Joblist (http://thelajoblist.blogspot.co.uk/2009/12/peru.html) compiled by an EL teacher, **Sharon Hinojosa**, who used to teach in Lima and researched all the schools. Although she has now left the continent to teach at a university in Korea, she still maintains the site (last updated 2012). She stresses how much easier it is to find teaching hours once you are in Peru than when you're trying to fix up a job from home.

Many temporary visitors to Peru who lack a TEFL background end up doing some English teaching once they have established a base in the capital, usually earning $5–$10 an hour. Some employers offer a free or subsidised training course to new potential recruits, at which native English speakers usually excel over the locals, whose knowledge of English is often very weak.

Ruain Burrows from Ireland turned himself from a long-term backpacker into a teacher in Lima working for Business Links (www.bl.com.pe) and English Life (see entry):

I had been travelling around South America for the best part of two years and was, inevitably, running out of money. I had just enough for a flight home, yet wasn't ready to go home, so decided to invest in a 120-hour online TEFL course (with i-to-i.com) after convincing myself that it was an easy way to continue living my dream. Three hundred US dollars and five weeks later, certificate in hand, I was ready to dive into the word of TEFLing.

The application process was as simple as typing up a cover email, attaching my CV along with my new qualification and sending it out in bulk to all the institutes, colleges and temping agencies with which Google provided me. The interviews were really easy, the main requisite being fluency in English (being Irish, I just squeezed into this category) and being in possession of some sort of TEFL certificate. The recurring question was concerning my availability, because apparently a lot of foreigners pass through the doors of the institutes just looking for short-term work to fund a flight home or to fill a gap between stages in their lives and they were sick of this. Fortunately they didn't expect teaching experience because prior to the application/interview stage, my teaching experience had been restricted to teaching my dog how to play fetch. Also, the institutes in Lima generally don't insist on permits or special visas but it is required if you intend on applying to the colleges or universities.

Ruain taught as many hours as his employers were willing to assign him, and earned decent money, up to 2,500 soles a month (when the minimum wage in Peru is 700 soles). He found the cost of living to be relatively low, particularly since he earned free hostel accommodation by working as a barman in the evenings.

One tip he offers is never to give out your telephone number to students. When he did this to one of his female students she used him as her personal dictionary whenever she felt like it. He really enjoyed seeing the progress his students made: *'When you take on a student who can't even count to five, then watch them progress through the levels and go on to pass an exam like the IELTS or CAE, that to me is amazing.'* It is not difficult for him to identify an even better highlight which was when he met his wife with whom he has settled in Peru. So his summation of the experience comes as no surprise: *'The rewards of being a TEFL teacher in Peru are that the Peruvian people are amazing, the food is next to none and it's an intriguing country'.*

FREELANCING

Setting up as a freelance tutor is potentially lucrative. A standard fee is $10–$20 a lesson, though this can be reduced for clients who want to book a whole course. James Gratton put a cheap advertisement (written in English) in the main daily *El Comercio* and signed up two clients. This was straightforward in his case since he was staying at his girlfriend's house where he had free accommodation and telephone. His new students were both employees of Petro-Peru, and soon other clients contacted James for lessons. He admits that freelancers do lose out to cancellations, though some of his students willingly paid for missed lessons. Freelancing is a continual process of advertising and getting new students to replace the ones that fall by the wayside.

REGULATIONS

Peruvian work visas are very rare and most people teach as tourists. British and Irish nationals, as well as US and EU citizens, do not require tourist visas for Peru, neither do nationals from EU countries. They are allowed to stay in Peru for up to 90 days, although they are required to possess an onward/return ticket. After that it is necessary to cross the Peruvian border. One reason which many people use to extend their stay is that they have formed a romantic attachment to a local woman/man.

In his quest for a work visa, **James Gratton** gathered together all the necessary documents, including contract, notarised certificates and documents translated into Spanish. All of this cost him a lot of money and time, and he still didn't succeed. He concluded that it would be possible only if you knew someone in the immigration department who could give your application a safe passage without having to pay fines (bribes) at every stage. Making key contacts is more important than gathering documentation. Care must be taken to keep on the right side of the tax office (SUNAT) to which about 15% of earnings are supposed to be paid. Many employers pay their staff under the table, sometimes by cash, personal cheque or via a *Recibo de Honorario* from a Peruvian friend, which uses their tax details and signature to receive your money.

LIST OF EMPLOYERS

ENGLISH LIFE

La Paz 434, Oficina 602, Miraflores, Lima

☎ +51 1 446 1968

✉ info@englishlifeperu.com

🖥 www.englishlifeperu.com

NUMBER OF TEACHERS: 20 on self-employed basis.

PREFERENCE OF NATIONALITY: None. School hires native English speakers only.

QUALIFICATIONS: TEFL certificate or similar, plus some experience is desirable.

CONDITIONS OF EMPLOYMENT: 6 months. Teachers are given part-time hours, on a class by class basis (3–15 per week).

SALARY: $8–$10 per hour.

FACILITIES/SUPPORT: No accommodation provided but advice can be given.

RECRUITMENT: People are invited for interview after submitting their CV. Interviews are essential and so applicants must be in Peru to qualify for an interview or employment.

CONTACT: Valerie Watson, Director General and Owner and Tracy Brylewski, Academic Director.

EXTREME LEARNING CENTER

Av Bolognesi 118, Yanahuara, Arequipa

☎ +51 54 250596

✉ teflperu@gmail.com

🖥 www.extreme.edu.pe and www.vialinguaperu.com

NUMBER OF TEACHERS: 28.

PREFERENCE OF NATIONALITY: USA and Canada.

QUALIFICATIONS: TEFL, TESOL or CELTA on-site course, a bachelor's degree plus experience of teaching. Candidates without experience must have excellent natural teaching ability and 'people' skills.

CONDITIONS OF EMPLOYMENT: 6 months. Normal working hours 7–9am and 5–9pm.

SALARY: Varies with experience.

FACILITIES/SUPPORT: Advice and contacts for accommodation given but teachers pay for their housing. Teachers come as legal TEFL interns.

RECRUITMENT: Paid ads online and university contacts in the USA. Interviews essential.

CONTACT: J C Larsen, B.S.Ed., M.A.Ed./TEFL, Executive Director.

INSTITUTO CULTURAL PERUANO NORTEAMERICANO
M.M.Izaga No. 807, Chiclayo
☎ +51 74 231241/233331
🖥 www.icpnachi.edu.pe

One of a dozen or so Bi-national Centres in Peru.

NUMBER OF TEACHERS: Fluctuating. North American students come as unpaid interns.

PREFERENCE OF NATIONALITY: American and Canadian preferred; others considered.

QUALIFICATIONS: University degree that qualifies candidate for teaching EFL/ESL. Experience not a necessity.

FACILITIES/SUPPORT: Can find apartments for teachers or arrange homestays. Help given with work permits for long-stay teachers.

RECRUITMENT: Via TESOL conferences and internet. Interviews not essential.

MAXIMO NIVEL INTERNATIONAL PERU
Avenida El Sol 612, Cusco
☎ +1 800 866 6358 (Florida contact number)
 instructors@maximonivel.com
🖥 www.maximonivel.com

NUMBER OF TEACHERS: 10–20.

PREFERENCE OF NATIONALITY: Must be native English speaker.

QUALIFICATIONS: Teachers must be TEFL, TESOL or CELTA certified from a training course of at least 100 hours with a minimum of 6 hours of practical teaching. Candidates must be dedicated, professional and passionate about teaching with a self-confident personality and a good sense of humour.

CONDITIONS OF EMPLOYMENT: 6-month contracts are the norm. Split shifts, generally with classes from 7am to 10am and 4pm to 9pm. Teachers teach 30 hours per week, Monday through Friday.

SALARY: $475 to $800 per month (net).

FACILITIES/SUPPORT: Teachers are responsible for their own accommodation, but school provides assistance in locating housing. Often the institute provides 5 days of free room and board in a family stay to a new arrival, while he or she finds more permanent housing. Work permits are available on a very limited basis, and only for long-term teachers.

RECRUITMENT: Via email and online advertising through GoAbroad.com, idealist.org, Dave's ESL Café and others. Many teachers are hired on graduating from Maximo Nivel's own TEFL/TESOL certification course in Cusco. In-person interviews are preferred, but interviews can be conducted via Skype or phone.

CONTACT: Ken Jones, Executive Director.

VENEZUELA

Proximity to the USA and the volume of business which is done with El Norte result in a strong preference for American accents and teaching materials in Venezuela. Oil wealth abounds in the business community and many corporations hire in-company language trainers through Caracas-based agencies. But work is not exclusively for Americans, as **Nick Branch** from St Albans discovered, nor is it confined to the capital:

> *Merida is very beautiful and a considerably more pleasant place to be than Caracas. The atmosphere and organisation of the institute where I worked were very good. But alas, as with all the English teaching institutes in Merida, the pay is very low. Merida is three times cheaper to live in than Caracas, but the salaries are 5–6 times lower.*

Nick investigated most of the schools and agencies in Venezuela and worked for several of them including one based in the Oriente coastal resort of Puerto la Cruz. Once again the pay was less than in Caracas but advantages such as easy access to the Mochima National Marine Park compensated. Opportunities for English teachers even exist on the popular resort island of Margarita. Check adverts in Caracas' main English language organ, the *Daily Journal*. Most give only a phone number. A typical advert might read:

> *We need English teachers and offer remuneration according to the market, stable incomes, paid training, organisation in the work, more earnings according to commissions. Excellent working condition. Work with best team. Punctual payment.*

The last item is worth noting, since many institutes do not pay as much or as often as they promise at the outset. In fact, Caracas has more than its fair share of shady characters running language schools, so that newcomers should take their time about signing any contracts.

Chris Morvan had been a professional writer in the UK for 20 years, in journalism, advertising and PR. But when the recession hit, some of his freelance work dried up and this is how he coped:

> *I'm living in Venezuela, baking in the streets of Caracas and swimming in the Caribbean even in the cooler months here, rather than shivering in the UK. I applied for literally hundreds of jobs by the miracle of the internet and got nowhere. I put it down mainly to my age – I'm in my 50s and that's not a fashionable age. Then I met a Venezuelan woman through a dating website and we got married. With no prospects in the UK we examined my options and decided on taking an online course in Teaching English as a Foreign Language (TEFL). There are lots to choose from and I went for a 100-hour course with i-to-i. This consisted of 20 hours of 'grammar awareness', 60 hours about the science of teaching and smaller modules on teaching large classes, young people, with limited resources etc. In the meantime I moved to Venezuela, applied for three part-time jobs with agencies and got them all. This was even before I finished the course, but they don't bother about formalities like that out here. I found that I loved teaching. Most of my classes are one-to-one with adults in their offices, so it's early mornings, lunchtimes and late afternoons. You can get gigs with schools, teaching bigger classes and younger people if you want. The money is not great, to say the least, but it's a new career in which I am in demand, and that makes a change from ungrateful old UK. The course cost me a couple of hundred quid, but it was money well spent. If you have a good command of English, doing this can open doors for you.*

REGULATIONS

Most people work on a tourist card which is valid for 90 days and non-extendable. It is also at least possible to apply for a multiple entry visa if you can provide proof of employment, sufficient funds and a return ticket. A combined work/study contract (internship in American parlance) is the solution which the Centro Venezolano Americano and Venusa have come up with (see entries) but this is available mainly to US citizens.

Most long-stay foreigners take brief trips to Curaçao or Trinidad and Tobago and get an extension of their tourist card when returning to Venezuela. Work permits are available only if the employer has obtained approval from the Ministry of Internal Affairs (DEX) and sent the necessary papers to a Venezuelan consulate in the teacher's country of residence. Even with a backer as well established as the British Council, the visa problem looms large.

Nick Branch describes the process of getting a work permit in Caracas as a nightmare:

> *On no account attempt to get one on your own, since this involves dealing with the DEX, a truly horrific organisation housed in what resembles a prison and with appalling disorganisation. I heard that they lost 3,000 passports of people who were applying for work permits. It was later discovered that they had been sold on the black market.*

James Gratton obtained a definite job offer from a university extension department on Margarita Island and presented the letter to the Venezuelan embassy in London. His application was turned down. His main complaint was that you hear a different story from every official. Even renewing his tourist card at the Immigration Office took a week and involved his having to present a typed letter in Spanish (and why would a bona fide tourist be expected to do that?) Yet he managed to stay legally in Venezuela for nine months, leaving the country when necessary and returning without once being asked to show a ticket home as proof of his intention to leave the country. His most serious problem occurred when one of his employers threatened to report his tourist status to the police if he quit to look for a better job. (James did quit and the police were not called.)

LIST OF EMPLOYERS

CENTRO VENEZOLANO AMERICANO DEL CARACAS

Av. Principal de las Mercedes, Edf CVA, Urbanización Las Mercedes, Caracas 1060-A

- +58 212 993 7911/8422
- cva@cva.org.ve or informacioncva@gmail.com
- www.cva.org.ve

CVA also located in the state of Zulia: Calle 63, No. 3E-60, Maracaibo, Estado Zulia

- +58 261 718 0842 5
- www.cevaz.org

NUMBER OF TEACHERS: 100+.

PREFERENCE OF NATIONALITY: American, Canadian, Venezuelan.

QUALIFICATIONS: Bachelor's degree or teachers with EFL/ESL experience. A written and oral test is given to all non-native English speaking applicants.

CONDITIONS OF EMPLOYMENT: Minimum 6 months with renewals up to 2 years. Choice of children's courses (for ages 9–11), teens (12–15) and regular and Saturday courses for adults. Minimum 30 academic hours per week.

SALARY: Hourly rate plus housing bonus.

FACILITIES/SUPPORT: Assistance with obtaining accommodation, health insurance and visas. 2-week pre-service training course for interns is paid. Free Spanish course. Computer lab and access to cultural centre activities.

INLINGUA VENEZUELA

Caracas: Av. San Ignacio de Loyola, Edif. Milano, piso 4, ofic. 401, Chacao, Caracas

- +58 212 421 90 33

Valencia: Av 97-C, Centro Comercial y Profeseional San José de Tarbes, Piso 8, Ofic 5–6, Urb. San José de Tarbes

- +58 241 823 99 35
- vzla@inlingua.com or info-caracas@inlingua.com
- www.inlingua.com or www.inlingua.com.ve

NUMBER OF TEACHERS: 40 (about 8 of whom are native English speakers).

PREFERENCE OF NATIONALITY: Native English speakers from major English-speaking countries: UK, USA, Canada, Australia or New Zealand.

QUALIFICATIONS: Formal qualifications are less important than enthusiasm, ability and business experience, which are assessed through the application process. Candidates must be dedicated to providing good quality contractual teaching hours and be adaptable and honest. A year's teaching experience in a non-English speaking country would be desirable as would TEFL/CELTA/TESOL or equivalent and business experience.

CONDITIONS OF EMPLOYMENT: 8-month commitment. To work irregular hours in 3 primary shifts, starting 7am, noon and 5pm. However, teachers must be available from 7am to 7pm, Monday to Friday.

SALARY: $650 gross per month, paid in the local currency (bolivares).

FACILITIES/SUPPORT: As part of the induction, training in the inlingua methodology is given. Airport pick-up on arrival. Accommodation in shared teachers' apartment when available or assistance in finding accommodation. Assistance in obtaining a cell phone. Internet access is provided at the school. Spanish language lessons are provided. Initial and ongoing training, assessment and support.

CONTACT: Academic Supervisor.

IOWA INSTITUTE

Avenida 4 con Calle 18, Merida Edo. Merida 5101

- +58 274 2526404
- cesar@iowainstitute.com
- www.iowainstitute.com

NUMBER OF TEACHERS: 7 native English speakers.

PREFERENCE OF NATIONALITY: None.

QUALIFICATIONS: University degree in Education, Linguistics, Modern Languages or some related field. If degree not in TEFL related field then a TEFL certificate or teaching experience is essential. All teachers must attend a 4-day seminar on school teaching methods held during September and again in January. Jobs for the less qualified (i.e. native English speakers who have not yet completed their degree) also possible. Those with experience working in children's camps for example, have been ideal for helping in the children's programme.

CONDITIONS OF EMPLOYMENT: Minimum 10 months. Full-time posts 6–8 hours a day. Part-time can be as few as 2 hours a day.

SALARY: By the hour, always a bit above the standard rate.

FACILITIES/SUPPORT: No accommodation assistance. Group Spanish lessons are free, private classes at cost price.

CONTACT: Cesar Gonzalez, through the web page.

NUMBER OF TEACHERS: 25–40 TESL internships a year.

PREFERENCE OF NATIONALITY: American, British and Canadian.

QUALIFICATIONS: TESL certification and experience preferred but not required.

CONDITIONS OF EMPLOYMENT: 3-month to 1-year contracts. Hours vary.

FACILITIES/SUPPORT: Homestay or room option offered (some meals included). Visa application and information provided.

RECRUITMENT: Internet, alumni. Interviews not essential. Apply electronically. $50 application fee.

NUMBER OF TEACHERS: As many as possible for branches throughout the country.

PREFERENCE OF NATIONALITY: None.

QUALIFICATIONS: Teaching degree not necessary but some experience teaching English as a second language is helpful. WSI trains all teachers in-house.

CONDITIONS OF EMPLOYMENT: No contract but minimum of 6 months. 8 teaching hours.

SALARY: Local average.

FACILITIES/SUPPORT: Assistance with work permits.

RECRUITMENT: Word of mouth, advertising in local papers and via AIESEC.

CENTRAL AMERICA AND THE CARIBBEAN

If you keep your ears open as you travel through this enormous isthmus squeezed between two great oceans, you may come across opportunities to teach English, especially if you are prepared to do so as a volunteer. Salaries on offer may be pitiful but if you find a congenial spot on the 'gringo trail' (for example, the lovely old colonial town of Antigua in Guatemala), you may decide to prolong your stay by helping the people you will inevitably meet who want to learn English. You might also find openings off the gringo trail. It is always interesting to hear from a part of the world that has never been included in this book before.

COSTA RICA

As the wealthiest country in Central America, Costa Rica is a good starting (and perhaps finishing) point for many native English teachers. The Education Ministry is pursuing a national plan to improve English instruction and produce a bilingual workforce for the nation's growing economy. Although such rhetoric can never be completely relied upon, it does at least suggest that English is seen as an important economic asset. The English language newspaper *Tico Times* corroborates this, and ran a series of articles headlined 'Learning English is a good investment' and 'Tourism will grow thanks to English speaking cops'. It is also government policy to teach English in primary schools, which has greatly increased the demand for English teachers. Although state schools can't usually afford to import expat teachers, they are often willing to accept an offer of voluntary assistance. The school year runs from 1 March to 1 December. The *Tico Times* publishes its job classified ads online at www.ticotimes.net.htm. A recent one ran: '*The Swan English Learning is looking for Native English Teachers, for Heredia, San José & Ciudad Colon. Part and full time. Call 2249 3598; info@theswanenglish.org*'. Other places to look for teaching job ads are www.costaricapages.com/jobs and Craigslist for Costa Rica.

The majority of teaching work is available in the capital San José. After four years of teaching at different institutes in Costa Rica and now working as a director at Intercultura in Heredia near San José (see entry), **Lindsay Fair** is an established expat who feels frustrated with American attitudes whenever she visits her home country. She describes teaching in the corporate market:

Teaching corporate in Costa Rica has advantages and disadvantages. The biggest disadvantage is having to travel by bus most of the day, especially during the rainy season, wearing business clothes. The benefits of working corporate includes nice working conditions and well-behaved students. Classes are paid for by employers and success is monitored by the bosses, so the students are for the most part very responsible. They come from the upper-middle class of Costa Rica, so are generally educated and, after having worked for North American companies, knowledgeable about North American culture. My colleagues have been almost all North Americans, and most around my age (23–28).

San José is not exactly what you think of when imagining Costa Rica; it's polluted, dirty and dangerous, and the closest beaches are a good two-hour bus ride away. But the company explained all that during the interview. Unfortunately, San José is where most of the work is, so the best part of living in Costa Rica is taking weekend trips to the beaches and national parks. Now that I know more about Costa Rica, I definitely recommend looking for jobs in Heredia instead of San José because it is much safer, nicer and an easier place to live for ex-pats.

Bryson Patterson made use of contacts from the TEFL course he did at ALI San Diego to get his first job in San José but eventually moved away from the city:

After working for a time in the capital, I moved to a town called Jaco on the Pacific Coast where I worked at a high school and then at the Marriott Hotel. I was teaching English first to high school students (that was hell) then to the hotel staff which was cool. A lot of people will tell you that there are no ESL jobs on the coast but they are wrong.

If you want to teach in Costa Rica and support eco-tourism, a government-sponsored organisation called English Volunteers for Change (EVOLC; www.evolc.org) places native speaker volunteers in various English-language teaching programmes for the tourism sector. Participants get a three-day weekend and plenty of cultural immersion. Programme costs are typically US$515 per month for a six-month commitment.

Work visas and residency permits (temporary as well as permanent) are very difficult to get. Immigration requires that you get your birth certificate and state background check from your home region, get them notarised by a public notary and send them to the Costa Rican Consulate in your country to be authenticated. Once the documents are sent on to Costa Rica, you have to take them to the foreign ministry to be authenticated again, get a background check, get fingerprinted by the OIJ and pay a lot of money. Once all these steps are taken (and they must be taken within six months before the birth certificate and background check expire), you can bring your documents to immigration, whereupon it can take up to 18 months to get your passport stamped, and that stamp will expire. Because the process requires so much time, energy and money, schools are not generally willing to assist teachers on standard one-year contracts who tend to opt for taking visa runs every 90 days to Nicaragua or Panama, making sure that they stay out of the country for at least 72 hours. Although it may be technically illegal for teachers to work without a work visa, the authorities routinely look the other way. Teachers with tourist visas only can register with the Caja Seguro Social (national health service), register with the *Tributación* (Home Office) as professional service providers, open bank accounts, get driver's licenses, etc.

Allen Tracey has pursued an alternative route by becoming an 'Independent Contractor' with Pro Language (see entry). Foreign teachers can independently contract with an institute (by starting a self-employed business) which means that employers do not take on the obligations of hiring an employee. No taxes are paid, no benefits are received and there is no binding contract. However, for each class an Assignment Sheet must be signed by the teacher, and the services outlined become the teacher's subcontracted responsibility. The system does mean that you don't really get to know other teachers unless your institute organises group training sessions which you attend.

I have been very fortunate to have been assigned a wide range of interesting and motivated students in my time teaching for Pro Language over the past three years, including top executives who are as eager to learn as trades people. Aside from teaching the essentials like grammar from the textbook, I do try to find ways to make each two-hour class fun and entertaining. I am always searching for viable new teaching games because students just love games. I just can't seem to find enough really good teaching games that work.

Of course, you get the occasional rotten apple students, who are there only because their employer requires it. A highlight was teaching a top Walmart executive who was a very interesting and appreciative student to invest time with. . .it's nice to be appreciated. A low point was having to deal with an extremely rude and controlling Venezuelan student who considered my lesson plans to be optional and negotiable.

LIST OF EMPLOYERS

CENTRO CULTURAL COSTARRICENSE NORTEAMERICANO

Apartado Postal 1489–1000, San José

✆ +506 2207 7500

✏ recruitmentacademic@centrocultural.cr

🖥 www.centrocultural.cr

NUMBER OF TEACHERS: Varies. Teachers also needed for centres in San Pedro, La Sabana, Alajuela and Cartago.

PREFERENCE OF NATIONALITY: None, but must be native English speaker.

QUALIFICATIONS: Experience in ESL and/or EFL is indispensable.

CONDITIONS OF EMPLOYMENT: Standard 1-year contract. Minimum 16 hours per week.

SALARY: About 4,000 colones ($7+) an hour. Deduction of about $15 a month for voluntary insurance.

FACILITIES/SUPPORT: No assistance with accommodation or work permits.

RECRUITMENT: Via newspaper adverts, work fairs and internal recommendations. Interviews carried out at CCCNCR sites in Costa Rica after applications have been processed centrally.

CONTACT: Carlos Vargas (carlos.vargas@centrocultural.cr).

ENGLISH TO GO - INGLES SIN FRONTERAS

Apartado Postal 271–3007, San Joaquin de Flores, Heredia

✆ +506 2588 2204

✏ academics@english2go.co.cr

🖥 www.english2go.co.cr

NUMBER OF TEACHERS: 15–25 contracted staff.

PREFERENCE OF NATIONALITY: Americans and Canadians, other native English speakers can also apply, as well as teachers of Spanish and Portuguese.

QUALIFICATIONS: 2 years' classroom experience teaching ESL in a foreign country; certified ESL through CELTA (preferred) TESOL, TEFL or others.

CONDITIONS OF EMPLOYMENT: Standard 6-month contract. Hours vary according to needs of students or companies with whom English to Go contracts.

SALARY: $8–$10 per classroom hour.

FACILITIES/SUPPORT: If needed on arrival, English to Go will help with finding housing but does not pay rent.

RECRUITMENT: Ads in craigslist, ESL sites, newspapers, and website. Interviews essential.

CONTACT: Robert Holloway, PhD, Academic Director (+506 2588 2204; mob +506 8914 1402; Skype: robaholloway).

EVOLC

English Volunteers for Change in Costa Rica, Apodo: 11062-–1000 San José

✆ +506 2248 0237 ext. 102

✏ evolc@aliarse.org

🖥 www.evolc.org

NUMBER OF TEACHERS: Constantly taking on new volunteers.

PREFERENCE OF NATIONALITY: Any native speaker of English.

QUALIFICATIONS: University degree, TEFL certified or with teaching experience. Volunteers should be independent, willing to adapt, be responsible and able to organise, have experience of living in another country, have commitment to service and volunteerism and have the ability to communicate well with others.

CONDITIONS OF EMPLOYMENT: 5 weeks to 1 year. 20 hours a week teaching, plus 20 hours preparing.

SALARY: Unpaid position. Volunteers pay a programme fee which covers homestay accommodation where they are given 3 meals per day.

FACILITIES/SUPPORT: EVOLC can arrange volunteer visa for those staying 6–12 months.

RECRUITMENT: Via adverts online. Interviews can be conducted over Skype.

CONTACT: Alexandra Johnson, EVOLC Programme Coordinator.

INTERCULTURA LANGUAGE AND CULTURAL CENTER

Apdo. 1952–3000, Heredia

✆ +506 2260 8480 (ext 21)

✏ info@interculturacostarica.com

🖥 www.interculturacostarica.com/ingles

NUMBER OF TEACHERS: 26–29 (depending on the semester).

PREFERENCE OF NATIONALITY: Native English speakers: American, British, Canadian, Irish, New Zealander and Australian.

QUALIFICATIONS: Minimum bachelor's degree, and TEFL/CELTA certification. At least 1 year's teaching experience is preferred.

CONDITIONS OF EMPLOYMENT: 1 year starting in July and January. Average 20–25 hours teaching per week. Classes last 1.5–3 hours and are held in mornings, evenings and some afternoons. Hours of teaching mainly Monday to Thursday evenings and Saturdays.

SALARY: $800–$1,100 per month net.

FACILITIES/SUPPORT: Local housing arrangements to help teachers find accommodation. Free Spanish lessons for full-time teachers. Mentor programme for new teachers, ongoing training and professional development opportunities.

RECRUITMENT: TEFL websites, local adverts and phone interviews. Applications should be sent in April and October in time for the start of the semester.

CONTACT: Lindsay Fair, English Department Director (lindsay@interculturacostarica.com).

MAXIMO NIVEL INTERNATIONAL COSTA RICA

De La Farmacia La Bomba, 75m South (left side), San Pedro-Montes de Oca, San José

☏ +1 800 866 6358 (Florida contact number)

✉ instructors@maximonivel.com

🖥 www.maximonivel.com

NUMBER OF TEACHERS: 10–20.

PREFERENCE OF NATIONALITY: Must be native English speaker.

QUALIFICATIONS: Teachers must be TEFL, TESOL or CELTA certified from a training course of at least 100 hours with a minimum of 6 hours of practical teaching. Candidates must be dedicated, professional and passionate about teaching with a self-confident personality and a good sense of humour.

CONDITIONS OF EMPLOYMENT: 6-month contracts are the norm. Split shifts, generally with classes from 7am to 10am and 4pm to 9pm. Teachers teach 30 hours per week, Monday through Friday.

SALARY: $475 to $800 per month (net).

FACILITIES/SUPPORT: Teachers are responsible for their own accommodation, but school provides assistance in locating housing. Often the institute provides 5 days of free room and board in a family stay to a new arrival, while he or she finds more permanent housing. Work permits are available on a very limited basis, and only for long-term teachers.

RECRUITMENT: Via email and online advertising through GoAbroad.com, idealist.org, Dave's ESL Café and others. Many teachers are hired on graduating from Maximo Nivel's own TEFL/TESOL certification course in San José. In-person interviews are preferred, but interviews can be conducted via Skype or phone.

CONTACT: Ken Jones, Executive Director.

PRO-LANGUAGE CORPORATE LANGUAGE SOLUTIONS

Edíficio Langer, Of. #3, Zapote, San José

☏ +506 2280 6053 ext 11

✉ info@prolanguage.org

🖥 www.prolanguage.org

NUMBER OF TEACHERS: 40 (for several branches including in Escazu and Heredia).

PREFERENCE OF NATIONALITY: None, but native English speakers.

QUALIFICATIONS: TEFL certification or equivalent and a minimum of 6 months' experience.

CONDITIONS OF EMPLOYMENT: Minimum 4 months. Lots of part-time opportunities.

SALARY: $8 per hour.

FACILITIES/SUPPORT: Assistance with accommodation and work permits. Free Spanish lessons and free training.

RECRUITMENT: Newspaper adverts, internet, alliances with teacher training organisations. Candidates already in Costa Rica strongly preferred.

CONTACT: Dawn Needham, Academic Co-ordinator or Mark Henker, Director.

SARAPIQUÍ CONSERVATION LEARNING CENTER

92–4001 Puerto Viejo de Sarapiquí, Heredia

☏ +506 2761 2082

✉ director@learningcentercostarica.org

🖥 www.learningcentercostarica.org

NUMBER OF TEACHERS: 3.

PREFERENCE OF NATIONALITY: English native speaking countries.

QUALIFICATIONS: TEFL, TESOL or CELTA certified, with teaching and group management experience. Intermediate level of Spanish, preferably with experience of community driven organisations.

CONDITIONS OF EMPLOYMENT: 6 months. 18 hours of teaching, 22 hours in lesson planning and other duties at the Center.

SALARY: Unpaid positions.

FACILITIES/SUPPORT: Room and board provided with a local family.

RECRUITMENT: Internet, volunteer websites, partnerships with language institutes in Costa Rica. Interviews can be by Skype.

CONTACT: Raquel Gómez Ramírez, Executive Director.

UNIVERSAL IDIOMAS

Avenida 2da, calle 9, San José

☏ +506 2223 9662; USA: +1 727 230 0563

✉ info@universal-edu.com

🖥 www.universal-edu.com

PREFERENCE OF NATIONALITY: American, British.

QUALIFICATIONS: TEFL/TESOL, University diploma, a couple of years of experience.

CONDITIONS OF EMPLOYMENT: 1 year. Teaching hours mainly in evenings and on Saturdays.

SALARY: About $8 per hour. 9% deductions for social security.

FACILITIES/SUPPORT: Most teachers find their own accommodation though homestay can be arranged at extra charge.

RECRUITMENT: Via internet ads. Local interview essential.

CONTACT: Patricia Jimenez, Academic Director.

WHITTEMORE DE COSTA RICA, S.A.

100 Oeste y 300 norte de Los Antojitos, Condominios Mantova #8, Rohrmoser

+506 2290 0837; Cell: + 506 8977 4809

mr_whittemore@yahoo.com

http://inglescostarica.weebly.com

New programme for 2013 yet to be confirmed for ESL teachers to work at public schools.

NUMBER OF TEACHERS: 4–6.

PREFERENCE OF NATIONALITY: North American only.

QUALIFICATIONS: Minimum age 30. Must be seasoned TESL teachers with a degree, ESL certification and 2 years' experience teaching ESL to children. Serious teachers only need apply.

CONDITIONS OF EMPLOYMENT: 1 year starting in February. 30–35 hours per week Monday to Friday.

SALARY: $7 per hour (net) paid in colones once a month. Bonus paid upon completing contract.

FACILITIES/SUPPORT: Initial hotel booking arranged and suitable condo at $300 per month fully furnished including colour TV, internet and cable.

RECRUITMENT: Via internet. Interviews essential via Skype. References will be checked.

CONTACT: Michael J. Whittemore, General Manager.

GUATEMALA AND HONDURAS

There are perhaps about a dozen institutes in the capital Guatemala City. But it is not nearly as appealing a destination as Antigua. Many travellers find that Lake Atitlán is the perfect place to use as a longer-term base. The small villages around the lake are all interconnected by launch boats, and the variety in atmosphere among these villages means that you can choose one that suits. Well known party town, San Pedro, attracts many foreigners who come to attend one of the many Spanish schools. Rooms are available for 15–35 quetzals (£1–£3) and food is also very cheap.

ANNA LING

Anna Ling, 20 years old and from Cambridge, headed to San Pedro last year on her world travels, as she pursues her main interests, writing and performing music. She decided to stay for a while.

I am based at the Iguana Perdida hostel (www.laiguanaperdida.com), the first building near the launch stop. The local village is a wonderful place and home to the Amigos (www.amigosdesantacruz.org), a charity that has brought medical care and an outreach programme to the more remote villages. They have also built a library and a school offering free education to all children under 12, and scholarship programmes for older children. They are in the process of building a large new centre for vocational education. I went up to the village to see Pam, the current brains behind the operation, and within the hour I was teaching an English class. I was soon given a classroom and started an enrichment afternoon with the local kids, doing arts, craft and music projects. The organisation is so well run that anyone willing to give some time will be put to good use, whether in teaching, construction or any other interests.

Visas are not a problem at all, neither for work nor volunteering. No one even asks to see a passport. Language is no problem either. Personally I'm trying to live very much on a tight budget and paid language lessons (25–50 quetzals per hour) would push me way over my daily price watch. But volunteering at the school has been the best opportunity for learning Spanish I could imagine. I take up a dictionary and the kids speak really slowly and clearly and it has helped so very much.

Volunteer teachers who wish to go to Honduras can arrange a placement in Ceiba, the third largest city, through the fee-charging agency Volunteering Solutions (http://volunteeringsolutions.com/honduras/volunteer_teaching_english_honduras.htm), helping local people to get ahead in the burgeoning tourist industry. The cost is $1,475 for eight weeks.

LIST OF EMPLOYERS

MAXIMO NIVEL INTERNATIONAL GUATEMALA

6a Avenida Norte #16–16A, La Antigua

✆ +1 800 866 6358 (Florida contact number)

✆ instructors@maximonivel.com

🖥 www.maximonivel.com

NUMBER OF TEACHERS: 10–20.

PREFERENCE OF NATIONALITY: Must be native English speaker.

QUALIFICATIONS: Teachers must be TEFL, TESOL or CELTA certified from a training course of at least 100 hours with a minimum of 6 hours of practical teaching. Candidates must be dedicated, professional and passionate about teaching with a self-confident personality and a good sense of humour.

CONDITIONS OF EMPLOYMENT: 6-month contracts are the norm. Split shifts, generally with classes from 7am to 10am and 4pm to 9pm. Teachers teach 30 hours per week, Monday through Friday.

SALARY: $475 to $800 per month (net).

FACILITIES/SUPPORT: Teachers are responsible for their own accommodation, but school provides assistance in locating housing. Often the institute provides 5 days of free room and board in a family stay to a new arrival, while he or she finds more permanent housing. Work permits are available on a very limited basis, and only for long-term teachers.

RECRUITMENT: Via email and online advertising through GoAbroad.com, idealist.org, Dave's ESL Café and others. Many teachers are hired on graduating from Maximo Nivel's own TEFL/TESOL certification course in Antigua. In-person interviews are preferred, but interviews can be conducted via Skype or phone.

CONTACT: Ken Jones, Executive Director.

NICARAGUA

LIST OF EMPLOYERS

ABC SCHOOL (American British School)

519 Calle El Consulado, Granada

✆ +505 55 2552 0812

✆ marlonabc@hotmail.com

NUMBER OF TEACHERS: 5 volunteers.

PREFERENCE OF NATIONALITY: North American.

QUALIFICATIONS: TEFL or equivalent, minimum 2 months' EFL teaching experience, some Spanish, some travel outside country of origin, interest in Nicaragua.

CONDITIONS OF EMPLOYMENT: Minimum stay 3 months. 20 hours per week on week days between 3pm and 8pm and 3-hour classes taught on Saturdays and Sundays. School open year round.

SALARY: Contribution of $160–$240 per month for housing.

FACILITIES/SUPPORT: Teachers are helped to find rooms to rent, or homestays.

RECRUITMENT: Internet (including Facebook page) and word of mouth. Phone interviews.

CONTACT: Marlon Gutierrez, Owner/Director.

EL SALVADOR

After finishing high school in his hometown of Flagstaff, Arizona, **Kellen Brandel** knew that he wanted to take a year out in 2010/2011. In his search for something affordable that would let him work on his Spanish, he settled on an NGO in the capital of El Salvador (see entry) which teaches English to local people and also supports some social justice projects around the country. Kellen spent a total of seven months in Central America and reflects on the benefits:

I mainly researched options using the internet and was most impressed with the one I chose (CIS – Center for Exchange and Solidarity) based on communication and quality of information, not to mention costs. I spent the first three months volunteer English teaching in CIS, a grassroots NGO founded by an American woman in the 1990s. I spent the next month backpacking through the countryside of El Salvador, Honduras, Guatemala and Belize before returning to San Salvador and spending an additional three months teaching again. While I volunteered abroad, I also studied the native language, Spanish, in a sister school at this particular NGO. The costs were quite reasonable. The average week consisted of spending about $80 for host family including meals and utilities, $57 for Spanish school, provided you were an English volunteer ($100 for programme fee) as well as a few additional expenses.

My volunteer position was that of an English teacher for adults, mainly in the evenings. The working conditions were great and the co-ordinators were very helpful in providing us with material, ideas, and support. At first I was wary about teaching adults, as most of my students were in their late twenties and thirties. But I think I established respect with them and was laid back to the extent that the age difference didn't seem to matter. After that we were able to relax and eventually make jokes about my young age. It was professional, but the atmosphere at the CIS is also really laid back. Over the course of seven months I got to know my students on a much more personal level than many teachers get to, and that to me was really special. The low point would probably be the amount of English spoken. For many the balance is good, but since I already had a strong foundation in the Spanish language, I found too much English spoken at the CIS. But once I became more involved with locals outside school, that improved.

LIST OF EMPLOYERS

CIS - CENTRO DE INTERCAMBIO Y SOLIDARIDAD (CIS)

Mélida Anaya Montes Language School, Avenida Aguilares y Avenida Bolivar #103, Colonia Libertad, San Salvador
US office: Los Olivos CIS, PO Box 76, Westmont, IL 60559–0076

✆ +503 2235 1330 / +503 2226 5362
✎ info@cis-elsalvador.org
💻 www.cis-elsalvador.org

NUMBER OF TEACHERS: 7–10 volunteer teachers at any one time.

PREFERENCE OF NATIONALITY: None.

QUALIFICATIONS: No teaching experience or certification needed. Must be committed to social justice and reciprocal learning between students and teacher.

CONDITIONS OF EMPLOYMENT: Minimum stay 10 weeks for complete English cycle. Time commitment includes teaching English 3 days a week (Monday, Tuesday and Thursday) 5.15pm–7pm, weekly 2 hour teachers meeting, plus time spent on lesson planning. Please contact for more details about rural volunteer placements and longer-term placements.

SALARY: None. Volunteers must also pay a one-time programme fee of $100.

FACILITIES/SUPPORT: The CIS has a host family network with whom volunteers can live: cost of homestay with breakfast and dinner is $80 a week. Training for teachers provided. Tourist visa ($10 at border) is sufficient. Volunteers are eligible to receive a half-price discount on Spanish classes.

RECRUITMENT: Word of mouth, internet, travel publications.

CONTACT: Emily Salava.

DOMINICAN REPUBLIC

A major tourist destination, the Dominican Republic (DR) provides some opportunities for native English teachers, although these may well be low paid (or volunteer positions) because the DR is still one of the poorest countries in the Caribbean. A useful resource is the Dominican Republic One news and information service (www.dr1.com) in English, which has a classified section and a messageboard where you can ask the online community for information. According to DR1:

> *If you would like to teach languages, particularly English, there are many immediate opportunities. For instance, the Instituto Cultural Dominico-Americano (tel +809 533 4199) is always looking for English teachers. Ditto for APEC's English Department (tel +809 686-0021). English Speaking Specialists (tel +809 547-7375) is an agency providing English teachers. It pays higher rates than the ICDA and provides all of the necessary materials. Look up language schools in the telephone book. Almost all of them will welcome you with open arms (if not pocketbooks) if you are a native, or a very good English speaker.*

ICDA carries teaching information on its web pages (www.icda.edu.do) and invites applicants to submit CVs to empleos@cda.edu.do.

The *Listín Diario* (www.listin.com.do), in Spanish, is a large circulation newspaper with a strong classified section, online and in print. There are also plenty of English speaking or bilingual schools that you can try.

A charity called Outreach 360 (6611 W Robert E Lee St, Glendale, AZ 85308; www.outreach360.org) sends volunteers to participate in conversational English programmes with children in the Dominican Republic (and Nicaragua). This doubles as a fund raiser for the organisation so for example an eight-week stay costs $2,800. In the rural areas where the organisation works, access to native speakers of English is very limited. Volunteers are also needed to attend English immersion summer camps.

LIST OF EMPLOYERS

ULAE ENGLISH PROGRAM

UCNE (Universidad Cathólica Nordestana), Calle Restauracion esq. 27 de Febrero, San Francisco de Macorís, Provincia Duarte, (Apartado Postal No. 239), Dominican Republic

- +1 809 588 3505; +1 809 588 3151 ext 233; +809 290 3355.
- ulae@ucne.edu; darling.ulae@gmail.com
- www.ulae.webs.com; www.ucne.edu

NUMBER OF TEACHERS: 30 volunteer professors of Language & Literature.

PREFERENCE OF NATIONALITY: English-speaking countries.

QUALIFICATIONS: Ages 21–38. Should be graduate in education-related subject or with experience working with children. Should be able to adapt to life in the Caribbean and have a love of multicultural life and tourism.

CONDITIONS OF EMPLOYMENT: 6 months or a year from beginning of terms (second Monday in September or early January). Working hours are 8am–3pm Monday to Friday with lunches provided at 1pm daily at school.

SALARY: US$650 per month (paid on the 10th of the month).

FACILITIES/SUPPORT: Shared apartment next to the school with utilities, phone and internet included; teachers have their own room. Access to beaches and aquatic sports on days off. Teachers meet regularly with the co-ordinator to prepare tests, evaluations and lesson plans.

RECRUITMENT: CVs to be submitted. Interviews by Skype.

CONTACT: Darling J. Perez, ULAE English Program.

NORTH AMERICA

Just about every university and college in the major cities has an ESL programme, as do a range of government and charitable organisations. Commercial schools offer a wide variety of classes but tend to focus on survival ESL and EAP (English for Academic Purposes) with writing as a major component. Berlitz and Inlingua are represented throughout the USA and are a completely different type of commercial school, concentrating on conversational skills and foreign languages for business people. Embassy CES (330 Seventh Avenue, New York 10001; +1 212 629 7300; www.embassyces.com) has adult English schools in Boston, New York, Fort Lauderdale, San Diego, Los Angeles and Seattle, plus new centres in Toronto and Victoria, Canada. These are worth applying to, although they often recruit locally. Details of summer teaching jobs in New York, Massachusetts, Florida and California can be found at www.embassysummer.com/PDFs/US_ESL_INSTRUCTOR.pdf.

Bilingual/bicultural classes are run in thousands of high schools across the country. Many require staff who are not only state-certified teachers but also bilingual in exotic languages like Hmong or Gujarati. Most larger cities have at least one free or low-cost workplace literacy/vocational ESL programme which caters for immigrants needing assistance with the basics of English. Some of these programmes operate in outposts (e.g. churches, libraries) and many depend on local volunteers as tutors. Volunteer positions can conceivably lead to better things.

GEMMA PIRELLI

Gemma Pirelli tried to think of ways of achieving her desire to travel after finishing a degree in psychology, and spend time with people from different cultures. She carried out lots of research on the internet and made contact with the director of Teachingenglishinltaly.com, Sheila Corwin, a fellow American. Not only did she enrol in a distance learning course, but took steps to get some practical experience.

In addition to putting together a portfolio of all coursework I'm doing for my distance TEFL course (the International Certificate for Applied Linguistics), I tried to find some volunteering opportunities and classroom observations here in New Jersey. Therefore I began to research local colleges/universities in my area as well as community centres accepting volunteers. I went back to my alma mater (Seton Hall University) and arranged a couple of classroom observations with the ESL adjunct. Because I wanted more involvement in the classroom, I decided to become a volunteer at a local community centre where they have programmes for adult learners. After connecting with the Director, she was able to accommodate me in a Monday evening class, and have me float around different classrooms to observe various levels. I was able to teach one class of learners at intermediate level which went very well and I was able to use my knowledge from the course as well as lesson planning guided by Sheila. Eventually I was put in charge of advanced learners (only one to three at a time). There are no set books and little structure so I had to arrange lessons on my own... There is no doubt in my mind that this experience will lead me to grand frontiers.

Although the demand for ESL teachers is enormous, it is very difficult for foreigners who do not have a 'green card' to obtain the necessary working visa. The J-1 visa is available to university students participating in an approved Exchange Visitor Programme (which are mainly for the summer) and to researchers and teachers whose applications are supported by their employing institution in the USA. Similarly it is extremely difficult to obtain the H-1B 'Temporary Worker' visa which is available for prearranged professional or highly skilled jobs for which there are no suitably qualified Americans, an increasingly unlikely circumstance as more and more Americans are becoming qualified to teach ESL/EFL. Although more US organisations now recognise the Cambridge CELTA Certificate than before, the MA in TESOL still dominates the American EFL scene. Even for qualified American teachers, part-time work is the norm, often referred to as being hired as an 'adjunct'. Many contracts are not renewed, creating a transient English teaching population. Pay is hourly and varies according to region, for example $25–$32 in Chicago, a little more in San Francisco. Part-timers almost never get benefits which means no health insurance or vacation pay. Even full-time teaching openings may be for just nine months with pay as little as $20,000 in the Midwest.

One possibility might be to teach at summer courses or work on summer camps attended by young people from overseas. For example, the Council on International Educational Exchange recruits ESL instructors for language camps on the east and west coasts, responsible for teaching English language classes to high school age international students in July and August. Even for such short appointments they look for an MA in TESOL or at least a strong background in ESL.

Canada has a flourishing ELT industry; however, the difficulty of getting a visa is a major stumbling block for foreign teachers. People with experience might have expected to be able to do some casual one-to-one tutoring of new immigrants, but stiff competition makes this difficult. When **David Hughes** arrived in Vancouver after a lengthy stint of teaching English in Taiwan, he felt fairly confident that with his experience he would be able to acquire a few fee-paying students from among the huge Chinese population in the area. But he didn't get a single reply to his advert. Two sources of possible contacts are Languages Canada (www.languagescanada.ca) and TESL Canada (www.tesl.ca). Member institutes will usually consider only Canadian citizens or those with work permits or landed immigrant status. The hourly wage starts at C$25 per hour.

AUSTRALASIA

While Europeans tend to have a somewhat Eurocentric view of the world, the Antipodean English language industry has built itself into a giant. TEFL has a very high profile in both Australia and New Zealand. There are no fewer than 17 Cambridge CELTA training centres in Australia and 10 in New Zealand, most of them attached to flourishing English language colleges. There are a further three Trinity TESOL centres in New Zealand, despite its tiny population of about four million. **Neil Preston** of International House Brisbane has kindly updated this assessment of the ELT scene in Australia.

PROSPECTS FOR TEACHERS IN AUSTRALIA

The growth in student numbers and ELT schools has resulted in strong job prospects for TESOL qualified teachers. Each year approximately 80,000 students study English in Australia on student visas and the Australian immigration department estimates that another 60,000 students studied on other visas, such as working holiday and tourist visas. This is an increase of 80% over the past 10 years although this growth has now slowed. For obvious reasons of geography, the majority of Australia's international students are from Asia, although there are a growing number of students coming from further away including Italy and elsewhere in Europe, plus a strong Latin America presence.

Australia has a strong market for longer-term students e.g. Academic English students (20+ weeks) and English for high school students (20–30 weeks) who need to improve their English skills for entry into an Australian university or high school. However, the average number of weeks overseas students study is 12. This longer-term student market has resulted in relatively steady student numbers year round. Whilst Australia does experience a peak in student numbers over the warmer months (September to May) due to an influx of study tours, there is not the same dramatic seasonal fluctuation as in Europe.

There are approximately 100 English language colleges in Sydney alone, around 70% of which are accredited by the National ELT Accreditation Scheme (NEAS). The profession is strictly regulated in Australia and standards are high in both the private and public sector. The minimum acceptable qualification to teach at an Australian NEAS-accredited language school is a degree in any discipline (or 3-year full-time diploma) plus a recognised TESOL qualification and 800 hours of teaching experience. Alternatively you may be considered with a higher-than-pass grade in the TESOL qualification or if you can show references from your TESOL course director about your performance.

An acceptable TESOL qualification must have a practical component including at least six hours supervised and assessed practice teaching in TESOL and involve no fewer than 100 contact hours in total (or the equivalent in Distance Education programmes). To check the current requirements and a list of accredited language schools see the NEAS website (www.neas.org.au). Some non-accredited schools will employ TESOL trained teachers who do not hold a degree or diploma. It is interesting to note that due to the strong demand for TEFL qualified teachers in Sydney, job-seekers with the CELTA but without a degree have still been offered positions by accredited schools.

Candidates (whether Australians or foreigners on working visas) are regularly offered employment in Sydney and in other Australian cities within a week or two of completing the Cambridge CELTA course. Generally teaching contracts are casual, as staffing is organised from one course period to the next, from week to week or month to month depending on the college. Once a relationship has been built between school and teacher the teacher can opt to work long term with one school or short term with a number of schools. Annual salaries range from around A$40,000 for a newly qualified graduate teacher without experience to A$60,000 for a head teacher. Fair Work Australia (www.fwa.gov.au) sets 'award rates' (agreed minimums) for different categories of TESOL teacher; these are normally reviewed in July.

Many foreigners teach English on a working holiday visa. Travellers aged between 18 and 30 years can apply for working holiday visas for up to 12 months (renewable for a further 12 months provided you do a minimum of 88 days of fruit-picking in a designated rural area). For further information visit www.immi.gov.au. When **Barry O'Leary** arrived in Sydney with a working holiday visa, he had very little money left so needed a job fast. He had emailed a number of language institutes in Sydney in advance and fixed up an interview the day after he arrived. In addition to walking round all the schools he could find, he used Australian search engines such as www.seek.com.au, www.jobsearch.gov.au and http://mycareer.com.au. Soon he found a job with a college in an outer suburb of Sydney:

This was my first full-time job and I was thrown in at the deep end. Initially I was doing maternity cover and working 15 hours a week, but this later increased to 45 including preparation time. The wages were fantastic, I wasn't paying any tax because I set myself up as a contractor and I was paid A$30 an hour (the going rate then) and $300 every two weeks for the evening business course I taught. I managed to save about A$8,000 in three months which paid for a brilliant trip up the east coast of Australia. There was always a laugh in the staff room and a lot of banter between England and Australia. I really enjoyed the mixed classes because there was such a range of opinions and at times more challenging because each nationality would have different weaknesses.

LIST OF EMPLOYERS

ACCESS LANGUAGE CENTRE
72 Mary Street, Surry Hills, New South Wales 2010
- +61 2 9281 6455
- english@access.nsw.edu.au
- www.access.nsw.edu.au

NUMBER OF TEACHERS: 16.
PREFERENCE OF NATIONALITY: None.
QUALIFICATIONS: Bachelor's degree plus TESOL certificate. Some experience essential.
CONDITIONS OF EMPLOYMENT: 4 weeks renewable to start.
SALARY: Depends on qualifications and experience.
FACILITIES/SUPPORT: No assistance with accommodation.
RECRUITMENT: Advertising and will respond to general enquiries about work while in Australia.
CONTACT: Blake Compton, Director of Studies.

AUSTRALIAN INTERNATIONAL COLLEGE OF ENGLISH
Level 3/303 Pitt St, Sydney 2000
- +61 2 9299 2400
- info@aice.nsw.edu.au
- www.aice.nsw.edu.au

NUMBER OF TEACHERS: 15.
PREFERENCE OF NATIONALITY: Any native-speaking country.
QUALIFICATIONS: Recognised TESOL Certificate/CELTA and a Bachelors or higher degree from a recognised university.

CONDITIONS OF EMPLOYMENT: 20 hours per week of teaching. Different class schedules, i.e. Monday to Thursday 9am–3pm or Monday–Friday 9am–1.30pm or 4.15pm–8.45pm.
SALARY: A$30–$45 per hour (gross), based on state salary scale for English teachers. Deductions are made for tax and compulsory superannuation contributions.
FACILITIES/SUPPORT: Candidates with working holiday visas are welcome. No help given with visas or accommodation.
RECRUITMENT: Local advertising. Face-to-face interviews.
CONTACT: Heidi Reid, Principal.

ENGLISH LANGUAGE COMPANY
495 Kent St, Sydney 2000
- +61 2 9267 5688
- recruitment@englishlanguagecompany.com
- www.englishlanguagecompany.com

NUMBER OF TEACHERS: 20.
PREFERENCE OF NATIONALITY: None but must already have right to work in Australia.
QUALIFICATIONS: University degree + CELTA or equivalent – though CELTA definitely preferred. (Under national industry regulations set down by NEAS, teaching qualifications must include 120 hours of face-to-face instruction and at least 6 hours of observed, assessed teaching.)
CONDITIONS OF EMPLOYMENT: Most teachers start with a short contract of 10 or 12 weeks as is common in Sydney. Teaching hours 8.15am–4.15pm.

SALARY: Teachers are paid on a national step-based award system. Qualifications and relevant experience are factored to give a salary step. Salaries range from approximately A$41,500 to A$60,000. Tax is deducted on a PAYE basis.

FACILITIES/SUPPORT: No help given with accommodation or visas.

RECRUITMENT: Applications with CV by email or post and then face-to-face interview is arranged. In certain cases the applicant is asked to do a demonstration lesson of 30–60 minutes using material given to them

CONTACT: Ian Aird, Director of Studies.

ENGLISH UNLIMITED

Level 3, 115 Queen Street Mall, Brisbane 4000, Queensland

✆ +61 7 3003 0088

🖱 info@englishunlimited.qld.edu.au

💻 www.englishunlimited.qld.edu.au

NUMBER OF TEACHERS: 5.

PREFERENCE OF NATIONALITY: Providing the applicant has the right to live and work in Australia and sufficient English language skills, teachers from any country of origin are encouraged to apply.

QUALIFICATIONS: Specific TESOL qualification, for example CELTA or Trinity CertTESOL are a requirement to teach within the private education industry, in colleges accredited by NEAS. TEFL training courses that are accepted must have a minimum number of hours input, and a practical teaching component, which excludes online courses. University degree also required (in any discipline).

CONDITIONS OF EMPLOYMENT: Teachers are employed on ongoing sessional contracts, mostly on a casual basis. Most teachers work approximately 20 hours a week, 8.30am–2.30pm Monday to Thursday (5 contact hours per day).

SALARY: Teachers are usually paid based on a national scheme, according to qualifications and experience. Unfortunately, the majority of overseas experience is not counted, so teachers may well find themselves starting at the bottom. Salary range is from A$42.02 per hour at Level 1 to A$55 at Level 12 (less superannuation payments of 9% and income tax).

FACILITIES/SUPPORT: Teachers source their own accommodation but advice is available. No visa sponsorship is available.

RECRUITMENT: Via adverts on www.seek.com.au and www.onestopenglish.com, walk-in applications and teacher recommendations. Interview prior to appointment is essential for all positions including voluntary; paid employees must teach a demonstration lesson.

CONTACT: Ms Rufus James, Academic Manager (rufus@englishunlimited.qld.edu.au).

INTERNATIONAL HOUSE BRISBANE

126 Adelaide St, Brisbane, Queensland 4000 (Postal address: PO Box 13393 George St, Brisbane 4003)

✆ +61 7 3229 3389

🖱 neil@ihbrisbane.com.au

💻 www.ihbrisbane.com.au

NUMBER OF TEACHERS: Approximately 20.

PREFERENCE OF NATIONALITY: Native English speakers.

QUALIFICATIONS: CELTA or equivalent and minimum 1 year's experience.

CONDITIONS OF EMPLOYMENT: Variable length contracts. Up to 25 hours per week.

SALARY: Australian award rates.

RECRUITMENT: CV and interview. Interviews occasionally conducted overseas.

CONTACT: Neil Preston, Director of Studies.

MILNER INTERNATIONAL COLLEGE OF ENGLISH

379 Hay Street, Perth, Western Australia 6000

✆ +61 8 9325 5444

🖱 dos@milner.wa.edu.au

💻 www.milner.wa.edu.au

NUMBER OF TEACHERS: 25–35.

PREFERENCE OF NATIONALITY: None. Teachers from the UK and Canada can come on a working holiday visa if they are under 30.

QUALIFICATIONS: Degree plus CELTA (or equivalent).

CONDITIONS OF EMPLOYMENT: No contracts for casual teachers. School hours 9am–3pm.

SALARY: There is an award scale for EL teachers ranging from A$38.55 to A$50.46 per hour.

FACILITIES/SUPPORT: Teachers find their own accommodation.

RECRUITMENT: CV and interview.

CONTACT: Deborah Pinder, Director of Studies.

PHOENIX ACADEMY

223 Vincent Street, West Perth, WA 6005

✆ +61 8 9227 5538

🖱 rwalsh@phoenixacademy.com.au

💻 www.phoenixacademy.com.au

NUMBER OF TEACHERS: 30–35 across all English programmes.

PREFERENCE OF NATIONALITY: None but candidates must have a working holiday visa or other appropriate visa.

QUALIFICATIONS: Minimum undergraduate degree in any discipline and a CELTA.

CONDITIONS OF EMPLOYMENT: Length of stay varies according to vacancy needs, e.g. it could be a 4-week summer course contract, a 12-week Business English or Cambridge course contract or a 6-month EAP contract. Permanent contracts occasionally available. Contact hours usually 20 per week plus 3–5 hours for other duties.

SALARY: Minimum starting salary A$42,000–A$53,000 per year. School usually pays above this award minimum according to skills and experience. Tax reduces salary by about 20%.

FACILITIES/SUPPORT: On-campus residence available for new arrivals at a cost of A$30 per night.

RECRUITMENT: Via teachers' websites and local advertising in newspaper media. Interviews essential and can be done by Skype for non-local applicants.

CONTACT: Robynne Walsh, Principal.

SYDNEY ENGLISH ACADEMY (SEA)
19/74–78 The Corso, Manly, NSW 2095
+61 2 9976 6988
info@sea-english.com
www.sea-english.com

NUMBER OF TEACHERS: 6–12 depending on time of year.

PREFERENCE OF NATIONALITY: None, provided they already have legal right to work.

QUALIFICATIONS: An undergraduate degree plus a CELTA or equivalent certificate (as an absolute minimum).

CONDITIONS OF EMPLOYMENT: Varies according to current needs but 12 weeks is typical. Hours normally 8.15am–3.45pm.

SALARY: Based on the New Federal Award. Depending on earnings, 25%–30% is deducted for income tax, and the employers adds on 9% of earnings to pay into the employee's Superannuation fund.

RECRUITMENT: Face-to-face or Skype interview necessary.

CONTACT: Samantha Milton, Director of Studies.

PROSPECTS FOR TEACHERS IN NEW ZEALAND

The English language teaching market in New Zealand is fairly similar to Australia; highly developed, although subject to demand fluctuation. Demand from Chinese, Korean and other Asian students is very high. Also there are plenty of Saudis, South Americans and many others who can see the appeal of learning a foreign language in this beautiful country. According to **Marty Pilott**, manager of the ETC Learning Centre in Wellington, plenty of local teaching applicants are available, which means that language schools are unlikely to hire teachers from abroad. However, anyone with a CELTA and several years' experience who goes to New Zealand to conduct a job hunt has a reasonable chance of success. One such a few years ago was **Rabindra Roy**:

When I came here, I'd never felt so popular. I was amazed how many jobs I got offered cold-calling with a CV. I entered the country on a visitor visa which, as a British passport holder, gave me six months in the country. Before coming here I had looked on the internet for the addresses of English language schools and I brought a stack of CVs with me too. I just typed 'English language schools New Zealand' into the Google search engine and clicked on the second link www.english-schools.co.nz/ which gave me some useful information. I didn't jump at the first three jobs I was offered in Auckland because I wanted to check out Christchurch, the other main centre for EFL schools. There I was offered a few more jobs and decided to take up a post at Aspect [now Kaplan] at 116 Worcester Street in the city centre. The students are mainly Chinese, Korean and Japanese but there are notable groups from Taiwan, Switzerland and South America too. My school was helpfully willing to aid me with the visa bureaucracy and now I have residency. My school has a core of staff with open-ended contracts and a larger number of casual/part-time staff including some British people with working holiday visas who work for some months and then continue travelling.

Private language schools are regulated by the New Zealand Qualifications Authority or NZQA (www.nzqa. govt.nz/providers/index.do). Its website lists all the educational establishments in New Zealand, but is worth looking through for leads (or search for 'language' to narrow it down). The national organisation of English language teachers, TESOLANZ, (www.tesolanz.org.nz) provides a free listing for job-seekers and institutions offering work, while English New Zealand (www.englishnewzealand.co.nz) is a group of schools which has its own accreditation process and a central contact for teacher recruitment (info@englishnewzealand.co.nz).

British citizens aged between 18 and 30 can work in New Zealand through the working holiday visa scheme for up to 23 months (www.immigration.govt.nz/migrant/stream/work/workingholiday).

LIST OF EMPLOYERS

DOMINION ENGLISH SCHOOLS

Auckland: PO Box 4217

☎ +64 9 377 3280

✐ dos@dominion.school.nz

Christchurch: PO Box 3908

✐ english@dominion.school.nz

💻 www.dominion.school.nz

NUMBER OF TEACHERS: Up to 20.

PREFERENCE OF NATIONALITY: None but must be native English speakers.

QUALIFICATIONS: Minimum Cambridge/RSA CELTA or Trinity CertTESOL or recognised equivalent. Preferably also university degree and experience.

CONDITIONS OF EMPLOYMENT: Flexible contracts. Part-time hours 12.5 per week from 9am to 12pm. Full-time hours 25 per week, 9am–4pm.

SALARY: Starting wage approximately NZ$30 per hour.

FACILITIES/SUPPORT: Applicants must hold a valid work visa/permit.

RECRUITMENT: Local interviews essential.

INDEX OF ADVERTISERS